BaseBall america®
2010 PROSPECT
HANDBOOK

BASEBALL AMERICA INC. · DURHAM, N.C.

Baseball america®

MAJORS ◆ MINORS ◆ PROSPECTS ◆ DRAFT ◆ COLLEGE ◆ HIGH SCHOOL

FOR GREAT PROSPECTS COVERAGE
ALL YEAR, VISIT ...

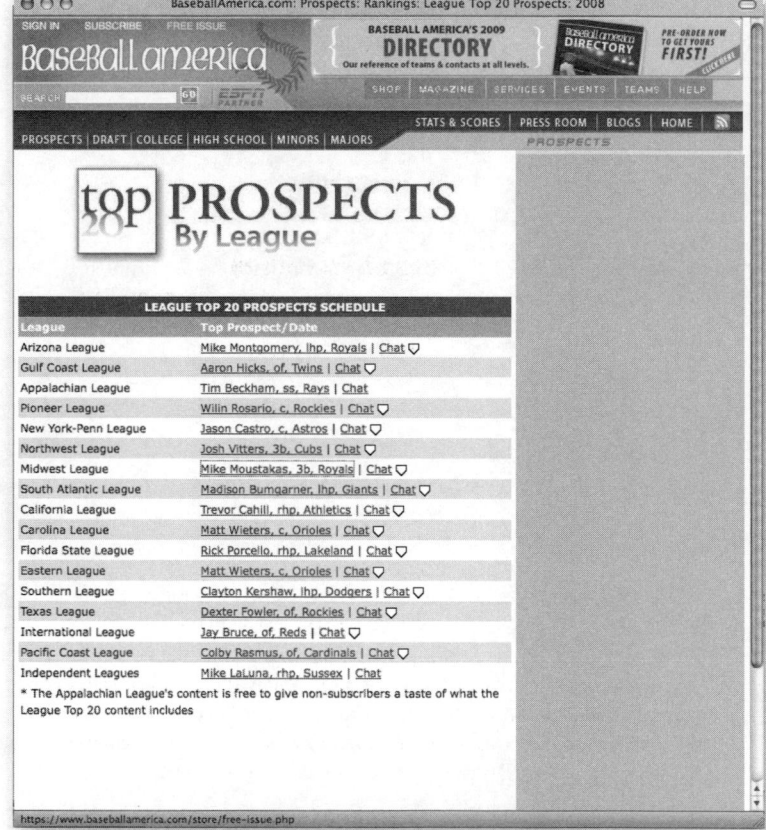

www.BaseballAmerica.com

BaseBall america
2010 PROSPECT
HANDBOOK

Editors
JIM CALLIS, WILL LINGO, JOHN MANUEL

Assistant Editors
BEN BADLER, J.J. COOPER, MATT EDDY, AARON FITT,
CONOR GLASSEY, JOSH LEVENTHAL, NATHAN RODE, JIM SHONERD

Database and Application Development
GREG LEVINE, BRENT LEWIS

Contributing Writers
ANDY BAGGARLY, BILL BALLEW, MIKE BERARDINO,
MATTHEW FORMAN, DERRICK GOOLD, TOM HAUDRICOURT,
JOHN PERROTTO, TRACY RINGOLSBY, PHIL ROGERS, ADAM RUBIN

Photo Editor
NATHAN RODE

Design & Production
SARA HIATT MCDANIEL, TIFFANY SCHWARZ, LINWOOD WEBB

Jacket Photos
JASON HEYWARD BY BRIAN BISSELL, STARLIN CASTRO BY JERRY HALE;
DESMOND JENNINGS BY CARL KLINE; BRIAN MATUSZ BY STEVE KING

BaseBall america

PRESIDENT/PUBLISHER: LEE FOLGER
EDITORS IN CHIEF: WILL LINGO, JOHN MANUEL
EXECUTIVE EDITOR: JIM CALLIS
DESIGN & PRODUCTION DIRECTOR: SARA HIATT MCDANIEL
TECHNOLOGY MANAGER: GREG LEVINE

BaseballAmerica.com

EDITOR'S NOTE: Transactions for this book go through Dec. 13, so the last significant player transactions included here came out of the Rule 5 draft. As always, you can find players even if they have changed organizations by using the handy index in the back. We also have scouting reports for Cuban defectors Noel Arguelles and Aroldis Chapman on Page 494. **>>** For the purposes of this book, a prospect is any player who has no more than 50 innings pitched, 30 relief appearances or 130 at-bats in the major leagues, regardless of service time. Finally, the grades you'll find for each team's drafts are based solely on the quality of the players signed, with no consideration for who players were traded for or how many picks a team might have lost.

FOREWORD

I remember that first copy of Baseball America I ever read. It was 1993 and Darren Dreifort was on the cover of an NL West Top 10 Prospects Issue. I was hooked. All in.

Little did I know, though, that my career path would begin to take shape that day. I became obsessed with prospect lists. It was easier for me to scrounge up a couple bucks in change every two weeks than it was to pony up for a subscription at the time, so I religiously made the trek to the bookstore at the mall every other Tuesday—and haven't missed an issue since. While I had always had an interest in prospects and rookies as a kid, Baseball America took it to a new level, and I was fascinated with the likes of Antonio Osuna, Josh Booty and of course "The Next Mickey Mantle," Ruben Rivera. I knew I had to infiltrate BA's headquarters.

Fast forward nearly a decade later and the opportunity of a lifetime came calling. BA was expanding their Top 10 lists to top 30s and the first Prospect Handbook was born, and I was asked to put the Phillies list together. I promptly ranked righthander Brad Baisley third, ahead of No. 5 prospect Chase Utley . . . oops. Nevertheless, a few months later I was on board full-time as an editor and headed for Durham, N.C.

I wasn't talented enough to play professional baseball and went to scout school instead of an Ivy League school (as if I had a choice), but I am proud that Baseball America became my training ground and was important in establishing my foundation for player evaluation, opening doors for me I never could have imagined. I witnessed the influence BA had in the industry and that motivated me, knowing I was being judged by the scouts, scouting directors, coaches, general managers and players who were all so generous with their time and information. I developed mentors in the scouting world, and lifelong friendships with many in the game, and many in the BA offices.

I like to think I've learned a lot since those days of ranking Drew Henson ahead of Nick Johnson and Robinson Cano, and Luis Terrero ahead of Jose Valverde and Brandon Webb. And what I've learned is that there is always more to learn in the world of scouting. As an eager reader back in 2001, or as a "baseball official" in 2010, the Prospect Handbook remains the standard in the industry for the most and best information on baseball's future stars.

Nearly two decades after reading my first Baseball America, I am truly honored to represent the Texas Rangers and lead off the 10th edition of the Prospect Handbook.

JOSH BOYD
DIRECTOR OF PRO SCOUTING
TEXAS RANGERS

TABLE OF CONTENTS

334

Domonic Brown changed the spelling of his first name this year, but what didn't change was his status as the Phillies' No. 1 prospect

Introduction	6
Profiling Prospects	7
Depth Chart Overview	8
Staff Top 50s	9
Organization Rankings	12
Arizona Diamondbacks	14
Atlanta Braves	30
Baltimore Orioles	46
Boston Red Sox	62
Chicago Cubs	78
Chicago White Sox	94
Cincinnati Reds	110
Cleveland Indians	126
Colorado Rockies	142
Detroit Tigers	158
Florida Marlins	174
Houston Astros	190
Kansas City Royals	206
Los Angeles Angels	222
Los Angeles Dodgers	238
Milwaukee Brewers	254
Minnesota Twins	270
New York Mets	286
New York Yankees	302
Oakland Athletics	318
Philadelphia Phillies	334
Pittsburgh Pirates	350
St. Louis Cardinals	366
San Diego Padres	382
San Francisco Giants	398
Seattle Mariners	414
Tampa Bay Rays	430
Texas Rangers	446
Toronto Blue Jays	462
Washington Nationals	478
APPENDIX: Extra scouting reports	494
2007-2009 Signing bonuses	495
2010 Draft Prospects	499
Minor League Top 20s	503
Index	506

INTRODUCTION

While most people are winding down their years and coasting through December, at Baseball America we are cranked into high gear. Beyond the Winter Meetings, it's Prospect Handbook season and that means getting our most daunting project completed before Christmas so you can have it in your hands before spring training.

The Prospect Handbook quickly became our signature publication because it pulls together key elements of everything we do. It's all there with each carefully crafted scouting report—all 900 of them. Amazingly enough, this is the 10th edition of the Prospect Handbook. I can still remember the first edition in 2001, featuring Corey Patterson on the cover. Doing 900 scouting reports seemed like a crazy idea, not to mention including their career statistics as well, and actually executing it proved to be more daunting than we had imagined.

What I don't remember is when we actually finished that first book. I think we targeted January as a completion date, but I don't think we actually sent it to the printer until the end of January or even the beginning of February. We severely underestimated the amount of information we were jamming into the book, both from a logistical point of view as well as something as simple as the number of pages we set aside for each team. Each organization got 14 pages for all of its information, and perhaps we just didn't realize how much we would have to say about all those prospects. When we thought about it conceptually, it seemed that maybe the players at the back of a Top 30 would be marginal guys about whom we wouldn't have much to say. In practice, however, we had plenty to say about all 30 guys, and sometimes the guys at the back of the list are even more interesting than the guys at the top.

In that first book, I remember fighting to get slugger Bucky Jacobsen at the back of the Brewers' list, both because of his back story—he had his own fan club, the Bucky Backers—as well as his power potential. That Jacobsen actually reached the major leagues with Seattle and hit nine home runs in 2004 made it all worthwhile. That's one of the many great fringe benefits of the Prospect Handbook. It gives you an appreciation for the complementary players who reach the major leagues, and helps you realize that finding a big league regular is an incredibly difficult and powerful achievement. It goes without saying that not all of the 900 players in any Prospect Handbook will reach the majors, but the number of players who will become stars is much smaller than you'd think. Reaching the big leagues at all remains a notable achievement for which players and teams probably don't get enough credit.

What's also notable about the first handbook is how little the format has changed over the next 10 editions. To me that shows just what a great idea the Prospect Handbook was to begin with. We have tweaked the idea, added to it and improved the way we execute it, but if you look back at the 2001 Prospect Handbook you wouldn't notice a huge difference in the format from what you see in 2010. The only significant difference is the addition of depth charts, which came in 2003.

Another great thing is that we have so many writers that were in the original book who remain with us now. Jim Callis, John Manuel and I have been fortunate enough to work for Baseball America for the whole run of the book, and I have written every Orioles list while Jim has handled the Cubs and Red Sox in every book. We did learn after the first book that asking Jim to do seven organizations—he originally planned to do 12—was probably a bit much, particularly since he also does a lot of the editorial heavy lifting, checking everyone's lists and making sure every one of the 900 writeups meets the same standard. John prides himself on being our utilityman, and this year is the first time in a long time that he has not added a new organization. He has written up 10 different organizations in the 10 editions of the book.

We've also had contributors Bill Ballew (Braves and Rays), Mike Berardino (Marlins), John Perrotto (Pirates), Tracy Ringolsby (Rockies) and Phil Rogers (White Sox) in every book. Tom Haudricourt also deserves a tip of the hat, having done the Brewers in the first book and returning a few years ago after an absence from the Brewers beat. That first book is also when we discovered a precocious young talent named Josh Boyd, who wrote the Phillies list as a freelancer and did such a good job that we hired him full-time. He was eventually hired away by the Padres as an actual scout, and he's now the Rangers' director of professional scouting.

That's probably the biggest change over the evolution of the Prospect Handbook. As our demands have grown, our staff has gotten better and now we do much more of the book with in-house writers. We think it's reflected in the quality of the book, and you have backed that up with your support of it. As we celebrate the 10th edition, we thank you for that and look forward to the next 10.

WILL LINGO
EDITOR IN CHIEF
BASEBALL AMERICA

PROFILING PROSPECTS

Among all the scouting lingo you'll come across in this book, perhaps no terms are more telling and prevalent than "profile" and "projection."

When scouts evaluate a player, their main objective is to identify—or project—what the player's future role will be in the major leagues. Each organization has its own philosophy when it comes to grading players, so we talked to scouts from several teams to provide general guidelines.

The first thing to know is what scouts are looking for. In short, tools. These refer to the physical skills a player needs to be successful in the major leagues. For a position player, the five basic tools are hitting, hitting for power, fielding, arm strength and speed. For a pitcher, the tools are based on the pitches he throws. Each pitch is graded, as well as a pitcher's control, delivery and durability.

The profiling system continues to evolve. Baseball is coming out of an era of historic offensive proportions, and in the first two years of the post-Mitchell Report era have featured no 40-home run hitters in the American League—the first time since 1992 that a league leader hasn't hit at least 40. While the emphasis in recent years has tilted profiles more and more towards offense, speed and defense have begun to creep higher up the list of priorities in coming years.

While more emphasis has been placed on hitting—which also covers getting on base—fielding and speed remain at a premium up the middle. As teams have sacrificed defense at the corner outfield slots, they continue to seek speedy center fielders to make up ground in the alleys. Most scouts prefer at least a 55 runner (on the 20-80 scouting scale; see chart) at short and center field, but as power increases at those two positions, running comes down.

Shortstops need range and at least average arm strength, and second basemen need to be quick on the pivot. Teams are more willing to put up with an immobile corner infielder if he can mash.

Arm strength is the one tool moving way down preference lists. For a catcher, it was always the No. 1 tool, though in today's game, scouts are looking for more offensive production from the position. Receiving skills, including game-calling, blocking pitches and release times, can make up for the lack of a plus arm.

On the mound, it doesn't just come down to pure stuff. While a true No. 1 starter on a first-division team should have a couple of 70 or 80 pitches in his repertoire, such as Zack Greinke and Tim Lincecum,

SCOUTING SCALE

When grading a player's tools, scouts use a standard 20-80 scale. When you read that a pitcher throws an above-average slider, it can be interpreted as a 60 pitch, or a plus pitch. Plus-plus is 70, or well-above-average, and so on. Scouts don't throw 80s around very freely. Here's what each grade means:

80	**OUTSTANDING**
70	**WELL-ABOVE-AVERAGE**
60	**ABOVE-AVERAGE**
50	**MAJOR LEAGUE AVERAGE**
40	**BELOW-AVERAGE**
30	**WELL-BELOW-AVERAGE**
20	**POOR**

they also need to produce 200-plus innings, 30 starts and 15-plus wins.

A player's overall future potential is also graded on the 20-80 scale, though some teams use a letter grade. This number is not just the sum of his tools, but rather a profiling system and a scout's ultimate opinion of the player.

70-80 (A): This category is reserved for the elite players in baseball. This player will be a perennial all-star, the best player at his position, one of the top five starters in the game or a frontline closer. Alex Rodriguez, Albert Pujols and Chase Utley reside here.

60-69 (B): You'll find all-star-caliber players here: No. 2 starters on a championship club and first-division players. See Jon Lester, Torii Hunter and Carl Crawford.

55-59 (C+): The majority of first-division starters are found in this range, including quality No. 2 and 3 starters, frontline set-up men and second-tier closers.

50-54 (C): Solid-average everyday major leaguers. Most are not first-division regulars. This group also includes No. 4 and 5 starters.

45-49 (D+): Fringe everyday players, backups, some No. 5 starters, middle relievers, pinch-hitters and one-tool players.

40-44 (D): Up-and-down roster fillers, situational relievers and 25th players.

38-39 (O): Organizational players who provide depth for the minor leagues but are not considered future major leaguers.

20-37 (NP): Not a prospect.

An Overview

Another feature of the Prospect Handbook is a depth chart of every organization's minor league talent. This shows you at a glance what kind of talent a system has and provides even more prospects beyond the top 30.

Players are usually listed on the depth charts where we think they'll ultimately end up. To help you better understand why players are slotted at particular positions, we show you here what scouts look for in the ideal candidate at each spot, with individual tools ranked in descending order.

LF	**CF**	**RF**
Power	Fielding	Hitting
Hitting	Hitting	Power
Fielding	Speed	Arm Strength
Arm Strength	Power	Fielding
Speed	Arm Strength	Speed

3B	**SS**	**2B**	**1B**
Hitting	Fielding	Hitting	Power
Power	Arm Strength	Fielding	Hitting
Fielding	Hitting	Power	Fielding
Arm Strength	Speed	Speed	Arm Strength
Speed	Power	Arm Strength	Speed

C
Fielding
Arm Strength
Hitting
Power
Speed

STARTING PITCHERS			
No. 1 starter	**No. 2 starter**	**No. 3 starter**	**No. 4-5 starters**
• Two plus pitches	• Two plus pitches	• One plus pitch	• Command of two major
• Average third pitch	• Average third pitch	• Two average pitches	league pitches
• Plus-plus command	• Average command	• Average command	• Average velocity
• Plus makeup	• Average makeup	• Average makeup	• Consistent breaking ball
			• Decent changeup

CLOSER
• One dominant pitch
• Second plus pitch
• Plus command
• Plus-plus makeup

TOP 50 PROSPECTS

When Baseball America ranks prospects, there's almost always a byline attributing who finally put the players in order, who decided, "OK, this guy's 6 and this guy's 7." But all our rankings are more than one person's opinion. They are most often a reflection of the consensus of sources on the subject—managers, coaches, scouts, front-office personnel, the whole spectrum.

Except here, really. In this section of the Handbook, we get personal. Sifting through all the information we've gathered to this point, three of our editors give their own personal takes on the game's top 50 prospects. This helps form the basis of the arguments that shape Baseball America's Top 100 Prospects. That list comes out during spring training, and we consider it the definitive guide to the best talent in the minor leagues.

The rules for these lists are the same for any prospect who appears in the Handbook: no more than 130 at-bats, 50 innings or 30 relief appearances in the major leagues. We do not consider service time in our eligibility requirements.

As with any prospect list, these rankings represent how each person regarded the top minor league talent in the game at a moment in time. Ask us again in a few months—or even tomorrow—how these prospects stack up, and you'll get a different answer.

JIM CALLIS

1. Stephen Strasburg, rhp, Nationals
2. Jason Heyward, of, Braves
3. Mike Stanton, of, Marlins
4. Jesus Montero, c, Yankees
5. Pedro Alvarez, 3b, Pirates
6. Dustin Ackley, of/1b, Mariners
7. Neftali Feliz, rhp, Rangers
8. Buster Posey, c, Giants
9. Brian Matusz, lhp, Orioles
10. Madison Bumgarner, lhp, Giants
11. Carlos Santana, c, Indians
12. Desmond Jennings, of, Rays
13. Starlin Castro, ss, Cubs
14. Alcides Escobar, ss, Brewers
15. Domonic Brown, of, Phillies
16. Justin Smoak, 1b, Rangers
17. Logan Morrison, 1b, Marlins
18. Kyle Drabek, rhp, Phillies
19. Ryan Westmoreland, of, Red Sox
20. Aaron Hicks, of, Twins
21. Casey Kelly, rhp, Red Sox
22. Tyler Matzek, lhp, Rockies
23. Jacob Turner, rhp, Tigers
24. Martin Perez, lhp, Rangers
25. Lonnie Chisenhall, 3b, Indians
26. Jarrod Parker, rhp, Diamondbacks
27. Mike Montgomery, lhp, Royals
28. Chris Carter, 1b/of, Athletics
29. Michael Taylor, of, Phillies
30. Kyle Gibson, rhp, Twins
31. Aaron Crow, rhp, Royals
32. Brett Wallace, 3b/1b, Athletics
33. Christian Friedrich, lhp, Rockies
34. Jeremy Hellickson, rhp, Rays
35. Dee Gordon, ss, Dodgers
36. Grant Green, ss, Athletics
37. Brett Lawrie, 2b, Brewers
38. Jason Castro, c, Astros
39. Todd Frazier, of/2b/3b, Reds
40. Matt Moore, lhp, Rays
41. Wade Davis, rhp, Rays
42. Casey Crosby, lhp, Tigers
43. Michael Saunders, of, Mariners
44. Yonder Alonso, 1b, Reds
45. Freddie Freeman, 1b, Braves
46. Josh Bell, 3b, Orioles
47. Donavan Tate, of, Padres
48. Tanner Scheppers, rhp, Rangers
49. Arodys Vizcaino, rhp, Yankees
50. Julio Teheran, rhp, Braves

Rangers righthander Neftali Feliz blazed a path to the big leagues last year

Yankees slugger Jesus Montero ranks among the minors' truly elite hitters

WILL LINGO

1. Jason Heyward, of, Braves
2. Stephen Strasburg, rhp, Nationals
3. Alcides Escobar, ss, Brewers
4. Mike Stanton, of, Marlins
5. Brian Matusz, lhp, Orioles
6. Pedro Alvarez, 3b, Pirates
7. Carlos Santana, c, Indians
8. Buster Posey, c, Giants
9. Dustin Ackley, of/1b, Mariners
10. Neftali Feliz, rhp, Rangers
11. Desmond Jennings, of, Rays
12. Justin Smoak, 1b, Rangers
13. Madison Bumgarner, lhp, Giants
14. Jesus Montero, c, Yankees
15. Martin Perez, lhp, Rangers
16. Starlin Castro, ss, Cubs
17. Lonnie Chisenhall, 3b, Indians
18. Jeremy Hellickson, rhp, Rays
19. Logan Morrison, 1b, Marlins
20. Chris Carter, 1b/of, Athletics
21. Casey Kelly, rhp, Red Sox
22. Aaron Hicks, of, Twins
23. Domonic Brown, of, Phillies
24. Jason Castro, c, Astros
25. Derek Norris, c, Nationals
26. Freddie Freeman, 1b, Braves
27. Wade Davis, rhp, Rays
28. Jared Mitchell, of, White Sox
29. Tyler Flowers, c, White Sox
30. Kyle Drabek, rhp, Phillies
31. Brett Wallace, 3b/1b, Athletics
32. Todd Frazier, of/2b/3b, Reds
33. Josh Bell, 3b, Orioles
34. Ryan Westmoreland, of, Red Sox
35. Tyler Matzek, lhp, Rockies
36. Michael Saunders, of, Mariners
37. Dan Hudson, rhp, White Sox
38. Donavan Tate, of, Padres
39. Shelby Miller, rhp, Cardinals
40. Wilson Ramos, c, Twins
41. Julio Teheran, rhp, Braves
42. Dee Gordon, ss, Dodgers
43. Peter Bourjos, of, Angels
44. Aaron Crow, rhp, Royals
45. Michael Taylor, of, Phillies
46. Brett Lawrie, 2b, Brewers
47. Grant Green, ss, Athletics
48. Hank Conger, c, Angels
49. Jarrod Parker, rhp, Diamondbacks
50. Mike Montgomery, lhp, Royals

Stephen Strasburg was the No. 1 pick in the 2009 draft and tops two editors' Top 50 lists

Athletic Marlins outfielder Mike Stanton has as much raw power as any prospect

JOHN MANUEL

1. Stephen Strasburg, rhp, Nationals
2. Jason Heyward, of, Braves
3. Mike Stanton, of, Marlins
4. Desmond Jennings, of, Rays
5. Jesus Montero, c/dh, Yankees
6. Brian Matusz, lhp, Orioles
7. Pedro Alvarez, 3b, Pirates
8. Neftali Feliz, rhp, Rangers
9. Buster Posey, c, Giants
10. Madison Bumgarner, lhp, Giants
11. Carlos Santana, c, Indians
12. Justin Smoak, 1b, Rangers
13. Domonic Brown, of, Phillies
14. Casey Kelly, rhp, Red Sox
15. Jeremy Hellickson, rhp, Rays
16. Kyle Drabek, rhp, Phillies
17. Alcides Escobar, ss, Brewers
18. Dustin Ackley, of/1b, Mariners
19. Aaron Hicks, of, Twins
20. Martin Perez, lhp, Rangers
21. Wade Davis, rhp, Rays
22. Ryan Westmoreland, of, Red Sox
23. Michael Taylor, of, Phillies
24. Tyler Matzek, lhp, Rockies
25. Lonnie Chisenhall, 3b, Indians
26. Chris Carter, 1b/dh, Athletics
27. Matt Moore, lhp, Rays
28. Brett Wallace, 3b/1b, Athletics
29. Starlin Castro, ss, Cubs
30. Wilson Ramos, c, Twins
31. Michael Saunders, of, Mariners
32. Nick Hagadone, lhp, Indians
33. Logan Morrison, 1b, Marlins
34. Jacob Turner, rhp, Tigers
35. Todd Frazier, 2b/3b/of, Reds
36. Freddie Freeman, 1b, Braves
37. Mike Montgomery, lhp, Royals
38. Kyle Gibson, rhp, Twins
39. Jared Mitchell, of, White Sox
40. Jarrod Parker, rhp, Diamondbacks
41. Tyler Flowers, c, White Sox
42. Aaron Crow, rhp, Royals
43. Tanner Scheppers, rhp, Rangers
44. Derek Norris, c, Nationals
45. Yonder Alonso, 1b, Reds
46. Jason Castro, c, Astros
47. Reid Brignac, ss, Rays
48. Christian Friedrich, lhp, Rockies
49. Shelby Miller, rhp, Cardinals
50. Jason Knapp, rhp, Indians

TALENT RANKINGS

		2009	2008	2007	2006	2005
1	**Tampa Bay Rays**	4	1	1	10	9

The Rays couldn't develop a pitcher for the first decade of their existence, and now they have more than they know what to do with. In Desmond Jennings, they have come up with yet another of their signatures: a toolsy, athletic outfielder in the Carl Crawford/B.J. Upton line.

		2009	2008	2007	2006	2005
2	**Texas Rangers**	1	4	28	16	16

The Rangers graduated a lot of talent to Arlington in 2009, and some of their lower-level pitchers didn't step forward as hoped. That's what pitching depth is for, though, and with Neftali Feliz and Martin Perez leading the way, the Rangers have plenty of impact players left on the farm.

		2009	2008	2007	2006	2005
3	**Cleveland Indians**	7	19	10	9	7

The song remains the same with Cleveland, which has primarily drafted for college players in the 2000s, with mixed results. Instead, most of their top prospects have come from trades. That's as true now as ever, though Lonnie Chisenhall and Alex White have more upside than past Tribe draft picks.

		2009	2008	2007	2006	2005
4	**San Francisco Giants**	5	23	20	18	17

These are not your big brother's Giants. Gone are the days of punting on a draft to sign a raft of free agents, as San Francisco has a surprisingly deep system. The Giants even figured out how to develop a hitter in Pablo Sandoval, and should have Buster Posey joining him soon.

		2009	2008	2007	2006	2005
5	**Philadelphia Phillies**	12	22	21	22	20

The Phillies traded four prospects off last year's Top 10 for Cliff Lee and graduated standout rookie J.A. Happ. Yet the organization held onto enough top prospects such as Domonic Brown, Michael Taylor and Kyle Drabek to restock or to make another blockbuster deal.

		2009	2008	2007	2006	2005
6	**Boston Red Sox**	13	2	9	8	21

Earlier in the decade, the Red Sox drafted heavily on the college side. Now their system is chock-full of high-upside international signees and high school draftees. A big reason for that is money—Boston has leveraged its revenue aggressively in both markets.

		2009	2008	2007	2006	2005
7	**Minnesota Twins**	22	15	8	6	4

Whether it was their consistent winning or the arrival of Target Field, the Twins were feeling spry in '09. They went over-slot for first-rounder Kyle Gibson and made huge strides internationally while getting strong seasons from top prospects Aaron Hicks and Wilson Ramos.

		2009	2008	2007	2006	2005
8	**Florida Marlins**	2	17	16	3	14

The Marlins have a homegrown ace in Josh Johnson but haven't been able to come up wtih in-house complements to join him in the rotation. Instead, they keep coming up with cheap players to fill out the lineup around their other superstar, Hanley Ramirez.

		2009	2008	2007	2006	2005
9	**Baltimore Orioles**	9	14	17	12	25

The Orioles' ranking gets a boost because Brian Matusz fell just short of exhausting his rookie eligibility. The O's still have an impressive core of talent considering how many pitchers the organization graduated to the majors in 2009.

		2009	2008	2007	2006	2005
10	**Colorado Rockies**	20	7	2	11	6

Whenever the Rockies have had a big league need, their farm system has come through to fill it, either through homegrown players such as Dexter Fowler, Ian Stewart and Seth Smith, or providing fodder for trades. A strong '09 draft effort should provide more of both.

		2009	2008	2007	2006	2005
11	**Seattle Mariners**	24	12	24	27	11

Poor seasons and injuries hampered Seattle's system, but Seattle added talent via the draft (No. 2 overall pick Dustin Ackley) and trades to buoy a flagging system. GM Jack Zduriencik accentuated defense at all levels, from the majors through the draft with picks Nick Franklin and Steve Baron.

		2009	2008	2007	2006	2005
12	**Oakland Athletics**	3	9	27	26	8

It's only natural for the A's to fall in the rankings somewhat, considering the pitching talent that graduated to the majors, led by Brett Anderson, Trevor Cahill and AL rookie of the year Andrew Bailey. Oakland reloaded with some trades and with an aggressive draft class.

		2009	2008	2007	2006	2005
13	**Atlanta Braves**	6	8	15	7	5

The end of Roy Clark's tenure as scouting director (he's now assistant GM in Washington) was marked by a shift to junior-college and college players in the draft. The Braves on a budget have drafted more conservatively than they used to, leading to a system with less depth than usual.

		2009	2008	2007	2006	2005
14	**Milwaukee Brewers**	10	21	7	5	3

The Brewers rank higher than they might have otherwise thanks to Alcides Escobar and Mat Gamel staying prospect-eligible. Milwaukee has proven it can develop hitters, but the Brewers still need to come up with some arms to complement homegrown ace Yovani Gallardo.

		2009	2008	2007	2006	2005
15	**Chicago Cubs**	27	18	18	15	10

After years of going backward, the Cubs farm system made significant progress in 2009. Top draft picks such as Andrew Cashner, Brett Jackson and Josh Vitters performed well, and shortstop Starlin Castro burst on the scene, jumping from Rookie ball to Double-A in one year.

	2009	2008	2007	2006	2005
16 Pittsburgh Pirates	18	26	19	19	18

Rather than tie up much of their budget in one pick as they did in '08 with Pedro Alvarez, the Pirates tried a portfolio approach in the '09 draft. Alvarez looks like an impact bat, and '09 first-rounder Tony Sanchez heads a class with strong early returns.

	2009	2008	2007	2006	2005
17 Kansas City Royals	11	24	11	23	28

Raised as a Brave, Royals GM Dayton Moore likes stockpiling young pitchers, and the Royals have an intriguing collection of arms. However, they're almost all at the lower levels. Moreover, the Royals got worrisome 2009 performances from first-round picks Mike Moustakas and Eric Hosmer.

	2009	2008	2007	2006	2005
18 New York Yankees	15	5	5	17	24

Jesus Montero broke through as one of the minors' best hitters, a bat so good the Yankees (probably) won't trade him. New York has spent aggressively to bring in its top pitching prospects, but can't feel good about Andrew Brackman's brutal 2009 season.

	2009	2008	2007	2006	2005
19 Chicago White Sox	16	30	25	14	12

Gordon Beckham flashed through the farm system in less than a year, and the White Sox traded talent to get Jake Peavy. The system still looks to be in good shape, though, thanks to productive drafts since the return of Doug Laumann as scouting director the last two years.

	2009	2008	2007	2006	2005
20 San Diego Padres	29	13	29	29	27

Many of the Padres' top prospects either graduated to the majors, such as Mat Latos and Will Venable, or had strong 2009 seasons, such as Cory Luebke and James Darnell. A rare high-risk, high-reward draft class was the last contribution made by fired scouting and farm director Grady Fuson.

	2009	2008	2007	2006	2005
21 Washington Nationals	21	9	30	24	26

The Esmailyn Gonzalez affair helped the Nats in the long run, as it forced Jim Bowden's resignation. New GM Mike Rizzo got No. 1 pick Stephen Strasburg signed, giving the Nationals an identity for the first time since the team moved from Montreal after the '04 season.

	2009	2008	2007	2006	2005
22 New York Mets	17	28	13	28	19

New York's aggressive international scouting has brought its top three prospects in Jenrry Mejia, Wilmer Flores and Fernando Martinez. When the Mets have had first-round picks, they've drafted fairly well, but they've had only two first-rounders (both in the '08 draft) in the last four years.

	2009	2008	2007	2006	2005
23 Cincinnati Reds	14	3	12	30	23

After aggressively pursuing talent in 2008—spending millions internationally and going over slot for first-rounder Yonder Alonso—the Reds played it straight in '09. They even traded prospects for third baseman Scott Rolen. At least top prospect Todd Frazier knows where he won't play in 2010.

	2009	2008	2007	2006	2005
24 Los Angeles Dodgers	23	6	6	?	?

No team has spent less on the draft the last two years than the Dodgers, and GM Ned Colletti isn't shy about trading prospects. Despite these handicaps, the Dodgers keep coming up with talent, and the farm system bounced back in 2009 with big years by Dee Gordon and Chris Withrow.

	2009	2008	2007	2006	2005
25 Los Angeles Angels	25	11	4	4	1

A homegrown core has helped the Angels to five playoff trips in the last six seasons. The Angels restocked their system with a draft bonanza last June, but they got more help when holdovers such as Hank Conger, Peter Bourjos and Trevor Bell had strong, bounceback seasons.

	2009	2008	2007	2006	2005
26 Detroit Tigers	28	27	14	13	29

Another year, another aggressive Tigers draft filled with power arms. Rick Porcello's success seems to have emboldened Detroit even more, which got a pair of hard throwers in Jacob Turner and Andy Oliver, plus toolsy Michigan prep product Daniel Fields.

	2009	2008	2007	2006	2005
27 Arizona Diamondbacks	26	20	3	1	13

Like the Angels, the Diamondbacks had extra picks to try to replenish a farm system that has graduated talent and has failed to replenish its stock of athletes. The draft class accounts for seven of the organization's Top 10 Prospects, an indictment of the talent that was on hand.

	2009	2008	2007	2006	2005
28 Toronto Blue Jays	19	25	26	25	15

It's the end of an error in Toronto, where J.P. Ricciardi got the hang of player development but not public relations or, in the end, winning. The Blue Jays' new approach under new GM Alex Anthopoulos is an attempt to go back to the future, emphasizing scouting.

	2009	2008	2007	2006	2005
29 St. Louis Cardinals	8	16	23	21	30

The Cardinals' stay among the top 10 farm systems was short-lived. St. Louis traded away several top-shelf prospects from last year's list, and saw other prospects graduate (Colby Rasmus). However, the rest of the system took a massive step backward, particularly on the mound.

	2009	2008	2007	2006	2005
30 Houston Astros	30	29	22	20	22

Houston's '07 draft class was a disaster, leaving a gaping hole in the system. The last two drafts under Bobby Heck's guidance have been marked by non-consensus selections that have included some finds such as Jason Castro and Jordan Lyles, but the system still lacks depth.

Arizona Diamondbacks

BY MATT FORMAN

How much can change in two years.
In 2007, the Diamondbacks were mentioned in tandem with the Rockies. Both National League West squads reached the NL Championship Series thanks to an influx of young, homegrown talent. Both missed the playoffs in 2008, and last season both fired their managers in May.

The paths diverged there. Colorado made it back to the postseason after promoting Jim Tracy to replace Clint Hurdle and surging to a 74-42 finish. Arizona, on the other hand, compiled the sixth-worst record in baseball at 70-92. A.J. Hinch's move from farm director to manager was controversial and yielded roughly the same results (58-75) as predecessor Bob Melvin (12-17).

What's more, the Rockies have more young talent, especially pitchers, ready to contribute in the big leagues. The Diamondbacks' best prospects reside in the lower levels of the minors. Baseball America ranked Arizona's farm system No. 1 in the game entering the 2006 season, but it has thinned as players such as Miguel Montero, Mark Reynolds and Justin Upton have graduated to the major leagues and others, such as Brett Anderson, Alberto Callaspo and Carlos Gonzalez, have been used in trades.

Given the strength of the Dodgers, Giants and Rockies, the Diamondbacks couldn't stand pat and traded more young talent away, giving up righthander Max Scherzer and lefthander Daniel Schlereth in a deal with the Tigers and Yankees that netted righthanders Edwin Jackson and Ian Kennedy. They needed the help after allowing more runs than all but five teams last season, and their best hope for immediate in-house help took a hit when righthander Jarrod Parker needed Tommy John surgery in October.

If there was a silver lining to Arizona's struggles in 2009—other than getting the No. 6 overall pick in the 2010 draft—it was being able to trade several veterans for prospects. Brandon Allen (acquired from the White Sox for Tony Pena) and Tony Abreu (picked up from the Dodgers for Jon Garland) could start on the right side of the major league infield in 2010. The Diamondbacks also added depth with outfielder Cole Gillespie and righthander Roque Mercedes (from the Brewers for Felipe Lopez), and righty Kevin Mulvey (from the Twins for Jon Rauch).

Arizona also tried to restock its system by cashing in eight of the first 95 picks in the 2009 draft. After focusing on pitching in previous drafts, the

Arizona turned to farm director A.J. Hinch as manager after firing Bob Melvin in May

MORRIS FOSTOFF

TOP 30 PROSPECTS

1. Jarrod Parker, rhp	**16.** Cole Gillespie, of
2. Bobby Borchering, 3b	**17.** Keon Broxton, of
3. A.J. Pollock, of	**18.** Kevin Eichhorn, rhp
4. Brandon Allen, 1b	**19.** David Nick, 2b
5. Chris Owings, ss	**20.** Matt Helm, 1b/3b
6. Mike Belfiore, lhp	**21.** Patrick Schuster, lhp
7. Marc Krauss, of	**22.** Rossmel Perez, c
8. Ryan Wheeler, 1b	**23.** Josh Collmenter, rhp
9. Collin Cowgill, of	**24.** Enrique Burgos, rhp
10. Matt Davidson, 3b	**25.** John Hester, c
11. Bryan Augenstein, rhp	**26.** Leyson Septimo, lhp
12. Reynaldo Navarro, ss	**27.** Pedro Ciriaco, ss/2b
13. Paul Goldschmidt, 1b	**28.** Roque Mercedes, rhp
14. Eric Smith, rhp	**29.** Jordan Norberto, lhp
15. Wade Miley, lhp	**30.** Zach Kroenke, lhp

Diamondbacks used their first four picks, and 11 of their 15 in the first 10 rounds, to select position players. Six of those hitters cracked the Top 10, as did lefthander Mike Belfiore (supplemental first).

Former Blue Jays professional scout Mike Berger will oversee the new talent after replacing Hinch as farm director. Arizona still doesn't have many athletic, up-the-middle prospects beyond A.J. Pollock and Chris Owings. That's an issue for a team that has an opening at second base and saw its shortstop (Stephen Drew) and center fielder (Chris Young) perform well below expectations in 2009.

General Manager: Josh Byrnes. **Farm Director:** Mike Berger. **Scouting Director:** Tom Allison.

Class	Team	League	W	L	PCT	Finish*	Manager(s)
Majors	Arizona Diamondbacks	National	70	92	.432	t-13th (16)	Bob Melvin/A.J. Hinch
Triple-A	Reno Aces	Pacific Coast	79	64	.552	3rd (16)	Brett Butler
Double-A	Mobile BayBears	Southern	66	74	.471	5th (10)	Hector de la Cruz
High A	Visalia Rawhide	California	64	76	.457	6th (10)	Mike Bell
Low A	South Bend Silver Hawks	Midwest	59	78	.431	10th (14)	Mark Haley
Short-season	Yakima Bears	Northwest	28	48	.368	8th (8)	Bob Didier
Rookie	Missoula Osprey	Pioneer	40	36	.526	5th (8)	Audo Vicente
Overall 2009 Minor League Record			336	376	.472	26th (30)	

*Finish in overall standings (No. of teams in league). †League champion.

LAST YEAR'S TOP 30

Player	Pos.		Status
1.	Jarrod Parker, rhp		No. 1
2.	Gerardo Parra, of		Majors
3.	Daniel Schlereth, lhp		(Tigers)
4.	Mark Hallberg, ss/2b		Dropped out
5.	Wade Miley, lhp		No. 15
6.	Kevin Eichhorn, rhp		No. 18
7.	Cesar Valdez, rhp		Dropped out
8.	Billy Buckner, rhp		Majors
9.	Collin Cowgill, of		No. 9
10.	Reynaldo Navarro, ss		No. 12
11.	Barry Enright, rhp		Dropped out
12.	Daniel Stange, rhp		Dropped out
13.	Trevor Harden, rhp		Dropped out
14.	Pedro Ciriaco, ss/2b		No. 27
15.	Rossmel Perez, c		No. 22
16.	Evan Frey, of		Dropped out
17.	Bryan Shaw, rhp		Dropped out
18.	Ryne White, 1b		(Cubs)
19.	Josh Whitesell, 1b		Majors
20.	Tony Barnette, rhp		Dropped out
21.	Wes Roemer, rhp		Dropped out
22.	Cyle Hankerd, of		Dropped out
23.	Clay Zavada, lhp		Majors
24.	Isaias Asencio, of		Dropped out
25.	Kyler Newby, rhp		Dropped out
26.	Leyson Septimo, lhp		No. 26
27.	James Skelton, c		Dropped out
28.	Brooks Brown, rhp		(Tigers)
29.	Ed Easley, c		Dropped out
30.	Tyrell Worthington, of		Dropped out

BEST TOOLS

Best Hitter for Average	A.J. Pollock
Best Power Hitter	Bobby Borchering
Best Strike-Zone Discipline	Ryan Wheeler
Fastest Baserunner	Antonio Sepulveda
Best Athlete	Keon Broxton
Best Fastball	Jarrod Parker
Best Curveball	Jarrod Parker
Best Slider	Jarrod Parker
Best Changeup	Josh Collmenter
Best Control	Bryan Augenstein
Best Defensive Catcher	Rossmel Perez
Best Defensive Infielder	Reynaldo Navarro
Best Infield Arm	Pedro Ciriaco
Best Defensive Outfielder	A.J. Pollock
Best Outfield Arm	Jeremia Gomez

PROJECTED 2013 LINEUP

Catcher	Miguel Montero
First Base	Bobby Borchering
Second Base	Chris Owings
Third Base	Mark Reynolds
Shortstop	Stephen Drew
Left Field	Gerardo Parra
Center Field	A.J. Pollock
Right Field	Justin Upton
No. 1 Starter	Dan Haren
No. 2 Starter	Jarrod Parker
No. 3 Starter	Brandon Webb
No. 4 Starter	Edwin Jackson
No. 5 Starter	Ian Kennedy
Closer	Chad Qualls

TOP PROSPECTS OF THE DECADE

Year	Player, Pos.	2009 Org.
2000	John Patterson, rhp	Out of baseball
2001	Alex Cintron, ss	Mariners
2002	Luis Terrero, of	Kansas City (Northern)
2003	Scott Hairston, 2b	Athletics
2004	Scott Hairston, 2b	Athletics
2005	Carlos Quentin, of	White Sox
2006	Stephen Drew, ss	Diamondbacks
2007	Justin Upton, of	Diamondbacks
2008	Carlos Gonzalez, of	Rockies
2009	Jarrod Parker, rhp	Diamondbacks

TOP DRAFT PICKS OF THE DECADE

Year	Player, Pos.	2009 Org.
2000	Mike Schultz, rhp (2nd)	Hiroshima (Japan)
2001	Jason Bulger, rhp	Angels
2002	Sergio Santos, ss	White Sox
2003	Conor Jackson, of	Diamondbacks
2004	Stephen Drew, ss	Diamondbacks
2005	Justin Upton, of	Diamondbacks
2006	Max Scherzer, rhp	Diamondbacks
2007	Jarrod Parker, rhp	Diamondbacks
2008	Daniel Schlereth, lhp	Diamondbacks
2009	Bobby Borchering, 3b	Diamondbacks

LARGEST BONUSES IN CLUB HISTORY

Travis Lee, 1996	$10,000,000
Justin Upton, 2005	$6,100,000
John Patterson, 1996	$6,075,000
Stephen Drew, 2004	$4,000,000
Max Scherzer, 2006	$3,000,000

ARIZONA DIAMONDBACKS

TOP 2010 ROOKIE: Brandon Allen, 1b. Acquired for Tony Pena in July, he hit four homers after a late-August callup and will push for a starting job in spring training.

BREAKOUT PROSPECT: Matt Helm, 1b/3b. Injuries truncated his high school senior season and dropped him to the seventh round of the 2009 draft, but he can really hit when healthy.

SLEEPER: Pat McAnaney, lhp. He's not overpowering, but he used a quality changeup and command of three pitches to finish third in the California League in strikeouts (146 in 147 innings) in his first full pro season.

SOURCE OF TOP 30 TALENT			
Homegrown	26	Acquired	4
College	11	Trades	3
Junior college	1	Rule 5 draft	1
High school	9	Independent leagues	0
Draft-and-follow	0	Free agents/waivers	0
Nondrafted free agents	0		
International	5		

Numbers in parentheses indicate prospect rankings

LF
Marc Krauss (7)
Cole Gillespie (16)
Cyle Hankerd
Bobby Stone
Chris Rahl

CF
A.J. Pollock (3)
Keon Broxton (17)
Ollie Linton
Evan Frye

RF
Collin Cowgill (9)

3B
Bobby Borchering (2)
Matt Davidson (10)
Matt Helm (20)
Justin Parker
Clayton Conner

SS
Reynaldo Navarro (12)
Pedro Ciriaco (27)
Antonio Sepulveda
Brent Greer
Raul Navarro

2B
Chris Owings (5)
David Nick (19)
Mark Hallberg
Rusty Ryal

1B
Brandon Allen (4)
Ryan Wheeler (8)
Paul Goldschmidt (13)
Sean Coughlin

C
Rossmel Perez (22)
John Hester (25)
Jae Yun Kim
Ed Easley
Tyson Van Winkle

RHP

Starters	Relievers
Jarrod Parker (1)	Roque Mercedes (28)
Bryan Augenstein (11)	Daniel Stange
Eric Smith (14)	T.J. Hose
Kevin Eichhorn (18)	Kyler Newby
Joshua Collmenter (23)	Jose Marte
Enrique Burgos (24)	Bryan Shaw
Matt Torra	Scottie Allen
Trevor Harden	Bradin Hagens
Barry Enright	Chase Anderson
Wes Roemer	Jake Hale
Kevin Mulvey	Reid Mahon
Cesar Valdez	
Charles Brewer	
Ryan Cook	

LHP

Starters	Relievers
Mike Belfiore (6)	Leyson Septimo (26)
Wade Miley (15)	Jordan Norberto (29)
Patrick Schuster (21)	Zach Kroenke (30)
Pat McAnaney	Ryan Robowski
Thomas Layne	

2009

BEST PURE HITTER: The Diamondbacks signed 10 quality bats in the first eight rounds, so there's no shortage of candidates. 1B Ryan Wheeler (5) had the most spectacular debut, hitting .361/.462/.540 while reaching low Class A, but the best pure hitter is OF A.J. Pollock (1), who batted .377 in the Cape Cod League last summer and .271 in low Class A.

BEST POWER HITTER: 3Bs Bobby Borchering (1) and Matt Davidson (1s) ranked first and third on BA's predraft list of the top high school power hitters. Davidson won the home run derby at the 2008 Aflac game at Dodger Stadium, though Borchering has better bat speed. Neither has as much present power as 1B Paul Goldschmidt (8), who led the Rookie-level Pioneer League in homers (18) and slugging (.638).

FASTEST RUNNER: OF Keon Broxton (3) showed off his plus speed by topping the Pioneer League with nine triples.

BEST DEFENSIVE PLAYER: Pollock has good speed and fine instincts in center field, but Broxton has the tools to be a superior defender there.

BEST FASTBALL: RHP Scottie Allen (11) put on 18 pounds after signing and hit 95 mph by the end of the summer. RHP Eric Smith (2) gets heavy sink on his 90-92 mph fastball and posted a 2.0 groundout/airout ratio in his pro debut.

BEST SECONDARY PITCH: LHP Mike Belfiore's (1s) hard breaking ball is slightly better than Smith's.

BEST PRO DEBUT: Wheeler, who led the short-season Northwest League in on-base percentage (.461) and OPS (.999), and Goldschmidt. RHP Charles Brewer (12) topped the Pioneer League with seven wins while showing a 90-93 mph fastball.

BEST ATHLETE: Broxton originally signed a football scholarship to play wide receiver at Florida Atlantic before deciding to attend Santa Fe (Fla.) CC.

MOST INTRIGUING BACKGROUND: LHP Patrick Schuster (13) threw four consecutive no-hitters this spring, two shy of the national high school record. 1B Jake Williams (29, Matt), 3B Cade Kreuter (41, Chad) and OF Beau Amaral (45, Rich) are all sons of former big leaguers. The area scout for SS Taylor Wrenn (25) was his father Luke, while OF Tim Sherlock's (40) dad Glenn is Arizona's bullpen coach. Of those players, only Sherlock turned pro.

CLOSEST TO THE MAJORS: Pollock's combination of hitting ability, all-around tools and drive should get him to the big leagues before Belfiore and OF Marc Krauss (2), an advanced hitter whose pro debut was cut short by a right ankle injury.

BEST LATE-ROUND PICK: The Diamondbacks like several pitchers from the later rounds, including Brewer, Schuster, LHP Ryan Robowski (16) and RHP Jake Hale (27).

THE ONE WHO GOT AWAY: Wrenn, Arizona's highest unsigned pick, is a slick fielder who will replace 2009 first-rounder Grant Green at Southern California after transferring from Manatee (Fla.) CC.

ASSESSMENT: The Diamondbacks had seven picks in the first two rounds, and no team added as many gifted position players. Thinned out by promotions and trades in recent year, Arizona's farm system needed a talent infusion—and got it.

2008

LHP Daniel Schlereth (1) raced to the majors before getting included in a three-team blockbuster that brought Edwin Jackson and Ian Kennedy to Arizona. LHP Wade Miley (1s), RHP Kevin Eichhorn (3) and OF Colin Cowgill (5) are the best of the rest of this bunch.

GRADE: C

2007

RHP Jarrod Parker (1) is the system's best prospect, but he may miss all of 2010 following Tommy John surgery. RHP Barry Enright (1s) and C Ed Easley (1s) have been disappointments, though RHP Bryan Augenstein (7) already has pitched in the majors.

GRADE: B

2006

The Diamondbacks landed a pair of potential stud pitchers in RHP Max Scherzer (1) and LHP Brett Anderson (2), but dealt them for present stud Dan Haren and veterans Jackson and Kennedy. RHP Clay Zavada (30) bolstered Arizona's bullpen last season, while C John Hester (13) homered in his first big league at-bat.

GRADE: A

2005

Arizona set a bonus spending record that lasted until 2008, investing $6.1 million in star-in-the-making Justin Upton (1). The club used RHP Micah Owings (3) in a trade for Adam Dunn, and LHP Greg Smith (6) in the Haren deal. INF Rusty Ryal (14) got big league time in 2009.

GRADE: A

Draft analysis by Jim Callis. Numbers in parentheses indicate draft rounds.

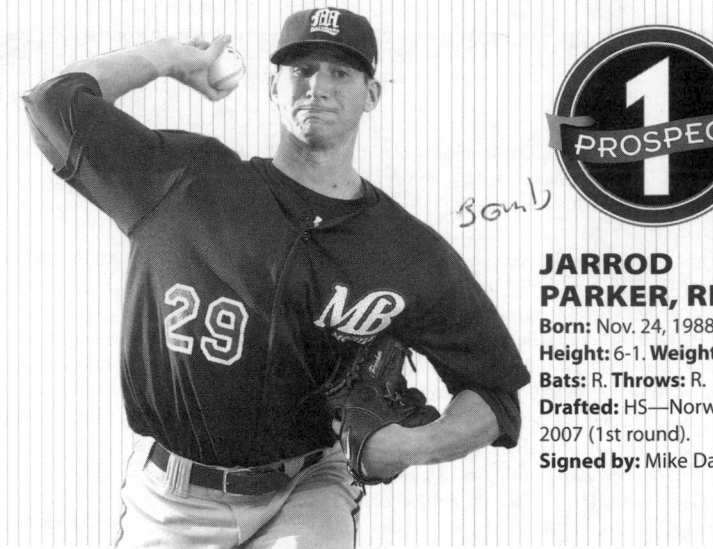

PROSPECT 1

JARROD PARKER, RHP

Born: Nov. 24, 1988.
Height: 6-1. **Weight:** 180.
Bats: R. **Throws:** R.
Drafted: HS—Norwell, Ind.,
2007 (1st round).
Signed by: Mike Daughtry.

If the Royals hadn't changed their minds on the day of the 2007 draft, they would have taken Josh Vitters second overall and the Cubs would have followed by selecting Parker. But Kansas City went with a different high school hitter, Mike Moustakas, so Vitters fell to Chicago and Parker fell to the Diamondbacks, who were thrilled to get him with the ninth overall pick. After signing late that summer for $2.1 million, Parker ranked as the low Class A Midwest League's No. 3 prospect in his 2008 pro debut. Parker needed just four starts at high Class A Visalia last April to earn a promotion to Double-A Mobile, and he rated as the Southern League's top pitching prospect despite being shut down for the season with elbow tightness in late July. He hoped rest and rehab would cure his elbow, and skipped planned stints with Team USA and in the Arizona Fall League. He started throwing side sessions again in September, but when his elbow didn't improve, he had Tommy John surgery in late October. Even if he misses all of 2010, Parker is still well ahead of the learning curve at age 21. His brother Justin, a third baseman, signed with Arizona as a sixth-round pick in 2008 and spent last season in low Class A.

When healthy, Parker sits at 93-95 mph and touches 97 with his fastball. His size and the ease with which he generates velocity earn him comparisons to Tim Lincecum. Parker offers three quality secondary pitches to go along with his heater. His 80-84 mph slider, a swing-and-miss pitch with late tilt and two-plane depth, rates a 70 on the 20-80 scouting scale. His curveball has classic 12-to-6 break. His changeup came a long way last season, showing flashes of becoming a plus pitch. He trusts his stuff, shows command of all four pitches and has a presence on the mound. He's athletic and repeats his delivery well. Though Parker needed reconstructive surgery, there are no red flags in his mechanics. Scouts always have been impressed with Parker's smooth, clean arm action and compact, easy delivery.

Outside of Parker's health, there's not much to quibble with. He'll miss all or most of the 2010 season, and may not regain his full stuff and command until mid-2011. He still needs to refine his overall feel for pitching, and he can get inconsistent with his location in the strike zone. He overthrows occasionally, leaving pitches up. His fastball doesn't have great late life and can get flat at times.

Before his elbow injury, Parker was on the verge of becoming the third high school pitcher to race from the 2007 draft to the majors, following Tigers righthander Rick Porcello and Giants lefthander Madison Bumgarner. Though it's obviously a setback, Tommy John surgery shouldn't have a long-term effect on Parker's value as a prospect because of the track record of pitchers recovering from elbow reconstruction. He still should be a bona fide top-of-the-rotation starter, it's just that his timetable will be delayed. If all goes well in his recovery, he could join the Diamondbacks late in the 2011 season.

Year	Club (League)	Class	W	L	ERA	G	GS	CG	SV	IP	H	R	ER	HR	BB	SO	AVG
2008	South Bend (MWL)	LoA	12	5	3.44	24	24	0	0	118	113	56	45	8	33	117	.251
2009	Visalia (CAL)	HiA	1	0	0.95	4	4	0	0	19	12	2	2	0	4	21	.179
	Mobile (SL)	AA	4	6	3.68	16	16	0	0	78	82	35	32	2	34	74	.272
MINOR LEAGUE TOTALS			17	11	3.31	44	44	0	0	215	207	93	79	10	71	212	.253

2 BOBBY BORCHERING, 3B

Buzz

BORN: Oct. 25, 1990. **B-T:** B-R. **HT.:** 6-4. **WT.:** 195. **DRAFTED:** HS—Fort Myers, Fla., 2009 (1st round). **SIGNED BY:** Ray Blanco.

In a deep 2009 high school draft class in Florida, Borchering was regarded as the best hitter available. The first of Arizona's five picks before the second round, he went 16th overall and signed for $1.8 million. He struggled early at Rookie-level Missoula, but went 9-for-28 with four doubles, two homers and 10 RBIs in six postseason games. Borchering draws comparisons to Chipper Jones because he's a Florida native with a similar frame who switch-hits and has a lot of pop in his bat. Borchering rated as the top prep power hitter in the draft and has the potential to be a middle-of-the-order force. Better from the left side of the plate, he has excellent bat speed and an advanced feel to hit. He has the arm strength to play third base. Borchering never will be a smooth defender. He'll have to work hard to stay at third base, though the Diamondbacks believe he can. His footwork has improved, but he'll have to get more consistent in fielding the ball cleanly and making accurate throws. He also needs to tighten his plate discipline, as he tends to chase high fastballs and low curveballs. Borchering will open his first full season at low Class A South Bend, probably alternating at third base and DH with supplemental first-rounder Matt Davidson. If Borchering has to eventually change positions, he'll have enough power to profile well at first base.

Year	Club (League)	Class	AVG	G	AB	R	H	2B	3B	HR	RBI	BB	SO	SB	OBP	SLG
2009	Missoula (PIO)	R	.241	22	87	10	21	8	1	2	11	5	27	0	.290	.425
MINOR LEAGUE TOTALS			.241	22	87	10	21	8	1	2	11	5	27	0	.290	.425

3 A.J. POLLOCK, OF

BORN: Dec. 5, 1987. **B-T:** R-R. **HT.:** 6-2. **WT.:** 200. **DRAFTED:** Notre Dame, 2009 (1st round). **SIGNED BY:** Mike Daughtry.

Pollock didn't have to make much of a transition after being drafted 17th overall in June, as both Notre Dame and Arizona's low Class A affiliate play in South Bend, Ind. Signed for $1.4 million, he first caught the Diamondbacks' attention by winning Cape Cod League MVP honors in the summer of 2008. Pollock's best tool is his bat, and his bat speed, strong hands and line-drive approach should allow him to hit for high average. He has gap power, slightly above-average speed and good instincts on the bases. He's a quality defender with an average arm in center field. In addition to his all-around athleticism, he also has strong makeup. Some scouts take a glass-half-empty view and say Pollock doesn't do anything particularly well beyond hit. He showed a tendency to get out on his front foot during the spring at Notre Dame, but he has a calmer approach with wood bats. His swing can get flat at times, limiting his power. Pollock projects as a solid major league leadoff hitter and center fielder, mostly because he knows how to affect games with his skill set. He could start 2010 in Double-A and will certainly get there at some point during the season. He's on the fast track to Arizona.

Year	Club (League)	Class	AVG	G	AB	R	H	2B	3B	HR	RBI	BB	SO	SB	OBP	SLG
2009	South Bend (MWL)	LoA	.271	63	255	36	69	12	3	3	22	16	36	10	.319	.376
MINOR LEAGUE TOTALS			.271	63	255	36	69	12	3	3	22	16	36	10	.319	.376

4 BRANDON ALLEN, 1B

Bomb

BORN: Feb, 12, 1986. **B-T:** L-R. **HT.:** 6-2. **WT.:** 235. **DRAFTED:** HS—Montgomery, Texas, 2004 (5th round). **SIGNED BY:** Paul Provas/Keith Staab (White Sox).

Allen looked like the White Sox's heir apparent to Paul Konerko after leading the high Class A Carolina League in slugging (.527) and homering twice off David Price in his first Double-A game in 2008. That changed in early July, when Chicago traded him for Tony Pena. Allen destroyed Triple-A pitching for six weeks, then hit four homers after the Diamondbacks called him up. A star linebacker in high school, Allen has huge raw power. For a big guy, he has some snap in his bat and doesn't have a long swing. He toned down his swing and hit more balls to the opposite field in 2009, allowing him to hit a career-high .298 in the minors. He does a good job of punishing mistakes. He has worked hard to improve his defense. Once Allen got to the major leagues, pitchers exploited him on the inner half. He's not fluid but manages to get the job done at first base, a far cry from the days when he projected as a DH. He has below-average speed, though he's not a baseclogger. Scouts compare him to Mike Jacobs, though Allen has much better plate discipline. He'll get a chance to win a job with the major league club in spring training.

ARIZONA DIAMONDBACKS

Year	Club (League)	Class	AVG	G	AB	R	H	2B	3B	HR	RBI	BB	SO	SB	OBP	SLG
2004	Bristol (APP)	R	.205	58	185	17	38	9	1	3	23	16	60	2	.280	.314
2005	Great Falls (PIO)	R	.264	66	231	41	61	11	2	11	42	32	69	7	.366	.472
2006	Kannapolis (SAL)	LoA	.213	109	395	36	84	17	2	15	68	22	126	6	.257	.380
2007	Kannapolis (SAL)	LoA	.283	129	516	84	146	39	5	18	93	39	124	7	.337	.483
2008	Winston-Salem (CAR)	HiA	.279	89	319	57	89	26	4	15	44	41	83	14	.372	.527
	Birmingham (SL)	AA	.275	41	153	30	42	6	2	14	31	19	41	3	.358	.614
2009	Birmingham (SL)	AA	.290	62	241	39	70	12	3	7	35	30	47	1	.372	.452
	Charlotte (IL)	AAA	.262	15	61	6	16	4	0	1	8	0	13	0	.262	.377
	Reno (PCL)	AAA	.324	38	145	33	47	8	1	12	32	20	25	6	.413	.641
	Arizona (NL)	MAJ	.202	32	104	13	21	7	0	4	14	12	40	0	.284	.385
MAJOR LEAGUE TOTALS			.202	32	104	13	21	7	0	4	14	12	40	0	.284	.385
MINOR LEAGUE TOTALS			.264	607	2246	343	593	132	20	96	376	219	588	46	.336	.469

5 CHRIS OWINGS, SS ✝

BORN: Aug. 12, 1991. **B-T:** R-R. **HT.:** 5-11. **WT.:** 170. **DRAFTED:** HS—Gilbert, S.C., 2009 (1st round supplemental). **SIGNED BY:** George Swain.

Owings moved up draft boards in the spring as he solidified himself as one of the best prep hitters available. Even more exciting than his bat, from the perspective of Arizona's scouts, was that he had the look of a young Craig Biggio. One of the youngest players in the draft, Owings signed for $950,000 as a sandwich pick and had no trouble with older competition, batting .306 in the Rookie-level Pioneer League. None of Owings' tools are outstanding, but they all grade out as solid across the board. He has a short swing and uses the whole field. As he has added strength, he has started to hit with more authority and should produce for average and gap power. He has drawn comparisons to Gordon Beckham and Aaron Hill, with less power. He's an average runner who shows soft hands and gets good carry on his throws. He plays with a full-throttle mentality at all times. Owings doesn't have traditional shortstop actions, and while he makes the routine plays, he may not make enough of the difficult ones to avoid a move to second base down the road. He'll have to show more plate discipline after drawing just three walks and striking out 25 times in his pro debut. Arizona will give Owings every chance to play shortstop, a position where it lacks a slam-dunk prospect. He'll begin his first full season in low Class A.

Year	Club (League)	Class	AVG	G	AB	R	H	2B	3B	HR	RBI	BB	SO	SB	OBP	SLG
2009	Missoula (PIO)	R	.306	24	108	20	33	5	1	2	10	3	25	3	.324	.426
MINOR LEAGUE TOTALS			.306	24	108	20	33	5	1	2	10	3	25	3	.324	.426

6 MIKE BELFIORE, LHP

BORN: Oct. 3, 1988. **B-T:** R-L. **HT.:** 6-3. **WT.:** 200. **DRAFTED:** Boston College, 2009 (1st round supplemental). **SIGNED BY:** Matt Merullo.

Belfiore was Boston College's first baseman and closer, at least until the team's 25-inning, 3-2 loss to Texas in last year's NCAA regionals. He pitched 9⅔ innings of scoreless relief, allowing three hits while striking out 11—and cementing himself as a potential starter. He had a successful pro debut in that role after signing for $725,000. Belfiore's best pitch is a heavy fastball that sits at 89-92 mph and tops out at 94. Opponents have a hard time lifting it, as shown by his 1.9 groundout/airout ratio and two homers allowed in 58 innings in the hitter-friendly Pioneer League. His 78-82 mph slider can be a plus pitch at times, and he started using his curveball more in instructional league. He has been mixing in more changeups after not throwing the pitch as a college reliever. He has a simple, repeatable delivery. Belfiore wore down at the end of the summer, but that should be less of an issue now that he's a full-time pitcher and will start to work deeper into games. He has a slight stab in the back of his arm swing, which costs him command. He needs to work on locating his pitches to both sides of the plate, and refine his curveball and changeup. If he can develop his secondary pitches, Belfiore can become a No. 3 starter in the big leagues. After exceeding Arizona's expectations in his pro debut, he'll jump to high Class A.

Year	Club (League)	Class	W	L	ERA	G	GS	CG	SV	IP	H	R	ER	HR	BB	SO	AVG
2009	Missoula (PIO)	R	2	2	2.17	14	11	0	0	58	59	29	14	2	13	55	.259
MINOR LEAGUE TOTALS			2	2	2.17	14	11	0	0	58	59	29	14	2	13	55	.259

7 MARC KRAUSS, OF

BORN: Oct. 5, 1987. **B-T:** L-R. **HT.:** 6-3. **WT.:** 235. **DRAFTED:** Ohio, 2009 (2nd round). **SIGNED BY:** Frankie Thon Jr.

Krauss exploded onto the prospect scene by leading the Cape Cod League in RBIs (34) and on-base percentage (.473) in the summer of 2008, and he nearly hit his way into the first round by batting .402 and setting Ohio school records for homers (27), RBIs (70) and slugging (.852) last spring. After signing for $550,000, he continued to hit in low Class A until he hurt his right ankle running into a wall in July, requiring surgery to remove bone chips. Krauss is a hitter first and a power threat second. His gap-to-gap approach yields consistent results, and he likes to hit the ball to the opposite field. He repeats his swing better than anyone in the system and consistently squares up pitches. Krauss also manages at-bats and identifies offspeed pitches well. Krauss isn't an instinctive defender, and a trial at third base in college didn't go well. His below-average speed and range limit him to left field or first base. He has some arm strength but needs to improve his throwing mechanics. Most of Krauss' value lies in his bat, but it should play at any level. He may return to South Bend to start 2010, but he won't remain there long. He could be the first player from Arizona's 2009 draft class to reach the majors.

Year	Club (League)	Class	AVG	G	AB	R	H	2B	3B	HR	RBI	BB	SO	SB	OBP	SLG
2009	South Bend (MWL)	LoA	.304	32	115	14	35	12	1	2	17	14	21	0	.377	.478
MINOR LEAGUE TOTALS			.304	32	115	14	35	12	1	2	17	14	21	0	.377	.478

8 RYAN WHEELER, 1B

BORN: July 10, 1988. **B-T:** L-R. **HT.:** 6-4. **WT.:** 220. **DRAFTED:** Loyola Marymount, 2009 (5th round). **SIGNED BY:** Hal Kurtzman.

A disappointing junior season at Loyola Marymount dropped Wheeler to the fifth round of the 2009 draft, where the Diamondbacks signed him for $160,000. Though he didn't enter the system until June, Wheeler was named Arizona's minor league player of the year. He led the short-season Northwest League in on-base percentage (.461) and OPS (.999), and topped those numbers after a late-season promotion to low Class A, where he batted cleanup in the Midwest League playoffs. Potentially the best offensive player in the system, Wheeler has a rhythmic, balanced swing. He has a feel for recognizing pitches and controls the strike zone well. He drives the ball from gap to gap and earns high marks for his plate coverage, particularly in his ability to drive the ball the other way. His offensive package reminds scouts of Joey Votto. An average defender at first base, Wheeler has solid hands and arm strength for the position. Wheeler's big body precludes a return to third base or left field, where he has dabbled in the past. He's a below-average runner. After his successful pro debut, there's no reason Wheeler can't open his first pro season in high Class A. His bat should enable him to move quickly.

Year	Club (League)	Class	AVG	G	AB	R	H	2B	3B	HR	RBI	BB	SO	SB	OBP	SLG
2009	Yakima (NWL)	SS	.363	64	234	44	85	20	3	5	36	37	28	7	.461	.538
	South Bend (MWL)	LoA	.345	8	29	4	10	1	1	1	5	5	4	0	.472	.552
MINOR LEAGUE TOTALS			.361	72	263	48	95	21	4	6	41	42	32	7	.462	.540

9 COLLIN COWGILL, OF

BORN: May 22, 1986. **B-T:** R-L. **HT.:** 5-9. **WT.:** 195. **DRAFTED:** Kentucky, 2008 (5th round). **SIGNED BY:** Matt Haas.

Cowgill missed the entire 2007 season at Kentucky with a broken hamate bone in his left hand, and he didn't play after June 14 last season because of a hamstring injury. In between, he led the Northwest League with 11 homers in just 20 games in his 2008 pro debut, and opened his first full pro season in high Class A. The Diamondbacks considered sending him to the Arizona Fall League but kept him in instructional league instead. For an undersized player, Cowgill has surprising power. He has great bat speed and takes advantage when pitchers make mistakes. One team official called Cowgill a gamer and compared him to Aaron Rowand with a better swing. Others compare him to Cody Ross. Cowgill has average speed and uses his instincts to steal bases and chase down balls in center field. His arm is solid. Already 23, Cowgill can't let injuries slow his development further. While he holds his own in center field, he ultimately projects as a right fielder. He can get overly aggressive at times and will chase pitches out of the zone, especially with two strikes. Cowgill earned the right to open 2010 in Double-A after hitting well in his two months at Visalia. On a contender, he profiles as a fourth outfielder who can provide righthanded pop and constant energy.

Year	Club (League)	Class	AVG	G	AB	R	H	2B	3B	HR	RBI	BB	SO	SB	OBP	SLG
2008	Yakima (NWL)	SS	.304	20	79	21	24	3	1	11	28	12	17	5	.415	.785
	South Bend (MWL)	LoA	.249	50	201	31	50	13	3	1	17	25	61	1	.346	.358
2009	Visalia (CAL)	HiA	.277	61	220	39	61	9	5	6	36	29	49	11	.373	.445
MINOR LEAGUE TOTALS			.270	131	500	91	135	25	9	18	81	66	127	17	.369	.464

10 MATT DAVIDSON, 3B

BORN: March 26, 1991. **B-T:** R-R. **HT.:** 6-3. **WT.:** 210. **DRAFTED:** HS—Yucaipa, Calif., 2009 (1st round supplemental). **SIGNED BY:** Jeff Mousser.

Davidson has been on scouts' radar screens since he started shining on the high school showcase circuit after his freshman year. He won the home run derby at the Aflac All-American High School Baseball Classic in the summer of 2008, and another at the National Classic tournament last spring. One of the best high school power hitters available in the draft, he went 35th overall and signed for $900,000. Because Arizona doesn't have a complex-based affiliate and first-round pick Bobby Borchering was assigned to Missoula, Davidson was sent to short-season Yakima. It was a tough assignment, as he hit .241/.312/.319 as the youngest regular in the Northwest League. He has plus-plus raw power, which he generates more with strength and leverage than bat speed. His swing mechanics, which feature a short backswing and a long follow-through, need refinement. He's a well below-average runner. Though Davidson has made significant defensive improvements since turning pro, some scouts whether he can stay at third base in the long run. His range, hands and footwork are questionable, but he does have the arm strength for the hot corner. He led NWL third basemen with a .934 fielding percentage. Davidson's potential to be a middle-of-the-order thumper has garnered him comparisons to Paul Konerko and Matt Williams. He'll open 2010 in low Class A South Bend, alternating with Borchering at third base and DH.

Year	Club (League)	Class	AVG	G	AB	R	H	2B	3B	HR	RBI	BB	SO	SB	OBP	SLG
2009	Yakima (NWL)	SS	.241	72	270	29	65	15	0	2	28	21	75	0	.312	.319
MINOR LEAGUE TOTALS			.241	72	270	29	65	15	0	2	28	21	75	0	.312	.319

11 BRYAN AUGENSTEIN, RHP

BORN: July 11, 1986. **B-T:** R-R. **HT.:** 6-6. **WT.:** 230. **DRAFTED:** Florida, 2007 (7th round). **SIGNED BY:** Luke Wrenn.

Augenstein raced through the minor leagues after signing as a seventh-round pick in 2007, making his major league debut last May. He got hit hard in two starts, then returned to the minors before resurfacing in Arizona's bullpen in September. Though Augenstein is 6-foot-6 and 230 pounds, he doesn't overpower hitters. He sits at 86-89 mph with his sinker, varying his arm angle and usually operating from a low slot. He also features a sweeping 76-79 mph slider and an improving 78-81 mph changeup. He pounds the strike zone and keeps the ball down in the zone, though big league hitters quickly realized that and were able to take advantage of him. Besides working higher in the zone on occasion, he also needs to add more bite to his slider so he can miss more bats. Those who like Augenstein's upside think he can be a solid fourth or fifth starter in the majors. Those who don't question whether he'll be able to get outs at the higher levels. Unless Augenstein wows the Diamondbacks in big league camp, he'll start 2010 in Triple-A.

Year	Club (League)	Class	W	L	ERA	G	GS	CG	SV	IP	H	R	ER	HR	BB	SO	AVG
2007	Missoula (PIO)	R	0	2	3.38	10	2	0	0	21	20	13	8	2	7	16	.250
2008	South Bend (MWL)	LoA	5	1	2.16	13	13	0	0	87	73	21	21	2	9	69	.224
	Visalia (CAL)	HiA	2	4	3.89	9	9	0	0	44	57	26	19	5	5	30	.318
2009	Reno (PCL)	AAA	2	5	5.50	8	7	0	0	36	43	23	22	2	7	29	.299
	Mobile (SL)	AA	5	0	0.99	9	9	0	0	46	27	5	5	0	8	36	.172
	Arizona (NL)	MAJ	0	1	7.94	7	2	0	0	17	23	16	15	2	6	6	.333
MAJOR LEAGUE TOTALS			0	1	7.94	7	2	0	0	17	23	16	15	2	6	6	.333
MINOR LEAGUE TOTALS			14	12	2.88	49	40	0	0	234	220	88	75	11	36	180	.248

12 REYNALDO NAVARRO, SS

BORN: Dec. 22, 1989. **B-T:** B-R. **HT.:** 5-10. **WT.:** 175. **DRAFTED:** HS—Gunabo, P.R., 2007 (3rd round). **SIGNED BY:** Ray Blanco.

After he spent his first two pro seasons in Rookie ball, the game started to slow down for Navarro in 2009. After making 66 errors in his first 128 games at shortstop, he made just 29 in 118 contests last season. A plus defender, he has good range to both sides, nimble feet and a solid-average arm. He still lays back on some balls he should charge and he'll rush plays at times, but he's much more consistent at shortstop. Though Navarro has yet to put up big offensive numbers, he showed improvement at the plate as well. Quiet and focused, he shows a repeatable swing and a line-drive approach from both sides. He did a better job of making contact in 2009, though he needs to further cut down his strikeouts and draw more walks. He's not very strong, but he can occasionally drive balls into the gaps and hit 25 doubles last year. A slightly above-average runner, he showed more savvy as a basestealer in 2009 than he had in a past. He projects as a quality defender who'll probably fit toward the bottom of a big league lineup. He's athletic enough to play a variety of positions if he's needed as a utilityman. He'll advance to high Class A in 2010.

Year	Club (League)	Class	AVG	G	AB	R	H	2B	3B	HR	RBI	BB	SO	SB	OBP	SLG
2007	Missoula (PIO)	R	.250	60	212	21	53	4	0	1	17	6	41	6	.274	.283
2008	Missoula (PIO)	R	.258	72	291	42	75	17	7	2	31	25	77	17	.323	.385
2009	South Bend (MWL)	LoA	.262	121	451	57	118	25	5	0	46	27	85	12	.308	.339
MINOR LEAGUE TOTALS			.258	253	954	120	246	46	12	3	94	58	203	35	.305	.341

13 PAUL GOLDSCHMIDT, 1B

BORN: Sept. 10, 1987. **B-T:** R-R. **HT.:** 6-4. **WT.:** 220. **DRAFTED:** Texas State, 2009 (8th round). **SIGNED BY:** Trip Couch.

Goldschmidt first stood out as a power-hitting corner infielder in 2006, when he teamed with Phillies prospect Kyle Drabek to lead The Woodlands (Texas) High to the national high school championship. Goldschmidt turned down the Dodgers as a 49th-rounder to attend Texas State, where he set a school record with 36 career homers and led NCAA Division I with 87 RBIs last spring. The Southland Conference's first repeat hitter of the year since future big leaguer Ben Broussard a decade earlier, he draws comparisons to Pete Incaviglia for his body type and massive raw power. After signing for $95,000 as an eighth-round pick, Goldschmidt led the Pioneer League in homers (18) and slugging (.638). He has a simple hitting approach and unloads on mistakes. He's an aggressive hitter who will have to prove he can make contact against more advanced pitching because his swing can get long and he can get pull-happy and spin off pitches on the outer half. He's a good athlete and runner for his size, but he's still a below-average runner and defender. His lack of range limits him to first base, and he's not smooth around the bag. Because the Diamondbacks have a number of corner-infield prospects—they selected four ahead of him in the 2009 draft—he may get a chance to play left field in the future. With Ryan Wheeler ticketed for high Class A, Goldschmidt figures to open 2010 in South Bend.

Year	Club (League)	Class	AVG	G	AB	R	H	2B	3B	HR	RBI	BB	SO	SB	OBP	SLG
2009	Missoula (PIO)	R	.334	74	287	51	96	27	3	18	62	36	74	4	.408	.638
MINOR LEAGUE TOTALS			.334	74	287	51	96	27	3	18	62	36	74	4	.408	.638

14 ERIC SMITH, RHP

BORN: Oct. 15, 1988. **B-T:** R-R. **HT.:** 6-3. **WT.:** 215. **DRAFTED:** Rhode Island, 2009 (2nd round). **SIGNED BY:** Matt Merullo.

When Smith first arrived at Rhode Island, he was a gangly freshman who looked like the basketball player he was in high school. Smith, who played on the same high school travel teams as A.J. Pollock, filled out his frame and added strength. He helped his cause in the 2009 draft with back-to-back strong outings against Miami and Cal State Fullerton, and wound up becoming the highest draft pick in Rams history when Arizona took him in the second round. Signed for $605,700, he capped his pro debut with three solid starts in low Class A. Smith pounds the zone with a 90-92 mph sinker that's difficult to lift. He features three secondary pitches: an 84-86 mph slider that's a plus offering at times, a solid-average changeup and a curveball. He needs to improve his feel with his secondary pitches, though he has shown the ability to add and subtract from his slider. He also must work on commanding his pitches to both sides of the plate and on building up his endurance. Smith, who has a ceiling as a No. 3 starter, will open his first full season in high Class A.

Year	Club (League)	Class	W	L	ERA	G	GS	CG	SV	IP	H	R	ER	HR	BB	SO	AVG
2009	Missoula (PIO)	R	0	3	4.21	9	7	0	0	26	22	14	12	1	16	21	.232
	South Bend (MWL)	LoA	0	0	2.76	3	3	0	0	16	16	7	5	2	6	10	.250
MINOR LEAGUE TOTALS			0	3	3.64	12	10	0	0	42	38	21	17	3	22	31	.239

15 WADE MILEY, LHP

BORN: Nov. 13, 1986. **B-T:** L-L. **HT.:** 6-2. **WT.:** 190. **DRAFTED:** Southeastern Louisiana, 2009 (1st round supplemental). **SIGNED BY:** Trip Couch.

Miley was one of four Louisiana prep lefties in 2005 who became supplemental first-round picks. Beau Jones (Braves) and Sean West (Marlins) signed out of high school, while Miley and Jeremy Bleich (Yankees) went in the sandwich round after three years of college. Signed for $887,000, Miley spent most of his first full-season in low Class A. His reviews, like his performance, were inconsistent. At his best, he showed three quality pitches in a 90-91 mph fastball that touched 93, a promising low-80s slider and a solid changeup with some fade and sink. At other times, his fastball sat at 87-88 mph, his slider became slurvy and his changeup lacked deception because he slowed his arm speed. Miley needs to do a more consistent job throwing strikes and locating his pitches, especially inside against righthanders. He throws across his body, which makes him deceptive but detracts from his command. Miley has the upside of a No. 3 starter but also could wind up as a reliever. He should reach

ARIZONA DIAMONDBACKS

Double-A at some point in 2010.

Year	Club (League)	Class	W	L	ERA	G	GS	CG	SV	IP	H	R	ER	HR	BB	SO	AVG
2008	Yakima (NWL)	SS	1	1	4.91	7	0	0	0	11	11	6	6	0	5	11	.250
2009	South Bend (MWL)	LoA	5	9	4.12	21	21	0	0	114	127	60	52	8	29	91	.287
	Visalia (CAL)	HiA	1	1	4.80	3	3	0	0	15	18	10	8	0	4	11	.295
MINOR LEAGUE TOTALS			7	11	4.25	31	24	0	0	140	156	76	66	8	38	113	.285

16 COLE GILLESPIE, OF

BORN: June 20, 1984. **B-T:** R-R. **HT.:** 6-1. **WT.:** 205. **DRAFTED:** Oregon State, 2006 (3rd round). **SIGNED BY:** Brandon Newell (Brewers).

Gillespie helped Oregon State win the 2006 College World Series and quickly became one of the Brewers' best outfield prospects after signing as a third-round pick that summer. When Milwaukee needed a second baseman last July, it packaged Gillespie and righthander Roque Mercedes to get Felipe Lopez from the Diamondbacks. Fellow July trade acquisition Brandon Allen and Gillespie are the most advanced position prospects in the system. He has a steady set of tools that rate as solid average across the board. He's a gap-to-gap hitter with decent power. He knows how to put together a professional at-bat and has good plate discipline, though he can get pull-happy at times. An average runner, he can swipe a few bases because of his baseball IQ. With average speed, athleticism and arm strength, he fits best in left field but saw time at all three outfield spots after he was traded. Gillespie doesn't figure to get the opportunity to play every day for Arizona, but he should be a solid fourth outfielder and could get that chance at some point in 2010.

Year	Club (League)	Class	AVG	G	AB	R	H	2B	3B	HR	RBI	BB	SO	SB	OBP	SLG
2006	Helena (PIO)	R	.344	51	186	49	64	12	1	8	31	40	34	18	.464	.548
2007	Brevard County (FSL)	HiA	.267	129	438	75	117	25	3	12	62	72	95	16	.378	.420
2008	Huntsville (SL)	AA	.281	131	462	73	130	38	4	14	79	75	102	17	.386	.472
2009	Brevard County (FSL)	HiA	.349	12	43	10	15	2	3	1	9	7	11	4	.431	.605
	Nashville (PCL)	AAA	.242	75	236	29	57	12	5	7	27	31	56	6	.332	.424
	Reno (PCL)	AAA	.304	42	138	33	42	6	4	5	27	27	31	8	.418	.514
MINOR LEAGUE TOTALS			.283	440	1503	269	425	95	20	47	235	252	329	69	.390	.466

17 KEON BROXTON, OF

BORN: May 7, 1990. **B-T:** R-R. **HT.:** 6-3. **WT.:** 187. **DRAFTED:** Santa Fe (Fla.) CC, 2009 (3rd round). **SIGNED BY:** Luke Wrenn.

Broxton originally signed a football scholarship to play wide receiver for Florida Atlantic, but decided to attend Sante Fe (Fla.) CC instead. After turning down the Phillies as a 29th-round pick in 2008, he returned for his sophomore season and starred as the Saints finished second at the Junior College World Series. The highest draft pick in Santa Fe history, he signed for $358,000 as a third-round pick. While Broxton still needs a lot of refinement, he's loaded with tools. He has a similar body type and similar tools to Chris Young, and Arizona hopes he develops into the Chris Young of 2007. Broxton has above-average raw power and speed. He has a quick bat that can handle most fastballs but he struggles with offspeed stuff. He has a maximum-effort approach and long swing that resulted in 93 strikeouts in 72 pro games. He's going to have to cut back on his stroke and avoid chasing pitches out of the zone. Broxton played shortstop in high school and has the ability to play all three outfield positions with his plus range and solid arm. He'll patrol center field this season in low Class A, where he'll have to show that he can make the necessary adjustments to hit.

Year	Club (League)	Class	AVG	G	AB	R	H	2B	3B	HR	RBI	BB	SO	SB	OBP	SLG
2009	Missoula (PIO)	R	.246	72	272	38	67	11	9	11	37	19	93	6	.302	.474
MINOR LEAGUE TOTALS			.246	72	272	38	67	11	9	11	37	19	93	6	.302	.474

18 KEVIN EICHHORN, RHP

BORN: Feb. 6, 1990. **B-T:** R-R. **HT.:** 6-0. **WT.:** 170. **DRAFTED:** HS—Aptos, Calif., 2008 (3rd round). **SIGNED BY:** Darold Brown.

Eichhorn went to the Little League World Series in 2002 with the Aptos, Calif., team that was coached by his father Mark, who pitched 11 seasons in the major leagues. A third-round pick in 2008, Kevin has pitched just 19 innings since signing late that summer for $500,000. He had an elbow hiccup in his first spring training, and minor surgery kept him from reporting to Missoula before late July. Eichhorn sits at 87-91 mph with his fastball, has a good three-quarters breaking ball and shows feel for a changeup. It's already a solid three-pitch mix, and he can add velocity once he puts on his lean body with more muscle. He's a quality athlete who also would have played shortstop had he attended Santa Clara. His repeatable delivery should allow him to throw strikes. He's mature for his age and shows good aptitude on the mound. Eichhorn is ready for full-season ball and should open 2010 in low Class A.

Year	Club (League)	Class	W	L	ERA	G	GS	CG	SV	IP	H	R	ER	HR	BB	SO	AVG
2008	Missoula (PIO)	R	0	0	6.75	2	0	0	0	3	2	2	2	0	1	2	.222
2009	Missoula (PIO)	R	0	2	3.38	10	0	0	0	16	13	7	6	1	9	25	.224
MINOR LEAGUE TOTALS			0	2	3.86	12	0	0	0	19	15	9	8	1	10	27	.224

19 DAVID NICK, 2B

BORN: Feb 3, 1990. **B-T:** R-R. **HT.:** 6-2. **WT.:** 175. **DRAFTED:** HS—Cypress, Calif., 2009 (4th round). **SIGNED BY:** Jeff Mousser.

Nick came out of the same Cypress (Calif.) High program that produced former big leaguer Troy O'Leary and first-round picks Scott Moore and Josh Vitters. A fourth-round pick in June, Nick received a $225,000 bonus. He has unorthodox hitting and throwing mechanics, but he gets the job done. At the plate, he uses a wide stance with little load or movement, then flicks violently at the ball to create pop. He stays inside the ball well and sprays the ball to all fields with decent authority. Nick moved from shortstop in high school to second base as a pro, in large part because of his below-average arm strength and unusual throwing motion. He does make accurate throws, but he needs to improve his footwork to get rid of the ball more quickly. Nick was old for a high school signee at 19, but he's well ahead of his years in baseball intelligence. He's a pesky, instinctive player who can steal a few bases with his average speed. None of his tools projects as better than average, but he profiles as an offensive-minded second baseman. He'll start the year in low Class A.

Year	Club (League)	Class	AVG	G	AB	R	H	2B	3B	HR	RBI	BB	SO	SB	OBP	SLG
2009	Missoula (PIO)	R	.286	66	273	46	78	18	3	6	35	22	49	16	.351	.440
MINOR LEAGUE TOTALS			.286	66	273	46	78	18	3	6	35	22	49	16	.351	.440

20 MATT HELM, 1B/3B

BORN: Sept. 1, 1990. **B-T:** R-R. **HT.:** 6-2. **WT.:** 190. **DRAFTED:** HS—Chandler, Ariz., 2009 (7th round). **SIGNED BY:** Rodney Davis.

Playing in the Diamondbacks' backyard, Helm was seen early and often by the club. That worked to Arizona's advantage because other teams didn't get much of a chance to evaluate him last spring, when knee and ankle injuries sidelined him for much of his high school senior season. The Diamondbacks took him in the seventh round and signed him at the Aug. 17 deadline for $500,000. Helm has present strength and the ability to put a charge in the baseball. His hitting ability and his power are his calling cards. His swing gets a little long at times, and he'll chase pitches out of the zone on occasion. Repetition and learning what pitches he can drive will be crucial to his development. Though Helm is a slightly below-average runner, he has a quick first step at third base and a strong arm. Arizona drafted him with the idea of playing him at the hot corner, but fellow 2009 draftees Bobby Borchering and Matt Davidson need reps there as well. For that reason, Helm played first base after joining Yakima in late August, and he saw time at second base and in the outfield during instructional league. Borchering, Davidson and Helm all figure to be at South Bend in 2010, so Helm may have to shuffle between several positions.

Year	Club (League)	Class	AVG	G	AB	R	H	2B	3B	HR	RBI	BB	SO	SB	OBP	SLG
2009	Yakima (NWL)	SS	.291	16	55	6	16	1	0	1	5	4	16	2	.339	.364
MINOR LEAGUE TOTALS			.291	16	55	6	16	1	0	1	5	4	16	2	.339	.364

21 PATRICK SCHUSTER, LHP

BORN: Oct. 30, 1990. **B-T:** R-L. **HT.:** 6-2. **WT.:** 165. **DRAFTED:** HS—New Port Richey, Fla., 2009 (13th round). **SIGNED BY:** Luke Wrenn.

Schuster became the center of national attention in the spring when he threw four consecutive no-hitters—two short of the national high school record—and generated nearly as much hype as No. 1 overall pick Stephen Strasburg. Besides the fanfare, there are few similarities between the two pitchers. Clubs weren't sure exactly what to make of Schuster's slingshot delivery or the prospect of signing him away from a commitment to Florida, so he was available for the Diamondbacks in the 13th round. They signed him shortly before the deadline for $450,000. Schuster has a lot of moving parts in his delivery and varies his arm slots, making it difficult for hitters to pick his pitches his up. His 89-92 mph sinker and lefty funk were tough for high schoolers to handle, but there are questions as to how well his stuff will translate against more advanced hitters. Schuster's fastball has sneaky carry and has touched 94 at times. He also throws an upper-70s curveball with good snap and a low-80s slider with sweeping bite from his low three-quarters arm slot. His changeup is a work in progress. Depending on how Schuster fills out physically, he could be a back-end starter or a lefty specialist. He'll open 2010 in low Class A.

Year	Club (League)	Class	W	L	ERA	G	GS	CG	SV	IP	H	R	ER	HR	BB	SO	AVG
2009	Missoula (PIO)	R	0	0	3.60	5	0	0	0	5	4	2	2	0	4	6	.211
MINOR LEAGUE TOTALS			0	0	3.60	5	0	0	0	5	4	2	2	0	4	6	.211

22 ROSSMEL PEREZ, C

BORN: Aug. 26, 1989. **B-T:** B-R. **HT.:** 5-10. **WT.:** 180. **SIGNED:** Venezuela, 2006. **SIGNED BY:** Miguel Nava.

The best defensive catcher in the system, Perez led the Midwest League by throwing out 44 percent of basestealers in 2009, his first year in full-season ball. He has above-average arm strength, recording pop times of 1.9 seconds, and is a good receiver. Despite his youth, he received strong reviews for his ability to handle a pitching staff. He has a good understanding of the game, embraces catching and brings energy to the position. The question with Perez is how much offense he'll be able to provide. His flat, line-drive stroke isn't conducive to power, and he slugged just .317 last season. He does control the strike zone and make consistent contact, so he should hit for a decent average. With his well-below-average speed and tendency to hit the ball on the ground, he hits into a lot of double plays. Perez has been likened to a switch-hitting version of Mike LaValliere, who carved out a 12-year career in the majors, and projects as a platoon player or backup in the majors. He'll get every opportunity to play in high Class A this year.

Year	Club (League)	Class	AVG	G	AB	R	H	2B	3B	HR	RBI	BB	SO	SB	OBP	SLG
2006	Diamondbacks (DSL)	R	.155	32	71	7	11	2	0	0	5	10	12	0	.307	.183
2007	Diamondbacks (DSL)	R	.306	39	111	8	34	4	1	0	5	28	19	2	.469	.360
2008	Missoula (PIO)	R	.243	43	144	15	35	8	0	0	11	16	13	0	.323	.299
2009	South Bend (MWL)	LoA	.272	97	353	29	96	16	0	0	35	30	31	1	.343	.317
MINOR LEAGUE TOTALS			.259	211	679	59	176	30	1	0	56	84	75	3	.358	.306

23 JOSH COLLMENTER, RHP

BORN: Feb. 7, 1986. **B-T:** R-R. **HT.:** 6-4. **WT.:** 235. **DRAFTED:** Central Michigan, 2007 (15th round). **SIGNED BY:** Matt Haas.

Collmenter doesn't look pretty and isn't overpowering, but he misses bats and has pitched his way into prospect status. Though he had a successful career at Central Michigan, his thick body and mixed signals about his signability dropped him to the 15th round of the 2007 draft, where he signed for $80,000. He led the Northwest League with a 2.71 ERA in his pro debut, and he topped the high Class A California League with 152 strikeouts in 145 innings last season. Collmenter's over-the-top delivery may make scouts cringe, but it creates deception because hitters don't see it very often. His fastball usually sits at 86-88 but it's hard to square up because of its natural cutting action. At times, his heater can reach the low 90s. His changeup is a strikeout pitch, and he also uses a slow curveball. Collmenter has tremendous feel for pitching, keeping hitters off balance by adding and subtracting from each of his pitches. He has been known to experiment on the mound, throwing an eephus pitch and knuckleball in college. Collmenter will have to prove himself again in 2010, this time in Double-A, but he's starting to look like a back-of-the-rotation option.

Year	Club (League)	Class	W	L	ERA	G	GS	CG	SV	IP	H	R	ER	HR	BB	SO	AVG
2007	Yakima (NWL)	SS	6	3	2.71	14	12	0	0	66	60	22	20	4	21	57	.244
2008	South Bend (MWL)	LoA	12	8	3.41	27	27	0	0	145	126	62	55	8	47	123	.230
2009	Visalia (CAL)	HiA	8	10	4.15	27	27	1	0	145	127	76	67	8	55	152	.238
MINOR LEAGUE TOTALS			26	21	3.58	68	66	1	0	357	313	160	142	20	123	332	.236

24 ENRIQUE BURGOS, RHP

BORN: Nov. 23, 1990. **B-T:** R-R. **HT.:** 6-4. **WT.:** 200. **DRAFTED:** Panama, 2007. **SIGNED BY:** Junior Noboa/Jose Diaz Perez.

The Diamondbacks shy away from big-bonus players in Latin America, preferring instead to spread their money among several players each summer. Burgos, who signed for $295,000 out of Panama in 2007, received the largest bonus Arizona has given to an international player since Josh Byrnes became general manager. His father Enrique Sr. pitched briefly in the majors. Burgos got hammered in his U.S. debut last summer, which was to be expected with an 18-year-old pitching in an extreme hitter's league against older competition. His stuff is much more impressive than his 6.26 ERA at Missoula. He sits at 90-94 mph with a fastball that flashes cutting and sinking action, not necessarily by design. He throws a 79-83 mph slurve with sharp three-quarters break. He also has a solid 80-83 mph changeup. Burgos has a loose arm and delivers the ball from a high three-quarters slot, creating good angle to the plate. He has long arms and his delivery can get awkward at times, costing him control. He'll have to polish his mechanics and avoid overthrowing. Burgos probably will open 2010 in extended spring training before reporting to Yakima or Missoula in June.

Year	Club (League)	Class	W	L	ERA	G	GS	CG	SV	IP	H	R	ER	HR	BB	SO	AVG
2008	Diamondbacks (DSL)	R	2	0	3.92	10	10	0	0	41	35	19	18	2	26	41	.238
2009	Missoula (PIO)	R	5	3	6.26	16	16	0	0	65	77	50	45	10	39	61	.292
MINOR LEAGUE TOTALS			7	3	5.35	26	26	0	0	106	112	69	63	12	65	102	.273

25 JOHN HESTER, C

BORN: Sept. 14, 1983. **B-T:** R-R. **HT.:** 6-3. **WT.:** 220. **DRAFTED:** Stanford, 2006 (13th round). **SIGNED BY:** Fred Castello.

Hester has gone from organizational player to big leaguer in just three short years, blasting a 420-foot homer to dead center at Chase Field in his first at-bat with the Diamondbacks last August. He sat for two seasons at Stanford behind future big leaguers Ryan Garko and Donny Lucy before becoming the Cardinal's starting catcher in 2005-06. The Diamondbacks signed Hester for $1,000 as a 13th-round pick, more for his big, physical frame than any standout tool. He made steady if unspectacular progress through the minors before taking his game up a notch in 2009. He has the strength for big-time pull power, though he employs an opposite-field approach. While his swing can get long at times, he did a better job of making contact last season. He's no blazer but runs well for a catcher, capable of taking an extra base or surprising opponents with an occasional steal. Hester has decent catch-and-throw skills and threw out 29 percent of basestealers last season. With Chris Snyder expected to be healthy again and back up Miguel Montero in 2010, Hester will return to Triple-A and wait for a call from Arizona.

Year	Club (League)	Class	AVG	G	AB	R	H	2B	3B	HR	RBI	BB	SO	SB	OBP	SLG
2006	Missoula (PIO)	R	.271	56	192	36	52	16	4	6	41	27	52	6	.370	.490
2007	Visalia (CAL)	HiA	.263	79	297	38	78	16	1	10	43	22	64	4	.316	.424
2008	Mobile (SL)	AA	.268	92	306	38	82	26	2	11	49	16	78	3	.302	.474
2009	Reno (PCL)	AAA	.328	92	329	61	108	31	5	9	66	22	65	13	.375	.535
	Arizona (NL)	MAJ	.250	15	28	4	7	2	0	1	4	2	7	0	.300	.429
MAJOR LEAGUE TOTALS			.250	15	28	4	7	2	0	1	4	2	7	0	.300	.429
MINOR LEAGUE TOTALS			.285	319	1124	173	320	89	12	36	199	87	259	26	.339	.481

26 LEYSON SEPTIMO, LHP

BORN: July 7, 1985. **B-T:** L-L. **HT.:** 6-0. **WT.:** 150. **SIGNED:** Dominican Republic, 2003. **SIGNED BY:** Junior Noboa.

Septimo had little success as a position player, batting .253/.312/.348 in five pro seasons and standing out mostly with his arm strength in right field. The Diamondbacks converted him to the mound after the 2007 season and have protected him on the 40-man roster after each of the last two seasons. Few lefthanders can throw as hard as Septimo, who has a 92-97 mph fastball that touches triple-digits. He has a loose arm with whip and fires the ball from a low three-quarters slot that makes it even tougher to pick up his pitches. If hitters look for his heat, Septimo can cross them up with a slider or changeup. While he has racked up 113 strikeouts in 98 innings, he understandably still is learning the nuances of pitching. He has trouble locating his pitches and getting ahead in the count, leading to too many baserunners. If he can put everything together, scouts envision him becoming a harder-throwing version of Damaso Marte. In 2010, Septimo will try to conquer Double-A after posting a 7.85 ERA there last season.

Year	Club (League)	Class	AVG	G	AB	R	H	2B	3B	HR	RBI	BB	SO	SB	OBP	SLG
2003	Diamondbacks (DSL)	R	.214	52	182	20	39	10	3	0	21	23	57	1	.319	.302
2004	Diamondbacks (DSL)	R	.276	63	221	29	61	9	3	2	25	14	41	8	.335	.371
2005	Yakima (NWL)	SS	.241	67	237	20	57	11	2	2	21	10	51	2	.272	.329
2006	South Bend (MWL)	LoA	.251	132	529	79	133	22	5	6	51	36	112	10	.310	.346
2007	Visalia (CAL)	HiA	.271	100	362	54	98	18	2	5	42	23	67	12	.322	.373
2009	Mobile (SL)	AA	1.000	12	1	0	1	0	0	0	0	0	0	0	1.000	1.000
MINOR LEAGUE TOTALS			.254	426	1532	202	389	70	15	15	160	106	328	33	.312	.349

Year	Club (League)	Class	W	L	ERA	G	GS	CG	SV	IP	H	R	ER	HR	BB	SO	AVG
2008	Visalia (CAL)	HiA	0	2	5.49	27	0	0	1	41	42	27	25	4	33	44	.263
2009	Visalia (CAL)	HiA	2	1	3.52	26	0	0	6	38	29	18	15	1	26	44	.212
	Mobile (SL)	AA	0	1	7.85	19	0	0	3	18	20	17	16	2	18	25	.278
MINOR LEAGUE TOTALS			2	4	5.16	72	0	0	10	98	91	62	56	7	77	113	.247

27 PEDRO CIRIACO, SS/2B

BORN: Sept. 27, 1985. **B-T:** R-R. **HT.:** 6-0. **WT.:** 160. **SIGNED:** Dominican Republic, 2003. **SIGNED BY:** Junior Noboa.

Ciriaco's package of raw tools has been among the best in the system since he signed in 2003, but it has been a slow process to refine them. He has the potential to impact with his glove and feet, but his offensive game is still a work in progress. Ciriaco had a career year when he repeated the hitter-friendly California League in 2008. While he hit .296 in Double-A last season, he totaled only 22 extra-base hits and 10 walks. After making good swing adjustments in 2008, he didn't hit the ball with much authority last year. He needs to refine his strike-zone judgment so he can take advantage of more hitter's counts and get on base more often. He's a plus runner and adept at stealing bases. Defense comes much more easily to Ciriaco than hitting. Managers rated him the best defensive shortstop and strongest infield arm in the Southern League in 2009. He has good range and soft hands. Ciriaco saw action at second base last season, preparing him for a possible future as a utilityman. He headed to the Arizona Fall League after the season but didn't show any improvements at the plate. He should open 2010 in Triple-A.

Year	Club (League)	Class	AVG	G	AB	R	H	2B	3B	HR	RBI	BB	SO	SB	OBP	SLG
2003	Diamondbacks (DSL)	R	.231	57	221	40	51	10	2	0	16	16	34	14	.290	.294
2004	Diamondbacks (DSL)	R	.349	67	252	45	88	11	4	1	18	19	33	29	.401	.437
2005	Missoula (PIO)	R	.240	69	254	28	61	9	4	2	31	7	50	7	.264	.331
2006	South Bend (MWL)	LoA	.264	128	550	77	145	15	5	2	32	32	96	19	.308	.320
2007	Visalia (CAL)	HiA	.251	119	463	61	116	14	5	3	39	20	81	20	.286	.322
2008	Visalia (CAL)	HiA	.310	124	520	85	161	26	5	5	61	18	89	40	.333	.408
2009	Mobile (SL)	AA	.296	121	469	56	139	15	3	4	54	16	71	38	.319	.367
MINOR LEAGUE TOTALS			.279	685	2729	392	761	100	28	17	251	128	454	167	.314	.355

28 ROQUE MERCEDES, RHP

BORN: Sept. 28, 1986. **B-T:** B-R. **HT.:** 6-3. **WT.:** 185. **SIGNED:** Dominican Republic, 2004. **SIGNED BY:** Fernando Arango/Fausto Sosa Pena (Brewers).

Along with Cole Gillespie, Mercedes joined the Diamondbacks in the Felipe Lopez trade with the Brewers last July. His career started to take off when Milwaukee moved him to the bullpen two months into the 2008 season. Working in relief, Mercedes sits at 89-93 mph with his sinker. He has a whip-like motion and gets tremendous dive on his sinker when he keeps it down in the zone. His low-80s slider has the chance to be a plus pitch if it gains more consistency. He also has a changeup, though he doesn't use it much as a reliever. Scouts have compared him physically to LaTroy Hawkins. Mercedes needs to work on repeating his delivery and commanding his pitches. He doesn't have the pure stuff to be a closer or set-up man, but he could develop into a seventh-inning reliever. After finishing last year in Double-A, he'll return there in 2010 and should reach Triple-A before season's end.

Year	Club (League)	Class	W	L	ERA	G	GS	CG	SV	IP	H	R	ER	HR	BB	SO	AVG
2005	Brewers (AZL)	R	2	3	6.60	14	8	0	0	44	53	42	32	5	34	45	.294
2006	Helena (PIO)	R	5	5	4.92	15	9	0	0	60	57	42	33	7	21	29	.243
2007	West Virginia (SAL)	LoA	0	4	7.26	12	8	0	0	40	51	38	32	7	18	23	.313
	Helena (PIO)	R	7	4	3.75	15	15	0	0	84	88	49	35	7	20	70	.263
2008	West Virginia (SAL)	LoA	5	5	4.30	30	13	0	3	113	112	59	54	14	27	111	.252
2009	Brevard County (FSL)	HiA	1	1	1.08	29	0	0	6	42	26	7	5	0	15	45	.179
	Mobile (SL)	AA	1	0	3.32	15	0	0	1	19	14	7	7	2	10	25	.200
MINOR LEAGUE TOTALS			21	22	4.44	130	53	0	10	401	401	244	198	42	145	348	.255

29 JORDAN NORBERTO, LHP

BORN: Dec. 8, 1986. **B-T:** L-L. **HT.:** 6-0. **WT.:** 195. **SIGNED:** Dominican Republic, 2004. **SIGNED BY:** Junior Noboa.

Norberto hit the wall as a starting pitcher in low Class A in 2007-08, but found more success after moving to the bullpen in July of the latter season. Last year, his first as a full-time reliever, he had mixed results, impressing in the hitter-friendly California League but scuffling after a promotion to Double-A. Norberto has good velocity for a lefthander, with a fastball that ranges from 89-95 mph and usually settles in around 92. It features late, sinking life. He's still searching for a reliable second pitch. His hard curveball is a fringe-average pitch, and he has mostly scrapped the changeup he used as a starter. He's still more thrower than pitcher and hasn't learned to control the strike zone. The Diamondbacks like Norberto's pure arm strength and competitiveness, and they think he can make a difference in their big league bullpen in the near future. Scouts compare him to a smaller version of J.C. Romero.

Year	Club (League)	Class	W	L	ERA	G	GS	CG	SV	IP	H	R	ER	HR	BB	SO	AVG
2004	Diamondbacks (DSL)	R	0	0	9.00	3	1	0	0	4	6	4	4	0	6	2	.353
2005	Diamondbacks (DSL)	R	8	4	2.24	15	14	1	0	68	37	24	17	0	38	102	.157
2006	Missoula (PIO)	R	3	2	3.09	16	16	0	0	76	59	30	26	4	40	64	.216
2007	South Bend (MWL)	LoA	6	7	5.28	21	21	0	0	102	102	67	60	10	46	111	.266
2008	South Bend (MWL)	LoA	5	7	5.31	31	18	0	0	102	108	72	60	15	56	109	.276
2009	Visalia (CAL)	HiA	4	1	1.61	29	0	0	2	45	36	9	8	1	22	59	.226
	Mobile (SL)	AA	0	2	7.99	19	0	0	2	24	29	23	21	4	18	30	.302
MINOR LEAGUE TOTALS			26	23	4.20	134	70	1	4	420	377	229	196	34	226	477	.242

30 ZACH KROENKE, LHP

BORN: April 21, 1984. **B-T:** R-L. **HT.:** 6-2. **WT.:** 212. **DRAFTED:** Nebraska, 2005 (5th round). **SIGNED BY:** Steve Lemke (Yankees).

Kroenke was a member of Nebraska's rotation for three years in college, often slotting in behind current big leaguers Brian Duensing and Joba Chamberlain. A fifth-round pick by the Yankees in 2005, Kroenke shifted to the bullpen two years later. He has been effective in the relief role, going 14-1 the last two seasons and showing enough to warrant getting pick in the major league phase of the last two Rule 5 drafts. The Marlins returned him to the Yankees after his fastball sat at 86-88 mph early in spring training last year. Kroenke pitched at 89-91 mph during the season and touched 93 in the Arizona Fall League, though he also posted a 5.28 ERA in 15 AFL innings. Kroenke commands his average slider fairly well and also throws a fringy changeup. Diamondbacks general manager Josh Byrnes said the club sees Kroenke as more than just a lefty specialist. He has a good chance to make Arizona's Opening Day roster and will become a free agent if he doesn't, because he was outrighted when Florida sent him back to New York last year.

Year	Club (League)	Class	W	L	ERA	G	GS	CG	SV	IP	H	R	ER	HR	BB	SO	AVG
2005	Yankees (GCL)	R	0	1	4.50	1	1	0	0	2	4	2	1	0	0	2	.400
	Staten Island (NYP)	SS	1	1	2.54	11	5	0	2	39	30	14	11	2	15	28	.219
2006	Tampa (FSL)	HiA	0	3	8.36	4	4	0	0	14	23	19	13	0	8	8	.354
	Charleston (SAL)	LoA	8	6	3.58	25	20	0	0	113	124	65	45	9	41	86	.277
2007	Trenton (EL)	AA	0	1	9.42	15	0	0	2	14	21	16	15	5	12	12	.344
	Tampa (FSL)	HiA	2	2	2.27	29	0	0	0	44	34	16	11	2	19	33	.209
2008	Trenton (EL)	AA	6	0	3.09	37	0	0	1	44	28	16	15	4	26	44	.187
	Scranton/W-B (IL)	AAA	1	0	1.80	4	0	0	0	10	7	3	2	0	2	10	.206
2009	Scranton/W-B (IL)	AAA	7	1	1.99	36	2	0	4	72	54	24	16	4	30	55	.213
MINOR LEAGUE TOTALS			25	15	3.30	162	32	0	9	352	325	175	129	26	153	278	.246

Atlanta Braves

BY BILL BALLEW

The Braves' recent rebuilding effort advanced to the next stage in 2009. They won 86 games, their most since their 14th straight and most recent playoff appearance in 2005, and contended into the final week of the season.

The offseason acquisitions of veterans Kenshin Kawakami, Derek Lowe and Javier Vazquez solidified the rotation. Atlanta took heat for releasing Tom Glavine after he completed a rehab assignment, but his departure led to the arrival of rookie righthander Tommy Hanson, who lived up to his billing as the organization's top prospect. The pitching additions helped the Braves improve from 12th in the National League in runs allowed in 2008 to fourth last year.

Atlanta retooled its lineup as well, with less effect, ranking sixth in the NL in scoring for the second straight season. The Braves reacquired Adam LaRoche at midseason after Casey Kotchman didn't provide enough production at first base, and Martin Prado proved ready for prime time when given the opportunity to play regularly while shuffling around the infield.

Two past No. 1 prospects in the outfield proved less effective. The insertion of rookie Jordan Schafer in center field didn't last, as Schafer struggled with a wrist injury that eventually required surgery following his demotion to Triple-A. Atlanta filled that hole by trading for Nate McLouth in June. A month later, the Braves pulled the plug on Jeff Francoeur, dealing him to the Mets.

The Braves will continue to evolve in 2010, which is expected to be manager Bobby Cox's swan song. The fourth-winningest manager of all time, he has skippered the team since mid-1990. Chipper Jones is also nearing the end of his Hall of Fame career, and he expressed frustration with his performance late last season.

While Jones has no obvious heir, more young talent is on the way. Jason Heyward, Baseball America's Minor League Player of the Year, will give the lineup a major jolt when he arrives in 2010. First baseman Freddie Freeman also should crack the lineup in the near future, and Atlanta still has high hopes for Schafer. Lefthander Mike Minor, the No. 7 overall pick in the 2009 draft, is expected to advance rapidly.

In another major change, scouting director Roy Clark left in October to become an assistant general manager with the Nationals. Clark had worked for the Braves for 20 years and had run their drafts since 2000. Atlanta promoted special assistant/major league scout Tony DeMacio to replace him.

Former No. 1 prospect Jordan Schafer endured a difficult rookie season in Atlanta

MORRIS FOSTOFF

TOP 30 PROSPECTS

1. Jason Heyward, of	16. Robinson Lopez, rhp
2. Freddie Freeman, 1b	17. Mycal Jones, ss
3. Julio Teheran, rhp	18. Brandon Hicks, ss
4. Mike Minor, lhp	19. Brett DeVall, lhp
5. Craig Kimbrel, rhp	20. Juan Abreu, rhp
6. Christian Bethancourt, c	21. Caleb Brewer, rhp
7. Randall Delgado, rhp	22. Richard Sullivan, lhp
8. Zeke Spruill, rhp	23. Cole Rohrbough, lhp
9. Cody Johnson, of	24. Kyle Cofield, rhp
10. Adam Milligan, of	25. Jose Ortegano, lhp
11. J.J. Hoover, rhp	26. Scott Diamond, lhp
12. Dimasther Delgado, lhp	27. Jesus Sucre, c
13. Brett Oberholtzer, lhp	28. Paul Clemens, rhp
14. David Hale, rhp	29. Riaan Spanjer-Furstenburg, 1b
15. Tyler Stovall, lhp	30. Jonny Venters, lhp

DeMacio had a mixed record as Orioles scouting director from 1999-2004, when he had 10 first-round choices (Brian Roberts and Nick Markakis among them) and five sandwich picks but had to contend with owner Peter Angelos' meddling and thriftiness.

The Braves increased their emphasis on the foreign front with the hiring of international scouting director Johnny Almaraz in 2006, and those efforts are about to bear fruit. Righthanders Julio Teheran and Randall Delgado, catcher Christian Bethancourt and lefty Dismather Delgado have proven to be as good as advertised. Atlanta opened a complex in the Canary Islands last February, in hopes of developing European talent.

General Manager: Frank Wren. **Farm Director:** Kurt Kemp. **Scouting Director:** Tony DeMacio.

Class	Team	League	W	L	PCT	Finish*	Manager(s)
Majors	Atlanta Braves	National	86	76	.531	7th (16)	Bobby Cox
Triple-A	Gwinnett Braves	International	81	63	.563	4th (14)	Dave Brundage
Double-A	Mississippi Braves	Southern	65	73	.471	4th (10)	Phillip Wellman
High A	Myrtle Beach Pelicans	Carolina	53	84	.387	8th (8)	Rocket Wheeler
Low A	Rome Braves	South Atlantic	66	73	.475	11th (16)	Randy Ingle
Rookie	Danville Braves	Appalachian	47	21	.691	†1st (10)	Paul Runge
Rookie	GCL Braves	Gulf Coast	26	34	.433	13th (16)	Luis Ortiz
Overall 2009 Minor League Record			338	348	.493	18th (30)	

*Finish in overall standings (No. of teams in league). †League champion.

LAST YEAR'S TOP 30

Player, Pos.		Status
1.	Tommy Hanson, rhp	Majors
2.	Jason Heyward, of	No. 1
3.	Jordan Schafer, of	Majors
4.	Gorkys Hernandez, of	(Pirates)
5.	Freddie Freeman, 1b	No. 2
6.	Cole Rohrbough, lhp	No. 23
7.	Jeff Locke, lhp	(Pirates)
8.	Julio Teheran, rhp	No. 3
9.	Kris Medlen, rhp	Majors
10.	Craig Kimbrel, rhp	No. 5
11.	Brandon Hicks, ss	No. 18
12.	Cody Johnson, of	No. 9
13.	Randall Delgado, rhp	No. 7
14.	Brett DeVall, lhp	No. 19
15.	Zeke Spruill, rhp	No. 8
16.	Tyler Stovall, lhp	No. 15
17.	Edgar Osuna, lhp	(Royals)
18.	Braeden Schlehuber, c	Dropped out
19.	Eric Campbell, 3b	(Released)
20.	Matt Kennelly, c	Dropped out
21.	Luis Sumoza, of	Dropped out
22.	Stephen Marek, rhp	Dropped out
23.	Paul Clemens, rhp	No. 28
24.	J.J. Hoover, rhp	No. 11
25.	Chad Rodgers, lhp	Dropped out
26.	Scott Diamond, lhp	No. 26
27.	Jacob Thompson, rhp	Dropped out
28.	James Parr, rhp	Dropped out
29.	Todd Redmond, rhp	Dropped out
30.	Christian Bethancourt, c	No. 6

BEST TOOLS

Best Hitter for Average	Jason Heyward
Best Power Hitter	Cody Johnson
Best Strike-Zone Discipline	Jason Heyward
Fastest Baserunner	Kyle Rose
Best Athlete	Mycal Jones
Best Fastball	Juan Abreu
Best Curveball	Caleb Brewer
Best Slider	Cory Gearrin
Best Changeup	Dimasther Delgado
Best Control	Mike Minor
Best Defensive Catcher	Christian Bethancourt
Best Defensive Infielder	Brandon Hicks
Best Infield Arm	Brandon Hicks
Best Defensive Outfielder	Jason Heyward
Best Outfield Arm	Jason Heyward

PROJECTED 2013 LINEUP

Catcher	Brian McCann
First Base	Freddie Freeman
Second Base	Martin Prado
Third Base	Mycal Jones
Shortstop	Yunel Escobar
Left Field	Nate McLouth
Center Field	Jordan Schafer
Right Field	Jason Heyward
No. 1 Starter	Tommy Hanson
No. 2 Starter	Jair Jurrjens
No. 3 Starter	Julio Teheran
No. 4 Starter	Mike Minor
No. 5 Starter	Javier Vazquez
Closer	Craig Kimbrel

TOP PROSPECTS OF THE DECADE

Year	Player, Pos.	2009 Org.
2000	Rafael Furcal, ss	Dodgers
2001	Wilson Betemit, ss	White Sox
2002	Wilson Betemit, ss	White Sox
2003	Adam Wainwright, rhp	Cardinals
2004	Andy Marte, 3b	Indians
2005	Jeff Francoeur, of	Mets
2006	Jarrod Saltalamacchia, c	Rangers
2007	Jarrod Saltalamacchia, c	Rangers
2008	Jordan Schafer, of	Braves
2009	Tommy Hanson, rhp	Braves

TOP DRAFT PICKS OF THE DECADE

Year	Player, Pos.	2009 Org.
2000	Adam Wainwright, rhp	Cardinals
2001	Macay McBride, lhp	Tigers
2002	Jeff Francoeur, of	Mets
2003	Luis Atilano, rhp (1st round supp.)	Nationals
2004	Eric Campbell, 3b (2nd round)	Braves
2005	Joey Devine, rhp	Athletics
2006	Cody Johnson, of	Braves
2007	Jason Heyward, of	Braves
2008	Brett DeVall, lhp (1st round supp.)	Braves
2009	Mike Minor, lhp	Braves

LARGEST BONUSES IN CLUB HISTORY

Mike Minor, 2009	$2,420,000
Jeff Francoeur, 2002	$2,200,000
Kenshin Kawakami, 2009	$2,000,000
Matt Belisle, 1998	$1,750,000
Jason Heyward, 2007	$1,700,000

ATLANTA BRAVES

TOP 2010 ROOKIE: Jason Heyward, of. Baseball's best prospect is ready to become the Braves' long-term answer in right field.

BREAKOUT PROSPECT: Robinson Lopez, rhp. The unheralded Dominican had no problem jumping to the United States for his pro debut.

SLEEPER: Cory Gearrin, rhp. The sidearmer is tough on righthanders with his slider and could wind up in the Atlanta bullpen in the near future.

SOURCE OF TOP 30 TALENT			
Homegrown	29	Acquired	1
College	5	Trades	0
Junior college	6	Rule 5 draft	0
High school	8	Independent leagues	0
Draft-and-follow	2	Free agents/waivers	1
Nondrafted free agents	1		
International	7		

Numbers in parentheses indicate prospect rankings.

LF
Cody Johnson (9)
Adam Milligan (10)
Willie Cabrera
Robby Hefflinger

CF
Matt Young
Cole Miles
Juan Flores
Kyle Rose
L.V. Ware

RF
Jason Heyward (1)
Luis Sumoza
Cory Harrilchak
Concepcion Rodriguez

3B
Donell Linares
Jordan Kreke

SS
Mycal Jones (17)
Brandon Hicks (18)
Matt Weaver
Chris Lovett

2B
Brooks Conrad
Diory Hernandez
Yoel Campusano
Travis Jones

1B
Freddie Freeman (2)
Riann Spanjer-Furstenburg (29)
Barbaro Canizares
Gerry Rodriguez
Alberto Odreman

C
Christian Bethancourt (6)
Jesus Sucre (27)
Matt Kennelly
Braeden Schlehuber
Clint Sammons
Jace Whitmer

RHP	
Starters	**Relievers**
Julio Teheran (3)	Craig Kimbrel (5)
Randall Delgado (7)	Juan Abreu (20)
Zeke Spruill (8)	Caleb Brewer (21)
J.J. Hoover (11)	Paul Clemens (28)
David Hale (14)	Stephen Marek
Robinson Lopez (16)	Cory Gearrin
Kyle Cofield (24)	Jaye Chapman
Ryan Weber	Thomas Berryhill
Todd Redmond	Cory Rasmus
Jacob Thompson	James Parr
Ryne Reynoso	Brandon Beachy
Erik Cordier	Michael Broadway
Aaron Northcraft	Jeff Lyman
	Tim Gustafson
	Brett Butts
	Rudy Darrow
	Deunte Heath
	Angelo Paulino
	Benino Pruneda

LHP	
Starters	**Relievers**
Mike Minor (4)	Jose Ortegano (25)
Dimasther Delgado (12)	Jonny Venters (30)
Brett Oberholtzer (13)	Lee Hyde
Tyler Stovall (15)	Kevin Gunderson
Brett DeVall (19)	
Richard Sullivan (22)	
Cole Rohrbough (23)	
Scott Diamond (26)	
Chris Masters	
Matt Crim	

2009   BONUSES: $4.4 MILLION

BEST PURE HITTER: OF Cory Harrilchak (14) hit .410 in 2008, making him the only Elon player to top .400 since the program moved to NCAA Division I in 2000. He batted .324/.401/.441 with 19 steals in the Rookie-level Appalachian League.

BEST POWER HITTER: Six-foot-2, 235-pound 1B Riann Spanjer-Furstenburg (16) has the most usable power right now, while 6-foot-5, 225-pound OF Robby Hefflinger (7) has more raw pop.

FASTEST RUNNER: OF Kyle Rose (8), who can cover 60 yards in 6.3 seconds, led the Rookie-level Gulf Coast League with 26 steals in 30 attempts. SS Mycal Jones (4) is a step behind with a 6.4 time in the 60 and led the Appy League in runs (50) and triples (six).

BEST DEFENSIVE PLAYER: With his smooth actions, good range and solid arm, Jones should develop into a quality shortstop. SS Matt Weaver (9) has good tools for the position, too.

BEST FASTBALL: RHP Thomas Berryhill (5) is just 5-foot-10, but he sits at 93-95 and maxes out at 98 coming out of the bullpen. RHP David Hale (3) works at 93-94 mph and touches 96, and the former Princeton two-way player may add more velocity now that he's concentrating on pitching.

BEST SECONDARY PITCH: LHP Mike Minor (1) had one of the best changeups in the draft, and his slider is plus at times. LHP Chris Masters' (11) curveball and Hale's slider are the best breaking pitches in this crop. Hale, Berryhill and Masters are products of the vaunted East Cobb program in suburban Atlanta, one of the Braves' favorite hunting grounds.

BEST PRO DEBUT: Spanjer-Furstenburg was the Appy League MVP and batting champ (.359). LHP Matt Crim (21), a strike thrower whose fastball reaches 93 mph, was the Appy pitcher of the year after leading the league in wins and going 10-2, 3.18. Masters went 8-4, 1.42 and topped the Appy League with 85 strikeouts (versus just nine walks) in 70 innings.

BEST ATHLETE: Jones.

MOST INTRIGUING BACKGROUND: Spanjer-Furstenburg is a native South African who was on his nation's provisional World Baseball Classic roster.

CLOSEST TO THE MAJORS: Minor was one of the most polished pitchers in the 2009 draft. He went straight to low Class A, where he had a 0.64 ERA and a 17-0 K-BB ratio in 14 innings, then headed to the Arizona Fall League.

BEST LATE-ROUND PICK: Spanjer-Furstenburg. RHP Ryan Weber (22) was the best pitcher on the 2008 U.S. national junior team, which also included 2009 first-rounders Matt Purke and Jacob Turner.

Weber is just 5-foot-11 and pitches in the high 80s with his fastball, but his changeup, slider and command are all assets.

THE ONE WHO GOT AWAY: OF Josh Conway (42), who will be a two-way player at Coastal Carolina.

ASSESSMENT: The Braves coveted Georgia high school righthander Zack Wheeler (who went one pick ahead of them) and were limited by financial constraints, but they still were thrilled to add Minor. Atlanta continued to mine junior colleges as much as any club, signing five juco players (Jones, Hefflinger, Rose, Weaver, SS Chris Lovett) in the first 12 rounds.

2008   BONUSES: $5.1 MILLION

The Braves' top three picks were high school arms who have yet to distinguish themselves: LHPs Brett DeVall (1s) and Tyler Stovall (2), and RHP Zeke Spruill (2). After that, they focused on juco players and found several interesting ones, led by RHP Craig Kimbrel (3) and OF Adam Milligan (6).

GRADE: C

2007   BONUSES: $4.9 MILLION

OF Jason Heyward (1) is the game's top prospect, and Atlanta plans on building its lineup around him and 1B Freddie Freeman (2) in the near future. 3B Jon Gilmore (1s) helped fetch Javier Vazquez in a trade last offseason.

GRADE: A

2006   BONUSES: $8.1 MILLION

The Braves had six choices in the top two rounds, but the only one with much promise is OF Cody Johnson (1), a slugger with contact issues. RHP Kris Medlen (10) shored up the big league bullpen as a rookie in 2009.

GRADE: C

2005   BONUSES: $4.2 MILLION*

Atlanta worked some draft-and-follow magic in the later rounds, finding a future ace in RHP Tommy Hanson (22) as well as slugging C Tyler Flowers (33), the key to the Vazquez deal. SS Yunel Escobar (2) is a career .301 hitter in the majors, while RHP Joey Devine (1) has flourished since being traded to the A's. The Braves still have hopes for OF Jordan Schafer (3), too.

GRADE: A

---

*Draft analysis by Jim Callis. Numbers in parentheses indicate draft rounds. *Bonuses for 2005 are first 10 rounds only.*

JASON HEYWARD, OF

Born: Aug. 9, 1989.
Height: 6-4. **Weight:** 220.
Bats: Left. **Throws:** Left.
Drafted: HS—McDonough, Ga., 2007 (1st round).
Signed by: Brian Bridges.

Bomb

DAVID STONER

The 14th overall pick in the 2007 draft, Heyward signed for $1.7 million and since has emerged as the top position prospect in baseball. He earned Baseball America's Minor League Player of the Year award after hitting .323/.408/.555 at three minor league stops, including a dominating performance at Double-A Mississippi. An oblique injury slowed him in early May, and he missed the Carolina League-California League All-Star game with a hip injury. Heyward recovered in time to play in the Futures Game and raised the issue about whether the Braves should call him up for the stretch drive shortly after his 20th birthday. He ranked as the No. 1 prospect in the high Class A Carolina and Double-A Southern leagues.

The main reason Heyward remained on the draft board so long in 2007 centered on the limited number of times he swung the bat as a high school senior. Opponents rarely pitched to him and he refused to compromise his impressive command of the strike zone. He has continued to demonstrate uncanny patience as he has climbed the ladder in pro ball. That type of feel for the game is just one of the many intangibles Heyward brings to the field. He has a plan every time he steps in the box and makes adjustments between at-bats.

Heyward has outstanding bat speed, uses the entire field well and can drive the ball to the opposite field. His short swing is a bit unorthodox, but it works and he should hit for a high average with a lot of power. Despite standing 6-foot-4, Heyward has solid-average speed. He has outstanding instincts on the basepaths and plus range in right field. His impressive body control allows him to make diving catches with relative ease, and his plus arm is one of the strongest in the minors with velocity, carry and accuracy on his throws. He also takes good routes on fly balls.

Heyward briefly struggled with quality changeups when he reached Double-A but quickly adapted. Injuries are the other concern. They've limited him to just 876 pro at-bats, and he played in just 99 games in 2009 because of the oblique and hip injuries, plus a jammed heel in August. Then his Arizona Fall League stint was cut short with a hamstring strain that was also causing back inflammation. He needs to prove he's not brittle.

Scouts who follow the Braves say Heyward was the best player they saw in the minor leagues last season. With the trade of former golden boy Jeff Francoeur in July and the expected free-agent departure of Garret Anderson, there are openings for Heyward to make his major league debut sooner rather than later. Atlanta wants to be patient, but he has improved every time he has been challenged at a higher level, including a stint in big league camp last spring as a non-roster invitee. Even if he opens 2010 at Triple-A Gwinnett, Heyward will be starting in Atlanta at some point during the year, and he has all the ability to emerge as one of the game's premier players.

Year	Club (League)	Class	AVG	G	AB	R	H	2B	3B	HR	RBI	BB	SO	SB	OBP	SLG
2007	Braves (GCL)	R	.296	8	27	1	8	4	0	1	5	2	4	1	.355	.556
	Danville (APP)	R	.313	4	16	3	5	1	0	0	1	1	5	0	.353	.375
2008	Rome (SAL)	LoA	.323	120	449	88	145	27	6	11	52	49	74	15	.388	.483
	Myrtle Beach (CAR)	HiA	.182	7	22	3	4	2	0	0	4	2	4	0	.240	.273
2009	Myrtle Beach (CAR)	HiA	.296	49	189	34	56	12	0	10	31	21	30	4	.369	.519
	Mississippi (SL)	AA	.352	47	162	32	57	13	4	7	30	28	19	5	.446	.611
	Gwinnett (IL)	AAA	.364	3	11	3	4	0	0	0	2	2	2	1	.462	.364
MINOR LEAGUE TOTALS			.318	238	876	164	279	59	10	29	125	105	138	26	.391	.508

2 FREDDIE FREEMAN, 1B   *Reach*

BORN: Sept. 12, 1989. **B-T:** L-R. **HT.:** 6-5. **WT.:** 220. **DRAFTED:** HS—Orange, Calif., 2007 (2nd round). **SIGNED BY:** Tom Battista.

The youngest player to sign out of the 2007 draft, Freeman continues to be Robin to Jason Heyward's Batman. He reached Double-A at age 19 last summer and hit .319/.354/.493 in his first month there before lingering soreness in his left wrist hampered his production. He missed the last two weeks, but didn't need surgery and headed to the Arizona Fall League. Freeman has been an RBI machine at every level, thriving with runners in scoring position. He drives the ball with consistency with a sweet, fluid swing, and scouts believe his doubles will become homers as he gains experience and strength. Comparisons to Keith Hernandez and Mark Grace with more power have become commonplace because of his defense, which managers rated the best among first basemen in both the Carolina and Southern leagues last season. Freeman runs well enough for a big man but never will be noted for his speed. His attacking approach at the plate doesn't lend itself to walks, but Atlanta gladly will sacrifice some on-base percentage for RBIs. The Braves will seek a stopgap solution at first base for 2010, with an eye on turning the position over to Freeman the next season. With him and Heyward, the Braves should be set at the right-side corners for the foreseeable future.

Year	Club (League)	Class	AVG	G	AB	R	H	2B	3B	HR	RBI	BB	SO	SB	OBP	SLG
2007	Braves (GCL)	R	.268	59	224	24	60	7	0	6	30	7	33	1	.295	.379
2008	Rome (SAL)	LoA	.316	130	491	70	155	33	7	18	95	46	84	5	.378	.521
2009	Myrtle Beach (CAR)	HiA	.302	70	255	43	77	19	0	6	34	26	41	1	.394	.447
	Mississippi (SL)	AA	.248	41	149	15	37	8	0	2	24	11	19	0	.308	.342
MINOR LEAGUE TOTALS			.294	300	1119	152	329	67	7	32	183	90	177	7	.356	.452

3 JULIO TEHERAN, RHP ⊣

BORN: Jan. 27, 1991. **B-T:** R-R. **HT.:** 6-2. **WT.:** 160. **SIGNED:** Colombia, 2007. **SIGNED BY:** Miguel Teheran/Carlos Garcia.

The Braves signed Teheran for $850,000, the largest bonus given to a pitcher on the international market in 2007. After pitching sparingly in 2008 because of shoulder tendinitis, Teheran returned to the Rookie-level Appalachian League last summer and ranked as the loop's top prospect. Teheran throws easy heat with plus command and mound presence beyond his years. His fastball resides at 92-96 mph and holds its velocity throughout the game. His sharp, mid-70s curveball has good depth and can be a plus pitch, particularly after he tightened its spin. His 79-82 mph changeup is also an above-average pitch at times, with depth, fade and screwball-like movement. He has impressive poise that some scouts believe borders on cockiness. Teheran is still learning how to pitch. His physical stamina needs some work, and scouts have some concerns about his mechanics, which aren't effortless. He has a long arm rotation in the back of his herky-jerky delivery that creates deception but attracts questions about his durability. Teheran has all the ingredients to develop into a frontline starter. He's expected to return to low Class A Rome to open the 2010 slate. While the Braves will be cautious due to his youth and lack of physical maturity, Teheran could accelerate his timetable.

Year	Club (League)	Class	W	L	ERA	G	GS	CG	SV	IP	H	R	ER	HR	BB	SO	AVG
2008	Danville (APP)	R	1	2	6.60	6	6	0	0	15	18	12	11	2	4	17	.305
2009	Danville (APP)	R	2	1	2.68	7	7	0	0	44	36	17	13	2	7	39	.229
	Rome (SAL)	LoA	1	3	4.78	7	7	0	0	38	42	20	20	2	11	28	.288
MINOR LEAGUE TOTALS			4	6	4.11	20	20	0	0	96	96	49	44	6	22	84	.265

4 MIKE MINOR, LHP ⊥

BORN: Dec. 26, 1987. **B-T:** R-L. **HT.:** 6-3. **WT.:** 200. **DRAFTED:** Vanderbilt, 2009 (1st round). **SIGNED BY:** Brian Bridges.

Drafted in the 13th round out of high school, Minor was the Southeastern Conference freshman of the year in 2007 and Baseball America's Summer Player of the Year in 2008. After a 6-6, 3.90 junior season, Minor signed for $2.42 million, a club record and the most ever for a No. 7 overall pick. Minor's repertoire consists of four pitches, with his plus changeup rating as his best offering. His fastball has excellent movement and sits in the upper 80s, and he is capable of increasing and reducing the velocity of the pitch to keep hitters off balance. Both his command and control are outstanding, and he didn't walk a batter in 14 innings after signing. His pickoff move is also a significant weapon. Minor still is trying to determine which breaking ball to work with. He threw an above-average slider with good depth during his first two years at Vanderbilt, but he had trouble snapping the pitch and locating it after adding a curveball last spring. He's not overpowering and his repertoire is similar to that of former Vanderbilt ace Jeremy Sowers, who hasn't been able to finesse his way past big league hitters. After pitching in the Arizona Fall League, Minor could open his first

RODGER WOOD

full season in Double-A. His greatest attribute is his overall pitching savvy, which should make him at least a middle-of-the-rotation starter in the big leagues.

Year	Club (League)	Class	W	L	ERA	G	GS	CG	SV	IP	H	R	ER	HR	BB	SO	AVG
2009	Rome (SAL)	LoA	0	1	0.64	4	4	0	0	14	10	1	1	0	0	17	.208
MINOR LEAGUE TOTALS			0	1	0.64	4	4	0	0	14	10	1	1	0	0	17	.208

5 CRAIG KIMBREL, RHP +

BORN: May 28, 1988. **B-T:** R-R. **HT.:** 5-11. **WT.:** 200. **DRAFTED:** Wallace State (Ala.) CC, 2008 (3rd round). **SIGNED BY:** Brian Bridges.

Kimbrel turned down $125,000 as a Braves 33rd-round pick in 2007 before signing for $391,000 as a third-rounder a year later. He overcame a slow start at high Class A Myrtle Beach—he had 18 walks and a 10.97 ERA in 11 innings—to save 18 games and rank second among minor league relievers with 15.5 strikeouts per nine innings. Kimbrel has the stuff and mentality to be a big league closer. He aggressively challenges hitters with his plus-plus fastball, which sits at 93-95 mph, touches 98 and has nasty life. He also throws an above-average breaking ball that he calls a curveball but looks more like a slider. He flashes a deceptive changeup, though he rarely used it in 2009. Kimbrel needs to pitch inside more often with his fastball. Though he showed marked improvement after April, he needs better command of his stuff. He spent most of his time in the AFL trying to hone his changeup. Kimbrel has moved quicker than expected and is Atlanta's closer of the future. More time in Triple-A wold benefit him, but he could make his major league debut in the second half of 2010.

Year	Club (League)	Class	W	L	ERA	G	GS	CG	SV	IP	H	R	ER	HR	BB	SO	AVG
2008	Danville (APP)	R	1	2	0.47	12	0	0	6	19	5	4	1	0	10	27	.076
	Rome (SAL)	LoA	2	0	0.71	10	0	0	4	13	6	1	1	0	4	26	.140
	Myrtle Beach (CAR)	HiA	0	0	0.00	2	0	0	0	4	5	0	0	0	1	3	.385
2009	Rome (SAL)	LoA	0	0	0.90	16	0	0	10	20	9	2	2	0	6	38	.132
	Myrtle Beach (CAR)	HiA	0	2	5.47	19	0	0	2	26	18	19	16	2	28	45	.200
	Mississippi (SL)	AA	2	1	0.77	12	0	0	6	12	3	1	1	0	7	17	.083
	Gwinnett (IL)	AAA	0	0	0.00	2	0	0	0	2	0	0	0	0	4	3	.000
MINOR LEAGUE TOTALS			5	5	1.98	73	0	0	28	95	46	27	21	2	60	159	.143

6 CHRISTIAN BETHANCOURT, C ↳

BORN: Sept. 2, 1991. **B-T:** R-R. **HT.:** 6-2. **WT.:** 175. **SIGNED:** Panama, 2008. **SIGNED BY:** Luis Ortiz.

Bethancourt starred for Panama at the 2004 Little League World Series, and four years later he signed with the Braves for $600,000 as the top catching talent on the international market. In his U.S. debut last season, he ranked as the No. 1 prospect in the Rookie-level Gulf Coast League and helped Danville win the Appalachian League title. Bethancourt stands out with his skills and presence behind the plate. He has soft hands, plus-plus arm strength and a quick release. His pop times to second have registered as low as 1.78 seconds, and he threw out 30 percent of basestealers in 2009. He swings the bat well with a short stroke and is expected to hit for some power as his body matures and he gains experience. While the raw abilities are obvious, Bethancourt is somewhat rough on the finer aspects of catching. He can improve his lateral movement and ability to block balls in the dirt. He's a free swinger who needs to gain better command of the strike zone. He's athletic for a catcher but a below-average runner. With his ideal frame and leadership abilities, Bethancourt could develop into a special player. At 18, he'll be one of the younger players in the low Class A South Atlantic League in 2010.

Year	Club (League)	Class	AVG	G	AB	R	H	2B	3B	HR	RBI	BB	SO	SB	OBP	SLG
2008	Braves (DSL)	R	.267	34	116	12	31	6	3	0	17	11	25	1	.328	.371
2009	Braves (GCL)	R	.284	32	116	22	33	9	1	2	19	11	22	7	.344	.431
	Danville (APP)	R	.260	14	50	10	13	5	0	2	8	6	16	1	.339	.480
MINOR LEAGUE TOTALS			.273	80	282	44	77	20	4	4	44	28	63	9	.336	.415

7 RANDALL DELGADO, RHP

BORN: Feb. 9, 1990. **B-T:** R-R. **HT.:** 6-3. **WT.:** 180. **SIGNED:** Panama, 2006.
SIGNED BY: Luis Ortiz.

Delgado was advanced enough for his age for the Braves to skip him to the Rookie-level Appalachian League (over the Gulf Coast League) in his first season in the U.S. He had a tale of two seasons in his introduction to full-season ball. He never hung his head while going 1-8, 5.45 in his first 16 starts at Rome. After improving his control, he dominated at times and finished second in the system with 141 strikeouts in 124 innings. Delgado throws on a sharp, downhill plane that helps produce electric stuff and allows him to overpower hitters with all three of his pitches at times. His explosive fastball sits in the low 90s and touches 96 mph, and his projectable frame could get stronger, giving him more velocity. His curveball and changeup improved once he made progress with his control. While Delgado threw more strikes in the second half of 2009, he still needs to upgrade his ability to command his pitches. He works up in the strike zone too often. His curve and changeup are potential plus pitches but still require more consistency. One of the youngest pitchers on a prospect-laden roster last season, Delgado made the greatest strides of any of Rome's pitchers. He'll open the 2010 season as a 20-year-old starter in high Class A and could move quickly if he continues to refine his command.

Year	Club (League)	Class	W	L	ERA	G	GS	CG	SV	IP	H	R	ER	HR	BB	SO	AVG
2007	Braves (DSL)	R	1	2	2.00	11	10	0	0	45	34	12	10	2	12	50	.213
2008	Danville (APP)	R	3	8	3.13	14	14	0	0	69	63	32	24	5	30	81	.249
2009	Rome (SAL)	LoA	5	10	4.35	25	25	1	0	124	123	70	60	9	49	141	.256
MINOR LEAGUE TOTALS			9	20	3.55	50	49	1	0	238	220	114	94	16	91	272	.246

8 ZEKE SPRUILL, RHP

BORN: Sept. 11, 1989. **B-T:** B-R. **HT.:** 6-4. **WT.:** 185. **DRAFTED:** HS—Marietta, Ga., 2008 (3rd round). **SIGNED BY:** Brian Bridges.

Spruill had to wonder what was so tough about pro ball after he went 7-0 in his pro debut and won his first six decisions in 2009. But he earned just three more wins the rest of the season, thanks mostly to poor run support. He also spent time on the disabled list and in Rookie ball with a non-physical issue the Braves have remained tight-lipped about. Spruill has an excellent feel for pitching and even at age 20, he's one of the more polished prospects in the system. He pounds the lower half of the strike zone with an 89-91 mph sinker that arrives on a steep downhill plane. He also does a good job of mixing his breaking ball and changeup. He's all business and tenacious on the mound. Spruill can't overpower opponents, so he'll have to mix and locate his pitches well to succeed. He has a mid-70s curveball with decent break and an upper-70s slider, and he probably needs to settle on one to have a reliable breaking ball. His changeup can be inconsistent. Spruill has the potential to move quickly and become a mid-rotation starter once he gains feel for all of his pitches. He'll spend 2010 in high Class A.

Year	Club (League)	Class	W	L	ERA	G	GS	CG	SV	IP	H	R	ER	HR	BB	SO	AVG
2008	Braves (GCL)	R	7	0	2.93	10	3	0	0	40	42	16	13	1	8	32	.268
2009	Braves (GCL)	R	1	0	4.58	4	4	0	0	20	24	15	10	2	5	23	.289
	Rome (SAL)	LoA	8	6	3.03	20	19	0	1	116	120	54	39	9	24	95	.261
MINOR LEAGUE TOTALS			16	6	3.18	34	26	0	1	176	186	85	62	12	37	150	.266

9 CODY JOHNSON, OF

BORN: Aug. 18, 1988. **B-T:** L-R. **HT.:** 6-4. **WT.:** 230. **DRAFTED:** HS—Lynn Haven, Fla., 2006 (1st round). **SIGNED BY:** Al Goetz.

The 30th overall pick in 2006, Johnson signed for $1.375 million and then hit .184 with one homer in his pro debut. He since has led the Appalachian League with 17 homers in 2007, ranked second in the Sally League with 26 in 2008 and topped the Carolina League with 32 last season. No CL hitter had reached the 30-homer plateau since Danny Peoples in 1997. A pure power hitter, Johnson has as much raw strength as anyone in the minor leagues. Nearly half of his hits have gone for extra bases, and he's developing more patience when pitchers refuse to challenge him. A better athlete than he gets credit for, he's a slightly above-average baserunner. Johnson has ranked second in the minors in strikeouts in each of the past two seasons. When he struggles, he starts trying to pull everything, and more advanced pitchers could really exploit his all-or-nothing swing and approach. He's just adequate in left field, where he needs to take better routes and has below-average arm strength and accuracy. Johnson has been a minor league version of Adam Dunn, albeit with significantly fewer walks. His ability to hit for enough average while maintaining his power will determine his future. A full season in Double-A awaits in 2010.

ATLANTA BRAVES

Year	Club (League)	Class	AVG	G	AB	R	H	2B	3B	HR	RBI	BB	SO	SB	OBP	SLG
2006	Braves (GCL)	R	.184	32	114	13	21	6	1	1	16	12	49	2	.260	.281
2007	Danville (APP)	R	.305	63	243	51	74	18	5	17	57	26	72	7	.374	.630
2008	Rome (SAL)	LoA	.252	127	468	62	118	26	1	26	89	40	177	8	.307	.479
2009	Myrtle Beach (CAR)	HiA	.242	122	422	59	102	18	1	32	84	64	171	10	.345	.517
	Mississippi (SL)	AA	.182	6	22	2	4	0	0	0	3	3	9	1	.280	.182
MINOR LEAGUE TOTALS			.251	350	1269	187	319	68	8	76	249	145	478	28	.328	.497

10 ADAM MILLIGAN, OF

BORN: March 14, 1988. **B-T:** L-R. **HT.:** 6-3. **WT.:** 210. **DRAFTED:** Walters State (Tenn.) CC, 2008 (6th round). **SIGNED BY:** Brian Bridges.

The Braves drafted Milligan three times before signing him for $600,000 in 2008. He originally committed to Austin Peay State to play football, then played two years of baseball at Walters State (Tenn.) CC. A knee injury delayed his pro debut until 2009, when he led the system with a .592 slugging percentage and slugged 13 homers in half a season. Milligan drives the ball to all fields and projects as a potential .280 hitter with 20-25 homers per season. He runs well for a big man, with solid-average speed, and he has a slightly above-average arm and good accuracy and carry on his throws. Though he shows some aptitude for working counts, Milligan doesn't exhibit much patience at the plate and will have to tighten his strike zone against better pitching. He has made strides in left field but still needs to make further improvements to his defense. He has enough bat to profile as a regular left fielder in the major leagues, though Cody Johnson is one step ahead of him. Milligan will open 2010 in high Class A but could advance quickly if he continues to produce.

Year	Club (League)	Class	AVG	G	AB	R	H	2B	3B	HR	RBI	BB	SO	SB	OBP	SLG
2009	Danville (APP)	R	.439	9	41	9	18	5	1	2	10	3	7	0	.500	.756
	Rome (SAL)	LoA	.345	52	197	28	68	14	2	10	33	12	43	4	.393	.589
	Myrtle Beach (CAR)	HiA	.167	6	24	2	4	1	0	1	6	0	8	0	.200	.333
MINOR LEAGUE TOTALS			.344	67	262	39	90	20	3	13	49	15	58	4	.393	.592

11 J.J. HOOVER, RHP

BORN: Aug. 13, 1987. **B-T:** R-R. **HT.:** 6-3. **WT.:** 230. **DRAFTED:** Calhoun (Ala.) CC, 2008 (10th round). **SIGNED BY:** Brian Bridges.

Aside from Zeke Spruill, Hoover has had as much success as any pitcher the Braves took in the 2008 draft. He signed for $400,000 as a 10th-round pick after being selected out of Calhoun (Ala.) CC—the alma mater of Jorge Posada—and putting together an impressive showing in the Cape Cod League. He opened 2009 in the bullpen but looked at home after a move to the rotation in early May. He didn't let playing for a weak offensive team at Rome hinder his performance, and he was one of the most consistent hurlers in the South Atlantic League. A workhorse with thick, strong thighs, a la Tom Seaver and Roger Clemens, Hoover keeps his pitches down in the zone while challenging hitters. He throws his fastball in the low 90s and complements it with a good changeup and curveball, both of which could become plus pitches with added refinement. He possesses impressive control that helped him limit his walks to 1.7 per nine innings in his first full pro season. While he has shown signs of being an innings-eater, Hoover also has the mentality and repertoire to pitch late in games, possibly even as a closer. The progress of his secondary pitches will determine which route he eventually takes. He should begin the 2010 campaign in high Class A, with a midseason promotion likely if he continues to produce like he did last season.

Year	Club (League)	Class	W	L	ERA	G	GS	CG	SV	IP	H	R	ER	HR	BB	SO	AVG
2008	Danville (APP)	R	1	0	0.00	2	0	0	0	5	4	0	0	0	1	6	.235
2009	Myrtle Beach (CAR)	HiA	0	0	9.00	1	1	0	0	3	3	3	3	1	5	2	.250
	Rome (SAL)	LoA	7	6	3.35	25	18	0	1	134	135	58	50	9	25	148	.259
MINOR LEAGUE TOTALS			8	6	3.36	28	19	0	1	142	142	61	53	10	31	156	.258

12 DIMASTHER DELGADO, LHP

BORN: March 9, 1989. **B-T:** L-L. **HT.:** 6-2. **WT.:** 180. **SIGNED:** Panama, 2007. **SIGNED BY:** Luis Ortiz.

Delgado has flown under the radar, overshadowed in the Braves system by Julio Teheran and Randall Delgado (no relation) and a host of early-round draft picks. Despite the lack of exposure, Delgado has emerged as a legitimate prospect after turning in a strong full-season debut in 2009. His changeup is one of the best in the organization and he does an excellent job of mixing it with his fastball, which peaks in the low 90s. His slow curveball lags behind his other two pitches and still needs a lot of work. Delgado has an advanced feel for pitching, working both sides of the plate and throwing inside with consistency. He also has a tremendous work ethic with the drive to get the most out of his ability. He has good athleticism and fields his position well. He needs to do a better job holding runners after giving up 14 steals in 16 attempts last season. If he improves his curveball, Delgado could become a mid-rotation starter in the majors. He'll serve a similar role in high Class A in 2010.

Year	Club (League)	Class	W	L	ERA	G	GS	CG	SV	IP	H	R	ER	HR	BB	SO	AVG
2007	Braves (DSL)	R	3	3	2.43	13	12	0	0	59	49	31	16	1	12	86	.217
2008	Braves (GCL)	R	5	1	4.31	11	3	0	0	40	51	22	19	2	9	39	.297
2009	Rome (SAL)	LoA	5	7	3.61	17	17	0	0	100	89	43	40	4	26	104	.237
MINOR LEAGUE TOTALS			13	11	3.40	41	32	0	0	199	189	96	75	7	47	229	.245

13 BRETT OBERHOLTZER, LHP

BORN: July 1, 1989. **B-T:** L-L. **HT.:** 6-2. **WT.:** 230. **DRAFTED:** Seminole (Fla.) CC, 2008 (8th round). **SIGNED BY:** Gregg Kilby.

Oberholtzer was the first player signed from the Braves' 2008 draft class, one year after he opted to attend Seminole (Fla.) CC instead of joining the Mariners as a 47th-round pick out of a Delaware high school. After a solid if unspectacular pro debut, he ranked fifth among pitchers in short-season and Rookie-leagues with a .191 opponent average last season. Employing a herky-jerky arm action that creates deception, Oberholtzer has good tailing life to his 86-92 mph fastball. His changeup and curveball are both average pitches, and he'll throw any of his offerings at any time in the count. Aggressive and able to work both sides of the plate, Oberholtzer has excellent command. He fields his position and holds runners very well. He showed the ability to pitch under pressure when he tossed a complete-game five-hitter in the opener of the Appy League championship series. His body still has some projectability, and scouts believe he will continue to improve as he gains experience and maturity. He'll pitch in the Rome rotation in 2010.

Year	Club (League)	Class	W	L	ERA	G	GS	CG	SV	IP	H	R	ER	HR	BB	SO	AVG
2008	Braves (GCL)	R	4	1	2.89	10	0	0	0	37	34	16	12	1	10	32	.241
2009	Danville (APP)	R	6	2	2.01	12	12	1	0	67	46	17	15	1	6	56	.191
MINOR LEAGUE TOTALS			10	3	2.33	22	12	1	0	104	80	33	27	2	16	88	.209

14 DAVID HALE, RHP

BORN: Sept. 27, 1987. **B-T:** R-R. **HT.:** 6-2. **WT.:** 195. **DRAFTED:** Princeton, 2009 (2nd round). **SIGNED BY:** Kevin Barry.

The third-highest pick ever out of Princeton, Hale signed for $405,000 as the 87th overall choice in the 2009 draft. A two-way player in college, he batted .291 as a center fielder over three seasons with the Tigers and pitched in only 26 games (22 starts). An excellent athlete, he has an ideal pitcher's frame and a lightning-quick arm. His fastball sits at 93-94 mph and repeatedly touches 96 mph, and he could gain more velocity now that he's not expending energy as an everyday player. His slider also has the makings of becoming a plus pitch while residing at 84-86 mph and touching 88. In order to remain a starter, he'll have to maintain consistent movement on his fastball and command his slider, which has nice bite at times but tends to hang and sweep. The development of his changeup, which he has shown some feel for, also will go a long way in determining his future role. Hale never dominated on the mound at Princeton or in the Cape Cod League, but he should improve now that he's focusing solely on pitching for the first time. He'll likely open his first full pro season in low Class A.

Year	Club (League)	Class	W	L	ERA	G	GS	CG	SV	IP	H	R	ER	HR	BB	SO	AVG
2009	Danville (APP)	R	2	1	1.13	7	1	0	1	16	7	4	2	0	5	12	.130
MINOR LEAGUE TOTALS			2	1	1.13	7	1	0	1	16	7	4	2	0	5	12	.130

15 TYLER STOVALL, LHP

BORN: Dec. 27, 1989. **B-T:** L-L. **HT.:** 6-1. **WT.:** 200. **DRAFTED:** HS—Hokes Bluff, Ala., 2008 (2nd round). **SIGNED BY:** Brian Bridges.

Stovall had a storied high school career in Alabama, winning four state titles in baseball and another as a quarterback in football. He set a national high school mark with 95 career doubles and numerous state standards, including marks for career wins (54) and strikeouts (683). He has battled his control in pro ball, leading the Appalachian League with 56 walks in 52 innings last year, but his potential is evident. Stovall does a good job of forcing batters to hit the ball on the ground, allowing only one home run in 2009, and he is capable of shutting down southpaw swingers, who batted just .147 against him last summer. When in rhythm, he works off an 89-91 mph fastball that features outstanding natural movement. The life on his fastball makes it difficult to control at times. His plus curveball is his best and most consistent offering, but he tends to rely on it too often when he can't locate his heater. He also has the makings of a quality changeup. Stovall's mechanics are a little rough, producing a maximum-effort delivery that needs to be honed in order to improve his accuracy and reduce his chances of injury. He's a work in progress, but he has the raw ingredients to be a mid-rotation starter. A promotion to low Class A is on the immediate horizon in 2010.

ATLANTA BRAVES

Year	Club (League)	Class	W	L	ERA	G	GS	CG	SV	IP	H	R	ER	HR	BB	SO	AVG
2008	Braves (GCL)	R	1	1	6.30	7	3	0	0	20	20	15	14	1	14	29	.250
2009	Danville (APP)	R	3	2	3.12	12	12	0	0	52	36	22	18	1	56	57	.202
MINOR LEAGUE TOTALS			4	3	4.00	19	15	0	0	72	56	37	32	2	70	86	.217

16 ROBINSON LOPEZ, RHP

BORN: March 2, 1991. **B-T:** R-R. **HT.:** 6-2. **WT.:** 190. **SIGNED:** Dominican Republic, 2008. **SIGNED BY:** Roberto Aquino.

Lopez may be the biggest sleeper in the system. After he signed out of the Dominican in 2008, his raw ability allowed him to come straight to the United States for his pro debut, during which he ranked fourth in the Gulf Coast League with a 1.29 ERA as an 18-year-old. Lopez's fastball resides at 90-92 mph and touches 94. He also has an above-average curveball and an average changeup. Lopez pounds the strike zone and competes very well on the mound while displaying a solid all-around feel for his craft. He needs to improve the consistency and the depth of his changeup as well as the overall command of his fastball, which is true for most teenagers. Based on his progress in 2009, Lopez could make the jump to low Class A with a solid showing in spring training.

Year	Club (League)	Class	W	L	ERA	G	GS	CG	SV	IP	H	R	ER	HR	BB	SO	AVG
2009	Braves (GCL)	R	3	1	1.29	11	8	0	0	49	41	13	7	1	12	42	.229
MINOR LEAGUE TOTALS			3	1	1.29	11	8	0	0	49	41	13	7	1	12	42	.229

17 MYCAL JONES, SS

BORN: May 30, 1987. **B-T:** R-R. **HT.:** 5-10. **WT.:** 165. **DRAFTED:** Miami Dade CC, 2009 (4th round). **SIGNED BY:** Buddy Hernandez.

Jones wasted no time making a name for himself after signing for $252,000 as a fourth-round pick last June. He went 3-for-6 with four RBIs in his first pro game, then helped turn a triple play in Danville's home opener. Undrafted out of high school, he attended North Florida for two years before transferring to Miami Dade CC, making him old for a juco draftee at age 22. Jones' best tool is his plus-plus speed, which he used to steal 19 bases in 23 attempts and lead the Appalachian League in runs (50) and triples (six). He tends to uppercut the ball and his swing can get long, which limited him to a .258 average in his pro debut. He flashed some power with metal bats in college, but the Braves believe he'll be better off with more of a line-drive approach that uses his speed to his greatest advantage. Jones has the quick-twitch athleticism and actions to excel on defense. He has good range and hands and an average arm, though his maximum-effort throws scare some scouts. Jones could move rapidly in a system that's not deep with shortstop talent. He'll open 2010 in low Class A.

Year	Club (League)	Class	AVG	G	AB	R	H	2B	3B	HR	RBI	BB	SO	SB	OBP	SLG
2009	Danville (APP)	R	.258	64	244	50	63	18	6	4	27	26	55	19	.337	.430
MINOR LEAGUE TOTALS			.258	64	244	50	63	18	6	4	27	26	55	19	.337	.430

18 BRANDON HICKS, SS

BORN: Sept. 14, 1985. **B-T:** R-R. **HT.:** 6-2. **WT.:** 200. **DRAFTED:** Texas A&M, 2007 (3rd round). **SIGNED BY:** John Barron.

In his 2007 pro debut, Hicks appeared to be on the fast track to Atlanta. He offered the possibility of hitting for both power and average, while also showing a plus arm at shortstop. Add in his determination and intensity, and he had the makings of becoming a top infield prospect. However, in his two full seasons since, he has struggled with strikeouts and been merely solid at shortstop. After hitting 20 homers in 2008, he dropped to 10 last year while batting .237 in Double-A. Hicks has tinkered with his batting stance in an effort to see the ball better and make better contact, but the results haven't been forthcoming. Despite his high strikeout totals, Hicks does have a good eye at the plate and draws some walks. He has slightly above-average speed and outstanding instincts, succeeding on 17 of his 18 steal attemps last year. A knack for being in the right place and a strong arm with a quick release are his strengths on defense, which help him compensate for fringe-average range. Hicks will be 24 next season, making it an important campaign for him. He's unlikely to unseat Yunel Escobar as the Braves' shortstop, but they're going to need to replace Chipper Jones in the near future. Hicks will move up to Triple-A in 2010.

Year	Club (League)	Class	AVG	G	AB	R	H	2B	3B	HR	RBI	BB	SO	SB	OBP	SLG
2007	Danville (APP)	R	.224	18	58	14	13	3	1	3	13	12	18	1	.370	.466
	Rome (SAL)	LoA	.313	37	128	26	40	11	0	4	15	27	26	5	.433	.492
2008	Mississippi (SL)	AA	.241	16	54	9	13	3	1	1	7	7	17	0	.333	.389
	Myrtle Beach (CAR)	HiA	.234	93	342	68	80	23	2	19	56	45	122	14	.335	.480
2009	Mississippi (SL)	AA	.237	128	464	63	110	25	4	10	48	53	131	17	.319	.373
MINOR LEAGUE TOTALS			.245	292	1046	180	256	65	8	37	139	144	314	37	.343	.428

19 BRETT DeVALL, LHP

BORN: Jan. 8, 1990. **B-T:** R-L. **HT.:** 6-4. **WT.:** 215. **DRAFTED:** HS—Niceville, Fla., 2008 (1st round supplemental). **SIGNED BY:** Brian Bridges.

When he has taken the mound, DeVall leaves no doubt as to why the Braves made him their top pick (40th overall) and handed him a $1 million bonus in 2008. Unfortunately, a lingering forearm ailment and an elbow strain have limited him to 63 pro innings. He opened 2009 in extended spring training before reporting to Rome in early May. He gave up a total of 10 earned runs in his first eight starts, then 11 in his next two before he was shut down until instructional league. DeVall felt strong and pain-free in the fall, but there's still concern that surgery may be in his future. He does have a clean delivery and good mechanics, which makes his arm problems puzzling. When healthy, DeVall has an 88-91 mph fastball that features good movement when he keeps it down in the zone. He's also developing a solid curveball and showing good feel for his changeup. His advanced knowledge of pitching helps him set up hitters, but the key is going to be whether he'll be available to pitch every fifth day. If he's 100 percent physically, he should open next season in high Class A.

Year	Club (League)	Class	W	L	ERA	G	GS	CG	SV	IP	H	R	ER	HR	BB	SO	AVG
2008	Braves (GCL)	R	0	0	0.93	4	3	0	0	10	4	1	1	1	2	7	.125
2009	Rome (SAL)	LoA	4	4	3.52	10	10	1	0	54	50	22	21	3	14	41	.245
MINOR LEAGUE TOTALS			4	4	3.13	14	13	1	0	63	54	23	22	4	16	48	.229

20 JUAN ABREU, RHP

BORN: April 8, 1985. **B-T:** R-R. **HT.:** 6-0. **WT.:** 170. **SIGNED:** Dominican Republic, 2003. **SIGNED BY:** Pedro Silverio (Royals).

Abreu has shown an intriguing arm since signing with the Royals out of the Dominican Republic in 2003, but a variety of hurdles, including an elbow injury that cost him all of the 2007 season, has prevented him from reaching his potential. He had the best stretch of his career at high Class A Wilmington in the first half of 2009, going 12-for-12 in save opportunities, but struggled in Double-A during the second half. Kansas City reached a deal to re-sign him as a minor league free agent after the season, but a contract snafu allowed him to hit the open market, and the Braves landed him by offering him a major league contract. Small and wiry, Abreu has a whippy arm action that produced a hard sinker that sits at 94-95 mph. Some teams have clocked his fastball as hard as 100 mph. His 78-80 mph curveball has an early break, shows good rotation and could develop into a plus pitch. He also has some feel for a changeup, but it's not as effective as his other two pitches. In addition to injuries, Abreu has battled a lack of command. If he can harness his live arm, he has a chance to be a solid setup man in the major leagues. After a stop in big league camp, he figures to open 2010 in Double-A.

Year	Club (League)	Class	W	L	ERA	G	GS	CG	SV	IP	H	R	ER	HR	BB	SO	AVG
2003	Royals (DSL)	R	0	2	2.25	5	2	0	0	16	16	12	4	0	7	10	.242
2004	Royals (DSL)	R	2	1	4.06	9	7	0	0	31	22	15	14	0	20	33	.198
2005	Royals (AZL)	R	2	5	6.88	14	13	0	0	52	72	49	40	4	27	52	.327
2006	Idaho Falls (PIO)	R	4	2	5.76	20	0	0	2	50	39	34	32	4	35	57	.223
2007	Did Not Play—Injured																
2008	Burlington (MWL)	LoA	4	4	3.66	22	4	0	7	76	59	40	31	6	42	104	.214
2009	Wilmington (CAR)	HiA	3	2	1.69	20	0	0	12	21	8	5	4	1	14	28	.114
	NW Arkansas (TL)	AA	2	2	5.75	16	0	0	4	20	19	15	13	3	22	25	.247
MINOR LEAGUE TOTALS			17	18	4.65	106	26	0	25	267	235	170	138	18	167	309	.236

21 CALEB BREWER, RHP

BORN: Feb. 2, 1989. **B-T:** R-R. **HT.:** 6-3. **WT.:** 205. **DRAFTED:** HS—Harris County, Ga., 2007 (14th round). **SIGNED BY:** Al Goetz.

A hip injury cost Brewer the 2008 season, but he made up for lost time by leading the Gulf Coast League with 65 strikeouts in 45 innings last summer. Though he was old for the GCL at age 20, he displayed one of the best arms in the league, highlighted by a fastball that sat at 91-93 mph and touched 95. He also showed a good overhand curveball with above-average spin and hard downward break. Scouts like his high arm slot and downhill plane from which he delivers the ball to the plate. Brewer's greatest need is to develop better fastball command. He also needs to refine a changeup and locate all of his pitches more consistently after ranking second in the GCL with 31 walks. Brewer's durability shouldn't be a factor in the future, as he had no further problems with his hip last year. He should move two steps up the organization ladder to Rome in 2010.

Year	Club (League)	Class	W	L	ERA	G	GS	CG	SV	IP	H	R	ER	HR	BB	SO	AVG
2007	Braves (GCL)	R	0	1	4.68	11	4	0	0	33	31	22	17	3	24	23	.248
2008	Did Not Play—Injured																
2009	Braves (GCL)	R	3	3	2.82	12	10	0	0	45	20	14	14	0	31	65	.132
MINOR LEAGUE TOTALS			3	4	3.61	23	14	0	0	77	51	36	31	3	55	88	.185

22 RICHARD SULLIVAN, LHP

BORN: April 14, 1987. **B-T:** L-L. **HT.:** 6-3. **WT.:** 235. **DRAFTED:** Savannah College of Art and Design, 2008 (11th round). **SIGNED BY:** Brian Bridges.

The Savannah College of Art and Design isn't a hotbed for major league prospects, but Sullivan has displayed promise after becoming just the second player drafted out of the NAIA school. After pitching well at Rome at the end of his 2008 pro debut and the start of 2009, he earned a quick promotion to high Class A. An extreme groundball pitcher, he was victimized by poor infield defense at Myrtle Beach, where he pitched better than his 2-12 record would indicate. He had six quality starts with the Pelicans but won only one of them—a complete game in which he fanned 10. Sullivan employs a heavy 87-93 mph sinker, a plus changeup and an average curveball. He doesn't miss a lot of bats and has to rely on his infielders, but he throws strikes, keeps the ball down and makes it difficult to lift the ball in the air. He does a good job of using his size to his advantage. He's still working on the nuances of pitching, and he's extremely vulnerable to the running game, especially for a lefthander. Sullivan made three starts in Double-A at midseason and will return there in 2010.

Year	Club (League)	Class	W	L	ERA	G	GS	CG	SV	IP	H	R	ER	HR	BB	SO	AVG
2008	Danville (APP)	R	2	0	1.40	4	4	0	0	19	10	4	3	1	0	22	.149
	Rome (SAL)	LoA	2	2	2.80	8	8	0	0	35	40	15	11	0	4	27	.282
2009	Rome (SAL)	LoA	4	1	3.72	5	5	1	0	29	37	18	12	2	5	27	.306
	Mississippi (SL)	AA	0	1	9.45	3	3	0	0	13	21	15	14	0	10	8	.389
	Myrtle Beach (CAR)	HiA	2	12	4.25	19	19	1	0	112	115	66	53	5	39	80	.266
MINOR LEAGUE TOTALS			10	16	4.00	39	39	2	0	209	223	118	93	8	58	164	.273

23 COLE ROHRBOUGH, LHP

BORN: May 23, 1987. **B-T:** L-L. **HT.:** 6-3. **WT.:** 215. **DRAFTED:** Western Nevada CC, D/F 2006 (22nd round). **SIGNED BY:** Tim Moore.

The Braves' final draft-and-follow sign before the process was eliminated with the 2007 draft, Rohrbough received a $675,000 bonus and ranked as the Appalachian League's top prospect in his pro debut. An ankle injury that begat a shoulder problem limited his performance in 2008. Last season, he struggled to find any consistency. After he made his first start, he spent a month on the disabled list with a hamstring injury. He gave up a total of six runs in his first four starts back, then got bombed for 10 runs in his next outing and had a 6.53 ERA from June on. When Rohrbough is on, he has a 92-94 mph fastball with plus movement and a power curveball with late, hard break. His changeup continues to need work, and he still tends to drop his arm angle on occasion, which flattens his pitches and makes them hittable. Rohrbough gets down on himself and dwells on his difficulties, and he wasn't able to snap out of it in 2009. He has electric stuff at times and the ability to be a solid major league starter, but Atlanta still isn't sure what it has in him. His 2010 performance in Double-A should help make his future more clear.

Year	Club (League)	Class	W	L	ERA	G	GS	CG	SV	IP	H	R	ER	HR	BB	SO	AVG
2007	Danville (APP)	R	3	2	1.08	8	7	0	0	33	20	8	4	1	8	58	.167
	Rome (SAL)	LoA	2	0	1.29	6	6	0	0	28	13	7	4	1	12	38	.138
2008	Rome (SAL)	LoA	3	4	4.94	13	12	0	0	58	55	37	32	3	31	76	.248
	Myrtle Beach (CAR)	HiA	2	2	3.41	5	5	1	0	32	27	16	12	0	8	28	.233
2009	Myrtle Beach (CAR)	HiA	6	8	5.77	23	22	0	0	117	129	80	75	12	48	100	.280
MINOR LEAGUE TOTALS			16	16	4.26	55	52	1	0	268	244	148	127	17	107	300	.241

24 KYLE COFIELD, RHP

BORN: Jan. 23, 1987. **B-T:** R-R. **HT.:** 6-5. **WT.:** 220. **DRAFTED:** HS—Rainbow City, Ala., 2005 (8th round). **SIGNED BY:** Al Goetz.

After splitting his time between the rotation and bullpen during his first three seasons in the organization, Cofield became a full-time starter in 2008 and ranked second in the Carolina League with a 3.26 ERA. Last year, he jumped to Double-A and tied for the system lead with 10 wins. He bordered on dominating in the first half of 2009, allowing three earned runs or less in 13 of his first 14 outings. The primary weakness preventing Cofield from being one of the Atlanta's premier prospects is his lack of control. He ranked second in the minors in 2009 by issuing 89 walks, which comes from an inconsistent feel for his pitches and a tendency to be too fine. A work in progress since turning pro in 2005, Cofield signed as a raw high school hurler out of Alabama and has struggled with his confidence. There's nothing wrong with his pure stuff. His fastball resides in the low 90s and touches 95 mph. His plus curveball is his best pitch, but he also struggles with commanding it in the strike zone. His changeup shows promise but lacks consistency as well. The Braves believe Cofield can be a valuable asset if and when he puts everything together, so much so that they added him to their 40-man roster to protect him from the Rule 5 draft. He'll work toward that goal this year in Triple-A.

Year	Club (League)	Class	W	L	ERA	G	GS	CG	SV	IP	H	R	ER	HR	BB	SO	AVG
2005	Braves (GCL)	R	0	0	7.31	10	0	0	2	16	16	15	13	0	6	15	.254
2006	Danville (APP)	R	2	3	6.21	13	8	0	0	42	50	31	29	2	22	29	.289
2007	Rome (SAL)	LoA	4	8	3.86	25	16	0	1	112	96	56	48	7	56	90	.236
2008	Myrtle Beach (CAR)	HiA	8	6	3.26	24	22	0	0	116	113	54	42	2	66	80	.260
2009	Mississippi (SL)	AA	10	5	3.90	26	24	1	0	141	122	74	61	9	89	87	.236
MINOR LEAGUE TOTALS			24	22	4.07	98	70	1	3	427	397	230	193	20	239	301	.249

25 JOSE ORTEGANO, LHP

BORN: Aug. 5, 1987. **B-T:** L-L. **HT.:** 6-1. **WT.:** 155. **SIGNED:** Venezuela, 2003. **SIGNED BY:** Rolando Petit.

Ortegano just concluded his sixth season in the organization, yet the crafty lefthander didn't celebrate his 22nd birthday until the final month of the campaign. He spent four years in Rookie ball, leading the Appalachian League with a 1.48 ERA in 2007, and battled shoulder tendinitis in his first taste of full-season ball in 2008. Normally a starter, he excelled early last year as a reliever at Myrtle Beach before finishing strong in the Mississippi rotation. Ortegano's strength is his ability to command three pitches. His fastball sits at 86-88 mph and occasionally touches 90. He also has a plus curveball and locates his changeup with precision. He has an excellent feel for pitching, keeping hitters off balance with his ability to mix his offerings and put them where he wants. The skinny Ortegano may not be physical enough to succeed as a starter in the big leagues, and his ultimate role may be as a crafty lefthanded reliever. Although he was added to the Braves' 40-man roster after the season, he'll likely return to Double-A to open 2010.

Year	Club (League)	Class	W	L	ERA	G	GS	CG	SV	IP	H	R	ER	HR	BB	SO	AVG
2004	Braves1 (DSL)	R	0	1	1.60	17	5	0	2	39	35	9	7	1	11	46	.252
2005	Braves2 (DSL)	R	5	2	2.58	13	10	0	0	52	49	22	15	3	12	55	.247
2006	Braves (GCL)	R	3	3	3.30	12	5	0	0	46	43	20	17	3	10	31	.247
2007	Danville (APP)	R	6	1	1.48	13	9	0	0	61	44	14	10	3	11	55	.199
2008	Braves (GCL)	R	0	0	0.00	2	2	0	0	3	1	0	0	0	0	4	.100
	Rome (SAL)	LoA	2	5	4.62	17	15	0	0	86	90	49	44	2	25	83	.275
2009	Myrtle Beach (CAR)	HiA	4	5	3.49	21	12	0	0	70	56	30	27	4	19	59	.220
	Mississippi (SL)	AA	5	2	2.83	8	8	1	0	48	46	19	15	2	15	42	.247
MINOR LEAGUE TOTALS			25	19	3.00	103	66	1	2	405	364	163	135	18	103	375	.241

26 SCOTT DIAMOND, LHP

BORN: July 30, 1986. **B-T:** L-L. **HT.:** 6-3. **WT.:** 210. **SIGNED:** Binghamton, NDFA 2007. **SIGNED BY:** Paul Faulk/Lonnie Goldberg.

Signed by the Braves as a nondrafted free agent for $50,000 after starring in the summer collegiate Coastal Plain League, Diamond was the surprise of the system in 2008. In his pro debut, he led the system with 15 wins and ranked fifth with 123 strikeouts in 153 innings. His numbers weren't as sexy last year, but he successfully made the jump to Double-A. The Canadian thrives by locating most of his pitches in the lower third of the strike zone. He mixes three offerings: an 89-91 mph fastball, an above-average curveball and a solid-average changeup. He isn't afraid of pitching to contact and does a good job of forcing opponents to hit the ball on the ground. Diamond's stuff isn't overwhelming, but he passed the test in Double-A. He'll get challenged again in Triple-A this year, with a big league callup awaiting afterward.

Year	Club (League)	Class	W	L	ERA	G	GS	CG	SV	IP	H	R	ER	HR	BB	SO	AVG
2008	Rome (SAL)	LoA	3	1	3.08	9	9	0	0	53	47	20	18	2	11	38	.240
	Myrtle Beach (CAR)	HiA	12	2	2.79	17	15	1	0	100	95	42	31	6	28	85	.245
2009	Mississippi (SL)	AA	5	10	3.50	23	23	0	0	131	152	68	51	5	53	111	.294
MINOR LEAGUE TOTALS			20	13	3.17	49	47	1	0	284	294	130	100	13	92	234	.267

27 JESUS SUCRE, C

BORN: April 30, 1988. **B-T:** R-R. **HT.:** 6-0. **WT.:** 200. **SIGNED:** Venezuela, 2005. **SIGNED BY:** Julian Perez/Rolando Petit/Jose Leon.

Since instructional league in 2008, Sucre has made greater strides than any prospect in the system. He entered 2009 with a career batting average of .223 over four pro seasons, including a paltry .182 performance at Danville in 2008. Yet a strong showing in spring training carried over into the regular season at Rome, where he hit for both power and average before making a midseason jump to Myrtle Beach. Pull-happy during his first few years as a pro, Sucre did a much better job putting the barrel of the bat on the ball in 2009, and he must continue to take pitches to the opposite field. He has possessed a cannon for an arm since signing as a 17-year-old, and he threw out 42 percent of basestealers last year. He still needs to continue smoothing out some rough areas with his defense, such as his footwork and lateral mobility. Sucre's offensive and defensive improvements have coincided with his diligent work and becoming more comfortable in speaking English. He has come a long way but still has a ways to go to serve as Brian McCann's backup in Atlanta. Spring training will determine whether Sucre starts the 2010 season in high Class A or Double-A.

Year	Club (League)	Class	AVG	G	AB	R	H	2B	3B	HR	RBI	BB	SO	SB	OBP	SLG
2005	Braves1 (DSL)	R	.214	19	70	6	15	0	0	2	7	5	10	0	.276	.300
2006	Braves (DSL)	R	.278	35	133	20	37	8	1	1	16	9	12	1	.331	.376
2007	Braves (GCL)	R	.221	40	104	8	23	5	0	0	14	7	10	1	.265	.269
2008	Danville (APP)	R	.182	44	154	14	28	2	0	3	15	7	24	1	.222	.253
2009	Rome (SAL)	LoA	.325	45	169	14	55	15	0	1	18	6	17	1	.352	.432
	Myrtle Beach (CAR)	HiA	.259	53	197	17	51	8	1	5	20	8	33	3	.286	.386
MINOR LEAGUE TOTALS			.253	236	827	79	209	38	2	12	90	42	106	7	.292	.347

28 PAUL CLEMENS, RHP

BORN: Feb. 14, 1988. **B-T:** R-R. **HT.:** 6-4. **WT.:** 180. **DRAFTED:** Louisburg (N.C.) JC, 2008 (7th round). **SIGNED BY:** Billy Best.

Clemens has been somewhat of an enigma over the past two years. He was so ineffective as a sophomore at Louisburg (N.C.) JC in 2008 that he lost his job in the rotation. The Braves still drafted him in the seventh round that June because of his live arm. He was effective in his pro debut but underachieved in low Class A last year. When he's right, Clemens' stuff is undeniable. He has a 91-94 mph fastball he can dial up to 97 and an above-average curveball. The problem, however, is inconsistency. In one game last year he couldn't top 93 mph or throw strikes, but two outings later he was hitting 97 and blowing hitters away with impressive command. Clemens has an ideal pitcher's build and the arm strength to develop into a mid-rotation starter or late-inning reliever. His ability to develop a changeup and refine his command will determine his ultimate role. Clemens still is learning how to harness his energy and improve his understanding of the game. His composure on the mound also needs work. His learning process will continue in high Class A this season.

Year	Club (League)	Class	W	L	ERA	G	GS	CG	SV	IP	H	R	ER	HR	BB	SO	AVG
2008	Braves (GCL)	R	1	0	0.00	1	0	0	0	3	1	0	0	0	0	2	.111
	Danville (APP)	R	3	3	3.39	12	8	0	1	58	57	33	22	6	18	57	.252
	Rome (SAL)	LoA	0	1	9.00	1	1	0	0	4	7	5	4	0	2	0	.412
2009	Rome (SAL)	LoA	6	5	5.91	26	11	0	3	85	105	67	56	7	49	64	.296
MINOR LEAGUE TOTALS			10	9	4.90	40	20	0	4	151	170	105	82	13	69	123	.280

29 RIAAN SPANJER-FURSTENBURG, 1B

BORN: Feb. 8, 1988. **B-T:** R-R. **HT.:** 6-2. **WT.:** 235. **DRAFTED:** Nova Southeastern (Fla.), 2009 (16th round). **SIGNED BY:** Buddy Hernandez.

Though Spanjer-Furstenburg was on South Africa's provisional World Baseball Classic roster and hit .393-15-67 at Nova Southeastern (Fla.) in the spring, he was a relative unknown when he signed for $75,000 as a 16th-round pick in June. That changed after he tore up the Appalachian League, hitting safely in his first 10 pro games en route to winning the MVP award and batting title (.359). Spanjer-Furstenburg has a sweet swing with a chance to hit for average and solid power. He has a lot of strength in his 6-foot-2, 235-pound frame. He doesn't have much speed or athleticism, which limits him to first base, where he's an average defender at best. With Freddie Freeman in the system, his lack of versatility may hurt him. He could end up as a solid bat off the bench and a caddy for Freeman on the major league roster in the future. Spanjer-Furstenburg's impressive debut could allow him to jump to high Class A in 2010.

Year	Club (League)	Class	AVG	G	AB	R	H	2B	3B	HR	RBI	BB	SO	SB	OBP	SLG
2009	Danville (APP)	R	.359	62	234	36	84	19	0	8	53	16	37	0	.411	.543
MINOR LEAGUE TOTALS			.359	62	234	36	84	19	0	8	53	16	37	0	.411	.543

30 JONNY VENTERS, LHP

BORN: March 20, 1985. **B-T:** L-L. **HT.:** 6-3. **WT.:** 195. **DRAFTED:** Indian River (Fla.) CC, D/F 2003 (30th round). **SIGNED BY:** Alex Morales, George Martin.

Injuries have highlighted Venters' career, including a torn elbow ligament that required Tommy John surgery and cost him the entire 2006 season, and elbow tendinitis that limited him to 34 innings in 2008. Healthy again last season, he didn't allow an earned run in half of his 12 starts at Mississippi before a promotion to Gwinnett in mid-June. Venters has solid overall stuff and is aggressive with all of his pitches. His fastball ranges from 88-94 mph, and he can add to and subtract from it at will. He also has a plus slider and an average curveball and changeup. Venters' stuff isn't as effective as it should be, because he doesn't throw strikes or locate his pitches consistently. He projects best as a late-inning lefty reliever and occasional spot starter. Venters will open 2010 back in Triple-A but he's been added to Atlanta's 40-man roster and should make his major league debut at some point during the season.

Year	Club (League)	Class	W	L	ERA	G	GS	CG	SV	IP	H	R	ER	HR	BB	SO	AVG
2004	Braves (GCL)	R	1	6	5.74	11	8	0	0	42	53	31	27	3	12	54	.296
2005	Rome (SAL)	LoA	8	6	3.93	23	12	0	3	103	100	51	45	4	52	66	.258
2006	Did Not Play—Injured																
2007	Myrtle Beach (CAR)	HiA	3	3	3.39	17	12	0	1	80	60	39	30	4	38	64	.210
2008	Braves (GCL)	R	0	0	4.70	4	4	0	0	8	10	6	4	1	2	10	.313
	Myrtle Beach (CAR)	HiA	1	2	4.08	5	3	0	1	18	21	12	8	0	7	7	.300
	Mississippi (SL)	AA	1	0	1.00	3	2	0	0	9	10	2	1	0	5	7	.270
2009	Mississippi (SL)	AA	4	4	2.76	12	12	1	0	65	60	24	20	2	35	40	.251
	Gwinnett (IL)	AAA	4	7	5.62	17	17	0	0	91	103	64	57	7	42	58	.285
MINOR LEAGUE TOTALS			22	28	4.15	92	70	1	5	416	417	229	192	21	193	306	.262

Baltimore Orioles

BY WILL LINGO

The 2000s were a decade to forget for the Orioles. But they finally can see enough legitimate big leaguers in place or on the horizon to believe there's hope for the future.

Since Baltimore won the American League East and went to the AL Championship Series in 1997, the team not only hasn't returned to the playoffs but also hasn't finished above .500—and it hasn't even been

particularly close. The Orioles finished fourth in the AL East nine times in 10 years before bottoming out in last place over the last two seasons.

The Orioles were able to keep their heads above water before the all-star break in 2009, but the second half was a disaster. They endured a 13-game losing streak in September, the third-longest in franchise history, on the way to a 64-98 record, the third-worst in baseball. Their offense and defense were middle of the road, but their pitchers put up the worst numbers in baseball, with a 5.16 ERA and 876 runs allowed.

And yet it's on that young and often overmatched pitching staff that the seeds of a turnaround have been planted. Chris Tillman and Brian Matusz, Baltimore's top pitching prospects coming into 2009, made their major league debuts, taking their lumps but showing flashes of their talent. Matusz now ranks as the system's top prospect, while Tillman no longer qualifies.

Several other pitchers graduated to the majors, including Brad Bergesen, Jason Berken, David Hernandez and Kam Mickolio. Others such as Jake Arrieta, Zach Britton and Troy Patton are expected to reach Baltimore soon. Not all of them will pan out—Berken's numbers in particular were ugly last year at 6-12, 6.54—but the volume of arms with legitimate promise finally gives the Orioles margin for error.

While the rookie position players couldn't match the pitchers in volume, their results were even more encouraging. Organization cornerstone Matt Wieters didn't put up overwhelming numbers in his big league debut, batting .288/.340/.412, but he showed enough that he's still expected to be one of baseball's best catchers in the near future. A more pleasant surprise was the performance of Nolan Reimold, whose 15 homers led AL rookies. With him, Adam Jones and Nick Markakis, the Orioles look set in the outfield.

Baltimore also found a building block for its infield at the trade deadline when it sent closer George Sherrill to the Dodgers for third baseman Josh Bell (as well as righthander Steve Johnson, who was lost in the

DAVID STONER

Chris Tillman led a wave of young pitching that began arriving in Baltimore in 2009

TOP 30 PROSPECTS

1. Brian Matusz, lhp	16. Brett Jacobson, rhp
2. Josh Bell, 3b	17. Brandon Cooney, rhp
3. Zach Britton, lhp	18. Brandon Waring, 1b/3b
4. Jake Arrieta, rhp	19. Cameron Coffey, lhp
5. Matt Hobgood, rhp	20. Kyle Hudson, of
6. Brandon Snyder, 1b	21. L.J. Hoes, 2b
7. Brandon Erbe, rhp	22. Oliver Drake, rhp
8. Kam Mickolio, rhp	23. Jake Cowan, rhp
9. Mychal Givens, ss	24. Ryan Berry, rhp
10. Caleb Joseph, c	25. Matt Angle, of
11. Luis Lebron, rhp	26. Ryan Adams, 2b
12. Pedro Florimon, ss	27. Garabez Rosa, ss
13. Xavier Avery, of	28. Chorye Spoone, rhp
14. Troy Patton, lhp	29. Eddie Gamboa, rhp
15. Michael Ohlman, c	30. Billy Rowell, of

major league Rule 5 draft). Bell got in better shape this year and really impressed scouts in the Arizona Fall League. He easily ranks as the best upper-level hitting prospect in the system.

Beyond Bell the position players are thin, however, as the Orioles have emphasized pitching as the way they're going to become a contender again. They did shell out their second- and third-largest bonuses to sign shortstop Mychal Givens and catcher Michael Ohlman in last year's draft, but used the fifth overall pick on high school righthander Matt Hobgood and spent big money on several pitchers in later rounds.

General Manager: Andy MacPhail. **Farm Director:** David Stockstill. **Scouting Director:** Joe Jordan.

Class	Team	League	W	L	PCT	Finish*	Manager(s)
Majors	Baltimore Orioles	American	64	98	.395	14th (14)	Dave Trembley
Triple-A	Norfolk Tides	International	71	71	.500	7th (14)	Gary Allenson
Double-A	Bowie Baysox	Eastern	73	69	.514	4th (12)	Brad Komminsk
High A	Frederick Keys	Carolina	64	75	.460	6th (8)	Richie Hebner
Low A	Delmarva Shorebirds	South Atlantic	66	70	.485	10th (16)	Orlando Gomez
Short-season	Aberdeen IronBirds	New York-Penn	30	44	.405	12th (14)	Gary Kendall
Rookie	Bluefield Orioles	Appalachian	33	35	.485	5th (10)	Einar Diaz
Rookie	GCL Orioles	Gulf Coast	30	26	.536	5th (16)	Ramon Sambo
Overall 2009 Minor League Record			367	390	.485	25th (30)	

*Finish in overall standings (No. of teams in league). †League champion.

LAST YEAR'S TOP 30

Player, Pos.	Status
1. Matt Wieters, c	Majors
2. Chris Tillman, rhp	Majors
3. Brian Matusz, lhp	No. 1
4. Jake Arrieta, rhp	No. 4
5. Nolan Reimold, of	Majors
6. Brandon Erbe, rhp	No. 7
7. Billy Rowell, 3b	No. 30
8. Troy Patton, lhp	No. 14
9. Brandon Snyder, 1b	No. 6
10. Kam Mickolio, rhp	No. 8
11. Chorye Spoone, rhp	No. 28
12. Zach Britton, lhp	No. 3
13. Xavier Avery, of	No. 13
14. L.J. Hoes, 2b	No. 21
15. Bobby Bundy, rhp	Dropped out
16. David Hernandez, rhp	Majors
17. Jason Berken, rhp	Majors
18. Brad Bergesen, rhp	Majors
19. Tyler Henson, 3b	Dropped out
20. Matt Angle, of	No. 25
21. Pedro Beato, rhp	Dropped out
22. Bob McCrory, rhp	(Free agent)
23. Greg Miclat, ss	Dropped out
24. Tony Butler, lhp	Dropped out
25. Brandon Cooney, rhp	No. 17
26. Brandon Waring, 3b	No. 18
27. Justin Turner, 2b	Dropped out
28. Ryan Adams, 2b	No. 26
29. Lou Montanez, of	Majors
30. Caleb Joseph, c	No. 10

BEST TOOLS

Best Hitter for Average	Brandon Snyder
Best Power Hitter	Brandon Waring
Best Strike-Zone Discipline	Matt Angle
Fastest Baserunner	Xavier Avery
Best Athlete	Mychal Givens
Best Fastball	Kam Mickolio
Best Curveball	Brian Matusz
Best Slider	Jake Arrieta
Best Changeup	Brian Matusz
Best Control	Brian Matusz
Best Defensive Catcher	Caleb Joseph
Best Defensive Infielder	Blake Davis
Best Infield Arm	Mychal Givens
Best Defensive Outfielder	Matt Angle
Best Outfield Arm	Billy Rowell

PROJECTED 2012 LINEUP

Catcher	Matt Wieters
First Base	Brandon Snyder
Second Base	Brian Roberts
Third Base	Josh Bell
Shortstop	Mychal Givens
Left Field	Nolan Reimold
Center Field	Adam Jones
Right Field	Nick Markakis
Designated Hitter	Brandon Waring
No. 1 Starter	Chris Tillman
No. 2 Starter	Brian Matusz
No. 3 Starter	Zach Britton
No. 4 Starter	Jake Arrieta
No. 5 Starter	Matt Hobgood
Closer	Brandon Erbe

TOP PROSPECTS OF THE DECADE

Year	Player, Pos.	2009 Org.
2000	Matt Riley, lhp	Out of baseball
2001	Keith Reed, of	Out of baseball
2002	Richard Stahl, lhp	Out of baseball
2003	Erik Bedard, lhp	Mariners
2004	Adam Loewen, lhp	Blue Jays
2005	Nick Markakis, of	Orioles
2006	Nick Markakis, of	Orioles
2007	Billy Rowell, 3b	Orioles
2008	Matt Wieters, c	Orioles
2009	Matt Wieters, c	Orioles

TOP DRAFT PICKS OF THE DECADE

Year	Player, Pos.	2009 Org.
2000	Beau Hale, rhp	Out of baseball
2001	Chris Smith, lhp	Out of baseball
2002	Adam Loewen, lhp	Blue Jays
2003	Nick Markakis, of	Orioles
2004	*Wade Townsend, rhp	Rays
2005	Brandon Snyder, c	Orioles
2006	Billy Rowell, 3b	Orioles
2007	Matt Wieters, c	Orioles
2008	Brian Matusz, lhp	Orioles
2009	Matt Hobgood, rhp	Orioles

*Did not sign.

LARGEST BONUSES IN CLUB HISTORY

Matt Wieters, 2007	$6,000,000
Adam Loewen, 2002	$3,200,000
Brian Matusz, 2008	$3,200,000
Matt Hobgood, 2009	$2,422,000
Beau Hale, 2000	$2,250,000

BALTIMORE ORIOLES

TOP 2010 ROOKIE: Brian Matusz, lhp. He got to the big leagues a year after the Orioles drafted him fourth overall, and he'll be a mainstay in their rotation from here on out.

BREAKOUT PROSPECT: Jake Cowan, rhp. If he can stay healthy, he has the stuff to rank among the best mound prospects in a system stacked with pitching.

SLEEPER: Randy Henry, rhp. He touched 96 mph last spring, just 18 months removed from Tommy John surgery.

SOURCE OF TOP 30 TALENT			
Homegrown	25	Acquired	5
College	9	Trades	5
Junior college	2	Rule 5 draft	0
High school	11	Independent leagues	0
Draft-and-follow	0	Free agents/waivers	0
Nondrafted free agents	0		
International	3		

Numbers in parentheses indicate prospect rankings

LF
Kieron Pope
Manuel Hernandez

CF
Xavier Avery (13)
Kyle Hudson (20)
Matt Angle (25)
Danny Figueroa
Brenden Webb
Kyle Hoppy

RF
Billy Rowell (30)
Robbie Widlansky

3B
Josh Bell (2)
Tyler Henson
Ty Kelly
Scott Moore
Corey Thomas

SS
Mychal Givens (9)
Pedro Florimon (12)
Garabez Rosa (27)
Greg Miclat
Blake Davis

2B
L.J. Hoes (21)
Ryan Adams (26)
Justin Turner
Miguel Abreu
Paco Figueroa

1B
Brandon Snyder (6)
Brandon Waring (18)
Rhyne Hughes
Tyler Townsend

C
Caleb Joseph (10)
Michael Ohlman (15)
Craig Tatum
Justin Dalles
Dashenko Ricardo

RHP

Starters	Relievers
Jake Arrieta (4)	Kam Mickolio (8)
Matt Hobgood (5)	Luis Lebron (11)
Brandon Erbe (7)	Brett Jacobson (16)
Oliver Drake (22)	Brandon Cooney (17)
Jake Cowan (23)	Ryan Berry (24)
Chorye Spoone (28)	Eddie Gamboa (29)
Randy Henry	Jose Duran
Bobby Bundy	Ryohei Tanaka
Pedro Beato	Pat Egan
Jesse Beal	Alfredo Simon
Josh Perrault	John Mariotti
David Pauley	Kevin Landry
Sean Gleason	
Tim Bascom	
Luis Noel	
David Baker	
Ryan Palsha	

LHP

Starters	Relievers
Brian Matusz (1)	Wilfrido Perez
Zach Britton (3)	Rick Zagone
Troy Patton (14)	Tony Butler
Cameron Coffey (19)	Chad Thall
Ashur Tolliver	
Aaron Wirsch	
Cole McCurry	
Jarret Martin	
Tim Berry	

2009 BONUSES: $8.7 MILLION

BEST PURE HITTER: The Orioles believe 1B Tyler Townsend (3) can hit for power and average. He struggled in his debut, due in part to a sore wrist, after hitting .426 in the spring at Florida International and .387 last summer in the Valley League.

BEST POWER HITTER: With his 6-foot-4, 200-pound frame, C Michael Ohlman (11) resembles Jayson Werth, whom the Orioles drafted in the first round in 1997. Ohlman has similar power potential. Townsend also has plus power.

FASTEST RUNNER: OF Brenden Webb (30), who spurned Southern California for a $250,000 bonus, is a well above-average runner with an athletic 6-foot-2, 190-pound frame.

BEST DEFENSIVE PLAYER: The Orioles drafted SS Mychal Givens (2) because they believe in his defense and athleticism. He has the first-step quickness, good hands and premium arm to be an above-average defender.

BEST FASTBALL: Scouting director Joe Jordan saw RHPs Matt Hobgood (1) and Randy Henry (4) hit 96 mph this spring. They do it very differently, as the burly Hobgood is listed at 245 pounds while Henry has a lithe, athletic body. Hobgood's velocity dipped after signing, and he topped out at 91 in instructional league. LHP Cameron Coffey (22) ran his heater up to 95 before having Tommy John surgery in March, while LHP Ashur Tolliver (5) has hit 96 in the past.

BEST SECONDARY PITCH: RHP Ryan Berry (9) has an excellent feel for his knuckle-curve, throwing it for strikes when needed and burying it at other times.

BEST PRO DEBUT: 3B/2B Ty Kelly (13) was a midseason New York-Penn League all-star but struggled in the second half for short-season Aberdeen, batting .265/.357/.310 overall. RHP Jake Cowan (10) pitched just 24 innings at Aberdeen, going 1-2, 2.25 with 27 strikeouts.

BEST ATHLETE: Givens, who ran his fastball up to 97 mph on the mound and has a quick bat at the plate, was a legitimate two-way prospect.

MOST INTRIGUING BACKGROUND: Like his father Al, a former Orioles all-star, Steve Bumbry (12) is a lefthanded-hitting center fielder. 1B/3B Mike Flacco (31), who hit .272/.325/.417 at Rookie-level Bluefield, is the younger brother of Ravens quarterback Joe. He missed two seasons of athletic competition with a stress fracture in his back.

CLOSEST TO THE MAJORS: Berry, if he's healthy after a muscle strain in his throwing shoulder slowed him last spring. The Orioles are wary of the track record of Rice pitchers, but their medical staff cleared him.

BEST LATE-ROUND PICK: Baltimore has high hopes for Ohlman ($995,000) and Coffey ($990,000) after giving them lavish bonuses.

THE ONE WHO GOT AWAY: RHP Garrett Bush (15) has a good frame and gained velocity after giving up catching in the spring, but he couldn't be signed away from his Auburn commitment.

ASSESSMENT: Hobgood may determine how this draft is remembered, but taking him at No. 5 allowed the Orioles to save money and take chances on Ohlman and Coffey. By diversifying, they got the impact up-the-middle talent they wanted in Givens and Ohlman while also adding some promising arms.

2008 BONUSES: $6.9 MILLION

The Orioles got the best pitcher in the draft with the fourth overall choice, and LHP Brian Matusz (1) has been as good as advertised. OFs Xavier Avery (2) and Kyle Hudson (4) are two of the best athletes in the system.

GRADE: A

2007 BONUSES: $8.0 MILLION

Baltimore got the best hitter in this draft with the fifth overall pick, and C Matt Wieters (1) is headed for stardom. Signed for $1.1 million, RHP Jake Arrieta (5) is almost ready for the big league rotation.

GRADE: A

2006 BONUSES: $5.4 MILLION

OF Billy Rowell (1) and RHP Pedro Beato (1s), the top picks in this crop, are flaming out quickly. That leaves LHP Zach Britton (3) to pick up the slack. RHP Jason Berksen (6) didn't look good in an extended big league trial last season.

GRADE: D

2005 BONUSES: $4.2 MILLION*

OF Nolan Reimold (2) topped American League rookies with 15 homers last year, and since-traded LHP Garrett Olson (1s) and RHP David Hernandez (16) also have reached the majors. 1B Brandon Snyder (1) and RHP Brandon Erbe (3) could join them soon.

GRADE: C+

*Draft analysis by John Manuel (2009) and Jim Callis (2005-08). Numbers in parentheses indicate draft rounds. *Bonuses for 2005 are first 10 rounds only.*

RODGER WOOD

BRIAN MATUSZ, LHP

Born: Feb. 11, 1987.
Height: 6-5. **Weight:** 200.
Bats: Left. **Throws:** Left.
Drafted: San Diego, 2008 (1st round).
Signed by: Mark Ralston.

The Orioles felt like they got a bargain when they took Matusz with the fourth overall pick in the 2008 draft and signed him to a major league contract worth $3,472,500. He did nothing but reinforce that opinion in his pro debut, going from the University of San Diego to pitching in Yankee Stadium in a year. After signing too late to pitch in 2008, Matusz opened at high Class A Frederick and dominated in 11 starts, then pitched even better at Double-A Bowie to earn an eight-start trial in Baltimore to wrap up the season. His 1.91 ERA between his two minor league stops ranked fourth overall in the minors. He ranked as the top pitching prospect in the Carolina League, and would have done the same in the Eastern League if he had enough innings to qualify for Baseball America's rankings. Matusz was the fourth-highest pick out of the 2005 draft not to sign, turning down the Angels in the fourth round out of an Arizona high school to spend three years at San Diego, where he set the school's career strikeout record (396) and led NCAA Division I in whiffs (146) during an All-America junior season in 2008. He went 12-2, 1.71 that spring. He was the highest-drafted player in Toreros history and the first pitcher drafted that year.

Matusz has three (and potentially four) above-average pitches and advanced command of his entire repertoire, yet most people say that his best trait might be his makeup. Team officials describe him as a winner and admire the way he made adjustments in his first pro season. He's both intelligent and determined, with a great feel for pitching and a strong will that allows him to deal with adversity and never give in to hitters. When an Orioles official told him that his changeup wasn't as good as it needed to be early in the year at Frederick, he went out and threw more than 20 times in his next start, commanding it and using it in a variety of counts and situations. He sits in the low 90s with his fastball, touching 95 mph, and complements it with both a curveball and a slider. The slider rates as the more effective pitch at this point. His changeup is the best in the system and could be well above-average in the future as he masters his command of it. He has a clean delivery and repeats it well.

While his command is advanced for his level of pro experience, sharpening it will be Matusz's final task. He has great control and usually is able to keep the ball low and work both sides of the plate at will, so he just needs more experience against big league hitters to develop the pinpoint command he'll require to get them out consistently.

A No. 1 starter isn't always the guy who has the best pure stuff. And while Matusz's pure stuff is plenty good, it's what's between his ears that could make him the Orioles' ace within the next couple of years. Having gotten his feet wet in Baltimore last season, he'll be expected to win a spot in the major league rotation in spring training as the Orioles fill in homegrown studs behind newly acquired veteran Kevin Millwood.

Year	Club (League)	Class	W	L	ERA	G	GS	CG	SV	IP	H	R	ER	HR	BB	SO	AVG
2009	Frederick (CAR)	HiA	4	2	2.16	11	11	0	0	67	56	22	16	5	21	75	.225
	Bowie (EL)	AA	7	0	1.55	8	8	1	0	46	31	9	8	2	11	46	.189
	Baltimore (AL)	MAJ	5	2	4.63	8	8	0	0	45	52	24	23	6	14	38	.292
MAJOR LEAGUE TOTALS			5	2	4.63	8	8	0	0	45	52	24	23	6	14	38	.292
MINOR LEAGUE TOTALS			11	2	1.91	19	19	1	0	113	87	31	24	7	32	121	.211

2 JOSH BELL, 3B

BORN: Nov. 13, 1986. **B-T:** B-R. **HT.:** 6-3. **WT.:** 235. **DRAFTED:** HS—Santaluces, Fla., 2005 (4th round). **SIGNED BY:** Manny Estrada (Dodgers).

Bell's prospect status had dimmed a bit with the Dodgers, but he got himself into better shape and had a bounceback season, becoming the key player in the deadline trade that sent reliever George Sherrill to Los Angeles. He showed no ill effects from a knee injury that had bothered him in 2008, and ranked as the No. 5 prospect in the Arizona Fall League after the season. In a system lacking in impact bats, Bell fills a huge need. He has above-average power and a good approach, showing the ability to work counts to get on base. While he's a below-average runner, Bell has worked hard to become an average defender at third base, with smooth actions, improved footwork and an above-average arm. Bell is a switch-hitter, but his lefthanded swing is much smoother and he has severe splits, batting .193 with one home run in 135 at-bats against lefthanders last year, and .339 with 19 homers in 313 at-bats against righthanders. He has shown enough promise that the Orioles will allow him to continue switch-hitting for now. The Orioles think they have found their third baseman of the future, and with Melvin Mora not returning the future could come soon. Garret Atkins will keep the position warm while Bell gets at-bats in Triple-A, but Bell should take over at some point in 2010.

Year	Club (League)	Class	AVG	G	AB	R	H	2B	3B	HR	RBI	BB	SO	SB	OBP	SLG
2005	Dodgers (GCL)	R	.318	45	157	26	50	7	1	1	21	20	33	5	.399	.395
2006	Ogden (PIO)	R	.308	64	250	45	77	17	3	12	53	23	72	4	.367	.544
2007	Great Lakes (MWL)	LoA	.289	108	398	65	115	21	3	15	62	39	109	5	.354	.470
	Inland Empire (CAL)	HiA	.173	20	75	4	13	2	1	2	9	3	19	0	.203	.307
2008	Inland Empire (CAL)	HiA	.273	51	187	34	51	12	2	6	21	31	56	4	.373	.455
2009	Chattanooga (SL)	AA	.296	94	334	47	99	30	2	11	52	50	70	3	.386	.497
	Bowie (EL)	AA	.289	33	114	18	33	5	0	9	24	11	28	0	.346	.570
MINOR LEAGUE TOTALS			.289	415	1515	239	438	94	12	56	242	177	387	21	.363	.478

3 ZACH BRITTON, LHP

BORN: Dec. 22, 1987. **B-T:** L-L. **HT.:** 6-2. **WT.:** 180. **DRAFTED:** HS—Weatherford, Texas, 2006 (3rd round). **SIGNED BY:** Jim Richardson.

When talking about quality pitching prospects in the Orioles organization, it's time to add Britton's name to the discussion. He was the pitcher of the year in the Carolina League last season, and his 2.70 ERA ranked second in the league. The Orioles shut him down a bit early with shoulder fatigue when he hit 140 innings, but he'll be at full speed for spring training. Britton seems like the typical sinker/slider pitcher, except that his fastball touches 94 mph. His velocity improved last season, and he usually works in the 88-92 range with his sinker, adding a four-seam fastball to go with it. His slider has become an effective weapon against lefthanded hitters, and his already-solid changeup improved as well, in part thanks to tips he got from Brian Matusz. Britton's command has improved and he does a good job of keeping the ball down in the zone, but he still needs to throw more strikes with his fastball and get himself ahead of hitters. His 55 walks led the Frederick staff, and his 21 wild pitches led the Carolina League. Britton is another Orioles pitcher who earns high marks for his makeup, and he could get a lot more attention in 2010 if he moves up to the Bowie rotation and pitches well. He projects as a solid No. 3 starter.

Year	Club (League)	Class	W	L	ERA	G	GS	CG	SV	IP	H	R	ER	HR	BB	SO	AVG
2006	Bluefield (APP)	R	0	4	5.29	11	11	0	0	34	35	22	20	4	20	21	.271
2007	Aberdeen (NYP)	SS	6	4	3.68	15	15	0	0	64	64	33	26	1	22	45	.256
2008	Delmarva (SAL)	LoA	12	7	3.12	27	27	1	0	147	118	68	51	9	49	114	.219
2009	Frederick (CAR)	HiA	9	6	2.70	25	24	0	0	140	123	64	42	6	55	131	.232
MINOR LEAGUE TOTALS			27	21	3.25	78	77	1	0	385	340	187	139	20	146	311	.234

4 JAKE ARRIETA, RHP

BORN: March 6, 1986. **B-T:** R-R. **HT.:** 6-4. **WT.:** 225. **DRAFTED:** Texas Christian, 2007 (5th round). **SIGNED BY:** Jim Richardson.

After leading the Carolina League in ERA and pitching in the Olympics for Team USA in 2008, Arrieta pitched his way to Triple-A in 2009 and led the organization (both major and minor leaguers) with 148 strikeouts. The Orioles signed him for a $1.1 million bonus in 2007. Arrieta is a bulldog who is willing to challenge hitters in the strike zone. His fastball sits in the 92-94 mph range, and has the action to generate swings and misses. His slider has become a solid second pitch and is plus at times, while his changeup is solid but needs the most improvement. He also occasionally throws a curve to lefthanded hitters. While Arrieta can throw strikes with all his pitches, he needs to do it more consistently and better command his pitches in the strike zone. His 56 walks last season were the most in the farm system. The Orioles worked to shorten his stride last season to give his pitches a better finish and keep them down. Arrieta's pure stuff compares with any of the Orioles' elite young pitchers, but his command puts him a notch behind them. While some scouts think that could eventually send Arrieta to the bullpen, the Orioles see him as a middle-of-the-rotation pitcher who can pile up 200 innings a year with no problems.

Year	Club (League)	Class	W	L	ERA	G	GS	CG	SV	IP	H	R	ER	HR	BB	SO	AVG
2008	Frederick (CAR)	HiA	6	5	2.87	20	20	0	0	113	80	44	36	7	51	120	.199
2009	Bowie (EL)	AA	6	3	2.59	11	11	2	0	59	45	21	17	4	23	70	.208
	Norfolk (IL)	AAA	5	8	3.93	17	17	0	0	92	97	46	40	9	33	78	.276
MINOR LEAGUE TOTALS			17	16	3.17	48	48	2	0	264	222	111	93	20	107	268	.229

5 MATT HOBGOOD, RHP

BORN: Aug. 3, 1990. **B-T:** R-R. **HT.:** 6-4. **WT.:** 245. **DRAFTED:** HS—Norco, Calif., 2009 (1st round). **SIGNED BY:** Mark Ralston.

The Orioles surprised some people when they made Hobgood the first high school pitcher drafted last June, taking him No. 5 overall. Most clubs rated him as a mid-first-round talent and he signed quickly for a slightly below-slot $2.422 million, but Baltimore insists he was the player it liked best. He began his pro career in the Rookie-level Appalachian League and finished as the league's No. 4 prospect. Hobgood is a big, burly power pitcher who has drawn physical comparisons to Goose Gossage and Curt Schilling. He was a two-way player in high school with plus power in his bat. With a 90-96 mph fastball, backed by a curveball and changeup that also could become plus pitches, his future clearly was on the mound. His frame and clean, repeatable mechanics should bode well for his durability. Hobgood still needs to refine his secondary pitches and command. His body is already mature, so there's not a lot of projection left. He topped out at 91 mph in instructional league, but the Orioles say he was just tired. It may take Hobgood some time to refine his arsenal, but the raw stuff is there. He'll get a chance to win a spot in the low Class A Delmarva rotation in spring training, though he could open the year in extended spring

Year	Club (League)	Class	W	L	ERA	G	GS	CG	SV	IP	H	R	ER	HR	BB	SO	AVG
2009	Bluefield (APP)	R	1	2	4.72	8	8	0	0	27	32	17	14	0	8	16	.305
MINOR LEAGUE TOTALS			1	2	4.72	8	8	0	0	27	32	17	14	0	8	16	.305

6 BRANDON SNYDER, 1B

BORN: Nov. 23, 1986. **B-T:** R-R. **HT.:** 6-2. **WT.:** 210. **DRAFTED:** HS—Centreville, Va., 2005 (1st round). **SIGNED BY:** Ty Brown.

The son of former big leaguer Brian Snyder, Brandon signed for $1.7 million as the 13th overall pick in the 2005 draft. He looked like he might wash out after shoulder problems limited his at-bats and forced him to move from behind the plate, but he has proven over the last two seasons that he can be a major league hitter. His .343 average would have led the Eastern League in 2009 had he stayed around long enough to qualify, and he further boosted his stock by batting .354 in the Arizona Fall League. Since Snyder got his swing and approach dialed in during the 2008 season, he has been productive at the plate. He's hitting more with his hands now, staying inside the ball and working it up the middle, as well as driving it to the opposite field more often. His defense at first base has improved significantly, and he shows good hands, footwork and arm strength for the position. Snyder doesn't have prototypical power for a first baseman, projecting to hit 15-20 homers per season, though some scouts think he could add more power down the line. He had trouble getting ahead in the count following his promotion to Triple-A last June. He's a fringe-average runner. Snyder struggled enough at Norfolk to show that he needs more experience against quality pitching. He'll open the season back in Triple-A and prepare himself for a major league opportunity. He looks like he'll profile as a righthanded-hitting Sean Casey.

Year	Club (League)	Class	AVG	G	AB	R	H	2B	3B	HR	RBI	BB	SO	SB	OBP	SLG
2005	Bluefield (APP)	R	.271	44	144	26	39	8	0	8	35	28	36	7	.380	.493
	Aberdeen (NYP)	SS	.393	8	28	4	11	2	0	0	6	2	7	0	.419	.464
2006	Delmarva (SAL)	LoA	.194	38	144	12	28	12	0	3	20	9	55	0	.237	.340
	Aberdeen (NYP)	SS	.234	34	124	14	29	8	1	1	11	5	43	2	.267	.339
2007	Delmarva (SAL)	LoA	.283	118	448	63	127	23	3	11	58	44	107	0	.354	.422
2008	Frederick (CAR)	HiA	.315	116	435	70	137	33	2	13	80	29	83	3	.358	.490
2009	Bowie (EL)	AA	.343	58	201	24	69	19	1	10	45	27	45	0	.421	.597
	Norfolk (IL)	AAA	.248	73	262	36	65	18	2	2	43	24	64	3	.316	.355
MINOR LEAGUE TOTALS			.283	489	1786	249	505	123	9	48	298	168	440	15	.346	.442

7 BRANDON ERBE, RHP

BORN: Dec. 25, 1987. **B-T:** R-R. **HT.:** 6-4. **WT.:** 180. **DRAFTED:** HS—Baltimore, 2005 (3rd round). **SIGNED BY:** Ty Brown.

The Orioles have taken a patient approach with Erbe because they've had do. After a strong 2008 when he led the Carolina League with 151 strikeouts, Erbe missed nearly two months last year with shoulder tendinitis. He returned to action in June and made three starts in the Arizona Fall League, and the Orioles added him to the 40-man roster. When he returned to action, he worked at 91-92 mph and touched 94 with good, hard late life down in the zone. He has thrown harder in the past. His slider should be an above-average pitch in time, and he made strides with his now-average changeup as well. Fastball command and durability remain the tipping points that will determine how good Erbe can be. He tends to pitch up in the strike zone, leaving him vulnerable to homers and walks. The Orioles smoothed out his mechanics a couple of years ago and will give him every opportunity to remain a starter. Erbe will compete for a spot in the Norfolk rotation in spring training. Because of his track record and the large group of starter candidates in the organization, it seems likely that he'll end up in the bullpen long-term.

Year	Club (League)	Class	W	L	ERA	G	GS	CG	SV	IP	H	R	ER	HR	BB	SO	AVG
2005	Bluefield (APP)	R	1	1	3.09	11	3	0	1	23	8	10	8	1	10	48	.103
	Aberdeen (NYP)	SS	1	1	7.71	3	1	0	0	7	6	6	6	0	4	9	.261
2006	Delmarva (SAL)	LoA	5	9	3.22	28	27	0	0	115	88	47	41	2	47	133	.217
2007	Frederick (CAR)	HiA	6	8	6.26	25	25	0	0	119	127	95	83	14	62	111	.273
2008	Frederick (CAR)	HiA	10	12	4.30	28	28	2	0	151	120	82	72	21	50	151	.216
2009	Aberdeen (NYP)	SS	0	1	4.61	4	4	0	0	14	13	9	7	3	2	11	.245
	Bowie (EL)	AA	5	3	2.34	14	14	2	0	73	44	27	19	5	35	62	.170
MINOR LEAGUE TOTALS			28	35	4.23	113	102	4	1	502	406	276	236	46	210	525	.221

8 KAM MICKOLIO, RHP

BORN: May 10, 1984. **B-T:** R-R. **HT.:** 6-9. **WT.:** 255. **DRAFTED:** Utah Valley State, 2006 (18th round). **SIGNED BY:** Phil Geisler (Mariners).

Though he'll play most of the 2010 season at 26, Mickolio is young in terms of his experience and his arm. He didn't play baseball until American Legion ball in 2001, before his senior year of high school in Montana, then he attended college in Utah for four years before the Mariners drafted him in 2006. He came to the Orioles in the Erik Bedard deal in February 2008 and has pitched in the majors in each of the last two seasons. Mickolio has a pure power arsenal and is an intimidating presence on the mound, driving fastballs down on a steep downhill plane. His fastball sits around 95 mph and peaks at 97-98, and he was much more consistent with his slider last season. He even had enough confidence in his changeup to throw it in the big leagues on occasion. The Orioles try to walk the line between tweaking his funky crossfire delivery and letting him do what works for him. He was shut down the last two Septembers with a tired arm. He needs to sharpen his command and must do a better job of understanding hitters and how to attack them. His changeup still grades as below-average. Mickolio has the stuff to pitch in the back of a major league bullpen, and if he develops a better feel he could be a closer. He should win a spot in the big league bullpen this spring.

Year	Club (League)	Class	W	L	ERA	G	GS	CG	SV	IP	H	R	ER	HR	BB	SO	AVG
2006	Everett (NWL)	SS	1	0	2.78	21	0	0	4	32	34	14	10	1	7	26	.264
2007	West Tenn (SL)	AA	3	1	1.82	18	0	0	2	30	24	9	6	0	12	27	.224
	Tacoma (PCL)	AAA	3	3	3.75	14	0	0	1	24	19	12	10	3	10	28	.213
2008	Bowie (EL)	AA	2	1	4.70	28	0	0	1	38	39	21	20	2	22	40	.262
	Norfolk (IL)	AAA	1	0	1.80	17	0	0	2	20	13	7	4	0	9	23	.173
	Baltimore (AL)	MAJ	0	1	5.87	9	0	0	0	8	8	5	5	0	4	8	.267
2009	Norfolk (IL)	AAA	3	3	3.50	35	0	0	0	44	32	21	17	4	16	52	.203
	Baltimore (AL)	MAJ	0	2	2.63	11	0	0	0	14	11	4	4	0	7	14	.220
MAJOR LEAGUE TOTALS			0	3	3.80	20	0	0	0	21	19	9	9	0	11	22	.238
MINOR LEAGUE TOTALS			13	8	3.21	133	0	0	10	188	161	84	67	10	76	196	.228

9 MYCHAL GIVENS, SS

BORN: May 13, 1990. **B-T:** R-R. **HT.:** 6-1. **WT.:** 190. **DRAFTED:** HS—Tampa, 2009 (2nd round). **SIGNED BY:** John Martin.

Givens jumped into the national amateur spotlight early and played in both the Aflac and Under Armour All-America games before his senior year of high school, and he was regarded as one of the best two-way prospects in the 2009 draft class. Eventually most scouts thought he would end up as a reliever on the mound and saw him more as a shortstop—as did the Orioles, who signed him for $800,000 as the 54th overall pick. Givens signed too late to make his professional debut last summer, but in instructional league he showed the athleticism the Orioles were looking for, with agility, balance, speed and strength. He has good bat speed and should be able to hit for power as he matures. He shows good actions at shortstop and has a plus arm, touching 97 mph when he was a pitcher. The Orioles expect Givens will need a good number of minor league at-bats and will need to tweak his swing to take advantage of his strength. He'll need repetitions at shortstop as well. While Givens has played a lot of baseball, he'll need refinement as a shortstop and hitter after spending a good bit of his high school career as a pitcher. He'll debut at a short-season stop after a stint in extended spring training.

Year	Club (League)	Class	AVG	G	AB	R	H	2B	3B	HR	RBI	BB	SO	SB	OBP	SLG
2009	Did Not Play—Signed Late															

10 CALEB JOSEPH, C

BORN: June 18, 1986. **B-T:** R-R. **HT.:** 6-3. **WT.:** 180. **DRAFTED:** Lipscomb, 2008 (7th round). **SIGNED BY:** Rich Morales.

When Joseph had a strong debut at Aberdeen in 2008, the Orioles jumped him a level and he spent all season at Frederick, finishing up as the catcher on the Carolina League's postseason all-star team. He wore down as the season went on and hit .156 in August, but still finished eighth in the league in batting. The more you see Joseph, the more you like him, and that seems to go for everyone from scouts to managers to pitchers, who love working with him. His tools grade out as average across the board, but his performance is consistently above-average. He understands his swing and knows how to hit, consistently centering the ball and hitting it where it's pitched. He's a good athlete and blocks and receives well. He has an average arm. Joseph's swing can get long and funky, and he'll have to hit with more power to stay out of the lower part of a batting order. He has to work on his footwork, and his release time is a bit slow. He'll need to get stronger to handle catching every day. Joseph has all the skills to be an everyday, workingman catcher. Unfortunately for him, the Orioles have Matt Wieters, who has all the skills to be a star catcher. A decision about his long-term future is still a couple of years away, though, so for now Joseph will move up to Double-A.

Year	Club (League)	Class	AVG	G	AB	R	H	2B	3B	HR	RBI	BB	SO	SB	OBP	SLG
2008	Aberdeen (NYP)	SS	.261	63	238	34	62	19	0	8	34	15	56	2	.303	.441
2009	Frederick (CAR)	HiA	.284	104	380	50	108	23	2	12	60	26	64	2	.337	.450
MINOR LEAGUE TOTALS			.275	167	618	84	170	42	2	20	94	41	120	4	.324	.447

11 LUIS LEBRON, RHP

BORN: March 13, 1985. **B-T:** R-R. **HT.:** 6-1. **WT.:** 172. **SIGNED:** Dominican Republic, 2004. **SIGNED BY:** Carlos Bernhardt.

Lebron made just seven pro starts in 2005 before the Orioles figured out his power arm worked best out of the bullpen, and he subsequently made quick progress until an elbow injury knocked him out for most of the 2008 season. He returned last season and put up the best numbers of his career, making the Carolina League all-star team before getting added to the 40-man roster after the season. His .137 opponent average ranked second among all minor league relievers last year, and his 13.6 strikeouts per nine innings ranked fifth. Lebron has lightning in his arm, with a fastball that sits at 94-96 mph and touches 97, but he's more than just a hard thrower. His slider is also a plus pitch and looked sharper than ever last year. His changeup even looked like a potentially above-average pitch after he never had shown any confidence in it in previous seasons. He generates a lot of swings and misses but needs to tighten up his command to avoid walks. Lebron showed the stuff to work at the back of a major league bullpen last season, and he should do that if he stays healthy and throws strikes. He'll likely open 2010 in Triple-A but will be an early candidate for a callup.

Year	Club (League)	Class	W	L	ERA	G	GS	CG	SV	IP	H	R	ER	HR	BB	SO	AVG
2004	Orioles (DSL)	R	0	2	4.76	14	0	0	1	17	19	15	9	0	21	22	.271
2005	Bluefield (APP)	R	2	4	11.16	14	7	0	0	25	34	37	31	2	22	45	.318
2006	Delmarva (SAL)	LoA	1	0	27.00	2	0	0	0	1	3	4	4	1	1	1	.500
	Aberdeen (NYP)	SS	0	2	1.17	32	0	0	20	31	17	6	4	2	15	46	.163
2007	Delmarva (SAL)	LoA	1	2	5.04	46	0	0	5	55	48	35	31	1	55	86	.233
	Bowie (EL)	AA	0	0	3.86	2	0	0	0	2	1	1	1	0	1	4	.125
2008	Orioles (GCL)	R	0	1	14.40	11	0	0	2	10	20	18	16	0	15	6	.426
	Aberdeen (NYP)	SS	0	0	6.52	10	0	0	0	10	11	7	7	0	12	11	.314
2009	Frederick (CAR)	HiA	2	3	3.00	28	0	0	11	33	20	11	11	2	20	52	.168
	Bowie (EL)	AA	1	0	1.98	24	0	0	9	27	8	6	6	3	13	39	.093
MINOR LEAGUE TOTALS			7	14	5.10	183	7	0	48	212	181	140	120	11	175	312	.226

12 PEDRO FLORIMON, SS

BORN: Dec. 10, 1986. **B-T:** B-R. **HT.:** 6-2. **WT.:** 165. **SIGNED:** Dominican Republic, 2004. **SIGNED BY:** Carlos Bernhardt.

Florimon may have been the most improved player in the system last year, putting his tools into action much more consistently and winning a spot on the 40-man roster after the season. A career .222 hitter entering 2009, he earned a spot in the Carolina League-California League all-star game by batting .310 in the first two months of the season, and team officials said he showed better pitch recognition and plate discipline than ever before. He fell back into bad habits in June and July but recovered to hit .312 in August. Florimon started to string together good at-bats last year, hitting the ball where it was pitched and using his hands to stay on pitches better. He still needs to cut down on his strikeouts. He's a switch-hitter with some pop and has gotten stronger in the last couple of seasons. He's an above-average runner with good instincts on the bases. Florimon's calling card remains his strong defense. He has plus range and arm strength, and he shows soft hands and fluid actions at shortstop. He also reacts well to to the ball off the bat. He has agility, quickness and an accurate slingshot throwing motion. He has to get more consistent on both offense and defense, and a player with his tools shouldn't have led the Carolina League with 35 errors last year. The Orioles were excited by his progress and would love to see him play his way into the big league picture with a good year in Double-A in 2010.

Year	Club (League)	Class	AVG	G	AB	R	H	2B	3B	HR	RBI	BB	SO	SB	OBP	SLG
2004	Orioles (DSL)	R	.204	52	167	33	34	5	5	0	19	34	59	17	.351	.293
2005	Orioles (DSL)	R	.200	63	170	35	34	4	2	0	8	41	55	19	.387	.247
2006	Bluefield (APP)	R	.333	33	120	23	40	6	1	1	8	28	29	7	.456	.425
	Aberdeen (NYP)	SS	.248	26	105	13	26	4	1	0	5	13	26	0	.336	.305
2007	Delmarva (SAL)	LoA	.197	111	371	50	73	14	1	4	34	28	107	16	.257	.272
2008	Delmarva (SAL)	LoA	.223	81	269	28	60	18	1	0	19	27	97	13	.298	.297
2009	Frederick (CAR)	HiA	.267	115	430	76	115	32	5	9	68	42	107	26	.336	.428
	Bowie (EL)	AA	.091	7	22	0	2	0	0	0	1	1	9	0	.130	.091
MINOR LEAGUE TOTALS			.232	488	1654	258	384	83	16	14	162	214	489	98	.328	.327

13 XAVIER AVERY, OF

BORN: Jan. 1, 1990. **B-T:** L-L. **HT.:** 6-0. **WT.:** 188. **DRAFTED:** HS—Ellenwood, Ga., 2008 (2nd round). **SIGNED BY:** Dave Jennings.

Orioles scouting director Joe Jordan loves athleticism and strong makeup, and Avery offers plenty of both, which is why he received a $900,000 bonus as a second-round pick in 2008. Also a standout football player in high school, he didn't put up good numbers in his first full season, but Baltimore was impressed with how hard he worked all season and started to see flashes of his ability translate into baseball performance. He's a tough young man who wants to be successful, and he told one Orioles official during the season, "I love baseball because it's so hard to be good." He's an exciting player who drew comparisons to Carl Crawford as an amateur and got Kenny Lofton comps last season because of his body and his speed. Avery's speed is at the top of the baseball scale, though he's still learning how to use it. His routes and angles are a bit shaky but he covers a lot of ground in center field. His arm is slightly below average now, though it could be average as he gets more baseball experience. He's also learning the technique of stealing bases, though he swiped 30 in 40 tries last year just on pure speed. Avery doesn't understand how to hit yet, with pitch recognition his main challenge. He swings defensively for now, though as his approach improves, his strong hands and bat speed could produce power. His ideal role is as a top-of-the-order hitter, where any pop would be a bonus. Baltimore says Avery exceeded its expectations by jumping to low Class A and holding his own last year. He'll take the next step to Frederick this season.

Year	Club (League)	Class	AVG	G	AB	R	H	2B	3B	HR	RBI	BB	SO	SB	OBP	SLG
2008	Orioles (GCL)	R	.280	47	175	27	49	8	1	0	7	10	51	13	.333	.337
2009	Delmarva (SAL)	LoA	.262	129	473	55	124	15	8	2	36	27	111	30	.306	.340
MINOR LEAGUE TOTALS			.267	176	648	82	173	23	9	2	43	37	162	43	.314	.340

14 TROY PATTON, LHP

BORN: Sept. 3, 1985. **B-T:** L-R. **Ht:** 6-5. **Wt:** 205. **DRAFTED:** HS—Magnolia, Texas, 2004 (9th round). **SIGNED BY:** Rusty Pendergrass (Astros).

When the Orioles unloaded Miguel Tejada to the Astros after the 2007 season, Patton was regarded as major league-ready and the most promising of the five players they got in return. But he dealt with shoulder problems that spring and had surgery to repair a labrum tear, missing all of 2008. When he returned last year, Baltimore's only real goal was to have him complete a healthy season, which he did by compiling 108 innings between Double-A and Triple-A. He dominated at Bowie but seemed to wear down at Norfolk, and his command wasn't sharp enough to get Triple-A hitters out consistently. Getting his pinpoint command back is the most important part of Patton's recovery, as he has always relied on moving his pitches around and keeping hitters off balance. The Orioles thought his command was good for his first year back. He pitches in the low 90s with his four-seam fastball and the high 80s with his two-seamer, and he also uses a slider and changeup. The Orioles expect to get their first real look at Patton this year, and he'll open the season in Triple-A with the expectation that he'll contribute in the big leagues at some point.

Year	Club (League)	Class	W	L	ERA	G	GS	CG	SV	IP	H	R	ER	HR	BB	SO	AVG
2004	Greeneville (APP)	R	2	2	1.93	6	6	0	0	28	23	8	6	1	5	32	.225
2005	Lexington (SAL)	LoA	5	2	1.94	15	15	0	0	79	59	24	17	3	20	94	.211

	Club (League)	Class	W	L	ERA	G	GS	CG	SV	IP	H	R	ER	HR	BB	SO	AVG
	Salem (CAR)	HiA	1	4	2.63	10	9	0	0	41	34	12	12	2	8	38	.227
2006	Salem (CAR)	HiA	7	7	2.93	19	19	1	0	101	92	49	33	4	37	102	.240
	Corpus Christi (TL)	AA	2	5	4.37	8	8	0	0	45	48	26	22	6	13	37	.271
2007	Corpus Christi (TL)	AA	6	6	2.99	16	16	0	0	102	96	38	34	10	33	69	.247
	Round Rock (PCL)	AAA	4	2	4.59	8	8	0	0	49	44	26	25	5	11	25	.247
	Houston (NL)	MAJ	0	2	3.55	3	2	0	0	13	10	6	5	3	4	8	.213
2008	Did Not Play—Injured																
2009	Bowie (EL)	AA	6	2	1.99	11	11	0	0	63	50	18	14	4	18	47	.211
	Norfolk (IL)	AAA	1	3	6.45	9	9	0	0	45	62	35	32	12	14	26	.337
MAJOR LEAGUE TOTALS			0	2	3.55	3	2	0	0	13	10	6	5	3	4	8	.213
MINOR LEAGUE TOTALS			34	33	3.17	102	101	1	0	554	508	236	195	47	159	470	.244

15 MICHAEL OHLMAN, C

BORN: Dec. 14, 1990. **B-T:** R-R. **HT.:** 6-4. **WT.:** 200. **DRAFTED:** HS—Bradenton, Fla., 2009 (11th round). **SIGNED BY:** John Martin.

While the Orioles signed 2009 first-round pick Matt Hobgood for less than MLB's slot recommendation, they made huge investments in late-round picks Ohlman ($995,000 in the 11th round) and Cameron Coffey ($990,000 in the 22nd). Ohlman draws comparisons to Jayson Werth, who had a similar build when Baltimore made him the 22nd overall pick in 1997. Like Werth, who moved from behind the plate to the outfield before he found major league success, Ohlman may not be able to stay at catcher long-term. He's long and slender and has limited experience behind the plate, so he'll have to make big strides with his blocking, footwork and ability to frame pitches. After instructional league, the Orioles believe he can make those improvements. He does have strength in his body and a plus arm, so the tools are there if he dedicates himself to getting through the steep learning curve. Ohlman has a good feel for hitting and above-average raw power, so if he can't make it behind the plate, he could have the bat for an outfield corner. He's athletic and a solid runner. Ohlman got just a handful of at-bats in the Rookie-level Gulf Coast League after signing late last summer, but Baltimore will give him a shot at making the Delmarva roster in the spring. His placement will also depend on where 2009 sixth-round pick Justin Dalles ends up, because the Orioles will want both to catch regularly.

Year	Club (League)	Class	AVG	G	AB	R	H	2B	3B	HR	RBI	BB	SO	SB	OBP	SLG
2009	Orioles (GCL)	R	.182	4	11	1	2	1	0	0	1	1	3	1	.250	.273
MINOR LEAGUE TOTALS			.182	4	11	1	2	1	0	0	1	1	3	1	.250	.273

16 BRETT JACOBSON, RHP

BORN: Nov. 9, 1986. **B-T:** R-R. **HT.:** 6-6. **WT.:** 205. **DRAFTED:** Vanderbilt, 2008 (4th round). **SIGNED BY:** Harold Zonder (Tigers).

When the Tigers went looking for a veteran bat to try to keep their sinking ship afloat last September, the Orioles were happy to oblige, sending them Aubrey Huff in exchange for Jacobson. His power repertoire always has been intriguing but has never added up to dominant results, which explains why he lasted until the fourth round in 2008 and why Detroit was willing to deal him just a year later. Jacobson's fastball runs from 89-95 mph, and he sits more at 92-95 when he's at his best. He throws straight over the top, giving hitters a different look and creating a good downward plane when he's on, but he left the ball up too often last year and had trouble repeating his delivery. His hard curveball offers a nice contrast to his fastball, and he uses his changeup against lefthanders. His changeup has sink and he throws it with good arm speed. Jacobson always has seemed best suited for a relief role, and kept ending up in the bullpen when he tried to start at Vanderbilt. He didn't work much on his secondary pitches while with Detroit, so Baltimore had him focus on those pitches and was impressed by his work ethic. He has the pure stuff to close games but probably profiles best as a setup man. He'll work in the Bowie bullpen to open 2010.

Year	Club (League)	Class	W	L	ERA	G	GS	CG	SV	IP	H	R	ER	HR	BB	SO	AVG
2008	West Michigan (MWL)	LoA	2	2	1.52	21	0	0	1	30	26	7	5	0	5	31	.236
2009	Lakeland (FSL)	HiA	1	3	3.74	35	0	0	6	55	51	30	23	6	17	44	.243
	Frederick (CAR)	HiA	1	2	6.30	7	0	0	0	10	7	7	7	1	9	11	.206
MINOR LEAGUE TOTALS			4	7	3.32	63	0	0	7	95	84	44	35	7	31	86	.237

17 BRANDON COONEY, RHP

BORN: Aug. 2, 1985. **B-T:** R-R. **HT.:** 6-6. **WT.:** 261. **DRAFTED:** Florida Atlantic, 2007 (30th round). **SIGNED BY:** John Martin.

Cooney slogged through the college ranks, never putting together a strong season at Broward (Fla.) CC or Florida Atlantic. He turned down the White Sox as a 33rd-rounder in 2004 and the Cardinals as a 20th-rounder two years later before signing with the Orioles for $1,000 as a 30th-round afterthought in 2007. Baltimore discovered he had a shoulder injury after signing him, but rest and rehab got Cooney back to full strength without surgery. The Orioles sent him to the bullpen in 2008 to keep his innings down, and he pitched so well in relief that they decided to keep him there. He converted 22 of 25 save opportunities between two Class A stops in 2009. Cooney is a big, intimidating presence on the mound, and he usually dials his baseball to 93-96 mph with heavy sink. He had a 2.1 groundout/airout ratio and gave up just two homers in 59 innings last season. He has flashed a slider that could be an above-average pitch, but it still needs a lot of work. He also needs to sharpen his command. Things finally seem to be coming together for Cooney, as he's staying healthy and has found a role he can thrive in. He's 24, so the Orioles won't hesitate to move him aggressively if he continues performing well. He'll could start 2010 as the closer in Bowie.

Year	Club (League)	Class	W	L	ERA	G	GS	CG	SV	IP	H	R	ER	HR	BB	SO	AVG
2007	Bluefield (APP)	R	4	2	4.58	11	10	0	0	53	63	33	27	4	14	36	.301
2008	Aberdeen (NYP)	SS	1	3	3.81	28	0	0	10	26	24	13	11	3	9	38	.242
2009	Delmarva (SAL)	LoA	2	5	2.68	38	0	0	16	44	39	22	13	2	17	36	.234
	Frederick (CAR)	HiA	0	2	0.60	12	0	0	6	15	7	3	1	0	2	12	.140
MINOR LEAGUE TOTALS			7	12	3.40	89	10	0	32	138	133	71	52	9	42	122	.253

18 BRANDON WARING, 1B/3B

BORN: Jan. 2, 1986. **B-T:** R-R. **HT.:** 6-3. **WT.:** 210. **DRAFTED:** Wofford, 2007 (7th round). **SIGNED BY:** Steve Kring (Reds).

The Orioles unloaded catcher Ramon Hernandez to the Reds before the 2009 season to clear the way for Matt Wieters, getting Waring, Ryan Freel and Justin Turner in return. Waring provides a power bat in an organization in need of them, and he led Baltimore farmhands with 27 homers and 96 RBIs in his first season in the system. He added two more homers in a nine-game stint in the Arizona Fall League. Waring's raw power is well above-average and he can drive the ball out of the ballpark in all directions. He also piles up a lot of strikeouts and will have to shorten his swing and adjust his approach to hit enough at higher levels. He needs to improve his pitch selection and understand game situations and counts better to avoid being an all-or-nothing hacker. He played mostly at first base last year so that Tyler Henson could play third at Frederick. While Waring has experience at the hot corner and has the arm to play there, concerns about his range and footwork may keep him at first base. He's a slightly below-average runner. If Waring can't change his approach to handle more advanced pitching—his primary task this year in Double-A—he'll wind up as no more than a power bat off a big league bench.

Year	Club (League)	Class	AVG	G	AB	R	H	2B	3B	HR	RBI	BB	SO	SB	OBP	SLG
2007	Billings (PIO)	R	.311	68	267	63	83	17	2	20	61	21	83	1	.369	.614
	Dayton (MWL)	LoA	1.000	1	1	0	1	0	0	0	2	0	0	0	1.000	1.000
2008	Dayton (MWL)	LoA	.270	119	441	63	119	23	2	20	71	43	156	1	.346	.467
2009	Frederick (CAR)	HiA	.273	128	473	70	129	35	2	26	90	51	121	5	.354	.520
	Bowie (EL)	AA	.292	8	24	4	7	3	0	1	6	3	9	0	.414	.542
MINOR LEAGUE TOTALS			.281	324	1206	200	339	78	6	67	230	118	369	7	.356	.522

19 CAMERON COFFEY, LHP

BORN: Sept. 20, 1990. **B-T:** L L. **HT.:** 6-5. **WT.:** 215. **DRAFTED:** HS—Houston, 2009 (22nd round). **SIGNED BY:** Rich Morales.

Coffey rode an incredible roller coaster in 2009, and at the end of the ride he found himself cashing a check for $990,000. He was regarded as nothing more than a solid college prospect in the summer before his last year of high school, when he threw in the mid-80s and committed early to Duke. But he touched 94 mph in a scrimmage last spring, then sat at 92-93 and hit 95 in his first game. That didn't last long, as he felt discomfort in his elbow and struggled to pitch in the mid-80s the next time out. The pain got worse and Coffey had Tommy John surgery in March. Teams still inquired about him, and the Angels reportedly offered $500,000, but he turned them down and seemed destined to end up at school when Baltimore took him in the 22nd round. Area scout Rich Morales had followed Coffey closely and the Orioles rated him as a top-two-rounds talent, so they broke the bonus record for a draftee coming off reconstructive elbow surgery, surpassing the $710,000 the Angels gave the late Nick Adenhart as a 14th-rounder in 2004. Based on the track record of pitchers like Adenhart, Baltimore invested in Coffey's talent, poise and projectable frame. In addition to a plus fastball, he has a solid breaking ball, though he'll have to work on a changeup. His rehabilitation has gone well and the Orioles expect him to be healthy in spring training, though they'll take a slow approach and send him to a short-season affiliate after time in extended spring.

Year	Club (League)	Class	W	L	ERA	G	GS	CG	SV	IP	H	R	ER	HR	BB	SO	AVG
2009	Did Not Play—Injured																

20 KYLE HUDSON, OF

BORN: Jan. 7, 1987. **B-T:** L-L. **HT.:** 5-10. **WT.:** 165. **DRAFTED:** Illinois, 2008 (4th round). **SIGNED BY:** Troy Hoerner.

Hudson hails from Mattoon, a small town in central Illinois that's a hotbed for youth baseball, having hosted numerous regional tournaments as well as the Cal Ripken World Series for 11- and 12-year-olds. Hudson was a four-sport standout in high school: football, basketball, baseball and track, where he won the 2004 state high jump. He first drew attention in college as a wide receiver at Illinois. He led the Illini in receiving yards as a freshman and sophomore, but as his role on the football team diminished, he focused more on baseball, breaking out in 2008 with a .398/.498/.482 season that put him among the national leaders in several offensive categories. The Orioles took him in the fourth round that June and signed him for $287,000, but he played in just 11 games because of a broken finger. Hudson is faster than any player in the organization besides Xavier Avery, the kind of player who can hit a ball four steps to the side of an outfielder and have a double. He's an above-average defender in center field with a slightly below-average arm. Hudson looked much stronger at the plate last season, and the ball started to jump off his bat. He has become a good bunter and stays inside the ball with a short, line-drive swing. He just needs to cut down on his strikeouts so he can let his speed put so much pressure on defenses. If he continues to make strides at the plate, he clearly has all the tools to be an everyday center fielder. He'll advance to high Class A this year.

Year	Club (League)	Class	AVG	G	AB	R	H	2B	3B	HR	RBI	BB	SO	SB	OBP	SLG
2008	Aberdeen (NYP)	SS	.216	11	37	5	8	1	0	0	5	8	12	4	.356	.243
2009	Delmarva (SAL)	LoA	.284	117	398	61	113	8	2	0	21	49	85	31	.365	.314
	Frederick (CAR)	HiA	.250	6	20	4	5	0	0	0	0	4	6	3	.400	.250
MINOR LEAGUE TOTALS			.277	134	455	70	126	9	2	0	26	61	103	38	.366	.505

21 L.J. HOES, 2B

BORN: March 5, 1990. **B-T:** R-R. **HT.:** 6-1. **WT.:** 190. **DRAFTED:** HS—Washington D.C., 2008 (3rd round). **SIGNED BY:** Dean Albany.

Baltimore took Hoes in the third round of the 2008 draft and signed him away from a North Carolina commitment, making a $490,000 bet on his advanced bat. A pitcher and outfielder in high school, he immediately moved to second base as a pro because his bat didn't profile for an outfield corner and his average speed wasn't enough for center field. He never had played second base before and continues to learn the position, from improving his footwork around the bag to working on turning the double play. He led low Class A South Atlantic League second basemen with 28 errors last year, and his .939 fielding percentage was the worst in the league among anyone who played at least 50 games at the position. But the Orioles rate his actions, range and arm as average, and they think he'll be able to hold down the position with experience. Hoes has a good swing and should be able to command the strike zone and hit for average, though he didn't produce good numbers at Delmarva in his first full season. Like Xavier Avery, though, Hoes jumped from Rookie ball to low Class A and the Orioles just liked seeing him battle every day. He needs more instruction and tons of innings as he refines his game, but Baltimore still believes in his as an offensive second baseman. He'll move up to high Class A in 2010.

Year	Club (League)	Class	AVG	G	AB	R	H	2B	3B	HR	RBI	BB	SO	SB	OBP	SLG
2008	Orioles (GCL)	R	.308	48	159	36	49	4	3	1	18	30	22	10	.416	.390
2009	Delmarva (SAL)	LoA	.260	119	431	42	112	19	0	2	47	23	80	20	.299	.318
MINOR LEAGUE TOTALS			.273	167	590	78	161	23	3	3	65	53	102	30	.333	.337

22 OLIVER DRAKE, RHP

BORN: Jan. 13, 1987. **B-T:** R-R. **HT.:** 6-4. **WT.:** 220. **DRAFTED:** Navy, 2008 (43rd round). **SIGNED BY:** Dean Albany.

The Orioles may have pulled off a steal when they got Drake near the end of the 2008 draft. He had been impressive in his first two seasons at Navy, but many teams apparently didn't know he was draft-eligible as a sophomore. Fewer still realized that if he dropped out of the Naval Academy he could bypass his military commitment, which has sidetracked the career of his former teammate Mitch Harris with the Mariners. Midshipmen don't make their five-year commitment until they start their junior year. Drake had a relationship with area scout Dean Albany and played for his team in the Cal Ripken Sr. Collegiate League, going 4-1, 1.00 in the summer after he was drafted before signing with Baltimore in July for $100,000. Drake has a nice feel for pitching, with a fluid motion and good life on his pitches. His fastball sits at 88-91 mph touches 92, and he complements it with a slider that's an above-average pitch at times. He's working on his changeup. Drake throws strikes and works quickly, and he still has some projection left in his big frame. The Orioles were pleased with his first full pro season and think he could take a big step forward in high Class A this year.

Year	Club (League)	Class	W	L	ERA	G	GS	CG	SV	IP	H	R	ER	HR	BB	SO	AVG
2008	Bluefield (APP)	R	1	0	0.77	7	0	0	0	12	7	2	1	1	2	11	.167
	Aberdeen (NYP)	SS	0	0	0.87	5	0	0	1	10	9	3	1	0	1	13	.214
2009	Delmarva (SAL)	LoA	8	9	4.34	25	24	0	0	131	138	72	63	6	42	104	.277
MINOR LEAGUE TOTALS			9	9	3.83	37	24	0	1	153	154	77	65	7	45	128	.264

23 JAKE COWAN, RHP

BORN: June 30, 1988. **B-T:** L-R. **HT.:** 6-3. **WT.:** 175. **DRAFTED:** San Jacinto (Texas) JC, 2009 (10th round). **SIGNED BY:** Rich Morales.

The Orioles are getting more aggressive in the later rounds of the draft as they are in the first few rounds, investing a lot of money and scouting resources in finding talent. They spent a slightly over-slot $175,000 to sign Cowan in the 10th round of the 2009 draft. The Red Sox made Cowan a 14th-round pick out of a Georgia high school in 2007, but he headed to Virginia instead. He transferred to San Jacinto (Texas) JC as a sophomore and led the Gators to the Junior College World Series for the sixth time in eight seasons, throwing a one-hitter in the regionals and then striking out 13 as San Jac beat Santa Fe (Fla.) JC to finish third in the tournament. Cowan usually pitches in the low 90s, but he worked in the high 80s for much of the spring and missed four weeks with elbow tendinitis. He didn't have any structural damage and his velocity bounced back a bit after he signed, though Baltimore handled him carefully. Cowan's fastball has late boring action, and his slider and changeup both have the potential to be plus pitches. He also has thrown a curveball, and the Orioles will make him choose one breaking ball to focus on this season. Scouts love the way Cowan competes, even without his best stuff, and think he could add velocity as he gets stronger. Baltimore is excited to see what he can do in the Aberdeen rotation in 2010.

Year	Club (League)	Class	W	L	ERA	G	GS	CG	SV	IP	H	R	ER	HR	BB	SO	AVG
2009	Aberdeen (NYP)	SS	1	2	2.25	8	4	0	0	24	15	7	6	1	11	27	.179
MINOR LEAGUE TOTALS			1	2	2.25	8	4	0	0	24	15	7	6	1	11	27	.179

24 RYAN BERRY, RHP

BORN: Oct. 1, 1991. **B-T:** R-R. **HT.:** 6-1. **WT.:** 195. **DRAFTED:** Rice, 2009 (9th round). **SIGNED BY:** Rich Morales.

At the start of last year, Berry's performance compared to that of any college pitcher not named Stephen Strasburg, but a strained shoulder muscle kept him out of action for five weeks in the middle of the season. He still put up a 7-2, 2.42 performance and returned to form in the postseason with a two-hitter against Alabama-Birmingham in the Conference USA tournament. He threw 126 pitches in a loss to Kansas State in regional play, then closed the Owls' regional-clinching game against the Wildcats two days later. Pro teams already take a hard look at Rice pitchers based on their history of elbow and shoulder problems as professionals, and Berry's shoulder woes and his herky-jerky delivery gave teams pause. Undaunted, Baltimore took him in the ninth round and signed him late in the summer for $417,600. Berry's fastball sits at 89-91 mph and touches 93, and his best pitch is his knuckle-curve. He also threw a slider and changeup in college. Berry's mechanics concerned some scouts because they appear to put stress on his arm, but the Orioles like the way the ball comes out of his hand and think he does a good job of repeating his delivery. He gets good life on his pitches and throws strikes. One club official compared him to Turk Wendell, who built a long major league career as a reliever, and that could be Berry's eventual role as well. He'll open his pro career in the Delmarva rotation.

Year	Club (League)	Class	W	L	ERA	G	GS	CG	SV	IP	H	R	ER	HR	BB	SO	AVG
2009	Did Not Play—Signed Late																

25 MATT ANGLE, OF

BORN: Sept. 10, 1985. **B-T:** L-R. **HT.:** 5-10. **WT.:** 175. **DRAFTED:** Ohio State, 2007 (7th round). **SIGNED BY:** Rich Morales.

Angle is the Orioles' most polished outfield prospect and put himself on the verge of major league consideration by advancing to Double-A and playing in the Arizona Fall League last year. He batted just .237 in the AFL, though he was focusing on improving his bunting and approach at the plate. Defense is Angle's strong suit, and most scouts think he could play defense in the major leagues now. He also has an above-average arm for a center fielder. Angle knows his game and embraces the leadoff role. He has a short swing and uses the entire field. Angle has above-average speed and good baserunning instincts, and he stole 42 bases last year while getting caught just 12 times in 2009. His only truly deficient tool is power, but if he can be a leadoff hitter that won't be a problem. He might not get the opportunity to be a big league regular in Baltimore, where the outfield is stacked with talented young players. Angle will open 2010 in Double-A and wait for an opportunity.

Year	Club (League)	Class	AVG	G	AB	R	H	2B	3B	HR	RBI	BB	SO	SB	OBP	SLG
2007	Aberdeen (NYP)	SS	.301	66	236	60	71	4	4	0	14	47	40	34	.421	.352
2008	Delmarva (SAL)	LoA	.287	126	478	82	137	22	5	4	35	71	86	37	.385	.379
2009	Frederick (CAR)	HiA	.289	123	478	78	138	17	4	1	32	59	72	40	.370	.347
	Bowie (EL)	AA	.357	8	28	6	10	1	0	0	1	4	5	2	.438	.393
MINOR LEAGUE TOTALS			.292	323	1220	226	356	44	13	5	82	181	203	113	.388	.361

26 RYAN ADAMS, 2B

BORN: April 21, 1987. **B-T:** R-R. **HT.:** 6-0. **WT.:** 195. **DRAFTED:** HS—New Orleans, 2006 (2nd round). **SIGNED BY:** Mike Tullier.

Adams put up the numbers to back up his projection as an offensive second baseman in 2008, but he followed it up with an injury-plagued 2009 season in which he was limited to 215 at-bats. He dealt with an abdominal strain and was bothered by a groin injury all year. He still has plenty of fans in the organization, though, who like his bat and all-around ability. Adams has strong hands at the plate, producing mostly doubles power. His plate discipline has improved consistently but still needs more work. He has solid speed and can steal an occasional base. Adams has backers who believe he can be a solid-average defender with good range, hands and arm strength at second base. But he struggles with his throwing, which could prompt a move to left field. Adams is a good athlete and an enthusiastic workout guy, though he may be wound too tight at this point. While he has been criticized for his mental approach in the past, he likes to work and takes instruction well. He'll probably return to high Class A to open the season, with some club officials predicting that 2010 will be his breakout year.

Year	Club (League)	Class	AVG	G	AB	R	H	2B	3B	HR	RBI	BB	SO	SB	OBP	SLG
2006	Bluefield (APP)	R	.256	34	133	24	34	8	1	2	7	19	32	2	.361	.376
	Aberdeen (NYP)	SS	.316	6	19	2	6	3	0	1	5	4	7	0	.458	.632
2007	Aberdeen (NYP)	SS	.236	67	246	29	58	10	2	3	22	18	63	8	.296	.329
2008	Delmarva (SAL)	LoA	.308	119	448	68	138	26	5	11	57	36	109	12	.367	.462
2009	Frederick (CAR)	HiA	.288	59	215	27	62	14	0	2	25	19	41	2	.349	.381
MINOR LEAGUE TOTALS			.281	285	1061	150	298	61	8	19	116	96	252	24	.348	.407

27 GARABEZ ROSA, SS

BORN: Oct. 12, 1989. **B-T:** R-R. **HT.:** 6-2. **WT.:** 166. **SIGNED:** Dominican Republic, 2006. **SIGNED BY:** Carlos Bernhardt.

The Orioles were encouraged by the progress of Pedro Florimon last year, and they see a similar player in Rosa, who just completed his second season in the United States. He was sent to Delmarva to get a couple of weeks of game action but stepped down to Aberdeen when the New York-Penn League season opened. Rosa's defensive tools are the equal of any player's in the system, including Florimon, with outstanding hands and actions at shortstop. He has good range and a strong arm, though he plays out of control at times and committed 14 errors in 64 games at Aberdeen. His progression will depend on how he comes along with the bat. Rosa has a good body to go with a quick bat and strong hands. He has easy power, even to center field, and he can sting fastballs. He has trouble with pitch recognition, though, and can't handle breaking balls. He cheats on fastballs because he has no Plan B, so his focus is on making more contact. Rosa needs to refine pretty much every aspect of his game, but the tools are there to make a big leap. He'll open 2010 in low Class A.

Year	Club (League)	Class	AVG	G	AB	R	H	2B	3B	HR	RBI	BB	SO	SB	OBP	SLG
2007	Orioles (DSL)	R	.275	58	200	31	55	10	2	2	17	3	44	7	.290	.375
2008	Orioles (GCL)	R	.330	49	185	24	61	8	3	4	29	1	26	4	.339	.470
	Aberdeen (NYP)	SS	.250	6	20	2	5	0	0	0	0	2	11	0	.318	.250
2009	Delmarva (SAL)	LoA	.125	11	32	2	4	0	0	1	5	1	7	0	.152	.219
	Aberdeen (NYP)	SS	.218	64	220	28	48	8	6	6	25	8	72	1	.263	.391
MINOR LEAGUE TOTALS			.263	188	657	87	173	26	11	13	76	15	160	12	.288	.396

28 CHORYE SPOONE, RHP

BORN: Sept. 16, 1985. **B-T:** R-R. **HT.:** 6-1. **WT.:** 215. **DRAFTED:** Catonsville (Md.) CC, 2005 (8th round). **SIGNED BY:** Ty Brown.

Spoone went from an unknown at a Maryland junior college to one of Baltimore's best pitching prospects in less than three years. Now he'll have to overcome a more significant obstacle—shoulder surgery—to complete the saga. After rest and rehab didn't work, he had an operation to repair a small tear in his labrum after the 2008 season. He saw only limited action last year as he worked his arm back into shape. The Orioles were cautious and focused on getting him through the season healthy, and they accomplished the mission as he had no setbacks. He throws a 93-95 mph fastball with good movement, a power curveball and an average changeup when he's healthy. Command never has been his strong suit, and the shoulder trouble led to even greater struggles. Baltimore expects to see a much truer indication of his velocity and command in 2010. Spoone didn't go to instructional league but is expected to be fully healthy for spring training. He's slotted for the Bowie rotation, and if he doesn't prove able to handle the rigors of starting he could take his two power pitches to the bullpen. The Orioles kept him on the 40-man roster despite their pitching depth, an indication that they still believe in his arm.

Year	Club (League)	Class	W	L	ERA	G	GS	CG	SV	IP	H	R	ER	HR	BB	SO	AVG
2005	Bluefield (APP)	R	2	5	8.03	15	3	0	0	25	27	25	22	3	13	27	.273
2006	Delmarva (SAL)	LoA	7	9	3.56	26	25	0	0	129	118	72	51	5	80	90	.241
2007	Frederick (CAR)	HiA	10	9	3.26	26	25	3	0	152	108	65	55	8	67	133	.200
2008	Bowie (EL)	AA	3	3	4.57	9	9	0	0	41	40	23	21	4	27	32	.252

2009	Orioles (GCL)	R	0	1	4.38	5	5	0	0	12	9	6	6	1	2	11	.220
	Aberdeen (NYP)	SS	0	0	0.00	1	1	0	0	3	1	0	0	0	3	3	.100
	Frederick (CAR)	HiA	0	2	9.42	4	4	0	0	14	17	16	15	3	14	12	.298
MINOR LEAGUE TOTALS			22	29	4.06	86	72	3	0	377	320	207	170	24	206	308	.229

29 EDDIE GAMBOA, RHP

BORN: Dec. 21, 1984. **B-T:** R-R. **HT.:** 6-2. **WT.:** 195. **DRAFTED:** UC Davis, 2008 (21st round). **SIGNED BY:** James Keller.

Gamboa doesn't have the same ceiling as most of the other pitchers on this list, but he's a great bet to get the most out of his ability. A 21st-round pick in 2008 as a fifth-year senior out of UC Davis, Gamboa is a durable pitcher who throws strikes. He jumped into full-season ball last year and blazed through the system, reaching Double-A and compiling a 1.08 ERA between three stops. He has walked just 31 batters in 146 pro innings and rates as the best strike-thrower in the system. Righthander Pat Egan has a similar profile, but Gamboa's stuff is a notch better. He has an 89-91 mph fastball with good life, also throws a changeup and has worked on both a curveball and slider as a pro. He relies heavily on his fastball, challenging opponents to hit it, and so far they haven't. He's athletic and fields his position well, and he has a good pickoff move. The Orioles love his makeup. Gamboa profiles strictly as a reliever, and at age 25 there's no reason to hold him back. He could open 2010 in Triple-A and get his first big league opportunity later in the year.

Year	Club (League)	Class	W	L	ERA	G	GS	CG	SV	IP	H	R	ER	HR	BB	SO	AVG
2008	Bluefield (APP)	R	1	7	3.63	12	12	1	0	62	64	31	25	6	14	41	.264
2009	Delmarva (SAL)	LoA	6	0	1.86	18	0	0	1	39	30	8	8	5	3	35	.219
	Frederick (CAR)	HiA	4	0	0.55	14	0	0	1	33	27	3	2	0	7	29	.227
	Bowie (EL)	AA	1	0	0.00	7	0	0	1	12	7	3	0	0	7	11	.167
MINOR LEAGUE TOTALS			12	7	2.16	51	12	1	3	146	128	45	35	11	31	116	.237

30 BILLY ROWELL, OF

BORN: Sept. 10, 1988. **B-T:** l-R **HT.:** 6-5. **WT.:** 220. **DRAFTED:** HS—Pennsauken, N.J., 2006 (1st round). **SIGNED BY:** Dean Albany.

Rowell was the first high school hitter selected in the 2006 draft, but he has struggled to fulfill expectations since signing for $2.1 million as the ninth overall pick. His average has gotten progressively worse each season, dipping to .225 when he repeated high Class A last season. Rowell has consistently been one of the youngest players in each league he has played in, and he has compounded his youth with immaturity. The Orioles would make recommendations on his swing, stance and bat path, but he always would revert to his old ways. As he continued to struggle last year, he finally realized he needed to make adjustments and began implementing instruction better. Though Rowell has as much raw power as anyone in the system, he never has shown it in games. He has a smooth swing and should be a good hitter, but he puts too much pressure on himself and doesn't let his ability take over. Baltimore finally decided to move him to the outfield in 2009 after he struggled at third base for three seasons. He has some athleticism and his plus arm should play in right field, but he's still learning the position. He's an average runner. Rowell hasn't earned a promotion, but the Orioles may send him to Double-A just for a change of scenery. He had a good instructional league and needs to carry that over into 2010 because he's running out of opportunities to prove himself.

Year	Club (League)	Class	AVG	G	AB	R	H	2B	3B	HR	RBI	BB	SO	SB	OBP	SLG
2006	Bluefield (APP)	R	.329	42	152	38	50	15	3	2	26	25	47	3	.422	.507
	Aberdeen (NYP)	SS	.326	11	43	8	14	4	0	1	6	4	12	0	.388	.488
2007	Delmarva (SAL)	LoA	.273	91	352	47	96	21	3	9	57	31	104	3	.335	.426
2008	Frederick (CAR)	HiA	.248	111	375	39	93	24	0	7	50	36	104	1	.315	.368
2009	Frederick (CAR)	HiA	.225	120	423	51	95	20	0	9	39	35	122	3	.284	.336
MINOR LEAGUE TOTALS			.259	375	1345	183	348	84	6	28	178	131	389	10	.326	.393

Boston Red Sox

BY JIM CALLIS

After winning the World Series in 2007 and losing in Game Seven of the American League Championship Series the following year, the Red Sox looked poised to make another title run in 2009.

They got off to a 51-34 start, the best first-half record in the AL, but didn't look like the same club after the all-star break. Boston went from three games up to eight games behind the eventual World Series champion Yankees, then got swept in Division Series by the Angels.

It was the Red Sox' least successful season since failing to make the playoffs in 2006. It also illustrated how high their expectations have become. Boston has won at least 95 games and advanced to the playoffs in six of the last seven years.

The Red Sox began the run with a team made up mostly of imports acquired through free agency and trades. As the decade progressed, they became much more self-sustaining. Since they ended an 86-year championship drought by winning the 2004 World Series, they've thrust several homegrown players into important roles.

All-stars Dustin Pedroia and Kevin Youkilis and major league stolen-base champ Jacoby Ellsbury were signed and developed by Boston, as were ace Jon Lester and closer Jonathan Papelbon. The farm system continued to provide in 2009, with Clay Buchholz helping solidify the rotation and rookie Daniel Bard handling set-up duties in the bullpen. The Red Sox also solved their catching problem by spinning three former sandwich or second-round picks (lefthander Nick Hagadone and righthanders Justin Masterson and Bryan Price) to the Indians for Victor Martinez in July.

Promotions and trades have thinned out the upper levels of the system a bit. However, the Red Sox' scouting and player development machine continues to roll on. The team has enviable depth at the lower levels, led by a pair of 2008 draft picks, outfielder Ryan Westmoreland and righthander Casey Kelly.

That's the Red Sox philosophy in a nutshell, to identify elite talent and spend what it takes to acquire it. Boston aggressively mined the draft and the international market once again in 2009, handing out seven-figure bonuses to Cuban shortstop Jose Iglesias ($6.25 million), Dominican shortstop Jose Vinicio ($1.95 million), third-round shortstop David Renfroe ($1.4 million) and first-round outfielder Reymond Fuentes ($1.134 million).

Papelbon's blown save in the Division Series finale was tough to stomach, but the Red Sox may have sus-

Hard-throwing Daniel Bard broke through as a top set-up man as a rookie in Boston

TOP 30 PROSPECTS

1. Ryan Westmoreland, of	16. Madison Younginer, rhp
2. Casey Kelly, rhp	17. Stephen Fife, rhp,
3. Josh Reddick, of	18. Felix Doubront, lhp
4. Lars Anderson, 1b	19. Will Middlebrooks, 3b
5. Ryan Kalish, of	20. Che-Hsuan Lin, of
6. Junichi Tazawa, rhp	21. Alex Wilson, rhp
7. Reymond Fuentes, of	22. Tim Federowicz, c
8. Anthony Rizzo, 1b	23. Roman Mendez, rhp
9. Jose Iglesias, ss	24. Luis Exposito, c
10. Derrik Gibson, ss/2b	25. Mark Wagner, c
11. Stolmy Pimentel, rhp	26. Kyle Weiland, rhp
12. Yamaico Navarro, ss	27. Dustin Richardson, lhp
13. Michael Bowden, rhp	28. Ryan Dent, 2b/ss
14. David Renfroe, ss	29. Jose Vinicio, ss
15. Drake Britton, lhp	30. Brandon Jacobs, of

tained a bigger loss right before the Winter Meetings. Scouting director Jason McLeod left to become vice president of scouting and player development for the Padres under new general manager Jed Hoyer, who had been Boston's assistant GM.

McLeod, who's from the San Diego area and spent a decade in the Padres front office before coming to Boston, presided over five strong drafts for the Sox. His first five picks from his first draft in 2005, highlighted by Ellsbury and Buchholz, have reached the majors. McLeod will be missed but has left the team well-stocked for the future.

General Manager: Theo Epstein. **Farm Director:** Mike Hazen. **Scouting Director:** Amiel Sawdaye.

Class	Team	League	W	L	PCT	Finish*	Manager(s)
Majors	Boston Red Sox	American	95	67	.586	3rd (14)	Terry Francona
Triple-A	Pawtucket Red Sox	International	61	82	.427	12th (14)	Ron Johnson
Double-A	Portland Sea Dogs	Eastern	67	74	.475	9th (12)	Arnie Beyeler
High A	Salem Red Sox	Carolina	67	72	.482	5th (8)	Chad Epperson
Low A	Greenville Drive	South Atlantic	73	65	.529	5th (16)	Kevin Boles
Short-season	Lowell Spinners	New York-Penn	45	30	.600	t-3rd (14)	Gary DiSarcina
Rookie	GCL Red Sox	Gulf Coast	26	27	.491	10th (16)	Dave Tomlin
Overall 2009 Minor League Record			339	350	.492	19th (30)	

*Finish in overall standings (No. of teams in league). †League champion.

LAST YEAR'S TOP 30

Player, Pos.		Status
1.	Lars Anderson, 1b	No. 4
2.	Michael Bowden, rhp	No. 13
3.	Nick Hagadone, lhp	(Indians)
4.	Daniel Bard, rhp	Majors
5.	Josh Reddick, of	No. 3
6.	Casey Kelly, rhp/ss	No. 2
7.	Junichi Tazawa, rhp	No. 6
8.	Ryan Westmoreland, of	No. 1
9.	Michael Almanzar, 3b	Dropped out
10.	Yamaico Navarro, inf	No. 12
11.	Stolmy Pimentel, rhp	No. 11
12.	Oscar Tejeda, ss/3b	Dropped out
13.	Ryan Kalish, of	No. 5
14.	Che-Hsuan Lin, of	No. 20
15.	Luis Exposito, c	No. 24
16.	Kris Johnson, lhp	Dropped out
17.	Argenis Diaz, ss	(Pirates)
18.	Will Middlebrooks, 3b	No. 19
19.	Pete Hissey, of	Dropped out
20.	Bryan Price, rhp	(Indians)
21.	Derrik Gibson, inf	No. 10
22.	Anthony Rizzo, 1b	No. 8
23.	Kyle Weiland, rhp	No. 26
24.	Zach Daeges, of	Dropped out
25.	Mitch Dening, of	Dropped out
26.	Richie Lentz, rhp	Dropped out
27.	Felix Doubront, lhp	No. 18
28.	Stephen Fife, rhp	No. 17
29.	Brock Huntzinger, rhp	Dropped out
30.	Mark Wagner, c	No. 25

BEST TOOLS

Best Hitter for Average	Ryan Westmoreland
Best Power Hitter	Lars Anderson
Best Strike-Zone Discipline	Che-Hsuan Lin
Fastest Baserunner	Wilfred Pichardo
Best Athlete	Ryan Westmoreland
Best Fastball	Casey Kelly
Best Curveball	Casey Kelly
Best Slider	Alex Wilson
Best Changeup	Casey Kelly
Best Control	Casey Kelly
Best Defensive Catcher	Tim Federowicz
Best Defensive Infielder	Jose Iglesias
Best Infield Arm	Will Middlebrooks
Best Defensive Outfielder	Che-Hsuan Lin
Best Outfield Arm	Josh Reddick

PROJECTED 2013 LINEUP

Catcher	Victor Martinez
First Base	Lars Anderson
Second Base	Dustin Pedroia
Third Base	Kevin Youkilis
Shortstop	Jose Iglesias
Left Field	Jacoby Ellsbury
Center Field	Reymond Fuentes
Right Field	Ryan Westmoreland
Designated Hitter	Josh Reddick
No. 1 Starter	Jon Lester
No. 2 Starter	Josh Beckett
No. 3 Starter	Clay Buchholz
No. 4 Starter	Casey Kelly
No. 5 Starter	John Lackey
Closer	Jonathan Papelbon

TOP PROSPECTS OF THE DECADE

Year	Player, Pos.	2009 Org.
2000	Steve Lomasney, c	Out of baseball
2001	Dernell Stenson, of/1b	Deceased
2002	Seung Song, rhp	Lotte (Korea)
2003	Hanley Ramirez, ss	Marlins
2004	Hanley Ramirez, ss	Marlins
2005	Hanley Ramirez, ss	Marlins
2006	Andy Marte, 3b	Indians
2007	Daisuke Matsuzaka, rhp	Red Sox
2008	Clay Buchholz, rhp	Red Sox
2009	Lars Anderson, 1b	Red Sox

TOP DRAFT PICKS OF THE DECADE

Year	Player, Pos.	2009 Org.
2000	Phil Dumatrait, lhp	Pirates
2001	Kelly Shoppach, c (2nd round)	Indians
2002	Jon Lester, lhp (2nd round)	Red Sox
2003	David Murphy, of	Rangers
2004	Dustin Pedroia, ss (2nd round)	Red Sox
2005	Jacoby Ellsbury, of	Red Sox
2006	Jason Place, of	Red Sox
2007	Nick Hagadone, lhp (1st round supp.)	Indians
2008	Casey Kelly, rhp/ss	Red Sox
2009	Reymond Fuentes, of	Red Sox

LARGEST BONUSES IN CLUB HISTORY

Jose Iglesias, 2009	$6,250,000
Casey Kelly, 2008	$3,000,000
Daisuke Matsuzaka, 2006	$2,000,000
Ryan Westmoreland, 2008	$2,000,000
Jose Vinicio, 2009	$1,950,000

BOSTON RED SOX

TOP 2010 ROOKIE: Dustin Richardson, lhp. There aren't many openings on the big league club, but he has the inside track to become the second lefty in the bullpen.

BREAKOUT PROSPECT: Drake Britton, lhp. Recovered from Tommy John surgery, he's topping out at 97 mph with his fastball and flashing a hard slider.

SLEEPER: Pete Hissey, of. He has the tools to become a Paul O'Neill-type right fielder once he adds strength.

SOURCE OF TOP 30 TALENT			
Homegrown	30	Acquired	0
College	6	Trades	0
Junior college	1	Rule 5 draft	0
High school	14	Independent leagues	0
Draft-and-follow	1	Free agents/waivers	0
Nondrafted free agents	0		
International	8		

Numbers in parentheses indicate prospect rankings

LF
Brandon Jacobs (30)
Zach Daeges
David Mailman
Shannon Wilkerson

CF
Ryan Westmoreland (1)
Reymond Fuentes (7)
Che-Hsuan Lin (20)
Jason Place
Jeremy Hazelbaker
Wilfred Pichardo
Keury de la Cruz
Felix Sanchez

RF
Josh Reddick (3)
Ryan Kalish (5)
Pete Hissey
Mitch Dening
Alex Hassan
Seth Schwindenhammer
Daniel Nava

3B
David Renfroe (14)
Will Middlebrooks (19)
Oscar Tejeda
Miles Head

SS
Jose Iglesias (9)
Yamaico Navarro (12)
Jose Vinicio (29)
Xander Bogaerts

2B
Derrik Gibson (10)
Ryan Dent (28)
Jason Thompson
Ken Roque
Tug Hulett

1B
Lars Anderson (4)
Anthony Rizzo (8)
Aaron Bates
Michael Almanzar
Chris McGuiness

C
Tim Federowicz (22)
Luis Exposito (24)
Mark Wagner (25)
Dusty Brown
Ryan Lavarnway
Oscar Perez
Michael Thomas
Carson Blair

RHP

Starters	Relievers
Casey Kelly (2)	Richie Lentz
Junichi Tazawa (6)	Jason Rice
Stolmy Pimentel (11)	Robert Manuel
Michael Bowden (13)	Ramon Ramirez
Madison Younginer (16)	Miguel Gonzalez
Stephen Fife (17)	Jordan Flasher
Alex Wilson (21)	
Roman Mendez (23)	
Kyle Weiland (26)	
Brock Huntzinger	
Ryne Miller	
Eammon Portice	
Kendal Volz	
Kyle Stroup	
Caleb Clay	
Renny Parthemore	
Juan Rodriguez	
Randy Consuegra	
Austin Bailey	

LHP

Starters	Relievers
Drake Britton (15)	Dustin Richardson (27)
Felix Doubront (18)	Fabio Castro
Fabian Williamson	Lance McClain
Kris Johnson	Mitch Herold
Manny Rivera	

DRAFT ANALYSIS

2009 — BONUSES: $7.1 MILLION

BEST PURE HITTER: OF Reymond Fuentes (1) has lots of speed and a line-drive approach, helping him bat .290 in the Rookie-level Gulf Coast League. OF Brandon Jacobs (10), SS Jason Thompson (11) and 3B Miles Head (26) are also gifted hitters.

BEST POWER HITTER: Though he was better known as a running back committed to Auburn, Jacobs is more advanced than most baseball players with football backgrounds. He has a strong 5-foot-11, 240-pound frame, plus some feel for hitting, giving him a lot of power potential.

FASTEST RUNNER: With 6.3-second speed in the 60-yard dash, Fuentes may be faster than major league stolen-base leader Jacoby Ellsbury.

BEST DEFENSIVE PLAYER: SS David Renfroe (3) has soft hands and a strong arm. He might wind up at third base but the Red Sox will give him every chance to stay at shortstop. Fuentes should be a fine center fielder. C Michael Thomas (12) has unbelievable arm strength but is otherwise raw defensively.

BEST FASTBALL: RHP Madison Younginer (7) had one of the best pure arms in the draft and can reach 97 mph. RHP Alex Wilson (2) sits at 92-93 mph and touches 95.

BEST SECONDARY PITCH: Wilson has a wipeout slider at times, while Younginer can spin a hard curve.

BEST PRO DEBUT: The latest Boston draftee to excel in brief stints at short-season Lowell, Wilson gave up two earned runs and struck out 33 in 36 innings. RHP Jordan Flasher (22), who's building back his velocity following Tommy John surgery in 2008, fanned 15 in 16 scoreless innings between two stops. OF Alex Hassan (20), considered more of a pitcher when the Red Sox drafted him, batted .328/.375/.472 and reached low Class A.

BEST ATHLETE: Renfroe does everything easily. Some teams liked him more as a pitcher, and he starred at quarterback for a South Panola High (Batesville, Miss.) team that won 89 straight games.

MOST INTRIGUING BACKGROUND: OF Mike Yastrzemski's (36) grandfather Carl is a franchise icon. RHP Luke Bard's (16) brother Daniel is a key component of Boston's bullpen. Fuentes is a cousin of Carlos Beltran. Renfroe's father Laddie and C Kyle Arnsberg's (45) dad Brad pitched in the majors. OF Gavin McCourt (39) is the son of Dodgers owner Frank McCourt. Bard, Yastrzemski, McCourt and Arnsberg all opted for college over pro ball.

CLOSEST TO THE MAJORS: Wilson, who should open his first full season in high Class A.

BEST LATE-ROUND PICK: Jacobs has the upside of becoming the next Kevin Mitchell.

THE ONE WHO GOT AWAY: The Red Sox never made a run at Virginia-bound RHP Branden Kline (6) because he didn't pitch during the summer. They were close to landing athletic OF Zeke DeVoss (38) but couldn't divert him from Miami.

ASSESSMENT: In Jason McLeod's final draft as scouting director, the Red Sox were as aggressive as any club. They targeted high-ceiling prospects and spent what it took to sign them. Renfroe ($1.4 million), Younginer ($975,000) and Jacobs ($750,000) all signed for well over MLB's slot recommendations.

2008 — BONUSES: $10.5 MILLION

The Red Sox spent $5 million to sign RHP Casey Kelly (1) and OF Ryan Westmoreland (5), and they have no regrets after seeing the early returns. They're nearly as excited by the offensive potential and speed of SS/2B Derrik Gibson (2). RHP Bryan Price (1s) was used in a trade for Victor Martinez.

GRADE: A

2007 — BONUSES: $4.8 MILLION

LHPs Nick Hagadone (1s), another piece of the Martinez deal, and Drake Britton (23) are making successful comebacks from Tommy John surgery. 1B Anthony Rizzo (6) has been even more impressive after beating cancer.

GRADE: C+

2006 — BONUSES: $8.6 MILLION

RHP Daniel Bard (1) became a weapon out of the Boston bullpen last year, as did RHP Justin Masterson (2) before he became part of the Martinez trade. Three other first-round or sandwich picks haven't panned out, but the Red Sox found quality bats in OFs Ryan Kalish (9) and Josh Reddick (17) and 1B Lars Anderson (18), and big leaguers in 1B Aaron Bates (3) and LHP Dustin Richardson (5).

GRADE: B+

2005 — BONUSES: $6.2 MILLION*

All five of Boston's picks before the second round have reached the majors, led by OF Jacoby Ellsbury (1) and RHP Clay Buchholz (1s). The Red Sox still have plans for SS Jed Lowrie (1s) and RHP Michael Bowden (1s), while RHP Craig Hansen (1) helped land Jason Bay in a three-team trade.

GRADE: A

*Draft analysis by Jim Callis. Numbers in parentheses indicate draft rounds. *Bonuses for 2005 are first 10 rounds only.*

RYAN WESTMORELAND, OF

Born: April 27, 1990.
Height: 6-2. **Weight:** 195.
Bats: L. **Throws:** R.
Drafted: HS—Portsmouth, R.I., 2008 (5th round).
Signed by: Ray Fagnant.

RODGER WOOD

Westmoreland drew relatively little interest as a high school senior in 2008. He showed interesting athleticism at the Area Code Games the summer before, but didn't stand out. His commitment to Vanderbilt, $2 million asking price and the weather-related difficulties of scouting a Rhode Island prep player meant that few teams focused on him in the spring. One of just four clubs to talk to him directly, Boston selected him in the fifth round. Westmoreland joined the Bayside Yankees, one of the nation's top amateur teams, for the summer, giving the Red Sox more time to evaluate him. After watching him hit .557/.658/.918 for Bayside, they considered him the equivalent of a top-five-overall pick and gladly paid him $2 million at the Aug. 15 signing deadline. A pre-existing injury to his throwing shoulder turned out to be a torn labrum and required surgery in November, so Boston had him mostly DH during his pro debut at short-season Lowell in 2009. Westmoreland rated as the New York-Penn League's top prospect after exuding five-tool potential. The only negative came on Aug. 28, when he broke his collarbone crashing into the outfield wall while making a catch. Westmoreland didn't do any further damage to his shoulder and should be healthy for spring training.

Former Red Sox scouting director Jason McLeod says Westmoreland has more upside than any player the club selected in his five years running its drafts. His skills are just as impressive as his considerable tools. Westmoreland has an advanced approach for a teenager, with a short stroke, control of the strike zone and a willingness to use the entire field. His hand-eye coordination allows him to barrel balls consistency, and he has above-average power potential. He has plus-plus speed and knows how to use it, swiping 19 bases without getting caught at Lowell. Westmoreland has above-average range and should be a quality defender in center field. He also starred as a pitcher in high school, and his arm should grade as at least average once it's back to 100 percent. He's an intelligent player with the makeup to succeed.

Westmoreland basically just needs to get healthy and soak up pro experience. An all-state soccer player and basketball star, he never concentrated on baseball year-round before turning pro. Boston has had him take it easy on his shoulder, so his arm isn't back to full strength yet. He used a low-three-quarters delivery when he pitched in high school and needs to raise his arm angle as an outfielder. While he has the tools for center field, he has yet to play there in pro ball.

After watching the hype get to their last two No. 1 prospects, Clay Buchholz and Lars Anderson, the Red Sox are trying to temper expectations for Westmoreland. That's hard to do with such a polished athlete, especially one with New England roots. He'll probably open 2010 at low Class A Greenville but is talented enough to force a promotion to high Class A Salem by season's end. He's a potential 30-30 player who one day could bat third in the Boston lineup.

Year	Club (League)	Class	AVG	G	AB	R	H	2B	3B	HR	RBI	BB	SO	SB	OBP	SLG
2009	Lowell (NYP)	SS	.296	60	223	38	66	15	3	7	35	38	49	19	.401	.484
MINOR LEAGUE TOTALS			.296	60	223	38	66	15	3	7	35	38	49	19	.401	.484

2 CASEY KELLY, RHP

BORN: Oct. 4, 1989. **B-T:** R-R. **HT.:** 6-3. **WT.:** 195. **DRAFTED:** HS—Sarasota, Fla., 2008 (1st round). **SIGNED BY:** Anthony Turco.

The Red Sox considered Kelly the most polished high school pitcher in the 2008 draft, and they spent the No. 30 pick and $3 million to sign him away from a Tennessee football scholarship. The son of former big leaguer Pat Kelly, Casey fancied himself a shortstop and played there in his pro debut and during the second half of 2009. Kelly's stuff and aptitude were on display at the Futures Game, where he needed just nine pitches to work a perfect inning, recording all three outs on 93-94 mph fastballs. His heater usually sits at 89-92 mph but plays up because he can cut it or sink it and command it to both sides of the plate. He throws his above-average changeup with the same arm speed and slot as his fastball. His 12-to-6 curveball has plus potential as well. He repeats his fluid, athletic delivery with ease. Advanced well beyond his years, Kelly mainly needs to throw his curveball more consistently for strikes. He lacks overpowering velocity, but he doesn't need it and should throw harder as he fills out. Kelly had much more success on the mound, and Boston would have pushed him to pitch if he hadn't come to that decision on his own in December. A future frontline starter, he's ticketed for Double-A and may not need more than another year in the minors.

Year	Club (League)	Class	W	L	ERA	G	GS	CG	SV	IP	H	R	ER	HR	BB	SO	AVG
2009	Salem (CAR)	HiA	1	4	3.09	8	8	0	0	47	33	21	16	4	7	35	.196
	Greenville (SAL)	LoA	6	1	1.12	9	9	0	0	48	32	9	6	0	9	39	.184
MINOR LEAGUE TOTALS			7	5	2.08	17	17	0	0	95	65	30	22	4	16	74	.190

Year	Club (League)	Class	AVG	G	AB	R	H	2B	3B	HR	RBI	BB	SO	SB	OBP	SLG
2008	Red Sox (GCL)	R	.173	27	98	10	17	5	0	1	9	6	34	1	.229	.255
	Lowell (NYP)	SS	.344	9	32	5	11	5	1	0	4	0	8	0	.344	.563
2009	Red Sox (GCL)	R	.214	8	28	4	6	1	0	2	6	3	10	1	.290	.464
	Greenville (SAL)	LoA	.224	32	134	18	30	7	1	1	10	16	39	0	.305	.313
MINOR LEAGUE TOTALS			.219	76	292	37	64	18	2	4	29	25	91	2	.282	.336

3 JOSH REDDICK, OF

BORN: Feb. 19, 1997. **B-T:** L-R. **HT.:** 6-2. **WT.:** 180. **DRAFTED:** Middle Georgia JC, 2006 (17th round). **SIGNED BY:** Rob English.

The Red Sox planned to make Reddick a draft-and-follow in 2006, but signed him for $140,000 after he homered against Team USA's Ross Detwiler (the sixth overall pick in 2007). A strained oblique last May couldn't stop him from reaching the majors. All five of Reddick's tools are average or better. He makes hard contact against pitches all over and outside the strike zone, and he has plus raw power and speed. He has improved defensively since signing and is capable of playing center field, though he really shines in right. He enhances slightly above-average arm strength with an unbelievable release and accuracy, allowing him to record 50 assists in 290 pro games. Reddick enjoys hitting so much that he has little patience at the plate, running into streaks where he gets himself out. He showed more selectivity in 2009 but regressed once he got to Boston. He's still learning to use his speed effectively on the bases and isn't much of a threat to steal. Reddick likely will open 2010 at Triple-A Pawtucket. Once he solves upper-level pitching, he could factor into the left-field mix if Boston doesn't re-sign Jason Bay.

Year	Club (League)	Class	AVG	G	AB	R	H	2B	3B	HR	RBI	BB	SO	SB	OBP	SLG
2007	Greenville (SAL)	LoA	.306	94	369	60	113	17	6	18	72	26	51	8	.352	.531
	Portland (EL)	AA	.000	1	1	0	0	0	0	0	0	0	0	0	.000	.000
2008	Greenville (SAL)	LoA	.340	14	53	7	18	4	2	0	9	5	8	2	.397	.491
	Lancaster (CAL)	HiA	.343	76	312	60	107	11	8	17	57	17	49	9	.375	.593
	Portland (EL)	AA	.214	34	117	22	25	4	2	6	25	12	25	3	.290	.436
2009	Portland (EL)	AA	.277	63	256	47	71	17	3	13	29	30	62	5	.352	.520
	Pawtucket (IL)	AAA	.127	18	71	1	9	0	2	0	6	6	13	0	.190	.183
	Boston (AL)	MAJ	.169	27	59	5	10	4	0	2	4	2	17	0	.210	.339
MAJOR LEAGUE TOTALS			.169	27	59	5	10	4	0	2	4	2	17	0	.210	.339
MINOR LEAGUE TOTALS			.291	300	1179	197	343	53	23	54	198	96	208	27	.343	.512

4 LARS ANDERSON, 1B

BORN: Sept. 25, 1987. **B-T:** L-L. **HT.:** 6-4. **WT.:** 215. **DRAFTED:** HS—Carmichael, Calif., 2006 (18th round). **SIGNED BY:** Blair Henry.

Signed for $825,000 after he dropped to the 18th round of the 2006 draft because of his price tag, Anderson hit .304/.404/.480 in his first two pro seasons. He tore up Double-A pitching at the end of 2008, earning the No. 1 spot on this list a year ago and prompting talk he was ready to help Boston if needed. Instead, he returned to Portland and struggled all year. With the loft in his swing and the leverage in his big frame, Anderson is still the system's best power-hitting prospect. Even when he slumped, he continued to draw walks and recognize pitches. Before 2009, he excelled at letting the ball travel deep and using his quick hands to punish pitches. He has worked hard to become an average defender at first base. When Anderson slumped, he tinkered with his swing, which became longer and more mechanical. After previously using the opposite field well, he became more pull-conscious, perhaps pressing to hit homers. Nothing worked, and he hit just .154 with one homer after the all-star break. He's a below-average runner. The Red Sox hope Anderson will learn from adversity, like Clay Buchholz and Daniel Bard did before him. They still think he has a difference-making bat, though they may have to send him back to Double-A to get it going again.

Year	Club (League)	Class	AVG	G	AB	R	H	2B	3B	HR	RBI	BB	SO	SB	OBP	SLG
2007	Greenville (SAL)	LoA	.288	124	458	69	132	35	3	10	69	71	112	2	.385	.443
	Lancaster (CAL)	HiA	.343	10	35	13	12	2	0	1	9	11	9	0	.489	.486
2008	Lancaster (CAL)	HiA	.317	77	306	58	97	19	1	13	50	46	64	0	.408	.513
	Portland (EL)	AA	.316	41	133	27	42	13	0	5	30	29	43	1	.436	.526
2009	Portland (EL)	AA	.233	119	447	50	104	23	0	9	51	63	114	2	.328	.345
MINOR LEAGUE TOTALS			.281	371	1379	217	387	92	4	38	209	220	342	5	.380	.436

5 RYAN KALISH, OF

BORN: March 28, 1988. **B-T:** L-L. **HT.:** 6-1. **WT.:** 205. **DRAFTED:** HS—Red Bank, N.J., 2006 (9th round). **SIGNED BY:** Ray Fagnant.

After a broken hamate bone truncated his 2007 season and affected him mentally in 2008, Kalish showed last year why he got a $600,000 bonus as a ninth-round pick out of high school. The Red Sox named him their minor league offensive player of the year after he set career highs in most categories and finished with a flourish, hitting .299 with 12 homers in the last two months in Double-A. No longer worried about his hand, Kalish turned his swing loose and hit hard line drives all over the field. He manages his at-bats as well as anyone in the system, waiting for pitches he can drive and taking walks if they don't come. He can steal and take extra bases with his slightly above-average speed and smarts. He gets good jumps on fly balls, allowing him to play center field, though he fits better in right. His arm is average. Kalish added loft to his swing and did a better job of using his legs at the plate in 2009, and the Red Sox would like to see more of that so he can bring out more power. Some scouts see him as a tweener without the defense to play center or the bat to profile on a corner. Kalish eventually may battle Josh Reddick for a corner-outfield job in Boston. They'll probably begin 2010 as teammates in Triple-A.

Year	Club (League)	Class	AVG	G	AB	R	H	2B	3B	HR	RBI	BB	SO	SB	OBP	SLG
2006	Red Sox (GCL)	R	.300	6	20	6	6	2	0	1	2	1	2	0	.333	.550
	Lowell (NYP)	SS	.200	11	35	8	7	0	1	0	4	2	14	2	.275	.257
2007	Lowell (NYP)	SS	.368	23	87	27	32	4	1	3	16	12	18	4	.471	.540
2008	Greenville (SAL)	LoA	.281	96	360	51	101	16	1	3	32	53	76	18	.376	.356
	Lancaster (CAL)	HiA	.233	18	73	6	17	6	0	2	14	8	23	1	.305	.397
2009	Salem (CAR)	HiA	.304	32	115	21	35	5	2	5	21	26	20	7	.434	.513
	Portland (EL)	AA	.271	103	391	63	106	19	4	13	56	42	87	14	.341	.440
MINOR LEAGUE TOTALS			.281	289	1081	182	304	52	9	27	142	148	234	60	.370	.421

6 JUNICHI TAZAWA, RHP

BORN: June 6, 1986. **B-T:** R-R. **HT.:** 5-11. **WT.:** 180. **SIGNED:** Japan, 2008. **SIGNED BY:** Craig Shipley/Jon Deeble.

A star in Japan's industrial league, Tazawa created a furor in his homeland when he asked Japanese big league clubs not to draft him so he could play in the United States. He signed a three-year, $3.3 million contract with the Red Sox in December 2008 and reached the majors eight months later. He gave up a game-winning homer to Alex Rodriguez in his first game with Boston but later blanked the Yankees for six innings in his third big league start. Tazawa aggressively goes after hitters with four pitches, and scouts can't agree which is the best. Some like his 88-92 fastball because he commands it so well, others point to his slider and others note that his splitter is a plus pitch at its best. He also throws a curveball. Though he's short, his clean delivery and strong frame give him the durability needed to start. Because he lacks a true plus pitch, Tazawa has to keep the ball down to succeed. He tends to miss up in the strike zone when his command is off, and that happened more frequently when he tired at the end of the season. He needs to get stronger. With no opening in Boston's rotation, Tazawa figures to open 2010 in Triple-A. He'll continue to develop as a starter, though his opportunity could come as a reliever.

Year	Club (League)	Class	W	L	ERA	G	GS	CG	SV	IP	H	R	ER	HR	BB	SO	AVG
2009	Portland (EL)	AA	9	5	2.57	18	18	0	0	98	80	31	28	8	26	88	.222
	Pawtucket (IL)	AAA	0	2	2.38	2	2	0	0	11	7	4	3	0	1	6	.184
	Boston (AL)	MAJ	2	3	7.46	6	4	0	0	25	43	23	21	4	9	13	.374
MAJOR LEAGUE TOTALS			2	3	7.46	6	4	0	0	25	43	23	21	4	9	13	.374
MINOR LEAGUE TOTALS			9	7	2.55	20	20	0	0	109	87	35	31	8	27	94	.219

7 REYMOND FUENTES, OF

DAVID STONER

BORN: Feb. 12, 1991. **B-T:** L-L. **HT.:** 6-0. **WT.:** 160. **DRAFTED:** HS—Manati, P.R., 2009 (1st round). **SIGNED BY:** Edgar Perez.

A cousin of Carlos Beltran, Fuentes drew Johnny Damon comparisons before going 28th overall in the 2009 draft and signing for $1.134 million. The sixth Puerto Rican ever drafted in the first round—and the first since the Blue Jays' Miguel Negron in 2000—Fuentes made a smooth transition to pro ball, hitting .290 and ranking as the No. 3 prospect in the Rookie-level Gulf Coast League. Fuentes has the polished bat and plus-plus speed to become a dynamic leadoff man. A track star in high school, he uses his quickness to make things happen on the bases and in center field, where he has Gold Glove potential. His swing is geared more for contact, but he has some power to his pull side and eventually could hit as many as 15 homers per season. Fuentes has much work to do on the nuances of the game. Offensively, he can do a better job of managing his at-bats and adding strength. He's learning as a basestealer and center fielder, with his speed making up for some of his mistakes. His arm strength is fringy but acceptable for a center fielder. Similar to Jacoby Ellsbury, Fuentes is a far better hitter at the same stage and projects as a better defender. He showed enough in his pro debut to make the jump to low Class A in 2010.

Year	Club (League)	Class	AVG	G	AB	R	H	2B	3B	HR	RBI	BB	SO	SB	OBP	SLG
2009	Red Sox (GCL)	R	.290	40	145	16	42	6	2	1	14	7	24	9	.331	.379
MINOR LEAGUE TOTALS			.290	40	145	16	42	6	2	1	14	7	24	9	.331	.379

8 ANTHONY RIZZO, 1B

BORN: Aug. 8, 1989. **B-T:** L-L. **HT.:** 6-3. **WT.:** 220. **DRAFTED:** HS—Parkland, Fla., 2007 (6th round). **SIGNED BY:** Laz Gutierrez.

Rizzo signed for an above-slot $325,000 bonus as a sixth-rounder in 2007 and was hitting .373 at Greenville the next April when he learned he had limited stage classical Hodgkin's lymphoma. He missed the rest of the season to get treatment. With his cancer in remission, he returned to hit .297/.368/.461 and conquer high Class A as a teenager in 2009. Rizzo has a smooth lefthanded stroke, keeps the bat in the zone for a long time and smokes liners to all fields. He already shows doubles power and should have 20-homer pop as he turns on more pitches. Managers rated him as the high Class A Carolina League's best defensive first baseman in 2009, and he has soft hands and a strong arm. His swing can get long, and when it does, pitchers can tie Rizzo up inside with good fastballs. He's a below-average runner whose speed could rate as a 35 on the 20-80 scouting scale as he gets older, though he does move well at first base. Rizzo will play one level behind Lars Anderson in 2010. They're competing to be the Red Sox' first baseman of the future, with Anderson having more power but Rizzo offering a more fluid swing, more consistent approach and better defense.

Year	Club (League)	Class	AVG	G	AB	R	H	2B	3B	HR	RBI	BB	SO	SB	OBP	SLG
2007	Red Sox (GCL)	R	.286	6	21	6	6	0	0	1	3	1	2	0	.375	.429
2008	Greenville (SAL)	LoA	.373	21	83	9	31	6	0	0	11	3	15	0	.402	.446
2009	Greenville (SAL)	LoA	.298	64	245	40	73	21	0	9	42	25	60	2	.365	.494
	Salem (CAR)	HiA	.295	55	200	23	59	16	0	3	24	25	39	2	.371	.420
MINOR LEAGUE TOTALS			.308	146	549	78	169	43	0	13	80	54	116	4	.373	.457

BOSTON RED SOX

9 JOSE IGLESIAS, SS

BILL MITCHELL

BORN: Jan. 5, 1990. **B-T:** R-R. **HT.:** 5-11. **WT.:** 175. **SIGNED:** Cuba, 2009. **SIGNED BY:** Craig Shipley/Johnny DiPuglia.

Iglesias broke into Cuba's top league as a 17-year-old and defected at the World Junior Championship in July 2008. He signed a four-year, $8.25 million big league contract last September that included a club-record $6.25 million bonus. He wowed observers with his defense and batted .275/.324/.420 in the Arizona Fall League. Scouts can't say enough about Iglesias' defensive ability, raving about his lightning-fast hands, quick feet and strong arm. He has a short swing and makes consistent contact. Though he's small, he has bat speed and pop and could become a 10-homer hitter down the road. Add in his slightly above-average speed, and he draws comparisons to a young Orlando Cabrera—with a better glove. He has the upside of a No. 2 hitter, but Iglesias' aggressive nature at the plate makes it more likely that he'll hit in the bottom third of the order. Much of his offensive value may come from his batting average because he doesn't project to contribute a lot of power, steals or walks. The Red Sox have had a revolving door at shortstop since Nomar Garciaparra began to decline, and they hope Iglesias can end that. He could make his pro debut in Double-A and be ready for Boston when Marco Scutaro's new contract expires after 2011.

Year	Club (League)	Class	AVG	G	AB	R	H	2B	3B	HR	RBI	BB	SO	SB	OBP	SLG
2009	Did Not Play—Signed 2010 Contract															

10 DERRIK GIBSON, SS/2B

RODGER WOOD

BORN: Dec. 5, 1989. **B-T:** R-R. **HT.:** 6-1. **WT.:** 170. **DRAFTED:** HS—Seaford, Del., 2008 (2nd round). **SIGNED BY:** Chris Calciano.

Gibson is the best baseball athlete and highest-drafted position player to come out of Delaware since Delino DeShields was an Expos first-round pick in 1989. Gibson has similar tools and turned down a North Carolina scholarship to sign for $600,000. The Red Sox minor league baserunner of the year in 2009, he stole 28 bases in 33 tries and led the New York-Penn League with 54 runs. A classic leadoff hitter, Gibson has plus-plus speed and supreme control of the strike zone. He has a quick bat, solid gap power and could realize his 15-homer potential once he adds strength to his broad-shouldered frame. He covers a lot of ground in the field and has solid arm strength. His instincts and makeup are off the charts. Gibson has a funny hitch in his throwing motion that eventually will lead him to a move from shortstop to second base or possibly center field. Though he doesn't take a big cut or give less than full effort, he doesn't always get a good jump out of the batter's box. Gibson is poised for a breakout 2010 season at Greenville. He'll still see time at shortstop, but a move is in his near future. The Red Sox don't need to rush him, but he may start to accelerate his timetable.

Year	Club (League)	Class	AVG	G	AB	R	H	2B	3B	HR	RBI	BB	SO	SB	OBP	SLG
2008	Red Sox (GCL)	R	.309	27	94	15	29	6	1	0	9	14	18	14	.411	.394
	Lowell (NYP)	SS	.086	14	35	4	3	0	0	0	3	6	11	2	.233	.086
2009	Lowell (NYP)	SS	.290	67	255	54	74	15	4	0	25	39	42	28	.395	.380
MINOR LEAGUE TOTALS			.276	108	384	73	106	21	5	0	37	59	71	44	.384	.357

11 STOLMY PIMENTEL, RHP

BORN: Feb. 1, 1990. **B-T:** R-R. **HT.:** 6-3. **WT.:** 185. **SIGNED:** Dominican Republic, 2006. **SIGNED BY:** Luis Scheker.

In contrast to the first 10 players on this list, who averaged $1.67 million in signing bonuses, Pimentel turned pro for just $25,000 as a 16-year-old. He has breezed through the lower levels of the minors, winning the organization's Latin program pitcher of the year award in his 2007 pro debut and having no trouble making the transition to the United States. He projects as a solid No. 3 pitcher, at least, with the potential for two plus pitches and a solid breaking ball. At his best, Pimentel sits at 90-92 mph and touches 95 with his four-seam fastball, which features explosive life up in the strike zone. He needs to do a better job of maintaining his velocity and may add a two-seamer to work lower in the zone. He has one of the best changeups in the system, with good movement and deception on the pitch. His curveball isn't as reliable as his other pitches, but he improved the shape of it in 2009. Pimentel always has thrown strikes, and the next step will be to locate his pitches with more precision. He's well ahead of most 20-year-olds and could reach the majors by 2012.

Year	Club (League)	Class	W	L	ERA	G	GS	CG	SV	IP	H	R	ER	HR	BB	SO	AVG
2007	Red Sox (DSL)	R	3	1	2.90	14	13	0	0	62	44	20	20	2	22	60	.202
2008	Lowell (NYP)	SS	5	2	3.14	13	11	0	0	63	51	25	22	7	17	61	.224
2009	Greenville (SAL)	LoA	10	7	3.82	24	23	1	0	118	135	62	50	12	29	103	.290
MINOR LEAGUE TOTALS			18	10	3.41	51	47	1	0	243	230	107	92	21	68	224	.252

12 YAMAICO NAVARRO, SS

BORN: Oct. 31, 1987. **B-T:** R-R. **HT.:** 5-11. **WT.:** 180. **SIGNED:** Dominican Republic, 2005. **SIGNED BY:** Pablo Lantigua.

Navarro signed for $20,000 and had established himself as the system's top shortstop prospect after hitting .304/.359/.447 and advancing to high Class A as a 20-year-old in 2008, but his encore went awry on Opening Day last season. He broke the hamate bone in his left hand, requiring surgery that knocked him out until mid-June. He hit better than ever when he returned, earning his first promotion to Double-A, but more advanced pitchers shut him down. Navarro has the best bat speed in the system and more pop than most middle infielders. The ball sounds different coming off his bat, and his plus raw power could make him an annual 15-20 homer threat. He usually makes consistent, hard contact to all fields, but he can fall into ruts where he gets out of control at the plate, taking huge hacks and chasing pitches. An average runner, Navarro has ordinary range at shortstop. His soft hands, strong arm and good instincts will allow him to shift to second or third base, and he should have enough bat for either position if he refines his approach. Navarro needs to work harder and deliver more consistent effort, but the tools are there for him to become a big league regular. He'll get another shot at Double-A in 2010, when he could move to second base and form a double-play combo with Jose Iglesias.

Year	Club (League)	Class	AVG	G	AB	R	H	2B	3B	HR	RBI	BB	SO	SB	OBP	SLG
2006	Red Sox (DSL)	R	.279	53	201	29	56	13	5	3	37	21	29	5	.344	.438
2007	Lowell (NYP)	SS	.289	62	225	36	65	10	1	5	37	22	52	12	.357	.409
2008	Greenville (SAL)	LoA	.280	83	325	46	91	14	4	7	54	29	73	3	.341	.412
	Lancaster (CAL)	HiA	.348	42	181	33	63	13	2	4	23	12	30	3	.393	.508
2009	Lowell (NYP)	SS	.238	5	21	1	5	1	0	0	2	3	0	.304	.286
	Salem (CAR)	HiA	.319	23	94	10	30	9	0	4	17	6	12	2	.373	.543
	Portland (EL)	AA	.185	39	135	16	25	6	2	2	11	14	28	5	.270	.304
MINOR LEAGUE TOTALS			.283	307	1182	171	335	66	14	25	181	106	227	30	.346	.426

13 MICHAEL BOWDEN, RHP

BORN: Sept. 9, 1986. **B-T:** R-R. **HT.:** 6-3. **WT.:** 215. **DRAFTED:** HS—Aurora, Ill., 2005 (1st round supplemental). **SIGNED BY:** Danny Haas.

All five of Boston's picks in the first and sandwich rounds of the 2005 draft have reached the majors, but while Jacoby Ellsbury, Clay Buchholz and Jed Lowrie have found long-term roles, Bowden still is looking for his niche. He has nothing left to prove in Triple-A after posting a 3.19 ERA there over the last two seasons, but big league hitters have torched him to the tune of .333/.381/.578. The key for Bowden is pitching downhill. He succeeds when he uses his strong frame and high three-quarters arm angle to keep his pitches down in the zone. He commands his 89-93 mph fastball to both sides of the plate, but it's not a swing-and-miss pitch and is vulnerable if he throws it thigh-high. He had a power curveball in high school but it has regressed, and he now relies more on a fringy slider to give him an offering that breaks away from righthanders. His changeup is better than either of his breaking balls. His long arm action bothers some scouts, though he has cleaned it up a little in recent years. Bowden faces a future as a middle reliever with the Red Sox, but could be a No. 3 or 4 starter if they use him as trade bait. He'll try again to crack the Boston staff in spring training.

Year	Club (League)	Class	W	L	ERA	G	GS	CG	SV	IP	H	R	ER	HR	BB	SO	AVG
2005	Red Sox (GCL)	R	1	0	0.00	4	2	0	0	6	4	0	0	0	4	10	.190
2006	Greenville (SAL)	LoA	9	6	3.51	24	24	0	0	108	91	50	42	9	31	118	.224
	Wilmington (CAR)	HiA	0	0	9.00	1	1	0	0	5	9	5	5	0	1	3	.391
2007	Lancaster (CAL)	HiA	2	0	1.37	8	8	0	0	46	35	10	7	1	8	46	.212
	Portland (EL)	AA	8	6	4.28	19	19	1	0	97	105	51	46	9	33	82	.279
2008	Portland (EL)	AA	9	4	2.33	19	19	0	0	104	72	31	27	5	24	101	.192
	Pawtucket (IL)	AAA	0	3	3.38	7	6	0	0	40	40	16	15	5	5	29	.261
	Boston (AL)	MAJ	1	0	3.60	1	1	0	0	5	7	2	2	0	1	3	.333
2009	Pawtucket (IL)	AAA	4	6	3.13	24	24	0	0	126	106	47	44	11	47	88	.228
	Boston (AL)	MAJ	1	1	9.56	8	1	0	0	16	23	17	17	3	6	12	.333
MAJOR LEAGUE TOTALS			2	1	8.14	9	2	0	0	21	30	19	19	3	7	15	.333
MINOR LEAGUE TOTALS			33	25	3.15	106	103	1	0	532	462	210	186	40	153	477	.233

14 DAVID RENFROE, SS

BORN: Nov. 16, 1990. **B-T:** R-R. **HT.:** 6-3. **WT.:** 200. **DRAFTED:** HS—Batesville, Miss., 2009 (3rd round). **SIGNED BY:** Danny Watkins.

Renfroe's background is similar to Casey Kelly's. Both were star prep quarterbacks (Renfroe's South Panola High team won 89 straight games) who could have played football in the Southeastern Conference (Mississippi wanted him to walk on), and both of their fathers had brief big league careers (Laddie Renfroe pitched four games for the 1991 Cubs). They both were outstanding two-way players, too. While Kelly will focus on pitching after dabbling as a shortstop, Renfroe will be a full-time position player. He dropped to the third round of the 2009 draft because of signability questions, and the Red Sox anted up $1.4 million to sign him—more than they gave first-rounder Reymond Fuentes. Renfroe packs power in his compact righthanded stroke, which he demonstrated by homering during the 2008 Under Armour All-America Game at Wrigley Field. He needs to improve his timing at the plate and use his lower half better, but those aren't major adjustments. Renfroe has a strong arm and soft hands, but he has just average range and speed and figures to lose a step as he matures. He'll get the opportunity to play shortstop but profiles better at third base. Renfroe prefers to play every day but could have a future on the mound if he desired. He touched 95 mph with his fastball in high school and showed feel for a curveball and changeup. He'll open 2010 in extended spring training and make his pro debut in Lowell in June.

Year	Club (League)	Class	AVG	G	AB	R	H	2B	3B	HR	RBI	BB	SO	SB	OBP	SLG
2009	Did Not Play—Signed Late															

15 DRAKE BRITTON, LHP

BORN: May 22, 1989. **B-T:** L-L. **HT.:** 6-2. **WT.:** 200. **DRAFTED:** HS—Tomball, Texas, 2007 (23rd round). **SIGNED BY:** Jim Robinson.

Britton was the top high school lefthander in Texas for the 2007 draft, but inconsistent velocity and a commitment to Texas A&M dropped him to the 23rd round. The Red Sox followed him during the summer, and after he repeatedly worked in the low 90s they signed him at the Aug. 15 deadline for $700,000. Britton didn't make his pro debut until 2008, and he blew out his elbow at the end of the New York-Penn League season, requiring Tommy John surgery that September. He worked diligently in his rehab and was ready for game action 11 months later. Elbow reconstruction didn't rob him of his stuff, as he came back dealing in the low 90s and topping out at 97. A pitcher's breaking ball and command are often the last two things to return after he has Tommy John surgery, and while that's true with Britton, he has the makings of a hard slider and should throw enough strikes. His changeup will give him a solid third pitch. Britton threw from a low arm slot in high school, but now he operates from a high three-quarters angle with clean arm action. He's a bulldog on the mound who loves to go after hitters, and he might fit best as a lefty set-up man for the long run. For now, Boston will continue to develop him as a starter, and because he'll open the season at age 20, there's no need to push him to make up for his lost year.

Year	Club (League)	Class	W	L	ERA	G	GS	CG	SV	IP	H	R	ER	HR	BB	SO	AVG
2008	Lowell (NYP)	SS	1	2	4.28	8	7	0	0	34	30	18	16	3	16	26	.234
2009	Red Sox (GCL)	R	0	0	0.00	4	4	0	0	7	2	0	0	0	4	11	.080
	Lowell (NYP)	SS	0	0	1.93	3	3	0	0	5	4	1	1	0	3	8	.235
MINOR LEAGUE TOTALS			1	2	3.38	15	14	0	0	45	36	19	17	3	23	45	.212

16 MADISON YOUNGINER, RHP

BORN: Nov. 3, 1990. **B-T:** R-R. **HT.:** 6-4. **WT.:** 195. **DRAFTED:** HS—Mauldin, S.C., 2009 (7th round). **SIGNED BY:** Quincy Boyd.

Younginer had one of the best pure arms in the 2009 draft, and one of the most difficult to see. His high school coach used him primarily as a reliever, making it impossible for scouts to know when he'd pitch, and his lone start drew a crowd of 75 evaluators from big league clubs. Younginer's lack of exposure, combined with his commitment to Clemson and concerns about his arm action, dropped him to the seventh round. Three days before the signing deadline, Boston anted up first-round money ($975,000) to sign him. He's a cousin of Orioles prospect Brandon Snyder. Younginer signed too late to pitch in the minors last summer but wowed scouts in instructional league. One saw him throw his fastball at 94-97 mph with good downhill plane in a matchup against Baltimore first-rounder Matt Hobgood, while another compared him to Justin Verlander and said, "He'll hit 100 mph one day. That's a great fastball and an awesome curveball, just wicked stuff." Younginer throws a power 12-to-6 curveball, and though he had little reason to use a changeup in high school, it's further along than expected. The Red Sox aren't worried about his arm action and won't try to change his mechanics, other than trying to help him find a consistent release point. They'll take their time with his development, and he'll probably make his pro debut in Lowell in June.

Year	Club (League)	Class	W	L	ERA	G	GS	CG	SV	IP	H	R	ER	HR	BB	SO	AVG
2009	Did Not Play—Signed Late																

17 STEPHEN FIFE, RHP

BORN: Oct. 4, 1986. **B-T:** R-R. **HT.:** 6-3. **WT.:** 210. **DRAFTED:** Utah, 2008 (3rd round). **SIGNED BY:** Matt Mahoney.

A member of a Boise team that played in the 1999 Little League World Series, Fife didn't start pitching regularly until he was a high school senior. He went undrafted out of high school and Everett (Wash.) CC, and didn't really get noticed until he dueled Stephen Strasburg in April 2008, losing 1-0 as Strasburg struck out 23. Fife pitched his way into the third round of the 2008 draft and had a solid first full season, though he spent the first two months building up his shoulder strength after tests detected weakness during spring training. He fills the strike zone with three pitches, starting with an 88-92 mph fastball that tops out at 94 mph and features plenty of sink. His changeup surpassed his curveball last season, showing splitter action at times. His curveball wasn't the hammer it was in 2008, but it's at least an average pitch. Fife does a nice job of using his strong frame to power balls down in the zone. He has the stuff, command and frame to get the job done as a No. 3 starter. He'll advance to Double-A at some point this season.

Year	Club (League)	Class	W	L	ERA	G	GS	CG	SV	IP	H	R	ER	HR	BB	SO	AVG
2008	Lowell (NYP)	SS	1	1	2.33	14	0	0	2	39	28	14	10	1	11	41	.196
2009	Greenville (SAL)	LoA	0	3	2.70	8	8	0	0	37	32	13	11	1	4	35	.230
	Salem (CAR)	HiA	3	2	4.44	10	10	0	0	51	58	28	25	7	10	51	.283
MINOR LEAGUE TOTALS			4	6	3.29	32	18	0	2	126	118	55	46	9	25	127	.242

18 FELIX DOUBRONT, LHP

BORN: Oct. 23, 1987. **B-T:** L-L. **HT.:** 6-2. **WT.:** 190. **SIGNED:** Venezuela, 2004. **SIGNED BY:** Miguel Garcia.

Doubront spent most of 2008 in low Class A but responded well when the Red Sox pushed him to Double-A last season. That wasn't a surprise considering his consistent success throughout his pro career—with the exception of 2007, when he fell victim to hernia surgery, a staph infection in his leg and a strained elbow. Since regaining his health, he has blossomed into the most advanced lefthanded starter in the system. Doubront touched 94 mph with his fastball during spring training last year and usually sits at 89-92 mph with good sink. He has added velocity through a long-toss program and other between-starts work, and Boston would like to see him continue to improve his strength. His changeup is better than his curveball, which explains why he has been more effective against righties than lefties. Doubront repeats his clean delivery well. He usually throws strikes but nibbled around the plate at times against Double-A hitters, and his command could use more consistency. He may not be more than a No. 4 starter if he can't improve his curveball, but he's ready for Triple-A at age 22.

Year	Club (League)	Class	W	L	ERA	G	GS	CG	SV	IP	H	R	ER	HR	BB	SO	AVG
2005	Red Sox/Padres (VSL)	R	7	1	0.97	13	13	0	0	65	32	11	7	0	29	58	.152
2006	Red Sox (GCL)	R	2	3	2.52	11	11	0	0	54	41	17	15	6	13	36	.212
	Lowell (NYP)	SS	2	0	4.91	2	2	0	0	11	7	6	6	1	3	7	.179
2007	Greenville (SAL)	LoA	3	7	8.93	11	11	0	0	42	63	49	42	8	17	22	.337
	Lowell (NYP)	SS	1	3	5.66	8	8	0	0	35	41	24	22	2	11	25	.283
2008	Greenville (SAL)	LoA	12	8	3.67	23	23	0	0	115	115	53	47	9	24	118	.260
	Lancaster (CAL)	HiA	1	1	3.86	3	3	0	0	14	15	6	6	1	4	20	.278
2009	Portland (EL)	AA	8	6	3.35	26	26	1	0	121	119	59	45	8	52	101	.255
MINOR LEAGUE TOTALS			36	29	3.74	97	97	1	0	457	433	225	190	35	153	387	.249

19 WILL MIDDLEBROOKS, 3B

BORN: Sept. 9, 1988. **B-T:** R-R. **HT.:** 6-3. **WT.:** 200. **DRAFTED:** HS—Texarkana, Texas, 2007 (5th round). **SIGNED BY:** Jim Robinson.

Middlebrooks hasn't developed as quickly as the Red Sox hoped he would when they signed him for $925,000 as a fifth-round pick in 2007, though they're pleased with his steady progress. He didn't play in his first pro summer because he signed late and had shoulder tendinitis, and he has started slow and finished strong in the two seasons since. Middlebrooks fits the scouting blueprint of a third baseman. He has a big league body and is loaded with raw power and arm strength. His power shows up more in batting practice, when he crushes balls to all fields, than it does in games. He falls behind in the count after passing up pitches he should drive. He can get confounded by breaking pitches, struggling against good ones and laying off hanging ones that are begging to be pounded. He's a below-average runner out of the box but average under way. Boston considered developing Middlebrooks at shortstop, his high school position, and he has good actions and a cannon arm at third base. He'll advance to high Class A this year, and if hitting doesn't work out, he has other career options. He drew interest as a pitcher in high school, showing a low-90s fastball and a promising curveball, and also had NFL potential as a punter.

Year	Club (League)	Class	AVG	G	AB	R	H	2B	3B	HR	RBI	BB	SO	SB	OBP	SLG
2008	Lowell (NYP)	SS	.254	59	209	21	53	17	2	1	21	12	73	10	.298	.368
2009	Greenville (SAL)	LoA	.265	103	374	53	99	25	3	7	57	48	123	7	.349	.404
MINOR LEAGUE TOTALS			.261	162	583	74	152	42	5	8	78	60	196	17	.331	.391

20 CHE-HSUAN LIN, OF

BORN: Sept. 21, 1988. **B-T:** R-R. **HT.:** 6-0. **WT.:** 180. **SIGNED:** Taiwan, 2007. **SIGNED BY:** Jon Deeble/ Louie Lin.

Signed for $400,000 out of high school in Taiwan, Lin was a national 100-meter and high jump champion. He remains a key member of the Taiwan national team, leading the club with four RBIs at the 2008 Olympics and going 3-for-7 at the World Baseball Classic last spring. He has a good mix of tools, but unless he shows more upside with the bat, he's going to have a hard time getting big league playing time in an organization that already has Jacoby Ellsbury, Ryan Westmoreland and Reymond Fuentes as center-field options. Lin is a special defender, blanketing the gaps better than anyone in the organization, including Ellsbury. He also has the best pure arm strength of any of the organization's outfielders, and he led the Carolina League with 18 outfield assists in 2009. He sometimes tries to do too much defensively, which resulted in 11 errors last year. Lin has good bat speed, shows power in batting practice and won MVP honors at the 2008 Futures Game when he homered off a 94 mph fastball from the Rockies' Ryan Mattheus. But he doesn't drive the ball in games, making consistent if relatively soft contact. Lin controls the strike zone better than any Red Sox farmhand, so it would be easy to project him as a big league regular if he showed more pop. He's a plus runner under way and has basestealing instincts. He'll move up to Double-A in 2010, with Westmoreland and Fuentes getting closer in his rearview mirror.

Year	Club (League)	Class	AVG	G	AB	R	H	2B	3B	HR	RBI	BB	SO	SB	OBP	SLG
2007	Red Sox (GCL)	R	.263	43	175	33	46	10	6	4	22	17	42	14	.330	.457
	Lowell (NYP)	SS	.163	11	43	7	7	2	0	0	3	5	10	3	.265	.209
2008	Greenville (SAL)	LoA	.249	91	362	60	90	13	6	5	37	43	62	33	.342	.359
2009	Salem (CAR)	HiA	.265	131	479	75	127	23	2	7	54	66	75	26	.355	.365
MINOR LEAGUE TOTALS			.255	276	1059	175	270	48	14	16	116	131	189	76	.343	.372

21 ALEX WILSON, RHP

BORN: Nov. 3, 1986. **B-T:** R-R. **HT.:** 6-1. **WT.:** 205. **DRAFTED:** Texas A&M, 2009 (2nd round). **SIGNED BY:** Jim Robinson.

Scouts viewed Wilson as a potential first-round pick for 2008 until he blew out his elbow in the Cape Cod League in the summer of 2007, right before he transferred from Winthrop to Texas A&M. He redshirted in 2008 but generated draft interest when he touched 94 mph in bullpen workouts. The Cubs selected him in the 10th round and scouted him in his return to the Cape, reportedly offering him $600,000, well short of his $1.5 million asking price. Wilson flashed first-round stuff last spring but tailed off before the draft, enabling the Red Sox to land him in the second round for $470,700. They like to break college pitchers into pro ball with short starts at Lowell, and he was spectacular in that role, limiting opponents to a .085 average. At his best, Wilson can carve up hitters with two pitches: a fastball that sits at 92-93 mph and peaks at 95, and a wipeout slider. Though there's some effort in his delivery, he repeats it well and throws strikes. He could move quickly as a reliever, but Boston hasn't ruled out developing him as a starter. To succeed in that role, he'll have to refine his changeup and prove he can maintain his stuff late into games and into the season. Wilson will spend his first full pro season in the Salem rotation.

Year	Club (League)	Class	W	L	ERA	G	GS	CG	SV	IP	H	R	ER	HR	BB	SO	AVG
2009	Lowell (NYP)	SS	0	1	0.50	13	13	0	0	36	10	3	2	0	7	33	.085
MINOR LEAGUE TOTALS			0	1	0.50	13	13	0	0	36	10	3	2	0	7	33	.085

22 TIM FEDEROWICZ, C

BORN: Aug. 5, 1987. **B-T:** R-R. **HT.:** 5-11. **WT.:** 200. **DRAFTED:** North Carolina, 2008 (7th round). **SIGNED BY:** Quincy Boyd.

The Red Sox have been searching for a while to find a successor to Jason Varitek, though they bought themselves some time by trading for Victor Martinez last summer. Their current best hope for a homegrown catcher of the future is Federowicz. He's the best defensive backstop in the system. With average arm strength and a quick transfer and release, he threw out 31 percent of basestealers last season. He got accustomed to handling quality stuff while catching for first-round pitchers Daniel Bard, Andrew Miller and Alex White at North Carolina, and he has improved his receiving mechanics since turning pro. He has strong leadership skills and calls a good game. How much Federowicz hits will determine whether he's a regular or a backup in the major leagues. Even after he batted .305/.341/.484 in his first full pro season—despite a 4-for-53 (.075) slump in July after he was promoted to high Class A—scouts still aren't sure how much he'll hit for average or power. He's a streaky hitter who can get pull-happy, but he has a short stroke and doesn't hook many balls foul. He has power to his pull side. He made good contact against Class A pitching, but more advanced hurlers can exploit his lack of patience at the plate. He runs better than many catchers but has below-average speed. Federowicz will return to Salem to start 2010, with an excellent chance for a midseason promotion.

Year	Club (League)	Class	AVG	G	AB	R	H	2B	3B	HR	RBI	BB	SO	SB	OBP	SLG
2008	Lowell (NYP)	SS	.244	36	127	14	31	6	0	1	15	19	24	10	.338	.315
2009	Greenville (SAL)	LoA	.345	55	226	34	78	19	0	10	34	15	42	1	.393	.562
	Salem (CAR)	HiA	.257	51	187	18	48	13	0	4	24	5	22	1	.276	.390
MINOR LEAGUE TOTALS			.291	142	540	66	157	38	0	15	73	39	88	12	.340	.444

23 ROMAN MENDEZ, RHP

BORN: July 25, 1990. **B-T:** R-R. **HT.:** 6-4. **WT.:** 195. **SIGNED:** Dominican Republic, 2007. **SIGNED BY:** Luciano del Rosario.

Signed for $125,000 out of the Dominican Republic in 2007, Mendez has breezed through the two lowest levels of the system. In his U.S. debut last year, he ranked fourth in the Gulf Coast League in opponent average (.184) and baserunners per nine innings (8.2). Mendez has one of the best arms in the system, sitting in the low 90s and reaching as high as 97 mph with his fastball. He's still growing into his 6-foot-4 frame and could have a plus-plus fastball when he's done filling out. His low-80s slider has some tilt but still has a ways to go, as does his changeup. While his secondary pitches lack polish, he throws them for strikes. Mendez has a sound delivery and operates from a high three-quarters arm slot. Scouts love his live, athletic body and praise his mound presence. Because Mendez has handled Rookie-level hitters so easily, Boston may send him to low Class A at age 19 this season.

Year	Club (League)	Class	W	L	ERA	G	GS	CG	SV	IP	H	R	ER	HR	BB	SO	AVG
2008	Red Sox (DSL)	R	3	1	2.65	11	11	0	0	51	43	19	15	1	16	46	.222
2009	Red Sox (GCL)	R	2	3	1.99	12	10	0	0	50	33	11	11	1	8	47	.184
MINOR LEAGUE TOTALS			5	4	2.32	23	21	0	0	101	76	30	26	2	24	93	.204

24 LUIS EXPOSITO, C

BORN: Jan. 20, 1987. **B-T:** R-R. **HT.:** 6-3. **WT.:** 220. **DRAFTED:** St. Petersburg (Fla.) JC, D/F 2005 (31st round). **SIGNED BY:** Jon Lukens.

Exposito has the best pure tools among Boston's catching prospects, starting with raw power and arm strength. The Red Sox were attracted to his defensive ability when they signed him for $150,000 as a draft-and-follow in 2006, but he stands out more with his offense now after clubbing 30 homers over the past two seasons. Exposito has a strong frame and can drive balls a long way, but he also has a long swing that leads scouts to question whether he'll be able to tap into his power potential. His aggressive approach results in some wasted at-bats. Exposito's size and lack of fast-twitch athleticism make him an easily below-average runner, which normally isn't a concern, but it eventually could affect his defense, which would be a problem. His arm features more strength than accuracy, and he threw out 27 percent of basestealers in 2009. He doesn't have soft hands but has worked hard on his defense and rates close to average as a receiver. He also has sought advice from Jason Varitek on how to lead a pitching staff. After finishing strong in Double-A last year, Exposito will return there to begin 2010. The Red Sox want to avoid having him share time on the same team with Tim Federowicz, who's a better defender but has less offensive potential.

Year	Club (League)	Class	AVG	G	AB	R	H	2B	3B	HR	RBI	BB	SO	SB	OBP	SLG
2006	Lowell (NYP)	SS	.250	57	200	10	52	13	0	1	23	13	44	1	.301	.327
2007	Greenville (SAL)	LoA	.233	9	30	3	7	0	0	0	2	2	5	0	.281	.233
2008	Greenville (SAL)	LoA	.283	49	191	34	54	8	1	11	31	12	42	1	.328	.508
	Lancaster (CAL)	HiA	.301	55	226	31	68	13	2	10	37	9	47	0	.331	.509
2009	Salem (CAR)	HiA	.271	76	288	28	78	24	1	6	45	23	49	3	.329	.424
	Portland (EL)	AA	.337	23	92	14	31	5	0	3	12	4	27	1	.371	.489
MINOR LEAGUE TOTALS			.280	269	1035	128	290	63	4	31	150	63	214	6	.326	.439

25 MARK WAGNER, C

BORN: June 11, 1984. **B-T:** R-R. **HT.:** 6-1. **WT.:** 205. **DRAFTED:** UC Irvine, 2005 (9th round). **SIGNED BY:** James Orr.

He gets overlooked in comparison to Tim Federowicz and Luis Exposito, but some club officials believe that Wagner is the organization's best catching prospect. He has a more consistent approach and is more effective at nabbing basestealers than Federowicz and Exposito. Wagner shook off a dreadful 2008 season at Portland and conquered Double-A pitching last year, though he missed three weeks with a strained hamstring and later struggled in his first taste of Triple-A. He controls the strike zone well, using a flat stroke to mainly serve line drives to the opposite field. He consistently gets on base and has some power, mostly to the gaps. Wagner enhances his average arm strength with a quick release and tremendous accuracy, allowing him to throw out 47 percent of basestealers in 2009. He has become an average receiver through hard work, and Jason Varitek lauded his blocking skills during spring training last year. Wagner could use more strength because he tends to get worn down late in the season. Typical of a catcher, he's a below-average runner. He's not dazzling, but Wagner should be at least a solid big league backup and possibly a regular. He'll spend this season in Triple-A, with a late-season callup a possibility.

BOSTON RED SOX

Year	Club (League)	Class	AVG	G	AB	R	H	2B	3B	HR	RBI	BB	SO	SB	OBP	SLG
2005	Lowell (NYP)	SS	.203	24	69	10	14	2	1	0	6	9	7	1	.309	.261
2006	Greenville (SAL)	LoA	.301	96	355	49	107	32	1	7	45	42	52	1	.386	.456
	Wilmington (CAR)	HiA	.169	17	65	8	11	4	0	1	5	7	9	0	.243	.277
2007	Lancaster (CAL)	HiA	.318	95	368	71	117	35	1	14	82	55	46	0	.406	.533
2008	Portland (EL)	AA	.219	94	342	44	75	19	0	10	48	38	78	0	.304	.363
2009	Portland (EL)	AA	.301	42	153	21	46	18	0	3	23	28	26	1	.410	.477
	Pawtucket (IL)	AAA	.214	43	154	12	33	12	0	3	20	11	29	0	.268	.351
MINOR LEAGUE TOTALS			.268	411	1506	215	403	122	3	38	229	190	247	3	.354	.428

26 KYLE WEILAND, RHP

BORN: Sept. 12, 1986. **B-T:** L-R. **HT.:** 6-4. **WT.:** 195. **DRAFTED:** Notre Dame, 2008 (3rd round). **SIGNED BY:** Chris Mears.

Weiland set single-season (16) and career (25) saves records at Notre Dame, but the Red Sox looked at his three-pitch mix and saw him as a starter when they drafted him in the third round in 2008. They sent him to high Class A for his first full pro season, and he recovered from a 1-5, 6.91 start to go 6-4, 1.81 over the final three months. Weiland's best pitch is a 91-94 mph turbo sinker, which has helped him post a 1.6 groundout/airout ratio as a pro. His hard three-quarters breaking ball can be a solid pitch, though it flattens out when he doesn't stay on top of it. He shows good feel for his changeup now that he's using it more as a starter. Weiland battled his control at times—he led the Carolina League with 16 hit batters and ranked third with 57 walks in 2009—so Boston has tried to help him tighten up his arm action and repeat his delivery better. He also has to work on controlling the running game after giving up 32 steals in 39 tries last year. Weiland ultimately may return to the bullpen, but he'll spend this season as a starter in Double-A.

Year	Club (League)	Class	W	L	ERA	G	GS	CG	SV	IP	H	R	ER	HR	BB	SO	AVG
2008	Lowell (NYP)	SS	3	3	1.50	15	10	0	0	60	36	17	10	1	10	68	.166
2009	Salem (CAR)	HiA	7	9	3.46	26	26	0	0	133	119	65	51	4	57	112	.240
MINOR LEAGUE TOTALS			10	12	2.85	41	36	0	0	193	155	82	61	5	67	180	.218

27 DUSTIN RICHARDSON, LHP

BORN: Jan. 9, 1984. **B-T:** L-L. **HT.:** 6-6. **WT.:** 220. **DRAFTED:** Texas Tech, 2006 (5th round). **SIGNED BY:** Jim Robinson.

Before he made three scoreless appearances for Boston last September, Richardson's claim to fame had been his participation on the ESPN reality show "Knight School," in which Texas Tech students tried to make basketball coach Bob Knight's team as a walk-on. Richardson would have won the competition if he had been able to join the team, but that would have conflicted with his baseball participation. A one-pitch pitcher when he signed as a fifth-rounder in 2006, Richardson spent his first two full pro seasons as a starter so he would get plenty of innings to work on his secondary offerings. After going 7-11, 6.45 in 2008, he moved to the bullpen last season and took off. He led Double-A Eastern League relievers with a .186 opponent average, consistently missing bats with a 90-95 mph fastball that plays up because he's deceptive. He has ditched a loopy curveball and developed a solid slider that he trusts. He also has a fringy changeup but uses it only sparingly. The last item on Richardson's to-do list is to cut down on his walks. If he can do that in spring training, he could make the Red Sox as the No. 2 lefty in the bullpen.

Year	Club (League)	Class	W	L	ERA	G	GS	CG	SV	IP	H	R	ER	HR	BB	SO	AVG
2006	Lowell (NYP)	SS	4	1	3.18	16	1	0	2	40	28	16	14	2	13	44	.199
2007	Greenville (SAL)	LoA	5	7	3.34	21	21	0	0	100	86	46	37	4	47	98	.235
	Lancaster (CAL)	HiA	4	0	2.74	4	4	0	0	23	14	8	7	1	5	25	.173
2008	Lowell (NYP)	SS	0	1	9.00	2	2	0	0	5	8	5	5	2	2	4	.333
	Portland (EL)	AA	7	10	6.33	22	22	0	0	107	108	76	75	17	51	114	.267
2009	Portland (EL)	AA	2	2	2.70	38	0	0	4	63	42	22	19	2	40	80	.186
	Pawtucket (IL)	AAA	0	0	1.69	7	0	0	0	11	8	2	2	1	2	16	.211
	Boston (AL)	MAJ	0	0	0.00	3	0	0	0	3	3	0	0	0	1	0	.250
MAJOR LEAGUE TOTALS			0	0	0.00	3	0	0	0	3	3	0	0	0	1	0	.250
MINOR LEAGUE TOTALS			22	21	4.11	110	50	0	6	348	294	175	159	29	160	381	.230

28 RYAN DENT, 2B/SS

BORN: March 15, 1989. **B-T:** R-R. **HT.:** 6 0. **WT.:** 190. **DRAFTED:** HS—Long Beach, 2007 (1st round supplemental). **SIGNED BY:** Jim Woodward.

Dent played with Twins top prospect Aaron Hicks on the Wilson High (Long Beach) team that won the 2007 national championship. The Red Sox rated Dent as a first-round talent that year and were delighted to get him with the 62nd-overall pick and sign him for $571,000. He had a miserable first full pro season in 2008, leading the New York-Penn League in strikeouts (87) and finishing with the worst batting average (.154) in the circuit. Dent made drastic improvements in 2009, recognizing pitches and managing his at-bats better, giving hope that he one day will take advantage of his tremendous bat speed and raw power. He still swings too often early in the count and pulls off too many pitches, so there's more work to be done. He has plus speed and basestealing aptitude, though he could be more aggressive on the bases. Boston's 2009 minor league defensive player of the year, Dent has split time between second base and shortstop as a pro. His actions, range and arm are all solid. The Red Sox think he plays better at shortstop, though he's destined to see more time at second base (and perhaps center field) after the Red Sox signed Jose Iglesias and Jose Vinicio on the international market last year. Dent will try to maintain his progress this year in high Class A.

Year	Club (League)	Class	AVG	G	AB	R	H	2B	3B	HR	RBI	BB	SO	SB	OBP	SLG
2007	Red Sox (GCL)	R	.371	10	35	7	13	1	2	1	2	5	5	4	.463	.600
	Lowell (NYP)	SS	.178	11	45	5	8	1	0	0	3	1	13	4	.196	.200
2008	Lowell (NYP)	SS	.154	58	201	33	31	7	2	6	21	29	87	17	.267	.299
2009	Greenville (SAL)	LoA	.252	99	345	59	87	24	3	6	48	49	112	17	.350	.391
	Salem (CAR)	HiA	.268	13	41	6	11	4	0	0	3	0	10	1	.279	.366
MINOR LEAGUE TOTALS			.225	191	667	110	150	37	7	13	77	84	227	43	.317	.360

29 JOSE VINICIO, SS

BORN: July 10, 1993. **B-T:** B-R. **HT.:** 6-0. **WT.:** 155. **SIGNED:** Dominican Republic, 2009. **SIGNED BY:** Craig Shipley/Johnny DiPuglia.

Vinicio celebrated his 16th birthday last July by signing with the Red Sox for $1.95 million. That set a franchise record for the largest bonus ever given to a foreign amateur, though Cuban defector Jose Iglesias shattered it when he got $6.25 million as part of an $8.25 million big league contract two months later. The top pure shortstop from the 2009 international signing class, Vinicio has terrific actions and hands, good range and a strong arm. A switch-hitter, he's better from the right side of the plate. Though he's skinny, he has a quick bat and can drive the ball, so he could grow into some power once he gets stronger. He has slightly above-average speed, and that too could improve as he matures physically. Vinicio will need plenty of time to develop his body and his skills, and Boston will give it to him. He'll make his pro debut in either the Rookie-level Dominican Summer League or the Gulf Coast League in June.

Year	Club (League)	Class	AVG	G	AB	R	H	2B	3B	HR	RBI	BB	SO	SB	OBP	SLG
2009	Did Not Play—Signed 2010 Contract															

30 BRANDON JACOBS, OF

BORN: Dec. 8, 1990. **B-T:** R-R. **HT.:** 5-11. **WT.:** 240. **DRAFTED:** HS—Lilburn, Ga., 2009 (10th round). **SIGNED BY:** Tim Hyers.

Jacobs is built like the New York Giants running back of the same name, and he was a top running-back recruit committed to Auburn, where his football counterpart played one season. Boston took him away from the gridiron, however, drafting him in the 10th round last June and signing him for $750,000. Jacobs is surprisingly advanced at the plate for someone who never was a full-time baseball player. He manages at-bats well and has a quick bat and plenty of raw strength, so he has the potential to hit for average and power. Jacobs will have to hit because he's not going to offer much else. He has solid-average speed once he gets going, but he lacks quickness. He's a poor defender in left field, and his arm lacks both strength and accuracy. The Red Sox recognize that he's an all-bat player, but if they dream they can envision him becoming another Kevin Mitchell. They could challenge him by sending him to low Class A in 2010.

Year	Club (League)	Class	AVG	G	AB	R	H	2B	3B	HR	RBI	BB	SO	SB	OBP	SLG
2009	Red Sox (GCL)	R	.250	8	24	1	6	2	0	0	0	2	8	0	.333	.333
MINOR LEAGUE TOTALS			.250	8	24	1	6	2	0	0	0	2	8	0	.333	.333

Chicago Cubs

BY JIM CALLIS

Cubs fans thought getting swept in consecutive Division Series in 2007 and 2008 was tough to swallow. But at least Chicago made back-to-back postseason appearances for the first time since 1906-08.

The franchise still was left seeking its first World Series appearance since 1945 and its first championship since 1908, though. To help end those droughts,

the Cubs decided their big addition would be mercurial Milton Bradley, who cost $30 million and was supposed to provide more balance to a predominantly righthanded-hitting lineup.

Instead, Bradley had his worst season since 2002 and damaged clubhouse chemistry. When he criticized the team in September, the Cubs suspended him for the final two weeks of the season. His play and behavior were the most disappointing aspects of a disappointing season for Chicago, which finished 83-78 and swiftly fell out of contention after the all-star break.

It was the third straight winning year for a franchise that hadn't accomplished that feat since 1970-72, which is a step forward, but much more was expected after the Cubs opened the season with a $135 million payroll, the third-highest in baseball.

The most significant Cubs news of the year came off the field, however, when on Oct. 27 the Ricketts family completed its $845 million purchase of the club, as well as Wrigley Field and 25 percent of Comcast SportsNet Chicago from the Tribune Co. The sale topped the major league record of $660 million paid for the Red Sox and related assets in 2002.

How much time the Ricketts family will give general manager Jim Hendry to get the Cubs back on track remains unclear, as does how Hendry will accomplish that task. Chicago dropped from first in the National League in scoring in 2008 to 10th last season, and has only one projected regular who will be younger than 30 in 2010. The rotation has holes to fill with Rich Harden departing as a free agent and Ted Lilly recovering from shoulder surgery. The bullpen is unsettled as well.

After contributing Jake Fox and Micah Hoffpauir, who combined for 21 homers, and surprise 12-game winner Randy Wells last season, the farm system doesn't appear to have any noteworthy reinforcements to offer for 2010. However, Cubs minor league talent is on the rise after a period of decline marked by weak drafts and the departure of top prospects in trades for veterans.

Recent first-round picks Josh Vitters (2007) and

Milton Bradley was one of many problems on a disappointing 2009 Cubs club

TOP 30 PROSPECTS

1. Starlin Castro, ss	16. Trey McNutt, rhp
2. Brett Jackson, of	17. Tyler Colvin, of
3. Josh Vitters, 3b	18. Darwin Barney, ss
4. Andrew Cashner, rhp	19. Jeffry Antigua, lhp
5. Jay Jackson, rhp	20. Blake Parker, rhp
6. Hak-ju Lee, ss	21. Brooks Raley, lhp
7. Logan Watkins, 2b	22. Esmailin Caridad, rhp
8. Chris Carpenter, rhp	23. Sam Fuld, of
9. Ryan Flaherty, 2b/ss/3b	24. Marcos Mateo, rhp
10. D.J. Lemahieu, ss/2b	25. Casey Coleman, rhp
11. Kyler Burke, of/1b	26. Robinson Chirinos, c
12. Dae-Eun Rhee, rhp	27. Welington Castillo, c
13. Rafael Dolis, rhp	28. David Cales, rhp
14. John Gaub, lhp	29. Junior Lake, ss/2b
15. Chris Archer, rhp	30. James Adduci, of

Brett Jackson (2009) have slugged their way through the lower minors. Five pitchers drafted in 2008 appeared in Double-A last summer, and the Cubs also are doing better work in Latin America and the Far East, as evidenced by shortstop phenoms Starlin Castro and Hak-Ju Lee. Still, most of Chicago's best farmhands are at least a couple of years away from making an impact in the major leagues.

Chicago may have to transition from trying to contend to trying to reload if it can't turn its fortunes around in 2010. That would mean more waiting for fans whose patience already has been stretched thin.

General Manager: Jim Hendry. **Farm Director:** Oneri Fleita. **Scouting Director:** Tim Wilken.

Class	Team	League	W	L	PCT	Finish*	Manager(s)
Majors	Chicago Cubs	National	83	78	.516	8th (16)	Lou Piniella
Triple-A	Iowa Cubs	Pacific Coast	72	72	.500	9th (16)	Bobby Dickerson
Double-A	Tennessee Smokies	Southern	71	69	.507	3rd (10)	Ryne Sandberg
High A	Daytona Cubs	Florida State	64	71	.474	9th (12)	Buddy Bailey
Low A	Peoria Chiefs	Midwest	81	57	.587	2nd (14)	Marty Pevey
Short-season	Boise Hawks	Northwest	34	42	.447	t-6th (8)	Casey Kopitzke
Rookie	AZL Cubs	Arizona	29	27	.518	4th (11)	Juan Cabreja
Overall 2009 Minor League Record			351	338	.509	12th (30)	

*Finish in overall standings (No. of teams in league). †League champion.

LAST YEAR'S TOP 30

Player, Pos.		Status
1.	Josh Vitters, 3b	No. 3
2.	Jeff Samardzija, rhp	Majors
3.	Andrew Cashner, rhp	No. 4
4.	Dae-Eun Rhee, rhp	No. 12
5.	Welington Castillo, c	No. 27
6.	Kevin Hart, rhp	(Pirates)
7.	Starlin Castro, ss/2b	No. 1
8.	Ryan Flaherty, ss	No. 9
9.	Jay Jackson, rhp	No. 5
10.	Hak-Ju Lee, ss	No. 6
11.	Steve Clevenger, c/1b	Dropped out
12.	Micah Hoffpauir, 1b/of	Majors
13.	Brandon Guyer, of	Dropped out
14.	Junior Lake, ss	No. 29
15.	Jovan Rosa, 3b/1b	Dropped out
16.	Tyler Colvin, of	No. 17
17.	Marcos Mateo, rhp	No. 24
18.	Chris Carpenter, rhp	No. 8
19.	Darwin Barney, ss	No. 18
20.	Marquez Smith, 3b/2b	Dropped out
21.	Mitch Atkins, rhp	Dropped out
22.	Esmailin Caridad, rhp	No. 22
23.	Tony Thomas, 2b	Dropped out
24.	Jake Fox, 1b/of	(Athletics)
25.	Ty Wright, of	Dropped out
26.	Blake Parker, rhp	No. 20
27.	Matt Cerda, c	Dropped out
28.	Logan Watkins, 2b	No. 7
29.	Alex Maestri, rhp	Dropped out
30.	Su-Min Jung, rhp	Dropped out

BEST TOOLS

Best Hitter for Average	Hak-Ju Lee
Best Power Hitter	Brett Jackson
Best Strike-Zone Discipline	Kyler Burke
Fastest Baserunner	Jose Valdez
Best Athlete	Brett Jackson
Best Fastball	Andrew Cashner
Best Curveball	Jay Jackson
Best Slider	Andrew Cashner
Best Changeup	Casey Coleman
Best Control	Casey Coleman
Best Defensive Catcher	Robinson Chirinos
Best Defensive Infielder	Starlin Castro
Best Infield Arm	Junior Lake
Best Defensive Outfielder	Sam Fuld
Best Outfield Arm	Kyler Burke

PROJECTED 2013 LINEUP

Catcher	Geovany Soto
First Base	Derrek Lee
Second Base	Starlin Castro
Third Base	Aramis Ramirez
Shortstop	Hak-Ju Lee
Left Field	Josh Vitters
Center Field	Brett Jackson
Right Field	Kyler Burke
No. 1 Starter	Carlos Zambrano
No. 2 Starter	Jay Jackson
No. 3 Starter	Chris Carpenter
No. 4 Starter	Ryan Dempster
No. 5 Starter	Randy Wells
Closer	Andrew Cashner

TOP PROSPECTS OF THE DECADE

Year	Player, Pos.	2009 Org.
2000	Corey Patterson, of	Brewers
2001	Corey Patterson, of	Brewers
2002	Mark Prior, rhp	Padres
2003	Hee Seop Choi, 1b	Kia (Korea)
2004	Angel Guzman, rhp	Cubs
2005	Brian Dopirak, 1b	Blue Jays
2006	Felix Pie, of	Orioles
2007	Felix Pie, of	Orioles
2008	Josh Vitters, 3b	Cubs
2009	Josh Vitters, 3b	Cubs

TOP DRAFT PICKS OF THE DECADE

Year	Player, Pos.	2009 Org.
2000	Lou Montanez, ss	Orioles
2001	Mark Prior, rhp	Padres
2002	Bobby Brownlie, rhp	Braves
2003	Ryan Harvey, of	Rockies
2004	Grant Johnson, rhp (2nd round)	Gary (Northern)
2005	Mark Pawelek, lhp	Reds
2006	Tyler Colvin, of	Cubs
2007	Josh Vitters, 3b	Cubs
2008	Andrew Cashner, rhp	Cubs
2009	Brett Jackson, of	Cubs

LARGEST BONUSES IN CLUB HISTORY

Mark Prior, 2001	$4,000,000
Kosuke Fukudome, 2007	$4,000,000
Corey Patterson, 1998	$3,700,000
Josh Vitters, 2007	$3,200,000
Luis Montanez, 2000	$2,750,000

CHICAGO CUBS

TOP 2010 ROOKIE: Esmailin Caridad, rhp. He touched 96 mph while turning in 11 scoreless appearances for Chicago last September.

BREAKOUT PROSPECT: Dae-Eun Rhee, rhp, With Tommy John surgery nearly two years behind him, he could emerge as the system's top pitching prospect.

SLEEPER: Alberto Cabrera, rhp. When he's not battling elbow problems, he can reach 94 mph and shows the potential for three solid or better pitches.

SOURCE OF TOP 30 TALENT			
Homegrown	25	Acquired	5
College	13	Trades	5
Junior college	1	Rule 5 draft	0
High school	2	Independent leagues	0
Draft-and-follow	0	Free agents/waivers	0
Nondrafted free agents	0		
International	9		

Numbers in parentheses indicate prospect rankings

LF
Matt Spencer
Ty Wright
Bobby Wagner
Smaily Borges

CF
Brett Jackson (2)
Sam Fuld (23)
James Adduci (30)
Brandon Guyer
Jose Valdez
Kyung-Min Na
Cody Shields

RF
Kyler Burke (11)
Tyler Colvin (17)
Nelson Perez
Dong-Yeop Kim
Blair Springfield

3B
Josh Vitters (3)
Ryan Flaherty (9)
Junior Lake (29)
Marquez Smith

SS
Starlin Castro (1)
Hak-Ju Lee (6)
Darwin Barney (18)
Matt Camp
Wes Darvill
Jonathan Mota

2B
Logan Watkins (7)
D.J. LeMahieu (10)
Tony Thomas
Nate Samson
Matt Cerda
Pin-Chieh Chen

1B
Rebel Ridling
Ryne White
Charles Thomas

C
Robinson Chirinos (26)
Welington Castillo (27)
Steve Clevenger
Richard Jones
Sergio Burruel
Michael Brenly

RHP

Starters
Andrew Cashner (4)
Jay Jackson (5)
Chris Carpenter (8)
Dae-Eun Rhee (12)
Rafael Dolis (13)
Chris Archer (15)
Trey McNutt (16)
Casey Coleman (25)
Alberto Cabrera
Ryan Searle
Dan McDaniel
Robert Hernandez
Ronny Morla
Su-Min Jung
Justin Bristow
Melvin Rosa
Tzu-An Wang
Yao-Lin Wang

Relievers
Blake Parker (20)
Esmailin Caridad (22)
Marcos Mateo (24)
David Cales (28)
Chris Huseby
Jeff Gray
Alex Maestri
Justin Berg
David Patton
Brian Schlitter
Jeff Stevens
Greg Reinhard
Marcus Hatley
Dionis Nunez
Jose Rosario

LHP

Starters
Jeffry Antigua (19)
Brooks Raley (21)
Austin Kirk
Chris Rusin
James Russell

Relievers
John Gaub (14)
Scott Maine
Jeffrey Beliveau
Jeremy Papelbon
Casey Lambert
James Leverton
John Mincone

2009   BONUSES: $4.0 MILLION

BEST PURE HITTER: SS D.J. LeMahieu (2) led College World Series champion Louisiana State with a .350 average, then hit .323 in his pro debut. The Cubs believe he's a late bloomer physically who will develop some pull power. SS/2B Wes Darvill (5) and 2B Blair Springfield (7) are two promising but raw high school bats.

BEST POWER HITTER: OF Brett Jackson (1) has the most usable power and slugged .545 with seven homers in 26 games in low Class A. He found more consistent success in pro ball after he stopped trying to do too much at the plate. 1B Charles Thomas (10) and 3B/OF Bobby Wagner (38) have more raw power than Jackson. Wagner, who's already 23, played in semipro leagues for several years in Canada before heading to Panola (Texas) JC in 2008.

FASTEST RUNNER: OF Cody Shields (15) has close to 80 speed on the 20-80 scouting scale, though he has yet to make his pro debut after having Tommy John surgery. OF Runey Davis (12) is a 70 runner, and LHP Brooks Raley 6) showed similar speed as a two-way player at Texas A&M.

BEST DEFENSIVE PLAYER: Jackson covers the gaps well in center field and has an average arm. Darvill has a chance to be a good defender at shortstop.

BEST FASTBALL: The Cubs spotted RHP Trey McNutt (32) when they saw him throwing 90-93 mph at the Junior College World Series. After signing for $115,000, he was up to 93-96 later in the summer. Thomas showed a 90-94 mph fastball as a two-way player in college.

BEST SECONDARY PITCH: McNutt's power curveball gives him a potential second plus pitch. LHP Austin Kirk's (3) curveball and Raley's slider are solid breaking pitches.

BEST PRO DEBUT: Jackson hit .318/.418/.488 with 13 steals before tweaking his right wrist swinging a bat, which knocked him out of the low Class A Midwest League playoffs. McNutt posted a 0.98 ERA, .143 opponent average and 28 strikeouts in 28 innings.

BEST ATHLETE: Jackson, though Darvill may push him once he fills out his 6-foot-2, 175-pound frame.

MOST INTRIGUING BACKGROUND: Unsigned 3B Joe Jocketty's (47) father Walt is general manager of the Reds. Springfield is a cousin of Jermaine Dye. Thomas is the first player ever drafted from Edward Waters (Fla.) College.

CLOSEST TO THE MAJORS: The Cubs are seeking a center fielder, so Jackson could move quickly. Raley and Chris Rusin (4) are polished college lefthanders who could beat him to Wrigley Field.

BEST LATE-ROUND PICK: McNutt.

THE ONE WHO GOT AWAY: SS Chad Taylor (13, now at South Florida) and OF Keenyn Walker (16, now at Central Arizona CC) were projectable high school athletes who opted for college.

ASSESSMENT: Jackson and LeMahieu were two of the better college position players in the draft and eventually could fill the two biggest holes in the Cubs' current big league lineup. Chicago also stocked up on lefties with solid stuff and good pitchability, adding Kirk, Rusin and Raley in the early rounds.

2008   BONUSES: $5.5 MILLION

This looks like the Cubs' deepest draft in years, led by RHPs Andrew Cashner (1), Chris Carpenter (3) and Jay Jackson (9), plus 2B/SS/3B Ryan Flaherty (1s) and 2B Logan Watkins (21). Those three pitchers, as well as RHPs Casey Coleman (15) and David Cales (24), already have reached Double-A.

GRADE: B+

2007   BONUSES: $6.1 MILLION

3B Josh Vitters (1) could be Chicago's best home grown hitter since Mark Grace, a 24th-round pick in 1985. SS Darwin Barney (4) keeps getting better, while C Josh Donaldson (1s) was part of the payment in the Rich Harden trade.

GRADE: C+

2006   BONUSES: $5.0 MILLION

The Cubs still hope for big things from OF Tyler Colvin (1) and $10 million RHP Jeff Samardzija (5), though scouts from other clubs aren't as high as on them. RHPs Chris Huseby (11) and Blake Parker (16) could provide bullpen help in the future.

GRADE: D

2005   BONUSES: $2.8 MILLION*

A truly dreadful draft started with LHP Mark Pawelek (1), who bombed after a promising pro debut. The only big leaguer is LHP Donald Veal (2), who stuck with the Pirates last season as a Rule 5 pick.

GRADE: F

---

*Draft analysis by Jim Callis. Numbers in parentheses indicate draft rounds. *Bonuses for 2005 are first 10 rounds only.*

PROSPECT 1

STARLIN CASTRO, SS

Born: March 24, 1990.
Height: 6-1. **Weight:** 175.
Bats: R. **Throws:** R.
Signed: Dominican Republic, 2006.
Signed by: Jose Serra.

Sand Lot

MIKE JANES

lubs rarely ask players to make the jump from Rookie ball to high Class A, but that's exactly the challenge the Cubs presented Castro with in 2009. After he and Junior Lake shared shortstop duties in the Rookie-level Arizona League in 2008, Chicago wanted both to play regularly and sent Lake to low Class A Peoria and Castro to Daytona—skipping two levels in the process. Simply holding his own as the youngest regular in the Florida State League would have been a significant accomplishment, but Castro did much more. He won MVP honors at the FSL all-star game by going 4-for-4 with an inside-the-park home run, and made the league's postseason all-star team. He singled in his lone at-bat in the Futures Game before earning an August promotion to Double-A Tennessee. Castro hit .303 in the Southern League playoffs, then moved on to the Arizona Fall League, where he continued to establish himself as an elite shortstop prospect. The Cubs, who signed him for $50,000 out of the Dominican Republic, thought Castro had all-star potential but never expected him to be this good this quickly.

Castro's performance has drawn him comparisons with the likes of Tony Fernandez, Edgar Renteria, Miguel Tejada—and even Derek Jeter. Castro covers the plate well for a young hitter and does a nice job of staying inside the ball and using the entire field. He consistently puts the barrel of the bat on the ball and has a knack for making adjustments. He has no trouble hitting breaking pitches, usually taking the first one from a pitcher he hasn't seen before, sizing it up and attacking the next. Though he had just 32 extra-base hits in 2009, Castro has the power potential to double that total once he matures physically. He has added 15 pounds in the last year and Chicago envisions him growing to 6-foot-3 and 195 pounds. He has strong hands and wrists, and he's starting to pull and drive more pitches. He has the plus speed to make things happen on the bases. Castro excels defensively as well, with range to both sides, body control and arm strength to make any play. Managers rated him the best defensive shortstop in the Florida State League. The Cubs also like his instincts, charisma and work ethic.

Castro just needs time to fill out and polish his game. He made 39 errors last season, which isn't a high number for a young shortstop but shows that he needs to play more under control. He makes so much contact that he doesn't draw many walks, though he does work counts. He's still learning to look for pitches he can drive in certain situations. He needs to hone his basestealing technique after getting caught in 11 of 39 tries in 2009, though he did go 6-for-6 in Double-A.

Castro's stellar AFL performance further accelerated his timetable. He'll probably open 2010 back in Tennessee because Darwin Barney is slated for Triple-A Iowa, but there's rumbling that Castro could be in Chicago by season's end. He has all the ingredients to become the Cubs' first all-star shortstop since Shawon Dunston in 1990.

Year	Club (League)	Class	AVG	G	AB	R	H	2B	3B	HR	RBI	BB	SO	SB	OBP	SLG
2007	Cubs (DSL)	R	.299	60	221	47	66	6	2	2	31	23	24	13	.371	.371
2008	Cubs (AZL)	R	.311	51	196	33	61	11	5	3	22	14	33	6	.364	.464
2009	Daytona (FSL)	HiA	.302	96	358	45	108	17	3	3	35	19	41	22	.340	.391
	Tennessee (SL)	AA	.288	31	111	11	32	6	3	0	14	10	12	6	.347	.396
MINOR LEAGUE TOTALS			.301	238	886	136	267	40	13	8	102	66	110	47	.354	.403

2 BRETT JACKSON, OF *Lez*

BORN: Aug. 2, 1988. **B-T:** L-R. **HT.:** 6-2. **WT.:** 210. **DRAFTED:** California, 2009 (1st round). **SIGNED BY:** John Bartsch.

The Cubs thought Jackson had the best bat speed and some of the best power in the 2009 draft class, but he lasted 31 picks because other teams questioned his ability to make contact. The Cubs took him with their first pick and he signed quickly for $972,000. He had a smashing pro debut until he tweaked his right wrist on a practice swing in late August. More than just a slugger, Jackson is the best athlete in the system. His quick bat and the loft in his swing give him well-above-average raw power. He uses his plus speed well on the bases and in center field, and he also has solid arm strength with good accuracy on his throws. He plays with constant energy. Jackson will accrue his share of strikeouts but can keep them under control if he doesn't get too aggressive. He has enough natural power that he doesn't have to chase pitches out of the zone or swing for the fences to produce home runs. After using five different regular center fielders in the last five years, the Cubs are seeking stability. They may send Jackson to Double-A to start his first full pro season, and he could reach Chicago by the end of 2011.

Year	Club (League)	Class	AVG	G	AB	R	H	2B	3B	HR	RBI	BB	SO	SB	OBP	SLG
2009	Cubs (AZL)	R	.455	3	11	6	5	0	1	0	4	3	4	0	.533	.636
	Boise (NWL)	SS	.330	24	88	14	29	1	1	1	15	17	20	2	.443	.398
	Peoria (MWL)	LoA	.295	26	112	30	33	5	1	7	17	11	32	11	.383	.545
MINOR LEAGUE TOTALS			.318	53	211	50	67	6	3	8	36	31	56	13	.418	.488

3 JOSH VITTERS, 3B *Lez*

BORN: Aug. 27, 1989. **B-T:** R-R. **HT.:** 6-2. **WT.:** 200. **DRAFTED:** HS—Cypress, Calif., 2007 (1st round). **SIGNED BY:** Denny Henderson/Tim Wilken.

The No. 3 overall pick in the 2007 draft, Vitters signed for $3.2 million. Managers rated him the best hitting and power prospect in the Midwest League last summer, when he arrived in low Class A a year behind schedule after developing tendinitis in his left hand in 2008. He struggled when promoted to high Class A at age 19. Vitters has a compact stroke for a power hitter, using his exceptional hand eye coordination to easily put the fat part of the barrel on balls. He's a potential .300 hitter who could have 25-30 homers a year. He has the hands and arm strength to play third base, and he has improved his agility and footwork since signing. Vitters makes contact almost too easily, as he rarely walks and gives away at-bats by putting balls in play that he should let go of. Though he has gotten better defensively, there's still concern that he doesn't have the quick first step and range to play third base. He's a below-average runner. The game comes so easily to him that some question how diligent he is about addressing his shortcomings. By pounding Arizona Fall League pitching, Vitters made a case for opening 2010 in Double-A. He's on course to hit the majors by the end of 2011.

Year	Club (League)	Class	AVG	G	AB	R	H	2B	3B	HR	RBI	BB	SO	SB	OBP	SLG
2007	Cubs (AZL)	R	.067	7	30	0	2	0	0	0	2	1	9	0	.094	.067
	Boise (NWL)	SS	.190	7	21	2	4	0	0	0	1	2	5	1	.261	.190
2008	Peoria (MWL)	LoA	.214	4	14	1	3	3	0	0	1	0	5	0	.214	.429
	Boise (NWL)	SS	.328	61	259	38	85	25	2	5	37	13	45	1	.365	.498
2009	Peoria (MWL)	LoA	.316	70	269	42	85	12	1	15	46	7	42	4	.351	.535
	Daytona (FSL)	HiA	.238	50	189	21	45	7	2	3	22	5	23	2	.260	.344
MINOR LEAGUE TOTALS			.286	199	782	104	224	47	5	23	109	28	129	8	.319	.448

4 ANDREW CASHNER, RHP +

BORN: Sept. 11, 1986. **B-T:** R-R. **HT.:** 6-6. **WT.:** 210. **DRAFTED:** Texas Christian, 2008 (1st round). **SIGNED BY:** Trey Forkerway.

Cashner turned down the Cubs as a 29th-round pick from Angelina (Texas) JC in 2007, then signed for $1.54 million as a first-round pick out of Texas Christian a year later. He won the Florida State League championship clincher in his pro debut and finished his first full season in Double-A. With his frame and power stuff, Cashner is reminiscent of Kerry Wood. His fastball sits at 92-95 mph and touches 98 when he starts, and he has operated in the upper 90s as a reliever. His 81-85 mph slider breaks like a power curveball. He works down in the zone, allowing just two homers in 120 pro innings. Chicago wants to develop Cashner as a starter, but some scouts believe he's destined to be a reliever. His delivery is sound but not fluid, and he often battles his command. His changeup has the potential to become an average pitch, but he needs to use it more often. The Cubs kept him on tight pitch counts after he missed the start of last season with a strained oblique, so he has yet to prove he can pitch deep into games. Whether he's a frontline starter or a closer, Cashner should be a big part of Chicago's future. He'll likely begin 2010 in Double-A and could make his big league debut later in the year.

Year	Club (League)	Class	W	L	ERA	G	GS	CG	SV	IP	H	R	ER	HR	BB	SO	AVG
2008	Cubs (AZL)	R	0	0	0.00	1	1	0	0	1	1	1	0	0	0	2	.333
	Boise (NWL)	SS	1	1	4.96	6	4	0	0	16	19	12	9	1	19	16	.302
	Daytona (FSL)	HiA	0	1	13.50	1	1	0	0	3	4	4	4	0	4	1	.364
2009	Daytona (FSL)	HiA	0	0	1.50	12	12	0	0	42	31	8	7	1	15	34	.201
	Tennessee (SL)	AA	3	4	3.39	12	12	0	0	58	45	30	22	0	27	41	.210
MINOR LEAGUE TOTALS			4	6	3.14	32	30	0	0	120	100	55	42	2	65	94	.225

5 JAY JACKSON, RHP ✝

BORN: Oct. 27, 1987. **B-T:** R-R. **HT.:** 6-1. **WT.:** 195. **DRAFTED:** Furman, 2008 (9th round). **SIGNED BY:** Antonio Grissom.

Jackson looks like one of the steals of the 2008 draft after lasting nine rounds and signing for $90,000. A two-way star at Furman, he breezed through his pro debut and opened his first full season in Double-A. His only speed bump came in late July, when he was demoted for violating an unspecified team policy. Jackson has good feel for four pitches that are average or better. His best offering is a fastball ranging from 90-95 mph. His mid-80s slider and high-70s curveball are distinct pitches that rate as above-average at times. He also has an effective changeup. He has a long arm action, but he's so athletic that he repeats his high-three-quarters delivery easily. He's fearless and fields his position well. Jackson sometimes overthrows, costing him command. Because he's not tall, he has to stay on top of his pitches to keep them down in the zone. His changeup lags behind his other pitches and could use refinement. The Cubs believe his indiscretion was a one-time incident, and he responded well, earning a late-season start in Triple-A. Once Jackson throws quality strikes on a more consistent basis, he'll be ready for the big league rotation. He'll probably return to Double-A to start 2010.

Year	Club (League)	Class	W	L	ERA	G	GS	CG	SV	IP	H	R	ER	HR	BB	SO	AVG
2008	Boise (NWL)	SS	0	0	5.00	3	1	0	0	9	7	5	5	1	1	14	.212
	Peoria (MWL)	LoA	2	2	3.00	6	1	0	0	24	22	8	8	3	5	37	.253
	Daytona (FSL)	HiA	2	0	1.59	4	3	0	0	17	11	4	3	0	7	21	.183
2009	Tennessee (SL)	AA	5	5	3.70	16	16	1	0	83	73	35	34	7	39	77	.236
	Daytona (FSL)	HiA	2	2	1.64	7	7	0	0	38	31	12	7	3	4	46	.218
	Iowa (PCL)	AAA	1	0	1.50	1	1	0	0	6	5	1	1	1	3	4	.227
MINOR LEAGUE TOTALS			12	9	2.95	37	29	1	0	177	149	65	58	15	59	199	.222

6 HAK-JU LEE, SS ✝

BORN: Nov. 4, 1990. **B-T:** L-R. **HT.:** 6-2. **WT.:** 170. **SIGNED:** Korea, 2008. **SIGNED BY:** Steve Wilson.

More active than most clubs in the Far East, the Cubs spent $725,000 to sign Lee out of Korea in June 2008. He injured his elbow before coming to the United States, requiring Tommy John surgery, delaying his professional debut. He recovered quickly, ranking as the top prospect in the short-season Northwest League. Lee has four above-average tools, starting with plus-plus speed that he used to lead the NWL with 25 steals. He's a gifted hitter who stays inside the ball and sprays line drives all over the field. His patience and quickness enhance his ability to get on base. He gets to balls that a lot of shortstops can't reach, and he has the actions, hands and arm strength to make difficult plays. Lee doesn't possess much power and needs to get stronger, though he does sting the ball with authority. For a player with his profile, he'll have to make more contact. He can get flashy and sloppy at times, especially on defense, where he led NWL shortstops with 27 errors. Lee is more athletic than Starlin Castro, which could push Castro to second base when they're double-play partners in Chicago. The Cubs haven't ruled out skipping Lee a level to high Class A in 2010.

Year	Club (League)	Class	AVG	G	AB	R	H	2B	3B	HR	RBI	BB	SO	SB	OBP	SLG
2009	Boise (NWL)	SS	.330	68	264	56	87	14	2	2	33	31	50	25	.399	.420
MINOR LEAGUE TOTALS			.330	68	264	56	87	14	2	2	33	31	50	25	.399	.420

7 LOGAN WATKINS, 2B ✌

BORN: Aug. 29, 1989. **B-T:** L-R. **HT.:** 5-11. **WT.:** 170. **DRAFTED:** HS—Goddard, Kan., 2008 (21st round). **SIGNED BY:** Brandon Mozley.

Watkins generated little predraft hype in 2008 and appeared headed to Wichita State out of high school before the Cubs selected him in the 21st round and gave him a stunning $500,000 bonus. He has been worth every penny so far, batting .326 in two pro seasons. He led the Northwest League in plate appearances per strikeout (10.3) in 2009. An all-state quarterback and defensive back in high school in Kansas, Watkins is a quality athlete. He has an unorthodox stance with high elbows, but whips the bat through the zone and makes contact easily. He uses the whole field and is a skilled bunter. He has plus-plus speed and an above-average arm, making him capable of playing almost anywhere on the diamond. He's a hard worker whose intensity rubs off on his teammates. Watkins needs to get stronger to hit the ball with more authority. He can get too aggressive running at times, and too passive at others. He waits on balls too much at second base, relying on his arm to make plays. Watkins merits a look at shortstop and center field, but Chicago hasn't figured out how to make that happen. The Cubs like the way he interacts with Hak-Ju Lee, and if they play together in low Class A in 2010, Watkins faces another season at second base.

Year	Club (League)	Class	AVG	G	AB	R	H	2B	3B	HR	RBI	BB	SO	SB	OBP	SLG
2008	Cubs (AZL)	R	.325	27	80	15	26	3	0	0	14	20	19	2	.462	.363
2009	Boise (NWL)	SS	.326	72	279	48	91	14	2	0	29	27	31	14	.389	.391
MINOR LEAGUE TOTALS			.326	99	359	63	117	17	2	0	43	47	50	16	.407	.384

8 CHRIS CARPENTER, RHP X-e(

BORN: Dec. 26, 1985. **B-T:** R-R. **HT.:** 6-4. **WT.:** 215. **DRAFTED:** Kent State, 2008 (3rd round). **SIGNED BY:** Lukas McKnight.

The highest-drafted prep pitcher in 2004 who opted for college, Carpenter turned down the Tigers as a seventh-rounder. He had Tommy John surgery as a Kent State freshman in 2005, then a second elbow procedure the next year. His medical history made him available to the Cubs in the third round in 2008. Carpenter throws his fastball at 91-94 mph and touches 97. It has very good life for a four-seamer, inducing lots of groundballs. He also has a mid-80s slurve that flashes the bite and depth of a slider. His changeup gives him a potential solid third pitch. He's a diligent worker with a frame built for innings. Carpenter's stuff can be so lively that he struggles to control it. He needs to stay on top of his breaking ball to make it a true slider, and his changeup will develop more quickly if he uses it more often. While his health may always be a concern, he has had no physical problems since a tired arm in the summer of 2007. As long as he stays healthy, Carpenter has a bright future. He'll return to Double-A to open 2010 and contend for a big league rotation spot the following year.

Year	Club (League)	Class	W	L	ERA	G	GS	CG	SV	IP	H	R	ER	HR	BB	SO	AVG
2008	Cubs (AZL)	R	0	0	18.00	1	1	0	0	1	2	2	2	0	1	1	.500
	Boise (NWL)	SS	4	2	4.22	10	6	0	0	32	32	21	15	2	22	24	.258
2009	Peoria (MWL)	LoA	4	3	2.44	15	15	1	0	74	55	23	20	4	33	60	.210
	Daytona (FSL)	HiA	2	1	1.44	5	5	0	0	25	15	7	4	1	8	33	.163
	Tennessee (SL)	AA	0	3	4.78	7	7	0	0	32	30	20	17	0	11	25	.246
MINOR LEAGUE TOTALS			10	9	3.19	38	34	1	0	164	134	73	58	7	75	143	.222

9 RYAN FLAHERTY, 2B/SS/3B

BORN: July 27, 1986. **B-T:** L-R. **HT.:** 6-3. **WT.:** 200. **DRAFTED:** Vanderbilt, 2008 (1st round supplemental). **SIGNED BY:** Antonio Grissom.

After playing second fiddle to Pedro Alvarez in the Vanderbilt lineup, Flaherty went 41st overall in the 2008 draft and signed for $1.5 million. He has ranked third in his league in homers in each of his two pro seasons. His father Ed has won two NCAA Division III College World Series as the head coach at Southern Maine. Flaherty made significant improvements in 2009. Formerly a dead-pull hitter, he started driving balls the other way, giving him solid power to all fields. He has a polished lefthanded swing and hit .309 in the second half. His arm strength went from subpar to average, and he did a better job of turning double plays. His instincts and makeup enhance his tools. Flaherty is seeking a defensive home after splitting 2009 between second base, shortstop and third base. He's a below-average runner who lacks the range for shortstop. He may not be quick enough for second base, and some scouts question whether he has enough power and arm to profile at third base. Chicago has yet to decide what level and what position Flaherty will play at in 2010. If he doesn't settle into one position, he could have value as a lefthanded-hitting version of Mark DeRosa.

Year	Club (League)	Class	AVG	G	AB	R	H	2B	3B	HR	RBI	BB	SO	SB	OBP	SLG
2008	Boise (NWL)	SS	.297	56	219	39	65	19	2	8	26	24	51	4	.369	.511
2009	Peoria (MWL)	LoA	.276	131	485	81	134	24	5	20	81	50	98	7	.344	.470
MINOR LEAGUE TOTALS			.283	187	704	120	199	43	7	28	107	74	149	11	.352	.483

10 D.J. LeMAHIEU, SS/2B

BORN: July 13, 1988. **B-T:** R-R. **HT.:** 6-4. **WT.:** 185. **DRAFTED:** Louisiana State, 2009 (2nd round). **SIGNED BY:** Steve Riha.

LeMahieu starred in the Cape Cod League in 2008, but his play slipped last spring. He played his way off shortstop and hit just five homers for Louisiana State, though he led the Tigers in batting (.350) as they won the College World Series. The Cubs took him in the second round and signed him for a $508,000 bonus. LeMahieu may be the purest hitter in the system, staying inside the ball and drilling line drives to the opposite field. He could develop average power as he fills out and turns on more pitches, which he started to do after Peoria hitting coach Barbaro Garbey helped him reduce the front arm bar in his swing. As a defender, he has a solid arm and good hands but doesn't have the range to stay at shortstop. Some scouts wonder if he'll have enough quickness for second base or provide enough offense to play regularly elsewhere. He's a fringe-average runner. LeMahieu has some similarities to Ryan Flaherty, and the two could shift around the infield together in high Class A in 2010. The Cubs believe in LeMahieu's bat, and he could move quickly if he finds a position.

Year	Club (League)	Class	AVG	G	AB	R	H	2B	3B	HR	RBI	BB	SO	SB	OBP	SLG
2009	Cubs (AZL)	R	.417	3	12	2	5	0	1	0	4	1	3	1	.429	.583
	Peoria (MWL)	LoA	.316	38	152	19	48	4	2	0	30	12	22	2	.371	.368
MINOR LEAGUE TOTALS			.323	41	164	21	53	4	3	0	34	13	25	3	.376	.384

11 KYLER BURKE, OF/1B

BORN: April 20, 1988. **B-T:** L-L. **HT.:** 6-3. **WT.:** 205. **DRAFTED:** HS—Ooltewah, Tenn., 2006 (1st round supplemental). **SIGNED BY:** Ash Lawson (Padres).

The Padres gave Burke $950,000 as the 35th overall pick in the 2006 draft, but soured on him when he hit just .210 in 107 games in the lower levels of their system. They traded him to the Cubs for Michael Barrett the following June. Chicago discussed using Burke on the mound before the 2009 season, but he insisted he could hit, and the Cubs told him it was time to prove it. He did just that, winning the organization's minor league player of the year award. Burke improved both his plate discipline and power. He has a short, direct lefthanded swing and stays inside pitches well. His power is to the gaps—he led the MWL with 43 doubles—and he could have plus power in time because he drives the ball well to left-center. He'll have to show more pop against lefthanders to become more than a platoon partner in the big leagues. He can be too patient, taking hittable pitches, but he has cut down on his tendency to chase pitches when he fell behind in the count. Though Burke has below-average speed, he runs the bases well. He played all three outfield positions and first base last year, fitting best in right field. His instincts give him slightly above-average range and reads on the corners, and he has one of the best outfield arms in the minors. On the 20-80 scouting scale, his arm strength rates a 70 and his accuracy an 80, allowing him to rack up 43 assists in 378 games in the outfield. Burke should see Double-A at some point in 2010.

Year	Club (League)	Class	AVG	G	AB	R	H	2B	3B	HR	RBI	BB	SO	SB	OBP	SLG
2006	Padres (AZL)	R	.209	45	163	24	34	3	4	1	15	26	56	1	.313	.294
2007	Fort Wayne (MWL)	LoA	.211	62	213	24	45	7	1	1	21	26	73	3	.305	.268
	Boise (NWL)	SS	.254	63	224	35	57	11	1	10	41	24	63	1	.340	.446
2008	Peoria (MWL)	LoA	.206	35	131	12	27	5	1	2	8	11	34	3	.278	.305
	Boise (NWL)	SS	.261	67	245	46	64	18	2	7	41	28	70	6	.336	.437
2009	Peoria (MWL)	LoA	.303	132	465	93	141	43	3	15	89	78	99	14	.405	.505
MINOR LEAGUE TOTALS			.255	404	1441	234	368	87	12	36	215	193	395	28	.347	.407

12 DAE-EUN RHEE, RHP

BORN: March 23, 1989. **B-T:** L-R. **HT.:** 6-2. **WT.:** 190. **SIGNED:** Korea, 2007. **SIGNED BY:** Steve Wilson.

The Cubs mine Korea as aggressively as any club. They gave seven-figure bonuses to Hee Seop Choi and Jae-Kuk Ryu, two of the 12 Koreans to reach the majors, and have another wave of Korean talent coming, led by Hak-Ju Lee and Rhee. who was signed for $525,000 as an 18-year-old in July 2007. Rhee was so advanced that the Cubs sent him to low Class A to make his pro debut the spring after he signed. He looked terrific before injuring his elbow in his fourth start, resulting in Tommy John surgery that sidelined him for most of 2009. During instructional league, Rhee showed that he's on the verge of regaining his feel and stuff. His fastball returned to the low 90s, and he flashed a solid curveball and a nifty changeup with splitter action. He threw well enough for the Cubs to consider sending him to high Class A to start 2010. He has a clean arm action and no red flags in his delivery, so there are no health concerns going forward. While rehabbing, he used his downtime to improve his English and his conditioning. With a chance for three plus pitches, Rhee could develop into a frontline starter.

Year	Club (League)	Class	W	L	ERA	G	GS	CG	SV	IP	H	R	ER	HR	BB	SO	AVG
2008	Peoria (MWL)	LoA	4	1	1.80	10	10	0	0	40	28	13	8	0	16	33	.194
2009	Cubs (AZL)	R	0	0	7.71	3	2	0	0	5	4	4	4	0	5	3	.235
	Boise (NWL)	SS	0	1	11.25	2	2	0	0	4	8	5	5	2	1	4	.421
MINOR LEAGUE TOTALS			4	2	3.14	15	14	0	0	49	40	22	17	2	22	40	.222

13 RAFAEL DOLIS, RHP

BORN: Jan. 10, 1988. **B-T:** R-R. **HT.:** 6-4. **WT.:** 215. **SIGNED:** Dominican Republic, 2004. **SIGNED BY:** Jose Serra/Marino Encarnacion.

The Cubs convert more position players to pitchers than most clubs. The best starter on their big league club last season was Randy Wells, an ex-catcher, and their closer down the stretch was Carlos Marmol, a former catcher/infielder. The talk of Chicago's instructional league camp was Dolis, originally signed as a shortstop. He became a pitcher before he made his U.S. debut in 2006, but he injured his elbow early in 2007 and missed 2008 while recovering from Tommy John surgery. The Cubs kept Dolis on short pitch counts when he returned last season, and he showed a 92-97 mph fastball and flashed a hard slider while averaging fewer than four innings per start. In instructional league, pitching coordinator Mark Riggins had Dolis start using a full windup. The results were immediate, as Dolis' fastball sat in the mid-90s and touched triple digits. His slider jumped to 86-87 mph and showed out-pitch potential. He also has a changeup with some fade, but at times he throws the pitch too hard. The full windup allowed Dolis to get better extension on his delivery and better finish on his pitches, and may be the key to improving his inconsistent command and control. If Dolis can throw more quality strikes, he has the stuff to be a frontline starter. If not, he could be a late-inning weapon out of the bullpen. After adding Dolis to the 40-man roster, the Cubs will send him to Double-A to open 2010.

Year	Club (League)	Class	W	L	ERA	G	GS	CG	SV	IP	H	R	ER	HR	BB	SO	AVG
2006	Cubs (AZL)	R	0	2	8.28	13	3	0	0	25	30	27	23	1	16	33	.294
2007	Peoria (MWL)	LoA	3	1	1.80	6	6	0	0	30	23	7	6	1	16	24	.223
2009	Daytona (FSL)	HiA	3	9	3.79	27	25	0	0	100	78	46	42	4	53	75	.221
MINOR LEAGUE TOTALS			6	12	4.13	46	34	0	0	155	131	80	71	6	85	132	.235

14 JOHN GAUB, LHP

BORN: April 28, 1985. **B-T:** R-L. **HT.:** 6-2. **WT.:** 210. **DRAFTED:** Minnesota, 2006 (21st round). **SIGNED BY:** Byron Ewing (Indians).

The Cubs acquired Gaub from the Indians in the Mark DeRosa deal. One pro scout with another organization said Gaub was the best lefthanded reliever he saw in the minors in 2009. He had shoulder surgery after his sophomore season at Minnesota and again in pro ball in 2007, and his stuff came all the way back last season, Gaub touched 93 mph and showed a good slider at the end of 2008, and last year he worked from 91-96 mph with his fastball and 84-90 mph with a wipeout slider. The deception in his three-quarters delivery makes him that much tougher to hit. Gaub needs to find more consistency with his slider, and an offspeed pitch would help him confound batters who are geared up for hard stuff. His top priority is to improve his control, though there are advantages to being effectively wild. He gets righthanders out, so he can work the late innings and be more than a lefty specialist. A November addition to Chicago's 40-man roster, Gaub likely will begin 2010 in Triple-A but should help the big league club later in the year.

Year	Club (League)	Class	W	L	ERA	G	GS	CG	SV	IP	H	R	ER	HR	BB	SO	AVG
2007	Indians (GCL)	R	0	0	2.25	4	0	0	0	4	4	1	1	0	4	4	.308
2008	Lake County (SAL)	LoA	1	1	3.38	34	0	0	2	64	44	30	24	3	32	100	.195
2009	Tennessee (SL)	AA	3	1	2.83	26	0	0	4	29	19	12	9	3	17	40	.188
	Iowa (PCL)	AAA	1	1	1.72	26	0	0	1	31	17	6	6	1	16	40	.157
MINOR LEAGUE TOTALS			5	3	2.81	90	0	0	7	128	84	49	40	7	69	184	.188

15 CHRIS ARCHER, RHP

BORN: Sept. 26, 1988. **B-T:** R-R. **HT.:** 6-3. **WT.:** 180. **DRAFTED:** HS—Clayton, N.C., 2006 (5th round). **SIGNED BY:** Bob Mayer (Indians).

Archer went just 5-18, 5.13 in three seasons in the Indians system but turned a corner after coming to the Cubs in the Mark DeRosa trade. He went 6-4, 2.81 in low Class A and didn't allow a homer in 109 innings. Archer turns bats into kindling with a 91-93 mph fastball and a hard breaking ball. His heater tops out at 96 mph, and while it can get straight because he uses an over-the-top delivery, it has some sink and armside run. His curve becomes slurvy at times, but it's a plus pitch when he commands it. It remains to be seen whether Archer will be a starter or reliever. To remain in the rotation, he'll need to improve his control and command and commit to using his changeup more often. He shies away from pitching to contact, and he has the stuff to challenge hitters more often without getting hit. He has an easy delivery without any obvious flaws, yet he has repeated trouble throwing strikes. Archer will seek more consistency in high Class A this season.

CHICAGO CUBS

Year	Club (League)	Class	W	L	ERA	G	GS	CG	SV	IP	H	R	ER	HR	BB	SO	AVG
2006	Indians (GCL)	R	0	3	7.45	7	6	0	0	19	17	22	16	1	17	21	.224
	Burlington (APP)	R	0	0	10.80	1	0	0	0	2	2	2	2	1	1	1	.333
2007	Indians (GCL)	R	1	7	5.64	12	11	0	0	53	56	36	33	4	21	48	.271
	Lake County (SAL)	LoA	0	0	9.00	1	0	0	0	4	5	4	4	0	3	5	.333
2008	Lake County (SAL)	LoA	4	8	4.29	27	27	0	0	115	92	64	55	8	84	106	.220
2009	Peoria (MWL)	LoA	6	4	2.81	27	26	0	0	109	78	41	34	0	66	119	.202
MINOR LEAGUE TOTALS			11	22	4.29	75	70	0	0	302	250	169	144	14	192	300	.225

16 TREY McNUTT, RHP

BORN: Aug. 2, 1989. **B-T:** R-R. **HT.:** 6-4. **WT.:** 205. **DRAFTED:** Shelton State (Ala.) CC, 2009 (32nd round). **SIGNED BY:** Al Geddes/Steve McFarland/Lukas McKnight/Jim Crawford.

Strange as it may sound, the Cubs benefited when their area scout for Alabama quit and they decided not to replace him. While other teams saw McNutt throw in the high 80s as as a freshman for Shelton State (Ala.) CC early last spring and moved on, Chicago didn't get its first look at him until the Junior College World Series, where he threw 90-93 mph despite getting knocked around by eventual champion Howard (Texas). After McNutt turned down an eighth-round offer from the Twins, he slid all the way to the 32nd round. The Cubs saw him reach the mid-90s in summer ball and signed him at the end of June for $115,000. They compare the big, strong, athletic righthander to a lesser version of Andrew Cashner. McNutt's fastball has climbed as high as 96 mph and features late riding action. His power curveball projects as a second plus pitch, and he has the makings of a good changeup. McNutt needs to cut down on his walks, but he dominated hitters in his pro debut. The 980th player drafted in 2009 looks like a steal, and the Cubs are looking forward to seeing how he fares in Class A World.

Year	Club (League)	Class	W	L	ERA	G	GS	CG	SV	IP	H	R	ER	HR	BB	SO	AVG
2009	Cubs (AZL)	R	0	1	0.00	6	4	0	0	7	5	5	0	0	3	7	.167
	Boise (NWL)	SS	3	0	1.33	7	2	0	0	20	9	7	3	1	12	21	.132
MINOR LEAGUE TOTALS			3	1	0.98	13	6	0	0	28	14	12	3	1	15	28	.143

17 TYLER COLVIN, OF

BORN: Sept. 5, 1985. **B-T:** L-L. **HT.:** 6-3. **WT.:** 190. **DRAFTED:** Clemson, 2006 (1st round). **SIGNED BY:** Antonio Grissom.

Now that Colvin has put elbow problems behind him, the Cubs believe they're seeing the player they expected when they drafted him 13th overall and signed him for $1.475 million in 2006. He first injured his left elbow in instructional league after his pro debut, and it repeatedly bothered him until he had Tommy John surgery following the 2008 season. Fully recovered by the time he joined Tennessee at the end of May, he put up the best offensive numbers of his career and tied a Southern League record with 11 consecutive hits in August. Colvin got the bat head through the zone quicker and did a better job of covering the plate, as it no longer hurt when he torqued his elbow extending his arms to hit pitches on the outer half. With his size, bat speed and the loft in his swing, he could develop 20-homer power. To deliver on his power potential, Colvin will need to show more discipline against more advanced pitchers. Some evaluators outside the organization aren't as high on him, criticizing his swing, lack of patience and tendency to roll over on pitches and hit soft grounders. He has lost a half-step since signing and has below-average speed out of the box, though he's a solid runner under way. He has good range and enough arm to play right field. When the Cubs suspended Milton Bradley at the end of the season, they promoted Colvin and gave him five starts in the final two weeks. He'll open 2010 by getting his first taste of Triple-A.

Year	Club (League)	Class	AVG	G	AB	R	H	2B	3B	HR	RBI	BB	SO	SB	OBP	SLG
2006	Boise (NWL)	SS	.268	64	265	50	71	12	6	11	53	17	55	12	.313	.483
2007	Daytona (FSL)	HiA	.306	63	245	38	75	24	3	7	50	10	47	10	.336	.514
	Tennessee (SL)	AA	.291	62	247	34	72	11	2	9	31	5	54	7	.313	.462
2008	Tennessee (SL)	AA	.256	137	540	68	138	27	11	14	80	44	101	7	.312	.424
2009	Daytona (FSL)	HiA	.250	32	112	18	28	5	2	1	10	13	27	3	.326	.357
	Tennessee (SL)	AA	.300	84	307	51	92	13	7	14	50	16	57	5	.334	.524
	Chicago (NL)	MAJ	.176	6	17	1	3	0	0	0	2	2	5	0	.250	.176
MAJOR LEAGUE TOTALS			.176	6	17	1	3	0	0	0	2	2	5	0	.250	.176
MINOR LEAGUE TOTALS			.277	442	1716	259	476	92	31	56	274	105	341	44	.320	.465

18 DARWIN BARNEY, SS

BORN: Nov. 8, 1985. **B-T:** R-R. **HT.:** 5-10. **WT.:** 180. **DRAFTED:** Oregon State, 2007 (4th round). **SIGNED BY:** John Bartsch.

It's no coincidence that Oregon State won College World Series championships in Barney's last two seasons there, or that Daytona won the Florida State League title in his first full pro season. He's not flashy but has a knack for doing what it takes to win in all phases of the game. Scouts both within and outside the organization think more highly of his tools than they did when he signed. He always handled the bat well, but he took a step forward when Daytona hitting coach Richie Zisk switched him to a 35-ounce bat in mid-2008. Barney's approach noticeably improved, as he stopped trying to pull everything and hit more hard liners and grounders than easy flyouts. He doesn't have any power and will have to bat toward the bottom of the order unless he starts taking more walks, but he makes consistent contact and isn't afraid to hit with two strikes or in clutch situations. His instincts allow his average speed to play up on the bases. Barney's range and arm are just a tick above-average, but he grades as a plus defender because he reads balls well and has soft hands and a quick release. Barney is nearly ready after spending the second half of 2009 in Triple-A, but it's uncertain how much of an opportunity he'll get in Chicago with incumbent Ryan Theriot, a similar player with more speed, ahead of him and Starlin Castro closing fast on both of them.

Year	Club (League)	Class	AVG	G	AB	R	H	2B	3B	HR	RBI	BB	SO	SB	OBP	SLG
2007	Cubs (AZL)	R	.444	5	18	6	8	3	0	0	2	4	0	0	.545	.611
	Peoria (MWL)	LoA	.273	44	176	27	48	9	3	2	21	11	22	5	.323	.392
2008	Daytona (FSL)	HiA	.262	123	409	46	107	22	4	3	51	38	58	8	.325	.357
2009	Tennessee (SL)	AA	.317	74	252	30	80	12	0	3	32	23	33	5	.368	.401
	Iowa (PCL)	AAA	.264	63	212	25	56	12	1	0	17	13	32	4	.304	.330
MINOR LEAGUE TOTALS			.280	309	1067	134	299	58	8	8	123	89	145	22	.335	.372

19 JEFFRY ANTIGUA, LHP

BORN: June 23, 1990. **B-T:** R-L. **HT.:** 6-1. **WT.:** 170. **SIGNED:** Dominican Republic, 2006. **SIGNED BY:** Jose Serra.

Looking to stock up on lefthanders, the Cubs drafted Austin Kirk, Chris Rusin, Brooks Raley in the first six rounds of the 2009 draft. The unheralded Antigua is younger and has better stuff than all of them. He has had steady success at each of his four pro stops and wasn't fazed by jumping to low Class A shortly after he turned 19 last summer. Antigua has very good feel for three pitches that project as average or better. His changeup is his best present offering, ranking ahead of his 89-92 mph fastball and his slider. He needs to get stronger so he can maintain his fastball velocity deeper into games and into the season, and his slider lacks consistent tilt. Antigua is advanced well beyond his years. He fills the strike zone, reads hitters well and has the ability to adjust to how good his individual pitches are on any given day. He can run his fastball to both sides of the plate and while he's not overpowering, he has swing and-miss stuff. He could do a better job of using his lower half in his delivery, but his mechanics are sound. Antigua has a realistic expectation of becoming a No. 3 starter and should reach high Class A by the end of 2010.

Year	Club (League)	Class	W	L	ERA	G	GS	CG	SV	IP	H	R	ER	HR	BB	SO	AVG
2007	Cubs (DSL)	R	7	2	3.15	14	14	0	0	71	72	33	25	2	14	55	.259
2008	Cubs (AZL)	R	2	3	3.05	14	6	0	0	41	42	22	14	2	16	32	.258
2009	Boise (NWL)	SS	2	1	2.30	7	5	0	0	31	19	8	8	3	10	35	.171
	Peoria (MWL)	LoA	4	0	3.62	7	7	0	0	37	30	16	15	4	9	33	.214
MINOR LEAGUE TOTALS			15	6	3.08	42	32	0	0	181	163	79	62	11	49	155	.236

20 BLAKE PARKER, RHP

BORN: June 19, 1985. **B-T:** R-R. **HT.:** 6-3. **WT.:** 225. **DRAFTED:** Arkansas, 2006 (16th round). **SIGNED BY:** Brian Milner.

Parker batted just .266 in three college seasons at Arkansas, and when he hit .224 in his pro debut, the Cubs promptly made him a pitcher. He took to the mound just as quickly, and his mound presence may be more impressive than his stuff, which is formidable. Parker can get hitters out with three different pitches: a low-90s sinker that touches 95, a slider that's a plus pitch at times and a changeup that he picked up from Dae-Eun Rhee when they were Peoria teammates in 2008. Parker needs more consistency with his pitches, as his fastball can get true and his slider can get flat. He doesn't use his changeup as much as he should. He gets himself into jams with walks, but gets out thanks to his competitiveness and fearlessness. He converted 25 of his 26 save opportunities in 2009. Parker projects as more of a sixth- or seventh-inning reliever than a closer in the majors, but don't be surprised if he exceeded expectations and becomes a setup man through sheer will. He figures to make his major league debut at some point this season.

Year	Club (League)	Class	W	L	ERA	G	GS	CG	SV	IP	H	R	ER	HR	BB	SO	AVG
2007	Cubs (AZL)	R	1	0	1.80	11	0	0	2	15	10	6	3	0	3	14	.185
	Boise (NWL)	SS	1	0	3.18	8	0	0	0	11	15	5	4	0	7	10	.319
2008	Peoria (MWL)	LoA	3	0	1.33	23	0	0	3	47	32	8	7	2	18	51	.193
	Iowa (PCL)	AAA	0	0	6.00	2	0	0	0	3	1	2	2	1	2	3	.091
	Daytona (FSL)	HiA	1	2	3.38	20	0	0	9	21	17	8	8	0	10	21	.221
2009	Tennessee (SL)	AA	0	0	1.46	10	0	0	3	12	8	2	2	0	8	19	.195
	Iowa (PCL)	AAA	2	3	3.00	45	0	0	22	51	36	20	17	3	27	58	.196
MINOR LEAGUE TOTALS			8	5	2.40	119	0	0	39	161	119	51	43	6	75	176	.205

21 BROOKS RALEY, LHP

BORN: June 29, 1988. **B-T:** L-L. **HT.:** 6-3. **WT.:** 185. **DRAFTED:** Texas A&M, 2009 (6th round). **SIGNED BY:** Trey Forkerway.

Though he was a sixth-round pick, Raley received the second-highest bonus among Cubs 2009 draftees, using his extra leverage as a draft-eligible sophomore to wrangle a $750,000 bonus. His talent should have placed him in the second or third round, but clubs couldn't get a handle on his signability before the draft. He was one of college baseball's best two-way players and would have drawn interest as a center fielder/leadoff hitter had it been his lone role. Teams preferred him on the mound because he commands several pitches and competes. Raley's best pitch is his solid slider, and his other primary offerings are his 87-90 mph sinker and his changeup. He can hit 93 mph when he opts for a four-seam fastball, and he also can throw a curveball. He's athletic and repeats his smooth delivery well, so he throws strikes with ease. The question is whether Raley's feel for his craft can overcome his lack of a plus pitch against advanced hitters. Scouts also wonder whether his wiry frame is durable enough. After working just 11 innings in his pro debut, he may start 2010 in low Class A, but he has the polish to move quickly.

Year	Club (League)	Class	W	L	ERA	G	GS	CG	SV	IP	H	R	ER	HR	BB	SO	AVG
2009	Cubs (AZL)	R	0	1	4.15	3	3	0	0	4	2	4	2	1	2	3	.125
	Boise (NWL)	SS	0	0	1.42	2	0	0	0	6	3	1	1	1	1	2	.150
MINOR LEAGUE TOTALS			0	1	2.53	5	3	0	0	11	5	5	3	2	3	5	.139

22 ESMAILIN CARIDAD, RHP

BORN: Oct. 28, 1983. **B-T:** R-R. **HT.:** 5-10. **WT.:** 195. **SIGNED:** Dominican Republic, 2007. **SIGNED BY:** Jose Serra.

Like Alfonso Soriano, Caridad signed with Japan's Hiroshima Carp out of the Dominican Republic and played briefly in the Japanese majors before becoming a free agent on a technicality. The Cubs beat out other U.S. clubs for Caridad during the 2007 offseason, thanks to a $175,000 bonus, an invitation to big league camp and a visit from general manager Jim Hendry during his trip to the team's Dominican complex. Caridad paid quick dividends, reaching the big leagues last August and winning manager Lou Piniella's trust by not allowing a run in 11 September appearances. A starter in the minors, Caridad was more effective in shorter stints as a reliever in the majors. Though he's just 5-foot-10, his quick arm and smooth mechanics allow him to throw his fastball in the low 90s with some sink. He can reach 96 mph, but his heater tends to flatten out when he throws harder. His curveball morphs between an average pitch and a slurve, and his changeup has some splitter action but is fringy. Chicago envisioned him as a reliever all along but started him in the minors to give him innings to work on his secondary pitches. He attacks hitters and throws strikes, though his delivery lacks deception. Caridad's strong finish in 2009 helps him stand out amidst the Cubs' slew of bullpen candidates and enhances his chances of making their Opening Day roster.

Year	Club (League)	Class	W	L	ERA	G	GS	CG	SV	IP	H	R	ER	HR	BB	SO	AVG
2008	Daytona (FSL)	HiA	6	4	4.41	14	13	0	0	69	64	35	34	3	17	38	.252
	Tennessee (SL)	AA	7	3	3.16	14	14	0	0	83	67	31	29	15	21	50	.218
2009	Iowa (PCL)	AAA	5	10	4.17	25	25	0	0	132	139	71	61	17	46	114	.271
	Chicago (NL)	MAJ	1	0	1.40	14	0	0	0	19	15	4	3	0	3	17	.221
MAJOR LEAGUE TOTALS			1	0	1.40	14	0	0	0	19	15	4	3	0	3	17	.221
MINOR LEAGUE TOTALS			18	17	3.93	53	52	0	0	284	270	137	124	35	84	202	.251

23 SAM FULD, OF

BORN: Nov. 20, 1981. **B-T:** L-L. **HT.:** 5-10. **WT.:** 185. **DRAFTED:** Stanford, 2004 (10th round). **SIGNED BY:** Steve Hinton/Steve Fuller.

Fuld finally avoided the disabled list and carved out a niche for himself in the major leagues in 2009. He's had to scrap his way through the minors since signing as a 10th-round pick in 2004, and after generating some momentum by winning Arizona Fall League MVP honors in 2008, he lost it by failing to hit in Triple-A at the start of the next season. Fuld conquered the Pacific Coast League last year, earning a callup in late June and coming up for good at the end of July. He doesn't have the tools to profile as a regular, but he's capable of helping a club win as a quality bench player. Fuld controls the strike zone and plays center field better than anyone on Chicago's big league team. He makes consistent line-drive contact and draws walks, and he improved his bunting last season. He has little home run power, so he focuses on getting on base. He has average speed, and his instincts make him a savvy baserunner and a quality center fielder. In his short time in Chicago, Fuld has made several highlight plays where he has gone crashing into the Wrigley Field bricks. That all-out style has led to a lengthy medical history, as he has missed time with shoulder, back, hip, hernia, oblique and thumb problems since turning pro. He has below-average arm strength but compensates with a quick release and good accuracy. He's a smart player, no surprise considering he graduated from Stanford with an economics degree, and gets the most out of his ability. Fuld has become an organization and fan favorite and should be the Cubs' fourth outfielder in 2010.

Year	Club (League)	Class	AVG	G	AB	R	H	2B	3B	HR	RBI	BB	SO	SB	OBP	SLG
2005	Peoria (MWL)	LoA	.300	125	443	82	133	32	6	5	37	50	44	18	.377	.433
2006	Daytona (FSL)	HiA	.300	89	353	63	106	19	6	4	40	40	54	22	.378	.422
2007	Iowa (PCL)	AAA	.269	14	52	13	14	4	1	1	2	9	5	2	.397	.442
	Tennessee (SL)	AA	.290	90	335	56	97	23	2	2	27	41	38	10	.372	.388
	Chicago (NL)	MAJ	.000	14	6	3	0	0	0	0	0	3	3	0	.333	.000
2008	Iowa (PCL)	AAA	.222	20	63	11	14	3	0	1	4	8	12	3	.310	.317
	Tennessee (SL)	AA	.271	85	339	48	92	16	3	5	48	50	40	7	.366	.381
2009	Iowa (PCL)	AAA	.284	84	328	62	93	17	10	2	33	38	24	23	.358	.415
	Chicago (NL)	MAJ	.299	65	97	17	29	6	1	1	2	17	10	2	.409	.412
MAJOR LEAGUE TOTALS			.282	79	103	20	29	6	1	1	2	20	13	2	.403	.388
MINOR LEAGUE TOTALS			.287	507	1913	335	549	114	28	20	191	236	217	85	.370	.407

24 MARCOS MATEO, RHP

BORN: April 18, 1984. **B-T:** R-R. **HT.:** 6-1. **WT.:** 160. **SIGNED:** Dominican Republic, 2004. **SIGNED BY:** Johnny Almaraz (Reds).

A cousin of former Cubs pitcher Juan Mateo, Marcos originally signed with the Reds and joined Chicago in an August 2007 trade for Buck Coats. The Cubs added Mateo to their 40-man roster after the 2008 season, but he responded by arriving in big league camp out of shape last spring. He struggled for most of the first two months of last season before recapturing his electric stuff after the all-star break. Chicago primarily used Mateo as a starter to get him innings before turning him loose as a reliever last July. At his best, he sits in the mid-90s and tops out at 98 mph with his fastball—and his high-80s slider may be more unhittable than his heater. He doesn't believe in throwing his changeup and has some effort in his delivery, though pitching coordinator Mark Riggins has helped him make his mechanics smoother than they once were. Mateo's command is still a work in progress and will determine his ultimate role. He has closer's stuff but will have to do a much better job of locating his pitches to ever get a chance to finish big league games. Ticketed for Triple-A to start 2010, he could make his major league debut by the end of the year.

Year	Club (League)	Class	W	L	ERA	G	GS	CG	SV	IP	H	R	ER	HR	BB	SO	AVG
2004	Reds (DSL)	R	4	2	2.61	15	8	1	0	69	62	25	20	2	17	57	.238
2005	Reds (GCL)	R	2	3	4.30	13	4	0	0	44	54	26	21	2	10	23	.309
2006	Billings (PIO)	R	5	1	3.20	18	0	0	1	45	43	17	16	2	20	30	.262
2007	Dayton (MWL)	LoA	2	4	3.50	41	0	0	6	72	68	29	28	2	24	63	.260
2008	Peoria (MWL)	LoA	1	0	1.20	8	0	0	1	15	4	3	2	1	7	20	.085
	Daytona (FSL)	HiA	4	3	3.57	25	16	0	0	88	87	42	35	6	29	65	.257
2009	Daytona (FSL)	HiA	0	0	0.00	3	3	0	0	9	4	0	0	0	2	7	.143
	Tennessee (SL)	AA	3	6	4.07	34	14	0	0	97	97	47	44	9	43	70	.258
MINOR LEAGUE TOTALS			21	19	3.40	157	45	1	8	440	419	189	166	24	152	335	.254

25 CASEY COLEMAN, RHP

BORN: July 3, 1987. **B-T:** L-R. **HT.:** 6-1. **WT.:** 180. **DRAFTED:** Florida Gulf Coast, 2008 (15th round). **SIGNED BY:** Rolando Pino.

Few players have better bloodlines than Coleman, whose grandfather and father (both named Joe) were all-star pitchers who combined for 194 big league wins. His background led to the polish that enabled him to jump to Double-A and win the organization's minor league pitcher of the year award in his first full pro season. Coleman led the Southern League with 14 wins, a testament to his craftiness. His 88-91 mph fastball plays up because he can spot it where he wants. His changeup is his best pitch and the best in the system, and his curveball is an above-average pitch at times. Coleman has a chance to have plus command, though he sometimes can try to be too fine with his pitches, resulting in walks. A two-way player who was a regular shortstop at Florida Gulf Coast, he's very athletic and helps himself by doing all of the little things well. He fields his position like an extra infielder and topped Southern League pitchers in total chances (43) and fielding percentage (1.000). He shuts down the running game, leading SL pitching qualifiers by giving up just three steals (in eight tries) in his 27 starts. He handles the bat better than most pitchers too. Coleman's primary tasks this year in Triple-A are to put on more weight and to be a bit more aggressive without catching too much of the plate. His feel for the game gives him a good chance of reaching his ceiling as a No. 4 or 5 starter.

Year	Club (League)	Class	W	L	ERA	G	GS	CG	SV	IP	H	R	ER	HR	BB	SO	AVG
2008	Boise (NWL)	SS	1	1	4.05	7	4	0	0	27	27	13	12	4	7	24	.257
	Peoria (MWL)	LoA	2	2	2.70	5	5	0	0	23	25	11	7	1	4	18	.272
	Daytona (FSL)	HiA	1	0	0.00	1	1	0	0	5	4	1	0	0	2	2	.222
2009	Tennessee (SL)	AA	14	6	3.68	27	27	1	0	149	142	63	61	8	58	84	.256
MINOR LEAGUE TOTALS			18	9	3.53	40	37	1	0	204	198	88	80	13	71	128	.257

26 ROBINSON CHIRINOS, C

BORN: June 5, 1984. **B-T:** R-R. **HT.:** 6-1. **WT.:** 185. **SIGNED:** Venezuela, 2000. **SIGNED BY:** Hector Ortega.

Signed in 2000 as an infielder, Chirinos bounced around the lower levels of the system for years, including three full seasons in low Class A. In the middle of 2008, his eighth pro season, the Cubs decided to try him behind the plate as a last resort. He has progressed so quickly that he has become the best catching prospect in the system. The move even jump-started Chirinos' bat, as he has hit .296/.416/.511 since the switch. His ability to handle the bat and his patient approach are nothing new, but now he's showing some solid pop as well. He runs better than most catchers and moves well behind the plate. Chirinos mitigates his arm strength with a long release, and he has thrown out 30 percent of basestealers in two years as a catcher. Though he needs to improve his receiving, he has soft hands and should be able to do so. Because he still needs more polish and has yet to prove he can hit Double-A pitching at age 25, the Cubs gambled on leaving Chirinos off its 40-man roster. They then sweated that decision when he ranked among the batting and home run leaders in the Venezuelan Winter League. Chirinos doesn't profile as a regular because he lacks a standout tool, but he does everything well for a catcher and could make a fine backup who's capable of playing all four infield positions in a pinch.

Year	Club (League)	Class	AVG	G	AB	R	H	2B	3B	HR	RBI	BB	SO	SB	OBP	SLG
2001	Cubs (AZL)	R	.234	47	154	15	36	12	0	2	15	10	42	4	.292	.351
2002	Boise (NWL)	SS	.247	62	231	35	57	15	2	8	38	16	66	5	.311	.433
2003	Lansing (MWL)	LoA	.232	108	362	51	84	27	1	7	39	28	82	10	.298	.370
2004	Lansing (MWL)	LoA	.241	84	319	56	77	18	6	7	39	25	70	7	.313	.401
2005	Daytona (FSL)	HiA	.273	74	231	30	63	6	0	7	27	16	42	3	.325	.390
2006	Peoria (MWL)	LoA	.242	126	433	74	105	30	2	9	47	69	79	19	.360	.383
2007	Daytona (FSL)	HiA	.259	79	239	35	62	14	2	3	20	37	48	8	.385	.372
	Tennessee (SL)	AA	.220	42	127	11	28	4	2	2	16	13	31	1	.298	.331
2008	Tennessee (SL)	AA	.243	38	103	12	25	7	3	0	8	10	18	0	.304	.369
	Cubs (AZL)	R	.462	4	13	5	6	1	1	0	3	6	2	1	.632	.692
	Daytona (FSL)	HiA	.283	37	120	22	34	4	2	5	18	26	21	3	.431	.475
2009	Daytona (FSL)	HiA	.300	69	227	40	68	13	5	11	47	35	40	2	.400	.546
	Tennessee (SL)	AA	.257	12	35	4	9	3	0	0	5	7	4	0	.372	.343
MINOR LEAGUE TOTALS			.252	782	2594	390	654	154	26	61	322	298	545	63	.342	.402

27 WELINGTON CASTILLO, C

BORN: April 24, 1987. **B-T:** R-R. **HT.:** 6-0. **WT.:** 200. **SIGNED:** Dominican Republic, 2004. **SIGNED BY:** Jose Serra.

The Cubs debated which of their catchers to protect on their 40-man roster during the offseason, and Castillo ultimately got the nod over Robinson Chirinos and Steve Clevenger. Castillo earned his spot due to his youth and upside rather than his performance. After appearing in the Futures Game the year before, he turned in the worst full season of his career in 2009. Castillo's swing deteriorated as he sold out for power, and while he matched a career high with 11 homers, he set career lows with a .232 average and .275 on-base percentage. He never has shown much plate discipline or the ability to solve breaking pitches, so he might be more of a platoon player against lefthanders or a backup than a starter. Castillo's best tool is his arm strength, and he led the Southern League by throwing out 44 percent of basestealers last season. But he's a sloppy receiver who loses his concentration too often. He also let his body get soft in 2009, costing him some agility behind the plate. He offers little speed, even by catcher standards. He used to draw Yadier Molina comparisons but those seem way too optimistic at this point. Castillo will advance to Triple-A and attempt to get back on track in 2010.

Year	Club (League)	Class	AVG	G	AB	R	H	2B	3B	HR	RBI	BB	SO	SB	OBP	SLG
2005	Cubs (DSL)	R	.289	60	204	29	59	14	0	1	28	19	28	1	.370	.373
2006	Boise (NWL)	SS	.167	3	6	1	1	0	0	0	0	1	0	0	.286	.167
	Cubs (AZL)	R	.192	7	26	4	5	0	0	0	0	1	6	0	.250	.192
2007	Peoria (MWL)	LoA	.271	98	317	41	86	11	2	11	44	23	77	1	.334	.423
2008	Daytona (FSL)	HiA	.273	33	121	15	33	8	0	0	12	4	23	1	.299	.339
	Tennessee (SL)	AA	.298	57	198	25	59	11	0	4	24	14	50	0	.362	.414
	Iowa (PCL)	AAA	.200	1	5	0	1	0	0	0	1	0	1	0	.200	.200
2009	Tennessee (SL)	AA	.232	95	319	27	74	16	0	11	39	15	71	1	.275	.386
MINOR LEAGUE TOTALS			.266	354	1196	142	318	60	2	27	148	77	256	4	.324	.387

28 DAVID CALES, RHP

BORN: July 27, 1987. **B-T:** R-R. **HT.:** 5-11. **WT.:** 200. **DRAFTED:** St. Xavier (Ill.), 2008 (24th round). **SIGNED BY:** Stan Zielinski.

Excuse Cales' family if they have a tinge of regret that he's on the verge of joining the Cubs. He grew up on Chicago's South Side and his mother Mary Weiss works in the White Sox ticket office. Of the five Cubs pitchers who jumped from the draft in 2008 to Double-A in 2009, he was the biggest surprise. Cales had a checkered college career, bouncing from Missouri to Illinois-Chicago to St. Xavier (Ill.), redshirting at that last stop in

2008. Familiar with the local kid, the Cubs drafted him in the 24th round and signed him for $52,500 after he pitched 11 scoreless innings in the summer collegiate Northwoods League. Cales got torched when he first joined Tennessee last May, allowing 14 runs in 12 innings, but dominated when he returned in August, permitting just one run in 13 frames. His stuff was noticeably better, as his fastball jumped from the high 80s to 91-92 with good armside run. His slider improved as well, rating as a plus-plus pitch at times. He's 5-foot-11 and throws from a low three-quarters angle, yet he gets good depth on his slider. He also flashes an effective changeup, though he often throws it too hard. Animated on the mound, Cales backs down from no one and aggressively challenges hitters. If he can carry over his late-2009 success to Triple-A this year, he won't be in the minors for much longer.

Year	Club (League)	Class	W	L	ERA	G	GS	CG	SV	IP	H	R	ER	HR	BB	SO	AVG
2008	Cubs (AZL)	R	0	1	5.87	6	1	0	0	8	9	6	5	1	3	11	.273
	Boise (NWL)	SS	3	0	1.84	8	0	0	1	15	11	4	3	1	4	15	.204
2009	Iowa (PCL)	AAA	0	0	5.40	1	0	0	0	2	4	5	1	2	2	2	.444
	Daytona (FSL)	HiA	3	0	0.78	37	0	0	14	46	29	5	4	1	11	43	.187
	Tennessee (SL)	AA	3	0	5.40	16	0	0	2	25	29	16	15	2	11	21	.302
MINOR LEAGUE TOTALS			9	1	2.65	68	1	0	17	95	82	36	28	7	31	92	.236

29 JUNIOR LAKE, SS/2B

BORN: March 27, 1990. **B-T:** R-R. **HT.:** 6-2. **WT.:** 200. **SIGNED:** Dominican Republic, 2007. **SIGNED BY:** Jose Serra.

While Starlin Castro thrived after being promoted from the Rookie-level Arizona League in 2008 to full-season ball as a 19-year-old in 2009, Lake struggled under the same circumstances. He still showed an intriguing package of tools but wasn't able to translate them into production against low Class A pitchers. He has the size, quick hands and snap in his swing to hit for more power than most infielders, but he also has a lot of holes in his stroke and approach. His swing gets long and he exhibits no patience. He improved his swing plane late in the season, though it didn't yield any noticeable results. Lake has average speed out of the box and is an above-average runner underway, and he's more adept at taking extra bases than basestealing. His single most impressive tool is his cannon arm, one of the strongest in the minors. It sometimes gets him in trouble because he'll attempt some throws he shouldn't. His hands aren't the softest and he also has lapses in concentration, all factors that led to 42 errors in 2009. He has good range but will outgrow shortstop as he gets stronger and slows down. Castro probably will see a lot of time at third base in 2010, because the Cubs have double-play combos set for Daytona (Ryan Flaherty, D.J. LeMahieu) and Peoria (Logan Watkins, Hak-Ju Lee).

Year	Club (League)	Class	AVG	G	AB	R	H	2B	3B	HR	RBI	BB	SO	SB	OBP	SLG
2007	Cubs (DSL)	R	.274	62	223	41	61	16	2	3	30	16	53	9	.341	.404
2008	Cubs (AZL)	R	.286	47	168	24	48	4	6	2	23	13	42	12	.335	.417
2009	Peoria (MWL)	LoA	.248	131	463	71	115	19	7	7	42	18	138	10	.277	.365
MINOR LEAGUE TOTALS			.262	240	854	136	224	39	15	12	95	47	233	31	.306	.385

30 JAMES ADDUCI, OF

BORN: May 15, 1985. **B-T:** L-L. **HT.:** 6-2. **WT.:** 185. **DRAFTED:** HS—Evergreen Park, Ill., 2003 (42nd round). **SIGNED BY:** Scot Engler (Marlins).

When the Cubs traded Todd Wellemeyer to the Marlins in 2006, they received pitchers Lincoln Holdzkom and Zach McCormack in return. McCormack would never pitch again because of a pre-existing injury, and Chicago returned him to Florida at the end of the 2006 season and received Adduci instead. The son of former big leaguer Jim Adduci, James got off to a slow start in pro ball. He attended some college classes in his first season, then played in just 25 games in 2005-06 while battling quad, knee and hand injuries. Healthy with the Cubs, he has improved in each of his three seasons in the organization. He's making more consistent line-drive contact and pulling more pitches, though he still doesn't exhibit much power. His speed rates as average out of the box and plus once he gets going, and he's a proficient basestealer. Adduci has gotten better defensively too, becoming a solid center fielder after playing first base and corner outfield. Though he has below-average arm strength, he recorded 14 assists in 2009 because he charges balls well, has a quick release and makes accurate throws. Adduci hasn't shown enough thump to be a big league regular, but he can be a valuable reserve with his on-base skills, speed and ability to play four positions. He'll move up to Triple-A after gaining a spot on the 40-man roster in November.

Year	Club (League)	Class	AVG	G	AB	R	H	2B	3B	HR	RBI	BB	SO	SB	OBP	SLG
2004	Marlins (GCL)	R	.207	49	164	21	34	4	1	0	27	24	42	6	.327	.244
2005	Marlins (GCL)	R	.378	11	37	3	14	3	1	0	7	3	5	1	.425	.514
2006	Marlins (GCL)	R	.286	12	35	3	10	2	1	1	5	5	8	1	.375	.486
	Greensboro (SAL)	LoA	.000	2	3	1	0	0	0	0	0	0	1	0	.000	.000
2007	Daytona (FSL)	HiA	.121	12	33	2	4	1	0	0	1	0	13	0	.121	.152
	Peoria (MWL)	LoA	.292	107	401	54	117	18	2	2	48	30	98	20	.345	.362
2008	Daytona (FSL)	HiA	.290	123	458	81	133	19	3	3	48	63	96	26	.380	.365
2009	Tennessee (SL)	AA	.300	131	467	63	140	21	4	4	51	58	76	35	.377	.388
MINOR LEAGUE TOTALS			.283	447	1598	228	452	68	12	10	187	183	339	89	.360	.359

Chicago White Sox

BY PHIL ROGERS

Before the White Sox selected Gordon Beckham with the eighth pick in the 2008 draft, 17 years had passed since they had a choice among the top 10. Beckham may have been worth the wait.

After taking righthander Alex Fernandez with the fourth overall pick in 1990, the Sox averaged picking 20th overall. They watched scores of no-brainer choices go elsewhere, without drafting a single position player who would develop into a homegrown all-star. Beckham should change that. In his first full season, the 2008 NCAA Division I home run leader jumped to the big leagues and hit .270/.347/.460. Beckham flashed leadership skills and unusual poise for a 22-year-old. It looks like he'll give the Sox something they have missed since the days of Frank Thomas and Robin Ventura: the chance to market and build a team around a hitter who could spend his entire career in Chicago.

While Ken Williams has made more trades during the last decade than any general manager, he would love to assemble a core around Beckham. Williams said he's excited about a couple of other hitters from the 2008 draft, third baseman Brent Morel and center fielder Jordan Danks, and was thrilled to add center fielder Jared Mitchell with the 23rd overall pick in the 2009 draft. Williams has used other means to acquire position players who could be building blocks, signing Cuban defectors Alexei Ramirez and Dayan Viciedo to major league contracts in the last couple of years, and acquiring catching prospect Tyler Flowers in a trade that sent Javier Vazquez to the Braves a year ago.

Flowers joined righthander Dan Hudson (another 2008 draft pick) as the most productive players in the White Sox farm system last year. He earned a promotion to Chicago in September. He offers the White Sox an alternative to re-signing veteran A.J. Pierzynski, whose contract expires after the 2010 season.

The arrival of young talent should please Sox owner Jerry Reinsdorf. He quietly cut the White Sox payroll by $8.3 million last season and will monitor it closely as he awaits an economic recovery. A year after winning the American League Central, Chicago dropped to third place at 79-83, the second-worst record of manager Ozzie Guillen's tenure.

Williams' flexibility to make major moves in preparation for 2010 was hampered by two moves he made 11 days apart last summer. He traded four young pitchers—Aaron Poreda, Clayton Richard, Adam Russell and Dexter Carter—to the Padres for Jake Peavy, then claimed Alex Rios off waivers from

Gordon Beckham provided dividends in Chicago less than a year after being drafted

TOP 30 PROSPECTS

1. Jared Mitchell, of	16. Carlos Torres, rhp
2. Tyler Flowers, c	17. Lucas Harrell, rhp
3. Dan Hudson, rhp	18. Santos Rodriguez, lhp
4. Brent Morel, 3b	19. Eduardo Escobar, ss
5. Jordan Danks, of	20. Nevin Griffith, rhp
6. Trayce Thompson, of	21. Christian Marrero, of/1b
7. Dayan Viciedo, 3b	22. Jhonny Nunez, rhp
8. David Holmberg, lhp	23. Dan Remenowsky, rhp
9. Clevelan Santeliz, rhp	24. Kyle Bellamy, rhp
10. Miguel Gonzalez, c	25. John Shelby, of
11. Josh Phegley, c	26. Nate Jones, rhp
12. John Ely, rhp	27. Charlie Leesman, lhp
13. Sergio Santos, rhp	28. Jon Link, rhp
14. Stefan Gartrell, of	29. Jose Martinez, of
15. C.J. Retherford, 2b	30. Justin Collop, rhp

the Blue Jays. The White Sox assumed $116 million in salary obligations in the two transactions.

Williams has developed a reputation for being willing to trade top prospects for veterans. He was at it again in 2009, dealing three of the top six players from this list a year ago (Poreda, Richard and first baseman Brandon Allen) and four former first-round picks (Brian Anderson, Josh Fields, Lance Broadway and Poreda). It's not always popular with his scouts and player-development staff, but that's how he built the 2005 World Series champions and he hasn't been badly burned by the youngsters he has traded away.

General Manager: Ken Williams. **Farm Director:** Buddy Bell. **Scouting Director:** Doug Laumann.

Class	Team	League	W	L	PCT	Finish*	Manager(s)
Majors	Chicago White Sox	American	79	83	.488	9th (14)	Ozzie Guillen
Triple-A	Charlotte Knights	International	67	76	.469	11th (14)	Chris Chambliss
Double-A	Birmingham Barons	Southern	92	47	.662	1st (10)	Ever Magallanes
High A	Winston-Salem Dash	Carolina	73	65	.529	3rd (8)	Joe McEwing
Low A	Kannapolis Intimidators	South Atlantic	82	57	.590	1st (16)	Ernie Young
Rookie	Great Falls Voyagers	Pioneer	42	34	.553	3rd (8)	Chris Cron
Rookie	Bristol White Sox	Appalachian	27	39	.409	8th (10)	Ryan Newman
Overall 2009 Minor League Record			383	318	.546	3rd (30)	

*Finish in overall standings (No. of teams in league). †League champion.

LAST YEAR'S TOP 30

Player, Pos.	Status
1. Gordon Beckham, ss	Majors
2. Dayan Viciedo, 3b	No. 7
3. Aaron Poreda, lhp	(Padres)
4. Tyler Flowers, c	No. 2
5. Clayton Richard, lhp	(Padres)
6. Brandon Allen, 1b	(Diamondbacks)
7. Jordan Danks, of	No. 5
8. Brent Lillibridge, ss	Majors
9. Chris Getz, 2b/ss/of	(Royals)
10. John Shelby, of	No. 25
11. John Ely, rhp	No. 12
12. Cole Armstrong, c	Dropped out
13. Eduardo Escobar, ss	No. 19
14. Clevelan Santeliz, rhp	No. 9
15. Jose Martinez, of	No. 29
16. Jhonny Nunez, rhp	No. 22
17. Brent Morel, 3b	No. 4
18. Santos Rodriguez, lhp	No. 18
19. Brian Omogrosso, rhp	Dropped out
20. Jeff Marquez, rhp	Dropped out
21. Jon Gilmore, 3b	Dropped out
22. Jon Link, rhp	No. 28
23. Dexter Carter, rhp	(Padres)
24. Dan Hudson, rhp	No. 3
25. Carlos Torres, rhp	No. 16
26. Jayson Nix, 2b	Majors
27. Adam Russell, rhp	(Padres)
28. Lance Broadway, rhp	Free agent
29. C.J. Retherford, 3b	No. 15
30. Gregory Infante, rhp	Dropped out

BEST TOOLS

Best Hitter for Average	Brent Morel
Best Power Hitter	Tyler Flowers
Best Strike-Zone Discipline	Tyler Flowers
Fastest Baserunner	Jared Mitchell
Best Athlete	Jared Mitchell
Best Fastball	Sergio Santos
Best Curveball	Nate Jones
Best Slider	Dan Hudson
Best Changeup	John Ely
Best Control	Dan Hudson
Best Defensive Catcher	Miguel Gonzalez
Best Defensive Infielder	Eduardo Escobar
Best Infield Arm	Brent Morel
Best Defensive Outfielder	Jared Mitchell
Best Outfield Arm	Jordan Danks

PROJECTED 2013 LINEUP

Catcher	Tyler Flowers
First Base	Paul Konerko
Second Base	Gordon Beckham
Third Base	Brent Morel
Shortstop	Alexei Ramirez
Left Field	Jordan Danks
Center Field	Jared Mitchell
Right Field	Alex Rios
Designated Hitter	Carlos Quentin
No. 1 Starter	Jake Peavy
No. 2 Starter	John Danks
No. 3 Starter	Mark Buehrle
No. 4 Starter	Gavin Floyd
No. 5 Starter	Dan Hudson
Closer	Bobby Jenks

TOP PROSPECTS OF THE DECADE

Year	Player, Pos.	2009 Org.
2000	Kip Wells, rhp	Reds
2001	Jon Rauch, rhp	Twins
2002	Joe Borchard, of	Giants
2003	Joe Borchard, of	Giants
2004	Joe Borchard, of	Giants
2005	Brian Anderson, of	Red Sox
2006	Bobby Jenks, rhp	White Sox
2007	Ryan Sweeney, of	Athletics
2008	Aaron Poreda, lhp	Padres
2009	Gordon Beckham, ss	White Sox

TOP DRAFT PICKS OF THE DECADE

Year	Player, Pos.	2009 Org.
2000	Joe Borchard, of	Giants
2001	Kris Honel, rhp	Out of baseball
2002	Royce Ring, lhp	Cardinals
2003	Brian Anderson, of	Red Sox
2004	Josh Fields, 3b	White Sox
2005	Lance Broadway, rhp	Mets
2006	Kyle McCulloch, rhp	White Sox
2007	Aaron Poreda, lhp	Padres
2008	Gordon Beckham, ss	White Sox
2009	Jared Mitchell, of	White Sox

LARGEST BONUSES IN CLUB HISTORY

Joe Borchard, 2003	$5,300,000
Dayan Viciedo, 2008	$4,000,000
Gordon Beckham, 2008	$2,600,000
Jason Stumm, 1999	$1,750,000
Royce Ring, 2002	$1,600,000

CHICAGO WHITE SOX

TOP 2010 ROOKIE: Dan Hudson, rhp. The White Sox signed Freddy Garcia to be their No. 5 starter, but the deceptive Hudson could take that job sooner rather than later.

BREAKOUT PROSPECT: Stefan Gartrell, of. The run producer doesn't attract much attention, even after hitting 23 homers in the upper minors last year.

SLEEPER: Ryan Buch, rhp. The eighth-round pick from the 2009 draft touched 97 mph with his fastball during instructional league, and he also flashes a plus curveball.

SOURCE OF TOP 30 TALENT			
Homegrown	24	Acquired	6
College	13	Trades	4
Junior college	0	Rule 5 draft	0
High school	4	Independent leagues	1
Draft-and-follow	1	Free agents/waivers	1
Nondrafted free agents	1		
International	5		

Numbers in parentheses indicate prospect rankings

LF
Nick Ciolli
Brady Shoemaker
Miguel Negron
Tyler Kuhn
Joe Persichina
Kyle Colligan
Ryan Lee

CF
Jared Mitchell (1)
Jordan Danks (5)
Trayce Thompson (6)
John Shelby (25)
Kent Gerst
Justin Greene

RF
Stefan Gartrell (14)
Christian Marrero (21)
Jose Martinez (29)
Sal Sanchez
Sergio Morales

3B
Brent Morel (4)
Dayan Viciedo (7)
Jon Gilmore

SS
Eduardo Escobar (19)
Greg Paiml
Juan Silverio

2B
C.J. Retherford (15)
Andrew Garcia
Dale Mollenhauer

1B
Jim Gallagher
Mark Fleisher
Jorge Castillo

C
Tyler Flowers (2)
Miguel Gonzalez (10)
Josh Phegley (11)
Donny Lucy
Ken Dubler
John Curtis
Adam Ricks
Logan Johnson

RHP

Starters	Relievers
Dan Hudson (3)	Clevelan Santeliz (9)
John Ely (12)	Sergio Santos (13)
Carlos Torres (16)	Jhonny Nunez (22)
Lucas Harrell (17)	Dan Remenowsky (23)
Nevin Griffith (20)	Kyle Bellamy (24)
Justin Collop (30)	Nate Jones (26)
Gregory Infante	Jon Link (28)
Brandon Hynick	Santo Luis
Ryan Buch	Miguel Socolovich
Jeff Marquez	Brian Omogrosso
Justin Cassel	Matthew Long
Johnnie Lowe	Henry Mabee
Kyle McCulloch	Ricky Brooks
Jacob Rasner	Derek Rodriguez
Charlie Shirek	Drew O'Neil
Stephen Sauer	Charlis Burdie
Steven Upchurch	
Matt Heidenreich	
Taylor Thompson	
Matt Hopps	

LHP

Starters	Relievers
David Holmberg (8)	Santos Rodriguez (18)
Charlie Leesman (27)	Hector Santiago
Wes Whisler	Kyle Aselton
Justin Edwards	Alex Farotto
Joe Serafin	Enrique Lechuga
Matt Wickswat	

2009   BONUSES: $4.2 MILLION

BEST PURE HITTER: OF Nick Ciolli (10) has the pretty swing path scouts look for, and his other tools are solid. He batted .317 at Rookie-level Great Falls.

BEST POWER HITTER: C Josh Phegley (2) slugged 32 homers in his last two seasons at Indiana, then hit nine at low Class A Kannapolis. He has adjustments to make receiving and in his stance, but the raw hitting and power tools are there.

FASTEST RUNNER: OF Jared Mitchell (1) has electric athleticism and is a 70 runner on the 20-80 scouting scale.

BEST DEFENSIVE PLAYER: Mitchell played mostly right field at Louisiana State despite his below-average arm. His speed and arm should play better in center.

BEST FASTBALL: RHP Ryan Buch (8) was inconsistent all spring at Monmouth and in the summer after signing, but his fastball touched 97 mph in instructional league. RHPs Nick Collop (6) and Taylor Thompson (44) pump heavy sinkers in the low 90s. RHP Kyle Bellamy (5) has plus life, sink and command of his upper-80s fastball from a submarine slot.

BEST SECONDARY PITCH: LHP David Holmberg (2) commands a plus curveball and has good feel for a changeup that's nearly as good. Buch's curve also can be a plus pitch when he repeats his mechanics.

BEST PRO DEBUT: OF Brady Shoemaker (19) led all Sox farmhands (minimum 250 plate appearances) with a .321 batting average, while Ciolli finished right behind him. Mitchell hit .296/.417/.435 at low Class A Kannapolis. Bellamy posted a 1.23 ERA and 32-2 K-BB ratio in 22 innings, mostly at Kannapolis.

BEST ATHLETE: Mitchell. OF Trayce Thompson (2) has an athletic, projectable 6-foot-4, 200-pound frame.

MOST INTRIGUING BACKGROUND: Trayce Thompson is the son of former NBA center Mychal Thompson. Mitchell was also wide receiver at Louisiana State and won national titles both in baseball and football. Chicago drafted three players whose fathers work for the club: Unsigned 3B Tyler Williams (43) is the son of general manager Ken; OF Harold Baines Jr.'s (45) dad is the first-base coach; and unsigned RHP Grant Monroe (46) is the son of longtime Sox scout/adviser Larry. All three fathers played for the White Sox, too, and Harold Baines was the No. 1 overall pick in 1977 and a six-time all star whose number was retired by the team.

CLOSEST TO THE MAJORS: Bellamy could get to Chicago in 2010 if everything breaks right for him.

BEST LATE-ROUND PICK: Taylor Thompson,

who went so low because he had a 6.65 ERA in 154 innings at Auburn. The White Sox drafted him in the 25th round in 2008, too.

THE ONE WHO GOT AWAY: After trading Aaron Poreda and Clayton Richard to the Padres, Chicago could have replenished its stock of lefthanders with LHP Bryan Morgado (3). A draft-eligible sophomore who shined in the Cape Cod League last summer, he returned to Tennessee.

ASSESSMENT: After striking gold with a deep 2008 draft headlined by Gordon Beckham, the White Sox were ecstatic to get Mitchell and his top-shelf tools with the 23rd overall pick. A hitter-heavy crop will become more well-rounded if college enigmas such as Buch and Thompson work out.

2008   BONUSES: $4.7 MILLION

3B/2B Gordon Beckham (1) already looks like a steal as the No. 8 overall pick, and the White Sox didn't stop there. 3B Brent Morel (3), RHP Dan Hudson (5) and OF Jordan Danks (7) all look like they'll be key components of future Chicago clubs.

GRADE: A

2007   BONUSES: $2.8 MILLION

It's unclear whether LHP Aaron Poreda (1) can be more than a reliever, but the White Sox don't worry about that anymore after using him in a trade for Jake Peavy. RHP Jon Ely (3) is the top prospect still in the system, but his stuff isn't as gaudy as his win totals.

GRADE: C

2006   BONUSES: $2.9 MILLION

OF Stefan Gartrell (31) was a nice find late in the draft, but it's not a good sign that he's the best prospect in this crop. RHP Kyle McCulloch (1) went undrafted in the 2009 Rule 5 draft.

GRADE: D

2005   BONUSES: $2.7 MILLION*

Chicago has dealt the six best players from this draft—most notably 2B Chris Getz (4), OF Aaron Cunningham (6), LHP Clayton Richard (8) and 1B/OF Chris Carter (15)—to get players such as Jake Peavy, Carlos Quentin and Mark Teahen. RHPs Lance Broadway (1), who has pitched briefly in the majors, and Dan Cortes (7) got traded too.

GRADE: C+

*Draft analysis by John Manuel (2009) and Jim Callis (2005-08). Numbers in parentheses indicate draft rounds. *Bonuses for 2005 are first 10 rounds only.*

PROSPECT 1

JARED MITCHELL, OF

Born: Oct. 31, 1988.
Height: 5-11. **Weight:** 192.
Bats: L. **Throws:** L.
Drafted: Louisiana State, 2009 (1st round).
Signed by: Warren Hughes.

TONY FARLOW

Mitchell is a winner. He won two national championships in his career at Louisiana State, one as a backup wide receiver on the football team that beat Ohio State in the BCS title game in January 2008, and another as an outfielder on the baseball team that won the 2009 College World Series. He was the Most Outstanding Player of the latter event, hitting .348 with two homers among his five extra-base hits. Mitchell flashed first-round talent in 2006, when he batted .506 for Westgate High outside New Orleans and was the Louisiana high school player of the year. He fell to the Twins in the 10th round of the draft, however, because he wanted $1 million to give up football. Minnesota made him a significant offer but didn't reach seven figures, so he went to Louisiana State. He joined the baseball team after spring football practice in his first two years, and got permission from Tigers football coach Les Miles to focus on baseball last spring. The extra work on the diamond paid off, not just with a national title but also with Mitchell going 23rd overall in the 2009 draft. The White Sox signed him for $1.2 million and sent him straight to low Class A Kannapolis, where he had few problems transitioning to pro ball.

Mitchell played football because his skills pushed him toward the field, but his real passion is baseball. He's a terrific athlete with plus-plus speed who projects as a center fielder and leadoff man. He has been clocked from the plate to third base in 10.3 seconds. He's a patient hitter who's willing to work counts, ranking fifth in NCAA Division I with 57 walks last year, yet he hit in the middle of Louisiana State's lineup because he also flashes power. He has the quickness to cover huge swaths of ground in center field. "He takes control in center field like he's been playing professionally for a while," Kannapolis manager Ernie Young said. Mitchell has impressive instincts, especially given that he hadn't focused solely on baseball before 2009. He loves the biggest stages.

Mitchell still has work to do at the plate, both in his technique and approach. Sox coaches are working to smooth out some uppercut in his swing, and he strikes out more than he should because he takes hittable pitches while trying to work counts. He's also working on getting better reads and jumps as a basestealer, as he has the speed to swipe bags more frequently and more successfully than he does now. Mitchell played right field in college but doesn't have the arm strength to stay there as a professional, and his arm is his only below-average tool. The White Sox will develop him as a center fielder, but like Carl Crawford he could eventually move to left. He drifts on fly balls at times.

Mitchell performed above expectations after signing, so Chicago could skip him to Double-A Birmingham to open his first full season. With Alex Rios and Jordan Danks ahead of him in the organization, Mitchell won't have to be rushed. He's exactly the kind of pure athlete that White Sox GM Ken Williams has exhorted his scouting staff to sign, though he'll require time to hone his skills after being distracted by football for so long.

Year	Club (League)	Class	AVG	G	AB	R	H	2B	3B	HR	RBI	BB	SO	SB	OBP	SLG
2009	Kannapolis (SAL)	LoA	.296	34	115	13	34	12	2	0	10	23	40	5	.417	.435
MINOR LEAGUE TOTALS			.296	34	115	13	34	12	2	0	10	23	40	5	.417	.435

2 TYLER FLOWERS, C

BORN: Jan. 24, 1986. **B-T:** R-R. **HT.:** 6-4. **WT.:** 220. **DRAFTED:** Chipola (Fla.) JC, D/F 2005 (33rd round). **SIGNED BY:** Al Goetz (Braves).

The headliner in the deal that sent Javier Vazquez to Atlanta for four young players, Flowers has been everything the White Sox hoped. He hit as expected and while many scouts thought he'd have to move to first base, he held his own behind the plate in Double-A and Triple-A last year. Chicago rewarded him with a September callup. Flowers combines light-tower power with plate discipline, making it easy to project his bat into the middle of a big league lineup. He generates his pop through his strength and size, and he has good hand-eye coordination and advanced pitch recognition. Pitchers like throwing to him because he's a good communicator and works hard on gameplans. Managers rated him the top defensive catcher in the Double-A Southern League last year. He has an average arm and has improved his footwork and release, thowing out 29 percent of basestealers last year. Flowers' size can be a problem behind the plate, limiting his quickness in blocking and handling tough pitches. One scout said Flowers "spent more time at the backstop than Bob Uecker" early in 2009, but that he improved throughout the season. Though he's athletic for a catcher, he's still a below-average runner. Flowers is ready to hit in the major leagues, but the White Sox have A.J. Pierzynski in the final year of his contract. They want Flowers playing every day and continuing to polish his defense, so he'll open 2010 at Triple-A Charlotte.

Year	Club (League)	Class	AVG	G	AB	R	H	2B	3B	HR	RBI	BB	SO	SB	OBP	SLG
2006	Danville (APP)	R	.279	34	129	24	36	9	0	5	16	16	30	0	.373	.465
2007	Rome (SAL)	LoA	.298	106	389	65	116	34	2	12	70	49	74	3	.378	.488
2008	Myrtle Beach (CAR)	HiA	.288	122	413	72	119	32	1	17	88	98	102	8	.427	.494
2009	Birmingham (SL)	AA	.302	77	248	54	75	18	2	13	43	57	76	3	.445	.548
	Charlotte (IL)	AAA	.286	31	105	13	30	10	0	2	13	10	32	0	.364	.438
	Chicago (AL)	MAJ	.188	10	16	3	3	1	0	0	0	3	8	0	.350	.250
MAJOR LEAGUE TOTALS			.188	10	16	3	3	1	0	0	0	3	8	0	.350	.250
MINOR LEAGUE TOTALS			.293	370	1284	228	376	103	5	49	230	230	314	14	.406	.495

3 DAN HUDSON, RHP

BORN: March 9, 1987. **B-T:** R-R. **HT.:** 6-4 **WT.:** 220. **DRAFTED:** Old Dominion, 2008 (5th round). **SIGNED BY:** Chuck Fox/Nick Hostetler.

After an up-and-down career at Old Dominion, Hudson went in the fifth round of the 2008 draft and signed for $180,000. In his first full season, he picked up wins at five different levels, including the big leagues. He ranked second in the minors in opponent average (.200), sixth in strikeouts (166 in 147 innings), seventh in wins (14) and ninth in ERA (2.32). Hudson throws three solid pitches from a three quarters arm slot with a crossfire delivery, a la Jered Weaver. His motion gives him natural deception, making his lively 91-93 mph fastball seem even quicker. His second-best pitch is his changeup, which elicits swings and misses. He also has a low-80s slider with average tilt, and he occasionally throws a slow curve. He pounds the strike zone and commands his fastball to both sides of the plate. Hudson's delivery can be high maintenance, sometimes requiring adjustments early in games. His pitches tend to flatten out when his arm drops below his preferred slot. Advanced hitters were able to elevate his pitches, which won't play well at U.S. Cellular Field. His defense and pickoff move are raw. Hudson could open the 2010 season in the big leagues, but with Freddy Garcia signing to fill out the rotation, there's no rush. The White Sox have developed starters with an apprenticeship in the big league bullpen, but Hudson would be better served by more regular work in Double-A.

Year	Club (League)	Class	W	L	ERA	G	GS	CG	SV	IP	H	R	ER	HR	BB	SO	AVG
2008	Great Falls (PIO)	R	5	4	3.36	14	14	0	0	70	52	30	26	6	22	90	.202
2009	Kannapolis (SAL)	LoA	1	2	1.23	4	4	0	0	22	15	5	3	0	2	30	.190
	Winston-Salem (CAR)	HiA	4	3	3.40	8	8	1	0	45	31	19	17	3	13	49	.195
	Birmingham (SL)	AA	7	0	1.60	9	9	0	0	56	37	11	10	1	10	63	.188
	Charlotte (IL)	AAA	2	0	3.00	5	5	0	0	24	22	10	8	1	9	24	.247
	Chicago (AL)	MAJ	1	1	3.38	6	2	0	0	19	16	9	7	3	9	14	.225
MAJOR LEAGUE TOTALS			1	1	3.38	6	2	0	0	19	16	9	7	3	9	14	.225
MINOR LEAGUE TOTALS			19	9	2.65	40	40	1	0	217	157	75	64	11	56	256	.201

4 BRENT MOREL, 3B

BORN: April 21, 1987. **B-T:** R-R. **HT.:** 6-1. **WT.:** 220. **DRAFTED:** Cal Poly, 2008 (3rd round). **SIGNED BY:** Gary Woods/Derek Valenzuela.

The White Sox rated Morel as a second-round talent in the 2008 draft, but they didn't have a pick in that round and were thrilled to get him in the third and sign him for $440,000. He's off to a good start as a pro, hitting .304/.361/.496 in the second half last year at high Class A Winston-Salem before winning the Arizona Fall League batting title with a .435 average. Morel is a manager's dream, with solid tools, outstanding instincts and a blue-collar work ethic. He's one of the system's top pure hitters, making good contact with a compact, line-drive swing. He has excellent pitch recognition and attacks fastballs. He has the power to hit 15 homers per year, and could show more as he matures. He runs well enough for a third baseman and is a good baserunner, but he doesn't project as a basestealer. He's a natural third baseman with first-step quickness and a plus arm. Morel's power is just borderline average for a third baseman. He can be overly aggressive at times, working himself into pitcher's counts. He would benefit from taking more pitches and drawing more walks, though he doesn't strike out a lot. Gordon Beckham's move to second base opens up third for the long term, and Morel could reach Chicago within the next two years. He'll open 2010 in Double-A.

Year	Club (League)	Class	AVG	G	AB	R	H	2B	3B	HR	RBI	BB	SO	SB	OBP	SLG
2008	Great Falls (PIO)	R	.375	15	64	11	24	0	2	0	3	6	7	7	.437	.438
	Kannapolis (SAL)	LoA	.297	45	172	26	51	6	2	6	24	16	28	5	.359	.459
2009	Winston-Salem (CAR)	HiA	.281	128	481	82	135	33	1	16	79	38	66	25	.335	.453
MINOR LEAGUE TOTALS			.293	188	717	119	210	39	5	22	106	60	101	37	.350	.453

5 JORDAN DANKS, OF

BORN: Aug. 7, 1986. **B-T:** L-R. **HT.:** 6-4. **WT.:** 210. **DRAFTED:** Texas, 2008 (7th round). **SIGNED BY:** Keith Staab/Derek Valenzuela.

John Danks turned down the White Sox's initial attempt to sign him to a multiyear contract last spring, but he may soon may have more motivation to stick around—the chance to play with his younger brother. Drafted by Chicago in the 19th round out of high school and then again in the seventh round out of Texas, Jordan signed for an above-slot $525,000. He needed just 40 games as a pro to reach Double-A, where wrist and thumb ailments sabotaged his production. Danks is an excellent athlete and a hard-nosed player. He's a natural hitter with good bat speed, gap power, surprising bunting ability and above-average speed. He has the range and instincts to play center field, and he also has a solid-average arm. His swing is sound, but Danks is prone to slumps when he gets pull-happy or faces a steady diet of breaking balls. He can struggle with pitch recognition at times, and he never has hit for the power projected for him coming out of high school. The White Sox filled their immediate need for a center fielder with Alex Rios. But he and Danks could play right field, so it's easy to project them playing side by side, perhaps even in the second half of 2010. After leading the Arizona Fall League with 31 runs and ranking fifth with a .458 on-base percentage, Danks figures to start the season in Double-A but shouldn't stay there long.

Year	Club (League)	Class	AVG	G	AB	R	H	2B	3B	HR	RBI	BB	SO	SB	OBP	SLG
2008	Kannapolis (SAL)	LoA	.325	10	40	10	13	4	1	2	7	4	14	1	.400	.625
2009	Winston-Salem (CAR)	HiA	.322	30	118	25	38	11	2	3	21	18	32	5	.409	.525
	Birmingham (SL)	AA	.243	73	284	50	69	12	1	6	20	37	73	7	.337	.356
MINOR LEAGUE TOTALS			.271	113	442	85	120	27	4	11	48	59	119	13	.362	.425

6 TRAYCE THOMPSON, OF

BORN: March 15, 1991. **B-T:** R-R. **HT.:** 6-4. **WT.:** 200. **DRAFTED:** HS—Santa Margarita, Calif., 2009 (2nd round). **SIGNED BY:** George Kachigian.

The White Sox haven't taken a lot of high-risk, high-reward picks in recent drafts, but Thompson is that kind of player. The son of Mychal Thompson, the No. 1 pick in the 1978 NBA draft, he turned down a scholarship at UCLA to sign for $625,000 as a second-round pick last summer. Thompson has everything scouts look for—athleticism, bat speed, power, speed and arm strength. He's unusually coordinated for his size. He can catch up to good fastballs and drive bad breaking pitches a long way. He has range to play center field and the arm to fit in right. He showed intensity and a competitive nature during his introduction to pro ball. Thompson has a lot of work to do as a hitter. He has a long swing and struggles against curveballs, often chasing pitches outside of the zone. He doesn't trust his bat speed, committing himself too soon. Chicago expects him to develop power but doesn't want him to force the issue at this stage in his development. He needs work at getting better jumps, both in the outfield and on the bases. Thompson could start his first full pro season in low Class A, but the White Sox may prefer to let him have some time in extended spring training before heading to Rookie-level Great Falls. He may wind up on an outfield corner but will remain in center field for the foreseeable future.

Year	Club (League)	Class	AVG	G	AB	R	H	2B	3B	HR	RBI	BB	SO	SB	OBP	SLG
2009	Bristol (APP)	R	.188	25	85	8	16	3	1	0	10	4	33	2	.247	.247
	Great Falls (PIO)	R	.238	7	21	2	5	0	0	0	0	3	8	1	.333	.238
MINOR LEAGUE TOTALS			.198	32	106	10	21	3	1	0	10	7	41	3	.265	.245

7 DAYAN VICIEDO, 3B

BORN: March 10, 1989. **B-T:** R-R. **HT.:** 6-1. Wt: 240. **SIGNED:** Cuba, 2008. **SIGNED BY:** Doug Laumann/Jose Ortega.

A Cuban defector who signed a four-year, $10 million major league contract in December 2008, Viciedo looked overmatched at times in his pro debut. The White Sox were generally pleased with his performance in Double-A, but some club officials felt he would have been better off at Winston-Salem. Elbow inflammation forced him to leave the Arizona Fall League after four games. Viciedo can drive the ball to all fields and possesses tremendous opposite-field power. He can put on a show in batting practice and punish fat pitches. He has soft hands and an average arm at third base. He took a serious approach to his conditioning, a major issue when he signed. He did a nice job of making adjustments on and off the field in his first season in the United States. Viciedo sits on fastballs to the point where he often looks helpless against offspeed pitches, doesn't consistently center hittable pitches and chases out of the strike zone too often. He doesn't look natural at third base, where he lacks range and has trouble on balls to his right and rollers in front of him. He's easily a below-average runner. He'll have to stay on top of his weight. Kendry Morales needed part of four seasons in the Angels system to make the climb from Cuba to the major leagues, and Viciedo is younger than Morales was. The White Sox hope he can stick at third, but he could be a candidate to replace first baseman Paul Konerko, whose contract expires after 2010.

Year	Club (League)	Class	AVG	G	AB	R	H	2B	3B	HR	RBI	BB	SO	SB	OBP	SLG
2009	Birmingham (SL)	AA	.280	130	504	72	141	20	0	12	78	23	89	5	.317	.391
MINOR LEAGUE TOTALS			.280	130	504	72	141	20	0	12	78	23	89	5	.317	.391

8 DAVID HOLMBERG, LHP

BORN: July 19, 1991. **B-T:** R-L. **HT.:** 6-4. **WT.:** 220. **DRAFTED:** HS—Port Charlotte, Fla., 2009 (2nd round). **SIGNED BY:** Joe Siers.

Holmberg led the Florida high school ranks in strikeouts as a junior, creating some first-round talk, but a soft body and a fastball that only occasionally hit 90 mph caused him to slip to the second round last June. He had committed to Florida but signed with the White Sox for $514,000 as the fourth of their four picks before the third round. Other young pitchers may have better velocity or nastier breaking pitches, but few are as skilled at pitching. Holmberg has great secondary stuff and an advanced feel for changing speeds and locating pitches. Using a classic overhand delivery, he throws a 12-to-6 curveball with plus break and depth, and his changeup is nearly as good. The quality of his secondary pitches allows him to get swings and misses with a fastball that sits at 86-88 mph. It has late movement, making it tough to square up. He's intelligent and an excellent learner. Scouts have described Holmberg's body as pear-shaped and raised questions about his conditioning, but his legs and core appear strong, like a young David Wells. Radar guns don't love him, but some club officials believe he could gain velocity as his body matures. He moves slowly off the mound and projects as a below-average fielder. Holmberg has some projection but looks like a middle-of-the-rotation workhorse at best. Because he's so young, Chicago will limit his innings in low Class A this season.

Year	Club (League)	Class	W	L	ERA	G	GS	CG	SV	IP	H	R	ER	HR	BB	SO	AVG
2009	Bristol (APP)	R	2	2	4.72	14	7	0	0	40	40	26	21	5	18	37	.256
MINOR LEAGUE TOTALS			2	2	4.72	14	7	0	0	40	40	26	21	5	18	37	.256

9 CLEVELAN SANTELIZ, RHP

BORN: Sept. 1, 1986. **B-T:** R-R. **HT.:** 6-0. **WT.:** 160. **SIGNED:** Venezuela, 2004. **SIGNED BY:** Roberto Espinoza.

Animated on the mound and armed with a fastball/slider combination that can be eye-popping, Santeliz is hard to miss. He served as a set-up man for Fernando Hernandez at the start of the season in Birmingham, then converted 10 of 11 save opportunities in the final month. He pitched well in the Venezuelan League during the winter. Santeliz models himself after fellow Venezuelan Francisco Rodriguez, daring hitters to dig in against him. His fastball sits in the low 90s but can climb to 95-96 mph. When he's on, he shows a plus slider with good depth and has the ability to locate his two pitches in the strike zone. The challenge for the White Sox is to help Santeliz stay under control without losing his flair. He still has trouble throwing strikes at times, and his slider lacks consistency. He never developed much of a changeup or much trust in the pitch. He hasn't had any serious injuries, but he has had trouble handling a full workload as a starter or reliever. The Sox would like to use Santeliz as a starter, but he believes he's a closer. Better suited to be a setup man unless he significantly improves his command, he'll open 2010 in Triple-A and could make his major league debut later in the year.

Year	Club (League)	Class	W	L	ERA	G	GS	CG	SV	IP	H	R	ER	HR	BB	SO	AVG
2004	White Sox (DSL)	R	0	1	7.71	13	1	0	0	16	19	16	14	1	13	19	.284
2005	White Sox (DSL)	R	2	3	3.03	15	1	0	2	33	27	18	11	0	13	34	.223
2006	Kannapolis (SAL)	LoA	0	2	6.85	16	0	0	0	24	30	19	18	4	15	21	.319
	Great Falls (PIO)	R	1	8	4.77	14	14	0	0	66	62	41	35	9	32	61	.248
2007	Kannapolis (SAL)	LoA	1	4	6.69	27	0	0	0	38	40	35	28	4	27	37	.274
	Winston-Salem (CAR)	HiA	2	1	4.30	14	0	0	0	15	10	7	7	3	9	18	.192
2008	Birmingham (SL)	AA	0	1	4.41	10	0	0	0	16	14	8	8	2	8	6	.246
	Winston-Salem (CAR)	HiA	3	6	4.90	15	15	0	0	68	55	47	37	8	48	60	.224
2009	Birmingham (SL)	AA	4	0	0.96	40	0	0	10	56	43	10	6	2	35	52	.216
MINOR LEAGUE TOTALS			13	26	4.45	164	31	0	12	332	300	201	164	33	200	308	.244

10 MIGUEL GONZALEZ, C

BORN: Dec. 3, 1990. **B-T:** R-R. **HT.:** 6-0. **WT.:** 200. **SIGNED:** Venezuela, 2008. **SIGNED BY:** Amador Arias.

There were no headlines when the White Sox signed Gonzalez, but he has grabbed attention with his play and approach ever since. He hit .302/.372/.481 in his U.S. debut last season, which included an emergency three-game stint in Triple-A in the final week. Gonzalez is a true two-way catcher, strong at the plate and behind it. He has the bat speed to hit a good fastball, prompting teams to pitch backward against him. He's a line-drive hitter who should add power as his thin upper body fills out to match his thick legs. He threw out 35 percent of basestealers last season with his plus arm, and he's a sound receiver with an advanced feel for running games. Gonzalez already has a thick lower half, and he'll have to maintain his conditioning to retain the agility to play behind the plate. He's working to quicken his release on throws. He only has 305 pro at-bats and much more advanced pitching awaits at higher levels. Gonzalez is on the fast track. He'll open 2010 in low Class A as a 19-year-old and could appear on the big league radar in the second half of 2011. Two large obstacles loom ahead in Tyler Flowers and 2009 sandwich pick Josh Phegley.

Year	Club (League)	Class	AVG	G	AB	R	H	2B	3B	HR	RBI	BB	SO	SB	OBP	SLG
2008	White Sox 1 (DSL)	R	.500	2	2	0	1	1	0	0	0	0	0	0	.500	1.000
	White Sox 2 (DSL)	R	.291	43	141	25	41	9	1	0	23	16	18	8	.388	.369
2009	Bristol (APP)	R	.311	45	151	24	47	15	1	4	19	16	25	2	.385	.503
	Charlotte (IL)	AAA	.182	3	11	1	2	0	0	0	1	0	2	0	.182	.182
MINOR LEAGUE TOTALS			.298	93	305	50	91	25	2	4	43	32	45	10	.380	.433

11 JOSH PHEGLEY, C

BORN: Feb. 12, 1988. **B-T:** R-R. **HT.:** 5-10. **WT.:** 215. **DRAFTED:** Indiana, 2009 (1st round supplemental). **SIGNED BY:** Mike Shirley.

Like Tyler Flowers, Phegley is an offensive-minded catcher who faces questions about his long-term future behind the plate. The White Sox thought enough of his potential as a hitter to take him with the 2009 sandwich pick they received for losing Orlando Cabrera to Oakland, and signed him for $858,600. While some organizations projected Phegley as a player who would need a position change, club officials say his arm gives him the chance to be at least an average catcher. He has repaid them for their faith so far, using his plus arm to throw out 58 percent of basestealers in his pro debut. He also had 11 passed balls in 47 games, however, showing the lack of receiving skills that caused other teams to pass on him. Some scouts also are bothered by his slow release. His thick body robs him of quickness behind the plate, and he had trouble handling premium 2009 draft picks Eric Arnett (first round, Brewers) and Matt Bashore (sandwich round, Twins) at Indiana. Phegley generates gap power has a good understanding of the strike zone. He hits from a crouch, making him tougher on pitches down in the strike zone than up. There are some questions about his bat speed and how well he'll handle quality fastballs. Ticketed for high Class A in his first full pro season, Phegley won't have to be rushed because Flowers is the heir apparent to A.J. Pierzynski.

Year	Club (League)	Class	AVG	G	AB	R	H	2B	3B	HR	RBI	BB	SO	SB	OBP	SLG
2009	Kannapolis (SAL)	LoA	.224	52	196	27	44	9	0	9	33	11	40	1	.277	.408
MINOR LEAGUE TOTALS			.224	52	196	27	44	9	0	9	33	11	40	1	.277	.408

12 JOHN ELY, RHP

BORN: May 17,1986. **B-T:** R-R. **HT.:** 6-1. **WT.:** 190. **DRAFTED:** Miami (Ohio), 2007 (3rd round). **SIGNED BY:** Mike Shirley/Keith Staab.

Few minor league pitchers had a better 2009 than Ely. He led the Southern League in wins (14) and strikeouts (125 in 156 innings), and no minor leaguer who worked at least 150 innings could match his ERA (2.82) or winning percentage (.875). He doesn't have the kind of pure stuff that excites scouts, but he has outstanding makeup and a history of winning. Going back to his days as a high school star in suburban Chicago, he has posted an 83-27 record. His preparation, intensity and poise are major assets, almost as important as his plus changeup. Ely's lack of a consistent 90 mph fastball makes scouts doubt if he can succeed against elite hitters, but his mid-70s changeup is an equalizer. He also knows how to add and subtract with his fastball, which sits at 87-89 mph. His command usually improves as the season goes on, and he had a 1.68 ERA in the second half of 2009. Ely's curveball remains a work in progress, in part because he has so much success with his fastball and changeup that he's reluctant to use a third pitch. He added a cut fastball last season, giving him another option when teams stack lefthanders against him. They hit .271 off him last season, compared to .217 by righthanders. Ely is durable and never has missed a start in college or pro ball. He'll try to prove himself yet again in Triple-A this season.

Year	Club (League)	Class	W	L	ERA	G	GS	CG	SV	IP	H	R	ER	HR	BB	SO	AVG
2007	Great Falls (PIO)	R	6	1	3.86	13	12	0	0	56	55	26	24	6	14	56	.259
2008	Winston-Salem (CAR)	HiA	10	12	4.71	27	27	0	0	145	142	83	76	18	46	134	.259
2009	Birmingham (SL)	AA	14	2	2.82	27	27	1	0	156	140	63	49	9	50	125	.241
MINOR LEAGUE TOTALS			30	15	3.75	67	66	1	0	358	337	172	149	33	110	315	.251

13 SERGIO SANTOS, RHP

BORN: July 4, 1983. **B-T:** R-R. **HT.:** 6-3. **WT.:** 225. **DRAFTED:** HS—Hacienda Heights, Calif., 2002 (1st round). **SIGNED BY:** Mark Baca (Diamondbacks).

Sometimes it takes awhile to find your true calling. After the White Sox signed him as a minor league infielder a year ago, Santos heads to spring training in 2010 with an outside chance to earn a spot in their big league bullpen. A first-round pick of the Diamondbacks in 2002, he never hit well enough to reach the big leagues but always had a cannon for an arm. Arizona traded him and Troy Glaus to get Orlando Hudson and Miguel Batista from the Blue Jays in December 2005, and the Twins claimed him off waivers in May 2008. Chicago approached Santos with the idea of pitching last spring, but he wasn't ready. The Sox traded him to the Giants at the end of spring training, but when San Francisco were about to release him, he returned with an open mind and tackled pitching at extended spring training. He reported to Kannapolis on May 31 and has moved quicker than even the Sox imagined—because he can pitch in the high 90s. He earned an assignment to the Arizona Fall League, where he worked out of the bullpen, and both his peak fastball velocity (99 mph) and average velocity (96 mph) were second only to Stephen Strasburg in the prospect-heavy circuit. Santos throws a slider and changeup, both of which need improvement, but he has a good feel for pitching given his inexperience. The White Sox added him to the 40-man roster after the season because they were sure another team would take him in the major league Rule 5 draft if they didn't protect him. He'll probably open 2010 in the Charlotte bullpen but could move up quickly.

Year	Club (League)	Class	AVG	G	AB	R	H	2B	3B	HR	RBI	BB	SO	SB	OBP	SLG
2002	Missoula (PIO)	R	.272	54	202	38	55	19	2	9	37	29	49	6	.367	.520
2003	Lancaster (CAL)	HiA	.287	93	341	55	98	13	2	8	49	41	64	5	.368	.408
	El Paso (TL)	AA	.255	37	137	13	35	7	1	2	16	8	25	0	.293	.365
2004	El Paso (TL)	AA	.282	89	347	53	98	19	5	11	52	24	89	3	.332	.461
2005	Tucson (PCL)	AAA	.239	132	490	55	117	21	3	12	68	34	108	2	.288	.367
2006	Syracuse (IL)	AAA	.214	128	481	48	103	24	1	5	38	24	96	1	.254	.299
2007	Syracuse (IL)	AAA	.191	13	47	4	9	2	0	0	4	1	10	2	.204	.234
	New Hampshire (EL)	AA	.250	113	432	63	108	34	2	20	62	43	97	2	.325	.477
2008	Syracuse (IL)	AAA	.183	26	93	7	17	5	0	0	4	5	13	2	.224	.237
	Rochester (IL)	AAA	.242	86	297	44	72	24	0	5	43	16	59	4	.279	.374
MINOR LEAGUE TOTALS			.248	771	2867	380	712	168	16	72	373	225	610	27	.305	.393

Year	Club (League)	Class	W	L	ERA	G	GS	CG	SV	IP	H	R	ER	HR	BB	SO	AVG
2009	Kannapolis (SAL)	LoA	0	1	7.36	8	0	0	0	7	8	6	6	0	3	10	.286
	Winston-Salem (CAR)	HiA	0	0	5.87	8	0	0	0	8	9	5	5	2	3	7	.290
	Birmingham (SL)	AA	0	1	10.38	7	0	0	0	9	15	10	10	0	7	6	.375
	Charlotte (IL)	AAA	0	1	9.00	3	0	0	0	5	5	5	5	0	7	7	.263
MINOR LEAGUE TOTALS			0	3	8.16	26	0	0	0	29	37	26	26	2	20	30	.314

14 STEFAN GARTRELL, OF

BORN: Jan. 14, 1984. **B-T:** R-R. **HT.:** 6-3. **WT.:** 230. **DRAFTED:** San Francisco, 2006 (31st round). **SIGNED BY:** Adam Virchis.

For a 31st-round draft pick, Gartrell already has proved himself a success just by getting added to the 40-man roster last fall. His consistent production and ability to hit for power could take him beyond the fringes of the big leagues. He has seemed like a reasonable facsimile of Jermaine Dye during his four minor league seasons and heads to his first big league camp as the White Sox are looking to replace the middle-of-the-order presence previously provided by Dye and Jim Thome. Gartrell is a solid athlete with good size and strength. He helped Birmingham establish itself as the best team in the Southern League before finishing 2010 at Triple-A, where his production dipped. He has a solid stroke that delivers power to all fields, and he drives balls to right-center when he's locked in. His plate discipline comes and goes, and he gets overly aggressive at times. He led the Rookie-level Appalachian League with 43 walks in 2006, but he has had trouble with pitch recognition since then. Gartrell has enough arm to play right field, but a lack of first-step quickness limits his range. He's an average baserunner and shouldn't become a baseclogger anytime soon. His immediate future will depend on whom the Sox acquire in the offseason, but he'll get a major league opportunity if he keeps hitting.

Year	Club (League)	Class	AVG	G	AB	R	H	2B	3B	HR	RBI	BB	SO	SB	OBP	SLG
2006	Bristol (APP)	R	.308	61	214	41	66	16	1	4	33	43	48	4	.438	.449
	Birmingham (SL)	AA	.200	5	15	4	3	1	0	0	0	3	6	1	.333	.267
2007	Kannapolis (SAL)	LoA	.301	95	339	67	102	20	3	12	57	37	77	12	.374	.484
	Winston-Salem (CAR)	HiA	.288	20	73	13	21	1	1	2	6	6	17	2	.358	.411
2008	Birmingham (SL)	AA	.254	122	409	54	104	22	2	14	52	45	106	7	.334	.421
2009	Birmingham (SL)	AA	.285	101	361	72	103	20	4	19	70	46	99	6	.371	.521
	Charlotte (IL)	AAA	.265	31	113	14	30	11	1	4	19	7	29	0	.314	.487
MINOR LEAGUE TOTALS			.281	435	1524	265	429	91	12	55	237	187	382	32	.367	.465

15 C.J. RETHERFORD, 2B

BORN: Aug. 14, 1985. **B-T:** R-R. **HT.:** 5-11. **WT.:** 190. **SIGNED:** Arizona State, NDFA 2007. **SIGNED BY:** Alan Regier.

Earning every at-bat he ever has gotten gotten, Retherford has climbed to the point where he's ready to prove he can play in the major leagues. He went undrafted for five straight years from 2003-07, despite being eligible each June out of high school, South Mountain (Ariz.) CC or Arizona State. A former walk-on with the Sun Devils, he has hit throughout his pro career and tied for the minor league lead with 46 doubles last season. Retherford helped Birmingham win 92 games in 2009 and then contributed to a championship team in the Arizona Fall League, hitting a game-winning homer in the title game. He has a .301 career minor league average, thanks to outstanding hand-eye coordination and bat control. He could hit 15 or more homers per year if he plays regularly. He has fringe-average speed and is a good baserunner. A third baseman in his first two seasons in the system, Retherford moved to second base last year. Birmingham hitting coach Andy Tomberlin said Retherford can be a Dustin Pedroia-like player, though others still project him as more of a utilityman. His range and arm are no better than average, but he positions himself well and makes all the routine plays. He improved on the pivot throughout last year. The move of Gordon Beckham from third base to second wasn't good for his upward mobility, but Retherford usually finds ways to create opportunities for himself.

Year	Club (League)	Class	AVG	G	AB	R	H	2B	3B	HR	RBI	BB	SO	SB	OBP	SLG
2007	Great Falls (PIO)	R	.318	61	261	53	83	30	4	13	48	24	45	2	.389	.613
2008	Winston-Salem (CAR)	HiA	.295	130	461	66	136	28	1	16	71	37	78	11	.350	.464
2009	Birmingham (SL)	AA	.297	128	478	70	142	46	4	10	76	30	70	3	.340	.473
MINOR LEAGUE TOTALS			.301	319	1200	189	361	104	9	39	195	91	193	16	.354	.500

16 CARLOS TORRES, RHP

BORN: Oct. 22, 1982. **B-T:** R-R. **HT.:** 6-1. **WT.:** 185. **DRAFTED:** Kansas State, 2004 (15th round). **SIGNED BY:** Paul Provas/Keith Staab.

You can find plenty of pitchers with better pure stuff than Torres, but he has made a career of outpitching them. He developed mental toughness while pitching for four colleges—Allan Hancock (Calif.) JC, Grossmont (Calif.) JC, San Jose State and Kansas State—and showed it by throwing seven scoreless innings in a start at Wrigley Field last September. He earned that opportunity by leading the Triple-A International League in ERA (2.39), opponent average (.207) and strikeouts per nine innings (9.1). Torres succeeds with a heavy 90-92 mph fastball and a plus cutter that frustrates lefthanders. He also throws a curveball and changeup. His fearlessness and durability make him an organizational favorite, and he'll compete for a job on the big league staff this spring. Torres profiles as a long reliever/sixth starter and could be helped by his ability to warm up quickly. His fate could hinge on whether the more hyped Daniel Hudson sticks in Chicago or continues his education in the minors.

Year	Club (League)	Class	W	L	ERA	G	GS	CG	SV	IP	H	R	ER	HR	BB	SO	AVG
2004	Bristol (APP)	R	2	2	4.74	19	0	0	1	38	43	30	20	2	12	28	.281
2005	Great Falls (PIO)	R	1	1	2.88	5	5	0	0	25	18	8	8	1	8	26	.205
	Kannapolis (SAL)	LoA	1	3	3.53	8	8	0	0	43	28	20	17	4	23	54	.179
2006	Winston-Salem (CAR)	HiA	3	8	4.69	25	20	0	1	94	116	66	49	7	55	76	.304
2007	Winston-Salem (CAR)	HiA	0	2	3.72	19	0	0	3	36	33	16	15	0	10	41	.248
	Birmingham (SL)	AA	2	2	3.70	36	0	0	1	56	57	26	23	3	22	59	.269
2008	Birmingham (SL)	AA	9	5	3.20	21	17	0	0	101	86	40	36	4	29	93	.234

	Club (League)	Class	W	L	ERA	G	GS	CG	SV	IP	H	R	ER	HR	BB	SO	AVG
	Charlotte (IL)	AAA	0	0	4.58	8	1	0	0	20	23	10	10	2	11	19	.295
2009	Charlotte (IL)	AAA	10	4	2.39	23	20	2	1	128	96	38	34	4	56	130	.207
	Chicago (AL)	MAJ	1	2	6.04	8	5	0	0	28	30	20	19	5	17	22	.286
MAJOR LEAGUE TOTALS			1	2	6.04	8	5	0	0	28	30	20	19	5	17	22	.286
MINOR LEAGUE TOTALS			28	27	3.52	164	71	2	7	542	500	254	212	27	226	526	.246

17 LUCAS HARRELL, RHP

BORN: June 3, 1985. **B-T:** B-R. **HT.:** 6-2. **WT.:** 200. **DRAFTED:** HS—Ozark, Mo. 2004 (4th round). **SIGNED BY:** Alex Slattery.

Harrell never has lacked for competitiveness. Now that his shoulder is sound again, he has the collection of pitches to back up his confidence. He missed all of 2007 following shoulder surgery, and also spent time on the disabled list in 2006 and 2008 with shoulder issues. Harrell flashed his potential for Team USA in the World Cup at the end of last season, throwing 10 scoreless innings in the tournament, including four against Cuba. He would have preferred to be in Chicago, but Daniel Hudson and Carlos Torres were summoned to the big leagues ahead of him. Harrell comes at hitters with two different fastballs: a low-90s sinker that gets a ton of groundouts and a 93-94 mph four-seamer that misses bats. Harrell also has a plus changeup, but his slider has a tendency to flatten out and lacks depth. Harrell has worked primarily as a starter as a pro, but his World Cup experience suggests he can function well as a multiple-inning reliever. He's likely to start 2010 back in Triple-A but will get a chance to make the big league club in spring training. There figures to be at least one spot open for a rookie, and Harrell will compete with Hudson, Torres, Sergio Santos, Clevelan Santeliz and Jon Link.

Year	Club (League)	Class	W	L	ERA	G	GS	CG	SV	IP	H	R	ER	HR	BB	SO	AVG
2004	Bristol (APP)	R	3	5	5.59	13	9	0	0	48	53	39	30	5	32	33	.282
2005	Kannapolis (SAL)	LoA	7	11	3.64	26	26	0	0	133	128	86	54	8	71	85	.248
2006	Winston-Salem (CAR)	HiA	7	2	2.45	17	17	0	0	92	58	29	25	3	44	70	.182
	Birmingham (SL)	AA	0	2	10.24	3	3	0	0	10	12	12	11	1	14	4	.316
2007	Did Not Play—Injured																
2008	Bristol (APP)	R	0	0	3.00	1	1	0	0	3	3	1	1	0	1	5	.273
	Kannapolis (SAL)	LoA	1	1	5.91	3	3	0	0	11	13	7	7	0	4	7	.302
	Birmingham (SL)	AA	3	3	3.46	11	10	0	0	55	56	30	21	3	19	34	.272
2009	Birmingham (SL)	AA	8	3	3.25	14	14	0	0	80	78	38	29	4	32	51	.264
	Charlotte (IL)	AAA	4	1	3.29	11	11	0	0	66	58	26	24	3	37	42	.246
MINOR LEAGUE TOTALS			33	28	3.66	99	94	0	0	497	459	268	202	27	254	331	.248

18 SANTOS RODRIGUEZ, LHP

BORN: Jan. 2, 1988. **B-T:** L-L. **HT.:** 6-6. **WT.:** 185. **SIGNED:** Dominican Republic, 2006. **SIGNED BY:** Roberto Aquino (Braves).

At 22, Rodriguez is old for a Latin American prospect who hasn't established himself in full-season ball, but his velocity is eye-popping. Along with catcher Tyler Flowers and infielders Brent Lillibridge and Jon Gilmore, the White Sox acquired him from the Braves in the Javier Vazquez trade after the 2008 season. Chicago hoped to start Rodriguez at Kannapolis last season, but he wasn't deemed ready to face low Class A hitters until September. He's a hard thrower with an impressive frame, and only now is he starting to put polish on his skills. At times last year, his fastball sat at 95 mph and spiked to 97, thanks to what one scout called "just ridiculous arm strength." Hitters hate facing him, and he hasn't given up a home run since 2007. Rodriguez slowly is learning to use three pitches, making major strides with his changeup last season and sharpening a slider that looks more like a slurve most of the time. His delivery is raw and inconsistent, and he also needs work on his fielding. The White Sox view Rodriguez as a reliever, and he could move fast if he gets his delivery locked in. At the very least he's a commodity that general Ken Williams can deal, as his fastball is the kind that intrigues almost any organization.

Year	Club (League)	Class	W	L	ERA	G	GS	CG	SV	IP	H	R	ER	HR	BB	SO	AVG
2007	Braves (GCL)	R	0	1	6.67	12	2	0	2	28	29	25	21	3	21	35	.248
2008	Braves (GCL)	R	1	2	2.79	14	0	0	5	29	16	12	9	0	13	45	.155
2009	Bristol (APP)	R	2	0	1.33	19	0	0	4	27	18	5	4	0	17	42	.189
	Kannapolis (SAL)	LoA	0	0	0.00	3	0	0	0	4	3	0	0	0	1	8	.200
MINOR LEAGUE TOTALS			3	3	3.46	48	2	0	11	88	66	42	34	3	52	130	.200

19 EDUARDO ESCOBAR, SS

BORN: Jan. 5, 1989. **B-T:** B-R. **HT.:** 5-10. **WT.:** 150. **SIGNED:** Venezuela, 2006. **SIGNED BY:** Amador Arias.

If you didn't have to hit to get noticed on defense, Escobar would project as a future Gold Glove shortstop. But it's unclear if he has enough bat to get to the big leagues. He was overmatched at the plate in 2009, as low Class A pitchers consistently challenged him and he didn't make them pay. A switch-hitter, Escobar doesn't make enough solid contact to put his plus speed to use. He's defensive at the plate, rarely looking to drive the ball despite having deceptive strength, but still struck out three times as much as he walked last season. He did a better job of reading pitchers last year and has improved his basestealing. He's fun to watch in the field, and Kannapolis' middle-infield combo of Escobar and Andrew Garcia was a major reason why the Intimidators went 82-57 and held opponents to 3.8 runs per game. Escobar has Omar Vizquel-like range, sure hands and a strong arm. He played in the Venezuelan League over the winter and will move up to high Class A this season.

Year	Club (League)	Class	AVG	G	AB	R	H	2B	3B	HR	RBI	BB	SO	SB	OBP	SLG
2006	Orioles/White Sox (VSL)	R	.236	46	123	21	29	3	1	0	17	14	25	7	.317	.276
2007	White Sox2 (DSL)	R	.291	64	247	56	72	5	4	0	18	22	45	19	.359	.344
2008	Great Falls (PIO)	R	.417	6	24	6	10	2	1	1	4	2	3	1	.464	.708
	Kannapolis (SAL)	LoA	.267	60	243	37	65	6	1	0	22	13	65	4	.302	.300
2009	Kannapolis (SAL)	LoA	.256	128	464	64	119	10	7	3	41	29	91	20	.300	.328
MINOR LEAGUE TOTALS			.268	304	1101	184	295	26	14	4	102	80	229	51	.320	.328

20 NEVIN GRIFFITH, RHP

BORN: March 23, 1989. **B-T:** R-R. **HT.:** 6-2. **WT.:** 165. **DRAFTED:** HS—Tampa, 2007 (2nd round). **SIGNED BY:** Scott Bikowski/Warren Hughes.

On one hand, it seems like the White Sox have been waiting forever for Griffith to pitch significant innings. On the other, he'll still only be 21 this season. One of the top high school pitchers in Florida in the 2007 draft, Griffith blew out his elbow a year after signing as a second-round pick and had Tommy John surgery. He has pitched just 98 innings in his first three pro seasons, but took a huge step forward by finishing 2009 as a full-time member of the Kannapolis rotation. He followed up with a strong showing in instructional league. Griffith has added strength to his frame and shortened a delivery that produces easy heat. He has a 92-95 mph fastball and a curveball that's a plus pitch at times but flattens out at others. His changeup is a work in progress. Improving his secondary pitches is Griffith's major challenge, as low Class A lefthanders hit .370 against him and he doesn't miss as many bats as he should. He'll move up to Winston-Salem in 2010 as Chicago waits for him to begin his long-awaited rise through the system.

Year	Club (League)	Class	W	L	ERA	G	GS	CG	SV	IP	H	R	ER	HR	BB	SO	AVG
2007	Bristol (APP)	R	0	0	5.19	8	1	0	0	9	14	8	5	0	6	7	.359
2008	Great Falls (PIO)	R	0	0	2.13	3	3	0	0	13	13	6	3	0	5	12	.245
2009	Bristol (APP)	R	0	1	5.00	2	2	0	0	9	10	7	5	0	7	7	.294
	Kannapolis (SAL)	LoA	5	5	3.86	13	12	0	0	68	69	35	29	4	26	35	.274
MINOR LEAGUE TOTALS			5	6	3.86	26	18	0	0	98	106	56	42	4	44	61	.280

21 CHRISTIAN MARRERO, OF/1B

BORN: July 30, 1986. **B-T:** L-L. **HT.:** 6-1. **WT.:** 185. **DRAFTED:** Broward CC, D/F 2005 (22nd round). **SIGNED BY:** Jose Ortega.

When Marrero arrived at Birmingham last June, he hit at the bottom of the order, but he migrated up to the No. 3 spot by the time the playoffs rolled around. He ended the season hitting .308/.348/.501 between Winston-Salem and Birmingham. The brother of former Nationals first-round pick Chris Marrero, Christian isn't a toolsy guy with a huge ceiling, but he has hit well to get close to big league consideration. Marrero generates excellent bat speed despite having an uppercut swing. He catches up to all but the very best fastballs and stays back on breaking pitches. He uses the entire field and holds his own against lefties. Marrero has solid knowledge of the strike zone but doesn't walk often. He has split time between the outfield and first base as a pro and is considered only adequate in both places. He played right field in Double-A, picking up eight outfield assists with his strong arm, but could wind up moving to left field as he advances. His range and speed are fringy. The ability to play first base and the outfield should eventually make it easier for Marrero to make a big league roster, and his passion for baseball could keep him there for years as a role player.

Year	Club (League)	Class	AVG	G	AB	R	H	2B	3B	HR	RBI	BB	SO	SB	OBP	SLG
2006	Great Falls (PIO)	R	.252	72	242	24	61	17	0	3	24	30	37	1	.337	.360
2007	Great Falls (PIO)	R	.305	69	269	53	82	21	6	12	63	36	43	3	.383	.561
2008	Kannapolis (SAL)	LoA	.273	124	436	53	119	29	5	10	61	54	89	11	.355	.431
2009	Winston-Salem (CAR)	HiA	.314	62	226	35	71	15	1	7	34	11	44	2	.357	.482
	Birmingham (SL)	AA	.301	65	229	28	69	15	1	11	40	18	50	1	.340	.520
MINOR LEAGUE TOTALS			.287	392	1402	193	402	97	13	43	222	149	263	18	.355	.466

22 JHONNY NUNEZ, RHP

BORN: Nov. 26, 1985. **B-T:** L-R. **HT.:** 6-3. **WT.:** 185. **SIGNED:** Dominican Republic, 2003. **SIGNED BY:** Andres Lopez (Dodgers).

While Jeff Marquez was the more prominent prospect in the deal that sent Nick Swisher to the Yankees after the 2008 season, Nunez has a much better chance to have a lasting impact in Chicago. He didn't show it last September, when he got his first chance with the White Sox, but scouts say he has the stuff to establish himself as a big league reliever. He worked exclusively in relief for the first time in 2009 and put up a 2.55 ERA in 42 appearances in the minors. Originally signed by the Dodgers and traded three times since 2006, Nunez has a two-seam fastball that parks in the low 90s and a four-seamer than spikes as high as 97. His plus slider is his best pitch. He can back-door it to lefthanders or wrap it around their back foot when they're expecting him to work outside. He didn't have a feel for a third pitch when the White Sox acquired him but improved his changeup working with Birmingham pitching coach J.R. Perdew. Nunez is unlikely to pitch his way onto the big league staff out of spring training, but he could get there as a midseason replacement. The key will be the sharpness of his slider and his ability to get outs against lefties.

Year	Club (League)	Class	W	L	ERA	G	GS	CG	SV	IP	H	R	ER	HR	BB	SO	AVG
2004	Dodgers1 (DSL)	R	2	1	1.73	7	7	0	0	36	30	8	7	1	6	23	.229
	Dodgers2 (DSL)	R	2	0	4.60	4	3	0	0	16	17	9	8	0	4	12	.262
2005	Dodgers (DSL)	R	4	3	1.92	15	8	1	0	52	29	13	11	0	13	40	.153
2006	Dodgers (GCL)	R	6	0	1.58	10	7	0	0	57	35	12	10	0	19	56	.177
2007	Hagerstown (SAL)	LoA	4	6	4.05	23	22	0	0	107	97	59	48	10	48	86	.239
2008	Potomac (CAR)	HiA	2	8	5.22	21	17	0	0	81	88	51	47	11	21	82	.276
	Harrisburg (EL)	AA	0	0	1.13	5	0	0	0	8	9	1	1	0	6	8	.300
	Trenton (EL)	AA	1	0	1.86	8	0	0	0	19	16	5	4	2	6	26	.229
2009	Birmingham (SL)	AA	3	0	2.14	26	0	0	3	46	38	12	11	3	21	57	.229
	Charlotte (IL)	AAA	2	0	3.33	16	0	0	1	24	19	9	9	3	5	22	.221
	Chicago (AL)	MAJ	0	0	9.53	7	0	0	0	6	10	6	6	1	2	3	.370
MAJOR LEAGUE TOTALS			0	0	9.53	7	0	0	0	6	10	6	6	1	2	3	.370
MINOR LEAGUE TOTALS			26	18	3.15	135	64	1	4	446	378	179	156	30	149	412	.228

23 DAN REMENOWSKY, RHP

BORN: April 7, 1986. **B-T:** R-R. **HT.:** 6-5. **WT.:** 245. **SIGNED:** Windy City (Frontier), 2008. **SIGNED BY:** Doug Laumann.

Joe Borowski nailed down 131 saves in parts of 12 major league seasons without ever making a scout snap to attention. He simply attacked the strike zone with an ordinary fastball and forced hitters to beat him. Remenowsky, who went undrafted after a four-year career at NCAA Division III Otterbein (Ohio), is the same kind of pitcher. The White Sox signed him after a brief stop with Windy City in the independent Frontier League, then sat back and watched him put up unbelievable numbers in 2009. His 15.5 strikeouts per nine innings led all minor league relievers. Remenowsky's delivery includes an unusually high leg kick, a la Paul Byrd. It allows him to get strikeouts with an 88-90 mph fastball, giving him an unusual amount of deception and late movement. He uses a splitter to keep hitters from sitting on his fastball. His changeup is in the low 80s, like his splitter, and he's working to get more separation between the pitches. He also has a spike curveball in his arsenal, though he doesn't use it working out of the bullpen. He isn't afraid to work inside. Remenowsky's delivery makes him an easy target for basestealers, so he's working to shorten it with men on base. At times last year, he threw exclusively out of the stretch. Chicago isn't afraid of moving effective pitchers quickly, so don't be surprised if he darts through the high minors in 2010.

Year	Club (League)	Class	W	L	ERA	G	GS	CG	SV	IP	H	R	ER	HR	BB	SO	AVG
2008	Windy City (FRN)	IND	1	0	1.69	2	1	0	0	11	10	2	2	1	3	12	.256
	Bristol (APP)	R	0	0	0.00	0	0	0	0	2	1	0	0	0	0	2	.143
	Great Falls (PIO)	R	4	0	0.48	11	0	0	3	19	17	2	1	0	6	18	.239
2009	Kannapolis (SAL)	LoA	7	3	1.99	54	0	0	24	63	40	18	14	3	16	109	.176
MINOR LEAGUE TOTALS			11	3	1.61	66	0	0	27	84	58	20	15	3	22	129	.190

24 KYLE BELLAMY, RHP

BORN: Oct. 25, 1987. **B-T:** R-R. **HT.:** 6-5. **WT.:** 215. **DRAFTED:** Miami, 2009 (5th round). **SIGNED BY:** Jose Ortega.

Talk about locked in. Bellamy has posted a 1.56 ERA in 103 appearances over the last two seasons between Miami, two minor league stops and the Arizona Fall League. He has worked as a set-up man and a closer during that span and could have a future in either role. A fifth-round pick who signed for $147,500 last June, he's poised to move fast through the system. A sidearmer, he has a high-80s sinker that is especially tough on righthanders. His Frisbee slider acts only as a deterrent to keep batters from sitting on his sinker. It breaks early, making it ineffective against lefthanders, which is why some scouts see Bellamy as more of a situational reliever. His fastball tends to lose velocity when he works on back-to-back days, which doesn't help his cause for a larger role. White Sox coaches praise Bellamy's confidence, but it will be interesting to see how he reacts to adversity because he hasn't encountered much of it since his freshman season at Miami. He could jump as high as Double-A to start his first full pro season, and a solid first half there could get him big league consideration by the end of 2010. He'd be best served by focusing on his slider, because that's the pitch that will determine if he has a future as a closer.

Year	Club (League)	Class	W	L	ERA	G	GS	CG	SV	IP	H	R	ER	HR	BB	SO	AVG
2009	Bristol (APP)	R	0	0	0.00	3	0	0	1	3	0	0	0	0	0	2	.000
	Kannapolis (SAL)	LoA	2	0	1.42	17	0	0	2	19	14	5	3	1	2	30	.189
MINOR LEAGUE TOTALS			2	0	1.23	20	0	0	3	22	14	5	3	1	2	32	.169

25 JOHN SHELBY, OF

BORN: Aug. 6, 1985. **B-T:** R-R. **HT.:** 5-10. **WT.:** 190. **DRAFTED:** Kentucky, 2006 (5th round). **SIGNED BY:** Mike Shirley.

As scouts debate whether he can be an everyday major leaguer, the son of former big leaguer John Shelby continues his steady rise toward the big leagues. Speed and versatility are his biggest assets, but his struggles against righthanders raise questions about whether he can ever be more than an extra outfielder. His hitting slipped when he moved to Double-A in 2009, though he did slowly dig himself out from a poor start. Shelby had been a bit of a free swinger in previous seasons but showed improved plate discipline in 2009. Deeper counts and better pitching contributed to a drop in his average, and he'll have to make more adjustments this season. He does have good pop, and he used his plus speed and instincts to steal 30 bases in 39 tries. A second baseman in college and in his first two years as a pro, Shelby played well in his second full season an outfielder. He got to more balls in center than he had in 2008, and continued to see action in left field. His fringe-average arm invites runners to challenge him, but he had 13 outfield assists, showing good accuracy. Shelby should advance to Triple-A in 2009.

Year	Club (League)	Class	AVG	G	AB	R	H	2B	3B	HR	RBI	BB	SO	SB	OBP	SLG
2006	Great Falls (PIO)	R	.272	66	250	37	68	12	3	8	36	18	55	8	.332	.440
2007	Kannapolis (SAL)	LoA	.301	122	488	83	147	35	9	16	79	35	77	19	.352	.508
2008	Winston-Salem (CAR)	HiA	.295	114	447	81	132	37	7	15	80	22	98	33	.331	.510
2009	Birmingham (SL)	AA	.243	115	428	64	104	32	3	10	49	49	77	30	.323	.402
MINOR LEAGUE TOTALS			.280	417	1613	265	451	116	22	49	244	124	307	90	.335	.470

26 NATE JONES, RHP

BORN: Jan. 28, 1986. **B-T:** R-R. **HT.:** 6-5. **WT.:** 190. **DRAFTED:** Northern Kentucky, 2007 (5th round). **SIGNED BY:** Mike Shirley.

Depending on whom you talk to, Jones is either the most exciting arm in the system or a complete longshot. He has moved slowly through the system and was used carefully between two Class A leagues last season, but when his mechanics and approach are right, he can be lights out. Jones is a long, lanky righthander who's all about power. His fastball can sit in the high 90s, spiking as high as 99 mph, and his curveball can be the same kind of hammer that helped Bobby Jenks have immediate success when he reached the big leagues. Jones' curveball is inconsistent, though, lacking depth at times and prompting some thought that he should turn it into a slider. He showed improved control last season and has made adjustments in his delivery, shortening it somewhat. He also worked mostly out of the stretch in 2009. While most see Jones as a possible late-inning reliever, it's unclear if he'll be able to handle the strain of getting ready quickly and pitching often. The White Sox may send him back to Winston-Salem and use him as a starter in 2010 to develop more consistency, especially with his curveball.

Year	Club (League)	Class	W	L	ERA	G	GS	CG	SV	IP	H	R	ER	HR	BB	SO	AVG
2007	Bristol (APP)	R	0	4	5.13	13	10	0	0	47	44	33	27	4	29	42	.250
2008	Bristol (APP)	R	1	0	1.35	4	1	0	0	7	6	4	1	0	2	12	.222
	Kannapolis (SAL)	LoA	1	7	6.83	18	10	1	0	57	63	45	43	8	35	71	.281
	Winston-Salem (CAR)	HiA	0	0	3.38	2	0	0	0	3	1	1	1	0	2	1	.111
2009	Kannapolis (SAL)	LoA	2	0	2.41	13	0	0	1	19	8	5	5	0	9	25	.129
	Winston-Salem (CAR)	HiA	2	1	3.65	32	0	0	0	49	44	20	20	4	13	43	.244
MINOR LEAGUE TOTALS			6	12	4.81	82	21	1	1	181	166	108	97	16	90	194	.245

27 CHARLIE LEESMAN, LHP

BORN: March 10, 1987. **B-T:** L-L. **HT.:** 6-4. **WT.:** 210. **DRAFTED:** Xavier, 2008 (11th round). **SIGNED BY:** Mike Shirley/Phil Gulley.

Led by Gordon Beckham, Brent Morel, Dan Hudson and Jordan Danks, the White Sox's 2008 draft is looking like a good one. It will be even better if Leesman can continue to make strides like he did last season, when he led the South Atlantic League with 13 wins. Leesman attended Xavier after the Twins selected him in the 40th round out of high school, and he showed more stuff than results in college. The White Sox drafted him in the 11th round mainly because he touched 93 mph with his fastball at Xavier's scout day. Leesman is only now really learning how to pitch. The Sox credit his strong showing in 2009 to improved command of his fastball, which sits in the low 90s and has exaggerated sink, producing a lot of grounders. That pitch alone makes him tough on lefthanders. Both his breaking ball and changeup are below-average offerings at this point, though his work in instructional league hinted that they may be coming around. With Aaron Poreda and Clayton Richard traded in the Jake Peavy deal, Leesman is the organization's most advanced lefthanded starter prospect. He's still raw in many ways, however, and shouldn't be rushed. He could open 2010 in Double-A if he has a strong spring training.

Year	Club (League)	Class	W	L	ERA	G	GS	CG	SV	IP	H	R	ER	HR	BB	SO	AVG
2008	Bristol (APP)	R	0	0	0.00	2	0	0	1	5	5	0	0	0	1	6	.263
	Kannapolis (SAL)	LoA	0	0	0.00	1	1	0	0	5	3	1	0	0	2	5	.188
2009	Kannapolis (SAL)	LoA	13	5	3.08	27	27	1	0	158	165	66	54	4	58	117	.275
MINOR LEAGUE TOTALS			13	5	2.90	30	28	1	1	168	173	67	54	4	61	128	.273

28 JON LINK, RHP

BORN: March 23, 1984. **B-T:** R-R. **HT.:** 6-1. **WT.:** 175. **DRAFTED:** Bluefield (Va.) JC, 2005 (26th round). **SIGNED BY:** Ash Lawson (Padres).

After leading the minor leagues with 35 saves in 2008, Link was positioned to reach the big leagues last season. Instead he took a step back, mostly because it took until July for him to throw his slider with the depth and command that he showed previously. While it wasn't as consistent, the slider remains one of the best in the organization, but Link seemed to lose confidence in it too quickly and went to his low-90s fastball too often. He can be hard on himself when he isn't having success. Though he struggled at times against Triple-A hitters, he still finished with more than a strikeout per inning. His command improved later in the season, after his big league window had closed, but he took advantage of a chance to work as a closer in the Venezuelan League, going 2-0, 2.95 with seven saves in 21 innings of work. Acquired in a 2007 trade that sent Rob Mackowiak to the Padres, Link remained on the the 40-man roster and will get a look for a bullpen job in spring training

Year	Club (League)	Class	W	L	ERA	G	GS	CG	SV	IP	H	R	ER	HR	BB	SO	AVG
2005	Eugene (NWL)	SS	3	3	4.42	25	7	0	0	59	67	33	29	5	8	44	.285
2006	Fort Wayne (MWL)	LoA	5	5	4.91	53	0	0	3	62	72	45	34	3	24	57	.283
2007	Lake Elsinore (CAL)	HiA	2	1	3.07	41	0	0	13	41	32	16	14	5	11	45	.209
	Winston-Salem (CAR)	HiA	1	0	2.55	14	0	0	3	18	16	5	5	1	4	19	.246
2008	Birmingham (SL)	AA	5	4	3.02	56	0	0	35	57	48	21	19	3	27	66	.223
2009	Charlotte (IL)	AAA	1	2	3.99	48	0	0	13	56	55	26	25	5	27	66	.256
MINOR LEAGUE TOTALS			17	15	3.87	237	7	0	67	293	290	146	126	22	101	297	.255

29 JOSE MARTINEZ, OF

BORN: July 25, 1988. **B-T:** R-R. **HT.:** 6-5. **WT.:** 180. **SIGNED:** Venezuela, 2006. **SIGNED BY:** Amador Arias/Dave Wilder.

A well-built package of potential, Martinez hopes to reacquaint himself with the diamond this season. He has played just 104 games over the last three seasons, missing all of last season and most of 2008 due to problems with a torn anterior cruciate ligament in his knee. He injured the knee early in 2008 and required microfracture surgery to repair the damage, resulting in an extended recovery. The son of the late Carlos Martinez, a former corner infielder for the White Sox, Jose was a productive hitter as a 17-year-old in the Rookie-level Venezuelan Summer League in 2006 and has shown the ability to be a run-producer everywhere he has played. He generates impressive bat speed from a swing that can get long at times, and he uses his size and strength to put on shows in batting practice. He had good speed before his surgeries but no longer projects to be a basestealer. He has good range in the outfield and enough arm for right field, which has been his primary position. The White Sox aren't giving up on him, in part because they appreciate his work ethic, and he'll probably return to Kannapolis to get his career going again.

Year	Club (League)	Class	AVG	G	AB	R	H	2B	3B	HR	RBI	BB	SO	SB	OBP	SLG
2006	Orioles/White Sox (VSL)	R	.278	54	158	26	44	8	0	4	30	25	29	5	.384	.405
2007	Bristol (APP)	R	.282	65	245	34	69	11	3	7	37	22	53	12	.348	.437
2008	Kannapolis (SAL)	LoA	.306	39	144	19	44	5	0	2	18	12	26	7	.359	.382
2009	Did Not Play—Injured															
MINOR LEAGUE TOTALS			.287	158	547	79	157	24	3	13	85	59	108	24	.362	.413

30 JUSTIN COLLOP, RHP

BORN: May 30, 1988. **B-T:** R-R. **HT.:** 6-1. **WT.:** 185. **DRAFTED:** Toledo, 2009 (6th round). **SIGNED BY:** Mike Shirley.

A good scout sometimes has to ignore what happens after the ball leaves a pitcher's hand. The White Sox did just that in regard to Collop last spring, and they may have made a solid investment by signing him for $122,500 in the sixth round. His junior season at Toledo was the poorest of his career, with the results becoming worse as the draft approached, but Chicago believed in the stuff it had seen earlier. Collop got his pro career off to a great start in the hitter-friendly Pioneer League, showing a clean delivery and a low-90s fastball with good life and movement. The fastball hit 94 mph at times and had boring sink, the result of his quick arm. His heater sets up his other pitches, the best of which is a splitter that misses bats. His slider is inconsistent, as is his changeup, but the naturally quick action in his delivery gives him the potential to turn both into solid offerings. He brings an athletic presence to the mound, in part the result of playing basketball in high school. It's no surprise that he's proving to be a quick learner, because he initially went to Toledo on an academic scholarship, not an athletic scholarship. Collop will open his first full season in low Class A but might force a quick promotion.

Year	Club (League)	Class	W	L	ERA	G	GS	CG	SV	IP	H	R	ER	HR	BB	SO	AVG
2009	Great Falls (PIO)	R	3	2	2.72	15	7	0	0	40	38	20	12	1	23	33	.257
MINOR LEAGUE TOTALS			3	2	2.72	15	7	0	0	40	38	20	12	1	23	33	.257

Cincinnati Reds

BY J.J. COOPER

The Reds have been in rebuilding mode for a decade, even if they don't realize it.

Cincinnati hasn't finished with a winning record since 2000, though it's hard to pinpoint a time at which the club truly cashed in and planned for tomorrow. A fallow farm system in the first half of the decade made it almost impossible to build from within. Even now that the system has started to produce players, the Reds have continued to teeter in the no-man's land between being competitive and building for the future.

It was much the same story in 2009. On July 4, the Reds sat a game above .500 and two games out of first place in the National League Central. For a moment, it appeared the Reds would be a part of a pennant race for the first time since Barry Larkin was their shortstop.

But it was just a mirage. Edinson Volquez went down in early July with an elbow injury that required Tommy John surgery. Jay Bruce broke his wrist in the middle of the month, and Chris Dickerson was lost soon afterward with back spasms. The team quickly fell apart, going 8-19 in July to drop to 10 games out of first place.

Owner Bob Castellini wants to see a winner sooner than later, so instead of being sellers at the trade deadline, Cincinnati decided to buy. The Reds traded their top pitching prospect (Zach Stewart) and their best relief pitching prospect (Josh Roenicke) to upgrade from 26-year-old Edwin Encarnacion to 34-year-old Scott Rolen at third base.

Predictably, the trade did nothing to turn around Cincinnati's season. The Reds finished 13 games behind the Cardinals, something they could have done without Rolen. But more importantly, the addition of the veteran third baseman strained the team's already tight budget. Cincinnati has $59.25 million committed to seven players (including Rolen's $11 million) for 2010—even though the team was expected to cut up to $5 million from its $71 million payroll.

That means that there is little choice but to look to the farm system to fill several glaring holes. While they weren't rebuilding, the Reds did try out 17 rookies in 2009 thanks to injuries and necessity. Veterans Ramon Hernandez and Willy Taveras were expensive busts, so Ryan Hanigan and Drew Stubbs had displaced them by season's end. Paul Janish and Adam Rosales got most of the playing time on the left side of the infield, with less success. Despite that,

Homer Bailey, the Reds' No. 1 prospect for three years, earned a spot in the rotation

TOP 30 PROSPECTS

1. Todd Frazier, of/2b/3b	16. Jordan Smith, rhp
2. Yonder Alonso, 1b	17. Miguel Rojas, ss
3. Mike Leake, rhp	18. Juan Duran, of
4. Chris Heisey, of	19. Enerio del Rosario, rhp
5. Juan Francisco, 3b	20. Kyle Lotzkar, rhp
6. Yorman Rodriguez, of	21. Donnie Joseph, lhp
7. Travis Wood, lhp	22. Pedro Viola, lhp
8. Matt Maloney, lhp	23. Phillippe Valiquette, lhp
9. Brad Boxberger, rhp	24. Mark Serrano, rhp
10. Zack Cozart, ss	25. Juan Carlos Sulbaran, rhp
11. Billy Hamilton, ss	26. Josh Fellhauer, of
12. Chris Valaika, ss/2b	27. Daniel Tuttle, rhp
13. Neftali Soto, 3b	28. Cody Puckett, 2b/ss
14. Logan Ondrusek, rhp	29. Byron Wiley, of
15. Mariekson Gregorius, ss	30. Devin Mesoraco, c

Janish headed into the offseason as the favorite to be the team's 2010 shortstop because of his steady glove. The most important development was the apparent breakthrough of Homer Bailey. He went 4-1, 2.08 over his final seven big league starts to secure a spot in the Reds' 2010 rotation.

With Bruce, Stubbs and Joey Votto forming the core of the lineup, and Bailey and Johnny Cueto headlining the pitching staff, Cincinnati has a good nucleus to build around. But with an owner and a fan base itching to move past a decade of losing and a surplus of prospects at already-occupied positions, the Reds may not have much patience.

General Manager: Walt Jocketty. **Farm Director:** Terry Reynolds. **Scouting Director:** Chris Buckley.

Class	Team	League	W	L	PCT	Finish*	Manager(s)
Majors	Cincinnati Reds	National	78	84	.481	10th (16)	Dusty Baker
Triple-A	Louisville Bats	International	84	58	.592	1st (14)	Rick Sweet
Double-A	Carolina Mudcats	Southern	65	74	.468	t-6th (10)	David Bell
High A	#Sarasota Reds	Florida State	54	83	.394	12th (12)	Joe Ayrault
Low A	Dayton Dragons	Midwest	59	80	.424	11th (14)	Todd Benzinger
Rookie	Billings Mustangs	Pioneer	24	52	.316	8th (8)	Julio Garcia
Rookie	#GCL Reds	Gulf Coast	28	27	.509	8th (16)	Pat Kelly
Overall 2009 Minor League Record			314	374	.456	27th (30)	

*Finish in overall standings (No. of teams in league). †League champion.
#High Class A affiliate will be in Lynchburg (Carolina) in 2010. Rookie affiliate will be in Arizona League in 2010.

LAST YEAR'S TOP 30

Player,	Pos.	Status
1.	Yonder Alonso, 1b	No. 2
2.	Todd Frazier, ss/3b/1b	No. 1
3.	Drew Stubbs, of	Majors
4.	Chris Valaika, ss	No. 12
5.	Yorman Rodriguez, of	No. 6
6.	Kyle Lotzkar, rhp	No. 20
7.	Neftali Soto, 3b	No. 13
8.	Juan Francisco, 3b	No. 5
9.	Juan Duran, of	No. 18
10.	Devin Mesoraco, c	No. 30
11.	Daryl Thompson, rhp	Dropped out
12.	Chris Dickerson, of	Majors
13.	Jordan Smith, rhp	No. 16
14.	Josh Roenicke, rhp	(Blue Jays)
15.	Zach Stewart, rhp	(Blue Jays)
16.	Ryan Hanigan, c	Majors
17.	Ramon Ramirez, rhp	(Red Sox)
18.	Matt Maloney, lhp	No. 8
19.	Zack Cozart, ss	No. 10
20.	Juan Carlos Sulbaran, rhp	No. 25
21.	Dallas Buck, rhp	Dropped out
22.	Chris Heisey, of	No. 4
23.	Danny Dorn, of	Dropped out
24.	Carlos Fisher, rhp	Majors
25.	Pedro Viola, lhp	No. 22
26.	Sean Watson, rhp	Dropped out
27.	Robert Manuel, rhp	(Red Sox)
28.	Craig Tatum, c	(Orioles)
29.	Adam Rosales, inf	Majors
30.	Alex Buchholz, 2b	Dropped out

BEST TOOLS

Best Hitter for Average	Yonder Alonso
Best Power Hitter	Juan Francisco
Best Strike-Zone Discipline	Yonder Alonso
Fastest Baserunner	Theodis Bowe
Best Athlete	Yorman Rodriguez
Best Fastball	Brad Boxberger
Best Curveball	Mike Leake
Best Slider	Mark Serrano
Best Changeup	Travis Wood
Best Control	Matt Maloney
Best Defensive Catcher	Chris McMurray
Best Defensive Infielder	Miguel Rojas
Best Infield Arm	Juan Francisco
Best Defensive Outfielder	David Sappelt
Best Outfield Arm	Yorman Rodriguez

PROJECTED 2013 LINEUP

Catcher	Ryan Hanigan
First Base	Yonder Alonso
Second Base	Brandon Phillips
Third Base	Todd Frazier
Shortstop	Zack Cozart
Left Field	Joey Votto
Center Field	Drew Stubbs
Right Field	Jay Bruce
No. 1 Starter	Johnny Cueto
No. 2 Starter	Homer Bailey
No. 3 Starter	Mike Leake
No. 4 Starter	Aaron Harang
No. 5 Starter	Bronson Arroyo
Closer	Brad Boxberger

TOP PROSPECTS OF THE DECADE

Year	Player, Pos.	2009 Org.
2000	Gookie Dawkins, ss	Marlins
2001	Austin Kearns, of	Nationals
2002	Austin Kearns, of	Nationals
2003	Chris Gruler, rhp	Out of baseball
2004	Ryan Wagner, rhp	Nationals
2005	Homer Bailey, rhp	Reds
2006	Homer Bailey, rhp	Reds
2007	Homer Bailey, rhp	Reds
2008	Jay Bruce, of	Reds
2009	Yonder Alonso, 1b	Reds

TOP DRAFT PICKS OF THE DECADE

Year	Player, Pos.	2009 Org.
2000	David Espinosa, ss	Mariners
2001	*Jeremy Sowers, lhp	Indians
2002	Chris Gruler, rhp	Out of baseball!
2003	Ryan Wagner, rhp	Nationals
2004	Homer Bailey, rhp	Reds
2005	Jay Bruce, of	Reds
2006	Drew Stubbs, of	Reds
2007	Devin Mesoraco, c	Reds
2008	Yonder Alonso, 1b	Reds
2009	Mike Leake, rhp	Reds

*Did not sign.

LARGEST BONUSES IN CLUB HISTORY

Chris Gruler, 2002	$2,500,000
Yorman Rodriguez, 2008	$2,500,000
Homer Bailey, 2004	$2,300,000
Mike Leake, 2009	$2,270,000
Drew Stubbs, 2006	$2,000,000
Juan Duran, 2008	$2,000,000
Yonder Alonso, 2008	$2,000,000

CINCINNATI REDS

TOP 2010 ROOKIE: Matt Maloney, lhp. His September performance gave him the inside track on the Reds' No. 5 starter job.

BREAKOUT PROSPECT: Billy Hamilton, ss. The Reds and Hamilton have to decide whether it's in his long-term interest to switch-hit, but he has the bat and speed to wreak havoc.

SLEEPER: Jamie Walczak, rhp. He hit .357 as an outfielder at NCAA Division II Mercyhurst (Pa.) last spring, but his future is on the mound, where he has a 92-94 mph fastball with a solid curveball.

SOURCE OF TOP 30 TALENT			
Homegrown	29	Acquired	1
College	12	Trades	1
Junior college	2	Rule 5 draft	0
High school	8	Independent leagues	0
Draft-and-follow	7	Free agents/waivers	0
Nondrafted free agents	0		
International	0		

Numbers in parentheses indicate prospect rankings

LF
Byron Wiley (29)
Danny Dorn
Alex Oliveras
Josh Garton

CF
Yorman Rodriguez (6)
Josh Fellhauer (26)
Junior Arias
Sean Henry
Dayne Read
David Sappelt
Andrew Means
Justin Reed
Juan Silva

RF
Chris Heisey (4)
Juan Duran (18)
Denis Phipps

3B
Todd Frazier (1)
Neftali Soto (13)

SS
Zack Cozart (10)
Billy Hamilton (11)
Mariekson Gregorius (15)
Miguel Rojas (17)
Huberto Valor

2B
Chris Valaika (12)
Cody Puckett (28)
Alex Buchholz

1B
Yonder Alonso (2)
Juan Francisco (5)
Dave Stewart
Logan Parker

C
Devin Mesoraco (30)
Kevin Coddington
Mark Fleury
Tucker Barnhart

RHP

Starters	Relievers
Mike Leake (3)	Logan Ondrusek (14)
Brad Boxberger (9)	Enerio del Rosario (19)
Jordan Smith (16)	Mark Serrano (24)
Kyle Lotzkar (20)	Daryl Thompson
Juan Carlos Sulbaran (25)	Derrik Lutz
Daniel Tuttle (27)	Brian Pearl
Matt Klinker	Ezequiel Infante
Sam Lecure	Daniel Corcino
Josh Ravin	Ramon Geronimo
Curtis Partch	Justin Freeman
Dallas Buck	Sean Watson
Tyler Cline	
Jacob Johnson	
Lance Janke	

LHP

Starters	Relievers
Travis Wood (7)	Donnie Joseph (21)
Matt Maloney (8)	Pedro Viola (22)
Matt Fairel	Philippe Valiquette (23)
Jeremy Horst	Alexander Smit
	Lee Tabor
	Joseph Krebs
	Aguido Gonzalez
	Mace Thurman

2009   BONUSES: $5.9 MILLION

BEST PURE HITTER: While several of the Reds' top draft choices struggled with the bat in their pro debuts, OF Josh Fellhauer (7) went directly to low Class A and hit .280/.351/.453. Fellhauer doesn't have a standout tool, but he does a little of everything and doesn't have a glaring weakness.

BEST POWER HITTER: 1B Dave Stewart (22) has a lot of strength and leverage in his 6-foot-5, 230-pound frame, though a wrist injury short-circuited his pro debut. OF Josh Garton (12) puts on a show in batting practice.

FASTEST RUNNER: SS Billy Hamilton (2) can get from the right side of the plate to first base in less than 4.0 seconds, and he covers 60 yards in 6.3 seconds.

BEST DEFENSIVE PLAYER: Hamilton covers a lot of ground and has a well above-average arm. He also led Rookie-level Gulf Coast League shortstops with a .955 fielding percentage.

BEST FASTBALL: RHPs Brad Boxberger (1s) and Daniel Tuttle (5) can pitch at 94-96 mph in short spurts, though the Reds aren't ruling out using Boxberger as a starter. RHP Mike Leake (1) doesn't have that kind of velocity, but his ability to sink, cut and command his 88-92 mph fastball make it play up.

BEST SECONDARY PITCH: Oral Roberts coach Rob Walton is noted for his ability to teach his pitchers a slider, and RHP Mark Serrano (6) is his latest star pupil. LHP Donnie Joseph (3) also has a nice slider, while Leake baffles hitters with his changeup.

BEST PRO DEBUT: Serrano went 3-1, 2.11 with 65 strikeouts in 55 innings, mostly at low Class A Dayton, where Fellhauer also performed well. RHP Brian Pearl (9) tied for the Rookie-level Pioneer League lead with eight saves, and he fanned 43 in 29 innings.

BEST ATHLETE: Hamilton had a football scholarship to play wide receiver for Mississippi State. Puerto Rican OF Juan Silva (8) has good all-around tools. RHP Jason Braun (29) played three seasons of basketball at Corban (Ore.) before committing to baseball full-time.

MOST INTRIGUING BACKGROUND: Boxberger's father Rod was the College World Series MVP and an Astros first-round pick in 1978. SS Deven Marrero (17) brother Chris was a Nationals first-rounder in 2006. Unsigned 2B Matt Valaika's (20) brother Chris is a prospect in the Reds system.

CLOSEST TO THE MAJORS: Leake is so polished that he should be the first player from this draft to reach Cincinnati, even if Boxberger and Joseph move quickly as relievers. Serrano is already 24, so the Reds will push him.

BEST LATE-ROUND PICK: OF Dayne Read (37) has drawn comparisons to Ryan Freel because he has plus speed, some pop and versatility.

THE ONE WHO GOT AWAY: A smooth defender, Marrero drew some draft interest late in the first round. He made good on his commitment to attend Arizona State.

ASSESSMENT: Finances played a part in the decision to draft Leake eighth overall, but he should bolster the Reds' rotation in short order. If Hamilton gets his bat going, he could be a dynamic leadoff man and shortstop.

2008   BONUSES: $4.8 MILLION

1B Yonder Alonso (1) could ascend to the majors in 2010 if he hits lefthanders, though the Reds still have to figure out how to get him and Joey Votto into the same lineup. RHP Zach Stewart (3) rates as the Blue Jays' No. 1 prospect after getting included in the Scott Rolen trade.

GRADE: B+

2007   BONUSES: $4.9 MILLION

OF/2B/1B Todd Frazier (1s) may not have a set position, but he is Cincinnati's top prospect. C Devin Mesoraco (1) has been a disappointment, and RHP Kyle Lotzkar (1s) and 3B Neftali Soto (3) took steps back in 2009, but SS Zack Cozart (2) is on the verge of a big league job.

GRADE: B

2006   BONUSES: $4.8 MILLION

With eight homers in 42 big league games, OF Drew Stubbs (1) showed more power than he had in the minors. RHP Josh Roenicke (10) and OF Chris Heisey (17) were two late-round steals, though Roenicke went to Toronto in the Rolen deal.

GRADE: C+

2005   BONUSES: $3.8 MILLION*

OF Jay Bruce (1) has hit 43 big league homers before his 23rd birthday. RHPs Jeff Stevens (6, since traded) and Carlos Fisher (11) and INF Adam Rosales (12) all have played in the majors, while LHP Travis Wood (2) and RHP Logan Ondrusek (13) improved significantly last season.

GRADE: B+

*Draft analysis by Jim Callis. Numbers in parentheses indicate draft rounds. *Bonuses for 2005 are first 10 rounds only.*

TODD FRAZIER, OF/2B/3B

Born: Feb. 12, 1986.
Height: 6-3. **Weight:** 215.
Bats: R. **Throws:** R.
Drafted: Rutgers, 2007 (1st round supplemental).
Signed by: Lee Seras.

Frazier first stood out on the diamond when he starred for 1998 Little League World Series champion Toms River (N.J.), going 4-for-4 with a homer in the championship game. He was the third brother in his family to play pro ball, following Charlie (a former outfielder in the Marlins system) and Jeff (a Triple-A outfielder for the Tigers last season). After he set records for single-season (22) and career (47) home runs at Rutgers, the Reds drafted him 34th overall in 2007 and signed him for $875,000. As a pro, Frazier has played all four infield spots as well as left field. In 2009, he impressed the big league coaching staff in spring training, leading to a decision to make him an everyday left fielder and shore up a position that appeared thin in Cincinnati. The emergence of Chris Dickerson and Johnny Gomes eased those concerns, so Frazier moved to second base full-time at the end of July. David Bell, his manager at Double-A Carolina, said Frazier was more advanced than Bell's former teammate Jeff Kent was at the same point in his transition to second base.

Frazier's excellent strength and line-drive stroke combine to produce bushels of doubles, and he tied for third in the minors with 45 last season. Though he has a pronounced arm bar in his swing, he has had no problems hitting inside pitches because he's strong and his hands work well. His ability to make adjustments should allow him to hit for average with solid-average power in the major leagues. Frazier has average arm strength that plays up both in the infield and outfield thanks to his quick release and accuracy. He positions himself well and has a knack for reading balls off the bat. His speed and range are average. The Reds have been willing to move him around because he has excellent makeup and is receptive to coaching.

Because he has changed positions so often, Frazier is a jack of all trades but a master of none. He doesn't have the range to be an everyday shortstop, though he makes plays on the balls he gets to. He's raw at second base, with problems turning double plays and playing around the bag. His doubles power doesn't fit the offensive profile for first base. His best position and destiny may be third base, but he has played just 18 games at the hot corner in his career, and just four in 2009 largely because he's been paired almost everywhere with third baseman Juan Francisco. The Reds believe he'll eventually be a solid defender wherever he winds up, but scouts from other clubs are reserving judgment.

The Reds sent Frazier to Puerto Rico for winter ball to continue his development as a second baseman. If he shows he can be even adequate defensively, his bat would make him a valuable regular there. He may be a better fit at third base, where he projects as a solid hitter and defender. With Scott Rolen's contract expiring after 2010 and Brandon Phillips locked up through 2011, Frazier's initial big league opportunity would seem to more likely come at third base or left field. He'll head to Triple-A Louisville in 2010 for some final polish.

Year	Club (League)	Class	AVG	G	AB	R	H	2B	3B	HR	RBI	BB	SO	SB	OBP	SLG
2007	Billings (PIO)	R	.319	41	160	29	51	6	5	5	25	18	22	3	.409	.513
	Dayton (MWL)	LoA	.318	6	22	4	7	3	0	2	5	2	4	0	.375	.727
2008	Dayton (MWL)	LoA	.321	30	112	25	36	10	0	7	20	15	28	4	.402	.598
	Sarasota (FSL)	HiA	.281	100	366	62	103	20	3	12	54	41	84	8	.357	.451
2009	Carolina (SL)	AA	.290	119	451	59	131	40	2	14	68	42	67	7	.350	.481
	Louisville (IL)	AAA	.302	16	63	9	19	5	0	2	9	6	12	2	.362	.476
MINOR LEAGUE TOTALS			.296	312	1174	188	347	84	10	42	181	124	217	24	.367	.491

2 YONDER ALONSO, 1B Busch

NIKOLAUS JOHNSON — CAROLINA MUDCATS

BORN: April 8, 1987. **B-T:** L-R. **HT.:** 6-2. **WT.:** 215. **DRAFTED:** Miami, 2008 (1st round). **SIGNED BY:** Tony Arias.

With the No. 7 overall pick in the 2008 draft, the Reds narrowed their choices to Alonso and Gordon Beckham. They chose Alonso in part because they considered him easier to sign, then watched Beckham sign more quickly for less money. While Beckham reached the big leagues in 2009, Alonso was slowed by a broken hamate bone. Alonso is the purest hitter in the system and has above-average power. He has a good understanding of the strike zone, working counts in his favor to get a pitch he wants. He has a balanced swing that allows him to drive the ball to all fields. Alonso has struggled to hit lefthanders in college and pro ball. Some scouts think he should be more aggressive, as he sometimes lays off pitches he could drive. His well-below-average speed (35 on the 20-80 scouting scale) limits him to first base. Cincinnati has toyed with playing him at third base, but his limited range would be a liability. The hamate injury sapped Alonso's power and slowed down his timetable, postponing a difficult decision. He plays the same position as Joey Votto, the Reds' best big league hitter, and Cincinnati will either have to move Votto to left field or trade one of them. Alonso likely will spend all or most of 2010 in the minors, but his bat could hasten his path.

Year	Club (League)	Class	AVG	G	AB	R	H	2B	3B	HR	RBI	BB	SO	SB	OBP	SLG
2008	Sarasota (FSL)	HiA	.316	6	19	1	6	1	0	0	2	5	5	0	.440	.368
2009	Reds (GCL)	R	.133	6	15	0	2	0	0	0	0	3	1	0	.278	.133
	Sarasota (FSL)	HiA	.303	49	175	21	53	13	0	7	38	24	30	0	.383	.497
	Carolina (SL)	AA	.295	29	105	12	31	11	0	2	14	14	15	1	.372	.457
MINOR LEAGUE TOTALS			.293	90	314	34	92	25	0	9	54	46	51	1	.378	.459

3 MIKE LEAKE, RHP Sand

BORN: Nov. 12, 1987. **B-T:** R-R. **HT.:** 6-1. **WT.:** 190. **DRAFTED:** Arizona State, 2009 (1st round). **SIGNED BY:** Clark Crist.

Leake didn't receive the hype of No. 1 overall pick Stephen Strasburg, but he was just as dominant during the spring, going 16-1, 1.71 at Arizona State. Sun Devils coach Pat Murphy said Leake could have been the team's best defensive third baseman or shortstop. The eighth overall pick in June, Leake signed at the Aug. 17 deadline for $2.27 million. Leake's feel for pitching and command are outstanding. He keeps hitters off balance by throwing five pitches (fastball, cutter, slider, curveball and changeup) for strikes. He can run his fastball up to 94 mph, but it's more effective when he pitches at 88-92 with better run and sink. His changeup is deceptive, and his curve and slider are two distinct breaking pitches that play well off each other. He fields his position like an extra infielder on the mound. At 6-foot-1 and with a mostly average fastball, Leake has little margin for error and a lower ceiling than his college dominance might indicate. Few pitchers can master a five-pitch arsenal, so it's possible he'll have to drop an offering or two as he moves through the minors. For now, Cincinnati will let him use his full repertoire. The Reds drafted Leake in part because he fit in their budget, but also because he was one of the most advanced pitchers in the draft. He likely will begin his pro career in high Class A and could challenge for a big league spot by the end of the season.

Year	Club (League)	Class	W	L	ERA	G	GS	CG	SV	IP	H	R	ER	HR	BB	SO	AVG
2009	Did Not Play—Signed Late																

4 CHRIS HEISEY, OF Cey

NIKOLAUS JOHNSON — CAROLINA MUDCATS

BORN: Dec. 14, 1984. **B-T:** R-R. **HT.:** 6-0. **WT.:** 200. **DRAFTED:** Messiah (Pa.) 2006, (17th round). **SIGNED BY:** Jeff Brookens.

Until he tagged along with a friend to tryout camps before his junior year at Division III Messiah (Pa.), Heisey wasn't assured of a baseball career. Four years later, he was playing in the Futures Game, earning a midseason promotion to Triple-A and ranking among the minor league leaders in hits (162) and total bases (269). Heisey could be termed a "cheap five-tool player." None of his tools is overwhelming, but all of them are at least fringe-average. At the plate, he uses the entire field and makes his living driving the ball back up the middle. He shows solid bat speed and surprising power, nearly equaling his previous career total with 22 homers in 2009. He's an above-average runner with instincts that enhance his speed, and he is 53-for-58 stealing bases in the past two years. He has a slightly above-average arm and makes accurate throws. He's a plus defender on the outfield corners. In Triple-A, Heisey struggled initially when veterans spotted their breaking balls for strikes. Though he played mostly in center field last season, he's better defensively as a corner outfielder. He'll have to maintain his newfound power to be a regular on a corner. After the Reds nontendered Johnny Gomes, Heisey, who was added to the 40-man roster, could compete for a spot in a left-field platoon with Chris Dickerson.

CINCINNATI REDS

Year	Club (League)	Class	AVG	G	AB	R	H	2B	3B	HR	RBI	BB	SO	SB	OBP	SLG
2006	Billings (PIO)	R	.286	70	245	46	70	10	0	6	37	28	33	11	.362	.400
2007	Dayton (MWL)	LoA	.289	104	374	60	108	24	2	9	46	25	57	19	.350	.436
	Sarasota (FSL)	HiA	.349	12	43	6	15	1	0	1	5	4	6	3	.396	.442
2008	Sarasota (FSL)	HiA	.287	117	436	77	125	31	7	7	51	57	69	27	.381	.438
	Chattanooga (SL)	AA	.316	19	79	11	25	6	1	2	10	3	15	5	.341	.494
2009	Carolina (SL)	AA	.347	71	271	54	94	18	2	13	40	34	34	13	.426	.572
	Louisville (IL)	AAA	.278	63	245	37	68	17	1	9	37	14	43	8	.323	.465
MINOR LEAGUE TOTALS			.298	456	1693	291	505	107	13	47	226	165	257	86	.369	.460

5 JUAN FRANCISCO, 3B $\mathcal{B}osch$

BORN: June 24, 1987. **B-T:** L-R. **HT.:** 6-2. **WT.:** 210. **SIGNED:** Dominican Republic, 2004. **SIGNED BY:** Juan Peralta.

Francisco gave the big league team a taste of his prodigious power in its preseason exhibition, crushing a Francisco Cordero fastball and clearing the visitor's clubhouse that sits beyond right field at Carolina's ballpark. Francisco has led the Reds system in home runs in each of the past two seasons. Francisco has plenty of strength and his hands work well at the plate. He can turn on most any fastball and his long arms not only generate excellent leverage, but they also let him reach pitches outside of the zone. He also has one of the strongest arms in the organization and has more athleticism than is readily apparent. Francisco still strikes out too much, though he has made more consistent contact the last two years. He has problems recognizing changeups and almost refuses to be walked. He showed improvement in his range at third base, but it's still below-average, as are his hands and speed. Francisco's best position may be first base, but that position is blocked by Joey Votto and Yonder Alonso. Third base currently belongs to Scott Rolen, so Francisco will spend 2010 in Triple-A, and he may see more time in left field.

Year	Club (League)	Class	AVG	G	AB	R	H	2B	3B	HR	RBI	BB	SO	SB	OBP	SLG
2005	Reds (DSL)	R	.228	49	158	7	36	10	1	4	10	14	26	2	.293	.380
2006	Reds (GCL)	R	.280	45	182	24	51	14	0	3	30	6	35	2	.305	.407
	Billings (PIO)	R	.333	9	36	6	12	3	0	0	2	0	8	2	.333	.417
2007	Dayton (MWL)	LoA	.268	135	534	69	143	21	4	25	90	23	161	12	.301	.463
2008	Sarasota (FSL)	HiA	.277	127	516	71	143	34	5	23	92	19	123	1	.303	.496
2009	Carolina (SL)	AA	.281	109	437	64	123	26	2	22	74	20	91	6	.317	.501
	Louisville (IL)	AAA	.359	22	92	17	33	5	1	5	19	4	24	0	.384	.598
	Cincinnati (NL)	MAJ	.429	14	21	4	9	1	0	1	7	3	7	0	.520	.619
MAJOR LEAGUE TOTALS			.429	14	21	4	9	1	0	1	7	3	7	0	.520	.619
MINOR LEAGUE TOTALS			.277	496	1955	258	541	113	13	82	317	86	468	25	.309	.474

6 YORMAN RODRIGUEZ, OF +

BORN: Aug. 15, 1992. **B-T:** R-R. **HT.:** 6-3. **WT.:** 175. **SIGNED:** Venezuela, 2008. **SIGNED BY:** Tony Arias.

The Reds made their biggest splash in Latin America in years when they signed Rodriguez for a Venezuela-record $2.5 million in 2008. Though the plan was to let him make his debut in the Rookie-level Gulf Coast League, Cincinnati felt comfortable promoting him when injuries left a void at Rookie-level Billings. Rodriguez is the system's best athlete. His arm and speed are plus tools, and he has excellent range and instincts in center field. He has the bat speed and frame to eventually hit for power. Because he's young and inexperienced, Rodriguez is raw in all phases of the game. At this point, there isn't a fastball, breaking ball or bowling ball that Rodriguez won't swing at. He struggles with pitch recognition and is often caught trying to pull pitches he should hit the other way. Though he's fast, his big swing slows him down coming out of the batter's box, so he doesn't get many infield hits. He must learn how to read pitchers to become a better basestealer. He needs to get a lot stronger, and there's room for another 50 pounds on his frame. Rodriguez will play most of the 2010 season at 17, so another year at Billings isn't out of the question. His ceiling is the highest among Reds farmhands, but he's a long way from fulfilling it.

Year	Club (League)	Class	AVG	G	AB	R	H	2B	3B	HR	RBI	BB	SO	SB	OBP	SLG
2009	Reds (GCL)	R	.274	22	84	9	23	2	1	0	2	10	23	5	.347	.321
	Billings (PIO)	R	.219	46	183	21	40	10	2	3	17	9	61	5	.259	.344
MINOR LEAGUE TOTALS			.236	68	267	30	63	12	3	3	19	19	84	10	.288	.33

7 TRAVIS WOOD, LHP

NIKOLAUS JOHNSON — CAROLINA MUDCATS

BORN: Feb. 6, 1987. **B-T:** L-L. **HT.:** 6-0. **WT.:** 165. **DRAFTED:** HS—Alexander, Ark., 2005 (2nd round). **SIGNED BY:** Mike Keenan.

Wood lost some of his luster as he battled shoulder problems and lost velocity. After posting a 7.09 ERA in the Double-A Southern League in 2008, he returned last season to win the circuit's ERA title (1.21) and pitcher of the year award. Wood's dramatic turnaround resulted from improved health and his mastery of a cutter. His fastball regained its previous 88-91 mph velocity, making it easier to set up his plus-plus changeup with fade. Righthanders used to crowd the plate and look for pitches on the outer half, but Wood now can bust them inside with his cutter. He also improved his command this season, which is necessary for a pitcher with average stuff. When the Reds signed Wood, he ran his fastball up to 94 mph at times, but he has struggled to gain weight and strength to maintain anywhere close to that velocity. Partly because of his thin frame, he has had durability problems. Scouts still wonder if he'll be more than a No. 5 starter because of his fringy velocity and his lack of a second plus pitch. His curveball is mediocre, so he doesn't project as a lefty specialist. Wood will go into spring training with a chance to make Cincinnati's rotation. The Reds don't have an established lefty starter (though he'll be battling fellow prospect Matt Maloney), which helps his chances.

Year	Club (League)	Class	W	L	ERA	G	GS	CG	SV	IP	H	R	ER	HR	BB	SO	AVG
2005	Reds (GCL)	R	0	0	0.75	8	7	0	0	24	13	3	2	0	7	45	.157
	Billings (PIO)	R	2	0	1.82	6	4	0	0	25	15	6	5	0	13	22	.174
2006	Dayton (MWL)	LoA	10	5	3.66	27	27	0	0	140	108	65	57	14	56	133	.215
2007	Sarasota (FSL)	HiA	3	2	4.86	12	12	0	0	46	49	33	25	6	27	54	.268
2008	Sarasota (FSL)	HiA	3	4	2.70	9	9	0	0	47	39	18	14	2	21	41	.222
	Chattanooga (SL)	AA	4	9	7.09	17	17	0	0	80	91	67	63	9	48	58	.289
2009	Carolina (SL)	AA	9	3	1.21	19	19	1	0	119	78	23	16	2	37	103	.189
	Louisville (IL)	AAA	4	2	3.14	8	8	0	0	49	43	17	17	4	16	32	.240
MINOR LEAGUE TOTALS			35	25	3.38	106	103	1	0	529	436	232	199	37	225	488	.225

8 MATT MALONEY, LHP

BORN: Jan. 16, 1984. **B-T:** L-L. **HT.:** 6-4. **WT.:** 220. **DRAFTED:** Mississippi, 2005 (3rd round). **SIGNED BY:** Mike Stauffer (Phillies).

A shoulder impingement in high school threatened Maloney's career. He ended up at Mississippi and blossomed into a third-round pick in 2005. Traded by the Phillies for Kyle Lohse in mid-2007, Maloney made his big league debut last June and earned his two major league victories in September. Though Maloney has piled up strikeouts throughout his career, he's not a power pitcher. He gets outs by locating and mixing his pitches: an 86-89 mph fastball that touches 91, a slow curveball, a slider and a changeup. Like several other Reds farmhands, he added a cut fastball in 2009. The cutter helped him reduce his ERA by 1.60 in his second full season in Triple-A. Lacking average velocity and a swing-and-miss pitch, Maloney has a slim margin for error. He threw strikes in the big leagues but saw that he can be hit hard when his command isn't there, giving up nine homers in 41 innings. Maloney will head into spring training as a candidate for the back of the Reds' rotation. His ceiling isn't much higher than that, but his 50 Triple-A starts make him a relatively finished product and give him an edge over Travis Wood for 2010.

Year	Club (League)	Class	W	L	ERA	G	GS	CG	SV	IP	H	R	ER	HR	BB	SO	AVG
2005	Batavia (NYP)	SS	2	1	3.89	8	8	0	0	37	38	20	16	2	15	36	.277
2006	Lakewood (SAL)	LoA	16	9	2.03	27	27	2	0	169	120	54	38	5	73	180	.194
2007	Reading (EL)	AA	9	7	3.94	21	21	1	0	126	117	70	55	13	45	115	.246
	Chattanooga (SL)	AA	2	2	2.57	4	4	0	0	28	17	9	8	4	3	39	.175
	Louisville (IL)	AAA	2	1	3.18	3	3	0	0	17	10	6	6	2	6	23	.169
2008	Reds (GCL)	R	1	0	0.00	1	0	0	0	6	1	0	0	0	0	9	.056
	Louisville (IL)	AAA	11	5	4.68	25	25	2	0	140	143	75	73	18	39	132	.264
2009	Louisville (IL)	AAA	9	9	3.08	22	22	3	0	143	143	56	49	11	24	125	.262
	Carolina (SL)	AA	0	0	1.29	1	1	0	0	7	3	1	1	1	2	5	.136
	Cincinnati (NL)	MAJ	2	4	4.87	7	7	0	0	41	43	22	22	9	8	28	.281
MAJOR LEAGUE TOTALS			2	4	4.87	7	7	0	0	41	43	22	22	9	8	28	.281
MINOR LEAGUE TOTALS			52	34	3.29	112	111	8	0	672	592	291	246	56	207	664	.235

9 BRAD BOXBERGER, RHP

BORN: May 27, 1988. **B-T:** R-R. **HT.:** 6-2. **WT.:** 200. **DRAFTED:** Southern California, 2009 (1st round supplemental). **SIGNED BY:** Rex de la Nuez.

Boxberger followed in his father Rod's footsteps by pitching at Southern California, for whom his dad was the College World Series MVP in 1978. He nearly emulated his dad as a first-round pick as well, going 43rd overall in the 2009 draft and signing at the Aug. 17 deadline for $857,000. Boxberger has the best fastball in the system. He sat at 91-93 mph as a starter and worked at 94-96 mph as a reliever in college. He has the makings of four pitches, with his slightly above-average slider his second-best offering. He also throws a spike curveball and is developing feel for a changeup. There's a lot of debate in scouting circles whether Boxberger profiles better in the rotation or bullpen. Like they did with since-traded Zach Stewart, the Reds will give him a chance to succeed as a starter. In that role, his velocity sometimes dips to 88-91 mph in later innings and he tends to battle his command. He hasn't proven yet that he can command his curve well enough to make pro hitters take it seriously. If Boxberger moved to the pen, his fastball would pave the way for a quick trip to the big leagues. After getting his feet wet in the Arizona Fall League, Boxberger is polished enough to begin 2010 in high Class A.

Year	Club (League)	Class	W	L	ERA	G	GS	CG	SV	IP	H	R	ER	HR	BB	SO	AVG
2009	Did Not Play—Signed Late																

10 ZACK COZART, SS

BORN: Aug. 12, 1985. **B-T:** R-R. **HT.:** 6-1. **WT.:** 185. **DRAFTED:** Mississippi, 2007 (2nd round). **SIGNED BY:** Jerry Flowers.

Like Todd Frazier, Cozart was an All-America shortstop in college and a member of the 2006 USA Baseball collegiate national team. Questions about his bat dropped Cozart to the second round of the 2007 draft, but he has eased those concerns by showing more pop than expected and improving his plate discipline. Cozart's defense remains his biggest asset. He has a quick first step, plus range, soft hands and average arm strength. He has worked hard to modify the all-or-nothing swing he had in college, and now uses the whole field and manages the strike zone better. His power should be close to average and is better than that of most shortstops. He's an average runner with the instincts to steal 15 bases annually in the majors. Despite his average arm and a quick release, Cozart doesn't get enough on his throws to make many highlight plays from deep in the hole. While he has improved his offensive profile, he's a career .265 hitter in pro ball and may never hit for a high average. Cincinnati needs a shortstop for 2010, but Cozart isn't refined enough at the plate to skip Triple-A and take the job. He's more likely to start the year at Louisville and could push for a midseason callup.

Year	Club (League)	Class	AVG	G	AB	R	H	2B	3B	HR	RBI	BB	SO	SB	OBP	SLG
2007	Dayton (MWL)	LoA	.239	53	184	28	44	7	2	2	18	11	36	3	.288	.332
2008	Dayton (MWL)	LoA	.280	109	418	57	117	20	6	14	49	24	77	3	.330	.457
2009	Carolina (SL)	AA	.262	131	462	72	121	29	2	10	59	63	87	10	.360	.398
MINOR LEAGUE TOTALS			.265	293	1064	157	282	56	10	26	126	98	200	16	.336	.410

11 BILLY HAMILTON, SS

BORN: Sept. 9, 1990. **B-T:** B-R. **HT.:** 6-1. **WT.:** 160. **DRAFTED:** HS—Taylorsville, Miss., 2009 (2nd round). **SIGNED BY:** Tyler Jennings.

Four years ago, the Reds drafted raw but athletic outfielder Justin Reed out of Jackson, Miss., and convinced him to give up a Mississippi football scholarship to sign as a fourth-round pick. That hasn't worked out so well, as Reed hasn't made it out of Class A. Cincinnati believes Hamilton will outdo Reed's career track after convincing the raw but athletic shortstop to turn down a Mississippi State football scholarship in exchange for a $623,600 bonus as a second-round pick last June. One of the fastest players in a system with several speedsters, he can get to first base in less than 4.0 seconds from the right side of the plate. He has the instincts to take extra bases and accumulate a lot of steals. Hamilton alleviated concerns about whether he could stick at shortstop by showing above-average range and a strong arm as a pro, though he needs to refine his footwork. Hamilton struggled at the plate in his debut, in part because he's trying to learn to switch-hit to take full advantage of his speed. His stroke from the left side shows some promise—it's not just a slap-and-dash swing—but he shows more balance and power from his natural right side. He has enough speed to get infield hits from the right side of the plate, so his decision to switch-hit isn't set in stone yet. Like many raw teenagers, he needs to learn to work counts and lay off breaking balls out of the zone. Hamilton is a long way from the big leagues, but he profiles as a top-of-the-order shortstop. Considering how raw he is, he'll likely begin 2010 in extended spring before heading to Billings.

Year	Club (League)	Class	AVG	G	AB	R	H	2B	3B	HR	RBI	BB	SO	SB	OBP	SLG
2009	Reds (GCL)	R	.205	43	166	19	34	6	3	0	11	11	47	14	.253	.277
MINOR LEAGUE TOTALS			.205	43	166	19	34	6	3	0	11	11	47	14	.253	.277

12 CHRIS VALAIKA, SS/2B

BORN: Aug. 14, 1985. **B-T:** R-R. **HT.:** 6-0. **WT.:** 215. **DRAFTED:** UC Santa Barbara, 2006 (3rd round). **SIGNED BY:** Rex de la Nuez.

Until last season, Valaika's trip through the minor leagues could not have been smoother. He was MVP of the Rookie-level Pioneer League in his 2006 debut and hit .306 over his first three pro seasons. But 2009 quickly tested Valaika more than he'd ever been tested as a pro. He hit .161 in his first 23 games and his frustration got the better of him. He punched a water cooler, breaking his right hand and leading to a five-week stint on the disabled list. Thanks to the ill-timed punch, Valaika didn't get his batting average above the Mendoza line until July, and he never really got going. The offensive struggles baffled the Reds, who believe that his bat speed and uncomplicated swing should allow him to hit for a solid average with average power. Valaika has always been on the edge of being too aggressive at the plate—he'll chase fastballs up and out of the zone—but 2009 was the first time that it caught up to him. He'll need to show that he can work counts to get better pitches in his second try at Triple-A this season. The bigger questions for Valaika have been on defense, where his range is below average for shortstop, though his hands work well and he has enough arm for the position. His long-term future is still at second base, where he should profile as a bat-first player whose defense is good enough. He's an average runner. With Brandon Phillips settled at second in Cincinnati and Todd Frazier trying to learn the position as well, Valaika's best shot in the short-term with Cincinnati may be as an offensive-minded utility player.

Year	Club (League)	Class	AVG	G	AB	R	H	2B	3B	HR	RBI	BB	SO	SB	OBP	SLG
2006	Billings (PIO)	R	.324	70	275	58	89	22	4	8	60	24	61	2	.387	.520
2007	Dayton (MWL)	LoA	.307	79	300	38	92	20	3	10	56	17	72	1	.353	.493
	Sarasota (FSL)	HiA	.253	57	217	26	55	9	1	2	23	13	42	0	.310	.332
2008	Sarasota (FSL)	HiA	.363	32	135	20	49	9	0	7	31	7	28	2	.393	.585
	Chattanooga (SL)	AA	.301	97	379	58	114	19	1	11	50	28	74	7	.352	.443
2009	Louisville (IL)	AAA	.235	95	366	32	86	20	1	6	36	16	76	1	.271	.344
MINOR LEAGUE TOTALS			.290	430	1672	232	485	99	10	44	256	105	353	13	.339	.440

13 NEFTALI SOTO, 3B

BORN: Feb. 28, 1989. **B-T:** R-R. **HT.:** 6-2. **WT.:** 180. **DRAFTED:** HS—Manati, P.R., 2007 (3rd round). **SIGNED BY:** Tony Arias.

One of the Reds' most promising hitting stars in his first two pro seasons, when he batted .327/.360/.522, Soto experienced his first taste of failure in 2009. He saw his strikeout rate jump, his power production plunge and his defense suffer at high Class A Sarasota. Soto possesses excellent hand-eye coordination and plus power potential, but his swing isn't particularly fluid and Florida State League pitchers took advantage of his tendency to chase pitches out of the zone. Soto was a high school shortstop but has thickened up since signing. He was never fast and is now a well below-average runner who has lost some first-step quickness at third base. He has the arm for the hot corner, but his actions and range are below average for the position. Cincinnati tried Soto at catcher in instructional league and he showed a receptiveness to make the move and picked up some of the essentials quickly. He would profile better behind the plate, though the Reds haven't decided whether he'll move there in 2010. Soto likely will return to high Class A, this time at Cincinnati's new Lynchburg affiliate, to open the season.

Year	Club (League)	Class	AVG	G	AB	R	H	2B	3B	HR	RBI	BB	SO	SB	OBP	SLG
2007	Reds (GCL)	R	.303	40	152	18	46	7	5	2	28	11	31	2	.355	.454
2008	Billings (PIO)	R	.388	15	67	12	26	10	1	4	11	4	10	1	.423	.746
	Dayton (MWL)	LoA	.326	52	218	26	71	15	1	7	36	7	36	1	.343	.500
2009	Sarasota (FSL)	HiA	.248	131	505	53	125	21	2	11	57	23	95	1	.282	.362
MINOR LEAGUE TOTALS			.285	238	942	109	268	53	9	24	132	45	172	5	.318	.436

14 LOGAN ONDRUSEK, RHP

BORN: Feb. 13, 1985. **B-T:** R-R. **HT.:** 6-7. **WT.:** 207. **DRAFTED:** McLennan (Texas) CC, 2005 (13th round). **SIGNED BY:** Brian Wilson.

No Reds pitcher made a bigger leap in 2009 than Ondrusek, who went from being a starting pitcher fighting for a minor league roster spot to a reliever on the cusp of a big league job. Thanks to his 6-foot-7 frame, he always has seemed to be right on top of hitters, but before last season his assortment of pitches never really worked. In spring training, the Reds found that his mediocre 87-91 mph fastball as a starter became a 92-94 mph heater that touches 96 out of the bullpen. More important, he also perfected a cut fastball that quickly turned him into an entirely different pitcher. After he had struggled trying to mix his pitches in the past, Cincinnati had him focus on throwing fastballs and cutters. While his cutter has only a little late movement, it's enough to ensure plenty of weak contact. Ondrusek allowed only one home run in 72 innings and got nearly two groundouts for every fly-out. Though 2009 was the first time he spent any appreciable time above Class A, Ondrusek did enough to earn a spot on the 40-man roster. He'll head to spring training with a chance to earn a spot in Cincinnati's bullpen..

Year	Club (League)	Class	W	L	ERA	G	GS	CG	SV	IP	H	R	ER	HR	BB	SO	AVG
2005	Billings (PIO)	R	1	6	6.02	15	9	0	0	55	72	49	37	9	19	46	.314
2006	Billings (PIO)	R	0	1	27.00	1	0	0	0	1	4	3	3	0	1	3	.571
	Chattanooga (SL)	AA	0	0	0.00	1	0	0	0	4	0	0	0	0	3	7	.000
	Dayton (MWL)	LoA	4	5	3.42	27	0	0	0	53	48	24	20	2	19	47	.240
2007	Sarasota (FSL)	HiA	7	10	4.43	31	22	0	1	124	131	72	61	4	48	86	.278
2008	Louisville (IL)	AAA	0	0	0.00	1	0	0	0	1	1	0	0	0	2	1	.250
	Sarasota (FSL)	HiA	1	7	4.97	40	3	0	1	80	93	47	44	5	32	58	.284
2009	Sarasota (FSL)	HiA	2	0	0.96	13	0	0	0	19	7	4	2	0	7	12	.117
	Carolina (SL)	AA	2	1	1.65	24	0	0	7	33	21	7	6	0	12	24	.184
	Louisville (IL)	AAA	0	0	1.74	19	0	0	12	21	16	4	4	1	2	11	.219
MINOR LEAGUE TOTALS			17	30	4.08	172	34	0	21	390	393	210	177	21	145	295	.263

15 MARIEKSON GREGORIUS, SS

BORN: Feb. 18, 1990. **B-T:** L-R. **HT.:** 6-1. **WT.:** 152. **SIGNED:** Netherlands Antilles, 2007. **SIGNED BY:** Jim Stoeckel.

Gregorius comes from a baseball family. The Curacao native was born in Amsterdam because his father Didi was pitching for the Amsterdam Pirates. At the 2009 World Cup, Mariekson played for the Dutch team while his father and brother Johnny played for the Netherland Antilles. Gregorius' baseball background explains why he was able to make the big leap from extended spring training to fill in as an injury replacement in high Class A last year. Considering the teenager's limited experience, he wasn't expected to do anything more than provide some solid defense. But Gregorius held his own, recovering from a 5-for-30 (.167) start to hit .317 over his final 13 games. He carried that success over to the Pioneer League, where his average never dipped below .309. Gregorius shows solid athleticism and good actions in the field as well as a feel for the little game. He's a solid bunter who uses his plus speed to his advantage, though he has to learn how to read pitchers to steal bases. He has very little power at this point, though he has room to add some strength on his frame. Gregorius has one of the best arms in the system, a cannon that ranks as a 65-70 on the 20-80 scouting scale. In a system stocked with shortstops, his ceiling is matched only by Billy Hamilton, and Gregorius is better defensively. After surviving in Sarasota, he shouldn't be overwhelmed by low Class A in 2010.

Year	Club (League)	Class	AVG	G	AB	R	H	2B	3B	HR	RBI	BB	SO	SB	OBP	SLG
2008	Reds (GCL)	R	.155	31	97	6	15	0	0	0	9	10	10	2	.241	.155
2009	Sarasota (FSL)	HiA	.254	22	71	8	18	4	0	0	2	1	9	0	.274	.310
	Billings (PIO)	R	.314	50	204	28	64	10	1	1	16	12	27	6	.363	.387
MINOR LEAGUE TOTALS			.261	103	372	42	97	14	1	1	27	23	46	10	.314	.312

16 JORDAN SMITH, RHP

BORN: Feb. 4, 1986. **B-T:** R-R. **HT.:** 6-4. **WT.:** 174. **DRAFTED:** CC of Southern Nevada, 2006 (6th round). **SIGNED BY:** Jeff Morris.

Poised to make a breakthrough in 2009, Smith got off to a solid start but went down when the same knee problems that have bothered him in past years flared up again. He had surgery to clear up torn cartilage in 2008 but had further knee pain and went on the disabled list last April. He tried to return quickly, but continued discomfort led to elbow pain from his attempts to compensate for his knee, and the Reds shut him down for good in early July. When healthy, Smith throws a 92-93 mph fastball that has plenty of sink, and he backs it up with an average slider. He doesn't have a true strikeout pitch, but he succeeds by working down in the zone and generating lots of grounders. Because his changeup is fringy and he has had trouble with injuries, Smith may eventually end up as a reliever, where his fastball could play up. He returned to the mound in instructional league and should start 2010 back in Double-A.

Year	Club (League)	Class	W	L	ERA	G	GS	CG	SV	IP	H	R	ER	HR	BB	SO	AVG
2006	Billings (PIO)	R	6	3	3.01	14	14	0	0	69	58	29	23	3	20	49	.227
2007	Dayton (MWL)	LoA	10	8	3.84	26	26	0	0	134	133	74	57	8	40	96	.258
2008	Sarasota (FSL)	HiA	7	2	2.55	10	10	0	0	67	61	23	19	2	7	44	.241
	Chattanooga (SL)	AA	2	6	5.40	11	11	0	0	55	72	42	33	6	17	42	.316
2009	Carolina (SL)	AA	5	3	3.44	13	13	0	0	73	77	37	28	4	21	39	.277
MINOR LEAGUE TOTALS			30	22	3.62	74	74	0	0	398	401	205	160	23	105	270	.262

17 MIGUEL ROJAS, SS

BORN: Feb. 24, 1989. **B-T:** R-R. **HT.:** 6-0. **WT.:** 150. **SIGNED:** Venezuela, 2005. **SIGNED BY:** Luis Baez/Maximo Rombley.

When Omar Vizquel was growing up, he wanted to follow in the footsteps of Dave Concepcion. Now Rojas is part of the new generation of young Venezuelan shortstops trying to emulate Vizquel. His defense draws some comparisons to Vizquel's. Rojas' hands are the best in the organization and some of the best scouts have seen in recent years. He has excellent hand-eye coordination and the kind of fluidity that can't be taught. Rojas manages to scoop and throw in one easy motion. He makes very few errors for a young shortstop and was the easy choice for managers as the best defensive shortstop in the Midwest League last season. His arm is a tick below average but that doesn't prevent him from making plays. He's an extremely hard worker who's a leader in the field. There are questions about Rojas' bat, and he never had hit better than .231 in any of his first three pro seasons. He did show significant improvement in 2009, batting .311/.357/.361 after the all-star break. Rojas handles the bat well and makes consistent contact, but he has very little power and a slight frame. Pitchers don't fear him enough to give him many walks, and he's an average runner who isn't a big basestealing threat. If he can show any offensive ability, his glove is good enough for him to make the big leagues. He'll move up to high Class A this season.

Year	Club (League)	Class	AVG	G	AB	R	H	2B	3B	HR	RBI	BB	SO	SB	OBP	SLG
2006	Reds (VSL)	R	.178	58	157	21	28	3	0	0	8	24	28	9	.317	.197
2007	Devil Rays/Reds (VSL)	R	.228	30	101	12	23	5	0	2	9	14	11	1	.336	.337
	Reds (DSL)	R	.250	7	16	3	4	1	0	0	0	3	0	1	.368	.313
2008	Billings (PIO)	R	.183	61	208	27	38	8	1	1	21	14	35	3	.248	.245
2009	Dayton (MWL)	LoA	.273	130	469	50	128	16	3	3	49	35	44	14	.326	.339
MINOR LEAGUE TOTALS			.232	286	951	113	221	33	4	6	87	90	118	28	.310	.294

18 JUAN DURAN, OF

BORN: Sept. 2, 1991. **B-T:** R-R. **HT.:** 6-7. **WT.:** 190. **SIGNED:** Dominican Republic, 2007. **SIGNED BY:** Tony Arias.

When the Reds cleverly found a loophole that allowed them to sign Duran months before everyone else thought he was eligible in 2007, they knew they were getting a tall outfielder with a projectable frame. But they didn't expect he'd grow into an NBA forward overnight. Six-foot-3 when Cincinnati signed him for $2 million, Duran has grown four inches since then, which hasn't been good for his development. Elbow problems in 2008 were related to his growth spurt, and minor knee surgery caused him to miss extended spring training last year. He has grown seven inches overall since he was 15 and hasn't gotten accustomed to his new frame yet. Duran struggles to stay balanced in his swing, a situation that isn't helped by the pronounced leg kick he uses as a timing mechanism. His calling card is his plus raw power and he puts on a show in batting practice, though his pop wasn't apparent in game action in 2009. Making contact was a serious problem for Duran, who must develop a better base to his batting stance and learn the strike zone to translate his power potential into production. He's a below-average runner coming out of the batter's box, though he does run better once under way. Because of his height—he has the frame to pack on 50 pounds as he matures—it's questionable whether he'll be able to stick in the outfield. His above-average arm fits well in right field. Duran isn't ready to jump to full-season ball in 2010, and he won't be 19 until the end of the season, so the Reds can be patient.

Year	Club (League)	Class	AVG	G	AB	R	H	2B	3B	HR	RBI	BB	SO	SB	OBP	SLG
2008	Reds (DSL)	R	.215	41	135	15	29	3	4	1	14	24	47	8	.340	.319
2009	Reds (GCL)	R	.177	45	164	15	29	7	4	0	17	8	52	0	.218	.268
MINOR LEAGUE TOTALS			.194	86	299	30	58	10	8	1	31	32	99	8	.277	.291

19 ENERIO DEL ROSARIO, RHP

BORN: Oct. 16, 1985. **B-T:** R-R. **HT.:** 6-2. **WT.:** 185. **SIGNED:** Dominican Republic, 2005. **SIGNED BY:** Luis Baez/Maximo Rombley.

Logan Ondrusek made the biggest jump from suspect to prospect of any Reds pitcher in 2009, with del Rosario right on his heels. The Reds altered his arm slot during spring training and the results were immediate and dramatic. Like Ondrusek, del Rosario jumped from high Class A to Triple-A and was added to the 40-man roster after the season. Signed out of the Dominican Republic as a 19-year-old in 2005, he didn't even make it to the United States until 2007 and didn't pitch in a full-season league until he was 22. He was at best a roster-filler with good command of an 87-89 mph fastball. But once he started pitching from a lower arm slot last season, del Rosario was able to generate increased velocity (90-92 mph, touching 93) with newfound sink. When he's on, as he was for most of 2009, his sinker generates plenty of grounders and broken bats. He also throws a slider and a changeup, but mainly relies on his sinker. Projecting as a set-up man, del Rosario figures to open this season back in Triple-A.

CINCINNATI REDS

Year	Club (League)	Class	W	L	ERA	G	GS	CG	SV	IP	H	R	ER	HR	BB	SO	AVG
2005	Reds (DSL)	R	4	4	3.12	13	6	0	1	52	47	22	18	0	14	35	.247
2006	Reds (DSL)	R	5	5	1.78	13	13	0	0	71	51	24	14	1	15	59	.200
2007	Billings (PIO)	R	5	4	3.97	15	15	0	0	70	77	40	31	6	30	40	.288
2008	Sarasota (FSL)	HiA	1	4	6.09	13	6	0	0	44	57	31	30	2	23	32	.318
	Dayton (MWL)	LoA	5	2	1.16	19	9	1	5	70	52	19	9	3	11	49	.208
2009	Sarasota (FSL)	HiA	2	1	1.98	31	0	0	7	50	40	14	11	2	6	33	.215
	Carolina (SL)	AA	0	0	1.59	4	0	0	1	6	2	1	1	0	0	9	.105
	Louisville (IL)	AAA	1	0	1.09	15	0	0	4	25	24	6	3	1	6	12	.258
MINOR LEAGUE TOTALS			23	20	2.72	123	49	1	18	388	350	157	117	15	105	269	.243

20 KYLE LOTZKAR, RHP

BORN: Oct. 24, 1989. **B-T:** L-R. **HT.:** 6-4. **WT.:** 200. **DRAFTED:** HS—Delta, B.C., 2007 (1st round supplemental). **SIGNED BY:** Bill Byckowski.

Whenever he has been healthy, Lotzkar has been one of the best pitching prospects in the system. But those times have been few and far between. He was held back in extended spring training with a sore neck to start 2008, then suffered a stress fracture in his elbow that August. Upon his return last spring, he blew out his elbow and required Tommy John surgery in mid-May. The combination of elbow injuries will require a longer rehab time than normal, and Lotzkar likely won't return to the mound until mid-2010. However, the Reds note that Francisco Cordero went through similar problems in 1998 and returned with no ill effects. Before the injuries, Lotzkar showed the potential for three plus pitches—a 91-93 mph fastball, a power curveball and a changeup—but needed to improve his command and consistency. Because he was drafted as a 17-year-old, Lotzkar hasn't fallen too far behind. He still has the potential to be a middle-of-the-rotation starter if he can stay healthy.

Year	Club (League)	Class	W	L	ERA	G	GS	CG	SV	IP	H	R	ER	HR	BB	SO	AVG
2007	Reds (GCL)	R	0	2	3.86	7	7	0	0	21	21	10	9	2	7	24	.263
	Billings (PIO)	R	0	0	1.13	2	2	0	0	8	1	1	1	1	3	12	.040
2008	Dayton (MWL)	LoA	2	3	3.58	10	10	0	0	38	29	19	15	2	24	50	.215
2009	Did Not Play—Injured																
MINOR LEAGUE TOTALS			2	5	3.37	19	19	0	0	67	51	30	25	5	34	86	.213

21 DONNIE JOSEPH, LHP

BORN: Nov. 1, 1987. **B-T:** L-L. **HT.:** 6-3. **WT.:** 180. **DRAFTED:** Houston, 2009 (3rd round). **SIGNED BY:** Jerry Flowers.

After two middling seasons as a midweek starter for Houston, Joseph won the Cougars' closer job as a junior and turned his college career around. After posting ERAs above 5.00 in each of his first two seasons, he went 3-1, 2.16 with 11 saves and 75 strikeouts in 50 innings. That impressed the Reds enough to draft him in the third round last June and sign him for $398,000. Before 2009, Joseph had to reduce his velocity to get the ball over the plate, but he sharpened his control and was able to locate his 90-93 mph fastball where he wanted. He also has a hard-biting 82-83 mph slider that shows flashes of being a plus pitch. His command and his lack of a changeup make it unlikely that he can transition to being a starter. He profiles best as a power reliever, though he has the stuff to retire righthanders and shouldn't be pigeonholed as a lefty specialist. Joseph pitched well while reaching low Class A in his pro debut. He may advance rapidly through the minors and should open his first full season in high Class A.

Year	Club (League)	Class	W	L	ERA	G	GS	CG	SV	IP	H	R	ER	HR	BB	SO	AVG
2009	Billings (PIO)	R	2	1	0.77	8	0	0	0	12	6	6	1	0	4	11	.146
	Dayton (MWL)	LoA	2	2	4.35	16	0	0	4	21	13	10	10	0	10	31	.176
MINOR LEAGUE TOTALS			4	3	3.06	24	0	0	4	32	19	16	11	0	14	42	.165

22 PEDRO VIOLA, LHP

BORN: June 29, 1983. **B-T:** L-L. **HT.:** 6-1. **WT.:** 185. **SIGNED:** Dominican Republic, 2005. **SIGNED BY:** Luis Baez/Maximo Rombley.

Originally signed by the Giants for $20,000 as an outfielder, Viola was cut after it was discovered that he had forged his birth certificate to appear three years younger. The Reds signed him as a 22-year-old lefthander for $1,000 and he quickly displayed one of the best arms in the system. But what once looked like a coup has proven to be less of one because his scouting report has changed little in his three seasons in the United States. Viola still displays a fastball that sits at 92-94 mph and runs up to 96. But he shows little feel for pitching, and his fringy slider and changeup haven't shown much improvement. His command is extremely inconsistent. He has outings where he can hit his spots, but too often he struggles to find the strike zone. Viola has tried starting, but his lack of secondary stuff and polish make him more suited for a bullpen role. Viola had his first taste of major league action in 2009 as a September callup, but he'll need to show more than just a blazing fastball to fit into Cincinnati's long-term plans. He's 26 now, and the Reds are starting to wonder if he'll ever add more polish.

Year	Club (League)	Class	W	L	ERA	G	GS	CG	SV	IP	H	R	ER	HR	BB	SO	AVG
2006	Reds (DSL)	R	3	5	2.04	15	12	0	0	62	50	25	14	0	20	77	.214
2007	Dayton (MWL)	LoA	3	1	1.87	22	0	0	2	43	29	14	9	3	17	49	.190
	Sarasota (FSI)	HiA	0	1	0.90	10	0	0	2	20	14	2	2	0	7	28	.187
	Chattanooga (SL)	AA	0	0	0.95	14	0	0	2	19	12	3	2	2	6	17	.176
2008	Chattanooga (SL)	AA	4	7	4.48	52	7	0	2	82	88	50	41	6	36	84	.278
2009	Louisville (IL)	AAA	2	2	5.47	54	0	0	8	49	48	30	30	7	33	57	.251
	Cincinnati (NL)	MAJ	0	0	5.14	9	0	0	0	7	7	4	4	2	3	5	.269
MAJOR LEAGUE TOTALS			0	0	5.14	9	0	0	0	7	7	4	4	2	3	5	.269
MINOR LEAGUE TOTALS			12	16	3.20	167	19	0	16	276	241	124	98	18	119	312	.232

23 PHILLIPPE VALIQUETTE, LHP

BORN: Feb. 14, 1987. **B-T:** L-L. **HT.:** 6-1. **WT.:** 175. **DRAFTED:** HS—Montreal, 2004 (7th round). **SIGNED BY:** Jason Baker.

A seventh-round pick in 2004, Valiquette is the only player left from that Reds draft who's still in the organization and hasn't made it to the big leagues. His path to Double-A involved several stops and starts. Promoted to low Class A in 2005 before he was ready, he was shelled on the mound and struggled to adjust to life as a full-time baseball player. The Quebec native spoke little English when he signed, which added to his struggles. He eventually went home during the 2006 season, but decided to return to the game the following year. He has shown improved maturity and a better ability to fit in with his teammates since coming back. As with Pedro Viola, Valiquette's success always has revolved around unusual velocity for a lefty and little else. He mostly sits at 93-94 mph and touches 96 with his fastball. He has improved his slider to the point where it's usable, but it's still below average. He also has fiddled with a changeup but with little success. His control and command also leaves something to be desired. Because he was drafted as a 17-year-old, Valiquette is still relatively young. He could fill a need as a low-cost lefty out of the pen before too long, but his ceiling is relatively low because of his inability to develop a solid second pitch.

Year	Club (League)	Class	W	L	ERA	G	GS	CG	SV	IP	H	R	ER	HR	BB	SO	AVG
2005	Dayton (MWL)	LoA	2	5	6.30	19	16	0	0	64	81	54	45	3	44	42	.315
	Billings (PIO)	R	2	1	6.43	7	3	0	0	21	23	16	15	1	10	18	.291
2006	Dayton (MWL)	LoA	2	4	7.54	12	9	0	0	37	52	39	31	5	21	24	.327
2007	Billings (PIO)	R	3	1	1.77	11	0	0	3	41	31	17	8	0	11	29	.214
	Dayton (MWL)	LoA	1	2	6.75	7	0	0	0	11	17	9	8	1	2	8	.347
2008	Dayton (MWL)	LoA	2	1	3.12	16	0	0	1	26	25	11	9	2	10	32	.250
	Sarasota (FSL)	HiA	2	2	3.92	31	0	0	2	39	45	18	17	4	18	33	.294
2009	Sarasota (FSL)	HiA	1	1	2.29	17	0	0	6	20	11	5	5	2	9	19	.175
	Carolina (SL)	AA	1	1	2.76	27	0	0	3	33	25	13	10	2	20	27	.217
MINOR LEAGUE TOTALS			14	18	4.58	147	28	0	15	291	310	182	148	20	145	232	.277

24 MARK SERRANO, RHP

BORN: Sept. 14, 1985. **B-T:** L-R. **HT.:** 6-1. **WT.:** 185. **DRAFTED:** Oral Roberts, 2009 (6th round). **SIGNED BY:** Mike Keenan.

Though he was eligible every year, Serrano went undrafted in two seasons at Cypress (Calif.) JC and as a junior at Oral Roberts. He took a huge leap forward in 2009, winning Summit League player and pitcher of the year honors while ranking second in NCAA Division I in strikeouts per nine innings (13.8) and sixth in whiffs (132). After signing him for $25,000 as a sixth-round pick, the Reds expected him to succeed against younger hitters, but his complete dominance was a pleasant surprise. Serrano blew through Rookie ball, then was even better for most of his stay in low Class A Dayton. He allowed two runs in three relief outings (spanning eight innings), then put together a 20-inning scoreless streak once he moved to the starting rotation. Serrano's tight slider is his best pitch. He commands it and his 89-90 mph fastball well, and he also uses a palmball grip to throw an effective changeup. In the long term, he profiles best as a reliever, a role in which his fastball could play up to give him a second plus pitch. Already 24, he'll have to prove he can succeed against hitters who are as advanced as he is, and Cincinnati will give him that chance in Double-A at some point in 2010.

Year	Club (League)	Class	W	L	ERA	G	GS	CG	SV	IP	H	R	ER	HR	BB	SO	AVG
2009	Billings (PIO)	R	0	0	1.42	3	0	0	0	6	3	2	1	0	3	8	.143
	Dayton (MWL)	LoA	3	1	2.20	11	8	0	0	49	37	14	12	2	12	57	.204
MINOR LEAGUE TOTALS			3	1	2.11	14	8	0	0	55	40	16	13	2	15	65	.198

25 JUAN CARLOS SULBARAN, RHP

BORN: Nov. 9, 1989. **B-T:** R-R. **HT.:** 6-2. **WT.:** 198. **DRAFTED:** HS—Plantation, Fla., 2008 (30th round). **SIGNED BY:** Tony Arias.

Though he's one of the younger pitchers in the system, Sulbaran already has more experience facing elite-level hitters than any Reds farmhand. Before he ever threw a professional pitch, he had faced Cuba's powerful national team twice, once in the Beijing Olympics and once in the Haarlem Honkbal tournament. And before he made his pro debut in 2009, he struck out Ivan Rodriguez and retired Yadier Molina and Carlos Beltran while pitching out of the pen for the Dutch team at the World Baseball Classic. Unfortunately for Sulbaran, a $500,000 bonus baby, his international success has been the highlight of his young pro career and made the day-to-day grind of the minor league season seem mundane by comparison. His first pro season was hampered by a blister problem and his own lack of focus. He was held back in extended spring until May 1 because of blisters, then struggled with them throughout the second half of the season. Sulbaran needs to prove that he can win when he doesn't have his best stuff. He sometimes sits at 89-92 mph with his lively fastball and complements it with a plus curveball and an average changeup. But at other times, he struggles to top 90 mph, fails to locate his curveball and doesn't believe in his changeup. Those days became more and more common as the season went along, and he finished with a 5.80 ERA in his final 12 starts. Sulbaran still has one of the better assortments of pitches in the system, but he'll need to take a step forward in 2010.

Year	Club (League)	Class	W	L	ERA	G	GS	CG	SV	IP	H	R	ER	HR	BB	SO	AVG
2009	Dayton (MWL)	LoA	5	5	5.24	21	21	0	0	93	94	68	54	19	51	100	.265
MINOR LEAGUE TOTALS			5	5	5.24	21	21	0	0	93	94	68	54	19	51	100	.265

26 JOSH FELLHAUER, OF

BORN: March 24, 1988. **B-T:** L-L. **HT.:** 5-11. **WT.:** 180. **DRAFTED:** Cal State Fullerton, 2009 (7th round). **SIGNED BY:** Mike Misuraca.

In scouting director Chris Buckley's first draft with the Reds in 2006, they drafted Justin Turner and Danny Dorn out of Cal State Fullerton. For the cost of just $51,000, Cincinnati signed one player who already has reached the big leagues (Turner, after going to the Orioles in a trade for Ramon Hernandez) and another who ended 2009 in Triple-A (Dorn). The Reds may get a similar return on investment from their latest Titan, Fellhauer, who signed for $125,000 as a seventh-round pick in June. Like Chris Heisey, Fellhauer is a well-rounded outfielder with no standout tool but also none that rates significantly below average. A gifted hitter who ranked second on USA Baseball's college team with a .299 average in 2008 and batted .396 at Fullerton last spring, he sprays the ball to all fields. His raw power is his worst tool, which makes his seven homers at Dayton (one more than he hit with metal bats as a junior) somewhat surprising. He has average speed, and his instincts allow him to steal a few bases and cover enough ground to play center field. Both his range and accurate arm earn 55 grades on the 20-80 scouting scale. If he can't do enough to win a job as a regular, he profiles as a solid reserve capable of playing all three outfield positions. He'll open his first full season in high Class A.

Year	Club (League)	Class	AVG	G	AB	R	H	2B	3B	HR	RBI	BB	SO	SB	OBP	SLG
2009	Dayton (MWL)	LoA	.280	57	236	31	66	16	2	7	23	19	34	7	.351	.453
MINOR LEAGUE TOTALS			.280	57	236	31	66	16	2	7	23	19	34	7	.351	.453

27 DANIEL TUTTLE, RHP

BORN: Aug. 21, 1990. **B-T:** R-R. **HT.:** 6-1. **WT.:** 175. **DRAFTED:** HS—Randleman, N.C., 2009 (5th round). **SIGNED BY:** Perry Smith.

Facing a cleanup hitter with the bases loaded doesn't seem like a life-or-death scenario to Tuttle because he already has been through the real thing. Two days after he turned 12, he was nearly killed in a car accident that forced him to spend five weeks in the hospital. He bounced back from that to become an intriguing prospect both as a shortstop and a pitcher, committing to North Carolina State as a two-way player before the Reds drafted him in the fifth round and persuaded him to turn pro for $200,000. Tuttle's improved velocity as a senior made it clear is future is on the mound. He mostly showed an 89-92 mph fastball in his pro debut, though he touched 94 mph and has hit 96 mph in high school. His low three-quarters arm angle makes it appear he's slinging the ball and isn't pretty, but it gives his fastball plenty of natural run and sink. Very few of Tuttle's pitches are straight, which is both a blessing and a minor curse, as it makes it hard for him to command his fastball. He throws strikes but has too much movement to paint the corners. He also sometimes struggles to maintain his release point. He has a sweepy slider that was effective in Rookie ball but will need tightening as he moves up the ladder. His changeup, like that of many young pitchers, is more an idea than a consistent pitch at this point. Tuttle's delivery makes some scouts cringe and leads some to think he'll end up as a reliever, but Cincinnati will give him plenty of time to prove he can start. He figures to pitch in low Class A this season.

Year	Club (League)	Class	W	L	ERA	G	GS	CG	SV	IP	H	R	ER	HR	BB	SO	AVG
2009	Reds (GCL)	R	1	2	1.67	9	7	0	0	32	32	14	6	1	10	30	.258
MINOR LEAGUE TOTALS			1	2	1.67	9	7	0	0	32	32	14	6	1	10	30	.258

28 CODY PUCKETT, 2B/SS

BORN: April 3, 1987. **B-T:** R-R. **HT.:** 5-10. **WT.:** 185. **DRAFTED:** Cal State Dominguez Hills, 2008 (8th round). **SIGNED BY:** Rex de la Nuez.

As the success of Chris Denorfia and Chris Heisey has shown, the Reds have a knack for finding small-college talent. Since signing for $80,000 as a 2008 eighth-round pick out of NCAA Division II Cal State Dominguez Hills, Puckett has slugged 27 homers and 72 extra-base hits in 183 pro games. Physically, he doesn't look like much of a prospect. He's generously listed at 5-foot-10, but when he steps into the batter's box, he shows the power and the approach of a much bigger man. He looks to drive the ball with a power-oriented swing that will pile up strikeouts as well as home runs. His combination of plus raw power and slightly above-average speed is intriguing, and it will be much more intriguing if Puckett can prove he can stick at second base. He has very limited range to go with hard hands, as his excellent strength at the plate actually works against his flexibility in the field. He has an average arm that would be enough for third base or left field if he had to make a move to an easier position. Cincinnati will give Puckett every opportunity to stick at second base as he spends 2010 in high Class A.

Year	Club (League)	Class	AVG	G	AB	R	H	2B	3B	HR	RBI	BB	SO	SB	OBP	SLG
2008	Sarasota (FSL)	HiA	.000	2	7	0	0	0	0	0	0	0	2	0	.000	.000
	Reds (GCL)	R	.269	18	67	11	18	1	0	2	10	10	19	6	.372	.373
	Billings (PIO)	R	.287	33	122	22	35	7	1	6	19	22	30	2	.401	.508
2009	Sarasota (FSL)	HiA	.056	5	18	1	1	0	0	0	1	2	4	1	.143	.056
	Dayton (MWL)	LoA	.263	125	482	76	127	35	1	19	67	39	138	19	.325	.459
MINOR LEAGUE TOTALS			.260	183	696	110	181	43	2	27	97	73	193	28	.336	.444

29 BYRON WILEY, OF

BORN: Dec. 12, 1986. **B-T:** L-L. **HT.:** 5-11. **WT.:** 205. **DRAFTED:** Kansas State, 2008 (22nd round). **SIGNED BY:** Mike Keenan.

Coming off of a .366 sophomore season at Kansas State, Wiley put himself in position to be an early-round pick for 2008. Then he hit .217 in the Cape Cod League and .227 as a junior, which caused him to drop to the 22nd round. Since then, he has done everything he can to prove that his struggles were an aberration, batting .289/.403/.507 in pro ball. Wiley shows natural strength in his stroke and good plate coverage. He has an excellent batting eye that allows him to draw walks, though he takes a full swing and sometimes sells out for power. Few pitchers can throw a fastball past him. Wiley will have to hit to make it to the majors because he's a poor defender. His arm is weak, even for a left fielder, and his below-average range plays down because he doesn't take good routes. Wiley has some athleticism, so there's hope that he can improve and become a passable corner outfielder. He has slightly above-average speed once he gets going, though he's just an average runner out of the box because of his big swing. He'll move up to high Class A this season.

Year	Club (League)	Class	AVG	G	AB	R	H	2B	3B	HR	RBI	BB	SO	SB	OBP	SLG
2008	Billings (PIO)	R	.328	39	137	29	45	17	5	5	37	24	49	3	.427	.635
2009	Dayton (MWL)	LoA	.275	110	382	62	105	25	5	12	64	76	114	9	.395	.461
MINOR LEAGUE TOTALS			.289	149	519	91	150	42	10	17	101	100	163	12	.403	.507

30 DEVIN MESORACO, C

BORN: June 19, 1988. **B-T:** R-R. **HT.:** 6-1. **WT.:** 200. **DRAFTED:** HS—Punxsutawney, Pa., 2007 (1st round). **SIGNED BY:** Lee Seras.

When the Reds drafted Mesoraco 15th overall and signed him for $1.4 million in 2007, they thought they were getting a catcher with a plus bat, defensive potential and excellent athleticism. Three years later, they're still waiting to see him turn his tools into production. His bat speed and athleticism have been less than expected. He battled an injury to his left wrist—his third hand or wrist injury in three pro seasons—but did show improved defense. After throwing out just two of the 23 basestealers who tested him in April, he caught 23 of 50 (46 percent) over the rest of the year. Mesoraco has hit just .240/.311/.368 as a pro, showing a lack of bat speed and discipline. His injuries may partly explain his lack of explosiveness. Not many scouts outside of the organization now see the same tools that made Mesoraco a first-round pick. The Reds don't have to place him on their 40-man roster until after the 2011 season, so they have every reason to be patient.

Year	Club (League)	Class	AVG	G	AB	R	H	2B	3B	HR	RBI	BB	SO	SB	OBP	SLG
2007	Reds (GCL)	R	.219	40	137	16	30	4	0	1	8	15	26	2	.310	.270
2008	Dayton (MWL)	LoA	.261	83	306	29	80	13	1	9	42	20	64	2	.311	.399
2009	Sarasota (FSL)	HiA	.228	92	312	32	71	22	1	8	37	35	76	0	.311	.381
MINOR LEAGUE TOTALS			.240	215	755	77	181	39	2	18	87	70	166	4	.311	.368

Cleveland Indians

BY BEN BADLER

The Indians thought a few better players or even better fortune would get them to the playoffs, after they scored more runs than they allowed in each of the previous five seasons, including a pair of 90-plus win campaigns. The 2009 season disabused them of that belief.

Cleveland tied Kansas City for last place in the American League Central with a 65-97 record, its worst mark since 1991 and a performance that cost manager Eric Wedge his job. The Indians went outside the organization for his replacement, hiring former Nationals manager Manny Acta.

Acta tried to oversee a rebuilding effort in Washington, and that's what he has on his hands in Cleveland. The 2009 Indians had a middle-of-the-road offense, but the Orioles and Nationals were the only teams in baseball that allowed more runs. Cleveland was plagued by poor pitching from both starters and relievers, and a defense that ranked 27th in the majors in defensive efficiency.

Things look better in the farm system, where the Indians have one of the deepest collections of prospects around. Much of that talent came via the trade market, including five of their top eight prospects: catcher Carlos Santana, lefthander Nick Hagadone, righthanders Jason Knapp and Carlos Carrasco, and outfielder Michael Brantley. Those players didn't come cheaply, as they were parts of deals including the two Game One starters in the 2009 World Series—Cliff Lee and C.C. Sabathia—as well as three-time all-star Victor Martinez and solid veteran Casey Blake.

Smaller deals that shipped off Rafael Betancourt, Mark DeRosa and Ryan Garko during the 2009 season provided additional depth.

The Indians are developing an intriguing group of homegrown Latin American players, most notably Venezuelan righthander Hector Rondon, Dominican lefty Kelvin de la Cruz and Venezuelan shortstop Carlos Rivero. But Cleveland was burned last year when it found out that Dominican shortstop Jose Ozoria, who was believed to be 16 when he signed for $575,000 in 2008, was three years older and named Wuali Bryan.

While the Indians have built an impressive farm system, trading away big leaguers in exchange for prospects every year isn't a sustainable model for competing. They realize they need to get more out of their drafts, especially now that they're picking fifth

Eric Wedge lost his job as Indians manager after the club finished with a 65-97 record

TOP 30 PROSPECTS

1. Carlos Santana, c	**16.** Zach Putnam, rhp
2. Lonnie Chisenhall, 3b	**17.** Carlos Rivero, ss
3. Nick Hagadone, lhp	**18.** Jess Todd, rhp
4. Jason Knapp, rhp	**19.** Josh Judy, rhp
5. Michael Brantley, of	**20.** Alexander Perez, rhp
6. Nick Weglarz, of	**21.** Jeanmar Gomez, rhp
7. Hector Rondon, rhp	**22.** Chen-Chang Lee, rhp
8. Carlos Carrasco, rhp	**23.** Abner Abreu, of
9. Alex White, rhp	**24.** Beau Mills, 1b
10. Jason Kipnis, of/2b	**25.** Jesus Brito, 3b
11. Lou Marson, c	**26.** Connor Graham, rhp
12. T.J. House, lhp	**27.** Wes Hodges, 3b
13. Kelvin de la Cruz, lhp	**28.** Bryan Price, rhp
14. Jordan Brown, of/1b	**29.** Scott Barnes, lhp
15. Jason Donald, ss	**30.** Eric Berger, lhp

overall in 2010. It's Cleveland's highest draft position since taking Paul Shuey second overall in 1992, and it will have to get more than the last time it had a top-10 choice and drafted Jeremy Sowers sixth overall in 2004.

The Indians have a strong nucleus of up-the-middle talent to build around with Grady Sizemore in center field, Asdrubal Cabrera at shortstop and Santana soon to arrive behind the plate. One of their most important tasks will be to improve their run prevention, with Rondon and Carrasco and several potentially useful bullpen arms nearly ready to help.

General Manager: Mark Shapiro. **Farm Director:** Ross Atkins. **Scouting Director:** Brad Grant.

Class	Team	League	W	L	PCT	Finish*	Manager(s)
Majors	Cleveland Indians	American	65	97	.401	t-12th (14)	Eric Wedge
Triple-A	Columbus Clippers	International	57	85	.401	13th (14)	Torey Lovullo
Double-A	Akron Aeros	Eastern	89	53	.627	†1st (12)	Mike Sarbaugh
High A	Kinston Indians	Carolina	60	78	.435	7th (8)	Chris Tremie
Low A	Lake County Captains	South Atlantic	71	66	.518	6th (16)	Aaron Holbert
Short-season	Mahoning Valley Scrappers	New York-Penn	49	27	.645	1st (14)	Travis Fryman
Rookie	AZL Indians	Arizona	24	32	.429	t-8th (11)	Ted Kubiak
Overall 2009 Minor League Record			350	341	.507	t-13th (30)	

*Finish in overall standings (No. of teams in league). †League champion.

LAST YEAR'S TOP 30

Player, Pos.		Status
1.	Carlos Santana, c	No. 1
2.	Matt LaPorta, of	Majors
3.	Nick Weglarz, of	No. 6
4.	Adam Miller, rhp	Dropped out
5.	Beau Mills, 1b	No. 24
6.	Lonnie Chisenhall, ss	No. 2
7.	Kelvin de la Cruz, lhp	No. 13
8.	David Huff, lhp	Majors
9.	Michael Brantley, of/1b	No. 5
10.	Luis Valbuena, 2b	Majors
11.	Carlos Rivero, ss	No. 17
12.	Wes Hodges, 3b	No. 27
13.	Hector Rondon, rhp	No. 7
14.	T.J. House, lhp	No. 12
15.	Trevor Crowe, of	Majors
16.	Abner Abreu, 3b/of	No. 23
17.	Tony Sipp, lhp	Majors
18.	Jon Meloan, rhp	(Athletics)
19.	Jeff Stevens, rhp	(Cubs)
20.	Trey Haley, rhp	Dropped out
21.	Scott Lewis, lhp	Dropped out
22.	Zach Putnam, rhp	No. 16
23.	Tim Fedroff, of	Dropped out
24.	Cord Phelps, 2b	Dropped out
25.	Jordan Brown, 1b	No. 14
26.	Delvi Cid, of	Dropped out
27.	Bryce Stowell, rhp	Dropped out
28.	Josh Tomlin, rhp	Dropped out
29.	John Gaub, lhp	(Cubs)
30.	Wuali Bryan, ss	Dropped out

BEST TOOLS

Best Hitter for Average	Michael Brantley
Best Power Hitter	Nick Weglarz
Best Strike-Zone Discipline	Carlos Santana
Fastest Baserunner	Delvi Cid
Best Athlete	Michael Brantley
Best Fastball	Nick Hagadone
Best Curveball	Alexander Perez
Best Slider	Nick Hagadone
Best Changeup	Carlos Carrasco
Best Control	Hector Rondon
Best Defensive Catcher	Carlos Santana
Best Defensive Infielder	Jason Donald
Best Infield Arm	Carlos Rivero
Best Defensive Outfielder	Jordan Henry
Best Outfield Arm	Matt Brown

PROJECTED 2013 LINEUP

Catcher	Carlos Santana
First Base	Matt LaPorta
Second Base	Luis Valbuena
Third Base	Lonnie Chisenhall
Shortstop	Asdrubal Cabrera
Left Field	Michael Brantley
Center Field	Grady Sizemore
Right Field	Shin-Soo Choo
Designated Hitter	Nick Weglarz
No. 1 Starter	Nick Hagadone
No. 2 Starter	Jason Knapp
No. 3 Starter	Hector Rondon
No. 4 Starter	Justin Masterson
No. 5 Starter	Carlos Carrasco
Closer	Alex White

TOP PROSPECTS OF THE DECADE

Year	Player, Pos.	2009 Org.
2000	C.C. Sabathia, lhp	Yankees
2001	C.C. Sabathia, lhp	Yankees
2002	Corey Smith, 3b	Royals
2003	Brandon Phillips, ss/2b	Reds
2004	Grady Sizemore, of	Indians
2005	Adam Miller, rhp	Indians
2006	Adam Miller, rhp	Indians
2007	Adam Miller, rhp	Indians
2008	Adam Miller, rhp	Indians
2009	Carlos Santana, c	Indians

TOP DRAFT PICKS OF THE DECADE

Year	Player, Pos.	2009 Org.
2000	Corey Smith, 3b	Royals
2001	Dan Denham, rhp	Angels
2002	Jeremy Guthrie, rhp	Orioles
2003	Michael Aubrey, 1b	Orioles
2004	Jeremy Sowers, lhp	Indians
2005	Trevor Crowe, of	Indians
2006	David Huff, lhp (1st round supp.)	Indians
2007	Beau Mills, 3b/1b	Indians
2008	Lonnie Chisenhall, ss	Indians
2009	Alex White, rhp	Indians

LARGEST BONUSES IN CLUB HISTORY

Danys Baez, 1999	$4,500,000
Jeremy Guthrie, 2002	$3,000,000
Jeremy Sowers, 2004	$2,475,000
Alex White, 2009	$2,250,000
Michael Aubrey, 2003	$2,010,000

CLEVELAND INDIANS

TOP 2010 ROOKIE: Michael Brantley, of. After batting .313 during a September callup, he's the frontrunner to win the left-field job.

BREAKOUT PROSPECT: Josh Judy, rhp. After a torrid second half and a strong Arizona Fall League, he could bring his 92-94 mph fastball to Cleveland at some point in 2010.

SLEEPER: Delvi Cid, of. He's quite raw but he's the fastest runner and one of the best athletes in the system.

SOURCE OF TOP 30 TALENT			
Homegrown	19	Acquired	11
College	9	Trades	11
Junior college	0	Rule 5 draft	0
High school	2	Independent leagues	0
Draft-and-follow	0	Free agents/waivers	0
Nondrafted free agents	0		
International	8		

Numbers in parentheses indicate prospect rankings

LF
Nick Weglarz (6)
Tim Fedroff
Chris Gimenez
Bo Greenwell
Greg Folgia

CF
Michael Brantley (5)
Delvi Cid
Jordan Henry

RF
Abner Abreu (23)
Jesus Brito (25)

3B
Lonnie Chisenhall (2)
Carlos Rivero (17)
Wes Hodges (27)
Kyle Bellows

SS
Jason Donald (15)
Kyle Smith

2B
Jason Kipnis (10)
Cord Phelps
Jairo Kelly
Josh Rodriguez
Karexon Sanchez

1B
Jordan Brown (14)
Beau Mills (24)
Matt McBride
Ben Carlson

C
Carlos Santana (1)
Lou Marson (11)
Alex Monsalve
Wyatt Toregas

RHP

Starters	Relievers
Jason Knapp (4)	Zach Putnam (16)
Hector Rondon (7)	Jess Todd (18)
Carlos Carrasco (8)	Josh Judy (19)
Alex White (9)	Chen-Chang Lee (22)
Alexander Perez (20)	Connor Graham (26)
Jeanmar Gomez (21)	Carlton Smith
Bryan Price (28)	Adam Miller
Joe Gardner	Yohan Pino
Hector Ambriz	Frank Herrmann
Marty Popham	Santo Frias
Josh Tomlin	Neil Wagner
Austin Adams	Rob Bryson
Trey Haley	Cory Burns
Bryce Stowell	Nick Sarianides
Kyle C. Smith	
Alex Morales	
Preston Guilmet	
Brett Brach	

LHP

Starters	Relievers
Nick Hagadone (3)	Danny Jimenez
T.J. House (12)	
Kelvin de la Cruz (13)	
Scott Barnes (29)	
Eric Berger (30)	
Chris Jones	
Ryan Morris	
Elvis Araujo	
Mike Rayl	

2009

BEST PURE HITTER: OF Jason Kipnis (2) used a compact swing and strong forearms to earn Pacific-10 Conference player of the year honors the last spring. He batted .384 with a .709 slugging percentage, then hit .306 at short-season Mahoning Valley. He has surprising pop for his size.

BEST POWER HITTER: 3B Kyle Bellows (4) got more aggressive and unlocked some of his above-average power potential in 2009, hitting 10 homers for San Jose State and adding seven more for Mahoning Valley. He's a solid athlete who played a lot of shortstop in college.

FASTEST RUNNER: OF Jordan Henry (7) has one true plus tool, as he's a well-above-average runner. He makes it work by controlling the strike zone and having just enough power to hit for average.

BEST DEFENSIVE PLAYER: Henry's speed allows him to play a shallow, daring center field, and he goes back well on balls hit over his head.

BEST FASTBALL: RHP Austin Adams (5) can sit at 95-97 mph at times, even as a starter. RHP Alex White (1) has good sink and life on his 91-95 mph fastball when he's at his best.

BEST SECONDARY PITCH: White came to college with a plus slider, and while he has lost the feel for it, he has gained a nasty splitter. RHP Cory Burns (8) uses a lower arm slot and gets swings and misses with his plus changeup.

BEST PRO DEBUT: Kipnis (.306/.388/.459), Henry (.286/.408/.335, 22 SB), Burns (3-2, 1.93, 11 SV) and RHP Brett Brach (10; 5-2, 2.19) helped lead Mahoning Valley to a 49-27 record, the best in the New York-Penn League.

BEST ATHLETE: Adams was drafted as a shortstop in 2008 and has the tools to play there. Among position players, OF Greg Folgia (40) has all-around tools and was a good high school wrestler.

MOST INTRIGUING BACKGROUND: The Tribe drafted and signed two Kyle Smiths. The shortstop (14) out of Cal Poly is a solid defender with no standout tools or glaring weaknesses, while the righthander (20) out of Kent State has a projectable 6-foot-6, 195-pound frame. Henry's brother Justin plays in Tigers system, as does Chris Carlson, brother of 1B Ben Carlson (6).

CLOSEST TO THE MAJORS: Kipnis and White, though Adams could vault past them if he moves to the bullpen.

BEST LATE-ROUND PICK: The Indians decided to follow RHP Nick Sarianides (28) in the Great Lakes League last summer and came away impressed enough

to sign him for $100,000. He bumped 93-94 mph with his fastball while flashing a solid slider.

THE ONE WHO GOT AWAY: The Indians made runs at prep RHPs Michael Hamann (24) and Blake Hauser (25) but couldn't get either deal done. Hamann, who headed to Toledo, may have more upside as a late bloomer physically with athleticism and promising secondary stuff. Hauser opted to attend Virginia Commonwealth.

ASSESSMENT: White didn't figure to last until the 15th pick early in the season, and he was an excellent talent value for that pick. He combines with sinker-balling RHP Joe Gardner (3), Adams, Brach and Sarianides to make this a pitching-heavy group, and there's strength in numbers.

2008

3B Lonnie Chisenhall (1) lasted 29 picks and quickly has developed into one of the game's top hot-corner prospects. LHP T.J. House (16) is the best of Cleveland's several above-slot signees, many of whom struggled in their first full pro season.

GRADE: B

2007

1B Beau Mills (1) hit the wall in Double-A last season, and the highest-ranking prospect from this crop is now RHP Josh Judy (34). Unsigned RHP Bryce Brentz (30) has blossomed into one of the top hitting prospects for the 2010 draft.

GRADE: D

2006

LHP David Huff (1s), the first pick, won 11 games for Cleveland in a rocky 2009 rookie season. 3B Wes Hodges (2) hasn't stayed healthy since signing for $1 million. RHP Chris Archer (5) and LHP John Gaub (21) took a big step forward last year after going to the Cubs in a trade for Mark DeRosa.

GRADE: C

2005

OFs Trevor Crowe (1) and John Drennen (1s) never delivered on their potential, and not signing RHP Tim Lincecum (42) and OF Desmond Jennings (18, now the Rays' No. 1 prospect) stings. The Tribe can take some solace in RHP Jensen Lewis (3) and OFs Nick Weglarz (3) and Jordan Brown (4).

GRADE: C

---

*Draft analysis by John Manuel (2009) and Jim Callis (2005-08). Numbers in parentheses indicate draft rounds. *Bonuses for 2005 are first 10 rounds only.*

CARLOS SANTANA, C

Born: April 8, 1986.
Height: 5-11. **Weight:** 190.
Bats: B. **Throws:** R.
Signed: Dominican Republic, 2004.
Signed by: Andres Lopez (Dodgers).

After signing with the Dodgers for $75,000 in 2004, Santana spent his first two seasons playing third base and the outfield. He made the transition to catcher during instructional league after the 2006 season, then broke out with an MVP season in the high Class A California League. Los Angeles traded Santana and Jonathan Meloan to the Indians that July in a deadline deal for third baseman Casey Blake, agreeing to send a higher-quality prospect if Cleveland covered the roughly $2 million remaining on Blake's contract. Santana added another MVP trophy last season in the Double-A Eastern League. The only negative for Santana came while playing winter ball in the Dominican Republic, where he broke the hamate bone in his right hand and had surgery in early December. He should be ready by the start of spring training.

Santana has a bat that would fit nicely at any position, making it a premium bat for a catcher. Showing the ability to draw walks at a high clip, Santana is selectively aggressive, not offering at pitches he can't handle on the edges and taking an aggressive swing at pitches in his zone. He has good balance at the plate and generally shows a compact swing. Though he's not a big catcher like Victor Martinez, Santana maximizes his swing from top to bottom to generate plus power from both sides of the plate. He uses a leg lift to incorporate his lower half into his swing. He has above-average bat speed and strong hands, and he gets late acceleration through the zone with his wrists. Santana is a solid defensive catcher, with an arm that gets plus grades or better, accuracy and a quick release. He threw out 30 percent of basestealers last year. His athleticism also helps his agility behind the dish.

Santana's swing gets long at times and he's still learning how to keep it under control. His stride can get him caught out on his front foot, and some EL observers questioned his ability to turn on hard stuff inside. His receiving skills have made progress, though as a converted catcher he still needs additional seasoning. Santana has the physical tools to be an above-average defensive catcher, but he's still learning nuances such as game management. After Santana finished with Akron, the Indians brought him to Cleveland—not to play but to be a part of pregame meetings and sit in the stands behind home plate with their advance scouts. He's a below-average runner.

With the Indians trading Martinez to the Red Sox last July and shipping Kelly Shoppach to the Rays in December, the door is open for Santana to take over in Cleveland at some point in 2010. His injury might set back his timetable, but he likely would have started the season at Triple-A Columbus regardless. He should be the Indians' full-time catcher by 2011 and has the potential to be a perennial all-star.

Year	Club (League)	Class	AVG	G	AB	R	H	2B	3B	HR	RBI	BB	SO	SB	OBP	SLG
2005	Dodgers (GCL)	R	.295	32	78	14	23	4	1	1	14	16	8	0	.412	.410
2006	Vero Beach (FSL)	HiA	.268	54	198	16	53	10	2	3	18	23	43	0	.345	.384
	Ogden (PIO)	R	.303	37	132	31	40	5	1	7	27	30	19	4	.423	.515
2007	Great Lakes (MWL)	LoA	.223	86	292	32	65	20	1	7	36	40	45	5	.318	.370
2008	Inland Empire (CAL)	HiA	.323	99	350	88	113	34	4	14	96	69	59	7	.431	.563
	Kinston (CAR)	HiA	.352	29	105	34	37	5	1	6	19	20	24	3	.452	.590
	Akron (EL)	AA	.125	2	8	3	1	0	0	1	2	0	2	0	.125	.500
2009	Akron (EL)	AA	.290	130	428	91	124	30	2	23	97	90	83	2	.413	.530
MINOR LEAGUE TOTALS			.287	469	1591	309	456	108	12	62	309	288	283	21	.395	.486

2 LONNIE CHISENHALL, 3B

CARL KLINE

BORN: Oct. 4, 1988. **B-T:** L-R. **HT.:** 6-1. **WT.:** 200. **DRAFTED:** Pitt (N.C.) CC, 2008 (1st round). **SIGNED BY:** Bob Mayer.

Baseball America rated Chisenhall as college baseball's top freshman for 2007, but South Carolina dismissed him after an arrest on charges of larceny. He emerged at Pitt (N.C.) CC and batted .410 with eight strikeouts in 219 plate appearances in 2008, going 29th overall in the draft and signing for $1.1 million. He finished his first full pro season by helping Akron win the Eastern League title, hitting .467 in the postseason. Chisenhall draws rave reviews for his simple, low-maintenance swing. He stays calm, quiet and balanced at the plate, using a short, compact stroke with good bat speed and length through the zone. He has a good approach at the plate, hanging in well against lefthanders, staying back to drive balls to the opposite field and using his hands to adjust to breaking balls. He has a strong arm, good hands and body control, plus solid range to both sides at third base, where he moved after playing shortstop in his pro debut. He's a good athlete with average speed. Chisenhall doesn't project to have plus raw power but he could develop average pop in time. He initially struggled at third base with his footwork and throwing, though the majority of his errors came at the beginning of the year. He had to make strides getting his feet lined up, using his lower body and keeping his arm angle up on his throws. One of the top third-base prospects in the minors, Chisenhall has the bat to be an above-average major leaguer. He should return to Double-A in 2010 as one of the EL's youngest players.

Year	Club (League)	Class	AVG	G	AB	R	H	2B	3B	HR	RBI	BB	SO	SB	OBP	SLG
2008	Mahoning Valley (NYP)	SS	.290	68	276	38	80	20	3	5	45	24	32	7	.355	.438
2009	Kinston (CAR)	HiA	.276	99	388	59	107	26	2	18	79	37	80	2	.346	.492
	Akron (EL)	AA	.183	24	93	13	17	5	1	4	13	7	16	1	.238	.387
MINOR LEAGUE TOTALS			.269	191	757	110	204	51	6	27	137	68	128	10	.336	.460

3 NICK HAGADONE, LHP

BORN: Jan. 1, 1986. **B-T:** L L. **HT.:** 6-5. **WT.:** 230. **DRAFTED:** Washington, 2007 (1st round supplemental). **SIGNED BY:** John Booher (Red Sox).

A 2007 sandwich pick of the Red Sox, Hagadone got off to a strong start in pro ball before blowing out his elbow in April 2008 and requiring Tommy John surgery. He returned to game action last June, showing an electric arm before Boston included him with Justin Masterson and another supplemental first-rounder, Bryan Price, in the Victor Martinez trade in July. Hagadone has outstanding arm strength for a lefthander, sitting at 93-94 mph with good life and touching 98. His slider is a plus pitch that flashes plus-plus with outstanding late bite. He also shows solid feel for a changeup, though he primarily pitches off his fastball/slider combination. Hagadone doesn't throw with much effort and his arm works well. He gets grounders at an above-average clip and didn't surrender a homer last year. Command is often the last thing to come back from Tommy John surgery, and Hagadone's wasn't strong even before he got hurt. Though he's athletic and able to pitch inside well, he's still learning to repeat his delivery and still has a tendency to rush toward the plate. His longest start in 2009 lasted three innings, so he'll have to prove his durability. The Indians plan to use Hagadone in the rotation this year at high Class A Kinston. He has the stuff to be a frontline starter, and he also could be a weapon as a power lefty reliever.

Year	Club (League)	Class	W	L	ERA	G	GS	CG	SV	IP	H	R	ER	HR	BB	SO	AVG
2007	Lowell (NYP)	SS	0	1	1.85	10	10	0	0	24	14	5	5	1	8	33	.163
2008	Greenville (SAL)	LoA	1	1	0.00	3	3	0	0	10	5	3	0	0	6	12	.135
2009	Greenville (SAL)	LoA	0	2	2.52	10	10	0	0	25	13	8	7	0	14	32	.149
	Lake County (SAL)	LoA	0	1	2.45	5	5	0	0	15	8	4	4	0	5	21	.163
	Kinston (CAR)	HiA	0	0	5.06	2	2	0	0	5	5	3	3	0	5	6	.250
MINOR LEAGUE TOTALS			1	5	2.16	30	30	0	0	79	45	23	19	1	38	104	.161

4 JASON KNAPP, RHP

BORN: Aug. 31, 1990. **B-T:** R-R. **HT.:** 6-5. **WT.:** 215. **DRAFTED:** HS—Annandale, N.J., 2008 (2nd round). **SIGNED BY:** Gene Schall (Phillies).

A second-round pick by the Phillies in 2008, Knapp is the best prospect in the four-player package that the Indians received in the Cliff Lee deal last summer. After missing time in 2008 with elbow fatigue, he was on the disabled list with biceps tendinitis at the time of the trade, then had arthroscopic surgery to remove loose bodies in his shoulder after the season. Knapp is a big, strong-bodied pitcher with a quick arm and an electric fastball, working at 93-95 mph with riding life and touching 98. He mixes in a sharp curveball with inconsistent but occasional 12-to-6 break that's in and out of the zone. It's a plus pitch on his best days. He shows feel for his changeup, which could become an average offering. While Knapp has improved his delivery, a major worry among scouts when he was in high school, it's still awkward. He needs to repeat his mechanics with greater frequency and his inverted arm action gives some scouts cause for concern, particularly for a player with a shoulder injury. Knapp was still rehabbing as 2009 came to a close, and the Indians plan to assess his status when he arrives at spring training. If he shows durability, he has the potential to be at least a frontline starter. If his health continues to hamper him, he could be a power closer instead. He should begin 2010 in high Class A.

Year	Club (League)	Class	W	L	ERA	G	GS	CG	SV	IP	H	R	ER	HR	BB	SO	AVG
2008	Phillies (GCL)	R	3	1	2.61	7	6	0	0	31	26	10	9	1	12	38	.228
2009	Lakewood (SAL)	LoA	2	7	4.01	17	17	0	0	85	63	45	38	3	39	111	.208
	Lake County (SAL)	LoA	0	0	5.40	4	4	0	0	12	10	10	7	0	8	12	.238
MINOR LEAGUE TOTALS			5	8	3.80	28	27	0	0	128	99	65	54	4	59	161	.216

5 MICHAEL BRANTLEY, OF

BORN: May 15, 1987. **B-T:** L-L. **HT.:** 6-2. **WT.:** 200. **DRAFTED:** HS—Fort Pierce, Fla. 2005 (7th round). **SIGNED BY:** Larry Pardo (Brewers).

The Indians picked Brantley over third baseman Taylor Green as the player to be named in the 2008 deal that sent C.C. Sabathia to Milwaukee. While Green stagnated last year in Double-A, Brantley had a solid year as one of the Triple-A International League's youngest players. The son of former major leaguer Mickey Brantley, he hit .313 during a September callup. Brantley is a career .300 hitter with a .387 on-base percentage in the minors because he has excellent plate discipline and plus speed from the left side. He has an easy, compact swing and a good two-strike approach. He pairs his speed with good instincts on the basepaths, tying for the IL lead with 46 steals while getting caught just five times, including a perfect 33-for-33 against righthanders. His speed is also an asset in center field, where he improved his reads and routes to become a solid-average defender with a chance to get better. Brantley has well-below-average power, though he has the size to develop more pop. He doesn't use his legs much in his swing, but more power could come once he learns to work his lower half, leverage the ball more consistently and learn what pitches he can drive. His arm is below-average. Brantley won't start in center field for Cleveland as long as Grady Sizemore is around, so he'll try to win the left-field job. He could make up for his lack of power with his on-base ability and defensive value.

Year	Club (League)	Class	AVG	G	AB	R	H	2B	3B	HR	RBI	BB	SO	SB	OBP	SLG
2005	Brewers (AZL)	R	.347	44	173	34	60	3	1	0	19	22	13	14	.426	.376
	Helena (PIO)	R	.324	10	34	8	11	2	0	0	3	6	4	2	.425	.382
2006	West Virginia (SAL)	LoA	.300	108	360	47	108	10	2	0	42	61	51	24	.402	.339
2007	West Virginia (SAL)	LoA	.335	56	218	41	73	15	1	2	32	31	22	18	.413	.440
	Huntsville (SL)	AA	.251	59	187	28	47	6	1	0	21	29	25	17	.353	.294
2008	Huntsville (SL)	AA	.319	106	420	80	134	17	2	4	40	50	27	28	.395	.398
2009	Columbus (IL)	AAA	.267	116	457	80	122	21	2	6	37	59	48	46	.350	.361
	Cleveland (AL)	MAJ	.313	28	112	10	35	4	0	0	11	8	19	4	.358	.348
MAJOR LEAGUE TOTALS			.313	28	112	10	35	4	0	0	11	8	19	4	.358	.348
MINOR LEAGUE TOTALS			.300	499	1849	318	555	74	9	12	194	258	190	149	.387	.369

6 NICK WEGLARZ, OF

BORN: Dec. 16, 1987. **B-T:** L-L. **HT.:** 6-3. **WT.:** 245. **DRAFTED:** HS—Stevensville, Ontario 2005 (3rd round). **SIGNED BY:** Les Pajari.

After playing sparingly for Canada as one of the youngest players in the World Baseball Classic, Weglarz got off to a brutal start in 2009, going 5-for-56 with one extra-base hit in April. He tore through Double-A pitching in May and June, but his numbers tailed off as a back injury took a toll, and he went on the disabled list with a stress fracture in his left shin. He went to the Arizona Fall League after the season but left early to have surgery on his shin. Weglarz is one of the most patient hitters in the minors and has the potential to draw 100 walks over a full season. He has a massive frame and outstanding raw power with the ability to hit the ball out to all fields. He has made strides with his hitting mechanics, using his legs more and doing a better job of getting the back half of his body through the ball. Weglarz could tighten his mechanics to hit for a better average, including a more consistent hand trigger. While his patience is a virtue, he could be more aggressive on certain pitches in the strike zone. Weglarz's size and injuries are a concern for some scouts. His fringy arm and well-below-average speed limit him to left field. The Indians expect Weglarz to be ready to play by the beginning of spring training. He could open 2010 in Triple-A, though at age 22 he could return to Akron for another season.

Year	Club (League)	Class	AVG	G	AB	R	H	2B	3B	HR	RBI	BB	SO	SB	OBP	SLG
2005	Burlington (APP)	R	.231	41	147	22	34	11	0	2	13	17	42	2	.313	.347
2006	Indians (GCL)	R	.000	1	2	0	0	0	0	0	0	0	2	0	.000	.000
2007	Lake County (SAL)	LoA	.276	125	439	75	121	28	0	23	82	82	129	1	.395	.497
	Kinston (CAR)	HiA	.143	2	7	1	1	0	0	1	1	1	2	0	.250	.571
2008	Kinston (CAR)	HiA	.272	106	375	68	102	20	5	10	41	71	78	9	.396	.432
2009	Akron (EL)	AA	.227	105	339	69	77	17	2	16	65	75	78	2	.377	.431
MINOR LEAGUE TOTALS			.256	380	1309	235	335	76	7	52	202	246	331	14	.381	.444

7 HECTOR RONDON, RHP

BORN: Feb. 26, 1988. **B-T:** R-R. **HT.:** 6-3. **WT.:** 180. **SIGNED:** Venezuela, 2004.
SIGNED BY: Stewart Ruiz.

KEN CARR

A Futures Gamer in 2008, Rondon cruised through his first five Double-A starts last year before the Indians moved him to the Akron bullpen, with an eye toward finding help for a beleaguered bullpen in Cleveland. He made just two relief appearances before the Indians nixed the experiment, sending him back into the rotation and giving him a promotion to Triple-A in July at age 21. Rondon's best pitch is his fastball, a lively low-90s heater that touches 96 mph. He commands it well to both sides of the plate and it has late life through the zone, making it a swing-and-miss pitch. His second-best offering is his average changeup, which could be a future 55 pitch on the 20-80 scouting scale. He repeats a clean delivery, and his athleticism helps him field his position well. Rondon has made strides with his secondary pitches, but he'll have to prove that they're good enough to keep big league hitters off his impressive fastball. His mid-80s slider is a fringe-average pitch. He experienced mild biceps soreness in June but didn't miss much time. Rondon profiles as a potential mid-rotation starter. He'll likely begin 2010 in the Columbus rotation and should be in line for a callup at some point.

Year	Club (League)	Class	W	L	ERA	G	GS	CG	SV	IP	H	R	ER	HR	BB	SO	AVG
2005	Indians1 (DSL)	R	3	3	1.65	15	12	1	1	65	60	24	12	2	8	55	.230
2006	Indians (GCL)	R	3	4	5.13	11	11	0	0	53	62	34	30	6	3	32	.286
2007	Lake County (SAL)	LoA	7	10	4.37	27	27	0	0	136	143	78	66	13	27	113	.269
2008	Kinston (CAR)	HiA	11	6	3.60	27	27	0	0	145	130	63	58	12	42	145	.239
2009	Akron (EL)	AA	7	5	2.75	15	13	1	0	72	60	23	22	3	16	73	.227
	Columbus (IL)	AAA	4	5	4.00	12	12	0	0	74	83	38	33	8	13	64	.282
MINOR LEAGUE TOTALS			35	33	3.65	107	102	2	1	545	538	260	221	44	109	482	.255

8 CARLOS CARRASCO, RHP

BORN: March 3, 1987. **B-T:** R-R. **HT.:** 6-3. **WT.:** 215. **SIGNED:** Venezuela, 2003.
SIGNED BY: Sal Agostinelli (Phillies).

The No. 1 prospect on our Phillies Top 10 before the 2007 and 2008 seasons, Carrasco struggled in Triple-A at the outset of last year. He got back on track after coming to the Indians in the Cliff Lee trade, but got crushed in five big league starts in September. Carrasco throws a 91-94 mph fastball that touches 96. He also throws his plus changeup with good arm speed and late action, and that could be one reason he has been more effective against lefthanders than righthanders over the last two seasons. He has a big frame, solid mechanics and arm action. Durable throughout his career, he has made at least 25 starts in each of the last four seasons. Carrasco has also been maddeningly inconsistent. His curveball comes and goes and is often a fringe-average pitch. He'll mix in a fringy slider with shorter, harder break. He throws strikes but has lapses with repeating his delivery and his command, often making mistakes up and over the middle of the plate. He has been hit hard with runners on base. Some believe it's a matter of wavering focus, while others say it's a mechanical issue when he pitches from the stretch, as he tends to sink on his backside, lower his release point and not stay as tall in his delivery. That causes him to throw from a lower slot and leaves his stuff a little bit flat, but it should be correctable. If Carrasco can refine his command and straighten out his inconsistencies, he has the stuff to be a mid-rotation starter. He'll compete for a spot in the major league rotation this spring.

Year	Club (League)	Class	W	L	ERA	G	GS	CG	SV	IP	H	R	ER	HR	BB	SO	AVG
2004	Phillies (GCL)	R	5	4	3.56	11	8	0	0	48	53	23	19	2	15	34	.276
2005	Lakewood (SAL)	LoA	1	7	7.04	13	13	1	0	63	78	50	49	11	28	46	.302
	Batavia (NYP)	SS	0	3	13.50	4	4	0	0	15	29	25	23	8	5	12	.392
	Phillies (GCL)	R	0	0	1.80	2	2	0	0	5	3	1	1	0	1	2	.176
2006	Lakewood (SAL)	LoA	12	6	2.26	26	26	2	0	159	103	50	40	6	65	159	.182
2007	Clearwater (FSL)	HiA	6	2	2.84	12	12	1	0	70	49	22	22	8	22	53	.199
	Reading (EL)	AA	6	4	4.86	14	13	1	0	70	65	42	38	9	46	49	.247
2008	Reading (EL)	AA	7	7	4.32	20	19	1	0	115	109	58	55	13	45	109	.254
	Lehigh Valley (IL)	AAA	2	2	1.72	6	6	0	0	37	37	15	7	1	13	46	.250
2009	Lehigh Valley (IL)	AAA	6	9	5.18	20	20	0	0	115	118	73	66	14	38	112	.262

Club (League)	Class	W	L	ERA	G	GS	CG	SV	IP	H	R	ER	HR	BB	SO	AVG
Columbus (IL)	AAA	5	1	3.19	6	6	0	0	42	31	18	15	3	7	36	.196
Cleveland (AL)	MAJ	0	4	8.87	5	5	0	0	22	40	23	22	6	11	11	.400
MAJOR LEAGUE TOTALS		0	4	8.87	5	5	0	0	22	40	23	22	6	11	11	.400
MINOR LEAGUE TOTALS		50	45	4.08	134	129	6	0	739	675	377	335	75	285	658	.241

9 ALEX WHITE, RHP

BORN: Aug. 29, 1988. **B-T:** R-R. **HT.:** 6-3. **WT.:** 200. **DRAFTED:** North Carolina, 2009 (1st round). **SIGNED BY:** Bob Mayer.

White passed on signing with the Dodgers as a 14th-round pick in 2006 to attend North Carolina, where he spent three years in the Tar Heels' weekend rotation and two years as their ace. White fell slightly in the 2009 draft because of inconsistency and sign-ability concerns, going 15th overall and signing for $2.25 million at the Aug. 17 deadline. An excellent athlete and competitor, White throws a heavy 91-95 mph fastball with plus sink. His out pitch is his plus splitter, a strong weapon with depth and deception to thwart lefties. His slider has been an inconsistent pitch—some feel he got away from it in college in deference to his splitter to miss more metal bats—but it's an above-average pitch at times. White focused on his slider in instructional league, trying to get more extension out front and later break instead of letting it get long. His command wavered at times in college, and his arm action in the back—which has changed since high school, when his slider was better—concerns some scouts. After initial talk of developing White as a reliever, the Indians plan to bring him through the system as a starter. If he can rediscover his slider he would have the pure stuff to be an above-average starter, though he also could also fit in as a future closer. He'll begin his pro career in high Class A.

Year	Club (League)	Class	W	L	ERA	G	GS	CG	SV	IP	H	R	ER	HR	BB	SO	AVG
2009	Did Not Play—Signed Late																

10 JASON KIPNIS, OF/2B

BORN: April 3, 1987. **B-T:** L-R. **HT.:** 5-10. **WT.:** 175. **DRAFTED:** Arizona State, 2009 (2nd round). **SIGNED BY:** Byron Ewing.

After a redshirt year and an uneven freshman season at Kentucky—one that ended with him kicked off the team—Kipnis transferred to Arizona State. He turned down a fourth-round offer from the Padres as a draft-eligible sophomore in 2008, then went 63rd overall last June after winning Pacific-10 Conference player of the year honors. After signing him for $575,000, the Indians asked him to work at second base in instructional league. Cleveland drafted Kipnis for his bat and advanced hitting approach. He has good bat speed, a quick trigger and a loose, flat swing that stays in the zone a long time. There's occasional length to his stroke, but he centers the ball consistently, uses the whole field and handles lefties and righties. An average runner, Kipnis immediately showed surprising skill at second base with good hands, foot-work, body control and the ability to make plays to both sides. Kipnis is a tweener as an outfielder. His average speed and fringe-average arm fit better in left field than center, and while he has surprising pop for his size, he'll likely max out at average power. Though he looked good at second base in instructional league and dabbled there in college, he hasn't played the position extensively. Kipnis will report to Cleveland's complex in Goodyear, Ariz., in January to get a head start preparing for second base, where he'll get more work in spring training. He'll be 23 at the start of the 2010 season, so he'll skip a level and advance to high Class A.

Year	Club (League)	Class	AVG	G	AB	R	H	2B	3B	HR	RBI	BB	SO	SB	OBP	SLG
2009	Mahoning Valley (NYP)	SS	.306	29	111	19	34	8	3	1	19	15	18	3	.388	.459
MINOR LEAGUE TOTALS			.306	29	111	19	34	8	3	1	19	15	18	3	.388	.459

11 LOU MARSON, C

BORN: June 26, 1986. **B-T:** R-R. **HT.:** 6-1. **WT.:** 200. **DRAFTED:** HS—Scottsdale, Ariz., 2004 (4th round). **SIGNED BY:** Therron Brockish (Phillies).

Marson made his major league debut with the Phillies in the final game of the 2008 season, then spent most of April 2009 with the big league club. He went down to Triple-A in May, missed a week in June with a bruised foot, then went to Cleveland just before the trading deadline in the Cliff Lee trade. Marson doesn't have a plus tool, but he's an instinctive player with above-average control of the strike zone and a solid feel for hitting. He has limited power, as his swing isn't conducive to loft and he still needs to add strength. A below-average runner, Marson is an athletic, solid defender who receives well and gets rid of the ball quickly to make up for fringe-average arm strength. He threw out 32 percent of basestealers last year. It's only a matter of time before Carlos Santana takes over as the Indians' catcher, but his offseason hamate injury means Marson should get a chance to open 2010 as Cleveland's starter. Future projections for him range from a quality backup to an average regular.

Year	Club (League)	Class	AVG	G	AB	R	H	2B	3B	HR	RBI	BB	SO	SB	OBP	SLG
2004	Phillies (GCL)	R	.257	38	113	18	29	3	0	4	8	13	18	4	.333	.389
2005	Batavia (NYP)	SS	.245	60	220	25	54	11	3	5	25	27	52	0	.329	.391
2006	Lakewood (SAL)	LoA	.243	104	350	44	85	16	5	4	39	49	82	4	.343	.351
2007	Clearwater (FSL)	HiA	.288	111	393	68	113	24	1	7	63	52	80	3	.373	.407
2008	Reading (EL)	AA	.314	94	322	55	101	18	0	5	46	68	70	3	.433	.416
	Philadelphia (NL)	MAJ	.500	1	4	2	2	0	0	1	2	0	2	0	.500	1.250
2009	Philadelphia (NL)	MAJ	.235	7	17	3	4	1	0	0	0	3	7	0	.350	.294
	Lehigh Valley (IL)	AAA	.294	63	211	32	62	13	0	1	24	30	40	3	.382	.370
	Columbus (IL)	AAA	.243	28	103	10	25	5	1	1	9	10	19	1	.319	.340
	Cleveland (AL)	MAJ	.250	14	44	6	11	6	0	0	4	7	14	0	.346	.386
MAJOR LEAGUE TOTALS			.262	22	65	11	17	7	0	1	6	10	23	0	.355	.415
MINOR LEAGUE TOTALS			.274	498	1712	252	469	90	10	27	214	249	361	18	.369	.386

12 T.J. HOUSE, LHP

BORN: Sept. 29, 1989. **B-T:** L-L. **HT.:** 6-2. **WT.:** 215. **DRAFTED:** HS—Picayune, Miss., 2008 (16th round). **SIGNED BY:** Chuck Bartlett.

Most teams figured House would attend Tulane, which is why he fell to the Indians in the 16th round of the 2008 draft. He turned pro, however, for a $750,000 bonus and made his pro debut in 2009 in low Class A. He proved to be Lake County's most consistent starter at age 19. House doesn't have a plus pitch, but he mixes three solid offerings with an advanced feel for pitching for his age. House has solid command of his fastball, which sits at 87-91 mph and touches 93 with sink. His changeup is his most advanced secondary offering, an average pitch with a chance to be plus in the future. His low-80s slider isn't an out pitch, but it has average potential. House is a good athlete with clean arm action and a compact delivery that he repeats, which helps him throw strikes and generally keep the ball down in the zone. He should open the year in the Kinston rotation.

Year	Club (League)	Class	W	L	ERA	G	GS	CG	SV	IP	H	R	ER	HR	BB	SO	AVG
2009	Lake County (SAL)	LoA	6	11	3.15	26	26	0	0	134	127	56	47	8	49	109	.250
MINOR LEAGUE TOTALS			6	11	3.15	26	26	0	0	134	127	56	47	8	49	109	.250

13 KELVIN DE LA CRUZ, LHP

BORN: Jan. 8, 1988. **B-T:** L-L. **HT.:** 6-5. **WT.:** 187. **SIGNED:** Dominican Republic, 2004. **SIGNED BY:** Johnny Martinez.

De la Cruz appeared to be a prime candidate for a breakout season in 2009, and his two brilliant starts to open the season with Kinston were a promising sign. Yet those would be the last starts he would make for the K-Tribe, as he came down with a strained ligament in his elbow that effectively ended his season. He made three rehab starts in the Rookie-level Arizona League at the end of August, and threw more in instructional league and in the team's Dominican instructional program, working as long as three innings against live hitters. His velocity hadn't fully returned, though he was throwing without restrictions and the Indians expect him to be ready to go for spring training. Cleveland still chose to protect de la Cruz from the Rule 5 draft by placing him on their 40-man roster after the season. He has the most upside of any lefthander in the system, starting with a 90-91 mph fastball that touches 94 when he's right. His mid- to high-70s curveball can be a plus pitch that he can throw to lefties and righties. He's still growing into his coordination and his delivery, and he'll need to throw his changeup more when he's healthy. There's a good chance de la Cruz will return to high Class A in 2010, and if he stays healthy he should end up in Akron at some point.

Year	Club (League)	Class	W	L	ERA	G	GS	CG	SV	IP	H	R	ER	HR	BB	SO	AVG
2005	Indians1 (DSL)	R	3	3	2.36	13	12	0	1	53	49	23	14	3	16	39	.234
2006	Indians (GCL)	R	1	2	10.98	9	4	0	0	20	32	29	24	2	13	15	.360
2007	Indians (GCL)	R	3	0	0.50	3	3	0	0	18	7	1	1	1	2	20	.117
	Mahoning Valley (NYP)	SS	2	4	3.98	12	12	0	0	54	41	27	24	5	34	53	.216
2008	Akron (EL)	AA	1	0	7.20	1	1	0	0	5	4	4	4	1	3	4	.222
	Lake County (SAL)	LoA	8	4	1.69	18	18	1	0	96	71	23	18	2	34	96	.207
	Kinston (CAR)	HiA	3	2	6.44	8	8	0	0	29	35	22	21	1	25	36	.292
2009	Kinston (CAR)	HiA	2	0	1.50	2	2	0	0	12	6	2	2	1	2	19	.146
	Indians (AZL)	R	0	2	9.39	3	3	0	0	8	10	8	8	1	5	5	.323
MINOR LEAGUE TOTALS			23	17	3.54	69	63	1	1	295	255	139	116	17	134	287	.232

14 JORDAN BROWN, OF/1B

BORN: Dec. 18, 1983. **B-T:** L-L. **HT.:** 6-0. **WT.:** 205. **DRAFTED:** Arizona, 2005 (4th round). **SIGNED BY:** Joe Graham.

Brown picked up MVP awards in the high Class A Carolina League in 2006 and in the Eastern League the following year, but a knee injury hampered him in 2008. Brown bounced back in 2009, winning the International League batting crown (.336) and ranking third in slugging (.532). He was added to the 40-man roster in

November and continued to hit well in winter ball for Caracas in the Venezuelan League. Brown's best attribute is his low-maintenance swing, as he's one of the better contact hitters in the organization. He has a tendency to chase high fastballs, though a shift in his hand position holding the bat helped keep him on top of the ball more. He used his lower half more in his swing last year and sacrificed some on-base ability for more power, though he projects to have only average pop. A below-average runner, Brown isn't the best athlete and is a subpar defensive first baseman. He also spent time with Columbus in left field and played there primarily in Venezuela. Brown will have the chance to compete for a job in Cleveland in spring training, though with the talent ahead of him, he seems likely head back to Triple-A.

Year	Club (League)	Class	AVG	G	AB	R	H	2B	3B	HR	RBI	BB	SO	SB	OBP	SLG
2005	Mahoning Valley (NYP)	SS	.253	19	75	15	19	1	0	3	7	3	7	2	.291	.387
2006	Kinston (CAR)	HiA	.290	125	473	71	137	26	7	15	87	51	59	4	.362	.469
2007	Akron (EL)	AA	.333	127	483	85	161	36	2	11	76	63	56	11	.421	.484
2008	Buffalo (IL)	AAA	.281	109	420	52	118	30	3	7	51	35	67	3	.337	.417
2009	Columbus (IL)	AAA	.336	111	417	65	140	35	1	15	67	30	64	2	.381	.532
MINOR LEAGUE TOTALS			.308	491	1868	288	575	128	13	51	288	182	253	22	.374	.472

15 JASON DONALD, SS

BORN: Sept. 4, 1984. **B-T:** R-R. **HT.:** 6-1. **WT.:** 195. **DRAFTED:** Arizona, 2008 (3rd round). **SIGNED BY:** Therron Brockish (Phillies).

Donald was teammates with Jordan Brown on Arizona's 2005 College World Series team and was signed by the same scout who signed Lou Marson. Donald had a breakout year in 2008, playing in the Futures Game, performing as one of Team USA's top players at the Olympics and finishing the season with a good effort in the Arizona Fall League. He couldn't replicate that success in 2009, when injuries limited him. With Jimmy Rollins and Chase Utley blocking Donald in Philadelphia, the Phillies included him in the four-player package to acquire Cliff Lee. Donald played just 10 games in Triple-A after the trade because of a strained back, after missing time earlier in the year with a torn meniscus in his left knee. Donald has solid but not spectacular tools across the board. When healthy, he shows a solid feel for hitting and for the strike zone, with good hands and strong forearms generating a tick below-average power. An average runner, Donald has an average arm but is a fringy defensive shortstop whose range and overall defensive skill set might be better suited for second base. He's also capable at third base. Added to the 40-man roster in November, Donald could get a chance to crack Cleveland's Opening Day roster, but the more likely scenario is a return to Triple-A. Some scouts see him as a utility player, but he has the upside of a solid starter if he regains his 2008 form.

Year	Club (League)	Class	AVG	G	AB	R	H	2B	3B	HR	RBI	BB	SO	SB	OBP	SLG
2006	Batavia (NYP)	SS	.263	63	213	33	56	14	2	1	24	23	42	12	.347	.362
2007	Lakewood (SAL)	LoA	.310	51	197	41	61	9	3	4	30	29	39	2	.409	.447
	Clearwater (FSL)	HiA	.300	83	293	48	88	22	5	8	41	35	70	3	.386	.491
2008	Reading (EL)	AA	.307	92	362	57	111	19	4	14	54	47	86	11	.391	.497
2009	Phillies (GCL)	R	.231	9	26	4	6	1	1	0	1	2	5	1	.286	.346
	Lehigh Valley (IL)	AAA	.236	51	208	26	49	15	1	1	16	14	53	6	.297	.332
	Columbus (IL)	AAA	.257	10	35	10	9	2	0	1	1	3	11	1	.350	.400
MINOR LEAGUE TOTALS			.285	359	1334	219	380	82	16	29	167	153	306	36	.369	.436

16 ZACH PUTNAM, RHP

BORN: July 3, 1987. **B-T:** R-R. **HT.:** 6-2. **WT.:** 225. **DRAFTED:** Michigan, 2008 (5th round). **SIGNED BY:** Derrick Ross.

Putnam was a highly touted prospect in high school, then starred for three years as a two-way player at Michigan. Always considered a better prospect on the mound, he came out college with polish and a wide array of pitches. One of several over-slot signings for the Tribe in the 2008 draft, he received $600,000 as a fifth-rounder. After opening last season in Kinston's rotation, Putnam advanced to Double-A in May and pitched out of the bullpen. He throws a heavy low-90s fastball that touches 94 mph. He generally commands the pitch to both sides of the plate, and the sink on his heater helps him get grounders at a high clip. His out pitch is a plus splitter with late tumble, and he has the ability to throw it for strikes or get hitters to chase it out of the zone. He'll also mix in a solid changeup with sink and fade, and a developing slider. At times his slider has cutter action, but it needs more depth to become an average pitch. Putnam has a strong, athletic body, though he still has inconsistencies with his delivery. He'll get another chance to start in 2010, but many scouts see his future as a power arm in the back of the bullpen, where his stuff plays up in shorter stints.

Year	Club (League)	Class	W	L	ERA	G	GS	CG	SV	IP	H	R	ER	HR	BB	SO	AVG
2008	Mahoning Valley (NYP)	SS	0	1	3.72	3	3	0	0	10	7	5	4	0	5	8	.206
2009	Kinston (CAR)	HiA	2	0	4.13	5	5	0	0	24	22	12	11	1	5	23	.247
	Akron (EL)	AA	4	2	4.13	33	0	0	2	57	59	29	26	2	18	57	.261
MINOR LEAGUE TOTALS			6	3	4.08	41	8	0	2	90	88	46	41	3	28	88	.252

17 CARLOS RIVERO, SS

BORN: May 20, 1988. **B-T:** R-R. **HT.:** 6-3. **WT.:** 210. **SIGNED:** Venezuela, 2005. **SIGNED BY:** Stewart Ruiz.

Rivero has shown flashes of breaking out but has yet to put it all together. After hitting .220/.290/.279 in the first half last season, he rebounded and hit .280/.340/.457 after the all-star break as Akron cruised to the Eastern League title. He also made strides at the plate in the Arizona Fall League, showing the ability to keep his bat in the zone longer. Rivero is bigger than most shortstops and showcases impressive raw power in batting practice that he's still learning to translate into game situations. He's still figuring out his swing, and he has made strides leveraging his legs better and not drifting with his hips as often, though it's still something he needs to monitor. While he's not a free swinger, Rivero can struggle to handle breaking balls. He's a reliable fielder on balls hit in his area, with soft hands and a plus arm, but he has below-average speed and lateral range, so he might ultimately end up at third base. Rivero likely will return to Double-A, and repeating the level could lead to the best offensive year of his career. The Indians protected him on their 40-man roster during the offseason.

Year	Club (League)	Class	AVG	G	AB	R	H	2B	3B	HR	RBI	BB	SO	SB	OBP	SLG
2005	Indians1 (DSL)	R	.257	66	237	21	61	6	0	0	31	12	26	7	.295	.283
2006	Indians (GCL)	R	.284	37	134	17	38	6	0	2	22	10	20	0	.338	.373
	Burlington (APP)	R	.212	16	66	3	14	3	0	1	7	5	11	0	.264	.303
2007	Lake County (SAL)	LoA	.261	115	436	59	114	26	0	7	62	47	84	1	.332	.369
2008	Kinston (CAR)	HiA	.282	108	411	46	116	27	1	8	64	36	84	1	.342	.411
2009	Akron (EL)	AA	.242	132	480	50	116	24	2	7	58	50	73	1	.309	.344
MINOR LEAGUE TOTALS			.260	474	1764	196	459	92	3	25	244	160	298	10	.321	.358

18 JESS TODD, RHP

BORN: April 20, 1986. **B-T:** R-R. **HT.:** 5-11. **WT.:** 210. **DRAFTED:** Arkansas, 2007 (2nd round). **SIGNED BY:** Roger Smith (Cardinals).

The Cardinals drafted Todd in the second round 2007, and he cruised through three levels to reach Triple-A in his first full pro season. Converted to a reliever last year, he was dominant before St. Louis traded him and Chris Perez to the Indians for Mark DeRosa in June. Todd soon joined the Cleveland bullpen for the rest of the year, and he got hit hard. He has come largely as advertised out of college, showing a solid fastball/slider mix that profiles well for middle relief. Todd has good control and throws his fastball at 88-92 mph. His go-to pitch is an above-average slider, a swing-and-miss offering with late break and two-plane depth at 83-86 mph. He doesn't have a reliable third pitch yet to combat lefthanders. Though he's not big, his durability is less of an issue in the bullpen and he has the resilient arm to pitch on consecutive days. Todd should compete for a job in the big league bullpen this spring.

Year	Club (League)	Class	W	L	ERA	G	GS	CG	SV	IP	H	R	ER	HR	BB	SO	AVG
2007	Batavia (NYP)	SS	4	1	2.78	16	7	0	0	58	48	23	18	2	14	69	.223
2008	Palm Beach (FSL)	HiA	3	0	1.65	7	4	0	1	27	18	7	5	0	7	35	.184
	Springfield, MO (TL)	AA	4	5	2.97	17	16	0	0	103	79	37	34	12	24	81	.216
	Memphis (PCL)	AAA	1	1	3.97	4	4	0	0	23	19	10	10	4	11	20	.232
2009	St. Louis (NL)	MAJ	0	0	10.80	1	0	0	0	2	3	2	2	1	2	2	.375
	Memphis (PCL)	AAA	4	2	2.20	41	0	0	24	49	39	13	12	3	13	59	.214
	Columbus (IL)	AAA	0	0	0.00	3	0	0	1	4	1	0	0	0	0	7	.077
	Cleveland (AL)	MAJ	0	1	7.40	19	0	0	0	21	31	17	17	3	7	18	.356
MAJOR LEAGUE TOTALS			0	1	7.66	20	0	0	0	22	34	19	19	4	9	20	.358
MINOR LEAGUE TOTALS			16	9	2.69	88	31	0	26	264	204	90	79	21	69	271	.214

19 JOSH JUDY, RHP

BORN: Feb. 9, 1986. **B-T:** R-R. **HT.:** 6-4. **WT.:** 200. **DRAFTED:** Indiana Tech, 2007 (34th round). **SIGNED BY:** Derrick Ross.

After getting his feet wet in Double-A for a couple of months, Judy was nearly unhittable from July through the end of the 2009 season, posting a 1.07 ERA and a 43-6 K-BB mark in 25 innings. He also pitched well in the Arizona Fall League, where he maintained a 1.59 ERA. Judy doesn't have a high ceiling, but he should help Cleveland's bullpen in the near future, possibly as soon as 2010. He struck out more than a batter per inning and induced grounders at an above-average clip with a solid two-pitch mix last season. Judy's fastball comes in at 92-94 mph with solid life and deception that make it a swing-and-miss pitch. He can throw his fastball to both sides of the plate and gets good sink on the pitch at times, which helps him keep the ball on the ground. He backs up his fastball with a solid-average slider that has the potential to be a plus pitch with depth and two-plane break. Judy should get a chance to begin 2010 in Triple-A and could pitch in Cleveland at some point this year.

Year	Club (League)	Class	W	L	ERA	G	GS	CG	SV	IP	H	R	ER	HR	BB	SO	AVG
2007	Indians (GCL)	R	1	2	0.63	9	0	0	0	14	11	4	1	0	8	14	.204
	Mahoning Valley (NYP)	SS	0	0	0.00	4	1	0	1	11	7	0	0	0	3	7	.194

2008	Lake County (SAL)	LoA	12	1	3.51	35	0	0	1	74	60	38	29	6	25	80	.223
	Kinston (CAR)	HiA	0	0	1.93	7	0	0	0	14	12	3	3	0	1	17	.226
2009	Kinston (CAR)	HiA	0	0	0.00	5	0	0	3	5	4	0	0	0	0	7	.235
	Akron (EL)	AA	4	3	3.10	36	1	0	11	49	35	19	17	2	18	63	.198
MINOR LEAGUE TOTALS			17	6	2.68	96	2	0	16	168	129	64	50	8	55	188	.213

20 ALEXANDER PEREZ, RHP

BORN: July 24, 1989. **B-T:** R-R. **HT.:** 6-2. **WT.:** 156. **SIGNED:** Dominican Republic, 2007. **SIGNED BY:** Junior Betances.

After coming to the United States in 2008, Perez made his full-season debut last year. He pitched well enough to earn a promotion to high Class A in July, but a sore shoulder limited him toward the end of the season. A lanky righthander, Perez has a fringe-average fastball that sits at 87-91 mph and touches 93. He mixes in two and four-seamers, though he still needs to improve his fastball command. His best pitch is his 78-80 mph curveball, a plus offering with sharp action that he commands well. He also shows good feel at times for his changeup, a potentially above-average pitch that he can use against both lefthanders and righthanders. Perez has a relatively loose delivery, though he needs to be more consistent with his mechanics and incorporate his lower half better. His body type has some similarities to Hector Rondon's at the same age, and he could add another 25-30 pounds and gain a few ticks on his fastball. Adding weight and strength is also important for him to improve his durability. Perez is expected to start the season back in Kinston, though he could end the year in Double-A.

Year	Club (League)	Class	W	L	ERA	G	GS	CG	SV	IP	H	R	ER	HR	BB	SO	AVG
2007	Indians (DSL)	R	1	2	2.90	13	10	0	0	50	41	18	16	3	13	64	.218
2008	Indians (GCL)	R	2	4	4.26	10	9	0	0	51	37	24	24	5	16	49	.204
2009	Lake County (SAL)	LoA	5	4	3.04	15	15	1	0	83	69	36	28	9	24	76	.223
	Kinston (CAR)	HiA	1	2	2.87	8	7	0	0	31	32	10	10	1	9	31	.264
MINOR LEAGUE TOTALS			9	12	3.27	46	41	1	0	215	179	88	78	18	62	220	.224

21 JEANMAR GOMEZ, RHP

BORN: Feb. 10, 1988. **B-T:** R-R. **HT.:** 6-4. **WT.:** 190. **SIGNED:** Venezuela, 2005. **SIGNED BY:** Henry Centeno.

A fringy prospect coming into last season, Gomez grabbed attention when he threw a nine-inning perfect game in May. Though he lacks a true out pitch, he's a good athlete who succeeds with deception and pounding the strike zone, and his pitching acumen has increased steadily over the last couple of seasons. He mixes two- and four-seam fastballs at 89-91 mph, touching 93. His slider made strides last season, morphing from a pitch that was in between a power curveball and a cutter and adding depth when it was at its best in May. The slider is still a bit short and usually isn't a true swing-and-miss pitch. Gomez throws a firm changeup that has splitter action in the zone and induces hitters to hit the top of the baseball. He still needs to improve his changeup to have a weapon to counteract lefthanders. He shortened his arm swing last year and did a better job of creating a more consistent arm circle in the back of his delivery, but some scouts aren't crazy about his arm action. A 40-man roster addition in the offseason, Gomez will get a chance to open 2010 in Triple-A. He should be a serviceable fifth starter or middle reliever in the future.

Year	Club (League)	Class	W	L	ERA	G	GS	CG	SV	IP	H	R	ER	HR	BB	SO	AVG
2005	Indians1 (DSL)	R	5	3	1.33	13	10	0	1	61	47	15	9	2	9	46	.210
2006	Indians (GCL)	R	4	3	2.48	11	9	0	0	54	50	24	15	2	12	34	.238
2007	Lake County (SAL)	LoA	11	7	4.80	27	27	1	0	141	152	84	75	19	46	94	.278
2008	Kinston (CAR)	HiA	5	9	4.55	27	27	0	0	138	154	76	70	14	46	110	.283
2009	Kinston (CAR)	HiA	2	2	2.63	4	4	0	0	24	17	8	7	2	5	15	.202
	Akron (EL)	AA	10	4	3.43	22	22	1	0	123	117	56	47	11	40	109	.249
MINOR LEAGUE TOTALS			37	28	3.71	104	99	2	1	542	537	263	223	50	158	408	.259

22 CHEN-CHANG LEE, RHP

BORN: Oct. 21, 1986. **B-T:** R-R. **HT.:** 5-11. **WT.:** 175. **SIGNED:** Taiwan, 2008. **SIGNED BY:** Jason Lee.

The Indians signed Lee for $400,000 in September 2008, but he had been on their radar for several years. They offered the Taiwanese righthander a contract out of high school, but he declined and went to college instead. He has experience on the international stage, pitching in the Olympics in 2008 and in the World Baseball Classic in 2009. Lee showcases above-average arm strength with a lively 92-93 mph fastball that has been clocked as high as 96. His solid-average slider is slurvy and has late downward bite at 82-84 mph. When he repeats his delivery and keeps his arm slot up, the slider has late depth off his fastball, though when he overthrows it breaks more side to side. Lee fits better in the bullpen than the rotation because of his low three-quarters arm slot. He still needs to develop his splitter, a work in progress, to combat lefthanders. Lee will head to Double-A for 2010 and could help Cleveland's bullpen by 2011.

Year	Club (League)	Class	W	L	ERA	G	GS	CG	SV	IP	H	R	ER	HR	BB	SO	AVG
2009	Kinston (CAR)	HiA	4	6	3.35	45	0	0	2	83	67	33	31	5	28	97	.220
MINOR LEAGUE TOTALS			4	6	3.35	45	0	0	2	83	67	33	31	5	28	97	.220

23 ABNER ABREU, OF

BORN: Oct. 24, 1989. **B-T:** R-R. **HT.:** 6-3. **WT.:** 170. **SIGNED:** Dominican Republic, 2006. **SIGNED BY:** Junior Betances.

Abreu's younger brother Esdras signed with the Rangers in 2008 for $550,000, but pales in comparison as a prospect to Abner, who signed for $75,000. He posted strong numbers for Lake County in 2009, but his season ended in June when he dislocated his shoulder diving for a ball in the outfield. Lean and athletic, Abreu has a high-waisted, slender build but already generates natural power with his bat speed and the natural loft in his swing. Despite his offensive tools, he remains raw at the plate. He has a long way to go in terms of patience, working the count and recognizing offspeed stuff. Getting himself into better hitter's counts and learning to lay off pitches up and out of the zone will allow Abreu to better translate his raw power into game situations. A third baseman in 2008, he moved to right field last season, where his skill set is better suited. His average speed plays up because he has good instincts in the field, giving him a chance to be a solid defender with an above-average arm. Abreu's injury set his timetable back, and he could return to low Class A in 2010.

Year	Club (League)	Class	AVG	G	AB	R	H	2B	3B	HR	RBI	BB	SO	SB	OBP	SLG
2007	Indians (DSL)	R	.303	56	228	34	69	13	7	4	41	18	46	5	.353	.474
2008	Indians (GCL)	R	.251	51	199	32	50	16	4	11	37	9	52	4	.289	.538
2009	Lake County (SAL)	LoA	.305	63	246	36	75	16	4	7	30	11	68	3	.351	.488
MINOR LEAGUE TOTALS			.288	170	673	102	194	45	15	22	108	38	166	12	.334	.498

24 BEAU MILLS, 1B

BORN: Aug. 15, 1986. **B-T:** R-R. **HT.:** 6-3. **WT.:** 220. **DRAFTED:** Lewis-Clark State (Idaho), 2007 (1st round). **SIGNED BY:** Greg Smith.

The son of new Astros manager Brad Mills, Beau went 13th overall in the 2007 draft after setting an NAIA record with 38 homers and leading Lewis-Clark State (Idaho) to a national title. Signed for $1.575 million, he won the Carolina League MVP award in his first full pro season, then struggled to get on base and tap into his raw power in 2009. Despite Mills' difficulties in Double-A, he still shows the aptitude for hitting and strength for power. He exhibits good baseball instincts and solid plate discipline, but he also has a tendency to chase with two strikes and needs to learn which pitches he can drive. Mills began pressing and became more pull-oriented later in the 2009 season, though toward the end of the year his numbers began to pick up as he started to use the whole field. With the leg lift he employs in his swing, he has trouble staying back at times, which gets him caught out on his front foot and takes away from his power. He has worked hard to decrease his leg kick, and when he stays back he's able to leverage the baseball for power to all fields. Considered a defensive liability coming into the season, Mills did make strides at first base, where he showed solid hands and improved footwork. A third baseman in his pro debut, he has some arm strength but his range always will be limited and some scouts see him as a bit stiff. He's a below-average runner. The Indians are deep with first base/left field types, so Mills will have to rebound in 2010.

Year	Club (League)	Class	AVG	G	AB	R	H	2B	3B	HR	RBI	BB	SO	SB	OBP	SLG
2007	Mahoning Valley (NYP)	SS	.179	8	28	5	5	2	0	0	1	3	7	0	.303	.250
	Lake County (SAL)	LoA	.271	44	177	32	48	12	1	5	36	14	38	0	.333	.435
	Kinston (CAR)	HiA	.275	10	40	7	11	6	0	1	5	4	8	0	.375	.500
2008	Kinston (CAR)	HiA	.293	125	482	78	141	34	3	21	90	54	105	2	.373	.506
2009	Akron (EL)	AA	.267	134	516	59	138	33	1	14	83	31	95	1	.308	.417
MINOR LEAGUE TOTALS			.276	321	1243	181	343	87	5	41	215	106	253	3	.340	.453

25 JESUS BRITO, 3B

BORN: December 25, 1987. **B-T:** R-R. **HT.:** 6-1. **WT.:** 160. **SIGNED:** Dominican Republic, 2005. **SIGNED BY:** Johnny Martinez.

Brito spent three years in the Rookie-level Dominican Summer League before coming to the United States last year and leading the Arizona League in hitting at .366. He also performed well after a promotion to short-season Mahoning Valley. Brito handles the bat well and hits to all fields. He's not the most physical player, but the ball comes off his bat well. He has room to add weight and get stronger, which could turn his gap power into home run pop down the road. He has a solid feel for the strike zone and doesn't strike out at a high clip. An outfielder prior to 2009, Brito moved to third base, where he has a strong, accurate arm. He made strides with his footwork, but he struggled with the transition to the hot corner, primarily with going to his right and getting throws off quickly. He made 19 errors in 47 games at third base and might ultimately end up back in the outfield. He's an average runner at best and not much of a basestealer. Brito could get a chance to make his full-season debut this year in Lake County.

Year	Club (League)	Class	AVG	G	AB	R	H	2B	3B	HR	RBI	BB	SO	SB	OBP	SLG
2006	Indians (DSL)	R	.223	69	229	32	51	12	2	2	33	39	66	5	.348	.319
2007	Indians (DSL)	R	.210	61	210	24	44	17	1	1	25	37	55	1	.335	.314
2008	Indians (DSL)	R	.239	68	230	45	55	5	1	1	19	44	32	20	.360	.283
2009	Indians (AZL)	R	.366	35	134	36	49	12	8	3	25	18	26	2	.439	.642
	Mahoning Valley (NYP)	SS	.333	25	90	16	30	7	2	0	18	14	15	0	.419	.456
MINOR LEAGUE TOTALS			.256	258	893	153	229	53	14	7	120	152	194	28	.368	.371

26 CONNOR GRAHAM, RHP

BORN: Dec. 30, 1985. **B-T:** R-R. **HT.:** 6-6. **WT.:** 235. **DRAFTED:** Miami (Ohio), 2007 (5th round). **SIGNED BY:** Ed Santa (Rockies).

Graham was a starter in the Rockies system and continued to pitch in the rotation after Colorado traded him to the Indians for Rafael Betancourt in July. The scouting consensus, however, is that he'll fit better in the bullpen, where he spent his first two years at Miami (Ohio). Graham throws a low-90s fastball that has been clocked up to 97 mph. With his size, he generates downhill plane, and the solid sink on his heater is aided by the angle and leverage he's able to create. Graham's slider bites downhill and flashes depth at times. It has a chance to be an average or better pitch with a bit of late tilt when it's on, but it's inconsistent right now. Some scouts question Graham's athleticism and have concerns about his body, and his results bear out those worries. He walked five batters per nine innings in 2009, showing his control needs quite a bit of work. He needs to be able to repeat his delivery to throw more strikes, and his corkscrew arm action doesn't make things easier for him. Graham will probably open this year in Double-A.

Year	Club (League)	Class	W	L	ERA	G	GS	CG	SV	IP	H	R	ER	HR	BB	SO	AVG
2007	Tri-City (NWL)	SS	1	0	2.37	6	4	0	0	19	23	7	5	2	6	18	.303
2008	Asheville (SAL)	LoA	12	6	2.26	26	26	2	0	147	99	50	37	3	83	138	.189
2009	Modesto (CAL)	HiA	7	4	3.14	16	16	0	0	80	68	35	28	2	41	87	.225
	Akron (EL)	AA	1	3	4.93	8	7	0	0	38	40	21	21	3	25	39	.268
MINOR LEAGUE TOTALS			21	13	2.87	56	53	2	0	285	230	113	91	10	155	282	.219

27 WES HODGES, 3B

BORN: Sept. 14, 1984. **B-T:** R-R. **HT.:** 6-2. **WT.:** 205. **DRAFTED:** Georgia Tech, 2006 (2nd round). **SIGNED BY:** Jerry Jordan.

It was hard for scouts to get a handle on Hodges in 2009, when wrist and shoulder injuries limited him to 91 games and often relegated him to DH. The injuries took a noticeable toll on his hitting and defense, getting him out of his rhythm and his routine. Staying healthy has been a longtime problem for Hodges. He broke a bone in his hand—and taught himself to hit lefthanded—as a high school senior in 2003, then had a stress fracture in his leg when he was draft-eligible again in 2006. Paid first-round money ($1 million) as a second-round pick, he broke a toe and strained a hamstring in his 2007 pro debut. At his best, Hodges has shown advanced feel for hitting and the ability to use the whole field with average power. Scouts are concerned about his body and his fielding, with many predicting a move off third base in the near future. He has decent hands and an average arm, but he's a below-average runner with limited range and first-step quickness. Cleveland showed its faith in Hodges by protecting him on its 40-man roster in November. He'll return to Triple-A to get back on track in 2010.

Year	Club (League)	Class	AVG	G	AB	R	H	2B	3B	HR	RBI	BB	SO	SB	OBP	SLG
2007	Kinston (CAR)	HiA	.288	104	393	60	113	22	3	15	71	44	90	0	.367	.473
2008	Akron (EL)	AA	.290	133	504	70	146	29	3	18	97	52	105	3	.354	.466
2009	Lake County (SAL)	LoA	.400	5	10	1	4	2	0	0	2	2	1	0	.538	.600
	Columbus (IL)	AAA	.265	86	332	33	88	24	0	5	38	19	64	8	.307	.383
MINOR LEAGUE TOTALS			.283	328	1239	164	351	77	6	38	208	117	260	11	.348	.447

28 BRYAN PRICE, RHP

BORN: Nov. 13, 1986. **B-T:** R-R. **HT.:** 6-4. **WT.:** 210. **DRAFTED:** Rice, 2008 (1st round supplemental). **SIGNED BY:** John Booher (Red Sox).

Price was a reliever at Rice, but the Red Sox signed him for $849,000 as a supplemental first-round pick in 2008 and began to develop him as a starter. He reached high Class A before Boston included him with Justin Masterson and Nick Hagadone in a trade for Victor Martinez last July. Price has a long, strong, angular body with long arms and fingers, and he mostly pitches off his strong fastball/slider combination. His fastball comes in the low 90s, and while it can be a little straight, he has made strides locating the pitch. His plus slider is his best offering, with hard, tight spin and downward angle that's tough for hitters to pick up. Price mixed in a curveball every now and then while with the Red Sox, though he mostly shelved the pitch to work on his mechanics and fastball location down in the zone. He's still trying to find a solid third pitch, as his changeup isn't a reliable weapon against lefthanders yet. Price has good arm action and a smooth delivery that he repeats. He might end up in the bullpen down the road, though the Indians plan to exhaust his options as a starter. He should make the jump to Double-A in 2010.

Year	Club (League)	Class	W	L	ERA	G	GS	CG	SV	IP	H	R	ER	HR	BB	SO	AVG
2008	Lowell (NYP)	SS	1	3	3.83	12	9	0	0	40	47	22	17	2	10	43	.281
2009	Greenville (SAL)	LoA	3	2	2.45	8	8	0	0	44	37	16	12	2	12	40	.223
	Salem (CAR)	HiA	1	6	6.54	11	11	0	0	52	62	43	38	4	19	57	.288
	Kinston (CAR)	HiA	2	4	4.95	7	7	0	0	36	38	22	20	9	10	30	.268
MINOR LEAGUE TOTALS			7	15	4.53	38	35	0	0	173	184	103	87	17	51	170	.267

29 SCOTT BARNES, LHP

BORN: Sept. 5, 1987. **B-T:** L-L. **HT.:** 6-4. **WT.:** 185. **DRAFTED:** St. John's, 2008 (8th round).
SIGNED BY: John DiCarlo (Giants)

A gangly lefthander, Barnes looked like a nifty sign for the Giants in the eighth round of the 2008 draft. He was part of a low Class A South Atlantic League championship team in his pro debut, then pitched well in high Class A last year before San Francisco traded him for Ryan Garko in late July. Barnes doesn't have top-shelf stuff, but he's deceptive, throws strikes and can finish hitters off with his above-average changeup. Pitching from the third-base side of the rubber, he repeats his mechanics and his arm works well out front. He has an unorthodox delivery and can get across his body a little, though that helps him hide the ball and aids in his deception. Barnes works at 89-90 mph and touches 92, spotting his fastball to both sides of the plate. He throws from a low three-quarters arm slot, which results in a slurvish slider that needs to improve. Barnes has the upside of a back-of-the-rotation starter and should begin 2010 in Double-A.

Year	Club (League)	Class	W	L	ERA	G	GS	CG	SV	IP	H	R	ER	HR	BB	SO	AVG
2008	Giants (AZL)	R	0	1	3.38	3	0	0	0	5	3	2	2	0	4	11	.167
	Salem-Keizer (NWL)	SS	0	0	4.76	2	1	0	0	6	6	3	3	0	1	11	.250
	Augusta (SAL)	LoA	3	2	1.38	6	6	0	0	33	15	6	5	0	7	41	.133
2009	San Jose (CAL)	HiA	12	3	2.85	18	18	0	0	98	82	36	31	7	29	99	.227
	Kinston (CAR)	HiA	0	0	2.13	3	3	0	0	13	14	3	3	1	6	10	.280
	Akron (EL)	AA	2	2	5.68	6	6	0	0	32	35	22	20	7	14	29	.292
MINOR LEAGUE TOTALS			17	8	3.10	38	34	0	0	186	155	72	64	15	61	201	.226

30 ERIC BERGER, LHP

BORN: April 22, 1986. **B-T:** L-L. **HT.:** 6-2. **WT.:** 205. **DRAFTED:** Arizona, 2008 (8th round).
SIGNED BY: Cesar Geronimo.

Berger had Tommy John surgery while at Arizona, costing him the 2007 season. An eighth-round pick as a redshirt junior the following year, he already has surpassed expectations while drawing raves for his competitiveness. He doesn't have overpowering stuff, but he's deceptive and keeps hitters off balance. Berger's fastball resides at 89-91 mph and touches 93. It has natural cutting life because of how he finishes his pitches, getting off to the side at times. He's still developing his secondary offerings, though his curveball has some promise. It has late bite to get the occasional swing and miss when he's able to release it out front, but he also leaves it up in the zone at times. His changeup has late sink that he's able to repeat with good arm speed, though it also lacks consistency. Berger is a good athlete, but there's a lot of effort in his delivery, and his arm action and over-the-top arm slot are deceptive but difficult to repeat. He's a solid strike thrower, but his unorthodox mechanics lead to difficulties with his secondary pitches and command. Berger has a chance be a back-of-the-rotation starter, and he also could crack the big league roster as a lefthanded reliever. He should open 2010 in Double-A.

Year	Club (League)	Class	W	L	ERA	G	GS	CG	SV	IP	H	R	ER	HR	BB	SO	AVG
2008	Mahoning Valley (NYP)	SS	2	0	2.12	8	8	0	0	34	26	11	8	2	9	41	.203
	Lake County (SAL)	LoA	0	0	2.08	2	1	0	0	4	3	1	1	0	2	4	.176
2009	Kinston (CAR)	HiA	7	8	2.45	21	21	0	0	110	93	38	30	4	45	100	.227
	Akron (EL)	AA	3	1	2.67	6	6	0	0	34	32	14	10	1	16	33	.250
MINOR LEAGUE TOTALS			12	9	2.42	37	36	0	0	182	154	64	49	7	72	178	.226

Colorado Rockies

BY TRACY RINGOLSBY

After making their first World Series appearance and winning Baseball America's Organization of the Year award in 2007, the Rockies plummeted to 74 wins as an encore. A month after their disappointing season ended, they traded their best player, Matt Holliday, a year before he became a free agent in a move that appeared to signal the beginning of a rebuilding process.

Colorado stumbled to an 18-28 start in 2009, costing manager Clint Hurdle his job as it appeared the club was headed for another underachieving season.

But the Rockies suddenly reversed course, going 74-42 after bench coach Jim Tracy replaced Hurdle. They won a franchise-record 92 games and advanced to the playoffs for the third time in club history.

Just as homegrown players had sparked the World Series run two years earlier, they keyed the turnaround this time. Colorado was the only team to field an Opening Day lineup consisting solely of players it had originally signed and developed.

Following an injury-plagued second season, Troy Tulowitzki reclaimed his place as one of baseball's elite shortstops. Ubaldo Jimenez blossomed into a legitimate ace. Rookie Dexter Fowler, who ranked No. 1 on this list a year ago, injected speed and athleticism into the lineup after claiming the center-field job.

More talent is on the way. Lefthander Christian Friedrich, who surprisingly lasted 25 picks in the 2008 draft, ranked second in the minor leagues in strikeouts per nine innings (12.0) and may push for a big league audition by the end of 2010. Righthanders Jhoulys Chacin and Esmil Rogers made cameos in Colorado, providing further evidence that pitching shouldn't be in short supply. Second baseman Eric Young Jr. earned a spot on the postseason roster with his speed and defensive versatility.

Rockies scouting director Bill Schmidt and his staff further stocked the system with a 2009 draft rated as the industry's best by Baseball America. Lefthander Tyler Matzek slipped through the first 10 picks primarily because he had let it be known that he was looking for "unprecedented money," and Schmidt pounced with the 11th overall choice. At the Aug. 17 signing deadline, Colorado was able to land Matzek for $3.9 million, the biggest bonus in franchise history but not an extraordinary sum for a player rated by some clubs as the second-best talent in the draft.

Dexter Fowler, Colorado's top prospect last year, added speed to a homegrown lineup

LARRY GOREN

TOP 30 PROSPECTS

1. Tyler Matzek, lhp	16. Chris Balcom-Miller, rhp
2. Christian Friedrich, lhp	17. Delta Cleary, of
3. Wilin Rosario, c	18. Jordan Pacheco, c
4. Jhoulys Chacin, rhp	19. Kent Matthes, of
5. Hector Gomez, ss	20. Al Alburquerque, rhp
6. Eric Young Jr., 2b/of	21. Parker Frazier, rhp
7. Tim Wheeler, of	22. Craig Baker, rhp
8. Rex Brothers, lhp	23. Shane Lindsay, rhp
9. Esmil Rogers, rhp	24. Chaz Roe, rhp
10. Nolan Arenado, 3b	25. Matt Reynolds, lhp
11. Samuel Deduno, rhp	26. Jonathan Vargas, lhp
12. Charlie Blackmon, of	27. Edgmer Escalona, rhp
13. Michael McKenry, c	28. Tyler Massey, of
14. Casey Weathers, rhp	29. Chris Nelson, ss
15. Juan Nicasio, rhp	30. Kiel Roling, 1b

Schmidt said he didn't think taking Matzek despite his questionable signability was a gamble, because the Rockies also owned the 32nd and 34th overall selections, compensation for the loss of free agent Brian Fuentes. They got two more talent values with those choices in a pair of college players with upside in outfielder Tim Wheeler and lefthander Rex Brothers.

In his decade on the job, Schmidt has proven to be conservative and productive in his drafting approach. The Rockies also continue to get a return on their modest investments in Latin America, including Jimenez, who has emerged as their No. 1 starter.

General Manager: Dan O'Dowd. **Farm Director:** Marc Gustafson. **Scouting Director:** Bill Schmidt.

Class	Team	League	W	L	PCT	Finish*	Manager(s)
Majors	Colorado Rockies	National	92	70	.568	3rd (16)	Clint Hurdle/Jim Tracy
Triple-A	Colorado Springs Sky Sox	Pacific Coast	73	69	.514	6th (16)	Tom Runnells/Stu Cole
Double-A	Tulsa Drillers	Texas	74	66	.529	2nd (8)	Stu Cole/Ron Gideon
High A	Modesto Nuts	California	75	65	.536	t-3rd (10)	Jerry Weinstein
Low A	Asheville Tourists	South Atlantic	68	70	.493	7th (16)	Joe Mikulik
Short-season	Tri-City Dust Devils	Northwest	47	29	.618	2nd (8)	Fred Ocasio
Rookie	Casper Ghosts	Pioneer	28	46	.378	7th (8)	Tony Diaz
Overall 2009 Minor League Record			365	345	.514	9th (30)	

*Finish in overall standings (No. of teams in league). †League champion.

LAST YEAR'S TOP 30

Rank	Player, Pos.	Status
1.	Dexter Fowler, of	Majors
2.	Jhoulys Chacin, rhp	No. 4
3.	Christian Friedrich, lhp	No. 2
4.	Wilin Rosario, c	No. 3
5.	Hector Gomez, ss	No. 5
6.	Casey Weathers, rhp	No. 14
7.	Esmil Rogers, rhp	No. 9
8.	Seth Smith, of	Majors
9.	Michael McKenry, c	No. 13
10.	Charlie Blackmon, of	No. 12
11.	Delta Cleary, of	No. 17
12.	Connor Graham, rhp	(Indians)
13.	Chris Nelson, ss	No. 29
14.	Tyler Massey, of	No. 28
15.	Parker Frazier, rhp	No. 21
16.	Aneury Rodriguez, rhp	(Rays)
17.	Shane Lindsay, rhp	No. 23
18.	Eric Young Jr., 2b/of	No. 6
19.	Ryan Mattheus, rhp	(Nationals)
20.	Darin Holcomb, 3b	Dropped out
21.	Aaron Weatherford, rhp	Dropped out
22.	Brandon Hynick, rhp	(White Sox)
23.	Juan Morillo, rhp	(Rakuten (Japan))
24.	Cory Riordan, rhp	Dropped out
25.	Chaz Roe, rhp	No. 24
26.	Corey Wimberly, 2b	(Athletics)
27.	Jonathan Herrera, 2b	Dropped out
28.	Christian Colonel, of/inf	Dropped out
29.	Joe Koshansky, 1b	(Brewers)
30.	Carlos Martinez, ss	Dropped out

BEST TOOLS

Best Hitter for Average	Nolan Arenado
Best Power Hitter	Kent Matthes
Best Strike-Zone Discipline	Darin Holcomb
Fastest Baserunner	Eric Young Jr.
Best Athlete	Eric Young Jr.
Best Fastball	Tyler Matzek
Best Curveball	Christian Friedrich
Best Slider	Rex Brothers
Best Changeup	Jhoulys Chacin
Best Control	Matt Reynolds
Best Defensive Catcher	Michael McKenry
Best Defensive Infielder	Jonathan Herrera
Best Infield Arm	Hector Gomez
Best Defensive Outfielder	Chris Frey
Best Outfield Arm	David Christensen

PROJECTED 2013 LINEUP

Catcher	Chris Iannetta
First Base	Brad Hawpe
Second Base	Hector Gomez
Third Base	Ian Stewart
Shortstop	Troy Tulowitzki
Left Field	Seth Smith
Center Field	Dexter Fowler
Right Field	Carlos Gonzalez
No. 1 Starter	Ubaldo Jimenez
No. 2 Starter	Tyler Matzek
No. 3 Starter	Aaron Cook
No. 4 Starter	Christian Friedrich
No. 5 Starter	Jorge de la Rosa
Closer	Rex Brothers

TOP PROSPECTS OF THE DECADE

Year	Player, Pos.	2009 Org.
2000	Choo Freeman, of	Out of baseball
2001	Chin-Hui Tsao, rhp	Royals
2002	Chin-Hui Tsao, rhp	Royals
2003	Aaron Cook, rhp	Rockies
2004	Chin-Hui Tsao, rhp	Royals
2005	Ian Stewart, 3b	Rockies
2006	Ian Stewart, 3b	Rockies
2007	Troy Tulowitzki, ss	Rockies
2008	Franklin Morales, lhp	Rockies
2009	Dexter Fowler, of	Rockies

TOP DRAFT PICKS OF THE DECADE

Year	Player, Pos.	2009 Org.
2000	*Matt Harrington, rhp	Out of baseball
2001	Jayson Nix, 2b (1st round supp.)	White Sox
2002	Jeff Francis, lhp	Rockies
2003	Ian Stewart, 3b	Rockies
2004	Chris Nelson, ss	Rockies
2005	Troy Tulowitzki, ss	Rockies
2006	Greg Reynolds, rhp	Rockies
2007	Casey Weathers, rhp	Rockies
2008	Christian Friedrich, lhp	Rockies
2009	Tyler Matzek, lhp	Rockies

*Did not sign.

LARGEST BONUSES IN CLUB HISTORY

Tyler Matzek, 2009	$3,900,000
Greg Reynolds, 2006	$3,250,000
Jason Young, 2000	$2,750,000
Troy Tulowitzki, 2005	$2,300,000
Chin-Hui Tsao, 1999	$2,200,000

COLORADO ROCKIES

TOP 2010 ROOKIE: Eric Young Jr., 2b/of. Game-changing speed got him on the postseason roster.

BREAKOUT PROSPECT: Shane Lindsay, rhp. He has big league stuff with a mid-90s fastball and a knuckle-curve, but he hasn't been able to stay healthy.

SLEEPER: Scott Beerer, of. A 2003 second-round pick as a pitcher, he retired after 2006 and came back last year as an outfielder, hitting .385/.443/.594.

SOURCE OF TOP 30 TALENT			
Homegrown	29	Acquired	1
College	11	Trades	1
Junior college	2	Rule 5 draft	0
High school	6	Independent leagues	0
Draft-and-follow	1	Free agents/waivers	0
Nondrafted free agents	0		
International	9		

Numbers in parentheses indicate prospect rankings

LF
Tyler Massey (28)
Scott Robinson
Scott Beerer
Cole Garner
Mike Zuanich

CF
Charlie Blackmon (12)
Delta Cleary (17)
Chris Frey
Avery Barnes

RF
Tim Wheeler (7)
Kent Matthes (19)
Matt Miller
David Christensen

3B
Nolan Arenado (10)
Joe Sanders
Darin Holcomb

SS
Hector Gomez (5)
Helder Velazquez
Jason Van Kooten
Joey Wong

2B
Eric Young Jr. (6)
Chris Nelson (29)
Daniel Mayora
Jonathan Herrera

1B
Kiel Roling (30)
Ben Paulsen
Brent Bowman
Jared Clark

C
Wilin Rosario (3)
Michael McKenry (13)
Jordan Pacheco (18)
Lars Davis
Dustin Garneau

RHP

Starters	Relievers
Jhoulys Chacin (4)	Casey Weathers (14)
Esmil Rogers (9)	Al Alburquerque (20)
Samuel Deduno (11)	Craig Baker (22)
Juan Nicasio (15)	Shane Lindsay (23)
Chris Balcom-Miller (16)	Edgmer Escalona (27)
Parker Frazier (21)	Aaron Weatherford
Chaz Roe (24)	Joey Williamson
Cory Riordan	Andrew Johnston
Bruce Billings	Kurt Yacko
Rob Scahill	Charlie Ruiz
Ethan Hollingsworth	Adam Jorgenson
Erik Stavert	
Jonnathan Aristil	
Dan Houston	

LHP

Starters	Relievers
Tyler Matzek (1)	Rex Brothers (8)
Christian Friedrich (2)	Matt Reynolds (25)
Jonathan Vargas (26)	Xavier Cedeno
Wes Musick	Brandon Durden
Keith Weiser	

DRAFT ANALYSIS

2009   BONUSES: $7.9 MILLION

BEST PURE HITTER: 3B Nolan Arenado (2), the most outstanding hitter at the National Classic high school tournament in April, batted .300 at Rookie-level Casper. The Rockies added four college position players in the first five rounds, and 1B Ben Paulsen (3) has the best bat among them.

BEST POWER HITTER: OF Kent Matthes (4) led NCAA Division I with 28 homers during the spring and topped the short-season Northwest League with 23 doubles during the summer.

FASTEST RUNNER: OF Avery Barnes (11), who hit .335 with 23 steals at Casper, has plus speed.

BEST DEFENSIVE PLAYER: Joey Wong (24) has no true plus tool but makes all the plays and led NWL shortstops with a .985 fielding percentage. C Dustin Garneau (19) threw out 16 of the 24 basestealers who tested him.

BEST FASTBALL: Colorado grabbed two lefthanders who can touch 98 mph in Tyler Matzek (1) and Rex Brothers (1s). Brothers will throw harder more often because the Rockies will use him as a reliever. RHP Rob Scahill (8) has recovered from labrum surgery in 2007 to top out at 95.

BEST SECONDARY PITCH: Brothers throws his slider in the mid-80s. Matzek's curveball and slider both have the potential to become plus pitches. RHP Charlie Ruiz (10) racks up outs with his splitter.

BEST PRO DEBUT: RHP Chris Balcom-Miller (6), who has three solid pitches, was the Rookie-level Pioneer League pitcher of the year after going 4-0, 1.58 with 60 strikeouts in 57 innings. Ruiz led the NWL with 17 saves and had a 1.14 ERA and 46 strikeouts in 32 innings.

BEST ATHLETE: OF Tim Wheeler (1) stands out the most for his hitting ability and has at least average tools across the board.

MOST INTRIGUING BACKGROUND: 1B Sterling Monfort's (47) father Dick and uncle Charles are the vice chairmen of the franchise. C Mark Tracy's (49) dad Jim is Colorado's big league manager, and his brother Chad plays in the Rangers system. C Jason Bagoly (40) is the nephew of Yankees scouting director Damon Oppenheimer. OF Franco Broyles (43) is the grandson of former Arkansas football coach Frank Broyles. None of the four players signed.

CLOSEST TO THE MAJORS: As a lefthanded reliever with power stuff, Brothers could rocket through the minors. Matzek will move quickly for a high schooler.

BEST LATE-ROUND PICK: 1B Jared Clark (12) reminds the Rockies of Ryan Shealy, who rode his raw power from the 11th round to the big leagues.

THE ONE WHO GOT AWAY: The Rockies signed all 30 of their picks in the first 28 rounds but couldn't corral OF Tym Pearson (35), the best athlete they drafted. He turned down a scholarship to play quarterback at Portland State to focus on baseball at Western Nevada CC.

ASSESSMENT: The Rockies got tremendous talent values by taking Matzek at No. 11, Wheeler at No. 32 and Brothers at No. 34. Some clubs rated Matzek the second-best player in the draft and several considered him unsignable, but Colorado landed him for a club-record $3.9 million.

2008   BONUSES: $4.2 MILLION

LHP Christian Friedrich (1) has dominated pro hitters since inexplicably lasting until the 25th overall pick. OFs Charlie Blackmon (2) and Delta Cleary (37) are two of the best athletes in the system.

GRADE: B

2007   BONUSES: $3.7 MILLION

The Rockies hoped to expedite RHP Casey Weathers (1) to the big leagues, but he had Tommy John surgery after his first full pro season. RHP Connor Graham (5) yielded Rafael Betancourt in a trade. RHP Parker Frazier (8), C Jordan Pacheco (9) and LHP Matt Reynolds (20) are sleeper prospects.

GRADE: C

2006   BONUSES: $6.2 MILLION

RHP Greg Reynolds (1) was a reach as the No. 2 overall pick, and persistent shoulder problems haven't helped. C Michael McKenry (7) is the best prospect from this crop, which included future first-round RHP Andrew Cashner (18) and sandwich-round LHP Aaron Miller (11).

GRADE: D

2005   BONUSES: $4.0 MILLION*

SS Troy Tulowitzki (1) does it all as a hitter, defender and leader. RHP Chaz Roe (1s) has developed slowly because of injuries.

GRADE: A

*Draft analysis by Jim Callis. Numbers in parentheses indicate draft rounds. *Bonuses for 2005 are first 10 rounds only.*

PROSPECT 1

TYLER MATZEK, LHP

Born: Oct. 19, 1990.
Height: 6-3. **Weight:** 210.
Bats: L. **Throws:** L.
Drafted: HS—Capistrano Valley, Calif., 2009 (1st round).
Signed by: John Lukens.

Matzek first gained the attention of scouts early in his junior season of high school in 2008, when he outpitched Gerrit Cole (who would become the Yankees' first-round pick that June) in a preseason matchup. Matzek entered 2009 as the top-rated pitcher in the high school draft crop, and he saved his best for last. After pitching a shutout in the California Interscholastic Federation Division I semifinals, he took the mound with the bases loaded and two out in the sixth inning of the finale. He pitched out of the jam, hit an opposite-field homer for a 1-0 lead in the bottom half, then got out of another bases-loaded situation in the seventh to preserve the victory. Matzek didn't allow a run in 18 ⅓ innings in the CIF playoffs while touching 97-98 mph and maintaining both his velocity and quality breaking stuff deep into his starts. With his strong finish, he pushed himself to as high as No. 2 on some clubs' draft boards, but he fell to the Rockies at No. 11 after stating that he was looking for "unprecedented money." At the Aug. 17 signing deadline, Matzek passed up a full scholarship and the opportunity to play both ways at Oregon in order to receive a club-record $3.9 million bonus.

Scouts thought he was the best high school lefthander to come out of Southern California since Cole Hamels in 2002, and Matzek has better stuff. He has a legitimate four-pitch arsenal, starting with a fastball that sat at 90-94 mph for most of the spring before jumping to the upper 90s right before the draft. His curveball and slider are two distinct breaking pitches and both have the potential to become plus offerings. He also shows feel for a changeup, though he didn't need the pitch very often as an amateur. Matzek has an exceedingly smooth delivery and the ball comes out of his hand easily. He's athletic and repeats his mechanics well, which bodes well for his future control and command. His leadership is another trait that has him destined to be a staff ace. While he hasn't faced much adversity on the mound, he proved his toughness after his father Jeff, who had coached him since T-ball, was diagnosed with throat cancer while Matzek was a sophomore. He didn't let his father's illness affect his performance, and Jeff's cancer is now in remission.

Matzek sometimes lands on a stiff front leg, causing his fastball to sail high and out of the strike zone. He'll need to improve his fastball command and use his changeup more often, but that should come with more innings. There's really little he needs more than experience, and he has the aptitude and confidence to make any adjustments that he'll need to address.

The Rockies are normally reluctant to push young players, particularly pitchers, but they were very impressed with how Matzek handled instructional league. The first high school pitcher they've picked in the first round since the Matt Harrington debacle in 2000, Matzek is ticketed for low Class A Asheville, which would make him the first high school player that Colorado has allowed to debut in full-season ball. He should move very fast for a prep product and projects as a frontline starter.

Year	Club (League)	Class	W	L	ERA	G	GS	CG	SV	IP	H	R	ER	HR	BB	SO	AVG
2009	Did Not Play—Signed Late																

2 CHRISTIAN FRIEDRICH, LHP $5/$ 𝑈𝑧

BORN: July 8, 1987. **B-T:** R-L. **HT.:** 6-4. **WT.:** 218. **DRAFTED:** Eastern Kentucky, 2008 (1st round). **SIGNED BY:** Scott Corman.

Friedrich went from undrafted as an Illinois high schooler to a first-round pick in 2008 after three years at Eastern Kentucky. The Rockies didn't expect him to be available with the 25th overall pick and gladly signed him for $1.35 million. In his first full pro season, he rated as the top prospect in the high Class A California League and ranked second in the minors in strikeouts per nine innings (12.0). Friedrich has added velocity, pitching consistently in the low 90s and topping out at 95 last season. He has a 12-to-6 curveball and a hard slider, both emerging as plus pitches. He rarely threw his changeup before pro ball, but it is becoming an average offering. He does a good job of throwing strikes, but Friedrich must continue to improve his fastball command. Once he can locate his fastball consistently, he'll be ready for the big leagues. He missed a month at midseason with left elbow inflammation, but it's not a long-term concern. Friedrich will open 2010 in Double-A Tulsa, where he would have finished last season if the Rockies hadn't decided to handle him carefully after his elbow problems. If he develops as quickly as he did in 2009, he could make his major league debut by the end of the season.

Year	Club (League)	Class	W	L	ERA	G	GS	CG	SV	IP	H	R	ER	HR	BB	SO	AVG
2008	Tri-City (NWL)	SS	2	1	3.25	8	8	0	0	36	31	16	13	2	8	50	.228
	Asheville (SAL)	LoA	0	1	7.50	3	3	0	0	12	14	10	10	2	7	15	.269
2009	Asheville (SAL)	LoA	3	3	2.18	8	8	0	0	45	35	14	11	2	15	66	.215
	Modesto (CAL)	HiA	3	2	2.54	14	14	0	0	74	59	25	21	3	28	93	.215
MINOR LEAGUE TOTALS			8	7	2.95	33	33	0	0	168	139	65	55	9	58	224	.222

3 WILIN ROSARIO, C ✝

BORN: Feb. 23, 1989. **B-T:** R-R. **HT.:** 5-11. **WT.:** 195. **SIGNED:** Dominican Republic, 2006. **SIGNED BY:** Rolando Fernandez/Felix Feliz.

Rosario and Hector Gomez are the first potential impact position players to come out of the Rockies' Latin American program, which initially emphasized finding pitching. After Rosario rated as the top prospect in the Rookie-level Pioneer League in 2008, Colorado jumped him to high Class A Modesto last season, where he worked with catching guru Jerry Weinstein. He missed all of August after hurting his left wrist on a tag at the plate, but returned to impress scouts in the Arizona Fall League. Rosario has the physical abilities to be the complete package behind the plate. He has a quick, compact swing and can drive the ball. He has a strong arm and threw out 47 percent of basestealers who tested him in 2009. He's agile behind the plate. In order to get the most out of his offensive potential, Rosario needs more discipline at the plate. He's too anxious to hit and tends to chase hard breaking balls out of the zone. He loses his concentration at times, affecting his receiving. He's a below-average runner, though he's not a baseclogger. With Chris Iannetta in the majors, the Rockies don't need to push Rosario more aggressively. He's scheduled for a full season in Double-A at age 21 and should battle Iannetta for the big league starting job in 2012.

Year	Club (League)	Class	AVG	G	AB	R	H	2B	3B	HR	RBI	BB	SO	SB	OBP	SLG
2006	Rockies (DSL)	R	.249	62	213	28	53	7	0	3	25	16	56	5	.309	.324
2007	Casper (PIO)	R	.209	34	115	11	24	4	0	2	9	11	38	2	.283	.296
2008	Casper (PIO)	R	.316	66	263	48	83	15	3	12	49	24	57	4	.371	.532
2009	Modesto (CAL)	HiA	.266	58	203	17	54	12	2	4	33	10	55	2	.297	.404
MINOR LEAGUE TOTALS			.270	220	794	104	214	38	5	21	116	61	206	13	.323	.409

4 JHOULYS CHACIN, RHP *Busch*

BORN: Jan. 7, 1988. **B-T:** R-R. **HT.:** 6-4. **WT.:** 218. **SIGNED:** Venezuela, 2004. **SIGNED BY:** Rolando Fernandez/Francisco Cartaya/Orlando Medina.

Chacin led the minors with 18 wins in 2008 before making his big league debut last July. He allowed just two runs in eight relief appearances with Colorado, though the Pirates roughed him up in his lone major league start. Chacin's size and athleticism allow him to throw a hard sinker that ranges from 89-92 mph. His best pitch is a changeup that negates lefthanders. He throws it with the same arm action that he uses for his fastball. His slider is a plus pitch at times. He's poised well beyond his years. His slider and curveball need refinement, but for some reason Chacin made them his primary pitches when he got to the big leagues. He fell behind in the count too often and fell prey to walks. He has to pitch off his fastball and changeup, and use his breaking pitches only intermittently, to be effective. He lacks fastball command at times, particularly when he overthrows. Chacin will open the season in the Triple-A Colorado Springs rotation, and figures to return to the big leagues to stay later in the year. His ultimate ceiling depends on his ability to develop a consistent breaking ball to complement his fastball and changeup.

COLORADO ROCKIES

Year	Club (League)	Class	W	L	ERA	G	GS	CG	SV	IP	H	R	ER	HR	BB	SO	AVG
2005	Rockies (DSL)	R	3	1	4.32	16	4	0	0	50	43	32	24	5	16	48	.219
2006	Rockies (DSL)	R	4	1	1.49	12	11	1	0	73	60	20	12	4	18	67	.226
2007	Casper (PIO)	R	6	5	3.13	16	16	0	0	92	85	45	32	5	26	77	.248
2008	Asheville (SAL)	LoA	10	1	1.86	16	16	2	0	111	82	30	23	3	30	98	.205
	Modesto (CAL)	HiA	8	2	2.31	12	12	0	0	66	61	20	17	3	12	62	.247
2009	Tulsa (TL)	AA	8	6	3.14	18	18	1	0	103	87	45	36	10	35	86	.227
	Colorado Springs (PCL)	AAA	1	2	3.77	4	4	0	0	14	11	7	6	2	13	11	.220
	Colorado (NL)	MAJ	0	1	4.91	9	1	0	0	11	6	6	6	1	11	13	.167
MAJOR LEAGUE TOTALS			0	1	4.91	9	1	0	0	11	6	6	6	1	11	13	.167
MINOR LEAGUE TOTALS			40	18	2.65	94	81	4	0	510	429	199	150	32	150	449	.228

5 HECTOR GOMEZ, SS +

BORN: March 5, 1988. **B-T:** R-R. **HT.:** 6-2. **WT.:** 185. **SIGNED:** Dominican Republic, 2004. **SIGNED BY:** Rolando Fernandez/Felix Feliz/Frank Roa.

A low Class A South Atlantic League all-star as a 19-year-old in 2007, Gomez has been slowed by injuries the last two years. In his first at-bat of 2008, he fouled a ball off his shin, sustaining a stress fracture, then hurt his elbow during his rehab and required Tommy John surgery. He returned to the diamond late last April, then missed almost all of June with a groin strain. Gomez has the tools to be an all-around shortstop. Managers rated him as having the California League's best infield arm last year, and he also has excellent range and soft hands. He has a quick bat that can catch up to quality fastballs, and the power to eventually hit 15 or more homers per season. He has plus speed. After losing so much development time the last two years, Gomez still needs work on the nuances of the game. His lack of plate discipline cuts into his power production. He has a tendency to chase breaking pitches, which the Rockies hope to alleviate by shortening his stroke. He's still learning how to steal bases and he sometimes gets careless in the field. Gomez got some much-needed at-bats in the AFL, paving the way for him to step up to Double-A. Troy Tulowitzki's presence in Colorado means there's no need to rush Gomez, and also could mean he'll move to second base when he's ready for the big leagues.

Year	Club (League)	Class	AVG	G	AB	R	H	2B	3B	HR	RBI	BB	SO	SB	OBP	SLG
2005	Rockies (DSL)	R	.335	67	242	49	81	16	1	6	43	24	38	15	.423	.483
2006	Casper (PIO)	R	.327	50	202	24	66	9	4	5	35	11	26	5	.364	.485
	Tri-City (NWL)	SS	.244	12	45	4	11	3	0	0	6	0	14	0	.255	.311
2007	Asheville (SAL)	LoA	.266	124	534	89	142	34	8	11	61	29	120	20	.309	.421
2008	Modesto (CAL)	HiA	.333	1	3	0	1	0	0	0	0	0	0	0	.333	.333
2009	Modesto (CAL)	HiA	.275	83	338	39	93	21	4	7	46	15	68	10	.310	.423
MINOR LEAGUE TOTALS			.289	337	1364	205	394	83	17	29	191	79	266	50	.337	.438

6 ERIC YOUNG JR., 2B/OF *Busch*

BORN: May 25, 1985. **B-T:** B-R. **HT.:** 5-10. **WT.:** 180. **DRAFTED:** Chandler-Gilbert (Ariz.) CC, D/F 2003 (30th round). **SIGNED BY:** Mike Garlatti/Mike Ericson.

Like his father Eric Sr., the Rockies' first starting second baseman and now an ESPN analyst, Eric Jr. could have played college football. Instead, he turned down Villanova and attended junior college to focus on baseball. Young has led his league in stolen bases three times in the last four years, topping the minors with 87 in 2006. Young's ability to disrupt a game with his plus-plus speed earned him a spot on Colorado's postseason roster. He embraces the value of small ball, though he does have some strength and can drive the ball if a pitcher makes a mistake, as he showed with a Futures Game home run in St. Louis. He's a tireless worker who has put in the effort to improve his defense. Young lacks soft hands and has fringy arm strength. He's just adequate at second base, where he'll make an occasional spectacular play but also get caught on his heels by a routine grounder. He has been given limited playing time in center field, and he still has a lot to learn there. At the plate, he needs to get more selective and make more contact. Young fits into the Rockies big league picture as a role player for now, serving as a pinch-runner, alternative at second base to Clint Barmes, and a double-switch candidate in the outfield.

Year	Club (League)	Class	AVG	G	AB	R	H	2B	3B	HR	RBI	BB	SO	SB	OBP	SLG
2004	Casper (PIO)	R	.264	23	87	20	23	5	1	0	7	20	13	14	.407	.345
2005	Casper (PIO)	R	.301	63	219	48	66	7	7	3	25	35	52	25	.404	.438
2006	Asheville (SAL)	LoA	.295	128	482	92	142	28	6	5	49	67	75	87	.391	.409
2007	Modesto (CAL)	HiA	.291	130	540	113	157	29	11	8	63	46	105	73	.359	.430
2008	Tulsa (TL)	AA	.290	105	403	74	117	24	4	3	33	61	77	46	.391	.392
2009	Colorado Springs (PCL)	AAA	.299	119	472	118	141	21	10	7	43	56	79	58	.387	.430
	Colorado (NL)	MAJ	.246	30	57	7	14	1	0	1	1	4	12	4	.295	.316
MAJOR LEAGUE TOTALS			.246	30	57	7	14	1	0	1	1	4	12	4	.295	.316
MINOR LEAGUE TOTALS			.293	568	2203	465	646	114	39	26	220	285	401	303	.385	.416

7 TIM WHEELER, OF ✝

BORN: Jan. 21, 1988. **B-T:** L-R. **HT.:** 6-4. **WT.:** 205. **DRAFTED:** Sacramento State, 2009 (1st round). **SIGNED BY:** Gary Wilson.

Wheeler led the Cape Cod League with 15 steals in the summer of 2008, then set Sacramento State records for single-season (72) and career (142) RBIs while batting .385 last spring. One of the best all-around college players in the 2009 draft, he surprisingly lasted until the 32nd overall choice, which made him the highest pick in Hornets history. Signed for $900,000, he finished his pro debut on a 12-game hitting streak. Wheeler has solid tools across the board. With a pretty lefthanded swing and a strong, athletic build, he has the potential to hit for a high average with 20 or more homers per season. His slightly above-average speed and strong arm give him a chance to play center field. He has a good feel for the game, allowing his tools to play up. Wheeler fits better defensively in right field, and to play regularly on a corner he'll have to deliver on his power potential, which currently is more evident in batting practice than in games. He expanded his strike zone and got under balls rather than squaring them up in his pro debut. He can improve his reads and routes on fly balls. If Wheeler has a strong spring training, he could skip a level and head to high Class A. Brad Hawpe's contract expires after 2011, and Wheeler could be ready to take over in right field by then if needed.

Year	Club (League)	Class	AVG	G	AB	R	H	2B	3B	HR	RBI	BB	SO	SB	OBP	SLG
2009	Tri-City (NWL)	SS	.256	68	273	44	70	13	3	5	35	29	60	10	.332	.381
MINOR LEAGUE TOTALS			.256	68	273	44	70	13	3	5	35	29	60	10	.332	.381

8 REX BROTHERS, LHP ✝

BORN: Dec. 18, 1987. **B-T:** L-L. **HT.:** 6-1. **WT.:** 205. **DRAFTED:** Lipscomb, 2009 (1st round supplemental). **SIGNED BY:** Scott Corman.

After setting a Lipscomb record with 132 strikeouts in 94 innings, Brothers projected to go in the middle of the first round of the 2009 draft. The Rockies gladly scooped him up with the No. 34 pick, making him the second-highest drafted player in school history behind Bo McLaughlin—who's now Colorado's minor league pitching coordinator. Brothers signed for $969,000. Though he was a starter in college, Colorado envisions him as a power lefthanded closer in the mold of Randy Myers. Brothers' fastball sits at 94-96 mph and touches 97, while his slider parks in the mid-80s and peaks at 89. He has plenty of life on his pitches to go with his velocity, making it very difficult for hitters to square him up. He has a resilient arm that will serve him well in the pen. Brothers' pitches move so much that he has trouble commanding them at times. He focused on developing his changeup during instructional league, though it will always be his third option and he won't need it as much as a starter. Brothers reached low Class A at the end of his pro debut and could advance to Double-A to start 2010. He should move very quickly as a reliever, and if he throws enough strikes, he has the type of stuff that could land him in Colorado by the end of the season.

Year	Club (League)	Class	W	L	ERA	G	GS	CG	SV	IP	H	R	ER	HR	BB	SO	AVG
2009	Tri-City (NWL)	SS	2	0	3.38	8	0	0	0	11	10	4	4	0	5	18	.256
	Asheville (SAL)	LoA	0	0	3.38	9	0	0	0	11	6	4	4	1	3	10	.171
MINOR LEAGUE TOTALS			2	0	3.38	17	0	0	0	21	16	8	8	1	8	28	.216

9 ESMIL ROGERS, RHP

BORN: Aug. 14, 1985. **B-T:** R-R. **HT.:** 6-1. **WT.:** 176. **SIGNED:** Dominican Republic, 2003. **SIGNED BY:** Rolando Fernandez/Felix Feliz/Frank Roa.

Originally signed as a shortstop, Rogers hit .209 in three years in the Rookie-level Dominican Summer League before moving to the mound in 2006. He dominated Double-A hitters in the first half of 2009 before getting knocked around in Triple-A and making his big league debut in September. Rogers made the transition to pitching more easily than most former position players, quickly developing smooth mechanics. His fastball ranges from 92-95 mph and features good life, and he can rack up strikeouts with his hard curveball. Until he got to Triple-A, he did a good job of challenging hitters. Rogers seemed intimidated when he got to Colorado Springs, consistently fell behind in the count and got hit harder than ever before. He just has to trust his power stuff. Lefthanders batted .367/.453/.608 against him in Triple-A, reinforcing his need to develop a changeup. Though he's a good athlete, he's still learning how to control the running game and has committed 18 errors the last three years. Rogers will return to Colorado Springs and try to conquer Triple-A to start 2010. If he can clean up his changeup, he'll be a starter. If not, his fastball and curveball are more than enough for him to succeed in a late-inning relief role.

Year	Club (League)	Class	AVG	G	AB	R	H	2B	3B	HR	RBI	BB	SO	SB	OBP	SLG
2003	Rockies (DSL)	R	.212	34	118	10	25	3	0	1	9	3	35	1	.230	.263
2004	Rockies (DSL)	R	.227	51	176	13	40	7	1	2	23	6	48	2	.259	.313
2005	Rockies (DSL)	R	.190	55	200	23	38	5	1	4	17	18	73	13	.268	.285
2009	Tulsa (TL)	AA	.091	6	11	2	1	0	0	0	1	1	7	0	.167	.091
	Colorado Springs (PCL)	AAA	.222	7	9	1	2	0	0	0	0	0	3	0	.222	.222
	Colorado (NL)	MAJ	.000	1	1	0	0	0	0	0	0	0	0	0	.000	.000
MAJOR LEAGUE TOTALS			.000	1	1	0	0	0	0	0	0	0	0	0	.000	.000
MINOR LEAGUE TOTALS			.206	153	514	49	106	15	2	7	50	28	166	16	.254	.284

Year	Club (League)	Class	W	L	ERA	G	GS	CG	SV	IP	H	R	ER	HR	BB	SO	AVG
2006	Casper (PIO)	R	3	6	6.96	15	15	1	0	63	78	53	49	8	24	40	.306
2007	Asheville (SAL)	LoA	7	4	3.75	19	18	1	0	118	125	60	49	6	42	90	.272
2008	Modesto (CAL)	HiA	9	7	3.95	25	25	0	0	144	146	73	63	9	45	116	.264
2009	Tulsa (TL)	AA	8	2	2.48	15	15	0	0	94	87	30	26	2	19	83	.243
	Colorado Springs (PCL)	AAA	3	5	7.42	12	11	0	0	61	77	50	50	9	35	46	.317
	Colorado (NL)	MAJ	0	0	4.50	1	1	0	0	4	3	2	2	0	2	3	.231
MAJOR LEAGUE TOTALS			0	0	4.50	1	1	0	0	4	3	2	2	0	2	3	.231
MINOR LEAGUE TOTALS			30	24	4.45	86	84	2	0	480	513	266	237	34	165	375	.275

10 NOLAN ARENADO, 3B

BORN: April 16, 1991. **B-T:** R-R. **HT.:** 6-2. **WT.:** 205. **DRAFTED:** HS—El Toro, Calif., 2009 (2nd round). **SIGNED BY:** Jon Lukens.

Arenado hit safely in 27 of 28 games as a high school senior last spring, batting .529 overall and earning most outstanding hitter honors at the National Classic tournament in April. After signing him for $625,000 as a second-round pick, the Rockies moved him from shortstop to third base. Their lack of a complex league team necessitated sending him to the Pioneer League, where he hit .300 despite being the second-youngest regular in the circuit. Arenado has the impact bat teams want from a corner infielder. He has a balanced approach, advanced plate discipline and excellent hand-eye coordination, so he should hit for average. His bat speed and strength should give him at least average power in the future, and he already drives balls into the gaps. He has good reactions and first-step quickness at the hot corner, along with soft hands and a strong arm. Some scouts think he could be an impact catcher if given the chance. He has strong leadership skills and work ethic. He's a below-average runner, though Arenado moves well enough for his size and has good instincts on the bases. He doesn't have a lot of range and will have to continue to work on his defense at his new position. The Rockies usually avoid rushing high school players, but they're excited about Arenado's bat. He could open 2010 in low Class A.

Year	Club (League)	Class	AVG	G	AB	R	H	2B	3B	HR	RBI	BB	SO	SB	OBP	SLG
2009	Casper (PIO)	R	.300	54	203	28	61	15	0	2	22	16	18	5	.351	.404
MINOR LEAGUE TOTALS			.300	54	203	28	61	15	0	2	22	16	18	5	.351	.404

11 SAMUEL DEDUNO, RHP

BORN: July 2, 1983. **B-T:** R-R. **HT.:** 6-3. **WT.:** 190. **SIGNED:** Dominican Republic, 2003. **SIGNED BY:** Rolando Fernandez/Felix Feliz/Frank Roa.

Deduno missed the 2008 season recovering from Tommy John surgery, and he returned looking better than ever. He won the Double-A Texas League pitching triple crown, going 12-4, 2.57 with 123 strikeouts in 133 innings. He finished so strong at Tulsa that the Rockies cleared him to pitch in his native Dominican Republic during the winter. Deduno has a quality fastball that sits at 92-93 mph, as well as a power curveball. He's still working on a changeup, which will be important for him to control lefthanded hitters. He has leverage in his delivery that gives him a good downhill plane and helps him keep the ball down in the zone. He allowed just three homers last season. The key for Deduno will be command. He almost won a quadruple crown in the Texas League, finishing second with 72 walks, and he has averaged 5.0 walks per nine innings as a pro. Deduno can be a solid major league starter if he sharpens his command and develops a changeup. His two strikeout pitches should make him a good bullpen arm regardless. He'll move to Triple-A in 2010, and could get a big league callup.

Year	Club (League)	Class	W	L	ERA	G	GS	CG	SV	IP	H	R	ER	HR	BB	SO	AVG
2003	Rockies (DSL)	R	3	4	2.47	12	12	0	0	69	53	26	19	1	26	61	.202
2004	Casper (PIO)	R	6	4	3.18	15	15	0	0	76	62	40	27	3	32	118	.219
2005	Asheville (SAL)	LoA	8	8	5.62	20	20	1	0	90	82	67	56	9	65	110	.248
2006	Modesto (CAL)	HiA	5	8	4.80	27	26	0	0	146	121	88	78	3	92	167	.222
2007	Modesto (CAL)	HiA	1	1	6.55	2	2	0	0	11	9	8	8	1	7	8	.214
	Tulsa (TL)	AA	5	8	5.44	21	21	1	0	124	120	90	75	13	66	121	.251
2008	Did Not Play—Injured																
2009	Tulsa (TL)	AA	12	4	2.57	24	24	1	0	133	94	48	38	3	72	123	.202
	Colorado Springs (PCL)	AAA	0	1	6.35	1	1	0	0	6	5	4	4	0	4	8	.250
MINOR LEAGUE TOTALS			40	38	4.19	122	121	3	0	655	546	371	305	33	364	716	.228

12 CHARLIE BLACKMON, OF

BORN: July 1, 1986. **B-T:** L-L. **HT.:** 6-3. **WT.:** 180. **DRAFTED:** Georgia Tech, 2008 (2nd round). **SIGNED BY:** Alan Matthews.

Blackmon was drafted out of high school (Marlins, 28th round, 2004) and out of Young Harris (Ga.) JC (Red Sox, 20th round, 2005)—both times as a lefthander. After he transferred to Georgia Tech and redshirted for a year, he pulled a joke on his coach in the summer Texas Collegiate League by playing in the outfield. It worked out well, and he stayed there for his junior season at Georgia Tech, playing his way into the second round of the 2008 draft. Blackmon has a simple, consistent stroke and a feel for driving the ball gap to gap. His splits are strikingly similar against lefthanders and righthanders, day and night, home and road. The Rockies think he could turn some of his doubles into homers as he gets older. His well above-average speed makes him a stolen-base threat, though he could improve his efficiency. Blackmon handles center field well despite his limited experience. He needs to improve his jumps and reads so he doesn't have to rely as much on his speed. He has a solid arm but tends to wind up rather than using a crow hop and quick release. He'll continue to refine his game as he moves up to Double-A in 2010.

Year	Club (League)	Class	AVG	G	AB	R	H	2B	3B	HR	RBI	BB	SO	SB	OBP	SLG
2008	Tri-City (NWL)	SS	.338	68	290	42	98	21	5	2	33	16	37	13	.390	.466
2009	Modesto (CAL)	HiA	.307	133	550	87	169	34	7	7	69	39	83	30	.370	.433
MINOR LEAGUE TOTALS			.318	201	840	129	267	55	12	9	102	55	120	43	.377	.444

13 MICHAEL McKENRY, C

BORN: March 4, 1985. **B-T:** R-R. **HT.:** 5-10. **WT.:** 210. **DRAFTED:** Tennessee State, 2006 (7th round). **SIGNED BY:** Scott Corman.

A freak injury slowed McKenry down late in the 2009 season after he made significant progress the last couple of years. USA Baseball had selected him to be one of its catchers for the World Cup in Europe, but the day before he was to leave Tulsa he was hit in the ear by a bat on a backswing, giving him a concussion and requiring stitches in his ear. He also had a negative reaction to the local anesthesia, but he has a clean bill of health for the 2010 season. Typically a slow starter, McKenry gets himself in trouble offensively when he becomes home run happy and tries to pull everything, opening up too quickly. At his best, though, he has a quality line-drive stroke and uses the middle of the field. He's also willing to work counts for walks. McKenry handles pitchers well and has strong makeup, intelligence and work habits. He moves well behind the plate and has a strong arm. When he focuses on his footwork and technique he can slow a running game. He sometimes tries to be too quick with his throws, wrapping his arm behind his head. He threw out 33 percent of basestealers last season. He has such a thick, strong body that it can inhibit him behind the plate and at bat, and he has well below-average speed. McKenry is ready for Triple-A and is knocking on the big league door, though his best role may be as a high-energy backup. The Rockies added him to the 40-man roster for the first time in November.

Year	Club (League)	Class	AVG	G	AB	R	H	2B	3B	HR	RBI	BB	SO	SB	OBP	SLG
2006	Tri-City (NWL)	SS	.216	66	245	28	53	16	1	4	23	22	49	3	.303	.339
2007	Asheville (SAL)	LoA	.287	113	408	79	117	35	1	22	90	66	84	8	.392	.539
2008	Modesto (CAL)	HiA	.258	111	400	59	103	28	1	18	75	55	101	2	.360	.468
2009	Tulsa (TL)	AA	.279	102	358	52	100	25	1	12	50	54	69	2	.376	.455
MINOR LEAGUE TOTALS			.264	392	1411	218	373	104	4	56	238	197	303	15	.363	.463

14 CASEY WEATHERS, RHP

BORN: June 10, 1985. **B-T:** R-R. **HT.:** 6-1. **WT.:** 200. **DRAFTED:** Vanderbilt, 2007 (1st round). **SIGNED BY:** Scott Corman.

When they drafted him eighth overall and paid him a $1.8 million bonus in 2007, the Rockies expected that Weathers could make their big league bullpen by last season. That was before he blew out his elbow in the Arizona Fall League after the 2008 season, causing him to miss all of 2009. He did throw bullpen sessions during instructional league and should be ready to go in the spring. Converted from an outfielder to a pitcher in junior college, Weathers has to re-establish his quality fastball. It's most effective in the low 90s, where it has late life, and can reach the mid-90s. He throws a late-breaking slider that sits in the mid-80s, giving him two swing-and-miss pitches. Weathers has the aggressive mentality that teams want from a closer, and he needs to show it more often against lefthanders, who at times appear to intimidate him. He has to refine the command of both of his pitches. The Rockies will take it slowly with him to open 2010. He's expected to spend the year in Triple-A, but it's not out of the question that he could start the season in Double-A.

Year	Club (League)	Class	W	L	ERA	G	GS	CG	SV	IP	H	R	ER	HR	BB	SO	AVG
2007	Asheville (SAL)	LoA	0	1	4.61	13	0	0	2	14	6	7	7	2	7	19	.130
	Modesto (CAL)	HiA	0	0	0.00	1	0	0	0	1	0	0	0	0	2	2	.000
2008	Tulsa (TL)	AA	2	1	3.05	44	0	0	2	44	34	18	15	1	28	54	.210
2009	Did Not Play—Injured																
MINOR LEAGUE TOTALS			2	2	3.36	58	0	0	4	59	40	25	22	3	37	75	.190

15 JUAN NICASIO, RHP

BORN: Aug. 31, 1986. **B-T:** R-R. **HT.:** 6-3. **WT.:** 190. **SIGNED:** Venezuela, 2006. **SIGNED BY:** Rolando Fernandez/Felix Feliz.

After three years of Rookie and short-season action, Nicasio had an eye-opening effort in low Class A last year, showing the ability to throw strikes and dominating hitters. He had a 5-1 strikeout-walk ratio and led the South Atlantic League with a 2.41 ERA, pitching his way onto the 40-man roster because the Rockies feared losing him in the Rule 5 draft. Nicasio sits in the low 90s with his fastball, which he complements with a plus changeup. He uses a curveball for his primary breaking pitch, but he'll probably refine a slider to use more than the curve. Nicasio's breakthrough year was the result of adjustments in his delivery, improving his downhill angle to the plate and giving him better sink on his pitches. He's a strike-thrower, though he becomes hittable if he flattens out his delivery. After his first summer with a heavy workload, the Rockies brought him to instructional league and then sent him to their Dominican academy, but they declined to have him pitch winter ball. Nicasio will open 2010 in high Class A, and Colorado will accelerate his progress if he continues to dominate.

Year	Club (League)	Class	W	L	ERA	G	GS	CG	SV	IP	H	R	ER	HR	BB	SO	AVG
2006	Rockies (DSL)	R	2	1	2.89	8	5	0	0	28	27	14	9	1	8	24	.250
2007	Casper (PIO)	R	0	3	4.36	13	8	0	0	43	48	32	21	3	13	33	.276
2008	Tri-City (NWL)	SS	2	4	4.50	12	12	0	0	54	46	30	27	1	19	61	.229
2009	Asheville (SAL)	LoA	9	3	2.41	18	18	1	0	112	110	44	30	6	23	115	.252
MINOR LEAGUE TOTALS			13	11	3.30	51	43	1	0	237	231	120	87	11	63	233	.251

16 CHRIS BALCOM-MILLER, RHP

BORN: March 3, 1989. **B-T:** R-R. **HT.:** 6-2. **WT.:** 210. **DRAFTED:** West Valley (Calif.) JC, 2009 (6th round). **SIGNED BY:** Gary Wilson.

Primarily a shortstop in high school, Balcom-Miller felt he had a future on the mound so he decided to focus on pitching. The Royals made him a 35th-round draft choice after his freshman year at West Valley (Calif.) JC, and he turned them down to return for his sophomore season. The gamble paid off when the Rockies picked him in the sixth round last June and signed him for $125,000. He debuted at Rookie-level Casper and went 4-0, 1.58 to win Pioneer League pitcher of the year honors. Returning to West Valley allowed Balcom-Miller to add velocity to his fastball, which is now a solid 89-91 mph pitch that hits 93 and shows good sink. The extra year in junior college also gave him time to develop an average changeup and refine a slider that has become his best pitch. His herky-jerky motion helps with his deception, and he has a bulldog approach. Balcom-Miller throws strikes, but he needs better command within the strike zone to consistently get outs as he moves to higher levels. He should jump to low Class A this year and has the ceiling of a solid middle-of-the-rotation starter.

Year	Club (League)	Class	W	L	ERA	G	GS	CG	SV	IP	H	R	ER	HR	BB	SO	AVG
2009	Casper (PIO)	R	4	0	1.58	11	11	1	0	57	37	13	10	3	10	60	.181
MINOR LEAGUE TOTALS			4	0	1.58	11	11	1	0	57	37	13	10	3	10	60	.181

17 DELTA CLEARY, OF

BORN: Aug. 14, 1989. **B-T:** B-R. **HT.:** 6-3. **WT.:** 180. **DRAFTED:** Louisiana State-Eunice JC, 2008 (37th round). **SIGNED BY:** Damon Iannelli.

Cleary is the kind of raw athlete whom Rockies scouting director Bill Schmidt looks for in the late rounds of the draft. He was a quarterback on his high school football team and a guard on the basketball team that won the Arkansas Class 6-A state title his junior year. Since signing for $250,000 as a 37th-rounder in 2008, Cleary often has been referred to as a poor man's Dexter Fowler, a testament to his exciting potential. The cousin of NBA forward Shawn Marion, Cleary has above-average speed and some raw power. A switch-hitter, he must continue to work on his lefthanded swing and his strength, because he too often gets overpowered by hard-throwing right-handers. He also has to tighten his strike zone and avoid getting overly anxious at the plate. He's still learning how to tap into his power and may be better off concentrating on putting the ball on the ground and getting on base to maximize his speed. Cleary can steal bases and cover a lot of ground in center field. He has a decent arm that should get stronger with more baseball repetitions. Cleary will spend 2010 in high Class A.

Year	Club (League)	Class	AVG	G	AB	R	H	2B	3B	HR	RBI	BB	SO	SB	OBP	SLG
2008	Casper (PIO)	R	.276	27	105	22	29	2	1	3	9	6	19	4	.321	.400
2009	Asheville (SAL)	LoA	.256	105	399	53	102	19	4	7	45	31	87	32	.315	.376
MINOR LEAGUE TOTALS			.260	132	504	75	131	21	5	10	54	37	106	36	.316	.381

18 JORDAN PACHECO, C

BORN: Jan. 30, 1986. **B-T:** R-R. **HT.:** 6-1. **WT.:** 190. **DRAFTED:** New Mexico, 2007 (9th round). **SIGNED BY:** Mike Ericson.

A middle infielder at New Mexico, Pacheco made the transition to catching in his first full pro season in 2008. He won the South Atlantic League MVP award last season, finishing second in the league batting race (.322). Pacheco's bat is what got him drafted, but he lacked the quickness to play second base and the power potential to profile as a corner infielder. The Rockies believed that if he could be an adequate defender behind the plate, he could hit his way to a backup/utility role in the big leagues. Now the thought is that Pacheco could be a regular catcher. He handles the bat well and knows the strike zone. He understands his limitations and looks to drive balls in the gaps. He's a below-average runner but moves well for a catcher. Pacheco has average arm strength, though he's still working on his throwing mechanics after throwing out just 16 percent of basestealers in 2009. His receiving also is a work in progress, though he made strides by committing just eight passed balls in 69 games after giving up 21 in 44 contests in 2008. He has the leadership qualities a team looks for in a catcher. Pacheco will advance to Modesto, where he'll benefit playing for catching guru Jerry Weinstein.

Year	Club (League)	Class	AVG	G	AB	R	H	2B	3B	HR	RBI	BB	SO	SB	OBP	SLG
2007	Casper (PIO)	R	.292	55	192	27	56	10	2	3	29	21	36	3	.380	.411
	Tri-City (NWL)	SS	.258	8	31	5	8	2	0	0	3	1	6	0	.324	.323
2008	Tri-City (NWL)	SS	.280	54	214	25	60	8	3	1	35	26	20	3	.368	.360
2009	Asheville (SAL)	LoA	.322	117	451	67	145	30	4	13	79	38	44	12	.379	.492
MINOR LEAGUE TOTALS			.303	234	888	124	269	50	9	17	146	86	106	18	.375	.437

19 KENT MATTHES, OF

BORN: Jan. 8, 1987. **B-T:** R-R. **HT.:** 6-2. **WT.:** 215. **DRAFTED:** Alabama, 2009 (4th round). **SIGNED BY:** Damon Iannelli.

Matthes was an Aflac All-American in high school and performed well as a sophomore and junior at Alabama, yet he went undrafted until putting up big numbers his senior season in 2009. Matthes became the first Alabama player to earn Southeastern Conference player of the year honors, hitting .358 with an NCAA Division I-leading 28 homers. After signing for $200,000 as a fourth-round pick, Matthes built on that success with a solid pro debut, topping the short-season Northwest League with 23 doubles. His power started to blossom when he began to improve his pitch-recognition skills during Alabama's tour of Cuba in the fall of 2008. He has a sound swing and drives the ball to all fields, but needs to be more selective. He's a solid athlete and runner who could become an above-average defender on an outfield corner. He has enough arm to play right field but would fit better in left. Given his age and performance record, Matthes could jump over Class A and open 2010 at Tulsa.

Year	Club (League)	Class	AVG	G	AB	R	H	2B	3B	HR	RBI	BB	SO	SB	OBP	SLG
2009	Tri-City (NWL)	SS	.289	63	239	39	69	23	1	5	35	21	77	6	.364	.456
MINOR LEAGUE TOTALS			.289	63	239	39	69	23	1	5	35	21	77	6	.364	.456

20 AL ALBURQUERQUE, RHP

BORN: June 10, 1986. **B-T:** R-R. **HT.:** 6-0. **WT.:** 195. **SIGNED:** Dominican Republic, 2003. **SIGNED BY:** Jose Serra (Cubs).

Alburquerque came to the Rockies from the Cubs in a trade last July for Jeff Baker, who had been squeezed out of the big league lineup by the arrival of Ian Stewart. Much like Baker, Alburquerque has had a career plagued by injury. He missed the entire 2005 season following Tommy John surgery and all of 2008 after a shoulder operation. Fully healthy again, he put up his best season yet in 2009, when he became a full-time reliever. The Rockies added him to the 40-man roster after he sat in the mid-90s and touched 99 mph in the Dominican Winter League. In addition to his overpowering fastball, he also has a quality slider with depth that sits at 87-88 mph. Alburquerque had better success against lefthanders following the trade, and if he can get lefties out consistently, he'll soon fit into the back of Colorado's bullpen. He'll open 2010 in Triple-A.

Year	Club (League)	Class	W	L	ERA	G	GS	CG	SV	IP	H	R	ER	HR	BB	SO	AVG
2004	Cubs (DSL)	R	4	1	1.57	13	6	0	1	46	33	15	8	0	9	43	.192
2005	Did Not Play—Injured																
2006	Cubs (AZL)	R	0	2	5.68	8	5	0	0	13	10	8	8	1	10	15	.233
2007	Boise (NWL)	SS	3	2	3.73	10	6	0	1	41	42	20	17	2	17	49	.266
	Peoria (MWL)	LoA	1	4	9.24	11	4	0	0	25	36	29	26	5	12	20	.330
2009	Daytona (FSL)	HiA	1	0	2.08	24	0	0	2	35	26	11	8	4	14	44	.203
	Tulsa (TL)	AA	1	3	3.76	23	0	0	0	26	23	13	11	0	13	31	.240
MINOR LEAGUE TOTALS			10	12	3.77	89	21	0	4	186	170	96	78	12	75	202	.257

21 PARKER FRAZIER, RHP

BORN: Nov. 11, 1988. **B-T:** R-R. **HT.:** 6-5. **WT.:** 180. **DRAFTED:** HS—Tulsa, 2007 (8th round). **SIGNED BY:** Dar Cox.

The son of former big leaguer and current Rockies broadcaster George Frazier, Parker was on the verge of jumping to high Class A as a 20-year-old last season before developing elbow problems. Following Tommy John surgery, he's expected to miss at least the first half of the 2010 season, though his rehab is progressing ahead of schedule over thanks to his conditioning and dedication to his rehab. Frazier operates primarily with two pitches, a low-90s sinker with late movement and a hard slider. He throws strikes and thrives off pitching to contact, generating plenty of grounders. His numbers should improve as he moves up the minor league ladder because he'll have better defenses behind him. Colorado will err on the side of caution with Frazier as he comes back from elbow surgery. But if he returns to form quickly, it's possible he could reach Double-A by the end of the season.

Year	Club (League)	Class	W	L	ERA	G	GS	CG	SV	IP	H	R	ER	HR	BB	SO	AVG
2007	Casper (PIO)	R	3	5	10.07	16	10	0	0	45	78	54	50	8	18	22	.386
2008	Tri-City (NWL)	SS	5	5	3.83	15	15	0	0	87	94	41	37	3	20	47	.281
2009	Asheville (SAL)	LoA	10	7	4.48	23	23	1	0	131	158	70	65	7	33	98	.303
MINOR LEAGUE TOTALS			18	17	5.21	54	48	1	0	262	330	165	152	18	71	167	.312

22 CRAIG BAKER, RHP

BORN: Jan. 31, 1985. **B-T:** R-R. **HT.:** 6-2. **WT.:** 210. **DRAFTED:** Cal State Northridge, 2006 (4th round). **SIGNED BY:** Jeff Hipps.

After Baker finished second in the minors with 33 saves last season, the Rockies sweated when they left him off their 40-man roster. But he went unpicked in the major league Rule 5 draft, so he'll continue his climb toward Colorado in 2010. Because of a heavy college workload and biceps tendinitis, Baker didn't pitch in his first pro summer after signing in 2006. Shoulder problems cost him the last month of the 2007 season, and he returned to low Class A in 2008 before taking off last season. Baker uses a high three-quarters delivery to his advantage in creating deception on his four-seam fastball, which ranges from 89-94 mph. He complements his heater with a 12-to-6 curveball. He has good control but will need to sharpen his command of both pitches as he moves up. He also has a slider but could use a pitch to combat lefthanders, perhaps a two-seamer. He's ready to advance to Double-A.

Year	Club (League)	Class	W	L	ERA	G	GS	CG	SV	IP	H	R	ER	HR	BB	SO	AVG
2007	Asheville (SAL)	LoA	3	1	3.35	36	0	0	5	51	58	23	19	6	18	48	.284
2008	Asheville (SAL)	LoA	7	5	2.22	52	0	0	6	57	49	16	14	5	11	70	.228
2009	Modesto (CAL)	HiA	4	2	2.30	62	0	0	33	63	49	23	16	1	21	75	.212
MINOR LEAGUE TOTALS			14	8	2.59	150	0	0	44	170	156	62	49	12	50	193	.240

23 SHANE LINDSAY, RHP

BORN: July 25, 1985. **B-T:** R-R. **HT.:** 6-1. **WT.:** 205. **SIGNED:** Australia, 2003. **SIGNED BY:** Phil Allen.

The biggest question about Lindsay is if he will ever stay healthy enough to capitalize on his raw ability. He tore his labrum late in 2006 and missed all of the following season. He then broke his hand in a barroom brawl, cutting short his comeback in 2008. A strong Arizona Fall League performance in 2008 renewed hope, but then he missed nearly three months last season with a strained ribcage. The Rockies wanted him to build up innings in winter ball, but he struggled in six appearances in the Dominican League and was sent home. Lindsay has worked just 256 innings since signing out of Australia in 2003, but he remains intriguing because he owns a mid-90s fastball that can touch 98 mph, as well as a knuckle-curve that he throws for quality strikes. His changeup never has materialized, but that's less of an issue after Colorado made him a full-time reliever in 2009. His two-pitch assortment gives him plenty with which to attack hitters coming out of the bullpen. Lindsay could open this season in Triple-A and finally get his first big league callup later in the year.

Year	Club (League)	Class	W	L	ERA	G	GS	CG	SV	IP	H	R	ER	HR	BB	SO	AVG
2004	Casper (PIO)	R	1	1	6.75	17	0	0	0	21	22	24	16	1	19	31	.256
2005	Tri-City (NWL)	SS	6	1	1.89	13	13	0	0	67	37	21	14	1	34	107	.163
2006	Tri-City (NWL)	SS	2	2	2.79	6	5	0	0	29	18	10	9	0	17	48	.176
	Asheville (SAL)	LoA	2	1	2.67	7	7	0	0	34	26	15	10	2	27	43	.211
2007	Did Not Play—Injured																
2008	Modesto (CAL)	HiA	2	3	3.99	10	10	0	0	47	33	29	21	1	34	56	.194
	Asheville (SAL)	LoA	1	2	5.55	6	6	0	0	24	30	16	15	1	12	26	.306
2009	Asheville (SAL)	LoA	1	1	1.59	5	0	0	0	6	4	1	1	0	4	7	.211
	Tulsa (TL)	AA	3	1	2.60	22	0	0	1	28	12	8	8	0	19	36	.129
MINOR LEAGUE TOTALS			18	12	3.31	86	41	0	1	256	182	124	94	6	166	354	.198

24 CHAZ ROE, RHP

BORN: Sept. 7, 1986. **B-T:** R-R. **HT.:** 6-3. **WT.:** 180. **DRAFTED:** HS—Louisville, 2005 (1st round supplemental). **SIGNED BY:** Scott Corman.

A quality athlete who could have followed in his father's footsteps and played quarterback at Kentucky, Roe instead chose to sign for $1.025 million as a sandwich pick in 2005. He made steady progress until he was slowed by arthroscopic surgery on his left knee in spring training in 2008. He missed time again in 2009 with a strained oblique and got little out of instructional league after coming down with a serious case of the flu. Nevertheless, Roe has reaffirmed his ability as a starting pitcher. He went back to his high school mechanics last season and regained velocity on his fastball, sitting in the low-90s. His curveball is a swing-and-miss pitch, yet he gets hit harder than his stuff would indicate he should because his command is very much a work in progress. He's still refining the changeup that will be a necessity for him to negate lefthanders. His command also remains very much a work in progress. After earning a spot on the 40-man roster, Roe will see how effective his curveball will be at high altitude when he gets to Colorado Springs this year.

Year	Club (League)	Class	W	L	ERA	G	GS	CG	SV	IP	H	R	ER	HR	BB	SO	AVG
2005	Casper (PIO)	R	5	2	4.17	12	12	0	0	50	31	25	23	2	36	55	.175
2006	Asheville (SAL)	LoA	7	4	4.06	19	19	0	0	100	105	54	45	4	47	80	.273
2007	Modesto (CAL)	HiA	7	11	4.33	29	29	2	0	170	148	93	82	17	73	131	.235
2008	Modesto (CAL)	HiA	2	1	5.49	3	3	0	0	20	24	17	12	1	3	16	.279
	Tulsa (TL)	AA	5	4	4.27	16	16	1	0	105	98	57	50	15	34	70	.248
2009	Tulsa (TL)	AA	7	3	3.15	20	20	1	0	117	105	47	41	7	43	77	.241
MINOR LEAGUE TOTALS			33	25	4.05	99	99	4	0	562	511	293	253	46	236	429	.243

25 MATT REYNOLDS, LHP

BORN: Oct. 2, 1984. **B-T:** L-L. **HT.:** 6-5. **WT.:** 240. **DRAFTED:** Austin Peay State, 2007 (20th round). **SIGNED BY:** Scott Corman.

An unheralded 20th-round pick in 2007, Reynolds has pitched well enough that the Rockies debated bringing him to the big leagues for their pennant drive last year until they were able to acquire veteran Joe Beimel. Reynolds has dominated at times as a lefty set-up man in the minors. His fastball sits at 90 mph and appears quicker because of the deception in his delivery, which is similar to that of Jeff Francis. Both southpaws use their height as leverage in getting quality downhill action. Reynolds has a curveball with good bite, and his splitter gives him an out pitch against righthanders. A starter at Austin Peay State, he has settled into a bullpen role, showing a resilient arm and the ability to get loose quickly. The plan is for Reynolds to open 2010 in Triple-A, but he could force himself into the big league equation with a strong spring.

Year	Club (League)	Class	W	L	ERA	G	GS	CG	SV	IP	H	R	ER	HR	BB	SO	AVG
2007	Tri-City (NWL)	SS	1	4	3.60	20	0	0	0	35	37	21	14	4	4	27	.264
2008	Asheville (SAL)	LoA	6	2	2.53	42	0	0	2	57	49	19	16	4	14	53	.226
2009	Modesto (CAL)	HiA	5	3	1.29	39	0	0	3	49	32	8	7	2	8	58	.190
	Tulsa (TL)	AA	1	2	4.21	21	0	0	1	26	23	12	12	3	9	29	.237
MINOR LEAGUE TOTALS			13	11	2.65	122	0	0	6	167	141	60	49	13	35	167	.227

26 JONATHAN VARGAS, LHP

BORN: May 29, 1989. **B-T:** L-L. **HT.:** 6-2. **WT.:** 210. **SIGNED:** Venezuela, 2005. **SIGNED BY:** Rolando Fernandez/Francisco Cartaya/Carlos Gomez.

After spending three years in the Dominican Summer League and dealing with a bout of appendicitis in 2000, Vargas finally came to the United States last season and pitched his way into the Rockies' long-term plans. After giving up 10 earned runs in his first two starts at Casper, he allowed just 19 more over his final 11 starts. Vargas has solid velocity for a lefthander, sitting in the low-90s with his fastball, and he has the makings of a good curveball and solid changeup. Having thrown just 145 innings in four pro seasons, Vargas needs more innings to refine his pitches and command. He has yet to pitch in a full-season league, yet Colorado will have to protect him on its 40-man roster after the 2010 season or risk losing him in the major league Rule 5 draft. He'll get a shot at making the Asheville club out of spring training.

Year	Club (League)	Class	W	L	ERA	G	GS	CG	SV	IP	H	R	ER	HR	BB	SO	AVG
2006	Rockies (DSL)	R	0	1	5.17	13	3	0	0	16	18	11	9	0	10	10	.281
2007	Rockies (DSL)	R	5	3	3.09	12	11	0	0	47	40	22	16	0	28	36	.238
2008	Rockies (DSL)	R	1	2	1.71	7	6	0	0	26	16	10	5	0	15	30	.172
2009	Casper (PIO)	R	4	5	4.61	13	13	0	0	57	58	36	29	5	32	31	.270
MINOR LEAGUE TOTALS			10	11	3.65	45	33	0	0	145	132	79	59	5	85	107	.244

27 EDGMER ESCALONA, RHP

BORN: Oct. 6, 1986. **B-T:** R-R. **HT.:** 6-4. **WT.:** 225. **SIGNED:** Venezuela, 2004. **SIGNED BY:** Rolando Fernandez/Francisco Cartaya.

Escalona has made tremendous strides in the last two seasons, improving his control while reaching Double-A as a 22-year-old. He has one of the best fastballs in the system, pitching at 92-96 mph and hitting 98 on occasion while coming out of the bullpen. He has good sink on his heater, inducing a lot of weak contact. Escalona has a decent slider, but to be more than a middle reliever he needs to refine his splitter to give him something offspeed that he can use against lefthanders. In a rarity for a pitching prospect, he never has started a game in five pro seasons. The Rockies gave him permission to pitch for Caracas in the second half of the Venezuelan League, and he continued to make progress. He'll get the chance to make the Colorado Springs roster out of spring training after getting added to the 40-man roster this offseason.

Year	Club (League)	Class	W	L	ERA	G	GS	CG	SV	IP	H	R	ER	HR	BB	SO	AVG
2005	Rockies (DSL)	R	2	2	1.64	20	0	0	2	38	28	9	7	1	9	13	.204
2006	Rockies (DSL)	R	0	2	7.11	14	0	0	0	19	22	15	15	1	11	17	.297
2007	Casper (PIO)	R	1	1	4.05	18	0	0	1	27	22	17	12	1	13	20	.212
2008	Asheville (SAL)	LoA	6	2	3.22	44	0	0	1	78	71	32	28	9	18	79	.242
2009	Modesto (CAL)	HiA	2	0	2.48	28	0	0	0	33	25	10	9	3	7	34	.207
	Tulsa (TL)	AA	1	2	2.45	31	0	0	4	37	33	12	10	5	11	32	.232
MINOR LEAGUE TOTALS			12	9	3.15	155	0	0	8	232	201	95	81	20	69	195	.231

28 TYLER MASSEY, OF

BORN: July 21, 1989. **B-T:** L-L. **HT.:** 6-0. **WT.:** 205. **DRAFTED:** HS—Chattanooga, 2008 (14th round). **SIGNED BY:** Scott Corman.

Massey played football for his father Phil at the Baylor School in Chattanoogan and could have played the sport in college as well. He accepted a baseball scholarship offer from Virginia, which scared teams away from him in the 2008 draft, but the Rockies persuaded him to turn pro with a $525,000 bonus in the 14th round. His pro debut was cut short when he ran into an outfield wall and tore the anterior cruciate ligament in his left knee, requiring surgery. Colorado challenged Massey with a jump to low Class A last season, and his numbers weren't pretty. Some scouts from other clubs question his feel for hitting after he posted the third-worst OPS (.551) among South Atlantic League regulars. The Rockies aren't as concerned. They point to his short stroke and ability to use the whole field, and believe he'll be more productive with more experience. He has good raw power but needs to do a better job with his plate discipline and pitch recognition. Massey has the drive to put in the work to make improvements. His arm is solid but his speed is average at best, so he fits best in left field or at first base. He may return to Asheville until his bat gets going.

Year	Club (League)	Class	AVG	G	AB	R	H	2B	3B	HR	RBI	BB	SO	SB	OBP	SLG
2008	Casper (PIO)	R	.257	19	70	7	18	4	0	1	5	1	18	5	.278	.357
2009	Asheville (SAL)	LoA	.220	110	404	31	89	12	5	2	38	23	100	8	.261	.290
MINOR LEAGUE TOTALS			.226	129	474	38	107	16	5	3	43	24	118	13	.263	.300

29 CHRIS NELSON, SS

BORN: Sept. 3, 1985. **B-T:** R-R. **HT.:** 5-11. **WT.:** 180. **DRAFTED:** HS—Decatur, Ga., 2004 (1st round). **SIGNED BY:** Damon Iannelli.

It was considered a coup when the Rockies landed Nelson with the ninth overall pick in the 2004 draft, but the $2.15 million bonus baby is starting to run out of time. A summer league teammate of Dexter Fowler when they were Georgia high schoolers, Nelson hit .299 with 19 homers at Modesto in 2007 but has been held back by injuries ever since. A broken hamate bone in his left hand limited him to 81 games and muted his bat in 2008, while a cartilage problem in his left wrist ended his 2009 season in late May. The bat speed that wowed scouts when Nelson came out of high school is still there, but he has lost too much playing time and has yet to develop plate discipline. He has plus speed and a terrific arm—he was clocked at 99 mph as a junior in high school before he had Tommy John surgery—but hasn't fulfilled his potential as a basestealer or defender. He gets careless at shortstop and likely will wind up at second base or center field. In light of his inability to put together a full season, Nelson is likely headed for a third stint in Double-A to start 2010.

Year	Club (League)	Class	AVG	G	AB	R	H	2B	3B	HR	RBI	BB	SO	SB	OBP	SLG
2004	Casper (PIO)	R	.347	38	147	36	51	6	3	4	20	20	42	6	.432	.510
2005	Asheville (SAL)	LoA	.241	79	315	51	76	13	3	3	38	25	88	7	.304	.330
2006	Asheville (SAL)	LoA	.260	118	466	69	121	38	1	11	76	32	101	14	.313	.416
2007	Modesto (CAL)	HiA	.289	133	529	97	153	42	7	19	99	55	92	27	.358	.503
2008	Modesto (CAL)	HiA	.167	8	30	2	5	1	0	1	5	2	8	0	.219	.300
	Tulsa (TL)	AA	.237	73	283	38	67	18	2	3	42	35	69	6	.324	.346
2009	Tulsa (TL)	AA	.280	29	107	21	30	5	2	4	17	12	21	5	.355	.477
MINOR LEAGUE TOTALS			.268	478	1877	314	503	123	18	45	297	181	421	65	.336	.425

30 KIEL ROLING, 1B

BORN: Jan. 23, 1987. **B-T:** R-R. **HT.:** 6-3. **WT.:** 240. **DRAFTED:** Arizona State, 2008 (6th round).
SIGNED BY: Mike Ericson.

Roling has as much raw power as anyone in the system, but whether he can find a position remains to be seen. A Colorado high school product who signed as a sixth-rounder out of Arizona State in 2008, he led the South Atlantic League in batting (.331) and slugging (.593) in his first full pro season. He uses his strength, bat speed and leverage to drive balls a long way. His swing can get long, but he has the ability to make adjustments. He needs better plate discipline. Though he's a decent athlete, Roling is bulky and slow. He had knee surgery in college and missed time with quadriceps and knee injuries last season. He did some catching at Arizona State but is raw behind the plate. He has soft hands but a below-average arm, and he's pretty much limited to first base. Roling will start 2010 in Modesto but could reach Tulsa before season's end.

Year	Club (League)	Class	AVG	G	AB	R	H	2B	3B	HR	RBI	BB	SO	SB	OBP	SLG
2008	Casper (PIO)	R	.344	18	64	10	22	7	0	4	17	8	11	0	.417	.641
2009	Asheville (SAL)	LoA	.331	94	344	54	114	26	2	20	66	39	92	0	.401	.593
MINOR LEAGUE TOTALS			.333	112	408	64	136	33	2	24	83	47	103	0	.403	.600

Detroit Tigers

BY CONOR GLASSEY

The Tigers spent most of the 2009 season looking down on the rest of the American League Central. They moved into first place on May 10 and held a seven-game lead after they won their first six games in September. Detroit then went just 11-16 the rest of the way, allowing the red-hot Twins to catch them on the final day of the season and force a one-game playoff.

That game turned out to be an epic 12-inning affair that Minnesota won 6-5. The loss was a bitter disappointment for the Tigers, obscuring many of the positive developments that happened during the season.

Eight players made their major league debut with Detroit before rosters expanded in September, led by Rick Porcello, who ranked No. 1 on this list a year ago. The Tigers drew the ire of Major League Baseball when they gave Porcello a $7 million big league contract as a first-round pick in 2007, matching the record guarantee for a high schooler established by Josh Beckett. The investment already has proven justified, as Porcello jumped from high Class A to win 14 games as a rookie and make a strong start in the final loss to the Twins.

Detroit also expedited the development of a pair of 2008 draftees. First-rounder Ryan Perry spent the entire season in the big league bullpen, striking out 60 in 62 innings and looking every bit like the club's closer of the future. Fifth-rounder Alex Avila, who joined the club in August to add another catcher and lefthanded bat, delivered five homers in 61 at-bats.

After setting a franchise record by spending $136 million on player salaries in 2008 and opening last season with a $115 million payroll, the Tigers entered the offseason looking to reduce their expenditures for 2010. Detroit has committed $65.5 million alone for the salaries of Magglio Ordonez, Carlos Guillen, Jeremy Bonderman, Dontrelle Willis and Nate Robertson, whose recent performance has rendered them virtually unmovable.

As a result, the Tigers had to deal one of their most popular players and one of their most effective starters. At the Winter Meetings, they sent Curtis Granderson to the Yankees and Edwin Jackson to the Diamondbacks in a three-team trade that brought back outfield prospect Austin Jackson and Phil Coke from New York and Max Scherzer and Daniel Schlereth from Arizona. The Tigers' hope is that Jackson, Scherzer and Schlereth will team with Miguel Cabrera, Porcello and Justin Verlander to

MORRIS FOSTOFF

Righthander Rick Porcello jumped from high Class A in 2008 to the big leagues in 2009

TOP 30 PROSPECTS

1. Jacob Turner, rhp	**16.** Casper Wells, of
2. Casey Crosby, lhp	**17.** Avisail Garcia, of
3. Austin Jackson, of	**18.** Brayan Villarreal, rhp
4. Andy Oliver, lhp	**19.** Jared Gayhart, rhp
5. Daniel Schlereth, lhp	**20.** Luke Putkonen, rhp
6. Alex Avila, c	**21.** Jay Sborz, rhp
7. Gustavo Nunez, ss	**22.** Tyler Stohr, rhp
8. Wilkin Ramirez, of	**23.** Melvin Mercedes, rhp
9. Daniel Fields, ss	**24.** Wade Gaynor, 3b
10. Scott Sizemore, 2b	**25.** Brennan Boesch, of
11. Ryan Strieby, 1b/of	**26.** Dusty Ryan, c
12. Robbie Weinhardt, rhp	**27.** Casey Fien, rhp
13. Cale Iorg, ss	**28.** Scott Green, rhp
14. Cody Satterwhite, rhp	**29.** James Robbins, 1b
15. Alfredo Figaro, rhp	**30.** Edwin Gomez, ss

give them a solid core around which they can build a contender at reduced rates.

Detroit may be trying to save money at the major league level, but it wasn't afraid to spend to acquire young talent in 2009. The Tigers went from the second-lowest draft bonus total ($3.7 million) in 2008 to the third-highest (a club-record $9.4 million) last summer. They gave a $4.7 million bonus (the largest ever for a high school pitcher) as part of a $5.5 million big league contract to first-rounder Jacob Turner, $1.495 million to second-rounder Andy Oliver and $1.625 million to sixth-rounder Daniel Fields.

General Manager: Dave Dombrowski. **Farm Director:** Dan Lunetta. **Scouting Director:** David Chadd.

Class	Team	League	W	L	PCT	Finish*	Manager(s)
Majors	Detroit Tigers	American	86	77	.528	6th (14)	Jim Leyland
Triple-A	Toledo Mud Hens	International	73	70	.510	6th (14)	Larry Parrish
Double-A	Erie SeaWolves	Eastern	71	70	.504	6th (12)	Tom Brookens
High A	Lakeland Flying Tigers	Florida State	55	75	.423	11th (12)	Andy Barkett
Low A	West Michigan Whitecaps	Midwest	81	59	.579	t-3rd (14)	Joe DePastino
Short-season	Oneonta Tigers	New York-Penn	35	39	.473	9th (14)	Howie Bushong
Rookie	GCL Tigers	Gulf Coast	29	30	.492	9th (16)	Basilio Cabrera
Overall 2009 Minor League Record			344	343	.501	16th (30)	

*Finish in overall standings (No. of teams in league). †League champion.

LAST YEAR'S TOP 30

Player, Pos.		Status
1.	Rick Porcello, rhp	Majors
2.	Ryan Perry, rhp	Majors
3.	Cale Iorg, ss	No. 13
4.	Casey Crosby, lhp	No. 2
5.	Jeff Larish, 1b/3b	Majors
6.	Wilkin Ramirez, of	No. 8
7.	Scott Sizemore, 2b	No. 10
8.	Cody Satterwhite, rhp	No. 14
9.	Dusty Ryan, c	No. 26
10.	Brett Jacobson, rhp	(Orioles)
11.	Casey Fien, rhp	No. 27
12.	Ryan Strieby, 1b	No. 11
13.	Casper Wells, of	No. 16
14.	Rudy Darrow, rhp	(Braves)
15.	Freddy Dolsi, rhp	Majors
16.	Alfredo Figaro, rhp	No. 15
17.	Luis Marte, rhp	Dropped out
18.	Scott Green, rhp	No. 28
19.	Jonathan Kibler, lhp	Dropped out
20.	Alex Avila, c	No. 6
21.	Clete Thomas, of	Majors
22.	Robbie Weinhardt, rhp	No. 12
23.	Brandon Douglas, ss	Dropped out
24.	Mauricio Robles, lhp	(Mariners)
25.	Michael Hollimon, 2b/ss	Dropped out
26.	Brandon Hamilton, rhp	Dropped out
27.	Danny Worth, ss	Dropped out
28.	Zach Simons, rhp	Dropped out
29.	Kyle Bloom, lhp	Dropped out
30.	Will Rhymes, 2b/ss	Dropped out

BEST TOOLS

Best Hitter for Average	Scott Sizemore
Best Power Hitter	Ryan Strieby
Best Strike-Zone Discipline	Scott Sizemore
Fastest Baserunner	Daniel Fields
Best Athlete	Daniel Fields
Best Fastball	Casey Crosby
Best Curveball	Jacob Turner
Best Slider	Brayan Villarreal
Best Changeup	Tyler Conn
Best Control	Austin Wood
Best Defensive Catcher	Alex Avila
Best Defensive Infielder	Gustavo Nunez
Best Infield Arm	Cale Iorg
Best Defensive Outfielder	Austin Jackson
Best Outfield Arm	Casper Wells

PROJECTED 2013 LINEUP

Catcher	Alex Avila
First Base	Miguel Cabrera
Second Base	Scott Sizemore
Third Base	Brandon Inge
Shortstop	Gustavo Nunez
Left Field	Wilkin Ramirez
Center Field	Austin Jackson
Right Field	Daniel Fields
Designated Hitter	Ryan Strieby
No. 1 Starter	Justin Verlander
No. 2 Starter	Rick Porcello
No. 3 Starter	Jacob Turner
No. 4 Starter	Max Scherzer
No. 5 Starter	Casey Crosby
Closer	Ryan Perry

TOP PROSPECTS OF THE DECADE

Year	Player, Pos.	2009 Org.
2000	Eric Munson, 1b/c	Athletics
2001	Brandon Inge, c	Tigers
2002	Nate Cornejo, rhp	Out of baseball
2003	Jeremy Bonderman, rhp	Tigers
2004	Kyle Sleeth, rhp	Out of baseball
2005	Curtis Granderson, of	Tigers
2006	Justin Verlander, rhp	Tigers
2007	Cameron Maybin, of	Marlins
2008	Rick Porcello, rhp	Tigers
2009	Rick Porcello, rhp	Tigers

TOP DRAFT PICKS OF THE DECADE

Year	Player, Pos.	2009 Org.
2000	Matt Wheatland, rhp	Out of baseball
2001	Kenny Baugh, rhp	Astros
2002	Scott Moore, ss	Orioles
2003	Kyle Sleeth, rhp	Out of baseball
2004	Justin Verlander, rhp	Tigers
2005	Cameron Maybin, of	Marlins
2006	Andrew Miller, lhp	Marlins
2007	Rick Porcello, rhp	Tigers
2008	Ryan Perry, rhp	Tigers
2009	Jacob Turner, rhp	Tigers

LARGEST BONUSES IN CLUB HISTORY

Jacob Turner, 2009	$4,700,000
Rick Porcello, 2007	$3,580,000
Andrew Miller, 2006	$3,550,000
Eric Munson, 1999	$3,500,000
Kyle Sleeth, 2003	$3,350,000

DETROIT TIGERS

TOP 2010 ROOKIE: Scott Sizemore, 2b. He should be fully recovered from a broken ankle in the Arizona Fall League and ready to replace Placido Polanco.

BREAKOUT PROSPECT: Robbie Weinhardt, rhp. Hitters don't pick up his 92-94 mph fastball or hard slider, which is why he has a 1.64 ERA in two pro seasons.

SLEEPER: Ramon Lebron, rhp. He's still raw, but he hit 97 mph with his fastball last season.

SOURCE OF TOP 30 TALENT

Homegrown	27	Acquired	3
College	15	Trades	2
Junior college	0	Rule 5 draft	0
High school	5	Independent leagues	0
Draft-and-follow	1	Free agents/waivers	1
Nondrafted free agents	0		
International	6		

Numbers in parentheses indicate prospect rankings

LF
Wilkin Ramirez (8)
Jeff Frazier

CF
Austin Jackson (3)
Casper Wells (16)
Andy Dirks
Jamie Johnson
Ben Guez
Michael Rockett

RF
Avisail Garcia (17)
Brennan Boesch (25)
Steven Moya
Alexis Espinoza
Deik Scram

3B
Wade Gaynor (24)
Edgar Corcino
Francisco Martinez
Brett Anderson

SS
Gustavo Nunez (7)
Daniel Fields (9)
Cale Iorg (13)
Edwin Gomez (30)
Audy Ciriaco
Brent Dlugach
Danny Worth

2B
Scott Sizemore (10)
Brandon Douglas
Alexander Nunez
Will Rhymes
Alden Carrithers
Chris Sedon

1B
Ryan Strieby (11)
James Robbins (29)
Michael Bertram
Rawley Bishop
Billy Nowlin
Chris Carlson

C
Alex Avila (6)
Dusty Ryan (26)
John Murrian
Jordan Newton
Gabriel Purroy

RHP

Starters	Relievers
Jacob Turner (1)	Robbie Weinhardt (12)
Alfredo Figaro (15)	Cody Satterwhite (14)
Brayan Villarreal (18)	Jared Gayhart (19)
Luke Putkonen (20)	Jay Sborz (21)
Luis Marte	Tyler Stohr (22)
Thad Weber	Melvin Mercedes (23)
L.J. Gagnier	Casey Fien (27)
Brandon Hamilton	Scott Green (28)
Brooks Brown	Ramon Lebron
Luis Sanz	Lester Oliveros
Nate Newman	Brett Jensen
	Freddy Dolsi
	Zach Simons
	Josh Rainwater
	Jose Ortega
	Anthony Shawler
	Michael Torrealba

LHP

Starters	Relievers
Casey Crosby (2)	Daniel Schlereth (5)
Andy Oliver (4)	Austin Wood
Charlie Furbush	Tyler Conn
Adam Wilk	
Matt Hoffman	
Jon Kibler	
Duane Below	
Giovanni Soto	
Jade Todd	

2009   BONUSES: $9.4 MILLION

BEST PURE HITTER: He's a bit raw as a Michigan prep product, but SS Daniel Fields (6) is the best position player the Tigers have drafted since Cameron Maybin in 2005.

BEST POWER HITTER: 3B Wade Gaynor (3) had a huge spring at Western Kentucky, turning in a 20-20 season. His plus raw power will keep playing in pro ball, and he runs well for a 6-foot-4, 215 pounder.

FASTEST RUNNER: Fields, whose speed rates a 65 on the 20-80 scouting scale.

BEST DEFENSIVE PLAYER: 3B Edgar Corcino (26) has the arm strength and athletic ability to be a plus defender at the hot corner. He tried his hand at catching in instructional league, and his bat would profile better behind the plate.

BEST FASTBALL: The Tigers' top two selections, RHP Jacob Turner (1) and LHP Andy Oliver (2), had two of the draft's best fastballs. Turner has reached 98 mph and works at 92-94 with command. Oliver has reached the upper 90s at times and sits 92-94.

BEST SECONDARY PITCH: Turner's curveball and changeup have plus potential. LHP Austin Wood (5), who was undrafted as a junior, moved from the rotation to the bullpen at Texas, allowing him to take advantage of his plus slider.

BEST PRO DEBUT: LHP Adam Wilk (11) used his pitchability to go 4-1, 1.47 with 67 strikeouts in 74 innings between short-season Oneonta and low Class A West Michigan.

BEST ATHLETE: Fields.

MOST INTRIGUING BACKGROUND: Wood starred for 12 1/3 scoreless innings and 169 pitches in Texas' 3-2, 25-inning win against Boston College in a 2009 regional game, the longest game in NCAA history. Fields leads a fleet of Tigers picks with big league ties. His father Bruce reached the majors as an outfielder and was the Tigers' hitting coach from 2003-2005. He's now the Indians' roving hitting coordinator. The group also includes: C Eric Roof (18), son of Gene, who is now Detroit's roving outfield/baserunning instructor; SS Jim Gulliver (20), son of Glenn; RHP Nick Avila (42), nephew of Tigers assistant GM Al Avila; 3B Andrew Allen (43), son of Tigers color analyst and former Detroit outfielder Rod; and RHP Jake Porcello (48), younger brother of Tigers rookie ace Rick. Avila, Allen and Porcello didn't sign.

CLOSEST TO THE MAJORS: Wood may zoom past Oliver as a situational, strike-throwing lefty.

BEST LATE-ROUND PICK: If he hits, Corcino will be a steal. 1B James Robbins (30) has raw power to

rival Gaynor and should move faster than Corcino.

THE ONE WHO GOT AWAY: Detroit knew it would be tough to woo RHP Mark Appel (15) away from Stanford. They took a longer look at sophomore-eligible RHP Craig Fritsch (8), who returned to Baylor.

ASSESSMENT: Oliver would have been in Detroit's mix at No. 9 overall had he shown any consistency with his breaking ball during the spring at Oklahoma State. If he, Turner and Fields click, this will be a draft class that features three first-round talents.

2008   BONUSES: $3.7 MILLION

RHP Ryan Perry (1) made Detroit's Opening Day roster 10 months after getting drafted, and C Alex Avila (5) got to the majors last August. RHPs Cody Satterwhite (2) and Robbie Weinhardt (10) could join Perry in the Tigers bullpen in the near future.

GRADE: B

2007   BONUSES: $8.0 MILLION

The Tigers gave RHP Rick Porcello (1) a high school-record $7 million contract, and it didn't take long for them to get their money's worth. Of their two other bonus babies, LHP Casey Crosby (5) is a budding star but SS Cale Iorg (6) is stalling.

GRADE: A

2006   BONUSES: $6.0 MILLION

LHP Andrew Miller (1) has fallen far short of expectations but was used as a key piece in the Miguel Cabrera/Dontrelle Willis trade. 2B Scott Sizemore (5) will be Detroit's second baseman in 2010, and 1B/OF Ryan Strieby (4) has some of the best power in the system. RHP Casey Fien (20) defied the odds and reached the majors.

GRADE: C+

2005   BONUSES: $3.8 MILLION*

Seven signees from this crop have reached the majors, most notably OF Cameron Maybin (1), part of the Cabrera/Willis deal. The Tigers also traded RHPs Anthony Claggett (11) and Burke Badenhop (19) and OF Matt Joyce (12), and they've held onto 1B Jeff Larish (5), OF Clete Thomas (6) and 3B Michael Hollimon (16).

GRADE: B+

---

*Draft analysis by John Manuel (2009) and Jim Callis (2005-08). Numbers in parentheses indicate draft rounds. *Bonuses for 2005 are first 10 rounds only.*

DAVID STONER

JACOB TURNER, RHP

Born: May 21, 1991.
Height: 6-5. **Weight:** 210.
Bats: R. **Throws:** R.
Drafted: HS—St. Louis, 2009 (1st round).
Signed by: Marty Miller.

After an excellent summer on the showcase circuit, which included striking out five straight batters at the Aflac All-America Game, Turner positioned himself as a mid-first-round pick for the 2009 draft. He looked sharper and sharper as the spring progressed, boosting his stock to where he was the consensus top high school righthander available in a standout class of prep arms. His price tag and choice of Scott Boras as his adviser scared some teams off, but the Tigers aren't afraid to gamble in the draft and selected him with the ninth overall pick. He signed at the Aug. 17 deadline, getting a $4.7 million bonus—the highest ever for a high school pitcher—as part of a $5.5 million major league contract. Signing that late didn't allow Turner to make his pro debut in 2009, but he enters the system more polished than most high schoolers. His pitching coach at Westminster Christian Academy (St. Louis) was former all-star Todd Worrell, and ex-big leaguers Andy Benes and Mike Matheny also had sons on the team. Turner's older brother Ben formed the other half of his battery growing up and now catches for Missouri. If Turner hadn't signed, he would have attended North Carolina, which also had a commitment from Missouri's top prep pitcher in 2008, Royals righthander Tim Melville.

At 6-foot-5 and 210 pounds, Turner has an ideal pitcher's frame and the stuff to match. He throws his four-seam fastball at 92-94 mph and will touch 97-98 multiple times per game. He gets good, late action on his fastball and locates it to both sides of the plate. He'll also mix in two-seamers on occasion. Turner's curveball isn't as good as his heater, but it projects as a future plus pitch. He throws it between 78-83 mph with good depth and sharp 12-to-6 break. His changeup should be a solid third pitch as he gets more experience with it. A good athlete, he has smooth mechanics and the ball comes out of his hand cleanly with explosive late life.

Turner is still a little inconsistent with his curveball, though that's typical for high school pitchers, especially those that can blow fastballs by their competition so easily. His changeup will need to be refined if he's going to turn over pro lineups a few times every five days. Mostly, Turner just needs to pitch more and face quality competition. He made just one outing in the instructional league because he developed some shoulder stiffness and the Tigers shut him down. They were just being cautious, and there are no major concerns about his health.

Detroit scouting director David Chadd historically favors college players. When he takes a high schooler with an early pick, he has made some terrific choices, including Jon Lester in the second round in 2002 (with the Red Sox) and Rick Porcello in the first round in 2007. Turner profiles as a top-of-the-rotation starter and likely will begin his pro career at low Class A West Michigan. He may not race to the majors as quickly as Porcello—who was regarded as a slightly better prospect at the same stage of his career—but Turner shouldn't require much seasoning either. He could be pitching in Detroit by the end of 2011.

Year	Club (League)	Class	W	L	ERA	G	GS	CG	SV	IP	H	R	ER	HR	BB	SO	AVG
2009	Did Not Play—Signed Late																

2 CASEY CROSBY, LHP

BORN: Sept. 17, 1988. **B-T:** R-L. **HT.:** 6-5. **WT.:** 200. **DRAFTED:** HS—Maple Park, Ill., 2007 (5th round). **SIGNED BY:** Marty Miller.

The Tigers signed Crosby for $748,500 as a fifth-round pick in 2007, only to see him hurt his elbow in instructional league and require Tommy John surgery. Because he entered 2009 with just five innings of pro experience, they limited him to five innings or 75-80 pitches per outing in low Class A. Crosby starred despite the short leash, going 5-2, 0.78 in the second half and drawing comparisons to Clayton Kershaw. Crosby has well-above-average velocity for a lefthander, sitting at 92-95 mph and getting as high as 98 with late life. He also throws a true curveball with sharp downward break and tight rotation. His curve has the potential to be a plus pitch, and when he misses with it, he misses down rather than in a hitter's wheelhouse. He also shows some feel for a changeup. He has some deception and uses his height and high three-quarters arm slot to throw on a steep downward plane. A very good athlete, he was an all-state wide receiver at his suburban Chicago high school. Crosby needs work on the consistency and command of all of his pitches. Because his offerings aren't fully developed, he relies on blowing his fastball by hitters. He lost a chance to work on his secondary pitches during instructional league, as he was shut down after a couple starts with shoulder tendinitis. Crosby has an electric arm and is one of the game's best lefthanded pitching prospects. Rick Porcello notwithstanding, Detroit typically moves its pitchers one step at a time, so Crosby figures to spend 2010 at high Class A Lakeland. If he can handle a full workload, he figures to accelerate his timetable.

Year	Club (League)	Class	W	L	ERA	G	GS	CG	SV	IP	H	R	ER	HR	BB	SO	AVG
2008	Tigers (GCL)	R	0	0	0.00	3	3	0	0	5	4	1	0	0	3	2	.211
2009	West Michigan (MWL)	LoA	10	4	2.41	24	24	0	0	105	70	36	28	3	48	117	.195
MINOR LEAGUE TOTALS			10	4	2.30	27	27	0	0	109	74	37	28	3	51	119	.196

3 AUSTIN JACKSON, OF

BORN: Feb. 1, 1987. **B-T:** R-R. **HT.:** 6-1. **WT.:** 185. **DRAFTED:** HS—Denton, Texas, 2005 (8th round). **SIGNED BY:** Mark Batchko (Yankees).

A former Georgia Tech point guard recruit, Jackson signed with the Yankees for a then-eighth-round-record $800,000 in 2005. He had a mixed performance when he reached Triple-A in 2009, hitting .300 but showing little power and slumping in the second half. He came to Detroit in December as part of the three-team trade that sent Curtis Granderson to New York and Edwin Jackson to Arizona. Jackson brings his athleticism to bear defensively in center field, where he glides to balls with good range, and offensively, where he repeats his swing to produce gap power. He has shown the ability to hit for average, batting .300 or better in three of his five pro seasons. He's a tick above-average runner underway who has improved his basestealing ability. His arm strength is above average for center field and allows him to play right field as well. In an attempt to hit for more power, Jackson lost his rhythm, stopped making contact and had just nine extra-base hits in the second half of last season. He has hit just 30 homers in 565 pro games, and he's likely to have average power at best. He's not selective enough to take walks consistently, and he needs a better two-strike approach. Jackson had reached a crossroads with the Yankees but will get the opportunity to replace Granderson in center field for the Tigers. He may be better suited to hit at the top of the lineup than Granderson was.

Year	Club (League)	Class	AVG	G	AB	R	H	2B	3B	HR	RBI	BB	SO	SB	OBP	SLG
2005	Yankees (GCL)	R	.304	40	148	32	45	11	2	0	14	18	26	11	.374	.405
2006	Charleston, SC (SAL)	LoA	.260	134	535	90	139	24	5	4	47	61	151	37	.340	.346
2007	Charleston, SC (SAL)	LoA	.260	60	235	33	61	16	1	3	25	24	59	19	.336	.374
	Tampa (FSL)	HiA	.345	67	258	53	89	15	6	10	34	22	48	13	.398	.566
	Scranton/W-B (IL)	AAA	.333	1	3	2	1	0	0	0	0	2	2	1	.600	.667
2008	Trenton (EL)	AA	.285	131	520	75	148	33	5	9	69	56	113	19	.354	.419
2009	Scranton/W-B (IL)	AAA	.300	132	504	67	151	23	9	4	65	40	123	24	.354	.405
MINOR LEAGUE TOTALS			.288	565	2203	352	634	123	28	30	254	223	522	124	.356	.410

4 ANDY OLIVER, LHP

BORN: Dec. 3, 1987. **B-T:** L-L. **HT.:** 6-3. **WT.:** 206. **DRAFTED:** Oklahoma State, 2009 (2nd round). **SIGNED BY:** Chris Wimmer.

The NCAA tried to make an example of Oliver in May 2008, suspending him for having an adviser present during negotiations with the Twins two years earlier, when they drafted him in the 17th round out of high school. Oliver sued the NCAA, was reinstated for the 2009 season and received a $750,000 settlement. He had an up and down junior season at Oklahoma State, but the Tigers loved his live left arm and gave him a $1.495 million bonus as a second-round pick. Oliver throws harder than most lefthanders, pitching at 92-94 mph and occasionally reaching the upper 90s. He throws strikes and gets average movement with his four-seam fastball, and Detroit is having him add a two-seamer and emphasizing pounding the bottom of the strike zone. He pitches with clean mechanics and an easy arm action. Part of the reason Oliver struggled last spring was that he was essentially operating with just one pitch, throwing 95 percent fastballs in some starts. He had shown a good curveball in the past but it was virtually non-existent. He also has a cutter/slider and a changeup, but he needs to throw them more to maximize his effectiveness. Oliver also has a few kinks to iron out in his delivery. He sometimes opens up too early and tends to land a little hard on his heel. The Tigers made some tweaks to help him use his strength and leverage more efficiently. If Oliver develops his secondary stuff, he has the potential to be a frontline starter. If not, he could wind up as a closer. After getting some experience in the Arizona Fall League, he could make his pro debut in high Class A.

Year	Club (League)	Class	W	L	ERA	G	GS	CG	SV	IP	H	R	ER	HR	BB	SO	AVG
2009	Did Not Play—Signed Late																

5 DANIEL SCHLERETH, LHP

BORN: May 9, 1986. **B-T:** L-L. **HT.:** 6-0. **WT.:** 210. **DRAFTED:** Arizona, 2008 (1st round). **SIGNED BY:** Rodney Davis (Diamondbacks).

The son of former NFL lineman and ESPN analyst Mark Schlereth, Daniel overcame Tommy John surgery in 2006 to go 26th overall in the draft two years later. Ten months after signing with the Diamondbacks for $1.33 million, he was in the big leagues. Arizona shipped him to Detroit in December in a deal that brought Edwin Jackson to the desert. Schlereth has the potential to be a rare power-pitching lefty closer. He has a 93-96 mph fastball with riding life, and he can buckle knees with his hard 82-84 mph curveball. Though he didn't need it in college, he also flashes a changeup that dives and floats. He's intense on the mound and wants the ball late in games. Schlereth struggled in the big leagues because he battled his command. He couldn't maintain a consistent release point, hurting his ability to locate his pitches. He needs to throw more strikes, and batters shouldn't tee off on his swing-and-miss stuff if he does. As soon as Schlereth works out his control issues, he'll be pitching in the late innings for the Tigers.

Year	Club (League)	Class	W	L	ERA	G	GS	CG	SV	IP	H	R	ER	HR	BB	SO	AVG
2008	Missoula (PIO)	R	0	0	0.00	3	0	0	0	3	3	1	0	0	2	6	.250
	South Bend (MWL)	LoA	1	0	2.00	7	0	0	0	9	3	2	2	0	4	14	.103
2009	Mobile (SL)	AA	0	0	1.01	21	0	0	4	27	14	3	3	1	16	39	.161
	Reno (PCL)	AAA	0	0	0.00	1	0	0	0	1	1	0	0	0	1	1	.250
	Arizona (NL)	MAJ	1	4	5.89	21	0	0	0	18	15	13	12	1	15	22	.221
MAJOR LEAGUE TOTALS			1	4	5.89	21	0	0	0	18	15	13	12	1	15	22	.221
MINOR LEAGUE TOTALS			1	0	1.13	32	0	0	4	40	21	6	5	1	23	60	.159

6 ALEX AVILA, C

BORN: Jan. 29, 1987. **B-T:** L-R. **HT.:** 5-11. **WT.:** 210. **DRAFTED:** Alabama, 2008 (5th round). **SIGNED BY:** Jim Rough.

The Tigers drafted both of assistant GM Al Avila's sons in 2008, Alex in the fifth round and Alan in the 47th. They signed Alex, who was in his first year as a full-time catcher, and he reached Detroit last year in surprisingly quick fashion. Not only did he get the call in August when the Tigers needed an extra catcher and lefty bat, but he responded with five homers in 61 at-bats. Avila can catch up to good fastballs and drive the ball to all fields, projecting as a possible .280 hitter with 15 homers in the big leagues. He has improved tremendously in a short time as a catcher, and one scout who saw him in 2009 couldn't believe Avila was the same guy he saw in college. He's agile and has solid catch-and-throw skills, and he led the Double-A Eastern League by throwing out 44 percent of basestealers last season. He has tremendous makeup and instincts after growing up around the game. Avila has yet to prove he can handle lefthanders, hitting .234/.316/.360 against them in 175 minor league at-bats. As is the case with most catchers, he's a below-average runner. Avila leapfrogged Dusty Ryan on the organizational depth chart and profiles as solid regular. He'll likely split time with Gerald Laird in 2010 as he prepares to become Detroit's full-time catcher in 2011.

Year	Club (League)	Class	AVG	G	AB	R	H	2B	3B	HR	RBI	BB	SO	SB	OBP	SLG
2008	West Michigan (MWL)	LoA	.305	58	213	21	65	14	0	1	22	27	41	0	.383	.385
2009	Erie (EL)	AA	.264	93	329	52	87	23	1	12	55	52	77	2	.365	.450
	Detroit (AL)	MAJ	.279	29	61	9	17	4	0	5	14	10	18	0	.375	.590
MAJOR LEAGUE TOTALS			.279	29	61	9	17	4	0	5	14	10	18	0	.375	.590
MINOR LEAGUE TOTALS			.280	151	542	73	152	37	1	13	77	79	118	2	.372	.424

7 GUSTAVO NUNEZ, SS

BORN: Feb. 8, 1988. **B-T:** B-R. **HT.:** 5-10. **WT.:** 168. **SIGNED:** Dominican Republic, 2007. **SIGNED BY:** Julian German/Ramon Perez.

After hitting .245/.304/.272 in high Class A in 2008, Nunez was much improved after taking a step back to West Michigan last season. He emerged as the system's best infield prospect, with the lone negative a July suspension for what the Tigers deemed "conduct detrimental to the organization." Nunez is a very good defender with smooth actions, fluid footwork and one of the best arms in the system. He has good bat control, grinds out at-bats and finds a way to get on base and score runs. His speed rates a 65 on the 20-80 scouting scale and he led Detroit farmhands with 48 steals last year. Despite the suspension, the Tigers regard him as a hard worker with great makeup. Nunez has a tendency to jump at the first pitch and get behind in the count. He's undersized and doesn't project to hit for much power. After getting caught stealing 25 times last year, he needs to work on getting better reads and jumps. At shortstop, he sometimes lets the ball play him instead of being more aggressive. One scout from outside the organization compared Nunez to Orlando Cabrera with less power. A top-of-the-order sparkplug and a terrific defender, he'll get a second crack at Lakeland in 2010.

Year	Club (League)	Class	AVG	G	AB	R	H	2B	3B	HR	RBI	BB	SO	SB	OBP	SLG
2007	Tigers (DSL)	R	.284	64	243	50	69	10	3	0	42	32	45	9	.370	.350
2008	Tigers (GCL)	R	.200	13	40	5	8	3	0	0	5	2	6	1	.233	.275
	Lakeland (FSL)	HiA	.245	45	147	14	36	4	0	0	15	11	29	1	.304	.272
2009	Tigers (GCL)	R	.190	6	21	5	4	0	0	1	4	1	5	3	.261	.333
	West Michigan (MWL)	LoA	.315	112	464	82	146	16	10	5	40	25	62	45	.360	.425
MINOR LEAGUE TOTALS			.287	240	915	156	263	33	13	6	106	71	147	59	.346	.372

8 WILKIN RAMIREZ, OF

BORN: Oct. 25, 1985. **B-T:** R-R. **HT.:** 6-2. **WT.:** 190. **SIGNED:** Dominican Republic, 2003. **SIGNED BY:** Ramon Pena.

Signed out of the Dominican Republic as a third baseman in 2003, Ramirez moved to left field in 2007 and made his way to the majors last season. He homered off Matt Harrison in his first big league game, but for the most part came back to earth a bit after having the best minor league season of his career in 2008. Although he's still a bit raw, Ramirez continues to show off tantalizing five-tool ability. Both his power and speed grade as above-average and he could be a 25-25 man in the majors. He has the bat speed to catch up with major league fastballs and the swing to hit .280-.300. Ramirez has a swing-hard-in-case-you-hit-it approach, so his power comes with a lot of strikeouts. His stroke can get a bit long at times and he's pull-oriented, leaving him vulnerable to breaking balls off the plate. He fits best in left field because he's still learning to play the outfield, but he has a strong arm. He needs to take better routes on flyballs and get better jumps on the bases. Detroit doesn't have an established left fielder, but Ramirez could use some more seasoning at Triple-A Toledo. He could push for a regular job in the majors by the end of 2010.

Year	Club (League)	Class	AVG	G	AB	R	H	2B	3B	HR	RBI	BB	SO	SB	OBP	SLG
2003	Tigers (GCL)	R	.275	54	200	34	55	6	7	5	35	13	51	6	.321	.450
2004	Did Not Play—Injured															
2005	West Michigan (MWL)	LoA	.262	131	493	69	129	21	2	16	65	35	143	21	.317	.410
2006	Lakeland (FSL)	HiA	.225	66	249	31	56	10	4	8	33	10	69	8	.259	.394
2007	Lakeland (FSL)	HiA	.273	88	319	48	87	7	4	10	41	20	86	28	.315	.414
	Erie (EL)	AA	.215	34	121	15	26	3	1	2	14	8	38	6	.273	.306
2008	Toledo (IL)	AAA	.083	11	36	2	3	1	0	0	1	1	11	1	.132	.111
	Erie (EL)	AA	.303	110	433	74	131	24	7	19	73	43	138	26	.371	.522
2009	Toledo (IL)	AAA	.258	113	434	69	112	18	6	17	51	41	143	33	.326	.445
	Detroit (AL)	MAJ	.364	15	11	6	4	0	1	1	3	1	3	0	.385	.818
MAJOR LEAGUE TOTALS			.364	15	11	6	4	0	1	1	3	1	3	0	.385	.818
MINOR LEAGUE TOTALS			.262	607	2285	342	599	90	31	77	312	171	679	129	.318	.430

9 DANIEL FIELDS, SS

BORN: Jan. 23, 1991. **B-T:** L-R. **HT.:** 6-2. **WT.:** 200. **DRAFTED:** HS—Detroit, 2009 (5th round). **SIGNED BY:** Tom Osowski.

Fields grew up around baseball, as his father Bruce won three minor league batting titles and reached the big leagues briefly with the Tigers and Mariners. He was Detroit's big league batting coach in 2003, when he let Daniel take batting practice at Comerica Park and the 12-year-old wowed onlookers by homering with a wood bat. The Tigers lured Fields away from a Michigan commitment with an over-slot bonus of $1.625 million after selecting him in the sixth round last June. Fields is a quality athlete with the strength and natural lift in his lefthanded swing to hit home runs. Though he's a below-average runner out of the box, he grades out as plus underway. He runs the 60-yard dash in 6.6 seconds and has the instincts to steal bases. His arm rates as average to a tick above. Detroit also praises his makeup and work ethic. Though he'll get every opportunity to stay at shortstop, Fields is big for the position and doesn't have a quick first step. He'll have to work hard to remain there, but most scouts project that he'll have to shift to third base or the outfield. The best athlete in the system, Fields excites the Tigers with his power-speed combination and good bloodlines. He'll get his pro career started in low Class A.

Year	Club (League)	Class	AVG	G	AB	R	H	2B	3B	HR	RBI	BB	SO	SB	OBP	SLG
2009	Did Not Play—Signed Late															

10 SCOTT SIZEMORE, 2B

BORN: Jan. 4, 1985. **B-T:** R-R. **HT.:** 6-0. **WT.:** 185. **DRAFTED:** Virginia Commonwealth, 2006 (5th round). **SIGNED BY:** Bill Buck.

A rare second-base prospect who was actually drafted at the position, Sizemore has batted .296 since signing as a fifth-round pick in 2006. He represented the Tigers at the Futures Game in 2009, when he easily handled the transition to Double-A and Triple-A and earned a spot on the 40-man roster. Sizemore is a blue-collar grinder who comes to the park ready to play every day. He has a compact swing and a knack for putting the barrel on the ball. His hitting ability grades as his lone plus tool, but his instincts help the rest of his game play up. He has average speed and a knack for stealing bases, succeeding in 21 of 25 attempts last season. The Tigers played Sizemore at shortstop in his pro debut, but gave up on that experiment after one season. Even at second base, his range is fringy and his arm is just adequate. He has trouble turning the double play, though he has shown improvement. Sizemore broke his left ankle on a double-play pivot in the Arizona Fall League in October. Expected to be healthy for spring training, he's the frontrunner to take over for departed free agent Placido Polanco in Detroit. Sizemore profiles as a steady if not spectacular regular.

Year	Club (League)	Class	AVG	G	AB	R	H	2B	3B	HR	RBI	BB	SO	SB	OBP	SLG
2006	Oneonta (NYP)	SS	.327	70	294	49	96	15	4	3	37	32	47	7	.394	.435
2007	West Michigan (MWL)	LoA	.265	125	438	78	116	33	5	4	48	73	60	16	.376	.390
2008	Lakeland (FSL)	HiA	.286	53	203	32	58	11	1	4	20	33	44	14	.365	.409
2009	Erie (EL)	AA	.307	59	228	39	70	17	4	9	33	35	46	7	.402	.535
	Toledo (IL)	AAA	.308	71	292	49	90	22	1	8	33	29	49	14	.378	.473
MINOR LEAGUE TOTALS			.296	378	1455	247	430	98	15	28	171	193	246	58	.383	.441

11 RYAN STRIEBY, 1B/OF

BORN: Aug. 9, 1985. **B-T:** R-R. **HT.:** 6-5. **WT.:** 235. **DRAFTED:** Kentucky, 2006 (4th round). **SIGNED BY:** Harold Zonder.

Strieby started his college career at Edmonds (Wash.) CC before transferring to Kentucky, where he was the Southeastern Conference player of the year in 2006. He broke Lakeland's franchise home run record with 29 in 2008, and he was on pace to break the Florida State League mark before a broken hamate bone in his left hand shut him down. He hasn't been able to show off his above-average power as much as he'd like since, as the injury continued to bother him last year. He missed three weeks to have a second surgery, nixing a trip to the Arizona Fall League. A sturdy 6-foot-5 and 235 pounds, Strieby stands out with his power. Double-A Erie's Jerry Uht Park measures just 312 feet down the left-field line, and while players routinely bounce balls off the hockey arena just beyond the wall, Strieby hits balls over the building. He has the bat speed to turn around major league fastballs. For a big man, he stays inside the ball well and can hit to all fields, but there are holes in his swing and he's an average hitter at best, projecting to hit around .250 in the major leagues. With Miguel Cabrera at first base in Detroit, Strieby has worked in left field, but scouts don't see that as a viable option because he has below-average athleticism, speed and arm strength. His best shot at regular playing time with the Tigers is probably as a DH. Added to the 40-man roster in the offseason, he's ready for Triple-A.

Year	Club (League)	Class	AVG	G	AB	R	H	2B	3B	HR	RBI	BB	SO	SB	OBP	SLG
2006	Oneonta (NYP)	SS	.241	61	224	26	54	9	0	4	25	25	58	1	.319	.335
2007	West Michigan (MWL)	LoA	.253	123	443	65	112	23	2	16	76	63	78	6	.347	.422
2008	Lakeland (FSL)	HiA	.278	112	421	65	117	19	7	29	94	46	101	0	.352	.563
2009	Erie (EL)	AA	.303	86	294	64	89	18	1	19	58	57	80	2	.427	.565
MINOR LEAGUE TOTALS			.269	382	1382	220	372	69	10	68	253	191	317	9	.362	.481

12 ROBBIE WEINHARDT, RHP

BORN: Dec. 8, 1985. **B-T:** R-R. **HT.:** 6-2. **WT.:** 205. **DRAFTED:** Oklahoma State, 2008 (10th round). **SIGNED BY:** Chris Wimmer.

After turning down the Astros as a 38th-round pick in 2007, Weinhardt was a $15,000 bargain for the Tigers the following year as a senior sign out of Oklahoma State, where he roomed with Andy Oliver, Detroit's 2009 second-round pick. After transferring from Hill (Texas) JC, Weinhardt was a swingman for the Cowboys as a sophomore before becoming a full-time reliever in his final two years of college. The bullpen role suits him best, and he has yet to start a game in pro ball. Weinhardt creates deception with a low, almost sidearm, slinging arm action. But he's not all smoke and mirrors, as his lively fastball sits at 92-94 mph and touches 95 every time out. He also has a hard, late-breaking slider and a changeup. Weinhardt capped off 2009 by leading the Arizona Fall League with 29 strikeouts in 18 innings. Some club officials wanted him in the big league bullpen at the end of last season, so it will be no surprise if he makes the team out of spring training this year.

Year	Club (League)	Class	W	L	ERA	G	GS	CG	SV	IP	H	R	ER	HR	BB	SO	AVG
2008	Tigers (GCL)	R	0	0	0.00	3	0	0	0	6	6	3	0	0	2	4	.261
	Lakeland (FSL)	HiA	3	1	2.04	21	0	0	4	35	19	11	8	1	11	44	.162
2009	Lakeland (FSL)	HiA	1	1	0.85	22	0	0	3	32	24	5	3	2	10	40	.200
	Erie (EL)	AA	0	1	2.30	20	0	0	2	31	28	9	8	0	16	32	.233
MINOR LEAGUE TOTALS			4	3	1.64	66	0	0	9	104	77	28	19	3	39	120	.203

13 CALE IORG, SS

BORN: Sept. 6, 1985. **B-T:** R-R. **HT.:** 6-2. **WT.:** 180. **DRAFTED:** Alabama, 2007 (6th round). **SIGNED BY:** David Chadd.

Iorg has good bloodlines, as his father Garth and uncle Dane both played in the big leagues. After a solid 2005 freshman season at Alabama, he spent two years in Portugal on a Mormon mission, but the Tigers believed enough in his talent to pay him $1.5 million as a sixth-round pick in 2007. Iorg has an athletic, physical frame and unquestionable tools. An above-average shortstop with plenty of range and arm strength, he's more advanced as a defender at this point. He has good bat speed, a nice swing and can put on a show in batting practice, but his hitting ability hasn't shown up consistently against live pitching. His career batting line as a pro is an underwhelming .235/.299/.364. He hit worse than that in 2009, and his anemic results last year were actually inflated by Erie's cozy home park, as he hit .205/.266/.307 on the road. His pitch recognition isn't good and he often gets himself out by swinging through pitches outside the strike zone. Iorg is a skilled defender, but the development of his bat will determine whether he becomes an everyday player or a utilityman. He batted .217 in the Arizona Fall League, so he'll return to Double-A to open 2010.

Year	Club (League)	Class	AVG	G	AB	R	H	2B	3B	HR	RBI	BB	SO	SB	OBP	SLG
2007	Tigers (GCL)	R	.182	3	11	1	2	0	0	0	0	1	6	0	.308	.182
	Lakeland (FSL)	HiA	.278	5	18	0	5	2	0	0	5	1	5	0	.316	.389
2008	Lakeland (FSL)	HiA	.251	99	383	61	96	15	7	10	47	35	111	22	.329	.405
2009	Erie (EL)	AA	.222	129	491	57	109	17	3	11	41	32	149	13	.274	.336
MINOR LEAGUE TOTALS			.235	236	903	119	212	34	10	21	93	69	271	35	.299	.364

14 CODY SATTERWHITE, RHP

BORN: Jan. 27, 1987. **B-T:** R-R. **HT.:** 6-4. **WT.:** 205. **DRAFTED:** Mississippi, 2008 (2nd round). **SIGNED BY:** Jim Rough.

Satterwhite struggled as a starter during his junior season at Mississippi, allowing the Tigers to get an electric arm in the second round of the 2008 draft. Detroit liked him better as a closer anyway, and he had shown he could handle that role in his first two years with the Rebels and with Team USA. Satterwhite has an overpowering fastball, sitting at 94-96 mph and dialing it up to 98 at times with late, nasty sink. He also throws a good slider that has a chance to be an above-average pitch. He'll flash a changeup from time to time, but he's mostly a two-pitch guy. Satterwhite has the big, physical presence teams like on the mound. While his frame helps him throw hard, he has long arms and legs and a lot of moving parts in his delivery, which causes him some command difficulties. He walked 27 batters and threw 12 wild pitches in 49 innings last year. He also had some shoulder soreness that limited him to three appearances in the final month and kept him out of the Arizona Fall League, though he's expected to be ready for spring training. If he stays healthy, Satterwhite has the stuff to pitch at the back of a major league bullpen. If his control improves, he could be an all-star closer, though some scouts believe his inability to repeat his delivery will limit him to a set-up role.

Year	Club (League)	Class	W	L	ERA	G	GS	CG	SV	IP	H	R	ER	HR	BB	SO	AVG
2008	Tigers (GCL)	R	0	0	0.00	3	0	0	1	2	4	0	0	0	1	2	.400
	Lakeland (FSL)	HiA	0	0	4.42	17	0	0	2	18	16	10	9	0	12	22	.232
2009	Erie (EL)	AA	4	6	3.47	34	0	0	12	49	46	22	19	5	27	52	.246
MINOR LEAGUE TOTALS			4	6	3.60	54	0	0	15	70	66	32	28	5	40	76	.248

15 ALFREDO FIGARO, RHP

BORN: July 7, 1984. **B-T:** R-R. **HT.:** 6-0. **WT.:** 175. **SIGNED:** Dominican Republic, 2004. **SIGNED BY:** Angel Santana (Dodgers)

The Dodgers originally signed Figaro in 2004 but released him after his first pro season. The Tigers signed him the following spring and he joined his cousin, Fernando Rodney, on their big league pitching staff last year. Figaro probably didn't gain many fans in Detroit, as he was thrust into the spotlight and was one of the goats in the Tigers' late-season collapse, but he has the stuff to warrant another chance. He has a power arm, with a sinker that sits at 92-95 mph and tops out at 98. He throws two hard breaking balls: a curveball that peaks at 80 mph, and a mid-80s slider that can get a little short and look more like a cutter at times. He also throws a changeup, but he doesn't use it much because it's his fourth-best offering. Figaro's offspeed stuff and command can be inconsistent, but he has a power arsenal and can get swings and misses with three of his pitches. While he has spent most of his career starting, the Tigers have a crowded rotation, so he could come out of the bullpen and get an occasional spot start until things clear out. Otherwise he'll move into the Triple-A rotation. He has the ceiling of a back-end starter.

Year	Club (League)	Class	W	L	ERA	G	GS	CG	SV	IP	H	R	ER	HR	BB	SO	AVG
2004	Dodgers1 (DSL)	R	0	0	9.82	5	0	0	0	7	10	10	8	0	7	6	.303
2005	Tigers (DSL)	R	8	2	1.87	14	13	0	1	77	51	29	16	0	31	100	.181
2006	Tigers (GCL)	R	3	1	0.70	14	4	0	1	38	29	7	3	0	12	31	.210
2007	Lakeland (FSL)	HiA	0	2	4.76	5	4	0	0	23	26	15	12	0	6	6	.292
	Oneonta (NYP)	SS	4	2	3.38	11	11	0	0	53	56	23	20	1	16	40	.269
2008	West Michigan (MWL)	LoA	12	4	2.05	19	19	2	0	123	99	35	28	0	30	96	.218
	Lakeland (FSL)	HiA	0	5	4.91	6	5	1	0	29	37	22	16	2	12	23	.311
2009	Erie (EL)	AA	6	3	3.60	16	11	0	0	80	67	36	32	8	23	69	.225
	Detroit (AL)	MAJ	2	2	6.35	5	3	0	0	17	23	13	12	3	10	16	.324
MAJOR LEAGUE TOTALS			2	2	6.35	5	3	0	0	17	23	13	12	3	10	16	.324
MINOR LEAGUE TOTALS			33	17	2.82	90	67	3	2	431	375	177	135	11	137	371	.231

16 CASPER WELLS, OF

BORN: Nov. 23, 1984. **B-T:** R-R. **HT.:** 6-2. **WT.:** 210. **DRAFTED:** Towson, 2005 (14th round). **SIGNED BY:** Bill Buck.

A former 14th-round pick, Wells didn't emerge as a prospect until 2008, his fourth pro season. He made the Midwest League all-star and Arizona Fall League all-prospect teams, and he joined the Mariners' Greg Halman as the only minor leaguers to reach 25 homers and 25 steals. Wells' hope for a strong encore was dashed when he broke the hamate bone in his left hand in the first week of the 2009 season, had surgery and didn't return until June 9. Hamate injuries can sap power, but Wells homered in his first game back and ended the season with 15 longballs. However, he also struck out in 27 percent of his plate appearances because his swing gets long and he doesn't have much of a two-strike approach. He also didn't show the same prowess on the basepaths that he did the year before. Wells is an above-average runner and sound defender with a cannon arm. He showed a low-90s fastball on the mound back in his college days at Towson. He'll try to recapture his 2008 form in Triple-A this season. Even he can't cut back on his strikeouts, he still has enough tools to play in the majors as a platoon or fourth outfielder.

Year	Club (League)	Class	AVG	G	AB	R	H	2B	3B	HR	RBI	BB	SO	SB	OBP	SLG
2005	Tigers (GCL)	R	.220	45	141	25	31	9	5	5	20	18	59	6	.341	.461
2006	Lakeland (FSL)	HiA	.152	11	33	4	5	1	0	1	4	4	9	1	.300	.273
	Oneonta (NYP)	SS	.229	35	105	19	24	8	0	1	14	9	27	1	.305	.333
2007	Lakeland (FSL)	HiA	.500	2	2	0	1	1	0	0	0	0	1	0	.500	1.000
	Oneonta (NYP)	SS	.265	67	260	46	69	18	11	9	47	18	64	8	.323	.523
2008	West Michigan (MWL)	LoA	.240	50	179	30	43	7	0	10	26	22	39	17	.351	.447
	Erie (EL)	AA	.289	75	270	60	78	18	6	17	53	30	66	8	.376	.589
2009	Erie (EL)	AA	.260	86	311	52	81	18	4	15	41	43	103	8	.369	.489
MINOR LEAGUE TOTALS			.255	371	1301	236	332	80	26	58	205	144	368	49	.349	.490

17 AVISAIL GARCIA, OF

BORN: June 12, 1991. **B-T:** R-R. **HT.:** 6-4. **WT.:** 210. **SIGNED:** Venezuela, 2007. **SIGNED BY:** Alejandro Rodriguez/Pedro Chavez.

After signing for $200,000 out of Venezuela as a 16-year-old, Garcia spent 2008 in the Rookie-level Venezuelan Summer League. He then made the leap to West Michigan for most of 2009, showing how much the usually conservative Tigers believe in his tools. He looked his age at times last year—both at the plate and in the field—but keeps a level head and loves playing the game. Garcia has a quick swing and good raw power for an 18-year-old. He also has plus speed and arm strength and has no discernible physical shortcoming. He still has a lot to learn in all aspects of the game, however, from plate discipline to basestealing jumps to outfield routes. Garcia has grown taller and added muscle since signing, and he now fits best in right field. He should have enough bat for the position if he can refine his approach. After playing briefly in high Class A last May, he'll return there to start 2010.

Year	Club (League)	Class	AVG	G	AB	R	H	2B	3B	HR	RBI	BB	SO	SB	OBP	SLG
2008	Tigers (VSL)	R	.298	63	245	33	73	12	2	7	34	15	39	7	.342	.449
2009	Lakeland (FSL)	HiA	.250	3	8	1	2	0	0	0	0	0	2	0	.250	.250
	West Michigan (MWL)	LoA	.264	81	299	36	79	11	2	1	31	8	70	8	.289	.324
MINOR LEAGUE TOTALS			.279	147	552	70	154	23	4	8	65	23	111	15	.312	.379

18 BRAYAN VILLARREAL, RHP

BORN: May 10, 1987. **B-T:** R-R. **HT.:** 6-0. **WT.:** 170. **SIGNED:** Venezuela, 2005. **SIGNED BY:** Ramon Pena.

Villarreal was an overlooked arm in his first few years in the system, and shoulder surgery didn't help his cause. After putting together an impressive 2009 season in low Class A, he finally started to get noticed. He began the year in the West Michigan bullpen before moving to the rotation for the second half of the season and finishing with numbers similar to Casey Crosby's. Villarreal doesn't quite have Crosby's stuff, but it's still very good. He throws a 93-94 mph fastball that he can locate to all quadrants of the strike zone, and he can pump it up to 97 on occasion. His slider is the best in the system, and he's working to hone a changeup. Villarreal pitches with good tempo, remains under control and has an authoritative presence on the mound. He profiles better as a reliever in the long run, but will continue getting starts and logging innings to help develop his pitches. He's slotted to spend all of 2010 in high Class A.

Year	Club (League)	Class	W	L	ERA	G	GS	CG	SV	IP	H	R	ER	HR	BB	SO	AVG
2006	Tigers/Marlins (VSL)	R	0	2	3.48	14	5	0	0	41	35	23	16	3	20	23	.233
2007	Tigers (GCL)	R	0	0	6.23	1	1	0	0	4	4	4	3	0	3	5	.235
2008	Tigers (GCL)	R	1	5	3.65	11	6	1	0	37	26	19	15	0	11	37	.197
	West Michigan (MWL)	LoA	0	1	16.20	1	1	0	0	3	7	7	6	1	1	0	.438
2009	West Michigan (MWL)	LoA	5	5	2.87	26	16	0	2	103	85	40	33	5	34	118	.231
MINOR LEAGUE TOTALS			6	13	3.47	53	29	1	2	189	157	93	73	9	69	183	.230

19 JARED GAYHART, RHP

BORN: April 11, 1986. **B-T:** L-R. **HT.:** 6-5. **WT.:** 220. **DRAFTED:** Rice, 2008 (13th round). **SIGNED BY:** Tim Grieve.

Gayhart was Rice's best outfielder and hit near the top of the lineup as a junior in 2008. He pitched in only four games, but that was enough to get him noticed, and the Tigers signed him as a pitcher for $125,000 in the 13th round. He dominated Class A hitters and held his own in Double-A during his first full pro season. Gayhart's fastball works at 92-93 mph with good life, and he holds that velocity on back-to-back days. Being relatively new to pitching, his secondary stuff has further to go than is the case with most 23-year-old pitchers. His slider improved significantly last year, and he flashes a changeup that has a chance to be effective. Gayhart is a hard worker and has impressive makeup. He attends all of the organization's classes for Latin players so he can give them support and learn Spanish. Gayhart got extra opportunity to work on his secondary pitches late in the year, when he took the mound as an emergency starter and the Tigers kept him in the Erie rotation to log more innings. He could start again this season in Double-A, but his long-term profile is as a reliever.

Year	Club (League)	Class	W	L	ERA	G	GS	CG	SV	IP	H	R	ER	HR	BB	SO	AVG
2008	Tigers (GCL)	R	1	0	4.82	10	0	0	2	9	11	6	5	0	6	6	.333
	Oneonta (NYP)	SS	0	1	11.57	3	0	0	0	2	2	5	3	0	7	4	.222
2009	West Michigan (MWL)	LoA	5	3	1.97	24	0	0	3	46	24	11	10	2	15	49	.156
	Lakeland (FSL)	HiA	0	0	0.77	7	0	0	0	12	5	1	1	0	0	10	.128
	Erie (EL)	AA	1	1	4.45	10	4	0	0	28	32	17	14	0	18	20	.294
MINOR LEAGUE TOTALS			7	5	3.05	54	4	0	5	97	74	40	33	2	46	89	.215

20 LUKE PUTKONEN, RHP

BORN: May 10, 1986. **B-T:** R-R. **HT.:** 6-6. **WT.:** 204. **DRAFTED:** North Carolina, 2007 (3rd round). **SIGNED BY:** Grant Brittain.

Born in Illinois, Putkonen grew up in suburban Atlanta, a hotbed for amateur baseball talent. He went undrafted out of high school and ended up at North Carolina, where he missed the 2005 season due to Tommy John surgery. The Tigers made him their third-round pick in 2007 and he has moved at a snail's pace since because of more arm problems. He missed nearly two months with a shoulder strain that required surgery in 2008, so he didn't reach low Class A until nearly two years after he was drafted. The towering righthander has long arms and legs but a smooth, effortless delivery that almost lulls hitters to sleep. He throws on a good downhill plane that generates a lot of grounders. Putkonen showed better poise on the mound last season, and his stuff was up a tick as well, as his fastball operated at 92-95 mph. He throws both a curveball and a slider, and he also has a feel for a changeup. Detroit would like to see him focus on one breaking ball and his better option is his slider, an 80-82 mph pitch with some bite that misses bats. Putkonen had a strong second half in 2009, encouraging the Tigers that he can become a big league starter. He'll move up to high Class A this year and try to accelerate his progress.

Year	Club (League)	Class	W	L	ERA	G	GS	CG	SV	IP	H	R	ER	HR	BB	SO	AVG
2007	Tigers (GCL)	R	0	1	4.15	3	3	0	0	9	8	5	4	0	0	9	.229
2008	Oneonta (NYP)	SS	2	1	3.65	6	6	0	0	25	24	10	10	1	8	17	.270
2009	West Michigan (MWL)	LoA	7	8	3.13	28	28	1	0	149	148	63	52	3	47	115	.260
MINOR LEAGUE TOTALS			9	10	3.25	37	37	1	0	183	180	78	66	4	55	141	.259

21 JAY SBORZ, RHP

BORN: Jan. 24, 1985. **B-T:** R-R. **HT.:** 6-4. **WT.:** 210. **DRAFTED:** HS—Great Falls, Va., 2003 (2nd round). **SIGNED BY:** Bill Buck.

Sborz won a gold medal with USA Baseball's youth team in 2001 and had a standout high school career in northern Virginia, pitching his way into the second round of the 2003 draft. Though he still hasn't reached the majors after seven pro seasons, he still has some prospect value. Though he missed much of the 2006 (shoulder), 2007 (elbow) and 2009 (oblique) seasons with injuries, the Tigers added him to their 40-man roster in November. When he's healthy, Sborz has some of the best stuff in the system. He throws a heavy fastball around 94 mph, and he can get it up to 98 at times. He also throws a hard curveball at 79-84 mph. Strictly a two-pitch guy, he has a lot of effort in his delivery, which contributes to control and health woes. He reached Double-A (and Triple-A) for the first time in 2009, and if he remains healthy he could be another power arm in the Detroit bullpen. He could earn his first big league callup this year if he performs well at Toledo.

Year	Club (League)	Class	W	L	ERA	G	GS	CG	SV	IP	H	R	ER	HR	BB	SO	AVG
2003	Tigers (GCL)	R	0	2	4.85	8	7	0	0	26	20	18	14	2	14	35	.206
2004	Tigers (GCL)	R	1	4	4.48	12	12	0	0	60	52	32	30	9	44	62	.230
2005	West Michigan (MWL)	LoA	1	1	7.90	21	0	0	0	27	36	27	24	2	23	31	.321
	Oneonta (NYP)	SS	1	3	4.34	9	7	0	0	29	24	15	14	1	27	25	.224
2006	West Michigan (MWL)	LoA	1	0	5.40	3	0	0	0	5	8	3	3	0	4	4	.364
2007	Tigers (GCL)	R	1	1	2.61	5	2	0	0	10	9	4	3	0	2	8	.237
	Oneonta (NYP)	SS	0	0	5.40	5	1	0	0	10	10	10	6	1	6	9	.263
2008	Lakeland (FSL)	HiA	3	2	2.87	40	0	0	7	53	44	22	17	3	25	48	.223
2009	Lakeland (FSL)	HiA	0	0	0.00	1	0	0	0	3	1	0	0	0	1	1	.125
	Erie (EL)	AA	1	2	2.52	14	1	0	0	25	16	9	7	3	13	29	.184
	Toledo (IL)	AAA	1	0	2.25	2	0	0	0	4	1	1	1	1	1	5	.077
MINOR LEAGUE TOTALS			10	15	4.23	120	30	0	7	253	221	141	119	22	160	257	.234

22 TYLER STOHR, RHP

BORN: Sept. 19, 1986. **B-T:** R-R. **HT.:** 6-2. **WT.:** 208. **DRAFTED:** North Florida, 2008 (6th round). **SIGNED BY:** Steve Nichols.

Stohr went in the sixth round of the 2008 draft, making him the highest pick from North Florida since Todd Dunn was a Brewers supplemental first-rounder 15 years earlier, Stohr first put himself on the map in 2007 as a closer in the Cape Cod League, where his father Keith (now a scout with the Cubs) used to manage. Stohr has a loose arm that delivers 93-94 mph fastballs with little effort. The ball jumps out of his hand, and his pitches have late life. He'll also mix in a two-seam fastball with good sink, a true curveball with deep break and a cutter that gets up to 88 mph. Stohr needs to get stronger, because he loses 2-3 mph off his pitches when he works on consecutive days. He also faded in the second half of 2009, posting a 5.46 ERA after the all-star break. The Tigers would like to see Stohr tighten his command and show greater confidence on the mound because he has what it takes to be a middle reliever in the big leagues. He'll move up to high Class A in 2010.

Year	Club (League)	Class	W	L	ERA	G	GS	CG	SV	IP	H	R	ER	HR	BB	SO	AVG
2008	Oneonta (NYP)	SS	0	1	3.98	21	0	0	12	20	17	10	9	0	15	24	.224
2009	West Michigan (MWL)	LoA	3	4	3.54	52	0	0	19	61	59	26	24	2	16	55	.254
MINOR LEAGUE TOTALS			3	5	3.65	73	0	0	31	81	76	36	33	2	31	79	.247

23 MELVIN MERCEDES, RHP

BORN: Nov. 2, 1990. **B-T:** R-R. **HT.:** 6-3. **WT.:** 240. **SIGNED:** Dominican Republic, 2008. **SIGNED BY:** Miguel Rodriguez/Ramon Perez.

Mercedes is a behemoth who gained about 50 pounds in the first year after he signed, though it looks like he'll be able to carry that amount of weight. He led the Rookie-level Gulf Coast League with 26 appearances and 16 saves in his U.S. debut last season. Mercedes throws a heavy fastball that parks at 92-93 mph and peaks at 95. He also throws a true slider in the low 80s. At times it has good tilt and misses bats, but at others it just spins without much break. Mercedes still is working to learn a changeup and almost never throws it in games at this point. Because his control is erratic, his outings tend to be interesting. Mercedes has the resilience to pitch on consecutive days and recover quickly from bad performances. If he can do a better job of throwing strikes and locating his pitches, he has a future as a late-inning reliever. He's ticketed to return to low Class A after getting a cameo there to finish 2009.

Year	Club (League)	Class	W	L	ERA	G	GS	CG	SV	IP	H	R	ER	HR	BB	SO	AVG
2008	Tigers (DSL)	R	2	2	3.19	24	0	0	6	37	28	19	13	1	24	33	.207
2009	Tigers (GCL)	R	1	1	1.82	26	0	0	16	25	19	9	5	0	14	20	.221
	West Michigan (MWL)	LoA	0	1	11.57	3	0	0	0	2	1	4	3	0	3	1	.125
MINOR LEAGUE TOTALS			3	4	2.97	53	0	0	22	64	48	32	21	1	41	54	.210

24 WADE GAYNOR, 3B

BORN: April 19, 1988. **B-T:** R-R. **HT.:** 6-4. **WT.:** 215. **DRAFTED:** Western Kentucky, 2009 (3rd round) **SIGNED BY:** Harold Zonder.

In 2009, Gaynor became the first player in Western Kentucky history to record a 20-20 season. He helped the Hilltoppers finish second in NCAA regional play, the best season in school history. He ranked third in Division I with 196 total bases, trailing only No. 2 overall pick Dustin Ackley (North Carolina) and top 2010 prospect Bryce Brentz (Middle Tennessee State). Gaynor's performance pushed him into the third round of the draft and earned him a $392,400 bonus. He can put a charge into a ball and had no problems putting balls in the seats at Comerica Park during a predraft workout. As a pro, he has looked impressive during batting practice but significantly less so against live pitching. There's a lot of noise in his swing that the Tigers are trying to calm down. He has a lot of preswing hand movement and uses a big leg kick, causing him to be late on balls. Gaynor has a big, physical body and is more athletic than most players his size, featuring average speed. He's not flashy, but he makes all the plays at third and has an average arm. His speed is average to a tick above, but it's his raw power that gets him noticed. Gaynor is a hard-nosed player with a strong work ethic, so if he can quiet his swing and utilize his power, he could develop into a big league regular. Given his struggles in his pro debut, he may open 2010 in low Class A.

Year	Club (League)	Class	AVG	G	AB	R	H	2B	3B	HR	RBI	BB	SO	SB	OBP	SLG
2009	Oneonta (NYP)	SS	.192	67	234	37	45	10	1	3	23	21	52	8	.281	.282
MINOR LEAGUE TOTALS			.192	67	234	37	45	10	1	3	23	21	52	8	.281	.282

25 BRENNAN BOESCH, OF

BORN: April 12, 1985. **B-T:** L-L. **HT.:** 6-6. **WT.:** 210. **DRAFTED:** California, 2006 (3rd round). **SIGNED BY:** Scott Cerny.

Boesch put up uninspiring numbers in his first three seasons before leading the Eastern League in homers in 2009. Scouts who saw him last year were skeptical, however, saying his numbers were inflated by Erie's cozy ballpark, where he hit 19 of his 28 longballs. Boesch does have considerable raw power, but it's produced with a stiff, mechanical uppercut swing. He has bat speed, but his stroke can get long and has an arm bar that results in a lot of holes. He has particular difficulty pulling his hands in when pitchers come inside with fastballs. Boesch is a fringe average runner but moves well for his size, and he has an adequate arm that's playable in right field. He struggles against lefthanders and may not be more than a platoon player, especially if he doesn't improve his approach and ability to make contact. He'll get his first Triple-A opportunity in 2010.

Year	Club (League)	Class	AVG	G	AB	R	H	2B	3B	HR	RBI	BB	SO	SB	OBP	SLG
2006	Oneonta (NYP)	SS	.291	70	292	27	85	15	6	5	54	21	42	3	.344	.435
2007	West Michigan (MWL)	LoA	.267	126	513	52	137	19	4	10	86	23	81	15	.297	.378
2008	Lakeland (FSL)	HiA	.249	111	417	46	104	17	8	7	64	36	90	3	.310	.379
2009	Erie (EL)	AA	.275	131	527	89	145	26	7	28	93	33	127	11	.318	.510
MINOR LEAGUE TOTALS			.269	438	1749	214	471	77	25	50	297	113	340	32	.314	.428

26 DUSTY RYAN, C

BORN: Sept. 2, 1984. **B-T:** R-R. **HT.:** 6-4. **WT.:** 220. **DRAFTED:** Merced (Calif.) JC, D/F 2003 (48th round). **SIGNED BY:** Tom Hinkle.

Not many 48th-round picks make it to the major leagues. Then again, not many 48th-round picks have power like Ryan does. Signed as a draft-and-follow out of Merced (Calif.) JC in 2004, Ryan staked a claim to Detroit's starting catching job when he hit .315/.370/.548 during a September callup in 2008. But the Tigers traded for Gerald Laird that offseason, and Ryan since has been leapfrogged by Alex Avila. Ryan projects more as a backup than a regular, but his power off the bench could be valuable. He went just 4-for-26 (.154) with Detroit last season, but one scout who saw him in the majors said he hit balls as far as Miguel Cabrera did during batting practice. Ryan's swing can get long and has some loop to it, which leads to difficulty making consistent contact, as does his pull-oriented approach. Big and lumbering, he doesn't move well laterally and is slow getting out of his crouch to make throws from behind the plate. He threw out just 25 percent of basestealers in 2009 and is just adequate defensively. Laird and Avila will handle the Tigers' catching duties in 2010, so Ryan faces more time in Triple-A.

DETROIT TIGERS

Year	Club (League)	Class	AVG	G	AB	R	H	2B	3B	HR	RBI	BB	SO	SB	OBP	SLG
2004	Oneonta (NYP)	SS	.274	54	157	20	43	11	1	4	26	24	52	6	.369	.433
2005	West Michigan (MWL)	LoA	.183	75	241	21	44	11	0	4	21	22	70	3	.255	.278
2006	West Michigan (MWL)	LoA	.245	98	322	49	79	13	2	6	35	44	102	3	.344	.354
2007	Tigers (GCL)	R	.063	6	16	1	1	0	0	0	1	4	5	0	.250	.063
	Lakeland (FSL)	HiA	.214	46	145	17	31	0	0	7	22	18	52	0	.310	.359
2008	Erie (EL)	AA	.253	82	296	46	75	17	2	15	50	38	95	2	.340	.476
	Toledo (IL)	AAA	.315	20	73	12	23	7	2	2	13	6	27	0	.370	.548
	Detroit (AL)	MAJ	.318	15	44	6	14	2	0	2	7	5	13	0	.380	.500
2009	Toledo (IL)	AAA	.257	63	202	25	52	8	1	10	35	29	64	2	.359	.455
	Detroit (AL)	MAJ	.154	12	26	1	4	1	0	0	4	4	12	0	.267	.192
MAJOR LEAGUE TOTALS			.257	27	70	7	18	3	0	2	11	9	25	0	.338	.386
MINOR LEAGUE TOTALS			.240	444	1452	191	348	67	8	48	203	185	467	16	.331	.396

27 CASEY FIEN, RHP

BORN: Oct. 21, 1983. **B-T:** R-R. **HT.:** 6-2. **WT.:** 195. **DRAFTED:** Cal Poly, 2006 (20th round). **SIGNED BY:** Tim McWilliam.

Several interesting players were selected in the 20th round of the 2006 draft. Righthanders Brad Boxberger and Billy Bullock didn't sign, instead heading to college and becoming premium picks in the 2009 draft. Outfielder Domonic Brown turned pro and has become the Phillies' top prospect. While Fien can't match their prospect status, he beat them all to the big leagues, pitching 2⅓ hitless innings of relief against the White Sox in his debut last July 26. Fien works primarily off his fastball, throwing a four-seamer at 91-93 mph and mixing in a two-seamer for more sink. He'll flash a promising slider but it's inconsistent, and his changeup lags behind his other pitches. Once he refines his secondary pitches, sharpens his command and learns to read hitters' swings, he'll get a longer look in Detroit. He profiles as a middle reliever.

Year	Club (League)	Class	W	L	ERA	G	GS	CG	SV	IP	H	R	ER	HR	BB	SO	AVG
2006	Oneonta (NYP)	SS	1	1	2.74	20	0	0	1	43	39	17	13	1	8	37	.248
2007	West Michigan (MWL)	LoA	6	1	3.10	39	0	0	6	61	55	28	21	4	10	77	.233
2008	Erie (EL)	AA	3	3	2.96	40	0	0	12	46	38	16	15	5	12	42	.226
	Toledo (IL)	AAA	2	1	2.40	12	0	0	1	15	14	4	4	2	4	17	.246
2009	Toledo (IL)	AAA	2	1	3.41	42	0	0	14	58	51	23	22	5	15	66	.237
	Detroit (AL)	MAJ	0	1	7.94	9	0	0	0	11	13	11	10	2	6	9	.289
MAJOR LEAGUE TOTALS			0	1	7.94	9	0	0	0	11	13	11	10	2	6	9	.289
MINOR LEAGUE TOTALS			14	6	3.04	153	0	0	34	222	197	88	75	17	49	239	.236

28 SCOTT GREEN, RHP

BORN: Aug. 10, 1985. **B-T:** R-R. **HT.:** 6-7. **WT.:** 240. **DRAFTED:** Kentucky, 2008 (3rd round). **SIGNED BY:** Harold Zonder.

Green missed the entire 2006 season at Kentucky after having Tommy John surgery and pitched just 18 innings for the Wildcats the next spring. The Red Sox took a chance on him in the 15th round, watched him star in the Cape Cod League and offered him $800,000. He turned them down and returned to school, which proved to be a costly decision when he struggled as a redshirt junior. He signed with the Tigers for $373,000 as a third-rounder in 2008 and hasn't made a lot of progress since. He tried to hide a shoulder injury last season, but the Tigers shut him down in late July. A physical specimen at a chiseled 6-foot-7 and 240 pounds, Green has an imposing presence on the mound. When he's right, his fastball sits at 94-95 mph and bumps 97 on a steep downward plane. He also has an 87-88 mph cutter and an adequate changeup. Green battles his command, so he gets hit harder than someone with his stuff should. He has worked just 54 innings in pro ball, none above Class A, at age 24, so 2010 figures to be a crucial year for him. If he's healthy, he'll start the season in Double-A.

Year	Club (League)	Class	W	L	ERA	G	GS	CG	SV	IP	H	R	ER	HR	BB	SO	AVG
2008	West Michigan (MWL)	LoA	1	2	3.57	15	0	0	2	18	14	9	7	1	5	15	.219
2009	Lakeland (FSL)	HiA	3	4	3.25	32	0	0	11	36	42	21	13	3	14	35	.296
MINOR LEAGUE TOTALS			4	6	3.35	47	0	0	13	54	56	30	20	4	19	50	.272

29 JAMES ROBBINS, 1B

BORN: Sept. 26, 1990. **B-T:** L-L. **HT.:** 6-1. **WT.:** 232. **DRAFTED:** HS—Shoreline, Wash., 2009 (30th round). **SIGNED BY:** Ryan Johnson.

Teams were split on Robbins heading into the 2009 draft. Some liked him as a pitcher because he showed a heavy 86-90 mph fastball from the left side, while others preferred him as a hitter. His commitment to Washington State, where he would have played both ways, muddled the situation further. He lasted 30 rounds but ultimately signed for $235,000. The Tigers like his power potential and will make him a full-time hitter. He's a big, strong kid who swings with authority. He has good bat speed and the ball jumps off his bat. With a stout, pudgy frame, Robbins never will be confused with an elite athlete, and the Tigers already have shifted him to first base. He has an above-average arm and is learning the nuances of the position. Robbins has more speed than most 6-foot-1, 232-pounders, and he even played some center field in high school. He should be able to maintain good conditioning if he works at it. He'll jump to low Class A for his first full pro season.

Year	Club (League)	Class	AVG	G	AB	R	H	2B	3B	HR	RBI	BB	SO	SB	OBP	SLG
2009	Tigers (GCL)	R	.361	9	36	4	13	0	1	2	7	2	9	0	.410	.583
MINOR LEAGUE TOTALS			.361	9	36	4	13	0	1	2	7	2	9	0	.410	.583

30 EDWIN GOMEZ, SS

BORN: Aug. 26, 1991. **B-T:** B-R. **HT.:** 6-4. **WT.:** 168. **DRAFTED:** HS—Gurabo, P.R., 2009 (4th round). **SIGNED BY:** Rolando Casanova/German Geigel.

A fourth-round pick who signed for $245,700, Gomez was the second of 26 Puerto Rican players drafted in 2009, a standout year for the island's baseball talent. He didn't perform well in the spring before the draft, nor after turning pro. Gomez is athletic and already bigger than his cousin Alex Cintron, who has played parts of nine seasons in the big leagues. His 6-foot-4 frame draws comparisons to a young Alex Rios and gives Gomez lots of room for projection. He's a switch-hitter whose swing works better from the left side at this point. He's more of a gap-to-gap hitter with the potential for 25 doubles and 10 homers per season. Currently a shortstop, Gomez may outgrow the position once he fills out his 6-foot-4 frame. He has a solid arm and plus speed, running the 60-yard dash in 6.6 seconds, so he may end up in center field. Every aspect of Gomez's game is a work in progress, so he'll start 2010 in extended spring training before reporting to short-season Oneonta in June.

Year	Club (League)	Class	AVG	G	AB	R	H	2B	3B	HR	RBI	BB	SO	SB	OBP	SLG
2009	Tigers (GCL)	R	.190	45	153	12	29	4	0	0	12	9	31	1	.233	.216
MINOR LEAGUE TOTALS			.190	45	153	12	29	4	0	0	12	9	31	1	.233	.216

Florida Marlins

BY MIKE BERARDINO

The Marlins have stayed competitive thanks to homegrown talent like Josh Johnson

At long last, after 16 years and countless failed attempts under three different ownership groups, the Marlins finally won approval for a publicly funded, baseball-only stadium in South Florida. They broke ground in July.

Scheduled to open in 2012 in Miami's Little Havana section, the $541 million park will feature a retractable roof and seat 37,000. More importantly, the stadium will get the Marlins out from perhaps the most one-sided lease in pro sports.

It should also allow owner Jeffrey Loria to sink a little more money into his team's payroll, which annually ranks at or near the bottom of the major leagues.

That was the case again in 2009, as the Marlins spent just $37 million, last in the majors. Yet they again managed to chase the National League wild card until the season's final week.

Shortstop Hanley Ramirez, just getting started on a contract that runs through 2014, enjoyed his best all-around season en route to the first batting title in franchise history. Josh Johnson, one of several Marlins to come through the farm system, went 15-5 and moved closer to a big-time payday once he reaches free agency after the 2011 season.

Finishing with 87 wins, the third-most in franchise history, Florida registered its second straight winning season under manager Fredi Gonzalez. Despite this achievement, Gonzalez still had to hear rumors that had the Marlins considering a switch to Bobby Valentine before the organization finally came back to its senses and stayed the course.

The farm system once again paid dividends, even with top prospect Cameron Maybin flopping in an attempt to secure the center-field job. His strong work at Triple-A New Orleans and during his September call-up gave the Marlins hope he'll stay for good in 2010. Sean West came up in May, made 20 solid starts and laid his claim to a permanent spot in the rotation.

But the best work, by far, came from Chris Coghlan, who not only jumped into the leadoff spot for the first time since high school but also made the move from second base to left field in seamless fashion. Coghlan batted .321, including .373 after the all-star break, to win the NL rookie of the year award.

In the minors, Marlins affiliates posted a combined 350-341 (.507) record. Just two of the six clubs posted winning records, but those two were Double-A

TOP 30 PROSPECTS

1. Mike Stanton, of	**16.** Jake Smolinski, 3b
2. Logan Morrison, 1b	**17.** Brad Hand, lhp
3. Chad James, lhp	**18.** Chris Leroux, rhp
4. Matt Dominguez, 3b	**19.** Bryan Berglund, rhp
5. Gaby Sanchez, 1b/3b	**20.** Tim Wood, rhp
6. Ryan Tucker, rhp	**21.** Jorge Jimenez, 3b
7. Kyle Skipworth, c	**22.** Graham Johnson, rhp
8. Isaac Galloway, of	**23.** Jay Voss, lhp
9. Scott Cousins, of	**24.** Brett Sinkbeil, rhp
10. Jhan Marinez, rhp	**25.** Kris Harvey, rhp
11. Bryan Petersen, of	**26.** Brett Hayes, c
12. Marcell Ozuna, of	**27.** Curtis Petersen, rhp
13. Dan Jennings, lhp	**28.** Jai Miller, of
14. Jose Ceda, rhp	**29.** Greg Burns, of
15. Edgar Olmos, lhp	**30.** Osvaldo Martinez, ss

Jacksonville, which won the Southern League championship, and the Rookie-level Gulf Coast League Marlins, who rolled to a .691 winning percentage. Top prospects such as right fielder Mike Stanton, first baseman Logan Morrison and third baseman Matt Dominguez continued their progress toward an eventual place in Miami.

After focusing on position players in the past several drafts, the Marlins went for pitching with three of their top four picks in 2009. Their top choice (18th overall) was Oklahoma high school lefthander Chad James, who signed for $1.7 million and immediately became their best pitching prospect.

General Manager: Michael Hill. **Farm Director:** Brian Chattin. **Scouting Director:** Stan Meek.

Class	Team	League	W	L	PCT	Finish*	Manager(s)
Majors	Florida Marlins	National	87	75	.537	6th (16)	Fredi Gonzalez
Triple-A	New Orleans Zephyrs	Pacific Coast	63	80	.441	14th (16)	Edwin Rodriguez
Double-A	Jacksonville Suns	Southern	82	58	.586	†2nd (10)	Brandon Hyde
High A	Jupiter Hammerheads	Florida State	67	70	.489	8th (12)	Tim Leiper
Low A	Greensboro Grasshoppers	South Atlantic	66	74	.471	13th (16)	Darin Everson
Short-season	Jamestown Jammers	New York-Penn	34	42	.447	11th (14)	Andy Haines
Rookie	GCL Marlins	Gulf Coast	38	17	.691	1st (16)	Jorge Hernandez
Overall 2009 Minor League Record			350	341	.507	t-13th (30)	

*Finish in overall standings (No. of teams in league). †League champion.

LAST YEAR'S TOP 30

Player, Pos.		Status
1.	Cameron Maybin, of	Majors
2.	Mike Stanton, of	No. 1
3.	Logan Morrison, 1b	No. 2
4.	Sean West, lhp	Majors
5.	Ryan Tucker, rhp	No. 6
6.	Matt Dominguez, 3b	No. 4
7.	Kyle Skipworth, c	No. 7
8.	Gaby Sanchez, 1b/3b	No. 5
9.	Chris Coghlan, 2b	Majors
10.	Jose Ceda, rhp	No. 14
11.	John Raynor, of	(Pirates)
12.	Brett Sinkbeil, rhp	No. 24
13.	Aaron Thompson, lhp	(Nationals)
14.	Scott Cousins, of	No. 9
15.	Isaac Galloway, of	No. 8
16.	Chris Leroux, rhp	No. 18
17.	Tim Wood, rhp	No. 20
18.	Brad Hand, lhp	No. 17
19.	Bryan Petersen, of	No. 11
20.	P.J. Dean, rhp	Dropped out
21.	Jesus Delgado, rhp	(Mariners)
22.	Hector Correa, rhp	Dropped out
23.	Eulogio de la Cruz, rhp	(Yakult Japan))
24.	Edgar Olmos, lhp	No. 15
25.	Jake Smolinski, 2b	No. 16
26.	Brett Hayes, c	No. 26
27.	Dan Meyer, lhp	Majors
28.	Greg Burns, of	No. 29
29.	Kyle Winters, rhp	Dropped out
30.	Graham Taylor, lhp	Dropped out

BEST TOOLS

Best Hitter for Average	Logan Morrison
Best Power Hitter	Mike Stanton
Best Strike-Zone Discipline	Logan Morrison
Fastest Baserunner	Marquise Cooper
Best Athlete	Mike Stanton
Best Fastball	Jhan Marinez
Best Curveball	Brad Hand
Best Slider	Dan Jennings
Best Changeup	Chad James
Best Control	Elih Villanueva
Best Defensive Catcher	Brett Hayes
Best Defensive Infielder	Matt Dominguez
Best Infield Arm	Matt Dominguez
Best Defensive Outfielder	Scott Cousins
Best Outfield Arm	Marcell Ozuna

PROJECTED 2013 LINEUP

Catcher	Kyle Skipworth
First Base	Logan Morrison
Second Base	Dan Uggla
Third Base	Matt Dominguez
Shortstop	Hanley Ramirez
Left Field	Chris Coghlan
Center Field	Cameron Maybin
Right Field	Mike Stanton
No. 1 Starter	Josh Johnson
No. 2 Starter	Chad James
No. 3 Starter	Ricky Nolasco
No. 4 Starter	Chris Volstad
No. 5 Starter	Sean West
Closer	Ryan Tucker

TOP PROSPECTS OF THE DECADE

Year	Player, Pos.	2009 Org.
2000	A.J. Burnett, rhp	Yankees
2001	Josh Beckett, rhp	Red Sox
2002	Josh Beckett, rhp	Red Sox
2003	Miguel Cabrera, 3b	Tigers
2004	Jeremy Hermida, of	Marlins
2005	Jeremy Hermida, of	Marlins
2006	Jeremy Hermida, of	Marlins
2007	Chris Volstad, rhp	Marlins
2008	Cameron Maybin, of	Marlins
2009	Cameron Maybin, of	Marlins

TOP DRAFT PICKS OF THE DECADE

Year	Player, Pos.	2009 Org.
2000	Adrian Gonzalez, 1b	Padres
2001	Garrett Berger, rhp (2nd round)	Out of baseball
2002	Jeremy Hermida, of	Marlins
2003	Jeff Allison, rhp	Marlins
2004	Taylor Tankersley, rhp	Marlins
2005	Chris Volstad, rhp	Marlins
2006	Brett Sinkbeil, rhp	Marlins
2007	Matt Dominguez, 3b	Marlins
2008	Kyle Skipworth, c	Marlins
2009	Chad James, lhp	Marlins

LARGEST BONUSES IN CLUB HISTORY

Josh Beckett, 1999	$3,625,000
Adrian Gonzalez, 2000	$3,000,000
Livan Hernandez, 1996	$2,500,000
Kyle Skipworth, 2008	$2,300,000
Jason Stokes, 2000	$2,027,000

FLORIDA MARLINS

TOP 2010 ROOKIE: Logan Morrison, 1b. If he can get to Florida by May, Morrison could give the Marlins back-to-back National League rookies of the year.

BREAKOUT PROSPECT: Marcell Ozuna, of. With five-tool potential that draws comparisons to Andre Dawson and Vladimir Guerrero, he's poised for a big year at hitter-friendly Greensboro.

SOURCE OF TOP 30 TALENT			
Homegrown	27	Acquired	3
College	8	Trades	2
Junior college	2	Rule 5 draft	1
High school	13	Independent leagues	0
Draft-and-follow	2	Free agents/waivers	0
Nondrafted free agents	0		
International	2		

SLEEPER: Jose Alvarez, lhp. His finesse stuff worked well enough to win him the New York-Penn League ERA title (1.52) last summer before the Red Sox sent him to Florida in the Jeremy Hermida trade.

Numbers in parentheses indicate prospect rankings.

LF
Tom Hickman
Brent Keys
Kevin Mattison
Jeremy Synan
Chad Cregar

CF
Isaac Galloway (8)
Scott Cousins (9)
Jai Miller (28)
Greg Burns (29)
Marquise Cooper
Rand Smith

RF
Mike Stanton (1)
Bryan Petersen (11)
Marcell Ozuna (12)
Kyle Jensen

3B
Matt Dominguez (4)
Jake Smolinski (16)
Jorge Jimenez (21)
Chase Austin

SS
Osvaldo Martinez (30)
Jose Torres
Chris Wade
Noah Perio

2B
Danny Pertusati
Brandon Turner
Ryan Curry

1B
Logan Morrison (2)
Gaby Sanchez (5)

C
Kyle Skipworth (7)
Brett Hayes (26)
Brad Davis
Chris Hatcher
Miguel Fermin
Jobduan Morales
David Peters

RHP

Starters	Relievers
Bryan Berglund (19)	Ryan Tucker (6)
Graham Johnson (22)	Jhan Marinez (10)
Curtis Petersen (27)	Jose Ceda (14)
Kyle Winters	Chris Leroux (18)
Tom Koehler	Tim Wood (20)
Kyle Kaminska	Brett Sinkbeil (24)
Josh Hodges	Kris Harvey (25)
Elih Villanueva	Jay Buente
Jose Rosario	Pete Andrelczyk
Dan Mahoney	Arquimedes Caminero
Daniel Gil	A.J. Battisto
Alvaro Estevez	Garrett Parcell
A.J. Ramos	Jared Yecker
Jeff Allison	Matt Montgomery

LHP

Starters	Relievers
Chad James (3)	Dan Jennings (13)
Edgar Olmos (15)	Jay Voss (23)
Brad Hand (17)	Stephen Richards
Jose Alvarez	Hunter Jones
Graham Taylor	Ricardo Hernandez
	Andy Loomis
	Kelvin Ferreira

2009

BEST PURE HITTER: Area scout Tim McDonnell got a steal in a California high school outfielder/football star two years ago (Mike Stanton) and may have another one in Brent Keys (17). A line-drive hitter with plus speed, Keys hit .288 with more walks (28) than strikeouts (20) in the Rookie-level Gulf Coast League.

BEST POWER HITTER: OFs Kyle Jensen (12) and Chad Cregar (15) both offer a lot of raw lefthanded power. Jensen has an easier stroke, while Cregar has more bat speed. Cregar got only 32 at-bats in his pro debut because he injured his right shoulder on a swing.

FASTEST RUNNER: OF Marquise Cooper (3) can get from the right side of the plate to first base in less than 4.0 seconds, giving him 80 speed on the 20-80 scouting scale.

BEST DEFENSIVE PLAYER: SS Chris Wade (11) has good actions, soft hands and a better arm than the Marlins realized. A draft-eligible sophomore, he began the summer in the Cape Cod League before signing for $150,000.

BEST FASTBALL: LHP Chad James (1) has the best combination of life and velocity, sitting at 90-92 mph and touching 95. RHP Josh Hodges (7), a giant at 6-foot-7 and 235 pounds, peaks at 96. RHP Dan Mahoney (4) reached 95 before requiring Tommy John surgery.

BEST SECONDARY PITCH: RHP Bryan Berglund (2) has a short, quick slider. James had one of the best changeups among high schoolers in the draft.

BEST PRO DEBUT: RHP A.J. Ramos (21) is just 5-foot-10, but he has a low-90s fastball and an average curveball. He went 2-2, 2.14 with 50 strikeouts in 34 innings at short-season Jamestown. LHP Jared Eskew (29) led the Rookie-level Gulf Coast League with seven wins.

BEST ATHLETE: Cooper attracted interest from college football programs as a tailback/linebacker.

MOST INTRIGUING BACKGROUND: Berglund is the first Swedish player ever drafted and seeks to become the first Swede to reach the majors since Eric Erickson in 1922. LHP Brett Bukvich's (18) brother Ryan pitched parts of six seasons in the big leagues.

CLOSEST TO THE MAJORS: LHP Stephen Richards (8), who throws strikes and has a solid slider, or RHP Matt Montgomery (10), a sinker/slider specialist.

BEST LATE-ROUND PICK: Keys. Others to watch include OF Rand Smith (20) and SS Noah Perio (39). Smith is a good athlete who hit safely in 42 of his final 43 games at Appalachian State. Florida signed Perio, who shows solid tools across the board except

for arm strength, away from the University of Texas for $150,000.

THE ONE WHO GOT AWAY: 1B Dustin Dickerson (6) signed and spent the whole summer at Jamestown, then had his contract voided during the offseason for reasons that haven't become public. RHP Tyler Curtis (13) hit 94 mph during the spring at the JC of Southern Idaho, but a physical revealed a torn elbow ligament and derailed contract talks with the Marlins. He's not academically eligible to play at a four-year school in 2010, so he won't pitch during the spring while rehabbing his elbow.

ASSESSMENT: The Marlins have an affinity for athletic, projectable high schoolers who will stick close to MLB's slot guidelines. This year was no exception, as their first three picks (James, Berglund, Cooper) all fit that profile.

2008   BONUSES: $5.4 MILLION

C Kyle Skipworth's (1) bat was supposed to be his strong suit, but he has hit just .208 in two pro seasons. OF Isaac Galloway (8) could be the best player from this crop, while LHP Dan Jennings (9) could be the first to reach the majors.

GRADE: C

2007   BONUSES: $3.7 MILLION

OF Mike Stanton (2) is one of the minors' top prospects and most physical presences. 3B Matt Dominguez (1) also should claim a spot in Florida's lineup of the future, and OF Bryan Petersen (4) could as well.

GRADE: A

2006   BONUSES: $5.1 MILLION

OF Chris Coghlan (1s) was the National League rookie of the year in 2009, helping atone for the disappointing career path of RHP Brett Sinkbeil (1). Scott Cousins (3) adds to the system's outfield depth, while LHP Graham Taylor (10) made three big league starts last season.

GRADE: B

2005   BONUSES: $7.7 MILLION*

This draft already has sent six players to the big leagues in RHPs Chris Volstad (1), Ryan Tucker (1s) and Chris Leroux (7), LHP Sean West (1s), C Brett Hayes (2s) and 1B/3B Gaby Sanchez (4). The best may be yet to come in 1B Logan Morrison (22).

GRADE: B+

*Draft analysis by Jim Callis. Numbers in parentheses indicate draft rounds. *Bonuses for 2005 are first 10 rounds only.*

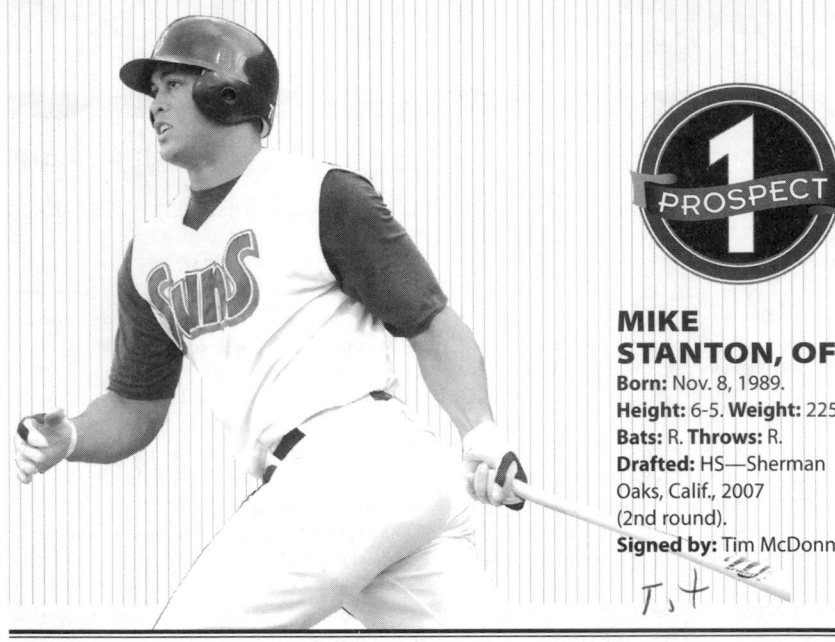

PROSPECT 1

MIKE STANTON, OF

Born: Nov. 8, 1989.
Height: 6-5. **Weight:** 225.
Bats: R. **Throws:** R.
Drafted: HS—Sherman Oaks, Calif., 2007 (2nd round).
Signed by: Tim McDonnell.

Notre Dame High has churned out a long list of accomplished athletes, with former No. 1 overall pick Tim Foli and Cy Young Award winner Jack McDowell its most distinguished baseball players. Stanton, a three-sport star, was considered the school's best athlete in at least a decade. Southern California offered him a baseball scholarship and Pete Carroll extended an opportunity to walk on as a receiver/defensive back in football. Nevada-Las Vegas wanted Stanton to play two sports as well, but the Marlins stole him for $475,000, thanks in large part to the work of area scout Tim McDonnell. Stanton struggled in summer showcases before his senior year, which caused him to drop to the 76th overall pick. Born Giancarlo Cruz-Michael Stanton, he has Puerto Rican ancestry. Stanton's reputation took off after the Marlins refused to include him in a deal for Manny Ramirez in July 2008, even with the Red Sox willing to pay the entire $7 million remaining on the future Hall of Famer's contract. After blasting his way to a 39-homer season at low Class A Greensboro in his first full year, Stanton followed up by reaching Double-A Jacksonville and playing in the Futures Game midway through 2009.

Stanton's power numbers predictably dropped off in the thick Florida air, but he again showed regular flashes of light-tower power. He has the ability to stay back on breaking balls and take them the other way with authority. He has a flat swing and keeps the barrel in the zone for a long time. His performance only brought more comparisons to a young Dave Winfield, while some liken his skill set to that of Jayson Werth or Jermaine Dye. All five tools are present, as his speed, right-field range and arm all grade as solid-average or better. Stanton's work ethic is tremendous, basically that of a far less talented player. Intelligent, inquisitive and driven, he never lets the hype go to his head.

His pitch recognition is improving, though Stanton still gets caught guessing too much. He must cut down on his strikeouts—297 during the past two seasons—but that's not a huge concern considering his power production. Though he has the speed to swipe 20 or more bases a year, Stanton has yet to develop basestealing instincts. A bout of shoulder tendinitis affected his throwing for a short time early in 2009, but he has worked hard to improve his arm. He left the Arizona Fall League with a sore back in mid-October, though it's not a major worry and he should be 100 percent for spring training.

The Marlins are determined not to rush Stanton, though some in the organization believe he could handle the jump to the majors sooner rather than later. An outfield featuring Cameron Maybin in center field and Stanton in right could become a reality by mid-2010, but Stanton should return to Double-A to start the season. Florida doesn't want him to experience the multiple big league failures that have dogged Maybin the past few seasons as he faced similar expectations.

Year	Club (League)	Class	AVG	G	AB	R	H	2B	3B	HR	RBI	BB	SO	SB	OBP	SLG
2007	Marlins (GCL)	R	.269	8	26	6	7	2	0	0	1	1	6	0	.321	.346
	Jamestown (NYP)	SS	.067	9	30	2	2	1	0	1	2	3	15	0	.147	.200
2008	Greensboro (SAL)	LoA	.293	125	468	89	137	26	3	39	97	58	153	4	.381	.611
2009	Jupiter (FSL)	HiA	.294	50	180	27	53	9	3	12	39	28	45	2	.390	.578
	Jacksonville (SL)	AA	.231	79	299	49	69	15	2	16	53	31	99	1	.311	.455
MINOR LEAGUE TOTALS			.267	271	1003	173	268	53	8	68	192	121	318	7	.354	.539

2 LOGAN MORRISON, 1B

BORN: Aug. 25, 1987. **B-T:** L-L. **HT.:** 6-2. **WT.:** 215. **DRAFTED:** Maple Woods (Mo.) CC, D/F 2005 (22nd round). **SIGNED BY:** Ryan Wardinsky.

Morrison turned down $95,000 out of high school so he could attend Maple Woods (Mo.) CC, Albert Pujols' alma mater. Morrison grew two inches and added 20 pounds of muscle, prompting the Marlins to sign him for $225,000 the following spring. After winning MVP honors in the high Class A Florida State League in 2008, he missed most of the first two months last season with a broken bone at the base of his right thumb. Morrison has the best plate discipline in the organization. He has a balanced, flat swing that enables him to keep his bat in the zone a long time. He has plus power and can put on a batting-practice show that nearly rivals those of Jacksonville teammate Mike Stanton, but Morrison reins it in during games and looks gap to gap. He projects as a classic No. 3 hitter, and his makeup and leadership skills are outstanding. His hands and arm are assets at first base. Morrison hit just .233 with one homer in 86 at-bats against lefties in 2009. While he has worked hard on his defense, he has limited range and speed. He continues to dabble in left field as the Marlins try to find ways to get both him and Gaby Sanchez into their lineup. Barring a huge spring, Morrison likely will head back to Double-A to start 2010, but he could get the call at any time.

Year	Club (League)	Class	AVG	G	AB	R	H	2B	3B	HR	RBI	BB	SO	SB	OBP	SLG
2006	Marlins (GCL)	R	.270	26	89	10	24	4	0	1	7	10	12	1	.343	.348
	Jamestown (NYP)	SS	.203	23	74	6	15	3	0	1	11	11	17	0	.295	.284
2007	Greensboro (SAL)	LoA	.267	128	453	71	121	22	2	24	86	48	96	2	.343	.483
2008	Jupiter (FSL)	HiA	.332	130	488	71	162	38	1	13	74	57	80	9	.402	.494
2009	Jupiter (FSL)	HiA	.273	3	11	0	3	1	0	0	2	1	2	0	.333	.364
	Jacksonville (SL)	AA	.277	79	278	48	77	18	2	8	47	63	46	9	.411	.442
MINOR LEAGUE TOTALS			.289	389	1393	206	402	86	5	47	227	190	253	21	.375	.459

3 CHAD JAMES, LHP

BORN: Jan. 23, 1991. **B-T:** L-L. **HT.:** 6-3. **WT.:** 190. **DRAFTED:** HS—Yukon, Okla., 2009 (1st round). **SIGNED BY:** Ryan Wardinsky.

Entering his senior season in high school, James got serious about his conditioning and the reward was his selection as the 18th overall pick in the 2009 draft. The latest Oklahoma product to hit the radar of Oklahoma-based Marlins scouting officials Jim Fleming and Stan Meek, he signed at the deadline for $1.7 million. His older brother Justin was a Blue Jays fifth-round pick in 2003. In addition to firming up his frame, James improved his fastball from the high 80s to 90-92 mph, and he can touch 95. His highly developed changeup was one of the best in the nation's prep class. His curveball went from mediocre as a junior to close to a plus pitch at times. A strong athlete with solid makeup, he's willing to learn. Like many young pitchers, James still has some minor delivery issues he needs to iron out. His curveball can get sharper and he needs to throw his changeup more often. James should make his pro debut at low Class A Greensboro, which won't be all that easy considering NewBridge Bank Park's well-earned reputation as a bandbox. The Marlins could be conservative and hold him back in extended spring training, but that seems unnecessary considering his physicality and advanced repertoire.

Year	Club (League)	Class	W	L	ERA	G	GS	CG	SV	IP	H	R	ER	HR	BB	SO	AVG
2009	Did Not Play—Signed Late																

4 MATT DOMINGUEZ, 3B

BORN: Aug. 28, 1989. **B-T:** R-R. **HT.:** 6-2. **WT.:** 180. **DRAFTED:** HS—Chatsworth, Calif., 2007 (1st round). **SIGNED BY:** Tim McDonnell.

Dominguez emerged from the same left side of the Chatsworth (Calif.) High infield that also produced No. 2 overall pick Mike Moustakas in 2007. A Cal State Fullerton signee chosen 12th overall, Dominguez signed for $1.8 million. After hitting .296 with 18 homers at Greensboro in 2008, he found the going tougher last season. Dominguez has smooth hands and actions in the field, along with a strong arm and a quick release, so comparisons to former Marlin Mike Lowell persist. His numbers weren't as strong in 2009, but he did show power in the dead air of the Florida State League. He has worked tirelessly with Florida hitting coordinator John Mallee on staying behind the ball and improving his strike-zone discipline, enabling him to do more damage when he connects. His makeup is an asset. Double-A pitchers exposed some of things Dominguez needs to work on. He can lunge at times and get jammed on the inner half. He needs to continue to add strength. His running is below-average, and some scouts question his range. Dominguez likely will return to Double-A, where he'll continue to lay the foundation for what should be a long run at third in Florida. Even if his power numbers don't improve, the Marlins believe Dominguez at least will be another Jeff Cirillo.

Year	Club (League)	Class	AVG	G	AB	R	H	2B	3B	HR	RBI	BB	SO	SB	OBP	SLG
2007	Marlins (GCL)	R	.100	5	20	0	2	0	0	0	2	1	2	0	.136	.100
	Jamestown (NYP)	SS	.189	10	37	3	7	2	0	1	4	1	12	0	.211	.324
2008	Greensboro (SAL)	LoA	.296	88	345	59	102	16	0	18	70	28	68	0	.354	.499
2009	Jupiter (FSL)	HiA	.262	103	381	49	100	25	1	11	53	38	68	1	.333	.420
	Jacksonville (SL)	AA	.186	31	97	10	18	7	0	2	9	14	24	0	.292	.320
MINOR LEAGUE TOTALS			.260	237	880	121	229	50	1	32	138	82	174	1	.328	.428

5 GABY SANCHEZ, 1B/3B

BORN: Sept. 2, 1983. **B-T:** R-R. **HT.:** 6-1. **WT.:** 234. **DRAFTED:** Miami, 2005 (4th round). **SIGNED BY:** John Martin.

Suspended his entire junior year at Miami, Sanchez was a fourth-round steal for the Marlins. He signed for $250,000, largely on the recommendation of East Coast scouting supervisor Mike Cadahia. He won the short-season New York-Penn League batting title (.355) in his pro debut and the Double-A Southern League MVP award in 2008. He was slowed last season by two separate minor injuries to his left knee, both from freak collisions. Sanchez's plate discipline is excellent, maybe a tick behind Logan Morrison's. He hits for average with a short swing and continues to show plenty of raw power, with the potential to hit as many as 25 homer annually. Defensively, he shows plus arm strength and good lateral quickness. Some scouts have questioned Sanchez's bat speed, noting he tends to dive for pitches and can struggle against top pitching. A strong work ethic keeps his conditioning in order, but his chunky body could be a problem down the road. He projects to be average at best defensively, and has settled back in at first base after trying catcher and third base. After failing to win a big league starting job last spring in a wide-open competition, Sanchez will try again in 2010. Morrison is just one level behind him, so it would behoove Sanchez to establish himself at first before the superior bat arrives.

Year	Club (League)	Class	AVG	G	AB	R	H	2B	3B	HR	RBI	BB	SO	SB	OBP	SLG
2005	Jamestown (NYP)	SS	.355	62	234	34	83	16	0	5	42	16	24	11	.401	.487
2006	Greensboro (SAL)	LoA	.317	55	189	43	60	12	0	14	40	39	20	6	.447	.603
	Marlins (GCL)	R	.333	3	6	1	2	1	0	0	3	5	0	0	.636	.500
	Jupiter (FSL)	HiA	.182	16	55	13	10	3	1	1	7	12	12	1	.324	.327
2007	Jupiter (FSL)	HiA	.279	133	473	89	132	40	3	9	70	64	74	6	.369	.433
2008	Carolina (SL)	AA	.314	133	478	70	150	42	1	17	92	69	70	17	.404	.513
	Florida (NL)	MAJ	.375	5	8	0	3	2	0	0	1	0	2	0	.375	.625
2009	New Orleans (PCL)	AAA	.289	85	318	55	92	11	0	16	56	41	44	5	.374	.475
	Florida (NL)	MAJ	.238	21	21	2	5	0	0	2	3	2	3	0	.304	.524
MAJOR LEAGUE TOTALS			.276	26	29	2	8	2	0	2	4	2	5	0	.323	.552
MINOR LEAGUE TOTALS			.302	487	1753	305	529	125	5	62	310	246	244	46	.392	.485

6 RYAN TUCKER, RHP

BORN: Dec. 6, 1986. **B-T:** R-R. **HT.:** 6-1. **WT.:** 205. **DRAFTED:** HS—Temple City, Calif., 2005 (1st round supplemental). **SIGNED BY:** John Cole.

The Marlins' fourth of five picks before the second round in 2005, Tucker signed for $975,000 as a sandwich pick. He reached the majors for three weeks midway through 2008, when he was Florida's minor league pitcher of the year. Surgery on his left knee limited him to six starts last season. At his best, Tucker shows an overpowering fastball that sits at 92-95 mph and touches 97. He likes throwing his changeup and isn't afraid to keep it in his arsenal, even as a reliever. At times, he'll show a tight, late-breaking slider. He's a bulldog on the mound. When things go wrong, Tucker tries to hump up with his fastball, a habit that big league hitters exploited during his brief trial in 2008. While he has learned to control his emotions since getting suspended in 2007 for a pair of confrontations with high Class A Jupiter pitching coach Reid Cornelius, he still needs to work on keeping his poise. His slider needs refinement, after he scrapped previous attempts at mastering a curveball and cutter. Tucker still profiles best as a short reliever but the Marlins have mostly kept him in their minor league rotations in order to help him hone his craft. With a big spring he could make the jump to the major league bullpen, but he will more likely head back to New Orleans as a starter for a second crack at the Pacific Coast League.

Year	Club (League)	Class	W	L	ERA	G	GS	CG	SV	IP	H	R	ER	HR	BB	SO	AVG
2005	Marlins (GCL)	R	3	3	3.69	8	7	0	0	32	35	13	13	0	16	23	.315
	Jamestown (NYP)	SS	1	1	8.36	4	4	0	0	14	21	14	13	3	8	18	.323
2006	Greensboro (SAL)	LoA	7	13	5.00	25	25	2	0	131	123	86	73	14	67	133	.246
2007	Jupiter (FSL)	HiA	5	8	3.71	24	24	1	0	138	142	64	57	6	46	104	.264
2008	Carolina (SL)	AA	5	3	1.58	25	12	0	0	91	64	17	16	2	37	74	.195
	Florida (NL)	MAJ	2	3	8.27	13	6	0	0	37	46	34	34	8	23	28	.305

2009	Marlins (GCL)	R	1	0	2.25	2	2	0	0	8	5	2	2	0	2	7	.179
	New Orleans (PCL)	AAA	1	2	8.04	4	4	0	0	16	18	14	14	1	14	7	.295
MAJOR LEAGUE TOTALS			2	3	8.27	13	6	0	0	37	46	34	34	8	23	28	.305
MINOR LEAGUE TOTALS			23	30	3.93	92	78	3	0	430	408	210	188	26	190	366	.250

7 KYLE SKIPWORTH, C *Chin*

BORN: March 1, 1990. **B-T:** L-R. **HT.:** 6-4. **WT.:** 207. **DRAFTED:** HS—Rubidoux, Calif., 2008 (1st round). **SIGNED BY:** Robby Corsaro.

Skipworth didn't become a full-time catcher until his junior season, but by the end of his prep career he was drawing comparisons to Joe Mauer, the only other prep catcher taken in the top 10 of the past 14 drafts. Skipworth set a California record with hits in 18 consecutive plate appearances, but has batted just .208/.263/.345 since signing for $2.3 million as the sixth overall pick. Despite his hitting woes, Skipworth has solid swing mechanics and the Marlins still believe in his offensive potential. He has been an advanced receiver from the moment he turned pro. He has outstanding hands and footwork, as well as toughness and intelligence. He has a strong, accurate arm, though he threw out just 20 percent of basestealers last season while playing through a hyperextension of his elbow. He earned points for his refusal to make excuses before getting shut down in early August. Skipworth has struggled with pitch recognition and will resort to guessing at times. Strikeouts have been a problem, and he needs to add strength. He hasn't shown power in games, though he has displayed loft power to his pull side in batting practice. Not since Charles Johnson in the mid-1990s have the Marlins had a catching prospect with such a high ceiling. Skipworth figures to repeat low Class A in hopes the Greensboro effect will get him going with the bat.

Year	Club (League)	Class	AVG	G	AB	R	H	2B	3B	HR	RBI	BB	SO	SB	OBP	SLG
2008	Marlins (GCL)	R	.208	43	159	22	33	6	0	5	21	13	46	2	.263	.340
2009	Greensboro (SAL)	LoA	.208	70	264	28	55	14	1	7	37	18	91	1	.263	.348
MINOR LEAGUE TOTALS			.208	113	423	50	88	20	1	12	58	31	137	3	.263	.345

8 ISAAC GALLOWAY, OF +

BORN: Oct. 10, 1989. **B-T:** R-R. **HT.:** 6-2. **WT.:** 190. **DRAFTED:** HS—Rancho Cucamonga, Calif., 2008 (8th round). **SIGNED BY:** Robby Corsaro.

Galloway looked like a first-round pick as a high school sophomore, but he pressed as a senior, leading to a disastrous season. The Marlins took him in the eighth round and signed him quickly for $245,000, and he has been motivated to prove his doubters wrong ever since. With the help of hitting coordinator John Mallee, Galloway has learned to stay inside the ball and make better use of his hips. A potential five-tool player, he has drawn comparisons to a young Torii Hunter with his lanky frame and long stride. He was clocked in the 6.5-second range in the 60-yard dash at prep showcases, but he's still learning to harness that raw speed. He has tremendous makeup and solid instincts. Strike-zone discipline remains Galloway's biggest bugaboo, as he gets himself out too often. He struggled with routes and jumps in center field but improved as the year went on. His arm is average but could improve with work. He remains fairly raw, but his willingness to work should help him smooth out the rough edges. With Cameron Maybin still trying to nail down the big league center-field job, the Marlins are tracking Galloway's progress closely. He should head to Class A Jupiter to start 2010 and continue to move one level at a time.

Year	Club (League)	Class	AVG	G	AB	R	H	2B	3B	HR	RBI	BB	SO	SB	OBP	SLG
2008	Marlins (GCL)	R	.286	48	199	29	57	13	5	1	23	4	33	4	.303	.417
2009	Greensboro (SAL)	LoA	.268	83	340	44	91	24	3	3	30	12	89	15	.293	.382
MINOR LEAGUE TOTALS			.275	131	539	73	148	37	8	4	53	16	122	19	.297	.395

9 SCOTT COUSINS, OF

BORN: Jan. 22, 1985. **B-T:** L-L. **HT.:** 6-1. **WT.:** 194. **DRAFTED:** San Francisco, 2006 (3rd round). **SIGNED BY:** John Hughes.

It has taken Cousins three pro seasons to break into the Marlins Top 10, but that's mostly because he was stuck in a highly talented system. A two-way star at the University of San Francisco, he signed for $407,500 and steadily has increased his profile. Managers voted him the most exciting player in the Florida State League in 2008, and he fit neatly into the No. 5 batting slot behind Logan Morrison and Mike Stanton as Double-A Jacksonville won the Southern League title in 2009. The best defensive outfielder in the system, Cousins is a tooled-up option at all three outfield spots. He has the ability to stay in center if necessary, and his plus arm profiles well for right. He shows the potential to hit for average and power, and he took a big step forward with his basestealing instincts last year. Cousins still struggles at times against lefties. His refusal to stay patient at the plate causes him to fall into some prolonged funks, and he needs to improve his consistency. With Jeremy Hermida traded to the Red Sox, Cousins could get a shot at winning the left field job this spring and he's already been added to Florida's 40-man roster. Some believe he has perhaps the highest ceiling of any Marlins position prospect besides Stanton.

Year	Club (League)	Class	AVG	G	AB	R	H	2B	3B	HR	RBI	BB	SO	SB	OBP	SLG
2006	Jamestown (NYP)	SS	.211	21	90	11	19	1	0	1	6	4	17	3	.253	.256
2007	Greensboro (SAL)	LoA	.292	110	421	69	123	25	0	18	74	38	92	16	.358	.480
2008	Marlins (GCL)	R	.000	2	6	0	0	0	0	0	0	0	5	0	.000	.000
	Jupiter (FSL)	HiA	.304	49	191	35	58	9	2	9	29	20	47	11	.370	.513
	Carolina (SL)	AA	.264	27	91	15	24	7	1	1	9	10	28	4	.350	.396
2009	Jacksonville (SL)	AA	.263	130	482	60	127	31	11	12	74	42	107	27	.323	.448
MINOR LEAGUE TOTALS			.274	339	1281	190	351	73	14	41	192	114	296	61	.338	.449

10 JHAN MARINEZ, RHP

BORN: Aug. 12, 1988. **B-T:** R-R. **HT.:** 6-1. **WT.:** 165. **SIGNED:** Dominican Republic, 2006. **SIGNED BY:** Sandy Nin.

Signed out of Santo Domingo in the Dominican Republic at age 17, Marinez developed slowly until experiencing a breakthrough season in 2009. He first came to the United States at the beginning of the 2007 season but was sent back to the Rookie-level Dominican Summer League after three poor outings, punctuated by bouts of immaturity. Marinez' slight frame and explosive fastball draw the inevitable comparisons to a young Pedro Martinez. He pitches with his fastball at 92-94 mph and has topped out at 98. He also has a two-seamer that he can work in to righthanders at 89-92 mph. He complements his fastball with a hard slider that clocks in at 85 mph. His makeup and work ethic were much better last season, though they remain works in progress. Marinez' slider requires more consistency and his changeup needs significant work. His frame and overall conditioning must improve if he is to improve his durability and move into a starting role, and just eight of his 69 career appearances have been starts. He remains raw in the secondary aspects of the game, such as holding runners and fielding his position. Some still wonder if his improved maturity is just a mirage. There's no need to rush Marinez, who figures to open 2010 back in high Class A. If everything clicks, he could earn an early promotion to Double-A.

Year	Club (League)	Class	W	L	ERA	G	GS	CG	SV	IP	H	R	ER	HR	BB	SO	AVG
2006	Marlins (DSL)	R	2	1	7.00	20	2	0	1	36	44	30	28	0	26	22	.324
2007	Marlins (GCL)	R	0	0	10.80	3	0	0	0	3	5	5	4	0	4	4	.357
	Marlins (DSL)	R	2	3	4.70	5	5	0	0	23	14	17	12	1	19	25	.163
2008	Marlins (GCL)	R	1	1	6.11	12	1	0	1	18	21	14	12	0	14	18	.296
2009	Jupiter (FSL)	HiA	1	1	3.14	29	0	0	1	43	28	17	15	4	20	42	.185
MINOR LEAGUE TOTALS			6	6	5.20	69	8	0	3	123	112	83	71	5	83	111	.252

11 BRYAN PETERSEN, OF

BORN: April 9, 1986. **B-T:** L-R. **HT.:** 6-0. **WT.:** 200. **DRAFTED:** UC Irvine, 2007 (4th round). **SIGNED BY:** Tim McDonnell.

It said plenty about Petersen's progress when he drew the nod to join the likes of Mike Stanton and Matt Dominguez in the 2009 crop of Marlins at the Arizona Fall League. Petersen responded by finishing fourth in the AFL batting race and hitting .379/.412/.600. His swing was inconsistent and full of holes when he signed as a fourth-round pick in 2007, but thanks to hard work with hitting coordinator John Mallee, Petersen was able to shorten his stroke and cut down on his strikeouts. Not overly blessed with power, he still projects to hit 15 homers per year in the majors. Lefties don't faze him as much as they used to. At worst, he'll hit enough to become a fourth outfielder. He's a plus runner who knows how to use that speed on the bases and via the bunt. A two-way player as a freshman at UC Irvine, Petersen has a strong arm and is an above-average defender on the outfield corners. He played mostly left field in Jacksonville last season, in deference to Stanton and Scott Cousins, but Petersen is fully capable of playing right field. His instincts are sound and he shows a flair for winning. He inspires his teammates with the way he plays all out and grinds out every at-bat. Set to open 2010 in Triple-A New Orleans, he may be closer to being ready for the majors than any outfielder in the system.

Year	Club (League)	Class	AVG	G	AB	R	H	2B	3B	HR	RBI	BB	SO	SB	OBP	SLG
2007	Jamestown (NYP)	SS	.250	57	216	27	54	13	1	5	24	18	53	11	.318	.389
2008	Greensboro (SAL)	LoA	.301	79	296	60	89	10	2	19	58	38	74	15	.381	.541
	Carolina (SL)	AA	.351	12	37	5	13	2	0	1	10	5	6	1	.409	.486
	Jupiter (FSL)	HiA	.265	40	155	23	41	5	0	3	12	15	29	7	.339	.355
2009	Jacksonville (SL)	AA	.297	121	431	64	128	15	7	7	49	50	66	13	.368	.413
MINOR LEAGUE TOTALS			.286	309	1135	179	325	45	10	35	153	126	228	47	.360	.436

12 MARCELL OZUNA, OF

BORN: Nov. 12, 1990. **B-T:** R-R. **HT.:** 6-2. **WT.:** 190. **SIGNED:** Dominican Republic, 2008. **SIGNED BY:** Sandy Nin.

A cousin of former Marlins utility player Pablo Ozuna, Marcell has a far more physical presence and a greater upside. Long-levered with a thin waist, he's reminiscent of a young Vladimir Guerrero, and not just in his ability to hit balls out of the zone with authority and to all fields. Ozuna uses a high leg kick and must fight a tendency to rush his stride, a flaw he has worked on with Marlins hitting coordinator John Mallee. For such a raw young player, he handles offspeed pitches surprisingly well and shows improving plate discipline. He's a plus runner who reminds some scouts of Marlins special assistant Andre Dawson, both in his gait and in his over-the-top throwing motion. Ozuna is still learning how to steal bases and working on the nuances of playing right field. A potential five-tool player, he displays infectious energy on the field. He figures to open the year in low Class A, where Greensboro's friendly confines should help him increase his confidence at the plate.

Year	Club (League)	Class	AVG	G	AB	R	H	2B	3B	HR	RBI	BB	SO	SB	OBP	SLG
2008	Marlins (DSL)	R	.279	63	233	33	65	14	0	6	43	23	61	8	.335	.416
2009	Marlins (GCL)	R	.313	55	214	32	67	22	0	5	39	22	52	4	.377	.486
MINOR LEAGUE TOTALS			.295	118	447	65	132	36	0	11	82	45	113	12	.355	.450

13 DAN JENNINGS, LHP

BORN: April 17, 1987. **B-T:** L-L. **HT.:** 6-3. **WT.:** 190. **DRAFTED:** Nebraska, 2008 (9th round). **SIGNED BY:** Bob Oldis.

Jennings' pro career got off to a slow start, as he had a middling debut in 2008 and then had his first spring training interrupted by an emergency appendectomy. But in his first full season, he turned in strong work at three levels, including a cameo in Double-A. Armed with the best slider in the organization, Jennings throws the pitch with two different breaks, one for lefties and the other for righties. Because he tended to rely too much on his slider, pitching coordinator Wayne Rosenthal got Jennings to throw more fastballs last season. The results were impressive, as his velocity improved from 88-90 mph to 91-94, and he now sprinkles in his slider as more of an out pitch. He has some deception as well as late arm speed, and the ball seems to jump out of his hand. Almost frail when he first signed, Jennings has gotten significantly stronger. With his solid mound presence and ability to get righthanders out, he profiles as a lefty set-up man. He'll probably return to Jacksonville to start 2010.

Year	Club (League)	Class	W	L	ERA	G	GS	CG	SV	IP	H	R	ER	HR	BB	SO	AVG
2008	Jamestown (NYP)	SS	1	4	3.53	13	13	0	0	59	79	31	23	2	18	62	.321
2009	Greensboro (SAL)	LoA	1	2	2.74	34	0	0	0	49	42	21	15	1	21	54	.237
	Jupiter (FSL)	HiA	0	0	0.00	8	0	0	6	12	5	0	0	0	4	13	.132
	Jacksonville (SL)	AA	0	0	0.00	3	0	0	0	2	2	0	0	0	1	2	.286
MINOR LEAGUE TOTALS			2	6	2.82	58	13	0	6	121	128	52	38	3	44	131	.274

14 JOSE CEDA, RHP

BORN: Jan. 28, 1987. **B-T:** R-R. **HT.:** 6-4. **WT.:** 280. **SIGNED:** Dominican Republic, 2004. **SIGNED BY:** Felix Francisco/Randy Smith (Padres).

The Marlins traded Kevin Gregg to the Cubs for Ceda in November 2008, and they have yet to see Ceda on the mound. Shut down after one brief outing in winter ball in his native Dominican Republic, he experienced shoulder problems early in his first Marlins spring training. This shouldn't have been a shock, considering he missed two months with shoulder stiffness in 2007, shortly after Chicago had acquired him in a mid-2006 deal that sent Todd Walker to the Padres. Ceda eventually had shoulder surgery, which is always a crapshoot, though Marlins officials hope he'll return early in 2010. They showed faith by adding him to the 40-man roster in November. At his best, Ceda's fastball sits at 95-97 mph and touches 100. He also has shown a hard slider that can be overpowering at times. Before mid-2008, Ceda split his time between starting and relieving. He has been much more dominant out of the bullpen, where his lack of an effective changeup or sharp control isn't as much of a handicap. With his hulking frame and power repertoire, he has drawn comparisons to a young Lee Smith or Armando Benitez. Ceda's conditioning was a problem even before his surgery and will remain a concern going forward.

Year	Club (League)	Class	W	L	ERA	G	GS	CG	SV	IP	H	R	ER	HR	BB	SO	AVG
2005	Padres (DSL)	R	4	2	1.50	13	9	2	2	60	38	18	10	2	29	83	.174
2006	Padres (AZL)	R	2	0	5.09	8	4	0	0	23	20	14	13	1	13	31	.235
	Cubs (AZL)	R	0	0	0.75	5	3	0	0	12	6	2	1	0	7	21	.154
	Boise (NWL)	SS	1	0	3.27	3	3	0	0	11	5	4	4	1	2	11	.139
2007	Cubs (AZL)	R	0	0	2.45	2	1	0	0	4	2	1	1	0	3	3	.182
	Peoria (MWL)	LoA	2	2	3.11	21	6	0	0	46	14	18	16	1	31	66	.093
2008	Daytona (FSL)	HiA	2	2	4.80	15	12	0	0	54	41	29	29	4	28	53	.212
	Tennessee (SL)	AA	2	1	2.08	22	0	0	9	30	26	8	7	2	14	42	.234
2009	Did Not Play—Injured																
MINOR LEAGUE TOTALS			13	7	3.03	89	38	2	11	241	152	94	81	11	127	310	.180

15 EDGAR OLMOS, LHP

BORN: April 12, 1990. **B-T:** L-L. **HT.:** 6-5. **WT.:** 180. **DRAFTED:** HS—Van Nuys, Calif., 2008 (3rd round). **SIGNED BY:** Tim McDonnell.

If Olmos could just stay healthy, the Marlins believe he could really take off. After spurning Arizona to sign for $478,000 as a third-round pick out of high school, he was shut down with shoulder tendinitis after one start in his 2008 pro debut. His second was interrupted by shoulder surgery that was initially expected to be serious but turned out to be minor. Some fraying of his labrum was repaired, and Olmos was back pitching at the end of the season in the Rookie-level Gulf Coast League. His fastball sits at 89 mph and touches 92, and the Marlins believe he could add velocity because he has a live, loose arm and lean, projectable frame. He throws from a high three-quarters arm slot, and his changeup has shown screwball rotation when it's working. He features both a slow curveball at 70-72 mph and a slider at 73-76 mph. His work ethic is unquestioned, as his body got stronger during his rehab period. Olmos is highly motivated to get rolling now that his health issues have been cleared up. Florida may take things slow with him, so he could begin 2010 in extended spring training and head to short-season Jamestown in June.

Year	Club (League)	Class	W	L	ERA	G	GS	CG	SV	IP	H	R	ER	HR	BB	SO	AVG
2008	Marlins (GCL)	R	0	0	0.00	1	1	0	0	2	2	0	0	0	0	5	.250
2009	Marlins (GCL)	R	0	0	0.00	2	2	0	0	5	1	0	0	0	2	5	.077
	Jamestown (NYP)	SS	0	0	2.25	1	1	0	0	4	3	1	1	0	2	4	.214
MINOR LEAGUE TOTALS			0	0	0.84	4	4	0	0	11	6	1	1	0	4	14	.171

16 JAKE SMOLINSKI, 3B

BORN: Feb. 9, 1989. **B-T:** R-R. **HT.:** 5-11. **WT.:** 185. **DRAFTED:** HS—Rockford, Ill., 2007 (2nd round). **SIGNED BY:** Steve Arnieri (Nationals).

Old school in his approach and crew-cut appearance, Smolinski is still working his way back from reconstructive left knee surgery that immediately preceded his inclusion in the trade that sent Scott Olsen and Josh Willingham to the Nationals in November 2008. Smolinski didn't join Greensboro until May, and it took him a while to get back up to speed. He shows strong plate discipline, a solid line-drive stroke and projects to add power. He can handle all pitch types in all areas within the zone, but he has a tendency to cut off his swing, which costs him power for now. His arm and speed are average, and scouts have loved him ever since he was ranked the best position prospect in Illinois as a high school senior in 2007. He rejected Clemson to sign for $452,500 out of the second round. The biggest question with Smolinski is where he'll fit defensively. He played left field and second base in two seasons in the Washington system, then moved to third base last year. At the hot corner, he struggles at times to read balls off the bat and gets caught on too many in-between hops. Some scouts believe he'll eventually have to return to left field, where he could fit into the Chris Coghlan mold. Smolinski needs to get a full season of at-bats, as he lost time in 2007 (broken foot when he fouled a ball off it) and 2008 (broken thumb before he tore up his knee when he got steamrolled turning a double play in instructional league). He'll advance to high Class A this season.

Year	Club (League)	Class	AVG	G	AB	R	H	2B	3B	HR	RBI	BB	SO	SB	OBP	SLG
2007	Nationals (GCL)	R	.305	28	105	18	32	8	0	1	16	13	24	7	.387	.410
2008	Hagerstown (SAL)	LoA	.261	50	184	28	48	12	1	4	22	19	33	1	.338	.402
	Nationals (GCL)	R	.111	3	9	0	1	0	0	0	2	1	1	0	.200	.111
	Vermont (NYP)	SS	.306	24	98	17	30	8	1	0	9	9	17	4	.370	.408
2009	Greensboro (SAL)	LoA	.283	77	279	50	79	25	0	7	31	38	45	2	.379	.448
MINOR LEAGUE TOTALS			.281	182	675	113	190	53	2	12	80	80	120	14	.366	.419

17 BRAD HAND, LHP

BORN: March 20, 1990. **B-T:** L-L. **HT.:** 6-2. **WT.:** 185. **DRAFTED:** HS—Chaska, Minn., 2008 (2nd round). **SIGNED BY:** Bob Oldis.

Having landed with an organization that values lefthanded pitching more than most, Hand's handedness should only speed his rise through the organization. Physical and country strong, he turned down Arizona State to sign with the Marlins for $760,000 after going early in the second round in 2008. He also played football and hockey in high school, where he showed two-way ability as a power-hitting first baseman. After pitching coordinator Wayne Rosenthal helped him make some early adjustments to what had been a stiff delivery, Hand got his fastball velocity back up to 93-94 mph last year after working at 88-91 mph in his pro debut. His 77-81 mph curveball and developing changeup also show the potential to become plus pitches. He uses a mid three-quarters arm slot and must fight a tendency to drop his arm, which causes his pitches to sail and leads to too many walks. Hand managed to survive at Greensboro, which has been known to chew up pitchers, and he should head to high Class A with a full head of steam in 2010.

Year	Club (League)	Class	W	L	ERA	G	GS	CG	SV	IP	H	R	ER	HR	BB	SO	AVG
2008	Marlins (GCL)	R	2	0	2.48	9	7	0	0	33	25	16	9	0	11	34	.212
	Jamestown (NYP)	SS	1	2	3.00	3	3	0	0	15	11	6	5	0	10	12	.208
2009	Greensboro (SAL)	LoA	7	13	4.86	26	26	0	0	128	130	83	69	12	66	122	.264
MINOR LEAGUE TOTALS			10	15	4.26	38	36	0	0	175	166	105	83	12	87	168	.250

18 CHRIS LEROUX, RHP

BORN: April 14, 1984. **B-T:** L-R. **HT.:** 6-6. **WT.:** 210. **DRAFTED:** Winthrop, 2005 (7th round). **SIGNED BY:** Joel Matthews.

Given a couple of shots at the big leagues in 2009, Leroux failed to generate results reflective of the quality of his stuff. That won't keep the Marlins from giving him additional chances, as they still see him as a late-inning piece for their bullpen. A converted catcher who overused his curveball at Winthrop and had Tommy John surgery shortly before the 2005 draft, Leroux went in the seventh round though he wouldn't be able to pitch for nearly a year. A member of Canada's World Baseball Classic club, Leroux can get his fastball to 94-96 mph, but it tends to flatten out when he tries to overthrow. He has ditched his curve and concentrated on a tight slider, which he throws at 87-88 mph. He has lowered his ERA and his walk rate in each of his four pro seasons, though he looked tentative in his brief big league exposure. Leroux has struggled to close games and a set-up role may work best for him in the short term. He could make a revamped Florida bullpen with a strong spring.

Year	Club (League)	Class	W	L	ERA	G	GS	CG	SV	IP	H	R	ER	HR	BB	SO	AVG
2006	Greensboro (SAL)	LoA	0	3	6.10	3	3	0	0	10	13	7	7	2	6	9	.325
	Marlins (GCL)	R	0	0	4.09	4	4	0	0	11	10	9	5	0	9	9	.250
	Jamestown (NYP)	SS	0	1	7.94	4	4	0	0	11	13	13	10	0	12	4	.283
2007	Greensboro (SAL)	LoA	2	3	4.14	46	0	0	0	72	72	38	33	6	29	76	.261
2008	Jupiter (FSL)	HiA	6	7	3.65	57	0	0	1	74	60	37	30	6	26	78	.225
2009	Florida (NL)	MAJ	0	0	10.80	5	0	0	0	7	11	8	8	0	4	2	.355
	Jacksonville (SL)	AA	5	3	2.70	46	0	0	2	60	59	19	18	0	17	55	.258
MAJOR LEAGUE TOTALS			0	0	10.80	5	0	0	0	7	11	8	8	0	4	2	.355
MINOR LEAGUE TOTALS			13	17	3.89	160	11	0	3	238	227	123	103	14	91	231	.253

19 BRYAN BERGLUND, RHP

BORN: Nov. 2, 1990. **B-T:** R-R. **HT.:** 6-4. **WT.:** 180. **DRAFTED:** HS—Simi Valley, Calif., 2009 (2nd round). **SIGNED BY:** Tim McDonnell.

Barely known, even in prospect-rich Southern California, Berglund saw his profile explode after a strong showing at a local all-star game last winter. He wound up signing late last summer for $572,500 out of the second round, spurning a scholarship to nearby Loyola Marymount. The first Swedish citizen ever drafted, he's fairly Americanized and flashes a dry wit. If he reaches the majors, he'll be the first Swede to do so since Eric Erickson in 1922. Like many high school pitchers, Berglund saw his velocity dip when he first entered pro ball. He worked at 87-89 mph and touched 90 after signing, down from 90-92 mph. Tall and lanky with a lean, projectable frame, he needs to add muscle but his work ethic and makeup are sound. His mechanics are solid and the Marlins saw no reason to tinker with him at their season-end minicamp. In-game durability remains a concern as his fastball often lost power by the middle innings during his prep career. Berglund's short slider will eventually be an out pitch, but for now he relies more heavily on his changeup. He figures to open his first full pro season in low Class A.

Year	Club (League)	Class	W	L	ERA	G	GS	CG	SV	IP	H	R	ER	HR	BB	SO	AVG
2009	Did Not Play—Signed Late																	

20 TIM WOOD, RHP

BORN: Nov. 16, 1982. **B-T:** R-R. **HT.:** 6-1. **WT.:** 185. **DRAFTED:** Pima (Ariz.) CC, D/F 2002 (44th round). **SIGNED BY:** Scott Stanley.

Having overcome Tommy John surgery in July 2005 and a minor shoulder issue in 2008, Wood has proven he's a survivor. After forcing his way onto the 40-man roster following the 2008 season, Wood turned in a strong showing in Triple-A and handled himself well in his first taste of the big leagues. Despite his slender frame and unassuming appearance, Wood can run his fastball up to 94-95 mph with sink. He tends to get a little too rotational at times, which takes his slider off the plate to his arm side. But when he stays in line to the plate, his slider can be an out pitch. He also shows a hard changeup with plus action down in the zone. He has matured significantly in recent years and those who have worked with him praise his bulldog mentality. While there were some hiccups, nine of Wood's last 10 outings in the majors were scoreless, giving him a leg up on securing a full-time set-up spot in 2010.

FLORIDA MARLINS

Year	Club (League)	Class	W	L	ERA	G	GS	CG	SV	IP	H	R	ER	HR	BB	SO	AVG
2003	Jamestown (NYP)	SS	0	2	5.35	16	4	0	2	39	44	33	23	2	28	32	.289
2004	Greensboro (SAL)	LoA	2	3	4.22	24	8	0	1	70	73	47	33	12	22	70	.263
2005	Greensboro (SAL)	LoA	1	2	9.28	5	5	0	0	21	29	23	22	2	15	10	.312
2006	Jupiter (FSL)	HiA	2	7	5.83	16	16	0	0	63	65	43	41	4	25	52	.273
2007	Jupiter (FSL)	HiA	0	2	3.81	17	0	0	0	26	24	14	11	1	8	26	.245
2008	Jupiter (FSL)	HiA	5	2	1.80	27	1	0	1	40	25	10	8	1	15	22	.182
	Carolina (SL)	AA	2	1	5.75	12	0	0	0	20	20	14	13	2	6	15	.250
2009	New Orleans (PCL)	AAA	1	2	3.18	31	0	0	0	40	42	16	14	1	17	37	.269
	Florida (NL)	MAJ	1	0	2.82	18	0	0	0	22	22	8	7	2	10	16	.272
MAJOR LEAGUE TOTALS			1	0	2.82	18	0	0	0	22	22	8	7	2	10	16	.272
MINOR LEAGUE TOTALS			13	21	4.65	148	34	0	4	320	322	200	165	25	136	264	.261

21 JORGE JIMENEZ, 3B

BORN: Sept. 12, 1984. **B-T:** L-R. **HT.:** 6-1. **WT.:** 210. **DRAFTED:** Porterville (Calif.) JC, 2006 (15th round). **SIGNED BY:** Jim Woodward (Red Sox).

Though the Red Sox spent the offseason looking to upgrade at third base and had Jimenez coming off a solid season in Double-A, they chose not to protect him on their 40-man roster. That left him available in the major league Rule 5 draft, where the Astros selected him and shipped him to Florida as the third prospect in a package for Matt Lindstrom. Jimenez controls the strike zone and hits for average with gap power. He has a cannon for an arm, but scouts are split on whether he'll be able to play third base at the big league level. A below-average runner, he doesn't cover much ground at third and his hands aren't the softest. The Marlins think he can handle the hot corner, and he might be a low-cost option for the big league club in 2010. If he can't stick on the 25-man roster, he'd have to clear waivers and be offered back to Boston for half the $50,000 draft price before Florida could send him to the minors.

Year	Club (League)	Class	AVG	G	AB	R	H	2B	3B	HR	RBI	BB	SO	SB	OBP	SLG
2006	Lowell (NYP)	SS	.257	41	136	19	35	3	0	0	9	18	17	1	.365	.279
2007	Lowell (NYP)	SS	.303	68	238	38	72	23	3	4	44	32	18	4	.412	.475
2008	Lancaster (CAL)	HiA	.352	70	267	47	94	20	1	4	42	26	31	1	.421	.479
	Portland (EL)	AA	.270	55	211	23	57	12	2	3	22	8	29	1	.305	.389
2009	Portland (EL)	AA	.289	133	498	63	144	23	2	13	87	52	70	3	.366	.422
MINOR LEAGUE TOTALS			.298	367	1350	190	402	81	8	24	204	136	165	10	.377	.423

22 GRAHAM JOHNSON, RHP

BORN: Oct. 13, 1989. **B-T:** R-R. **HT.:** 6-6. **WT.:** 215. **DRAFTED:** HS—Westlake Village, Calif., 2008 (6th round). **SIGNED BY:** Tim McDonnell.

Johnson wasn't a regular on the high school showcase circuit and was overshadowed at Westlake High (Westlake Village, Calif.) by the likes of Lenny Dykstra's son Cutter. A late bloomer as a senior, Johnson spurned a Fresno State scholarship to sign for $150,000 out of the sixth round in 2008. Tall and lanky, he needs to refine his command and gain more strength, but the raw materials are here. He pitches at 88-90 mph and touches 92 mph with his fastball, and the Marlins believe he'll add velocity as he fills out. With the help of pitching coordinator Wayne Rosenthal, Johnson has revamped his delivery to take better advantage of his natural leverage. He has moved his arm slot from low three-quarters to a full three-quarters and stands taller on the mound. In turn, that has helped his slider get more bite. He continues to refine his changeup, which has some cut to it and is a plus pitch at times. Quiet and hard-working, Johnson could move quickly once everything clicks for him. He figures to open 2010 in high Class A.

Year	Club (League)	Class	W	L	ERA	G	GS	CG	SV	IP	H	R	ER	HR	BB	SO	AVG
2008	Marlins (GCL)	R	0	0	5.40	3	2	0	0	5	6	3	3	1	0	8	.286
2009	Greensboro (SAL)	LoA	6	7	4.83	20	20	0	0	91	100	59	49	8	47	52	.277
MINOR LEAGUE TOTALS			6	7	4.86	23	22	0	0	96	106	62	52	9	47	60	.277

23 JAY VOSS, LHP

BORN: April 22, 1987. **B-T:** L-L. **HT.:** 6-4. **WT.:** 195. **DRAFTED:** Kaskaskia (Ill.) CC, 2007 (8th round). **SIGNED BY:** Scot Engler.

Voss dabbled as a starter in his first two pro seasons before coming into his own with a move to full-time relief in 2009. He worked his way up to Double-A, where he averaged a strikeout per inning and held opponents to a .200 average. Tall and solidly built, Voss pitches at 89-91 mph and touches 93 with his fastball. He has two different sliders, a sweeping version for lefties and one with splitter action for righties. He still throws his changeup, which is developing. A hard worker with a soft-spoken personality, he went along with mechanical changes suggested by pitching coordinator Wayne Rosenthal early in his career to smooth out his delivery. Voss struggled in August last year after returning home to help his father recover from a fall off a ladder, then turned in a decent showing in the Arizona Fall League. Voss will bid for a lefty-specialist role in Florida's bullpen in spring training, but more likely will head to Triple-A to sharpen his game at the outset of 2010.

Year	Club (League)	Class	W	L	ERA	G	GS	CG	SV	IP	H	R	ER	HR	BB	SO	AVG
2007	Jamestown (NYP)	SS	0	7	7.63	15	11	0	0	48	78	45	41	5	21	35	.364
2008	Greensboro (SAL)	LoA	3	6	6.39	26	11	0	0	69	106	56	49	8	24	55	.355
2009	Jupiter (FSL)	HiA	0	1	2.03	10	0	0	0	13	14	5	3	0	3	10	.269
	Jacksonville (SL)	AA	3	0	2.97	30	0	0	1	36	26	14	12	2	15	36	.200
MINOR LEAGUE TOTALS			6	14	5.66	81	22	0	1	167	224	120	105	15	63	136	.322

24 BRETT SINKBEIL, RHP

BORN: Dec. 26, 1984. **B-T:** R-R. **HT.:** 6-2. **WT.:** 205. **DRAFTED:** Missouri State, 2006 (1st round). **SIGNED BY:** Ryan Wardinsky.

Having invested $1.525 million and the 16th overall pick in the 2006 draft in Sinkbeil, the Marlins still hope to see some return. A series of nagging injuries have slowed him through the years, including a strained oblique, a minor elbow problem and a herniated disk in his back. His fastball velocity dropped all the way down to 90-93 mph before a move to the bullpen last May in Triple-A seemed to revive him. Soon he was back to touching 96 mph with his fastball and his 86-87 mph slider got tighter and harder. He struggled with the slider out of the full windup, but he stopped getting around the pitch once he opted for the stretch on a full-time basis. He still throws from a high three-quarters arm slot, but his simplified delivery allows him to stay more on target with his body. He still needs to cut down on his walks and miss more bats, but with his work ethic and new momentum, Sinkbeil could bid for a role in the big league bullpen sometime in 2010. Florida added him to its 40-man roster for the first time in November.

Year	Club (League)	Class	W	L	ERA	G	GS	CG	SV	IP	H	R	ER	HR	BB	SO	AVG
2006	Jamestown (NYP)	SS	2	0	1.23	5	5	0	0	22	14	4	3	1	8	22	.192
	Greensboro (SAL)	LoA	1	1	4.99	8	8	0	0	40	45	22	22	5	14	32	.290
2007	Jupiter (FSL)	HiA	6	4	3.42	14	14	1	0	79	82	41	30	8	14	49	.268
2008	Carolina (SL)	AA	5	9	5.02	26	26	1	0	143	172	84	80	12	51	66	.306
2009	New Orleans (PCL)	AAA	2	8	6.07	47	8	0	0	83	106	65	56	9	44	52	.315
MINOR LEAGUE TOTALS			16	22	4.68	100	61	2	0	367	419	216	191	35	131	221	.292

25 KRIS HARVEY, RHP

BORN: Jan. 5, 1984. **B-T:** R-R. **HT.:** 6-2. **WT.:** 195. **DRAFTED:** Clemson, 2005 (2nd round). **SIGNED BY:** Joel Matthews.

The son of original Marlins closer Bryan Harvey came to the club as a power-hitting outfield prospect. Coming off a 25-homer season at Clemson in 2005, he signed for $575,000 as a second-round pick and rose as high as Double-A. However, problems with hitting the breaking ball eventually prompted Florida to convert him back to the mound, where he had touched 97 mph in college. It didn't take long after his late-season conversion in 2008 for the switch to start paying dividends. Harvey's fastball was back up to 95-96 mph at its peak in his first full pro season on the mound, though he became fatigued toward the end of the year. His splitter should eventually become a solid No. 2 offering, just like it was for his father. For now, Harvey also features a slider, curveball and changeup. Quiet and hard-working, he has the right mentality for short relief, though he probably profiles more in a set-up role than as a closer. Added to the 40-man roster for the first time, he figures to open 2010 in Double-A. From there, it might not take long before he reaches the majors and forges the first father-son combo in Marlins history.

Year	Club (League)	Class	W	L	ERA	G	GS	CG	SV	IP	H	R	ER	HR	BB	SO	AVG
2008	Marlins (GCL)	R	1	0	6.23	4	0	0	0	4	3	3	3	1	3	5	.200
	Greensboro (SAL)	LoA	0	2	7.50	4	0	0	0	6	10	8	5	0	7	2	.400
2009	Jupiter (FSL)	HiA	6	7	4.38	37	3	0	1	72	67	39	35	3	34	54	.248
MINOR LEAGUE TOTALS			7	9	4.70	45	3	0	1	82	80	50	43	4	44	61	.258

Year	Club (League)	Class	AVG	G	AB	R	H	2B	3B	HR	RBI	BB	SO	SB	OBP	SLG
2005	Jamestown (NYP)	SS	.300	65	263	34	79	14	3	9	38	9	60	4	.320	.479
2006	Greensboro (SAL)	LoA	.245	96	367	46	90	18	2	15	60	24	82	9	.291	.428
2007	Jupiter (FSL)	HiA	.238	116	420	52	100	16	3	12	55	34	100	6	.301	.376
2008	Carolina (SL)	AA	.148	74	209	24	31	9	1	6	18	21	71	1	.228	.287
MINOR LEAGUE TOTALS			.238	351	1259	156	300	57	9	42	171	88	313	20	.290	.398

26 BRETT HAYES, C

BORN: Feb. 13, 1984. **B-T:** R-R. **HT.:** 6-1. **WT.:** 200. **DRAFTED:** Nevada, 2005 (2nd round supplemental). **SIGNED BY:** John Hughes.

Hayes attended the same Notre Dame High (Sherman Oaks, Calif.) program as top Marlins prospect Mike Stanton, then attended Nevada before signing for $450,000 as a supplemental second-round pick. He doesn't carry nearly the same potential impact as Stanton, but Hayes continues to make steady progress both at the plate and behind it. Plagued by nagging injuries early in his career, he has worked hard with catching coordinator Tim Cossins to improve his game-calling and footwork. Blocking balls in the dirt is no longer the weakness it once was, and his fiery touch with pitchers remains impressive. His arm is average and accurate, and he threw out 27 percent of basestealers in Triple-A last year. With the help of hitting coordinator John Mallee, Hayes has learned to avoid overstriding and stays behind the ball much better. This also has helped improve his pitch recognition. His power is below-average, but he's intelligent and competitive enough to hold his own at the plate. He's a below-average runner. Brought to the majors for the first time in 2009, Hayes served mainly as a pinch-hitter and delivered a homer off Victor Garate.

Year	Club (League)	Class	AVG	G	AB	R	H	2B	3B	HR	RBI	BB	SO	SB	OBP	SLG
2005	Marlins (GCL)	R	.417	3	12	2	5	1	0	0	2	0	2	0	.417	.500
	Jamestown (NYP)	SS	.239	36	117	11	28	6	1	1	12	12	21	3	.313	.333
2006	Greensboro (SAL)	LoA	.245	82	278	39	68	13	1	9	38	29	61	4	.321	.396
2007	Jupiter (FSL)	HiA	.338	17	65	10	22	3	1	1	11	9	10	2	.413	.462
	Carolina (SL)	AA	.234	74	273	22	64	16	0	3	31	18	51	2	.280	.326
2008	Carolina (SL)	AA	.232	54	181	19	42	8	0	6	18	10	43	1	.275	.376
	Albuquerque (PCL)	AAA	.293	37	116	21	34	3	1	5	17	4	23	1	.331	.466
2009	New Orleans (PCL)	AAA	.240	90	321	27	77	15	0	4	20	20	66	2	.281	.324
	Florida (NL)	MAJ	.273	14	11	5	3	1	0	1	2	0	4	0	.333	.636
MAJOR LEAGUE TOTALS			.273	14	11	5	3	1	0	1	2	0	4	0	.333	.636
MINOR LEAGUE TOTALS			.249	393	1363	151	340	65	4	29	166	102	277	15	.303	.367

27 CURTIS PETERSEN, RHP

BORN: Aug. 28, 1989. **B-T:** R-R. **HT.:** 6-3. **WT.:** 180. **DRAFTED:** HS—Denton, Texas, 2008 (4th round). **SIGNED BY:** Dennis Cardoza.

Signed away from a Nebraska commitment for $350,000 out of the fourth round in 2008, Petersen came in with a tall, projectable frame and a smooth delivery. He struggled in his first pro summer, but came back strong in 2009 after getting his legs under him at extended spring training. His fastball sat at 86-89 mph in high school but now works at 90-91 with a peak of 94. His 12-to-6 curveball can be a plus pitch for him, but it's his changeup that has shown the most progress. It now has serious downward bite and he throws it with much better arm speed. A quiet competitor with a bulldog mentality, the late-blooming Texan is considered one of the hardest workers in the system. Rare is the day his pitching coach doesn't have to chase him off the bullpen mound between starts. He more than held his own in the New York-Penn League at age 19. He figures to open 2010 in low Class A, where he'll continue to pile up innings and momentum.

Year	Club (League)	Class	W	L	ERA	G	GS	CG	SV	IP	H	R	ER	HR	BB	SO	AVG
2008	Marlins (GCL)	R	0	2	9.64	5	4	0	0	14	19	16	15	0	13	9	.352
2009	Jamestown (NYP)	SS	3	5	4.29	15	15	0	0	63	61	41	30	3	31	50	.250
MINOR LEAGUE TOTALS			3	7	5.26	20	19	0	0	77	80	57	45	3	44	59	.268

28 JAI MILLER, OF

BORN: Jan. 17, 1985. **B-T:** R-R. **HT.:** 6-3. **WT.:** 205. **DRAFTED:** HS—Selma, Ala., 2003 (4th round). **SIGNED BY:** Dave Dangler.

Miller warrants a spot on this list almost on sheer perseverance alone. The first three-sport all-star athlete in Alabama high school history, he turned down a Stanford scholarship to sign for $250,000 as a fourth-round pick in 2003. His stock steadily dipped as he failed to hit better than .209 in any of his first four pro seasons. Too many strikeouts were the problem, too many holes in his swing. To his credit, Miller has kept working to tighten up that swing and close those holes. The result is an on-base percentage that steadily climbed from a low of .273 in 2004 all the way to the .360 figure he posted in 2009. Miller can now take pitches out over the plate to the opposite field with authority. He has plus raw power, plus speed and keeps getting more reliable in center field, where his routes are no longer an adventure. He has more arm strength than most center fielders, though his accuracy wavers. He's still learning how to translate his quickness into stolen bases. Some in the organization still see him as a late bloomer with Mike Cameron characteristics. Should Cameron Maybin falter in center yet again, Miller could be there to pick up the pieces.

Year	Club (League)	Class	AVG	G	AB	R	H	2B	3B	HR	RBI	BB	SO	SB	OBP	SLG
2003	Marlins (GCL)	R	.199	46	146	17	29	4	1	1	15	15	45	9	.279	.260
	Jamestown (NYP)	SS	.233	11	43	5	10	3	0	0	6	3	15	1	.292	.302
2004	Greensboro (SAL)	LoA	.205	113	390	51	80	15	3	12	49	32	163	11	.273	.351
2005	Greensboro (SAL)	LoA	.207	115	415	69	86	14	2	13	34	57	139	16	.305	.345
2006	Jupiter (FSL)	HiA	.209	111	344	40	72	16	2	0	24	45	115	24	.308	.267
2007	Carolina (SL)	AA	.261	129	406	54	106	26	2	14	58	55	127	12	.354	.438
2008	Florida (NL)	MAJ	.000	1	1	0	0	0	0	0	0	0	1	0	.000	.000
	Albuquerque (PCL)	AAA	.267	117	434	67	116	22	5	19	56	52	133	20	.349	.472
2009	New Orleans (PCL)	AAA	.289	102	343	55	99	24	2	16	52	38	106	6	.360	.510
MAJOR LEAGUE TOTALS			.000	1	1	0	0	0	0	0	0	0	1	0	.000	.000
MINOR LEAGUE TOTALS			.237	744	2521	358	598	124	17	75	294	297	843	99	.322	.389

29 GREG BURNS, OF

BORN: Nov. 7, 1986. **B-T:** L-L. **HT.:** 6-2. **WT.:** 185. **DRAFTED:** HS—West Covina, Calif., 2004 (3rd round). **SIGNED BY:** Robby Corsaro.

Sent back to high Class A for a second crack at the Florida State League in 2009, Burns led the league with 163 strikeouts but still made progress in other areas. He set a career high in walks and attempted the most stolen bases of his career and displayed flashes of raw power. After six seasons, Burns remains one of the best athletes in the system—he turned down a football scholarship to play wide receiver at Hawaii—but still needs more strength and refinement. Burns struggles against lefties and must improve his bunting, and his lower half continues to betray him at times at the plate. As a result, he can't take full advantage of his plus-plus speed. He has tremendous range and closing speed in center field, and he doesn't shy away from walls. He also shows an average arm with good accuracy. Burns continues to add strength to his frame and has a strong work ethic, and he's only 23. But the clock is ticking with the depth of outfield prospects in the system. Burns figures to open 2010 in Double-A as the Marlins continue to wait patiently for him to take off.

Year	Club (League)	Class	AVG	G	AB	R	H	2B	3B	HR	RBI	BB	SO	SB	OBP	SLG
2004	Marlins (GCL)	R	.243	42	136	28	33	5	4	0	7	26	48	7	.372	.338
2005	Jamestown (NYP)	SS	.257	65	241	43	62	5	2	1	11	39	84	17	.366	.307
2006	Greensboro (SAL)	LoA	.231	105	342	44	79	13	8	2	23	38	109	20	.307	.333
2007	Greensboro (SAL)	LoA	.280	120	434	70	116	21	4	7	54	40	122	39	.347	.401
2008	Jupiter (FSL)	HiA	.244	121	377	55	92	12	5	3	28	61	143	34	.351	.326
2009	Jupiter (FSL)	HiA	.242	132	475	64	115	20	7	4	35	64	163	37	.335	.339
MINOR LEAGUE TOTALS			.250	585	1985	304	497	76	30	17	158	268	669	154	.342	.345

30 OSVALDO MARTINEZ, SS

BORN: May 7, 1988. **B-T:** R-R. **HT.:** 5-10. **WT.:** 170. **DRAFTED:** Porterville (Calif.) JC, 2006 (11th round). **SIGNED BY:** Carlos Berroa.

Martinez is a lucky man. Shot three times in a drive-by, mistaken-identity shooting on Sept. 30 in his hometown of Carolina, Puerto Rico, he not only survived but is expected to make a full recovery that will enable him to resume a promising baseball career. Finally given a chance to play every day, Martinez took a big leap forward in 2009. He puts the ball in play thanks to excellent hand-eye coordination but needs to draw more walks because he has limited power. He swings hard and makes the most of his strong hands and forearms. He has learned to punish mistake offspeed pitches and projects to hit .265 with 10-15 homers annually should he reach the majors. He doesn't have blazing speed but has proven to be a smart basestealer. Martinez lacks quick feet, but he makes up for that at shortstop with positioning and anticipation. His plus arm and instincts help as well. Coachable and fearless, he's the sort of leader whom teammates gravitate toward.

Year	Club (League)	Class	AVG	G	AB	R	H	2B	3B	HR	RBI	BB	SO	SB	OBP	SLG
2006	Marlins (GCL)	R	.263	49	171	21	45	4	1	1	21	19	21	7	.335	.316
2007	Jupiter (FSL)	HiA	—	1	0	0	0	0	0	0	0	1	0	0	1.000	—
	Jamestown (NYP)	SS	.184	38	114	8	21	5	0	0	6	11	25	8	.262	.228
2008	Greensboro (SAL)	LoA	.296	85	304	44	90	11	3	6	29	13	46	5	.331	.411
2009	Jupiter (FSL)	HiA	.254	130	433	54	110	16	5	1	45	41	51	16	.323	.321
MINOR LEAGUE TOTALS			.260	303	1022	127	266	36	9	8	101	85	143	36	.321	.337

Houston Astros

BY BEN BADLER

Want to build a farm system overnight? One glance at Baseball America's organization talent rankings suggests a proven template.

The Rangers went from 28th entering 2007 to fourth in 2008 to first in 2009, getting a boost from the prospects they received by trading Mark Teixeira, not to mention Eric Gagne and Kenny Lofton. The Athletics spent three years near the bottom of the rankings before zooming from No. 27 in 2008 to No. 3 in 2009, thanks largely to the talent they received in deals for Joe Blanton, Rich Harden, Dan Haren and Nick Swisher.

At the July 31 trading deadline, the Astros had a .500 record and ranked sixth in the National League wild-card race. Despite having the oldest roster in baseball and a run differential that suggested the team was due for regression, Houston stood pat rather than trade big leaguers and rebuild a farm system that ranked last entering 2009.

The Astros tanked afterward, finishing 74-88. Despite the eighth-highest Opening Day payroll ($103 million), Houston ranked 27th in baseball in scoring and 23rd in runs allowed.

Focusing on the big league club and neglecting their farm system, the Astros haven't acquired a significant prospect via trade in years. Instead, their strategy has been to sign veteran free agents (costing them draft picks as compensation) and to deal prospects for veterans. That philosophy proved painful last season when Ben Zobrist emerged as one of the game's better players, three years after Houston sent him to the Rays in a deal for Aubrey Huff. Zobrist wasn't highly regarded at the time but has proven a costly loss.

After years of poor drafts that culminated with fifth-rounder Collin DeLome being their highest signed pick in 2007, the Astros restructured their scouting department. Bobby Heck's first draft as scouting director in 2008 has yielded two promising prospects, catcher Jason Castro and righthander Jordan Lyles, neither of whom were consensus choices at their draft slots.

Castro has the potential to be the franchise's most successful first-round choice since Brad Lidge in 1998. Houston's only other first-rounder to reach the big leagues since then was Chris Burke, the 10th overall pick in 2001, and he never developed as hoped.

Houston's 2009 first-rounder, shortstop Jiovanni Mier, also had a promising debut. After Castro, Mier

Instead of dealing prospects like Ben Zobrist, the Astros could use an infusion of talent

TOP 30 PROSPECTS

1. Jason Castro, c	16. Chris Johnson, 3b
2. Jiovanni Mier, ss	17. Telvin Nash, of
3. Jordan Lyles, rhp	18. Jonathan Meyer, 3b
4. Sammy Gervacio, rhp	19. Arcenio Leon, rhp
5. Chia-jen Lo, rhp	20. Koby Clemens, c/of
6. Ross Seaton, rhp	21. Brian Bogusevic, of
7. Tanner Bushue, rhp	22. Wilton Lopez, rhp
8. Jay Austin, of	23. Evan Englebrook, rhp
9. Jon Gaston, of	24. Dallas Keuchel, lhp
10. T.J. Steele, of	25. Collin DeLome, of
11. Tommy Manzella, ss	26. Polin Trinidad, lhp
12. Danny Meszaros, rhp	27. Henry Villar, rhp
13. J.B. Shuck, of	28. Ashton Mowdy, rhp
14. Fernando Abad, lhp	29. Brad Dydalewicz, lhp
15. Matt Nevarez, rhp	30. Kyle Greenwalt, rhp

and Lyles, the talent drops off precipitously.

Where do the Astros go from here? Heck was a regional crosschecker for the Brewers when they built through the draft and jumped from No. 30 to No. 1 in BA's talent rankings from 2001 to 2004. Houston will have an opportunity to add to its system with the eighth overall pick in the 2010 draft, its highest selection since taking Phil Nevin No. 1 overall in 1992.

Dealing their big leaguers for youngsters could accelerate an Astros turnaround as well. But under owner Drayton McLane, the team has shied away from committing to rebuilding.

General Manager: Ed Wade. **Farm Director:** Ricky Bennett. **Scouting Director:** Bobby Heck.

Class	Team	League	W	L	PCT	Finish*	Manager(s)
Majors	Houston Astros	National	74	88	.457	12th (16)	C. Cooper/D. Clark
Triple-A	Round Rock Express	Pacific Coast	63	81	.438	15th (16)	Marc Bombard
Double-A	Corpus Christi Hooks	Texas	61	79	.436	t-7th (8)	Luis Pujols
High A	Lancaster JetHawks	California	56	84	.400	10th (10)	Wes Clements
Low A	Lexington Legends	South Atlantic	68	72	.486	9th (16)	Tom Lawless
Short-season	Tri-City ValleyCats	New York-Penn	27	48	.360	13th (14)	Jim Pankovits
Rookie	Greeneville Astros	Appalachian	27	40	.403	9th (10)	Rodney Linares
Rookie	GCL Astros	Gulf Coast	18	38	.321	16th (16)	Omar Lopez
Overall 2009 Minor League Record			320	442	.420	30th (30)	

*Finish in overall standings (No. of teams in league). †League champion.

LAST YEAR'S TOP 30

Player, Pos.		Status
1.	Jason Castro, c	No. 1
2.	Bud Norris, rhp	Majors
3.	Ross Seaton, rhp	No. 6
4.	Brian Bogusevic, of	No. 21
5.	Chris Johnson, 3b	No. 16
6.	Jordan Lyles, rhp	No. 3
7.	Felipe Paulino, rhp	Majors
8.	Drew Sutton, 2b/ss	(Reds)
9.	Collin DeLome, of	No. 25
10.	Jay Austin, of	No. 8
11.	Tommy Manzella, ss	No. 11
12.	Chia-Jen Lo, rhp	No. 5
13.	Sergio Perez, rhp	Dropped out
14.	Brad Dydalewicz, lhp	No. 29
15.	Brad James, rhp	Dropped out
16.	Josh Flores, of	Dropped out
17.	David Duncan, lhp	Dropped out
18.	Chris Hicks, rhp	Dropped out
19.	Sammy Gervacio, rhp	No. 4
20.	Federico Hernandez, c	Dropped out
21.	Gilbert de la Vara, lhp	(Royals)
22.	T.J. Steele, of	No. 10
23.	Eli Iorg, of	(Free agent)
24.	Polin Trinidad, lhp	No. 26
25.	Chris Blazek, lhp	Dropped out
26.	Jerrod Holloway, lhp	Dropped out
27.	Phil Disher, 1b	Dropped out
28.	Leandro Cespedes, rhp	Dropped out
29.	Lou Palmisano, c	Dropped out
30.	Luis Cruz, lhp	Dropped out

BEST TOOLS

Best Hitter for Average	Jason Castro
Best Power Hitter	Jon Gaston
Best Strike-Zone Discipline	J.B. Shuck
Fastest Baserunner	Jay Austin
Best Athlete	Jay Austin
Best Fastball	Arcenio Leon
Best Curveball	Ashton Mowdy
Best Slider	Sammy Gervacio
Best Changeup	Jordan Lyles
Best Control	Fernando Abad
Best Defensive Catcher	Jason Castro
Best Defensive Infielder	Jiovanni Mier
Best Infield Arm	Jiovanni Mier
Best Defensive Outfielder	T.J. Steele
Best Outfield Arm	Yordany Ramirez

PROJECTED 2013 LINEUP

Catcher	Jason Castro
First Base	Lance Berkman
Second Base	Tommy Manzella
Third Base	Chris Johnson
Shortstop	Jiovanni Mier
Left Field	Carlos Lee
Center Field	Michael Bourn
Right Field	Hunter Pence
No. 1 Starter	Roy Oswalt
No. 2 Starter	Wandy Rodriguez
No. 3 Starter	Jordan Lyles
No. 4 Starter	Bud Norris
No. 5 Starter	Ross Seaton
Closer	Sammy Gervacio

TOP PROSPECTS OF THE DECADE

Year	Player, Pos.	2009 Org.
2000	Wilfredo Rodriguez, lhp	Out of baseball
2001	Roy Oswalt, rhp	Astros
2002	Carlos Hernandez, lhp	Rays
2003	John Buck, c	Royals
2004	Taylor Buchholz, rhp	Rockies
2005	Chris Burke, 2b	Braves
2006	Jason Hirsh, rhp	Yankees
2007	Hunter Pence, of	Astros
2008	J.R. Towles, c	Astros
2009	Jason Castro, c	Astros

TOP DRAFT PICKS OF THE DECADE

Year	Player, Pos.	2009 Org.
2000	Robert Stiehl, rhp	Out of baseball
2001	Chris Burke, ss	Braves
2002	Derick Grigsby, rhp	Out of baseball
2003	Jason Hirsh, rhp (2nd round)	Yankees
2004	Hunter Pence, rhp (2nd round)	Astros
2005	Brian Bogusevic, lhp	Astros
2006	Max Sapp, c	Astros
2007	*Derek Dietrich, 3b (3rd round)	Georgia Tech
2008	Jason Castro, c	Astros
2009	Jiovanni Mier, ss	Astros

*Did not sign

LARGEST BONUSES IN CLUB HISTORY

Chris Burke, 2001	$2,125,000
Jason Castro, 2008	$2,070,000
Max Sapp, 2006	$1,400,000
Brian Bogusevic, 2005	$1,375,000
Jiovanni Mier, 2009	$1,358,000

HOUSTON ASTROS

TOP 2010 ROOKIE: Sammy Gervacio, rhp. He already made a big league impact in the final two months of the 2009 season, posting a 2.14 ERA and 25 strikeouts in 21 innings.

BREAKOUT PROSPECT: Fernando Abad, lhp. He has a low-90s fastball with enough pitches to transition from reliever to starter, and he'll significantly boost his value if he can handle the role.

SLEEPER: Edgar Ferreira, lhp. The 17-year-old Dominican is still very raw, but he already throws 90 mph and has hit 93-94.

SOURCE OF TOP 30 TALENT			
Homegrown	28	Acquired	2
College	11	Trades	1
Junior college	1	Rule 5 draft	0
High school	10	Independent leagues	0
Draft-and-follow	0	Free agents/waivers	1
Nondrafted free agents	0		
International	6		

Numbers in parentheses indicate prospect rankings.

LF
Jon Gaston (9)
Telvin Nash (17)
Koby Clemens (20)
Brian Bogusevic (21)
Collin DeLome (25)
Drew Locke
J.D. Martinez
Jake Goebbert

CF
Jay Austin (8)
T.J. Steele (10)
J.B. Shuck (13)
Grant Hogue

RF
Yordany Ramirez
Mitch Einertson
Garen Wright

3B
Chris Johnson (16)
Jonathan Meyer (18)
Chan-Jong Moon
Yonathan Mejia
Erik Castro

SS
Jiovanni Mier (2)
Tommy Manzella (11)
Wladimir Sutil
Brandon Wikoff
Luis Bryan

2B
Jose Vallejo
Enrique Hernandez
Ben Orloff
Jose Altuve

1B
Jimmy Van Ostrand
Brian Pellegrini

C
Jason Castro (1)
Federico Hernandez

RHP

Starters	Relievers
Jordan Lyles (3)	Sammy Gervacio (4)
Ross Seaton (6)	Chia-Jen Lo (5)
Tanner Bushue (7)	Danny Meszaros (12)
Wilton Lopez (22)	Matt Nevarez (15)
Henry Villar (27)	Arcenio Leon (19)
Kyle Greenwalt (30)	Evan Englebrook (23)
Brandt Walker	Ashton Mowdy (28)
B.J. Hyatt	Juri Perez
Brad James	Ryan McKeller
Sergio Perez	Erick Abreu
Leando Cespedes	Chris Hicks
Jose Cisnero	Mike Schurz
R.J. Alaniz	J.B. MacDonald

LHP

Starters	Relievers
Fernando Abad (14)	Pat Urckfitz
Dallas Keuchel (24)	Doug Arguello
Polin Trinidad (26)	Jeff Icenogle
Brad Dydalewicz (29)	
Edgar Ferreira	
David Duncan	

2009   BONUSES: $4.2 MILLION

BEST PURE HITTER: Compared to his stellar defense, SS Jiovanni Mier's (1) bat was considered a question mark. Hitting .276/.380/.484 at Rookie-level Greeneville put a lot of those concerns to rest. OF J.D. Martinez (20) hit .428 as a Nova Southeastern (Fla.) junior and won the short-season New York-Penn League batting title with a .326 average. SS Brandon Wikoff (5) also handles the bat well and ranked second in NCAA Division I in at-bats per strikeout (32.6) last spring.

BEST POWER HITTER: A high school teammate of 2008 No. 1 overall pick Tim Beckham at Griffin (Ga.) High, OF Telvin Nash (3) has plus-plus raw power. He's still recovering from a shoulder injury from football, where the 6-foot-1, 230-pounder played defensive end and tight end.

FASTEST RUNNER: OF Grant Hogue (35) used his well-above-average speed to steal 17 bases at Greeneville.

BEST DEFENSIVE PLAYER: Mier was the best pure shortstop in the draft. He covers a lot of ground and has a plus-plus arm. 3B Jonathan Meyer (3s) has the quickness and arm strength to be a quality defender.

BEST FASTBALL: RHPs B.J. Hyatt (4) and Brandt Walker (8) both can touch 96 mph. Neither had much success in college, but the Astros like their upside if they can develop command.

BEST SECONDARY PITCH: RHP Tanner Bushue's (2) power curveball or LHP Dallas Keuchel's (7) changeup. Bushue is projectable and his 88-90 mph fastball should develop into a plus pitch.

BEST PRO DEBUT: Mier and Martinez.

BEST ATHLETE: Mier also starred in soccer and football (as a wide receiver and defensive back) in high school. Bushue averaged 18.2 points per game in basketball as a high school senior.

MOST INTRIGUING BACKGROUND: Unsigned RHP Raul Rivera's (37) brother Saul pitched in the Nationals bullpen last season. Mier's brother Jessie plays in the Dodgers system. GM Ed Wade's clubs drafted LHP Mike Modica (24) three times (Phillies in 2005, Astros the last two years) before signing him this summer.

CLOSEST TO THE MAJORS: Keuchel, who earned both of Arkansas' victories at the 2009 College World Series, throws four pitches for strikes and gets outs with his sinker and changeup.

BEST LATE-ROUND PICK: Martinez is a decent athlete who consistently puts the barrel on the ball. RHP Mike Schurz (44) overcame Tommy John surgery in 2007 and comes out of the bullpen with a low-90s fastball and a low-80s slider.

THE ONE WHO GOT AWAY: Houston liked RHP Geoff Thomas' (12, Southern Mississippi) fastball and SS Justin Gonzalez's (46, Florida State) bat, but couldn't sign either away from college.

ASSESSMENT: For the second time in two years as scouting director, Bobby Heck addressed an up-the-middle position in the first round (C Jason Castro preceded Mier in 2008). The Astros put more faith in predraft workouts than the industry consensus on players, and it used its top four picks on high schoolers Mier, Bushue, Nash and Meyer.

2008   BONUSES: $6.5 MILLION

The Astros finally found their catcher of the future when they made Jason Castro (1) somewhat of a surprise pick at No. 10 overall. They also restocked a thin system with the likes of RHPs Jordan Lyles (1s) and Ross Seaton (3), and OFs. Jay Austin (2), T.J. Steele (4) and Jon Gaston (7).

GRADE: B

2007   BONUSES: $1.6 MILLION

Houston forfeited its picks in the first two rounds to sign free agents, then failed to sign SS Derek Dietrich (3) and RHP/OF Brett Eibner (4) and RHP Chad Bettis (8), all of whom should be early round choices in 2010. OF Collin DeLome (5) and RHP Kyle Greenwalt (20) are the only things close to prospects from this crop.

GRADE: F

2006   BONUSES: $3.6 MILLION

RHP Bud Norris (6) is the big league club's most promising young starter, and 3B Chris Johnson (4) will have a chance to win a job in spring training. C Max Sapp (1) batted .224 in three seasons before viral meningitis has left his baseball future is in doubt.

GRADE: C

2005   BONUSES: $2.2 MILLION*

OF Brian Bogusevic (1) was drafted and failed as a pitcher, while OF Eli Iorg (1s) drew his release last summer. SS Tommy Manzella (3) could be the Astros' next starting shortstop. C/OF Koby Clemens (8) has exceeded expectations and led the minors with 123 RBIs last summer.

GRADE: F

*Draft analysis by Jim Callis. Numbers in parentheses indicate draft rounds. *Bonuses for 2005 are first 10 rounds only.*

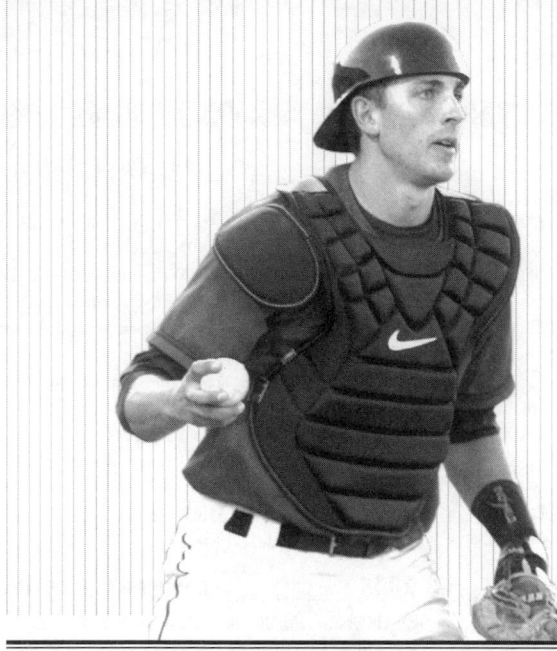

JASON CASTRO, C

Born: June 18, 1987.
Height: 6-3. **Weight:** 210.
Bats: L. **Throws:** R.
Drafted: Stanford, 2008 (1st round).
Signed by: Joe Graham/Bobby Heck.

LARRY GOREN

Castro was the first building block in the Astros' effort to rebuild their farm system after hiring Bobby Heck as scouting director. Mostly a reserve at first base and DH his first two years at Stanford, Castro finished second in the Cape Cod League batting race (.341) in 2007, often playing the outfield in deference to teammate Buster Posey but also displaying his athleticism. He then led Stanford to the College World Series in 2008 as the Cardinal's starting catcher, leading the Pacific-10 Conference with 105 hits. Houston drafted him 10th overall that June and signed him for $2.07 million, the second-largest bonus in franchise history. While some clubs thought Castro was a bit of a reach at No. 10, the Astros took him with the expectation that he'd move quickly through the system and solidify a premium position. So far, so good for Castro, who has established himself as one of the top catching prospects in the game while batting .300/.380/.446 in his first full pro season. After opening 2009 at high Class A Lancaster, he advanced to Double-A Corpus Christi in June, then left the Hooks in August to help Team USA win a gold medal at the World Cup. He also participated in the Futures Game in July, when he homered on a breaking ball from Blue Jays lefty Luis Perez.

Castro has a sound approach at the plate, showing good feel for the strike zone with a knack for staying inside the ball. He makes consistent contact and gets on base by working the count and putting the ball in play to all fields. While he's not a power hitter, he has a solid swing and is able to generate loft. He doesn't show a discernible platoon split, hitting well against both lefties and righties. Castro is solid behind the plate in every regard. He has a solid-average arm and makes accurate throws, recording 2.0-second pop times thanks to his athleticism, quick release and footwork. He threw out 45 percent of basestealers last season. He has soft hands and receives the ball well.

Castro isn't likely to become a big power threat, projecting to have fringe-average to average power and hit 10-15 homers a season. He runs better than most catchers, but he still has below-average speed. He appeared worn down in the Arizona Fall League after his first full pro season. Astros officials noted that he lost about 15 pounds since the beginning of the year, so he'll need to learn to stay stronger throughout the course of a season while catching in the Texas heat.

While Castro doesn't have one overwhelming tool, he's solid in nearly every phase of the game. He profiles as an average to a tick above-average starting catcher in the big leagues, along the lines of a more selective A.J. Pierzynski, who is a similarly built, lefthanded hitting catcher. Castro's future home run power is the biggest variable in his projection. He figures to start 2010 at Triple-A Round Rock but has a chance to reach Houston at some point during the season. He should establish himself as the Astros' catcher by 2011, shoring up a position where the club has seen recent first-round picks (Max Sapp) and No. 1 prospects (J.R. Towles) fizzle.

Year	Club (League)	Class	AVG	G	AB	R	H	2B	3B	HR	RBI	BB	SO	SB	OBP	SLG
2008	Tri-City (NYP)	SS	.275	39	138	10	38	9	0	2	12	22	32	0	.383	.384
2009	Lancaster (CAL)	HiA	.309	56	207	27	64	20	1	7	44	30	41	1	.399	.517
	Corpus Christi (TL)	AA	.293	63	239	38	70	11	1	3	29	25	35	2	.362	.385
MINOR LEAGUE TOTALS			.295	158	584	75	172	40	2	12	85	77	108	3	.380	.432

2 JIOVANNI MIER, SS ✝

BORN: Aug. 26, 1990. **B-T:** R-R. **HT.:** 6-2. **WT.:** 175. **DRAFTED:** HS—Bonita, Calif. 2009 (1st round). **SIGNED BY:** Doug Deutsch.

Mier was the first prep shortstop drafted in 2009, going 21st overall and signing for $1,358,000. He signed quickly and impressed pro scouts with a strong showing in the Rookie-level Appalachian League, where he ranked as the top position prospect. Mier has an advanced feel for the game at the plate and in the field. He has a good eye, works deep counts and shows good pitch recognition. He has a smooth, loose, line-drive stroke with quick hands and solid bat speed. He projects to stay at shortstop with a plus arm, great actions, good hands and above-average range to both sides. He's an average runner, and he'll show faster times from home to first because he gets out of the box quickly. Mier has below-average power, though some think he could eventually hit as many as 15 homers a season because he shows some ability to lift the ball. Shortening his stride has helped his timing at the plate, though on occasion he'll still lunge and get out on his front leg. He needs to improve his basestealing and tone down his aggressiveness on the basepaths. Like many young shortstops, he has a tendency to rush his actions in the field. Though Mier has yet to play full-season ball, he has a higher ceiling than Jason Castro and could be a perennial all-star who provides value in both run creation and prevention. He should start 2010 at low Class A Lexington.

Year	Club (League)	Class	AVG	G	AB	R	H	2B	3B	HR	RBI	BB	SO	SB	OBP	SLG
2009	Greeneville (APP)	R	.276	51	192	32	53	7	6	7	32	30	45	10	.380	.484
MINOR LEAGUE TOTALS			.276	51	192	32	53	7	6	7	32	30	45	10	.380	.484

3 JORDAN LYLES, RHP ✝

BORN: Oct. 19, 1990. **B-T:** R-R. **HT.:** 6-4. **WT.:** 185. **DRAFTED:** HS—Hartsville, S.C., 2009 (1st round supplemental). **SIGNED BY:** J.D. Alleva/Clarence Johns.

Few teams saw Lyles, South Carolina's top prep talent in 2008, as an early round pick. He excelled in a predraft workout for the Astros, who drafted him 38th overall and signed him for $930,000. He justified Houston's faith by finishing second in the South Atlantic League with 167 strikeouts last season. Lyles' fastball sits at 89-91 mph, touches 93-94 and has late life in the zone. He has a lot of confidence in his changeup, which has fade and heavy sink at its best and could be a plus offering down the road. He adds and subtracts from his curveball, throwing it in the mid-70s for an early count strike and burying it at 77-80 mph when he gets ahead. He has clean arm action and repeats his athletic, easy delivery. He hides the ball well behind his back shoulder, adding deception. He has advanced control for his age and keeps hitters off balance by working both sides of the plate. The development of Lyles' breaking balls will determine his ceiling. He didn't have a good one in high school, and his curve is still inconsistent, getting hammered when he leaves it up in the zone. He also added a slider late in the season. The Astros might move Lyles past Lancaster's launching pad and send him to Double-A. He has the repertoire and control to fit in the middle of a big league rotation, and each of his pitches has enough projection for him to become a potential frontline starter.

Year	Club (League)	Class	W	L	ERA	G	GS	CG	SV	IP	H	R	ER	HR	BB	SO	AVG
2008	Greeneville (APP)	R	3	3	3.99	13	13	0	0	50	44	26	22	4	10	64	.228
	Tri-City (NYP)	SS	0	0	6.35	2	2	0	0	6	7	5	4	2	7	4	.292
2009	Lexington (SAL)	LoA	7	11	3.24	26	26	0	0	145	134	56	52	5	38	167	.247
MINOR LEAGUE TOTALS			10	14	3.51	41	41	0	0	200	185	87	78	11	55	235	.243

4 SAMMY GERVACIO, RHP *m ut*

BORN: Jan. 10, 1985. **B-T:** R-R. **HT.:** 6-0. **WT.:** 175. **SIGNED:** Dominican Republic, 2002. **SIGNED BY:** Julio Linares.

Used exclusively as a reliever since signing in 2002, Gervacio has struck out more than a batter per inning at each of his stops in pro ball. He was effective after joining the Astros last August, recording six holds and allowing runs in just four of his 29 outings. Gervacio's best pitch is his slider, a plus pitch in the mid-80s. He trusts his slider and uses it more than his fastball, an 89-93 mph offering that touches 95. Hitters have a difficult time picking up the ball out of his crossfire delivery from a low three-quarters arm slot, making him tough on righthanders. He does a good job of inducing groundballs and has allowed just 30 homers in 448 pro innings. His changeup can be a solid pitch at times, but Gervacio uses it sparingly, leaving him more vulnerable against lefthanders. He throws across his body, but durability isn't as much of a concern with him working out of the bullpen. Gervacio was prepping for the 2010 season with a stint in the Dominican League. Barring a disastrous spring, Gervacio has claimed a middle-relief role in Houston's bullpen. If free agent Jose Valverde doesn't re-sign with the Astros, Gervacio could get an opportunity to close games, though he'll have to prove he can get lefties out with the game on the line.

Year	Club (League)	Class	W	L	ERA	G	GS	CG	SV	IP	H	R	ER	HR	BB	SO	AVG
2003	Astros (DSL)	R	4	0	2.01	24	0	0	6	45	34	13	10	3	14	50	.206
2004	Astros (DSL)	R	1	4	1.92	29	0	0	13	52	30	18	11	2	29	81	.160
2005	Greeneville (APP)	R	3	2	2.67	21	0	0	8	34	24	10	10	1	6	53	.190
	Lexington (SAL)	LoA	1	0	0.96	5	0	0	0	9	4	1	1	0	1	11	.125
2006	Lexington (SAL)	LoA	7	5	2.58	47	0	0	10	84	58	28	24	8	28	89	.197
2007	Salem (CAR)	HiA	1	3	2.44	39	0	0	18	55	42	16	15	1	15	80	.204
	Corpus Christi (TL)	AA	3	2	1.99	13	0	0	0	23	15	7	5	1	11	24	.197
2008	Corpus Christi (TL)	AA	2	5	4.13	47	0	0	5	65	69	36	30	8	26	82	.275
	Round Rock (PCL)	AAA	1	0	2.25	3	0	0	0	8	6	2	2	0	3	14	.207
2009	Round Rock (PCL)	AAA	2	2	4.82	39	0	0	0	52	43	30	28	5	21	58	.223
	Houston (NL)	MAJ	1	1	2.14	29	0	0	0	21	16	5	5	1	8	25	.219
MAJOR LEAGUE TOTALS			1	1	2.14	29	0	0	0	21	16	5	5	1	8	25	.219
MINOR LEAGUE TOTALS			25	23	2.87	267	0	0	60	427	325	161	136	29	154	542	.208

5 CHIA-JEN LO, RHP +

BORN: April 7, 1986. **B-T:** R-R. **HT.:** 5-11. **WT.:** 181. **SIGNED:** Taiwan, 2008.
SIGNED BY: Glen Barker.

The Astros are trying to raise their profile in Asia, and Lo was the first major acquisition of Pacific Rim scouting director Glen Barker. Signed out of Taiwan for $250,000 in November 2008, Lo pitched for his nation in the Beijing Olympics and was on its World Baseball Classic roster but didn't see any game action. He survived Lancaster and reached Double-A in his first pro season. The Astros initially talked about using Lo as a starter but wound up deploying him as a reliever in part because his fastball sits at 93-96 mph when he works out of the bullpen. Both his short curveball and his changeup can be average pitches. Throwing from a high three-quarters slot, he creates deception that causes hitters to see the ball late. Lo has extreme confidence in his fastball, to the point where he sometimes doesn't use his secondary pitches enough. His control needs improvement after he walked 4.6 batters per nine innings in his pro debut. Shoulder tendinitis caused him to miss the last two weeks of May, but he was healthy afterward. Houston thinks Lo could be ready to help its bullpen at some point in 2010, though he'll probably begin the season in Triple-A. If he refines and trusts a second pitch, he could be the Astros' closer of the future.

Year	Club (League)	Class	W	L	ERA	G	GS	CG	SV	IP	H	R	ER	HR	BB	SO	AVG
2009	Lancaster (CAL)	HiA	1	0	1.78	12	0	0	1	25	10	6	5	1	13	36	.120
	Corpus Christi (TL)	AA	0	2	2.31	30	0	0	2	39	30	12	10	1	20	39	.213
MINOR LEAGUE TOTALS			1	2	2.10	42	0	0	3	64	40	18	15	2	33	75	.179

6 ROSS SEATON, RHP +

BORN: Sept. 18, 1989. **B-T:** L-R. **HT.:** 6-4. **WT.:** 213. **DRAFTED:** HS—Houston, 2008 (3rd round supplemental). **SIGNED BY:** Rusty Pendergrass/Mike Burns.

Seaton's velocity and draft stock skyrocketed during his senior high school season in 2008. Teams backed off him because he was a valedictorian strongly committed to Tulane, but the Astros signed the local product for $700,000 as a supplemental third-round pick. He had a solid 2009 season as a teenager in low Class A, but his stuff wasn't as good as it was in high school. At Lexington, Seaton stood out more with his size and control than his stuff. His fastball was down about 3 mph from high school, sitting at 87-91 mph and touching 93. Houston hopes he'll recover velocity after getting acclimated to the long pro season. He also throws an 81-83 mph slider that flashes average tilt, though it's not a true out pitch. Seaton's delivery lacks fluidity and can become mechanical, creating issues with his rhythm and timing. He doesn't fully incorporate his lower half, which he worked on in instructional league. He didn't throw a curveball in high school, but the Astros made him use one in the first half of last season and it was slurvy. His changeup also needs work. Seaton wasn't as good as advertised in his first full pro season, which isn't unusual for a high schooler pitching every fifth day for the first time. Houston believes smoothing out his mechanics will help him in 2010, when he'll open the season in high Class A.

Year	Club (League)	Class	W	L	ERA	G	GS	CG	SV	IP	H	R	ER	HR	BB	SO	AVG
2008	Greeneville (APP)	R	0	0	13.50	3	3	0	0	4	8	7	6	1	2	4	.381
2009	Lexington (SAL)	LoA	8	10	3.29	24	24	1	0	137	137	69	50	11	39	88	.261
MINOR LEAGUE TOTALS			8	10	3.58	27	27	1	0	141	145	76	56	12	41	92	.266

7 TANNER BUSHUE, RHP ✛

BORN: June 20, 1991. **B-T:** R-R. **HT.:** 6-4. **WT.:** 180. **DRAFTED:** HS—Farina, Ill., 2009 (2nd round). **SIGNED BY:** Troy Hoerner.

After missing most of his high school junior season with a sprained right knee, Bushue blossomed into Illinois' top prep prospect in 2009. A strong predraft workout sold the Astros, who took him in the second round and signed him for $530,000. Bushue shows a good feel for pitching and the ability to work both sides of the plate. His fastball currently sits at 88-90 mph, but he's so athletic—he was a high school basketball standout—and generates velocity with such little effort that it's easy to project his heater as a future plus pitch. He already touches 94 mph on occasion, and his athleticism also should allow him to repeat his delivery and throw strikes. He also shows the ability to spin a breaking ball, with the makings of a power curveball. Bushue needs to stay healthy so he can soak up more experience. He hasn't had any arm problems, but he had the knee injury in 2008 and had his pro debut ended by stress fractures in his lower back in July. That also limited him in instructional league. He shows aptitude for a changeup, but it's still a work in progress. He also throws a slider, though it's not as promising as his curve. The Astros expect Bushue to be healthy and able to handle a full season of starts in low Class A in 2010. He's just beginning to scratch the surface of his ability and has the potential to develop the best stuff among Houston's starting pitching prospects.

Year	Club (League)	Class	W	L	ERA	G	GS	CG	SV	IP	H	R	ER	HR	BB	SO	AVG
2009	Astros (GCL)	R	1	0	2.42	5	5	0	0	22	18	8	6	2	5	19	.220
MINOR LEAGUE TOTALS			1	0	2.42	5	5	0	0	22	18	8	6	2	5	19	.220

8 JAY AUSTIN, OF ⌿

BORN: Aug. 10, 1990. **B-T:** L-L. **HT.:** 5-11. **WT.:** 170. **DRAFTED:** HS—Atlanta, 2008 (2nd round). **SIGNED BY:** Lincoln Martin/Clarence Johns.

Some Astros officials thought Austin might begin 2009 in extended spring training after he struggled mightily in his pro debut. Instead, he broke camp with Lexington and was the youngest everyday player in the South Atlantic League. After he batted .245/.296/.308 in the first half, he hit .291/.346/.418 after the all-star break. Austin is the best athlete in the system. He has well-above-average pure speed, which gives him the potential to be a quality basestealer and center fielder. At the plate, he has a compact stroke and good bat speed. Austin's bat is a major question mark, as he has issues with pitch recognition and doesn't adjust against breaking balls. His power is well-below-average, and he lacks the strength and loft in his swing to project that he'll add much more. His speed doesn't play as well in game situations because he doesn't get out of the box quickly or have much feel for stealing bases or getting good jumps and routes in the outfield. He has a fringe-average arm. Austin will begin 2010 in high Class A, where he'll try to build on his second-half success. He has enticing tools, but he has a lot of refining to do if he's going to be more than an extra outfielder in the major leagues.

Year	Club (League)	Class	AVG	G	AB	R	H	2B	3B	HR	RBI	BB	SO	SB	OBP	SLG
2008	Greeneville (APP)	R	.198	55	212	31	42	4	2	0	14	19	69	14	.277	.236
2009	Lexington (SAL)	LoA	.267	101	397	49	106	22	6	1	33	31	78	23	.320	.360
MINOR LEAGUE TOTALS			.243	156	609	80	148	26	8	1	47	50	147	37	.305	.317

9 JON GASTON, OF

BORN: Oct. 13, 1986. **B-T:** L-R. **HT.:** 6-0. **WT.:** 210. **DRAFTED:** Arizona, 2008 (7th round). **SIGNED BY:** Mark Ross.

One year after hitting .193 with two homers in his first taste of pro ball, Gaston took advantage of the hitter-friendly winds at Lancaster's Clear Channel Stadium. He hit .308/.397/.692 at home en route to leading the minors in runs (119), homers (35), extra-base hits (81) and total bases (310). He continued to show power in the Arizona Fall League after the season. The Astros helped Gaston tap into his power by getting his hands deeper and into a better position to drive the ball. When teams pitch around him, he's willing to take a walk. Though his bat will have to carry him, he has more athleticism than his stocky build might indicate, with fringe-average speed and a solid arm. Gaston uses a big-load mechanism, angling his bat to get into a launch position and tilting his back side to turn and drive the ball. It's an all-or-nothing approach, which is why he struck out 164 times, and more advanced pitchers in less favorable hitting environments could exploit the holes in his swing. He'll have to work to become an adequate defender on an outfield corner, and if he loses a step he might be destined for first base. In Double-A, Gaston will get the chance to prove his 2009 numbers weren't entirely a product of Lancaster. If he does, he'll be on the fast track to Houston.

Year	Club (League)	Class	AVG	G	AB	R	H	2B	3B	HR	RBI	BB	SO	SB	OBP	SLG
2008	Tri-City (NYP)	SS	.193	62	207	18	40	11	1	2	25	25	65	0	.292	.285
2009	Lancaster (CAL)	HiA	.278	139	518	119	144	31	15	35	100	71	164	14	.367	.598
MINOR LEAGUE TOTALS			.254	201	725	137	184	42	16	37	125	96	229	14	.346	.509

10 T.J. STEELE, OF

BORN: Sept. 21, 1986. **B-T:** R-R. **HT.:** 6-3. **WT.:** 185. **DRAFTED:** Arizona, 2008 (4th round). **SIGNED BY:** Mark Ross.

He outperformed former college teammate Jon Gaston at Arizona and in 2009 at Lancaster, but Steele couldn't stay in the JetHawks' lineup. He injured his hamstring in spring training and missed the first two weeks of the season, then appeared in just 50 games because he kept tweaking the muscle. Steele is one of the toolsiest players in the system. He's an excellent defensive center fielder with plus speed and arm strength. He has above-average bat speed and average raw power, and there's also projection remaining in his athletic frame. He shows ability to put backspin on a ball and has cut down on his propensity to swing and miss since college. Despite Steele's tools and college pedigree, he remains raw and his offensive game is still a question mark. He lacks pitch recognition and is too impatient at the plate to get on base at a high clip. He has drawn just 15 walks in 90 pro games. He hasn't shown much home run power yet, partly because he doesn't get himself into hitter's counts. Steele could become an everyday center fielder if he becomes more selective at the plate. That's his top priority when he advances to Double-A in 2010.

Year	Club (League)	Class	AVG	G	AB	R	H	2B	3B	HR	RBI	BB	SO	SB	OBP	SLG
2008	Tri-City (NYP)	SS	.283	40	159	18	45	8	1	3	21	6	51	6	.320	.403
2009	Lancaster (CAL)	HiA	.345	50	194	41	67	11	8	5	40	9	40	8	.385	.562
MINOR LEAGUE TOTALS			.317	90	353	59	112	19	9	8	61	15	91	14	.355	.490

11 TOMMY MANZELLA, SS

BORN: April 16, 1983. **B-T:** R-R. **Ht.:** 6-2. **Wt.:** 200. Drafted: Tulane, 2005 (3rd round). Signed by: Mike Rosamond.

Manzella has stood out with his glove ever since the Astros made him a third-round pick in 2005, but it took him four years to climb to the majors. A strong second half in Triple-A earned him a September callup, though he didn't get much of a chance to audition for the departing Miguel Tejada's shortstop job. Manzella is a defense-first shortstop who positions himself well and shows good instincts. His hands and feet work well together and he has a strong, accurate arm. Manzella isn't much of a threat at the plate, where he's mostly a spray hitter with a little bit of gap power. He makes decent contact but doesn't draw many walks. An average runner, he's not much of a threat on the basepaths either. He's somewhat similar to Adam Everett, who spent five seasons in the minors before becoming Houston's starting shortstop. Offering more offense but not quite the same defense as Everett, Manzella could replace Tejada in 2010. He'll bat toward the bottom of the order and have to prove he can hit enough to warrant regular playing time.

Year	Club (League)	Class	AVG	G	AB	R	H	2B	3B	HR	RBI	BB	SO	SB	OBP	SLG
2005	Tri-City (NYP)	SS	.232	53	220	24	51	6	4	0	18	9	39	5	.260	.295
2006	Lexington (SAL)	LoA	.275	99	338	50	93	22	1	7	43	33	80	16	.340	.408
2007	Salem (CAR)	HiA	.238	57	223	28	53	13	0	0	24	19	30	5	.305	.296
	Corpus Christi (TL)	AA	.289	64	228	35	66	12	3	1	15	19	40	10	.343	.382
2008	Corpus Christi (TL)	AA	.299	54	224	27	67	11	5	4	34	17	35	4	.346	.446
	Round Rock (PCL)	AAA	.219	61	228	19	50	15	1	0	15	17	39	0	.273	.294
2009	Round Rock (PCL)	AAA	.289	133	530	68	153	31	5	9	56	40	99	12	.339	.417
	Houston (NL)	MAJ	.200	7	5	0	1	0	0	0	0	0	4	0	.200	.200
MAJOR LEAGUE TOTALS			.200	7	5	0	1	0	0	0	0	0	4	0	.200	.200
MINOR LEAGUE TOTALS			.268	521	1991	251	533	110	19	21	205	154	362	52	.321	.374

12 DANNY MESZAROS, RHP

BORN: Sept. 6, 1985. **B-T:** R-R. **Ht.:** 6-0. **Wt.:** 170. Drafted: Charleston, 2008 (48th round). **SIGNED BY:** J.D. Alleva.

After missing the 2007 season rehabbing from shoulder surgery, Meszaros posted a 9.63 ERA in seven starts for Charleston as a redshirt junior. Area scout J.D. Alleva pushed for the Astros to draft Meszaros based on what he saw prior to his injury. Houston took him in the 48th round and signed him for $25,000 in July after he performed well in the Cape Cod League. Meszaros commands his fastball to both sides of the plate, sitting at 91-93 mph and touching 94. He throws strikes with an above-average curveball ranging from 75-79 mph with good depth and bite. He mixes in an occasional 81-84 mph changeup, though it's more of a show-me pitch to get hitters off his fastball and breaking ball. Meszaros has a compact, repeatable delivery and throws from a high three-quarters to overhand slot. He learned to mix his offspeed offerings better upon his promotion to Double-A last May. Durability is a concern given his injury history, though it's not a major issue in the bullpen. Meszaros doesn't have a high ceiling, but he figures to fit into the Astros' bullpen picture, possibly sometime this year.

Year	Club (League)	Class	W	L	ERA	G	GS	CG	SV	IP	H	R	ER	HR	BB	SO	AVG
2008	Tri-City (NYP)	SS	1	3	4.44	12	0	0	1	26	21	14	13	2	8	46	.212
2009	Lexington (SAL)	LoA	0	0	0.71	14	0	0	9	13	5	1	1	0	3	19	.116
	Corpus Christi (TL)	AA	3	3	3.36	37	0	0	1	62	63	25	23	7	17	48	.268
MINOR LEAGUE TOTALS			4	6	3.31	63	0	0	11	101	89	40	37	9	28	113	.236

13 J.B. SHUCK, OF

BORN: June 18, 1987. B-T: L-L. Ht.: 5-11. Wt.: 185. Drafted: Ohio State, 2008 (6th round). Signed by: Nick Venuto.

Shuck was a two-way standout at Ohio State, making the all-Big 10 Conference team as both an outfielder and a pitcher. Now a full-time hitter, he ranked second in the minors with 175 hits in 2009, his first full pro season. Playing in Lancaster helped, but he's a talented hitter who does an excellent job controlling the strike zone. His swing has a short, flat path to the ball, spraying liners to all fields. He has limited power and hit just one homer despite playing in an extreme hitter's park. More advanced pitchers won't hesitate to challenge him if he doesn't develop more pop. He hit markedly better against righthanders last year, so he'll have to prove that he can hit southpaws. Shuck has plus-plus speed under way, but it doesn't play quite that well in the outfield or on the basepaths. He needs to improve his jumps and leads to become a basestealing threat. Shuck could be an average defender in center field, but his routes to the ball need work and he shows better instincts in left field. Though he pitched in college, he has a fringe-average arm. He'll head to Double-A in 2010.

Year	Club (League)	Class	AVG	G	AB	R	H	2B	3B	HR	RBI	BB	SO	SB	OBP	SLG
2008	Tri-City (NYP)	SS	.300	65	263	51	79	12	5	4	24	35	34	8	.385	.430
2009	Lancaster (CAL)	HiA	.315	133	556	98	175	30	11	1	36	64	55	18	.389	.414
MINOR LEAGUE TOTALS			.310	198	819	149	254	42	16	5	60	99	89	26	.388	.419

14 FERNANDO ABAD, LHP

BORN: Dec. 17, 1985. B-T: L-L. Ht.: 6-2. Wt.: 170. Signed: Dominican Republic, 2002. **SIGNED BY:** Julio Linares/Adriano Rodriguez.

Abad's career started slowly, as he spent four seasons in the Rookie-level Dominican Summer League and didn't advance to full-season ball until he was 22 and in his sixth year as a pro. He improved his stock so much in 2009 that the Astros added him to their 40-man roster after the season and plan to make him a starter this year. Though he pitched almost exclusively in relief last year, many of his appearances lasted multiple innings. Abad pitches at 90-91 mph and touches 93-94 with his fastball. He complements his heater with a heavy, running changeup and a solid curveball. Abad's crossfire delivery and his short, quick arm stroke give him some deception, making it difficult for hitters to pick up the ball out of his hand. Abad pitched well as a starter in the Dominican League and will open 2010 in Double-A, where he made three short if solid starts at the end of last season.

Year	Club (League)	Class	W	L	ERA	G	GS	CG	SV	IP	H	R	ER	HR	BB	SO	AVG
2003	Astros (DSL)	R	6	2	1.61	14	14	0	0	78	55	24	14	0	7	87	.190
2004	Astros (DSL)	R	4	1	1.29	8	8	0	0	42	24	10	6	0	7	39	.155
2005	Astros (DSL)	R	0	0	3.00	1	1	0	0	3	4	2	1	0	0	2	.308
2006	Astros (DSL)	R	5	2	1.32	15	11	0	1	61	50	18	9	1	7	64	.221
2007	Greeneville (APP)	R	6	4	4.14	17	4	0	1	50	47	29	23	6	12	54	.246
	Tri-City (NYP)	SS	0	0	6.00	2	0	0	0	3	2	2	2	0	2	5	.182
2008	Lexington (SAL)	LoA	2	7	3.30	45	0	0	3	76	78	31	28	9	13	94	.259
2009	Lancaster (CAL)	HiA	4	6	4.14	41	0	0	6	83	78	42	38	8	8	79	.252
	Corpus Christi (TL)	AA	0	1	3.21	3	3	0	0	14	12	7	5	1	3	13	.222
MINOR LEAGUE TOTALS			27	23	2.76	146	41	0	11	411	350	165	126	25	59	437	.226

15 MATT NEVAREZ, RHP

BORN: Feb. 26, 1987. B-T: R-R. Ht.: 6-4. Wt.: 220. Drafted: HS—San Fernando, Calif., 2005 (10th round). **SIGNED BY:** Todd Guggiana (Rangers).

Though Nevarez was old for low Class A as a 22-year-old in 2009, his power arm intrigued the Astros enough that they asked for him in the Ivan Rodriguez trade that also yielded second-base prospect Jose Vallejo last August. After the deal, Nevarez struck out 13 in eight scoreless innings. A good athlete for his size, he throws 93-95 mph fastballs on a steep downhill plane. His best secondary pitch is a short 82-83 mph slider, and he'll mix in an occasional changeup. Nevarez has a compact delivery, but there's some stiffness and effort involved. His control improved significantly in 2009 but remains below-average. Added to the 40-man roster in November, he could be a useful big league reliever if he improves his slider. He'll tackle high Class A in 2010.

HOUSTON ASTROS

Year	Club (League)	Class	W	L	ERA	G	GS	CG	SV	IP	H	R	ER	HR	BB	SO	AVG
2005	Rangers (AZL)	R	2	1	1.61	10	3	0	0	28	18	7	5	1	13	24	.184
2006	Rangers (AZL)	R	0	0	9.00	1	0	0	0	1	2	1	1	1	0	2	.400
2007	Did not play--Injured																
2008	Spokane (NWL)	SS	4	2	4.36	16	7	0	0	43	39	26	21	3	43	50	.238
2009	Hickory (SAL)	LoA	1	4	2.83	34	0	0	9	35	22	14	11	1	15	50	.177
	Lexington (SAL)	LoA	1	0	0.00	8	0	0	4	8	3	0	0	0	0	13	.103
MINOR LEAGUE TOTALS			8	7	2.96	69	10	0	13	116	84	48	38	6	71	139	.200

16 CHRIS JOHNSON, 3B

BORN: Oct. 1, 1984. B-T: R-R. Ht.: 6-3. Wt.: 220. Drafted: Stetson, 2006 (4th round). **SIGNED BY:** Jon Bunnell.

Though Johnson was one of the most big league-ready prospects in the system and the Astros got little production from their third basemen, he didn't get much of a chance to show what he could do. An errant pitch broke his hand in April, costing him a month on the disabled list, and he never got going upon his return. The son of former big leaguer and current Red Sox first-base coach Ron Johnson, Chris shows flashes of ability to hit for average and power, but he chases too many pitches and doesn't work into enough hitter's counts or draw enough walks. He has tinkered with his stance, trying to find the best approach, but tends to become too pull-oriented. At third base, Johnson has soft hands and a strong arm. He needs to work on his footwork and agility, particularly his lateral movement. He has a thick lower half and below-average speed. Houston's third-base situation is still wide open, so Johnson could win the job if he plays well in spring training. He'll have to show more plate discipline to do so.

Year	Club (League)	Class	AVG	G	AB	R	H	2B	3B	HR	RBI	BB	SO	SB	OBP	SLG
2006	Tri-City (NYP)	SS	.212	60	222	18	47	7	1	1	29	11	35	7	.251	.266
2007	Lexington (SAL)	LoA	.259	64	255	37	66	14	0	8	44	17	38	3	.304	.408
	Salem (CAR)	HiA	.263	60	224	24	59	11	0	6	38	8	41	1	.292	.393
2008	Corpus Christi (TL)	AA	.324	84	330	43	107	24	0	12	58	20	61	5	.364	.506
	Round Rock (PCL)	AAA	.218	30	101	10	22	2	1	1	9	5	25	0	.252	.287
2009	Lancaster (CAL)	HiA	.438	4	16	5	7	5	0	0	6	1	3	0	.471	.750
	Round Rock (PCL)	AAA	.281	104	384	48	108	20	5	13	42	21	90	2	.323	.461
	Houston (NL)	MAJ	.091	11	22	1	2	0	0	0	1	1	6	0	.130	.091
MAJOR LEAGUE TOTALS			.091	11	22	1	2	0	0	0	1	1	6	0	.130	.091
MINOR LEAGUE TOTALS			.272	406	1532	185	416	83	7	41	226	83	293	18	.311	.415

17 TELVIN NASH, OF

BORN: Feb. 20, 1991. B-T: R-R. Ht.: 6-1. Wt.: 230. Drafted: HS—Griffin, Ga., 2009 (3rd round). **SIGNED BY:** Lincoln Martin.

Nash jumped on to the Astros' radar as a junior at Griffin (Ga.) High in 2008, when he played with No. 1 overall pick Tim Beckham. Houston drafted Nash in the third round a year later, signing him for $330,300. He has imposing size and strength, and he's a good athlete for a 6-foot-1, 230-pounder. His strength and leverage help him generate plus-plus raw power, as he can hit the ball out to all fields. Pitchers in the Rookie-level Gulf Coast League were able to exploit Nash's aggressiveness in his pro debut. He swings and misses quite a bit and chases too many pitches out of the strike zone. Nash's defensive value is already slim, as he's limited to an outfield corner and might end up moving to first base. A football-related shoulder injury relegated him to left field in his debut. He has a funky throwing motion, but he could have an average arm and possibly shift to right field when he's fully healthy. His below-average speed limits his range, and he still needs to work on getting better jumps off the bat. Nash lacks polish in all phases of the game, so he might open 2010 in extended spring rather than low Class A.

Year	Club (League)	Class	AVG	G	AB	R	H	2B	3B	HR	RBI	BB	SO	SB	OBP	SLG
2009	Astros (GCL)	R	.218	40	142	15	31	10	1	1	20	12	45	1	.280	.324
MINOR LEAGUE TOTALS			.218	40	142	15	31	10	1	1	20	12	45	1	.280	.324

18 JONATHAN MEYER, 3B

BORN: Nov. 1, 1990. B-T: R-R. Ht.: 6-1. Wt.: 195. Drafted: HS—Simi Valley, Calif., 2009 (3rd round supplemental). **SIGNED BY:** Tim Costic.

A natural righthanded hitter, Meyer took up switch-hitting prior to his senior year in high school. After the Astros signed him for $274,500 as a supplemental third-round pick last June, he moved from shortstop to third base and returned to hitting exclusively righthanded. He struggled mightily in his pro debut and struck out excessively, looking especially vulnerable against breaking balls from righties. Meyer does have good bat speed, strong hands and patience, as he led the Appalachian League with 36 walks. He's more of a gap hitter than a significant power threat. Meyer is an instinctive player with good reactions and first-step quickness at third base. He has below-average speed but moves well laterally, goes back well on foul balls down the line and profiles as an above-average defender with a plus arm. Some scouts believe he has the tools to move behind the plate, but the Astros have no such plans for now. They hope his bat will catch up to his glove this year in low Class A.

Year	Club (League)	Class	AVG	G	AB	R	H	2B	3B	HR	RBI	BB	SO	SB	OBP	SLG
2009	Greeneville (APP)	R	.190	62	221	27	42	9	3	3	27	36	69	1	.301	.299
MINOR LEAGUE TOTALS			.190	62	221	27	42	9	3	3	27	36	69	1	.301	.299

19 ARCENIO LEON, RHP

BORN: Sept. 22, 1986. B-T: R-R. Ht.: 6-1. Wt.: 162. Signed: Venezuela, 2005. **SIGNED BY:** Andres Reiner/ Orlando Fernandez.

Signed out of Venezuela at age 18, Leon spent two summers in the Rookie-level Venezuelan Summer League and two more in the Appalachian League. When he finally made it to low Class A in 2009, he showed perhaps the best pure stuff among Astros farmhands. He sits at 93-95 mph with his fastball, topping out at 96. He mixes in a slider that can be an electric pitch at 86-88 mph, a swing-and-miss offering with sharp, late break and depth. As good as Leon's stuff is, his control prevents him from having success. He struggles to throw strikes, often failing to come close to the zone as he struggles to repeat his delivery. Leon often has to dial his fastball down just to get the ball over the plate, and he gets behind in the count so often that he's unable to use his slider as a put-away pitch. If he ever can harness his control, Leon has the potential to be an excellent reliever. That's a fairly sizable "if," however. He may need to repeat another level again and return to Lexington this season.

Year	Club (League)	Class	W	L	ERA	G	GS	CG	SV	IP	H	R	ER	HR	BB	SO	AVG
2005	Astros (VSL)	R	3	1	1.42	20	0	0	8	32	17	5	5	1	16	16	.172
2006	Astros (VSL)	R	0	5	5.87	19	0	0	5	23	26	22	15	0	14	14	.286
2007	Greeneville (APP)	R	0	7	4.67	15	9	0	0	54	56	37	28	1	27	43	.267
2008	Greeneville (APP)	R	3	1	3.33	15	2	0	0	49	55	34	18	2	19	42	.285
2009	Lexington (SAL)	LoA	4	2	5.86	41	4	0	0	71	82	53	46	6	49	52	.287
MINOR LEAGUE TOTALS			10	16	4.42	110	15	0	13	228	236	151	112	10	125	167	.268

20 KOBY CLEMENS, C/OF

BORN: Dec. 4, 1986. B-T: R-R. Ht.: 5-11. Wt.: 193. Drafted: HS—Houston, 2005 (8th round). **SIGNED BY:** Rusty Pendergrass.

When Houston made Clemens a surprise eighth-round pick in 2005, it was as much to persuade his father Roger to extend his career with the Astros than it was a belief that Koby might one day play in the big leagues. Clemens has exceeded expectations and had the best year of his career in 2009, leading the minors in RBIs (123) while ranking second in extra-base hits (73) and slugging (.620), third in doubles (45) and fourth in batting (.341). He was repeating high Class A and benefited from playing at the launching pad in Lancaster, but he also performed well on the road in the California League. Clemens made strides at the plate last season, shortening his actions in his hitting approach. He did a better job keeping his head still and maintaining a stronger foundation underneath him. He's adept at working the right-center field gap and handles pitches on the outer half well. Despite his gaudy numbers, he projects more as a doubles hitter with a chance for average power in the future. Clemens' chances of reaching Houston would be better if he weren't a well-below-average catcher. He threw out just 26 percent of basestealers in 2009, allowing 72 steals and 19 passed balls in 71 games. He also spent time in left field, where he's also below-average. He played third base in his first three pro seasons, but lacked range and consistency there. He does have arm strength. Headed for Double-A, Clemens will have to prove his 2009 performance was more than a Cal League aberration. The Astros may move him off catcher, which could enhance the development of his bat.

Year	Club (League)	Class	AVG	G	AB	R	H	2B	3B	HR	RBI	BB	SO	SB	OBP	SLG
2005	Greeneville (APP)	R	.297	33	111	14	33	8	0	4	17	18	26	4	.398	.477
	Tri-City (NYP)	SS	.281	9	32	3	9	1	2	0	6	4	5	1	.361	.438
2006	Lexington (SAL)	LoA	.229	91	306	40	70	19	1	5	39	32	67	2	.313	.346
2007	Lexington (SAL)	LoA	.252	115	413	65	104	21	0	15	56	53	112	8	.344	.412
2008	Salem (CAR)	HiA	.268	109	388	54	104	29	5	7	52	61	99	1	.369	.423
2009	Corpus Christi (TL)	AA	.235	5	17	2	4	0	0	0	2	3	2	0	.333	.235
	Lancaster (CAL)	HiA	.345	116	423	74	146	45	6	22	121	51	109	4	.419	.636
MINOR LEAGUE TOTALS			.278	478	1690	252	470	123	14	53	293	222	420	20	.367	.462

21 BRIAN BOGUSEVIC, OF

BORN: Feb. 18, 1984. B-T: L-L. Ht.: 6-3. Wt.: 215. Drafted: Tulane, 2005 (1st round). **SIGNED BY:** Mike Rosamond.

Drafted 24th overall and paid a $1.375 million bonus in 2005 as a lefthander, Bogusevic never could overcome command issues and posted a 5.05 ERA in four seasons. A two-way star at Tulane, he made a full-time switch to the outfield in July 2008 at the Astros' behest. He has responded with solid results, showing a quick stroke and solid knowledge of the strike zone. He has good size and is adept at driving the ball to the opposite field. He'll need to learn how to pull the ball for power with more regularity. Bogusevic's transition to the outfield was relatively easy. He opened 2009 in center field, though he spent most of his time in left field as the season progressed. His solid speed and plus arm could make him an above-average defender on an outfield corner, but he'll have to hit more to have value there. He shows sharp instincts on the basepaths, both for stealing bases and going first to third. Bogusevic should return to Triple-A in 2010, when he'll try to show he has enough power to warrant a big league promotion.

Year	Club (League)	Class	W	L	ERA	G	GS	CG	SV	IP	H	R	ER	HR	BB	SO	AVG
2005	Tri-City (NYP)	SS	0	2	7.59	13	0	0	3	21	30	20	18	2	9	17	.316
2006	Tri-City (NYP)	SS	0	0	4.09	3	3	0	0	11	10	8	5	1	5	6	.233
	Lexington (SAL)	LoA	2	5	4.73	17	17	0	0	70	76	44	37	6	24	60	.274
2007	Salem (CAR)	HiA	9	7	4.01	21	21	1	0	114	133	57	51	7	39	91	.296
	Corpus Christi (TL)	AA	1	1	7.40	6	6	0	0	24	29	21	20	1	14	17	.296
2008	Corpus Christi (TL)	AA	2	6	5.50	17	17	0	0	88	94	56	54	15	32	34	.275
MINOR LEAGUE TOTALS			14	21	5.05	77	64	1	3	330	372	206	185	32	123	225	.285

Year	Club (League)	Class	AVG	G	AB	R	H	2B	3B	HR	RBI	BB	SO	SB	OBP	SLG
2007	Corpus Christi (TL)	AA	.500	2	2	0	1	0	0	0	0	0	0	0	.500	.500
2008	Salem (CAR)	HiA	.217	8	23	4	5	2	0	1	6	4	1	1	.357	.435
	Corpus Christi (TL)	AA	.371	42	124	21	46	10	2	3	20	16	24	8	.447	.556
2009	Round Rock (PCL)	AAA	.271	138	520	68	141	25	3	6	53	53	118	22	.342	.365
MINOR LEAGUE TOTALS			.288	190	669	93	193	37	5	10	79	73	143	31	.363	.404

22 WILTON LOPEZ, RHP

BORN: July 19, 1983. B-T: R-R. Ht.: 6-0. Wt.: 200. Signed: Nicaragua, 2002. Signed by: Edgar Rodriguez (Yankees).

Originally signed by the Yankees, Lopez pitched sparingly before being placed on the voluntarily retired list prior to the 2005 season. Reinstated and released by the Yankees before the 2007 season, he then signed with the Padres. Claimed off waivers by the Astros last April, he made his major league debut in August and stayed in Houston the rest of the year, though he didn't quite look big league ready. Lopez shows good command of a lively low-90s sinker, which he leans on heavily to get grounders. He throws a solid 82-84 mph changeup but lacks a reliable breaking ball. His 82-84 mph slider is a fringy pitch. Lopez also doesn't miss many bats, which limits his ceiling to a possible back-of-the-rotation starter. After getting additional work in the Arizona Fall League, he's ticketed for Triple-A in 2010, though he could win a big league job out of spring training.

Year	Club (League)	Class	W	L	ERA	G	GS	CG	SV	IP	H	R	ER	HR	BB	SO	AVG
2004	Tampa (FSL)	HiA	0	0	4.50	1	0	0	0	2	2	1	1	0	1	2	.250
	Battle Creek (MWL)	LoA	0	1	0.00	2	0	0	0	2	4	5	0	0	1	2	.444
	Staten Island (NYP)	SS	0	0	12.00	2	0	0	0	3	5	5	4	2	1	2	.357
	Yankees (GCL)	R	1	0	0.00	4	0	0	1	6	2	0	0	0	0	6	.100
2005	Did Not Play																
2006	Did Not Play																
2007	Fort Wayne (MWL)	LoA	1	0	3.30	22	0	0	0	30	34	11	11	2	2	17	.291
	Lake Elsinore (CAL)	HiA	2	1	6.10	22	0	0	3	21	35	16	14	3	1	19	.372
2008	Portland (PCL)	AAA	0	0	9.00	1	0	0	0	1	1	1	1	0	2	1	.250
	San Antonio (TL)	AA	0	2	4.93	27	0	0	0	38	41	21	21	2	9	24	.272
	Lake Elsinore (CAL)	HiA	2	1	2.64	30	0	0	12	31	34	10	9	0	4	26	.283
2009	Corpus Christi (TL)	AA	4	5	4.73	29	15	1	0	110	133	62	58	8	13	69	.297
	Houston (NL)	MAJ	0	2	8.38	8	2	0	0	19	32	21	18	4	8	9	.386
MAJOR LEAGUE TOTALS			0	2	8.38	8	2	0	0	19	32	21	18	4	8	9	.386
MINOR LEAGUE TOTALS			10	10	4.40	140	15	1	16	243	291	132	119	17	34	168	.295

23 EVAN ENGLEBROOK, RHP

BORN: April 28, 1982. B-T: R-R. Ht.: 6-8. Wt.: 225. Drafted: Shippensburg (Pa.), 2004 (8th round). Signed by: Nick Venuto.

Taller pitchers sometimes take longer to develop, and that has been the case with Englebrook, an eighth-round pick out of NCAA Division II Shippensburg in 2004. He throws in the mid-90s and tops out at 97 mph. Despite his velocity, he's more of a groundball guy than a strikeout pitcher. Englebrook's fastball is his only above-average pitch. His short slider doesn't miss bats, and he tends to get underneath the ball, causing his stuff to flatten out. He started pitching exclusively out of the stretch midway through 2008, as the Astros shortened up his leg kick to simplify his mechanics and help him repeat his delivery. His height and high three-quarters arm slot give him good downhill angle toward the plate. After missing the last month of the 2008 season with a shoulder injury, he stayed healthy last season. Though he got hammered in the Arizona Fall League, the Astros still believe he could help them in the near future. After winning a spot on the 40-man roster in November, he'll probably open 2010 in Triple-A.

Year	Club (League)	Class	W	L	ERA	G	GS	CG	SV	IP	H	R	ER	HR	BB	SO	AVG
2004	Tri-City (NYP)	SS	2	4	3.94	14	14	0	0	62	58	30	27	5	28	71	.260
2005	Lexington (SAL)	LoA	8	6	4.32	30	17	0	0	115	103	69	55	10	65	101	.238
2006	Salem (CAR)	HiA	9	4	3.31	36	10	0	0	109	95	46	40	6	46	82	.235
2007	Corpus Christi (TL)	AA	1	3	9.15	11	0	0	0	20	27	22	20	2	18	14	.329
	Salem (CAR)	HiA	4	3	1.90	21	3	0	1	52	47	16	11	1	14	40	.242
2008	Corpus Christi (TL)	AA	2	2	3.90	34	2	0	4	55	54	26	24	3	25	33	.257
2009	Round Rock (PCL)	AAA	1	1	6.97	9	0	0	0	10	14	8	8	1	3	8	.326
	Corpus Christi (TL)	AA	2	0	3.16	21	0	0	9	26	19	12	9	2	9	16	.207
MINOR LEAGUE TOTALS			29	23	3.90	176	46	0	14	448	417	229	194	30	208	365	.248

24 DALLAS KEUCHEL, LHP

BORN: Jan. 1, 1988. B-T: L-L. Ht.: 6-3. Wt.: 200. Drafted: Arkansas, 2009 (7th round). **SIGNED BY:** Jim Stevenson.

The Astros believe Keuchel could be one of the steals of the 2009 draft, a seventh-rounder signed for $150,000. He succeeded throughout his college career at Arkansas and in the Cape Cod League, and he earned both of the Razorbacks' victories at last year's College World Series. His polish was evident in his pro debut, as he cruised through the short-season New York-Penn League. Keuchel is a finesse lefthander who relies on his control, mixing locations and pitch sequences to keep hitters off balance. He pitched in the high 80s and touched 91 mph at Arkansas, though after a long college season he worked more at 85-88 in pro ball. His fastball has sink and he commands it well. His changeup is his bread and butter, a plus offering that keeps hitters off his fastball. His curveball is a fringe-average pitch, and he also toys around with a slider that he can add and subtract from. Keuchel's stuff gives him little margin for error, but his command, feel and poise could make him a back-of-the-rotation starter. He could reach high Class A at some point in 2010 and could be the first 2009 Astros draftee to reach the majors.

Year	Club (League)	Class	W	L	ERA	G	GS	CG	SV	IP	H	R	ER	HR	BB	SO	AVG
2009	Tri-City (NYP)	SS	2	3	2.70	11	10	0	0	57	52	18	17	2	9	44	.240
MINOR LEAGUE TOTALS			2	3	2.70	11	10	0	0	57	52	18	17	2	9	44	.240

25 COLLIN DeLOME, OF

BORN: Dec. 18, 1985. B-T: L-R. Ht.: 6-2. Wt.: 195. Drafted: Lamar, 2007 (5th round). **SIGNED BY:** Rusty Pendergrass.

The Astros had one of the worst drafts in recent baseball history in 2007. They gave up their first two choices as free agent compensation and failed to sign their third- or fourth-rounders. That left fifth-rounder DeLome as the earliest pick they signed. He's athletic and has an intriguing combination of above-average raw power and speed, yet he has an unrefined offensive approach for a 24-year-old. Houston wanted him to focus on developing his plate discipline in 2009, but it remains an area of concern. He's a free swinger, his stroke is long and he needs to do a better job of recognizing breaking balls. Though he runs well, DeLome lacks instincts on the bases and in the outfield. With his average arm, he fits best in left field. He figures to spend 2010 in Triple-A, where he'll have to show more discipline at the plate if he's to be anything more than an extra outfielder at the big league level.

Year	Club (League)	Class	AVG	G	AB	R	H	2B	3B	HR	RBI	BB	SO	SB	OBP	SLG
2007	Tri-City (NYP)	SS	.300	65	243	31	73	17	6	6	28	23	65	9	.374	.494
2008	Lexington (SAL)	LoA	.261	61	226	41	59	9	6	12	36	18	71	7	.329	.513
	Salem (CAR)	HiA	.232	68	237	40	55	14	3	10	35	17	57	7	.305	.443
2009	Corpus Christi (TL)	AA	.255	125	467	79	119	18	10	20	61	37	141	15	.323	.465
MINOR LEAGUE TOTALS			.261	319	1173	191	306	58	25	48	160	95	334	38	.331	.476

26 POLIN TRINIDAD, LHP

BORN: Nov. 19, 1984. B-T: L-L. Ht.: 6-3. Wt.: 195. Signed: Venezuela, 2002. **SIGNED BY:** Julio Linares/Rick Aponte.

Another pitcher the Astros have nurtured patiently, Trinidad spent three years in the Dominican Summer League and has toiled for eight seasons in the minors without reaching Houston. His best pitch is his changeup, which can be an out pitch at times. His fastball resides in the high 80s and touches as high as 93. His loose slider is a below-average offering that he has tried to improve without success. Trinidad throws strikes but still needs to refine his ability to command his fastball to both sides of the plate. He doesn't miss many bats, and without much margin for error he must learn to keep his pitches down in the zone. He gave up 25 homers last year, including six in one five-inning start in July. He's a good athlete who fields his position and holds runners well, allowing just three steals last season. If Trinidad pitches well in Triple-A in 2010, he finally should make his big league debut later in the year. He profiles as a No. 5 starter or long reliever.

Year	Club (League)	Class	W	L	ERA	G	GS	CG	SV	IP	H	R	ER	HR	BB	SO	AVG
2002	Astros (DSL)	R	2	1	4.74	17	7	0	0	49	59	32	26	1	6	49	.286
2003	Astros (DSL)	R	0	1	2.57	2	2	0	0	7	7	5	2	0	2	6	.219
2004	Astros (DSL)	R	1	0	1.38	5	1	0	0	13	9	4	2	0	3	12	.184
2005	Greeneville (APP)	R	1	2	4.89	14	8	0	2	50	65	34	27	5	11	47	.308
2006	Greeneville (APP)	R	4	4	2.39	13	13	0	0	75	59	24	20	2	10	66	.208
	Tri-City (NYP)	SS	0	0	4.50	2	1	0	0	8	14	4	4	0	3	5	.389
2007	Lexington (SAL)	LoA	6	8	4.18	23	23	1	0	131	118	62	61	16	35	120	.242
	Salem (CAR)	HiA	2	1	2.81	4	4	0	0	26	23	9	8	4	3	23	.237
2008	Salem (CAR)	HiA	4	2	2.32	10	10	0	0	62	46	18	16	2	11	34	.202
	Corpus Christi (TL)	AA	6	5	3.61	18	18	0	0	107	109	47	43	13	21	75	.263
2009	Corpus Christi (TL)	AA	7	5	2.94	13	12	2	1	83	87	36	27	7	10	53	.272
	Round Rock (PCL)	AAA	6	5	4.53	13	12	0	0	87	90	46	44	18	25	59	.260
MINOR LEAGUE TOTALS			39	34	3.61	134	111	3	3	699	686	321	280	68	140	549	.253

27 HENRY VILLAR, RHP

BORN: May 24, 1987. B-T: R-R. Ht.: 5-11. Wt.: 150. Signed: Dominican Republic, 2005. Signed by: Julio Linares/Ricardo Aponte.

Villar has performed well in four seasons in the lower levels of the system, posing a career 2.93 ERA and 5.4-to-1 strikeout-to-walk ratio. He made a smooth transition to full-season ball in 2009, impressing the Astros enough to give him a spot on the 40-man roster. After switching him to the bullpen in low Class A last season, he'll get a trial as a starter in 2010. Villar's stuff doesn't quite align with his numbers. His fastball sits at 89-91 mph and he can reach 93 on occasion. His heater is more notable for its heavy sink than its velocity, and he succeeds by throwing first-pitch strikes. Villar also mixes in an 83-84 mph slider and a changeup. Both pitches need work, as he sometimes struggles to finish his slider and tends to throw his changeup too hard. He's a good athlete who repeats his delivery and fields his position well. It remains to be seen whether Villar can duplicate his performance at higher levels, but he has the upside of a No. 4 or 5 starter.

Year	Club (League)	Class	W	L	ERA	G	GS	CG	SV	IP	H	R	ER	HR	BB	SO	AVG
2006	Astros (DSL)	R	1	1	2.16	13	7	0	0	42	33	15	10	1	9	32	.217
2007	Astros (DSL)	R	4	4	2.45	13	13	0	0	73	64	26	20	4	12	69	.233
2008	Greeneville (APP)	R	3	6	4.41	13	13	0	0	65	69	32	32	6	12	65	.272
2009	Lexington (SAL)	LoA	3	4	2.60	43	3	0	5	90	80	36	26	6	18	109	.235
MINOR LEAGUE TOTALS			11	15	2.93	82	36	0	5	270	246	109	88	17	51	275	.241

28 ASHTON MOWDY, RHP

BORN: June 21, 1986. B-T: R-R. Ht.: 6-0. Wt.: 185. Drafted: Eastern Oklahoma State JC, 2008 (19th round). Signed by: Jim Stevenson.

Jason Castro and Jordan Lyles headline a 2008 draft that restocked a thin Astros system, but Houston also may have found a sleeper in the 19th round in Mowdy. Signed for $35,000, he owns the system's best breaking ball, a plus curveball that grades as a 70 on the 20-80 scouting scale at times. He can throw his curve for a strike or use it as a knockout pitch to get batters to swing and miss. Mowdy has an 89-91 mph fastball, and the Astros have tried to add a two-seamer to his repertoire to get more sink on his heater. He has a changeup, though it's mostly a show pitch and isn't as needed as much as it would be if he were a starter. After pitching well in Lexington's bullpen, he struggled after a promotion to the hitter-friendly California League in July. If he can make the necessary adjustments when he returns to high Class A this year, he could put himself in position to challenge for a job in Houston's bullpen by 2012.

Year	Club (League)	Class	W	L	ERA	G	GS	CG	SV	IP	H	R	ER	HR	BB	SO	AVG
2008	Tri-City (NYP)	SS	4	3	4.10	21	2	0	1	42	39	21	19	5	21	48	.242
2009	Lexington (SAL)	LoA	0	0	1.72	26	0	0	3	37	21	14	7	4	8	33	.157
	Lancaster (CAL)	HiA	1	1	9.30	15	0	0	0	20	32	26	21	5	11	21	.337
MINOR LEAGUE TOTALS			5	4	4.29	62	2	0	4	99	92	61	47	14	40	102	.236

29 BRAD DYDALEWICZ, LHP

BORN: March 24, 1990. B-T: L-L. Ht.: 6-1. Wt.: 180. Drafted: HS—Austin, 2008 (8th round). Signed by: Rusty Pendergrass/Bobby Heck.

When the Astros couldn't sign their 2008 third-round pick, Chase Davidson, it freed up the money to bring in eighth-rounder Dydalewicz for an above-slot $425,000 bonus just before the signing deadline. He flew under the radar after he missed the 2007 season following knee surgery to repair a football injury. Dydalewicz threw 90-94 mph as a high school senior but pitched more at 88-92 mph in his full-season debut last year. His curveball also lost sharpness and bite, and his changeup passed his curve as his most reliable secondary pitch. Dydalewicz had a lot of moving parts in his delivery, so the Astros spent instructional league trying to streamline his mechanics, which knocked his velocity down a little more. Houston expects that his stuff will bounce back now that he has gotten acclimated to the grind of the long pro season. Dydalewicz could benefit from heading back to low Class A for the first half of 2010.

Year	Club (League)	Class	W	L	ERA	G	GS	CG	SV	IP	H	R	ER	HR	BB	SO	AVG
2008	Greeneville (APP)	R	0	0	2.70	4	4	0	0	10	7	3	3	1	3	6	.206
2009	Lexington (SAL)	LoA	8	5	3.93	22	22	0	0	110	93	58	48	6	51	78	.221
MINOR LEAGUE TOTALS			8	5	3.83	26	26	0	0	120	100	61	51	7	54	84	.220

30 KYLE GREENWALT, RHP

BORN: Sept. 29, 1988. B-T: R-R. Ht.: 6-0. Wt.: 200. Drafted: HS—Souderton, Pa., 2007 (20th round). **SIGNED BY:** Ed Edwards.

Greenwalt is one of the few bright spots from Houston's disastrous 2007 draft. He pitches at 88-93 mph with his fastball, throwing it for strikes but not always commanding it as well as he needs to. He flashes an average 75-78 mph curveball, though he needs more consistency with its quality and his control of it. In his full-season debut last year, he held righthanders in check but lefties pounded him to the tune of an .815 OPS. His struggles against lefthanders result because he has been slow to bring his below-average changeup up to par. Greenwalt has a solid delivery with good arm action, and his quick footwork gives him a good pickoff move. Some scouts think he might be better off as a reliever because his stuff would play up and his changeup would be less crucial, but the Astros plan on exhausting his potential as a starter. He'll get a stiff test at Lancaster in 2010.

Year	Club (League)	Class	W	L	ERA	G	GS	CG	SV	IP	H	R	ER	HR	BB	SO	AVG
2007	Greeneville (APP)	R	0	7	7.53	12	8	0	0	35	55	40	29	1	12	28	.353
2008	Greeneville (APP)	R	6	4	3.14	13	13	0	0	72	77	27	25	2	14	53	.274
	Tri-City (NYP)	SS	1	0	1.50	2	1	0	0	6	3	1	1	0	2	5	.143
2009	Lexington (SAL)	LoA	8	13	4.20	25	25	0	0	139	154	72	65	7	28	90	.278
MINOR LEAGUE TOTALS			15	24	4.29	52	47	0	0	252	289	140	120	10	56	176	.286

Kansas City Royals

BY J.J. COOPER

Every day that Cy Young Award winner Zack Greinke wasn't pitching was a disaster for the 2009 Royals. There's hope for the future, but the bad news for Kansas City fans is that the club's rebuilding effort will need more time.

The Royals thought they were fielding a team ready to take a significant step toward contending last season. They traded away young relievers Leo Nunez and Ramon Ramirez to acquire veterans Mike Jacobs and Coco Crisp, and signed free-agent relievers Juan Cruz and Kyle Fansworth. The result was 65 wins, which marked the seventh time in the past nine years that Kansas City has won fewer than 70 games.

At least the organization recognizes now that it's planning for the future. General manager Dayton Moore says his team will focus on acquiring young major leaguers who are years away from free agency. That would seem to fit with the state of the farm system, which has plenty of talent but little to contribute in 2010.

The Royals at least deserve credit for trying a different approach. Unlike many smaller-revenue teams that save money by sticking to slot bonus recommendations in the draft, Kansas City has spent money.

The problem is that the Royals haven't always gotten what they paid for. They gave a $4 million bonus to Alex Gordon, the No. 2 overall pick in 2005, and a $5.25 million contract to Luke Hochevar, the top choice in 2006. Gordon (.250/.331/.415 in three big league seasons) and Hochevar (13-26, 5.88 in three years) have massively underperformed, and no other player from those drafts has made the majors.

Those failed drafts have left the upper levels of the system system barren, which became a significant problem when injuries struck in 2009. When Crisp went down with a shoulder injury early in the season, the Royals were forced to get Josh Anderson from the Tigers. When Mike Aviles' arm injury ended any chance of an encore to his outstanding rookie season, they traded for Yuniesky Betancourt.

Despite injuries to Crisp, Aviles, Gordon, Gil Meche and Joakim Soria, and a record that quickly made it clear that they were playing for the future, Kansas City had only two marginal rookies (Mitch Maier and Brayan Pena) see playing time before September. The system simply lacked upper-level prospects worth promoting.

At the lower levels, the Royals have a bounty of pitching prospects that few organizations can

Former No. 1 pick Luke Hochevar has yet to live up to his $5.25 million big league deal

TOP 30 PROSPECTS

1. Mike Montgomery, lhp	16. Johnny Giavotella, 2b
2. Aaron Crow, rhp	17. Cheslor Cuthbert, 3b
3. Wil Myers, c	18. Kelvin Herrera, rhp
4. Mike Moustakas, 3b	19. Jordan Parraz, of
5. Eric Hosmer, 1b	20. Salvador Perez, c
6. Tim Melville, rhp	21. Jose Bonilla, c
7. John Lamb, lhp	22. Derrick Robinson, of
8. Danny Duffy, lhp	23. Keaton Hayenga, rhp
9. Chris Dwyer, lhp	24. Blake Wood, rhp
10. David Lough, of	25. Patrick Keating, rhp
11. Jeff Bianchi, ss	26. Crawford Simmons, lhp
12. Louis Coleman, rhp	27. Edgar Osuna, lhp
13. Carlos Rosa, rhp	28. Matt Mitchell, rhp
14. Tyler Sample, rhp	29. Cole White, rhp
15. Kila Ka'aihue, 1b	30. Hilton Richardson, of

match, led by lefthander Mike Montgomery. Their willingness to exceed MLB's slot recommendations landed five of their 10 best prospects (catcher Wil Myers, third baseman Mike Moustakas, first baseman Eric Hosmer, righthander Tim Melville, lefty Chris Dwyer) and they gave a major league contract to a sixth (righty Aaron Crow).

Moore came to Kansas City from Atlanta, and his farm system reflects the Braves' emphasis on developing pitching. The Royals can dream of similar success, but their promising youngsters are going to need a few more years to develop.

General Manager: Dayton Moore. **Farm and Scouting Director:** J.J. Picollo.

Class	Team	League	W	L	PCT	Finish*	Manager(s)
Majors	Kansas City Royals	American	65	97	.401	t-12th (14)	Trey Hillman
Triple-A	Omaha Royals	Pacific Coast	64	80	.444	13th (16)	Mike Jirschele
Double-A	Northwest Arkansas Naturals	Texas	73	67	.521	3rd (8)	Brian Poldberg
High A	Wilmington Blue Rocks	Carolina	84	55	.604	1st (8)	Brian Rupp
Low A	Burlington (Iowa) Bees	Midwest	64	75	.460	8th (14)	Jim Gabella
Rookie	Idaho Falls Chukars	Pioneer	43	31	.581	2nd (8)	Darryl Kennedy
Rookie	Burlington (N.C.) Royals	Appalachian	24	44	.353	10th (10)	Nelson Liriano
Rookie	AZL Royals	Arizona	20	35	.364	11th (11)	Julio Bruno
Overall 2009 Minor League Record			372	387	.490	21st (30)	

*Finish in overall standings (No. of teams in league). †League champion.

LAST YEAR'S TOP 30

Rank	Player, Pos.	Status
1.	Mike Moustakas, 3b	No. 4
2.	Eric Hosmer, 1b	No. 5
3.	Daniel Cortes, rhp	(Mariners)
4.	Mike Montgomery, lhp	No. 1
5.	Tim Melville, rhp	No. 6
6.	Danny Duffy, lhp	No. 8
7.	Danny Gutierrez, rhp	(Rangers)
8.	Carlos Rosa, rhp	No. 13
9.	Kila Ka'aihue, 1b	No. 15
10.	Blake Wood, rhp	No. 24
11.	Johnny Giavotella, 2b	No. 16
12.	Kelvin Herrera, rhp	No. 18
13.	Henry Barrera, rhp	Dropped out
14.	Tyler Sample, rhp	No. 14
15.	David Lough, of	No. 10
16.	Derrick Robinson, of	No. 22
17.	Jason Taylor, 3b/1b	Dropped out
18.	Julio Pimentel, rhp	Dropped out
19.	Salvador Perez, c	No. 20
20.	Carlos Fortuna, rhp	Dropped out
21.	Matt Mitchell, rhp	No. 28
22.	Adrian Ortiz, of	Dropped out
23.	Mitch Maier, of	Majors
24.	Joe Dickerson, of	(Retired)
25.	Juan Abreu, rhp	(Braves)
26.	Jose Bonilla, c	No. 21
27.	Kyle Martin, ss/3b	(Retired)
28.	Sam Runion, rhp	Dropped out
29.	Yowill Espinall, ss	Dropped out
30.	Keaton Hayenga, rhp	No. 23

BEST TOOLS

Best Hitter for Average	Wil Myers
Best Power Hitter	Mike Moustakas
Best Strike-Zone Discipline	Kila Ka'aihue
Fastest Baserunner	Jarrod Dyson
Best Athlete	Derrick Robinson
Best Fastball	Aaron Crow
Best Curveball	Chris Dwyer
Best Slider	Aaron Crow
Best Changeup	Edgar Osuna
Best Control	John Lamb
Best Defensive Catcher	Salvador Perez
Best Defensive Infielder	Mario Lisson
Best Infield Arm	Mike Moustakas
Best Defensive Outfielder	Derrick Robinson
Best Outfield Arm	Jordan Parraz

PROJECTED 2013 LINEUP

Catcher	Wil Myers
First Base	Eric Hosmer
Second Base	Alberto Callaspo
Third Base	Alex Gordon
Shortstop	Jeff Bianchi
Left Field	David DeJesus
Center Field	David Lough
Right Field	Mike Moustakas
Designated Hitter	Billy Butler
No. 1 Starter	Zack Greinke
No. 2 Starter	Mike Montgomery
No. 3 Starter	Gil Meche
No. 4 Starter	Aaron Crow
No. 5 Starter	Tim Melville
Closer	Joakim Soria

TOP PROSPECTS OF THE DECADE

Year	Player, Pos.	2009 Org.
2000	Dee Brown, of	Nationals
2001	Chris George, lhp	Orioles
2002	Angel Berroa, ss	Mets
2003	Zack Greinke, rhp	Royals
2004	Zack Greinke, rhp	Royals
2005	Billy Butler, of	Royals
2006	Alex Gordon, 3b	Royals
2007	Alex Gordon, 3b	Royals
2008	Mike Moustakas, 3b	Royals
2009	Mike Moustakas, 3b	Royals

TOP DRAFT PICKS OF THE DECADE

Year	Player, Pos.	2009 Org.
2000	Mike Stodolka, lhp	Out of baseball
2001	Colt Griffin, rhp	Out of baseball
2002	Zack Greinke, rhp	Royals
2003	Chris Lubanski, of	Royals
2004	Billy Butler, of	Royals
2005	Alex Gordon, 3b	Royals
2006	Luke Hochevar, rhp	Royals
2007	Mike Moustakas, 3b	Royals
2008	Eric Hosmer, 1b	Royals
2009	Aaron Crow, rhp	Royals

LARGEST BONUSES IN CLUB HISTORY

Eric Hosmer, 2008	$6,000,000
Alex Gordon, 2005	$4,000,000
Mike Moustakas, 2007	$4,000,000
Luke Hochevar, 2006	$3,500,000
Jeff Austin, 1998	$2,700,000

KANSAS CITY ROYALS

TOP 2010 ROOKIE: Carlos Rosa, rhp. One of the few big league-ready prospects in the system, he should help in the bullpen.

BREAKOUT PROSPECT: Keaton Hayenga, rhp. In his first season back after two years off from shoulder surgery, he showed a promising fastball and curve.

SLEEPER: Justin Trapp, ss. The former Coastal Carolina quarterback recruit has the athleticism and work ethic to be an impact up-the-middle defender.

SOURCE OF TOP 30 TALENT			
Homegrown	28	Acquired	2
College	7	Trades	1
Junior college	0	Rule 5 draft	1
High school	15	Independent leagues	0
Draft-and-follow	0	Free agents/waivers	0
Independent/Drafted	1		
International	5		

Numbers in parentheses indicate prospect rankings

LF
David Lough (10)
Tim Smith

CF
Derrick Robinson (22)
Hilton Richardson (30)
Adrian Ortiz
Jarrod Dyson
Alex Llanos

RF
Jordan Parraz (19)
Geulin Beltre
Lane Adams

3B
Mike Moustakas (4)
Cheslor Cuthbert (17)
Jason Taylor

SS
Jeff Bianchi (11)
Yowill Espinall
Deivy Batista
Justin Trapp
Mario Lisson

2B
Johnny Giavotella (16)
Kurt Mertins

1B
Eric Hosmer (5)
Kila Ka'aihue (15)
Clint Robinson
Geoff Baldwin

C
Wil Myers (3)
Salvador Perez (20)
Jose Bonilla (21)
Manuel Pina
Shin-Jin-Ho
Fernando Cruz
Sean McCauley
Ben Theriot

RHP

Starters	Relievers
Aaron Crow (2)	Louis Coleman (12)
Tim Melville (6)	Carlos Rosa (13)
Tyler Sample (14)	Blake Wood (24)
Kelvin Herrera (18)	Patrick Keating (25)
Keaton Hayenga (23)	Cole White (29)
Matt Mitchell (28)	Henry Barrera
Anthony Lerew	Chris Hayes
Sam Runion	Dusty Odenbach
Greg Billo	Greg Holland
Blake Johnson	Edward Cegarra
Chase Hentges	Eric Basurto
Alex Caldera	Ryan Wood
	Aaron Hartsock

LHP

Starters	Relievers
Mike Montgomery (1)	Edgar Osuna (27)
John Lamb (7)	Brandon Sisk
Danny Duffy (8)	Dusty Hughes
Chris Dwyer (9)	Ben Swaggerty
Crawford Simmons (26)	Blaine Hardy
Buddy Baumann	Brendan Lafferty
Brian Peacock	Gilbert de la Vara
	Claudio Bavera

2009
BONUSES: $6.7 MILLION

BEST PURE HITTER: The Royals thought about taking C Wil Myers (3) 12th overall because of his polished bat. He has a smooth swing he repeats well and quick, strong hands that help him catch up to good fastballs.

BEST POWER HITTER: Myers has the potential to hit 20-25 home runs down the line, if not more, thanks to the leverage generated by his sturdy 6-foot-3 frame.

FASTEST RUNNER: SS Justin Trapp (34) committed to play quarterback at Coastal Carolina, but his 6.6-second speed over 60 yards plays well on the baseball diamond as well.

BEST DEFENSIVE PLAYER: Another two-sport athlete, OF Lanc Adams (13), has the present speed and plus arm to fit in center field. Kansas City expects the 6-foot-4, 190-pounder to fill out and be an above-average right fielder in time.

BEST FASTBALL: Velocity, command and life on his heater made RHP Aaron Crow (1) a two-time first-round pick. He can pitch at 91-96 mph with hard sink.

BEST SECONDARY PITCH: Crow uses a plus slider as a strikeout pitch. LHP Chris Dwyer (4) signed for $1.45 million as a freshman out of Clemson thanks to a 90-94 mph heater and a curveball that at times is a true hammer.

BEST PRO DEBUT: Myers hit .369/.427/.679 overall in 84 at-bats at two Rookie-level stops. RHP Patrick Keating (20) struck out 47 in 33 innings and had nine saves, finishing at high Class A Wilmington. Venezuelan LHP Claudio Bavera (33) went 4-0, 0.44 with 21 strikeouts in 21 innings in the Rookie-level Arizona League.

BEST ATHLETE: Trapp and Adams, who had a Missouri State basketball scholarship. A shooting guard, Adams averaged 32 points a game as a senior to lead Red Oak High to an Oklahoma state championship and ranks fifth in state history with 3,251 points. LHP Crawford Simmons (14) was a talented high school golfer.

MOST INTRIGUING BACKGROUND: RHP Cole White (6), a drummer and singer who also happens to throw 95 mph at times, co-wrote a song that was submitted for Grammy Award consideration. RHP Josh Worrell's (30) father Todd was an all-star closer, and his uncle Tim also pitched in the majors. Unsigned SS Kevin Kuntz's (48) dad Rusty played in the big leagues and is Kansas City's first-base coach.

CLOSEST TO THE MAJORS: Crow could join the Royals at some point during his first pro season. RHP Louis Coleman (5), who helped pitched Louisiana State to the College World Series title, may not be far behind.

BEST LATE-ROUND PICK: Keating struggled as a college starter but saw his fastball peak at 95 mph as a pro reliever. Lane and Tripp have a ways to go but higher upsides due to their athleticism. Simmons also bears watching.

THE ONE WHO GOT AWAY: RHP Mike Morin (40) improved his stock as the No. 1 prospect in the MINK League last summer, hitting 93 mph with his fastball and showing a good curveball, but North Carolina swooped in late to add him to its recruiting class.

ASSESSMENT: After their record $11.1 million draft outlay last year, the Royals gave Crow a big league contract and went well over slot to sign Myers and Dwyer. Their late-round finds add more depth to a strong draft.

2008
BONUSES: $11.1 MILLION

Kansas City couldn't be happier with a pitching crop that includes LHPs Matt Montgomery (1s) and John Lamb (5) and RHPs Tyler Sample (3) and Tim Melville (4). If 1B Eric Hosmer (1) gets his bat going, this group could be special.

GRADE: B

2007
BONUSES: $6.6 MILLION

Like Hosmer, 3B Mike Moustakas (1) hit a rough patch in 2009. LHP Danny Duffy (3) and OF David Lough (11) continue to put up dazzling numbers.

GRADE: B

2006
BONUSES: $6.7 MILLION

RHP Luke Hochevar (1) is looking like one of the worst No. 1 overall picks in draft history. No one else from this draft offers any hope.

GRADE: D

2005
BONUSES: $6.0 MILLION*

3B Alex Gordon (1), the No. 2 overall pick, has underachieved, though not to the extent of Hochevar. SS Jeff Bianchi (2) finally stayed healthy last year and soon could push for a big league job. Draft-and-follow RHP Danny Gutierrez (22) has a lot of talent, but repeated off-field problems prompted his trade to the Rangers.

GRADE: C+

*Draft analysis by John Manuel (2009) and Jim Callis (2005-08). Numbers in parentheses indicate draft rounds. *Bonuses for 2005 are first 10 rounds only.*

PROSPECT 1

BILL MITCHELL

MIKE MONTGOMERY, LHP

Born: July 1, 1989.
Height: 6-5. **Weight:** 180.
Bats: L. **Throws:** L.
Drafted: HS—Newhall, Calif., 2008 (1st round supplemental).
Signed by: Dan Ontiveros.

The Royals knew they were getting a fierce competitor when they drafted Montgomery 36th overall in 2008 and signed him for a slot $988,000 bonus. He had been kicked off his high school basketball team as a senior for picking up too many technical fouls. They saw it up close during spring training last year, when they tried to limit his long-toss program. He balked, saying long-tossing was vital to keeping up his arm strength. They agreed to compromise, allowing Montgomery to throw at a longer distance than they usually prescribe for young pitchers, but with less frequency than he was used to. He wanted to long-toss because he believed it could help his fastball jump to the 95-97 mph range, while Kansas City already was happy with his heater and didn't want him to risk injury by throwing too much. The Royals are happy to live with Montgomery's drive because he carries it to the mound. They held him out of the April chill at low Class A Burlington, Iowa, but once got into games in mid-May, he blazed through two levels, allowing more than three earned runs only once in 21 starts.

For a 20-year-old lefty, Montgomery is close to a complete package. His fastball is already a plus pitch that sits at 90-92 mph and touches 94-95. Considering his lanky frame, there's a good chance he'll add velocity as he fills out. When his fastball was on last year, he buzzed through lineups even when he was struggling to control his offspeed pitches. When he located his curveballs, he was untouchable. He throws two different types, a traditional downer that he's still mastering and a palm-curve that he's been throwing for years. While some scouts question how effective the palm-curve will be at higher levels, Class A hitters struggled to pick it up and took lots of ugly swings. The true curveball has the potential to be more effective in the long term. When he gets on top of it, it grades as slightly above-average. His changeup shows flashes of being a plus pitch that some scouts believe has more potential than his curveball. Montgomery's mechanics are solid. He shows the ability to repeat his delivery and has excellent arm speed.

The Royals want Montgomery to develop the regular curveball, but when he's struggling he falls back on the palm version. They've considered asking him to completely shelve his palm-curve, at least temporarily, to hasten the development of his other pitches. He won't consistently succeed at the upper levels until he becomes more consistent with his changeup and curve. He throws strikes but still needs to sharpen his command.

Montgomery is the best of Kansas City's deep crop of young pitchers, among whom rests the franchise's hope to return to contention. He lived up to all of the Royals' expectations in his first full pro season and could open 2010 at Double-A Northwest Arkansas. He could be ready for the big leagues by mid-2011 and won't be satisfied just to get there.

Year	Club (League)	Class	W	L	ERA	G	GS	CG	SV	IP	H	R	ER	HR	BB	SO	AVG
2008	Royals (AZL)	R	2	1	1.69	12	9	0	0	43	31	12	8	2	12	34	.211
2009	Burlington (MWL)	LoA	2	3	2.17	12	12	0	0	58	42	19	14	1	24	52	.206
	Wilmington (CAR)	HiA	4	1	2.25	9	9	0	0	52	38	15	13	0	12	46	.196
MINOR LEAGUE TOTALS			8	5	2.06	33	30	0	0	153	111	46	35	3	48	132	.204

2 AARON CROW, RHP

BORN: Nov. 11, 1986. **B-T:** R-R. **HT.:** 6-3. **WT.:** 195. **DRAFTED:** Fort Worth (American Association), 2009 (1st round). **SIGNED BY:** Scott Melvin.

Undrafted out of high school, Crow blossomed into the top college righthander in the 2008 draft and went ninth overall to the Nationals. When the two sides couldn't bridge a $500,000 gap ($3.5 million vs. $4 million), he signed with the independent Fort Worth Cats. The Royals, who considered him with the No. 3 pick in 2008, jumped at a second chance to take the Kansas native. After going 12th overall, he signed Sept. 17 for a $3 million big league contract that included a $1.5 million bonus. Crow made four starts in the Arizona Fall League, and his stuff wasn't far off what the Royals saw back in 2008. His fastball sits between 91-94 mph with plus movement, and he has touched 96 in the past. He commands his fastball well and pairs it with a tight slider that's a strikeout pitch. Crow has a wrist wrap in his delivery and sometimes collapses his back side, but those flaws don't cause many problems because he throws downhill and maintains proper alignment to the plate. He repeats his delivery well and shows good arm speed, but some scouts worry about the effort in his delivery. His changeup lags behind his other pitches, but he trusts it enough to throw it in key situations. Crow likely will make his pro debut in Double-A and could reach Kansas City by the end of the season. If he refines his changeup, he could be a worthy No. 2 starter behind Zack Greinke. His fallback position would be as a closer with two plus pitches.

Year	Club (League)	Class	W	L	ERA	G	GS	CG	SV	IP	H	R	ER	HR	BB	SO	AVG
2009	Did Not Play—Signed Late																

3 WIL MYERS, C

BORN: Dec. 10, 1990. **B-T:** R-R. **HT.:** 6-3. **WT.:** 190. **DRAFTED:** HS—High Point, N.C., 2009 (3rd round). **SIGNED BY:** Steve Connelly.

The Royals considered Myers for the 12th pick in the 2009 draft before settling on Aaron Crow. They didn't have a second-round choice, but his $2 million price tag made him available at No. 91 in the third round. After Kansas City met his asking price, he ranked as the No. 1 prospect in the Rookie-level Pioneer League. Capable of turning around a quality fastball with a flick of his wrists, Myers has excellent raw power. His swing isn't textbook and he'll sometime shift his weight to his front foot too early, but he manages to keep his hands back and hit line drives all over the park. He should hit for average as well as power. He has a plus arm and can rip off 1.85-second pop times even when his footwork isn't perfect. He threw out five of the 12 basestealers who tested him in his pro debut. He has average speed and is a better athlete than most catchers. Myers played a variety of positions as an amateur, so he's inexperienced and inconsistent as a catcher. He gets too upright coming out of his crouch and sometimes struggles to block pitches in the dirt. He committed six passed balls in just 10 games. Myers' rangy body draws comparisons to Dale Murphy and Jayson Werth—two tall catchers who ended up moving to the outfield. He has the raw tools to handle the position, but his advanced bat could tempt the Royals to move him. They're committed to trying to develop him as a catcher, however, which is where he'll play in low Class A this year.

Year	Club (League)	Class	AVG	G	AB	R	H	2B	3B	HR	RBI	BB	SO	SB	OBP	SLG
2009	Burlington (APP)	R	.125	4	16	1	2	0	1	1	4	0	3	0	.125	.438
	Idaho Falls (PIO)	R	.426	18	68	18	29	7	1	4	14	9	15	2	.488	.735
MINOR LEAGUE TOTALS			.369	22	84	19	31	7	2	5	18	9	18	2	.427	.679

4 MIKE MOUSTAKAS, 3B

BORN: Sept. 11, 1988. **B-T:** L-R. **HT.:** 6-0. **WT.:** 195. **DRAFTED:** HS—Chatsworth, Calif., 2007 (1st round). **SIGNED BY:** John Ramey.

After he went second overall in the 2007 draft and signed for $4 million, Moustakas led the low Class A Midwest League with 22 homers in his first full pro season. He seemed get swallowed up by high Class A Wilmington's pitcher-friendly Frawley Stadium last season. He posted the fourth-lowest on-base percentage (.297) among Carolina League qualifiers, thanks in large part to his .205/.266/.373 numbers at home. Moustakas has two well above-average tools in his raw power and arm. He has good hand-eye coordination and quick wrists to go with a mechanically sound swing, helping his power play in game situations. He has the bat speed to catch up to good fastballs. He made strides last year to become a more complete third baseman. Moustakas' approach at the plate got him into all kinds of trouble in 2009. The word got out to throw him offspeed stuff early in the count, and he struggled to adjust. He was too pull-happy and didn't hit his first opposite-field homer until August. He's so aggressiveness that he may never post high on-base percentages. Some scouts are skeptical that he can stay at third base because his hands are only adequate, his footwork is still raw and his body has thickened, costing him agility. He's a tick below-average runner who will get slower as he fills out. Most of Moustakas' problems in 2009 were apparent before the season began. He'll need to prove that he can make the adjustments needed to get back on track, and the hitter-friendly Texas League should help ease that transition.

Year	Club (League)	Class	AVG	G	AB	R	H	2B	3B	HR	RBI	BB	SO	SB	OBP	SLG
2007	Idaho Falls (PIO)	R	.293	11	41	6	12	4	1	0	10	4	8	0	.383	.439
2008	Burlington (MWL)	LoA	.272	126	496	77	135	25	3	22	71	43	86	8	.337	.468
2009	Wilmington (CAR)	HiA	.250	129	492	66	123	32	2	16	86	32	90	10	.297	.421
MINOR LEAGUE TOTALS			.262	266	1029	149	270	61	6	38	167	79	184	18	.320	.444

5 ERIC HOSMER, 1B

RODGER WOOD

BORN: Oct. 24, 1989. **B-T:** L-L. **HT.:** 6-4. **WT.:** 215. **DRAFTED:** HS—Plantation, Fla., 2008 (1st round). **SIGNED BY:** Alex Mesa.

Hosmer received a $6 million bonus as the No. 3 overall pick in 2008, but wound up ensnared in the Pedro Alvarez signing grievance with the Pirates and was limited to three games after signing. He got off to a slow start in 2009 after doctors diagnosed him with astigmatism during spring training. The eye condition apparently developed over the off-season, as Kansas City's vision tests in 2008 showed no such problems. He also sustained a hairline fracture on a knuckle on his right hand, limiting him to DH duty in June. He hit just .241/.334/.361 between two Class A stops. Hosmer's outstanding raw power is still apparent in batting practice, even if it seemed absent in games last year. His balanced swing is pure enough that he should hit for average as well. He has a plus arm that rarely comes into play at first base, but he's an average defender with soft hands. The Royals hope most of Hosmer's troubles can be blamed on his vision problems and knuckle injury. He wore contact lenses for a while, switched to glasses and eventually opted for laser eye surgery in August. Whatever the reason, he struggled with pitch recognition and batted a feeble .155/.202/.207 against lefthanders. He was also less athletic than advertised, with heavy feet and below-average speed. Hosmer will head back to high Class A, where he'll look to prove that the 2009 season was a fluke and not foreshadowing. Kansas City still envisions him as its No. 3 hitter of the future.

Year	Club (League)	Class	AVG	G	AB	R	H	2B	3B	HR	RBI	BB	SO	SB	OBP	SLG
2008	Idaho Falls (PIO)	R	.364	3	11	2	4	2	0	0	2	3	2	0	.533	.545
2009	Burlington (MWL)	LoA	.254	79	280	31	71	17	2	5	49	44	68	3	.352	.382
	Wilmington (CAR)	HiA	.206	27	97	9	20	2	2	1	10	9	22	0	.280	.299
MINOR LEAGUE TOTALS			.245	109	388	42	95	21	4	6	61	56	92	3	.341	.366

6 TIM MELVILLE, RHP

BORN: Oct. 9, 1989. **B-T:** R-R. **HT.:** 6-5. **WT.:** 210. **DRAFTED:** HS—Wentzville, Mo., 2008 (4th round). **SIGNED BY:** Phil Huttman.

Melville was the top high school pitching prospect entering 2008, but didn't quite live up to expectations and scared teams off with his desire for upper-first-round money. He was willing to give Kansas City a home-state discount, and signed for $1.25 million as a fourth-round pick. Because he signed late and the Royals wanted to keep him out of cold weather, he didn't make his pro debut until May 20. With his raw stuff, Melville has the potential to be a frontline starter. His 92-93 mph fastball touches 95, with boring action that makes it effective against lefthanders. His fastball generates strikeouts, but it's most effective as a heavy pitch that forces weak grounders. His curveball is a true 12-to-6 downer that's a plus pitch when he can command it. He has a clean arm action and a pitcher's body that should give him plenty of durability. Melville struggles when he loses his tempo in his delivery. He sometimes slows his arm down, leaving his curveball and changeup up in the zone and making him vulnerable to homers. He has adequate athleticism but has to work to keep his delivery in sync. Because of his inconsistent mechanics, his command and control aren't where they need to be. He lacks conviction in his changeup. Melville could be a No. 2 or No. 3 starter someday. He'll head to Wilmington, where a pitcher-friendly park should give him a chance to get on a roll.

Year	Club (League)	Class	W	L	ERA	G	GS	CG	SV	IP	H	R	ER	HR	BB	SO	AVG
2009	Burlington (MWL)	LoA	7	7	3.79	21	21	0	0	97	89	57	41	10	43	96	.245
MINOR LEAGUE TOTALS			7	7	3.79	21	21	0	0	97	89	57	41	10	43	96	.245

7 JOHN LAMB, LHP

BORN: July 10, 1990. **B-T:** L-L. **HT.:** 6-3. **WT.:** 195. **DRAFTED:** HS—Laguna Hills, Calif., 2008 (5th round). **SIGNED BY:** Gary Johnson/John Ramey.

The Royals selected Lamb in the fifth round in 2008, even though he had missed his high school senior season with a fractured elbow that was traced to a car accident. Kansas City followed his recovery, then signed him for $165,000 just before the signing deadline. He made his pro debut last June as the Opening Day starter at Rookie-level Burlington before earning a promotion to Rookie-level Idaho Falls. As good as Lamb's stuff is, the Royals are even more excited about his demeanor. He's a 19-year-old who pitches like a major league veteran, never getting rattled. His stuff is pretty good as well, and he could end up with three average or better pitches. His fastball sits at 88-91 mph and frequently touches 94. His compact delivery adds to his fastball's effectiveness because hitters struggle to pick it up. He does a good job of keeping the ball down in the zone. His velocity is easy and his control is good for his age, products of his repeatable delivery. Like most young pitchers, Lamb sometimes is too reliant on his fastball when he should be using his changeup and curveball. He's still learning how to consistently break off the curve, and his changeup needs further refinement. Lamb should be the ace of the low Class A Burlington staff in 2010. With his makeup and stuff, he projects as a solid No. 3 starter.

Year	Club (League)	Class	W	L	ERA	G	GS	CG	SV	IP	H	R	ER	HR	BB	SO	AVG
2009	Burlington (APP)	R	2	2	3.95	6	6	0	0	27	24	14	12	4	9	25	.238
	Idaho Falls (PIO)	R	3	1	3.70	8	8	0	0	41	33	20	17	4	11	46	.217
MINOR LEAGUE TOTALS			5	3	3.80	14	14	0	0	69	57	34	29	8	20	71	.225

8 DANNY DUFFY, LHP

BORN: Dec. 21, 1988. **B-T:** L-L. **HT.:** 6-2. **WT.:** 185. **DRAFTED:** HS—Lompac, Calif., 2007 (3rd round). **SIGNED BY:** Rick Schroeder.

In a system filled with pitching prospects, Duffy had the best season—while posting the worst numbers of his young career. He led Royals farmhands with a 2.98 ERA, finished second with 125 strikeouts and earned spots in the Futures Game and Carolina-California League all-star game. He's now 19-10, 2.49 with 290 strikeouts in 246 pro innings. Duffy's solid stuff plays up because he does a good job of messing with hitters' timing. His 88-92 mph fastball has good downward plane and seems to get in on opponents before they expect it, while his slow, big-breaking curveball keeps them off fastball. He's not afraid to pitch inside. He improved his delivery by shortening his stride. Duffy's changeup got better last year, but he still hasn't fully embraced it. While most pitchers have to learn to pitch in to hitters, he's learning the effectiveness of a down-and-away changeup. His delivery is less than ideal because he throws across his body and his bottom half isn't always in sync with his upper half. The Royals are working on keeping him centered over the rubber longer. He sometimes struggles to put bad starts behind him. Though he'll pitch the entire 2010 season at age 21, Duffy isn't that far away from the majors. One of the last remaining tests for the potential No. 3 starter is finding out how he handles adversity—because he hasn't encountered any.

Year	Club (League)	Class	W	L	ERA	G	GS	CG	SV	IP	H	R	ER	HR	BB	SO	AVG
2007	Royals (AZL)	R	2	3	1.45	11	9	0	0	37	24	14	6	0	17	63	.178
2008	Burlington (MWL)	LoA	8	4	2.20	17	17	0	0	82	56	26	20	4	25	102	.193
2009	Wilmington (CAR)	HiA	9	3	2.98	24	24	1	0	127	108	49	42	6	41	125	.230
MINOR LEAGUE TOTALS			19	10	2.49	52	50	1	0	246	188	89	68	10	83	290	.210

9 CHRIS DWYER, LHP

BORN: April 10, 1988. **B-T:** R-L. **HT.:** 6-3. **WT.:** 210. **DRAFTED:** Clemson, 2009 (4th round). **SIGNED BY:** Steve Connelly.

Dwyer was the rarest of rarities, a draft-eligible college freshman. Because he had been held back in elementary school and attended prep school—where he played with Phillies first-round pick Anthony Hewitt and was drafted by the Yankees in the 36th round in 2008—he was 21 and thus eligible as a Clemson freshman last spring. The Royals rated him as a late-first-round talent and gave him late-first-round money ($1.45 million) to sign him as a fourth-rounder. Dwyer's arm speed gives him a 90-94 mph fastball and a power curveball, both of which should be consistent plus pitches once he matures. His changeup is an advanced pitch that could end up being above average as well. A star as a high school quarterback, he's an excellent athlete. Dwyer was susceptible to big innings at Clemson. When he got into a jam, he battled his command and nibbled more than someone with his stuff should. His control suffers if he lands stiff on his front leg and struggles to stay aligned with the plate. He doesn't always maintain his quality stuff from start to start. Dwyer is less polished than the typical college pitcher but still could move quickly. He'll likely start his first full season in high Class A.

Year	Club (League)	Class	W	L	ERA	G	GS	CG	SV	IP	H	R	ER	HR	BB	SO	AVG
2009	Idaho Falls (PIO)	R	0	0	4.15	4	4	0	0	9	12	5	4	1	8	15	.324
MINOR LEAGUE TOTALS			0	0	4.15	4	4	0	0	9	12	5	4	1	8	15	.324

10 DAVID LOUGH, OF

DAVID GLAZIER

BORN: Jan. 20, 1986. **B-T:** L-L. **HT.:** 6-0. **WT.:** 180. **DRAFTED:** Mercyhurst (Pa.), 2007 (11th round). **SIGNED BY:** Jason Bryans.

Lough played soccer and football as well as baseball in high school, and he accepted a football scholarship at NCAA Division II Mercyhurst (Pa.), where he caught scout Jason Bryans' eye as a baseball walk-on. Since signing for $49,500 as an 11th-round pick, Lough has hit better than .320 at three of his four stops, and he led all Royals minor leaguers with a .325 average last year. Lough's above-average speed is his best tool, but what stands out most is his lack of a clear weakness. The rest of his tools all project to be right around major league average. He showed a more advanced approach at the plate in 2009. His swing is short and direct, which allows him to hit for average and rarely strike out. Thanks to his strong wrists, he projects to hit for average power, though he's most comfortable lining doubles into the gaps. He's an average defender in center field who usually has played in left because he has been alongside quality center fielders. Considering his speed, Lough should be a better basestealer. He's not particularly aggressive on the bases and doesn't get good jumps. His arm is a tick below-average but accurate. He has yet to show that he can hit lefties, with a .627 career OPS against them compared to .901 versus righthanders. Kansas City limped through much of the 2009 season without a true center fielder. Lough won't win any Gold Gloves out there, but his offensive potential could make up for it. If he can't handle center, he could be David DeJesus' eventual replacement in left. For now, he'll head to Triple-A Omaha for more seasoning.

Year	Club (League)	Class	AVG	G	AB	R	H	2B	3B	HR	RBI	BB	SO	SB	OBP	SLG
2007	Burlington (APP)	R	.337	24	86	15	29	6	0	2	12	4	13	6	.380	.477
2008	Burlington (MWL)	LoA	.268	126	488	76	131	21	11	16	62	35	70	12	.329	.455
2009	Wilmington (CAR)	HiA	.320	65	222	28	71	15	2	5	30	12	34	6	.370	.473
	NW Arkansas (TL)	AA	.331	61	236	41	78	13	2	9	31	12	30	13	.371	.517
MINOR LEAGUE TOTALS			.299	276	1032	160	309	55	15	32	135	63	147	37	.351	.475

11 JEFF BIANCHI, SS

BORN: Oct. 5, 1986. **B-T:** R-R. **HT.:** 6-0. **WT.:** 175. **DRAFTED:** HS—Lampeter, Pa., 2005 (2nd round). **SIGNED BY:** Sean Rooney.

Bianchi's career was nearly derailed by a series of injuries, but he regained his prospect status with a solid 2009 season that saw him fully healthy for the first time in his five-year career. A back strain ended his 2005 pro debut, then he missed almost all of 2006 with a torn labrum in his shoulder, which also cut into his 2007 season. That led to a move to second base in 2008, when he was slowed by a groin injuy, but he moved back to shortstop last season and looked like he had never left. Bianchi has a tick above-average arm at shortstop, and he showed average range thanks to his great footwork. He's the surest-handed fielder in the system and has picture-perfect fundamentals. He committed just 12 errrors in 120 games at short in 2009. Bianchi has a short swing that won't ever produce more than fringe-average power, but he does use the entire field. His aggressiveness costs him on-base opportunities and keeps him from exploiting what power he does have. He's a good basestealer despite being only an average runner, and he knows when to challenge outfielders for an extra base. To stay at shortstop, Bianchi must stay healthy because he doesn't have any range to lose. He could slide over to second base if needed, but his bat fits better at short. His solid all-around game makes him the likely successor to Yuniesky Betancourt before too long. Added to the 40-man roster in November, he'll challenge for a job in Triple-A during spring training.

Year	Club (League)	Class	AVG	G	AB	R	H	2B	3B	HR	RBI	BB	SO	SB	OBP	SLG
2005	Royals (AZL)	R	.408	28	98	29	40	7	4	6	30	16	22	5	.484	.745
2006	Royals (AZL)	R	.429	12	42	13	18	4	0	2	6	9	3	1	.537	.667
2007	Burlington (MWL)	LoA	.247	99	368	43	91	19	0	2	36	25	72	15	.296	.315
2008	Wilmington (CAR)	HiA	.255	104	396	57	101	34	5	10	61	20	95	13	.290	.442
2009	Wilmington (CAR)	HiA	.300	60	220	32	66	12	2	4	28	20	47	12	.360	.427
	NW Arkansas (TL)	AA	.315	68	270	42	85	17	1	5	42	19	58	10	.356	.441
MINOR LEAGUE TOTALS			.288	371	1394	216	401	93	12	29	203	109	297	56	.339	.434

12 LOUIS COLEMAN, RHP

BORN: April 4, 1986. **B-T:** R-R. **HT.:** 6-4. **WT.:** 195. **DRAFTED:** Louisiana State, 2009 (5th round). **SIGNED BY:** Scott Nichols.

After taking three pricy talents with its first three picks in the 2009 draft, Kansas City may have found a bargain in Coleman, a $100,000 senior sign in the fifth-round out of Louisiana State. After turning down the Nationals as a 14th-round pick as a junior, he not only improved his draft stock but also was a cornerstone of the Tigers' run to the national title. Coleman was on the mound for the final out of the College World Series just two days after starting the championship-series opener against Texas. He didn't have his best stuff after signing with the Royals following a long college season, yet still dominated in short stints. Coleman's fastball sat at 88-90 mph and touched 92 after signing, but at his best he works at 92-93 and peaks at 95 from a low-three-quarters arm slot. The combination of his delivery and a solid slider should allow him to move quickly as a reliever. Coleman's biggest hurdle is improving the consistency of his slider. He sometimes struggles to stay on top of it because of his low slot, but when he does it has enough bite and tilt to be a quality second pitch. His control is solid despite a less-than-ideal delivery. He throws across his body, which seems to add to his deception. Coleman is ready for Double-A and could help out the major league bullpen by 2011.

Year	Club (League)	Class	W	L	ERA	G	GS	CG	SV	IP	H	R	ER	HR	BB	SO	AVG
2009	Burlington (MWL)	LoA	1	0	2.45	4	0	0	1	7	2	2	2	0	1	6	.091
	Wilmington (CAR)	HiA	3	1	1.26	10	0	0	1	14	8	3	2	0	3	16	.157
MINOR LEAGUE TOTALS			4	1	1.66	14	0	0	2	22	10	5	4	0	4	22	.137

13 CARLOS ROSA, RHP

BORN: Sept. 21, 1984. **B-T:** R-R. **HT.:** 6-1. **WT.:** 210. **SIGNED:** Dominican Republic, 2001. **SIGNED BY:** Luis Silverio/Pedro Silverio.

The Royals originally included Rosa in the October 2008 trade for Mike Jacobs, but the Marlins' concerns about his elbow led to Leo Nunez taking his place. Rosa moved to the bullpen last season, and the transition didn't go as well as the Kansas City hoped. He struggled to get warmed up on short notice and went 0-3, 10.43 in May before settling into his new role over the second half of the season. He made it back up to Kansas City for another September callup, finishing the season with three straight solid outings in which he allowed one hit in six scoreless innings. Rosa's fastball continues to rank as one of the best in the system. After the move to the pen he consistently hit 94-96 mph with a good downhill angle. But Rosa needs to prove that he's more than just a one-pitch pitcher. His slider is still too inconsistent as he struggles to stay on top of it. He used his changeup more last season, but it's a fringy pitch. His lack of feel necessitated the move to the bullpen. The Royals want Rosa to serve as a big league long reliever who could eventually grow into a setup role. He'll have to refine his changeup to do so because he lacks any other weapons to keep lefthanders honest.

Year	Club (League)	Class	W	L	ERA	G	GS	CG	SV	IP	H	R	ER	HR	BB	SO	AVG
2002	Royals (GCL)	R	0	4	6.19	10	9	0	0	32	52	32	22	3	12	11	.361
	Royals (DSL)	R	1	0	1.80	1	1	0	0	5	3	1	1	0	0	2	.167
2003	Royals (AZL)	R	5	3	3.63	15	11	0	0	69	79	36	28	4	18	54	.288
2004	Royals (AZL)	R	0	0	4.91	4	4	0	0	11	14	6	6	1	9	8	.326
	Burlington (MWL)	LoA	0	5	4.67	8	8	0	0	35	41	24	18	1	17	23	.297
2005	Did Not Play—Injured																
2006	Burlington (MWL)	LoA	8	6	2.53	24	24	1	0	139	121	50	39	6	54	102	.239
	High Desert (CAL)	HiA	0	1	7.15	3	3	0	0	11	20	12	9	1	4	13	.392
2007	Wilmington (CAR)	HiA	1	0	0.39	4	4	0	0	23	18	2	1	0	3	15	.209
	Wichita (TL)	AA	6	6	4.36	21	17	0	1	97	101	50	47	8	43	70	.272
2008	NW Arkansas (TL)	AA	4	2	1.20	8	8	0	0	45	30	8	6	2	7	42	.189
	Kansas City (AL)	MAJ	0	0	2.70	2	0	0	0	3	3	1	1	0	0	3	.250
	Omaha (PCL)	AAA	4	3	4.09	11	11	0	0	51	51	24	23	3	12	44	.267
2009	Omaha (PCL)	AAA	2	8	4.56	43	0	0	7	71	69	40	36	6	32	80	.258
	Kansas City (AL)	MAJ	0	0	3.38	7	0	0	1	11	10	4	4	1	3	4	.256
MAJOR LEAGUE TOTALS			0	0	3.21	9	0	0	1	14	13	5	5	1	3	7	.255
MINOR LEAGUE TOTALS			32	39	3.61	152	100	1	8	589	599	285	236	35	211	464	.266

14 TYLER SAMPLE, RHP

BORN: June 27, 1989. **B-T:** L-R. **HT.:** 6-7. **WT.:** 245. **DRAFTED:** HS—Denver, 2008 (3rd round). **SIGNED BY:** Ken Munoz.

Sample's longer stride helped him take a big step forward as a prospect. He signed for slot money ($500,000) as a third-round pick in 2008, then quickly learned that he wasn't ready for pro ball. He allowed a run an inning in his debut in the Arizona League, thanks to his inability to repeat his delivery and his complete lack of control. But the Royals got Sample to lengthen his stride, which helped him begin to drive off the mound. His fastball sat consistently at 91-93 mph last season, and he significantly improved his control. His velocity and downhill angle make his fastball a potential plus pitch. He also throws a big-breaking knuckle-curve. Many pitchers struggle to use the knuckle-curve at more advanced levels because it becomes useful only as a chase pitch, but Kansas City is willing to let him continue to use his because he has shown an ability to throw it for strikes. His changeup still has a long way to go, which isn't a surprise considering he's still a relatively raw prospect. Sample has made rapid progress, which should allow him to join a talented Wilmington rotation this season.

Year	Club (League)	Class	W	L	ERA	G	GS	CG	SV	IP	H	R	ER	HR	BB	SO	AVG
2008	Royals (AZL)	R	0	5	9.00	10	8	0	0	27	30	36	27	0	29	39	.270
2009	Royals (AZL)	R	0	1	6.75	2	2	0	0	4	7	4	3	0	2	5	.412
	Burlington (APP)	R	4	2	2.84	12	9	0	1	51	34	22	16	2	20	44	.184
MINOR LEAGUE TOTALS			4	8	5.07	24	19	0	1	82	71	62	46	2	51	88	.227

15 KILA KA'AIHUE, 1B

BORN: March 29, 1984. **B-T:** L-R. **HT.:** 6-3. **WT.:** 220. **DRAFTED:** HS—Honolulu, 2002 (15th round). **SIGNED BY:** Eric Tokunaga.

When the Royals traded for Mike Jacobs before last season, it was a clear sign they were worried that Ka'aihue's Double-A Texas League MVP season in 2008 might be a fluke. Jacobs didn't work out, as he eventually was benched and later non-tendered, but Ka'aihue didn't help his own cause last year by putting up stats that seemed right in line with his pre-2008 production. Ka'aihue's best asset is an ability to get on base, a skill largely missing in Kansas City's big league lineup. He has a career .383 on-base percentage in the minors, thanks to his patience and excellent understanding of the strike zone. But where his patience gave him pitches he could drive in 2008, he became too focused on hitting homers last year, which predictably led to a power outage. Ka'aihue's bat speed always had been questioned before 2008, and it regressed last season. Power is the key to his production because he's a well below-average runner who's also a below-average defender at first base. The Royals rewarded his outstanding 2008 season with a September callup, but they left him in Triple-A last year even though he was already on the 40-man roster. It's likely he'll return to Omaha to serve again as insurance.

Year	Club (League)	Class	AVG	G	AB	R	H	2B	3B	HR	RBI	BB	SO	SB	OBP	SLG
2002	Royals (GCL)	R	.259	43	139	15	36	8	0	3	21	26	35	0	.381	.381
2003	Burlington (MWL)	LoA	.238	114	395	53	94	21	1	11	63	67	87	1	.355	.380
2004	Burlington (MWL)	LoA	.246	125	390	57	96	23	2	15	62	64	98	1	.361	.431
2005	High Desert (CAL)	HiA	.304	132	493	84	150	31	2	20	90	97	97	2	.428	.497
2006	Wichita (TL)	AA	.199	103	327	40	65	15	0	6	45	49	73	0	.303	.300
2007	Wilmington (CAR)	HiA	.251	60	207	28	52	8	0	9	42	35	38	1	.360	.420
	Wichita (TL)	AA	.246	70	244	37	60	13	0	12	40	41	40	0	.359	.447
2008	NW Arkansas (TL)	AA	.314	91	287	64	90	11	0	26	79	80	41	3	.463	.624
	Omaha (PCL)	AAA	.316	33	114	27	36	4	0	11	21	24	26	0	.439	.640
	Kansas City (AL)	MAJ	.286	12	21	4	6	0	0	1	1	3	2	0	.375	.429
2009	Omaha (PCL)	AAA	.252	131	441	83	111	27	1	17	57	102	85	0	.392	.433
MAJOR LEAGUE TOTALS			.286	12	21	4	6	0	0	1	1	3	2	0	.375	.429
MINOR LEAGUE TOTALS			.260	902	3037	488	790	161	6	130	520	585	620	8	.383	.446

16 JOHNNY GIAVOTELLA, 2B

BORN: July 10, 1987. **B-T:** R-R. **HT.:** 5-8. **WT.:** 185. **DRAFTED:** New Orleans, 2008 (2nd round). **SIGNED BY:** Scott Nichols.

Like fellow Wilmington infielders Mike Moustakas and Eric Hosmer, Giavotella found the Carolina League much less inviting than the Midwest League. But at least Giavotella did make an impressive turnaround during the second half, hitting .292/.355/.423. He still projects as an offensive second baseman with solid on-base skills and adequate power. He's a constant tinkerer at the plate, adjusting his feet and hands from slump to slump, but his hands generally work well with a short stroke. He has a good knowledge of the strike zone. None of that will matter if he doesn't improve defensively, though. After making significant strides during instructional league in 2008, Giovatella regressed last season. He seemed to take bad at-bats into the field and showed a slower first step and shoddy footwork. His range, especially to his right, was poor. His best tool on defense is his slightly above-average arm. Even at his best, Giavotella projected as a fringe-average defender whose bat would carry him. He looked more like a below-average defender last year, and his bat isn't good enough to carry that kind of glove. He's a slightly below-average runner but is aggressive on the basepaths. Giavotella will head to Double-A to continue to work on his defense.

Year	Club (League)	Class	AVG	G	AB	R	H	2B	3B	HR	RBI	BB	SO	SB	OBP	SLG
2008	Burlington (MWL)	LoA	.299	68	278	50	83	18	2	4	26	25	34	10	.355	.421
2009	Wilmington (CAR)	HiA	.258	133	476	84	123	24	8	6	52	66	54	26	.351	.380
MINOR LEAGUE TOTALS			.273	201	754	134	206	42	10	10	78	91	88	36	.352	.395

17 CHESLOR CUTHBERT, 3B

BORN: Nov. 16, 1992. **B-T:** R-R. **HT.:** 6-1. **WT.:** 190. **SIGNED:** Nicaragua, 2009. **SIGNED BY:** Orlando Esteves/Juan Lopez.

The Royals have shown a willingness to spend money in the draft in recent years, and they widened the net to place more emphasis on Latin America as well in 2009. That focus paid off with Cuthbert, a resident of the Corn Islands off the Nicaraguan coast. Scout Orlando Esteves had been following him for a couple of years and developed such a strong relationship with Cuthbert that several other teams backed off their pursuit, figuring it was fruitless. The difficult travel to the islands probably helped that decision. Cuthbert signed for $1.35 million, a bonus record for a Nicaraguan. The Corn Islands have a population of just 7,000, so he understandably has not faced much top-level competition. Scouts still consider him an advanced hitter for his age. He has a relatively mature body that gives him solid present power as well as good bat speed. Defensively, the biggest question is whether he'll have quick enough feet to stay at third base. He projects as a below-average runner as he matures, but he has a solid-average arm and good hands. The Corn Islands used to be under U.S. control, so its residents speak English, giving Cuthbert one less obstacle to overcome. He's years from Kansas City, but his upside ranks with just about any hitter's in the system. He'll likely debut in the Rookie-level Arizona League in 2010.

Year	Club (League)	Class	AVG	G	AB	R	H	2B	3B	HR	RBI	BB	SO	SB	OBP	SLG
2009	Did Not Play—Signed 2010 Contract															

18 KELVIN HERRERA, RHP

BORN: Dec. 31, 1989. **B-T:** R-R. **HT.:** 5-10. **WT.:** 162. **SIGNED:** Dominican Republic, 2006. **SIGNED BY:** Daurys Nin/Rafael Vasquez.

Poised for a breakout year in 2009, Herrera instead missed all but one start with a strained elbow ligament. He didn't require surgery, but his rehab stretched into August, at which point the Royals decided to shut him down for the season. He threw in the Dominican during the fall and is expected to be ready for spring training. The elbow injury stemmed from a change in his delivery. Herrera had been landing on his heel, and Kansas City wanted him to land on the ball of his foot. He overcompensated and shortened his stride to land on his toe, which produced the same jarring effect the Royals were trying to eliminate. They'll be patient with him because his stuff ranks with the best in the system. He is 5-foot-10 but showed a 91-92 mph fastball that touched 95 before the injury, with excellent armside run. He also throws a slurve and an advanced changeup for his age. His overall command is excellent for a teenager. He likely will start the season in low Class A, but if Herrera can stay healthy, it wouldn't be surprising to see him earn a quick promotion to Wilmington.

Year	Club (League)	Class	W	L	ERA	G	GS	CG	SV	IP	H	R	ER	HR	BB	SO	AVG
2007	Royals (DSL)	R	4	1	0.84	11	5	0	1	43	30	6	4	1	15	50	.197
2008	Burlington (APP)	R	2	2	1.42	11	8	0	0	51	48	17	8	0	5	45	.254
	Burlington (MWL)	LoA	2	0	2.13	3	1	0	0	13	4	3	0	2	7	.265
2009	Burlington (MWL)	LoA	1	0	0.00	1	1	0	0	5	3	0	0	0	0	1	.176
MINOR LEAGUE TOTALS			9	3	1.22	26	15	0	1	111	94	27	15	1	22	103	.231

19 JORDAN PARRAZ, OF

BORN: Oct. 8, 1984. **B-T:** R-R. **HT.:** 6-3. **WT.:** 212. **DRAFTED:** CC of Southern Nevada, 2004 (3rd round). **SIGNED BY:** Doug Deutsch (Astros).

The Royals traded disappointing lefthander Tyler Lumsden to the Astros for Parraz just after the 2008 Winter Meetings, and Parraz earned a spot on the 40-man roster this offseason after a solid year that was interrupted by a series of hamstring injuries. Parraz had an outstanding first half and was on the verge of a promotion to Triple-A when he pulled his left hamstring in a game in late June. After a stint on the disabled list, he got that promotion and continued to hit, but then he pulled his right hamstring, which ended his season in early August. Parraz moved his hands closer to his shoulders at the plate, which seemed to free up his swing last year. Whether it was that tweak or just a fresh start with a different team, he hit a career-high .348 in the Royals system last season. He always has been a gap-to-gap hitter with below-average usable power, even though he shows above-average raw power in batting practice. Parraz's best attribute is his strong, accurate arm, which rates as a 70 on the 20-80 scouting scale. He was drafted by the Phillies as a pitcher in the sixth round in 2003 but didn't sign. He doesn't run well enough to be an everyday center fielder, but he has enough athleticism to fill in there. The Royals held Parraz out of winter ball to make sure his legs are healthy, and he should be back in Omaha for Opening Day in 2010.

Year	Club (League)	Class	AVG	G	AB	R	H	2B	3B	HR	RBI	BB	SO	SB	OBP	SLG
2004	Greeneville (APP)	R	.244	53	180	35	44	6	5	4	21	24	44	8	.349	.400
2005	Vancouver (NWL)	SS	.250	26	76	10	19	3	0	0	6	10	20	2	.360	.289
	Tri-City (NYP)	SS	.262	71	282	31	74	11	2	5	35	12	45	17	.310	.369
2006	Tri-City (NYP)	SS	.336	70	253	46	85	18	2	6	38	33	44	23	.421	.494
2007	Lexington (SAL)	LoA	.281	122	462	69	130	28	3	14	76	47	89	33	.364	.446
2008	Salem (CAR)	HiA	.289	114	425	82	123	31	3	6	42	64	79	21	.399	.419

2009	NW Arkansas (TL)	AA	.358	64	226	35	81	17	3	7	42	29	25	4	.451	.553
	Idaho Falls (PIO)	R	.353	4	17	4	6	3	0	1	5	0	4	0	.353	.706
	Omaha (PCL)	AAA	.298	13	47	6	14	6	0	0	5	4	14	0	.358	.426
MINOR LEAGUE TOTALS			.293	537	1968	318	576	123	18	43	270	223	364	108	.381	.439

20 SALVADOR PEREZ, C

BORN: May 10, 1990. **B-T:** R-R. **HT.:** 6-3. **WT.:** 175. **SIGNED:** Venezuela, 2006. **SIGNED BY:** Juan Indiago.

The Royals faced a logjam of catching prospects at low Class A Burlington last year with Perez, Jose Bonilla and Sean McCauley. Rather than leave one of them back in extended spring training, the organization tried to spread the work between the trio and send the less-polished Bonilla back to Idaho Falls once the Pioneer League started in June. It proved tough for any of the three to get into a groove offensively or defensively with such irregular work, but Bonilla had a hot June so the Royals decided to demote Perez instead. The move worked wonders for Perez, who proved to be one of the better catchers in the Pioneer League, showing a solid gap-to-gap approach at the plate as well as above-average defense. His catch-and-throw skills make it likely he'll be a big leaguer. He has a tick above-average arm, receives the ball well and handles a pitching staff like a veteran. He threw out 33 percent of basestealers in 2009. What he lacks is athleticism and projection at the plate, which may just make him a solid backup at the big league level. He's a well below-average runner. Kansas City must deal with another catching surplus in 2010, with Wil Myers ready for low Class A. It's possible that Perez will jump to Wilmington because his defensive skills may be best-suited for handling what should be a talented pitching staff.

Year	Club (League)	Class	AVG	G	AB	R	H	2B	3B	HR	RBI	BB	SO	SB	OBP	SLG
2007	Royals (AZL)	R	.244	30	86	10	21	3	0	0	10	5	10	1	.320	.279
2008	Burlington (APP)	R	.325	13	40	4	13	0	1	0	10	5	5	0	.404	.375
	Idaho Falls (PIO)	R	.395	12	43	7	17	3	1	1	6	2	5	0	.413	.581
2009	Burlington (MWL)	LoA	.189	36	127	10	24	6	0	0	7	6	15	0	.230	.236
	Idaho Falls (PIO)	R	.309	59	233	35	72	14	3	2	38	19	25	0	.357	.421
MINOR LEAGUE TOTALS			.278	150	529	66	147	26	5	3	71	37	60	1	.329	.363

21 JOSE BONILLA, C

BORN: Aug. 4, 1988. **B-T:** R-R. **HT.:** 5-10. **WT.:** 180. **SIGNED:** Dominican Republic, 2006. **SIGNED BY:** Ramon Martinez.

If Salvador Perez is the safer bet as a catching prospect, Bonilla is more of a high-risk, high-reward type. Bonilla's first-half play earned him more regular work in low Class A last summer, but he seemed to press as the year went along. By the end of the season, he was chasing pitches well out of the zone and had become one of the easier outs in the Midwest League. He was in over his head, but his plus bat speed and arm strength still give him more upside than Perez. He has to learn the strike zone, but Bonilla's swing is solid and he projects to have average power. Behind the plate, he has all the tools, with soft hands and good feet, but he suffers concentration lapses where balls clank off his glove. He erased 34 percent of basestealers in 2009. Bonilla could flame out at Double-A, but he also has the potential to be an everyday big league catcher if he harnesses his considerable tools. He's likely to head back to Burlington, where he'll share time behind the plate with Wil Myers.

Year	Club (League)	Class	AVG	G	AB	R	H	2B	3B	HR	RBI	BB	SO	SB	OBP	SLG
2007	Royals (AZL)	R	.000	3	5	0	0	0	0	0	0	0	2	0	.000	.000
2008	Royals (AZL)	R	.357	34	112	20	40	9	3	5	24	5	22	5	.405	.625
2009	Burlington (MWL)	LoA	.217	100	351	43	76	12	3	5	36	29	92	6	.281	.311
MINOR LEAGUE TOTALS			.248	137	468	63	116	21	6	10	60	34	116	11	.307	.382

22 DERRICK ROBINSON, OF

BORN: Sept. 28, 1987. **B-T:** B-L. **HT.:** 5-11. **WT.:** 170. **DRAFTED:** HS—Gainesville, Fla., 2006 (4th round). **SIGNED BY:** Cliff Pastornicky.

At the end of last July, the Royals were about ready to give up on having Robinson switch-hit. He never had been comfortable hitting from the left side, though he never had really proven he could hit from the right side either. But when Kansas City approached him about batting solely righthanded, he asked if he could try one adjustment first. The Royals had spread out his stance, so he asked if he could move his feet closer together, partly because he felt it would allow him to get out of the box better. The results were convincing. After hitting three home runs in his first 1,475 pro at-bats, Robinson hit five in August as part of a .311/.362/.513 month—his first .300 or better month as a pro. The new stance allowed Robinson to get his hands through the strike zone quicker with more bat speed, and restored speed he had lost from home to first. He again started recording the sub-4.0-second times to first that were expected out of the former University of Florida quarterback recruit. He's a burner who ranked fifth in the minors with 69 stolen bases. Robinson still doesn't walk as much as a potential top-of-the-order speedster should, however. His speed does make him a well above-average center fielder, and his arm has improved to the point where it's now fringe-average. After two full seasons in Wilmington, Robinson will finally move up to Double-A in 2010. He'll have to prove that his hot August wasn't a fluke.

Year	Club (League)	Class	AVG	G	AB	R	H	2B	3B	HR	RBI	BB	SO	SB	OBP	SLG
2006	Royals (AZL)	R	.233	54	176	25	41	6	3	1	24	24	55	20	.335	.318
2007	Burlington (MWL)	LoA	.243	102	407	42	99	11	3	2	26	32	100	34	.299	.300
	Wilmington (CAR)	HiA	.385	3	13	1	5	1	0	0	0	1	0	1	.429	.462
2008	Wilmington (CAR)	HiA	.245	124	497	69	122	22	8	0	34	51	97	62	.316	.322
2009	Wilmington (CAR)	HiA	.239	128	522	72	125	19	5	5	47	35	90	69	.290	.324
MINOR LEAGUE TOTALS			.243	411	1615	209	392	59	19	8	131	143	342	186	.307	.318

23 KEATON HAYENGA, RHP

BORN: July 10, 1988. **B-T:** R-R. **HT.:** 6-4. **WT.:** 190. **DRAFTED:** HS—Eastlake, Wash., 2007 (31st round). **SIGNED BY:** Scott Ramsay.

The Royals paid Hayenga $300,000 as a 31st-round pick in 2007, then waited nearly two years to see him in a real game. He missed his first season and a half recovering from a torn labrum he sustained in high school. He showed flashes of being the same pitcher he was before the injury when he returned. Hayenga has the long arms and lanky frame to get good downward angle on his pitches and flashed a plus fastball, but he mostly pitched at 89-91 mph. During instructional league in 2008 and extended spring training in 2009, he had flashed a 92-94 mph fastball. His 12-to-6 curveball was also inconsistent, but it's a plus pitch with good depth when he snaps it off well. He throws a developing changeup. Now he just needs to get stronger and put the shoulder surgery behind him. He made every scheduled start last year, but he'll need to show he can maintain his best stuff more consistently in his second season back. A fine basketball player in high school, he has excellent athleticism, plus the feel and command scouts look for in a starting pitcher. If Hayenga gains just a tick more consistent velocity, he could have a breakout season in 2010. He should reach low Class A at some point this season.

Year	Club (League)	Class	W	L	ERA	G	GS	CG	SV	IP	H	R	ER	HR	BB	SO	AVG
2007	Did Not Play—Injured																
2008	Did Not Play—Injured																
2009	Burlington (APP)	R	4	7	3.66	13	13	0	0	66	68	40	27	2	16	34	.249
MINOR LEAGUE TOTALS			4	7	3.66	13	13	0	0	66	68	40	27	2	16	34	.249

24 BLAKE WOOD, RHP

BORN: Aug. 9, 1985. **B-T:** R-R. **HT.:** 6-4. **WT.:** 225. **DRAFTED:** Georgia Tech, 2005 (3rd round). **SIGNED BY:** Spencer Graham.

Wood continues to be proof that a huge radar gun reading isn't enough to be successful. He throws a 93-94 mph fastball that touches 97, as well as a power curveball that can be a strikeout pitch and an average changeup. Yet he has posted ERAs above 5.00 in Double-A in each of the past two seasons. He had even less success in the Arizona Fall League, going 1-1, 6.75 in 15 innings. Injuries have been part of Wood's problem. He had back surgery in 2007 to repair a herniated disc and missed the start of the 2009 season with more back problems. He returned quickly but missed another two months later in the season with elbow inflammation. Wood's delivery also doesn't do him any favors. He opens up too early, giving hitters a good look at his fastball. His struggles as a starter have led the Royals to look at him as a reliever, where his inability to repeat his delivery may be less of a problem. Kansas City added him to the 40-man roster in the offseason and still hopes that he could be a solid big league contributor, but his struggles have lowered his ceiling from a middle-of-the-rotation starter to more of a setup man. He should get his first taste of Triple-A in 2010.

Year	Club (League)	Class	W	L	ERA	G	GS	CG	SV	IP	H	R	ER	HR	BB	SO	AVG
2006	Idaho Falls (PIO)	R	3	1	4.50	12	12	0	0	52	50	28	26	1	15	46	.258
2007	Royals (AZL)	R	0	0	0.00	4	4	0	0	10	9	2	0	0	0	15	.250
	Burlington (MWL)	LoA	2	1	3.03	7	7	0	0	36	32	12	12	3	14	26	.239
	Wilmington (CAR)	HiA	0	1	4.66	2	2	0	0	10	9	5	5	1	3	11	.257
2008	Wilmington (CAR)	HiA	3	2	2.67	10	10	0	0	57	32	17	17	3	15	63	.168
	NW Arkansas (TL)	AA	5	7	5.30	18	18	2	0	87	96	55	51	7	32	76	.283
2009	Royals (AZL)	R	0	1	0.00	3	2	0	0	4	4	1	0	0	1	4	.250
	NW Arkansas (TL)	AA	2	8	5.83	17	13	1	0	79	92	52	51	8	28	49	.309
MINOR LEAGUE TOTALS			15	21	4.37	73	68	3	0	334	324	172	162	23	108	290	.261

25 PATRICK KEATING, RHP

BORN: June 9, 1987. **B-T:** R-R. **HT.:** 6-2. **WT.:** 215. **DRAFTED:** Florida, 2009 (20th round). **SIGNED BY:** Colin Gonzalez.

When the Royals drafted Keating in the 20th round and signed him for $1,000, they had little reason to think they were getting a sleeper. Keating went 4-4, 5.12 as a senior at Florida, losing his spot in the rotation. But area scout Colin Gonzalez and crosschecker Greg Kilby liked his stuff and pushed for Kansas City to draft him. The Royals persuaded Keating to throw his four-seam fastball more often, and it worked as he sat at 91-93 mph on most nights and touched 95. He also throws a hard-breaking slurve, which isn't a plus pitch but works when hitters are looking for the fastball. Keating dominated the Pioneer League and looked good in a short stint in high Class A. He doesn't have a high ceiling but could move quickly as a reliever. Keating could return to Wilmington to start his first full pro season.

Year	Club (League)	Class	W	L	ERA	G	GS	CG	SV	IP	H	R	ER	HR	BB	SO	AVG
2009	Idaho Falls (PIO)	R	5	1	1.78	22	0	0	8	30	20	8	6	1	10	46	.187
	Wilmington (CAR)	HiA	1	0	0.00	2	0	0	1	3	1	0	0	0	0	1	.125
MINOR LEAGUE TOTALS			6	1	1.64	24	0	0	9	33	21	8	6	1	10	47	.183

26 CRAWFORD SIMMONS, LHP

BORN: June 10, 1991. **B-T:** R-L. **HT.:** 6-2. **WT.:** 185. **DRAFTED:** HS—Statesboro, Ga., 2009 (14th round). **SIGNED BY:** Sean Gibbs.

The Royals knew they would have to pay big money to sign each of their top three 2009 draft picks, so they were mostly conservative afterward. They did take some late-round fliers on two-sport stars Lane Adams (13th round), Simmons (14th) and Justin Trapp (34th). Simmons is the best of that bunch. Area scout Sean Gibbs had an inkling that Kansas City could buy him out of his Georgia Tech scholarship, which it did for $450,000. Because he had the potential to play golf in college, the Royals spread his bonus payments over four years per MLB provisions for two-sport athletes. Simmons is a relatively polished young lefty, with an 86-90 mph fastball that touches 91, as well as a 12-to-6 curveball and solid feel for a changeup. His arm speed doesn't necessarily indicate that there's a lot more velocity to come, but Kansas City really likes his delivery, his command and his ability to snap off a plus curveball. He has a chance to develop into a solid fourth or fifth starter. Simmons signed too late to make his pro debut last summer, and he figures to open 2010 in extended spring training before reporting to Rookie ball in June.

Year	Club (League)	Class	W	L	ERA	G	GS	CG	SV	IP	H	R	ER	HR	BB	SO	AVG
2009	Did Not Play—Signed Late																

27 EDGAR OSUNA, LHP

BORN: Nov. 25, 1987. **B-T:** L-L. **HT.:** 6-1. **WT.:** 185. **SIGNED:** Mexico, 2004. **SIGNED BY:** Julian Perez/Manuel Samaniego (Braves).

Osuna may not be able to break bottles at the county fair, not to mention light up a radar gun, but he knows how to pitch. He keeps batters off balance with curveballs and one of the best changeups in the game. The Braves made him a full-time starter for the first time in his five pro seasons last year, and his performances seemed to be either outstanding or mediocre, with little in between. At his best, Osuna has a Bugs Bunny changeup that he mixes with a mid-80s fastball and a plus curveball. He does a good job of locating his pitches and despite his lack of velocity, he's not afraid to challenge hitters. Osuna gets in trouble when his pitches lack bite, causing them to hang and become in-game batting practice. The Royals picked him in the major league Rule 5 draft with the hope of using him out of the bullpen, though he's more suited to pitching multiple innings than serving as a one-out lefty because he succeeds by mixing his assortment of pitches. He had success as a reliever in the Mexican Pacific League over the winter and has a decent shot at sticking in Kansas City. If he doesn't, he has to clear waivers and get offered back to Atlanta for half of his $50,000 draft price.

Year	Club (League)	Class	W	L	ERA	G	GS	CG	SV	IP	H	R	ER	HR	BB	SO	AVG
2005	Braves1 (DSL)	R	3	1	0.94	13	8	0	0	48	34	10	5	0	7	57	.202
2006	Braves (GCL)	R	0	1	0.92	6	2	0	2	20	15	4	2	0	1	18	.217
2007	Danville (APP)	R	5	3	2.47	13	6	0	2	55	55	19	15	4	11	66	.258
2008	Rome (SAL)	LoA	10	5	3.38	30	14	2	5	125	122	53	47	9	31	135	.253
2009	Myrtle Beach (CAR)	HiA	3	6	4.33	14	14	1	0	73	82	40	35	4	14	56	.275
	Mississippi (SL)	AA	4	4	3.72	13	12	0	0	77	74	38	32	7	21	49	.251
MINOR LEAGUE TOTALS			25	20	3.08	89	56	3	9	397	382	164	136	24	85	381	.250

28 MATT MITCHELL, RHP

BORN: March 31, 1989. **B-T:** R-R. **HT.:** 6-2. **WT.:** 205. **DRAFTED:** HS—Barstow, Calif., 2007 (14th round). **SIGNED BY:** John Ramey.

When Mitchell led the Arizona League with a 1.80 ERA during his 2007 pro debut, it immediately made him one of the top pitching prospects in a thin system. Two years later as he works his way back from Tommy John surgery, he faces much less pressure to perform immediately because the Royals now have plenty of depth ahead of him. He returned to the mound last fall, showing the same 89-90 mph he had before his elbow reconstruction. Before he got hurt, he showed an average curveball and a developing changeup. His delivery is smooth, he does a good job of hiding the ball from hitters and he works both sides of the plate. Mitchell had excellent command for a teenager, though he lacked a strikeout pitch. He'll probably spend the 2010 season in low Class A trying to regain his curve and command, often the last two things to return after Tommy John surgery. He'll be 21 all season, so he still has plenty of time to develop.

Year	Club (League)	Class	W	L	ERA	G	GS	CG	SV	IP	H	R	ER	HR	BB	SO	AVG
2007	Royals (AZL)	R	5	1	1.80	14	7	0	1	55	34	16	11	0	25	72	.183
2008	Burlington (MWL)	LoA	8	8	3.47	25	21	0	0	117	116	55	45	9	25	77	.260
2009	Did Not Play—Injured																
MINOR LEAGUE TOTALS			13	9	2.94	39	28	0	1	172	150	71	56	9	50	149	.237

29 COLE WHITE, RHP

BORN: Jan. 22, 1988. **B-T:** R-R. **HT.:** 6-2. **WT.:** 195. **DRAFTED:** New Mexico, 2009 (6th round). **SIGNED BY:** Ken Munoz.

If White makes it to a major league bullpen, he may be the only big leaguer who gets to run to the mound as a song he wrote blares on the stadium loudspeakers. He has been playing drums and singing in bands since high school. The song "Fight A Storm," which White wrote with his old band Turning Point, was considered for the 2008 Grammy ballot for song of the year and best rock song. It didn't make the final cut, but being considered meant the Grammy judges regarded it as one of the top 100 rock songs of 2008. White now plays drums for the band FM South. His talent on the mound got him drafted in the sixth round last June, and he signed for $100,000. He's more raw than the typical college reliever, mostly because he was mostly a third baseman in high school and didn't start pitching regularly until he got to Paris (Texas) JC. While his delivery isn't particularly clean and there's some effort to it, White throws a 92-93 mph fastball that touches 95 mph. His three-quarters arm slot helps him get good sink on his fastball and allows him to succeed at times with only one pitch. His slider is below average because it's more of a sweeping pitch than a true two-planer. He profiles as a hard-throwing setup man and should spend 2010 in Class A.

Year	Club (League)	Class	W	L	ERA	G	GS	CG	SV	IP	H	R	ER	HR	BB	SO	AVG
2009	Idaho Falls (PIO)	R	3	2	1.29	12	0	0	3	21	15	7	3	1	13	23	.205
	Burlington (MWL)	LoA	0	0	2.16	8	0	0	0	17	16	5	4	1	9	13	.258
MINOR LEAGUE TOTALS			3	2	1.67	20	0	0	3	38	31	12	7	2	22	36	.230

30 HILTON RICHARDSON, OF

BORN: Jan. 10, 1989. **B-T:** L-L. **HT.:** 6-3. **WT.:** 200. **DRAFTED:** HS—Kirkland, Wash., 2007 (7th round). **SIGNED BY:** Scott Ramsay.

When the Royals decided to field three Rookie-level affiliates, it was with players like Richardson in mind. A 2007 high school draftee, he had struggled at the plate in each of his first two seasons in Rookie ball. But he moved through the Arizona, Appalachian and Pioneer leagues one step at a time, and he showed signs at Idaho Falls last season that he's figuring out how to use his considerable tools. The first thing scouts notice when watching Richardson is his speed. He's a well above-average runner from home to first and a threat to steal every time he reaches base. His quickness helps him in the outfield as well, where he covers plenty of ground as an above-average center fielder. His arm is below average. Richardson has a solid, muscular frame, but he's a tablesetter, not a power threat. He showed a better sense of the strike zone last season and took more walks. His swing mechanics partly explain his lack of pop because he doesn't extend his arms, instead cutting his swing off short. That helps him make contact but also ensures that he doesn't hit many stinging line drives. Richardson will get a chance to add some polish in his first shot at full season ball in 2010.

Year	Club (League)	Class	AVG	G	AB	R	H	2B	3B	HR	RBI	BB	SO	SB	OBP	SLG
2007	Royals (AZL)	R	.199	48	191	36	38	2	3	4	15	20	66	12	.295	.304
2008	Burlington (APP)	R	.229	54	205	36	47	7	5	1	16	17	61	10	.293	.327
	Royals (AZL)	R	.474	5	19	3	9	1	0	1	2	1	4	0	.500	.684
2009	Idaho Falls (PIO)	R	.313	48	166	34	52	12	2	1	17	19	44	20	.392	.428
	Burlington (MWL)	LoA	.154	8	26	2	4	2	0	0	2	1	10	2	.185	.231
MINOR LEAGUE TOTALS			.247	163	607	111	150	24	10	7	52	58	185	44	.323	.354

Los Angeles Angels

BY MATT EDDY

Tragedy descended on the Angels during the first week of the season, but they rebounded to win 97 games, third-most in franchise history. Nick Adenhart, the organization's reigning No. 1 prospect, and two others died in a collision with a suspected drunken driver on April 8. The 22-year-old had just thrown six shutout innings against the Athletics in his first appearance of the season. Los Angeles players wore a No. 34 patch on their jersey sleeves throughout the regular season and playoffs and voted the Adenhart family a full $138,038 playoff share after the season.

Beyond that tragedy, injuries sabotaged the club early in the season. The Angels hovered near .500 until John Lackey's return in mid-May helped stabilize the rotation. Because of injuries to Lackey, Kelvim Escobar and Ervin Santana, manager Mike Scioscia gave 36 starts to five righthanders—four of them rookies—who weren't expected to be major contributors. Trevor Bell, Anthony Ortega and Sean O'Sullivan came from within the organization, while 30-year-olds Shane Loux and Matt Palmer had signed as minor league free agents.

That quintet compiled an unsightly 5.45 ERA behind the homegrown trio of Lackey, Jered Weaver and Joe Saunders, so Los Angeles traded for Rays lefthander Scott Kazmir on Aug. 28 in advance of the playoffs. The acquisition cost them slugging Triple-A second baseman Sean Rodriguez, as well as a pair of promising high Class A talents in lefty Alex Torres and third baseman Matt Sweeney.

That the Angels cruised to their third straight American League West title—and their fifth in six years—in spite of all that adversity is yet another feather in Scioscia's cap. In a decade at the helm, he has guided the club to a 900-720 (.556) record, highlighted by the 2002 World Series championship.

Los Angeles finally vanquished the Red Sox in the AL Division Series after Boston had won three previous matchups in 2004, 2007 and 2008. The run came to an end against the Yankees, who beat them in a six-game AL Championship Series.

Even after losing Mark Teixeira as a free agent to the Yankees, the Angels scored more runs than any AL team besides New York after finishing 10th in the league in 2008. Los Angeles reaped the benefits of sticking with young players who had experienced growing pains at the big league level. Slick-fielding Erick Aybar hit .312 and posted the fourth-best OPS

LARRY GOREN

Kendry Morales helped carry the offense to new heights, rewarding the Angels' patience

TOP 30 PROSPECTS

1. Hank Conger, c	16. Chris Pettit, of
2. Peter Bourjos, of	17. Alexi Amarista, 2b
3. Mike Trout, of	18. Tyler Kehrer, lhp
4. Trevor Reckling, lhp	19. Jon Bachanov, rhp
5. Garrett Richards, rhp	20. Carlos Ramirez, c
6. Fabio Martinez, rhp	21. Ryan Chaffee, rhp
7. Randal Grichuk, of	22. Rafael Rodriguez, rhp
8. Tyler Skaggs, lhp	23. Bobby Mosebach, rhp
9. Jordan Walden, rhp	24. Mason Tobin, rhp
10. Trevor Bell, rhp	25. Rolando Gomez, ss
11. Mark Trumbo, 1b/of	26. Bobby Wilson, c
12. Pat Corbin, lhp	27. Andrew Romine, ss
13. Jean Segura, 2b	28. Ryan Mount, 2b
14. Tyler Chatwood, rhp	29. Clay Fuller, of
15. Will Smith, lhp	30. Michael Kohn, rhp

(.776) among AL shortstops, while Kendry Morales rocked 34 home runs and slugged .569.

The Angels also reversed their recent history of unsigned draft picks, investing $6.8 million in a crop that included five selections before the second round, all compensation choices for the loss of free agents Teixeira, Francisco Rodriguez and Jon Garland.

The extra picks helped bolster a farm system on the mend, and the Angels could be in store for another draft bonanza in 2010. They'll get two compensation picks for the loss of Chone Figgins to the Mariners, and two more for John Lackey signing with Boston.

General Manager: Tony Reagins. **Farm Director:** Abe Flores. **Scouting Director:** Eddie Bane.

Class	Team	League	W	L	PCT	Finish*	Manager(s)
Majors	Los Angeles Angels	American	97	65	.599	2nd (14)	Mike Scioscia
Triple-A	Salt Lake Bees	Pacific Coast	72	71	.503	8th (16)	Bobby Mitchell
Double-A	Arkansas Travelers	Texas	61	79	.436	t-7th (8)	Bobby Magallanes
High A	Rancho Cucamonga Quakes	California	61	79	.436	t-7th (10)	Keith Johnson
Low A	Cedar Rapids Kernels	Midwest	78	60	.565	5th (14)	Bill Mosiello
Rookie	Orem Owlz	Pioneer	51	25	.671	†1st (8)	Tom Kotchman
Rookie	AZL Angels	Arizona	38	18	.679	2nd (11)	Tyrone Boykin
Overall 2009 Minor League Record			361	332	.521	6th (30)	

*Finish in overall standings (No. of teams in league). †League champion.

LAST YEAR'S TOP 30

Player, Pos.		Status
1.	Nick Adenhart, rhp	Deceased
2.	Jordan Walden, rhp	No. 9
3.	Peter Bourjos, of	No. 2
4.	Trevor Reckling, lhp	No. 4
5.	Sean O'Sullivan, rhp	Majors
6.	Kevin Jepsen, rhp	Majors
7.	Hank Conger, c	No. 1
8.	Mark Trumbo, 1b	No. 11
9.	Anthony Ortega, rhp	Dropped out
10.	Mason Tobin, rhp	No. 24
11.	Tyler Chatwood, rhp	No. 14
12.	Will Smith, lhp	No. 15
13.	Bobby Wilson, c	No. 26
14.	Ryan Mount, 2b	No. 28
15.	Rafael Rodriguez, rhp	No. 22
16.	Clay Fuller, of	No. 29
17.	Chris Pettit, of	No. 16
18.	Matt Sweeney, 3b	(Rays)
19.	Manuarys Correa, rhp	Dropped out
20.	Robert Fish, lhp	Dropped out
21.	Ryan Chaffee, rhp	No. 21
22.	Andrew Romine, ss	No. 27
23.	Rolando Gomez, ss	No. 25
24.	Alex Torres, lhp	(Rays)
25.	Matt Brown, 3b/1b	Dropped out
26.	Luis Jimenez, 3b	Dropped out
27.	Terrell Alliman, of/3b	Dropped out
28.	David Herndon, rhp	(Phillies)
29.	Nick Green, rhp	(Brewers)
30.	Hainley Statia, ss	Dropped out

BEST TOOLS

Best Hitter for Average	Hank Conger
Best Power Hitter	Mark Trumbo
Best Strike-Zone Discipline	Hank Conger
Fastest Baserunner	Peter Bourjos
Best Athlete	Mike Trout
Best Fastball	Garrett Richards
Best Curveball	Garrett Richards
Best Slider	Fabio Martinez
Best Changeup	Trevor Reckling
Best Control	Trevor Bell
Best Defensive Catcher	Bobby Wilson
Best Defensive Infielder	Andrew Romine
Best Infield Arm	Rolando Gomez
Best Defensive Outfielder	Peter Bourjos
Best Outfield Arm	Angel Castillo

PROJECTED 2013 LINEUP

Catcher	Mike Napoli
First Base	Kendry Morales
Second Base	Howie Kendrick
Third Base	Brandon Wood
Shortstop	Erick Aybar
Left Field	Torii Hunter
Center Field	Peter Bourjos
Right Field	Mike Trout
Designated Hitter	Hank Conger
No. 1 Starter	Jered Weaver
No. 2 Starter	Scott Kazmir
No. 3 Starter	Joe Saunders
No. 4 Starter	Ervin Santana
No. 5 Starter	Trevor Reckling
Closer	Kevin Jepsen

TOP PROSPECTS OF THE DECADE

Year	Player, Pos.	2009 Org.
2000	Ramon Ortiz, rhp	Giants
2001	Joe Torres, lhp	Dodgers
2002	Casey Kotchman, 1b	Red Sox
2003	Francisco Rodriguez, rhp	Mets
2004	Casey Kotchman, 1b	Red Sox
2005	Casey Kotchman, 1b	Red Sox
2006	Brandon Wood, ss	Angels
2007	Brandon Wood, ss	Angels
2008	Brandon Wood, ss	Angels
2009	Nick Adenhart, rhp	Deceased

TOP DRAFT PICKS OF THE DECADE

Year	Player, Pos.	2009 Org.
2000	Joe Torres, lhp	Dodgers
2001	Casey Kotchman, 1b	Red Sox
2002	Joe Saunders, lhp	Angels
2003	Brandon Wood, ss	Angels
2004	Jered Weaver, rhp	Angels
2005	Trevor Bell, rhp (1st round supp.)	Angels
2006	Hank Conger, c	Angels
2007	Jon Bachanov, rhp (1st round supp.)	Angels
2008	Tyler Chatwood, rhp (2nd round)	Angels
2009	Randal Grichuk, of	Angels

LARGEST BONUSES IN CLUB HISTORY

Jered Weaver, 2004	$4,000,000
Kendry Morales, 2004	$3,000,000
Troy Glaus, 1997	$2,250,000
Joe Torres, 2000	$2,080,000
Casey Kotchman, 2001	$2,075,000

LOS ANGELES ANGELS

TOP 2010 ROOKIE: Trevor Bell, rhp. Command and composure could help him erase memories of a poor big league debut last year.

BREAKOUT PROSPECT: Jean Segura, 2b. The young Dominican has supreme feel for hitting and the potential to hit for power and steal bases.

SLEEPER: Johnny Hellweg, rhp. The Angels already have fielded trade offers for hard-throwing, 6-foot-7 relief prospect.

SOURCE OF TOP 30 TALENT

Homegrown	30	Acquired	0
College	6	Trades	0
Junior college	5	Rule 5 draft	0
High school	13	Independent leagues	0
Draft-and-follow	2	Free agents/waivers	0
Nondrafted free agents	0		
International	4		

Numbers in parentheses indicate prospect rankings

LF
Randal Grichuk (7)
Chris Pettit (16)

CF
Peter Bourjos (2)
Mike Trout (3)
Clay Fuller (29)
Travis Witherspoon
P.J. Phillips
Tyson Auer
Jake Locker

RF
Terry Evans
Jeremy Moore
Angel Castillo
Terrell Alliman

3B
Freddy Sandoval
Luis Jimenez
Casey Haerther

SS
Rolando Gomez (25)
Andrew Romine (27)
Hainley Statia
Jon Karcich

2B
Jean Segura (13)
Alexi Amarista (17)
Ryan Mount (28)
Nate Sutton
Ivan Contreras
Wes Hatton

1B
Mark Trumbo (11)
Dillon Baird
Gabe Jacobo
Roberto Lopez
Jamie Mallard

C
Hank Conger (1)
Carlos Ramirez (20)
Bobby Wilson (26)
Ryan Budde
Ben Johnson
Anel de los Santos

RHP

Starters	Relievers
Garrett Richards (5)	Jon Bachanov (19)
Fabio Martinez (6)	Ryan Chaffee (21)
Jordan Walden (9)	Rafael Rodriguez (22)
Trevor Bell (10)	Bobby Mosebach (23)
Tyler Chatwood (14)	Michael Kohn (30)
Mason Tobin (24)	Johnny Hellweg
Anthony Ortega	Rich Thompson
Tommy Mendoza	Fernando Rodriguez
Tim Kiely	Ismael Carmona
Pil-Joon Jang	Eddie McKiernan
Manaurys Correa	Francisco Rodriguez
Jeremy Thorne	David Carpenter
Young-Il Jung	Nick Pugliesse
Danny Reynolds	Marco Albano
	Jeremy Haynes

LHP

Starters	Relievers
Trevor Reckling (4)	Drew Taylor
Tyler Skaggs (8)	Robert Fish
Pat Corbin (12)	Josh Blanco
Will Smith (15)	Barret Browning
Tyler Kehrer (18)	
Manuel Flores	
Michael Anton	

DRAFT ANALYSIS

2009

BEST PURE HITTER: The Angels considered OF Mike Trout (1) one of the draft's few potential five-tool players and were impressed by his offensive polish. He's not afraid to use the whole field and legs out hits with his speed.

BEST POWER HITTER: OF Randal Grichuk (1) has well above-average raw power, which made him a first-rounder. 1B Jamie Mallard (18) has similar pop but must trim up his 5-foot-11, 270-pound frame.

FASTEST RUNNER: Trout has plus-plus speed, going from home to first in 3.9 seconds from the right side of the plate.

BEST DEFENSIVE PLAYER: Trout has the tools to be a plus center fielder. C Carlos Ramirez (8) stands out with his receiving skills and intangibles, but his modest arm strength keeps him from being an elite defender.

BEST FASTBALL: RHP Garrett Richards (1s) has touched 97 mph and sits at 93-95 with his fastball. LHP Tyler Kehrer (1s) also has reached 95.

BEST SECONDARY PITCH: LHP Tyler Skaggs (1s) has two breaking balls and the Angels prefer his slider to his big, slow curve.

BEST PRO DEBUT: 1B Dillon Baird (11) won the Pioneer League batting title at Rookie-level Orem, batting .372/.452/.567. That came on the heels of him leading the Pacific-10 Conference batting, on-base percentage and slugging during the spring. Ramirez fell short of qualifying for the Pioneer League title but was even better, hitting .376/.500/.638. Trout ranked as the Rookie-level Arizona League's No. 1 prospect after batting .360/.418/.506 with 13 stolen bases.

BEST ATHLETE: Jake Locker (10) will play for the Angels—if he ever plays baseball. He hasn't played baseball at Washington and is an NFL first-round prospect as a quarterback. Los Angeles considered him the best athlete available in the draft. Trout wasn't far behind. LHP Pat Corbin (2) is a lithe 6-foot-3, 170-pounder who played one year of basketball at Mohawk Valley (N.Y.) CC before transferring to Chipola (Fla.) JC.

MOST INTRIGUING BACKGROUND: Unsigned C Asaad Ali (40) is the son of boxing great Muhammad Ali. Unsigned LHP Josh Spence (3) is the highest-drafted Australian in history. RHP Taylor Kinzer (24) learned from his high school pitching coach and father Matt, who reached the big leagues in 1989-90. 2B Phil Bando's (45) father Chris and uncle Sal played in the majors.

CLOSEST TO THE MAJORS: Richards, especially if he shifts to the bullpen, though the Angels expect him to remain a starter. Ramirez also could move quickly at a premium position.

BEST LATE-ROUND PICK: Baird's bat should help him move, but he has to add loft to his line-drive swing to profile at first base.

THE ONE WHO GOT AWAY: Spence, a finesse specialist. Late-blooming LHP Sam Selman (14) has a projectable frame and a fastball that hits 94 mph, but he chose to attend Vanderbilt.

ASSESSMENT: After not having a first-round choice since Hank Conger in 2006, the Angels had two last June, as well as three sandwich picks. Trout excites Los Angeles on his own, and the club also envisions Grichuk, Skaggs, Richards and Kehrer making a significant impact.

2008

The Angels lacked a first-round pick, and handicapped themselves further by not signing OF Zach Cone (3) and OF Khiry Cooper (5). RHP Tyler Chatwood (2) and LHP Will Smith (7) are the best players who turned pro from this crop.

GRADE: D

2007

Los Angeles surrendered its first- and second-rounder as free agent compensation, top pick RHP Jon Bachanov (1s) blew out his elbow almost immediately and RHP Matt Harvey (3) failed to sign. LHP Trevor Reckling (8) is carrying this crop by himself.

GRADE: D

2006

C Hank Conger (1) finally stayed healthy last season, but draft-and-follow RHP Jordan Walden (12) battled a forearm strain. 3B Matt Sweeney's (8) potent bat helped the Angels land Scott Kazmir via trade, while OF Chris Pettit (19) reached the majors last September.

GRADE: C+

2005

OF Peter Bourjos (10) is Torii Hunter's heir apparent in center field. RHPs Trevor Bell (1s), Sean O'Sullivan (3) and Bobby Mosebach (9) made their big league debuts in 2009, though none has a huge ceiling. LHP Brian Matusz (4) and C Buster Posey (50) went on to become top five picks in the 2008 draft.

GRADE: C

*Draft analysis by John Manuel (2009) and Jim Callis (2005-08). Numbers in parentheses indicate draft rounds. *Bonuses for 2005 are first 10 rounds only.*

BILL MITCHELL

HANK CONGER, C

Born: Jan. 29, 1988.
Height: 6-1. **Weight:** 220.
Bats: B. **Throws:** R.
Drafted: HS—Huntington Beach, Calif., 2006 (1st round).
Signed by: Bobby DeJardin.

High school catchers historically have been the riskiest of first-round gambles. For every Joe Mauer, taken with the No. 1 pick in 2001, teams end up with a dozen players like Max Sapp, who hasn't advanced past low Class A since the Astros selected him 23rd overall in 2006. Conger, taken two picks after Sapp, is starting to live up to expectations after battling injuries early in his career. A second-generation Korean-American, he was nicknamed in honor of his grandfather's favorite player, Hank Aaron. Considered the top prep power hitter in the 2006 draft, Conger signed quickly for $1.35 million and rated as the Rookie-level Arizona League's No. 1 prospect in his pro debut. However, he missed time with a broken hamate bone in his right hand, setting the tone for injury-shortened seasons in 2007 (lower back and hamstring issues) and 2008 (a torn labrum in his throwing shoulder). Healthy last season, Conger caught 87 games for Double-A Arkansas, nearly doubling his career total.

With his well above-average bat speed and power from both sides of the plate, Conger's potential as a run producer has been readily apparent since he signed. He makes more consistent hard contact than many power hitters. He lets the ball travel deep in the hitting zone and his swing plane suggests increased power output as he matures. Conger remains a more dangerous hitter from the left side of the plate, but he closed that gap in 2009, posting a higher OPS from the right side (.840 versus .772). His overall plate discipline took a step forward too, as he logged more pro plate appearances than ever before. Behind the plate, Conger draws compliments for his game management skills. He's a leader who receives and blocks well, and he has above-average arm strength. He threw out 30 percent of basestealers last season.

The power-suppressing dimensions of Little Rock's Dickey-Stephens Park initially got in Conger's head. But when he focused on stroking line drives in the second half, his productivity soared and he batted .305/.404/.457. Some scouts think he can unlock more power by leveling his swing path slightly and producing more backspin on the ball. Conger lacks accuracy on his throws because of shaky footwork that cuts off his extension. Despite his arm strength and an improved transfer, there's some question as to how much he'll be able to deter big league basestealers. A well below-average runner who's more agile than his bulky frame suggests, Conger will need to maintain flexibility to stay behind the plate.

The Angels have a lot riding on Conger, their only first-round pick in four drafts from 2005-08. Big league manager Mike Scioscia demands much from his catchers, and Conger has much work to do on the defensive side before he's ready to play in Los Angeles. He may return to Double-A, at least to begin 2010. He has all-star potential if he can stay healthy and behind the plate.

Year	Club (League)	Class	AVG	G	AB	R	H	2B	3B	HR	RBI	BB	SO	SB	OBP	SLG
2006	Angels (AZL)	R	.319	19	69	11	22	3	4	1	11	7	11	1	.382	.522
2007	Angels (AZL)	R	.267	3	15	2	4	1	0	0	3	0	3	0	.267	.333
	Cedar Rapids (MWL)	LoA	.290	84	290	33	84	20	0	11	48	21	48	9	.336	.472
2008	R. Cucamonga (CAL)	HiA	.303	73	294	47	89	20	2	13	75	14	55	2	.333	.517
2009	Arkansas (TL)	AA	.295	123	458	61	135	20	3	11	68	55	68	4	.369	.424
MINOR LEAGUE TOTALS			.297	302	1126	154	334	64	9	36	205	97	185	16	.351	.465

2 PETER BOURJOS, OF

BORN: March 31, 1987. **B-T:** R-R. **HT.:** 6-1. **WT.:** 180. **DRAFTED:** HS—Scottsdale, Ariz., 2005 (10th round). **SIGNED BY:** John Gracio.

The Angels signed Bourjos for $325,000 as a 10th-rounder out of high school, gambling on his athleticism and bloodlines. His father Chris played professionally for seven seasons, reaching San Francisco for a cup of coffee in 1980, and now scouts for the Brewers. Bourjos led the Texas League with 14 triples last season, but he tailed off in the second half as he played through a ligament tear in his left wrist that required postseason surgery. Bourjos claims that no one ever has bested him in a footrace. Managers rated him the TL's most exciting player as well as its best defensive outfielder. He ranges well into both gaps, and his long legs belie his plus-plus speed. His solid-average arm strength gives him an advantage over most center fielders. He has a quick bat and made significant improvement at the plate in 2009, more notably with his discipline and pitch recognition. Though Bourjos ranked fifth in the TL with 32 stolen bases, Los Angeles would like him to run more frequently and improve his success rate (which dipped to 73 percent last year). He shows gap power when he stays balanced and gets his arms extended, but he still tends to open early and leave himself vulnerable to offspeed stuff away. Injuries to his left arm, first a broken finger and then a hyperextended elbow, cost him some much-needed at-bats in 2007 and 2008. Bourjos has game-changing defensive ability, and his progress at the plate has boosted his stock. The Angels added him to the 40-man roster in the offseason, but with Torii Hunter under contract for three more seasons, Bourjos still has plenty of time to develop.

Year	Club (League)	Class	AVG	G	AB	R	H	2B	3B	HR	RBI	BB	SO	SB	OBP	SLG
2006	Orem (PIO)	R	.292	65	250	42	73	16	7	5	28	22	67	13	.354	.472
2007	Angels (AZL)	R	.313	4	16	3	5	0	1	0	2	1	2	0	.353	.438
	Cedar Rapids (MWL)	LoA	.274	63	237	37	65	9	6	5	29	20	53	19	.335	.426
2008	R. Cucamonga (CAL)	HiA	.295	121	509	83	150	29	10	9	51	19	96	50	.326	.444
2009	Arkansas (TL)	AA	.281	110	437	72	123	16	14	6	51	49	77	32	.354	.423
MINOR LEAGUE TOTALS			.287	363	1449	237	416	70	38	25	161	111	295	114	.341	.440

3 MIKE TROUT, OF

BORN: Aug. 7, 1991. **B-T:** R-R. **HT.:** 6-1. **WT.:** 200. **DRAFTED:** HS—Millville, N.J., 2009 (1st round). **SIGNED BY:** Greg Morhardt.

A favorite of area scouts in the Northeast for his talent and makeup, Trout was the only player to appear at MLB Network's studios for the television broadcast of the draft last June. It wasn't a wasted trip. The Angels selected him 26th overall and signed him for $1.215 million. He rated as the Rookie-level Arizona League's No. 1 prospect and finished second in the batting race at .360. Trout has a line-drive stroke, the ability to make adjustments and a refined batting eye. His strength and bat speed give him the potential for average power. As good as his feel for hitting is, his plus-plus speed stands out even more. He gets from home to first in 3.9 seconds from the right side, enabling him to leg out infield hits. Built like a football defensive back, he has above-average range and instincts in center field. His arm is average. Trout hit only one home run in his pro debut and has yet to learn to pull the ball consistently. When using the opposite field, he tends to push the ball rather than drive through it. Already listed at 200 pounds, he might fill out, slow down and move to an outfield corner. The Angels haven't developed a starting outfielder since Darin Erstad, so they were thrilled to grab Trout, believing he was overlooked as a high schooler from the Northeast. He'll take his well-rounded game and five-tool potential to low Class A Cedar Rapids in 2010.

Year	Club (League)	Class	AVG	G	AB	R	H	2B	3B	HR	RBI	BB	SO	SB	OBP	SLG
2009	Angels (AZL)	R	.360	39	164	29	59	7	7	1	25	18	28	13	.418	.506
	Cedar Rapids (MWL)	LoA	.267	5	15	1	4	0	0	0	0	4	6	0	.421	.267
MINOR LEAGUE TOTALS			.352	44	179	30	63	7	7	1	25	22	34	13	.419	.486

4 TREVOR RECKLING, LHP

BORN: May 22, 1989. **B-T:** L-L. **HT.:** 6-1. **WT.:** 195. **DRAFTED:** HS—Newark, N.J., 2007 (8th round). **SIGNED BY:** Greg Morhardt.

Injuries at the big league level unleashed a wave of premature promotions in the system last year. Reckling, then 19, raced to Double-A after just three starts at high Class A Rancho Cucamonga. He had no problem adjusting, ranking fourth in the Texas League with a 2.93 ERA and 7.1 strikeouts per nine innings. He pitched in the Futures Game in July and for Team USA at the World Cup in September, but an oblique injury shelved him after two appearances. Reckling's best pitch is a sweepy slider-curve hybrid that sits at 78-82 mph with good spin and hard tilt. That weapon makes him a nightmare for lefthanders, who hit just .165 with four extra-base hits in 121 at-bats against him in 2009. His fastball ranges from 87-93 mph with run to his glove side. He works quickly and delivers the ball from a herky-jerky, high three-quarters delivery, which provides steep angle and terrific deception to his pitches. He took quickly to a changeup, commanding it with deceptive arm speed from the get-go. He'll throw any of his pitches at any point in the count. Because his delivery features a lot of moving parts and he loses his release point, Reckling's fastball command isn't where it needs to be. He led the TL with 75 walks and 14 wild pitches. He continues to shy away from his heater at times, favoring his quality secondary stuff. Despite rushing him last year, the Angels will give Reckling plenty of time to develop as a mid-rotation starter. If he can't iron out his command, his breaking ball would make him a nasty reliever.

Year	Club (League)	Class	W	L	ERA	G	GS	CG	SV	IP	H	R	ER	HR	BB	SO	AVG
2007	Angels (AZL)	R	3	1	2.75	9	5	0	2	36	33	13	11	2	7	55	.236
2008	Cedar Rapids (MWL)	LoA	10	7	3.37	26	26	1	0	152	137	64	57	8	59	128	.246
2009	R. Cucamonga (CAL)	HiA	1	2	0.95	3	3	0	0	19	9	3	2	2	3	16	.138
	Arkansas (TL)	AA	8	7	2.93	23	23	1	0	135	118	50	44	4	75	106	.244
MINOR LEAGUE TOTALS			22	17	2.99	61	57	2	2	343	297	130	114	16	144	305	.239

5 GARRETT RICHARDS, RHP

BORN: May 27, 1988. **B-T:** R-R. **HT.:** 6-3. **WT.:** 210. **DRAFTED:** Oklahoma, 2009 (1st round supplemental). **SIGNED BY:** Arnold Brathwaite.

Scouts left Richards' college starts at Oklahoma shaking their heads. He ran up a 6.57 ERA in three years for the Sooners, but his electric arm and strong finish in 2009 got him drafted 42nd overall. After signing for $802,000, he threw strikes and didn't allow a homer in 35 innings at Rookie-level Orem. Minor shoulder tightness scrapped a plan to have him make a start in low Class A at the end of the year. Richards' fastball explodes out of his hand at 90-97 mph, usually sitting at 93-94 down in the zone with average life and sink. He throws an average-to-plus curveball with depth and tilt, and a solid-average slider in the mid-80s with late break. If that weren't enough, he also throws a fading, sinking changeup that's a plus pitch at times. His arm is quick and his delivery is clean. Despite his strong debut, Richards' lack of consistent amateur success can't be ignored. He had trouble throwing strikes and hitters got a good look at his pitches, though those problems weren't an issue in pro ball. Richards has the size, stuff and command to pitch at the top of a rotation. If he spends time at Cedar Rapids in 2010, it probably won't be for long. He stands a good chance of finishing the year in Double-A.

Year	Club (League)	Class	W	L	ERA	G	GS	CG	SV	IP	H	R	ER	HR	BB	SO	AVG
2009	Orem (PIO)	R	3	1	1.53	8	8	0	0	35	37	6	6	0	4	30	.278
MINOR LEAGUE TOTALS			3	1	1.53	8	8	0	0	35	37	6	6	0	4	30	.278

6 FABIO MARTINEZ, RHP

BORN: Oct. 29, 1989. **B-T:** R-R. **HT.:** 6-3. **WT.:** 190. **SIGNED:** Dominican Republic, 2007. **SIGNED BY:** Leo Perez.

The Angels discreetly signed Martinez as a 17-year-old in April 2007, but more than a year elapsed before anybody took notice. Following up on a forgettable pro debut, he dominated Rookie-level Dominican Summer League competition in 2008 with 93 strikeouts in 76 innings. Martinez took another giant step forward in 2009, leading the Arizona League with 92 strikeouts and a .197 opponent average. Arm strength separates Martinez from the pack. He pitches at 93 mph, touches 96 with his four-seamer and holds that velocity deep into games. Tall, lean and projectable, he generates good downhill plane from his high three-quarters arm slot. He has the potential to have an average two-seam fastball and a plus slider. Martinez's command comes and goes. He gets a lot of swings and misses on high fastball that more advanced hitters will lay off. He could get more lateral movement on his fastball if he lowered his arm slot slightly. He needs to stay on top of his slider more consistently, and his workable changeup needs more refinement than any of his pitches. Slow and deliberate to the plate, he's vulnerable to basestealers. He could improve his composure on the mound by not wearing his emotions on his sleeve. If Martinez refines his command, he has true top-of-the-rotation stuff. He'll make the jump to low Class A in 2010.

Year	Club (League)	Class	W	L	ERA	G	GS	CG	SV	IP	H	R	ER	HR	BB	SO	AVG
2007	Angels (DSL)	R	1	2	6.75	13	3	0	1	25	27	22	19	0	26	30	.270
2008	Angels (DSL)	R	6	1	1.53	13	13	1	0	76	55	17	13	1	32	93	.202
2009	Angels (AZL)	R	3	2	3.26	14	13	0	0	61	45	33	22	1	36	92	.197
	Orem (PIO)	R	1	0	3.86	2	2	0	0	7	5	4	3	2	2	10	.192
MINOR LEAGUE TOTALS			11	5	3.03	42	31	1	1	169	132	76	57	4	96	225	.211

7 RANDAL GRICHUK, OF

GAINS DuVALL

BORN: Aug. 13, 1991. **B-T:** R-R. **HT.:** 6-1. **WT.:** 195. **DRAFTED:** HS—Rosenberg, Texas, 2009 (1st round). **SIGNED BY:** Kevin Ham.

Grichuk thrived on the showcase circuit, bashed 21 homers in 75 at-bats as a high school senior and then dazzled the Angels at a predraft workout. Using the first of its five picks before the second round, Los Angeles selected him 24th overall and signed him quickly for $1.242 million. He led the Arizona League with 76 hits and 10 triples and ranked second with 30 extra-base hits and 53 RBIs in his pro debut. A noted pull hitter in high school—he blasted a 475-foot shot at Tropicana Field during one show-case—Grichuk showed impressive opposite-field power in his debut. His strong hands and leveraged, quick swing should produce above-average power. His work ethic and passion are quite strong, allaying concerns about his fringe-average range and arm. To hit for average, Grichuk will have to improve his plate discipline and pitch recognition. He'll continue to see a steady diet of breaking balls until he proves he can hit them. He's just a fair athlete who figures to lose a bit of his fringy speed as he ages, so his bat will have to carry the day. Though he played some center field in the AZL, his future is in left. He doesn't look comfortable running the bases and needs to use his legs more in making throws. The Angels view Grichuk as a premium hitter with power. He and fellow first-rounder Mike Trout will advance together to low Class A in 2010 and could form the heart of Los Angeles' lineup of the future.

Year	Club (League)	Class	AVG	G	AB	R	H	2B	3B	HR	RBI	BB	SO	SB	OBP	SLG
2009	Angels (AZL)	R	.322	53	236	47	76	13	10	7	53	9	64	6	.352	.551
MINOR LEAGUE TOTALS			.322	53	236	47	76	13	10	7	53	9	64	6	.352	.551

8 TYLER SKAGGS, LHP

BRIAN FLEMING PHOTOGRAPHY

BORN: July 13, 1991. **B-T:** L-L. **HT.:** 6-4. **WT.:** 180. **DRAFTED:** HS—Santa Monica, Calif., 2009 (1st round supplemental). **SIGNED BY:** Bobby DeJardin.

The first of a run of tall, loose-armed pitchers drafted by the Angels in their 2009 draft bonanza, Skaggs signed for $1 million in early August as the 40th overall pick. A three-sport star at Santa Monica (Calif.) High, where his mother Debbie is volleyball coach, he grew up an Angels fan and passed on a Cal State Fullerton scholarship to turn pro. He consistently pitched well in front of scouts, but an ankle injury during the spring helped drop him out of the first round. Skaggs is the textbook definition of projectable. He's long-limbed, athletic and blessed with incredible arm speed. He delivers a lively 88-91 mph fastball down in the zone, and he could sit more comfortably at 92-93 with armside run when his upper body matures. His hard 75-78 mph slider is a knockout offering that features two-plane break. He likes to mix in a slow curveball as a surprise third pitch. He maintains a free and easy motion that reminds the Angels of Brian Matusz, whom they let slip away as a fourth-rounder out of high school in 2005. Los Angeles wants Skaggs to develop his below-average changeup at the expense of the slow curve. He shows some feel for the changeup, but it's a long ways away. Because he logged just 10 innings after signing, Skaggs may stay behind in extended spring training at the start of 2010. He projects as a solid mid-rotation starter.

Year	Club (League)	Class	W	L	ERA	G	GS	CG	SV	IP	H	R	ER	HR	BB	SO	AVG
2009	Angels (AZL)	R	0	0	0.00	3	2	0	0	6	4	0	0	0	1	7	.182
	Orem (PIO)	R	0	0	4.50	2	0	0	0	4	5	4	2	0	1	6	.278
MINOR LEAGUE TOTALS			0	0	1.80	5	2	0	0	10	9	4	2	0	2	13	.225

9 JORDAN WALDEN, RHP

BORN: Nov. 16, 1987. **B-T:** R-R. **HT.:** 6-5. **WT.:** 240. **DRAFTED:** Grayson County (Texas) CC, D/F 2006 (12th round). **SIGNED BY:** Arnold Brathwaite.

The Angels signed Walden for $1 million in May 2007 as a draft-and-follow out of Grayson County (Texas) CC, the same program that produced John Lackey. Walden had entered 2006 as the top high school prospect in the draft, but a poor showing dropped him to the 12th round. He dominated in his first two pro seasons, but a strained forearm limited him to 13 mostly ineffective starts in 2009. Though Walden clearly was not at his best last year, he never completely lost his heavy 90-94 mph fastball. Facing it has been likened to trying to hit a brick. Batters struggle to lift his fastball when it's down in the zone, and he has surrendered just 14 homers in 281 pro innings. His mid-80s slider has occasional tilt. Walden's forearm injury sapped him of his peak velocity and negatively affected his control. His changeup still lags behind his other pitches, and inconsistent mechanics also played a role in his poor command. He didn't pitch with his usual chutzpah while dealing with failure for the first time as a pro. After effectively losing a year of development, Walden rehabbed throughout instructional league in an effort to be ready for spring training. If his command doesn't improve, his power fastball/slider combo appears tailored to a late-inning relief role.

Year	Club (League)	Class	W	L	ERA	G	GS	CG	SV	IP	H	R	ER	HR	BB	SO	AVG
2007	Orem (PIO)	R	1	1	3.08	15	15	0	0	64	49	27	22	3	17	63	.209
2008	Cedar Rapids (MWL)	LoA	4	6	2.18	18	18	1	0	107	80	32	26	3	32	91	.207
	R. Cucamonga (CAL)	HiA	5	2	4.04	9	9	0	0	49	42	30	22	4	24	50	.226
2009	Arkansas (TL)	AA	1	5	5.25	13	13	0	0	60	72	39	35	4	29	57	.301
MINOR LEAGUE TOTALS			11	14	3.37	55	55	1	0	281	243	128	105	14	102	261	.232

10 TREVOR BELL, RHP

BORN: Oct. 12, 1986. **B-T:** L-R. **HT.:** 6-2. **WT.:** 186. **DRAFTED:** HS—La Crescenta, Calif., 2005 (1st round supplemental). **SIGNED BY:** Tim Corcoran.

Bell signed for $925,000 as the 37th overall pick in 2005 but was toiling in relief in high Class A three years later. He risked being better known as the grandson of Bob Bell, who starred as Bozo the Clown for 24 years on Chicago television, than for his pitching. But he grew up and improved his command in 2009, notched the system's second-best ERA at 2.70 and finished the season in the majors. Bell's first pitch in the big leagues registered at 94 mph, and he sits at 88-92 with life down in the zone. He works fast, relying on the cutting and sinking action on his fastball to pitch to both sides of the plate and induce weak contact. When it's on, his mid-70s slider features late tilt. He's a bulldog on the mound who seems to execute best when his back is against the wall. If he's not hitting spots with his fastball, Bell gets knocked around because the quality of his stuff is merely average. His slider is inconsistent, and while his changeup has improved, it's still wasn't good enough to keep big league lefties at bay. They batted .469/.526/.673 against him. Bell will need above-average command to thrive in the big leagues, and it's a trait he's shown at most every stop in his minor league career. The Angels view him as a back-of-the-rotation starter or a bullpen arm who will compete for a big league job in spring training.

Year	Club (League)	Class	W	L	ERA	G	GS	CG	SV	IP	H	R	ER	HR	BB	SO	AVG
2005	Angels (AZL)	R	0	0	4.50	4	4	0	0	8	10	4	4	0	3	7	.313
2006	Orem (PIO)	R	4	2	3.50	16	16	0	0	82	82	35	32	8	15	53	.261
2007	Cedar Rapids (MWL)	LoA	8	4	4.14	21	21	0	0	115	136	64	53	8	23	90	.292
2008	Cedar Rapids (MWL)	LoA	1	0	2.12	3	2	1	0	17	13	4	4	0	4	13	.232
	R. Cucamonga (CAL)	HiA	6	8	4.22	36	12	2	0	100	106	60	47	8	39	80	.274
2009	Arkansas (TL)	AA	4	3	2.23	11	11	0	0	69	54	24	17	1	20	51	.212
	Salt Lake (PCL)	AAA	3	4	3.15	11	11	2	0	71	67	27	25	5	15	38	.250
	Los Angeles (AL)	MAJ	1	2	9.74	8	4	0	0	20	40	25	22	3	11	14	.412
MAJOR LEAGUE TOTALS			1	2	9.74	8	4	0	0	20	40	25	22	3	11	14	.412
MINOR LEAGUE TOTALS			26	21	3.54	102	77	5	0	463	468	218	182	30	119	332	.263

11 MARK TRUMBO, 1B/OF

BORN: Jan. 16, 1986. **B-T:** R-R. **HT.:** 6-4. **WT.:** 220. **DRAFTED:** HS—Villa Park, Calif., 2004 (18th round). **SIGNED BY:** Tim Corcoran.

Trumbo spent one season in Rookie ball and then two more in low Class A after signing in 2004 for an 18th-round record $1.425 million. The slow development wasn't terribly surprising, considering most teams preferred him on the mound when he was an amateur. But he muscled his way onto the prospect map in 2008 by bashing 32 homers, and he ranked third in the Texas League with 35 doubles and fourth with 53 extra-base hits last year. Trumbo has plus-plus raw power to all fields—the best in the system—but hasn't shown the selectivity necessary for it to play consistently in games. To enhance plate coverage, he employs a wide stance with virtually no stride. He doesn't like to strike out and often swings early in counts rather than waiting for a cookie he can crush. Thus he makes a lot of contact for a slugger but figures to hit about .260. Trumbo is a substandard first baseman and lacks the range to be an asset in the outfield, where he saw time in the second half of 2009. He features plus arm strength, a vestige of his pitching days. He led all TL batters by grounding into 22 double plays, a testament to his below-average speed. With Kendry Morales' emergence, Trumbo's introduction to right field took on added significance. He'll move on to the Triple-A Pacific Coast League, a hitter's haven, in 2010.

Year	Club (League)	Class	AVG	G	AB	R	H	2B	3B	HR	RBI	BB	SO	SB	OBP	SLG
2005	Orem (PIO)	R	.274	71	299	45	82	23	1	10	45	21	67	2	.322	.458
2006	Cedar Rapids (MWL)	LoA	.220	118	428	43	94	19	0	13	59	44	99	5	.293	.355
2007	Cedar Rapids (MWL)	LoA	.272	128	471	57	128	27	2	14	76	34	98	10	.326	.427
2008	R. Cucamonga (CAL)	HiA	.283	103	407	70	115	28	2	26	68	26	67	7	.329	.553
	Arkansas (TL)	AA	.276	32	123	13	34	7	1	6	25	7	29	1	.311	.496
2009	Arkansas (TL)	AA	.291	137	533	54	155	35	3	15	88	37	100	6	.333	.452
MINOR LEAGUE TOTALS			.269	589	2261	282	608	139	9	84	361	169	460	31	.320	.450

12 PAT CORBIN, LHP

BORN: July 19, 1989. **B-T:** L-L. **HT.:** 6-3. **WT.:** 170. **DRAFTED:** Chipola (Fla.) JC, 2009 (2nd round). **SIGNED BY:** Tom Kotchman.

Corbin graduated from high school in upstate New York in 2007 and headed to nearby Mohawk Valley (N.Y.) CC to play both baseball and basketball. He transferred to Chipola (Fla.) JC for the 2009 season to focus on pitching and showed so much improvement that he was regarded as Florida's top juco pitching prospect. He won over observers in the Rookie-level Pioneer League after signing for $450,000 as a second-round pick. Corbin can dunk a basketball from a standstill, and his premium athleticism and loose arm portend more velocity down the road. He pitches downhill at 90 mph with natural sink now, and he ranges from the high 80s to 93. One thing remains consistent: the natural cutting or tailing action on his fastball. Corbin's hard slurve ranges from 75-82 mph and features sharp, deep tilt at its best. His aptitude and clean arm stroke enabled him to flash a plus changeup. Corbin's athleticism makes him a standout defender on the mound. He's around the plate, but his command suffers because he can't predict how his lively fastball will behave. He needs to improve the balance in his delivery because he tends to lean toward the plate with his upper body, which causes his arm to drag. Corbin is tall and skinny, with much of his future value tied to the development of his fastball. His mound presence and willingness to pitch in on righthanders could make him a mid-rotation starter. He's ready for low Class A.

Year	Club (League)	Class	W	L	ERA	G	GS	CG	SV	IP	H	R	ER	HR	BB	SO	AVG
2009	Orem (PIO)	R	4	2	5.05	13	12	0	0	46	59	34	26	6	11	46	.291
MINOR LEAGUE TOTALS			4	2	5.05	13	12	0	0	46	59	34	26	6	11	46	.291

13 JEAN SEGURA, 2B

BORN: March 17, 1990. **B-T:** R-R. **HT.:** 5-11. **WT.:** 193. **SIGNED:** Dominican Republic, 2007. **SIGNED BY:** Leo Perez.

Segura's U.S. debut in 2008 was marred by an infield collision that ended his season after 11 games and resulted in a pin being inserted in his ankle. More bad luck followed last year, when he broke a finger in an Aug. 5 game sliding headfirst into second base. The injuries can't mute his intriguing blend of tools, headlined by a feel for hitting that could give him a chance to win a batting title one day. Hitting appears to come easy to Segura, who features exceptional bat speed and a compact, slashing approach that produces line drives to all fields. He hits both fastballs and breaking balls, showing advanced barrel awareness and a knack for contact. Short but with powerful legs, Segura is a plus-plus runner who could fit at the top of a lineup if he matures as a basestealer. He has a chance to develop above-average power for a second baseman. Segura is limited to second, where his arm is above-average but his range and defensive instincts are a bit short. He's cocky and wears his emotions on his sleeve, so he would benefit from a toned-down approach. He's ready for full-season ball and the Angels would love to see him stay healthy for the entire year in low Class A.

Year	Club (League)	Class	AVG	G	AB	R	H	2B	3B	HR	RBI	BB	SO	SB	OBP	SLG
2007	Angels (DSL)	R	.324	61	219	39	71	5	2	2	31	22	28	22	.392	.393
2008	Angels (AZL)	R	.250	11	36	13	9	0	0	0	4	6	5	1	.372	.250
2009	Salt Lake (PCL)	AAA	.421	7	19	2	8	2	0	0	2	0	4	0	.421	.526
	Orem (PIO)	R	.346	36	162	33	56	10	4	3	21	11	11	11	.392	.512
MINOR LEAGUE TOTALS			.330	115	436	87	144	17	6	5	58	39	48	34	.391	.431

14 TYLER CHATWOOD, RHP

BORN: Dec. 16, 1989. **B-T:** R-R. **HT.:** 5-11. **WT.:** 175. **DRAFTED:** HS—Redlands, Calif., 2008 (2nd round). **SIGNED BY:** Tim Corcoran.

A two-way standout in high school, Chatwood missed his sophomore season because he had surgery to tighten an elbow ligament. He played center field as a junior and returned the mound as a senior. Passing on a chance to play both ways at UCLA, he signed with the Angels for $547,000 as a second-round pick in 2008. Chatwood began last season in extended spring training so he could work on throwing strikes, but his competitiveness soon won out and he ended up making 24 starts for Cedar Rapids. He ranked fifth in the Midwest League in both strikeouts per nine innings (8.2) and opponent average (.237). Chatwood could have turned pro as a shortstop, and his athleticism should allow him to overcome the stigma of being a short righthander. He has electric arm strength, firing 92-94 mph riding fastballs and touching the mid-90s from his over-the-top arm slot. He'll drop in a mid-70s overhand curveball featuring depth and downward bite, giving him two plus pitches when he's going well. He struggles to command his stuff—including a below-average changeup—because he doesn't repeat his delivery. The Angels think Chatwood's best role will be as a starter, but he'll need to throw a lot more strikes. He's coachable with a bulldog demeanor, and he's ready for high Class A.

Year	Club (League)	Class	W	L	ERA	G	GS	CG	SV	IP	H	R	ER	HR	BB	SO	AVG
2008	Angels (AZL)	R	1	2	3.08	11	11	0	0	38	25	15	13	1	36	48	.195
2009	Cedar Rapids (MWL)	LoA	8	7	4.02	24	24	0	0	116	99	60	52	3	66	106	.237
MINOR LEAGUE TOTALS			9	9	3.79	35	35	0	0	154	124	75	65	4	102	154	.227

15 WILL SMITH, LHP

BORN: July 10, 1989. **B-T:** R-L. **HT.:** 6-5. **WT.:** 235. **DRAFTED:** Gulf Coast (Fla.) CC, 2008 (7th round). **SIGNED BY:** Tom Kotchman.

Though he may be most famous for unearthing Howie Kendrick, area scout Tom Kotchman's track record with pitchers in Florida is more impressive. He scouted and signed a quartet of righthanders selected in the past two major league Rule 5 drafts: Bobby Cassevah, David Herndon, Bobby Mosebach and Darren O'Day. Enter Smith, a tall, physical lefthander who commands three pitches. He followed an outstanding pro debut in Rookie ball with a solid 2009 season in low Class A. He showed excellent control of both the strike zone and the running game, limiting basestealers to just six steals in 14 attempts. Smith pitches aggressively for someone without a knockout pitch, working his fastball to both sides of the plate at 88-90 mph and touching 92. His average curveball draws more strength from a range of velocities—from 72-80 mph—than from pure break. He adds and subtracts from his sinking fastball, too. The Angels lack pitchers with refined changeups, and Smith is no exception. Pitchability lefties often carve up low-level batters, so he'll have to keep proving himself. A hamstring pull and a lower back injury limited him to 19 starts last year, but if he comes to camp in shape he should advance to high Class A. His ceiling is as a No. 4 starter.

Year	Club (League)	Class	W	L	ERA	G	GS	CG	SV	IP	H	R	ER	HR	BB	SO	AVG
2008	Orem (PIO)	R	8	2	3.08	16	14	0	0	73	73	28	25	6	6	76	.253
2009	Cedar Rapids (MWL)	LoA	10	5	3.76	20	19	0	0	115	109	61	48	11	24	95	.249
MINOR LEAGUE TOTALS			18	7	3.49	36	33	0	0	188	182	89	73	17	30	171	.251

16 CHRIS PETTIT, OF

BORN: Aug. 15, 1984. **B-T:** R-R. **HT.:** 6-0. **WT.:** 194. **DRAFTED:** Loyola Marymount, 2006 (19th round). **SIGNED BY:** Bobby DeJardin.

Pettit has provided incredible value as a 19th-round senior sign, as long as he's been healthy. After winning the organization's minor league player of the year award in 2007, he broke his foot while chasing a fly ball on Opening Day in 2008 and struggled when he returned. He redeemed himself with a strong showing in the Arizona Fall League and an impressive Triple-A debut in 2009—until he broke his left wrist and required surgery. Pettit placed sixth in the Pacific Coast League batting race last season with a .321 average, and his feel for hitting stands as his only plus tool. He lines the ball into both gaps, showing quality bat speed and enough strength to pop 10-12 home runs per year. He's not a masher though, and leaves himself open to breaking stuff away when he gets pull-happy. Pettit always has handled lefties, batting .341/.404/.554 against them over 327 plate appearances in full-season leagues. He plays all three outfield spots but is best suited to a corner. He takes good routes, makes all the routine plays and has a solid-average arm. Despite his thick build, he's an average runner who can steal a base. Pettit will vie with Gary Matthews Jr. and Reggie Willits for playing time as an extra outfielder in Los Angeles this year, and that's the role for which he seems best suited.

Year	Club (League)	Class	AVG	G	AB	R	H	2B	3B	HR	RBI	BB	SO	SB	OBP	SLG
2006	Orem (PIO)	R	.336	68	226	41	76	25	3	7	54	31	48	5	.445	.566
2007	Cedar Rapids (MWL)	LoA	.346	64	228	47	79	24	1	9	41	23	41	17	.429	.579
	R. Cucamonga (CAL)	HiA	.309	69	265	54	82	20	2	9	54	36	48	13	.395	.502
2008	Angels (AZL)	R	.231	3	13	3	3	1	0	0	2	2	2	0	.333	.308
	Arkansas (TL)	AA	.248	61	222	27	55	12	2	6	26	16	39	5	.320	.401
2009	Angels (AZL)	R	.357	4	14	2	5	1	0	0	1	3	6	1	.471	.429
	Salt Lake (PCL)	AAA	.321	96	371	70	119	30	3	8	58	31	62	18	.383	.482
	Los Angeles (AL)	MAJ	.286	10	7	2	2	0	0	0	0	0	1	0	.286	.286
MAJOR LEAGUE TOTALS			.286	10	7	2	2	0	0	0	0	0	1	0	.286	.286
MINOR LEAGUE TOTALS			.313	365	1339	244	419	113	11	39	236	142	246	59	.395	.501

17 ALEXI AMARISTA, 2B

BORN: April 6, 1989. **B-T:** R-R. **HT.:** 5-8. **WT.:** 150. **SIGNED:** Venezuela, 2007. **SIGNED BY:** Denny Suarez.

Amarista hit .319 last season to become the first Cedar Rapids player to win the Midwest League batting title since Howie Kendrick hit .367 in 2004. He signed in January 2007 and hit .340 in his pro debut in the Dominican Summer League. Amarista showed more power than expected for a player listed at 5-foot-8—and he may be a full three inches shorter than that—ranking second in the MWL with 39 doubles and 10 triples. He makes a lot of hard contact and knows the strike zone, wearing down pitchers for walks if he gets nothing to hit. Amarista is an average runner who stole 38 bases in 2009 but was too aggressive, getting thrown out 20 times. He sports a poor 66 percent success rate in three pro seasons. MWL managers recognized Amarista as the league's best defensive second baseman, though his range and arm are just average and prevent him from playing on the left side of the infield. He played center field in 2008 and ultimately might fit best as a utility player. The high Class A California League awaits.

Year	Club (League)	Class	AVG	G	AB	R	H	2B	3B	HR	RBI	BB	SO	SB	OBP	SLG
2007	Angels (DSL)	R	.340	65	241	52	82	14	4	5	39	25	23	16	.408	.494
2008	Angels (AZL)	R	.332	51	202	46	67	6	4	2	21	29	20	22	.416	.431
	Cedar Rapids (MWL)	LoA	.000	1	2	0	0	0	0	0	0	0	1	0	.000	.000
2009	Cedar Rapids (MWL)	LoA	.319	125	477	84	152	39	10	4	49	50	61	38	.390	.468
MINOR LEAGUE TOTALS			.326	242	922	182	301	59	18	11	109	104	105	76	.400	.465

18 TYLER KEHRER, LHP

BORN: March 23, 1988. **B-T:** L-L. **HT.:** 6-3. **WT.:** 210. **DRAFTED:** Eastern Illinois, 2009 (1st round supplemental). **SIGNED BY:** Joel Murrie.

Kehrer generated draft buzz as a sophomore in 2008 when he stood toe-to-toe with the Ohio Valley Conference's top two arms, Eastern Kentucky lefty Christian Friedrich (a Rockies first-rounder in 2008) and Jacksonville State righty Ben Tootle (a Twins third-rounder in 2009). He showed steady progress throughout his junior year, then went to the Angels with the 48th overall pick and signed for $728,100. Kehrer's plus tailing fastball sits at 92-94 mph and touches 95, and the Orem staff encouraged him to develop his two-seam fastball. He has no trouble maintaining his velocity, having relied on his fastball to strike out an OVC-leading 90 batters as a junior, and threw 24 straight heaters to begin his first pro start. More thrower than pitcher now, he has erratic command of his fastball and slider, which flashes plus potential with its occasional sharp, three-quarters break. The slider will be key to Kehrer's development as a starter, because at its best it dives toward the ankles of righthanders. When it's not, it backs up over the heart of the plate. Kehrer lacks feel for a changeup but has flashed a quality one in brief glimpses. He sometimes flies open in his delivery, which leaves his pitches up in the zone. With uncommon arm strength and size for a lefthander, Kehrer could reach high Class A by the end of the season.

Year	Club (League)	Class	W	L	ERA	G	GS	CG	SV	IP	H	R	ER	HR	BB	SO	AVG
2009	Orem (PIO)	R	3	3	4.75	14	14	0	0	55	57	36	29	6	22	57	.266
MINOR LEAGUE TOTALS			3	3	4.75	14	14	0	0	55	57	36	29	6	22	57	.266

19 JON BACHANOV, RHP

BORN: Jan. 30, 1989. **B-T:** R-R. **HT.:** 6-4. **WT.:** 210. **DRAFTED:** HS—Orlando, 2007 (1st round supplemental). **SIGNED BY:** Tom Kotchman.

Bounceback seasons by both Trevor Bell and Bachanov, the Angels' first picks in the '05 and '07 drafts, boosted players who were forgotten men entering the 2009 season. Questions surrounding Bachanov's makeup dogged him during his draft year—his MySpace page featured a "countdown 'til I get paid" clock—followed by Tommy John surgery shortly after he signed for $553,300. After a slow recovery, he debuted as a reliever last summer. Bachanov has a big league fastball, pitching with command at 92-93 mph and touching 96 with modest life. He's a top-flight competitor who comes out of the bullpen firing strikes from a three-quarters arm slot. Even after the injury, he shows uncanny feel and control of a low-80s power slider that has above-average potential. He threw a curveball and a changeup in high school, but those pitches gathered dust in the bullpen. Bachanov finished the year in Orem under manager Tom Kotchman, who's also the scout who signed him in 2007. Kotchman said the improvements in Bachanov's delivery and arm action were dramatic. He no longer throws across his body, though the Angels will continue to stress balance as well as direction and time to the plate. Bachanov probably will remain in the bullpen in order to expedite his development. If it all comes together, he profiles as a potential setup man.

Year	Club (League)	Class	W	L	ERA	G	GS	CG	SV	IP	H	R	ER	HR	BB	SO	AVG
2007	Did Not Play—Injured																
2008	Did Not Play—Injured																
2009	Angels (AZL)	R	4	0	3.14	16	0	0	0	29	26	10	10	0	4	47	.239
	Orem (PIO)	R	0	0	2.70	2	0	0	0	3	5	1	1	0	1	5	.333
MINOR LEAGUE TOTALS			4	0	3.09	18	0	0	0	32	31	11	11	0	5	52	.250

20 CARLOS RAMIREZ, C

BORN: March 19, 1988. **B-T:** R-R. **HT.:** 5-11. **WT.:** 205. **DRAFTED:** Arizona State, 2009 (8th round). **SIGNED BY:** John Gracio.

The Angels first selected Ramirez in the 34th round of the 2008 draft, after he had spent two years at Chandler-Gilbert (Ariz.) CC. He led the summer collegiate Northwoods League with 10 homers and won league MVP honors, then declined to sign before heading to Arizona State. His draft stock soared as he helped the Sun Devils reach the College World Series, and he signed as an eighth-rounder last June for $110,000. Ramirez hit .376 and topped the Pioneer League with a .500 on-base percentage, leading Orem to the league's best record and playoff title. He shows a patient, polished approach but has no better than fringe-average bat speed. His swing is short and he's more of a gap hitter than a slugger. Ramirez called his own games in college and relished assuming a leadership role with the Owlz, developing a great rapport with his pitchers. Despite his well below-average speed and athleticism, Ramirez blocks and receives well. He features an average arm with a quick release, typically completing throws to second base in 1.9-2.0 seconds. He threw out 32 percent of basestealers in his pro debut. Ramirez, who draws body comparisons to Bengie Molina, could reach high Class A at some point in 2010.

Year	Club (League)	Class	AVG	G	AB	R	H	2B	3B	HR	RBI	BB	SO	SB	OBP	SLG
2009	Orem (PIO)	R	.376	42	149	34	56	18	0	7	36	35	26	0	.500	.638
MINOR LEAGUE TOTALS			.376	42	149	34	56	18	0	7	36	35	26	0	.500	.638

21 RYAN CHAFFEE, RHP

BORN: May 18, 1988. **B-T:** R-R. **HT.:** 6-2. **WT.:** 200. **DRAFTED:** Chipola (Fla.) JC, 2008 (3rd round). **SIGNED BY:** Tom Kotchman.

As a freshman in 2007, Chaffee helped pitch Chipola (Fla.) JC to its first Junior College World Series title. He broke a bone in his foot the following March, requiring surgery to insert a screw, then returned in time to pitch the Indians to a Florida state championship. He went in the third round and signed for $338,000 in 2008, though he reinjured the same foot in the Juco World Series and didn't make his pro debut until 2009. He proved to be worth the wait, leading low Class A Midwest League pitchers with a .206 opponent average and finishing second with 9.4 strikeouts per nine innings. He also took a walk on the wild side, hitting a league-high 16 batters and walking 65. Chaffee seems to have taken a cue from Orlando Hernandez in that he pitches from three distinct arm angles, ranging from sidearm to high three-quarters. He uses an old-fashioned full windup and throws everything but the kitchen sink at his opponents. His low-90s fastball has some life, while his curveball features good spin and is most often his best offering. His slider has lateral movement but not much tilt, while his changeup is an average pitch at times. If Chaffee is to remain a starter he'll need to focus on refining one arm slot—the Angels prefer three-quarters, from which his fastball and curve show the most life—because he doesn't repeat his delivery well enough to throw strikes. Other righthanded relievers have had success with multiple arm angles, and that might be the best way to utilize Chaffee's unique profile. He'll move up to high Class A this season.

Year	Club (League)	Class	W	L	ERA	G	GS	CG	SV	IP	H	R	ER	HR	BB	SO	AVG
2009	Cedar Rapids (MWL)	LoA	8	8	4.33	23	23	0	0	116	84	63	56	6	65	121	.206
MINOR LEAGUE TOTALS			8	8	4.33	23	23	0	0	116	84	63	56	6	65	121	.206

22 RAFAEL RODRIGUEZ, RHP

BORN: Sept. 24, 1984. **B-T:** R-R. **HT.:** 6-1. **WT.:** 175. **SIGNED:** Dominican Republic, 2001. **SIGNED BY:** Leo Perez.

Rodriguez looked like a $780,000 washout when he went 0-6, 4.16 with a diminished strikeout rate in Double-A in 2007. Because he had dealt with intermittent elbow trouble, he was making the move into a full-time relief role. He muscled his way back on the prospect map with a huge 2008, when he set up Kevin Jepsen in the Arkansas bullpen, and the Angels added him to the 40-man roster after the season. He dominated Triple-A hitters but got knocked around in his first exposure to major leaguers in 2009. An intelligent pitcher, Rodriguez learned to speak English quickly and at his best features two plus pitches. He challenges batters with a 91-93 mph fastball with sink and above-average lateral movement. His loose, quick arm gives him natural angle to the plate. Rodriguez fares much better against righthanders because his sharp, mid-80s slider with three-quarters tilt is a true out pitch. He'll mix in a changeup that features splitter action, but it's only an occasional weapon to combat lefties. Like most relievers who yo-yo between Triple-A and the big leagues, Rodriguez sometimes struggles to find the strike zone. When he elevates his sinker he gets hit hard. He's 25 and has completed eight pro seasons, but he still has two minor league options remaining. The Angels will evaluate his readiness for a big league job in spring training.

Year	Club (League)	Class	W	L	ERA	G	GS	CG	SV	IP	H	R	ER	HR	BB	SO	AVG
2002	Angels (AZL)	R	2	1	3.99	8	8	0	0	38	37	19	17	4	20	50	.255
	Provo (PIO)	R	1	1	5.96	6	6	0	0	26	26	17	17	3	14	25	.268
2003	Cedar Rapids (MWL)	LoA	10	11	4.31	26	26	1	0	144	129	85	69	7	59	100	.236
2004	Angels (AZL)	R	0	2	6.46	4	4	0	0	15	18	12	11	1	5	13	.295
	Cedar Rapids (MWL)	LoA	1	5	6.48	7	7	0	0	33	36	27	24	5	19	35	.273
2005	Cedar Rapids (MWL)	LoA	5	2	2.78	13	13	0	0	74	61	24	23	5	27	74	.220
	R. Cucamonga (CAL)	HiA	4	4	6.75	14	14	0	0	72	84	58	54	11	33	44	.292
2006	R. Cucamonga (CAL)	HiA	3	0	0.53	3	3	0	0	17	15	1	1	0	2	20	.234
	Arkansas (TL)	AA	5	10	6.63	24	24	0	0	133	175	111	98	28	55	83	.321
2007	Arkansas (TL)	AA	0	6	4.16	46	1	0	0	71	79	36	33	6	30	42	.287
2008	Salt Lake (PCL)	AAA	2	0	6.28	9	0	0	0	14	20	12	10	2	6	8	.351
	Arkansas (TL)	AA	2	4	1.86	42	0	0	11	53	46	11	11	3	11	48	.237
2009	Salt Lake (PCL)	AAA	1	0	1.85	22	0	0	3	34	27	7	7	3	10	23	.225
	Los Angeles (AL)	MAJ	0	1	5.58	18	0	0	0	31	47	22	19	4	9	10	.356
MAJOR LEAGUE TOTALS			0	1	5.58	18	0	0	0	31	47	22	19	4	9	10	.356
MINOR LEAGUE TOTALS			36	46	4.65	224	106	1	14	726	753	420	375	78	291	565	.269

23 BOBBY MOSEBACH, RHP

BORN: Sept. 14, 1984. **B-T:** R-R. **HT.:** 6-4. **WT.:** 195. **DRAFTED:** Hillsborough (Fla.) CC, 2005 (9th round). **SIGNED BY:** Tom Kotchman.

Intrigued by Mosebach's raw arm strength, the Phillies selected him in the 2008 major league Rule 5 draft, but they couldn't find a place for him and returned him to the Angels last spring. As a full-time reliever for the first time, he reached the majors in July and made a positive impression despite pitching in just three games. He further bolstered his standing with a solid showing in the Dominican League. Mosebach is a hard-throwing sinkerballer in the vein of Rafael Rodriguez. While he throws harder than Rodriguez, Mosebach's breaking ball isn't nearly as advanced. His fastball averaged nearly 94 mph in the big leagues, and he peaks at 96 while rarely dipping below 92. His heater features hard, late sink, and he has improved his command to his arm side, which will be crucial to neutralizing lefthanders. His groundball-inducing, mid-80s slider features sharp tilt when he stays on top of it, but that's often a 50-50 proposition. Like any sinkerballer, he gets hit when he leaves the ball up. Mosebach limited minor leaguers to a .197 average while allowing only one home run in 67 innings last season, though he tends to walk too many lefthanders. Mosebach is 25 and has two minor league options remaining, just like Rodriguez, whom he'll battle for a bullpen job in spring training.

Year	Club (League)	Class	W	L	ERA	G	GS	CG	SV	IP	H	R	ER	HR	BB	SO	AVG
2005	Orem (PIO)	R	3	3	4.57	15	13	0	0	65	69	36	33	6	18	52	.280
2006	Cedar Rapids (MWL)	LoA	10	6	3.04	24	24	3	0	160	166	67	54	5	29	97	.273
	R. Cucamonga (CAL)	HiA	1	1	6.35	4	4	0	0	23	23	17	16	1	8	15	.258
2007	R. Cucamonga (CAL)	HiA	11	7	4.28	25	23	1	0	156	171	88	74	16	49	93	.285
	Arkansas (TL)	AA	1	1	5.14	2	2	0	0	14	16	9	8	1	8	3	.302
2008	Arkansas (TL)	AA	9	12	4.62	29	29	2	0	177	209	106	91	6	69	88	.305
2009	Arkansas (TL)	AA	2	0	0.34	19	0	0	6	26	12	1	1	0	9	16	.140
	Los Angeles (AL)	MAJ	0	0	7.71	3	0	0	0	2	4	3	2	0	3	2	.364
	Salt Lake (PCL)	AAA	2	2	2.23	33	0	0	7	40	33	11	10	1	18	31	.232
MAJOR LEAGUE TOTALS			0	0	7.71	3	0	0	0	2	4	3	2	0	3	2	.364
MINOR LEAGUE TOTALS			39	32	3.91	151	95	6	13	661	699	335	287	36	208	395	.278

24 MASON TOBIN, RHP

BORN: July 8, 1987. **B-T:** R-R. **HT.:** 6-4. **WT.:** 220. **DRAFTED:** Everett (Wash.) CC, 2007 (16th round). **SIGNED BY:** Casey Harvie.

Taken by the Braves in both the 2005 and '06 drafts, Tobin finally signed for $125,000 as the Angels' 16th-round selection in 2007. Making a cameo in big league camp last year to fill in for World Baseball Classic participants, he impressed the coaching staff by showing a fastball that one Angels official called well above-average for both its velocity and life. That buzz lasted all of three relief outings, after which Tobin had Tommy John surgery. He made just eight starts in 2008 before succumbing to a shoulder strain. So as it stands, his combined innings count for the past two seasons is just 40. Prior to his run of injuries, Tobin fired 93-95 mph fastballs with heavy sink and plenty of armside run. He throws from a low three-quarters arm slot, so while his low-80s slider shows short, late break at times, it also flattens out when he gets under it. All the lost time has precluded him from throwing his rudimentary changeup. At 6-foot-4 and 220 pounds, Tobin looks the part of a power pitcher, but his delivery is neither fluid nor effortless. A shift to the bullpen seems like the best bet for his future health. He's expected to return to the mound around midseason, but 2010 will essentially be another lost developmental year, his third in a row.

Year	Club (League)	Class	W	L	ERA	G	GS	CG	SV	IP	H	R	ER	HR	BB	SO	AVG
2007	Angels (AZL)	R	2	0	0.95	8	7	0	0	28	17	5	3	1	7	32	.177
	Orem (PIO)	R	2	1	3.21	6	6	0	0	28	23	10	10	0	7	23	.230
2008	Cedar Rapids (MWL)	LoA	2	3	3.13	8	8	1	0	37	29	13	13	2	18	18	.225
2009	R. Cucamonga (CAL)	HiA	0	0	0.00	3	0	0	1	3	2	4	0	0	2	2	.167
MINOR LEAGUE TOTALS			6	4	2.43	25	21	1	1	96	71	32	26	3	34	75	.211

25 ROLANDO GOMEZ, SS

BORN: June 18, 1989. **B-T:** L-R. **HT.:** 5-7. **WT.:** 145. **DRAFTED:** HS—Pembroke Pines, Fla., 2008 (11th round). **SIGNED BY:** Demetrius Figgins.

The Angels thought enough of Gomez's pro potential that they signed him for $450,000 as an 11th-round pick in 2008, buying him out of a Miami commitment. He didn't play much during his pro debut after being sidelined by a hand injury. Gomez features plus defensive instincts just like his cousin Tony Fernandez, a four-time Gold Glove winner with the Blue Jays, but that comparison goes only so far. Listed at 5-foot-7, he's at least seven inches shorter than Fernandez. Gomez runs well and covers more ground than most shortstops, showing enough arm strength to make plays in the hole. His throwing mechanics need refinement, though, as he tends to flip the ball across the infield and sometimes fails to set his feet properly. A lefthanded batter, Gomez finished second in the Rookie-level Arizona League with 48 runs and third with 32 walks last year, showing that he understands his offensive strengths rest with his tablesetting ability. He bunts well and shows enough bat speed and strength to hit for occasional gap power. The Angels would like to see Gomez remove a bit of the loop from his swing and concentrate on hitting the ball on the ground or on a line. A hard-nosed player, he's on track to tackle low Class A, where he'll probably play middle infield in tandem with Jean Segura.

Year	Club (League)	Class	AVG	G	AB	R	H	2B	3B	HR	RBI	BB	SO	SB	OBP	SLG
2008	Angels (AZL)	R	.133	4	15	2	2	0	1	0	2	1	3	0	.188	.267
2009	Angels (AZL)	R	.304	45	181	48	55	13	5	2	19	32	43	12	.408	.464
	Cedar Rapids (MWL)	LoA	.111	5	18	1	2	1	0	0	1	1	4	0	.150	.167
MINOR LEAGUE TOTALS			.276	54	214	51	59	14	6	2	22	34	50	12	.373	.425

26 BOBBY WILSON, C

BORN: April 8, 1983. **B-T:** R-R. **HT.:** 6-0. **WT.:** 220. **DRAFTED:** St. Petersburg (Fla.) JC, D/F 2002 (48th round). **SIGNED BY:** Tom Kotchman.

Wilson was a high school teammate of Casey Kotchman, the organization's first-round pick in 2001 and son of longtime Angels scout and manager Tom. Wilson has worked hard to refine his defensive tools and keep his weight in check over the course of seven pro seasons, and it paid off when he made the Angels' playoff roster last year as a third catcher. Nothing about Wilson's game is aesthetically pleasing. A righthanded hitter, he has a stiff, arm-oriented, uppercut swing that produces below-average bat speed. He knows the strike zone and can put the ball in play. He has batted .290/.345/.425 in three seasons with Triple-A Salt Lake, though he can get tied up by good fastballs inside and has almost no power. While stocky, he's agile behind the plate, with soft hands and average arm strength. Wilson shines on defense, leading the Pacific Coast League by throwing out 38 percent of basestealers last year. He excels at calling games and running a pitching staff, drawing praise from big league manager Mike Scioscia, who demands a lot from his catchers. The Angels face a decision this season with Wilson, who's out of options and probably would be claimed if exposed to waivers, but also is unlikely to supplant Mike Napoli or Jeff Mathis in Los Angeles. In all likelihood, Wilson will serve as some big league club's backup catcher in 2010.

Year	Club (League)	Class	AVG	G	AB	R	H	2B	3B	HR	RBI	BB	SO	SB	OBP	SLG
2003	Provo (PIO)	R	.284	57	236	36	67	12	0	6	62	18	31	0	.329	.411
2004	Cedar Rapids (MWL)	LoA	.268	105	396	45	106	23	0	8	64	30	55	5	.320	.386
2005	R. Cucamonga (CAL)	HiA	.290	115	466	66	135	32	1	14	77	30	61	2	.333	.453
2006	Arkansas (TL)	AA	.286	103	374	45	107	26	0	9	53	33	47	1	.350	.428
2007	Arkansas (TL)	AA	.271	50	181	24	49	9	0	6	27	22	26	5	.348	.420
	Salt Lake (PCL)	AAA	.295	40	132	15	39	13	1	3	22	8	18	1	.336	.477
2008	Salt Lake (PCL)	AAA	.312	72	260	33	81	20	0	4	45	29	45	0	.386	.435
	Los Angeles (AL)	MAJ	.167	7	6	0	1	0	0	0	1	1	3	0	.286	.167
2009	Salt Lake (PCL)	AAA	.271	97	354	38	96	19	1	8	55	22	56	0	.316	.398
	Los Angeles (AL)	MAJ	.200	12	5	0	1	1	0	0	0	0	1	0	.200	.400
MAJOR LEAGUE TOTALS			.182	19	11	0	2	1	0	0	1	1	4	0	.250	.273
MINOR LEAGUE TOTALS			.283	639	2399	302	680	154	3	58	405	192	339	14	.338	.423

27 ANDREW ROMINE, SS

BORN: Dec. 24, 1985. **B-T:** B-R. **HT.:** 6-1. **WT.:** 190. **DRAFTED:** Arizona State, 2007 (5th round). **SIGNED BY:** John Gracio.

Baseball is in Romine's blood. His father Kevin spent seven seasons as a reserve outfielder for the Red Sox, while his younger brother Austin is a promising catching prospect in the Yankees system. Andrew succeeded Dustin Pedroia as Arizona State's shortstop, and since turning pro he has shown strong defensive chops while mixing in a dash of plate discipline and speed. A switch-hitter, he has more power and is more selective from the left side. But that power is relative—he has hit just three home runs in his two years of full-season ball, and only one in the high-octane California League. He improved from the right side last season, keeping his bat in the zone longer and better covering the outer half of the plate. Romine paced the Midwest League with 62 stolen bases in 2008 and is an above-average runner. In the field, he has plus actions, hands, range and plenty of arm strength for shortstop. The Angels don't expect Romine to be better than a fringe-average hitter, but his premium defensive tools, speed and feel for situational hitting will keep him alive as a prospect. He'll move to Double-A in 2010.

Year	Club (League)	Class	AVG	G	AB	R	H	2B	3B	HR	RBI	BB	SO	SB	OBP	SLG
2007	Orem (PIO)	R	.286	56	231	38	66	6	6	5	35	16	38	12	.337	.429
2008	Cedar Rapids (MWL)	LoA	.260	126	461	79	120	21	4	2	34	55	76	62	.347	.336
2009	R. Cucamonga (CAL)	HiA	.278	131	479	68	133	13	9	1	36	51	83	26	.351	.349
MINOR LEAGUE TOTALS			.272	313	1171	185	319	40	19	8	105	122	197	100	.346	.360

28 RYAN MOUNT, 2B

BORN: Aug. 17, 1986. **B-T:** L-R. **HT.:** 6-0. **WT.:** 190. **DRAFTED:** HS—Chino Hills, Calif., 2005 (2nd round). **SIGNED BY:** Tim Corcoran.

Mount went in the second round of the 2005 draft and signed for $615,000 after a breakout high school senior season, but in each of the last three years, injuries have relegated him to roughly half a season on the disabled list. His lost development time meant the Angels felt comfortable leaving him off the 40-man roster, and no team selected him in the Rule 5 draft. Mount had surgery on the hamate bone in his right hand in May and missed two months. He previously dealt with a sprained knee in 2007 and hamstring and quadriceps trouble in 2008. Mount has above-average raw power for a second baseman, but when he gets pull-happy he becomes vulnerable to pitches away. He just hasn't gotten enough repetitions to become comfortable against lefthanders, who continue to suffocate him (.492 OPS last year). That and an undisciplined approach suggest that power, and not average, will be his calling card. Though he was drafted as a shortstop, Mount's fringe-average speed necessitated a move across the keystone, where he turns the double play well but sometimes flubs the routine play because of poor positioning on hops. He has above-average arm strength. A healthy season in Double-A could restore his prospect status.

Year	Club (League)	Class	AVG	G	AB	R	H	2B	3B	HR	RBI	BB	SO	SB	OBP	SLG
2005	Angels (AZL)	R	.216	29	102	15	22	7	1	1	17	17	31	4	.325	.333
2006	Orem (PIO)	R	.285	69	277	54	79	14	2	9	38	36	67	10	.370	.448
2007	Angels (AZL)	R	.333	3	12	0	4	0	0	0	0	1	1	0	.429	.333
	Cedar Rapids (MWL)	LoA	.251	85	303	47	76	11	3	7	36	29	70	19	.320	.376
2008	R. Cucamonga (CAL)	HiA	.290	82	338	68	98	17	5	16	49	23	67	10	.337	.512
2009	Angels (AZL)	R	.375	4	16	5	6	0	0	0	1	2	4	0	.444	.375
	Arkansas (TL)	AA	.252	84	305	36	77	16	0	4	31	20	64	5	.301	.344
MINOR LEAGUE TOTALS			.268	356	1353	225	362	65	11	37	172	128	304	48	.334	.414

29 CLAY FULLER, OF

BORN: June 17, 1987. **B-T:** B-R. **HT.:** 6-2. **WT.:** 190. **DRAFTED:** HS—Spring Branch, Texas, 2006 (4th round). **SIGNED BY:** Kevin Ham.

Fuller was a nominal switch-hitter when he signed four years ago for $227,500, though his high school coach never let him bat from the left side. It took him two years in Rookie ball to iron out his lefthanded swing. Fuller is yet another member of the organization with athletic bloodlines. His father and two brothers played football at Texas Tech, and brother Cody, an Angels 48th-round pick in 2005, retired prior to last season having topped out at Double-A. Clay demonstrates more bat control from the right side, but he has shown more power and better strike-zone judgment from the left. He refuses to give away at-bats, ranking fourth in the California League with 71 walks, and isn't afraid to work deep counts, as evidenced by his 127 strikeouts. Wiry strong with a bit of projection remaining, Fuller projects to have fringe-average power at best, looking more like a doubles hitter than a true home run threat. He doesn't make enough contact to hit for a high average. A plus runner, Fuller has swiped a combined 66 bases the past two seasons at a 79 percent success rate. He's a strong defender in center field with an average arm. Fuller's raw tools suggest he could take a leap forward, but he'll have to show offensive improvement with Arkansas in 2010 to do that.

Year	Club (League)	Class	AVG	G	AB	R	H	2B	3B	HR	RBI	BB	SO	SB	OBP	SLG
2006	Angels (AZL)	R	.268	45	157	28	42	3	5	0	10	25	47	14	.383	.350
	Orem (PIO)	R	.000	1	2	0	0	0	0	0	0	1	2	1	.333	.000
2007	Angels (AZL)	R	.301	45	103	55	55	10	4	5	30	24	52	21	.398	.481
2008	Cedar Rapids (MWL)	LoA	.260	125	438	77	114	19	13	9	47	68	122	36	.379	.425
2009	R. Cucamonga (CAL)	HiA	.232	129	452	89	105	18	4	9	48	71	127	30	.341	.350
MINOR LEAGUE TOTALS			.256	345	1232	249	316	50	26	23	135	189	350	102	.368	.395

30 MICHAEL KOHN, RHP

BORN: June 26, 1986. **B-T:** R-R. **HT.:** 6-2. **WT.:** 200. **DRAFTED:** Charleston, 2008 (13th round). **SIGNED BY:** Chris McAlpin.

Kohn's trajectory could best be described as atypical. He transferred from South Carolina-Upstate to the College of Charleston for the 2007 season, but he did so as a heavy-hitting first baseman. He took up pitching the following year, saving four games while a bruised shoulder limited him to 13 innings. Because he showed 95-mph velocity and the makings of a slider, the Angels took a 13th-round flier on the senior. Featuring an extremely short arm stroke in back, Kohn combines deception with above-average velocity, making him a strikeout machine. Last year, he ranked fourth among minor league relievers with 14.1 whiffs per nine innings and sixth with a .153 opponent average. The ball seems to jump out of Kohn's hand at 90-96 mph, sitting at 93. Though his fastball is straight and usually elevated, it explodes up in the zone and generates a plethora of awkward swings. He allowed just eight extra-base hits and one homer all year. He throws a fringe-average slider for strikes to keep batters honest. The Angels teach the splitter to their relievers who lack feel for a changeup, and Kohn is no exception. He has a good chance to open 2010 in Double-A.

Year	Club (League)	Class	W	L	ERA	G	GS	CG	SV	IP	H	R	ER	HR	BB	SO	AVG
2008	Orem (PIO)	R	2	0	1.93	16	0	0	0	23	11	5	5	1	11	44	.134
2009	Cedar Rapids (MWL)	LoA	4	1	2.19	28	0	0	6	37	20	9	9	1	12	60	.161
	R. Cucamonga (CAL)	HiA	2	0	0.94	22	0	0	3	29	13	3	3	0	14	43	.141
MINOR LEAGUE TOTALS			8	1	1.72	66	0	0	9	89	44	17	17	2	37	147	.148

Los Angeles Dodgers

BY JOHN PERROTTO

The Dodgers' back-to-back National League West titles in 2008 and 2009 were in many ways a tribute to their scouting and player-development departments, even if the spotlight always seemed to shine on the antics of Manny Ramirez and the sage wisdom of manager Joe Torre.

Key players such as Chad Billingsley, Jonathan Broxton, Matt Kemp, Clayton Kershaw, James Loney, Russell Martin and James McDonald were drafted and developed by Los Angeles. Ten of the 25 players on the NL Championship Series roster were homegrown, while Ronnie Belliard, Casey Blake, Jon Garland, Ramirez, George Sherrill and Jim Thome all were acquired in trades for prospects.

It's a tribute to the work of assistant general manager for scouting Logan White and assistant GM for player development DeJon Watson that the Dodgers were able to win consecutive division crowns for the first time since 1977-78.

In order to avoid picking up the salaries of their mid-season trade acquisitions the last two years, the Dodgers were willing to sacrifice more in the way of talent. They traded catcher Carlos Santana and righthander John Meloan to the Indians for Blake; third baseman Andy LaRoche and righty Bryan Morris to the Pirates in the three-way deal for Ramirez; and third baseman Josh Bell and righty Steven Johnson to the Orioles for Sherrill.

Fortunately for the Dodgers, they don't need a lot of help from their farm system right now. The Dodgers have never made three consecutive playoff appearances, much less won three straight division titles, but they are poised to contend for a third straight NL West championship and make another run at their first World Series appearance since 1988.

The biggest question surrounding them is how divorce proceedings between owners Frank and Jamie McCourt will play out and affect the franchise financially. Los Angeles had a 2009 Opening Day payroll of $100 million, the highest figure in its division and the ninth-highest in baseball.

The Dodgers don't have cheaper players ready to step in if the divorce leads to budget slashing. The only potential rookies who could make much of an impact in Los Angeles in 2010 are lefty Scott Elbert and righty Josh Lindblom. They could try young big leaguers Blake DeWitt and McDonald at second base and in the rotation if in-house options are needed.

However, they're starting to replenish the lower levels of the system with athletic position players and

The Dodgers held onto Matt Kemp, and he has emerged as a team centerpiece

TOP 30 PROSPECTS

1. Dee Gordon, ss
2. Chris Withrow, rhp
3. Aaron Miller, lhp
4. Ethan Martin, rhp
5. Josh Lindblom, rhp
6. Scott Elbert, lhp
7. Andrew Lambo, of
8. Ivan Dejesus Jr., ss
9. Trayvon Robinson, of
10. Allen Webster, rhp
11. Garrett Gould, rhp
12. Kyle Russell, of
13. Nathan Eovaldi, rhp
14. Kenley Jansen, rhp
15. Pedro Baez, 3b
16. Javy Guerra, rhp
17. Lucas May, c
18. Alfredo Silverio, of
19. Scott Van Slyke, of
20. Brett Wallach, rhp
21. Austin Gallagher, 1b/3b
22. Blake Smith, of
23. Xavier Paul, of
24. Jonathan Garcia, of
25. Jerry Sands, of/1b
26. Brian Cavazos-Galvez, of
27. Daigoro Rondon, rhp
28. Tommy Giles, of
29. Danny Danielson, rhp
30. Gorman Erickson, c

live-armed pitchers from recent drafts, led by shortstop Dee Gordon, righthanders Chris Withrow and Ethan Martin, and lefty Aaron Miller.

Los Angeles rarely exceeds the bonus recommendations from the commissioner's office—its total of $8.5 million spent on bonuses in 2008-09 ranks last in MLB—yet has a knack for finding talent in the later rounds. The two best position players in the system, Gordon and outfielder Andrew Lambo, were fourth-round picks. Two of the better power arms, righthanders Allen Webster and Nathan Eovaldi, were 18th- and 11th-round choices in 2008.

General Manager: Ned Colletti. **Farm Director:** DeJon Watson. **Scouting Director:** Tim Hallgren.

Class	Team	League	W	L	PCT	Finish*	Manager(s)
Majors	Los Angeles Dodgers	National	95	67	.586	1st (16)	Joe Torre
Triple-A	Albuquerque Isotopes	Pacific Coast	80	64	.556	2nd (16)	Tim Wallach
Double-A	Chattanooga Lookouts	Southern	65	74	.468	t-6th (10)	John Wallach
High A	Inland Empire 66ers	California	59	81	.421	9th (10)	Carlos Subero
Low A	Great Lakes Loons	Midwest	81	59	.579	t-3rd (14)	Juan Bustabad
Rookie	Ogden Raptors	Pioneer	42	34	.553	4th (8)	Damon Berryhill
Rookie	AZL Dodgers	Arizona	24	32	.429	t-8th (11)	Jeff Carter
Overall 2009 Minor League Record			351	344	.505	15th (30)	

*Finish in overall standings (No. of teams in league). †League champion.

LAST YEAR'S TOP 30

Player, Pos.		Status
1.	Andrew Lambo, of	No. 7
2.	James McDonald, rhp	Majors
3.	Ethan Martin, rhp	No. 4
4.	Josh Lindblom, rhp	No. 5
5.	Scott Elbert, lhp	No. 6
6.	Ivan DeJesus Jr., ss/2b	No. 8
7.	Dee Gordon, ss	No. 1
8.	Josh Bell, 3b	(Orioles)
9.	Chris Withrow, rhp	No. 2
10.	Nathan Eovaldi, rhp	No. 13
11.	Austin Gallagher, 3b	No. 21
12.	Ramon Troncoso, rhp	Majors
13.	Pedro Baez, 3b	No. 15
14.	Travis Schlicting, rhp	Dropped out
15.	Steve Johnson, rhp	(Orioles)
16.	Xavier Paul, of	No. 23
17.	Kyle Russell, of	No. 12
18.	Jon Michael Redding, rhp	Dropped out
19.	Tony Delmonico, c/2b	Dropped out
20.	Justin Miller, rhp	Dropped out
21.	Brent Leach, lhp	Majors
22.	Jamie Hoffmann, of	(Yankees)
23.	Daigoro Rondon, rhp	No. 27
24.	Victor Garate, lhp	(Nationals)
25.	Javy Guerrra, rhp	No. 16
26.	James Adkins, lhp	Dropped out
27.	Alfredo Silverio, of	No. 18
28.	Lucas May, c	No. 17
29.	Josh Wall, rhp	Dropped out
30.	Jordan Pratt, rhp	Dropped out

BEST TOOLS

Best Hitter for Average	Dee Gordon
Best Power Hitter	Kyle Russell
Best Strike-Zone Discipline	A.J. Ellis
Fastest Baserunner	Dee Gordon
Best Athlete	Dee Gordon
Best Fastball	Kenley Jansen
Best Curveball	Ethan Martin
Best Slider	Josh Lindblom
Best Changeup	Scott Elbert
Best Control	Tim Sexton
Best Defensive Catcher	A.J. Ellis
Best Defensive Infielder	Dee Gordon
Best Infield Arm	Pedro Baez
Best Defensive Outfielder	Scott Van Slyke
Best Outfield Arm	Xavier Paul

PROJECTED 2013 LINEUP

Catcher	Russell Martin
First Base	James Loney
Second Base	Ivan DeJesus Jr.
Third Base	Blake DeWitt
Shortstop	Dee Gordon
Left Field	Andrew Lambo
Center Field	Matt Kemp
Right Field	Andre Ethier
No. 1 Starter	Clayton Kershaw
No. 2 Starter	Chad Billingsley
No. 3 Starter	Chris Withrow
No. 4 Starter	Aaron Miller
No. 5 Starter	Ethan Martin
Closer	Jonathan Broxton

TOP PROSPECTS OF THE DECADE

Year	Player, Pos.	2009 Org.
2000	Chin-Feng Chen, of	La New (Taiwan)
2001	Ben Diggins, rhp	Out of baseball
2002	Ricardo Rodriguez, rhp	Saltillo (Mexico)
2003	James Loney, 1b	Dodgers
2004	Edwin Jackson, rhp	Tigers
2005	Joel Guzman, ss/of	Nationals
2006	Chad Billingsley, rhp	Dodgers
2007	Andy LaRoche, 3b	Pirates
2008	Clayton Kershaw, lhp	Dodgers
2009	Andrew Lambo, of	Dodgers

TOP DRAFT PICKS OF THE DECADE

Year	Player, Pos.	2009 Org.
2000	Ben Diggins, rhp	Out of baseball
2001	Brian Pilkington, rhp (2nd round)	Out of baseball
2002	James Loney, 1b	Dodgers
2003	Chad Billingsley, rhp	Dodgers
2004	Scott Elbert, lhp	Dodgers
2005	*Luke Hochevar, rhp (1st round supp.)	Royals
2006	Clayton Kershaw, lhp	Dodgers
2007	Chris Withrow, rhp	Dodgers
2008	Ethan Martin, rhp	Dodgers
2009	Aaron Miller, lhp (1st round supp.)	Dodgers

*Did not sign.

LARGEST BONUSES IN CLUB HISTORY

Hiroki Kuroda, 2007	$7,300,000
Clayton Kershaw, 2006	$2,300,000
Joel Guzman, 2001	$2,255,000
Ben Diggins, 2000	$2,200,000
Hideo Nomo, 1995	$2,000,000

LOS ANGELES DODGERS

TOP 2010 ROOKIE: Josh Lindblom, rhp. His sinker-curveball mix almost won him an Opening Day roster spot in 2009 and should get the job done this spring.

BREAKOUT PROSPECT: Kenley Jansen, rhp. The former catcher is reaching 98 mph with his fastball and is only scratching the surface of his pitching potential.

SOURCE OF TOP 30 TALENT			
Homegrown	30	Acquired	0
College	7	Trades	0
Junior college	2	Rule 5 draft	0
High school	16	Independent leagues	0
Draft-and-follow	1	Free agents/waivers	0
Nondrafted free agents	0		
International	4		

SLEEPER: Rubby de la Rosa, rhp. His fastball hit 98 mph last summer before he was sent home to the Dominican Republic for disciplinary reasons.

Numbers in parentheses indicate prospect rankings.

LF
Andrew Lambo (7)
Alfredo Silverio (18)
Brian Cavazos-Galvez (26)
Tommy Giles (28)
Angelo Songco
Nick Akins

CF
Trayvon Robinson (9)
Xavier Paul (23)
Jonathan Garcia (24)
Nick Buss

RF
Kyle Russell (12)
Scott Van Slyke (19)
Blake Smith (22)
Jerry Sands (25)

3B
Pedro Baez (15)
Jeff Hunt
Brian Ruggiano

SS
Dee Gordon (1)
Ivan DeJesus Jr. (8)
Bryant Hernandez

2B
Jaime Pedroza

1B
Austin Gallagher (21)
Steven Caseres
Russ Mitchell

C
Lucas May (17)
Gorman Erickson (30)
Tony Delmonico
J.T. Wise
A.J. Ellis
Jan Vazquez

RHP

Starters	Relievers
Chris Withrow (2)	Josh Lindblom (5)
Ethan Martin (4)	Kenley Jansen (14)
Allen Webster (10)	Javy Guerra (16)
Garrett Gould (11)	Daigoro Rondon (27)
Nathan Eovaldi (13)	Carlos Monasterios
Brett Wallach (20)	Travis Schlichting
Danny Danielson (29)	Jordan Pratt
Justin Miller	Josh Walter
Carlos Frias	Steven Ames
Jon Michael Redding	Luis Vasquez
Josh Wall	Paul Koss
Tim Sexton	Robert Boothe
Elisaul Pimentel	
Brandon Martinez	

LHP

Starters	Relievers
Aaron Miller (3)	Cole St. Clair
Scott Elbert (6)	Geison Aguasviva
Alberto Bastardo	Andy Suiter
James Adkins	Greg Wilborn
Cody White	

DRAFT ANALYSIS

2009
BONUSES: $4.0 MILLION

BEST PURE HITTER: C J.T. Wise (5) or OF Brian Cavazos-Galvez (12). Wise hit .338/.401/.566 at Rookie-level Ogden, while Cavazos-Galvez batted .322/.353/.618 there.

BEST POWER HITTER: OF Blake Smith (2) needs to cut down on his strikeouts, but he crushes balls when he makes contact. OF Angelo Songco (4), Wise and Cavazos-Galvez all have good power.

FASTEST RUNNER: SS/2B Casio Grider (14) has plus-plus speed and stole 22 bases in 24 tries in the Rookie-level Arizona League.

BEST DEFENSIVE PLAYER: OF Jonathan Garcia (8) has good range and arm strength in center field. C Jan Vazquez (6), a fellow Puerto Rican, shifts and blocks well but needs to improve his throwing mechanics in order to take advantage of his above-average arm.

BEST FASTBALL: LHP Aaron Miller (1) was primarly an outfielder in his first two years at Baylor, but his 91-95 mph fastball means his future is on the mound. RHPs Garrett Gould (2) and Steven Ames (17) and LHPs Andy Suiter (10) and Greg Wilborn (18) all top out around 94 mph.

BEST SECONDARY PITCH: Gould has a plus fastball, but it's his filthy curveball that's his best pitch. Miller has a hard 82-83 mph slider.

BEST PRO DEBUT: Cavazos-Galvez was the Rookie-level Pioneer League MVP and topped the circuit in runs (59), hits (97), doubles (29), homers (18) and extra-base hits (50). Despite his inexperience on the mound, Miller went 3-1, 2.75 with 48 strikeouts in 36 innings between two stops, and he was outstanding in the low Class A Midwest League playoffs.

BEST ATHLETE: Miller has all-around tools as a right fielder and had the chance to go in the first round as a position player coming out of high school. Gould, who would have been a two-way player at Wichita State, was a star quarterback and basketball forward in high school. Among the position players, OF Nick Akins (19) stands out with his strength and slightly above-average speed.

MOST INTRIGUING BACKGROUND: RHP Brett Wallach's (3) father Tim is a former all-star third baseman who manages the Dodgers' Triple-A Albuquerque affiliate, and his brother Matt is a catcher in the system. Wise's great uncle, Bobby Richardson, was the 1960 World Series MVP. Cavazos-Galvez' father Balvino Galvez pitched briefly for Los Angeles. OF Stetson Banks' (22) uncle Brian also played in the majors. C Stephen Cilladi's (33) dad Dave was a former big league trainer with the Cubs and Rockies.

CLOSEST TO THE MAJORS: Miller, whose development should take off now that he's focusing solely on pitching. Ames, who backs up his fastball with a good slider, may reach the big league bullpen in a hurry.

BEST LATE-ROUND PICK: Cavazos-Galvez and Ames.

THE ONE WHO GOT AWAY: SS Chad Kettler (24), an athletic switch-hitter, opted for Oklahoma over pro ball.

ASSESSMENT: Lefthanders with stuff like Miller's don't usually last until the No. 36 pick, and if his debut is any indication, he could be a steal. The Dodgers rarely venture over MLB's slot recommendations, but they paid Gould more than Miller ($900,000 vs. $889,200) to make sure they got him.

2008
BONUSES: $4.4 MILLION

SS Dee Gordon (4) has been a revelation and become the system's best prospect. The three players drafted ahead of him—RHPs Ethan Martin (1) and Josh Lindblom (2) and OF Kyle Russell (3)—are off to good starts as well, as are RHPs Nathan Eovaldi (11) and Allen Webster (18).

GRADE: B+

2007
BONUSES: $3.6 MILLION

RHP Chris Withrow (1) came back strong after missing most of 2008 with finger and elbow injuries. Though OF Andrew Lambo (7) had a lackluster 2009, he's still the Dodgers' best position prospect.

GRADE: B

2006
BONUSES: $5.7 MILLION

LHP Clayton Kershaw (1) has been everything Los Angeles hoped for and more. That's good, because RHP Bryan Morris (1) went to the Pirates in the Manny Ramirez trade, OF Preston Mattingly (1s) has been a huge bust and the club gave up its second- and third-rounders as free-agent compensation.

GRADE: A

2005
BONUSES: $2.2 MILLION*

This draft didn't start well, as the Dodgers didn't have a first-rounder and failed to sign RHP Luke Hochevar (1s), who would go No. 1 overall in 2006. But they did manage to find quality prospects in SS Ivan DeJesus Jr. (2), 3B Josh Bell (4) and OF Trayvon Robinson (10); and big leaguers in RHP John Meloan (5) and LHP Brent Leach (6).

GRADE: C+

*Draft analysis by Jim Callis. Numbers in parentheses indicate draft rounds. *Bonuses for 2005 are first 10 rounds only.*

BILL MITCHELL

DEE GORDON, SS

Born: April 22, 1988.
Height: 5-11. **Weight:** 150.
Bats: L. **Throws:** R.
Drafted: Seminole (Fla.) CC, 2008 (4th round).
Signed by: Scott Hennessey.

G ordon's father Tom has spent 22 seasons pitching in the major leagues with eight clubs, including the Diamondbacks in 2009. Dee's first love as a youngster was basketball, though. He didn't play baseball until his senior year of high school in Avon Park, Fla., but he quickly learned to like the sport. Undrafted and lightly recruited out of high school, Gordon attended NAIA Southeastern (Fla.) and hit .378 with 45 steals as a freshman in 2007. He planned to transfer to Seminole (Fla.) CC in 2008 to increase his exposure, but he had to sit out the season because of issues with his high school transcript. While scouts couldn't see him in game action, Tom Gordon tipped off Dodgers assistant general manager for player development DeJon Watson, who was his roommate in the Royals system when Dee was born. Gordon threw too much in predraft workouts for a handful of clubs and showed a below-average arm when he auditioned for the Dodgers. Intrigued by his speed and athleticism, however, they took him in the fourth round and signed him for $250,000.

Gordon showed little rust from his layoff, batting .331 in his pro debut. For an encore he shared the MVP award in the low Class A Midwest League with Great Lakes teammate Kyle Russell in 2009. Gordon led the MWL with 73 steals—22 more than his nearest competitor—and 12 triples while ranking second with 96 runs and 162 hits. He also won the Dodgers' Branch Rickey minor league player of the year award.

Gordon is the best athlete Los Angeles has signed since Logan White took charge of the club's drafts in 2002. His most impressive tool is his game-changing speed. He has been clocked at 6.3 seconds in the 60-yard dash and has the raw ability to lead the majors in steals one day. Despite his inexperience, he's an adept hitter who crowds the plate and uses his quick bat to hit line drives from gap to gap. He's not just a slap hitter and should have decent pop for a middle infielder once he adds strength. His range is outstanding, as he gets to balls few other shortstops do. He has good actions and a solid arm. His tools also would make him a plus defender in center field.

Gordon is still raw in all phases of the game. He needs to learn how to recognize pitches better and show more discipline at the plate to be a truly effective leadoff hitter. He steals bases strictly on speed at this point, and he led the minors by getting caught 25 times in 2009. He topped MWL shortstops with 34 errors, with many coming on throws because he tends to drop down his arm angle. He also needs to be more aggressive at shortstop and let fewer grounders play him. He has tried, so far in vain, to gain weight despite often eating five or six meals a day last season. However, his broad shoulders suggest he has the frame to add strength.

Gordon has only scratched the surface of his potential. Considering his lack of experience, he has made amazing progress. He'll begin 2010 at high Class A Inland Empire and should be ready to become the Dodgers' starting shortstop and leadoff hitter at some point in 2012.

Year	Club (League)	Class	AVG	G	AB	R	H	2B	3B	HR	RBI	BB	SO	SB	OBP	SLG
2008	Ogden (PIO)	R	.331	60	251	45	83	13	3	2	27	16	29	18	.371	.430
2009	Great Lakes (MWL)	LoA	.301	131	538	96	162	17	12	3	35	43	90	73	.362	.394
MINOR LEAGUE TOTALS			.311	191	789	141	245	30	15	5	62	59	119	91	.365	.406

2 CHRIS WITHROW, RHP *Broke*

JON SOOHOO-LA DODGERS

BORN: April 1, 1989. **B-T:** R-R. **HT.:** 6-3. **WT.:** 195. **DRAFTED:** HS—Midland, Texas, 2007 (1st round). **SIGNED BY:** Calvin Jones.

The 20th overall pick in the 2007 draft, Withrow pitched just 13 innings in his first two pro seasons after signing for $1.35 million. He sustained a deep cut on his right index finger in a snorkeling accident during spring training in 2008, then was bothered by elbow tenderness for most of that season. Healthy again, he rocketed to Double-A Chattanooga as a 20-year-old in 2009. Withrow has a live arm, routinely throwing his fastball in the 92-96 mph range while being clocked as high as 99. His curveball is an above-average pitch with good late bite. He has very good mechanics, which he learned from his father Mike, who pitched in the White Sox system and coached him in high school. Withrow's changeup is a work in progress, and he needs to throw it more consistently for strikes. He also will have to command his fastball and curve better to reach his potential. He's prone to the occasional big inning because he tends to press with men on base. Withrow fared well in his late-season promotion to Double-A and will begin 2010 there. Despite his lack of experience, he's on track to reach the major leagues by the second half of 2011 and looks like a potential top-of-the-rotation starter.

Year	Club (League)	Class	W	L	ERA	G	GS	CG	SV	IP	H	R	ER	HR	BB	SO	AVG
2007	Dodgers (GCL)	R	0	0	5.00	6	4	0	0	9	5	5	5	0	4	13	.167
2008	Inland Empire (CAL)	HiA	0	0	4.50	4	0	0	0	4	2	2	2	0	6	1	.182
2009	Inland Empire (CAL)	HiA	6	6	4.69	19	16	0	0	86	80	50	45	3	45	105	.252
	Chattanooga (SL)	AA	2	2	3.95	6	6	0	0	27	24	14	12	2	12	26	.240
MINOR LEAGUE TOTALS			8	8	4.55	35	26	0	0	127	111	71	64	5	67	145	.242

3 AARON MILLER, LHP +

LOONS.COM

BORN: Sept. 18, 1987. **B-T:** L-L. **HT.:** 6-3. **WT.:** 200. **DRAFTED:** Baylor, 2009 (1st round supplemental). **SIGNED BY:** Chris Smith.

Highly regarded as a right fielder coming out of high school, Miller resisted pitching as a Baylor freshman but became a full-fledged two-way player as a junior last spring. Though he batted .310 with 12 homers, he was more impressive as a power lefthander and pitched his way into the supplemental first round. He signed for $889,200, finished his first pro summer by starring in the Midwest League playoffs and pitched briefly in the Arizona Fall League. Miller routinely pitches at 91-95 mph, and he could pick up velocity now that he's a full-time pitcher. His hard, 82-83 mph slider is tough on lefthanders. He's an outstanding athlete who fields his position well and has a good pickoff move despite his lack of experience. Command was an issue in college, but he has cleaned up his mechanics and started to throw strikes more consistently. More than anything, Miller just needs to accumulate innings and continue getting used to being a pitcher. He needs to fine tune his changeup in order to remain a starter, and he can make further refinements to his command. If Miller can master a changeup, he could be a No. 2 starter. If not, his stuff would play well in a late-innings relief role. He'll open 2010 in high Class A and should move quickly, possibly reaching Los Angeles toward the end of 2011.

Year	Club (League)	Class	W	L	ERA	G	GS	CG	SV	IP	H	R	ER	HR	BB	SO	AVG
2009	Dodgers (AZL)	R	0	0	6.35	3	3	0	0	6	8	5	4	0	2	10	.320
	Great Lakes (MWL)	LoA	3	1	2.08	7	7	0	0	30	22	7	7	3	10	38	.208
MINOR LEAGUE TOTALS			3	1	2.75	10	10	0	0	36	30	12	11	3	12	48	.229

4 ETHAN MARTIN, RHP *Son,/*

JON SOOHOO-LA DODGERS

BORN: June 6, 1989. **B-T:** R-R. **HT.:** 6-2. **WT.:** 195. **DRAFTED:** HS—Toccoa, Ga., 2008 (1st round). **SIGNED BY:** Lon Joyce.

Baseball America's High School Player of the Year and the first prep pitcher drafted in 2008, Martin tore the meniscus in his right knee during a fielding drill shortly after signing for $1.73 million. He had arthroscopic surgery, delaying his pro debut until last April. Many teams considered drafting him as a power-hitting third baseman. Martin's fastball sits at 93-95 mph and occasionally touches 97. He has good movement on the pitch, and he can make it sink or cut. His big-breaking curveball is a potential plus second pitch. He's very athletic and does a good job of repeating his delivery. Martin lacks command of his pitches, particularly his curveball, which he bounces in the dirt too frequently. Though his fastball usually has good life, it flattens out on him at times. He has struggled to get the feel for a changeup because of inconsistent arm speed with the pitch. His arm action is long in back, leading some scouts to project him as a reliever. Martin should move up to high Class A Inland Empire in 2010. The Dodgers won't rush him because of his inexperience, but he has the stuff to move quickly once he harnesses it. He projects as a No. 2 starter or dominant late-game reliever with a major league ETA of 2012.

Year	Club (League)	Class	W	L	ERA	G	GS	CG	SV	IP	H	R	ER	HR	BB	SO	AVG
2009	Great Lakes (MWL)	LoA	6	8	3.87	27	19	0	1	100	85	55	43	4	61	120	.232
MINOR LEAGUE TOTALS			6	8	3.87	27	19	0	1	100	85	55	43	4	61	120	.232

5 JOSH LINDBLOM, RHP +

JON SOOHOO-LA DODGERS

BORN: June 15, 1987. **B-T:** R-R. **HT.:** 6-5. **WT.:** 240. **DRAFTED:** Purdue, 2008 (2nd round). **SIGNED BY:** Chet Sergo.

Lindblom was one of the biggest stories of Dodgers spring training last March. The organization promoted him from minor league camp midway through the exhibition season, and he pitched so well that he nearly made the big league club nine months after signing as a second-round pick. He opened the season as a starter in Double-A and finished it as a reliever in Triple-A Albuquerque. Lindblom blows hitters away with a heavy sinker that breaks bats and sits at 94 mph when he pitches in short stints. He can dial his heater up another notch when he needs a strikeout. His No. 2 pitch is a power curveball. He's aggressive and attacks the strike zone. He has a resilient arm and a strong, durable body. Lindblom has good arm speed on his changeup but doesn't consistently keep it in the strike zone. That shouldn't matter as much now that the Dodgers have decided to develop him as a reliever, which was his college role at Purdue. He also had trouble pacing himself as a starter. The Dodgers resisted the temptation to call up Lindblom in 2009 because they had a deep bullpen. He's a strong candidate to make their Opening Day roster in 2010, however, and is a possible future closer.

Year	Club (League)	Class	W	L	ERA	G	GS	CG	SV	IP	H	R	ER	HR	BB	SO	AVG
2008	Great Lakes (MWL)	LoA	0	0	1.86	8	8	0	0	29	14	6	6	2	4	33	.137
	Jacksonville (SL)	AA	0	0	3.60	1	1	0	0	5	5	2	2	0	1	4	.263
2009	Chattanooga (SL)	AA	3	5	4.71	14	11	0	0	57	55	35	30	4	14	46	.250
	Albuquerque (PCL)	AAA	3	0	2.54	20	3	0	1	39	34	11	11	3	12	36	.236
MINOR LEAGUE TOTALS			6	5	3.38	43	23	0	1	130	108	54	49	9	31	119	.223

6 SCOTT ELBERT, LHP +

JON SOOHOO-LA DODGERS

BORN: Aug. 13, 1985. **B-T:** L-L. **HT.:** 6-1. **WT.:** 215. **DRAFTED:** HS—Seneca, Mo., 2004 (1st round). **SIGNED BY:** Mitch Webster.

Completely healthy for the first time since he had arthroscopic shoulder surgery in 2007, Elbert won the organization's minor league pitcher of the year award last season. The Dodgers called him up four separate times and placed him on their National League Championship Series roster. The 15th overall pick in the 2004 draft, he signed for $1.575 million. Elbert has regained the stuff he had before he had scar tissue removed from his labrum. His fastball sits at 92-94 mph and reaches 95. He complements it with a late-breaking, mid-80s slider that lefthanders find unhittable. His changeup keeps righthanders at bay. Though Elbert has enough pitches to start, he may not have the command or durability to succeed in that role. There's some effort in his delivery, he overthrows at times and shoots for strikeouts too often. All of that leads to walks and high pitch counts. Using him as a reliever may be the best way to keep him healthy. With George Sherill, Hong-Chih Kuo and Brent Leach, the Dodgers have enough big league lefty relievers to allow Elbert to start 2010 in Triple-A. His long-term role still remains to be determined.

Year	Club (League)	Class	W	L	ERA	G	GS	CG	SV	IP	H	R	ER	HR	BB	SO	AVG
2004	Ogden (PIO)	R	2	3	5.26	12	12	0	0	50	47	33	29	5	30	45	.270
2005	Columbus (SAL)	LoA	8	5	2.66	25	24	1	0	115	83	37	34	8	57	128	.200
2006	Vero Beach (FSL)	HiA	5	5	2.37	17	15	0	0	84	57	27	22	4	41	97	.193
	Jacksonville (SL)	AA	6	4	3.61	11	11	0	0	62	40	26	25	11	44	76	.187
2007	Jacksonville (SL)	AA	0	1	3.86	3	3	0	0	14	6	6	6	0	10	24	.128
2008	Jacksonville (SL)	AA	4	1	2.40	25	1	0	0	41	22	14	11	2	20	46	.157
	Los Angeles (NL)	MAJ	0	1	12.00	10	0	0	0	6	9	8	8	2	4	8	.346
2009	Chattanooga (SL)	AA	2	3	3.90	12	11	0	0	62	59	32	27	5	30	87	.248
	Albuquerque (PCL)	AAA	2	1	3.74	8	7	1	0	34	34	16	14	2	14	38	.262
	Los Angeles (NL)	MAJ	2	0	5.03	19	0	0	0	20	19	11	11	4	7	21	.253
MAJOR LEAGUE TOTALS			2	1	6.66	29	0	0	0	26	28	19	19	6	11	29	.277
MINOR LEAGUE TOTALS			29	23	3.27	113	84	2	0	462	348	191	168	37	246	541	.210

7 ANDREW LAMBO, OF

BORN: Aug. 11, 1988. **B-T:** L-L. **HT.:** 6-3. **WT.:** 190. **DRAFTED:** HS—Newbury Park, Calif., 2007 (4th round). **SIGNED BY:** Chuck Crim.

Lambo lasted until the fourth round of the 2007 draft because clubs questioned his makeup after he got caught smoking marijuana as a high school sophomore. He's had no problems since turning pro and ranked No. 1 on this list a year ago, when he reached Double-A shortly after turning 20. He had a lackluster 2009 season in Chattanooga but did bounce back to hit .330/.365/.484 in the Arizona Fall League. A pure hitter, Lambo has a short swing and uses the whole field. He's more of a gap hitter at this point, but his doubles should translate into more homers as he learns to turn on pitches. He played first base in high school and sporadically in his first two years as a pro, and he's a plus defender at that position. He has average arm strength and makes accurate throws from left field. Lambo is a below-average athlete whose lack of speed and range make him a substandard outfielder. Though he gets good jumps on balls, he may not be quick enough to avoid a return to first base. He has a tendency to get easily frustrated, which leads him to chase pitches out of the zone. Lambo could return for a third stint in Double-A to begin 2010, but he's still ahead of most 21-year-olds. He could be Manny Ramirez's successor in Los Angeles when the slugger's contract expires after next season.

Year	Club (League)	Class	AVG	G	AB	R	H	2B	3B	HR	RBI	BB	SO	SB	OBP	SLG
2007	Dodgers (GCL)	R	.343	54	181	38	62	15	1	5	32	29	34	1	.440	.519
2008	Great Lakes (MWL)	LoA	.288	123	472	58	136	33	2	15	79	41	110	5	.346	.462
	Jacksonville (SL)	AA	.389	8	36	7	14	2	1	3	12	2	9	0	.421	.750
2009	Chattanooga (SL)	AA	.256	130	492	70	126	39	1	11	61	39	95	4	.311	.407
MINOR LEAGUE TOTALS			.286	315	1181	173	338	89	5	34	184	111	248	10	.349	.456

8 IVAN DeJESUS JR., SS

BORN: May 1, 1987. **B-T:** R-R. **HT.:** 5-11. **WT.:** 190. **DRAFTED:** HS—Guaynabo, P.R., 2005 (2nd round). **SIGNED BY:** Manny Estrada.

After being chosen as the Dodgers' 2008 minor league player of the year, DeJesus had his 2009 season effectively end March 2, when he broke the lower part of the tibia in his right leg while being thrown out at the plate in a spring-training "B" game. He was limited to four late-season games in the Rookie-level Arizona League. DeJesus has an advanced approach at the plate, with good discipline and a willingness to use the whole field. He has average speed and keen baserunning instincts. He's a good defender with solid range and arm strength. He gets high marks for his baseball IQ, not surprising since his father Ivan Sr. was a major league shortstop for 15 seasons and is a coach with the Cubs. DeJesus doesn't have a lot of power and hits too many grounders for someone lacking plus speed. He has a knack for getting on base but won't provide many extra-base hits or steals. There will be questions about how his speed and range will be affected by his leg injury until he returns to playing every day. Had he spent last season in Triple-A, DeJesus might be ready to make the jump to Los Angeles. Instead, he'll open 2010 in Albuquerque, although he has been added to the Dodgers' 40-man roster. He's not as dynamic as Dee Gordon and may move to second base if they're in the same big league lineup one day.

Year	Club (League)	Class	AVG	G	AB	R	H	2B	3B	HR	RBI	BB	SO	SB	OBP	SLG
2005	Dodgers (GCL)	R	.339	33	121	18	41	5	0	0	11	10	22	8	.389	.380
	Ogden (PIO)	R	.208	20	72	4	15	1	0	0	3	6	18	3	.296	.222
2006	Columbus (SAL)	LoA	.277	126	483	65	134	17	2	1	44	63	85	16	.361	.327
2007	Inland Empire (CAL)	HiA	.287	121	428	69	123	22	3	4	52	57	64	11	.371	.381
2008	Jacksonville (SL)	AA	.324	128	463	91	150	21	2	7	58	76	81	16	.419	.423
2009	Dodgers (AZL)	R	.200	4	10	1	2	1	0	0	3	1	6	0	.308	.300
MINOR LEAGUE TOTALS			.295	432	1577	248	465	67	7	12	171	213	276	54	.380	.369

9 TRAYVON ROBINSON, OF

BORN: Sept. 1, 1987. **B-T:** B-R. **HT.:** 5-10. **WT.:** 175. **DRAFTED:** HS—Los Angeles, 2005 (10th round). **SIGNED BY:** Bobby Darwin.

Robinson played at Los Angeles' Crenshaw High, alma mater of former all-stars Chris Brown, Darryl Strawberry and Ellis Valentine. He earned a spot on the Dodgers' 40-man roster in November after setting career highs in most categories and ranking second in the high Class A California League with 43 steals. A veritable tool shed, Robinson boosted his stock by showing power for the first time last season, hitting 17 homers after totaling 12 in his first four pro seasons. He has made significant improvements with his swing from the left side and his approach. His plus-plus speed makes him a stolen-base threat and gives him range in center field. Robinson needs more discipline at the plate to avoid being exploited by more advanced pitchers. He chases too many pitches out of the zone and falls in love with his newfound power at times. His arm is slightly below-average, though that's not a problem in center field. He can have a hot temper, though his outbursts are becoming fewer. After taking a major step forward last season, Robinson will open 2010 back in Double-A with the chance for a midseason promotion. He's been added to the 40-man roster and if he continues his rapid progress, he'll be knocking on the door of the major leagues in 2011.

Year	Club (League)	Class	AVG	G	AB	R	H	2B	3B	HR	RBI	BB	SO	SB	OBP	SLG
2005	Dodgers (GCL)	R	.296	40	115	19	34	7	2	3	15	8	25	6	.357	.470
	Ogden (PIO)	R	.217	8	23	2	5	0	0	1	2	0	9	0	.217	.348
2006	Dodgers (GCL)	R	.254	39	134	24	34	7	2	2	20	16	48	5	.340	.381
	Vero Beach (FSL)	HiA	.400	3	5	1	2	0	0	0	1	0	2	1	.400	.400
2007	Great Lakes (MWL)	LoA	.253	110	396	50	100	9	4	2	31	32	119	22	.314	.311
2008	Inland Empire (CAL)	HiA	.276	112	439	67	121	20	8	4	42	33	104	22	.328	.385
2009	Inland Empire (CAL)	HiA	.306	117	470	82	144	28	9	15	54	50	125	43	.375	.500
	Chattanooga (SL)	AA	.246	19	57	8	14	1	2	2	10	10	18	4	.358	.439
MINOR LEAGUE TOTALS			.277	448	1639	253	454	72	27	29	175	149	450	103	.341	.407

10 ALLEN WEBSTER, RHP

BORN: Feb. 10, 1990. **B-T:** R-R. **HT.:** 6-2. **WT.:** 165. **DRAFTED:** HS—Madison, N.C., 2008 (18th round). **SIGNED BY:** Lon Joyce.

An unheralded 18th-round pick who signed for $20,000 and walked 17 in 18 innings during his pro debut, Webster improved as much as anyone in the system last season. He ranked third in the Arizona League in ERA (2.08) and opponent average (.197), and was impressive after a late promotion to Rookie-level Ogden. The Diamondbacks brought him up in trade talks when they shipped Jon Garland to Los Angeles. Webster's fastball sits in the low 90s and often touches 94-95 mph. It looks even quicker because he throws it so effortlessly after putting in extensive work on his delivery during extended spring training. His hard three-quarters breaking ball is a plus pitch at times, and he has fairly good command of his changeup. Webster is extremely thin and will have to add significant strength to have the durability to remain a starter. He's hesitant to throw his changeup right now, particularly when behind in the count or with less than two strikes. His breaking ball could use more consistency. Ticketed for low Class A, Webster will get his first taste of full-season ball in 2010. His raw stuff and ability to make adjustments could allow him to advance rapidly.

Year	Club (League)	Class	W	L	ERA	G	GS	CG	SV	IP	H	R	ER	HR	BB	SO	AVG
2008	Dodgers (GCL)	R	1	1	3.44	12	0	0	1	18	12	9	7	1	17	13	.197
2009	Dodgers (AZL)	R	2	1	2.08	12	8	0	0	48	35	19	11	0	14	56	.197
	Ogden (PIO)	R	2	0	3.00	4	3	0	0	21	23	8	7	1	4	21	.277
MINOR LEAGUE TOTALS			5	2	2.59	28	11	0	1	87	70	36	25	2	35	90	.217

11 GARRETT GOULD, RHP

BORN: July 19, 1991. **B-T:** R-R. **HT.:** 6-4. **WT.:** 190. **DRAFTED:** HS—Maize, Kan., 2009 (2nd round). **SIGNED BY:** Scott Little.

The Dodgers rarely exceed bonus recommendations from the commissioner's office, but they gave Gould $900,000—$337,500 over the slot value for the No. 65 pick last year and more than they gave their top choice, Aaron Miller. Gould impressed scouts at the World Wood Bat Championship in October 2008, striking out 18 and allowing only one hit in eight shutout innings, and followed up by breaking Nate Robertson's Maize (Kan.) High record with 95 strikeouts in 57 innings last spring. Gould's best pitch is a hard curveball that he throws from a high three-quarters arm slot, giving righthanders the impression it's coming straight at their batting helmet's earhole. He also has a quality fastball that sits in the low 90s and touches 94. His changeup is a work in progress. Extremely athletic, Gould was a star quarterback and basketball forward in high school and would have been a two-way player had he attended Wichita State. Despite just three innings of pro experience, he's advanced enough to begin 2010 in low Class A.

Year	Club (League)	Class	W	L	ERA	G	GS	CG	SV	IP	H	R	ER	HR	BB	SO	AVG
2009	Ogden (PIO)	R	0	1	10.13	3	3	0	0	3	4	5	3	1	2	4	.333
MINOR LEAGUE TOTALS			0	1	10.13	3	3	0	0	3	4	5	3	1	2	4	.333

12 KYLE RUSSELL, OF

BORN: June 27, 1986. **B-T:** L-L. **HT.:** 6-5. **WT.:** 195. **DRAFTED:** Texas, 2008 (3rd round). **SIGNED BY:** Chris Smith.

Russell holds the single-season and career home run records at Texas, connecting for 28 as a sophomore and 57 in his three-year career. He took a calculated gamble and turned down a reported $800,000 offer from the Cardinals after they selected him in 2007's fourth round as a draft-eligible sophomore. Russell wound up getting $410,000 from the Dodgers a year later as a third-rounder. He had a fine first full pro season in 2009, sharing

Midwest League MVP honors with Great Lakes teammate Dee Gordon. Russell led the MWL in homers (26), RBIs (102), extra-base hits (72) and slugging (.545). His calling card is his light-tower power, as he has the bat speed and strength to hit the ball out to all fields when he gets his long arms uncoiled. He always has been prone to strikeouts—he ranked second in the minors with 180 last year—and is trying to strike that delicate balance between being more patient at the plate without losing his aggressiveness. Russell is athletic enough to play center field with slightly above-average speed, but he's better in right field, where he has a plus arm. Russell is 23 and Los Angeles may begin pushing him more. He'll start 2010 in high Class A but could finish the year in Chattanooga. He has a chance to be a middle-of-the-order hitter in the majors but needs to cut down on his strikeouts.

Year	Club (League)	Class	AVG	G	AB	R	H	2B	3B	HR	RBI	BB	SO	SB	OBP	SLG
2008	Ogden (PIO)	R	.279	61	219	46	61	13	5	11	46	27	82	4	.365	.534
2009	Great Lakes (MWL)	LoA	.272	133	481	90	131	39	7	26	102	72	180	20	.371	.545
MINOR LEAGUE TOTALS			.274	194	700	136	192	52	12	37	148	99	262	24	.369	.541

13 NATHAN EOVALDI, RHP

BORN: Feb. 13, 1990. **B-T:** R-R. **HT.:** 6-3. **WT.:** 195. **DRAFTED:** HS—Alvin, Texas, 2008 (11th round). **SIGNED BY:** Chris Smith.

Eovaldi hails from Alvin, Texas, the same hometown as Hall of Famer Nolan Ryan. A fireballer in his own right, Eovaldi lasted 11 rounds in the 2008 draft because he was coming off Tommy John surgery the previous spring and was strongly committed to Texas A&M. The Dodgers persuaded him to sign with a $250,000 bonus and telephone sales pitches from manager Joe Torre and big leaguers Chad Billingsley and Jonathan Broxton. Eovaldi's game is all about heat, as he throws his fastball at 93-96 mph. He has developed a curveball since coming into pro ball but is inconsistent with it. He threw a slider in high school but shelved it because he felt it might have been the cause of his elbow problems. He has yet to gain a good feel for the changeup. There are some concerns about Eovaldi's durability because on his injury history. The Dodgers have been very careful with him and used him in tandem with 2008 first-rounder Ethan Martin in several outings at Great Lakes last season. Eovaldi will move to high Class A Inland Empire this season. If he doesn't develop his other pitches and work out as a starter, he still has the fastball to be an effective late-inning reliever.

Year	Club (League)	Class	W	L	ERA	G	GS	CG	SV	IP	H	R	ER	HR	BB	SO	AVG
2008	Dodgers (GCL)	R	0	1	1.13	6	0	0	1	8	6	1	1	0	3	9	.207
	Ogden (PIO)	R	0	0	0.00	1	0	0	0	3	1	0	0	0	0	2	.125
2009	Great Lakes (MWL)	LoA	3	5	3.27	26	16	0	1	96	95	48	35	2	41	71	.265
MINOR LEAGUE TOTALS			3	6	3.03	33	16	0	2	107	102	49	36	2	44	82	.258

14 KENLEY JANSEN, RHP

BORN: Sept. 30, 1987. **B-T:** B-R. **HT.:** 6-2. **WT.:** 220. **SIGNED:** Curacao, 2004. **SIGNED BY:** Camilo Pascual/Rolando Chirino.

Jansen had quite an eventful 2009. In March, he was the starting catcher for the Netherlands in the World Baseball Classic and helped seal a 3-2 upset of the Dominican Republic by throwing out Willy Taveras trying to steal third base in the ninth inning. By November, was the talk of the Arizona Fall League—as a reliever. In five seasons as a catcher, Jansen batted .229/.311/.337 and played just eight games above Class A. The Dodgers decided to utilize his cannon arm on the mound in late July and by the time he got to the AFL, he was routinely throwing his fastball at 95 mph and occasionally getting it to 98. He also has the makings of a good slider with two-plane break and a peak velocity of 82 mph. Los Angeles will keep him in the bullpen, so his learning curve won't be as sharp. Developing a changeup won't be as important as it would be if he were a starter, though he still has a ways to go to harness his electric stuff. Protecting him on the 40-man roster was an easy decision for the Dodgers. Jansen might be ready to start 2010 in Double-A, though he's young enough at 22 that there's no reason to rush him.

Year	Club (League)	Class	AVG	G	AB	R	H	2B	3B	HR	RBI	BB	SO	SB	OBP	SLG
2005	Dodgers (GCL)	R	.304	34	102	16	31	9	1	1	18	6	19	1	.339	.441
	Ogden (PIO)	R	.182	3	11	2	2	1	0	0	1	1	5	0	.250	.273
2006	Dodgers (GCL)	R	.248	35	117	14	29	2	1	1	10	19	32	1	.362	.308
2007	Great Lakes (MWL)	LoA	.102	20	59	5	6	1	0	1	6	7	18	0	.214	.169
	Ogden (PIO)	R	.240	53	183	26	44	5	1	2	22	28	50	0	.346	.311
2008	Great Lakes (MWL)	LoA	.227	79	247	31	56	15	0	9	27	23	72	3	.298	.397
2009	Albuquerque (PCL)	AAA	.185	8	27	1	5	0	0	0	2	1	7	0	.214	.185
	Inland Empire (CAL)	HiA	.202	26	89	7	18	6	0	1	11	7	21	0	.268	.303
MINOR LEAGUE TOTALS			.229	258	835	102	191	39	3	15	97	92	224	5	.311	.337

Year	Club (League)	Class	W	L	ERA	G	GS	CG	SV	IP	H	R	ER	HR	BB	SO	AVG
2009	Inland Empire (CAL)	HiA	0	0	4.63	12	0	0	0	12	14	6	6	1	11	19	.298
MINOR LEAGUE TOTALS			0	0	4.63	12	0	0	0	12	14	6	6	1	11	19	.298

15 PEDRO BAEZ, 3B

BORN: March 11, 1988. **B-T:** R-R. **HT.:** 6-2. **WT.:** 195. **SIGNED:** Dominican Republic, 2007. **SIGNED BY:** Elvio Jimenez.

The first time Dodgers assistant GM for scouting Logan White saw Baez work out, he was reminded of Adrian Beltre. There's more than a little irony to that because the Dodgers have been looking for a long-term solution at third base since Beltre bolted as a free agent after the 2004 season. The path has been cleared for Baez to eventually be that guy, as third-base prospect Josh Bell was sent to Baltimore last July in a trade for George Sherrill. After failing to stick in low Class A in 2008, Baez handled high Class A pitching last season and earned a spot in the Futures Game. He injured his knee at the end of July, however, and required season-ending surgery. Baez has big-time power potential. He can crush the best fastballs and the ball jumps off his bat. However, he lacks strike-zone discipline and pitchers can get him to chase offspeed pitches far off the plate. Baez has the tools to be an above-average defensive third baseman, though he lacks consistency. He has a strong arm, good range and outstanding body control. His speed is fringe average and he may lose a step after his surgery. Baez will begin the year in Double-A and be in position to take over in Los Angeles when Casey Blake's contract expires at the end of the 2011 season.

Year	Club (League)	Class	AVG	G	AB	R	H	2B	3B	HR	RBI	BB	SO	SB	OBP	SLG
2007	Dodgers (GCL)	R	.274	53	201	35	55	14	2	3	39	17	40	3	.341	.408
2008	Great Lakes (MWL)	LoA	.178	59	185	23	33	10	1	1	16	17	45	3	.244	.259
	Ogden (PIO)	R	.267	61	247	37	66	20	1	12	50	18	69	2	.317	.502
2009	Inland Empire (CAL)	HiA	.286	79	308	48	88	17	1	10	61	16	84	5	.326	.445
MINOR LEAGUE TOTALS			.257	252	941	143	242	61	5	26	166	68	238	13	.311	.416

16 JAVY GUERRA, RHP

BORN: Oct. 31, 1985. **B-T:** R-R. **HT.:** 6-1. **WT.:** 195. **DRAFTED:** HS—Denton, Texas, 2004 (4th round). **SIGNED BY:** Mike Leuzinger.

The Dodgers steered Guerra away from an Arizona scholarship with a $275,000 bonus in 2004 and have patiently waited for him to blossom. After he spent the previous two seasons in high Class A, Guerra was demoted to Great Lakes to begin 2009. He reacted positively, getting selected to play in the Midwest League all-star game before earning a two-level promotion to Double-A and eventually a spot on the 40-man roster in November. Guerra's power arm always has made him intriguing, but his development has been slow since he had Tommy John surgery in 2005. He throws his fastball at 94-96 mph range and also has a sharp slider. He'll throw an occasional changeup, but it's mainly for show as he doesn't need a consistent third pitch as a reliever. His control was better last year than it had been at any time since his elbow reconstruction, but he still averaged 4.0 walks per nine innings. He'll have to do a better job of throwing strikes and locating his pitches to keep advancing. Guerra, who kept a blog for MLB.com during the 2009 season, will return to Chattanooga to open this year.

Year	Club (League)	Class	W	L	ERA	G	GS	CG	SV	IP	H	R	ER	HR	BB	SO	AVG
2004	Dodgers (GCL)	R	4	1	3.38	11	9	0	0	40	31	18	15	3	19	36	.214
2005	Columbus (SAL)	LoA	2	5	4.96	11	11	0	0	53	51	35	29	3	23	40	.249
2006	Ogden (PIO)	R	1	3	4.82	7	7	0	0	28	37	18	15	1	20	22	.330
2007	Inland Empire (CAL)	HiA	6	9	6.27	27	24	0	1	118	139	98	82	10	80	121	.296
2008	Inland Empire (CAL)	HiA	5	4	4.07	31	3	0	2	66	68	34	30	0	44	63	.262
2009	Great Lakes (MWL)	LoA	3	1	1.54	28	0	0	16	41	23	7	7	1	15	55	.161
	Chattanooga (SL)	AA	3	1	4.13	23	0	0	0	28	32	15	13	2	16	29	.291
MINOR LEAGUE TOTALS			24	24	4.60	138	54	0	19	374	381	225	191	20	217	366	.264

17 LUCAS MAY, C

BORN: Oct. 24, 1984. **B-T:** R-R. **HT.:** 5-11. **WT.:** 195. **DRAFTED:** HS—Ballwin, Mo., 2003 (8th round). **SIGNED BY:** Mitch Webster.

The Dodgers have an affinity for converting players to catchers, with Russell Martin and since-traded Carlos Santana among their recent success stories. Another of their projects is May, who moved from shortstop to outfielder in mid-2005 before shifting to catcher during instructional league in 2006. May's development was slowed last season when he broke a wrist in mid-May and missed six weeks, though he showed few ill effects of the injury when he returned. He starred for gold-medal champion Team USA at the World Cup in September, hitting .355 in eight starts and driving in four runs in the clincher against Cuba. May has some power and can turn on the best of fastballs, but he struggles with breaking and offspeed pitches, particularly on the outer half of the plate. He did a better job of controlling the strike zone last year than he had in the past. He's a tick above-average as a runner, a tool that sets him apart from most catchers. May has improved in his three seasons behind the plate and has the tools to possibly become a plus defender, but he's still a work in progress. He has an above-average arm and threw out a career-best 35 percent of basestealers in 2009. He's still inconsistent with his receiving, with 75 passed balls in 239 games behind the plate, and doesn't frame pitches well. He's learning the nuances of calling a game and guiding his pitchers through jams. Ticketed for Triple-A in 2010, he could make his major league debut later in the year.

Year	Club (League)	Class	AVG	G	AB	R	H	2B	3B	HR	RBI	BB	SO	SB	OBP	SLG
2003	Dodgers (GCL)	R	.252	48	159	19	40	8	0	0	10	19	38	11	.350	.302
2004	Ogden (PIO)	R	.286	34	147	25	42	5	2	5	30	8	37	4	.329	.449
2005	Columbus (SAL)	LoA	.229	99	385	46	88	14	2	9	53	16	92	5	.267	.345
2006	Columbus (SAL)	LoA	.273	119	450	76	123	27	9	18	82	35	130	14	.332	.493
2007	Inland Empire (CAL)	HiA	.256	128	507	81	130	25	3	25	89	36	107	5	.313	.465
2008	Jacksonville (SL)	AA	.230	107	392	54	90	27	1	13	54	32	112	6	.294	.403
2009	Chattanooga (SL)	AA	.306	68	235	32	72	18	1	6	32	31	58	3	.390	.468
MINOR LEAGUE TOTALS			.257	603	2275	333	585	124	18	76	350	177	574	48	.318	.428

18 ALFREDO SILVERIO, OF

BORN: May 6, 1987. **B-T:** R-R. **HT.:** 6-1. **WT.:** 185. **SIGNED:** Dominican Republic, 2003. **SIGNED BY:** Angel Santana.

Silverio was signed as a 16-year-old and his progress has been predictably slow. He won the Rookie-level Gulf Coast League batting title in 2007 by hitting .373 but hasn't made the same impact in two seasons in low Class A. Silverio has the makings of a good hitter with gap power to all fields. He doesn't get pull-happy like many young hitters, but he'll need to look to turn on more inside pitches if he wants to fully realize his power potential. While he prefers fastballs, he's learning to stay back on breaking balls and offspeed pitches. A free swinger, Silverio has walked just 33 times in 227 games at Great Lakes. If he doesn't show more patience, more advanced pitchers will have little problem exploiting him. Silverio played all three outfield positions last year and is best suited for left field because of below-average range. He has plus arm strength. A slow runner, Silverio is not a threat on the bases. He'll continue polishing his many rough edges in high Class A this year.

Year	Club (League)	Class	AVG	G	AB	R	H	2B	3B	HR	RBI	BB	SO	SB	OBP	SLG
2004	Dodgers2 (DSL)	R	.240	59	192	18	46	6	2	1	16	7	36	5	.273	.307
2005	Dodgers (DSL)	R	.244	25	82	11	20	2	0	1	14	10	15	2	.316	.305
2006	Dodgers (DSL)	R	.276	61	225	36	62	12	6	6	48	18	44	6	.335	.462
2007	Dodgers (GCL)	R	.373	51	193	38	72	9	3	6	46	11	32	5	.406	.544
2008	Great Lakes (MWL)	LoA	.263	95	376	37	99	15	4	10	45	7	83	6	.279	.404
2009	Great Lakes (MWL)	LoA	.284	132	490	75	139	34	6	13	61	26	104	2	.320	.457
MINOR LEAGUE TOTALS			.281	423	1558	215	438	78	21	37	230	79	314	26	.317	.429

19 SCOTT VAN SLYKE, OF

BORN: July 24, 1986. **B-T:** R-R. **HT.:** 6-5. **WT.:** 195. **DRAFTED:** HS—Ladue, Mo., 2005 (14th round). **SIGNED BY:** Mitch Webster.

Van Slyke has outstanding baseball bloodlines as his father Andy played in the majors for 13 seasons, winning five Gold Gloves as a center fielder and being selected to three All-Star Games. Scott's older brother A.J. played in the Cardinals system, and his younger brother Jared is a safety on the University of Michigan football team. Like his dad, Scott didn't get his bat going until his third year in full-season ball. Van Slyke set career highs in virtually every category last season. Playing in the hitter-friendly California League helped, but he also learned how to work the count and hit the ball where it's pitched. Van Slyke also got comfortable with the idea of turning the bat loose instead of concentrating on just making contact. He doesn't possess the speed and range that his father did but has become a solid right fielder thanks to his instincts and strong, accurate arm. He'll steal an occasional base, more on smarts than speed. Five years after being drafted, Van Slyke finally is ready for Double-A, and his performance there should be a good barometer of what his future holds.

Year	Club (League)	Class	AVG	G	AB	R	H	2B	3B	HR	RBI	BB	SO	SB	OBP	SLG
2005	Dodgers (GCL)	R	.282	24	85	15	24	4	1	2	15	4	19	4	.330	.424
2006	Ogden (PIO)	R	.256	45	156	18	40	5	2	2	17	14	41	5	.320	.353
2007	Great Lakes (MWL)	LoA	.254	104	351	38	89	18	1	2	35	27	68	4	.310	.328
2008	Great Lakes (MWL)	LoA	.148	22	61	4	9	4	0	0	7	12	11	0	.280	.213
	Inland Empire (CAL)	HiA	.261	48	176	29	46	9	2	5	26	11	35	7	.309	.420
2009	Inland Empire (CAL)	HiA	.294	132	496	75	146	42	4	23	100	61	128	10	.373	.534
	Albuquerque (PCL)	AAA	.167	3	6	1	1	0	0	0	0	2	1	0	.375	.167
MINOR LEAGUE TOTALS			.267	378	1331	180	355	82	10	34	200	131	303	30	.335	.420

20 BRETT WALLACH, RHP

BORN: Dec. 2, 1988. **B-T:** R-R. **HT.:** 6-2. **WT.:** 180. **DRAFTED:** Orange Coast (Calif.) CC, 2009 (3rd round). **SIGNED BY:** Brian Stephenson.

Wallach's father Tim was a major league third baseman for 17 seasons and now manages the Dodgers' Albuquerque farm club, while his brother Matt is a catcher in the system. Brett joined them in the organization last summer, signing for $351,900 as a third-round pick after leading Orange Coast CC to its first California community college state championship since 1980. He started and won the playoff semifinal, then saved the clincher a day later. Wallach's fastball sits at 90-91 mph and tops out at 94 with good sink. His changeup is his best pitch, and he also has a slider that's inconsistent. Primarily a shortstop in high school, Wallach pitched just two innings as a senior and pulled double duty at Orange Coast, batting cleanup while playing first base and shortstop. He's still learning the art of pitching, though he has a very smooth delivery that he repeats easily. Wallach has come a long way in a short time as a pitcher and will begin his first full pro season in low Class A. He could blossom into a No. 3 starter in the majors.

Year	Club (League)	Class	W	L	ERA	G	GS	CG	SV	IP	H	R	ER	HR	BB	SO	AVG
2009	Ogden (PIO)	R	0	1	5.23	12	12	0	0	31	34	20	18	4	15	38	.279
MINOR LEAGUE TOTALS			0	1	5.23	12	12	0	0	31	34	20	18	4	15	38	.279

21 AUSTIN GALLAGHER, 1B/3B

BORN: Nov. 16, 1988. **B-T:** L-R. **HT.:** 6-5. **WT.:** 210. **DRAFTED:** HS—Lancaster, Pa., 2007 (3rd round). **SIGNED BY:** Clair Rierson.

After holding his own as a 19-year-old in high Class A in 2008, taking over at third base for Inland Empire when Josh Bell went down with a knee injury, little went right for Gallagher last season. He strained his throwing shoulder during spring training, and the Dodgers decided to have him take it easy by playing first base and serving as the DH in low Class A. He continued to reaggravate his shoulder and never got his bat going before getting shut down in July to have surgery. Gallagher's frame and bat speed suggest he could blossom into a power hitter, but he has yet to develop loft in his swing and instead focuses on hitting line drives to all fields. Pitchers were able to beat him by working him inside in 2009. Los Angeles still has hopes that Gallagher can stay at third base, but his lack of mobility and his shoulder problems seem to make it inevitable that he'll wind up at first base. He's a below-average runner. Gallagher likely will begin this season at Inland Empire, though the Dodgers want to see how he performs in spring training before making a decision.

Year	Club (League)	Class	AVG	G	AB	R	H	2B	3B	HR	RBI	BB	SO	SB	OBP	SLG
2007	Ogden (PIO)	R	.284	55	197	28	56	11	0	4	17	19	33	1	.346	.401
2008	Inland Empire (CAL)	HiA	.293	78	307	36	90	33	1	5	55	29	73	1	.349	.456
2009	Great Lakes (MWL)	LoA	.257	60	226	28	58	11	0	3	30	21	43	1	.319	.345
MINOR LEAGUE TOTALS			.279	193	730	92	204	55	1	12	102	69	149	3	.339	.407

22 BLAKE SMITH, OF

BORN: Dec. 9, 1987. **B-T:** L-R. **HT.:** 6-2. **WT.:** 220. **DRAFTED:** California, 2009 (2nd round). **SIGNED BY:** Fred Costello.

Smith excelled as both a pitcher and an outfielder at California and for Team USA's college team, leading to split opinion among scouts as to what his future should be in pro ball. The Dodgers liked him more as a hitter and became even more convinced that he had more upside with the bat when he put on a power display during a predraft workout at Dodger Stadium. They drafted him in the second round last June and signed him for $643,500. However, Smith struggled mightily in his pro debut and looked overmatched, even in the Arizona League. Club officials believe he tried too hard to make an impression as a high draft pick, causing him to overswing and hook a lot of balls because of his impatience. Smith has a long stroke with some uppercut, which leaves him prone to strikeouts, but he also has the raw power to hit 25 or more homers a year in the major leagues. He has a chance to be an above-average right fielder because of his strong arm. He's a good athlete with average speed. If Smith flops as a hitter, the Dodgers always can try him on the mound. He has a 92-94 mph fastball and his curveball and changeup show flashes of being plus pitches as well. He has more pure stuff than polish, so he may be more of a reliever than a starter if he becomes a full-time pitcher. But Los Angeles isn't close to giving up on his bat, which they hope will show more signs of life this year in low Class A.

Year	Club (League)	Class	AVG	G	AB	R	H	2B	3B	HR	RBI	BB	SO	SB	OBP	SLG
2009	Dodgers (AZL)	R	.227	6	22	3	5	1	0	0	2	2	9	0	.346	.273
	Ogden (PIO)	R	.212	30	104	14	22	7	0	1	12	13	38	0	.311	.308
MINOR LEAGUE TOTALS			.214	36	126	17	27	8	0	1	14	15	47	0	.317	.302

23 XAVIER PAUL, OF

BORN: Feb. 25, 1985. **B-T:** L-R. **HT.:** 5-9. **WT.:** 205. **DRAFTED:** HS—Slidell, La., 2003 (4th round). **SIGNED BY:** Clarence Johns.

Paul appeared to have a golden opportunity last May 7 when Major League Baseball suspended Manny Ramirez for 50 games for using a performance-enhancing drug. Recalled from Triple-A, he never got a chance to play regularly in left field because he developed a staph infection in his right knee that forced him to the disabled list. Once he recovered from the infection, he began feeling pain in his left ankle and was found to have microfractures that kept him on the DL for the remainder of the season. Paul has plenty of raw talent but never has quite refined it during his seven pro seasons. He has a nice line-drive stroke, yet his free-swinging ways result in high strikeout totals without enough home run power to compensate. He has plus speed but his lack of baserunning savvy keeps him from stealing more bases. Paul is a good defensive outfielder with the range to play center field and the arm to play right. He'll return to Triple-A to being this season, as the Dodgers' outfield is set after Ramirez exercised the player option in his contract.

Year	Club (League)	Class	AVG	G	AB	R	H	2B	3B	HR	RBI	BB	SO	SB	OBP	SLG
2003	Ogden (PIO)	R	.307	69	264	60	81	15	6	7	47	34	58	11	.384	.489
2004	Columbus (SAL)	LoA	.262	128	465	69	122	26	6	9	72	56	127	10	.341	.402
2005	Vero Beach (FSL)	HiA	.247	85	288	42	71	15	3	7	41	32	81	1	.328	.392
2006	Vero Beach (FSL)	HiA	.285	120	470	62	134	23	3	13	49	38	114	22	.343	.430
2007	Jacksonville (SL)	AA	.291	118	422	64	123	21	2	11	50	48	112	17	.366	.429
2008	Las Vegas (PCL)	AAA	.316	115	443	82	140	28	5	9	68	43	96	17	.378	.463
2009	Los Angeles (NL)	MAJ	.214	11	14	3	3	1	0	1	1	2	4	0	.313	.500
	Albuquerque (PCL)	AAA	.328	31	116	13	38	10	2	2	16	10	22	8	.378	.500
MAJOR LEAGUE TOTALS			.214	11	14	3	3	1	0	1	1	2	4	0	.313	.500
MINOR LEAGUE TOTALS			.287	666	2468	392	709	138	27	58	343	261	610	86	.357	.436

24 JONATHAN GARCIA, OF

BORN: Nov. 11, 1991. **B-T:** R-R. **HT.:** 5-11. **WT.:** 175. **DRAFTED:** HS—Yauco, P.R., 2009 (8th round).
SIGNED BY: Manny Estrada.

The Dodgers liked Garcia enough to give him $120,000 as an eighth-round pick in 2009, but even they were surprised at how well he performed in his pro debut. As a Puerto Rican high schooler, he developed the reputation of looking great in workouts but not being able to perform well in games. However, he hit .304/.362/.500 in the Arizona League and finished on a .371 tear with eight doubles in his last 17 games. Garcia has outstanding raw power, and some of the doubles he hit in his initial taste of pro ball figure to turn into homers as his body matures and he gets a better feel for facing advanced pitching. He's a smart hitter, which gives hope that he'll be able to increase his walk total and lower his strikeouts as he gains experience. The Dodgers consider Garcia the best defender from their 2009 draft. Though his speed is average, his instincts give him good range in center field. If he loses a step, he has the strong arm to make the move to right field. Garcia receives high marks for his work ethic and that, coupled with his baseball IQ, means he should be ready to make the jump to low Class A in 2010.

Year	Club (League)	Class	AVG	G	AB	R	H	2B	3B	HR	RBI	BB	SO	SB	OBP	SLG
2009	Dodgers (AZL)	R	.304	41	138	22	42	16	1	3	21	10	37	4	.362	.500
MINOR LEAGUE TOTALS			.304	41	138	22	42	16	1	3	21	10	37	4	.362	.500

25 JERRY SANDS, OF/1B

BORN: Sept. 28, 1987. **B-T:** R-R. **HT.:** 6-4. **WT.:** 210. **DRAFTED:** Catawba (N.C.), 2008 (25th round).
SIGNED BY: Lon Joyce.

After setting school records at NCAA Division II Catawba (N.C.) for homers (61), walks (132) and slugging (.752), Sands lasted 25 rounds in the 2008 draft and signed for $5,000. His best tool clearly is his power. Capable of hitting the ball out to the deepest part of just about any park, he has 29 homers in 119 pro games. He's more than just a one-dimensional slugger, too. He hits the ball to all fields and shows good patience at the plate. He also has decent speed and is capable of taking an extra base if he catches the defense napping. He moves well enough to have played some center field in 2009, though his range is below average and will dictate that he plays on a corner. He has a solid arm, so right field likely will be his future home. Sands initially struggled when he got to low Class A but came on at the end of the season. He'll go back to Great Lakes to begin this season.

Year	Club (League)	Class	AVG	G	AB	R	H	2B	3B	HR	RBI	BB	SO	SB	OBP	SLG
2008	Dodgers (GCL)	R	.205	46	146	29	30	4	0	10	33	29	43	5	.346	.438
2009	Ogden (PIO)	R	.350	41	163	41	57	9	2	14	39	22	28	0	.427	.687
	Great Lakes (MWL)	LoA	.260	32	104	22	27	7	2	5	19	15	32	1	.361	.510
MINOR LEAGUE TOTALS			.276	119	413	92	114	20	4	29	91	66	103	6	.380	.554

26 BRIAN CAVAZOS-GALVEZ, OF

BORN: May 17, 1987. **B-T:** R-R. **HT.:** 6-0. **WT.:** 215. **DRAFTED:** New Mexico, 2009 (12th round).
SIGNED BY: Calvin Jones.

The son of former Dodgers pitcher Balvino Galvez, with whom he lost contact when he was 10 years old, Cavazos-Galvez had a huge pro debut after signing for $15,000 as a 12th-round pick in June. He has a long track record as a hitter, having batted .495 in two seasons at New Mexico JC and and .379 in two seasons at New Mexico. He then won MVP honors in the Rookie-level Pioneer League after leading the league in runs (59), hits (97), doubles (29) and homers (18). He was a two-time all-Mountain West Conference selection at New Mexico, which shares a stadium with the Dodgers' Albuquerque farm club. Cavazos-Galvez has the ability to hit for average and power because of his outstanding bat speed. He can turn on inside pitches and is willing to hit to all fields. He's prone to strikeouts, though, because he becomes impatient at the plate and has a swing that tends to get long. Cavazos-Galvez has above average speed and is a threat to steal a base, though he needs to refine his technique after getting caught eight times in 25 tries at Ogden. He played all three outfield positions in his debut but has a below-average arm and takes bad routes to balls, so he'll wind up as a left fielder. Cavazos-Galvez's big 2009 debut was tempered by the fact he was quite old for the Pioneer League at 22. Los Angeles may jump him to high Class A for his first full pro season.

Year	Club (League)	Class	AVG	G	AB	R	H	2B	3B	HR	RBI	BB	SO	SB	OBP	SLG
2009	Ogden (PIO)	R	.322	71	301	59	97	29	3	18	63	10	43	17	.353	.618
MINOR LEAGUE TOTALS			.322	71	301	59	97	29	3	18	63	10	43	17	.353	.618

27 DAIGORO RONDON, RHP

BORN: Nov. 4, 1986. **B-T:** R-R. **HT.:** 6-2. **WT.:** 163. **SIGNED:** Dominican Republic, 2004. **SIGNED BY:** Ezequiel Sepulveda/Andres Lopez.

Rondon is 23 and has yet to prove he can handle full-season ball, having posted a 6.75 ERA in stints at Great Lakes and Inland Empire during the last two seasons. But there's no denying his live fastball, which sits at 92-93 mph and tops out at 95. Hitters have difficulty squaring up his heater, which generates plenty of strikeouts and grounders. Rondon has yet to master a second pitch, however, which is why he became a full-time reliever in 2009. He flashes a power slider with good depth but doesn't always get on top of it, causing it to flatten out and become very hittable. The bottom falls out of his changeup, much like a splitter, but he has a hard time keeping it in the strike zone. The biggest knock on Rondon is his attitude, as he's quite the showman and likes drawing attention to himself while riling opponents with his antics. Rondon also gained quite a bit of weight last offseason, not all of it muscle, and is significantly heavier than his listed weight of 163 pounds. He'll give high Class A another try in 2010.

Year	Club (League)	Class	W	L	ERA	G	GS	CG	SV	IP	H	R	ER	HR	BB	SO	AVG
2004	Dodgers 1 (DSL)	R	0	6	9.35	7	6	0	0	17	36	24	18	2	12	20	.409
2005	Dodgers (DSL)	R	4	3	3.04	13	12	0	0	56	47	22	19	3	19	56	.229
2006	Dodgers (DSL)	R	6	4	3.07	14	12	0	1	67	58	33	23	3	21	53	.226
2007	Dodgers (GCL)	R	7	2	2.77	12	7	1	1	65	68	22	20	1	4	59	.275
2008	Great Lakes (MWL)	LoA	4	11	6.96	21	11	0	0	74	113	64	57	7	28	82	.345
	Ogden (PIO)	R	1	0	1.17	5	0	0	0	8	6	1	1	0	2	11	.207
2009	Inland Empire (CAL)	HiA	1	2	7.62	10	0	0	1	13	17	11	11	2	8	10	.315
	Ogden (PIO)	R	3	4	3.98	19	0	0	7	20	24	11	9	1	7	24	.286
	Great Lakes (MWL)	LoA	0	0	0.00	3	0	0	0	4	3	0	0	0	0	5	.214
MINOR LEAGUE TOTALS			26	32	4.38	104	48	1	10	325	372	188	158	19	101	320	.285

28 TOMMY GILES, OF

BORN: Aug. 28, 1983. **B-T:** L-L. **HT.:** 6-0. **WT.:** 190. **DRAFTED:** Miami, 2006 (8th round). **SIGNED BY:** Manny Estrada.

Giles was a small part of the organization long before he was drafted. He grew up in Vero Beach, Fla., where the Dodgers held spring training from 1948-2008, and served as a bat boy for their big league club in the spring and their Florida State League affiliate during the season. He's a licensed pilot, though the team turned down his request to fly his family's six-seat plane from city to city when he broke into pro ball in the Pioneer League in 2006. Giles has slugged .500 or better in three of his four pro seasons, and last year he made significant strides in his ability to handle offspeed pitches. He still has yet to prove he can hit lefthanders well enough to be more than a platoon player. He has average speed on the bases. Giles has slightly above-average range and a good arm, enabling him to play all three outfield spots, though he's a bit stretched in center and profiles more as a right fielder. He finished last season in Double-A and likely will begin 2010 there, though Los Angeles could push him to Triple-A if he has a good spring.

Year	Club (League)	Class	AVG	G	AB	R	H	2B	3B	HR	RBI	BB	SO	SB	OBP	SLG
2006	Ogden (PIO)	R	.291	33	110	14	32	6	1	5	23	4	22	3	.314	.500
2007	Great Lakes (MWL)	LoA	.320	34	125	24	40	8	3	6	18	11	30	3	.381	.576
	Jacksonville (SL)	AA	.181	25	72	4	13	4	0	2	7	5	22	2	.231	.319
2008	Inland Empire (CAL)	HiA	.280	126	471	78	132	30	5	22	100	53	117	5	.357	.505
2009	Inland Empire (CAL)	HiA	.344	16	64	8	22	4	0	4	17	6	14	1	.389	.594
	Chattanooga (SL)	AA	.251	82	179	30	45	11	0	11	31	32	58	0	.364	.497
MINOR LEAGUE TOTALS			.278	316	1021	158	284	63	9	50	196	111	263	14	.350	.504

29 DANNY DANIELSON, RHP

BORN: Dec. 12, 1988. **B-T:** R-R. **HT.:** 6-4. **WT.:** 220. **DRAFTED:** HS—Seale, Ala., 2007 (7th round). **SIGNED BY:** Dennis Moeller.

Danielson comes from the Russell County High (Seale, Ala.) program that produced three first- or sandwich-round picks from 2006-07 in Colby (Cardinals) and Cory Rasmus (Braves) and Kasey Kiker (Rangers). A seventh-rounder in 2007, Danielson has spent all three of his pro seasons in Rookie ball. However, he took a major step forward last year when he reported to spring training having shed 30 pounds after ballooning to 250 by the end of the 2008 season. The Dodgers would like to see him continue to improve his strength and conditioning, believing that would add velocity to a fastball that sometimes touches 93 mph but usually sits at 88-89. He has an outstanding changeup, rare for a pitcher so inexperienced, and a curveball that gets loopy at times. He worked on a slider during instructional league at end of last season. Danielson has good command of all his pitches and is noted for his willingness to be coached. The time has come for him to step up to full-season ball, and he'll start 2010 in low Class A.

Year	Club (League)	Class	W	L	ERA	G	GS	CG	SV	IP	H	R	ER	HR	BB	SO	AVG
2007	Dodgers (GCL)	R	1	1	3.48	9	6	0	0	21	17	8	8	2	6	21	.224
2008	Dodgers (GCL)	R	0	0	5.59	9	0	0	0	10	11	6	6	0	4	8	.282
2009	Dodgers (AZL)	R	5	2	3.08	14	9	0	0	61	65	30	21	5	12	77	.257
MINOR LEAGUE TOTALS			6	3	3.44	32	15	0	0	92	93	44	35	7	22	106	.253

30 GORMAN ERICKSON, C

BORN: March 11, 1988. **B-T:** B-R. **HT.:** 6-3. **WT.:** 205. **DRAFTED:** San Diego Mesa JC, D/F 2006 (15th round). **SIGNED BY:** Gerric Waller.

The Dodgers selected Erickson in the 15th round out of a San Diego high school in 2006, then signed him for $35,000 as a draft-and-follow the next spring after he spent a year at San Diego Mesa JC. He has yet to advance past Rookie ball (for more than emergency cameos) in three pro seasons, yet he has shed the label of organizational player and is a legitimate prospect. A big switch-hitter, Erickson hits line drives from both sides of the plate, though he has trouble catching up to quality fastballs. With his big frame and solid plate discipline, he has the potential to hit for power. Like most catchers, he's not a good runner. Erickson has improved greatly behind the plate. He has a strong arm and erased 28 percent of basestealers last season. His receiving and blocking skills are decent, and he calls a good game. Moving up to low Class A in 2010 will provide a test to see if the gains he made in 2009 were real or the result of playing against less advanced competition.

Year	Club (League)	Class	AVG	G	AB	R	H	2B	3B	HR	RBI	BB	SO	SB	OBP	SLG
2007	Dodgers (GCL)	R	.163	18	49	10	8	0	0	0	5	8	16	0	.311	.163
	Las Vegas (PCL)	AAA	.000	1	1	0	0	0	0	0	0	0	0	0	.000	.000
2008	Dodgers (GCL)	R	.261	29	92	11	24	5	0	2	7	12	17	0	.349	.380
	Las Vegas (PCL)	AAA	.000	1	5	0	0	0	0	0	0	0	2	0	.000	.000
2009	Ogden (PIO)	R	.305	55	197	40	60	18	1	5	36	24	36	0	.378	.482
MINOR LEAGUE TOTALS			.267	104	344	61	92	23	1	7	48	44	71	0	.354	.401

Milwaukee Brewers

BY TOM HAUDRICOURT

Under former scouting director Jack Zduriencik, who's now the Mariners' general manager, the Brewers focused on hitters in the draft and succeeded in advancing several to the big leagues. Ryan Braun and Prince Fielder form the heart of Milwaukee's lineup, and J.J. Hardy, Corey Hart and Rickie Weeks have played strong supporting roles. Another position player, Matt LaPorta, was the key player in a 2008 deal for C.C. Sabathia, who led the club to its first playoff berth in 26 years that season.

However, concentrating on bats came at the expense of developing arms. The Brewers dropped to 80-82 in 2009, finishing with the second-worst starters ERA (5.37) in the majors and the fourth-worst overall mark (4.84).

Of the pitchers who saw regular action with Milwaukee, only three—Yovani Gallardo, Manny Parra and Mitch Stetter—were originally drafted by the club.

The Brewers suffered a major setback when right-hander Jeremy Jeffress, their top-rated pitching prospect entering the season and one of the hardest throwers in the minors, was suspended for a second time after testing positive for marijuana. He received a 100-game suspension that carries well into the 2010 season and leaves him one positive test away from a lifetime ban.

Other pitchers took steps forward, though they're all at least a year away from being ready to help Milwaukee. Righthander Mark Rogers, the fifth overall pick in 2004, was back throwing upper-90s fastballs after missing two seasons following multiple shoulder surgeries. Lefty Zach Braddock, who also had been plagued by injuries, advanced to Double-A and prospered after moving to the bullpen with the idea of limiting his workload. Righties Evan Anundsen, Jake Odorizzi and Amaury Rivas also showed promise.

In the first draft conducted by scouting director Bruce Seid, a former crosschecker under Zduriencik, the Brewers moved to address their lack of pitching depth. They took righthander Eric Arnett in the first round and added righty Kyle Heckathorn in the supplemental first round, giving them a pair of big-bodied hard throwers who might advance quickly. Another righty, fourth-rounder Brooks Hall, also has a big arm but will need more time to develop.

Nevertheless, the best prospects in the system are still position players. Alcides Escobar wrested the starting shortstop job away from Hardy, who was traded to the Twins for Carlos Gomez in November.

Yovani Gallardo went 13-12, 3.73 as a key member of Milwaukee's starting rotation

TOP 30 PROSPECTS

1. Alcides Escobar, ss	**16.** Amaury Rivas, rhp
2. Brett Lawrie, 2b	**17.** Caleb Gindl, of
3. Mat Gamel, 3b	**18.** D'Vontrey Richardson, of
4. Eric Arnett, rhp	**19.** Eric Farris, 2b
5. Jonathan Lucroy, c	**20.** Taylor Green, 3b/1b
6. Kentrail Davis, of	**21.** Jeremy Jeffress, rhp
7. Zach Braddock, lhp	**22.** Del Howell, lhp
8. Lorenzo Cain, of	**23.** John Axford, rhp
9. Jake Odorizzi, rhp	**24.** Josh Butler, rhp
10. Kyle Heckathorn, rhp	**25.** Alex Periard, rhp
11. Mark Rogers, rhp	**26.** Evan Anundsen, rhp
12. Logan Schafer, of	**27.** Brooks Hall, rhp
13. Cody Scarpetta, rhp	**28.** Max Walla, of
14. Wily Peralta, rhp	**29.** Nick Bucci, rhp
15. Angel Salome, c	**30.** Maverick Lasker, rhp

Brett Lawrie moved to second base and reached Double-A as a teenager.

Mat Gamel got his first extended stay in the the majors and Jonathan Lucroy is close to making a push to become Milwaukee's catcher.

Powered by Braun and Fielder, the most productive pair of teammates with 255 RBIs between them, the Brewers scored more runs in 2009 than they did during their wild-card run the year before. With Escobar, Gamel and Lucroy almost ready to step in, Milwaukee has the ammunition to trade bats for arms while waiting for more homegrown pitchers to develop.

ORGANIZATION OVERVIEW

General Manager: Doug Melvin. **Farm Director:** Reid Nichols. **Scouting Director:** Bruce Seid.

Class	Team	League	W	L	PCT	Finish*	Manager(s)
Majors	Milwaukee Brewers	National	80	82	.494	9th (16)	Ken Macha
Triple-A	Nashville Sounds	Pacific Coast	75	69	.521	5th (16)	Don Money
Double-A	Huntsville Stars	Southern	63	75	.457	9th (10)	Bobby Miscik
High A	Brevard County Manatees	Florida State	79	48	.622	1st (12)	Mike Guerrero
Low A	Wisconsin Timber Rattlers	Midwest	58	81	.417	12th (14)	Jeff Isom
Rookie	AZL Brewers	Arizona	25	31	.446	t-6th (11)	Tony Diggs
Rookie	Helena Brewers	Pioneer	32	44	.421	6th (8)	Rene Gonzales
Overall 2009 Minor League Record			332	348	.488	22nd (30)	

*Finish in overall standings (No. of teams in league). †League champion.

LAST YEAR'S TOP 30

Player, Pos.		Status
1.	Alcides Escobar, ss	No. 1
2.	Mat Gamel, 3b	No. 3
3.	Brett Lawrie, c/3b	No. 2
4.	Jeremy Jeffress, rhp	No. 21
5.	Angel Salome, c	No. 15
6.	Lorenzo Cain, of	No. 8
7.	Cutter Dykstra, of	Dropped out
8.	Taylor Green, 3b	No. 20
9.	Cole Gillespie, of	(Diamondbacks)
10.	Jonathan Lucroy, c	No. 5
11.	Jake Odorizzi, rhp	No. 9
12.	Zach Braddock, lhp	No. 7
13.	Alexandre Periard, rhp	No. 25
14.	Caleb Gindl, of	No. 17
15.	Cody Scarpetta, rhp	No. 13
16.	Lee Haydel, of	Dropped out
17.	Brent Brewer, ss	Dropped out
18.	R.J. Seidel, rhp	Dropped out
19.	Eduardo Morlan, rhp	(Rays)
20.	Seth Lintz, rhp	Dropped out
21.	Omar Aguilar, rhp	Dropped out
22.	Wily Peralta, rhp	No. 14
23.	Efrain Nieves, lhp	Dropped out
24.	Evan Frederickson, lhp	Dropped out
25.	Luis Pena, rhp	(Mariners)
26.	Amaury Rivas, rhp	No. 16
27.	Eric Farris, 2b	No. 19
28.	Cody Adams, rhp	Dropped out
29.	Logan Schafer, of	No. 12
30.	Tim Dillard, rhp	Dropped out

BEST TOOLS

Best Hitter for Average	Brett Lawrie
Best Power Hitter	Brett Lawrie
Best Strike-Zone Discipline	Jonathan Lucroy
Fastest Baserunner	Lee Haydel
Best Athlete	D'Vontrey Richardson
Best Fastball	Jeremy Jeffress
Best Curveball	Cody Scarpetta
Best Slider	Zach Braddock
Best Changeup	Amaury Rivas
Best Control	Amaury Rivas
Best Defensive Catcher	Carlos Corporan
Best Defensive Infielder	Alcides Escobar
Best Infield Arm	Alcides Escobar
Best Defensive Outfielder	Logan Schafer
Best Outfield Arm	Brendan Katin

PROJECTED 2013 LINEUP

Catcher	Jonathan Lucroy
First Base	Prince Fielder
Second Base	Brett Lawrie
Third Base	Casey McGehee
Shortstop	Alcides Escobar
Left Field	Ryan Braun
Center Field	Carlos Gomez
Right Field	Mat Gamel
No. 1 Starter	Yovani Gallardo
No. 2 Starter	Eric Arnett
No. 3 Starter	Jake Odorizzi
No. 4 Starter	Kyle Heckathorn
No. 5 Starter	Cody Scarpetta
Closer	Zach Braddock

TOP PROSPECTS OF THE DECADE

Year	Player, Pos.	2009 Org.
2000	Nick Neugebauer, rhp	Out of baseball
2001	Ben Sheets, rhp	Free agent (injured)
2002	Nick Neugebauer, rhp	Out of baseball
2003	Brad Nelson, 1b	Mariners
2004	Rickie Weeks, 2b	Brewers
2005	Rickie Weeks, 2b	Brewers
2006	Prince Fielder, 1b	Brewers
2007	Yovani Gallardo, rhp	Brewers
2008	Matt LaPorta, of	Indians
2009	Alcides Escobar, ss	Brewers

TOP DRAFT PICKS OF THE DECADE

Year	Player, Pos.	2009 Org.
2000	Dave Krynzel, of	Orioles
2001	Mike Jones, rhp	Brewers
2002	Prince Fielder, 1b	Brewers
2003	Rickie Weeks, 2b	Brewers
2004	Mark Rogers, rhp	Brewers
2005	Ryan Braun, 3b	Brewers
2006	Jeremy Jeffress, rhp	Brewers
2007	Matt LaPorta, of	Indians
2008	Brett Lawrie, c/3b	Brewers
2009	Eric Arnett, rhp	Brewers

LARGEST BONUSES IN CLUB HISTORY

Rickie Weeks, 2003	$3,600,000
Ben Sheets, 1999	$2,450,000
Ryan Braun, 2005	$2,450,000
Prince Fielder, 2002	$2,400,000
Mark Rogers, 2004	$2,200,000

MILWAUKEE BREWERS

TOP 2010 ROOKIE: Alcides Escobar, ss. With J.J. Hardy out of the picture, Escobar is ready to step up.

BREAKOUT PROSPECT: Logan Schafer, of. The Brewers' 2009 minor league player of the year has a line-drive bat and fine instincts that could take him quickly to the majors.

SLEEPER: Rob Wooten, rhp. His fastball is fringy, but he converted 29 of 31 saves and reached Double-A in 2009.

SOURCE OF TOP 30 TALENT			
Homegrown	28	Acquired	2
College	8	Trades	1
Junior college	1	Rule 5 draft	0
High school	13	Independent leagues	0
Draft-and-follow	3	Free agents/waivers	1
Nondrafted free agents	0		
International	3		

Numbers in parentheses indicate prospect rankings.

LF
Kentrail Davis (6)
Caleb Gindl (17)
Drew Anderson
Chris Dennis
Khris Davis
Chuckie Caufield
Demetrius McKelvie
Scott Krieger

CF
Lorenzo Cain (8)
Logan Schafer (12)
D'Vontrey Richardson (18)
Lee Haydel
Chad Stang
Franklin Romero

RF
Max Walla (28)
Trent Oeltjen
Brendan Katin

3B
Mat Gamel (3)
Taylor Green (20)
Adam Heether
Zelous Wheeler
Mike Brownstein
Juan Sanchez

SS
Alcides Escobar (1)
Yohannis Perez
Brent Brewer
Josh Prince

2B
Brett Lawrie (2)
Eric Farris (19)
Cutter Dykstra
Hernan Iribarren
Scooter Gennett

1B
Joe Koshansky
Steffan Wilson
Chris Errecart
Brock Kjeldgaard
Corey Kemp

C
Jonathan Lucroy (5)
Angel Salome (15)
Cameron Garfield
George Kottaras
Carlos Corporan
Tyler Roberts

RHP

Starters	Relievers
Eric Arnett (4)	Mark Rogers (11)
Jake Odorizzi (9)	John Axford (23)
Kyle Heckathorn (10)	Robert Wooten
Cody Scarpetta (13)	Omar Aguilar
Wily Peralta (14)	Tim Dillard
Amaury Rivas (16)	Chris Smith
Jeremy Jeffress (21)	Michael Fiers
Josh Butler (24)	Robert Hinton
Alex Periard (25)	Cody Adams
Evan Anundsen (26)	Dave Johnson
Brooks Hall (27)	Jim Henderson
Nick Bucci (29)	Nick Tyson
Maverick Lasker (30)	Ruben Flores
Trey Watten	
R.J. Seidel	
Seth Lintz	
Hiram Burgos	

LHP

Starters	Relievers
Del Howell (22)	Zach Braddock (7)
Efrain Nieves	Chuck Lofgren
Evan Frederickson	Jon Pokorny
Dan Merklinger	Brandon Ritchie
Chris Cody	Bobby Bramhall
Caleb Thielbar	Rafael Lluberes
Chase Wright	Dan Meadows
David Welch	

2009

BEST PURE HITTER: OF Kentrail Davis (1s) had a disappointing spring after he got impatient when teams pitched around him, but he got back on track in instructional league.

BEST POWER HITTER: Davis and OFs Max Walla (2), D'Vontrey Richardson (5), Khris Davis (7) and Demetrius McKelvie (25) all have plus raw power. Kentrail Davis and Walla should have the most usable pop down the road.

FASTEST RUNNER: The Brewers stocked up on speed, with Richardson leading the way with a 6.4-second time in the 60-yard dash. Davis, SS Josh Prince (3) and OFs Chad Stang (8) and Franklin Romero (20) run in the 6.6-6.7 range. Prince led NCAA Division I with 48 steals and the Rookie-level Pioneer League with 26 in just 36 games.

BEST DEFENSIVE PLAYER: C Cameron Garfield (2) showed advanced receiving and game-running skills in his pro debut. He threw out just 16 percent of basestealers in his pro debut, but he has a strong arm and just needs some mechanical adjustments.

BEST FASTBALL: RHPs Eric Arnett (1) and Kyle Heckathorn (1s) both sit at 91-94 mph, with Arnett topping out at 97 and Heckathorn peaking at 98. RHP Brooks Hall (4) already reaches 95 mph and has a lot of projection remaining on his 6-foot-5 frame.

BEST SECONDARY PITCH: Arnett's mid-80s slider grades as a plus-plus pitch at times. Heckathorn's slider has more velocity but less consistency. LHP Del Howell (15) also has a quality slider.

BEST PRO DEBUT: LHP Caleb Thielbar (18) led the Rookie-level Arizona League in wins (six) and ERA (1.59). RHP Michael Fiers (22), who topped NCAA Division II with 145 strikeouts in 109 innings at Nova Southeastern (Fla.) in the spring, led the Rookie-level Pioneer League with eight saves.

BEST ATHLETE: Richardson is a raw athlete who played quarterback at Florida State and holds the school record for longest run by a QB (55 yards). Kentrail Davis has all-around tools and more polish than Richardson. Arnett suited up but didn't play for Indiana's shorthanded basketball team last winter.

MOST INTRIGUING BACKGROUND: RHP Kyle Hansen's (40) brother Craig pitches for the Pirates. C Richard Stock's (45) brother Robert signed with the Cardinals as a second-round pick. Neither player signed.

CLOSEST TO THE MAJORS: Arnett, Kentrail Davis and Heckathorn—whoever can harness his considerable physical gifts first. Fiers is a longshot candidate.

BEST LATE-ROUND PICK: Howell wasn't at his best this spring while battling mononucleosis, one of the reasons he dropped to the 15th round. When he's right, he flashes three plus pitches in his 88-94 mph sinker, his slider and his changeup. SS Scooter Gennett (16) is an offensive-minded middle infielder. Both signed for $260,000.

THE ONE WHO GOT AWAY: LHP Lex Rutledge (26) reminded Milwaukee of Ted Lilly but couldn't be signed away from Samford.

ASSESSMENT: Arnett (the No. 26 pick) and Heckathorn (No. 47) both lasted longer than expected, a boon for the pitching-needy Brewers. Milwaukee also stocked up on position players, as Davis and Walla have potentially dangerous bats.

2008

Brett Lawrie (1) won't be a catcher, but his bat is as good as the Brewers hoped. With the exception of RHP Jake Odorizzi (1s), most of the early-round pitchers took a step back last season. OF Logan Schafer (3) won the high Class A Florida State League batting title (.313).

GRADE: B

2007

Milwaukee used OF/1B Matt LaPorta (1) as the key player in the 2008 C.C. Sabathia trade that resulted in its first playoff berth in 26 years. Jonathan Lucroy (3) looks like the franchise's catcher of the future. RHP Cody Scarpetta (11) could provide some of the rotation help that the Brewers need.

GRADE: B

2006

RHP Jeremy Jeffress (1) can hit 100 mph with his fastball, but he's one more failed drug test away from a lifetime ban. That leaves OF Cole Gillespie (3) as the best player from this crop, and he was traded for Felipe Lopez last summer.

GRADE: D

2005

By the time his career is over, OF Ryan Braun (1) could be the most devastating hitter in franchise history. Milwaukee also has hopes for 3B Mat Gamel (4) and draft-and-follow LHP Zach Braddock (18).

GRADE: A

*Draft analysis by Jim Callis. Numbers in parentheses indicate draft rounds. *Bonuses for 2005 are first 10 rounds only.*

ALCIDES ESCOBAR, SS

Born: Dec. 16, 1986.
Height: 6-1. **Weight:** 185.
Bats: R. **Throws:** R.
Signed: Venezuela, 2003.
Signed by: Epy Guerrero.

In an organization that focused for years on procuring offensive players, Escobar quickly established himself as a defensive whiz while climbing the ranks of the farm system. Signed by legendary scout Epy Guerrero out of Venezuela for a mere $33,000 in 2003, Escobar wowed scouts with eye-popping web gems. As his bat caught up to his glove, he switched jobs with slumping shortstop J.J. Hardy last August, when Hardy was demoted to Triple-A Nashville. While making some rookie mistakes in the field, Escobar showed why he's considered a special defender by making several remarkable plays. He also handled himself quite nicely at the plate while coming within two at-bats of losing his rookie eligibility.

Much of Escobar's game revolves around his legs. He uses them for quickness and amazing range to both sides in the field, allowing him to get to balls out of the grasp of most shortstops. At the plate, his speed makes him a threat for a hit every time he smacks a ball on the ground. When he tops a slow roller, even right at an infielder, he's almost impossible to throw out. He's a constant threat to steal bases, swiping 42 in 52 attempts at Nashville, though the Brewers seldom run under manager Ken Macha. Beyond his legs, Escobar owes his defensive prowess to long arms, soft hands, arm strength and natural instincts. In short, he was born to play shortstop. As a hitter, he covers the plate well and generally uses the whole field. Though he won't hit for power, he has some bat speed and leverage in his stroke.

Escobar sometimes gets lazy with throws on routine grounders and makes sloppy errors. He has exercised more patience at the plate in recent seasons but still has a long way to go in that department. He drew just four walks in 134 big league plate appearances last season, and getting on base needs to be his primary offensive goal. Though he has more pop than his thin frame might suggest, hitting the ball in the air does no good for him. He'll go through bouts where he becomes pull-conscious and tries to hit for power.

The transition from Hardy to Escobar took place ahead of schedule. Though Hardy had been one of the Brewers' core players during their resurgence, it was evident that Escobar's time had come, prompting a trade of Hardy to the Twins for Carlos Gomez in November. The youngster will start at shortstop for Milwaukee in 2010 and be a prime Rookie of the Year candidate, with the hope that he'll develop into the club's leadoff man of the future.

Year	Club (League)	Class	AVG	G	AB	R	H	2B	3B	HR	RBI	BB	SO	SB	OBP	SLG
2004	Helena (PIO)	R	.281	68	231	38	65	8	0	2	24	20	44	20	.348	.342
2005	West Virginia (SAL)	LoA	.271	127	520	80	141	25	8	2	36	20	90	30	.305	.362
2006	Brevard County (FSL)	HiA	.257	87	350	47	90	9	1	2	33	19	56	28	.296	.306
2007	Brevard County (FSL)	HiA	.325	63	268	37	87	8	3	0	25	7	35	18	.345	.377
	Huntsville (SL)	AA	.283	62	226	27	64	5	4	1	28	11	36	4	.314	.354
2008	Huntsville (SL)	AA	.328	131	546	95	179	24	5	8	76	31	82	34	.363	.434
	Milwaukee (NL)	MAJ	.500	9	4	2	2	0	0	0	0	0	1	0	.500	.500
2009	Nashville (PCL)	AAA	.298	109	430	76	128	24	6	4	34	32	65	42	.353	.409
	Milwaukee (NL)	MAJ	.304	38	125	20	38	3	1	1	11	4	18	4	.333	.368
MAJOR LEAGUE TOTALS			.310	47	129	22	40	3	1	1	11	4	19	4	.338	.372
MINOR LEAGUE TOTALS			.293	647	2571	400	754	103	27	19	256	140	408	176	.333	.377

2 BRETT LAWRIE, 2B

BORN: Jan. 18, 1990. **B-T:** R-R. **HT.:** 5-11. **WT.:** 200. **DRAFTED:** HS—Langley, B.C., 2008 (1st round). **SIGNED BY:** Marty Lehn.

After the Brewers signed him for $1.7 million as the 16th pick in the 2008 draft—making him the highest-drafted Canadian hitter ever—Lawrie planned on becoming a full-time catcher. He later changed his mind and asked to move to second base. He didn't make his pro debut in 2008 because he saw action with Canada's junior and Olympic teams. He returned to international play at the World Cup in 2009. Lawrie is an aggressive hitter with good pop. He made the adjustment to pro ball easily because he used wood bats regularly as an amateur. With strong hands and the quickest bat in the system, he drives the ball to all fields. He's more athletic than his stocky build would indicate, which is why Milwaukee agreed to let him play second base. He has average speed and good arm strength. He needs to show more interest in defense if he's going to stay at second base and become a player in the mold of Jeff Kent. Lawrie improved as the season progressed but will have to work to make his hands softer and his footwork smoother. Lawrie will get to the big leagues quicker now than he would have as a catcher, but some scouts think he's destined for an outfield corner. He has a potent bat that should profile at just about any position. Though he jumped to Double-A Huntsville last summer to prepare for the World Cup, he could open 2010 in high Class A.

Year	Club (League)	Class	AVG	G	AB	R	H	2B	3B	HR	RBI	BB	SO	SB	OBP	SLG
2009	Wisconsin (MWL)	LoA	.274	105	372	48	102	18	5	13	65	41	70	19	.348	.454
	Huntsville (SL)	AA	.269	13	52	6	14	0	1	0	0	0	14	0	.283	.308
MINOR LEAGUE TOTALS			.274	118	424	54	116	18	6	13	65	41	84	19	.340	.436

3 MAT GAMEL, 3B

BORN: July 26, 1985. **B-T:** L-R. **HT.:** 6-0. **WT.:** 205. **DRAFTED:** Chipola (Fla.) JC, 2005 (4th round). **SIGNED BY:** Doug Reynolds.

The Brewers figured both they and Gamel would profit from a midseason promotion to the majors, with his primary role as DH in interleague road games. But he had trouble adjusting to irregular playing time, lost his stroke and never got going again, even after returning to Triple-A. He batted .267 in 2009, down 39 points from his previous career average. When he's on his game, Gamel uses a compact stroke to spray the ball to all fields, mainly from gap to gap. He has enough pop in his bat to hit 20 homers annually in the majors. He normally hangs in well against lefties, taking breaking balls the other way. He has average speed and plenty of arm strength at third base. Gamel made strides defensively in 2009, but scouts still doubt his ability to handle the hot corner in the majors. He's not as bad as he was when he led the minors with 53 errors in 2007, but he still has flawed footwork that leads to erratic throws. He needs a better two-strike approach after whiffing a career-high 143 times last season. In an attempt to recapture his stroke, Gamel played winter ball in Venezuela. The Brewers have no plans to move him to first base or the outfield, but his status as their third baseman of the future became clouded when Casey McGehee turned in a strong rookie season in 2009. The 2010 season will determine where Gamel fits in Milwaukee.

Year	Club (League)	Class	AVG	G	AB	R	H	2B	3B	HR	RBI	BB	SO	SB	OBP	SLG
2005	West Virginia (SAL)	LoA	.174	8	23	2	4	0	0	1	1	5	9	0	.321	.304
	Helena (PIO)	R	.327	50	199	34	65	15	2	5	37	12	49	7	.375	.497
2006	West Virginia (SAL)	LoA	.288	129	493	65	142	28	5	17	88	52	81	9	.359	.469
2007	Brevard County (FSL)	HiA	.300	128	466	78	140	37	8	9	60	58	98	14	.378	.472
2008	Huntsville (SL)	AA	.329	127	508	96	167	35	7	19	96	55	111	6	.395	.537
	Nashville (PCL)	AAA	.238	5	21	3	5	0	0	1	3	2	10	0	.304	.381
	Milwaukee (NL)	MAJ	.500	2	2	0	1	0	0	0	0	0	1	0	.500	1.000
2009	Nashville (PCL)	AAA	.278	75	273	42	76	18	1	11	48	38	89	1	.367	.473
	Milwaukee (NL)	MAJ	.242	61	128	11	31	6	1	5	20	18	54	1	.338	.422
MAJOR LEAGUE TOTALS			.246	63	130	11	32	7	1	5	20	18	55	1	.340	.431
MINOR LEAGUE TOTALS			.302	522	1983	320	599	133	23	63	333	222	447	37	.374	.488

4 ERIC ARNETT, RHP

BORN: Jan. 25, 1988. **B-T:** R-R. **HT.:** 6-6. **WT.:** 220. **DRAFTED:** Indiana, 2009 (1st round). **SIGNED BY:** Mike Farrell.

Needing to bolster their stock of pitching prospects, the Brewers were pleasantly surprised Arnett was available with the No. 26 overall pick in June. Just the second first-rounder ever from Indiana University, he came out of nowhere to set Hoosiers records for wins (12) and strikeouts (109) last spring. He signed for $1.197 million. After battling command problems earlier in his college career, Arnett put it all together as a junior. He threw his fastball at 91-94 mph and touched 97, and he tightened a mid-80s slider to give him a second out pitch. He got better at using his big frame to throw on a downhill plane. He showed his athleticism by suiting up for Indiana's basketball practice squad but didn't play in regular games. At times, Arnett loses his arm slot and his command. He needs to refine his below-average changeup to give him an offspeed pitch that will keep hitters off balance. His fastball dipped into the high 80s at the end of his short pro outings, though he may just have been tired after a heavy college workload. The Brewers would love to move Arnett through their system as quickly as possible, which may mean that he'll start his first full season in high Class A. They want to be careful not to get too ambitious, but they'd be thrilled if he could get to Milwaukee before the end of 2011.

Year	Club (League)	Class	W	L	ERA	G	GS	CG	SV	IP	H	R	ER	HR	BB	SO	AVG
2009	Helena (PIO)	R	0	4	4.41	14	9	0	0	35	33	30	17	1	21	35	.228
MINOR LEAGUE TOTALS			0	4	4.41	14	9	0	0	35	33	30	17	1	21	35	.228

5 JONATHAN LUCROY, C †

BORN: June 13, 1986. **B-T:** R-R. **HT.:** 6-1. **WT.:** 206. **DRAFTED:** Louisiana-Lafayette, 2007 (3rd round). **SIGNED BY:** Brian Sankey.

In his third pro season, Lucroy bypassed Angel Salome as the Brewers' top catching prospect. Lucroy ranked second in the Double-A Southern League in walks (78) and throwing out basestealers (41 percent), then headed to the Arizona Fall League to expedite his development. Lucroy's offense has been more advanced than his defense since he turned pro. He has a good approach and a short swing, squares the ball up and has solid gap power. He has a career .380 on-base percentage and walked more than he struck out in 2009. He bolsters his average arm strength with a quick release and has recorded pop times as low as 1.8 seconds. Lucroy sometimes struggles behind the plate, boxing balls and losing his release point on throws, causing them to sail. He also needs to improve his game-calling skills. His batting average (.267) and slugging percentage (.418) in 2009 were easily career lows, though he still projects as a good offensive threat for a catcher. He has below-average speed but doesn't clog the bases. Scouts are divided over whether Lucroy projects as a regular or backup in the majors. He should hit enough but must continue to polish his overall defensive skills. He'll move up to Triple-A to start 2010 and could see his first big league action later in the year.

Year	Club (League)	Class	AVG	G	AB	R	H	2B	3B	HR	RBI	BB	SO	SB	OBP	SLG
2007	Helena (PIO)	R	.342	61	234	35	80	18	2	4	39	16	37	0	.383	.487
2008	West Virginia (SAL)	LoA	.310	65	239	45	74	16	1	10	33	30	39	8	.391	.510
	Brevard County (FSL)	HiA	.292	64	236	31	69	12	1	10	44	28	45	1	.364	.479
2009	Huntsville (SL)	AA	.267	125	419	61	112	32	2	9	66	78	66	1	.380	.418
MINOR LEAGUE TOTALS			.297	315	1128	172	335	78	6	33	182	152	187	10	.380	.465

6 KENTRAIL DAVIS, OF †

BORN: June 29, 1988. **B-T:** L-R. **HT.:** 5-9. **WT.:** 195. **DRAFTED:** Tennessee, 2009 (1st round supplemental). **SIGNED BY:** Joe Mason.

Davis entered 2009 as a potential top 10 draft pick, but he had a rough sophomore season while trying to do too much for a poor Tennessee team. Remembering his standout play for Team USA the previous summer, the Brewers took him with the 39th overall pick in June and signed him at the Aug. 17 deadline for $1.2 million. Davis' combination of hitting ability, power and speed, not to mention his stocky frame, have drawn comparisons to a lefthanded-hitting Kirby Puckett. He has a short swing with plenty of bat speed. He has plus speed and the potential to become at least a 20-20 player. At times, Davis gets pull-happy, his swing gets long and his strikeouts pile up. When he got pitched around with the Volunteers, he got frustrated and chased pitches out of the strike zone. He can run the 60-yard dash in 6.6 seconds, though he has yet to translate that quickness into stolen bases. Though his speed gives him average range in center field, he lacks top-notch instincts and ultimately may fit better in left field. His arm strength is fringe-average. The Brewers felt even better about Davis after watching him excel in instructional league. He could make his pro debut in high Class A and prove to be one of the steals of the 2009 draft.

Year	Club (League)	Class	AVG	G	AB	R	H	2B	3B	HR	RBI	BB	SO	SB	OBP	SLG
2009	Did Not Play—Signed Late															

7 ZACH BRADDOCK, LHP ↓

BORN: Aug. 23, 1987. **B-T:** L-L. **HT.:** 6-3. **WT.:** 230. **DRAFTED:** Burlington (N.J.) CC, D/F 2005 (18th round). **SIGNED BY:** Tony Blengino.

Braddock had Tommy John surgery in high school, and repeated elbow and shoulder issues made it a struggle for the Brewers to keep him on the mound as a starter. So they moved him to the bullpen in 2009. While he had two monthlong stints on the disabled list, he was dominant when healthy, posting a 62-7 strikeout-walk ratio in 40 innings. Braddock has a live arm, consistently throwing at 91-94 mph while topping out at 96. He also features a sharp slider that gives lefthanders nightmares, and he has dabbled with an improving cutter. He pounds the strike zone, using his size to throw on a steep downward plane. He has an effective changeup, though he doesn't throw it much, especially as a reliever. The biggest issue with Braddock is his health. Aside from his surgery in high school, he has pitched just 198 innings in four pro seasons. He also has dealt with emotional issues that required medication, though he seems to have those under control. To continue Braddock's transition from starter to reliever and to get him more innings, the Brewers sent him to the Arizona Fall League. If he can avoid more physical setbacks, he could join Milwaukee's bullpen at some point in 2010. It's tempting to think of what he might do as a starter, but he hasn't proven he can hold up in that role.

Year	Club (League)	Class	W	L	ERA	G	GS	CG	SV	IP	H	R	ER	HR	BB	SO	AVG
2006	Helena (PIO)	R	2	2	5.49	14	8	0	0	39	32	26	24	3	31	30	.227
2007	West Virginia (SAL)	LoA	3	1	1.15	10	9	0	0	47	28	6	6	1	15	68	.168
2008	West Virginia (SAL)	LoA	0	0	0.00	2	2	0	0	6	2	1	0	0	3	13	.095
	Brevard County (FSL)	HiA	4	7	5.51	21	11	0	0	65	55	44	40	7	42	80	.226
2009	Brevard County (FSL)	HiA	1	1	1.09	14	0	0	0	25	12	3	3	2	4	40	.143
	Huntsville (SL)	AA	2	1	2.87	12	0	0	0	16	16	9	5	2	3	22	.262
MINOR LEAGUE TOTALS			12	12	3.55	73	30	0	0	198	145	89	78	15	98	253	.202

8 LORENZO CAIN, OF ✝

BORN: April 13, 1986. **B-T:** R-R. **HT.:** 6-2. **WT.:** 192. **DRAFTED:** Tallahassee (Fla.) CC, D/F 2004 (17th round). **SIGNED BY:** Doug Reynolds.

The Brewers had hoped that Cain would put himself in position to take over from Mike Cameron in center field in 2010. But Cain seriously sprained his left knee diving for a fly ball in April and missed half the 2009 season. He wasn't the same, at the plate or in the field, when he returned in late June. Cain stands out most with his athleticism and speed. Moved from right field to center in 2008, he uses his quickness and long legs to gobble up ground in the field and on the basepaths. Still filling out and getting stronger, he shows flashes of power but is mostly a gap hitter. He has a strong arm, especially for a center fielder. Cain still has to work on his plate discipline, though it has improved. He didn't play baseball until high school and therefore lacks advanced instincts, but his athletic ability helps cover him. He could be a more prolific and successful basestealer. Cain's lost season left the Brewers in a quandary about what to do in center field for 2010, one they addressed by trading J.J. Hardy to the Twins for Carlos Gomez. Cain has yet to prove himself in Triple-A, and now Gomez could block him for the long term.

Year	Club (League)	Class	AVG	G	AB	R	H	2B	3B	HR	RBI	BB	SO	SB	OBP	SLG
2005	Brewers (AZL)	R	.356	50	205	45	73	18	5	5	37	20	32	12	.418	.566
	Helena (PIO)	R	.208	6	24	4	5	0	0	0	1	1	6	0	.321	.208
2006	West Virginia (SAL)	LoA	.307	132	527	91	162	36	4	6	60	58	104	34	.384	.425
2007	Brevard County (FSL)	HiA	.276	126	482	67	133	21	3	2	44	37	97	24	.338	.344
2008	Nashville (PCL)	AAA	.158	6	19	0	3	0	0	0	2	3	6	0	.273	.158
	Brevard County (FSL)	HiA	.287	80	317	50	91	22	4	7	41	29	68	19	.358	.448
	Huntsville (SL)	AA	.277	40	148	21	41	9	5	4	17	19	41	6	.363	.486
2009	Brewers (AZL)	R	.444	3	9	1	4	1	0	0	1	1	0	0	.455	.556
	Wisconsin (MWL)	LoA	.192	15	52	3	10	4	0	0	3	9	15	0	.311	.269
	Huntsville (SL)	AA	.214	42	145	17	31	6	0	4	15	10	35	3	.277	.338
MINOR LEAGUE TOTALS			.287	500	1928	299	553	117	21	28	221	187	404	98	.359	.413

9 JAKE ODORIZZI, RHP

BORN: March 27, 1990. **B-T:** R-R. **HT.:** 6-2. **WT.:** 180. **DRAFTED:** HS—Highland, Ill., 2008 (1st round supplemental). **SIGNED BY:** Harvey Kuenn Jr.

The Brewers liked Odorizzi's athleticism—which he put on display as a pitcher, short-stop and all-league wide receiver in high school—before signing him for $1.06 million as the 32nd overall pick in the 2008 draft. Some clubs rated him the best high school pitcher in that draft. Milwaukee has brought him along slowly, limiting him to 68 innings in two years of Rookie ball. Milwaukee believes Odorizzi will fill out and gain velocity as he matures. He currently pitches at 88-91 mph and touches 93 with his fastball, maintaining that zip throughout his outings. His free and easy delivery and good extension allow his heater to get in on hitters quickly, and it features good sink and armside run. He also features a curveball that's a plus pitch at times. He throws strikes and shows good poise and competitiveness. Odorizzi needs to continue refining his secondary pitches. His curveball is inconsistent, and his slider and changeup are less reliable. While he's consistently around the plate, he needs to do a better job of locating his pitches in the strike zone. If he adds velocity and improves his secondary offerings, Odorizzi could become a No. 2 or 3 starter. He'll probably begin 2010 at low Class A Wisconsin, with a chance for a midseason promotion.

Year	Club (League)	Class	W	L	ERA	G	GS	CG	SV	IP	H	R	ER	HR	BB	SO	AVG
2008	Brewers (AZL)	R	1	2	3.48	11	4	0	0	21	18	10	8	2	9	19	.220
2009	Helena (PIO)	R	1	4	4.40	12	10	0	0	47	55	27	23	3	9	43	.296
MINOR LEAGUE TOTALS			2	6	4.12	23	14	0	0	68	73	37	31	5	18	62	.272

10 KYLE HECKATHORN, RHP

BORN: June 17, 1988. **B-T:** R-R. **HT.:** 6-6. **WT.:** 235. **DRAFTED:** Kennesaw State, 2009 (1st round supplemental). **SIGNED BY:** Ryan Robinson.

After selecting Eric Arnett in the first round of the 2009 draft, the Brewers tabbed another big-bodied power pitcher in Heckathorn with the 47th overall choice. He would have been the highest pick in Kennesaw State history if the Blue Jays hadn't taken team-mate Chad Jenkins 27 selections earlier. After signing for $776,000, Heckathorn worked on tight pitch counts in his pro debut. His raw stuff is outstanding and rivaled anyone's in the 2009 draft. His fastball sits at 91-94 mph and peaks at 98. His slider also can be devastating, registering in the high 80s. Even with his live arm and big frame, Heckathorn doesn't have any problems throwing strikes. Heckathorn is learning how to use his stuff. He doesn't know how to set up batters and actually throws too many hittable strikes at times. He must come up with a reliable changeup so hitters can't sit on his hard stuff, and he'll have to locate his pitches better in the strike zone. He won just 12 games in three college seasons, when he had limited exposure to top-level competition, and got hit hard in his brief introduction to pro ball. The Brewers will keep Heckathorn in a starting role for now, though some scouts project him as an overpowering closer. He'll likely begin his first full season in low Class A.

Year	Club (League)	Class	W	L	ERA	G	GS	CG	SV	IP	H	R	ER	HR	BB	SO	AVG
2009	Helena (PIO)	R	0	1	6.04	6	5	0	0	22	30	18	15	4	4	15	.326
MINOR LEAGUE TOTALS			0	1	6.04	6	5	0	0	22	30	18	15	4	4	15	.326

11 MARK ROGERS, RHP

BORN: Jan. 30, 1986. **B-T:** R-R. **HT.:** 6-2. **WT.:** 224. **DRAFTED:** HS—Mount Ararat, Maine, 2004 (1st round). **SIGNED BY:** Tony Blengino.

After not throwing a pitch for two seasons while recovering from multiple shoulder surgeries, Rogers resurfaced with a healthy, productive 2009 season in high Class A. The Brewers were understandably cautious with Rogers, who signed for $2.2 million as the fifth overall pick in the 2004 draft, limiting his workload to a few innings at a time and resisting the urge to promote him. They emphasized the importance of using his legs more in his delivery to take stress off his shoulder, and he accomplished that mission. Rogers, who touched the upper 90s with his fastball before he got hurt, sat at 93-96 mph last year, with the ball coming out of his hand easily. He also showed a sharp-breaking curveball and a deceptive changeup, which were good pitches when he threw them for strikes. Working in short stints, he didn't need to rely on his secondary pitches as much as if he pitched deep into games. Rogers still throws across his body, which compromises his command. He walked 4.0 batters per nine innings in 2009, a marked improvement from his previous career rate of 6.2. Given his difficulty staying healthy and throwing multiple pitches for strikes, Rogers fits best as a reliever and could move quickly once Milwaukee shifts him to that role. He should see Double-A for the first time in 2010.

Year	Club (League)	Class	W	L	ERA	G	GS	CG	SV	IP	H	R	ER	HR	BB	SO	AVG
2004	Brewers (AZL)	R	0	3	4.72	9	6	0	0	27	30	21	14	0	14	35	.294
2005	West Virginia (SAL)	LoA	2	9	5.11	25	20	0	1	99	87	65	56	11	70	109	.238
2006	Brevard County (FSL)	HiA	1	2	5.07	16	16	0	0	71	68	46	40	6	53	96	.253
	Brewers (AZL)	R	0	0	2.25	3	3	0	0	4	5	1	1	0	2	5	.294
2007	Did Not Play—Injured																
2009	Brevard County (FSL)	HiA	1	3	1.67	23	22	0	0	65	46	16	12	2	29	67	.201
MINOR LEAGUE TOTALS			4	17	4.18	76	67	0	1	265	236	149	123	19	168	312	.240

12 LOGAN SCHAFER, OF

BORN: Sept. 8, 1986. **B-T:** L-L. **HT.:** 6-1. **WT.:** 175. **DRAFTED:** Cal Poly, 2008 (3rd round). **SIGNED BY:** Corey Rodriguez.

The Brewers were so impressed with Schafer's skills and poise in spring training, less than a year after they made him a third-round pick, that they kept him with the big league club for its final exhibition games in Los Angeles. Milwaukee's major league coaching staff predicted good things for him, and he fulfilled those expectations. He won the high Class A Florida State League batting title (.313) and the organization's minor league player of the year award, finishing his first full pro season in Double-A. A contact hitter who draws a decent number of walks, Schafer isn't blessed with raw strength or speed. He has gap power and can steal an occasional base, but some scouts wonder if he'll produce enough offense to become a big league regular. Where Schafer shines is as a fly chaser in center field. He uses his instincts and quickness to run down balls from gap to gap, and he committed just one error in 2009. He also has an average, accurate arm. Schafer has drawn comparisons to Steve Finley and Mark Kotsay, and he could move quickly because the Brewers are looking for center-field help. His individual tools are not overwhelming, but his total package, combined with his confidence and maturity, bode well for his future. He'll start 2010 in Double-A and could reach Milwaukee by season's end.

Year	Club (League)	Class	AVG	G	AB	R	H	2B	3B	HR	RBI	BB	SO	SB	OBP	SLG
2008	Helena (PIO)	R	.240	8	25	4	6	0	1	2	8	5	4	1	.355	.560
	West Virginia (SAL)	LoA	.276	43	181	25	50	13	2	0	20	8	42	3	.306	.370
2009	Huntsville (SL)	AA	.217	7	23	4	5	0	1	0	0	4	3	1	.379	.304
	Brevard County (FSL)	HiA	.313	113	457	76	143	31	6	6	58	38	53	16	.369	.446
MINOR LEAGUE TOTALS			.297	171	686	109	204	44	10	8	86	55	102	21	.353	.426

13 CODY SCARPETTA, RHP

BORN: Aug. 25, 1988. **B-T:** R-R. **HT.:** 6-3. **WT.:** 242. **DRAFTED:** HS—Guilford, Ill., 2007 (11th round). **SIGNED BY:** Harvey Kuenn Jr.

Scarpetta might have been selected higher than his father Dan, a 1982 Brewers third-round pick, had he not torn the flexor tendon at the base of his right index finger six weeks before the 2007 draft. He had surgery before the Brewers made him an 11th-round choice, and he signed for $325,000. Milwaukee voided that deal when he needed a second operation, re-signing him for $125,000. To keep his rights, the Brewers had to put Scarpetta on their 40-man roster last winter, ahead of schedule, but he'll be worth it if he continues to progress as he did in 2009. A big-bodied pitcher, Scarpetta maintains velocity and downward tilt on his 90-94 mph fastball. Managers rated his curveball as the best in the low Class A Midwest League in 2009, and his improved changeup gives him a chance to have three solid or better pitches. Scarpetta isn't athletic and could use better conditioning, which might help him repeat his mechanics more easily. When he doesn't get out in front with his delivery, his pitches come up in the zone and are more hittable. Scarpetta was so impressive in 2009 that the Brewers promoted him to Huntsville for the Southern League playoffs. He could return to Double-A to open this season.

Year	Club (League)	Class	W	L	ERA	G	GS	CG	SV	IP	H	R	ER	HR	BB	SO	AVG
2008	Brewers (AZL)	R	1	0	0.57	6	5	0	0	16	8	1	1	0	8	27	.154
	Helena (PIO)	R	1	0	3.48	6	3	0	0	21	18	10	8	2	8	31	.237
2009	Wisconsin (MWL)	LoA	4	11	3.43	26	18	0	0	105	83	53	40	5	55	116	.217
	Huntsville (SL)	AA	0	0	5.40	1	1	0	0	5	5	3	3	1	1	1	.263
MINOR LEAGUE TOTALS			6	11	3.20	39	27	0	0	146	114	67	52	8	72	175	.215

14 WILY PERALTA, RHP

BORN: May 8, 1989. **B-T:** R-R. **HT.:** 6-2. **WT.:** 225. **SIGNED:** Dominican Republic, 2005. **SIGNED BY:** Fausto Sosa Pena/Fernando Arango.

Peralta sat out the 2007 season following Tommy John surgery, and Milwaukee continued to protect him by using him in a tandem-starter system at Wisconsin last year. He worked as many as six innings in a game just three times, though his 104 total innings eclipsed his previous career total of 72. Peralta has one of the best arms in the system. He easily throws his fastball at 92-94 mph and touches 96, and it features cutting and tailing action. He augments his heater with a low-80s slider that has good tilt. He has worked hard on his changeup and impressed coaches with it during instructional league. His improving changeup allows the Brewers to continue to project him as a starter in the majors, though some scouts have touted him as closer material. He has command issues at times, usually when he doesn't stay on top of his pitches. His thick build should lend itself to durability, though his delivery isn't very smooth and he'll need to maintain his conditioning. The Brewers are shy of quality starting pitchers at the upper levels of the system, so Peralta has a chance to carve a niche for himself. He should reach Double-A at some point in 2010.

Year	Club (League)	Class	W	L	ERA	G	GS	CG	SV	IP	H	R	ER	HR	BB	SO	AVG
2006	Brewers (AZL)	R	2	5	6.63	14	6	0	0	38	51	37	28	5	20	28	.319
2007	Did Not Play—Injured																
2008	Helena (PIO)	R	1	1	3.07	15	2	0	2	29	23	14	10	4	8	36	.209
	West Virginia (SAL)	LoA	0	1	10.80	2	2	0	0	5	6	6	6	0	3	3	.316
2009	Wisconsin (MWL)	LoA	4	4	3.47	27	15	0	1	104	91	45	40	5	46	118	.235
MINOR LEAGUE TOTALS			7	11	4.30	58	25	0	3	176	171	102	84	14	77	185	.253

15 ANGEL SALOME, C

BORN: Oct. 11, 1985. **B-T:** R-R. **HT.:** 5-7. **WT.:** 199. **DRAFTED:** HS—New York, 2004 (5th round). **SIGNED BY:** Tony Blengino.

Salome hit .360 in Double-A in 2008, but has struggled to build on that performance. He left the Arizona Fall League after just one appearance with an ailing shoulder, then missed much of his first time in big league camp with back issues last spring. He had trouble staying on the field in Triple-A last season, put up the worst numbers of his four full minor league seasons and caught just 72 games, stunting his defensive growth. Salome has an unorthodox style at the plate, stepping in the bucket but staying on the ball long enough to use the entire field. He's powerfully built and has strong hands, though he didn't drive the ball as consistently in 2009 as he had in the past. While he's aggressive at the plate and doesn't walk much, he does make consistent contact. Salome has well-above-average arm strength, but his throws tend to tail off and he threw out just 26 percent of basestealers at Nashville. He needs to pay more attention to detail behind the plate, focusing on his footwork and improving his concentration. He has the tools to be a solid catcher if he makes defense a priority. He's a well-below-average runner, typical for a catcher. Jonathan Lucroy has passed Salome as Milwaukee's best catching prospect, and they both could open 2010 in Triple-A.

Year	Club (League)	Class	AVG	G	AB	R	H	2B	3B	HR	RBI	BB	SO	SB	OBP	SLG
2004	Brewers (AZL)	R	.235	20	81	7	19	7	0	0	8	4	14	2	.271	.321
2005	West Virginia (SAL)	LoA	.254	29	118	15	30	7	1	4	21	8	17	1	.302	.432
	Helena (PIO)	R	.415	37	159	34	66	17	0	8	50	15	16	6	.469	.673
2006	West Virginia (SAL)	LoA	.292	105	418	63	122	31	2	10	85	39	63	7	.349	.447
2007	Brevard County (FSL)	HiA	.318	68	258	33	82	20	0	6	53	12	32	1	.341	.465
2008	Huntsville (SL)	AA	.360	98	367	67	132	30	2	13	83	33	57	3	.415	.559
	Milwaukee (NL)	MAJ	.000	3	3	0	0	0	0	0	0	0	1	0	.000	.000
2009	Nashville (PCL)	AAA	.286	82	283	32	81	14	2	6	44	22	55	0	.334	.413
MAJOR LEAGUE TOTALS			.000	3	3	0	0	0	0	0	0	0	1	0	.000	.000
MINOR LEAGUE TOTALS			.316	439	1684	251	532	126	7	47	344	133	254	20	.364	.483

16 AMAURY RIVAS, RHP

BORN: Dec. 20, 1985 **B-T:** R-R. **HT.:** 6-2. **WT.:** 204. **SIGNED:** Dominican Republic, 2005. **SIGNED BY:** Fernando Arango/Fausto Sosa Pena.

One club official refers to Rivas as a "carnivore" because of the tenacious fashion with which he attacks hitters. He used that approach to win the Brewers' minor league pitcher of the year award in 2009, when he ranked second in the Florida State League in wins (13), third in strikeouts (123) and fifth in ERA (2.98). Rivas has regained his stuff since having Tommy John surgery in December 2006. He throws his fastball in the low 90s, touching 95 at times. Before last season, some thought he projected best as a reliever because his secondary stuff lagged behind his heater, but he improved his slider and refined his changeup into a plus pitch. The combination of three pitches, command, confidence and aggression makes Rivas one of the most efficient pitchers in the system. He should begin 2010 in Double-A with the chance for a midseason promotion.

Year	Club (League)	Class	W	L	ERA	G	GS	CG	SV	IP	H	R	ER	HR	BB	SO	AVG
2005	Brewers (AZL)	R	2	3	6.91	14	6	0	0	42	56	36	32	1	16	34	.326
2006	Brewers (AZL)	R	1	0	6.43	4	2	0	0	14	17	12	10	1	3	12	.293
	Helena (PIO)	R	5	4	3.02	10	10	0	0	54	48	28	18	6	16	36	.236
2007	Brewers (AZL)	R	0	0	3.12	6	6	0	0	9	3	4	3	1	4	10	.107
2008	West Virginia (SAL)	LoA	8	3	3.50	19	15	0	0	90	83	41	35	11	32	70	.239
	Brevard County (FSL)	HiA	1	2	4.20	7	6	0	0	30	35	16	14	2	11	20	.294
2009	Brevard County (FSL)	HiA	13	7	2.98	26	23	0	0	133	109	55	44	11	43	123	.220
MINOR LEAGUE TOTALS			30	19	3.78	86	68	0	0	371	351	192	156	33	125	305	.247

17 CALEB GINDL, OF

BORN: Aug. 31, 1988. **B-T:** L-L. **HT.:** 5-9. **WT.:** 185. **DRAFTED:** HS—Milton, Fla., 2007 (5th round).
SIGNED BY: Doug Reynolds.

Because his individual tools don't stand out and he has an unusual body type—think a squattier Brian Giles—scouts have trouble figuring out where Gindl might play in the majors. The consensus is that he can hit and will find a spot somewhere. Gindl won the Rookie-level Pioneer League batting title with a .372 average in his 2007 pro debut and has kept producing since. He has a compact stroke and good hand-eye coordination. He drives the ball into the gaps and has average home run power. He has consistently improved his strike-zone discipline since entering pro ball. Almost all of Gindl's value lies in his bat. He's a below-average runner, though he has good instincts and is aggressive on the bases. As a left fielder, he's just an adequate defender, though he does have arm strength. The Brewers like the way Gindl competes and will keep moving him up the ladder until pitchers start getting him out. His next assignment will be Double-A.

Year	Club (League)	Class	AVG	G	AB	R	H	2B	3B	HR	RBI	BB	SO	SB	OBP	SLG
2007	Helena (PIO)	R	.372	55	207	40	77	22	3	5	42	20	38	4	.420	.580
2008	West Virginia (SAL)	LoA	.307	137	508	86	156	38	4	13	81	63	144	14	.388	.474
2009	Brevard County (FSL)	HiA	.277	112	394	61	109	15	3	17	71	57	92	18	.363	.459
MINOR LEAGUE TOTALS			.308	304	1109	187	342	75	10	35	194	140	274	36	.385	.489

18 D'VONTREY RICHARDSON, OF

BORN: July 30, 1988. **B-T:** R-R. **HT.:** 6-2. **WT.:** 215. **DRAFTED:** Florida State, 2009 (5th round). **SIGNED BY:** Ryan Robinson.

Though Richardson had sporadic success playing baseball at Florida State, he wowed the Brewers in a predraft workout. They grabbed him in the fifth round and signed him for $400,000, spreading his bonus over multiple years under baseball's provisions for two-sport athletes. Richardson attended Florida State on a football scholarship, showing electrifying speed. He set a Seminoles record for the longest run by a quarterback with a 55-yard touchdown in 2008, and he would have become a defensive back had he not signed with Milwaukee. On the diamond, Richardson hit .351 as a freshman, but sat out 2008 to focus on his classwork and played sparingly last spring. His raw tools are undeniable, however, and his ceiling is huge. He's the best athlete in the system and the fastest of several speedsters whom the Brewers drafted in June, capable of covering 60 yards in 6.4 seconds. Though he hit just two homers in 210 college at-bats, Richardson has power and the ball jumps off his bat. Making consistent contact and controlling the strike zone are the main skills he's still working on. His speed gives him the range to play center field, and he has an above-average arm. The Brewers realize they'll need to be patient and he'll need at-bats. Richardson will likely make his pro debut in low Class A in April.

Year	Club (League)	Class	AVG	G	AB	R	H	2B	3B	HR	RBI	BB	SO	SB	OBP	SLG
2009	Did Not Play—Signed Late															

19 ERIC FARRIS, 2B

BORN: March 3, 1986. **B-T:** R-R. **HT.:** 5-10. **WT.:** 170. **DRAFTED:** Loyola Marymount, 2007 (4th round).
SIGNED BY: Corey Rodriguez.

Farris became one of the most disruptive baserunners in the minors last season, ranking third in the minors with 70 steals and getting caught just six times. Despite his gaudy steal total, he doesn't have eye-popping speed. He's an above-average runner who excels at reading pitchers and getting good jumps. He doesn't have much power and needs to focus on getting on base, so he'll have to improve his plate discipline after drawing just 29 walks in 2009. He's an adept bunter who led the minors with 26 sacrifices last season. Farris is a quality defender at second base, showing good instincts, nice range, soft hands and a decent arm. In short, he knows how to play the game and gives consistent performances night in and night out. Farris probably will begin 2010 in Double-A, though a good spring might get him a shot at Triple-A. He may be more of a utility player in the long run, but he could start at second base for the Brewers while they wait for Brett Lawrie.

Year	Club (League)	Class	AVG	G	AB	R	H	2B	3B	HR	RBI	BB	SO	SB	OBP	SLG
2007	Helena (PIO)	R	.326	63	239	34	78	16	2	1	34	16	22	21	.369	.423
2008	West Virginia (SAL)	LoA	.293	103	454	73	133	21	4	3	54	24	50	32	.332	.377
2009	Brevard County (FSL)	HiA	.298	124	473	68	141	18	1	7	49	29	46	70	.341	.385
MINOR LEAGUE TOTALS			.302	290	1166	175	352	55	7	11	137	69	118	123	.343	.389

20 TAYLOR GREEN, 3B/1B

BORN: Nov. 2, 1986. **B-T:** L-R. **HT.:** 5-10. **WT.:** 185. **DRAFTED:** Cypress (Calif.) CC, D/F 2005 (25th round). **SIGNED BY:** Bruce Seid.

A pitch hit Green on the left wrist near the end of the 2008 season, but it wasn't until well into the offseason that tests revealed a compression fracture that required a bone graft. The Brewers worried he would miss all of 2009, but self-motivation and an aggressive rehab program got him back on the field by mid-May. He wasn't 100 percent, however, and didn't hit as he had in the past. He still controlled the strike zone but rarely drove the ball with any authority. Hitters often take a long time to regain their power following a wrist injury, but whether Green would have the pop desired in a third baseman already was in question before he got hurt. He's more of a line-drive, contact hitter. His bat profiles better at second base, but he's a below-average runner and may lack the quickness to move there. He has decent range and an adequate arm at third base. Scouts love his competitive nature. Green, who was on the short list of potential players to be named in the 2008 C.C. Sabathia trade, will return to Double-A in 2010.

Year	Club (League)	Class	AVG	G	AB	R	H	2B	3B	HR	RBI	BB	SO	SB	OBP	SLG
2006	Helena (PIO)	R	.231	62	221	36	51	12	1	1	23	29	35	0	.328	.308
2007	West Virginia (SAL)	LoA	.327	111	397	68	130	29	2	14	86	51	65	0	.406	.516
2008	Brevard County (FSL)	HiA	.289	114	418	46	121	19	0	15	73	61	59	4	.382	.443
2009	Wisconsin (MWL)	LoA	.400	6	20	6	8	1	0	1	5	4	4	0	.538	.600
	Huntsville (SL)	AA	.258	87	306	34	79	15	0	5	43	33	37	0	.330	.356
MINOR LEAGUE TOTALS			.286	380	1362	190	389	76	3	36	230	178	200	4	.372	.425

21 JEREMY JEFFRESS, RHP

BORN: Sept. 21, 1987. **B-T:** R-R. **HT.:** 6-1. **WT.:** 185. **DRAFTED:** HS—South Boston, Va., 2006 (1st round). **SIGNED BY:** Tim McIlvaine.

Jeffress has as much sheer talent as any prospect in the system. But his continued pattern of substance abuse casts doubt that he'll ever make it to the majors. He failed multiple drug tests before drawing a 50-game suspension for testing positive for marijuana near the end of the 2007 season. After another positive test last June, he received a 100-game penalty that will carry over into 2010 and leaves him one more strike away from a lifetime ban. The 16th overall pick in the 2006 draft and recipient of a $1.55 million bonus, Jeffress has one of the most powerful arms in the minors. His fastball sits in the mid-90s and has reached 100 mph. His heater lacks life, but he throws it so hard and with such an easy motion that he blows it by hitters before they know what happened. Jeffress throws from a high three-quarters angle that makes his big-breaking curveball tough to hit when he throws it for strikes. He has yet to come close to mastering his changeup, control or command, so his future may lie in the bullpen. He had such difficulty throwing strikes in Double-A last season that the Brewers demoted him as a wakeup call before he was hit with the suspension. Milwaukee had hoped Jeffress would be on the brink of the majors by now, but he spent much of the offseason in a treatment program and his future lies in doubt.

Year	Club (League)	Class	W	L	ERA	G	GS	CG	SV	IP	H	R	ER	HR	BB	SO	AVG
2006	Brewers (AZL)	R	2	5	5.88	13	4	0	0	34	30	26	22	0	25	37	.227
2007	West Virginia (SAL)	LoA	9	5	3.13	18	18	0	0	86	62	43	30	8	44	95	.201
2008	Brevard County (FSL)	HiA	4	6	4.08	15	14	1	0	79	65	39	36	5	41	102	.226
	Huntsville (SL)	AA	2	1	5.52	4	4	0	0	15	17	9	9	2	11	13	.298
2009	Huntsville (SL)	AA	1	3	7.57	8	8	0	0	27	26	29	23	1	33	34	.255
	Brevard County (FSL)	HiA	2	1	2.18	6	5	1	0	33	16	13	8	2	22	36	.145
MINOR LEAGUE TOTALS			20	21	4.20	64	53	2	0	274	216	159	128	18	176	317	.217

22 DEL HOWELL, LHP

BORN: Sept. 6, 1987. **B-T:** L-L. **HT.:** 6-4. **WT.:** 200. **DRAFTED:** Alabama, 2009 (15th round). **SIGNED BY:** Joe Mason.

The Brewers think they got an absolute steal in Howell, a 15th-round pick in June who signed for $260,000. Poised to go in the early rounds after ranking as the top prospect in the Texas Collegiate League the previous summer, he was hampered by a bout with mononucleosis during the spring and went 5-3, 6.33. When he's 100 percent, Howell shows the potential for three plus pitches. He operates with an 88-92 mph sinker that touches 94, and he complements it with a sharp slider. He also has an effective changeup. Howell needs a bit more deception and sometimes has problems keeping his front side closed in his delivery. When he has his mechanics in order, he keeps hitters off balance. Howell signed at the end of July and worked just 12 innings in his pro debut. A two-way player at Alabama, he pitched just 83 innings in college and needs experience. He figures to open his first full season in low Class A.

Year	Club (League)	Class	W	L	ERA	G	GS	CG	SV	IP	H	R	ER	HR	BB	SO	AVG
2009	Brewers (AZL)	R	1	0	0.00	2	0	0	0	3	3	0	0	0	1	2	.273
	Helena (PIO)	R	0	0	1.04	3	3	0	0	9	7	1	1	0	2	7	.219
MINOR LEAGUE TOTALS			1	0	0.77	5	3	0	0	12	10	1	1	0	3	9	.233

23 JOHN AXFORD, RHP

BORN: April 1, 1983. **B-T:** R-R. **HT.:** 6-5. **WT.:** 195. **SIGNED:** Canisius, NDFA 2006. **SIGNED BY:** Mike Gibbons (Yankees).

It seemed like Axford came out of nowhere as he shot from high Class A to a September callup in 2009. And he certainly did take an unorthodox route to the majors. He started his college career at Notre Dame and was on track to being an early-round pick in the 2004 draft before he had Tommy John surgery in December 2003. After sitting out 2004 and barely pitching in 2005, he transferred to Canisius but went undrafted after a lackluster senior season in 2006. Axford returned home to Canada to pitch in the summer collegiate Western Major Baseball League. After he struck out 19 in a seven-inning game and fanned 66 in 36 innings, the Yankees signed him as an nondrafted free agent. New York released him after the 2007 season, and he hooked on with the Brewers the following spring. He led the Florida State League with 73 walks in just 95 innings in 2008, so Milwaukee shifted him to the bullpen and had him lower his arm angle slightly last season in hopes it would help with his control. The changes worked, though Axford still has stretches when he struggles to find the zone. When he throws strikes, he can overpower hitters with his 92-96 mph fastball. His sharp curveball is his No. 2 pitch, and he also mixes in a slider on occasion. Axford saved Milwaukee's final game of the 2009 season, and he should make the Opening Day roster if he throws enough strikes in big league camp.

Year	Club (League)	Class	W	L	ERA	G	GS	CG	SV	IP	H	R	ER	HR	BB	SO	AVG
2007	Scranton/W-B (IL)	AAA	0	0	13.50	1	0	0	0	1	2	1	1	0	1	1	.500
	Staten Island (NYP)	SS	1	1	2.22	8	0	0	2	24	13	8	6	0	15	30	.153
	Charleston, SC (SAL)	LoA	0	3	4.39	13	5	0	0	27	29	20	13	2	22	21	.276
	Tampa (FSL)	HiA	0	0	2.38	5	0	0	2	11	6	5	3	2	7	15	.162
2008	Brevard County (FSL)	HiA	5	10	4.55	26	14	0	0	95	86	58	48	5	73	89	.246
2009	Brevard County (FSL)	HiA	4	1	1.63	19	0	0	0	28	14	5	5	0	16	43	.151
	Huntsville (SL)	AA	0	0	3.52	4	0	0	1	8	7	3	3	1	3	9	.250
	Nashville (PCL)	AAA	5	0	3.55	22	0	0	0	33	23	13	13	2	19	37	.197
	Milwaukee (NL)	MAJ	0	0	3.52	7	0	0	1	8	5	3	3	0	6	9	.179
MAJOR LEAGUE TOTALS			0	0	3.52	7	0	0	1	8	5	3	3	0	6	9	.179
MINOR LEAGUE TOTALS			15	15	3.66	98	19	0	5	226	180	113	92	12	156	245	.220

24 JOSH BUTLER, RHP

BORN: Dec. 11, 1984. **B-T:** R-R. **HT.:** 6-5. **WT.:** 200. **DRAFTED:** San Diego, 2006 (2nd round). **SIGNED BY:** Dan Drake (Devil Rays).

Obtained from Tampa Bay in an April 2008 trade for Gabe Gross, Butler struggled at high Class A in his first season with his new organization. But after returning to Brevard County in 2009, he put his game back together and rose through the minors, making his major league debut in September. If he hadn't been shut down with a strained oblique in July, he probably would have gotten an earlier opportunity with the Brewers when the big league rotation was thinned by injuries. Tall with long arms, Butler gets good movement on a fastball that sits in the low 90s. His breaking ball is a cross between a curveball and a slider, but it's a solid pitch. His changeup lags behind his other two pitches. Butler throws strikes and has deception in his delivery. He figures to open 2010 in Triple-A, ready to serve the Brewers in the majors if they need help in their rotation or long relief.

Year	Club (League)	Class	W	L	ERA	G	GS	CG	SV	IP	H	R	ER	HR	BB	SO	AVG
2006	Hudson Valley (NYP)	SS	0	3	5.40	5	2	0	0	13	13	9	8	0	7	12	.265
2007	Columbus (SAL)	LoA	5	1	2.33	13	13	0	0	77	63	25	20	3	20	54	.224
	Vero Beach (FSL)	HiA	4	3	4.93	10	9	1	0	49	51	31	27	9	21	34	.273
2008	Vero Beach (FSL)	HiA	0	2	6.35	3	3	0	0	17	18	13	12	1	5	10	.269
	Brevard County (FSL)	HiA	2	8	5.36	20	20	0	0	82	86	53	49	10	40	63	.271
2009	Brevard County (FSL)	HiA	6	0	2.47	9	9	0	0	51	44	16	14	0	23	32	.235
	Nashville (PCL)	AAA	1	1	3.60	3	3	0	0	15	15	6	6	2	1	15	.263
	Brewers (AZL)	R	0	1	4.76	4	3	0	0	11	15	6	6	0	6	16	.319
	Huntsville (SL)	AA	2	1	2.85	8	8	0	0	41	37	17	13	2	13	33	.242
	Milwaukee (NL)	MAJ	0	0	9.00	3	0	0	0	4	7	4	4	0	6	3	.368
MAJOR LEAGUE TOTALS			0	0	9.00	3	0	0	0	4	7	4	4	0	6	3	.368
MINOR LEAGUE TOTALS			20	20	3.90	75	70	1	0	358	342	176	155	27	136	269	.254

25 ALEX PERIARD, RHP

BORN: June 15, 1987. **B-T:** L-R. **HT.:** 6-1. **WT.:** 185. **DRAFTED:** HS—St. Eustache, Quebec, 2004 (16th round). **SIGNED BY:** Jay Lapp.

The Brewers expected big things from Periard after a strong 2008 season, but he showed up for his first big league camp with shoulder tightness and never threw a pitch there. He opened the year on the disabled list and didn't pitch well when he returned to the mound in mid-June. The good news was that Periard was healthy by season's end, though his fastball didn't sit in the low 90s as it had the year before. When he's 100 percent, Periard uses his strong lower half to pound the bottom of the zone with lively fastballs. He also has a nice slider and a decent changeup. He does a good job of staying ahead in the count, inducing grounders and letting his infield go to work for him. He's still learning the nuances of setting up hitters and using both sides of the plate. Milwaukee likes his confidence and poise. Had things gone as expected in 2009, Periard would be vying for a spot in the big league rotation this spring. Instead, he'll be trying to make the Hunstville staff. Though he has taken a step back, he's still just 22.

Year	Club (League)	Class	W	L	ERA	G	GS	CG	SV	IP	H	R	ER	HR	BB	SO	AVG
2005	Brewers (AZL)	R	0	1	5.08	11	4	0	1	28	43	23	16	1	10	22	.358
2006	Brewers (AZL)	R	3	1	4.64	13	4	0	1	43	45	31	22	1	18	25	.266
2007	West Virginia (SAL)	LoA	7	7	3.55	23	18	0	2	109	115	49	43	8	21	55	.271
2008	Brevard County (FSL)	HiA	9	6	3.51	19	18	1	0	113	114	52	44	6	30	76	.256
	Huntsville (SL)	AA	2	4	5.68	8	8	0	0	38	42	25	24	3	16	20	.288
2009	Wisconsin (MWL)	LoA	0	0	3.18	3	3	0	0	11	14	5	4	0	2	5	.298
	Brevard County (FSL)	HiA	3	2	5.23	9	9	0	0	31	37	20	18	1	13	22	.296
MINOR LEAGUE TOTALS			24	21	4.13	86	64	1	4	373	410	205	171	20	110	225	.278

26 EVAN ANUNDSEN, RHP

BORN: May 17, 1988. **B-T:** R-R. **HT.:** 6-3. **WT.:** 200. **DRAFTED:** HS—Littleton, Colo., 2006 (4th round). **SIGNED BY:** Kevin Clouser.

Anundsen showed he was primed for a breakthrough season by throwing a no-hitter in April for Brevard County, and he took off from there. He finished the season with the third-best ERA (2.69) in the Florida State League, and second in both opponent average (.216) and baserunners per nine innings (10.7). With his tall frame and long arms, he throws on a downhill plane and pounds sinkers at hitters to induce groundballs. He has below-average velocity and often sits at 84-88 mph, but he isn't afraid to work inside and jam hitters. He's still maturing physically, so there's hope he can grow into at least average velocity. His slider and changeup are average pitches, and he also mixes in an occasional curve. Anundsen keeps hitters on the defensive by staying ahead in the count and using all of his pitches. A workhorse who pitches deep into games, he projects to fit in the back end of a major league rotation. Though Anundsen took a big step forward in 2009, the Brewers won't rush him. He should open 2010 at Double-A Huntsville.

Year	Club (League)	Class	W	L	ERA	G	GS	CG	SV	IP	H	R	ER	HR	BB	SO	AVG
2006	Brewers (AZL)	R	2	3	4.50	12	4	0	0	32	36	22	16	0	7	22	.273
2007	Helena (PIO)	R	7	5	4.77	15	15	0	0	77	81	50	41	6	20	59	.265
2008	West Virginia (SAL)	LoA	12	8	4.28	28	28	0	0	145	158	80	69	8	38	102	.283
2009	Brevard County (FSL)	HiA	10	8	2.69	24	23	2	0	130	101	51	39	2	41	118	.216
MINOR LEAGUE TOTALS			31	24	3.86	79	70	2	0	385	376	203	165	16	106	301	.257

27 BROOKS HALL, RHP

BORN: June 25, 1990. **B-T:** R-R. **HT.:** 6-5. **WT.:** 200. **DRAFTED:** HS—Anderson, S.C., 2009 (4th round). **SIGNED BY:** Ryan Robinson.

Hall pitched just five innings as a high school junior and 20 as a senior, but the Brewers saw enough to give him a $700,000 bonus after drafting him in the fourth round last June. He was shooting up draft boards thanks to his projectable frame and a perfect game that he threw in March, but he didn't pitch again after coming down with biceps tendinitis in April. He had committed to South Carolina as a two-way player who would have also been a power-hitting third baseman at the college level, but his future definitely was on the mound. Tall and lean, Hall uses his size to drive his 88-92 mph fastball down in the zone. He touches 95 at times and should do so with more regularity as he fills out. He also flashes a hard slider that could give him a second plus pitch. Like most young pitchers, Hall needs to develop a changeup, refine his command and improve his consistency. Because he hasn't logged a lot of innings on the mound, the Brewers could take it slow with him and allow him to make his pro debut in Rookie ball after opening 2010 in extended spring training.

Year	Club (League)	Class	W	L	ERA	G	GS	CG	SV	IP	H	R	ER	HR	BB	SO	AVG
2009	Did Not Play—Signed Late																

28 MAX WALLA, OF

BORN: April 12, 1991. **B-T:** L-L. **HT.:** 5-11. **WT.:** 200. **DRAFTED:** HS—Albuquerque, 2009 (2nd round). **SIGNED BY:** Kevin Clouser.

Walla put on buzzworthy power displays in high school, and between his junior season at Albuquerque Academy and the summer showcase circuit in 2008, he socked 51 homers. At a workout last spring, he hit 18 homers in 25 swings with a metal bat, then 18 more in 25 swings with wood. He found the going a little more difficult in pro ball after signing for $499,000 as a second-round pick, hitting just two homers while striking out 82 times in 186 at-bats. Scouts said he got off to a bad start and started pressing, and he may have been tired after participating in an aggressive schedule of workouts for clubs prior to the draft. When Walla is going well, he has a compact stroke and lets his strong hands and wrists do the work. He has the upper-body strength that comes with being a competitive swimmer, and he was part of a high school relay team that broke two New Mexico state records in his senior year. Though he struggled, he impressed scouts with his aggressiveness and makeup. Walla is a below-average runner, but he plays hard and gets the job done in left field. He has arm strength and makes accurate throws. The Brewers aren't concerned by his debut and believe in his offensive upside. His next stop could be the low Class A Midwest League, one of the tougher hitter's leagues in the minors.

Year	Club (League)	Class	AVG	G	AB	R	H	2B	3B	HR	RBI	BB	SO	SB	OBP	SLG
2009	Brewers (AZL)	R	.199	48	186	18	37	5	2	2	19	15	82	4	.283	.280
	Helena (PIO)	R	.250	4	8	2	2	0	0	0	0	0	5	0	.250	.250
MINOR LEAGUE TOTALS			.201	52	194	20	39	5	2	2	19	15	87	4	.282	.278

29 NICK BUCCI, RHP

BORN: Aug. 16, 1990. **B-T:** R-R. **HT.:** 6-2. **WT.:** 180. **DRAFTED:** HS—Sarnia, Ont., 2008 (18th round). **SIGNED BY:** Jay Lapp.

A somewhat raw pitcher who came to pro ball with limited experience out of Canada, Bucci worked just 11 innings in his 2008 pro debut. Bumped up a notch to Rookie-level Helena last season, he opened eyes by ranking second in the Pioneer League in wins (six), fourth in strikeouts (66) and fifth in ERA (4.41). He also threw five shutout innings to beat Korea at the World Cup in September. Bucci pitches regularly at 88-92 mph with his four-seam fastball, and he has room to fill out and add velocity. He also has an effective curveball and a changeup with sink. He mixes in cutters and two-seamers to keep hitters guessing. Athletic on the mound, Bucci has good balance and extension with his delivery. He stays on line to the plate but will have to do a better job of throwing strikes as he advances. He didn't turn 19 until late in the season, so he has plenty of time to develop. Most scouts think he projects as a back-of-the-rotation starter. He'll move up to low Class A in 2010.

Year	Club (League)	Class	W	L	ERA	G	GS	CG	SV	IP	H	R	ER	HR	BB	SO	AVG
2008	Brewers (AZL)	R	0	3	7.36	5	4	0	0	11	12	9	9	2	2	14	.273
2009	Huntsville (SL)	AA	1	0	6.75	3	0	0	0	4	3	3	3	2	2	3	.231
	Helena (PIO)	R	6	3	4.41	13	12	0	0	69	59	39	34	7	21	66	.231
MINOR LEAGUE TOTALS			7	6	4.91	21	16	0	0	84	74	51	46	11	25	83	.237

30 MAVERICK LASKER, RHP

BORN: Feb. 17, 1990. **B-T:** R-R. **HT.:** 6-2. **WT.:** 190. **DRAFTED:** HS—Phoenix, 2008 (5th round). **SIGNED BY:** Kevin Clouser.

Lasker strained his back strain shortly after signing as a fifth-round pick in 2008, which delayed his professional debut until 2009. The Brewers eased him into pro ball in the Rookie-level Arizona League, where he quickly caught the eye of scouts with his aggressive style of pitching. He performed so well in Arizona that Milwaukee promoted him to low Class A before the season ended, and he threw seven scoreless innings in his first start there. Lasker pounds the strike zone with an 88-92 mph fastball that touches 93 and has plus movement. There's still projection remaining in his frame, so he could throw harder down the road. His breaking ball is a slurvy slider that's improving in terms of depth and tilt. His changeup can be a good third pitch, but he needs more confidence in throwing it. He's not overpowering, but he doesn't hurt himself by walking hitters, either. The Brewers love Lasker's makeup and dedication to his craft. He should return to Wisconsin to open 2010.

Year	Club (League)	Class	W	L	ERA	G	GS	CG	SV	IP	H	R	ER	HR	BB	SO	AVG
2009	Brewers (AZL)	R	5	1	3.26	13	1	0	0	47	43	19	17	2	9	39	.246
	Wisconsin (MWL)	LoA	1	1	5.00	2	2	0	0	9	9	7	5	0	5	4	.257
MINOR LEAGUE TOTALS			6	2	3.54	15	3	0	0	56	52	26	22	2	14	43	.248

Minnesota Twins

BY JOHN MANUEL

The Twins experienced a slew of firsts and lasts in 2009, most notably wrapping up the final season in the Metrodome with a dramatic playoff run.

The hermetically sealed Dome had its warts, but it also provided one of sport's great home-field advantages. It gives way to Target Field and its open air and natural grass for 2010. Minnesota extended the dome's run by a couple of games by charging through September.

Minnesota was 68-68 on Sept. 6 and trailed the Tigers by seven games before rallying to catch Detroit on the second-to-last day of the regular season, forc-

ing a 163rd game for a second straight season. After losing 1-0 to the White Sox in 2008, the Twins won in walkoff fashion, 6-5 in a 12-inning thriller.

That would have been a tremendous sendoff for the Metrodome, but Minnesota came back home for one more game, the finale of a Division Series sweep at the hands of the Yankees. New York won all 10 meetings between the two clubs.

The Twins ranked fourth in the American League in runs thanks to a homegrown group of hitters, with AL MVP and three-time batting champion Joe Mauer leading the way with an epic .365/.444/.587 season. Michael Cuddyer hit 32 homers, Justin Morneau added 30 and Mauer and Jason Kubel belted 28 each.

They needed all that offense because Minnesota didn't pitch or defend up to previous standards, posting a 4.50 ERA (11th in the AL) with much the same cast of characters that put up a 4.18 mark in 2008. Even closer Joe Nathan looked mortal down the stretch and blew Game Two against the Yankees, which the Twins led 3-1 entering the ninth inning.

To settle the rotation and infield, general manager Bill Smith made two August deals, trading minor leaguers for Carl Pavano (who will return in 2010) and Orlando Cabrera. Cabrera was a stopgap, and Minnesota acquired J.J. Hardy in November after the season as a more long-term answer at shortstop.

Those moves should improve Smith's trade track record, sullied early in his tenure when he gave Jason Bartlett and Matt Garza to the Rays in a deal for Delmon Young and sent Johan Santana to the Mets for four players who have done little since. Minnesota gave up the best player in that foursome, Carlos Gomez, to get Hardy from the Brewers.

The Twins were active acquiring talent all summer. With the 22nd overall pick in June, they drafted Missouri righthander Kyle Gibson, a projected top-10

Joe Mauer's performance is unprecedented, and his future is crucial to the Twins

TOP 30 PROSPECTS

1. Aaron Hicks, of	**16.** Tyler Robertson, lhp
2. Wilson Ramos, c	**17.** Alex Burnett, rhp
3. Kyle Gibson, rhp	**18.** Oswaldo Arcia, of
4. Miguel Sano, ss/3b	**19.** Anthony Slama, rhp
5. Ben Revere, of	**20.** Jeff Manship, rhp
6. Danny Valencia, 3b	**21.** B.J. Hermsen, rhp
7. Carlos Gutierrez, rhp	**22.** Deolis Guerra, rhp
8. Angel Morales, of	**23.** Estarlin de los Santos, ss/2b
9. David Bromberg, rhp	**24.** Trevor Plouffe, ss
10. Max Kepler, of	**25.** Daniel Santana, ss
11. Adrian Salcedo, rhp	**26.** Matt Bashore, lhp
12. Rene Tosoni, of	**27.** Jose Morales, c
13. Joe Benson, of	**28.** Ben Tootle, rhp
14. Chris Parmelee, 1b/of	**29.** Loek Van Mil, rhp
15. Billy Bullock, rhp	**30.** James Beresford, ss

pick choice who was available because he had a stress reaction in his right forearm. Gibson signed at the Aug. 17 deadline for $1.85 million, marking the first time Minnesota took a premier talent who slid and paid him a seven-figure, above-slot bonus.

In another first, the Twins paid the highest bonus on the international market in 2009 and the highest for an international player in franchise history when infielder Miguel Sano signed in September for $3.15 million. Minnesota had kicked off the international period by signing German outfielder Max Kepler for $800,000, the largest bonus ever given to a European player.

General Manager: Bill Smith. **Farm Director:** Jim Rantz. **Scouting Director:** Deron Johnson.

Class	Team	League	W	L	PCT	Finish*	Manager(s)
Majors	Minnesota Twins	American	87	76	.534	5th (14)	Ron Gardenhire
Triple-A	Rochester Red Wings	International	70	74	.486	10th (14)	Stan Cliburn
Double-A	New Britain Rock Cats	Eastern	72	69	.511	5th (12)	Tom Nieto
High A	Fort Myers Miracle	Florida State	80	58	.580	2nd (12)	Jeff Smith
Low A	Beloit Snappers	Midwest	57	83	.407	13th (14)	Nelson Prada
Rookie	Elizabethton Twins	Appalachian	45	23	.662	2nd (10)	Ray Smith
Rookie	GCL Twins	Gulf Coast	34	21	.618	3rd (16)	Jake Mauer
Overall 2009 Minor League Record			358	328	.522	5th (30)	

*Finish in overall standings (No. of teams in league). †League champion.

LAST YEAR'S TOP 30

Player, Pos.		Status
1.	Aaron Hicks, of	No. 1
2.	Ben Revere, of	No. 5
3.	Wilson Ramos, c	No. 2
4.	Jose Mijares, lhp	Majors
5.	Danny Valencia, 3b	No. 6
6.	Anthony Swarzak, rhp	Majors
7.	Shooter Hunt, rhp	Dropped out
8.	Kevin Mulvey, rhp	(Diamondbacks)
9.	Carlos Gutierrez, rhp	No. 7
10.	Angel Morales, of	No. 8
11.	Jeff Manship, rhp	No. 20
12.	Tyler Robertson, lhp	No. 16
13.	Trevor Plouffe, ss	No. 24
14.	Chris Parmelee, 1b/of	No. 14
15.	Joe Benson, of	No. 13
16.	Brian Duensing, lhp	Majors
17.	Luke Hughes, 3b/of	Dropped out
18.	Rene Tosoni, of	No. 12
19.	David Bromberg, rhp	No. 9
20.	Deolis Guerra, rhp	No. 22
21.	Deibinson Romero, 3b	Dropped out
22.	Matt Tolbert, ss/2b	Majors
23.	Steven Tolleson, inf/of	Dropped out
24.	Rob Delaney, rhp	Dropped out
25.	Anthony Slama, rhp	No. 19
26.	Philip Humber, rhp	Dropped out
27.	Michael McCardell, rhp	Dropped out
28.	David Winfree, of	(Free agent)
29.	Loek Van Mil, rhp	No. 29
30.	Michael Tonkin, rhp	Dropped out

BEST TOOLS

Best Hitter for Average	Ben Revere
Best Power Hitter	Wilson Ramos
Best Strike-Zone Discipline	Aaron Hicks
Fastest Baserunner	Ben Revere
Best Athlete	Aaron Hicks
Best Fastball	Carlos Gutierrez
Best Curveball	Tyler Robertson
Best Slider	Kyle Gibson
Best Changeup	Deolis Guerra
Best Control	Bradley Tippett
Best Defensive Catcher	Wilson Ramos
Best Defensive Infielder	Jorge Polanco
Best Infield Arm	Estarlin de los Santos
Best Defensive Outfielder	Aaron Hicks
Best Outfield Arm	Aaron Hicks

PROJECTED 2013 LINEUP

Catcher	Joe Mauer
First Base	Justin Morneau
Second Base	Alexi Casilla
Third Base	Danny Valencia
Shortstop	J.J. Hardy
Left Field	Delmon Young
Center Field	Denard Span
Right Field	Aaron Hicks
Designated Hitter	Jason Kubel
No. 1 Starter	Kyle Gibson
No. 2 Starter	Scott Baker
No. 3 Starter	Kevin Slowey
No. 4 Starter	Nick Blackburn
No. 5 Starter	Brian Duensing
Closer	Carlos Gutierrez

TOP PROSPECTS OF THE DECADE

Year	Player, Pos.	2009 Org.
2000	Michael Cuddyer, 3b	Twins
2001	Adam Johnson, rhp	Out of baseball
2002	Joe Mauer, c	Twins
2003	Joe Mauer, c	Twins
2004	Joe Mauer, c	Twins
2005	Joe Mauer, c	Twins
2006	Francisco Liriano, lhp	Twins
2007	Matt Garza, rhp	Rays
2008	Nick Blackburn, rhp	Twins
2009	Aaron Hicks, of	Twins

TOP DRAFT PICKS OF THE DECADE

Year	Player, Pos.	2009 Org.
2000	Adam Johnson, rhp	Out of baseball
2001	Joe Mauer, c	Twins
2002	Denard Span, of	Twins
2003	Matt Moses, 3b	Twins
2004	Trevor Plouffe, ss	Twins
2005	Matt Garza, rhp	Rays
2006	Chris Parmelee, of/1b	Twins
2007	Ben Revere, of	Twins
2008	Aaron Hicks, of	Twins
2009	Kyle Gibson, rhp	Twins

LARGEST BONUSES IN CLUB HISTORY

Joe Mauer, 2001	$5,150,000
Miguel Sano, 2009	$3,150,000
B.J. Garbe, 1999	$2,750,000
Adam Johnson, 2000	$2,500,000
Ryan Mills, 1998	$2,000,000

MINNESOTA TWINS

TOP 2010 ROOKIE: Danny Valencia, 3b. If the Twins don't block him with a veteran, he could win their third-base job in spring training.

BREAKOUT PROSPECT: Adrian Salcedo, rhp. He's projectable, he already throws 90-94 mph at age 18 and he had a 58-3 K-BB ratio last season.

SLEEPER: Michael Gonzales, 1b. The former California junior college home run champ has hit .314/.373/.481 in two pro seasons.

SOURCE OF TOP 30 TALENT

Homegrown	29	Acquired	1
College	7	Trades	1
Junior college	0	Rule 5 draft	0
High school	10	Independent leagues	0
Draft-and-follow	3	Free agents/waivers	0
Nondrafted free agents	0		
International	9		

Numbers in parentheses indicate prospect rankings

LF
Luke Hughes
Juan Portes
Steve Liddle

CF
Aaron Hicks (1)
Ben Revere (5)
Max Kepler (10)
Joe Benson (13)
Jason Pridie
Dustin Martin

RF
Angel Morales (8)
Rene Tosoni (12)
Oswaldo Arcia (18)
Nick Freitas

3B
Miguel Sano (4)
Danny Valencia (6)
Deibinson Romero

SS
Estarlin de los Santos (23)
Trevor Plouffe (24)
Daniel Santana (25)
James Beresford (30)
Jorge Polanco
Brian Dozier

2B
Steven Tolleson
Steve Singleton
Brian Dinkelman
Derek McCallum
Nick Lockwood

1B
Chris Parmelee (14)
Michael Gonzales
Brock Peterson

C
Wilson Ramos (2)
Jose Morales (27)
Josmil Pinto
Danny Rams
Tobias Streich
Chris Hermann

RHP

Starters	Relievers
Kyle Gibson (3)	Billy Bullock (15)
Carlos Gutierrez (7)	Alex Burnett (17)
David Bromberg (9)	Anthony Slama (19)
Adrian Salcedo (11)	Ben Tootle (28)
Jeff Manship (20)	Loek Van Mil (29)
B.J. Hermsen (21)	Rob Delaney
Deolis Guerra (22)	Chris Province
Michael Tonkin	Steve Hirschfield
Michael McCardell	Bobby Lanigan
Shooter Hunt	Dakota Watts
Blayne Weller	Bruce Pugh
Tim Stuifbergen	
Liam Hendriks	
Brad Stillings	

LHP

Starters	Relievers
Tyler Robertson (16)	Jose Lugo
Matt Bashore (26)	Spencer Steedley
Dan Osterbrock	Joe Testa
Martire Garcia	
Edgar Ibarra	

2009 BONUSES: $4.7 MILLION

BEST PURE HITTER: 2B Derek McCallum (4) hit just .241 in his debut but was gassed after carrying Minnesota to a 40-19 season. He's got a short, strong swing and surprising strength for his 5-foot-11, 175-pound frame.

BEST POWER HITTER: Sophomore-eligible OF Steve Liddle (20), who signed for $200,000, has a short, direct swing with a strong frame and raw power potential.

FASTEST RUNNER: The Twins didn't sign a burner. OF Nick Freitas (33) is a slightly above-average runner. He has interesting tools, including bat speed and a plus arm, but he remains raw after four years of college split between Miami's bench and Southern Utah.

BEST DEFENSIVE PLAYER: SS Brian Dozier (8) profiles better at second base, but his instincts and excellent hands could keep him on the left side of the diamond. He has solid arm strength and just enough range to go with good infield actions.

BEST FASTBALL: RHP Ben Tootle (4) reached 98 mph consistently in the Cape Cod League in 2008 and sat at 93-96 after signing. RHPs Billy Bullock (2) and Dakota Watts (16) pitched at 93-95 mph all summer.

BEST SECONDARY PITCH: RHP Kyle Gibson (1) has an 82-85 mph slider with power, tilt and feel. It's such an out pitch that at times he relied on it too much as an amateur, but he can pitch at 91-92 mph with his heavy sinker as well. LHP Matt Bashore (1s) has a plus curveball.

BEST PRO DEBUT: Dozier finished second in the Rookie level Appalachian League batting race at .353/.417/.431. OF Chris Herrmann (6) hit .297/.391/.453 at the same stop and worked out at catcher in instructional league. He has good hitting tools and the strength to hit for power.

BEST ATHLETE: Dozier and Freitas are the best of a below-average crop by Twins standards.

MOST INTRIGUING BACKGROUND: Liddle's father Steven had an eight-year minor league playing career and is the Twins' big league bench coach. Unsigned 3B Cody Martin's (31) older brother Ethan was the first high school pitcher drafted in 2008, going 15th overall to the Dodgers. SS Nick Lockwood's (9) older brother Ryan went in the 39th round to the Athletics, but opted to return to South Florida.

CLOSEST TO THE MAJORS: Bullock could outpace Gibson because he's in the bullpen. If Gibson is healthy after having a forearm stress fracture develop just before the draft, he should move quickly.

BEST LATE-ROUND PICK: Watts (16) is strictly a reliever but he has size and a big fastball.

THE ONE WHO GOT AWAY: The Twins wanted SS Ronnie Richardson (11), an explosive 5-foot-6 Chone Figgins clone who was the best athlete they drafted. They couldn't keep him from headlining Central Florida's recruiting class.

ASSESSMENT: Usually picking in the bottom of the first round, Minnesota doesn't often get a shot at elite college pitchers like Gibson. Getting him, Bashore, Bullock and Tootle injected four quality arms into a system well-versed in developing pitchers.

2008 BONUSES: $7.3 MILLION

Minnesota knew OF Aaron Hicks (1) was loaded with tools, but he has been more polished than expected. RHP Carlos Gutierrez (1) has one of the best sinkers in the minors, though RHP Shooter Hunt's (1s) command has disintegrated. SS Tyler Ladendorf (2) brought back Orlando Cabrera in a key trade last summer.

GRADE: B

2007 BONUSES: $2.2 MILLION

One of the biggest surprise first-round picks in recent drafts, OF Ben Revere (1) has justified the selection by hitting .337 in pro ball. OF Angel Morales (3) has some of the best tools in the system.

GRADE: B

2006 BONUSES: $3.9 MILLION

1B/OF Chris Parmelee (1), OF Joe Benson (2) and LHP Tyler Robertson (3) show promise but are developing slowly. RHP Jeff Manship (14) reached the majors last year, and 3B Danny Valencia (19) could start for the Twins in 2010.

GRADE: C

2005 BONUSES: $5.2 MILLION*

Minnesota regrets trading away RHP Matt Garza (1) and selecting 1B Henry Sanchez (1s). But it still found two members of its rotation in RHP Kevin Slowey (2) and LHP Brian Duensing (3), and a pair of good draft-and-follows in RHP David Bromberg (32) and OF Rene Tosoni (36).

GRADE: A

*Draft analysis by John Manuel (2009) and Jim Callis (2005-08). Numbers in parentheses indicate draft rounds. *Bonuses for 2005 are first 10 rounds only.*

AARON
HICKS, OF

Born: Oct. 2, 1989.
Height: 6-2. **Weight:** 170.
Bats: B. **Throws:** R.
Drafted: HS—Long Beach,
2008 (1st round).
Signed by: John Leavitt.

DAVID STONER

Hicks is a product of Long Beach's Wilson High, alma mater of such baseball luminaries as Hall of Famer Bob Lemon, 1974 American League MVP Jeff Burroughs and all-stars Bud Daley and Bobby Grich. Focusing on baseball after showing tremendous talent as a teenager golfer, Hicks was a two-way star at Wilson. He ran his fastball up to 97 mph and could have been a first-round pick as a pitcher. However, the Twins considered him the best athlete available in the 2008 draft and liked his competitiveness, as he led Wilson to a No. 1 national ranking and its first California district title in 50 years as a junior. They drafted him 14th overall—their highest first-round pick since Joe Mauer went No. 1 in 2001—and signed him for $1.78 million. Hicks ranked as the No. 1 prospect in the Rookie-level Gulf Coast League in his pro debut, then started 2009 in extended spring training. One he was assigned to low Class A Beloit in mid-June, he overcame a slow start to establish himself as the Midwest League's No. 1 prospect as well.

Hicks combines five-tool athleticism with a surprisingly advanced approach at the plate. He has dynamic tools, starting with an arm that some scouts rate as an 80 on the 20-80 scale. His speed rates at least above-average if not better, and he has the tools to be a premium defender in center field. His hitting tools are in some ways similar to those of top Phillies prospect Domonic Brown, though Hicks has more explosiveness in his hands and may have more raw power. Like Brown, Hicks is more patient than most young, developing five-tool players. He repeats his swing and he recognizes pitches fairly well. He has good bat speed, especially from the left side of the plate.

The questions with Hicks revolve more around how high the ceiling will be, and how quickly he arrives there. At times he was too patient for his own good last year, letting pitches he could drive go by in hitter's counts. However, it's easier to learn to unload on those pitches than to learn patience, and he has the leverage in his swing and wiry strength to take advantage in the future. He's inexperienced in baserunning and basestealing, as well as other subtle aspects of the game. He's stronger from the left side than from the right, like most switch-hitters, and his swing tends to get long from the right side.

Denard Span taught the Twins some lessons. First, they want all of their center fielders to experience playing the corners in the minors, rather than learning in the majors as Span did. Expect Hicks to work in all three spots in 2010. Second, Span's development reiterated the lesson that power is often the last tool to develop. With his patience and aptitude, Hicks could move quicker than Span but come into his power down the line, perhaps like Span's predecessor, Torii Hunter. Hicks won't challenge Span anytime soon, and he may even return to low Class A to start this season. But when his skills and experience level catch up to his tools, he could take off, making his big league ETA of 2012 look conservative.

Year	Club (League)	Class	AVG	G	AB	R	H	2B	3B	HR	RBI	BB	SO	SB	OBP	SLG
2008	Twins (GCL)	R	.318	45	173	32	55	10	4	4	27	28	32	12	.409	.491
2009	Beloit (MWL)	LoA	.251	67	251	43	63	15	3	4	29	40	55	10	.353	.382
MINOR LEAGUE TOTALS			.278	112	424	75	118	25	7	8	56	68	87	22	.376	.427

2 WILSON RAMOS, C

GEORGE PETRO

BORN: Aug. 10, 1987. **B-T:** R-R. **HT.:** 6-0. **WT.:** 220. **SIGNED:** Venezuela, 2004.
SIGNED BY: Jose Leon.

When he wasn't hurt in 2009, Ramos was Double-A New Britain's best player, but he missed a month with a broken tip of his left middle finger and nearly two months with a hamstring injury. He hit .341 (including the playoffs) after he returned, then made up for lost time with another strong showing in winter ball. After helping Venezuela to the Caribbean Series championship in 2009, he was leading the Venezuelan League in RBIs and slugging in mid-December. Ramos fits the catcher profile almost perfectly. He is physical and strong, with plus raw power and the ability to get the barrel to the ball. He's aggressive but covers the plate well, has natural hitting actions and shows power to all fields. He's agile for his size, receives well and has a cannon for an arm, throwing out 42 percent of basestealers last year. His hamstring injury and physical maturity have left Ramos a below-average runner, and he's on his way to being a baseclogger if he's not careful. He gained weight during his layoff but was getting back in shape in winter ball, where he also improved his pedestrian walk rate. He's a slow starter who doesn't always play with energy, though that improved in 2009. Ramos is insurance in case the Twins can't re-sign Joe Mauer. If Mauer locks up a long-term deal, though, Ramos becomes a valuable trade chip as a catcher who's almost big league-ready and has significant upside. He's likely headed for Triple-A Rochester in 2010.

Year	Club (League)	Class	AVG	G	AB	R	H	2B	3B	HR	RBI	BB	SO	SB	OBP	SLG
2005	Twins (DSL)	R	.252	39	127	16	32	5	1	1	15	8	13	1	.295	.331
2006	Twins (GCL)	R	.286	46	154	18	44	12	1	3	26	12	14	4	.339	.435
2007	Beloit (MWL)	LoA	.291	73	292	40	85	17	1	8	42	19	61	1	.345	.438
2008	Fort Myers (FSL)	HiA	.288	126	452	50	130	23	2	13	78	37	103	1	.346	.434
2009	Twins (GCL)	R	.316	5	19	4	6	1	1	3	6	0	0	0	.316	.947
	New Britain (EL)	AA	.317	54	205	31	65	16	0	4	29	6	23	0	.341	.454
MINOR LEAGUE TOTALS			.290	343	1249	159	362	74	6	32	196	82	214	6	.338	.436

3 KYLE GIBSON, RHP

BORN: Oct. 23, 1987. **B-T:** R-R. **HT.:** 6-6. **WT.:** 208. **DRAFTED:** Missouri, 2009 (1st round). **SIGNED BY:** J.R. DiMercurio.

Gibson was the third Missouri pitcher drafted in the first round of the last four drafts, joining Max Scherzer (2006) and Aaron Crow (2008). In his final college start, an NCAA regional game against Monmouth, his fastball velocity dipped into the mid-80s. Doctors diagnosed a stress fracture in his right forearm, which dropped him down many draft boards. The Twins snagged him with the 22nd overall pick and signed him for an above-slot $1.85 million bonus. Gibson has premium secondary stuff that sometimes diverts attention from how good his fastball can be. He pitches at 91-92 mph with sinking life and commands his fastball to both sides of the plate. He'll run his four-seamer up to 94 mph, and scouts think there's more velocity to come. Minnesota believes his fastball will be a swing-and-miss pitch, as his plus slider already is. It sits at 82-85 mph when he's at his best and has sharp movement and good depth. His changeup gives him a third pitch with plus potential, and at times it's as good as his slider. The forearm injury scared off some clubs, as it's often a precursor to elbow damage. Some scouts thought Gibson trusted his offspeed stuff so much that he didn't learn to pitch off his fastball, so the Twins will emphasize that in his first pro season. Gibson threw well in instructional league, airing it out for four innings in his last start, and reported no problems. Minnesota is bullish on his health and will start his career at high Class A Fort Myers, putting him on a fast track. A strong, healthy season would put him in the mix for the big league rotation in 2011, and his upside is as a true No. 1 starter.

Year	Club (League)	Class	W	L	ERA	G	GS	CG	SV	IP	H	R	ER	HR	BB	SO	AVG
2009	Did Not Play—Injured																

4 MIGUEL SANO, SS/3B

BORN: May 11, 1993. **B-T:** R-R. **HT.:** 6-3. **WT.:** 195. **SIGNED:** Dominican Republic, 2009. **SIGNED BY:** Fred Guerrero.

Sano was the consensus top prospect available in the international amateur signing period last summer. While the Pirates were considered the leader to sign him for most of the summer, the Twins landed him for $3.15 million in September. It was the second-largest bonus in franchise history, trailing only Joe Mauer's $5.15 million as the No. 1 overall draft pick in 2001. Sano's tools fit perfectly with the profile major league clubs look for at third base. He's a physical, aggressive hitter who should hit for average and power. He has thunder in his hands and forearms and could hit 30 homers annually down the line.

His arm strength is well above-average, and he has the hands to stay in the infield. Sano is already too big for shortstop, and it's possible he could outgrow the infield altogether and end up in right field. He has no obvious physical limitations, so he'll just have to prove that his obvious tools will play against pro competition. The last significant hurdle for Sano was to get his work visa, which he did in December. After getting the stamp of approval from Major League Baseball's investigations unit, he's cleared to play. The Twins like to handle prospects conservatively and likely will keep him in extended spring training before starting his career in Rookie ball.

Year	Club (League)	Class	AVG	G	AB	R	H	2B	3B	HR	RBI	BB	SO	SB	OBP	SLG
2009	Did Not Play—Signed 2010 Contract															

5 BEN REVERE, OF

BORN: May 3, 1988. **B-T:** L-R. **HT.:** 5-9. **WT.:** 166. **DRAFTED:** HS—Lexington, Ky., 2007 (1st round). **SIGNED BY:** Billy Corrigan.

Revere's father John was a 19th-round pick in 1972, and his brother J.R. was a 49th-round pick of the Rockies in 2001. Ben was the first Revere to ink a contract, though, signing for $750,000, the second-lowest first-round bonus of the decade. Since signing, he has made the Twins look smart, batting .337 with nearly as many walks (80) as strikeouts (85). Revere is the best pure hitter in the organization and one of the best in the minors. He lashes line drives from pole to pole when he's locked in, and handles lefthanded pitchers well. His hand-eye coordination and plus-plus speed allow him to make contact and beat out even routine grounders for infield hits, and he also has shown gap power. He can be a disruptive force on the basepaths and has plus range in the outfield. Revere's power and arm grade out as below average, and his arm has had to improve to even get to that point. He may have a well below-average arm when all is said and done. His power is strictly to the gaps, and he'll have to keep proving he can handle hard stuff in. His routes and jumps in the outfield are rough, though he has the speed to make up for them. He has had left knee problems, missing two weeks after getting fluid drained last July. His overall game still needs polish, but Revere has a chance to be an impact leadoff hitter. With Denard Span ahead of him and Aaron Hicks behind him, the Twins have other center-field options, making him possible trade bait. He'll advance to Double-A this year.

Year	Club (League)	Class	AVG	G	AB	R	H	2B	3B	HR	RBI	BB	SO	SB	OBP	SLG
2007	Twins (GCL)	R	.325	50	191	46	62	6	10	0	29	13	20	21	.388	.461
2008	Beloit (MWL)	LoA	.379	83	340	51	129	17	10	1	43	27	31	44	.433	.497
2009	Fort Myers (FSL)	HiA	.311	121	466	75	145	13	4	2	48	40	34	45	.372	.369
MINOR LEAGUE TOTALS			.337	254	997	172	336	36	24	3	120	80	85	110	.396	.430

6 DANNY VALENCIA, 3B

BORN: Sept. 19, 1984. **B-T:** R-R. **HT.:** 6-2. **WT.:** 210. **DRAFTED:** Miami, 2006 (19th round). **SIGNED BY:** Hector Otero.

The Twins started four different third basemen for at least 20 games in 2009 and have used 17 players at the position since Corey Koskie left following the 2004 season. Valencia has evolved into their best in-house option, reaching Triple-A last June and earning a spot on the 40-man roster in November. With good strength in his hands and wrists plus leverage in his swing, Valencia has plus raw power and tied for the organization lead with 38 doubles in 2009. He has the bat speed to get to good fastballs and trusts his hands, staying back on breaking balls and using the whole field. He has the defensive tools to play third base, with average hands, solid first-step quickness and plus arm strength. Valencia committed 20 errors in 124 games last year, which scouts attribute to his subpar concentration and footwork. He's just not consistent defensively. His plate discipline regressed in Triple-A, which bears watching. His brash, cocky demeanor has turned off some club officials and teammates in the past, but he has matured in the last year. He's a below-average runner. Now 25, Valencia will challenge for the third-base job in Minnesota in 2010. Defense will be the determining factor for a team that started Matt Tolbert twice at the hot corner in the playoffs.

Year	Club (League)	Class	AVG	G	AB	R	H	2B	3B	HR	RBI	BB	SO	SB	OBP	SLG
2006	Elizabethton (APP)	R	.311	48	190	30	59	13	0	8	29	15	34	0	.365	.505
2007	Beloit (MWL)	LoA	.302	66	242	44	73	15	0	11	35	28	54	3	.374	.500
	Fort Myers (FSL)	HiA	.291	61	230	28	67	8	2	6	31	16	48	1	.332	.422
2008	Fort Myers (FSL)	HiA	.336	60	220	35	74	19	3	5	44	27	43	2	.402	.518
	New Britain (EL)	AA	.289	69	266	40	77	18	2	10	32	18	70	2	.334	.485
2009	New Britain (EL)	AA	.284	57	218	44	62	14	4	7	29	31	40	0	.373	.482
	Rochester (IL)	AAA	.286	71	269	35	77	24	0	7	41	8	37	0	.305	.454
MINOR LEAGUE TOTALS			.299	432	1635	256	489	111	11	54	241	143	326	8	.354	.480

7 CARLOS GUTIERREZ, RHP

BORN: Sept. 22, 1986. **B-T:** R-R. **HT.:** 6-3. **WT.:** 205. **DRAFTED:** Miami, 2008 (1st round). **SIGNED BY:** Hector Otero.

Gutierrez helped lead Miami to the 2008 College World Series and was one of three Hurricanes first-rounders in 2008, along with Yonder Alonso and Jemile Weeks. His younger brother David, a righthander, still pitches for the Hurricanes. Carlos closed for the 2008 club, but the Twins liked him as a starter and used him in that role for most of 2009, until he reached his innings limit. Gutierrez's hard sinker delivers groundouts by the bushel. It's a 92-94 mph bowling ball that produced a 3.45 groundout/airout ratio, the best of any minor leaguer with 100 innings last year. He's difficult to elevate when he commands his sinker, and it helps his average changeup and slider both play up. He's athletic, controls the running game and fields his position well. The Twins were cautious with Gutierrez's workload after he had Tommy John surgery in 2007 and pitched just 80 innings between college and pro ball in 2008. He'll need to get stretched out even more to be ready to start in the majors. Command is his other big obstacle, as his ball moves too much for him to keep it in the strike zone at times. If Gutierrez can improve his command, he has a chance to make good on the Derek Lowe comparisons he has earned. He's headed back to Double-A as a starter, but if he falters in that role, he should be able to make a big league impact as a setup man or possibly a closer.

Year	Club (League)	Class	W	L	ERA	G	GS	CG	SV	IP	H	R	ER	HR	BB	SO	AVG
2008	Fort Myers (FSL)	HiA	3	1	2.10	16	0	0	1	26	23	7	6	0	7	19	.240
2009	Fort Myers (FSL)	HiA	2	3	1.32	11	10	0	0	55	37	20	8	1	22	33	.192
	New Britain (EL)	AA	1	3	6.19	22	6	0	0	52	62	36	36	6	24	32	.300
MINOR LEAGUE TOTALS			6	7	3.39	49	16	0	1	133	122	63	50	7	53	84	.246

8 ANGEL MORALES, OF

BORN: Nov. 24, 1989. **B-T:** R-R. **HT.:** 6-1. **WT.:** 180. **DRAFTED:** HS—Caguas, P.R., 2007 (3rd round). **SIGNED BY:** Hector Otero.

Morales dazzled scouts with his tools prior to the 2007 draft, then led the Rookie-level Appalachian League with 15 homers in 2008. He led Beloit in homers (13), RBIs (62) and steals (19) in his full-season debut last year, despite missing time with several nagging injuries. With more than a dozen Twins farmhands in Europe for the World Cup, Morales moved up for the Eastern League playoffs, going 0-for-5 with an error. Only Aaron Hicks and Max Kepler rival Morales for raw five-tool ability in the system. He has four plus tools now, with his arm and speed grading out the highest. He's athletic enough to play center field and may stay there, though as he fills out he's more likely to move to right, where he should be a strong defender. His raw power also grades out as above-average. Morales has an aggressive approach that has led to contact issues. He ranked second in the system with 104 strikeouts last season, though he trimmed his whiff rate to 28 percent of his at-bats from 39 percent in 2008. The twin culprits are pitch recognition—he doesn't identify breaking balls early enough—and a two-part swing. While he's lowered his hands and gets through the zone quicker, he doesn't have a classic swing path and has holes that even Class A pitchers have been able to exploit. Morales has an all-star ceiling if he continues to cut down his strikeouts. He'll advance to high Class A in 2010.

Year	Club (League)	Class	AVG	G	AB	R	H	2B	3B	HR	RBI	BB	SO	SB	OBP	SLG
2007	Twins (GCL)	R	.256	38	121	18	31	6	3	2	15	12	44	11	.357	.405
2008	Elizabethton (APP)	R	.301	54	183	33	55	12	1	15	28	26	72	7	.413	.623
2009	Beloit (MWL)	LoA	.266	115	376	63	100	22	5	13	62	30	104	19	.329	.455
MINOR LEAGUE TOTALS			.274	207	680	114	186	40	9	30	105	68	220	37	.358	.491

9 DAVID BROMBERG, RHP

BORN: Sept. 14, 1987. **B-T:** L-R. **HT.:** 6-5. **WT.:** 241. **DRAFTED:** Santa Ana (Calif.) JC, D/F 2005 (32nd round). **SIGNED BY:** Dan Cox.

Signed for $40,000 as a draft-and-follow in 2006, Bromberg already has given the Twins value. In his last three seasons, he has led three leagues in strikeouts and topped the minors with 177 in 2008. Last year, he started the high Class A Florida State League all-star game and was Minnesota's minor league pitcher of the year. Bromberg chews up innings with a durable body and four pitches he can throw for strikes. He usually uses a two-seam fastball that sits at 89-92 mph, but he can run a four-seamer up to 95 when needed. He keeps the ball in the ballpark and pitches downhill. His curveball is his next-best pitch, and at times it has sharp downward break. He has confidence in his changeup and slider and pitches with a good tempo. He stays poised when in a jam, minimizing damage. His fastball command comes and goes, as Bromberg finished third in the FSL with 63 walks. He's not a great athlete, which can get his delivery out of whack. Because he doesn't command his fastball and his curve is a bit slurvy, he doesn't own a true plus pitch. Bromberg profiles as a No. 3

to No. 5 starter who will eat innings. He's headed for Double-A this year.

Year	Club (League)	Class	W	L	ERA	G	GS	CG	SV	IP	H	R	ER	HR	BB	SO	AVG
2006	Twins (GCL)	R	3	3	2.66	10	10	2	0	51	42	21	15	2	18	31	.230
2007	Elizabethton (APP)	R	9	0	2.78	13	11	0	0	58	45	19	18	4	32	81	.211
2008	Beloit (MWL)	LoA	9	10	4.44	27	27	0	0	150	149	81	74	10	54	177	.262
2009	Fort Myers (FSL)	HiA	13	4	2.70	27	26	1	0	153	125	52	46	6	63	148	.224
MINOR LEAGUE TOTALS			34	17	3.34	77	74	3	0	412	361	173	153	22	167	437	.237

10 MAX KEPLER, OF

BORN: Feb. 10, 1993. **B-T:** L-L. **HT.:** 6-3. **WT.:** 192. **SIGNED:** Germany, 2009. **SIGNED BY:** Howard Norsetter.

The Twins long have scouted Europe more actively than most clubs, and that groundwork paid off with Kepler, whose $800,000 bonus is the largest ever for a European position player. His Polish father and American mother met as ballet dancers in Berlin. He attended instructional league in September and enrolled at Fort Myers (Fla.) High, across the street from the Twins' Florida facility. Kepler has fast-twitch athleticism and graceful actions in the field. He does everything easily—running with plus speed, swinging the bat with authority and gliding after balls in the outfield. He has good hand-eye coordination and excellent size, projecting as every bit the five-tool athlete. He has plus raw power and the makings of a sound swing. Projecting 16-year-olds already is tough, and there's no precedent for Kepler, who's trying to become the first German amateur to reach the major leagues. The Twins' track record with European players has hits and misses, but their experience should help them ease Kepler's adjustment to the United States. He'll have to prove he can hit much better pitching than he saw in Germany. The Twins didn't sign many athletes in the 2009 draft, so the door is open for Miguel Sano and Kapler to establish themselves in Rookie ball in 2010. Kepler will report to extended spring training and play in the Gulf Coast League as a 17-year-old until high school starts again in the fall. He probably won't make it to full-season ball until after he graduates from high school in 2011.

Year	Club (League)	Class	AVG	G	AB	R	H	2B	3B	HR	RBI	BB	SO	SB	OBP	SLG
2009	Did Not Play—Signed 2010 Contract															

11 ADRIAN SALCEDO, RHP

BORN: April 24, 1991. **B-T:** R-R. **HT.:** 6-4. **WT.:** 175. **SIGNED:** Dominican Republic, 2007. **SIGNED BY:** Fred Guerrero.

The Twins have become prolific winners in Rookie ball, thanks in part to their ability to get their pitchers to throw strikes. Ivan Arteaga, their Gulf Coast League pitching coach the last five seasons, has fashioned impressive pitching staffs that pound the zone. His 2009 staff averaged 2.2 walks per nine innings and led the GCL with a 2.47 ERA, and had four starters who pitched at least 50 innings and walked fewer than 10 batters. Salcedo had the best ratios, with just three walks and 58 strikeouts in his first season in the United States. He also has the highest upside of the group, which also included B.J. Hermsen, Michael Tonkin and Blayne Weller. It's hard not to get excited about Salcedo, who has a projectable build at 6-foot-4 at 175 pounds, as well as a 90-94 mph fastball. He flashes a power curveball with plus potential that reaches 84-85 mph at times. He shows the makings of solid changeup as well. Salcedo has a loose, quick arm and a sound delivery that accounted for his miniscule walk total. He's a workout monster who outruns and outworks many of his peers. Salcedo has yet to make the jump to full-season ball and hold up over the course of 100-plus innings. He'll get that chance in 2010 in low Class A.

Year	Club (League)	Class	W	L	ERA	G	GS	CG	SV	IP	H	R	ER	HR	BB	SO	AVG
2008	Twins (DSL)	R	4	4	1.65	12	12	0	0	65	47	18	12	1	8	50	.198
2009	Twins (GCL)	R	3	2	1.46	11	10	0	0	62	60	25	10	1	3	58	.241
MINOR LEAGUE TOTALS			7	6	1.56	23	22	0	0	127	107	43	22	2	11	108	.220

12 RENE TOSONI, OF

BORN: July 2, 1986. **B-T:** L-R. **HT.:** 6-0. **WT.:** 195. **DRAFTED:** Chipola (Fla.) JC, D/F 2005 (36th round). **SIGNED BY:** Jim Ridley.

A Canadian who followed the path of countrymen such as Russell Martin and Adam Loewen to Chipola (Fla.) JC, Tosoni has impressed the Twins with his hitting skills and solid tools. He missed time after signing in 2006 because of visa restrictions (he worked out at the Twins' Dominican complex instead), and in 2008 with a broken left foot. He had the game-winning hit in the 2009 Futures Game and was named MVP of the prospect showcase, and he led Canada to a bronze medal in the World Cup, batting .357 with 11 extra-base hits in 56 at-bats. Tosoni has one of the system's best swings and should hit for average. He's short to the ball and long through the hitting zone, and he has the patience to get into good hitter's counts. Tosoni's other tools all grade out as solid-average, and his power emerged in 2009 for the first time. He has enough speed and savvy to play center field, and enough arm to fit into right field. He's a grinder who plays hard and earns praise for his makeup. Nothing

Tosoni does stands out, however. His average speed won't play on the bases at higher levels, and he doesn't have the profile power for a corner. He seemed gassed in the Arizona Fall League, where he hit just .218. He struggles against lefthanders and hit just .185/.293/.315 against them in 2009, compared to .308/.389/.515 against right-handers. Tosoni may not be more than a second-division regular or a quality fourth outfielder, but he could fit in soon in Minnesota, which could use his lefty bat and defensive versatility. He'll start 2010 in Triple-A.

Year	Club (League)	Class	AVG	G	AB	R	H	2B	3B	HR	RBI	BB	SO	SB	OBP	SLG
2006	Did Not Play—Restricted															
2007	Elizabethton (APP)	R	.301	63	236	58	71	13	4	3	31	32	48	13	.407	.428
	Beloit (MWL)	LoA	.273	2	11	1	3	1	0	0	1	0	2	0	.273	.364
2008	Twins (GCL)	R	.667	2	6	3	4	0	0	1	3	0	1	0	.667	1.167
	Fort Myers (FSL)	HiA	.300	42	140	27	42	7	3	1	19	21	30	3	.408	.414
2009	New Britain (EL)	AA	.271	122	425	64	115	25	4	15	71	45	98	8	.360	.454
MINOR LEAGUE TOTALS			.287	231	818	153	235	46	11	20	125	98	179	24	.383	.444

13 JOE BENSON, OF

BORN: March 5 1988. **B-T:** R-R. **HT.:** 6-2. **WT.:** 211. **DRAFTED:** HS—Joliet, Ill., 2006 (2nd round). **SIGNED BY:** Billy Milos.

Ranked as high as No. 2 on this list in 2008, Benson still has the potential for five plus tools. His problem remains staying healthy. He had a fractured vertebra in 2008, then missed two months last year when he broke his right hand punching a wall. Benson returned to help Fort Myers to the Florida State League playoffs and stayed hot with a 4-for-11 postseason showing and strong instructional league. He has improved his hitting ability, trusting his quick hands and waiting on pitches more often. While his strikeout rate remains a steady 28 percent—he has an all-out swing and problems with pitch recognition—he nearly set a career high in walks last season. Benson's power is still raw, as he has size, bat speed and strength but hasn't learned to loft the ball yet. He's a plus-plus runner who goes home to first in 4.0 seconds, allowing him to play a capable center field. His plus arm makes right field his likely future home. Benson's injuries haven't hurt his athleticism, but they have cost him development time. He's a cold-weather kid who committed to play football at Purdue before the Twins signed him for $575,000 as second-round pick in 2006. His strong instructional league likely will push him to Double-A in 2010.

Year	Club (League)	Class	AVG	G	AB	R	H	2B	3B	HR	RBI	BB	SO	SB	OBP	SLG
2006	Twins (GCL)	R	.260	52	196	30	51	11	5	5	28	21	41	9	.335	.444
	Beloit (MWL)	LoA	.263	8	19	2	5	0	0	0	1	0	6	1	.263	.263
2007	Beloit (MWL)	LoA	.255	122	432	73	110	18	8	5	38	49	124	18	.347	.368
2008	Beloit (MWL)	LoA	.248	69	254	39	63	16	3	4	27	24	73	17	.326	.382
2009	Twins (GCL)	R	.200	2	5	1	1	0	0	0	0	2	0	1	.429	.200
	Fort Myers (FSL)	HiA	.285	80	263	46	75	10	3	5	29	46	74	14	.414	.403
MINOR LEAGUE TOTALS			.261	333	1169	191	305	55	19	19	123	142	318	60	.356	.389

14 CHRIS PARMELEE, 1B/OF

BORN: Feb. 24, 1988. **B-T:** L-L. **HT.:** 6-1. **WT.:** 223. **DRAFTED:** HS—Chino Hills, Calif., 2006 (1st round). **SIGNED BY:** John Leavitt.

Parmelee and Joe Benson have been linked since the Twins drafted them in the first two rounds of the 2006 draft. The 20th overall pick that year and recipient of a $1.5 million bonus, Parmelee is an atypical Twins prospect in that he's not well-rounded and most of his value is tied up in his bat. He had his best season as a pro last year, considering he was coming off a broken left wrist and moved up to the pitcher-friendly Florida State League. He was one of the league's better sluggers, ranking first in walks (65), second in RBIs (73) and third in homers (16). He has strength and has worked hard to shorten his swing and make more contact. Parmelee can hit homers to all fields and has done a better job of using the opposite field. He made more progress in the Arizona Fall League, where he was among the league's younger players and continued to hit for power. Some scouts maintain that his bat speed is insufficient for him to catch up to good fastballs. Parmelee has a plus arm, but his below-average speed and range make him a better fit at first base than on an outfield corner. He'll get his first exposure to Double-A in 2010.

Year	Club (League)	Class	AVG	G	AB	R	H	2B	3B	HR	RBI	BB	SO	SB	OBP	SLG
2006	Twins (GCL)	R	.279	45	154	29	43	7	4	8	32	23	47	3	.369	.532
	Beloit (MWL)	LoA	.227	11	22	2	5	1	0	0	2	5	9	0	.370	.273
2007	Beloit (MWL)	LoA	.239	128	447	56	107	23	5	15	70	46	137	8	.313	.414
2008	Beloit (MWL)	LoA	.239	69	226	41	54	10	3	14	49	52	83	5	.385	.496
2009	Fort Myers (FSL)	HiA	.258	123	422	61	109	27	1	16	73	65	109	2	.359	.441
MINOR LEAGUE TOTALS			.250	376	1271	189	318	68	13	53	226	191	385	16	.350	.449

15 BILLY BULLOCK, RHP

BORN: Feb. 27, 1988. **B-T:** R-R. **HT.:** 6-6. **WT.:** 235. **DRAFTED:** Florida, 2009 (2nd round). **SIGNED BY:** Billy Corrigan.

The Twins have had success of late drafting college relievers, getting big league contributions from the likes of Pat Neshek and Jesse Crain, and strong early returns from 2008 first-rounder Carlos Gutierrez. Bullock is a bit different, with a physical 6-foot-6 frame and a bigger fastball. He was a tease throughout his college career and didn't have consistent success until his junior season, when Florida coach Kevin O'Sullivan—a former Twins minor league pitching coach—shifted him into the closer role. Bullock led the Gators to the NCAA super-regionals, where he lost a lead to Southern Mississippi. He gathered himself and had a strong pro debut after signing for $522,000 as a second-round pick. Bullock's fastball sits at 93-95 mph, peaks at 97-98 and can have explosive late life up in the zone when he's at his best. He changes hitters' eye level with a hard slider that made significant progress in 2009, as he added depth and tilt to the pitch. Both could be plus-plus pitches, though his command would have to improve markedly for that to happen. Bullock was homer-prone in college but overwhelmed lower-level hitters in his debut. He was gassed in instructional league, when his velocity dipped to around 90 mph. His fastball is one of the system's best in terms of velocity, giving him a chance to rocket through the system. He'll start his first full pro season in Fort Myers, about two hours south of where he went to high school in the Tampa area.

Year	Club (League)	Class	W	L	ERA	G	GS	CG	SV	IP	H	R	ER	HR	BB	SO	AVG
2009	Elizabethton (APP)	R	1	0	1.23	7	0	0	3	7	3	2	1	0	1	10	.125
	Beloit (MWL)	LoA	3	0	2.73	26	0	0	8	26	25	11	8	0	12	35	.253
MINOR LEAGUE TOTALS			4	0	2.41	33	0	0	11	34	28	13	9	0	13	45	.228

16 TYLER ROBERTSON, LHP

BORN: Dec. 23, 1987. **B-T:** L-L. **HT.:** 6-5. **WT.:** 220. **DRAFTED:** HS—Fair Oaks, Calif., 2006 (3rd round). **SIGNED BY:** Kevin Bootay.

The Twins' pitching-development philosophy was bound to change with Rick Knapp leaving to become the Tigers' big league pitching coach. His replacement, Eric Rasmussen, is more flexible about long-toss programs, which is music to Robertson's ears. His father Jay brought new pitching ideas to the Rangers as a scout before moving on to work as a special assistant to Nationals general manager Mike Rizzo, and Tyler was a long-toss devotee as an amateur. Keeping to Minnesota's 120-foot dictum as a pro, his arm strength has dipped a bit, though one club official says Robertson never was expected to have plus velocity. He has adjusted, creating angle on his fastball and pitching downhill from his 6-foot-5 frame. His funky arm action scares off some scouts but also creates deception. He sits at 85-88 mph and touches 90-91 with his fastball, pounding the bottom of the strike zone. His curveball is his best pitch and baffles lefthanders, who batted just .197/.292/.268 against him in 2009. His slider is more of a cutter and helps him work inside. He also throws a changeup, which would have greater effect if it had more separation from his fastball. Robertson made every start at Fort Myers last year. He'll move up to Double-A for 2010, and the Twins will see if long-tossing will bring back some of Robertson's lost velocity.

Year	Club (League)	Class	W	L	ERA	G	GS	CG	SV	IP	H	R	ER	HR	BB	SO	AVG
2006	Twins (GCL)	R	4	2	4.25	11	10	0	0	49	54	23	23	2	15	54	.280
2007	Beloit (MWL)	LoA	9	5	2.29	18	16	2	1	102	87	33	26	3	33	123	.226
2008	Fort Myers (FSL)	HiA	5	3	2.72	15	15	1	0	83	78	36	25	3	31	73	.247
2009	Fort Myers (FSL)	HiA	8	8	3.33	26	26	0	0	143	139	64	53	7	51	103	.259
MINOR LEAGUE TOTALS			26	18	3.03	70	67	3	1	377	358	156	127	15	130	353	.250

17 ALEX BURNETT, RHP

BORN: July 26, 1987. **B-T:** R-R. **HT.:** 6-0. **WT.:** 190. **DRAFTED:** HS—Huntington, Calif., 2005 (12th round). **SIGNED BY:** John Leavitt.

After making solid progress through the low minors, Burnett hit a speed bump in 2008 and the Twins responded by shifting the smallish righthander to the bullpen. He responded with the best season of his pro career in 2009, earning a trip to the Arizona Fall League and a spot on the 40-man roster. Burnett had average fastball velocity and decent life as a starter, and he cranked his heater up coming out of the bullpen, sitting at 93-94 mph and reaching 95 consistently. He gets strikeouts by going up the ladder with his heater. Burnett still uses his average straight changeup out of the pen and has success with it against lefthanders. They hit .150 off him during the 2009 regular season, then went 1-for-18 in the AFL. Burnett will become a big league bullpen factor when he improves his breaking ball command. He has thrown a hard, slurvy breaking ball, a true curveball with a bit less power and a big, slow curve in the past. He ditched the slow curve as a reliever and focused on the harder version, which is a strikeout pitch. Burnett's ability to retire lefthanders gives him a chance to be a future closer, but he must refine his fastball command and his breaking ball first. He's in line to close at New Britain in 2010 if Anthony Slama advances to Rochester, and Burnett's changeup could give him an edge over Slama in the long term.

Year	Club (League)	Class	W	L	ERA	G	GS	CG	SV	IP	H	R	ER	HR	BB	SO	AVG
2005	Twins (GCL)	R	4	2	4.10	13	8	0	0	48	50	25	22	6	14	33	.267
2006	Elizabethton (APP)	R	4	3	4.04	13	13	1	0	71	66	41	32	6	13	71	.242
2007	Beloit (MWL)	LoA	9	8	3.02	27	27	1	0	155	140	60	52	9	38	117	.239
2008	Fort Myers (FSL)	HiA	8	6	3.76	28	25	0	0	144	151	72	60	12	36	84	.269
2009	Fort Myers (FSL)	HiA	2	1	1.99	18	0	0	4	23	14	6	5	0	7	26	.175
	New Britain (EL)	AA	1	2	1.79	40	0	0	9	55	36	14	11	2	19	52	.187
MINOR LEAGUE TOTALS			28	22	3.30	139	73	2	13	496	457	218	182	35	127	383	.243

18 OSWALDO ARCIA, OF

BORN: May 9, 1991. **B-T:** B-R. **HT.:** 6-0. **WT.:** 210. **SIGNED:** Venezuela, 2007. **SIGNED BY:** Jose Leon.

The Twins don't have a great track record of developing players from the Dominican Republic, but they've had their share of success in Venezuela, from Luis Rivas to Jose Mijares to top catching prospect Wilson Ramos. Their latest find is Arcia, a strong hitter who could wind up fitting the right-field profile. Arcia thrived in the Gulf Coast League, as he's physically mature and has a fairly advanced hitting approach. He has plus raw power and current usable power but still was the third-toughest GCL regular to strike out. He has shown the ability to use the whole field, though he can get pull-happy. He impressed Twins coaches by adjusting as the season went along to constantly getting pitched away, hitting the ball with authority to the opposite field. Club officials laud his makeup. Arcia is an average runner with good instincts in the outfield. He has played center field on occasion, though he should slow down as he ages and wind up in right. His arm grades out as above average. He struggled in his first exposure to professional-quality lefthanded pitching, hitting just .194. Arcia has five average or better tools, and his hitting is advanced enough for the Twins to have high expectations. He could be the system's breakout player in 2010, when he's slated for low Class A.

Year	Club (League)	Class	AVG	G	AB	R	H	2B	3B	HR	RBI	BB	SO	SB	OBP	SLG
2008	Twins (DSL)	R	.293	61	229	38	67	12	4	4	36	16	27	8	.343	.432
2009	Twins (GCL)	R	.275	44	167	20	46	11	2	5	24	15	18	8	.337	.455
MINOR LEAGUE TOTALS			.285	105	396	58	113	23	6	9	60	31	45	16	.340	.442

19 ANTHONY SLAMA, RHP

BORN: Jan. 6, 1984. **B-T:** R-R. **HT.:** 6-3. **WT.:** 207. **DRAFTED:** San Diego, D/F 2006 (39th round). **SIGNED BY:** John Leavitt.

The Twins got 107 excellent innings over parts of two seasons out of Pat Neshek, a low-angle righthander who relied as much on deception as on stuff. Slama is his heir, putting up great minor league numbers and reaching Triple-A in his second full pro season. He has 68 saves in 140 career appearances, and he's the rare minor league closer who actually is a prospect. Slama's recipe for success has remained consistent. He pounds the bottom of the strike zone with two average pitches, an 89-92 mph sinker that tops out at 93, and a slider that he can throw for strikes or bury. Neither pitch has exceptional velocity, but he has above-average late life, throws strikes and misses down when he misses. Better hitters chased his pitches less and he made a few more mistakes in the strike zone last year. He gave up his first five regular-season homers of his career, and his strikeout rate dipped from 14.9 per nine innings in 2008 (best among minor league relievers that season) to 12.4 last year. He set a career best and ranked second in the minors with 62 appearances, proving his durability. Slama could use a better changeup or a splitter to combat lefthanders, who hit .292 with four homers in 120 at-bats against him in 2009. The Twins have moved him slowly, but few other minor league relievers have done more to earn a chance. He'll open 2010 as Rochester's closer.

Year	Club (League)	Class	W	L	ERA	G	GS	CG	SV	IP	H	R	ER	HR	BB	SO	AVG
2007	Elizabethton (APP)	R	0	0	2.45	6	0	0	4	7	2	2	2	0	1	10	.091
	Beloit (MWL)	LoA	1	1	1.48	21	0	0	10	24	15	4	4	0	9	39	.172
2008	Fort Myers (FSL)	HiA	4	1	1.01	51	0	0	25	71	43	12	8	0	24	110	.173
2009	New Britain (EL)	AA	4	2	2.48	51	0	0	25	65	46	18	18	5	32	93	.201
	Rochester (IL)	AAA	0	2	3.45	11	0	0	4	16	11	6	6	0	8	19	.212
MINOR LEAGUE TOTALS			9	6	1.86	140	0	0	68	184	117	42	38	5	74	271	.183

20 JEFF MANSHIP, RHP

BORN: Jan. 16, 1985. **B-T:** R-R. **HT.:** 6-2. **WT.:** 200. **DRAFTED:** Notre Dame, 2006 (14th round). **SIGNED BY:** Billy Milos.

Manship made his major league debut in 2009, becoming yet another success story for Tommy John surgery and the Twins' pitching-development program. He had the operation back in 2003, prior to his first college season at Notre Dame, and has proved his durability every year as a pro. He pitched at least 149 innings for the third straight season and maintained his success in the minors before running into trouble in Minnesota. Manship is a fairly finished product who has a good curveball and has continued to improve his sinker, which sits at 89-91 mph. He runs his four-seamer up to 94 in shorter stints. He has yielded just 20 homers in his last 430 minor league innings, and he gets his share of groundballs. He throws a solid changeup and fringe-average slider, and both pitches are at their best down in the strike zone. In the majors, though, Manship's average stuff and fringy command proved insufficient. He lacks true fastball command and has found big league hitters less apt to chase. He doesn't have swing-and-miss stuff in the zone, so he must be more precise to succeed as a back-of-the-rotation starter. Minnesota bolstered the depth of its rotation by bringing Carl Pavano back, and Manship has little chance to earn a starting role in 2010. Instead, he'll head back to Triple-A as insurance and could contribute to the Twins as a middle reliever later in the year.

MINNESOTA TWINS

Year	Club (League)	Class	W	L	ERA	G	GS	CG	SV	IP	H	R	ER	HR	BB	SO	AVG
2006	Twins (GCL)	R	0	0	0.00	2	0	0	0	6	3	0	0	0	1	10	.150
	Fort Myers (FSL)	HiA	0	0	2.08	4	3	0	0	9	7	3	2	0	2	12	.212
2007	Beloit (MWL)	LoA	7	1	1.51	13	13	0	0	78	51	15	13	4	9	77	.185
	Fort Myers (FSL)	HiA	8	5	3.15	13	13	0	0	71	77	38	25	5	25	59	.270
2008	Fort Myers (FSL)	HiA	7	3	2.86	13	13	1	0	79	68	31	25	0	20	63	.231
	New Britain (EL)	AA	3	6	4.46	14	14	0	0	77	90	47	38	8	24	62	.292
2009	New Britain (EL)	AA	6	4	4.28	13	13	0	0	76	72	37	36	2	20	45	.249
	Rochester (IL)	AAA	4	2	3.22	8	8	0	0	50	53	23	18	1	17	30	.277
	Minnesota (AL)	MAJ	1	1	5.68	11	5	0	0	32	39	21	20	4	15	21	.310
MAJOR LEAGUE TOTALS			1	1	5.68	11	5	0	0	32	39	21	20	4	15	21	.310
MINOR LEAGUE TOTALS			35	21	3.18	80	77	1	0	445	421	194	157	20	118	358	.248

21 B.J. HERMSEN, RHP

BORN: Dec. 1, 1989. **B-T:** R-R. **HT.:** 6-6. **WT.:** 230. **DRAFTED:** HS—Manchester, Iowa, 2008 (6th round). **SIGNED BY:** Mark Wilson.

Hermsen was the top pitching prospect in Iowa in 2008, despite breaking his collarbone the previous fall while playing quarterback for his high school football team. Iowa has no spring baseball at the high school level, so the Twins followed him through the summer after drafting him in the sixth round, buying him away from Oregon State for a $650,000 bonus. He pitched in instructional league and then had to wait until June 2009 to make his pro debut as part of a talented Gulf Coast League rotation. Some club officials say Hermsen had the most upside on the GCL staff, including Adrian Salcedo. Hermsen's fastball velocity is just average, as he sat in the upper 80s and touched the low 90s last season. But he throws downhill with good plane and pounds the bottom of the strike zone, helping him finish second in the GCL by allowing 7.4 baserunners per nine innings and fifth with a 1.35 ERA. He projects to have plus command if he continues his low-maintenance delivery, which will require staying in good shape and not getting too big. He repeats his mechanics well for a young 6-foot-6, 230-pounder, leading to his excellent 42-4 K-BB ratio. His slider is another pitch geared to get early contact, and he has made progress adding a changeup. Hermson has earned Nick Blackburn comparisons for his durable build and ability to work off his fastball. He should join Salcedo in the Beloit rotation this year.

Year	Club (League)	Class	W	L	ERA	G	GS	CG	SV	IP	H	R	ER	HR	BB	SO	AVG
2009	Twins (GCL)	R	6	2	1.35	10	10	1	0	53	32	12	8	0	4	42	.171
MINOR LEAGUE TOTALS			6	2	1.35	10	10	1	0	53	32	12	8	0	4	42	.171

22 DEOLIS GUERRA, RHP

BORN: April 17, 1989. **B-T:** R-R. **HT.:** 6-5. **WT.:** 200. **SIGNED:** Venezuela, 2005. **SIGNED BY:** Rafael Bournigal (Mets).

The most notable product of the Johan Santana trade for the Twins has been more trades. Minnesota got Kevin Mulvey, whom they traded to the Diamondbacks for Jon Rauch; and Carlos Gomez, whom they traded to the Brewers for J.J. Hardy in November. Philip Humber departed as a minor league free agent, leaving Guerra the last player from the deal still with the Twins. He signed with the Mets for $700,000 in 2005, but some scouts and managers who saw him last year can't get past the fact that a big, physical righty is essentially a finesse pitcher. Guerra has one plus pitch, a changeup with sink and good arm speed. His fastball is fringy, sitting at 89-90 mph and touching 92 with modest life, and his curveball is no better. His heater reached 94-95 mph in the Mets system but he didn't command it, and now he has lost life and velocity, with the Twins unsure if they'll come back. They say he uses his fastball and curve enough, but admit he gets predictable and leans on the changeup as an out pitch. He retires lefthanders (.234 opponent average in 2009) much more easily than righthanders (.305), evidence of just how much stronger his changeup is than his fastball and curve. He has improved his control but needs better fastball command to become more than just a piece of trade trivia. Added to the 40-man roster in November, Guerra will return to Double-A in 2010 after pitching in the Venezuelan League over the winter.

Year	Club (League)	Class	W	L	ERA	G	GS	CG	SV	IP	H	R	ER	HR	BB	SO	AVG
2006	Hagerstown (SAL)	LoA	6	7	2.20	17	17	0	0	82	59	22	20	3	37	64	.208
	St. Lucie (FSL)	HiA	1	1	6.14	2	2	0	0	7	9	6	5	1	6	5	.290
2007	St. Lucie (FSL)	HiA	2	6	4.01	21	20	0	0	90	80	44	40	9	25	66	.240
2008	Fort Myers (FSL)	HiA	11	9	5.47	26	25	1	0	130	138	85	79	12	71	71	.272
2009	Fort Myers (FSL)	HiA	6	8	4.69	16	15	0	0	86	95	52	45	6	25	57	.278
	New Britain (EL)	AA	6	3	5.17	12	11	1	0	63	62	38	36	4	17	49	.258
MINOR LEAGUE TOTALS			32	34	4.42	94	90	2	0	458	443	247	225	35	181	312	.255

23 ESTARLIN DE LOS SANTOS, SS/2B

BORN: Jan. 20, 1987. **B-T:** B-R. **HT.:** 5-10. **WT.:** 165. **SIGNED:** Dominican Republic, 2005. **SIGNED BY:** Fred Guerrero.

De los Santos has battled injuries over the last two seasons but showed the Twins enough to merit inclusion on the 40-man roster in the offseason. An elbow injury that didn't require surgery sidelined him until June in 2008, and a stress fracture in his leg kept him out of the lineup for two months last year. The leg injury cost him speed and upside, as he now projects more as a bottom-of-the-lineup hitter rather than as a tablesetting leadoff hitter. He lacks the patience for such a role anyway. De los Santos does have a quick bat and a line-drive swing, and he's still an above-average runner with the range, hands and plus-plus arm to play shortstop at the big league level. He's the best of the system's shortstops who have reached the full-season level. A switch-hitter, he has performed better from the right side. He needs to improve his consistency in the field and his short game (basestealing, bunting, etc.), and could evolve into an effective utility player. He already plays second base well enough, and the outfield and third base shouldn't be a stretch considering his tools and arm strength. His solid start to winter ball in the Dominican cemented his 40-man spot. Now de los Santos will try to stay healthy for a full season, likely at Double-A.

Year	Club (League)	Class	AVG	G	AB	R	H	2B	3B	HR	RBI	BB	SO	SB	OBP	SLG
2005	Twins (DSL)	R	.261	42	138	25	36	8	0	0	19	16	33	11	.373	.319
2006	Twins (GCL)	R	.195	24	82	12	16	1	2	0	2	8	18	8	.290	.256
2007	Elizabethton (APP)	R	.264	67	284	60	75	13	6	1	41	26	66	27	.341	.363
2008	Beloit (MWL)	LoA	.242	66	236	33	57	4	3	2	25	19	55	15	.304	.309
2009	Twins (GCL)	R	.250	2	8	1	2	0	0	0	0	0	1	1	.250	.250
	Fort Myers (FSL)	HiA	.290	68	262	33	76	11	7	1	23	13	49	11	.330	.397
MINOR LEAGUE TOTALS			.259	269	1010	164	262	37	18	4	110	82	222	73	.329	.344

24 TREVOR PLOUFFE, SS

BORN: June 15, 1986. **B-T:** R-R. **HT.:** 6-2. **WT.:** 195. **DRAFTED:** HS—Northridge, Calif., 2004 (1st round). **SIGNED BY:** Bill Mele.

The Twins had six of the first 61 selections in the 2004 draft, and a group that included pitchers Glen Perkins and Anthony Swarzak, who have reached the majors. Plouffe was Minnesota's top choice that year, signing for $1.5 million as the No. 20 overall pick, but he has yet to make the big leagues.. He was on the 40-man roster in 2009, but instead of getting a September callup, the Twins allowed Plouffe to play for the U.S. national team in the World Cup. Team USA won 14 straight games and the gold medal, and manager Eddie Rodriguez praised Plouffe's steady defensive play as a key to victory. His shortstop defense hasn't been good enough as a pro, despite a plus-plus arm that remains his best tool. He made 26 errors last year at Rochester, consistent with the 29 he made in Fort Myers in 2006 and 32 in '07 at New Britain. He was more of a utility infielder in 2008, but he lacks the energy or speed to play that role in the majors. His supporters in the organization believe in his power, and Plouffe made more contact while driving the ball with more regularity last year. He lacks the patience and the leverage in his swing, though, to ever hit for more than average power. Plouffe still could be a second-division regular, but now he's blocked by J.J. Hardy. He'll go back for another stint at Triple-A.

Year	Club (League)	Class	AVG	G	AB	R	H	2B	3B	HR	RBI	BB	SO	SB	OBP	SLG
2004	Elizabethton (APP)	R	.283	60	237	29	67	7	2	4	28	19	34	2	.340	.380
2005	Beloit (MWL)	LoA	.223	127	466	58	104	18	0	13	60	50	78	8	.300	.345
2006	Fort Myers (FSL)	HiA	.246	125	455	60	112	26	4	4	45	58	93	8	.333	.347
2007	New Britain (EL)	AA	.274	126	497	75	136	37	2	9	50	38	89	12	.326	.410
2008	New Britain (EL)	AA	.269	58	227	32	61	17	3	3	21	16	43	4	.325	.410
	Rochester (IL)	AAA	.256	66	250	34	64	17	3	6	39	14	47	1	.292	.420
2009	Rochester (IL)	AAA	.260	118	430	53	112	23	5	10	60	34	68	3	.313	.407
MINOR LEAGUE TOTALS			.256	680	2562	341	656	145	19	49	303	229	452	38	.318	.385

25 DANIEL SANTANA, SS

BORN: Nov. 7, 1990. **B-T:** B-R. **HT.:** 5-11. **WT.:** 150. **SIGNED:** Dominican Republic, 2007. **SIGNED BY:** Fred Guerrero.

Santana is one of several young shortstops who excite the Twins, a group that includes Australian James Beresford and 2009 Dominican signee Jorge Polanco. Santana has performed the best so far, showing impressive tools in the Gulf Coast League last summer. One club official said he had the highest ceiling of any middle infielder the club has had since acquiring Cristian Guzman from the Yankees in the Chuck Knoblauch trade in 1998. Santana is raw in terms of his approach at the plate, but he has electric ability. He has registered top-of-the-line 3.6-3.7 second times to first on drag bunts and hit grand slams in back-to-back games in August—one over the center-field fence, the other an inside-the-park job. His defensive ability also helps him stand out, as he has soft hands to go with above-average arm strength and range. While he has a feel for making contact, Santana is too aggressive at the plate and needs overall refinement and polish. His emergence and the system's overall depth at the position enabled the Twins to trade 2008 second-round pick Tyler Ladendorf to the Athletics for Orlando Cabrera, a key acquisition for last year's playoff drive. Santana has a chance to earn the Beloit shortstop job in 2010, provided Beresford moves up to Fort Myers.

Year	Club (League)	Class	AVG	G	AB	R	H	2B	3B	HR	RBI	BB	SO	SB	OBP	SLG
2008	Twins (DSL)	R	.274	51	190	37	52	6	10	1	27	20	38	15	.343	.426
2009	Twins (GCL)	R	.265	44	170	30	45	7	5	3	25	8	27	12	.302	.418
MINOR LEAGUE TOTALS			.269	95	360	67	97	13	15	4	52	28	65	27	.324	.422

26 MATT BASHORE, LHP

BORN: May 5, 1987. **B-T:** L-L. **HT.:** 6-2. **WT.:** 200. **DRAFTED:** Indiana, 2009 (2nd round). **SIGNED BY:** Jeff Pohl.

The Twins have had success developing college pitchers in recent years, from Kevin Slowey and Glen Perkins to more recent picks such as Carlos Gutierrez. They took four more college arms with their first four draft picks in 2009, starting with Kyle Gibson and followed by Bashore, one of the top lefthanded starters available. He signed for $751,500 as a sandwich pick. Bashore was a three-year starter for Indiana and teamed with Brewers first-rounder Eric Arnett to lead the Hoosiers to their second-ever regional appearance last spring. After flashing a 94-mph fastball as a sophomore, Bashore pitched more at 88-91 mph at the beginning of his junior season. His velocity perked back up late in the season and he touched 94-95 at times. The Twins grade his fastball as slightly above average because of its movement, velocity and control. Bashore throws both a plus curveball and an average slider, and he tends to blend the two when he gets in trouble. His arm action and sound delivery should allow him to pound the strike zone once he makes some refinements. He's physical and resembles Perkins, a fellow Big 10 Conference alum, in size and repertoire, though he has a better body than Perkins had at a similar stage. Bashore wound up having bone chips removed from his elbow after his brief pro debut but is expected to be ready for spring training. He may start in extended spring to ease his way back from surgery.

Year	Club (League)	Class	W	L	ERA	G	GS	CG	SV	IP	H	R	ER	HR	BB	SO	AVG
2009	Elizabethton (APP)	R	0	0	0.00	1	0	0	0	2	3	0	0	0	0	2	.375
MINOR LEAGUE TOTALS			0	0	0.00	1	0	0	0	2	3	0	0	0	0	2	.375

27 JOSE MORALES, C

BORN: Feb. 20, 1983. **B-T:** B-R. **HT.:** 5-11. **WT.:** 195. **DRAFTED:** HS—Rio Piedras, P.R., 2001 (3rd round). **SIGNED BY:** Hector Otero.

Morales' patience was rewarded in 2009. He made it to the major leagues in his ninth season in the organization, and it looks like he'll stay as Joe Mauer's backup. Morales earned significant playing time in the September stretch run and got a spot on the playoff roster, six years after the move that made his career—switching from infielder to catcher. His defensive shortcomings have kept him off prospect lists in the past, and he's still not an ideal backup from a defensive standpoint. He's a solid receiver with a fringy arm that produces 2.0-2.1 second pop times. He used to run OK for a catcher before left ankle injuries that ended his 2007 and 2008 seasons. Morales stands out more at the plate. In parts of four seasons in Triple-A, he has hit .317 in 791 at-bats. He continued to make contact in the majors, batting .311 and drawing walks as well. He has good hands, trusts them and isn't afraid to let the ball get deep. He uses the whole field and has the bat speed to keep pitchers honest when they try to come inside. He doesn't have a lot of power, though he can drive some balls to the gaps. Morales is cheap and has useful skills as a switch-hitter who can contribute offensively.

Year	Club (League)	Class	AVG	G	AB	R	H	2B	3B	HR	RBI	BB	SO	SB	OBP	SLG
2001	Twins (GCL)	R	.248	35	117	13	29	6	2	0	18	6	26	4	.296	.333
2002	Twins (GCL)	R	.309	53	175	25	54	7	2	0	28	7	28	3	.347	.371
2003	Fort Myers (FSL)	HiA	.357	12	42	6	15	3	1	0	2	1	5	0	.372	.476
	Quad City (MWL)	LoA	.271	48	170	14	46	10	1	2	25	5	32	0	.302	.376
2004	Fort Myers (FSL)	HiA	.287	91	331	30	95	13	4	4	46	29	77	0	.340	.387
2005	New Britain (EL)	AA	.250	7	20	1	5	1	0	0	0	1	3	0	.286	.300
2006	New Britain (EL)	AA	.211	80	251	23	53	14	1	3	26	19	56	2	.276	.311
	Rochester (IL)	AAA	.143	2	7	0	1	0	0	0	0	0	0	0	.143	.143
2007	Rochester (IL)	AAA	.311	108	376	42	117	25	1	2	37	30	44	1	.366	.399
	Minnesota (AL)	MAJ	1.000	1	3	1	3	1	0	0	0	0	0	0	1.000	1.333
2008	Rochester (IL)	AAA	.315	54	197	18	62	8	1	4	15	8	28	0	.348	.426
2009	Rochester (IL)	AAA	.336	58	211	30	71	13	1	2	26	28	27	1	.413	.436
	Minnesota (AL)	MAJ	.311	54	119	14	37	6	0	0	7	14	22	0	.381	.361
MAJOR LEAGUE TOTALS			.328	55	122	15	40	7	0	0	7	14	22	0	.394	.385
MINOR LEAGUE TOTALS			.289	548	1897	202	548	100	14	17	223	134	326	11	.340	.383

28 BEN TOOTLE, RHP

BORN: Jan. 9, 1988. **B-T:** R-R. **HT.:** 6-1. **WT.:** 180. **DRAFTED:** Jacksonville State, 2009 (4th round). **SIGNED BY:** Jack Powell.

Tootle is trying to top Todd Jones as the best Jacksonville State alumnus in major league history. He was the Ohio Valley Conference pitcher of the year in 2008 and then ranked as the No. 4 prospect in the Cape Cod League that summer, showing a fastball that reached 98 mph regularly. However, he missed a month last spring with a stomach virus that caused him to lose at least 10 pounds. He was never at his best, allowing Minnesota to grab him in the fourth round and sign him for $324,900. Tootle is a hard worker and long-toss fan with a quick arm who holds his above-average velocity deep into games when he's physically right. It took him a couple of starts last spring to get his velocity back, and he still couldn't maintain more than 92-96 mph velocity past the fifth inning. Pitching in relief and using his fastball almost exclusively, Tootle racked up groundouts in his brief pro debut. His fastball is far ahead of his secondary pitches, so he may be destined for the bullpen anyway. His slider is average at best, and he slows his arm noticeably when he throws his below-average changeup. The Twins plan to have him start in 2010 to further develop his secondary stuff, but even Tootle told club officials that he sees himself as a reliever in the long term.

Year	Club (League)	Class	W	L	ERA	G	GS	CG	SV	IP	H	R	ER	HR	BB	SO	AVG
2009	Elizabethton (APP)	R	0	0	0.00	6	0	0	2	6	4	0	0	0	2	1	.190
MINOR LEAGUE TOTALS			0	0	0.00	6	0	0	2	6	4	0	0	0	2	1	.190

29 LOEK VAN MIL, RHP

BORN: Sept. 15, 1984. **B-T:** R-R. **HT.:** 7-1. **WT.:** 232. **SIGNED:** Netherlands, 2005. **SIGNED BY:** Howard Norsetter.

Every bit of 7-foot-1, Van Mil remains both a curiosity and a potential impact reliever. The Twins have invested a lot of time in him, working with before he signed at age 20, and added him to the 40-man roster for the first time after the 2009 season. Van Mil passed through the Rule 5 draft unprotected in 2008, thanks in part to an elbow injury. He heard a pop in his elbow while warming up to pitch for the Netherlands in the Beijing Olympics. He wound up passing on surgery and rehabbed the ligament strain, sat out the World Baseball Classic in the spring and got back into game action by the end of May. Van Mil remains inconsistent with his stuff and delivery, as might be expected with his size. While he's coordinated and has a sound delivery, it's still hard to repeat. At his best, Van Mil sits in the mid-90s and touches 97 mph with his fastball. At times his slider is the best in the system (before Kyle Gibson's arrival), reaching as high as 88 mph. He doesn't command either pitch but really doesn't need pinpoint accuracy. He does need to throw more strikes to reach the big leagues, though. In a sign of his dedication, Van Mil skipped the World Cup at the end of last summer even though it was an opportunity to play in his homeland and more than 20 current and former Twins were involved. He finished up the season Double-A and figures to return there for 2010, though he could start in the warmer weather of Fort Myers if his elbow gives him any trouble.

Year	Club (League)	Class	W	L	ERA	G	GS	CG	SV	IP	H	R	ER	HR	BB	SO	AVG
2006	Twins (GCL)	R	1	2	3.30	10	8	0	0	44	51	31	16	3	17	24	.290
2007	Elizabethton (APP)	R	2	2	2.63	13	0	0	0	24	14	10	7	0	17	23	.171
2008	Beloit (MWL)	LoA	2	2	3.22	28	0	0	3	45	36	21	16	5	25	42	.221
2009	Fort Myers (FSL)	HiA	0	0	2.86	25	0	0	5	35	29	11	11	3	17	23	.236
	New Britain (EL)	AA	1	1	2.45	8	0	0	1	7	7	2	2	0	6	5	.269
MINOR LEAGUE TOTALS			6	7	3.03	84	8	0	9	154	137	75	52	11	82	117	.240

30 JAMES BERESFORD, SS

BORN: Jan. 19, 1989. **B-T:** L-R. **HT.:** 6-1. **WT.:** 155. **SIGNED:** Australia, 2005. **SIGNED BY:** Howard Norsetter.

The Twins loaded up on young infielders in 2009, from international signees Miguel Sano and Jorge Polanco to fifth-round pick Derek McCallum. Beresford, signed in 2005 to a contract that allowed him to stay home to finish high school, remains a factor in the organization because of his tools and makeup. He started for Australia during the World Baseball Classic and showcased his sound, fundamental swing by lashing a double to left field off flamethrowing Cuban lefty Aroldis Chapman. Beresford has good hands that work at the plate, giving him feel for the barrel of the bat, and with the glove. He's a capable defender at either position up the middle. Also scouted as a pitcher as an amateur, Beresford has had shoulder surgery and doesn't throw quite like he used to. He still has enough arm for shortstop, and it would be above average at second base. He has a rail-thin body, but Twins scouts believe there's projection left, especially considering how physical his father and older siblings are. He's a plus runner who needs work on his jumps to become a better basestealer. Beresford's makeup sets him apart, as he has leadership qualities and competitiveness that endear him to coaches, teammates and front-office officials. Beresford likely will repeat Beloit in 2010, teaming with McCallum and 2009 draft sleeper Brian Dozier in the middle infield.

Year	Club (League)	Class	AVG	G	AB	R	H	2B	3B	HR	RBI	BB	SO	SB	OBP	SLG
2006	Did Not Play															
2007	Twins (GCL)	R	.288	45	139	22	40	2	0	0	14	12	23	7	.349	.302
2008	Elizabethton (APP)	R	.246	55	179	26	44	5	1	0	23	25	35	1	.345	.285
2009	Beloit (MWL)	LoA	.289	114	450	52	130	11	0	0	38	34	70	15	.342	.313
MINOR LEAGUE TOTALS			.279	214	768	100	214	18	1	0	75	71	128	23	.344	.305

New York Mets

BY ADAM RUBIN

After being eliminated from the playoffs on the final day of the regular season in 2007 and 2008, the Mets continued to generate drama in 2009—though this time it was primarily off the field. New York christened Citi Field by going 70-92, the third-worst record in the National League, after they were expected to contend.

General manager Omar Minaya fired vice president of player development Tony Bernazard, whom he viewed as a trusted friend, on July 27 after Bernazard had a series of over-the-top confrontations with members of the organization. The incidents included Bernazard

removing his shirt and challenging Double-A Binghamton players to a fight after a game there, and getting into a heated exchange on a team bus with Francisco Rodriguez after a lopsided loss in Atlanta.

The front-office turnover continued after the season as well. The team fired Ramon Pena, a special assistant who oversaw Latin American operations, as well as field coordinator Luis Aguayo. Vice president for scouting Sandy Johnson opted for a reduced role as a special adviser. Former Reds GM Wayne Krivsky was hired as a special assistant to Minaya.

Minaya and manager Jerry Manuel got a reprieve after injuries wracked the big league roster, with Carlos Delgado (hip) and Jose Reyes (hamstring) not playing after May and John Maine (shoulder) and Oliver Perez (knee) missing significant portions of the season.

The farm system showed its weakness at the upper levels and provided little in the way of reinforcements, which prompted Minaya to acquire plug-ins such as Anderson Hernandez, Pat Misch and Wilson Valdez.

The biggest player-development success story was Bobby Parnell, who set a franchise rookie record with 68 appearances and at one point emerged as the primary set-up man to Rodriguez. Parnell's audition as a starter (1-5, 7.93 in eight starts) didn't go as well. Josh Thole batted .321 during a September callup and looked better than the Mets' other catching options.

After hitting .313 in New York in 2008, Daniel Murphy flopped as a left fielder, eventually succeeded Delgado at first base. He didn't hit as hoped. Fernando Martinez, the No. 1 prospect in the organization previous two years, got a chance to replace Murphy and hit .176 before tearing the meniscus in his right knee, requiring season-ending surgery in July. Jon Niese's chance to claim a spot in the big league rotation went awry when he tore a tendon in his upper right hamstring and needed surgery in early August.

Hard-throwing rookie Bobby Parnell thrived in a relief role but floundered as a starter

TOP 30 PROSPECTS

1. Jennry Mejia, rhp	16. Robert Carson, lhp
2. Wilmer Flores, ss	17. Cesar Puello, of
3. Fernando Martinez, of	18. Scott Moviel, rhp
4. Ike Davis, 1b	19. Robbie Shields, ss
5. Brad Holt, rhp	20. Zach Dotson, lhp
6. Jon Niese, lhp	21. Zach Lutz, 3b/1b
7. Reese Havens, ss	22. Sean Ratliff, of
8. Josh Thole, c	23. Dillon Gee, rhp
9. Ruben Tejada, ss/2b	24. Eric Niesen, lhp
10. Juan Urbina, lhp	25. Eddie Kunz, rhp
11. Steve Matz, lhp	26. Josh Stinson, rhp
12. Jefry Marte, 3b	27. Eric Beaulac, rhp
13. Kirk Nieuwenhuis, of	28. Brant Rustich, rhp
14. Kyle Allen, rhp	29. Tobi Stoner, rhp
15. Jeurys Familia, rhp	30. Jordany Valdespin, 2b/ss

Like the Mets, the clubs at the upper levels of their system performed dismally. Buffalo, in its first season as the organization's Triple-A affiliate, went 56-87, the worst record in the International League. At 54-86, Binghamton had the worst record of any full-season team in the minors.

The Mets continued to remain conservative in the draft, spending just $3.1 million in 2009, the lowest figure in baseball. New York forfeited its first-round pick as compensation for Rodriguez and used its top choice (second round) on Long Island high school lefthander Steve Matz.

General Manager: Omar Minaya. **Farm Director:** Adam Wogan. **Scouting Director:** Rudy Terrasas.

Class	Team	League	W	L	PCT	Finish*	Manager(s)
Majors	New York Mets	National	70	92	.432	t-13th (16)	Jerry Manuel
Triple-A	Buffalo Bisons	International	56	87	.392	14th (14)	Ken Oberkfell
Double-A	Binghamton Mets	Eastern	54	86	.386	12th (12)	Mako Oliveras
High A	St. Lucie Mets	Florida State	66	68	.493	7th (12)	Tim Teufel
Low A	Savannah Sand Gnats	South Atlantic	65	72	.474	12th (16)	Edgar Alfonzo
Short-season	Brooklyn Cyclones	New York-Penn	45	30	.600	t-3rd (14)	Pedro Lopez
Rookie	Kingsport Mets	Appalachian	30	35	.462	6th (10)	Mike DiFelice
Rookie	GCL Mets	Gulf Coast	22	34	.393	14th (16)	Julio Franco
Overall 2009 Minor League Record			338	412	.451	29th (30)	

*Finish in overall standings (No. of teams in league). †League champion.

LAST YEAR'S TOP 30

Player, Pos.		Status
1.	Fernando Martinez, of	No. 3
2.	Wilmer Flores, ss	No. 2
3.	Jon Niese, lhp	No. 6
4.	Brad Holt, rhp	No. 5
5.	Bobby Parnell, rhp	Majors
6.	Jefry Marte, 3b	No. 12
7.	Jenrry Mejia, rhp	No. 1
8.	Reese Havens, ss	No. 7
9.	Nick Evans, 1b/of	Majors
10.	Eddie Kunz, rhp	No. 25
11.	Ike Davis, 1b	No. 4
12.	Cesar Puello, of	No. 17
13.	Scott Moviel, rhp	No. 18
14.	Zach Lutz, 3b	No. 21
15.	Mike Antonini, lhp	Dropped out
16.	Ruben Tejada, ss	No. 9
17.	Dillon Gee, rhp	No. 23
18.	Scott Shaw, rhp	Dropped out
19.	Tobi Stoner, rhp	No. 29
20.	Lucas Duda, 1b	Dropped out
21.	Francisco Pena, c	Dropped out
22.	Greg Veloz, 2b	(Nationals)
23.	Josh Thole, c	No. 8
24.	Brant Rustich, rhp	No. 28
25.	Nathan Vineyard, lhp	(Retired)
26.	Elvin Ramirez, rhp	Dropped out
27.	Darren O'Day, rhp	(Rangers)
28.	Dylan Owen, rhp	Dropped out
29.	Javier Rodriguez, of	Dropped out
30.	Aderlin Rodriguez, 3b	Dropped out

BEST TOOLS

Best Hitter for Average	Josh Thole
Best Power Hitter	Ike Davis
Best Strike-Zone Discipline	Reese Havens
Fastest Baserunner	Alonzo Harris
Best Athlete	Jordany Valdespin
Best Fastball	Jenrry Mejia
Best Curveball	Jon Niese
Best Slider	Brant Rustich
Best Changeup	Mike Antonini
Best Control	Chris Schwinden
Best Defensive Catcher	Kai Gronauer
Best Defensive Infielder	Ruben Tejada
Best Infield Arm	Jefry Marte
Best Defensive Outfielder	Kirk Nieuwenhuis
Best Outfield Arm	Cesar Puello

PROJECTED 2013 LINEUP

Catcher	Josh Thole
First Base	Ike Davis
Second Base	Reese Havens
Third Base	David Wright
Shortstop	Jose Reyes
Left Field	Fernando Martinez
Center Field	Carlos Beltran
Right Field	Wilmer Flores
No. 1 Starter	Johan Santana
No. 2 Starter	Mike Pelfrey
No. 3 Starter	Jenrry Mejia
No. 4 Starter	Brad Holt
No. 5 Starter	Jon Niese
Closer	Francisco Rodriguez

TOP PROSPECTS OF THE DECADE

Year	Player, Pos.	2009 Org.
2000	Alex Escobar, of	Out of baseball
2001	Alex Escobar, of	Out of baseball
2002	Aaron Heilman, rhp	Cubs
2003	Jose Reyes, ss	Mets
2004	Kazuo Matsui, ss	Astros
2005	Lastings Milledge, of	Pirates
2006	Lastings Milledge, of	Pirates
2007	Mike Pelfrey, rhp	Mets
2008	Fernando Martinez, of	Mets
2009	Fernando Martinez, of	Mets

TOP DRAFT PICKS OF THE DECADE

Year	Player, Pos.	2009 Org.
2000	Billy Traber, lhp	Red Sox
2001	Aaron Heilman, rhp	Cubs
2002	Scott Kazmir, lhp	Angels
2003	Lastings Milledge, of	Pirates
2004	Philip Humber, rhp	Twins
2005	Mike Pelfrey, rhp	Mets
2006	Kevin Mulvey, rhp (2nd round)	Diamondbacks
2007	Eddie Kunz, rhp (1st round supp.)	Mets
2008	Ike Davis, 1b	Mets
2009	Steve Matz, lhp (2nd round)	Mets

LARGEST BONUSES IN CLUB HISTORY

Mike Pelfrey, 2005	$3,550,000
Philip Humber, 2004	$3,000,000
Scott Kazmir, 2002	$2,150,000
Lastings Milledge, 2003	$2,075,000
Geoff Goetz, 1997	$1,700,000

NEW YORK METS

TOP 2010 ROOKIE: Fernando Martinez. He didn't make the most of his first big league opportunity before hurting his knee in 2009, but the left-field job is still open.

BREAKOUT PROSPECT: Kyle Allen, rhp. A 24th-round pick, he can reach 95 mph with his fastball and has an advanced changeup.

SLEEPER: Aderlin Rodriguez, 3b. The organization's top international addition in 2008 with a $600,000 bonus, he has a big frame and bat.

SOURCE OF TOP 30 TALENT			
Homegrown	30	Acquired	0
College	13	Trades	0
Junior college	0	Rule 5 draft	0
High school	8	Independent leagues	0
Draft-and-follow	0	Free agents/waivers	0
Nondrafted free agents	0		
International	9		

Numbers in parentheses indicate prospect rankings.

LF
Fernando Martinez (3)
Nick Santomauro
Pedro Zapata
Juan Lagares
Julio Concepcion

CF
Javier Rodriguez
Darrell Ceciliani
R.J. Harris
Chase Greene

RF
Kirk Nieuwenhuis (13)
Cesar Puello (17)
Sean Ratliff (22)
Carlos Guzman
Chris Carter
Andres Perez
Kurt Steinhauer

3B
Jefry Marte (12)
Zach Lutz (21)
Aderlin Rodriguez
Richard Lucas
Shawn Bowman

SS
Wilmer Flores (2)
Ruben Tejada (9)
Robbie Shields (19)
Jose Coronado
Wilfredo Tovar

2B
Reese Havens (7)
Jordany Valdespin (30)
Alonzo Harris

1B
Ike Davis (4)
Lucas Duda
Jeff Flagg
Stefan Welch
Eddie Lora
Alexander Sanchez

C
Josh Thole (8)
Francisco Pena
Nelfi Zapata
Taylor Freeman
Jeff Glenn

RHP

Starters	Relievers
Jenrry Mejia (1)	Eddie Kunz (25)
Brad Holt (5)	Josh Stinson (26)
Kyle Allen (14)	Eric Beaulac (27)
Jeurys Familia (15)	Brant Rustich (28)
Scott Moviel (18)	Tobi Stoner (29)
Dillon Gee (23)	Stephen Clyne
Brandon Moore	
Scott Shaw	
Dylan Owen	
Jeff Kaplan	
Collin McHugh	

LHP

Starters	Relievers
Jon Niese (6)	Eric Niesen (24)
Juan Urbina (10)	Mike Antonini
Steve Matz (11)	Angel Calero
Robert Carson (16)	
Zach Dotson (20)	
Mark Cohoon	
Darin Gorski	
Jim Fuller	

2009 — BONUSES: $3.1 MILLION

BEST PURE HITTER: It should be SS Robbie Shields (3), though he hit just .178 at short-season Brooklyn while nursing a sore elbow. He eventually may move to second or third base, so he'll have to pick it up offensively.

BEST POWER HITTER: OF Nick Santomauro (10), who holds the Darmouth single-season home run record (10) and led Brooklyn with six homers. The Mets bought him away from his senior season for just $82,000.

FASTEST RUNNER: OFs Chase Greene (16) and ZeErika Hall (29) both have well above-average speed.

BEST DEFENSIVE PLAYER: OF Darrell Ceciliani (4) has plus speed and range to go with a slightly above-average arm in center field. OF R.J. Harris (14) also does a nice job in center, albeit with a lesser arm. C Nelfi Zapata (19) threw out 45 percent of basestealers in his pro debut, though his receiving needs more polish.

BEST FASTBALL: The Mets signed just three pitchers in the first 20 rounds, which limits the number of candidates. LHP Stephen Matz (2), New York's top pick, works at 90-91 mph and maxes out at 94. Five-foot-10 RHP Michael Johnson (24) had a quick arm capable of reaching 96, but he blew out his elbow eight innings into this pro career and required Tommy John surgery.

BEST SECONDARY PITCH: Matz and LHP Zach Dotson (13) both have promising curveballs and changeups, but none is a consistent plus pitch at this point.

BEST PRO DEBUT: OF Kurt Steinhauer (27) batted .328/.428/.525 between two Rookie-level clubs. He set a Point Loma Nazarene (Calif.) record with 19 homers in the spring and won the Charlie Hustle Award at the NAIA World Series, where the Sea Lions finished second.

BEST ATHLETE: In addition to his speed, Greene has strong hands and bat speed that bode well for future power once he fills out. Ceciliani and Harris also have decent to solid tools.

MOST INTRIGUING BACKGROUND: OF Joey August's (20) father Bill once held the junior college football record for passing yards in a game with 619 at Chabot (Calif.) in 1970.

CLOSEST TO THE MAJORS: The Mets didn't draft an NCAA Division I player until C Taylor Freeman in the eighth round, and he's not especially close. If Shields plays like he did in the Cape Cod League in the summer of 2008, he could take New York's second-base job quickly.

BEST LATE-ROUND PICK: Dotson, who was ticketed for Georgia until the Mets signed him at the deadline for $500,000. Harris and Greene are two of the better athletes from this draft, while Zapata offers some raw power to go with his arm strength.

THE ONE WHO GOT AWAY: New York though it had met the asking price for raw RHPs Damien Magnifico (5) and David Buchanan (6), but both deals fell apart in the end. Magnifico, who's now at Howard (Texas) JC, hit 98 mph during summer ball. Buchanan, now at Georgia State, tops out at 96.

ASSESSMENT: Though they're wealthier than most clubs, the Mets don't press their financial advantage in the draft. They went over slot to sign Matz ($895,000) and Dotson, but otherwise were conservative and didn't add much depth to a thin farm system.

2008 — BONUSES: $6.5 MILLION

1B Ike Davis (1), SS Reese Havens (1) and RHP Brad Holt (1s) all are off to good starts in their pro careers and rank among the system's best prospects. OF Kirk Nieuwenhuis (3) exceeded expectations in his first full year.

GRADE: B

2007 — BONUSES: $3.8 MILLION

This crop took a huge step back last season. RHP Eddie Kunz (1s) was totally ineffective, LHP Nathan Vineyard (1s) retired, and RHPs Scott Moviel (2) and Brant Rustich (2) had physical problems.

GRADE: D

2006 — BONUSES: $2.5 MILLION

The Mets' best pick was 1B/OF Daniel Murphy (13), who had mixed results as a big league regular in 2009. Their first choice was RHP Kevin Mulvey (2), who hasn't distinguished himself beyond being part of the Johan Santana deal. RHP Joe Smith (3) rushed to the majors and was traded for J.J. Putz.

GRADE: C

2005 — BONUSES: $4.7 MILLION*

New York's best draft in recent years may have landed them 40 percent of a starting rotation in RHP Mike Pelfrey (1) and LHP Jon Niese (7), as well as a possible setup man in RHP Bobby Parnell (9) and a potential starting catcher in Josh Thole (13).

GRADE: C+

*Draft analysis by Jim Callis. Numbers in parentheses indicate draft rounds. *Bonuses for 2005 are first 10 rounds only.*

JENRRY MEJIA, RHP

Born: Oct. 11, 1989.
Height:: 6-0. **Weight:** 162.
Bats: R. **Throws:** R.
Signed: Dominican Republic, 2007.
Signed by: Ramon Pena/ Ismael Cruz/Sandy Rosario/ Juan Mercado.

JERRY HALE

O n the day Mejia auditioned for the Mets in 2007, he felt ill and stiff, and told his representative he didn't think he could register more than 86 mph with his fastball. Mejia outperformed his own expectations that day, throwing 91-92. He agreed to a $16,500 bonus before leaving the organization's complex in Boca de Niqua, Dominican Republic, and since has proven to be a bargain. Mejia emerged as the organization's top prospect in 2009, when he opened the season by dominating at high Class A St. Lucie before earning a promotion to Double-A Binghamton that made him the youngest pitcher in the Eastern League. He missed seven weeks with a strained right middle finger, the result of overthrowing a fastball in late June when he got upset after surrendering one of only two homers he served up all year. The injury cost him a trip to the Futures Game. The Mets eased him back on short pitch counts when he returned to the mound in August, then sent him to the Arizona Fall League.

Mejia's fastball ranges from 90-96 mph, and it hit 98 on a handful of occasions in 2009. He's able to maintain his velocity late into games, and his fastball has so much cutting and sinking action that it befuddles hitters. He induces a lot of groundouts and broken bats. "They're asking me if it's a slider," said Josh Thole, who caught Mejia with Binghamton. "I said, 'It's 94 (mph), guys. I don't think that's a slider.' " Mejia's changeup is a plus pitch at times, resembling a splitter with its 81-84 velocity and drop. Though he's not particularly tall by right-hander standards, he has a good angle to the plate and throws downhill. In 210 pro innings, he has allowed just six homers. Mejia does a good job of pitching inside, and he generally stays composed with traffic on the bases. Stocky and muscular, he has impeccable conditioning.

Mejia's slider needs a lot of work. He throws it with an inconsistent release point and arm speed, often leaving it up in the strike zone. He sometimes throws his changeup too hard and doesn't achieve enough separation form his fastball. His fastball command also can stand to improve, and even he acknowledges he doesn't quite know where the pitch is headed when he releases it. He just aims for the middle and lets the movement work for him.

Manager Jerry Manuel watched Mejia pitch in the AFL to gauge whether he could contribute out of the major league bullpen to open 2010, though that may be a bit premature. Mejia instead may return to Double-A, where he has made just 10 starts and has yet to record a win. He has more value as a potential frontline starter, and his fastball life is so good that he probably could succeed by throwing mostly heaters. Regardless of his role, he has a good chance to reach New York at some point during the season. "Somebody told me if you play in the big leagues at 20 years old, that's good," Mejia said. "I said, 'I know. But I wanted to play in the big leagues last year.' "

Year	Club (League)	Class	W	L	ERA	G	GS	CG	SV	IP	H	R	ER	HR	BB	SO	AVG
2007	Mets (DSL)	R	2	3	2.47	14	7	0	1	44	24	17	12	0	27	47	.160
2008	Mets (GCL)	R	2	0	0.60	3	3	1	0	15	9	1	1	0	3	15	.164
	Brooklyn (NYP)	SS	3	2	3.49	11	11	0	0	57	42	22	22	4	23	52	.209
2009	St. Lucie (FSL)	HiA	4	1	1.97	9	9	0	0	50	41	18	11	0	16	44	.217
	Binghamton (EL)	AA	0	5	4.47	10	10	0	0	44	44	28	22	2	23	47	.263
MINOR LEAGUE TOTALS			11	11	2.91	47	40	1	1	210	160	86	68	6	92	205	.210

2 WILMER FLORES, SS ✝

BORN: Aug. 6, 1991. **B-T:** R-R. **HT.:** 6-3. **WT.:** 175. **SIGNED:** Venezuela, 2007.
SIGNED BY: Robert Alfonzo/Ismael Cruz.

Flores signed with the Mets for $750,000 in 2007 after honing his skills at the same Venezuelan academy (Agua Linda) that produced Pablo Sandoval. He became the youngest player ever to compete for short-season Brooklyn when he finished the 2008 season there as a 17-year-old. Flores continued to face older competition in 2009, when he was the youngest player in the low Class A South Atlantic League, and started at second base in the Futures Game. Flores makes consistent hard contact, thanks to his quick bat and ability to put the barrel on the ball. Though he launched just three homers in 2009, he's projected to hit for power to all fields as he matures. Even before signing, he displayed opposite-field power potential. He has a plus arm and soft hands at shortstop. Flores is a below-average runner with a slow first step and below-average range. He has a thick lower half and is expected to move to third base or an outfield corner as he fills out. He needs to get stronger and develop more patience at the plate to maximize his offensive potential. Flores won't turn 19 until late in 2010, and the Mets may be less inclined to push young players in the wake of their front-office turnover. He could begin 2010 back at low Class A Savannah with the chance for a midseason promotion.

Year	Club (League)	Class	AVG	G	AB	R	H	2B	3B	HR	RBI	BB	SO	SB	OBP	SLG
2008	Kingsport (APP)	R	.310	59	245	36	76	12	4	8	41	12	28	2	.352	.490
	Savannah (SAL)	LoA	.400	1	5	1	2	0	0	0	0	0	2	0	.400	.400
	Brooklyn (NYP)	SS	.267	8	30	3	8	1	0	0	1	1	7	0	.290	.300
2009	Savannah (SAL)	LoA	.264	125	488	44	129	20	2	3	36	22	72	3	.305	.332
MINOR LEAGUE TOTALS			.280	193	768	84	215	33	6	11	78	35	109	5	.320	.382

3 FERNANDO MARTINEZ, OF *Busch*

BORN: Oct. 10, 1988. **B-T:** L-R. **HT.:** 6-1. **WT.:** 200. **SIGNED:** Dominican
Republic, 2005. **SIGNED BY:** Rafael Bournigal/Sandy Johnson/Eddy Toledo.

The highest-profile Latin American signing in Omar Minaya's five years as GM, Martinez received a $1.3 million bonus and ranked No. 1 on this list the two previous years. He made his big league debut in 2009, but injuries continued to undermine his career. He had season-ending right knee surgery in July. He also has dealt with persistent hamstring trouble and a broken bone in his right hand in recent years. Martinez has power potential to all fields, though he has gone to left-center less frequently than when he was younger. He slugs mammoth home runs on occasion that offer a reminder as to why he was so highly touted. His bat speed and improved ability to make contact should allow him to hit for a solid average. He has average arm strength and good range for a corner outfielder after moving from center last season. Martinez's once solid-average speed has declined as he has matured and his lower half has become thicker. His throws are inaccurate—some cut, others tail, some are launched, others go into the ground—because his body gets ahead of his arm and his arm slot varies. Though Martinez's stock has slipped, he's still just 21. "He'll show you nothing for four days and you're ready to give up on him," a scout said, "and then out of nowhere he'll do something and you'll go, 'Hmmm, OK. That's what they've been talking about.' " Given the Mets' need for outfield help, Martinez will compete for a big league job in spring training.

Year	Club (League)	Class	AVG	G	AB	R	H	2B	3B	HR	RBI	BB	SO	SB	OBP	SLG
2006	Mets (GCL)	R	.250	1	4	1	1	0	0	0	0	0	1	0	.250	.250
	Hagerstown (SAL)	LoA	.333	45	192	24	64	14	2	5	28	15	36	7	.389	.505
	St. Lucie (FSL)	HiA	.193	30	119	18	23	4	2	5	11	6	24	1	.254	.387
2007	Binghamton (EL)	AA	.271	60	236	32	64	11	1	4	21	20	51	3	.336	.377
	Mets (GCL)	R	.111	3	9	1	1	0	1	0	1	1	6	0	.200	.333
2008	Mets (GCL)	R	.429	4	14	2	6	1	1	0	0	0	2	0	.467	.643
	Binghamton (EL)	AA	.287	86	352	48	101	19	4	8	43	27	73	6	.340	.432
2009	Buffalo (IL)	AAA	.290	45	176	24	51	16	2	8	28	11	33	2	.337	.540
	New York (NL)	MAJ	.176	29	91	11	16	6	0	1	8	5	14	2	.242	.275
MAJOR LEAGUE TOTALS			.176	29	91	11	16	6	0	1	8	5	14	2	.242	.275
MINOR LEAGUE TOTALS			.282	274	1102	150	311	65	13	30	132	80	226	19	.338	.446

4 IKE DAVIS, 1B

BORN: March 22, 1987. **B-T:** L-L. **HT.:** 6-5. **WT.:** 195. **DRAFTED:** Arizona State, 2008 (1st round). **SIGNED BY:** Mike Brown.

The son of former major league pitcher Ron Davis, Ike went homerless in his first 215 at-bats after signing for $1.575 million as the 18th pick in the 2008 draft. He rebounded with 20 homers while reaching Double-A in his first full season. He hit .333 with three homers in eight games to help Team USA win the World Cup in Italy in September. Davis has quick hands and lift in his swing, giving him plus power. He has the bat speed to catch up to good fastballs. Also a pitcher and right fielder at Arizona State, he's an above-average defender with good hands and a strong arm at first base. He has exceptional makeup and isn't in awe of big league surroundings. Davis has somewhat of a long swing and can become pull-conscious, leaving him vulnerable to pitches on the outer half and prone to strikeouts. While he hit .298 last season, he'll have to adjust his approach to hit for average in the majors. Though he's agile at first base, he's a below-average runner. The Mets entered the offseason with Daniel Murphy set to open 2010 as their first baseman and Davis headed to Triple-A Buffalo. He should make his big league debut later in the year and eventually supplant Murphy as New York's starter.

Year	Club (League)	Class	AVG	G	AB	R	H	2B	3B	HR	RBI	BB	SO	SB	OBP	SLG
2008	Brooklyn (NYP)	SS	.256	58	215	17	55	15	0	0	17	23	43	0	.326	.326
2009	St. Lucie (FSL)	HiA	.288	59	222	28	64	17	3	7	28	31	52	0	.376	.486
	Binghamton (EL)	AA	.309	55	207	30	64	14	0	13	43	26	60	0	.386	.565
MINOR LEAGUE TOTALS			.284	172	644	75	183	46	3	20	88	80	155	0	.363	.458

5 BRAD HOLT, RHP

BORN: Oct. 13, 1986. **B-T:** R-R. **HT.:** 6-4. **WT.:** 194. **DRAFTED:** UNC Wilmington, 2008 (1st round supplemental). **SIGNED BY:** Marlin McPhail.

The 33rd choice in the 2008 draft (a supplemental pick received when Tom Glavine returned to the Braves), Holt signed for $1.04 million. He allowed three homers and nine runs in his first start of 2009, then gave up just seven runs over his next eight starts to earn a promotion to Double-A. He injured his ankle after his first outing with Binghamton, missed three weeks and wasn't the same afterward. Holt has the stuff to be a No. 3 or No. 4 starter. He has a solid four-seam fastball, which ranges from 88-93 mph and tops out at 95, as well as a hard 75-78 mph curveball and a 79-81 mph changeup. He gets good extension to the plate and drive from his legs. Once he fills out, his frame should lend itself to durability. Holt's biggest problem is a tendency to overthrow. He's infatuated with strikeouts and tries to power his way out of jams, which costs him command. Maintaining a more consistent release point also will help him locate his pitches better. He throws his changeup too hard at times, and it's his least effective pitch. Though he'll attend big league camp, Holt isn't ready to compete for a rotation spot in New York. He could return to Double-A, teaming with Jenrry Mejia once again, then advance to Triple-A during the year.

Year	Club (League)	Class	W	L	ERA	G	GS	CG	SV	IP	H	R	ER	HR	BB	SO	AVG
2008	Brooklyn (NYP)	SS	5	3	1.87	14	14	0	0	72	43	18	15	3	33	96	.171
2009	St. Lucie (FSL)	HiA	4	1	3.12	9	9	0	0	43	34	16	15	5	13	54	.215
	Binghamton (EL)	AA	3	6	6.21	11	11	0	0	58	58	42	40	9	23	45	.270
MINOR LEAGUE TOTALS			12	10	3.63	34	34	0	0	174	135	76	70	17	69	195	.216

6 JON NIESE, LHP

BORN: Oct. 27, 1986. **B-T:** L-L. **HT.:** 6-4. **WT.:** 215. **DRAFTED:** HS—Defiance, Ohio, 2005 (7th round). **SIGNED BY:** Erwin Bryant.

Niese went 0-6, 7.36 in his first nine starts at Buffalo to open the season, then went on a 5-0, 0.72 tear to earn a big league callup. He tore a tendon in his right hamstring doing a split while receiving a throw at first base on Aug. 5, and then ripped it off the bone on a warmup pitch. He dropped to the ground in agony and required season-ending surgery. Niese's signature pitch is a 12-to-6 curveball, though he sometimes has difficulty getting it called for strikes. He can run his fastball into the low 90s, and he uses its natural cutting and sinking action to battle righthanders. He also has a solid changeup and he consistently throws strikes. Niese gets into trouble when he struggles with his fastball command. When that happens, he can't overpower hitters with sheer velocity and they sit on his curveball. Because he relies on his lower half with his drop-and-drive delivery, Niese will need to trust in the integrity of his surgically-repaired hamstring. When Niese visited the clubhouse at Citi Field in late September, he already had shed crutches and a brace, a sign that his hamstring should be 100 percent by spring training. He's a favorite to win the last spot in the New York's rotation for 2010, and he projects as an eventual No. 3 or 4 starter.

Year	Club (League)	Class	W	L	ERA	G	GS	CG	SV	IP	H	R	ER	HR	BB	SO	AVG
2005	Mets (GCL)	R	1	0	3.65	7	5	0	0	25	23	10	10	1	10	24	.245
2006	Hagerstown (SAL)	LoA	11	9	3.93	25	25	1	0	124	121	67	54	7	62	132	.256
	St. Lucie (FSL)	HiA	0	2	4.50	2	2	0	0	10	8	8	5	0	5	10	.216
2007	St. Lucie (FSL)	HiA	11	7	4.29	27	27	2	0	134	151	78	64	9	31	110	.285
2008	Binghamton (EL)	AA	6	7	3.04	22	22	2	0	124	118	53	42	5	44	112	.253
	New Orleans (PCL)	AAA	5	1	3.40	7	7	0	0	40	34	15	15	4	14	32	.231
	New York (NL)	MAJ	1	1	7.07	3	3	0	0	14	20	11	11	2	8	11	.333
2009	Buffalo (IL)	AAA	5	6	3.82	16	16	2	0	94	95	47	40	7	26	82	.258
	New York (NL)	MAJ	1	1	4.21	5	5	0	0	26	27	12	12	1	9	18	.276
MAJOR LEAGUE TOTALS			2	2	5.22	8	8	0	0	40	47	23	23	3	17	29	.297
MINOR LEAGUE TOTALS			39	32	3.76	106	104	7	0	551	550	278	230	33	192	502	.260

7 REESE HAVENS, SS ✝

BORN: Oct. 20, 1986. **B-T:** L-R. **HT.:** 6-1. **WT.:** 195. **DRAFTED:** South Carolina, 2008 (1st round). **SIGNED BY:** Marlin McPhail.

Havens passed on seven-figure signing offers out of high school, attended South Carolina, then went 22nd overall in 2008 and signed for $1.419 million. He has had nagging health issues since. Elbow trouble and a groin pull limited him to 85 at-bats in his pro debut, and he missed nearly four weeks in 2009 after pulling a quadriceps muscle in late May. He returned on June 23 but was hit in the right hand with a pitch a week later. He sustained a deep bone bruise and missed an additional three weeks Havens has good power for a middle infielder and slugged 14 homers in the pitcher-friendly Florida State League. He also has an advanced idea of the strike zone and recognizes pitches well, though he has batted just .247 in each of his two seasons. Defensively, he's a sound fielder with good hands and arm strength. Havens has slightly below-average speed and lacks the range for shortstop. He trimmed down during the 2009 season in an attempt to improve, but it probably won't stave off a position switch. He worked out at second base in the Arizona Fall League, where some scouts wonder if he has the footwork to stick. Havens will open 2010 in Double-A. The best-case scenario is that he becomes an offensive-minded second baseman. If that doesn't work out, third base is blocked in New York by David Wright, so Havens might have to become a corner outfielder.

Year	Club (League)	Class	AVG	G	AB	R	H	2B	3B	HR	RBI	BB	SO	SB	OBP	SLG
2008	Brooklyn (NYP)	SS	.247	23	85	13	21	6	2	3	11	11	27	3	.340	.471
2009	St. Lucie (FSL)	HiA	.247	97	360	53	89	19	1	14	52	55	73	3	.361	.422
MINOR LEAGUE TOTALS			.247	120	445	66	110	25	3	17	63	66	100	6	.357	.431

8 JOSH THOLE, C

BORN: Oct. 28, 1986. **B-T:** L-R. **HT.:** 6-1. **WT.:** 205. **DRAFTED:** HS—Breese, Ill., 2005 (13th round). **SIGNED BY:** Quincy Boyd.

A catcher in high school, Thole played just 26 games behind the plate in his first three years as a pro. When Sean McCraw couldn't get his bat going in 2008, Thole replaced him as St. Lucie's catcher a month into the season. He has hit .315 over the last two years, including .321 during a September callup with the Mets. Thole essentially takes a two-strike approach on all counts, choking up on the bat to punch line drives to both gaps. He hits for average and is difficult to strike out. He's receptive to coaching and showed defensive improvement after working with catching instructor Sandy Alomar Jr. in September. The downside of Thole's approach is that he hits for little power and rarely works deep enough counts to walk. His receiving is just adequate, his arm strength is below-average and he drops his arm slot, causing his throws to tail. However, he did throw out 30 percent of basestealers in 2009. He's a below-average runner. Though Thole received the bulk of the September playing time at the expense of pending free agent Brian Schneider, he likely will require more seasoning. He doesn't profile well at another position, and even at catcher he projects more as a platoon player or backup than an everyday player.

Year	Club (League)	Class	AVG	G	AB	R	H	2B	3B	HR	RBI	BB	SO	SB	OBP	SLG
2005	Mets (GCL)	R	.269	35	104	14	28	2	1	1	12	20	11	1	.406	.337
2006	Kingsport (APP)	R	.235	36	98	13	23	4	0	1	12	7	25	1	.300	.306
2007	Savannah (SAL)	LoA	.267	117	389	46	104	17	0	0	36	61	57	4	.372	.311
2008	St. Lucie (FSL)	HiA	.300	111	347	49	104	25	2	5	56	45	38	2	.382	.427
2009	Binghamton (EL)	AA	.328	103	384	48	126	29	2	1	46	42	34	8	.395	.422
	New York (NL)	MAJ	.321	17	53	2	17	2	1	0	9	4	5	1	.356	.396
MAJOR LEAGUE TOTALS			.321	17	53	2	17	2	1	0	9	4	5	1	.356	.396
MINOR LEAGUE TOTALS			.291	402	1322	170	385	77	5	8	162	175	165	16	.379	.375

9 RUBEN TEJADA, SS/2B

BORN: Oct. 27, 1989. **B-T:** R-R. **HT.:** 6-0. **WT.:** 160. **SIGNED:** Panama, 2006. **SIGNED BY:** Ismael Cruz/Wilfredo Blanco/Alex Zapata.

One of several international players whom New York has promoted aggressively, Tejada set career highs in most offensive categories last season while playing as 19-year-old in Double-A. A sparkplug who can play either middle-infield position, he started the year by representing Panama in the World Baseball Classic. The Mets considered calling him up when injuries decimated their middle infield, but decided against it because they didn't want to tie up a 40-man roster spot. Tejada is an above-average defender with the arm strength to make plays from the hole at shortstop. He has slightly above-average speed and the potential to steal 20-25 bases a season. He makes good contact at the plate and could grow into gap power as he matures physically. Tejada's bat may prevent him from becoming an everyday player. Even when he gets stronger, power won't be a major part of his game, and he'll need to do a better job of drawing walks. At shortstop, he can improve his ability to go to his right and make backhand plays. Tejada figures to open 2010 in Triple-A, with the potential for a callup if injuries strike the Mets again. With Jose Reyes entrenched at shortstop, Tejada and Reese Havens figure to battle to become New York's second baseman of the future.

Year	Club (League)	Class	AVG	G	AB	R	H	2B	3B	HR	RBI	BB	SO	SB	OBP	SLG
2007	Mets (VSL)	R	.364	32	121	32	44	5	0	3	25	19	19	16	.466	.479
	Mets (GCL)	R	.283	35	120	13	34	4	3	0	16	19	16	2	.401	.367
2008	St. Lucie (FSL)	HiA	.229	131	497	55	114	19	4	2	37	41	77	8	.293	.296
2009	Binghamton (EL)	AA	.289	134	488	59	141	24	3	5	46	37	59	19	.351	.381
MINOR LEAGUE TOTALS			.272	332	1226	159	333	52	10	10	124	116	171	45	.346	.355

10 JUAN URBINA, LHP

BORN: May 31, 1993. **B-T:** L-L. **HT.:** 6-2. **WT.:** 170. **SIGNED:** Venezuela, 2009. **SIGNED BY:** Sandy Johnson/Ramon Pena/Ismael Cruz/Robert Alfonzo.

The son of former big league righthander Ugueth Urbina, who's serving a 14-year jail sentence in Venezuela, Juan signed with the Mets in July for $1.2 million. It was the largest bonus the Mets bestowed on any amateur player in 2009, as the organization had no first-round draft pick in June after signing free agent closer Francisco Rodriguez. Unlike his father, who made two all-star teams as a closer, Juan projects as a starter, at least at this early stage of his career. He threw a bullpen session in New York after signing but has yet to make his pro debut. Urbina has a loose, quick arm and already sits at 88-89 mph and tops out at 91 with his fastball. He has plenty of projection remaining in his lean, athletic frame and figures to develop at least a consistent low-90s heater. He commands his fastball well and sets it up with a changeup that features good sink. His clean mechanics should minimize his risk of injury. He pitches like the son of a former big league pitcher, as he shows advanced feel for pitching and the ability to throw strikes. Urbina's slider lags behind his other two pitches, though it does show some promise. Thanks to his bloodlines, he's more advanced than most pitchers his age, but he still has a long ways to go and will require a lot of innings to develop. He'll need all three of his pitches if he's to remain a starter. The Mets expect that Urbina likely will begin his pro career in the Rookie-level Gulf Coast League. Whether the Mets will push him as quickly as they've moved other recent signees such as Jennry Mejia, Wilmer Flores, Fernando Martinez and Ruben Tejada remains to be seen.

Year	Club (League)	Class	W	L	ERA	G	GS	CG	SV	IP	H	R	ER	HR	BB	SO	AVG
Did Not Play—Signed 2010 Contract																	

11 STEVE MATZ, LHP

BORN: Dec. 29, 1991. **B-T:** L-L. **Ht.:** 6-4. **Wt.:** 195. **DRAFTED:** HS—East Setauket, N.Y., 2009 (2nd round). **SIGNED BY:** Larry Izzo Jr.

In a rare move for the Mets, they exceeded MLB's slot recommendations to sign Matz, their top pick (second round) in the 2009 draft. The 72nd overall choice, he turned down a commitment to Coastal Carolina to sign at the Aug. 17 deadline for $895,000—well over the $506,700 guideline from the commissioner's office. He joined the Rookie-level Gulf Coast League Mets at the end of the season bit didn't appear in a game. Director of amateur scouting Rudy Terrasas loves Matz's frame, arm action, athleticism and the way he competes. Matz likes to pitch inside with his fastball, which ranges from 89-94 mph and settles in at 90-91. His velocity took a significant jump from the Area Code Games in August 2008 to his high school senior season, which helped boost his stock. Both his curveball and changeup are promising pitches but lack consistency, and the latter is the better pitch at this point. He also started working on a slider with former big league pitcher Neal Heaton last winter, though it's still a work in progress. Matz has a projectable frame but there are questions about his durability. He didn't have a completely healthy year before 2009, and there's some effort in his delivery. Matz could make his pro debut in low Class A next April.

Year	Club (League)	Class	W	L	ERA	G	GS	CG	SV	IP	H	R	ER	HR	BB	SO	AVG
2009	Did Not Play—Signed Late																

12 JEFRY MARTE, 3B

BORN: June 21, 1991. **B-T:** R-R. **HT.:** 6-1. **WT.:** 187. **SIGNED:** Dominican Republic, 2007. **SIGNED BY:** Ramon Pena/Ismael Cruz/Marciano Alvarez.

The Mets signed Marte for $550,000 in 2007 and challenged him by sending him to low Class A before he turned 18 last season. The organization is expected to be less inclined to make that type of move now that Tony Bernazard is out as vice president of player development. The second-youngest regular in the South Atlantic League (behind only teammate Wilmer Flores), Marte struggled against older competition after excelling in his 2008 pro debut in Rookie ball. He projects as an average hitter with above average power. Mets international scouting director Ismael Cruz thought Marte had the quickest bat on the 2007 international amateur market, but he needs to stop trying to pull everything and let his natural strength take over. His approach and difficulties with breaking balls contributed to 117 strikeouts in 485 at-bats last season. He's a slightly below-average runner with decent instincts on the bases. Marte's hands and arm strength are solid at third base, but he likely faces an eventual move to first base. He doesn't always make routine plays or accurate throws, and he led the SAL with 49 errors. New York figures to take him off the fast track and send him back to Savannah in 2010.

Year	Club (League)	Class	AVG	G	AB	R	H	2B	3B	HR	RBI	BB	SO	SB	OBP	SLG
2008	Mets (GCL)	R	.325	44	154	29	50	14	3	4	24	13	30	2	.398	.532
2009	Savannah (SAL)	LoA	.233	123	485	58	113	21	6	6	41	25	117	5	.279	.338
MINOR LEAGUE TOTALS			.255	167	639	87	163	35	9	10	65	38	147	7	.309	.385

13 KIRK NIEUWENHUIS, OF

BORN: Aug. 7, 1987. **B-T:** L-R. **HT.:** 6-3. **WT.:** 210. **DRAFTED:** Azusa Pacific (Calif.), 2008 (3rd round). **SIGNED BY:** Fred Mazuca.

The top NAIA prospect in the 2008 draft, Nieuwenhuis signed as a third-round pick after leading Azusa Pacific (Calif.) to consecutive NAIA World Series. He matched former big leaguers Paul Moskau and Jeff Robinson as the highest-drafted players in school history. Nieuwenhuis had a strong first full pro season, leading the Florida State League in runs (91), doubles (35), extra-base hits (56) and slugging (.467) and finishing the year in Double-A when World Cup assignments left Binghamton shorthanded. Early in the year, he pounded fastballs but needed to improve at recognizing breaking balls and laying off pitches in the dirt. He made quality adjustments and displayed solid opposite-field power. He's a potential 20-20 player with his strength and slightly above-average speed, though some scouts worry about his ability to make consistent contact. Nieuwenhuis once rushed for 267 yards in a snowstorm in a Colorado Class 2-A football championship game, and he takes that mentality into the outfield. He has no fear of the wall and has a slightly above average arm. He played center field in 2009 but lacks classic range for the position, so he'll probably wind up in right. He'll return to Double-A to begin 2010 and could push for a September callup.

Year	Club (League)	Class	AVG	G	AB	R	H	2B	3B	HR	RBI	BB	SO	SB	OBP	SLG
2008	Brooklyn (NYP)	SS	.277	74	285	34	79	15	5	3	29	29	70	11	.348	.396
2009	St. Lucie (FSL)	HiA	.274	123	482	91	132	35	5	16	71	53	118	16	.357	.467
	Binghamton (EL)	AA	.406	8	32	8	13	3	1	1	2	4	9	1	.472	.656
MINOR LEAGUE TOTALS			.280	205	799	133	224	53	11	20	102	86	197	28	.358	.449

14 KYLE ALLEN, RHP

BORN: Feb. 12, 1990. **B-T:** R-R. **HT.:** 6-3. **WT.:** 195. **DRAFTED:** HS—Brandenton, Fla., 2008 (24th round). **SIGNED BY:** Les Parker.

Allen is the best unheralded prospect in the system. The nephew of former big leaguer Ray Semproch, Allen was a two-way star at The Pendleton School, part of the IMG Academy in Bradenton, Fla. He dropped to the 24th round in the 2008 draft because of concerns about his commitment to North Carolina State as well as his maturity, but the Mets insist the latter hasn't been a factor since he signed for $150,000. Allen arrived with an advanced changeup, and his slider has since improved to the point where some Mets officials think it's his best pitch. His fastball is a solid offering as well, usually sitting at 91-92 mph and peaking at 95. He has a project-able frame, so he could add more velocity in the future. Allen has spurts where he has trouble commanding his pitches, but he generally does a good job of throwing strikes and keeping the ball down in the zone. He's ready to advance to high Class A in 2010.

Year	Club (League)	Class	W	L	ERA	G	GS	CG	SV	IP	H	R	ER	HR	BB	SO	AVG
2008	Mets (GCL)	R	1	1	2.12	11	5	0	2	34	24	13	8	1	10	45	.194
2009	Savannah (SAL)	LoA	9	6	3.45	25	19	0	2	125	109	57	48	8	51	111	.234
MINOR LEAGUE TOTALS			10	7	3.16	36	24	0	4	159	133	70	56	9	61	156	.225

15 JEURYS FAMILIA, RHP

BORN: Oct. 10, 1989. **B-T:** R-R. Ht.: 6-3. Wt.: 185. **SIGNED:** Dominican Republic, 2007. **SIGNED BY:** Ramon Pena/Ismael Cruz/Marcelino Vallejo.

Familia has had no problems making the transition to the United States. After leading the GCL Mets with a 2.79 ERA in his 2008 pro debut, he encored by winning the organization's minor league pitcher of the year award. He ranked third in the South Atlantic League in ERA (2.69) and fourth in wins (10) and opponent average (.221). Familia's primary asset is his arm strength, which allows him to deliver fastballs in the low 90s and top out at 95 mph. He has a strong frame and is heavier than his listed 185 pounds. Familia's future success depends on his ability to improve his secondary pitches and his mechanics. His slider is better than his changeup, and while both offerings have gotten better in the last year, they're still a long ways from being major league caliber. He lacks balance in his delivery, which restricts him from consistently following through and driving balls down in the strike zone. Nevertheless, he overmatched SAL hitters and the Mets look forward to seeing what he can do in high Class A this season.

Year	Club (League)	Class	W	L	ERA	G	GS	CG	SV	IP	H	R	ER	HR	BB	SO	AVG
2008	Mets (GCL)	R	2	2	2.79	11	11	0	0	52	46	20	16	2	13	38	.232
2009	Savannah (SAL)	LoA	10	6	2.69	24	23	0	0	134	109	49	40	3	46	109	.221
MINOR LEAGUE TOTALS			12	8	2.71	35	34	0	0	186	155	69	56	5	59	147	.224

16 ROBERT CARSON, LHP

BORN: Jan. 23, 1989. **B-T:** L-L. Ht.: 6-3. Wt.: 220. **DRAFTED:** HS—Hattiesburg, Miss., 2007 (14th round). **SIGNED BY:** Benny Latino.

Carson flew under the radar in his first two pro seasons, signing as an unheralded 14th-round pick in 2007 and missing most of that summer after a line drive hit him in the head. He finally reached full-season ball in 2009, joining Kyle Allen and Jeurys Familia in Savannah's talented rotation. Carson's main weapon is his fastball, which sits at 88-92 mph and reaches 95. He can make his heater cut or sink, and he allowed just four homers and posted a 1.7 groundout/airout ratio last season. He also throws a low-80s slider and a high-70s changeup, both of which remain works in progress but aren't as raw as Familia's. Though he has a strong build, Carson tired late in the year and posted a 6.68 ERA in his final eight starts. He's expected to open 2010 in high Class A.

Year	Club (League)	Class	W	L	ERA	G	GS	CG	SV	IP	H	R	ER	HR	BB	SO	AVG
2007	Mets (GCL)	R	1	0	5.00	4	1	0	0	9	8	7	5	1	5	9	.216
2008	Mets (GCL)	R	1	0	1.57	5	5	0	0	23	11	5	4	0	6	25	.143
	Kingsport (APP)	R	2	3	1.76	6	6	0	0	31	29	12	6	1	18	21	.274
2009	Savannah (SAL)	LoA	8	10	3.21	25	25	2	0	132	139	68	47	4	45	90	.270
MINOR LEAGUE TOTALS			12	13	2.87	40	37	2	0	194	187	92	62	6	74	145	.255

17 CESAR PUELLO, OF

BORN: April 1, 1991. **B-T:** R-R. Ht.: 6-2. Wt.: 195. **SIGNED:** Dominican Republic, 2007. **SIGNED BY:** Ramon Pena/Ismael Cruz/Marciano Alvarez.

Part of a Mets 2007 international class that also included Wilmer Flores, Jefry Marte and Jeurys Familia, Puello signed for $400,000 out of the Dominican Republic. He has the potential to have five average or better tools. His plus speed is his biggest asset at this point, and he has stolen 28 bases in 38 attempts over 89 pro games. Puello uses an unconventional batting stance that looks like he's sitting in a chair, but he has a line-drive stroke and some natural feel for hitting. While his plate discipline needs to improve, he has shown natural power to the opposite field. Puello is an average defender in right field, with a solid arm and a penchant for charging the ball. Some managers in the Rookie-level Appalachian League questioned his maturity this summer, but the Mets have no concerns. After two solid seasons in Rookie ball, he's ticketed for low Class A in 2010.

Year	Club (League)	Class	AVG	G	AB	R	H	2B	3B	HR	RBI	BB	SO	SB	OBP	SLG
2008	Mets (GCL)	R	.305	40	151	24	46	6	0	1	17	5	32	13	.350	.364
2009	Kingsport (APP)	R	.296	49	196	37	58	10	0	5	23	10	51	15	.373	.423
MINOR LEAGUE TOTALS			.300	89	347	61	104	16	0	6	40	15	83	28	.363	.398

18 SCOTT MOVIEL, RHP

BORN: May 7, 1988. **B-T:** R-R. Ht.: 6-11. Wt.: 235. **DRAFTED:** HS—Berea, Ohio, 2007 (2nd round). **SIGNED BY:** Erwin Bryant.

Moviel's 2009 season didn't start until late June. He had surgery in January after tearing the meniscus in his right knee during offseason conditioning drills. While nearing a May return, he popped some stitches and experienced inflammation in the knee and required a second procedure to clean it out. When he returned to the mound, Moviel continued to show that he has a high ceiling and a ways to go to reach it. A former Michigan basketball recruit who signed to play two sports at North Carolina State before the Mets drafted him, Moviel is still growing into his body but is a good athlete and is less awkward than many tall pitchers. He hit 94 mph with his fastball last summer and usually pitches in the low 90s, though his velocity was down at times. At the suggestion of St. Lucie pitching coach Phil Regan, Moviel added a slider that has become his best secondary pitch. His curveball and changeup still require a lot of work. He throws strikes and uses his height to throw on a tough downward plane. Moviel, whose brothers Greg and Paul also pitched professionally, should get his first shot at Double-A this season.

Year	Club (League)	Class	W	L	ERA	G	GS	CG	SV	IP	H	R	ER	HR	BB	SO	AVG
2007	Mets (GCL)	R	0	2	3.38	12	12	0	0	40	45	23	15	2	11	37	.281
2008	Savannah (SAL)	LoA	9	8	4.43	24	24	0	0	120	128	75	59	9	36	82	.271
	St. Lucie (FSL)	HiA	1	0	0.00	1	1	0	0	5	2	0	0	0	1	2	.133
2009	Mets (GCL)	R	0	0	1.00	2	2	0	0	9	10	2	1	0	0	10	.270
	St. Lucie (FSL)	HiA	4	5	3.92	13	13	0	0	64	61	37	28	1	24	46	.250
MINOR LEAGUE TOTALS			14	15	3.89	52	52	0	0	238	246	137	103	12	72	177	.265

19 ROBBIE SHIELDS, SS

BORN: Dec. 7, 1987. **B-T:** R-R. Ht.: 6-1. Wt.: 195. **DRAFTED:** Florida Southern, 2009 (3rd round). **SIGNED BY:** Tommy Jackson.

Shields had a history of performing well at Pasco High (Dade City, Fla.) and NCAA Division II Florida Southern, but he really opened eyes with his play in the Cape Cod League in the summer of 2008. He looked like a potential first-round pick before injuring his right wrist on a headfirst slide, but he let the draft affect his performance last spring. The Mets were able to grab Shields in the third round and sign him for $315,000. He had a disappointing pro debut, batting .178 with little power at Brooklyn. The Mets blamed a sore elbow, which required Tommy John surgery after the season. A baseball rat, Shields should put up solid batting averages and on-base percentages. He uses the whole field, and his strong hands should enable him to hit for some power once he does a better job of incorporating his lower half into his swing. He has average speed and good instincts, so he may steal a few bases. Shields will remain at shortstop for now, though he has just average range and arm strength. He may slide over to second base in the future. His surgery is not expected to keep him out for all of 2010, and when he returns to the diamond in mid-2010, he'll head to low Class A.

Year	Club (League)	Class	AVG	G	AB	R	H	2B	3B	HR	RBI	BB	SO	SB	OBP	SLG
2009	Brooklyn (NYP)	SS	.178	44	146	14	26	4	3	1	9	16	32	2	.273	.267
MINOR LEAGUE TOTALS			.178	44	146	14	26	4	3	1	9	16	32	2	.273	.267

20 ZACH DOTSON, LHP

BORN: Oct. 10, 1990. **B-T:** L-L. Ht.: 6-3. Wt.: 200. **DRAFTED:** HS—Springfield, Ga., 2009 (13th round). **SIGNED BY:** Marlin McPhail.

The Mets considered selecting Dotson with their third-round pick, but when they couldn't agree to terms before the draft, they passed. New York eventually selected him in the 13th round and signed him at the Aug. 17 deadline for $500,000—or $185,000 more than they gave third-rounder Robbie Shields. Dotson, the best high school pitcher in Georgia's 2010 recruiting class, used a distance-running program to drop 25 pounds before his senior season, but he saw his velocity dip as well. After working mostly in the high 80s during the spring, he improved his fastball to the low 90s during the summer, improving his stock with the Mets. His best secondary pitch is his slider, and he also throws a changeup. He's athletic and has a strong body, which bodes well for his durability. Dotson didn't pitch in a game after signing, and could make his pro debut at Rookie-level Kingsport next summer. When he reaches Savannah, he'll be pitching just 25 minutes from his Springfield, Ga., home.

Year	Club (League)	Class	W	L	ERA	G	GS	CG	SV	IP	H	R	ER	HR	BB	SO	AVG
2009	Did Not Play—Signed Late																

21 ZACH LUTZ, 3B/1B

BORN: June 3, 1986. **B-T:** R-R. Ht.: 6-1. Wt.: 220. **DRAFTED:** Alvernia (Pa.), 2007 (5th round). **SIGNED BY:** Scott Hunter.

Lutz's professional career literally got off on the wrong foot in the first inning of his first game. He rolled over his left foot while making a backhand play on a grounder, fracturing the navicular bone on the top of his foot. The injury left him on crutches for six months and has stalled his development. He didn't make it to a full-season team until 2009 and his speed and range have suffered. The NCAA Division III player of the year as a senior in 2007, Lutz's value lies solely in his bat. He has a compact swing and the ball sounds different coming off his bat. He has a chance to hit for average and at least gap power, and he controls the strike zone well. Lutz is a poor runner, doesn't move well laterally and fields balls too close to his body. His arm and overall ability at third base are just adequate, and he started to see action at first base last season. "He could be a role player," a scout said. "He reminded me of Ron Coomer, a stockier guy who can swing the bat, drive in runs, make the routine play." Lutz finished 2009 with eight games in Double-A and will return there this season, a pivotal year in determining whether his bat can propel him to at least a major league bench role.

NEW YORK METS

Year	Club (League)	Class	AVG	G	AB	R	H	2B	3B	HR	RBI	BB	SO	SB	OBP	SLG
2007	Brooklyn (NYP)	SS	.000	1	2	0	0	0	0	0	0	0	0	0	.000	.000
2008	Brooklyn (NYP)	SS	.333	24	72	9	24	4	0	3	12	14	12	0	.442	.514
2009	St. Lucie (FSL)	HiA	.284	99	356	46	101	19	2	11	62	50	72	1	.381	.441
	Binghamton (EL)	AA	.207	8	29	0	6	1	0	0	2	5	7	0	.324	.241
MINOR LEAGUE TOTALS			.285	132	459	55	131	24	2	14	76	69	91	1	.385	.438

22 SEAN RATLIFF, OF

BORN: Feb. 24, 1987. **B-T:** L-L. Ht.: 6-3. Wt.: 185. **DRAFTED:** Stanford, 2008 (4th round). **SIGNED BY:** Doug Thurman.

Ratliff was primarily a pitcher as a Stanford freshman before becoming a full-time outfielder in his final two seasons. As a junior in 2008, he tied for the Pacific-10 Conference lead with 22 homers, and his power is what led the Mets to draft him in the fourth round that June. He's strong and gets tremendous leverage from his 6-foot-3 frame, but it's uncertain that he'll make enough consistent contact to be an everyday player. He's too aggressive at the plate, trying to pull every pitch and rarely drawing walks. His bat doesn't stay in the strike zone for long, and he particularly struggles on pitches away from him. Ratliff is a good athlete with average speed. He was clocked up to 92 mph as a college pitcher, and his arm is accurate as well as strong. He saw most of his time in 2009 in center field, but he gets late jumps at times and fits better in right field. He'll be old for high Class A this year at age 23 and needs to start moving more quickly.

Year	Club (League)	Class	AVG	G	AB	R	H	2B	3B	HR	RBI	BB	SO	SB	OBP	SLG
2008	Brooklyn (NYP)	SS	.229	59	201	32	46	9	1	7	22	18	67	1	.300	.388
2009	Savannah (SAL)	LoA	.265	122	468	64	124	28	7	15	68	31	131	11	.312	.451
	St. Lucie (FSL)	HiA	.286	7	28	3	8	2	0	0	6	0	10	0	.286	.357
MINOR LEAGUE TOTALS			.255	188	697	99	178	39	8	22	96	49	208	12	.308	.429

23 DILLON GEE, RHP

BORN: April 28, 1986. **B-T:** R-R. Ht.: 6-1. Wt.: 200. **DRAFTED:** Texas-Arlington, 2007 (21st round). **SIGNED BY:** Ray Corbett.

Mets manager Jerry Manuel praised Gee during spring training for his impeccable control. He was just hitting his stride in his first taste of Triple-A when he went down with a slight labrum tear, which ended his season on May 25. He addressed his shoulder problems with rehab rather than surgery, and he was throwing off a mound by the end of September. The Mets suspect that overwork led to Gee's shoulder problems. He pitched 154 innings during the 2008 season, then 49 more in the Puerto Rican winter league, where he was named pitcher of the year. Before the injury, Gee had fringe-average stuff. His solid changeup is his best pitch, and he throws an 88-90 mph fastball that tops out at 92. He also mixes in a cutter, slider and a slow curveball. Gee has little margin for error, so he's liable to get hit hard when he can't locate his pitches. He'll return to Triple-A in 2010.

Year	Club (League)	Class	W	L	ERA	G	GS	CG	SV	IP	H	R	ER	HR	BB	SO	AVG
2007	Brooklyn (NYP)	SS	3	1	2.47	14	11	0	0	62	57	17	17	1	9	56	.249
2008	St. Lucie (FSL)	HiA	8	6	3.25	21	21	0	0	127	117	49	46	6	19	94	.245
	Binghamton (EL)	AA	2	0	1.33	4	4	0	0	27	18	4	4	1	5	20	.194
2009	Buffalo (IL)	AAA	1	3	4.10	9	9	1	0	48	47	22	22	5	16	42	.253
MINOR LEAGUE TOTALS			14	10	3.03	48	45	1	0	265	239	92	89	13	49	212	.243

24 ERIC NIESEN, LHP

BORN: Sept. 4, 1985. **B-T:** L-L. Ht.: 6-0. Wt.: 192. **DRAFTED:** Wake Forest, 2007 (3rd round). **SIGNED BY:** Marlin McPhail.

Overshadowed by Jenrry Mejia and Brad Holt at St. Lucie and Binghamton in 2009, Niesen made significant improvements after reaching Double-A. When he first got to Binghamton, he overthrew too much and struggled working out of the stretch with runners on base. But he toned down his mechanics and grew more comfortable, which showed as he went 3-1, 2.40 in his last seven starts. He led the organization with 134 strikeouts. Niesen is a live-armed lefthander with an 88-92 mph fastball that peaks at 94 and has good arm-side run. He uses his 76-78 mph curveball as a strikeout pitch against lefties, and late last season he began jamming righties with it. His 81-82 mph changeup is inconsistent, but he's starting to get better separation from his fastball. Despite his progress, Niesen projects as a reliever. There's still a lot of effort in his delivery, with some stabbing action in his backswing. He'll overthrow and spin off his pitches, which leads to too many walks. He figures to return to Double-A to open 2010.

Year	Club (League)	Class	W	L	ERA	G	GS	CG	SV	IP	H	R	ER	HR	BB	SO	AVG
2007	Brooklyn (NYP)	SS	0	3	3.30	9	9	0	0	30	30	19	11	1	25	27	.268
	St. Lucie (FSL)	HiA	0	0	0.00	1	1	0	0	3	3	0	0	0	1	3	.273
2008	St. Lucie (FSL)	HiA	6	12	4.64	26	24	0	0	118	136	75	61	10	46	77	.286
2009	St. Lucie (FSL)	HiA	3	4	3.28	11	11	0	0	58	52	25	21	5	16	49	.237
	Binghamton (EL)	AA	4	7	4.66	16	16	1	0	83	75	46	43	6	41	85	.246
MINOR LEAGUE TOTALS			13	26	4.19	63	61	1	0	292	296	165	136	22	129	241	.264

25 EDDIE KUNZ, RHP

BORN: April 8, 1986. **B-T:** R-R. Ht.: 6-6. Wt.: 265. **DRAFTED:** Oregon State, 2007 (1st round supplemental). **SIGNED BY:** Jim Reeves.

A former Oregon State closer who was part of two College World Series championships, Kunz was the Mets' top draft pick (42nd overall) and signed for $720,000 in 2007. New York rushed him to the big leagues in August 2008, but he floundered in four appearances and has struggled in Triple-A ever since. He has been snubbed for September callups each of the past two seasons as his stock has plummeted in team officials' eyes. Kunz battles his command, leaves too many pitches over the plate appears overly concerned by radar gun readings. After working at 94-95 mph and touching 97 in the second half of 2008, he mostly settled in at 91-93 last season. His fastball also lost some sink, and he gave up eight homers in 61 innings at Buffalo after surrendering just two longballs in 69 previous frames. His slider, once a mid-80s pitch with good bite, has regressed into more of a slurve. He flies open too quickly in his low three-quarters delivery, making it difficult to stay on top of his pitches. In addition to improving his mechanics and consistency, Kunz also needs to address his conditioning. He'll return to Triple-A to try to pitch his way back into the Mets' plans.

Year	Club (League)	Class	W	L	ERA	G	GS	CG	SV	IP	H	R	ER	HR	BB	SO	AVG
2007	Brooklyn (NYP)	SS	0	1	6.75	12	0	0	5	12	8	9	9	0	8	9	.190
2008	Binghamton (EL)	AA	1	4	2.79	44	0	0	27	48	39	19	15	0	25	43	.222
	New York (NL)	MAJ	0	0	13.50	4	0	0	0	3	5	4	4	1	1	1	.455
	New Orleans (PCL)	AAA	0	1	7.94	6	0	0	0	6	9	5	5	1	2	4	.346
2009	Buffalo (IL)	AAA	4	5	5.02	40	0	0	1	61	54	35	34	8	31	38	.241
MAJOR LEAGUE TOTALS			0	0	13.50	4	0	0	0	3	5	4	4	1	1	1	.455
MINOR LEAGUE TOTALS			5	11	4.46	102	0	0	33	127	110	68	63	9	66	94	.235

26 JOSH STINSON, RHP

BORN: March 14, 1988. **B-T:** R-R. Ht.: 6-4. Wt.: 210. **DRAFTED:** HS—Shreveport, La., 2006 (37th round). **SIGNED BY:** Benny Latino.

The Mets jumped Stinson to low Class A shortly after signing him for $125,000 as a 37th-round pick in 2006. After he struggled as a starter in his first full season, New York gave him some time in the bullpen in 2008 and made him a full-time reliever last year. He prefers working out of the bullpen because he can air out his fastball without worrying about pacing himself. He gets groundballs with his 89-92 mph two seamer and reaches 96 with his four-seamer. Stinson's best secondary pitch is a hard curveball, and he also throws a slider and changeup. He's still seeking more consistency with his mechanics and battles his command at times. Though he posted a 1.98 ERA at St. Lucie in the final two months of the season, he walked 19 in 36 innings. Stinson, who started each of the last three seasons at Savannah, will open 2010 in Double-A after getting extra work in the Arizona Fall League during the offseason.

Year	Club (League)	Class	W	L	ERA	G	GS	CG	SV	IP	H	R	ER	HR	BB	SO	AVG
2006	Mets (GCL)	R	1	2	2.00	9	4	0	0	27	27	10	6	0	5	14	.273
	Hagerstown (SAL)	LoA	0	1	1.35	3	3	0	0	13	11	2	2	0	4	5	.239
2007	Savannah (SAL)	LoA	3	11	4.86	26	21	0	0	109	131	77	59	13	33	52	.294
2008	Savannah (SAL)	LoA	3	6	3.52	21	6	0	3	72	78	36	28	7	32	46	.280
	St. Lucie (FSL)	HiA	0	2	6.14	7	2	0	0	15	17	12	10	0	5	14	.293
2009	Savannah (SAL)	LoA	3	2	3.61	25	1	0	2	42	45	17	17	1	10	49	.287
	St. Lucie (FSL)	HiA	3	1	1.98	25	0	0	6	36	22	12	8	0	19	35	.168
MINOR LEAGUE TOTALS			12	25	3.72	116	37	0	11	315	331	166	130	21	108	215	.272

27 ERIC BEAULAC, RHP

BORN: Nov. 13, 1986. **B-T:** R-R. Ht.: 6-5. Wt.: 190. **DRAFTED:** LeMoyne, 2008 (9th round). **SIGNED BY:** Scott Hunter.

Beaulac grew up in Troy, N.Y., rooting for the Mets. He ranked as the No. 1 prospect in the New York Collegiate League after his sophomore season and set a LeMoyne record with 113 strikeouts as a junior in 2008, after which New York drafted him in the ninth round. He advanced quickly to low Class A in his pro debut and pitcher there last season, ranking fifth in the South Atlantic League in strikeouts per nine innings (10.3). The questions with Beaulac are how much of his success is the result of his deceptive mechanics, and how well his stuff will play at higher levels. He throws excessively across his body, which could lead to injuries down the road. Low Class A hitters were unaccustomed to his delivery, but advanced hitters won't be as flummoxed by a fastball that flashes at 91-92 mph in the early innings before dropping into the low 90s. He backs up his fastball with a slider, also throws a curveball and is working to develop a changeup. Relying on two pitches and featuring a delivery that leads to durability question means that Beaulac profiles better as a reliever, and he was outstanding in a brief stint in that role last season. He'll open 2010 in high Class A.

Year	Club (League)	Class	W	L	ERA	G	GS	CG	SV	IP	H	R	ER	HR	BB	SO	AVG
2008	Brooklyn (NYP)	SS	0	0	9.82	2	0	0	0	4	1	4	4	0	2	6	.091
	Kingsport (APP)	R	1	0	1.89	6	2	0	1	19	15	5	4	1	6	23	.214
	Savannah (SAL)	LoA	1	2	3.55	6	6	0	0	25	22	13	10	1	18	31	.239
2009	Savannah (SAL)	LoA	7	7	2.95	26	19	0	2	116	110	53	38	6	41	133	.250
MINOR LEAGUE TOTALS			9	9	3.07	40	27	0	3	164	148	75	56	8	67	193	.241

28 BRANT RUSTICH, RHP

BORN: Jan. 23, 1985. **B-T:** R-R. Ht.: 6-6. Wt.: 230. **DRAFTED:** UCLA, 2007 (2nd round). **SIGNED BY:** Steve Leavitt.

The Mets invested $373,500 in Rustich, their second-round pick, even after a tough redshirt junior year at UCLA in which he lost his job as closer. Prior to that 2007 season, he had surgery to repair a ruptured tendon in the middle finger of his pitching hand. Two and a half pro seasons later, Rustich hasn't been able to shake the injury bug. He continued to succeed on the mound in 2009, but he also continued to be undermined by a stress fracture in his humerus bone. Pitching with pain, he has a 2.77 career ERA in three pro seasons but has been limited to just 120 innings. He was sidelined twice last summer before being shut down in late August. The Mets hope that new medication will allow the bone to finally heal. Even with his physical problems, Rustich showed two power pitches in his 91-97 mph fastball and a slider that's his signature pitch. Though his delivery can get a little mechanical, he has good fastball command. He has dabbled as a starter in the last two seasons, but Rustich's future is as a set-up man. If he can put his health issues behind him, he'll begin 2010 in Double-A.

Year	Club (League)	Class	W	L	ERA	G	GS	CG	SV	IP	H	R	ER	HR	BB	SO	AVG
2007	Kingsport (APP)	R	1	0	0.87	5	2	0	0	10	6	1	1	0	1	10	.158
	Brooklyn (NYP)	SS	2	0	2.13	10	0	0	2	13	4	3	3	2	1	11	.095
2008	Savannah (SAL)	LoA	3	4	3.62	20	8	0	0	50	42	26	20	1	16	48	.231
2009	St. Lucie (FSL)	HiA	1	1	2.45	19	3	0	2	48	44	20	13	0	17	46	.240
MINOR LEAGUE TOTALS			7	5	2.77	54	13	0	4	120	96	50	37	3	35	115	.216

29 TOBI STONER, RHP

BORN: Dec. 3, 1984. **B-T:** R-R. Ht.: 6-2. Wt.: 190. **DRAFTED:** Davis & Elkins (W.Va.), 2006 (16th round). **SIGNED BY:** Matt Wondolowski.

Stoner became the 29th German-born player to reach the majors, and the first since Mickey Scott in 1972, when the Mets called him up in September. He was born in Landstuhl, near the Air Force base where his father Neil served as an intelligence officer. The Mets discovered him by accident, as he struck out 15 in a college game that area scout Matt Wondolowski attended to check out his opponent. Stoner spent his entire minor league career as a starter but pitched for the Mets as a reliever, and he fits better in that role. His fastball sits at 88-90 mph when he works out of the rotation, and plays up to 91-92 when he comes out of the bullpen. His average changeup is his best secondary pitch, while his curveball and slider are both fringy. New York will give Stoner a look in spring training, but he likely will get some more Triple-A seasoning at the start of the season.

Year	Club (League)	Class	W	L	ERA	G	GS	CG	SV	IP	H	R	ER	HR	BB	SO	AVG
2006	Brooklyn (NYP)	SS	6	2	2.15	14	14	1	0	84	66	25	20	1	17	62	.219
2007	Savannah (SAL)	LoA	3	5	3.61	11	11	0	0	57	59	32	23	1	17	50	.259
	St. Lucie (FSL)	HiA	4	5	4.90	16	16	0	0	83	90	57	45	9	25	57	.280
2008	St. Lucie (FSL)	HiA	1	5	2.60	9	9	0	0	52	46	17	15	3	9	48	.238
	Binghamton (EL)	AA	4	6	4.33	15	15	0	0	79	80	39	38	7	29	59	.267
2009	Binghamton (EL)	AA	2	2	2.68	7	7	1	0	47	28	15	14	5	13	28	.170
	Buffalo (IL)	AAA	7	7	3.96	16	16	1	0	98	92	45	43	9	34	64	.249
	New York (NL)	MAJ	0	0	4.00	4	0	0	0	9	9	4	4	2	3	5	.281
MAJOR LEAGUE TOTALS			0	0	4.00	4	0	0	0	9	9	4	4	2	3	5	.281
MINOR LEAGUE TOTALS			27	32	3.57	88	88	3	0	499	461	230	198	35	144	368	.245

30 JORDANY VALDESPIN, 2B/SS

BORN: Dec. 23, 1987. **B-T:** L-R. Ht.: 6-0. Wt.: 174. **SIGNED:** Dominican Republic, 2007. **SIGNED BY:** Ramon Pena/Ismael Cruz/Marciano Alvarez.

Valdespin hit .385/.406/.615 in the first three weeks of the 2009 season, but he had numerous clashes with Savannah's coaching staff. In late April, the Mets sent him to extended spring for two weeks to get his act together. He immediately went 0-for-25 after rejoining the Sand Gnats, and his average plummeted to .280 by late May. Valdespin was just heating up again, going on a 14-for-27 tear, when he badly sprained his ankle on June 2. He missed two months before spending August with the Rookie-level Dominican Summer League Mets, the GCL Mets and Brooklyn. Though Valdespin has a lot of movement at the plate and an aggressive approach, he has a quick bat and makes consistent hard contact. He has the potential to hit for average with a bit of gap power. He has average to slightly above-average speed and some basestealing ability. Though he saw some time at shortstop in 2009, his average arm and range fit better at second base. Valdespin has a lot to prove this season. He was old for low Class A at age 21 last season, and his history of insubordination doesn't help his cause.

Year	Club (League)	Class	AVG	G	AB	R	H	2B	3B	HR	RBI	BB	SO	SB	OBP	SLG
2007	Mets (DSL)	R	.245	43	139	23	34	4	3	1	16	24	26	8	.369	.338
2008	Mets (GCL)	R	.284	34	134	23	38	6	3	3	22	7	10	9	.319	.440
2009	Savannah (SAL)	LoA	.322	39	152	30	49	9	3	3	18	11	32	7	.366	.480
	Mets (DSL)	R	.333	4	15	0	5	0	2	0	5	3	1	1	.421	.600
	Mets (GCL)	R	.174	6	23	0	4	0	0	0	0	1	3	1	.208	.174
	Brooklyn (NYP)	SS	.279	18	68	10	19	3	1	1	5	5	16	4	.338	.397
MINOR LEAGUE TOTALS			.281	144	531	86	149	22	12	8	66	51	88	30	.347	.412

New York Yankees

BY JOHN MANUEL

MORRIS FOSTOFF

David Robertson led a group of homegrown players who contributed in the bullpen

Every Yankees team is measured against the amazing, rich history of the franchise, the most championship-laden in American team sports. The standard for success is clear. Anything less than a World Series title is a failure.

For the first time since 2000, New York had a season it could consider a success, beating the Phillies in six games for their 27th World Series championship. The Yankees started the year under the cloud of Alex Rodriguez's admitted steroid use, but he and the team put that behind them. The club got off to a 13-15 start before Rodriguez returned from hip surgery on

May 8, then won at a .672 clip for the remainder of the regular season before going 11-4 in the playoffs.

Investing $423.5 million in free agents Mark Teixeira, C.C. Sabathia and A.J. Burnett paid huge dividends, while Derek Jeter had one of the best seasons of his storied career. Despite playing in just 124 games, Rodriguez reached 30 homers and 100 RBIs for the 12th-straight season. Better yet, he erased memories of previous playoff failures by batting .365 with six homers in the postseason, earning his first championship ring.

While the Yankees continued to wield their financial muscle when putting together their big league club, they also got contributions from young homegrown players as well. Brett Gardner shared time in center field and provided a jolt with his speed. Joba Chamberlain failed to convince anyone that he's better suited as a starter than as a reliever, yet he still held down the fourth slot in the rotation. Phil Hughes shined as a setup man, and rookies Alfredo Aceves, Phil Coke and David Robertson helped further shore up the bullpen.

Senior vice president of baseball operations Mark Newman, who has overseen scouting and player development in the organization for the better part of the last 13 years, says the Yankees aspire to more.

"We're not in this to develop relievers, but starters, starting pitchers and impact hitters," he says. To that end, both Chamberlain and Hughes are likely to be given another shot at the rotation in 2010.

As for impact bats, New York points to Jesus Montero, the Venezuelan catcher they signed for a $1.65 million bonus in 2006. Montero took a significant leap forward last season, dominating Double-A pitching at age 19. The Yankees had similar hopes for outfielder Austin Jackson, who ranked No. 1 on this list a year ago. But after he hit .300 with just four homers in Triple-A, they included him, as well as Coke and

TOP 30 PROSPECTS

1. Jesus Montero, c	16. Ivan Nova, rhp
2. Austin Romine, c	17. D.J. Mitchell, rhp
3. Arodys Vizcaino, rhp	18. Melky Mesa, of
4. Slade Heathcott, of	19. Kelvin DeLeon, of
5. Zach McAllister, rhp	20. Jose Ramirez, rhp
6. Manny Banuelos, lhp	21. Graham Stoneburner, rhp
7. Gary Sanchez, c	22. David Adams, 2b/3b
8. J.R. Murphy, c	23. Caleb Cotham, rhp
9. Jeremy Bleich, lhp	24. Hector Noesi, rhp
10. Andrew Brackman, rhp	25. David Phelps, rhp
11. Bryan Mitchell, rhp	26. Adam Warren, rhp
12. Mike Dunn, lhp	27. Kevin Russo, 2b/3b
13. Corban Joseph, 2b/3b	28. Dellin Betances, rhp
14. Eduardo Nunez, ss	29. Jairo Heredia, rhp
15. Mark Melancon, rhp	30. Jamie Hoffmann, of

2006 first-rounder Ian Kennedy, in a three-team trade that netted Curtis Granderson from the Tigers.

Several of the system's top pitching prospects had down years, with 2007 first-rounder Andrew Brackman having a truly awful season, and Dellin Betances, among others, succumbing to injuries. But Newman said that on the whole, the Yankees' pitching injuries were down, and those setbacks were offset by the emergence of arms such as Arodys Vizcaino and Manny Banuelos, plus aggressive spending in the draft and internationally that landed prospects such as outfielder Slade Heathcott and catchers Gary Sanchez and J.R. Murphy.

General Manager: Brian Cashman. **Farm Director:** Pat Roessler. **Scouting Director:** Damon Oppenheimer.

Class	Team	League	W	L	PCT	Finish*	Manager(s)
Majors	New York Yankees	American	103	59	.636	†1st (14)	Joe Girardi
Triple-A	Scranton/Wilkes-Barre Yankees	International	81	60	.574	3rd (14)	Dave Miley
Double-A	Trenton Thunder	Eastern	69	72	.489	8th (12)	Tony Franklin
High A	Tampa Yankees	Florida State	77	56	.579	†3rd (12)	Luis Sojo
Low A	Charleston RiverDogs	South Atlantic	74	65	.532	4th (16)	Torre Tyson
Short-season	Staten Island Yankees	New York-Penn	47	29	.618	†2nd (14)	Josh Paul
Rookie	GCL Yankees	Gulf Coast	33	27	.550	4th (16)	Jody Reed
Overall 2009 Minor League Record			381	309	.552	2nd (30)	

*Finish in overall standings (No. of teams in league). †League champion.

LAST YEAR'S TOP 30

Player, Pos.		Status
1.	Austin Jackson, of	(Tigers)
2.	Jesus Montero, c	No. 1
3.	Andrew Brackman, rhp	No. 10
4.	Austin Romine, c	No. 2
5.	Dellin Betances, rhp	No. 28
6.	Zach McAllister, rhp	No. 5
7.	Alfredo Aceves, rhp	Majors
8.	Phil Coke, lhp	(Tigers)
9.	Mark Melancon, rhp	No. 15
10.	Bradley Suttle, 3b	Dropped out
11.	Jeremy Bleich, lhp	No. 9
12.	Jairo Heredia, rhp	No. 29
13.	Brett Gardner, of	Majors
14.	Manny Banuelos, lhp	No. 6
15.	David Robertson, rhp	Majors
16.	Mike Dunn, lhp	No. 12
17.	Christian Garcia, rhp	Dropped out
18.	Arodys Vizcaino, rhp	No. 3
19.	Wilkins de la Rosa, lhp	Dropped out
20.	Juan Miranda, 1b	Dropped out
21.	Francisco Cervelli, c	Dropped out
22.	Brett Marshall, rhp	Dropped out
23.	George Kontos, rhp	Dropped out
24.	D.J. Mitchell, rhp	No. 17
25.	Alan Horne, rhp	Dropped out
26.	Anthony Claggett, rhp	(Pirates)
27.	Kelvin DeLeon, of	No. 19
28.	Carmen Angelini, ss	Dropped out
29.	Steven Jackson, rhp	(Pirates)
30.	Abraham Almonte, of	Dropped out

BEST TOOLS

Best Hitter for Average	Jesus Montero
Best Power Hitter	Jesus Montero
Best Strike-Zone Discipline	Reegie Corona
Fastest Baserunner	Melky Mesa
Best Athlete	Melky Mesa
Best Fastball	Andrew Brackman
Best Curveball	Arodys Vizcaino
Best Slider	Mike Dunn
Best Changeup	Manny Banuelos
Best Control	Zach McAllister
Best Defensive Catcher	Francisco Cervelli
Best Defensive Infielder	Ramiro Pena
Best Infield Arm	Eduardo Nunez
Best Defensive Outfielder	Jamie Hoffmann
Best Outfield Arm	Melky Mesa

PROJECTED 2013 LINEUP

Catcher	Austin Romine
First Base	Mark Teixeira
Second Base	Robinson Cano
Third Base	Alex Rodriguez
Shortstop	Derek Jeter
Left Field	Curtis Granderson
Center Field	Brett Gardner
Right Field	Slade Heathcott
Designated Hitter	Jesus Montero
No. 1 Starter	C.C. Sabathia
No. 2 Starter	Phil Hughes
No. 3 Starter	A.J. Burnett
No. 4 Starter	Arodys Vizcaino
No. 5 Starter	Zach McAllister
Closer	Joba Chamberlain

TOP PROSPECTS OF THE DECADE

Year	Player, Pos.	2009 Org.
2000	Nick Johnson, 1b	Marlins
2001	Nick Johnson, 1b	Marlins
2002	Drew Henson, 3b	Out of baseball
2003	Jose Contreras, rhp	Rockies
2004	Dioner Navarro, c	Rays
2005	Eric Duncan, 3b	Yankees
2006	Phil Hughes, rhp	Yankees
2007	Phil Hughes, rhp	Yankees
2008	Joba Chamberlain, rhp	Yankees
2009	Austin Jackson, of	Yankees

TOP DRAFT PICKS OF THE DECADE

Year	Player, Pos.	2009 Org.
2000	David Parrish, c	Out of baseball
2001	John-Ford Griffin, of	Cubs
2002	Brandon Weeden, rhp (2nd round)	Out of baseball
2003	Eric Duncan, 3b	Yankees
2004	Phil Hughes, rhp	Yankees
2005	C.J. Henry, ss	Out of baseball
2006	Ian Kennedy, rhp	Yankees
2007	Andrew Brackman, rhp	Yankees
2008	*Gerrit Cole, rhp	UCLA
2009	Slade Heathcott, of	Yankees

*Did not sign.

LARGEST BONUSES IN CLUB HISTORY

Hideki Irabu, 1997	$8,500,000
Jose Contreras, 2002	$6,000,000
Andrew Brackman, 2007	$3,350,000
Gary Sanchez, 2009	$3,000,000
Willy Mo Pena, 1999	$2,440,000

NEW YORK YANKEES

TOP 2010 ROOKIE: Mike Dunn, lhp. The former outfielder should replace Phil Coke in the bullpen.

BREAKOUT PROSPECT: Graham Stoneburner, rhp. His injury history is scary, but his fastball and slider are plus pitches.

SLEEPER: Jimmy Paredes, ss. A speedster, he could enhance his stock if his improving arm allows him to move to shortstop.

SOURCE OF TOP 30 TALENT

Homegrown	29	Acquired	1
College	10	Trades	0
Junior college	0	Rule 5 draft	1
High school	7	Independent leagues	0
Draft-and-follow	1	Free agents/waivers	0
Nondrafted free agents	0		
International	11		

Numbers in parentheses indicate prospect rankings.

LF
Colin Curtis
Shelley Duncan
DeAngelo Mack

CF
Slade Heathcott (4)
Abraham Almonte
Eduardo Sosa

RF
Melky Mesa (18)
Kelvin DeLeon (19)
Jamie Hoffmann (30)
Dan Brewer
Neil Medchill

3B
David Adams (22)
Bradley Suttle

SS
Eduardo Nunez (14)
Ramiro Pena
Jose Pirela

2B
Corban Joseph (13)
Kevin Russo (27)
Reegie Corona
Jimmy Paredes
Damon Sublett

1B
Juan Miranda
Brandon Laird
Rob Lyerly

C
Jesus Montero (1)
Austin Romine (2)
Gary Sanchez (7)
J.R. Murphy (8)
Francisco Cervelli
Kyle Higashioka

RHP

Starters	Relievers
Arodys Vizcaino (3)	Mark Melancon (15)
Zach McAllister (5)	Graham Stoneburner (21)
Andrew Brackman (10)	Romulo Sanchez
Bryan Mitchell (11)	Kevin Whelan
Ivan Nova (16)	Jonathan Hovis
D.J. Mitchell (17)	Grant Duff
Juan Ramirez (20)	Manny Barreda
Caleb Cotham (23)	
Hector Noesi (24)	
David Phelps (25)	
Adam Warren (26)	
Dellin Betances (28)	
Jairo Heredia (29)	
George Kontos	
Brett Marshall	
Chris Garcia	
Lance Pendleton	
Brett Gerritse	
Sean Black	
Shane Greene	

LHP

Starters	Relievers
Manny Banuelos (6)	Mike Dunn (12)
Jeremy Bleich (9)	Wilkins de la Rosa
Evan DeLuca	Gavin Brooks
	Sam Elam

RHP/LHP
Pat Venditte

DRAFT ANALYSIS

2009   BONUSES: $7.6 MILLION

BEST PURE HITTER: The Yankees drafted C J.R. Murphy (2) for his quick bat and feel for hitting, which helped him bat .627 as a high school senior. He has enough bat and athletic ability to move to another position, but New York is confident he can remain behind the plate.

BEST POWER HITTER: OF Slade Heathcott (1) has all five tools, and his premium bat speed gives him plus raw power. OF Neil Medchill (11) has more present power and led the short-season New York-Penn League with 14 homers.

FASTEST RUNNER: Heathcott has well above-average speed and has been timed at 4.0 seconds home to first from the left side.

BEST DEFENSIVE PLAYER: Heathcott had a shoulder injury in the spring but still has a plus arm and the speed to play center field.

BEST FASTBALL: RHP Adam Warren (4) added velocity as a college senior, hitting 94 mph, then touched 96 in pro ball. His ability to throw quality strikes with his fastball gives him the edge over RHP Graham Stoneburner (14), who has touched 97 and throws consistently in the mid-90s.

BEST SECONDARY PITCH: RHP Bryan Mitchell (16), who signed for $800,000, has a power curveball that scrapes the low 80s. He throws his 88-92 fastball downhill and soon could have two plus pitches.

BEST PRO DEBUT: Warren helped Staten Island to the NY-P championship, with two dominant playoff starts after a 4-2, 1.43 regular season. LHP Gavin Brooks (9) shined in a relief role, going 5-1, 0.62 with 48 strikeouts in 43 innings. Medchill led the league in homers and slugging (.551), while OF DeAngelo Mack (13) ranked second with 30 extra-base hits during .306/.372/.513 campaign.

BEST ATHLETE: Heathcott's injuries and makeup questions kept him on the board long enough for him to get to the Yankees at No. 29 overall. His hitting and athletic ability certainly would have dictated a higher draft slot otherwise.

MOST INTRIGUING BACKGROUND: OF Justin Milo (37) signed and played this summer, then returned to Vermont to continue his college hockey career. He scored 12 goals and had 14 assists for the Catamounts last winter. His 5-foot-8, 175-pound frame works better in hockey than baseball. 1B Luke Murton's (19) brother Matt played for the Rockies in 2009.

CLOSEST TO THE MAJORS: RHP Caleb Cotham (5) could be a power sinker/slider guy if he's healthy after knee surgery. He has a low-90s sinker and touches 87 mph with his slider.

BEST LATE-ROUND PICK: Mitchell has good present stuff and more projection remaining.

THE ONE WHO GOT AWAY: New York reached its budget and couldn't sign LHP Tyler Lyons (10), who should be a fine senior sign after returning to Oklahoma State.

ASSESSMENT: Heathcott is the toolsiest player the Yankees have drafted in years, at least since C.J. Henry and Austin Jackson in 2005. A generous budget bought plenty of insurance if he doesn't pan out, and Mitchell could wind up as this crop's best pitcher.

2008   BONUSES: $5.1 MILLION

This draft took a huge hit when the Yankees failed to sign RHPs Gerrit Cole (1), the possible No. 1 overall pick for 2011, and Scott Bittle (2). The best player they nabbed, LHP Jeremy Bleich (1s), reached Double-A in his first full season.

GRADE: C

2007   BONUSES: $8.0 MILLION

RHP Andrew Brackman (1) is healthy but he's still not living up to a big league contract worth a potential $13 million. C Austin Romine (2), the MVP of the high Class A Florida State League in 2009, could be Jorge Posada's successor.

GRADE: C

2006   BONUSES: $6.7 MILLION

Even after an up-and-down season, RHP Joba Chamberlain (1s) still qualifies as a steal. RHP David Robertson (17) is a key part of the big league bullpen and could be joined by RHP Mark Melancon (9) in 2010. More RHPs: Zach McAllister (5) is one of the system's best prospects, while Ian Kennedy (1) and Daniel McCutchen (13) helped land Curtis Granderson, Damaso Marte and Xavier Nady in trades.

GRADE: A

2005   BONUSES: $3.7 MILLION*

New York invested heavily in two basketball stars: SS C.J. Henry (1), who's now playing hoops at Kansas, and OF Austin Jackson (8), the key to the Granderson trade. OF Brett Gardner (3) was a key reserve on last season's World Series champions.

GRADE: C+

*Draft analysis by John Manuel (2009) and Jim Callis (2005-08). Numbers in parentheses indicate draft rounds. *Bonuses for 2005 are first 10 rounds only.*

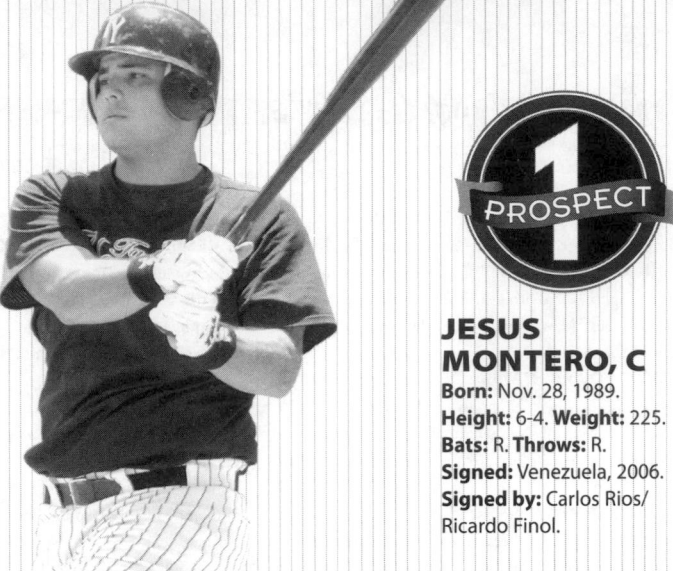

PROSPECT 1

JESUS MONTERO, C

Born: Nov. 28, 1989.
Height: 6-4. **Weight:** 225.
Bats: R. **Throws:** R.
Signed: Venezuela, 2006.
Signed by: Carlos Rios/
Ricardo Finol.

Montero ranked with corner infielders Balbino Fuenmayor and Angel Villalona, shortstops Esmailyn Gonzalez and Carlos Triunfel and catcher Francisco Pena as the top talents available on the international market in 2006. All signed big-money deals, and three years later, Montero is far and away the best prospect of the group. He got off to the roughest start. He initially signed for $2 million, but his bonus was renegotiated down to $1.65 million for reasons that never have been fully disclosed. He was overmatched in his first instructional league but has punished pitchers ever since. Montero broke out by finishing second in the low Class A South Atlantic League batting race at .326 in 2008 and was even better last season. He hit .337/.389/.562 and reached Double-A Trenton at age 19. A fractured left middle finger cost him the last six weeks of the season, and his rust showed with a poor start to winter ball in Venezuela.

Montero doesn't have a classic swing or textbook rhythm, but he's gifted with hand-eye coordination, keen pitch recognition, a knack for barreling balls and tremendous strength. He can be out front or off balance on a pitch and still crush it. He covers the plate well and makes excellent contact. Montero hasn't delivered completely on his raw power, but he's close to projecting as an 80 hitter with 80 power on the 20-80 scouting scale. One veteran scout called him the best young hitter he has seen in years. Montero has solid to plus arm strength and threw out 32 percent of basestealers in Double-A, success the Yankees ascribe to his improved transfer and pitchers doing a better job holding runners. He even showed some 1.9-second pop times, according to one club official.

Montero has improved under the tutelage of catching coordinator Julio Mosquera, but he still grades out as a below-average defender. The Yankees no longer talk about him as an everyday major league catcher. His defense frequently is compared to Mike Piazza's, though he's a bit more athletic. Montero is somewhat stiff and lacks agility behind the plate, leading to 11 passed balls in 59 games last year. He also threw out just 13 percent of basestealers at high Class A Tampa, and they tested him 108 times overall—nearly two attempts per game. While he improved, he has a long arm stroke that slows his transfer and detracts from his arm strength. His modest athleticism and below-average speed probably preclude a move to the outfield or third base, a position he played prior to signing.

In a different organization, Montero probably would just move to first base and mash, like Paul Konerko did when he came up through the Dodgers system in the mid-1990s. However, Mark Teixeira just finished the first year of an eight-year contract and isn't going anywhere. With an older roster, the Yankees aren't likely to break Montero into the lineup as strictly a DH. He's expected to catch at Triple-A Scranton/Wilkes-Barre in 2010, mixing in time at DH and perhaps first base. He's prime trade bait but also could be a complement to New York's veteran sluggers in short order—if the Yankees can find a lineup spot for him.

Year	Club (League)	Class	AVG	G	AB	R	H	2B	3B	HR	RBI	BB	SO	SB	OBP	SLG
2007	Yankees (GCL)	R	.280	33	107	13	30	6	0	3	19	12	18	0	.366	.421
2008	Charleston, SC (SAL)	LoA	.326	132	525	86	171	34	1	17	87	37	83	2	.376	.491
2009	Tampa (FSL)	HiA	.356	48	180	26	64	15	1	8	37	14	26	0	.406	.583
	Trenton (EL)	AA	.317	44	167	19	53	10	0	9	33	14	21	0	.370	.539
MINOR LEAGUE TOTALS			.325	257	979	144	318	65	2	37	176	77	148	2	.379	.509

2 AUSTIN ROMINE, C

BORN: Nov. 22, 1988. **B-T:** R-R. **HT.:** 6-2. **WT.:** 210. **DRAFTED:** HS—Lake Forest, Calif., 2007 (2nd round). **SIGNED BY:** David Keith.

Romine's brother Andrew is an Angels shortstop prospect, while his father Kevin played seven seasons in the major leagues. Austin had his best pro season in 2009, winning MVP honors in the high Class A Florida State League and helping lead Tampa to the league title. A minor thumb injury forced him to leave the Arizona Fall League after just four games. Romine has the tools to be an average or plus defender behind the plate, especially with his above-average arm. He threw out 30 percent of basestealers even though the Yankees don't emphasize holding runners for their Class A pitchers. His best offensive tool is his plus raw power, and he's a good athlete and runner for a catcher. Romine must get stronger to maintain his skills, both offensive and defensive, over the course of an entire season. At times he struggles handling velocity, being a little late getting his glove to pitches on the corners. He still could add polish, and his arm strength sometimes gets him in trouble, as he led FSL catchers with 10 errors. He lacks patience at the plate and his swing tends to get long. The Yankees view him as their eventual replacement for Jorge Posada, though Romine is at least two years away from the majors. With Jesus Montero moving up to Triple-A in 2010, Romine will open the season as the everyday catcher in at Double-A.

Year	Club (League)	Class	AVG	G	AB	R	H	2B	3B	HR	RBI	BB	SO	SB	OBP	SLG
2007	Yankees (GCL)	R	.500	1	2	2	1	0	0	1	1	1	1	0	.667	1.000
2008	Charleston (SAL)	LoA	.300	104	407	66	122	24	1	10	49	25	56	3	.344	.437
2009	Tampa (FSL)	HiA	.276	118	442	61	122	28	3	13	72	29	78	11	.322	.441
MINOR LEAGUE TOTALS			.288	223	851	129	245	53	4	23	122	55	135	14	.334	.441

3 ARODYS VIZCAINO, RHP

BORN: Nov. 13, 1990. **B-T:** R-R. **HT.:** 6-0. **WT.:** 189. **SIGNED:** Dominican Republic, 2007. **SIGNED BY:** Alfredo Dominguez.

When the Yankees spend big money during the international summer signing season, they usually give it to position players, such as Gary Sanchez, Wily Mo Pena and Jesus Montero. Vizcaino received the largest signing bonus the club has given a pitcher in that market, signing for $800,000 out of the Dominican Republic in 2007. He dominated the short-season New York-Penn League last summer before a muscle strain in his back ended his season in August. Vizcaino has the most electric arm in the system outside of Andrew Brackman, and he's much more polished. Vizcaino sits at 90-94 mph with his fastball and regularly runs it up to 96. His quick arm generates easy velocity, and the ball seems to explode out of his hand. His best pitch is a hammer curveball that he throws with solid command. Club officials say his curve is second only to A.J. Burnett's in the organization. He has a sturdy, durable body. Vizcaino's changeup has improved but still grades as below average. He's raw and has plenty of work to do on subtle skills such as setting up hitters, fielding his position and holding runners. He also could have a more mature mound presence. Given Vizcaino's youth and ceiling, New York will handle him carefully. He figures to go to low Class A Charleston for 2010, starting in the first half and relieving in the second half to keep his innings from piling up.

Year	Club (League)	Class	W	L	ERA	G	GS	CG	SV	IP	H	R	ER	HR	BB	SO	AVG
2008	Yankees (GCL)	R	3	2	3.68	12	6	0	0	44	38	22	18	5	13	48	.222
2009	Staten Island (NYP)	SS	2	4	2.13	10	10	0	0	42	34	18	10	2	15	52	.211
MINOR LEAGUE TOTALS			5	6	2.92	22	16	0	0	86	72	40	28	7	28	100	.217

4 SLADE HEATHCOTT, OF

BORN: Sept. 28, 1990. **B-T:** L-L. **HT.:** 6-1. **WT.:** 190. **DRAFTED:** HS—Texarkana, Texas, 2009 (1st round). **SIGNED BY:** Mark Batchko/Tim Kelly.

Heathcott was one of the few true five-tool players available in the 2009 draft, but knee and shoulder injuries limited him last spring and makeup concerns scared some clubs off him completely. The Yankees pounced on him and signed him for $2.2 million, the largest bonus they've ever given to a hitter or a high schooler out of the draft. Heathcott has strength and fast-twitch athleticism. He offers big raw power from the left side of the plate and the bat speed to catch up to quality fastballs. He's a plus-plus runner with a strong arm that delivered 94-mph fastballs during his prep pitching career, and New York believes he can play center field. Heathcott will need at-bats to translate his tools into consistent performance. His all-out playing style has made him injury-prone, leading to November 2008 surgery to repair a torn anterior cruciate ligament in his left knee and a jammed throwing shoulder that limited him to DH for most of his senior season. His home life was unsettled and his immaturity has kept him off the field at times. The Yankees believe in Heathcott's talent and growing maturity, and he could become a superstar if he can stay on the field. He'll spend his first full pro season in low Class A.

Year	Club (League)	Class	AVG	G	AB	R	H	2B	3B	HR	RBI	BB	SO	SB	OBP	SLG
2009	Yankees (GCL)	R	.100	3	10	0	1	0	0	0	0	1	2	0	.182	.100
MINOR LEAGUE TOTALS			.100	3	10	0	1	0	0	0	0	1	2	0	.182	.100

5 ZACH McALLISTER, RHP

DAVID SCHOFIELD

BORN: Dec. 8, 1987. **B-T:** R-R. **HT.:** 6-6. **WT.:** 230. **DRAFTED:** HS—Chillicothe, Ill., 2006 (3rd round). **SIGNED BY:** Steve Lemke.

McAllister has been a test case for an organization that favors power fastballs and curveballs. The Yankees tried to raise his arm slot and have him pitch more with a four-seamer and curve instead of his normal sinker/slider repertoire. Though he posted a 2.08 ERA at two Class A levels in 2008, the changes didn't suit him. He returned to his previous style last season and led the Double-A Eastern League with a 2.23 ERA. His father Steve is the Midwest crosschecker for the Diamondbacks. McAllister has the best command of any pitcher in the system. He throws his two-seamer with solid armside life, sitting at 89-91 mph and touching 93. He commands his sinker well enough to get inside on hitters effectively. His slider gives him another pitch that helps him get groundouts, and at times he can get swings and misses with it. He throws his curve and changeup for strikes. Only McAllister's slider grades as a plus pitch, and his fastball sometimes sits in the upper 80s. He must be precise with his fringy curveball and changeup. He missed time with a tired arm in 2009, but New York doesn't consider it a long-term concern. McAllister has a ceiling of an innings-eating No. 4 starter. If the Yankees move Phil Hughes back to the rotation, there's little chance of McAllister squeezing his way in anytime soon. He might just be trade bait as he anchors the Scranton rotation in 2010.

Year	Club (League)	Class	W	L	ERA	G	GS	CG	SV	IP	H	R	ER	HR	BB	SO	AVG
2006	Yankees (GCL)	R	5	2	3.09	11	1	0	0	35	35	14	12	1	12	28	.259
2007	Staten Island (NYP)	SS	4	6	5.17	16	15	0	0	71	80	42	41	3	28	75	.286
2008	Charleston (SAL)	LoA	6	3	2.45	10	10	0	0	62	59	28	17	3	8	53	.245
	Tampa (FSL)	HiA	8	6	1.83	15	14	1	1	89	74	24	18	6	13	62	.225
2009	Trenton (EL)	AA	7	5	2.23	22	22	0	0	121	98	39	30	4	33	96	.220
MINOR LEAGUE TOTALS			30	22	2.81	74	62	1	1	378	346	147	118	17	94	314	.242

6 MANNY BANUELOS, LHP

BORN: March 13, 1991. **B-T:** L-L. **HT.:** 5-10. **WT.:** 155. **SIGNED:** Mexico, 2008. **SIGNED BY:** Lee Sigman.

Just a year after signing out of Mexico, Banuelos has become the system's top lefthanded pitching prospect. He jumped from Rookie ball to low Class A as an 18-year-old and was Charleston's best starter in the first half before tiring and moving to the bullpen down the stretch. He was so good in that role he was promoted to Tampa for its playoff run. Banuelos has two potential plus pitches and pitching savvy well beyond his years. His fastball sits at 88-92 mph when he's at his best as a starter, and reached 94 mph in relief late in the season. He uses his fastball inside well and throws strikes to all quadrants of the plate. His changeup already rates as solid average after making more progress than his other pitches in 2009. The Yankees laud his mound presence, poise and makeup. While his curveball is currently fringy, Banuelos has the hand speed to add power to it and make it an average pitch in time. Some scouts who saw him sit at 86-88 mph with his fastball consider him more of a fifth starter. He's just a fair athlete and needs to improve his ability to field his position and hold runners. While other pitchers in the system have higher ceilings, Banuelos is on the fast track to becoming a No. 3 starter. He'll start 2010 in Tampa and could reach Double-A as a teenager by season's end.

Year	Club (League)	Class	W	L	ERA	G	GS	CG	SV	IP	H	R	ER	HR	BB	SO	AVG
2008	Yankees (GCL)	R	4	1	2.57	12	3	0	0	42	32	14	12	3	13	37	.208
2009	Charleston (SAL)	LoA	9	5	2.67	25	19	0	0	108	88	40	32	4	28	104	.219
	Tampa (FSL)	HiA	0	0	0.00	1	0	0	0	1	0	0	0	0	0	2	.000
MINOR LEAGUE TOTALS			13	6	2.62	38	22	0	0	151	120	54	44	7	41	143	.215

7 GARY SANCHEZ, C

CLIFF WELCH

BORN: Dec. 2, 1992. **B-T:** R-R. **HT.:** 6-2. **WT.:** 190. **SIGNED:** Dominican Republic, 2009. **SIGNED BY:** Raymon Sanchez/Victor Mata.

Sanchez was one of the top players available on the international market last summer, and the Yankees scouted him so extensively that they were widely believed to be the front-runners to sign him. They landed him in July for $3 million, the fourth-largest bonus in franchise history. It's the third-largest for a Dominican teen after Michael Ynoa ($4.25 million from the Athletics in 2008) and Miguel Sano ($3.15 million from the Twins in 2009). Sanchez's raw power rates at least a 60 on the 20-80 scouting scale. New York is confident he'll realize that power potential because he uses the whole field and recognizes breaking balls, two indications that he'll make consistent contact. He has a plus-plus arm with the athletic ability to remain a catcher. Just 17, Sanchez has plenty of work to do to clean up his receiving skills and he'll need to get used to catching velocity. He was overmatched at the plate in instructional league by older pitchers, but that's to be expected. He didn't significantly alter his approach, an encouraging sign. He has average speed now but projects as a below-average runner once he fills out and catching takes a toll on him. Sanchez has some similarities to Jesus Montero, with better defensive tools as a bonus. He also obviously has a long way to go. He'll likely start his career in the Rookie-level Gulf Coast League in June.

Year	Club (League)	Class	AVG	G	AB	R	H	2B	3B	HR	RBI	BB	SO	SB	OBP	SLG
2009	Did Not Play—Signed 2010 Contract															

8 J.R. MURPHY, C

CLIFF WELCH

BORN: May 13, 1991. **B-T:** R-R. **HT.:** 6-0. **WT.:** 190. **DRAFTED:** HS—Bradenton, Fla. (2nd round). **SIGNED BY:** Jeff Deardorff/Brian Barber.

After missing his junior season in high school following knee surgery, Murphy moved to catcher as a prep senior and hit .627 with 11 home runs last spring. The Yankees bought him away from a Miami commitment with a $1.25 million bonus. The Yankees love Murphy's blend of hitting ability and athleticism, which is above-average for a catcher. He has a feel for hitting and knows his swing well. He generates good bat speed and pairs a low-maintenance, line-drive stroke with a polished offensive approach. He should hit for average and eventually should add solid power. He augments his plus arm with a quick transfer. Murphy is raw defensively and lacks experience handling velocity. The Yankees were encouraged with his rapid improvement after signing, but he'll have to polish his receiving and learn how to call games and handle a staff. He's a fringe-average runner who figures to slow down with the grind of catching. The Yankees have spent $7.35 million on six highly touted amateur catchers since 2006. Murphy has as much athletic ability as any of them, which may prompt him to switch positions down the road. For now, New York will develop him as a catcher and could send him to low Class A in 2010.

Year	Club (League)	Class	AVG	G	AB	R	H	2B	3B	HR	RBI	BB	SO	SB	OBP	SLG
2009	Yankees (GCL)	R	.333	9	33	4	11	2	0	1	7	3	8	0	.405	.485
MINOR LEAGUE TOTALS			.333	9	33	4	11	2	0	1	7	3	8	0	.405	.485

9 JEREMY BLEICH, LHP

BORN: June 18, 1987. **B-T:** L-L. **HT.:** 6-2. **WT.:** 195. **DRAFTED:** Stanford, 2008 (1st round supplemental). **SIGNED BY:** Mike Thurman.

An elbow injury sidelined Bleich for much of the 2008 college season, but he returned in May to help Stanford reach the College World Series. The Yankees were impressed enough to make him a supplemental first-round pick and signed him for $700,000. He became their top signee from the 2008 draft when first-rounder Gerrit Cole opted to attend UCLA. In his first full pro season, Bleich stayed healthy and reached Double-A. Bleich sat at 90-92 mph and touched 94 with his four-seam fastball last season His curveball and changeup are solid-average, with his curve grading as a plus pitch at times. He added a two-seam fastball and started to control it better as the year progressed. Bleich's four-seamer is true and his changeup tends to straighten out, though he's learning to add some sink to it. He lost some feel for the strike zone last year, in part because he threw harder. He doesn't have the weapons to pitch from behind in count and paid for it at Trenton. He needs better control of his two-seamer and change to combat righthanders. New York thought it was getting a pitchability guy in Bleich and hopes he regains some of his feel while retaining his added velocity. He'll have to fix what ailed him in Double-A when he returns there for 2010.

Year	Club (League)	Class	W	L	ERA	G	GS	CG	SV	IP	H	R	ER	HR	BB	SO	AVG
2008	Staten Island (NYP)	SS	0	0	6.00	1	1	0	0	3	2	2	2	1	0	4	.182
2009	Tampa (FSL)	HiA	6	4	3.40	14	14	0	0	79	79	34	30	4	22	56	.257
	Trenton (EL)	AA	3	6	6.65	13	13	0	0	65	84	54	48	6	34	60	.318
MINOR LEAGUE TOTALS			9	10	4.89	28	28	0	0	147	165	90	80	11	56	120	.284

10 ANDREW BRACKMAN, RHP

BORN: Dec. 4, 1985. **B-T:** R-R. **HT.:** 6-10. **WT.:** 240. **DRAFTED:** North Carolina State, 2007 (1st round). **SIGNED BY:** Steve Swail.

Brackman juggled basketball and baseball for two seasons at North Carolina State before giving up hoops to focus on the 2007 draft. Though he injured his elbow that May, his huge frame and ceiling enticed the Yankees to draft him 30th overall. He had Tommy John surgery shortly after signing at the Aug. 15 deadline for the largest draft bonus ($3.35 million) in franchise history, part of a major league contract worth a guaranteed $4.55 million and as much as $13 million with incentives. The elbow reconstruction, coupled with an appendectomy the following spring, pushed back his pro debut to Hawaii Winter Baseball in October 2008. The results from his first pro season were less than encouraging, as he ranked second in the minors in wild pitches (26) and 13th in walks (76). He did stay off the disabled list all season and closed with 10 scoreless, walkless relief innings and continued to throw strikes in instructional league. Brackman's combination of arm strength, size and athleticism can translate into premium stuff. His fastball, which touched 99 mph when he was an amateur, peaked at 95 when he started in 2009 and sat at 92-96 in shorter relief stints. His curveball also shows flashes of being a plus-plus pitch. In his first fully healthy year since Tommy John surgery, Brackman had little control and no command, however. He showed little feel for his delivery, or for using his curveball or rudimentary changeup. His late hot streak happened when the Yankees shelved his knuckle-curve, having him focus on a conventional grip, and his changeup. He'll need the changeup back to remain a starter. His velocity was unpredictable, at times sitting in the upper 80s. Brackman is a unique prospect in terms of his size, contract and lack of experience for his age. He could be an expensive bust, or suddenly figure it all out and move rapidly through the system. New York hasn't given up on him as a starter and will promote him to high Class A for 2010.

Year	Club (League)	Class	W	L	ERA	G	GS	CG	SV	IP	H	R	ER	HR	BB	SO	AVG
2009	Charleston (SAL)	LoA	2	12	5.91	29	19	0	0	107	106	79	70	8	76	103	.266
MINOR LEAGUE TOTALS			2	12	5.91	29	19	0	0	107	106	79	70	8	76	103	.266

11 BRYAN MITCHELL, RHP

BORN: April 19, 1991. **B-T:** L-R. **HT.:** 6-2. **WT.:** 175. **DRAFTED:** HS—Reidsville, N.C., 2009 (16th round). **SIGNED BY:** Scott Lovekamp.

Committed to North Carolina, Mitchell told teams before the 2009 draft that it would take "life-changing money" for him to turn down his home-state Tar Heels. Undaunted, the Yankees selected him in the 16th round and changed his plans by signing him for $800,000. Mitchell signed late and didn't pitch until instructional league, but he arrived with a more polished repertoire and better present stuff than most of the high school pitchers New York has signed of late. Mitchell throws a four-seam fastball that sits at 88-92 mph and touches 94. He's loose-armed and projectable with excellent hand speed, which helps him throw a snapdragon curve that's his best pitch. His curve was the best breaking ball the organization found in the 2009 draft and one of the best in the organization already. Mitchell's mechanics are fairly clean and repeatable, and he already throws a two-seam fastball, which the Yankees require for pitchers to advance past Class A. He also shows a feel for his nascent changeup. Mitchell could jump on the fast track, particularly if he performs well at Charleston in 2010.

Year	Club (League)	Class	W	L	ERA	G	GS	CG	SV	IP	H	R	ER	HR	BB	SO	AVG
2009	Did Not Play—Signed Late																

12 MIKE DUNN, LHP

BORN: May 23, 1985. **B-T:** L-L. **HT.:** 6-1. **WT.:** 195. **DRAFTED:** CC of Southern Nevada, D/F 2004 (33rd round). **SIGNED BY:** Jeff Patterson.

Dunn finished last season in the major leagues, quite an accomplishment for the former two-way player at CC of Southern Nevada. He converted to the mound full-time in 2006 after batting .160/.269/.230 in 66 games as an outfielder. He quickly established himself as a power arm, and his strong 2009 season—his first as a full-time reliever—made the Yankees comfortable enough to include Phil Coke in the Curtis Granderson trade. Dunn has a better raw arm than Coke, sitting at 90-94 mph and touching 98 with his fastball. Along with his heater, his slider also gained velocity when he moved to the bullpen, and he now throws it in the mid-80s. It's usually an average pitch but is a plus offering when he gets good depth on it. While he's aggressive and attacks hitters, Dunn can get inconsistent with his delivery and release point, putting him into hitter's counts as he struggles to throw strikes. The Yankees say he's athletic enough to have serviceable control, which should be enough with his stuff. Like Coke, Dunn figures to carry the load as a cheap, durable reliever, though he won't often be counted on for late-game outs. He'll get the opportunity to earn a big league bullpen spot in 2010.

Year	Club (League)	Class	AVG	G	AB	R	H	2B	3B	HR	RBI	BB	SO	SB	OBP	SLG
2005	Yankees (GCL)	R	.194	24	62	4	12	2	2	0	9	8	16	0	.284	.290
	Tampa (FSL)	HiA	.167	28	90	8	15	5	0	0	6	11	28	2	.265	.222
2006	Charleston, SC (SAL)	LoA	.086	14	35	7	3	2	0	0	2	8	13	1	.256	.143
MINOR LEAGUE TOTALS			.160	66	187	19	30	9	2	0	17	27	57	3	.269	.230

Year	Club (League)	Class	W	L	ERA	G	GS	CG	SV	IP	H	R	ER	HR	BB	SO	AVG
2006	Yankees (GCL)	R	3	0	0.73	11	0	0	4	25	13	2	2	0	9	26	.155
	Staten Island (NYP)	SS	0	0	5.68	3	0	0	0	6	3	6	4	0	7	7	.125
2007	Charleston, SC (SAL)	LoA	12	5	3.42	27	27	0	0	145	136	69	55	14	45	138	.253
2008	Tampa (FSL)	HiA	4	7	4.55	30	22	0	1	125	124	70	63	10	58	118	.266
	Trenton (EL)	AA	1	0	0.00	1	0	0	0	2	1	0	0	0	1	2	.167
2009	Trenton (EL)	AA	3	3	3.71	26	0	0	2	53	41	23	22	3	32	76	.211
	Scranton/W-B (IL)	AAA	1	0	2.25	12	0	0	0	20	17	5	5	1	14	23	.230
	New York (AL)	MAJ	0	0	6.75	4	0	0	0	4	3	3	3	1	5	5	.200
MAJOR LEAGUE TOTALS			0	0	6.75	4	0	0	0	4	3	3	3	1	5	5	.200
MINOR LEAGUE TOTALS			24	15	3.62	110	49	0	7	375	335	175	151	28	166	390	.242

13 CORBAN JOSEPH, 2B/3B

BORN: Oct. 28, 1988. **B-T:** L-R. **HT.:** 6-0. **WT.:** 168. **DRAFTED:** HS—Franklin, Tenn., 2008 (4th round). **SIGNED BY:** D.J. Svihlik.

The best draft-eligible hitter in Tennessee in 2008, Joseph went in the fourth round—66 picks ahead of his older brother Caleb, a Lipscomb catcher whom the Orioles took in the seventh round of the same draft. Joseph opened 2009 in extended spring training, but an injury to Garrison Lassiter opened a spot for him in low Class A and he seized the opportunity, finishing second on Charleston with 57 RBIs. Joseph has one of the purest swings in the system. He's short to the ball and long through the zone, and he has the strength to drive the ball. He has an advanced approach for a high school hitter and shows a willingness to take a walk. He has good gap power and could have average home run power down the road. Joseph also shows the ability to hang in against lefthanders, batting .302 against them in 2009. Some scouts still question his bat, though, as his swing gets long and they aren't sure how much power he'll produce. The bat comes first for Joseph, who probably doesn't have enough arm to be a regular third baseman. He has rough edges at second base, his more natural position, but profiles better there. His hands, athleticism and arm work at second, but he'll need repetitions and agility work to become an average defender. He's an average runner. The Yankees have a glut of second basemen, with Kevin Russo at Triple-A and David Adams ready for Double-A. Joseph's pure lefthanded swing puts him atop the list and makes him the most likely to be a regular, though he may never displace Robinson Cano in New York. He's slated for high Class A in 2010.

Year	Club (League)	Class	AVG	G	AB	R	H	2B	3B	HR	RBI	BB	SO	SB	OBP	SLG
2008	Yankees (GCL)	R	.277	49	159	25	44	15	2	2	18	20	24	2	.359	.434
2009	Charleston (SAL)	LoA	.300	100	380	39	114	17	8	4	57	49	61	8	.381	.418
MINOR LEAGUE TOTALS			.293	149	539	64	158	32	10	6	75	69	85	10	.374	.423

14 EDUARDO NUNEZ, SS

BORN: June 15, 1987. **B-T:** R-R. **HT.:** 6-0. **WT.:** 155. **SIGNED:** Dominican Republic, 2004. **SIGNED BY:** Victor Mata.

Nunez ranked No. 6 on this list after his first year in the United States in 2005, when he starred as the third-youngest position player in the New York-Penn League. He faltered for the next three seasons before finding success again in 2009, when most scouts considered him Trenton's best position player. The Yankees added him to their 40-man roster after the season. Nunez has athletic ability and good all-around tools. He's a free swinger who may not have the plate discipline to bring his solid power out on a consistent basis. He made good strides with the bat last season, though, making more consistent contact. He has above-average speed but doesn't always make the best decisions on the basepaths. Nunez has the size, strength and quickness to play shortstop. His arm is his best tool, though it sometimes gets him into trouble on defense when he tries to make plays he shouldn't. His lack of concentration also contributed to 33 errors in 120 games at short last year, and he must improve at making routine plays to be an everyday option there. Nunez profiles better as a utilityman at the big league level. He'll work on polishing his rough edges in Triple-A this year, when he could see more time at second base, third base and the outfield.

Year	Club (League)	Class	AVG	G	AB	R	H	2B	3B	HR	RBI	BB	SO	SB	OBP	SLG
2004	Yankees1 (DSL)	R	.215	57	191	29	41	9	5	3	20	27	41	16	.324	.361
2005	Staten Island (NYP)	SS	.313	73	281	37	88	11	6	3	46	20	43	6	.365	.427
2006	Tampa (FSL)	HiA	.184	37	147	17	27	5	3	4	26	8	28	6	.223	.340
	Charleston (SAL)	LoA	.227	90	344	36	78	11	3	2	40	23	48	16	.278	.294

2007	Charleston (SAL)	LoA	.238	91	328	36	78	10	2	1	28	25	42	20	.293	.290
	Tampa (FSL)	HiA	.285	30	123	16	35	5	0	1	13	7	18	9	.336	.350
2008	Tampa (FSL)	HiA	.271	94	373	45	101	18	3	6	42	19	48	14	.305	.383
2009	Trenton (EL)	AA	.322	123	497	70	160	26	1	9	55	22	63	19	.349	.433
MINOR LEAGUE TOTALS			.266	595	2284	286	608	95	23	29	270	151	331	106	.314	.366

15 MARK MELANCON, RHP

BORN: March 28, 1985. **B-T:** R-R. **HT.:** 6-2. **WT.:** 215. **DRAFTED:** Arizona, 2006 (9th round). **SIGNED BY:** Andy Stankiewicz.

The Yankees bullpen should be quite different in 2010, following the trades of Brian Bruney and Phil Coke and the planned move of Phil Hughes back to the rotation. Melancon is in position to take advantage of that opportunity after making 13 appearances for New York last season, including two scoreless innings at Fenway Park in his big league debut. It was just the second fully healthy pro year for Melancon, who had a bad elbow when he signed for $600,000 as a ninth-round pick in 2006 and required Tommy John surgery shortly thereafter. He might have made a bigger impact in the majors had his fastball command not become an issue. He still throws hard, mostly in the low 90s with a peak of 95 mph, but didn't throw enough strikes with his heater. It's crucial for him to get ahead of hitters with his fastball, because his secondary pitches are designed to get hitters to chase. His power curveball is a low-80s hammer and his changeup has splitter action, but he doesn't throw them in the strike zone often enough. Melancon worked in a setup role at Triple-A last season, but he still has a closer's mentality and no one questions his makeup. His delivery always has had some effort, so he has to tone it down while maintaining his stuff.

Year	Club (League)	Class	W	L	ERA	G	GS	CG	SV	IP	H	R	ER	HR	BB	SO	AVG
2006	Staten Island (NYP)	SS	0	1	3.52	7	0	0	2	8	9	7	3	0	2	8	.281
2007	Did Not Play—Injured																
2008	Tampa (FSL)	HiA	1	0	2.84	13	0	0	0	25	26	9	8	2	6	20	.265
	Trenton (EL)	AA	6	0	1.81	19	0	0	2	50	32	14	10	3	12	47	.183
	Scranton/W-B (IL)	AAA	1	1	2.70	12	0	0	1	20	11	7	6	1	4	22	.162
2009	Scranton/W-B (IL)	AAA	4	0	2.89	32	0	0	3	53	37	22	17	3	11	54	.196
	New York (AL)	MAJ	0	1	3.86	13	0	0	0	16	13	8	7	0	10	10	.217
MAJOR LEAGUE TOTALS			0	1	3.86	13	0	0	0	16	13	8	7	0	10	10	.217
MINOR LEAGUE TOTALS			12	2	2.54	83	0	0	8	156	115	59	44	9	35	151	.205

16 IVAN NOVA, RHP

BORN: Jan. 12, 1987. **B-T:** R-R. **HT.:** 6-4. **WT.:** 210. **SIGNED:** Dominican Republic, 2005. **SIGNED BY:** Victor Mata/Carlos Rios.

The Yankees left Nova off the 40-man roster in 2008, and the Padres picked him in the major league Rule 5 draft. He yielded 11 runs in nine innings in big league camp, so San Diego returned him to New York. Nova then put together his most consistent season as a pro, earning a promotion to Triple-A, where he was Scranton's top starter in the playoffs. The Yankees protected him on the 40-man roster this time, and he's now good trade bait or an option if they need a fill-in starter. Nova always had stuff and added consistency in 2009, throwing his 89-93 mph fastball downhill and for strikes more often. His command now grades as fringe-average, and scouts still see room for projection with his loose arm and long frame. Nova is at his best when he throws his curve with power in the upper 70s. His changeup is a fringy pitch but he shows decent feel for it. He still doesn't have a true plus offering that would help him generate more swings and misses. Nova finally started to close the gap between his upside and production last year, and he could be a No. 4 starter in the big leagues if his command and secondary stuff improve.

Year	Club (League)	Class	W	L	ERA	G	GS	CG	SV	IP	H	R	ER	HR	BB	SO	AVG
2005	Yankees1 (DSL)	R	0	1	2.29	11	7	0	0	39	29	11	10	2	11	38	.200
2006	Yankees (GCL)	R	3	0	2.72	10	5	0	1	43	36	13	13	5	7	36	.229
2007	Charleston (SAL)	LoA	6	8	4.98	21	21	0	0	99	121	64	55	8	31	54	.306
2008	Tampa (FSL)	HiA	8	13	4.36	26	24	0	0	149	168	81	72	6	46	109	.294
2009	Trenton (EL)	AA	5	4	2.36	12	12	0	0	72	65	27	19	3	31	47	.244
	Scranton/W-B (IL)	AAA	1	4	5.10	12	12	1	0	67	72	39	38	4	28	43	.285
MINOR LEAGUE TOTALS			23	30	3.97	92	81	1	1	470	491	235	207	28	154	327	.274

17 D.J. MITCHELL, RHP

BORN: May 13, 1987. **B-T:** R-R. **HT.:** 6-0. **WT.:** 170. **DRAFTED:** Clemson, 2008 (10th round). **SIGNED BY:** Scott Lovekamp.

An outfielder for most of his first two seasons at Clemson, Mitchell moved into the Tigers rotation as a sophomore, then gave up hitting altogether that summer in the Cape Cod League and the next spring in preparation for pro ball. He signed for a $450,000 bonus as a 10th-round pick in 2008, and ranked second in the system in wins (12) and strikeouts (125 in 140 innings) and third in ERA (2.63) in his 2009 pro debut. With his repertoire and athleticism, he reminds club officials of Ramiro Mendoza. Mitchell came to the Yankees with a good 89-91 mph sinker, and he has excelled at producing groundouts (2.89 groundout/airout ratio last season) and keeping the ball in the park (no homers allowed in his last 98 innings). Since turning pro, he has switched from a slider to a hard, tight curveball that gives him a strikeout pitch. His changeup hasn't made as much progress, and lefthanders batted .293 against him. Mitchell has time to improve his changeup, but if he doesn't he'll wind up in a middle-relief role. He'll pitch in Trenton's rotation in 2010.

Year	Club (League)	Class	W	L	ERA	G	GS	CG	SV	IP	H	R	ER	HR	BB	SO	AVG
2009	Charleston (SAL)	LoA	4	1	1.95	6	6	0	0	37	31	16	8	1	6	42	.228
	Tampa (FSL)	HiA	8	6	2.87	19	18	1	0	103	93	41	33	1	38	83	.245
MINOR LEAGUE TOTALS			12	7	2.63	25	24	1	0	140	124	57	41	2	44	125	.241

18 MELKY MESA, OF

BORN: Jan. 31, 1987. **B-T:** R-R. **HT.:** 6-1. **WT.:** 165. **SIGNED:** Dominican Republic, 2003. **SIGNED BY:** Victor Mata/Carlos Rios.

Mesa was one of the Yankees' success stories in 2009, raising the possibility of a two-Melky outfield in New York. (In Mesa's case, Melky is short for Melquisedec, an Old Testament non-Hebrew priest.) Mesa was Charleston's most explosive player in 2009, and he could be the system's top five-tool player, with a lean, wiry frame and loads of athletic ability. The problem is that most scouts consider him a below-average hitter. Mesa is a free swinger who is overly aggressive, no matter what the count. One scout said pitch recognition wasn't the problem, which gave him hope that Mesa would make enough contact to be a regular. The ball jumps off his bat thanks to elite bat speed, and he crushes fastballs. He has the ability to put backspin on the ball, turning line drives into home runs. He's a plus runner who'll have average speed once he fills out, and he has an above-average arm that should fit in right field. Mesa can play center field in a pinch but doesn't have the range or instincts to be an everyday player there. The Yankees want to see him reach what senior vice president of baseball operations Mark Newman calls "that happy convergence of impact and contact" more often. They'll see if Mesa can make the necessary adjustments in high Class A this year.

Year	Club (League)	Class	AVG	G	AB	R	H	2B	3B	HR	RBI	BB	SO	SB	OBP	SLG
2004	Yankees 2 (DSL)	R	.146	49	144	13	21	5	0	3	10	12	67	2	.279	.243
2005	Yankees 1 (DSL)	R	.304	8	23	3	7	2	0	2	6	3	7	1	.407	.652
2006	Yankees (GCL)	R	.207	40	145	20	30	7	2	3	22	11	45	3	.266	.345
2007	Yankees (GCL)	R	.235	49	153	27	36	10	2	3	13	9	55	5	.293	.386
2008	Staten Island (NYP)	SS	.221	46	122	19	27	5	2	7	23	4	38	4	.252	.467
2009	Charleston (SAL)	LoA	.225	133	497	76	112	24	7	20	74	51	168	18	.309	.423
MINOR LEAGUE TOTALS			.215	325	1084	158	233	53	13	38	148	90	380	33	.293	.393

19 KELVIN DELEON, OF

BORN: Oct. 29, 1990. **B-T:** R-R. **HT.:** 6-2. **WT.:** 180. **SIGNED:** Dominican Republic, 2007. **SIGNED BY:** Carlos Rios/Ramon Valdivia.

DeLeon signed out of the Dominican Republic in 2007 for a $1.1 million bonus, but the two scouts who signed him were fired by the Yankees after accusations that they each took $100,000 cuts, part of the Dominican bonus-skimming epidemic. DeLeon has been on a slow track, spending his first two seasons in Rookie ball. He grinded his way through his U.S. debut in 2009, showing his talent as well as his rough edges. His raw power is the second in the system only to Jesus Montero's, and it's usable, as he ranked third in the Gulf Coast League with seven homers last summer. He's wiry strong and has shortened his swing while retaining his power. He's still too aggressive at the plate but has the bat speed to catch up to good fastballs. He fits the right-field profile, with solid athleticism, plus arm strength and average speed. DeLeon is quite raw, with contact issues (he ranked fourth in the GCL with 61 strikeouts) and below-average defensive skills. He'll need a good spring to earn a job in low Class A, but he's also just 19 and has plenty of time to add polish.

Year	Club (League)	Class	AVG	G	AB	R	H	2B	3B	HR	RBI	BB	SO	SB	OBP	SLG
2008	Yankees 2 (DSL)	R	.289	63	235	43	68	16	2	9	43	34	74	8	.399	.489
2009	Yankees (GCL)	R	.269	56	201	28	54	13	0	7	31	16	61	5	.330	.438
MINOR LEAGUE TOTALS			.280	119	436	71	122	29	2	16	74	50	135	13	.369	.466

20 JOSE RAMIREZ, RHP

BORN: Jan. 21, 1990. **B-T:** R-R. **HT.:** 6-1. **WT.:** 155. **SIGNED:** Dominican Republic, 2007. **SIGNED BY:** Victor Mata.

Ramirez emerged as one of the system's more electric arms in 2009. He led the Gulf Coast League in opponent average (.159) and fewest baserunners per nine innings (7.23), and his only defeat was a 2-1 decision in the first round of the playoffs. Working with GCL Yankees pitching coach Carlos Chantres, Ramirez made significant progress with his delivery, getting his energy moving more toward the plate. That helped his fastball velocity, which jumped to 92-95 mph on a consistent basis. He commands his heater well. He has a quick arm and room to fill out physically, though his velocity isn't likely to increase much more. Ramirez's second-best pitch is his changeup, which is average now and has plus potential. He doesn't have much of a breaking ball and focused on a curveball during the Yankees' Dominican instructional program. His curve still has a ways to go, as does Ramirez. His fastball and changeup might be enough to earn him a spot in Charleston's 2010 rotation.

Year	Club (League)	Class	W	L	ERA	G	GS	CG	SV	IP	H	R	ER	HR	BB	SO	AVG
2008	Yankees 2 (DSL)	R	0	3	4.15	12	10	0	0	39	35	23	18	2	18	39	.238
2009	Yankees (GCL)	R	6	0	1.48	11	10	0	0	61	33	12	10	5	16	53	.159
	Tampa (FSL)	HiA	0	0	0.00	1	0	0	0	3	1	0	0	0	0	2	.100
MINOR LEAGUE TOTALS			6	3	2.45	24	20	0	0	103	69	35	28	7	34	94	.189

21 GRAHAM STONEBURNER, RHP

BORN: Sept. 29, 1987. **B-T:** R-R. **HT.:** 6-1. **WT.:** 190. **DRAFTED:** Clemson, 2009 (14th round). **SIGNED BY:** Scott Lovekamp.

The younger brother of Rangers minor league infielder Davis Stoneburner, Graham was a better prospect out of high school but went undrafted after a stress fracture in his back kept him off the field as a senior in 2006. He redshirted the following season at Clemson after tearing the anterior cruciate ligament in his left knee. Stoneburner pitched with D.J. Mitchell in the Tigers rotation in 2008 but had more success working out of the bullpen last spring. His relief role, medical history and extra leverage as a draft-eligible sophomore helped drive him down in the 2009 draft, but the Yankees gave him a $675,000 bonus in the 14th round. Stoneburner has a compact, athletic build and generates electric stuff. His fastball sat in the mid-90s during the spring and again in instructional league. His slider was inconsistent at Clemson and the Yankees made it a point of emphasis after he turned pro. The slider looked nasty in instructional league, and he'll stick with it rather than developing a curve. Scouts who aren't high on Stoneburner consider him homer-prone because they think his four-seam fastball lacks life and his changeup lacks consistency. The Yankees have a hard time containing their enthusiasm, however. He'll get innings as a starter in low Class A this year but eventually will fit better as a power-armed reliever.

Year	Club (League)	Class	W	L	ERA	G	GS	CG	SV	IP	H	R	ER	HR	BB	SO	AVG
2009	Staten Island (NYP)	SS	0	0	0.00	1	0	0	0	1	1	0	0	0	0	2	.250
MINOR LEAGUE TOTALS			0	0	0.00	1	0	0	0	1	1	0	0	0	0	2	.250

22 DAVID ADAMS, 2B/3B

BORN: May 15, 1987. **B-T:** R-R. **HT.:** 6-2. **WT.:** 205. **DRAFTED:** Virginia, 2008 (3rd round). **SIGNED BY:** Scott Lovekamp.

Adams has been a prospect dating back to his high school days in Florida. A 21st-round pick of the Tigers in 2005, he spurned them to attend Virginia, where he started most of his three seasons at second base. He had draftitis in 2008, hitting .286 as a junior after batting .372 as a sophomore, and didn't quite snap out of his funk until his first full pro season, when he led the system with 40 doubles and slugged .498 after a midseason promotion to high Class A. Adams needed mechanical adjustments to his swing, which the Yankees made in instructional league after his 2008 pro debut. Hitting coordinator James Rowson adjusted his exaggerated load, allowing Adams to unleash his bat speed and improve his balance. He showed excellent gap power and could have average home run power as he learns to put backspin on the ball. Adams played mostly second base last year, but he could move to third base because he has a plus arm and the Yankees have a glut of second basemen. He's a fringe-average runner and his range is a shade below average for second, though he does turn the double play well. Adams will play in Double-A in 2010.

Year	Club (League)	Class	AVG	G	AB	R	H	2B	3B	HR	RBI	BB	SO	SB	OBP	SLG
2008	Staten Island (NYP)	SS	.257	67	257	45	66	19	2	4	31	32	57	8	.350	.393
2009	Charleston, SC (SAL)	LoA	.290	67	259	32	75	23	2	0	34	35	49	8	.385	.394
	Tampa (FSL)	HiA	.281	65	231	37	65	17	6	7	41	26	39	3	.360	.498
MINOR LEAGUE TOTALS			.276	199	747	114	206	59	10	11	106	93	145	19	.365	.426

23 CALEB COTHAM, RHP

BORN: Nov. 6, 1987. **B-T:** R-R. **HT.:** 6-3. **WT.:** 215. **DRAFTED:** Vanderbilt, 2009 (5th round). **SIGNED BY:** D.J. Svihlik.

The Yankees used the draft-and-follow approach with junior college players for years. With that system gone thanks to the August signing deadline, the Yankees have shifted to summer follows, with Cotham a prime example in 2009. An injury to his right knee interrupted his season at Vanderbilt in the spring, and the sophomore-eligible pitcher went to the Cape Cod League after the Yankees drafted him in the fifth round. He struck out 15 in 13 scoreless innings for Brewster, earning a $675,000 bonus. He wound up having knee surgery and didn't throw much in instructional league, but he has shown two plus pitches when healthy. His fastball sits in the low 90s with excellent sink, and when he's right he has solid command of the pitch. His slider improved greatly last spring, and he pushed its velocity into the upper 80s while maintaining depth. Cotham's knee is the biggest question about him going forward. He's one more Yankees pitching prospect working to improve his changeup, an area of emphasis for the organization. He'll begin his first full pro season in low Class A.

Year	Club (League)	Class	W	L	ERA	G	GS	CG	SV	IP	H	R	ER	HR	BB	SO	AVG
2009	Yankees (GCL)	R	0	0	0.00	1	1	0	0	2	2	0	0	0	0	5	.250
	Staten Island (NYP)	SS	0	1	4.50	2	2	0	0	6	5	3	3	1	3	8	.217
MINOR LEAGUE TOTALS			0	1	3.38	3	3	0	0	8	7	3	3	1	3	13	.226

24 HECTOR NOESI, RHP

BORN: Jan. 26, 1987. **B-T:** R-R. **HT.:** 6-2. **WT.:** 174. **SIGNED:** Dominican Republic, 2004. **SIGNED BY:** Victor Mata.

One of the best stories in the system last year, Noesi rebounded after missing parts of 2007 and 2008 because of Tommy John surgery. His stuff was as good as ever, and his command was surprisingly good for a pitcher who recently had his elbow reconstructed. He started 2009 in Charleston's bullpen before graduating into the rotation in May. He didn't give up a run in his first 27 1/3 innings last year, including seven no-hit frames against Lexington on May 13. After a successful promotion to high Class A, he was added to New York's 40-man roster. Noesi pounds the strike zone with three potential average pitches. His 88-92 mph fastball has good life up in the zone, and some scouts project more velocity because he has a low-effort delivery. He has good arm speed on his changeup and the hand speed to spin a breaking ball. His curveball got tighter in 2009, though it still gets loopy at times and isn't a strikeout pitch. Both should become average pitches. Noesi repeats his delivery and arm action, though they don't give him any deception. His 117 innings last season represented a career high, so he's far from ready to handle a major league workload, and his size raises doubts about his durability. He'll be part of the Trenton rotation in 2010.

Year	Club (League)	Class	W	L	ERA	G	GS	CG	SV	IP	H	R	ER	HR	BB	SO	AVG
2005	Yankees (DSL)	R	5	3	1.60	13	10	0	0	51	34	19	9	2	8	36	.178
2006	Yankees (GCL)	R	0	0	1.29	5	0	0	1	7	5	1	1	0	1	11	.192
2007	Charleston (SAL)	LoA	1	1	4.50	5	5	0	0	20	25	10	10	2	8	11	.309
2008	Yankees (GCL)	R	2	1	3.65	9	2	0	0	25	23	11	10	2	3	24	.253
	Staten Island (NYP)	SS	1	1	3.00	5	5	0	0	24	20	12	8	5	7	31	.227
2009	Charleston (SAL)	LoA	3	4	2.38	17	11	0	0	76	62	24	20	3	11	78	.218
	Tampa (FSL)	HiA	3	0	3.92	9	9	0	0	41	34	18	18	3	4	40	.224
MINOR LEAGUE TOTALS			15	10	2.81	63	42	0	1	243	203	95	76	17	42	231	.222

25 DAVID PHELPS, RHP

BORN: Oct. 9, 1986. **B-T:** R-R. **HT.:** 6-3. **WT.:** 190. **DRAFTED:** Notre Dame, 2008 (14th round). **SIGNED BY:** Mike Gibbons.

The Yankees like to draft college arms and turn them over to pitching coordinator Nardi Contreras. Phelps emerged from the pack last season, as he led the system with 13 wins, ranked second with a 2.38 ERA and third with 122 strikeouts while logging 151 innings. New York stole him in the 14th round of the 2008 draft, signing him for $150,000 after he slumped as a junior at Notre Dame. His brother Mike, a former Cubs farmhand, pitched in independent ball last year. Phelps has size and stuff, taking his four-seam fastball from 91-92 mph in college to 92-95 as a pro. He threw his fastball for strikes and consistently got ahead of Class A hitters last year. He throws his four-seamer on a good downhill plane and locates his 90-mph two-seamer in the bottom of the strike zone. Phelps' ceiling is tied to his secondary stuff, which isn't special. He throws a changeup that has made progress but is still below average. He also has a fringy slider that's more of a groundball pitch than a strikeout offering, plus a curveball that has flashes average potential. Phelps' fastball makes him intriguing, but he'll have to show more when he gets to Double-A this year.

Year	Club (League)	Class	W	L	ERA	G	GS	CG	SV	IP	H	R	ER	HR	BB	SO	AVG
2008	Staten Island (NYP)	SS	8	2	2.72	15	15	0	0	73	67	28	22	4	18	52	.245
2009	Charleston (SAL)	LoA	10	3	2.80	19	19	0	0	113	117	48	35	9	25	90	.272
	Tampa (FSL)	HiA	3	1	1.17	7	7	0	0	38	34	9	5	1	6	32	.234
MINOR LEAGUE TOTALS			21	6	2.49	41	41	0	0	224	218	85	62	14	49	174	.257

26 ADAM WARREN, RHP

BORN: Aug. 25, 1987. **B-T:** R-R. **HT.:** 6-2. **WT.:** 200. **DRAFTED:** North Carolina, 2009 (4th round). **SIGNED BY:** Scott Lovekamp.

Warren went 32-4 in his career at North Carolina, pitching in three College World Series. His fastball velocity gradually increased with the Tar Heels, peaking at 94 mph last spring, but the Yankees were unprepared for his breakout performance after he signed for $195,000 as a fourth-round pick last June. Not only did Warren help pitch Staten Island to the New York-Penn League championship, but his four-seam fastball sat at 93-95 mph at times. He's not likely to sit at that velocity in the long term, but his customary 90-92 mph velocity from college would be more than enough. He commands his two-seam and four-seam fastballs very well, and he adds adds deception with a little hesitation in his delivery. Warren has added a cutter to give him a pitch with a wrinkle. His solid-average changeup is his best secondary pitch, and he'll use a slow curveball early in the count. He could jump to high Class A in 2010 as the Yankees are eager to see exactly what they have in him.

Year	Club (League)	Class	W	L	ERA	G	GS	CG	SV	IP	H	R	ER	HR	BB	SO	AVG
2009	Staten Island (NYP)	SS	4	2	1.43	12	12	0	0	57	49	12	9	1	10	50	.236
MINOR LEAGUE TOTALS			4	2	1.43	12	12	0	0	57	49	12	9	1	10	50	.236

27 KEVIN RUSSO, 2B/3B

BORN: July 8, 1984. **B-T:** R-R. **HT.:** 5-11. **WT.:** 190. **DRAFTED:** Baylor, 2006 (20th round). **SIGNED BY:** Mark Batchko.

Russo continues to grind his way toward the big leagues, despite injuries and holes in his game. He suffered facial fractures in June 2008, when he was hit in the face by a batted ball during a practice, and has dealt with hamstring pulls the last two seasons. Russo's hitting ability, speed and arm all rate as plus tools, with his defense grading out as average at both second base and third base. He clearly knows what kind of player he is and led the system in batting (.326) in his first try at Triple-A with a slashing, contact-oriented approach. He uses the whole field and has some modest gap power. He's willing to take a walk and would be a future leadoff option if he were a better basestealer. He's a streaky defender and has just fair hands. His arm helps him turn the double play at second, and he's better defensively at third. He can play shortstop in a pinch and also has experience playing the outfield corners. Russo has hit in Double-A, the Arizona Fall League and now Triple-A. He could be an everyday infielder on a second-division team and fits a utility profile for the Yankees. He'll compete with Reegie Corona for that role in 2010 after joining the 40-man roster in the offseason.

Year	Club (League)	Class	AVG	G	AB	R	H	2B	3B	HR	RBI	BB	SO	SB	OBP	SLG
2006	Yankees (GCL)	R	.273	45	150	23	41	10	0	3	23	20	18	6	.383	.400
2007	Tampa (FSL)	HiA	.281	109	385	47	108	22	3	2	45	15	66	19	.311	.369
2008	Trenton (EL)	AA	.307	71	267	46	82	17	3	2	33	23	42	8	.363	.416
2009	Scranton/W-B (IL)	AAA	.326	90	353	51	115	18	2	5	31	42	55	13	.397	.431
MINOR LEAGUE TOTALS			.300	315	1155	167	346	67	8	12	132	100	181	46	.360	.403

28 DELLIN BETANCES, RHP

BORN: March 23, 1988. **B-T:** R-R. **HT.:** 6-8. **WT.:** 215. **DRAFTED:** HS—New York, 2006 (8th round). **SIGNED BY:** Cesar Presbott/Brian Barber.

Betances was a high-risk, high-reward pick whose $1 million bonus in 2006 set a record for an eighth-round pick. He has progressed slowly, and after seeming to turn the corner in 2008, adversity struck him last year. He was having an inconsistent season when he had elbow pain in late May. He tried rest but got hit hard when he pitched again and went back on the disabled list. His injury eventually was diagnosed as a ligament tear that required Tommy John surgery in August. Even before he got hurt, Betances showed little sign of improving the balance in his delivery or loosening up what can be a stiff landing. His lack of athletic ability and size prompted some scouts to compare him to Daniel Cabrera, who always had plus stuff but never learned how to use it successfully. Betances has a fastball that sits at 93-94 mph and touches 97, and he backs it up with a plus curveball. His poor command last year could have stemmed from his elbow trouble, but throwing quality strikes never has been his strong suit. Following a lost year, he'll miss most of another and have to be protected on the 40-man roster or exposed to the Rule 5 draft after the season.

Year	Club (League)	Class	W	L	ERA	G	GS	CG	SV	IP	H	R	ER	HR	BB	SO	AVG
2006	Yankees (GCL)	R	0	1	1.16	7	7	0	0	23	14	5	3	1	7	27	.173
2007	Staten Island (NYP)	SS	1	2	3.60	6	6	0	0	25	24	11	10	0	17	29	.255
2008	Yankees (GCL)	R	0	1	8.53	3	2	0	0	6	13	7	6	0	3	6	.406
	Charleston, SC (SAL)	LoA	9	4	3.67	22	22	0	0	115	87	57	47	9	59	135	.208
2009	Tampa (FSL)	HiA	2	5	5.48	11	11	0	0	44	48	29	27	2	27	44	.277
MINOR LEAGUE TOTALS			12	13	3.91	49	48	0	0	214	186	109	93	12	113	241	.233

29 JAIRO HEREDIA, RHP

BORN: Oct. 8, 1989. **B-T:** R-R. **HT.:** 6-1. **WT.:** 189. **SIGNED:** Dominican Republic, 2006. **SIGNED BY:** Victor Mata/Carlos Rios.

Signed for $350,000 out of the Dominican Republic in 2006, Heredia seemed on the verge of a breakout last season after a promising 2008 performance in low Class A. But he came to spring training out of shape and pitched just 38 innings in 2009. His lack of conditioning was particularly disappointing because the Yankees have stressed that he needs to get stronger for years. He came down with a sore shoulder and didn't pitch in a game until July. Heredia has the pitches to reach the major leagues if he can stay healthy. His 90-91 mph fastball touches 93 and features sink and armside run. His changeup also has sink, and his curveball can be a plus pitch at times. While Heredia throws strikes, he doesn't always throw quality strikes. With his stuff, he needs to be more precise and improve his pitch sequencing. Heredia is still just 20, so he has plenty of time to get back on track, starting with an assignment to high Class A this year.

Year	Club (League)	Class	W	L	ERA	G	GS	CG	SV	IP	H	R	ER	HR	BB	SO	AVG
2007	Yankees (GCL)	R	2	2	2.72	11	6	0	0	46	39	15	14	4	11	52	.228
2008	Charleston (SAL)	LoA	6	7	3.25	21	21	0	0	102	99	58	37	7	43	95	.249
2009	Yankees (GCL)	R	0	0	1.80	2	2	0	0	5	3	2	1	0	2	5	.167
	Charleston (SAL)	LoA	1	1	2.37	4	4	0	0	19	14	6	5	1	1	17	.203
	Tampa (FSL)	HiA	2	2	6.91	4	4	1	0	14	25	14	11	2	5	10	.373
MINOR LEAGUE TOTALS			11	12	3.27	42	37	1	0	187	180	95	68	14	62	179	.249

30 JAMIE HOFFMANN, OF

BORN: Aug. 20, 1984. **B-T:** R-R. **HT.:** 6-4. **WT.:** 230. **SIGNED:** HS—New Ulm, Minn., NDFA 2003. **SIGNED BY:** Jeff Schugel (Dodgers).

The Yankees don't usually need low-cost reserves, but they have stated their desire to lower their payroll in 2010. To that end, they traded Brian Bruney to the Nationals for the No. 1 pick in the major league Rule 5 draft, then used that choice to grab Hoffmann. He'll compete for a backup outfield job on the big league roster, and if he doesn't stick with New York, he'd have to clear waivers and get offered back to the Dodgers for half his $50,000 draft price. Hoffmann was drafted in the eighth round in 2003—by the NHL's Carolina Hurricanes. Like former all-star catcher Terry Steinbach, Hoffmann excelled in hockey and baseball at New Ulm (Minn.) High. Unselected in the baseball draft, he signed with Los Angeles as a free agent and reached the majors in his sixth pro season. Hoffman is a physical player with 55 speed on the 20-80 scouting scale, which along with his solid-average throwing arm allows him to play all three outfield spots. His defense is ahead of his offense, and despite his size he never has quite tapped into his raw power. The Yankees had hitting coordinator Kevin Long check out Hoffmann on film prior to selecting him and believe he has a foundation for hitting that just needs to be tweaked, not overhauled. His defense, speed and contact ability—plus the inclusion of Austin Jackson in a trade for Curtis Granderson—should help Hoffman win a bench job with the Yankees. That's his ceiling on a contending club.

Year	Club (League)	Class	AVG	G	AB	R	H	2B	3B	HR	RBI	BB	SO	SB	OBP	SLG
2004	Dodgers (GCL)	R	.310	60	229	40	71	8	7	4	36	24	38	14	.374	.459
2005	Columbus (SAL)	LoA	.308	79	321	53	99	13	9	1	24	39	73	10	.383	.414
	Vero Beach (FSL)	HiA	.241	46	166	26	40	6	2	1	10	10	45	3	.287	.319
2006	Vero Beach (FSL)	HiA	.252	121	433	50	109	16	0	5	29	35	94	15	.309	.323
	Las Vegas (PCL)	AAA	.300	4	10	0	3	0	0	0	0	1	3	1	.417	.300
2007	Inland Empire (CAL)	HiA	.309	116	433	67	134	22	7	9	81	47	70	19	.378	.455
2008	Jacksonville (SL)	AA	.278	133	478	64	133	20	3	10	71	54	73	28	.350	.395
2009	Chattanooga (SL)	AA	.307	29	101	25	31	9	2	2	16	22	18	5	.457	.495
	Los Angeles (NL)	MAJ	.182	14	22	2	4	2	0	1	7	0	5	0	.167	.409
	Albuquerque (PCL)	AAA	.284	68	257	44	73	14	3	8	48	32	37	10	.360	.455
MAJOR LEAGUE TOTALS			.182	14	22	2	4	2	0	1	7	0	5	0	.167	.409
MINOR LEAGUE TOTALS			.285	656	2428	369	693	108	33	40	315	264	451	105	.357	.407

Oakland Athletics

BY JIM SHONERD

The Athletics returned to prominence in the 2000s, claiming four division titles and making the playoffs five times in seven seasons from 2000-06. But the decade ended on a down note as they posted their third consecutive losing season in 2009, going 75-87 for their worst record and first last-place finish in 11 years.

Only a few holdovers remain from Oakland's run in the early part of the decade, most notably oft-injured third baseman Eric Chavez. The A's are trying to rebuild around young pitching and last year's team featured the majors' youngest rotation, with all six of its regular members age 25 or younger.

Foremost among that group were Brett Anderson and Trevor Cahill, the team's top two prospects entering last year. Both held their own as 21-year-olds making their big league debuts, and they were the only Oakland pitchers to post double-digit win totals. Anderson was especially impressive, going 6-4, 3.48 with 86 strikeouts in 88 innings after the all-star break.

Another rookie, Andrew Bailey, took over as the A's closer in later May. He went on to win the American League rookie of the year award after converting 26 of 30 save opportunities and leading all major league relievers in opponent average (.167) and strikeouts per nine innings (9.8).

While Oakland's pitching kept the team competitive, ranking fourth in the AL with a 4.29 ERA, the same couldn't be said of the hitting (ninth in scoring, last in home runs) and defense (second-most unearned runs allowed). General manager Billy Beane traded for Matt Holliday last offseason, but the slugger couldn't match his production with the Rockies. Beane flipped Holliday to the Cardinals in July for a package of three prospects headlined by corner infielder Brett Wallace.

Wallace adds to a mix of nearly ready hitters the A's hope will give their offense the punch it has lacked. Others on the verge of helping the big league club include first baseman Chris Carter (the system's No. 1 prospect), infielder Adrian Cardenas and outfielder Sean Doolittle. With all the graduations to the majors, the pool of pitching prospects at the top of the system has thinned out.

Oakland has invested heavily in scouting and player development the last two years, spending a record $4.25 million in 2008 on Dominican righthander Michael Ynoa—who didn't pitch last season because of elbow problems—and $13 million on the last two drafts. The A's have aggressively signed several players

Andrew Bailey saved 26 games for Oakland and won the AL rookie of the year award

BILL NICHOLS

TOP 30 PROSPECTS

1. Chris Carter, of/1b	16. Ian Krol, lhp
2. Brett Wallace, 3b/1b	17. Fautino de los Santos, rhp
3. Grant Green, ss	18. Tommy Everidge, 1b/3b
4. Max Stassi, c	19. Arnold Leon, rhp
5. Pedro Figueroa, lhp	20. Justin Souza, rhp
6. Tyson Ross, rhp	21. Ryan Ortiz, c
7. Jemile Weeks, 2b	22. Connor Hoehn, rhp
8. Grant Desme, of	23. Jonathan Joseph, rhp
9. Adrian Cardenas, inf	24. Julio Ramos, lhp
10. Sean Doolittle, of	25. Andrew Carignan, rhp
11. Michael Ynoa, rhp	26. Bobby Cassevah, rhp
12. Corey Brown, of	27. Justin Marks, lhp
13. Henry Rodriguez, rhp	28. Tyreace House, of
14. Josh Donaldson, c/3b	29. Josh Leyland, c
15. Clayton Mortensen, rhp	30. Brett Hunter, rhp

for more than MLB's slot recommendations, including shortstop Grant Green (first round), catcher Max Stassi (fourth) and lefthander Ian Krol (seventh) for a combined $5.125 million last August.

The A's may have to continue a budget-minded approach in the big leagues, however, after abandoning plans to build a new ballpark in Fremont, Calif. The project met heavy resistance from local groups, and with the ballpark's opening continually delayed, the team decided to look elsewhere. San Jose appears to be the new leading candidate, but territorial issues involving the Giants may hamper that plan.

General Manager: Billy Beane. **Farm Director:** Keith Lieppman. **Scouting Director:** Eric Kubota.

Class	Team	League	W	L	PCT	Finish*	Manager(s)
Majors	Oakland Athletics	American	75	87	.463	t-10th (14)	Bob Geren
Triple-A	Sacramento River Cats	Pacific Coast	86	57	.601	1st (16)	Tony DeFrancesco
Double-A	Midland RockHounds	Texas	78	62	.557	†1st (8)	Darren Bush
High A	Stockton Ports	California	61	79	.436	t-7th (10)	Aaron Nieckula
Low A	Kane County Cougars	Midwest	76	64	.543	6th (14)	Steve Scarsone
Short-season	Vancouver Canadians	Northwest	36	40	.474	5th (8)	Rick Magnante
Rookie	AZL Athletics	Arizona	22	34	.393	10th (11)	Marcus Jensen
Overall 2009 Minor League Record			359	336	.517	7th (30)	

*Finish in overall standings (No. of teams in league). †League champion.

LAST YEAR'S TOP 30

Rank	Player, Pos.	Status
1.	Brett Anderson, lhp	Majors
2.	Trevor Cahill, rhp	Majors
3.	Michael Ynoa, rhp	No. 11
4.	Aaron Cunningham, of	Majors
5.	Adrian Cardenas, ss/2b	No. 9
6.	Chris Carter, 1b/3b/of	No. 1
7.	Gio Gonzalez, lhp	Majors
8.	Vin Mazzaro, rhp	Majors
9.	Jemile Weeks, 2b	No. 7
10.	James Simmons, rhp	Dropped out
11.	Sean Doolittle, 1b/of	No. 10
12.	Josh Outman, lhp	Majors
13.	Josh Donaldson, c	No. 14
14.	Henry Rodriguez, rhp	No. 13
15.	Tyson Ross, rhp	No. 6
16.	Corey Brown, of	No. 12
17.	Cliff Pennington, ss	Majors
18.	Fautino de los Santos, rhp	No. 17
19.	Brett Hunter, rhp	No. 30
20.	Jerry Blevins, lhp	Majors
21.	Rashun Dixon, of	Dropped out
22.	Dusty Coleman, ss	Dropped out
23.	Andrew Bailey, rhp	Majors
24.	Craig Italiano, rhp	(Padres)
25.	Andrew Carignan, rhp	No. 25
26.	Sam Demel, rhp	Dropped out
27.	Jared Lansford, rhp	Dropped out
28.	Matt Sulentic, of	Dropped out
29.	Arnold Leon, rhp	No. 19
30.	Grant Desme, of	No. 8

BEST TOOLS

Best Hitter for Average	Brett Wallace
Best Power Hitter	Chris Carter
Best Strike-Zone Discipline	Josh Horton
Fastest Baserunner	Tyreace House
Best Athlete	Rashun Dixon
Best Fastball	Henry Rodriguez
Best Curveball	Michael Ynoa
Best Slider	Tyson Ross
Best Changeup	James Simmons
Best Control	Mickey Storey
Best Defensive Catcher	Max Stassi
Best Defensive Infielder	Grant Green
Best Infield Arm	Gregorio Petit
Best Defensive Outfielder	Tyreace House
Best Outfield Arm	Robin Rosario

PROJECTED 2013 LINEUP

Catcher	Max Stassi
First Base	Brett Wallace
Second Base	Jemile Weeks
Third Base	Adrian Cardenas
Shortstop	Grant Green
Left Field	Grant Desme
Center Field	Rajai Davis
Right Field	Sean Doolittle
Designated Hitter	Chris Carter
No. 1 Starter	Brett Anderson
No. 2 Starter	Trevor Cahill
No. 3 Starter	Pedro Figueroa
No. 4 Starter	Tyson Ross
No. 5 Starter	Vin Mazzaro
Closer	Andrew Bailey

TOP PROSPECTS OF THE DECADE

Year	Player, Pos.	2009 Org.
2000	Mark Mulder, lhp	Free agent (injured)
2001	Jose Ortiz, 2b	Saltillo (Mexico)
2002	Carlos Pena, 1b	Rays
2003	Rich Harden, rhp	Cubs
2004	Bobby Crosby, ss	Athletics
2005	Nick Swisher, of	Yankees
2006	Daric Barton, 1b	Athletics
2007	Travis Buck, of	Athletics
2008	Daric Barton, 1b	Athletics
2009	Brett Anderson, lhp	Athletics

TOP DRAFT PICKS OF THE DECADE

Year	Player, Pos.	2009 Org.
2000	Freddie Bynum, ss (2nd round)	Nationals
2001	Bobby Crosby, ss	Athletics
2002	Nick Swisher, of	Yankees
2003	Brad Sullivan, rhp	Out of baseball
2004	Landon Powell, c	Athletics
2005	Cliff Pennington, ss	Athletics
2006	Trevor Cahill, rhp (2nd round)	Athletics
2007	James Simmons, rhp	Athletics
2008	Jemile Weeks, 2b	Athletics
2009	Grant Green, ss	Athletics

LARGEST BONUSES IN CLUB HISTORY

Michael Ynoa, 2008	$4,250,000
Mark Mulder, 1998	$3,200,000
Grant Green, 2009	$2,750,000
Jemile Weeks, 2008	$1,910,000
Nick Swisher, 2002	$1,780,000

OAKLAND ATHLETICS

TOP 2010 ROOKIE: Brett Wallace, 3b/1b. A hitting machine, he'll be more valuable if he can handle the hot corner.

BREAKOUT PROSPECT: Jonathan Joseph, rhp. His 92-94 mph fastball and his hammer curve have him poised for a big year in low Class A—if he throws enough strikes.

SLEEPER: Steve Parker, 1b/3b. The 2009 fifth-rounder has power to all fields and some pure hitting ability.

SOURCE OF TOP 30 TALENT

Homegrown	22	Acquired	8
College	11	Trades	7
Junior college	2	Rule 5 draft	1
High school	3	Independent leagues	0
Draft-and-follow	0	Free agents/waivers	0
Nondrafted free agents	0		
International	6		

Numbers in parentheses indicate prospect rankings

LF
Rashun Dixon
Shane Peterson
Matt Sulentic

CF
Tyreace House (28)
Myrio Richard
Robin Rosario

RF
Grant Desme (8)
Sean Doolittle (10)
Corey Brown (12)
Jeremy Barfield
Alfredo Sosa
Jose Crisotomo

3B
Mike Spina
Junior Martinez
Leonardo Gil
Alex Valdez

SS
Grant Green (3)
Wilfredo Solano
Dusty Coleman
Jason Christian
Tyler Ladendorf
Gregorio Petit
Michael Gilmartin

2B
Jemile Weeks (7)
Adrian Cardenas (9)
Corey Wimberly
Conner Crumbliss
Kent Walton

1B
Chris Carter (1)
Brett Wallace (2)
Tommy Everidge (18)
Steve Parker

C
Max Stassi (4)
Josh Donaldson (14)
Ryan Ortiz (21)
Josh Leyland (29)
Anthony Recker

RHP

Starters	Relievers
Tyson Ross (6)	Henry Rodriguez (13)
Michael Ynoa (11)	Andrew Carignan (25)
Clay Mortensen (15)	Bobby Cassevah (26)
Fautino de los Santos (17)	Brett Hunter (30)
Arnold Leon (19)	Sam Demel
Justin Souza (20)	Mickey Storey
Connor Hoehn (22)	John Meloan
Jonathan Joseph (23)	Jared Lansford
James Simmons	Rob Gilliam
Ken Smalley	Paul Smyth
Graham Godfrey	Justin Friend
Argenis Paez	Lance Sewell

LHP

Starters	Relievers
Pedro Figueroa (5)	Brad Kilby
Ian Krol (16)	Ben Hornbeck
Julio Ramos (24)	
Justin Marks (27)	
Anthony Capra	
Omar Duran	
Anvioris Ramirez	

2009   BONUSES: $6.4 MILLION

BEST PURE HITTER: SS Grant Green (1) hit .390 and .374 in his final two college seasons at Southern California, sandwiched around a .348 campaign in the Cape Cod League. He has a quick bat and a knack for barreling balls. 1B/3B Steve Parker (5) also has a sound swing from the left side.

BEST POWER HITTER: Cs Max Stassi (4) and Josh Leyland (16) both have plus raw power, with the edge going to Leyland. He's short to the ball and long afterward.

FASTEST RUNNER: Green has above-average speed, as does 2B/OF Conner Crumbliss (28).

BEST DEFENSIVE PLAYER: Stassi had a reputation for having a polished bat, but the A's always have held his glove in high regard. He's an adept, polished receiver with good footwork and a strong, accurate arm.

BEST FASTBALL: RHP Connor Hoehn (12) worked with a consistent 92-96 mph fastball as a reliever.

BEST SECONDARY PITCH: LHP Ian Krol (7) shines because of his secondary stuff. On some days, his hard curveball is a plus pitch with two-plane break. On others, his changeup grades as plus.

BEST PRO DEBUT: RHP Paul Smyth (35) didn't allow a run in 25 outings covering 36⅓ innings, saving 11 games and posting a 44-4 K-BB ratio between short-season Vancouver and low Class A Kane County. He confounds hitters with his low-three-quarters arm slot, and his out pitch is his slider. Hoehn replaced Smyth as Vancouver's closer and saved seven games while fanning 25 in 18 innings.

BEST ATHLETE: Green stands out with his combination of speed, strength and body control.

MOST INTRIGUING BACKGROUND: Stassi's great-great uncle Myril Hoag played 13 seasons in the majors, including a stint in the Yankees outfield with Babe Ruth. 3B Blake Crosby's (42) brother Bobby won the 2004 American League rookie of the year award for the A's, while his father Ed scouted for the team after his big league career ended. Unsigned OF Dylan Brown's (34) brother Corey is one of the system's top outfield prospects.

CLOSEST TO THE MAJORS: Green should move quickly, as should LHP Justin Marks (3), a four-pitch southpaw who missed time with a groin injury after signing.

BEST LATE-ROUND PICK: Hoehn, Leyland or Crumbliss. Crumbliss has an excellent utility profile as a versatile defender with a decent lefthanded bat and good speed.

THE ONE WHO GOT AWAY: The A's hoped to add RHP Sam Dyson (10), the hardest thrower they drafted, but his bonus demands and track record of shoulder problems were too much to overcome. He returned to South Carolina.

ASSESSMENT: Green and Stassi could provide Oakland with a pair of up-the-middle cornerstones. The A's emphasized hitting but still added some interesting pitchers such as Krol and Hoehn.

2008   BONUSES: $6.5 MILLION

2B Jemile Weeks (1) and RHP Tyson Ross (2) already have reached Double-A and are on the verge of helping the A's. RHP Brett Hunter (7) hasn't thrown strikes since signing for a round-record $1.1 million.
GRADE: B

2007   BONUSES: $4.2 MILLION

RHP James Simmons (1) hit the wall hard in Triple-A last year, but OFs Sean Doolittle (1s), Corey Brown (1s) and Grant Desme (2) are three of the better hitters in the system.
GRADE: C

2006   BONUSES: $2.0 MILLION

The A's didn't have a first-round pick, but didn't need one to find the 2009 American League rookie of the year, RHP Andrew Bailey (6). The top choice, RHP Trevor Cahill (2), has frontline starter potential and won 10 games as a 21-year-old rookie.
GRADE: B+

2005   BONUSES: $4.8 MILLION*

Five members of this draft have played in the big leagues: SS Cliff Pennington (1), OF Travis Buck (1s), RHP Vin Mazzaro (3), 3B Jeff Baisley (12) and LHP Brad Kilby (29). But none has become a regular, and Buck has gone backwards the last two years.
GRADE: C+

*Draft analysis by John Manuel (2009) and Jim Callis (2005-08). Numbers in parentheses indicate draft rounds. *Bonuses for 2005 are first 10 rounds only.*

PROSPECT 1

CHRIS CARTER, 1B/OF

Born: Dec. 18, 1986.
Height: 6-4. **Weight:** 225.
Bats: R. **Throws:** R.
Drafted: HS—Las Vegas, 2005 (15th round).
Signed by: George Kachigian/Joe Butler (White Sox).

JOHN WILLIAMSON

Carter has found a home with the Athletics. The White Sox drafted him in 2005, then traded him to the Diamondbacks for Carlos Quentin in December 2007. He spent 11 days in the Arizona organization before getting shipped to the Athletics in the Dan Haren deal, part of a six-player package that also included Brett Anderson and Carlos Gonzalez. After Carter finished second in the minor leagues with 39 home runs in 2008 but batted just .259, he worked hard to shed his reputation as an all-or-nothing slugger. The results were spectacular, as Carter posted a .329 average last season, leading the minors in hits (179) and ranking second in RBIs (115). His power didn't go away either, as he posted his third straight 25-homer season and managers rated him as his league's best power prospect for the third consecutive year. Named MVP of the Double-A Texas League, he led the league in doubles (41), extra-base hits (67), on-base percentage (.435) and slugging (.576). He capped his year with four homers in the Triple-A Pacific Coast League playoffs for Sacramento.

Home runs always will be Carter's calling card. However, he dedicated himself to becoming a more complete hitter and stopping from giving at-bats away. He lowered his hands slightly and eliminated a small bat wrap from his swing, giving himself a more compact stroke. With his pure strength and explosive wrists, he still produces light-tower power. Carter can hit balls out of any part of any ballpark, and he's strong enough to do so without having to sell out for power. He's willing to take walks when pitchers won't challenge him, and he did a better job of handling offspeed pitches in 2009. He also made strides defensively at first base, where he should be at least adequate and possibly average, a big step up from years past. He has a strong arm for the position.

Though Carter reduced his strikeout rate in 2009, whiffs always will come with the territory with him. He's still learning to control the strike zone and not be overanxious. He needs to stay on breaking balls better, so the A's dispatched him to play in the Mexican Pacific League, well known for being chock full of junkballers. That venture was short-lived, as he returned home with what was believed to be appendicitis but turned out to be the flu. Carter still isn't the most agile first baseman and he has given up playing third base. He played some left field after his promotion to Sacramento, and that might be an option if he can get more experience, improve his instincts and stay in good shape. He has some athleticism for his size, but his first-step quickness and speed are below-average.

Carter can add power to an Oakland offense that sorely needs it. He has a great opportunity to make the A's in spring training and should bat in the middle of their lineup for years to come. The final question is where he plays. First base, left field and DH are all possibilities, but his best position is the batter's box.

Year	Club (League)	Class	AVG	G	AB	R	H	2B	3B	HR	RBI	BB	SO	SB	OBP	SLG
2005	Bristol (APP)	R	.283	65	233	33	66	17	0	10	37	17	64	2	.350	.485
2006	Kannapolis (SAL)	LoA	.130	13	46	4	6	3	0	1	5	5	17	0	.231	.261
	Great Falls (PIO)	R	.299	69	251	37	75	21	1	15	59	34	70	4	.398	.570
2007	Kannapolis (SAL)	LoA	.291	126	467	84	136	27	3	25	93	67	112	3	.383	.522
2008	Stockton (CAL)	HiA	.259	137	506	101	131	32	4	39	104	77	156	4	.361	.569
2009	Midland (TL)	AA	.337	125	490	108	165	41	2	24	101	82	119	13	.435	.576
	Sacramento (PCL)	AAA	.259	13	54	7	14	2	0	4	14	3	14	0	.293	.519
MINOR LEAGUE TOTALS			.290	548	2047	374	593	143	10	118	413	285	552	26	.383	.542

2 BRETT WALLACE, 3B/1B

BORN: Aug. 26, 1986. **B-T:** L-R. **HT.:** 6-2. **WT.:** 205. **DRAFTED:** Arizona State, 2008 (1st round). **SIGNED BY:** Chuck Fick (Cardinals).

The A's loved Wallace heading into the 2008 draft but elected to go with Jemile Weeks with the 12th overall pick. Wallace went one pick later to the Cardinals, signed for $1.84 million and had reached Triple-A when St. Louis traded him, Clayton Mortensen and outfield prospect Shane Peterson for Matt Holliday last July. A natural hitter, Wallace has a strong lower half and an inside-out stroke that allows him to drive balls to all fields. He has outstanding bat control and knows to how to get in favorable counts where he can do the most damage, allowing him to project for 20 homers per year despite not having outstanding raw power. His recognizes pitches well and puts together relentless at-bats. He has the hands and arm strength to play third base. Though he has worked hard at third base, Wallace lacks the agility and athleticism for the position. Most scouts think he'll have to move across the diamond to first base. He's a below-average runner. Oakland has a logjam of potential first basemen, while Eric Chavez has played just 32 games the last two seasons. Ideally, Wallace would be ready to play third base in the majors this year, but more than likely he'll compete for playing time with Chris Carter and Daric Barton at first base. He has the talent to win a big league batting title some day.

Year	Club (League)	Class	AVG	G	AB	R	H	2B	3B	HR	RBI	BB	SO	SB	OBP	SLG
2008	Quad Cities (MWL)	LoA	.327	41	153	28	50	8	1	5	25	17	32	0	.418	.490
	Springfield (TL)	AA	.367	13	49	13	18	5	0	3	11	2	7	0	.456	.653
2009	Springfield (TL)	AA	.281	32	128	22	36	5	0	5	16	18	34	0	.403	.438
	Memphis (PCL)	AAA	.293	62	222	22	65	11	0	6	19	15	42	0	.346	.423
	Sacramento (PCL)	AAA	.302	44	182	32	55	10	0	9	28	14	40	1	.365	.505
MINOR LEAGUE TOTALS			.305	192	734	117	224	39	1	28	99	66	155	1	.384	.475

3 GRANT GREEN, SS

BORN: Sept. 27, 1987. **B-T:** R-R. **HT.:** 6-3. **WT.:** 170. **DRAFTED:** Southern California, 2009 (1st round). **SIGNED BY:** J.T. Stotts.

A top prospect since high school, Green shot up draft boards with an outstanding showing in the Cape Cod League in the summer of 2008, hitting .340 on his way to being named the league's top prospect. He struggled early last spring but recovered to bat .374/.435/.569 for Southern California. Oakland landed him with the 13th overall pick and signed him at the Aug. 17 deadline for $2.75 million. Green has a short, compact stroke with a natural feel for hitting and an up-the-middle approach. Lean and athletic, he shows smooth actions and strong instincts at shortstop. He has good range and a solid arm, and his hands work well. He's also a plus runner. The A's laud his competitive makeup and how hard he plays the game. Green's bat isn't as explosive as his Cape showing seemed to indicate. He could project for average power once he develops physically, but he doesn't always maintain a good swing plane. His defense could use refinement, and scouts outside the organization weren't sold that he'd be more than an average defender at shortstop. Green has the offensive upside and playmaking ability to be an all-star shortstop, perhaps a lesser version of Troy Tulowitzki. He'll begin his first full pro season at high Class A Stockton, where he made his brief debut, and easily could reach Double-A Midland by the end of the year.

Year	Club (League)	Class	AVG	G	AB	R	H	2B	3B	HR	RBI	BB	SO	SB	OBP	SLG
2009	Stockton (CAL)	HiA	.316	5	19	2	6	1	0	0	3	1	5	1	.350	.368
MINOR LEAGUE TOTALS			.316	5	19	2	6	1	0	0	3	1	5	1	.350	.368

4 MAX STASSI, C

BORN: March 15, 1991. **B-T:** R-R. **HT.:** 5-10. **WT.:** 205. **DRAFTED:** HS Yuba City, Calif., 2009 (4th round). **SIGNED BY:** Jermaine Clark.

Stassi comes from a baseball family. He's the great-great nephew of former big league outfielder Myril Hoag, and his father Jim played in the minors and was his high school coach. A first-round talent who slipped last June because of his price tag, Stassi landed the largest bonus ever given to a fourth-rounder, $1.5 million. Stassi has good leverage in his swing and plus raw power to all fields. He's an advanced hitter for his age, with a balanced setup and quick hands. Against older competition at short-season Vancouver, he showed he could lay off breaking pitches out of the zone and wasn't afraid to go deep in counts. He's a secure receiver and shows a feel for calling pitches, and he has a strong, accurate arm. The A's consider him a future plus defender behind the plate. A shoulder injury limited Stassi to DH duty for part of the high school season. His arm should play once healthy, but it bears watching. As with most young hitters, his stroke can get long at times. Oakland wants him to use his legs a little better in his swing. His speed is already below-average, but he's not a baseclogger. Stassi is mature enough to open his first full pro season at low Class A Kane County. He's still a few years away from the majors, but he appears to be the closest thing to a sure bet a high school catcher can be.

Year	Club (League)	Class	AVG	G	AB	R	H	2B	3B	HR	RBI	BB	SO	SB	OBP	SLG
2009	Athletics (AZL)	R	.000	1	1	0	0	0	0	0	0	1	1	0	.500	.000
	Vancouver (NWL)	SS	.286	13	49	3	14	4	0	0	8	2	11	0	.340	.367
MINOR LEAGUE TOTALS			.280	14	50	3	14	4	0	0	8	3	12	0	.345	.360

5 PEDRO FIGUEROA, LHP

BORN: Nov. 23, 1985. **B-T:** L-L. **HT.:** 6-1. **WT.:** 165. **SIGNED:** Dominican Republic, 2003. **SIGNED BY:** Juan Carlos de la Cruz.

Figueroa's development had proceeded so slowly that he needed five years in Rookie and short-season ball and went unpicked in the 2008 Rule 5 draft. He broke though in 2009, winning Oakland's minor league pitcher of the year award after going 13-6, 3.38 with 145 strikeouts in 152 innings between two Class A stops. From a low-three-quarters delivery, Figueroa whips lively fastballs that sit at 93-95 mph and touch 97. He can throw his fastball with natural sink or give it cutting action. His breaking ball was big and sloppy in the past, but he has tightened it into a mid-80s slider with depth. His changeup still is developing but shows some promise and he's not afraid to throw it. Command is Figueroa's biggest downfall, a result of sometimes rushing his delivery. That causes him to throw too many hittable pitches and hand out too many walks. He may be a late bloomer, but he's 24 and has yet to pitch above Class A. Figueroa will have the stuff to be a frontline starter if he throws more strikes. If not, he could be a weapon out of the bullpen, with one A's official comparing him to Damaso Marte. Added to the 40-man roster this offseason, Figueroa should begin 2010 in Double-A.

Year	Club (League)	Class	W	L	ERA	G	GS	CG	SV	IP	H	R	ER	HR	BB	SO	AVG
2004	Athletics2 (DSL)	R	2	2	2.90	15	2	0	1	50	52	21	16	3	11	40	.261
2005	Athletics2 (DSL)	R	3	0	2.27	13	3	0	1	36	29	14	9	0	12	25	.215
2006	Athletics1 (DSL)	R	1	0	4.50	1	1	0	0	6	5	3	3	1	1	1	.227
	Athletics (AZL)	R	1	6	6.07	13	8	0	0	43	59	39	29	4	11	27	.321
2007	Vancouver (NWL)	SS	2	2	4.30	17	7	0	1	44	41	26	21	2	31	35	.252
2008	Vancouver (NWL)	SS	2	5	3.93	15	15	0	0	69	62	37	30	3	32	77	.238
2009	Kane County (MWL)	LoA	10	2	3.23	16	16	0	0	86	89	37	31	6	31	78	.267
	Stockton (CAL)	HiA	3	4	3.56	11	11	0	0	66	62	27	26	3	35	67	.251
MINOR LEAGUE TOTALS			24	21	3.72	101	63	0	3	399	399	204	165	22	164	350	.259

6 TYSON ROSS, RHP

BORN: April 22, 1987. **B-T:** R-R. **HT.:** 6-5. **WT.:** 215. **DRAFTED:** California, 2008 (2nd round). **SIGNED BY:** Jermaine Clark.

A travel-ball teammate of Brett Wallace in northern California, Ross looked like a potential first-round pick entering 2008. An up-and-down junior season at California dropped him to the second round, but he got back on track in his first full season, pitching well down the stretch in Double-A and starring in the Texas League playoffs as Midland won the championship. The A's lengthened Ross' previous short stride by about a foot last year, with spectacular results. His sinking fastball now sits at 93-94 mph and touches 97, helping him induce groundouts. He throws a cutter that usually comes in around 90 mph and a slider with tilt at 82-84, both of which are above-average pitches. He cuts an imposing figure on the mound and is a good athlete for his size. Ross' command needs tightening and his changeup lags behind his other offerings, though he shows a feel for it. He has an upright finish to his delivery and his motion is hard on his shoulder. He missed time in his 2008 pro debut with a shoulder strain as well as a couple of starts last April with biceps tendinitis. Durability may always be a concern with Ross and eventually could dictate a move to the bullpen, but Oakland will continue developing him as a starter. He has middle-of-the-rotation stuff, and possibly more. He may open 2010 back in Double-A, but should reach Sacramento by the end of the year.

Year	Club (League)	Class	W	L	ERA	G	GS	CG	SV	IP	H	R	ER	HR	BB	SO	AVG
2008	Kane County (MWL)	LoA	0	1	4.66	6	4	0	0	19	16	11	10	1	5	16	.219
2009	Stockton (CAL)	HiA	5	6	4.17	18	18	0	0	86	78	49	40	10	33	82	.237
	Midland (TL)	AA	5	4	3.96	9	9	1	0	50	40	22	22	3	20	31	.225
MINOR LEAGUE TOTALS			10	11	4.16	33	31	1	0	156	134	82	72	14	58	129	.231

7 JEMILE WEEKS, 2B

BORN: Jan. 26, 1987. **B-T:** B-R. **HT.:** 5-10. **WT.:** 175. **DRAFTED:** Miami, 2008 (1st round). **SIGNED BY:** Trevor Schaffer.

Weeks and his brother Rickie, the No. 2 choice in the 2003 draft, are the eighth pair of siblings to become first-round picks. Jemile signed for $1.91 million as the 12th overall selection in 2008. A hip-flexor injury cut short his pro debut and lingered into the spring, delaying his arrival at Stockton until late May. He struggled after an August promotion to Double-A but recovered to hit .290 with two homers in the Texas League playoffs. Weeks has good pitch recognition and a line-drive swing that produces surprising power for a player his size. He has the speed to steal bases, though leg injuries cut into his ability to run last year. He's athletic enough for the middle of the diamond and has a strong arm. Injuries have been Weeks' biggest obstacle going back to his college career, when hamstring and groin woes derailed his sophomore season. In addition to his hip, he had hamstring and Achilles problems in 2009. His hands aren't always smooth at second base and he sometimes rushes himself turning double plays, though that should improve with experience. He can fall in love with his power and try to hit home runs, lengthening his swing. Staying healthy will be Weeks' top priority in 2010. The A's are grooming him to be their leadoff hitter of the future, so it will be important for him to maintain a disciplined approach. He'll return to Midland to open the season.

Year	Club (League)	Class	AVG	G	AB	R	H	2B	3B	HR	RBI	BB	SO	SB	OBP	SLG
2008	Kane County (MWL)	LoA	.297	19	74	11	22	3	1	1	8	13	12	6	.422	.405
2009	Stockton (CAL)	HiA	.299	50	201	29	60	9	2	7	31	26	40	5	.385	.468
	Midland (TL)	AA	.238	30	105	10	25	5	0	2	13	10	16	4	.303	.343
MINOR LEAGUE TOTALS			.282	99	380	50	107	17	3	10	52	49	68	15	.370	.421

8 GRANT DESME, OF

BORN: April 4, 1986. **B-T:** R-R. **HT.:** 6-2. **WT.:** 205. **DRAFTED:** Cal Poly, 2007 (2nd round). **SIGNED BY:** Rick Magnante.

Desme broke a bone in his wrist late in the 2007 college season, then separated his shoulder in minor league camp in 2008 and wasn't fully healthy again until last spring. He showed off his all-around talents at two Class A stops, becoming the only 30-30 player in the minors last year. He continued his torrid play in the Arizona Fall League, hitting a league-leading 11 home runs and winning MVP honors. Desme has average to plus tools across the board. He has a quick bat and good leverage, providing power to all fields. A good athlete with average speed, his instincts allowed him to steal 40 bases and play mostly center field in 2009. He also has the arm strength for right field. He also earns praise for his leadership. Desme has trouble with pitch recognition and breaking balls, leading to 148 strikeouts last season and questions as to how much he'll hit for average. He'll lapse into trying to do too much at the plate and overswing. He needs to improve his routes on balls in the outfield, and he'll probably wind up on a corner in the long run. If Desme can make more consistent contact, he could bat in the heart of Oakland's lineup in a couple of years. For now, he'll advance to Double-A and try to keep his momentum going from 2009.

Year	Club (League)	Class	AVG	G	AB	R	H	2B	3B	HR	RBI	BB	SO	SB	OBP	SLG
2007	Vancouver (NWL)	SS	.261	12	46	6	12	3	0	1	6	6	21	2	.358	.391
2008	Athletics (AZL)	R	.333	2	3	2	1	0	0	1	2	0	0	0	.500	1.333
2009	Kane County (MWL)	LoA	.274	69	259	49	71	19	2	11	38	21	81	24	.334	.490
	Stockton (CAL)	HiA	.304	62	227	49	69	12	4	20	51	33	67	16	.398	.656
MINOR LEAGUE TOTALS			.286	145	535	106	153	34	6	33	97	60	169	42	.365	.557

9 ADRIAN CARDENAS, INF

BORN: Oct. 10, 1987. **B-T:** L-R. **HT.:** 6-0. **WT.:** 185. **DRAFTED:** HS—Miami, 2006 (1st round supplemental). **SIGNED BY:** Miguel Machado (Phillies).

Baseball America's High School Player of the Year in 2006, Cardenas went 37th overall in that draft to the Phillies and signed for $925,000. The A's acquired him along with Josh Outman and outfield prospect Matt Spencer in exchange for Joe Blanton in July 2008. In his first full year in the Oakland system, Cardenas reached Triple-A at age 21 while playing second base, third base and shortstop. A natural hitter with a compact swing, Cardenas has a keen sense for putting the barrel on the ball. He has gap power and controls the strike zone well for a player his age. He has an all-fields approach and always looks like he has a plan at the plate. He has the hands and arm to play anywhere in the infield, as well as average speed. A high school shortstop, Cardenas lacks range and quickness there. He can handle the defensive responsibilities at third base, but doesn't have the home run power for the position. He profiles best at second base. With Jemile Weeks looking like Oakland's second baseman of the future, Cardenas' long-term future with the organization may hinge on his ability to fit at third base, especially if Brett Wallace can't stay there. Most of Cardenas' value stems from his bat though, so the A's will find a place for him as long as he keeps hitting. He'll likely return to Sacramento to open 2010.

Year	Club (League)	Class	AVG	G	AB	R	H	2B	3B	HR	RBI	BB	SO	SB	OBP	SLG
2006	Phillies (GCL)	R	.318	41	154	22	49	5	4	2	21	17	28	13	.384	.442
2007	Lakewood (SAL)	LoA	.295	127	499	70	147	30	2	9	79	47	80	20	.354	.417
2008	Clearwater (FSL)	HiA	.307	68	261	44	80	11	6	4	23	28	42	16	.371	.441
	Stockton (CAL)	HiA	.278	15	72	11	20	1	0	1	10	1	14	1	.297	.333
	Midland (TL)	AA	.279	26	86	12	24	4	0	0	7	15	10	0	.392	.326
2009	Midland (TL)	AA	.326	79	325	56	106	26	2	3	55	38	44	5	.392	.446
	Sacramento (PCL)	AAA	.251	51	183	23	46	15	2	1	24	17	29	3	.317	.372
MINOR LEAGUE TOTALS			.299	407	1580	238	472	92	16	20	219	163	247	58	.363	.415

10 SEAN DOOLITTLE, OF

BORN: Sept. 26, 1986. **B-T:** L-L. **HT.:** 6-3. **WT.:** 190. **DRAFTED:** Virginia, 2007 (1st round supplemental). **SIGNED BY:** Neil Avent.

A two-way standout as a first baseman and lefthander at Virginia, Doolittle signed for $742,500 as a sandwich pick in 2007. After a strong first full pro season, he hit .329/.441/.724 with 11 RBIs in big league camp last spring, setting the stage for a big league callup later in the year. But tendinitis in both knees ruined his season, which ended in early May. His left knee eventually required surgery. Doolittle has bulked up and become more power-oriented since turning pro. He has a disciplined, all-fields approach and hangs in well against lefthanders. His swing is short to the ball and sound mechanically. A first baseman until last year, he moved to right field to take advantage of his above-average arm strength. The A's think he's athletic enough to handle the position, and always can move back to first, where he was an above-average defender with smooth actions. Though Doolittle has gotten stronger as a pro, scouts still don't project him to have more than fringe to average power. He's a below-average runner who isn't a threat on the bases. If he loses a step after knee problems, he won't be able to stay in right field. Following his surgery, Doolittle may not be ready for the start of spring training. Nevertheless, he looks like a safe bet to be a solid big league hitter, and he could develop more power. He'll return to Triple-A once he's healthy.

Year	Club (League)	Class	AVG	G	AB	R	H	2B	3B	HR	RBI	BB	SO	SB	OBP	SLG
2007	Vancouver (NWL)	SS	.283	13	46	6	13	3	0	0	4	9	10	0	.421	.348
	Kane County (MWL)	LoA	.233	55	193	23	45	10	0	4	29	24	40	1	.320	.347
2008	Stockton (CAL)	HiA	.305	86	334	64	102	25	3	18	61	46	99	7	.385	.560
	Midland (TL)	AA	.254	51	201	25	51	15	0	4	30	17	54	1	.311	.388
2009	Sacramento (PCL)	AAA	.267	28	105	17	28	5	1	4	14	15	23	0	.364	.448
MINOR LEAGUE TOTALS			.272	233	879	135	239	58	4	30	138	111	226	9	.354	.449

11 MICHAEL YNOA, RHP

BORN: Sept. 24, 1991. **B-T:** R-R. **HT.:** 6-7. **WT.:** 210. **SIGNED:** Dominican Republic, 2008. **SIGNED BY:** Raymond Abreu.

Ynoa was the crown jewel of the 2008 international free agent class, and the A's landed him for $4.25 million, the largest bonus in franchise history and the biggest any team has given a Latin American amateur. He still has yet to make his pro debut, however, because elbow tendinitis derailed his first year in pro ball. The A's didn't want to take any chances and kept him on the shelf all season. He was back throwing on flat ground during instructional league and returned to the mound at the A's Dominican camp in November. Ynoa looked like he hadn't missed a beat, effortlessly unleashing lively fastballs in the low 90s. He also showed a hammer curveball with late break that came in as hard as 79 mph, as well as an average changeup. Ynoa is plenty athletic with a fluid arm action and cohesive delivery that he repeats well for someone his size and age. He still has to tighten up other aspects of his craft, such as holding runners and fielding his position, but Ynoa's potential remains considerable. Losing a year of development time didn't help him but he's still just 18. His health will bear watching in 2010, when he should make his pro debut with Vancouver or the Rookie-level Arizona League club.

Year	Club (League)	Class	W	L	ERA	G	GS	CG	SV	IP	H	R	ER	HR	BB	SO	AVG
2009	Did Not Play—Injured																

12 COREY BROWN, OF

BORN: Nov. 26, 1985. **B-T:** L-L. **HT.:** 6-2. **WT.:** 210. **DRAFTED:** Oklahoma State, 2007 (1st round supplemental). **SIGNED BY:** Blake Davis.

Brown could have played college football as a wide receiver but chose baseball at Oklahoma State, where he starred for three years with the Cowboys, slugging 48 home runs. A supplemental first-round pick in 2007, he signed for $554,500. After hitting another 30 home runs between two Class A stops in his first full pro season,

Brown missed much of 2009 with a knee strain. He rallied with a terrific showing in the Arizona Fall League, leading the league in RBIs (28) while batting .333. Brown shows five-tool potential, with his upside drawing comparisons to Jim Edmonds'. He has gap-to-gap power, with the bat speed and leverage in his swing to drive balls out of the park. He runs well, has a strong arm and may be able to stick in center field, though some scouts think he's destined for right. Brown started putting together better at-bats and improved his contact rate last year, but strikeouts remain an issue. Though he's willing to use the whole field, he lacks a consistent approach. Sometimes he'll look willing to drive the ball to the opposite field, while at other times he looks like he's trying to cheat on fastballs and pull pitches down the line. He plays the game with a laid-back attitude that frustrates some observers as well. He'll try to apply some polish to his game this year in Triple-A.

Year	Club (League)	Class	AVG	G	AB	R	H	2B	3B	HR	RBI	BB	SO	SB	OBP	SLG
2007	Vancouver (NWL)	SS	.268	59	213	31	57	18	4	11	48	37	77	5	.379	.545
2008	Kane County (MWL)	LoA	.270	85	300	44	81	18	2	14	49	41	96	12	.359	.483
	Stockton (CAL)	HiA	.260	49	196	34	51	9	0	16	34	17	72	4	.322	.551
2009	Midland (TL)	AA	.268	66	250	46	67	20	4	9	43	27	69	5	.349	.488
MINOR LEAGUE TOTALS			.267	259	959	155	256	65	10	50	174	122	314	26	.354	.512

13 HENRY RODRIGUEZ, RHP

BORN: Feb. 25, 1987. **B-T:** R-R. **HT.:** 6-0. **WT.:** 210. **SIGNED:** Venezuela, 2003. **SIGNED BY:** Julio Franco.

Last season marked Rodriguez' first year as a full-time reliever, but the control problems that hampered his career as a starter were as bad as ever. It's hard not to be awestruck by his lightning arm, as he routinely fires fastballs in the upper 90s and can hit 100 mph, as he did in the 2008 Futures Game. His slider is overpowering as well, and he shows flashes of an effective changeup. He's nearly unhittable when he throws strikes, as his three-pitch mix is good enough that batters can't sit on his fastball. He just doesn't throw strikes nearly enough. Rodriguez still is trying to figure out his mechanics, working on staying closed and separating his hands before he comes to the plate. He tends to overthrow and has trouble repeating his delivery. Rodriguez did have success during a brief callup to Oakland late last season. He sometimes looked like he had trouble staying motivated in the minors and would pitch to the level of his competition. Based on his performance last year, Rodriguez should repeat Triple-A in 2010. However, he could pitch his way into the big league bullpen in the spring, especially if he responds to the challenge of facing big league hitters. Rodriguez has the potential to be a major league closer, but he has to rein in his command if he's going to earn that role.

Year	Club (League)	Class	W	L	ERA	G	GS	CG	SV	IP	H	R	ER	HR	BB	SO	AVG
2005	Athletics1 (DSL)	R	0	2	4.03	8	3	0	0	22	14	19	10	1	14	27	.163
2006	Athletics (AZL)	R	5	2	7.42	15	4	0	1	44	46	39	36	1	50	59	.284
2007	Kane County (MWL)	LoA	6	8	3.07	20	18	1	0	100	75	38	34	2	58	106	.214
2008	Stockton (CAL)	HiA	2	3	3.96	20	13	0	2	75	57	38	33	5	40	104	.208
	Midland (TL)	AA	2	7	7.46	14	9	0	0	41	51	39	34	1	44	43	.302
2009	Stockton (CAL)	HiA	0	0	0.00	3	0	0	0	5	3	0	0	0	1	11	.167
	Sacramento (PCL)	AAA	2	1	5.77	37	0	0	4	44	38	28	28	4	38	71	.228
	Oakland (AL)	MAJ	0	0	2.25	3	0	0	0	4	4	2	1	0	2	4	.235
MAJOR LEAGUE TOTALS			0	0	2.25	3	0	0	0	4	4	2	1	0	2	4	.235
MINOR LEAGUE TOTALS			17	23	4.77	117	47	1	7	330	284	201	175	14	245	421	.231

14 JOSH DONALDSON, C/3B

BORN: Dec. 8, 1985. **B-T:** R-R. **HT.:** 6-1. **WT.:** 215. **DRAFTED:** Auburn, 2007 (1st round supplemental). **SIGNED BY:** Bob Rossi (Cubs).

Donaldson didn't take up catching until his sophomore season at Auburn and quickly boosted his draft stock by showing some feel for working behind the plate and hitting .348 as a junior. The Cubs took him with the 48th overall pick in the 2007 draft and signed him for $652,500, but his career in their organization was short lived. Donaldson got off to a slow start at low Class A and was included with Sean Gallagher, Matt Murton and Eric Patterson in the July 2008 deal that sent Rich Harden and Chad Gaudin to Chicago. After rediscovering his stroke in the A's system in 2008, Donaldson advanced to Double-A and held his own last year, backstopping the RockHounds to the Texas League title. He has toned down the aggressive stride he had in college to give himself a more compact swing, and he has an outstanding feel for the strike zone. The A's are confident Donaldson's power will continue developing, and he has the strength to hit balls out to all fields. His power is primarily geared to his pull side now, though, as all but one of his nine homers last year went to left field. Donaldson is athletic and shows soft hands, a strong arm and a quick release behind the plate. He threw out 40 percent of basestealers last year, but he's by no means a finished product. His receiving needs some tightening up after he allowed a TL-high 17 passed balls and committed 16 errors. He's a below-average runner but moves better than most catchers, and he saw some action at third base last year. Donaldson doesn't have Max Stassi's potential, but he's the best catching option in the upper levels of the system. He'll be the everyday catcher at Sacramento in 2010.

Year	Club (League)	Class	AVG	G	AB	R	H	2B	3B	HR	RBI	BB	SO	SB	OBP	SLG
2007	Cubs (AZL)	R	.182	4	11	1	2	2	0	0	0	2	4	0	.308	.364
	Boise (NWL)	SS	.346	49	162	37	56	11	2	9	35	37	34	6	.470	.605
2008	Peoria (MWL)	LoA	.217	63	235	27	51	13	0	6	23	17	41	7	.276	.349
	Stockton (CAL)	HiA	.330	47	188	37	62	13	2	9	39	17	29	0	.391	.564
2009	Midland (TL)	AA	.270	124	455	67	123	37	1	9	91	80	92	7	.379	.415
MINOR LEAGUE TOTALS			.280	287	1051	169	294	76	5	33	188	153	200	20	.374	.456

15 CLAYTON MORTENSEN, RHP

BORN: April 10, 1985. **B-T:** R-R. **HT.:** 6-4. **WT.:** 180. **DRAFTED:** Gonzaga, 2007 (1st round supplemental). **SIGNED BY:** Jay North (Cardinals).

The Cardinals signed Mortensen for $650,000 as a sandwich pick in 2007, then promoted him aggressively, as he reached Triple-A in his first full pro season. He made his big league debut for St. Louis last June, then was shipped to the A's as part of the Matt Holliday deal just before the trade deadline. Mortensen induces plenty of groundballs thanks to his sinker, which sits at 89-91 mph and peaks at 92. His slider gives him a second weapon, rating as a plus pitch at times. He has a changeup as well, but he struggles to throw it for strikes and needs to refine his command with all his pitches. His biggest hurdle to clear is repeating his delivery. His arm action is long in the back and he has trouble staying on top of the ball and finding a consistent release point, causing his pitches to flatten out. He has had maturity issues in the past and that cropped up again in October, when he was arrested on suspicion of drunken driving. Though Mortensen has been used almost exclusively as a starter in pro ball, he might fit better as a set-up man who could focus on using his sinker and slider. After earning his first two big league wins last September, he'll get another chance to make the A's in spring training.

Year	Club (League)	Class	W	L	ERA	G	GS	CG	SV	IP	H	R	ER	HR	BB	SO	AVG
2007	Batavia (NYP)	SS	1	1	1.77	6	4	0	0	20	13	4	4	0	11	23	.188
	Quad Cities (MWL)	LoA	0	2	3.12	10	10	0	0	40	44	17	14	2	8	45	.275
2008	Springfield, MO (TL)	AA	3	4	4.22	11	11	0	0	60	59	31	28	6	22	48	.257
	Memphis (PCL)	AAA	5	6	5.51	15	14	0	0	80	87	50	49	12	42	57	.281
2009	St. Louis (NL)	MAJ	0	0	6.00	1	0	0	0	3	5	6	2	1	1	2	.417
	Memphis (PCL)	AAA	7	6	4.37	17	17	1	0	105	103	58	51	11	34	82	.259
	Sacramento (PCL)	AAA	2	2	4.45	6	6	0	0	32	40	20	16	2	14	18	.310
	Oakland (AL)	MAJ	2	4	7.81	6	6	0	0	28	37	28	24	5	12	11	.319
MAJOR LEAGUE TOTALS			2	4	7.63	7	6	0	0	31	42	34	26	6	13	13	.328
MINOR LEAGUE TOTALS			18	21	4.32	65	62	1	0	338	346	180	162	33	131	273	.267

16 IAN KROL, LHP

BORN: May 9, 1991. **B-T:** L-L. **HT.:** 6-1. **WT.:** 180. **DRAFTED:** HS—Naperville, Ill., 2009 (7th round). **SIGNED BY:** Kevin Mello.

Krol was the first high school pitcher to sign with Oakland since 2006, though his journey to the A's system wasn't without tumult. He was suspended from his high school team for the entire season last spring after being found in the presence of alcohol, his second violation of the school's athletic code of conduct. Krol pitched in a scout league in Wisconsin on the weekends, and the A's saw enough to nab him in the seventh round and sign him for $925,000. Krol shows command of three average pitches. His fastball dipped to 86-88 mph last spring, but he previously pitched at 89-92 mph and still features good sink. He doesn't project to add much more velocity, but if he can regain what he had, he'll be in good shape because his secondary pitches already grade as average and have a chance to become plus His curveball has good spin and two-plane break, and his changeup is effective. Krol is a feisty competitor and has an advanced feel for pitching for his age. He has a chance to be a solid big league starter, though he'll have to prove his off-the-field issues are a thing of the past. He could spend his first full pro season at Kane County, about 15 minutes from his hometown of Naperville, Ill.

Year	Club (League)	Class	W	L	ERA	G	GS	CG	SV	IP	H	R	ER	HR	BB	SO	AVG
2009	Athletics (AZL)	R	0	0	0.00	1	1	0	0	1	0	0	0	0	0	0	.000
	Vancouver (NWL)	SS	0	1	8.10	3	1	0	0	3	6	5	3	0	1	4	.375
MINOR LEAGUE TOTALS			0	1	6.23	4	2	0	0	4	6	5	3	0	1	4	.316

17 FAUTINO DE LOS SANTOS, RHP

BORN: Feb. 15, 1986. **B-T:** R-R. **HT.:** 6-0. **WT.:** 205. **SIGNED:** Dominican Republic, 2005. **SIGNED BY:** Denny Gonzalez (White Sox).

De los Santos burst onto the scene in 2007, going a combined 10-5, 2.65 between two Class A stops in the White Sox system, overpowering hitters with a mid-90s fastball and earning a trip to the Futures Game. After the season, Chicago dealt him, Gio Gonzalez and Ryan Sweeney to the A's in exchange for Nick Swisher. While Gonzalez and Sweeney have logged big league time, Oakland barely has been able to evaluate de los Santos since the trade. He has pitched just 35 innings over the last two seasons, having been shut down early in the 2008 season because he needed Tommy John surgery and not getting back on the mound until late in 2009. Still, the

A's remain excited about his potential. De los Santos was throwing in the mid-90s and touching 98 mph in the team's Dominican instructional league in November. His changeup showed encouraging signs as well, coming out with great hand speed around 84 mph with some depth. His slider was a plus pitch before the surgery, and he featured a curveball as well, and working those two pitches back into his arsenal will be the next step in his progression back from the surgery. The A's added de los Santos to their 40-man roster to protect him from the Rule 5 draft. He should be fully healthy for 2010, when he'll resume his career in high Class A.

Year	Club (League)	Class	W	L	ERA	G	GS	CG	SV	IP	H	R	ER	HR	BB	SO	AVG
2006	White Sox (DSL)	R	3	3	1.86	10	9	0	0	48	44	20	10	0	10	61	.232
2007	Kannapolis (SAL)	LoA	9	4	2.40	21	15	0	0	98	49	33	26	5	36	121	.148
	Winston-Salem (CAR)	HiA	1	1	3.65	5	5	0	0	25	20	12	10	3	7	32	.220
2008	Stockton (CAL)	HiA	2	2	5.87	5	5	0	0	23	29	17	15	3	11	26	.309
2009	Athletics (AZL)	R	0	1	3.86	7	7	0	0	12	12	6	5	0	4	16	.279
MINOR LEAGUE TOTALS			15	11	2.89	48	41	0	0	205	154	88	66	11	68	256	.205

18 TOMMY EVERIDGE, 1B/3B

BORN: April 20, 1983. **B-T:** R-R. **HT.:** 6-0. **WT.:** 240. **DRAFTED:** Sonoma State (Calif.), 2004 (10th round). **SIGNED BY:** Scott Kidd.

Everidge was one of the revelations in Oakland's farm system last season, beginning the year with his third stint in Double-A before earning his way to the big leagues by late July. His power and on-base skills make him a bit of a throwback to the kind of hitters the A's were known for early in the decade. A fairly complete hitter when drafted in the 10th round out of NCAA Division II power Sonoma State, Everidge started selling out for power as time went on, believing that was the way for him to advance. He never had hit better than .279 over a full season before last year, but he dialed back his approach, shortened his swing and focused on putting together better at-bats. The adjustments paid off in the form of a .335 average between two minor league stops, and he still hit 20 homers for the fourth consecutive season. Everidge has legitimate all-fields power and knows the strike zone. He's not especially agile and is an average defender at best, so he'll be anchored to first base as a big leaguer. He has some arm strength and played some third base in the minors, but that's not a realistic option. He's a well-below-average runner. Everidge enjoyed some success with Oakland—both of his homers came against all-stars, C.C. Sabathia and Joakim Soria—though big league pitchers eventually began exploiting him with breaking balls and changeups. He'll compete for Oakland's first base and DH jobs in spring training, but could find himself back in Triple-A.

Year	Club (League)	Class	AVG	G	AB	R	H	2B	3B	HR	RBI	BB	SO	SB	OBP	SLG
2004	Vancouver (NWL)	SS	.275	74	291	42	80	13	1	6	52	23	72	0	.333	.388
2005	Kane County (MWI)	LoA	.279	114	365	59	102	26	3	14	66	56	73	1	.370	.482
2006	Stockton (CAL)	HiA	.252	133	504	89	127	32	2	20	83	44	116	5	.323	.442
2007	Stockton (CAL)	HiA	.258	124	461	75	119	13	3	26	90	66	103	2	.354	.469
	Midland (TL)	AA	.361	10	36	7	13	4	0	4	2	5	0	.395	.472
2008	Midland (TL)	AA	.279	136	531	89	148	34	0	22	115	55	133	0	.346	.467
2009	Midland (TL)	AA	.306	55	229	41	70	18	0	8	53	28	34	0	.380	.489
	Oakland (AL)	MAJ	.224	24	85	13	19	6	0	2	7	8	17	0	.302	.365
	Sacramento (PCL)	AAA	.368	52	201	39	74	15	1	12	41	23	34	0	.428	.632
MAJOR LEAGUE TOTALS			.224	24	85	13	19	6	0	2	7	8	17	0	.302	.365
MINOR LEAGUE TOTALS			.280	698	2618	441	733	155	10	108	504	297	570	8	.355	.471

19 ARNOLD LEON, RHP

BORN: Sept. 6, 1988. **B-T:** R-R. **HT.:** 6-1. **WT.:** 205. **SIGNED:** Mexico, 2007. **SIGNED BY:** Randy Johnson/Craig Weissmann.

Athletics roving infield instructor Juan Navarrete discovered Leon while he was pitching for Saltillo of the Mexican League. The A's signed Leon after the 2007 season but he didn't spend a full year in their system until 2009. Part of Oakland's agreement with Saltillo stipulated that Leon would be loaned back for the second half of the 2008 season. He spent most of last season in Midland's bullpen in order to keep his innings down after he had pitched almost non-stop for two years between the A's, Saltillo and winter ball. He did make seven starts toward the end of the year and posted a 1-2, 1.76 record. Leon comes after hitters with a low-90s fastball that tops out at 93 mph and has cutting action. He throws both a hard slider and a slow 12-to-6 curveball, though both breaking balls lack consistency. His best secondary offering is his changeup, which has depth and is effective against lefthanders. Leon has a drop-and-drive delivery and sometimes has trouble staying on top of the ball. When he does, he gets a lot of movement down in the zone. Leon was a reliever throughout his career in Mexico and again in winter ball there, but the A's will attempt to develop him as a starter. They could choose to ease him into the role by returning him to Double-A.

Year	Club (League)	Class	W	L	ERA	G	GS	CG	SV	IP	H	R	ER	HR	BB	SO	AVG
2006	Saltillo (MEX)	AAA	0	0	2.70	4	0	0	0	3	2	1	1	0	2	2	.167
2007	Saltillo (MEX)	AAA	3	0	1.94	35	0	0	1	42	31	11	9	2	24	38	.217
2008	Stockton (CAL)	HiA	0	0	2.86	20	0	0	2	28	25	12	9	1	9	28	.238

	Saltillo (MEX)	AAA	2	1	4.30	13	0	0	0	15	12	7	7	0	2	21	.235
2009	Midland (TL)	AA	2	3	3.51	33	7	0	1	74	71	35	29	3	28	63	.247
MINOR LEAGUE TOTALS			7	4	3.05	105	7	0	4	162	141	66	55	6	65	152	.245

20 JUSTIN SOUZA, RHP

BORN: Oct. 22, 1985. **B-T:** R-R. **HT.:** 6-1. **WT.:** 185. **DRAFTED:** Sacramento CC, 2006 (9th round). **SIGNED BY:** Stacey Pettis (Mariners).

Souza arrived from the Mariners in a trade for Jack Hannahan last July and was one of the stars of Oakland's instructional league. His four-seam fastball sits at 93-95 mph with natural cutting action, and the A's helped him develop a true cutter at 88-89 that was electric in the fall. He has a two-seamer with sink as well, and three varieties of offspeed pitches to complement the fastballs. The best of the bunch is his hard slider, which has tilt and looks like a fastball coming out of his hand. He shows a feel for his changeup, and the A's are working with him on slowing down his curveball to give it more differentiation from his slider. There's some effort in Souza's delivery and he has had shoulder problems in the past. He both started and relieved in the Seattle system, and Oakland hasn't committed to a long-term path for him. The A's thought highly enough of Souza to add him to their 40-man roster after the season. He'll have a chance to prove himself against big league hitters in spring training but figures to open 2010 in Triple-A. He still could start but looks more likely to contribute as a power reliever.

Year	Club (League)	Class	W	L	ERA	G	GS	CG	SV	IP	H	R	ER	HR	BB	SO	AVG
2006	Everett (NWL)	SS	2	2	4.99	17	0	0	1	31	32	21	17	5	13	33	.267
2007	Wisconsin (MWL)	LoA	5	5	4.73	49	3	0	2	91	119	65	48	12	8	58	.304
2008	Wisconsin (MWL)	LoA	3	3	3.69	30	0	0	4	39	36	20	16	3	13	40	.247
	Tacoma (PCL)	AAA	0	0	2.08	2	0	0	0	4	4	1	1	0	0	3	.235
	High Desert (CAL)	HiA	2	1	4.31	12	5	0	0	40	46	20	19	5	13	39	.293
2009	West Tenn (SL)	AA	6	6	3.35	20	14	0	0	78	73	34	29	4	18	62	.247
	Midland (TL)	AA	0	2	10.35	5	5	0	0	20	32	28	23	1	10	13	.368
MINOR LEAGUE TOTALS			18	19	4.54	135	27	0	7	303	342	189	153	30	75	248	.281

21 RYAN ORTIZ, C

BORN: Sept. 29, 1987. **B-T:** R-R. **HT.:** 6-3. **WT.:** 205. **DRAFTED:** Oregon State, 2009 (6th round). **SIGNED BY:** Jim Coffman.

Ortiz was a little-used freshman on Oregon State's 2007 national championship squad, then took over as the Beavers' everyday catcher and shined for two seasons. After leading Oregon State in hitting for two years with a .351 average in 2008 and .352 last spring, Ortiz found the going tougher in pro ball after signing for $125,000 as a sixth-round pick. He made adjustments to his stance in instructional league, trying to eliminate a head tilt that caused him to pull off balls. The A's also want him to use his legs more and believe the changes should help him unlock at least average raw power. He hit just 10 home runs during his collegiate career. One scout compared Ortiz's swing to Jayson Werth's, and he has already shown good pitch recognition and a willingness to work the count. His defense is a work in progress. He's athletic and has an average arm, and he threw out 35 percent of basestealers last summer. But his footwork and receiving need improvement after he led the short-season Northwest League with 13 passed balls. Oakland believes Ortiz has enough athleticism to play other positions should the need arise, but in the short term he's expected to share Kane County's catching duties with Max Stassi.

Year	Club (League)	Class	AVG	G	AB	R	H	2B	3B	HR	RBI	BB	SO	SB	OBP	SLG
2009	Vancouver (NWL)	SS	.258	48	151	25	39	12	1	4	24	26	29	3	.388	.430
MINOR LEAGUE TOTALS			.258	48	151	25	39	12	1	4	24	26	29	3	.388	.430

22 CONNOR HOEHN, RHP

BORN: July 5, 1989. **B-T:** R-R. **HT.:** 6-1. **WT.:** 205. **DRAFTED:** St. Petersburg (Fla.) JC, 2009 (12th round). **SIGNED BY:** Trevor Schaffer.

The Brewers took Hoehn in the 21st round out of high school in 2007, but he opted to head to Alabama instead. He made five appearances for the Crimson Tide as a freshman in 2008, then transferred to St. Petersburg (Fla.) JC for his sophomore season. The A's paid him $75,000 as a 12th-round pick last June, and he turned in a dominant stint with Vancouver in his pro debut. After allowing two runs in his first game with the Canadians, he gave up only one the rest of the season and went 7-for-7 in save opportunities. Hoehn has a sturdy, physical frame and attacks hitters with a hard, sinking fastball that sits at 92-94 mph and tops out at 96. His secondary offerings both show promise as well. He has a hard slurve with late, darting movement and he can throw it for strikes. He gets nice fade on his changeup. Hoehn features deception in his delivery and it's hard to pick up his pitches, but he has trouble repeating his mechanics at times and there's some effort there as well. The A's employed him out of the bullpen mostly to limit his innings, and they plan to develop him as a starter going forward. Hoehn should advance to Kane County, where he'll be part of a prospect-laden rotation.

Year	Club (League)	Class	W	L	ERA	G	GS	CG	SV	IP	H	R	ER	HR	BB	SO	AVG
2009	Athletics (AZL)	R	0	1	4.50	2	1	0	0	2	1	1	1	0	2	3	.143
	Vancouver (NWL)	SS	0	1	1.00	15	0	0	7	18	9	3	2	0	7	25	.143
MINOR LEAGUE TOTALS			0	2	1.35	17	1	0	7	20	10	4	3	0	9	28	.143

23 JONATHAN JOSEPH, RHP

BORN: May 17, 1988. **B-T:** R-R. **HT.:** 6-1. **WT.:** 180. **SIGNED:** Dominican Republic, 2006. **SIGNED BY:** Amaurys Reyes.

The A's had been developing Joseph as a reliever, but they had him transition to the Vancouver rotation midway through 2009. He didn't put up spectacular numbers, but his stuff is much better than his stats indicate. Joseph features two above-average pitches in his fastball and curveball. The fastball sits at 92-94 mph and can touch 96. It's straight, but he generates good downhill plane from his high three-quarters delivery. Joseph complements his heater with a power curveball at 75-79 mph with 12-to-6 break. His changeup rates behind his other pitches, but he does get good differential between its velocity and his fastball's. Joseph's biggest shortcoming is his command, which he needs to improve on all of his pitches. He does a good job of repeating his delivery and maintaining a consistent arm slot, so he should be able to throw strikes more consistently. He was outstanding in instructional league and was praised for his work ethic, though the language barrier is something he's still overcoming. Joseph will have a chance to earn a spot in the Kane County rotation this spring.

Year	Club (League)	Class	W	L	ERA	G	GS	CG	SV	IP	H	R	ER	HR	BB	SO	AVG
2006	Athletics1 (DSL)	R	4	1	3.53	11	8	0	0	43	43	21	17	4	18	36	.259
2007	Athletics1 (DSL)	R	1	0	1.23	2	1	0	0	7	3	1	1	0	3	5	.120
	Athletics (AZL)	R	1	3	7.62	16	1	0	2	39	55	37	33	4	13	38	.327
2008	Athletics 2 (DSL)	R	1	1	4.50	3	2	0	0	10	9	6	5	0	4	13	.231
	Athletics (AZL)	R	1	1	4.56	16	0	0	4	24	30	17	12	1	11	37	.300
2009	Vancouver (NWL)	SS	0	2	4.94	16	8	0	0	55	65	40	30	4	25	35	.300
MINOR LEAGUE TOTALS			8	8	4.96	64	20	0	6	178	205	122	98	13	74	164	.287

24 JULIO RAMOS, LHP

BORN: Feb. 13, 1988. **B-T:** L-L. **HT.:** 6-1. **WT.:** 220. **SIGNED:** Dominican Republic, 2006. **SIGNED BY:** Amaurys Reyes.

Ramos posted a 1.41 ERA in his first extended domestic stint in 2008, then carried that success over into last season. He allowed three earned runs or fewer in all but one of his 13 starts for Vancouver, finished second in the Northwest League with a 2.38 ERA and won his last six outings after beginning the season 0-5. Ramos' fastball isn't overpowering at 88-91 mph, but it has some armside sink and he pounds the bottom half of the strike zone with it. He throws with an easy, fluid delivery that could allow him to add velocity as he develops. Ramos' changeup is his go-to pitch. He actually throws two varieties, a tumbling knuckle-change and a circle change with sink and fade. The A's scrapped his curveball before the season and switched him to a slider. He used to raise his arm more when throwing the curve, making it easy for batters to pick up, but he uses the same release point with his slider as with his fastball. The slider is a below-average pitch for now, but it has shown promising tilt and depth. Ramos should advance to low Class A in 2010.

Year	Club (League)	Class	W	L	ERA	G	GS	CG	SV	IP	H	R	ER	HR	BB	SO	AVG
2006	Athletics1 (DSL)	R	4	1	2.13	13	3	0	0	38	31	13	9	1	11	50	.225
2007	Athletics1 (DSL)	R	0	0	5.68	2	1	0	0	6	7	5	4	0	3	6	.292
	Athletics (AZL)	R	0	1	5.40	2	2	0	0	8	9	6	5	2	3	5	.300
2008	Athletics 1 (DSL)	R	0	1	1.50	2	1	0	0	6	6	2	1	0	2	7	.240
	Athletics (AZL)	R	3	2	1.41	14	7	0	0	51	56	17	8	0	12	36	.279
2009	Vancouver (NWL)	SS	6	5	2.38	13	13	0	0	72	67	30	19	4	18	64	.248
	Stockton (CAL)	HiA	0	1	3.75	2	2	0	0	12	12	5	5	0	3	11	.267
MINOR LEAGUE TOTALS			13	11	2.37	48	29	0	0	194	188	78	51	7	52	179	.256

25 ANDREW CARIGNAN, RHP

BORN: July 23, 1986. **B-T:** R-R. **HT.:** 5-11. **WT.:** 205. **DRAFTED:** North Carolina, 2007 (5th round). **SIGNED BY:** Neil Avent.

The closer for the North Carolina squads that made it to the College World Series in 2006 and 2007, Carignan looked like he was on the fast track to the big leagues when he reached Double-A in his first full pro season. That fast track took a detour last season, when he came down with a sore forearm in spring training and never saw regular action, though he avoided surgery. He was back on the mound in the fall and should be fine going forward. Carignan's main pitch is a fastball that sits at 92-93 mph and peaks at 94. The A's switched him from a slider to a curveball, which comes in hard with 12-to-6 break. He also has a straight changeup. Oakland gives Carignan high marks for his toughness and swagger on the mound. He has a little deception in his delivery, though at 5-foot-11, he doesn't generate much downhill plane. Provided he stays healthy, Carignan should advance to Triple-A in 2010 and could get a big league look before the end of the season.

Year	Club (League)	Class	W	L	ERA	G	GS	CG	SV	IP	H	R	ER	HR	BB	SO	AVG
2007	Kane County (MWL)	LoA	1	1	2.03	12	0	0	4	13	6	7	3	0	11	19	.136
2008	Stockton (CAL)	HiA	1	1	0.90	9	0	0	4	10	5	1	1	0	5	17	.147
	Midland (TL)	AA	3	3	2.22	46	0	0	24	53	36	15	13	4	39	67	.196
2009	Stockton (CAL)	HiA	0	0	4.50	2	0	0	0	2	1	1	1	0	3	2	.167
MINOR LEAGUE TOTALS			5	5	2.08	69	0	0	32	78	48	24	18	4	58	105	.179

26 BOBBY CASSEVAH, RHP

BORN: Sept. 11, 1985. **B-T:** R-R. **HT.:** 6-3. **WT.:** 195. **DRAFTED:** HS—Milton, Fla., 2004 (34th round). **SIGNED BY:** Tom Kotchman (Angels).

Coming off a season in which he was one of the Texas League's best relievers, the Angels expected they might lose Cassevah when they left him unprotected in the Rule 5 draft last December. Sure enough, the A's popped him. Now they have to keep him on their big league roster throughout 2010, and if they can't then they'll have to place him on waivers and offer him back to Los Angeles for half his $50,000 draft price. Cassevah's primary weapon is a heavy 92-94 mph sinker. He can pepper the bottom of the zone with the sinker, as evidenced by his 4.0 groundout/airout ratio in Double-A last year. He also features a splitter and a slider, both of which are average offerings. The splitter gives him a strikeout pitch, but he has a tendency to fall too much in love with his slider. He struggles somewhat against lefthanders, who hit .295 against him last year compared to .199 for righties. His biggest obstacle to finding a niche in Oakland is his control, as he gets himself in trouble with walks. He could be a serviceable middle reliever as a rookie if he throws enough strikes.

Year	Club (League)	Class	W	L	ERA	G	GS	CG	SV	IP	H	R	ER	HR	BB	SO	AVG
2005	Angels (AZL)	R	2	5	5.40	15	4	0	0	45	57	28	27	2	14	27	.318
2006	Orem (PIO)	R	2	5	6.80	16	10	0	0	41	57	40	31	1	38	32	.337
2007	Orem (PIO)	R	0	0	4.32	6	0	0	0	8	9	6	4	0	5	9	.290
	Cedar Rapids (MWL)	LoA	2	1	2.32	18	0	0	1	31	25	9	8	0	13	25	.227
2008	R. Cucamonga (CAL)	HiA	2	3	3.79	44	0	0	1	71	67	33	30	1	40	52	.250
2009	Arkansas (TL)	AA	3	7	3.68	57	0	0	4	73	64	40	30	2	37	45	.236
MINOR LEAGUE TOTALS			11	21	4.33	156	14	0	6	270	279	156	130	6	147	190	.271

27 JUSTIN MARKS, LHP

BORN: Jan. 12, 1988. **B-T:** L-L. **HT.:** 6-3. **WT.:** 170. **DRAFTED:** Louisville, 2009 (3rd round). **SIGNED BY:** Matt Ranson.

Marks helped pitch Louisville to the 2007 College World Series as a freshman, going 9-2, 2.67, and he went on to become the program's all-time leader in wins (29), ERA (2.96) and strikeouts (305) in three seasons. He also set a school single-season record with 11 wins in 2009 before signing with Oakland for $375,300 as a third-round pick. Marks is a polished lefthander with command of four average pitches, though none looks like a plus offering. He comes after hitters with a 90-92 mph fastball, a three-quarters curveball, a slider and a changeup. He shows moxie on the mound and has a physical frame, though there's some effort in his delivery. A groin injury cost him a chance to see much action in his pro debut and he eventually needed a hernia operation, though he should be ready to go in the spring. Marks' upside isn't as high as some of the other pitchers in the system, but he has the potential to move quickly and be a dependable back-of-the-rotation starter. He should open his first full pro season at one of Oakland's Class A affiliates.

Year	Club (League)	Class	W	L	ERA	G	GS	CG	SV	IP	H	R	ER	HR	BB	SO	AVG
2009	Athletics (AZL)	R	0	1	—	1	1	0	0	0	3	6	6	1	4	0	1.000
MINOR LEAGUE TOTALS			0	1	—	1	1	0	0	0	3	6	6	1	4	0	1.000

28 TYREACE HOUSE, OF

BORN: March 1, 1988. **B-T:** R-R. **HT.:** 5-10. **WT.:** 175. **DRAFTED:** JC of the Canyons (Calif.), 2008 (6th round). **SIGNED BY:** J.T. Stotts.

The Braves drafted House twice—in the 40th round out of high school in 2006 and in the 49th round after his freshman season at JC of the Canyons (Calif.) in 2007—before the A's took him in the sixth round in 2008 and signed him for $130,000. House hit .371 and stole 40 bases over his two-year junior-college career, and he has the tools to be an effective top-of-the-order hitter. He has a short, slashing swing, doesn't try to do too much and isn't afraid to go deep in counts. He has plus-plus speed on the bases and in center field, where he can be a highlight-reel defender. However, his game is still plenty raw. He's sometimes patient to a fault, still is learning to control the zone and isn't immune to chasing balls outside it. He also needs to improve his bunting ability, as well as his reads and breaks when stealing bases. He offers little power, though the A's are trying to get him to incorporate his lower half more and stay through the ball better, which could help. His arm strength is fringy but enough to get by in center field. House should advance to low Class A to open the year.

Year	Club (League)	Class	AVG	G	AB	R	H	2B	3B	HR	RBI	BB	SO	SB	OBP	SLG
2008	Athletics (AZL)	R	.263	29	99	25	26	1	0	0	10	18	22	12	.378	.273

2009	Vancouver (NWL)	SS	.291	56	196	31	57	3	0	0	16	17	38	19	.365	.306
MINOR LEAGUE TOTALS			.281	85	295	56	83	4	0	0	26	35	60	31	.370	.295

29 JOSH LEYLAND, C

BORN: July 6, 1991. **B-T:** L-R. **HT.:** 6-1. **WT.:** 220. **DRAFTED:** HS—San Dimas, Calif., 2009 (16th round). **SIGNED BY:** Eric Martins.

Leyland batted .506 with 11 home runs to lead San Dimas High to a southern California sectional championship as a senior. The A's thought he had some of the best raw power in the 2009 draft, so they were thrilled he only cost them a 16th-round pick and a $75,000 bonus. A physical specimen, Leyland is balanced and generates leverage in his swing. He has excellent timing to go with his strength, though he's still refining his approach at the plate. Leyland's defense has a long ways to go He needs plenty of work behind the plate, where he lacks quickness and athleticism. He does have arm strength, but he'll have to clean up his receiving and throwing mechanics. First base is the lone option if catching doesn't work out, because he doesn't run well enough to play anywhere else in the field. The A's can give Leyland time to develop because they have catching prospects at higher levels of the system. He'll probably begin 2010 in extended spring training before heading to Vancouver in June.

Year	Club (League)	Class	AVG	G	AB	R	H	2B	3B	HR	RBI	BB	SO	SB	OBP	SLG
2009	Athletics (AZL)	R	.150	7	20	3	3	0	0	0	1	4	11	0	.370	.150
MINOR LEAGUE TOTALS			.150	7	20	3	3	0	0	0	1	4	11	0	.370	.150

30 BRETT HUNTER, RHP

BORN: July 27, 1987. **B-T:** R-R. **HT.:** 6-4. **WT.:** 215. **DRAFTED:** Pepperdine, 2008 (7th round). **SIGNED BY:** J.T. Stotts.

Hunter was one of the best college pitching prospects in the nation entering 2008, but elbow pain limited him to just five appearances for Pepperdine. The A's still believed enough in him to give him a $1.1 million bonus, a record for a seventh-round pick, but his first full pro season couldn't have gone much worse. He struggled mightily to find the strike zone with Kane County, earning a demotion in July. Hunter still has one of the best arms in the system, but his delivery seemingly changed every outing last year. Oakland revamped his delivery In the fall, lowering his arm slot and making his motion similar to Carlos Marmol's. Hunter throws hard sinkers that sit at 92-94 mph and touch 96. His slider doesn't have as much rilt as it once did because of the lower arm angle, but it still comes in at 83-85 mph. He flashes a good changeup at times and it has some sink, but it's not as good as his slider. The A's will develop him as a reliever going forward, and Hunter has the potential to move quickly if his new delivery helps him throw more strikes. If he shows improved command in the spring, he could open 2010 in high Class A.

Year	Club (League)	Class	W	L	ERA	G	GS	CG	SV	IP	H	R	ER	HR	BB	SO	AVG
2008	Athletics (AZL)	R	0	0	0.00	1	1	0	0	1	1	0	0	0	0	2	.250
	Kane County (MWL)	LoA	0	0	5.40	2	0	0	0	2	0	1	1	0	2	1	.000
2009	Kane County (MWL)	LoA	0	1	6.85	21	8	0	0	47	38	42	36	2	59	55	.225
	Athletics (AZL)	R	0	1	1.93	4	3	0	0	5	0	2	1	0	1	5	.000
	Vancouver (NWL)	SS	0	0	7.20	4	0	0	0	5	10	5	4	0	3	4	.435
MINOR LEAGUE TOTALS			0	2	6.34	32	12	0	0	60	49	50	42	2	65	67	.229

Philadelphia Phillies

BY JOHN MANUEL

The first Philadelphia entry in the National League, known as the Quakers, went 17-81 way back in 1883. The franchise became the Phillies in 1890 and took 25 years to win its first pennant. Before the franchise captured its first World Series title in 1980, it had won just two pennants and only one World Series game.

The tradition of losing included 13 losing seasons out of 14 from 1987-2000. In July 2007, the Phillies became the first franchise in pro sports history to reach 10,000 losses. Well, those days are over. No organization transformed its image in the 2000s more than the Phillies, BA's 2009 Organization of the Year.

After winning a second World Series championship in 2008, Philadelphia figured out how to put together a strong encore. The Phillies won the National League East for the third straight season, reaching three straight postseasons for the second time in franchise history, and the NL pennant, marking the first time they played in consecutive World Series. Their success came under new general manager Ruben Amaro Jr., who replaced veteran executive Pat Gillick, who stepped down to make way for his former assistant. Gillick remains with the organization as an adviser.

Amaro faced immediate challenges, and most of his moves worked well. He kept the roster mostly intact, replacing departed free agent Pat Burrell with Raul Ibanez, who produced 34 home runs and 93 RBIs.

Amaro held onto prospects last offseason and had plenty on hand when his rotation took a step back, allowing him to trade righthanders Carlos Carrasco and Jason Knapp, catcher Lou Marson and shortstop Jason Donald to the Indians for Cliff Lee. They ranked second, 10th, third and fourth on this list last year.

The Phillies went 850-769 in the regular season from 2000-2009, good for a .525 winning percentage that's the franchise's best ever for a decade. They've sustained success by blending the added revenue from Citizens Bank Park with a commitment to player development that began in the 1990s.

Their homegrown core starts with Ryan Howard, Jimmy Rollins and Chase Utley, the heart of their explosive offense. Philadelphia also drafted and developed 40 percent of its rotation in 2008 World Series MVP Cole Hamels and rookie sensation J.A. Happ, while Ryan Madson has emerged as an elite setup man. Panamanian Carlos Ruiz is an underrated, cost-effective product of the club's international efforts.

J.A. Happ broke through as a rookie to help the Phillies win the National League

TOP 30 PROSPECTS

1. Domonic Brown, of	16. Mike Stutes, rhp
2. Kyle Drabek, rhp	17. Yohan Flande, lhp
3. Michael Taylor, of	18. Vance Worley, rhp
4. Travis D'arnaud, c	19. Heitor Correa, rhp
5. Trevor May, rhp	20. Jonathan Singleton, 1b
6. Anthony Gose, of	21. Joe Savery, lhp
7. Sebastian Valle, c	22. Jonathan Villan, ss
8. Jarred Cosart, rhp	23. Mike Cisco, rhp
9. Antonio Bastardo, lhp	24. B.J. Rosenberg, rhp
10. Domingo Santana, of	25. Leandro Castro, of
11. Jiwan James, of	26. Edgar Garcia, rhp
12. Brody Colvin, rhp	27. Kelly Dugan, of
13. Freddy Galvis, ss	28. Matt Way, lhp
14. Kyrell Hudson, of	29. Justin DeFratus, rhp
15. Scott Mathieson, rhp	30. Zach Collier, of

The Phillies have used prospects in trades, as was the case in 2009 with Lee, 2008 with Joe Blanton and after the 2007 season with Brad Lidge. The deals have thinned out the system, yet Amaro made sure to keep his top position prospect (outfielder Domonic Brown) and pitching prospect (righthander Kyle Drabek) out of the Lee trade. Throw in catchers Travis d'Arnaud and Sebastian Valle, Triple-A outfielder Michael Taylor and young, power arms Jarred Cosart and Trevor May, and Philadelphia still has impact talent on the farm.

Drink it in, Phillies fans. You just had your Best Decade Ever.

ORGANIZATION OVERVIEW

General Manager: Ruben Amaro Jr. **Farm Director:** Steve Noworyta. **Scouting Director:** Marti Wolever.

Class	Team	League	W	L	PCT	Finish*	Manager(s)
Majors	Philadelphia Phillies	National	93	69	.574	†2nd (16)	Charlie Manuel
Triple-A	Lehigh Valley IronPigs	International	71	73	.493	8th (14)	Dave Huppert
Double-A	Reading Phillies	Eastern	75	67	.528	3rd (12)	Steve Roadcap
High A	Clearwater Threshers	Florida State	67	69	.493	6th (12)	Ernie Whitt
Low A	Lakewood BlueClaws	South Atlantic	78	54	.574	†2nd (16)	Dusty Wathan
Short-season	Williamsport Crosscutters	New York-Penn	42	34	.553	5th (14)	Chris Truby
Rookie	GCL Phillies	Gulf Coast	31	28	.525	6th (16)	Rolando de Armas
Overall 2009 Minor League Record			364	329	.525	4th (30)	

*Finish in overall standings (No. of teams in league). †League champion.

LAST YEAR'S TOP 30

Player, Pos.		Status
1.	Domonic Brown, of	No. 1
2.	Carlos Carrasco, rhp	(Indians)
3.	Lou Marson, c	(Indians)
4.	Jason Donald, ss	(Indians)
5.	Kyle Drabek, rhp	No. 2
6.	Michael Taylor, of	No. 3
7.	Travis d'Arnaud, c	No. 4
8.	Zach Collier, of	No. 30
9.	J.A. Happ, lhp	Majors
10.	Jason Knapp, rhp	(Indians)
11.	Antonio Bastardo, lhp	No. 9
12.	Julian Sampson, rhp	Dropped out
13.	Drew Naylor, rhp	Dropped out
14.	Anthony Hewitt, 3b/of	Dropped out
15.	Anthony Gose, of	No. 6
16.	Vance Worley, rhp	No. 18
17.	Mike Stutes, rhp	No. 16
18.	Freddy Galvis, ss	No. 13
19.	Edgar Garcia, rhp	No. 26
20.	Joe Savery, lhp	No. 21
21.	Travis Mattair, 3b	Dropped out
22.	Drew Carpenter, rhp	Dropped out
23.	Jarred Cosart, rhp	No. 8
24.	John Mayberry Jr., of	Dropped out
25.	Quintin Berry, of	Dropped out
26.	Pat Overholt, rhp	Dropped out
27.	Sergio Escalona, lhp	Dropped out
28.	Trevor May, rhp	No. 5
29.	Mike Cisco, rhp	No. 23
30.	Colby Shreve, rhp	Dropped out

BEST TOOLS

Best Hitter for Average	Domonic Brown
Best Power Hitter	Michael Taylor
Best Strike-Zone Discipline	Domonic Brown
Fastest Baserunner	Jiwan James
Best Athlete	Jiwan James
Best Fastball	Scott Mathieson
Best Curveball	Kyle Drabek
Best Slider	Mike Stutes
Best Changeup	Yohan Flande
Best Control	Justin DeFratus
Best Defensive Catcher	Travis d'Arnaud
Best Defensive Infielder	Freddy Galvis
Best Infield Arm	Freddy Galvis
Best Defensive Outfielder	Anthony Gose
Best Outfield Arm	Domonic Brown

PROJECTED 2013 LINEUP

Catcher	Travis d'Arnaud
First Base	Ryan Howard
Second Base	Chase Utley
Third Base	Sebastian Valle
Shortstop	Jimmy Rollins
Left Field	Jayson Werth
Center Field	Shane Victorino
Right Field	Domonic Brown
No. 1 Starter	Cole Hamels
No. 2 Starter	Cliff Lee
No. 3 Starter	Kyle Drabek
No. 4 Starter	J.A. Happ
No. 5 Starter	Trevor May
Closer	Ryan Madson

TOP PROSPECTS OF THE DECADE

Year	Player, Pos.	2009 Org.
2000	Pat Burrell, 1b/of	Rays
2001	Jimmy Rollins, ss	Phillies
2002	Marlon Byrd, of	Rangers
2003	Gavin Floyd, rhp	White Sox
2004	Cole Hamels, lhp	Phillies
2005	Ryan Howard, 1b	Phillies
2006	Cole Hamels, lhp	Phillies
2007	Carlos Carrasco, rhp	Indians
2000	Carlos Carrasco, rhp	Indians
2009	Domonic Brown, of	Phillies

TOP DRAFT PICKS OF THE DECADE

Year	Player, Pos.	2009 Org.
2000	Chase Utley, 2b	Phillies
2001	Gavin Floyd, rhp	White Sox
2002	Cole Hamels, lhp	Phillies
2003	Tim Moss, 2b (3rd round)	Out of baseball
2004	Greg Golson, of	Rangers
2005	Mike Costanzo, 3b (2nd round)	Orioles
2006	Kyle Drabek, rhp	Phillies
2007	Joe Savery, lhp	Phillies
2008	Anthony Hewitt, 3b/of	Phillies
2009	Kelly Dugan, of (2nd round)	Phillies

LARGEST BONUSES IN CLUB HISTORY

Gavin Floyd, 2001	$4,200,000
Pat Burrell, 1998	$3,150,000
Brett Myers, 1999	$2,050,000
Cole Hamels, 2002	$2,000,000
Chase Utley, 2000	$1,780,000

PHILADELPHIA PHILLIES

TOP 2010 ROOKIE: Antonio Bastardo, lhp. He should have a full-time job in the big league bullpen after pitching in the Division Series last fall.

BREAKOUT PROSPECT: Jiwan James, of. A pitcher for the first two years of his pro career, he has a brighter future as a five-tool outfielder.

SLEEPER: Sergio Escalona, lhp. His ceiling isn't as high as Bastardo's, but he'll challenge him for a spot in Philadelphia's bullpen.

SOURCE OF TOP 30 TALENT			
Homegrown	30	Acquired	0
College	7	Trades	0
Junior college	1	Rule 5 draft	0
High school	13	Independent leagues	0
Draft-and-follow	0	Free agents/waivers	0
Nondrafted free agents	0		
International	9		

Numbers in parentheses indicate prospect rankings

LF
Michael Taylor (3)
Leandro Castro (25)
Kelly Dugan (27)
Zach Collier (30)
Aaron Altherr
Anthony Hewitt
Steve Susdorf

CF
Anthony Gose (6)
Jiwan James (11)
Kyrell Hudson (14)
Quintin Barry
D'Arby Myers

RF
Domonic Brown (1)
Domingo Santana (10)
John Mayberry Jr.

3B
Cody Overbeck
Travis Mattair

SS
Freddy Galvis (13)
Jonathan Villan (22)
Troy Hanzawa
Fidel Hernandez
Jeremy Barnes

2B
Harold Garcia
Cesar Hernandez
Adam Buschini

1B
Jonathan Singleton (20)
Jim Murphy

C
Travis d'Arnaud (4)
Sebastian Valle (7)
Tim Kennelly
Marlon Mitchell

RHP

Starters	Relievers
Kyle Drabek (2)	Scott Mathieson (15)
Trevor May (5)	B.J. Rosenberg (24)
Jarred Cosart (8)	Justin DeFratus (29)
Brody Colvin (12)	Michael Schwimer
Mike Stutes (16)	David Herndon
Vance Worley (18)	Austin Hyatt
Heitor Correa (19)	Freddy Ballestas
Mike Cisco (23)	
Edgar Garcia (26)	
Drew Carpenter	
Drew Naylor	
Tyler Cloyd	
Jon Pettibone	
Colby Shreve	
Julian Sampson	
Steven Inch	

LHP

Starters	Relievers
Yohan Flande (17)	Antonio Bastardo (9)
Joe Savery (21)	Sergio Escalona
Matt Way (28)	
Nick Hernandez	
Ryan Sasaki	

2009

BEST PURE HITTER: The Phillies first zeroed in on 1B Jonathan Singleton (8) in the summer of 2008 and always have thought he'd hit. His bat speed and plate discipline set him apart from most high school hitters, and he walked more than he struck out in his debut while batting .290.

BEST POWER HITTER: OF Kelly Dugan (2), the team's top pick, has average to plus power from both sides of the plate. Singleton's swing and maturing 6-foot-2, 215-pound frame should allow him to grow into plus power as well.

FASTEST RUNNER: OF Kyrell Hudson (3) fits with the Phillies' profile as a raw, toolsy speedster, with top-of-the-scale 6.4-second 60 times. His speed doesn't always play up to that level in games, but the Phillies have no questions with his makeup or effort.

BEST DEFENSIVE PLAYER: SS Jeremy Barnes (11) likely will move to second base, but he has good hands and his arm strength will help him turn the double play.

BEST FASTBALL: RHP Brody Colvin (7), signed for $900,000, sits in the low 90s and touches the mid-90s. He should throw harder when he fills out his 6-foot-4, 190-pound body.

BEST SECONDARY PITCH: LHPs Matt Way (5) and Nick Hernandez (12) and RHP Austin Hyatt (15) all have solid-average to plus changeups. Way's grades out just a bit ahead of the others.

BEST PRO DEBUT: Hyatt's slider made progress at short-season Williamsport and he ranked third in the New York-Penn League in strikeouts (81) despite pitching in relief. He went 3-0, 0.66 in 54 innings, giving up just 26 hits. Hernandez went 8-1, 2.70 for the Crosscutters, giving up just two home runs in 80 innings. Way advanced to low Class A Lakewood, going 6-4, 2.39 overall with an 85-12 K-BB ratio in 75 innings.

BEST ATHLETE: Hudson could have played football and baseball at Oregon State. OF Aaron Altherr (9) is a long, lanky 6-foot-5 athlete with a huge ceiling but relatively little baseball experience.

MOST INTRIGUING BACKGROUND: Dugan's father Dennis is an actor, director and producer who has worked on such films as "You Don't Mess with the Zohan" with Adam Sandler. Unsigned 3B Rob Amaro's (40) uncle Ruben is the Phillies' general manager, while unsigned RHP Stephen Kohlscheen's (30) father Brian is their Midwest crosschecker. 1B Cory Wine (39) is the grandson of ex-big league player and manager Bobby Wine, and played for his dad Robby at Penn State.

CLOSEST TO THE MAJORS: Hyatt, especially if he remains a reliever, and Way.

BEST LATE-ROUND PICK: Hyatt and Hernandez.

THE ONE WHO GOT AWAY: OF Jacob Stewart (14) has premium strength and athleticism, albeit with a swing that needs a lot of work. He's exactly the type of player the Phillies love, but they couldn't sway him away from Stanford.

ASSESSMENT: The Phillies again mixed solid college pitchers with raw, toolsy high school hitters. The organization's track record over the last decade at developing raw bats is solid, and Philadelphia has the big league roster to be patient.

2008

The Phillies focused on raw upside even more than usual. Their top two picks, 3B Anthony Hewitt (1) and OF Zach Collier (1s), have struggled at the plate. OF Anthony Gose (2) led the minors in steals last season and RHP Jason Knapp (2) was a key component to the Cliff Lee trade. RHPs Trevor May (4) and Jared Cosart (38) made nice progress as well.

GRADE: B

2007

LHP Joe Savery (1) has regressed, but C Travis d'Arnaud (2) and OF Michael Taylor (5) are keepers. OF Jiwan James (22), a converted pitcher, has stunning athleticism. OF Matt Spencer (3) helped land Joe Blanton in a deal for the 2008 World Series run.

GRADE: B

2006

This draft produced the system's top two prospects in OF Domonic Brown (20) and RHP Kyle Drabek (1), as well as pieces of the Blanton and Lee trades in INF Adrian Cardenas (1s) and SS Jason Donald (3). RHP Drew Carpenter (2) has pitched briefly in the majors.

GRADE: A

2005

The Phillies didn't have a first-rounder and moved their top pick, 3B/1B Mike Costanzo (2), and the best two players in this crop, LHPs Matt Maloney (3) and Josh Outman (10), in deals for Brad Lidge, Kyle Lohse and Blanton. RHP Mike Zagurski (12) looks like the only player who will ever contribute in Philadelphia.

GRADE: C

Draft analysis by John Manuel (2009) and Jim Callis (2005-08). Numbers in parentheses indicate draft rounds.

1 PROSPECT

DOMONIC BROWN, OF

Born: Sept. 3, 1987. **Height:** 6-5. **Weight:** 204.
Bats: Left. **Throws:** Left.
Drafted: HS—Redan, Ga.,
2006 (20th round).
Signed by: Chip Lawrence.

Brown attended Redan (Ga.) High, a big-time program in one of the most heavily scouted areas of the country. He'd attended top showcases—even playing on Team Baseball America at the 2005 World Wood Bat tournament in Jupiter, Fla.—yet wasn't considered an elite prospect. Brown's athletic ability was obvious, as he had an opportunity to play football (as a wide receiver) and baseball at Miami. But the fact that he was raw, combined with his bonus demands, prompted few clubs to even crosscheck him enough to consider drafting him with a early-round pick in 2006. Phillies area scout Chip Lawrence followed him closely, though, getting to know the family and bringing him to the club's predraft workout in Atlanta. After selecting him in the 20th round, scouting director Marti Wolever and national crosschecker Mike Ledna got a long look at Brown in an Atlanta-area tournament at the East Cobb complex and signed him for $200,000. Brown had a breakthrough year in 2008, won the Hawaii Winter Baseball (.389) batting title in the offseason and took another step forward last season. He shook off a broken finger on his right hand to finish with a flourish at Double-A Reading.

Brown is a physical specimen, long, lean and muscular, which earns him physical comparisons to Darryl Strawberry. While he doesn't have Strawberry's raw thunder, he has true five-tool ability. His work ethic has allowed him to translate his athletic ability into baseball skills, starting with above-average hitting ability. A free swinger as an amateur, Brown has developed a solid eye at the plate and recognizes pitches well. His buggy-whip swing and growing strength give him plus raw power, and he's starting to translate it into production. He has the bat speed and strength to drive mistakes and take advantage when he's ahead in the count. Brown's other tools grade out as well or better than his bat. He's a plus runner with an arm that grades out as high as a 70 on the 20-80 scouting scale.

The biggest question on Brown's upside revolves around how much power he'll develop. Some Double-A Eastern League observers thought his power would be average at best and would limit him to hitting at the top of the lineup, rather than being a middle-of-the-lineup factor. He's still raw in several aspects offensively, compensating with his athleticism. He needs to keep improving with his pitch recognition and ability to lay off chasing pitches out of the zone. He also needs to take better routes in right field.

The Phillies have productive corner outfielders in Raul Ibanez (signed through 2011) and Jayson Werth (2010), but refused to part with Brown at the trade deadline in a deal for Roy Halladay or Cliff Lee because they consider him a future star. The presence of Ibanez and Werth makes it easy to give Brown another year of at-bats and experience in the minors. He should reach Triple-A Lehigh Valley for the first time and earn at least a September callup in 2010.

Year	Club (League)	Class	AVG	G	AB	R	H	2B	3B	HR	RBI	BB	SO	SB	OBP	SLG
2006	Phillies (GCL)	R	.214	34	117	13	25	3	0	1	7	12	30	13	.292	.265
2007	Clearwater (FSL)	HiA	.444	3	9	2	4	1	0	1	7	2	0	0	.545	.889
	Williamsport (NYP)	SS	.295	74	285	43	84	11	5	3	32	27	49	14	.356	.400
2008	Lakewood (SAL)	LoA	.291	114	444	77	129	23	3	9	54	64	72	22	.382	.417
2009	Phillies (GCL)	R	.500	3	10	4	5	0	2	0	0	1	1	0	.583	.900
	Clearwater (FSL)	HiA	.303	66	238	41	72	12	3	11	44	34	48	15	.386	.517
	Reading (EL)	AA	.279	37	147	20	41	9	4	3	20	14	37	8	.346	.456
MINOR LEAGUE TOTALS			.288	331	1250	200	360	59	17	28	164	154	237	72	.368	.430

2 KYLE DRABEK, RHP

DAVID SCHOFIELD

BORN: Dec. 8, 1987. **B-T:** R-R. **HT.:** 6-0. **WT.:**185. **DRAFTED:** HS—The Woodlands, Texas, 2006 (1st round). **SIGNED BY:** Steve Cohen.

The son of 1990 Cy Young Award winner Doug Drabek, Kyle blew out his elbow early in his first full pro season, costing him parts of 2007 and 2008. He used his off time to improve his body, refine his delivery and grow up a bit with the help of minor league veteran Mike Zagurski, his rehab roommate and fellow TJ alumnus. Drabek broke out in 2009, dazzling in the Futures Game and pitching well in Double-A. Drabek has the organization's best curveball, a power downer that he can bury or throw for strikes. Some scouts rate it a 70 on the 20-80 scouting scale. His fastball sits at 88-93 mph, usually at the top end of that range, and has solid-average life. His competitiveness helps him maximize his stuff. Athletic and coordinated, he's effective holding runners, fielding his position and hitting. Drabek's changeup is his third-best pitch and still needs refinement, as Double-A lefthanders showed by bashing him for a .924 OPS (compared to .521 by righties). He has to improve his arm speed and his command with his changeup. Drabek could be a power reliever in the Tom Gordon mode, particularly if the Phillies need him in 2010. His aptitude and athleticism make it more likely that he'll improve that pitch and fulfill his profile as a No. 2 or 3 starter. He'll open the season in Triple-A.

Year	Club (League)	Class	W	L	ERA	G	GS	CG	SV	IP	H	R	ER	HR	BB	SO	AVG
2006	Phillies (GCL)	R	1	3	7.71	6	6	0	0	23	33	24	20	2	11	14	.333
2007	Lakewood (SAL)	LoA	5	1	4.33	11	10	0	0	54	50	29	26	9	23	46	.239
2008	Phillies (GCL)	R	0	1	2.25	4	4	0	0	12	6	3	3	0	6	6	.150
	Williamsport (NYP)	SS	1	2	2.21	4	4	0	0	20	11	6	5	1	6	10	.159
2009	Clearwater (FSL)	HiA	4	1	2.48	10	9	1	0	62	49	19	17	0	19	74	.218
	Reading (EL)	AA	8	2	3.64	15	14	0	0	96	92	40	39	9	31	76	.252
MINOR LEAGUE TOTALS			19	10	3.70	50	47	1	0	268	241	121	110	21	96	226	.239

3 MICHAEL TAYLOR, OF

LAVIE SCHOFIELD

BORN: Dec. 19, 1985. **B-T:** R-R. **HT.:** 6-6. **WT.:**250. **DRAFTED:** Stanford, 2007 (5th round). **SIGNED BY:** Joey Davis.

Taylor played a season of high school baseball as Zack Greinke's teammate, and his size and athleticism made him a top high school prospect. His grades helped lead him to Stanford, where he came around as a college junior, and he's been unstoppable the last two seasons, clubbing 39 homers and batting .334. Despite his size, Taylor has few holes and has become an excellent hitter, squaring up balls consistently and smashing line drives to all fields. Pitchers try to tie him up inside, and while he can be vulnerable there, he has shown the ability to make adjustments. He has excellent raw power, average speed and good baserunning instincts. He's a solid defender with an average-to-plus arm who grades as above average in left field. Taylor could stand to be more selective to get to his power more consistently. He needs to learn to loft the ball to become a true 30-homer threat. Conditioning probably will be a long-term issue for Taylor, who does a good job of staying on top of his juvenile diabetes. With Raul Ibanez and Jayson Werth ahead of him and Domonic Brown coming on, Taylor seems like ideal trade bait. He also could be a replacement for Ibanez, whose contract doesn't expire until after 2011. He's slated for Triple-A in 2010.

Year	Club (League)	Class	AVG	G	AB	R	H	2B	3B	HR	RBI	BB	SO	SB	OBP	SLG
2007	Williamsport (NYP)	SS	.227	66	233	30	53	14	0	6	33	23	53	8	.300	.365
2008	Lakewood (SAL)	LoA	.361	67	249	40	90	12	3	10	50	31	43	10	.441	.554
	Clearwater (FSL)	HiA	.329	65	243	36	80	27	1	9	38	19	46	5	.380	.560
2009	Reading (EL)	AA	.333	86	318	59	106	22	4	15	65	35	51	18	.408	.569
	Lehigh Valley (IL)	AAA	.282	30	110	15	31	6	1	5	19	13	19	3	.359	.491
MINOR LEAGUE TOTALS			.312	314	1153	180	360	81	9	45	205	121	212	44	.383	.515

4 TRAVIS D'ARNAUD, C

DAVID SCHOFIELD

BORN: Feb. 10, 1989. **B-T:** R-R. **HT.:** 6-2. **WT.:**195. **DRAFTED:** HS—Lakewood, Calif., 2007 (1st round supplemental). **SIGNED BY:** Tim Kissner.

The 37th overall pick in 2007, d'Arnaud played against his brother Chase, a shortstop in the Pirates system, in two four-game sets in the low Class A South Atlantic League last May. Chase was caught stealing just three times in the SAL, twice by his brother in the second series. The strong-bodied d'Arnaud got better as 2009 wore on, clubbing 25 doubles in his last 224 at-bats. He led the SAL in doubles and is tapping into his plus raw power. He has strength in his hands and generates good bat speed. D'Arnaud understands the importance of defense for a catcher and works hard at managing a staff. He has above-average arm strength, soft hands and good agility. Footwork can get d'Arnaud in trouble in both blocking balls and with the accuracy of his throws. He threw out just 40 of 172 basestealers (23 percent) last season, though opponents ran wild on Lakewood's pitching staff. He needs more at-bats against good breaking balls, against which he tends to lunge and get long with his swing. The Phillies were confident enough in their young catchers to include Lou Marson in the Cliff Lee trade. D'Arnaud is ahead of Sebastian Valle defensively and in his development, but will have to keep improving to maintain that lead. He's slated to move up to high Class A Clearwater in 2010 and should be ready for Philadelphia by 2012.

Year	Club (League)	Class	AVG	G	AB	R	H	2B	3B	HR	RBI	BB	SO	SB	OBP	SLG
2007	Phillies (GCL)	R	.241	41	141	18	34	3	0	4	20	4	23	4	.278	.348
2008	Williamsport (NYP)	SS	.309	48	175	21	54	13	1	4	25	18	29	1	.371	.463
	Lakewood (SAL)	LoA	.297	16	64	12	19	5	0	2	5	5	10	0	.357	.469
2009	Lakewood (SAL)	LoA	.255	126	482	71	123	38	1	13	71	41	75	8	.319	.419
MINOR LEAGUE TOTALS			.267	231	862	122	230	59	2	23	121	68	137	13	.326	.420

5 TREVOR MAY, RHP ✝

DAVID SCHOFIELD

BORN: Sept. 23, 1989. **B-T:** R-R. **HT.:** 6-5. **WT.:**215. **DRAFTED:** HS—Kelso, Wash., 2008 (4th round). **SIGNED BY:** Dave Ryles.

The Phillies have gone to the Pacific Northwest well several times in recent years, and May has outpaced such prospects as third baseman Travis Mattair and righthander Julian Sampson from that region. After starting 2009 in extended spring training, May jumped into Lakewood's rotation and stumbled at first before becoming the Blue Claws' ace. He finished the season with 24 scoreless innings, 11 coming in the playoffs as Lakewood won the South Atlantic League title. Big and strong, May has gained fastball velocity as a pro and now ranges from 88-95 mph. His heater features heavy sink at times, and he uses its armside run to pitch inside effectively. He has solid command of his upper-70s curveball, which has solid if slurvy break. His solid-average changeup features fade when thrown down in the zone. Still raw, May can lose his command suddenly. He needs work on all facets of pitching out of the stretch, as he tends to fly open with his shoulder and doesn't hold runners well. His curve remains inconsistent because he gets under it at times, and it's easier to identify out of his hand than his changeup. May has No. 3 starter potential and took a giant step with his strong finish last season. He still has a ways to go, however, and will begin 2010 in high Class A with the goal of surpassing 100 innings for the first time.

Year	Club (League)	Class	W	L	ERA	G	GS	CG	SV	IP	H	R	ER	HR	BB	SO	AVG
2008	Phillies (GCL)	R	1	1	3.75	5	2	0	0	12	11	7	5	0	7	11	.256
2009	Lakewood (SAL)	LoA	4	1	2.56	15	15	0	0	77	58	24	22	3	43	95	.211
MINOR LEAGUE TOTALS			5	2	2.72	20	17	0	0	89	69	31	27	3	50	106	.217

6 ANTHONY GOSE, OF ✝

RODGER WOOD

BORN: Aug. 10, 1990. **B-T:** L-L. **HT.:** 6-1. **WT.:**190. **DRAFTED:** HS—Bellflower, Calif., 2008 (2nd round). **SIGNED BY:** Tim Kissner.

Gose had as much arm strength as any high school lefthander this decade, reaching 97 mph at times, but had no desire to pitch as a professional. He also had a shoulder problem as a senior, so the Phillies popped him as an outfielder and paid him a $772,000 bonus. His tools were evident in 2009, as managers rated him the best and fastest baserunner, best defensive outfielder and most exciting player in the South Atlantic League. Gose earns 70 grades on the 20-80 scouting scale for three tools: his arm, his center-field defense and his speed. He led the minor leagues with 76 steals in 96 attempts, and he'll be even more dangerous as he gets on base more often and refines his basestealing instincts. His arm helped him rack up 13 assists, third among SAL outfielders. Despite hitting just two homers in 2009, he has solid-average raw power. His weakest tool is his bat, and Gose will need time to rework his offensive approach and improve his pitch recognition. His power gets him in trouble as he takes wild hacks at times. He gives away too many at-bats and lacks a two-strike approach. The Phillies believe in Gose and will give him plenty of time to learn and improve, but he may need 2,000 minor league at-bats. Some scouts liken his offensive upside to that of Carl Crawford, and Gose would have more defensive value. He'll advance to high Class A in 2010.

Year	Club (League)	Class	AVG	G	AB	R	H	2B	3B	HR	RBI	BB	SO	SB	OBP	SLG
2008	Phillies (GCL)	R	.256	11	39	4	10	2	1	0	3	1	12	3	.293	.359
2009	Lakewood (SAL)	LoA	.259	131	510	72	132	24	9	2	52	35	110	76	.323	.353
MINOR LEAGUE TOTALS			.259	142	549	76	142	26	10	2	55	36	122	79	.321	.353

7 SEBASTIAN VALLE, C ⟩⟨

BORN: July 24, 1990. **B-T:** R-R. **HT.:** 6-1. **WT.:**170. **SIGNED:** Mexico, 2006. **SIGNED BY:** Sal Agostinelli.

The Phillies saw Valle shine in international competitions for Mexico at the 16-and-under level, ripping hits against top pitchers from Cuba and the United States. They signed him for $30,000. Playing for his hometown team in Los Mochis, he was one of the youngest players in the Mexican Pacific League this winter and was the season's first player of the week. Valle has natural hitting instincts and plus raw power that stems from his pure bat speed. He has excellent timing and a good load in his swing, as well as the strength to drive the ball to all fields. He has a good plan at the plate for a teenager and is an average runner, though he figures to slow down. Valle's defensive tools are average across the board. Low Class A pitchers overwhelmed Valle a bit in 2009 as he got pull-happy and impatient, though he adjusted after a move down to short-season Williamsport. He needs to polish his footwork and throwing accuracy, and he'll never have a cannon for an arm. He threw out just 18 percent of basestealers last season. With Travis d'Arnaud ahead of him, Valle could move a level at a time, working to polish his defense. Both players have taken grounders at third base as the Phillies look ahead. Valle will stay behind the plate and take another shot at low Class A in 2010.

Year	Club (League)	Class	AVG	G	AB	R	H	2B	3B	HR	RBI	BB	SO	SB	OBP	SLG
2007	Phillies (DSL)	R	.284	54	176	29	50	13	1	2	25	29	26	4	.398	.403
2008	Phillies (GCL)	R	.281	48	167	27	47	15	0	2	18	12	31	0	.341	.407
2009	Williamsport (NYP)	SS	.307	50	192	25	59	15	5	6	40	10	41	0	.335	.531
	Lakewood (SAL)	LoA	.223	45	157	16	35	12	1	1	15	16	37	1	.313	.331
MINOR LEAGUE TOTALS			.276	197	692	97	191	55	7	11	98	67	135	5	.348	.423

8 JARRED COSART, RHP ✛

BORN: May 25, 1990. **B-T:** R-R. **HT.:** 6-3. **WT.:**180. **DRAFTED:** HS—League City, Texas, 2008 (38th round). **SIGNED BY:** Steve Cohen.

Noted for his bat as much as for his arm in high school, Cosart committed to Missouri as a two-way player. The Phillies drafted him in the 38th round as a summer follow, then paid him $550,000 after seeing him dominate American Legion competition. His father negotiated the deal in the stands during a Legion game in Enid, Okla. The Phillies love Cosart's pitcher's frame, athleticism and quick arm. He generates the hand speed to have a power fastball and to spin a potentially above-average breaking ball. His fastball sits at 92-94 mph while touching 96, and there should be more velocity in there as he fills out. His 12-to-6 curveball is presently average but should be a plus pitch as it gains consistency. A lack of maturity has held Cosart back. He needs to prepare better in the offseason as well as between starts, and he must improve his work ethic. Shoulder soreness delayed his pro debut until July, and he needs innings to hone his command. His changeup is in its nascent stages. With Trevor May and Cosart on hand, the Phillies were more comfortable parting with Jason Knapp's power arm in the Cliff Lee deal. Cosart has front-of-the-rotation potential and is a breakout candidate for 2010. He'll make his full-season debut at Lakewood.

Year	Club (League)	Class	W	L	ERA	G	GS	CG	SV	IP	H	R	ER	HR	BB	SO	AVG
2009	Phillies (GCL)	R	2	2	2.22	7	5	0	0	24	12	8	6	0	7	25	.143
MINOR LEAGUE TOTALS			2	2	2.22	7	5	0	0	24	12	8	6	0	7	25	.143

9 ANTONIO BASTARDO, LHP

BORN: Sept. 21, 1985. **B-T:** L-L. **HT.:** 5-11. **WT.:**195. **SIGNED:** Dominican Republic, 2005. **SIGNED BY:** Sal Agostinelli.

Bastardo earned a victory in his big league debut in June, shoving 92-95 mph fastballs past the Padres. A left shoulder strain cut his first big league stint short, but Bastardo returned to the majors in October and earned a spot on the Division Series roster. Bastardo has grown into a power repertoire. His fastball regularly sits at 91-93 mph, and he throws it for consistent quality strikes when he's going well. His changeup remains an average-to-plus pitch. His slider has its moments, as when he struck out Jason Giambi in the Division Series. Though it has its moments, Bastardo's slider usually is a below-average pitch and needs to be more consistent for him to remain a starter or succeed as a left-on-left reliever. Shoulder woes have interrupted each of his last two seasons, casting doubt on his durability. While he could be a fourth starter, Bastardo has a better chance to fill the Phils' immediate need for a lefty reliever if he shows an improved slider in spring training.

Year	Club (League)	Class	W	L	ERA	G	GS	CG	SV	IP	H	R	ER	HR	BB	SO	AVG
2005	Phillies (DSL)	R	2	2	2.13	11	5	0	1	38	22	14	9	0	22	63	.162
2006	Phillies (GCL)	R	1	2	3.91	9	2	0	0	23	20	16	10	1	14	27	.220
2007	Lakewood (SAL)	LoA	9	0	1.87	15	15	0	0	92	63	23	19	3	42	98	.189
	Clearwater (FSL)	HiA	1	0	7.20	1	1	0	0	5	5	4	4	0	3	12	.250
2008	Clearwater (FSL)	HiA	2	0	1.17	5	5	0	0	31	20	4	4	2	10	47	.183
	Reading (EL)	AA	2	5	3.76	14	14	0	0	67	56	35	28	13	37	62	.223
2009	Lehigh Valley (IL)	AAA	1	0	2.08	2	2	0	0	13	11	3	3	1	3	12	.234
	Phillies (GCL)	R	0	0	0.00	3	2	0	0	4	2	1	0	0	2	3	.133
	Clearwater (FSL)	HiA	0	0	27.00	1	0	0	0	1	4	3	3	0	0	0	.800
	Reading (EL)	AA	2	2	1.75	11	5	0	3	36	22	7	7	1	7	41	.179
	Philadelphia (NL)	MAJ	2	3	6.46	6	5	0	0	24	26	18	17	4	9	19	.274
MAJOR LEAGUE TOTALS			2	3	6.46	6	5	0	0	24	26	18	17	4	9	19	.274
MINOR LEAGUE TOTALS			20	11	2.53	72	51	0	4	310	225	110	87	21	140	365	.199

10 DOMINGO SANTANA, OF

RODGER WOOD

BORN: Aug. 5, 1992. **B-T:** R-R. **HT.:** 6-5. **WT.:**200. **SIGNED:** Dominican Republic, 2008. **SIGNED BY:** Sal Agostinelli.

Philadelphia's instructional league program featured a plethora of athletic, high-upside outfielders such as Santana, converted pitcher Jiwan James and 2009 draftees Kelly Dugan, Kyrell Hudson and Alston Altherr. Santana still stands out in that crowd. Born in the Bahamas, Santana signed for a $330,000 bonus—big money for Sal Agostinelli's budget-conscious international department—and had a strong debut in the Rookie-level Gulf Coast League despite being its second-youngest player at age 16. Santana is a physical monster and yet can run the 60-yard dash in 6.7 seconds. He has reached 90 mph off the mound and has a plus arm in right field. His hitting tools are more advanced than even the Phillies expected. Add in his raw power, and his total package evokes Jermaine Dye. Santana also speaks English well. Santana may lose some athleticism, speed and looseness as he fills out physically. Mostly, he just needs at-bats to learn how to adjust to hard stuff inside and to improve his pitch recognition. Santana's upside, performance and age give him a slight edge over his fellow toolsy outfielders. He should move up to Williamsport next season, but could jump to low Class A with a strong spring.

Year	Club (League)	Class	AVG	G	AB	R	H	2B	3B	HR	RBI	BB	SO	SB	OBP	SLG
2009	Phillies (GCL)	R	.288	37	118	17	34	6	1	6	28	15	44	3	.388	.508
MINOR LEAGUE TOTALS			.288	37	118	17	34	6	1	6	28	15	44	3	.388	.508

11 JIWAN JAMES, OF

BORN: April 11, 1989. **B-T:** B-R. **HT.:** 6-4. **WT.:**180. **DRAFTED:** HS—Williston, Fla., 2007 (22nd round). **SIGNED BY:** Chip Lawrence.

James has tremendous upside and is the best athlete in a system loaded with toolsy players. One scout said his pure tools are better than Anthony Gose's across the board except for his throwing arm. He was signed by the same scout, Chip Lawrence, who unearthed Domonic Brown in the 20th round. James was a quarterback, wide receiver and safety in football and an all-state shooting guard in basketball at Williston (Fla.) High, where he doubled as an outfielder and pitcher in baseball. He signed for $150,000 as a 22nd-round pick in 2007—notable because he was the first over-slot signing in that summer—and made nine appearances as a pitcher, posting a 7.71 ERA. He missed all of 2008 with a stress reaction in his forearm, and when that didn't heal well enough for him to return to the mound, he became an outfielder. Just as he was getting caught up in 2009, James missed a month with a left wrist injury. But he put on a show at instructional league, jumping out with his switch-hitting ability, blazing speed and surprising raw power. He has a chance to be a plus defender in center field with a plus arm, though his arm is just average now. James is raw and essentially missed two years trying to pitch. The Phillies are eager to get him to low Class A for his first full season as a hitter.

Year	Club (League)	Class	W	L	ERA	G	GS	CG	SV	IP	H	R	ER	HR	BB	SO	AVG
2007	Phillies (GCL)	R	0	4	7.71	9	8	0	0	33	45	32	28	7	15	14	.321
2008	Did Not Play—Injured																
MINOR LEAGUE TOTALS			0	4	7.71	9	8	0	0	33	45	32	28	7	15	14	.321

Year	Club (League)	Class	AVG	G	AB	R	H	2B	3B	HR	RBI	BB	SO	SB	OBP	SLG
2009	Williamsport (NYP)	SS	.264	30	121	15	32	4	3	1	13	11	22	7	.336	.372
MINOR LEAGUE TOTALS			.264	30	121	15	32	4	3	1	13	11	22	7	.336	.372

12 BRODY COLVIN, RHP

BORN: Aug. 14, 1990. **B-T:** R-R. **HT.:** 6-4. **WT.:**190. **DRAFTED:** HS—Lafayette, La., 2009 (7th round). **SIGNED BY:** Mike Stauffer.

Philadelphia paid Colvin considerably more than any of its other 2009 draft picks, signing him for $900,000 in the seventh round. While many clubs were concerned that he couldn't be signed away from a Louisiana State commitment, the Phillies were confident they knew the family well enough to know that he wanted to play pro ball. They landed one of the best fastballs in the draft and one of the best arms in the system. Colvin's fastball touches 96 mph and he could sit at 92-96 mph range eventually as he grows into his lean frame. Like most young pitchers, he'll have to work to clean up his mechanics. He's athletic enough to repeat his delivery, so a small adjustment or two should help him improve his command. He'll also need to harness his breaking ball. While his curveball at times has power and depth, it's inconsistent. His changeup remains in its early phases. Colvin should be able to start his first full pro season in low Class A, but it wouldn't be a surprise if Philadephia held him back in extended spring training and sent him to Williamsport instead.

Year	Club (League)	Class	W	L	ERA	G	GS	CG	SV	IP	H	R	ER	HR	BB	SO	AVG
2009	Phillies (GCL)	R	0	0	0.00	1	0	0	0	2	0	1	0	0	1	2	.000
MINOR LEAGUE TOTALS			0	0	0.00	1	0	0	0	2	0	1	0	0	1	2	.000

13 FREDDY GALVIS, SS

BORN: Nov. 14, 1989. **B-T:** B-R. **HT.:** 5-10. **WT.:**168. **SIGNED:** Venezuela, 2006. **SIGNED BY:** Sal Agostinelli.

Venezuelan glove-first shortstops inevitably get compared to Omar Vizquel, and that has happened a few times to Galvis, whose defense prompted his promotion to Double-A at age 19. His career path and ceiling are much closer to fellow Venezuelan shortstop Cesar Izturis, whose glove is excellent and whose bat has been just good enough to make him a big league regular. The Phillies believe in Galvis' offensive potential for several reasons. He centers the ball, he has a balanced swing that he repeats, he has hand-eye coordination and he has solid offensive instincts. He has improved at bunting and at moving runners. He lost two months of at-bats last spring with a broken right hand. He has just average speed and won't be a basestealing factor. If his bat reaches his ceiling—and he'll have to mature physically and get stronger before that happens—he still profiles as a No. 7 or 8 hitter. Defensively, Galvis has few peers and might be the best shortstop in the minor leagues. He has top-flight instincts, plus range and arm strength and excellent hands. He makes more plays than most short-stops, and he's more reliable on routine plays than most young shortstops. Galvis figures to return to Reading in 2010. It remains unclear where he'll fit in Philadelphia with Jimmy Rollins and Chase Utley starring in the middle infield.

Year	Club (League)	Class	AVG	G	AB	R	H	2D	3B	HR	RBI	BB	SO	SB	OBP	SLG
2007	Williamsport (NYP)	SS	.203	38	143	20	29	5	1	0	7	10	20	9	.255	.252
2008	Lakewood (SAL)	LoA	.238	127	458	59	109	12	1	3	42	39	58	14	.300	.288
2009	Phillies (GCL)	R	.276	7	29	6	8	1	0	0	0	1	4	1	.300	.310
	Clearwater (FSL)	HiA	.247	63	251	29	62	8	2	1	15	10	43	6	.280	.307
	Reading (EL)	AA	.197	16	61	6	12	0	0	1	5	2	7	0	.222	.246
MINOR LEAGUE TOTALS			.234	251	942	120	220	26	4	5	69	62	132	30	.283	.286

14 KYRELL HUDSON, OF

BORN: Dec. 6, 1990. **B-T:** R-R. **HT.:** 6-1. **WT.:**190. **DRAFTED:** HS—Vancouver, Wash., 2009 (3rd round). **SIGNED BY:** Tim Kissner.

The Phillies have an eye for athletes and the patience to develop them. For every Greg Golson who doesn't work out, they find a Domonic Brown who looks like he will. They targeted Hudson in the third round and signed him for $475,000 in 2009 because they considered him the best athlete in the draft class. He turned down a football scholarship from Oregon State, where he would have played both sports. His speed is his best tool, as he covers 60 yards in 6.4 seconds. He's just as fast as minor league stolen base leader Anthony Gose, and Philadelphia may have them race in spring training. Like Gose, Hudson pitched in high school and has a plus arm in center field. He also has strength in his frame, and he has a chance to hit and hit for power. His tools aren't in question, but area scouts in the Pacific Northwest questioned Hudson's desire and makeup. He was suspended for two football games as a senior for breaking team rules and showed inconsistent effort during the spring. That's why a player with his tools was available with the 106th overall pick. The Phillies hope to channel Hudson's competitiveness in the proper direction and were encouraged by his offensive progress and behavior in instructional league. His spring performance will determine whether he opens 2010 in low Class A or extended spring training.

Year	Club (League)	Class	AVG	G	AB	R	H	2B	3B	HR	RBI	BB	SO	SB	OBP	SLG
2009	Phillies (GCL)	R	.162	10	37	3	6	2	0	0	6	3	9	2	.225	.216
MINOR LEAGUE TOTALS			.162	10	37	3	6	2	0	0	6	3	9	2	.225	.216

15 SCOTT MATHIESON, RHP

BORN: Feb. 27, 1984. **B-T:** R-R. **HT.:** 6-3. **WT.:** 190. **DRAFTED:** HS—Aldergrove, B.C., 2002 (17th round). **SIGNED BY:** Tim Kissner.

Everyone in the organization is rooting for Mathieson, the son of a prominent Canadian amateur coach. He's still trying to complete his comeback after injuring his elbow during his first taste of the majors in September 2006. He had Tommy John surgery, then needed a second elbow reconstruction after he came back the following summer. He got back on the mound last June and showed power stuff again in the lower minors and the Arizona Fall League. Mathieson reached the big leagues as starter, but he was somewhat miscast in that role because he lacked command and feel for a changeup. Now a reliever, he still doesn't command his fastball well enough to project as future closer. He can be an asset as a set-up man if he can stay healthy, as he has a 93-97 mph fastball and a solid slider that's a plus pitch at times. He gets more life on his changeup than on his fastball, and it's a solid third pitch. His fastball can be straight, so he'll need to locate it with more precison against big league hitters. If he can avoid injuries, Mathieson could help Philadelphia at some point in 2010.

Year	Club (League)	Class	W	L	ERA	G	GS	CG	SV	IP	H	R	ER	HR	BB	SO	AVG
2002	Phillies (GCL)	R	0	2	5.40	7	2	0	0	17	24	11	10	0	6	14	.338
2003	Phillies (GCL)	R	2	7	5.52	11	11	0	0	59	59	42	36	5	13	51	.247
	Batavia (NYP)	SS	0	0	0.00	2	0	0	1	6	0	0	0	0	0	7	.000
2004	Lakewood (SAL)	LoA	8	9	4.32	25	25	1	0	131	130	73	63	7	50	112	.260
2005	Clearwater (FSL)	HiA	3	8	4.14	23	23	1	0	122	111	62	56	17	34	118	.241
2006	Reading (EL)	AA	7	2	3.21	14	14	0	0	93	73	35	33	8	29	99	.221
	Scranton/W-B (IL)	AAA	3	1	3.93	5	5	0	0	34	26	16	15	2	10	36	.208
	Philadelphia (NL)	MAJ	1	4	7.47	9	8	0	0	37	48	36	31	8	16	28	.312
2007	Phillies (GCL)	R	0	0	0.00	2	2	0	0	2	0	0	0	0	1	3	.000
	Clearwater (FSL)	HiA	0	0	4.50	3	2	0	0	4	3	3	2	0	3	5	.214
	Reading (EL)	AA	0	0	9.00	2	0	0	0	2	3	3	2	1	2	1	.333
2008	Did Not Play—Injured																
2009	Phillies (GCL)	R	2	0	0.00	4	0	0	0	6	3	1	0	0	2	8	.130
	Clearwater (FSL)	HiA	0	0	0.00	5	0	0	1	7	4	0	0	0	3	9	.167
	Reading (EL)	AA	2	0	1.40	13	0	0	1	19	10	6	3	1	7	17	.149
MAJOR LEAGUE TOTALS			1	4	7.47	9	8	0	0	37	48	36	31	8	16	28	.312
MINOR LEAGUE TOTALS			27	29	3.95	116	84	2	3	502	446	252	220	41	160	480	.236

16 MIKE STUTES, RHP

BORN: Sept. 4, 1986. **B-T:** R-R. **HT.:** 6-1. **WT.:** 185. **DRAFTED:** Oregon State, 2008 (11th round). **SIGNED BY:** Dave Ryles.

The Phillies jumped three of their 2008 college draft picks to Double-A last season. Stutes and Vance Worley began the year in Reading, while Mike Cisco joined them in August. A member of Oregon State's back-to-back national championship teams in 2006-07, Stutes threw five scoreless innings in his Double-A debut but endured an up-and-down season. His best pitch is a plus slider that he throws in the low 80s. He also flashes an above-average fastball, sitting at 89-93 mph with his two-seamer and peaking at 95 with his four-seamer. He's a long-toss devotee who has regained some of the arm strength he lost by throwing too many breaking balls as a college senior. His changeup is below-average, and he doesn't change speeds or locate his pitches well. Those shortcomings hurt him against lefthanders, who batted .307/.393/.512 against him in 2009, and he'll have to address them to remain a starter. Most scouts think he's better suited to focusing on two pitches and working as a reliever. He'll remain in the rotation in Triple-A this season.

Year	Club (League)	Class	W	L	ERA	G	GS	CG	SV	IP	H	R	ER	HR	BB	SO	AVG
2008	Williamsport (NYP)	SS	2	1	1.33	6	6	0	0	27	16	5	4	2	11	31	.172
	Lakewood (SAL)	LoA	5	1	1.48	7	7	0	0	43	20	8	7	1	18	53	.139
2009	Reading (EL)	AA	8	8	4.26	27	27	0	0	146	147	78	69	15	58	109	.265
MINOR LEAGUE TOTALS			15	10	3.34	40	40	0	0	215	183	91	80	18	87	193	.231

17 YOHAN FLANDE, LHP

BORN: Jan. 27, 1986. **B-T:** L-L. **HT.:** 6-2. **WT.:** 170. **SIGNED:** Dominican Republic, 2004. **SIGNED BY:** Sal Agostinelli.

Few prospects came as far as fast as Flande did last season. He spent three years in the Rookie-level Dominican Summer League and another in the Rookie-level Gulf Coast League before reaching Double-A and pitching in the Futures Game in 2009. The Phillies have pushed their minor leaguers more aggressively since Chuck LaMar took control of their farm system, and Flande responded positively when challenged. His work ethic and athleticism also helped. Signed for $10,000 at age 18, he took a while to mature physically. His previously average fastball pushed up a tick or two last year, sitting at 91-92 mph at times. His best pitch is his plus changeup, which gains deception from his stiff, unconventional arm action. Flande is tough to profile because he doesn't throw a true breaking ball, relying more on a cutter/slider that lacks depth. That makes him more of a back-of-the-rotation starter and limits his effectiveness as a potential left-on-left reliever. He's already something of an overachiever, and the Phillies don't want to limit him. After getting added to the 40-man roster in the offseason, he figures to return to Double-A to open 2010.

Year	Club (League)	Class	W	L	ERA	G	GS	CG	SV	IP	H	R	ER	HR	BB	SO	AVG
2005	Phillies (DSL)	R	3	6	2.76	14	8	2	1	59	69	40	18	1	20	50	.276
2006	Phillies (DSL)	R	6	1	2.08	13	10	0	0	65	55	24	15	1	12	60	.217
2007	Phillies (DSL)	R	3	2	2.36	13	12	1	0	72	61	27	19	2	27	62	.223
2008	Phillies (GCL)	R	4	1	2.19	10	9	0	0	53	41	19	13	5	11	39	.200
2009	Clearwater (FSL)	HiA	7	1	2.52	13	13	1	0	82	72	27	23	2	24	67	.238
	Reading (EL)	AA	4	4	4.58	13	13	1	0	71	81	38	36	5	21	50	.296
MINOR LEAGUE TOTALS			27	15	2.78	76	65	5	1	402	379	175	124	16	115	328	.243

18 VANCE WORLEY, RHP

BORN: Sept. 25, 1987. **B-T:** R-R. **HT.:** 6-2. **WT.:** 205. **DRAFTED:** Long Beach State, 2008 (3rd round). **SIGNED BY:** Tim Kissner.

The Phillies drafted Worley in the 20th round out of high school in 2005, and he spent three seasons in the Long Beach State rotation before they drafted him again in the third round in 2008. His profile has changed since his days at McClatchy High in Sacramento, and if he joins Larry Bowa and Nick Johnson among the school's big league alumni, he'll do it as a back-of-the-rotation starter rather than a premium power pitcher. Worley's 88-92 mph fastball has solid life and he controls it well. He maintains his velocity deep into games and deep into the season. He generally throws strikes with his secondary pitches, which include an average slider and changeup. He also uses a slow curveball as an early-count, get-me-over pitch. Worley had elbow issues as a high school senior and college sophomore, but he threw 172 innings between college and pro ball in 2008, then logged 153 in Double-A last season. While he has shown he can shoulder a heavy load, Worley tailed off in the second half of 2009, losing seven of his last eight decisions as his command deteriorated. He got tired and didn't finish his pitches, getting pounded when he left the ball up in the zone. Worley lacks a pitch to put hitters away with, and he could wind up in middle relief. He'll move up to Triple-A this season.

Year	Club (League)	Class	W	L	ERA	G	GS	CG	SV	IP	H	R	ER	HR	BB	SO	AVG
2008	Williamsport (NYP)	SS	0	0	1.13	2	2	0	0	8	3	1	1	0	1	8	.120
	Lakewood (SAL)	LoA	3	2	2.66	11	11	0	0	61	58	25	18	4	7	53	.247
2009	Reading (EL)	AA	7	12	5.34	27	27	0	0	153	163	102	91	17	49	100	.275
MINOR LEAGUE TOTALS			10	14	4.45	40	40	0	0	222	224	128	110	21	57	161	.263

19 HEITOR CORREA, RHP

BORN: Aug. 25, 1989. **B-T:** R-R. **HT.:** 6-3. **WT.:** 200. **SIGNED:** Brazil, 2006. **SIGNED BY:** Sal Agostinelli.

The Phillies signed Correa in 2006 as the highlight of their first Brazilian signing class. He lost much of his prospect luster in 2008, when Philadelphia suspended him and sent him home to Brazil for disciplinary reasons. Correa returned last season and became the best starter on Lakewood's staff before he tired and lost his last five decisions. A back injury kept him out of the South Atlantic playoffs, but he got in 124 innings of needed work. Correa's fastball reached 94 mph consistently when he signed as a 16-year-old, and he touched that peak in 2009 while sitting at 89-93 mph. He has solid secondary pitches, with one of the system's better breaking balls. Alternately described as a slider or power curve, it arrives in the low 80s with some depth. His changeup gives him a third average-or-better pitch. Correa's control is his biggest issue. He doesn't throw enough quality strikes and hasn't learned how to control the armside run on his fastball, leading to 21 hit batsmen—19 against right-handers. He creates decent plane to the plate and gave up just six homers last season. Correa's inexperience means he'll move a step at a time, heading to high Class A for 2010. His ceiling is the highest among Philadelphia's international pitchers and ranks among the best in the system.

Year	Club (League)	Class	W	L	ERA	G	GS	CG	SV	IP	H	R	ER	HR	BB	SO	AVG
2006	Phillies (GCL)	R	0	3	7.83	8	4	0	0	23	35	21	20	1	7	14	.365
2007	Phillies (GCL)	R	3	3	3.74	13	11	0	0	65	58	33	27	4	20	49	.230
2008	Did Not Play—Suspended																
2009	Lakewood (SAL)	LoA	7	8	4.13	22	21	2	0	124	128	64	57	6	50	89	.266
MINOR LEAGUE TOTALS			10	14	4.41	43	36	2	0	212	221	118	104	11	77	152	.267

20 JONATHAN SINGLETON, 1B

BORN: Sept. 18, 1991. **B-T:** L-L. **HT.:** 6-2. **WT.:** 215. **DRAFTED:** HS—Long Beach, 2009 (8th round). **SIGNED BY:** Demerius Pittman.

It's possible that the best players the Phillies drafted in 2009 were taken with consecutive picks in the seventh and eighth rounds: Brody Colvin and Singleton. The latter is the most advanced hitter Philadelphia has drafted since taking Adrian Cardenas (since traded to the Athletics) in 2006's sandwich round. The team continued a trend with Singleton, making it the fifth straight draft in which they took a first baseman with a single-digit pick.

His feel for hitting makes him the best prospect on the bunch. He made a strong impression on 2008 showcase circuit, but didn't stand out as much last spring, batting just .321 as a high school senior. The Phillies trusted their scouting reports and got him for a $200,000 bonus. Singleton had a good pro debut, showing off plus bat speed and a disciplined approach. His swing can get long at times, but he has improved his stroke since signing, reducing the length of his trigger. He's not as athletic as his father Herb, a former quarterback at Oregon, and has below-average speed but isn't a slug. He shows promise as a defender, deftly picking balls out of the dirt and exhibiting some feel for plays around the bag. Singleton will spend his first full season in low Class A, and he may anchor the Lakewood lineup with Sebastian Valle.

Year	Club (League)	Class	AVG	G	AB	R	H	2B	3B	HR	RBI	BB	SO	SB	OBP	SLG
2009	Phillies (GCL)	R	.290	31	100	12	29	9	0	2	12	18	13	1	.395	.440
MINOR LEAGUE TOTALS			.290	31	100	12	29	9	0	2	12	18	13	1	.395	.440

21 JOE SAVERY, LHP

BORN: Nov. 4, 1985. **B-T:** L-L. **HT.:** 6-3. **WT.:** 215. **DRAFTED:** Rice, 2007 (1st round). **SIGNED BY:** Steve Cohen.

Nine Rice pitchers have been drafted in the first round or the supplemental first round since Wayne Graham took over the Owls program in the early 1990s. After just one full big league season, Jeff Niemann already has as many victories (15) as any pitcher in the group, which has a track record of injuries and modest success. Savery is trying to buck that trend and is coming off his best pro year, rising to Triple-A and leading Phillies farmhands with 16 wins. But he isn't the same guy the Phillies drafted with the 19th overall pick and signed for $1,372,500 in 2007. He seems to have left his velocity in college, now touching 91-92 mph with his fastball at his best after sitting there at Rice. The athleticism that produced excellent command early in his college career also has regressed. The hope was that Savery's velocity and command would improve after he put college shoulder problems behind him and gave up hitting (he played first base and batted third for much of his time at Rice). To his credit, Savery still creates angle and plane with his fastball, which usually peaks at 90 mph. At times, he can spot his changeup with solid fade to both sides of the plate. His slider is below-average, limiting his usefulness as a potential reliever. He'll spend 2010 in Triple-A unless his stuff and command improve.

Year	Club (League)	Class	W	L	ERA	G	GS	CG	SV	IP	H	R	ER	HR	BB	SO	AVG
2007	Williamsport (NYP)	SS	2	3	2.73	7	7	0	0	26	22	9	8	0	13	22	.214
2008	Clearwater (FSL)	HiA	9	10	4.13	27	24	0	0	150	171	84	69	10	60	122	.286
2009	Reading (EL)	AA	12	4	4.41	21	20	1	0	112	111	55	55	13	53	77	.262
	Lehigh Valley (IL)	AAA	4	2	4.38	7	7	1	0	39	42	23	19	0	24	19	.286
MINOR LEAGUE TOTALS			27	19	4.14	62	58	2	0	328	346	171	151	23	150	240	.272

22 JONATHAN VILLAN, SS

BORN: May 2, 1991. **B-T:** B-R. **HT.:** 6-1. **WT.:**180. **SIGNED:** Dominican Republic, 2008. **SIGNED BY:** Sal Agostinelli.

Villan has as much upside as any Phillies infield prospect. Signed for $105,000 in 2008, he has plus tools across the board except for power. He earned a promotion to the short-season New York-Penn League in his first season in the United States, showing impressive polish. While he has a plus arm suited for shortstop, Villan may end up at second base as he continues to fill out. He might have enough bat for the move. A natural righthander, he's now better from the left side and has solid gap power, though he'll probably never be a home run threat. Villan has a willingness to take walks but must make more contact. He takes a big hack at the plate but is a plus runner once under way. He's also a smart, aggressive basestealer for his age and experience level. His excellent hands work well at the plate and in the field. He has solid range at shortstop. The Phillies will see if Villan can handle low Class A in 2010.

Year	Club (League)	Class	AVG	G	AB	R	H	2B	3B	HR	RBI	BB	SO	SB	OBP	SLG
2008	Phillies (DSL)	R	.271	62	214	37	58	6	3	1	21	30	56	27	.367	.341
2009	Phillies (GCL)	R	.277	31	94	14	26	7	1	0	14	13	24	11	.364	.372
	Williamsport (NYP)	SS	.231	11	39	6	9	1	1	0	5	4	14	6	.302	.308
MINOR LEAGUE TOTALS			.268	104	347	57	93	14	5	1	40	47	94	44	.359	.346

23 MIKE CISCO, RHP

BORN: May 23, 1987. **B-T:** R-R. **HT.:** 5-11. **WT.:**190. **DRAFTED:** South Carolina, 2008 (36th round). **SIGNED BY:** Roy Tanner.

The grandson of former big leaguer and former Phillies pitching coach Galen Cisco, Mike is trying to beat his brother Drew—a top high school prospect for the 2010 draft—to the big leagues. Cisco isn't as tall or as talented as his younger brother, but he has a head start and has fared better than most scouts expected after his modest four-year college career at South Carolina. After sitting at 89-92 mph and touching 94 with his fastball during his 2008 pro debut, Cisco opened last season on the disabled list with a strained oblique and didn't have quite the same velocity. He worked at 88-90 mph, which wasn't a problem because he still got outs with his plus changeup and mound savvy. Cisco throws strikes with his curveball and has a modest slider that's more of a cutter. He depends on his fine command, because when he gets too much of the plate, he's vulnerable to homers. Cisco's velocity could spike back up with a move to the bullpen, but he's likely to anchor the Reading rotation in 2010.

Year	Club (League)	Class	W	L	ERA	G	GS	CG	SV	IP	H	R	ER	HR	BB	SO	AVG
2008	Williamsport (NYP)	SS	1	0	1.86	9	1	0	0	19	18	5	4	1	5	22	.240
	Lakewood (SAL)	LoA	2	1	0.51	8	6	0	0	35	22	4	2	0	0	30	.173
2009	Clearwater (FSL)	HiA	7	3	3.31	15	14	0	0	73	69	32	27	9	15	51	.246
	Reading (EL)	AA	2	4	4.58	7	7	0	0	39	44	21	20	4	9	20	.282
MINOR LEAGUE TOTALS			12	8	2.86	39	28	0	0	167	153	62	53	14	29	123	.239

24 B.J. ROSENBERG, RHP

BORN: Sept. 17, 1985. **B-T:** R-R. **HT.:** 6-2. **WT.:** 215. **DRAFTED:** Louisville, 2008 (13th round). **SIGNED BY:** Paul Murphy.

Rosenberg had an eventful first full pro season in 2009. He opened the year as Lakewood's closer and thrived, not giving up an earned run in his final 20 appearances. The Phillies decided to aggressively jump him to Double-A, and he responded well before missing the Eastern League playoffs to pitch in Team USA's bullpen at the World Cup. He won a gold medal, striking out 11 in six innings. Rosenberg started for much of his college career at Louisville until he tore a labrum, which cost him his 2007 season, and he has shown the ability to pitch more than one inning at a time. He relies heavily on his fastball, which often sits at 93-95 mph in shorter stints. He needs to spot his fastball better at upper levels because it's more notable for its velocity than for its life. He also has a solid-average slider, which is a bit inconsistent but can be a strikeout pitch. Rosenberg turned 24 during the World Cup and will be pushed accordingly. With Scott Mathieson ahead of him and starters such as Mike Stutes, Vance Worley and Mike Cisco all potential future relievers, Rosenberg may best serve the Philadelphia as trade bait. He's likely to close at Lehigh Valley this season.

Year	Club (League)	Class	W	L	ERA	G	GS	CG	SV	IP	H	R	ER	HR	BB	SO	AVG
2008	Williamsport (NYP)	SS	3	1	1.00	21	0	0	10	36	26	9	4	2	15	52	.205
2009	Lakewood (SAL)	LoA	7	2	0.89	37	0	0	19	50	37	7	5	0	10	65	.200
	Reading (EL)	AA	0	1	2.53	10	0	0	3	11	10	3	3	0	4	8	.263
MINOR LEAGUE TOTALS			10	4	1.11	68	0	0	32	97	73	19	12	2	29	125	.209

25 LEANDRO CASTRO, OF

BORN: June 15, 1989. **B-T:** R-R. **HT.:** 5-11. **WT.:** 185. **SIGNED:** Dominican Republic, 2007. **SIGNED BY:** Sal Agostinelli.

Castro sticks out among the Phillies' lower-level outfield prospects because his bat is his best tool and his athleticism is merely good. He's advanced enough as a hitter that Philadelphia sent him to low Class A as a teenager to open 2009. After struggling there, he regrouped in extended spring training and went on to lead the New-York Penn League with 81 hits and 31 extra-base hits. Castro doesn't have a pretty swing—he uses a pronounced arm bar—but he squares balls up consistently and has good power. He has strength in his hands and forearms, giving him plus bat speed. An above-average runner now, Castro figures to slow down a bit down the line. He played all three outfield positions last season and projects as an eventual left fielder with an average arm. Unless he develops true plus power, he's more of a second-division regular or a fourth outfielder on a contender. His speed and arm give him an edge in the system over Steve Susdorf, who has a similar bat and has reached Double-A. Castro figures to return to Lakewood in 2010 but could advance to high Class A with a strong spring.

Year	Club (League)	Class	AVG	G	AB	R	H	2B	3B	HR	RBI	BB	SO	SB	OBP	SLG
2007	Phillies (DSL)	R	.278	59	223	41	62	3	5	6	37	26	39	24	.362	.417
2008	Phillies (GCL)	R	.298	44	161	25	48	9	1	3	19	4	25	9	.317	.422
2009	Lakewood (SAL)	LoA	.152	22	66	9	10	4	0	0	6	5	15	2	.230	.212
	Williamsport (NYP)	SS	.316	66	256	48	81	19	5	7	43	13	49	18	.351	.512
MINOR LEAGUE TOTALS			.285	191	706	123	201	35	11	16	105	48	128	53	.336	.433

26 EDGAR GARCIA, RHP

BORN: Sept. 20, 1987. **B-T:** R-R. **HT.:** 6-2. **WT.:** 190. **SIGNED:** Dominican Republic, 2004. **SIGNED BY:** Sal Agostinelli/Wil Tejada.

Garcia and Carlos Carrasco often were mentioned in tandem because they signed a year apart for significant money. They once were also two of the best righthanders in the system, but Carrasco went to Cleveland in the Cliff Lee trade last summer and Garcia wasn't protected on the 40-man roster after performing poorly in the Arizona Fall League. Garcia flashes the stuff that earned him a $500,000 signing bonus, but not on a consistent basis. He had a 92-94 mph fastball when he signed and worked at 93-96 during the high Class A Florida State League all-star game in 2008. But after he had visa problems in 2009 and didn't take the mound until late July, his arm strength was down. His fastball was average at best in the AFL, flattening out at times and getting hammered. His slider remains his best pitch, peaking in the mid-80s with depth, and he has a solid-average changeup. He has a good feel for using his secondary pitches and can get on a roll if he throws strikes with his fastball. Garcia still has a high ceiling, but his chances of reaching it keep getting smaller—which is why he didn't find any takers in the Rule 5 draft. He'll give Double-A another try after getting torched there in 2008.

Year	Club (League)	Class	W	L	ERA	G	GS	CG	SV	IP	H	R	ER	HR	BB	SO	AVG
2005	Phillies (GCL)	R	4	4	3.56	10	10	0	0	56	63	26	22	4	13	42	.284
2006	Batavia (NYP)	SS	3	5	2.98	12	12	1	0	66	62	28	22	5	10	46	.243
2007	Williamsport (NYP)	SS	1	0	2.16	2	1	0	0	8	6	2	2	0	2	11	.200
	Lakewood (SAL)	LoA	4	9	4.12	20	20	0	0	114	119	61	52	10	32	83	.268
2008	Clearwater (FSL)	HiA	8	2	3.97	14	13	0	0	79	80	36	35	7	20	70	.267
	Reading (EL)	AA	1	7	8.22	11	11	0	0	58	70	56	53	10	29	34	.299
2009	Phillies (GCL)	R	1	0	0.00	1	0	0	0	4	1	0	0	0	0	4	.083
	Clearwater (FSL)	HiA	1	4	4.32	8	8	0	0	42	38	24	20	3	9	27	.239
MINOR LEAGUE TOTALS			23	31	4.34	78	75	1	0	427	439	233	206	39	115	317	.265

27 KELLY DUGAN, OF

BORN: Sept. 18, 1990. **B-T:** B-R. **HT.:** 6-3. **WT.:**195. **DRAFTED:** HS—Sherman Oaks, Calif., 2009 (2nd round). **SIGNED BY:** Shane Bowers.

Dugan's father Dennis is a Hollywood actor, director and producer who often works with Adam Sandler, directing him in comedies such as "Big Daddy" and "You Don't Mess With the Zohan." His son has made a name for himself in baseball, where he was the first player the Phillies drafted (second round) in 2009 after giving up their first pick for signing free agent Raul Ibanez. His advanced bat and strong predraft workout prompted Philadelphia to buy him away from a Pepperdine scholarship with a $485,000 bonus. Dugan started switch-hitting as an 8-year-old and recognizes pitches well from both sides of the plate. A slightly better hitter as a lefty, he has average to plus raw power from both sides, thanks to good strength and a fairly mature, physical frame. He has average speed and arm strength, making right field a viable option. The Phillies are encouraged by his competitive streak and believe he'll do what it takes to get the most out of his ability. He's probably headed to Williamsport in 2010 because Lakewood's projected outfield is already crowded with Leandro Castro, Zach Collier, Jiwan James and perhaps Anthony Hewitt.

Year	Club (League)	Class	AVG	G	AB	R	H	2B	3B	HR	RBI	BB	SO	SB	OBP	SLG
2009	Phillies (GCL)	R	.233	45	150	18	35	8	1	0	8	12	30	9	.297	.300
MINOR LEAGUE TOTALS			.233	45	150	18	35	8	1	0	8	12	30	9	.297	.300

28 MATT WAY, LHP

BORN: Jan. 25, 1987. **B-T:** L-L. **HT.:** 6-1. **WT.:**195. **DRAFTED:** Washington State, 2009 (5th round). **SIGNED BY:** Tim Kissner.

For the second straight year, the Phillies got strong early returns from the college pitchers in their draft. Nick Hernandez (12th round) and Austin Hyatt (15th) tore up the New York-Penn League, while Way did the same before earning a promotion and easily handling low Class A hitters. A fifth-rounder who signed for $40,000 as a college senior, the Alaska native turned down the Giants as a 36th-round pick in 2008. He led Washington State to its first NCAA regional berth since 1990 in the spring, and capped his pro debut by contributing two fine playoff starts to Lakewood's championship run. He reached 190 innings between college and pro ball, but Philadelphia isn't overly concerned. Way relies on a downhill fastball that sits in the upper 80s touches 90-91 mph, and a solid to plus changeup that locks up righthanders. They hit just .197 against him in pro ball, with one home run in 234 at-bats. His slider has been short throughout his career, which hinders his chances of moving into a lefty specialist role if he can't stick as a starter. His sinker and changeup may be good enough to keep in the rotation, however. He'll open his first full season in high Class A.

Year	Club (League)	Class	W	L	ERA	G	GS	CG	SV	IP	H	R	ER	HR	BB	SO	AVG
2009	Williamsport (NYP)	SS	2	3	1.67	8	8	0	0	38	28	11	7	2	8	43	.197
	Lakewood (SAL)	LoA	4	1	3.11	6	6	1	0	38	32	15	13	0	4	42	.221
MINOR LEAGUE TOTALS			6	4	2.39	14	14	1	0	75	60	26	20	2	12	85	.209

29 JUSTIN DeFRATUS, RHP

BORN: Oct. 21, 1987. **B-T:** B-R. **HT.:** 6-4. **WT.:**217. **DRAFTED:** Ventura (Calif.) JC, 2007 (11th round).
SIGNED BY: Tim Kissner.

The Phillies drafted DeFratus out of Ventura (Calif.) JC, where he showed raw arm strength but was green in terms of pitching experience. He has advanced slowly in pro ball, but he has made improvements with his conditioning and delivery. DeFratus does a better job now of maintaining his velocity, sitting at 88-92 mph with his fastball and regularly touching 94-95 mph out of the bullpen. His command is among the best in the system, and he locates his fastball down in the zone consistently. He didn't allow a walk last year until May 12, and was so good out of Lakewood's bullpen that he became a starter in the second half. Though he was much more hittable working out of the rotation, his command didn't waver. His slider also continued to improve, giving him a second average to plus pitch. His changeup remains below-average in terms of life and his arm speed, but he does throw it for strikes and generally keeps it down. DeFratus finished strong before an oblique strain shut him down for the playoffs. His long-term future is likely as a reliever, but he'll pitch in the Clearwater rotation in 2010.

Year	Club (League)	Class	W	L	ERA	G	GS	CG	SV	IP	H	R	ER	HR	BB	SO	AVG
2007	Phillies (GCL)	R	2	3	4.30	10	8	0	0	46	51	25	22	1	3	34	.273
2008	Williamsport (NYP)	SS	6	5	3.67	14	14	1	0	83	87	39	34	1	25	74	.260
2009	Lakewood (SAL)	LoA	5	6	3.19	36	12	0	3	110	108	44	39	3	16	101	.258
MINOR LEAGUE TOTALS			13	14	3.57	60	34	1	3	239	246	108	95	5	44	209	.261

30 ZACH COLLIER, OF

BORN: Sept. 8, 1990. **B-T:** L-L. **HT.:** 6-2. **WT.:**190. **DRAFTED:** HS—Chino Hills, Calif., 2008 (1st round supplemental). **SIGNED BY:** Darrell Conner.

Collier ranked eighth on this list a year ago, after he signed for $1.02 million as a sandwich pick and enjoyed a solid pro debut. He moved to full-season ball in 2009 and was one of Lakewood's few disappointments. Considered a fairly polished hitter coming out of high school, he failed to make adjustments and lost his confidence last year. A midseason demotion to Williamsport didn't help. The biggest concern was his lack of power, as Collier hit only one home run. He didn't make frequent or hard contact, and scouts have started to question his explosiveness. He also was overmatched by lefthanders. Collier remains athletic and has a projectable body that should get stronger, but he may top out with just gap power. He's a plus runner, and his average arm gives him flexibility to play any outfield spot, though he fits best in left. He needs to show more in his second tour of low Class A this year to regain some of his lost luster.

Year	Club (League)	Class	AVG	G	AB	R	H	2B	3B	HR	RBI	BB	SO	SB	OBP	SLG
2008	Phillies (GCL)	R	.271	37	129	15	35	9	1	0	19	17	28	5	.347	.357
2009	Lakewood (SAL)	LoA	.218	82	298	40	65	16	7	0	32	23	80	13	.275	.319
	Williamsport (NYP)	SS	.226	34	137	21	31	10	1	1	13	9	42	7	.280	.336
MINOR LEAGUE TOTALS			.232	153	564	76	131	35	9	1	64	49	150	25	.293	.332

Pittsburgh Pirates

BY JOHN PERROTTO

I t didn't take Neal Huntington long after he became Pirates general manager late in the 2007 season to understand what the organization needed: young talent and lots of it. Pittsburgh not only had a bad major league team, but it also had little talent in the farm system. It made for a deadly mix that appeared to sentence the franchise to losing into perpetuity.

While the Pirates have become the only major North American pro sports team to endure 17 straight losing seasons after finishing 62-99 (the second-worst record in baseball) in 2009, their talent base has improved. Huntington has almost completely stripped the major league roster, trading away as many parts as he could in an effort to acquire prospects. He made seven trades last June and July, sending away eight players and getting 15 in return.

By the time the season ended, just five players remained on the major league roster who were on the major league club when Huntington was hired: Matt Capps, Ryan Doumit, Zach Duke, Paul Maholm and Steve Pearce. On the minor league side, just six of the players in the Pirates' Top 30 were in the organization when Huntington took over.

Owner Bob Nutting, noted for his penny-pinching ways in his other business holdings, has held the line on major league salaries. After all the trades, Pittsburgh's payroll was approximately $25 million by the end of last season. However, Nutting has given Huntington expanded budgets in the areas of scouting and player development.

The Pirates have spent more money ($18.7 million) on the last two drafts than any team. They gave out their first major league contract to a draftee, a $6.335 million deal to land No. 2 overall pick Pedro Alvarez in 2008. While they stuck to Major League Baseball's slot recommendation for their first-round pick last June, catcher Tony Sanchez, they gave seven-figure bonuses to sixth-round pick Zack Von Rosenberg and eighth-rounder Colton Cain. In fact, the Pirates have continually exceeded MLB's bonus recommendations under their new administration, ironic considering that club president Frank Coonelly helped to enforce the slotting system when he worked for MLB.

Pittsburgh also opened a $5 million Dominican Republic academy last April and has further expanded its international horizons by signing amateurs from Africa, Asia and Europe since Huntington arrived. Relievers Dinesh Patel and Rinku Singh became the first natives of India to play professional baseball when

GEORGE GOJKOVICH

Rookie of the Year Andrew McCutchen is now the face of a young franchise

TOP 30 PROSPECTS

1. Pedro Alvarez, 3b	**16.** John Raynor, of
2. Jose Tabata, of	**17.** Ramon Aguero, rhp
3. Tony Sanchez, c	**18.** Robbie Grossman, of
4. Brad Lincoln, rhp	**19.** Hunter Strickland, rhp
5. Chase d'Arnaud, ss/2b	**20.** Jarek Cunningham, 3b/ss
6. Sterling Marte, of	**21.** Daniel McCutchen, rhp
7. Tim Alderson, rhp	**22.** Jordy Mercer, ss/3b
8. Zack Von Rosenberg, rhp	**23.** Evan Chambers, of
9. Rudy Owens, lhp	**24.** Donnie Veal, lhp
10. Gorkys Hernandez, of	**25.** Brett Lorin, rhp
11. Colton Cain, lhp	**26.** Neil Walker, 3b
12. Victor Black, rhp	**27.** Brock Holt, ss/2b
13. Jeff Locke, lhp	**28.** Brian Friday, ss
14. Quinton Miller, rhp	**29.** Josh Harrison, of/2b/3b
15. Bryan Morris, rhp	**30.** Daniel Moskos, lhp

they made their debuts in the Rookie-level Gulf Coast League last summer. South African infielder Gift Ngoepe became a sensation when he hit two triples off veteran big leaguer Elmer Dessens in the World Baseball Classic, then later was featured in a lengthy Sports Illustrated profile.

Rookie of the Year Andrew McCutchen has the Pirates believing they're starting to get the franchise turned around. Pittsburgh drew just 1.58 million fans last season, the fewest since PNC Park opened in 2001. Fans will have to wait a little longer for the moves below the majors to pay off.

General Manager: Neal Huntington. **Farm Director:** Kyle Stark. **Scouting Director:** Greg Smith.

Class	Team	League	W	L	PCT	Finish*	Manager(s)
Majors	Pittsburgh Pirates	National	62	99	.385	15th (16)	John Russell
Triple-A	Indianapolis Indians	International	70	73	.490	9th (14)	Frank Kremblas
Double-A	Altoona Curve	Eastern	62	80	.437	11th (12)	Matt Walbeck
High A	#Lynchburg Hillcats	Carolina	73	66	.525	†4th (8)	P.J. Forbes
Low A	West Virginia Power	South Atlantic	67	70	.489	8th (16)	Gary Green
Short-season	State College Spikes	New York-Penn	38	38	.500	7th (14)	Gary Robinson
Rookie	GCL Pirates	Gulf Coast	29	31	.483	11th (16)	Tom Prince
Overall 2009 Minor League Record			339	358	.486	23rd (30)	

*Finish in overall standings (No. of teams in league). †League champion.
#High Class A affiliate will be in Bradenton (Florida State) in 2010.

LAST YEAR'S TOP 30

Player, Pos.		Status
1.	Pedro Alvarez, 3b	No. 1
2.	Andrew McCutchen, of	Majors
3.	Jose Tabata, of	No. 2
4.	Brad Lincoln, rhp	No. 4
5.	Bryan Morris, rhp	No. 15
6.	Neil Walker, 3b	No. 26
7.	Jeff Sues, rhp	Dropped out
8.	Shelby Ford, 2b	Dropped out
9.	Daniel McCutchen, rhp	No. 21
10.	Robbie Grossman, of	No. 18
11.	Jamie Romak, of/1b	Dropped out
12.	Jimmy Barthmaier, rhp	(Free agent)
13.	Jarek Cunningham 3b/ss	No. 20
14.	Brian Friday, ss	No. 28
15.	Jordy Mercer, ss	No. 22
16.	Quinton Miller, rhp	No. 14
17.	Chase d'Arnaud, ss	No. 5
18.	Ronald Uviedo, rhp	Dropped out
19.	Daniel Moskos, lhp	No. 30
20.	Wesley Freeman, of	Dropped out
21.	Steve Lerud, c	Dropped out
22.	Evan Meek, rhp	Majors
23.	Matt Hague, 3b/1b	Dropped out
24.	Jim Negrych, 3b/2b	Dropped out
25.	Romulo Sanchez, rhp	(Yankees)
26.	Donnie Veal, lhp	No. 24
27.	Brian Bixler, ss/2b	Majors
28.	Jason Jaramillo, c	Majors
29.	Justin Wilson, lhp	Dropped out
30.	Nelson Pereira, rhp	Dropped out

BEST TOOLS

Best Hitter for Average	Jose Tabata
Best Power Hitter	Pedro Alvarez
Best Strike-Zone Discipline	Chase d'Arnaud
Fastest Baserunner	Jose de los Santos
Best Athlete	Chase d'Arnaud
Best Fastball	Ramon Aguero
Best Curveball	Brad Lincoln
Best Slider	Victor Black
Best Changeup	Daniel McCutchen
Best Control	Rudy Owens
Best Defensive Catcher	Tony Sanchez
Best Defensive Infielder	Argenis Diaz
Best Infield Arm	Argenis Diaz
Best Defensive Outfielder	Gorkys Hernandez
Best Outfield Arm	Starling Marte

PROJECTED 2013 LINEUP

Catcher	Tony Sanchez
First Base	Jeff Clement
Second Base	Akinori Iwamura
Third Base	Pedro Alvarez
Shortstop	Chase d'Arnaud
Left Field	Lastings Milledge
Center Field	Andrew McCutchen
Right Field	Jose Tabata
No. 1 Starter	Brad Lincoln
No. 2 Starter	Charlie Morton
No. 3 Starter	Ross Ohlendorf
No. 4 Starter	Zach Duke
No. 5 Starter	Paul Maholm
Closer	Victor Black

TOP PROSPECTS OF THE DECADE

Year	Player, Pos.	2009 Org.
2000	Chad Hermansen, of	Out of baseball
2001	J.R. House, c	Royals
2002	J.R. House, c	Royals
2003	John Van Benschoten, rhp	White Sox
2004	John Van Benschoten, rhp	White Sox
2005	Zach Duke, lhp	Pirates
2006	Neil Walker, c	Pirates
2007	Andrew McCutchen, of	Pirates
2008	Andrew McCutchen, of	Pirates
2009	Pedro Alvarez, 3b	Pirates

TOP DRAFT PICKS OF THE DECADE

Year	Player, Pos.	2009 Org.
2000	Sean Burnett, lhp	Nationals
2001	John Van Benschoten, rhp	White Sox
2002	Bryan Bullington, rhp	Blue Jays
2003	Paul Maholm, lhp	Pirates
2004	Neil Walker, c	Pirates
2005	Andrew McCutchen, of	Pirates
2006	Brad Lincoln, rhp	Pirates
2007	Daniel Moskos, lhp	Pirates
2008	Pedro Alvarez, 3b	Pirates
2009	Tony Sanchez, c	Pirates

LARGEST BONUSES IN CLUB HISTORY

Pedro Alvarez, 2008	$6,000,000
Bryan Bullington, 2002	$4,000,000
Brad Lincoln, 2006	$2,750,000
Tony Sanchez, 2009	$2,500,000
Daniel Moskos, 2007	$2,475,000

PITTSBURGH PIRATES

TOP 2010 ROOKIE: Daniel McCutchen, rhp. He's no kid at 27, but he has the stuff and savvy to help the Pirates at the back end of their starting rotation.

BREAKOUT PROSPECT: Jeff Locke, lhp. Part of the Nate McLouth trade, he finished strong in high Class A last season and noticeably gained confidence with each outing.

SLEEPER: Ramon Cabrera, c. The son of Japanese League slugger Alex Cabrera hit .291/.372/.417 in his 2009 U.S. debut.

SOURCE OF TOP 30 TALENT			
Homegrown	19	Acquired	11
College	9	Trades	9
Junior college	1	Rule 5 draft	2
High school	6	Independent leagues	0
Draft-and-follow	1	Free agents/waivers	0
Nondrafted free agents	0		
International	2		

Numbers in parentheses indicate prospect rankings

LF
John Raynor (16)
Robbie Grossman (18)
Rogelios Noris
Quincy Latimore

CF
Starling Marte (6)
Gorkys Hernandez (10)
Evan Chambers (23)

RF
Jose Tabata (2)
Wesley Freeman

3B
Pedro Alvarez (1)
Neil Walker (26)
Elevys Gonzalez
Walker Gourley

SS
Chase d'Arnaud (5)
Jarek Cunningham (20)
Jordy Mercer (22)
Brian Friday (28)
Argenis Diaz
Benji Gonzalez

2B
Brock Holt (27)
Josh Harrison (29)
Gift Ngoepe
Jim Negrych
Shelby Ford

1B
Miles Durham
Calvin Anderson
Matt Hague
Aaron Baker
Jamie Romak

C
Tony Sanchez (3)
Ramon Cabrera
Robinzon Diaz
Joey Schoenfeld
Kris Watts

RHP

Starters	Relievers
Brad Lincoln (4)	Victor Black (12)
Tim Alderson (7)	Ramon Aguero (17)
Zack Von Rosenberg (8)	Nathan Adcock
Quinton Miller (14)	Jeff Sues
Bryan Morris (15)	Mike Dubee
Hunter Strickland (19)	Tom Boleska
Daniel McCutchen (21)	Diego Moreno
Brett Lorin (25)	Anthony Claggett
Brock Pounders	Brian Leach
Trent Stevenson	Zach Foster
Aaron Pribanic	Jared Hughes
Jeff Inman	Ryan Kelly
Brent Klinger	
Phillip Irwin	
Ronald Uviedo	
Kyle McPherson	
Derek Hankins	
Mike Crotta	

LHP

Starters	Relievers
Rudy Owens (9)	Donnie Veal (24)
Colton Cain (11)	Daniel Moskos (30)
Jeff Locke (13)	Justin Thomas
Justin Wilson	Zac Fuesser
Zack Dodson	
Nate Baker	
Nelson Pereira	

2009   BONUSES: $8.9 MILLION

BEST PURE HITTER: While some teams questioned C Tony Sanchez's (1) bat, the Pirates didn't. He became less pull-conscious after switching from metal to wood bats and hit .309/.409/.539 while reaching high Class A.

BEST POWER HITTER: 1B Aaron Baker (11) led the short-season New York-Penn League with seven triples, and the 6-foot-3, 232-pounder didn't do that with blazing speed. Sanchez and OF Evan Chambers (3) have a chance for solid or better power.

FASTEST RUNNER: Chambers and SS/2B Brock Holt (9) have plus speed, but Pittsburgh didn't sign any burners.

BEST DEFENSIVE PLAYER: The top defensive catcher in the 2009 draft, Sanchez has plus arm strength, soft hands and quick feet.

BEST FASTBALL: RHP Victor Black (1s) maintained his 96-mph peak velocity through instructional league. RHP Jeff Inman (12), who had a rough spring at Stanford, worked at 93-95 mph during instructional league.

BEST SECONDARY PITCH: Black's slider is the best in the organization. As for the top curveball, LHP Zack Dodson's (4) rates a slight edge over LHP Zac Fuesser's (34).

BEST PRO DEBUT: Sanchez did everything the Pirates wanted to see offensively and defensively.

BEST ATHLETE: Chambers' athleticism and stocky 5-foot-9, 215-pound frame have prompted physical comparisons to Hall of Famer Kirby Puckett. RHP Zack Von Rosenberg (6) and LHP Colton Cain (8) had pro potential as position players.

MOST INTRIGUING BACKGROUND: Unsigned C Wes Luquette (27) is the grandson of Tabasco tycoon Paul McIlhenny. Luquette also starred as a quarterback at the Isidore Newman School (New Orleans), the alma mater of Peyton and Eli Manning. Von Rosenberg won Louisiana state titles and pitched the clincher in each of his four years of high school. Baker's grandfather Jerry Mays played in two Super Bowls and was an all-American Football League performer as an offensive and defensive lineman.

CLOSEST TO THE MAJORS: Sanchez could be Pittsburgh's Opening Day starter behind the plate in 2011. LHP Nate Baker (5), who commands three average pitches, also could jump on the fast track.

BEST LATE-ROUND PICK: Inman has shown three promising pitches and improved competitiveness, and now he needs to bring them to the mound on a consistent basis. RHP Phillip Irwin (21), Nate Baker's teammate at Mississippi, does a nice job of locating all three of his pitches down in the zone.

THE ONE WHO GOT AWAY: OF Matt den Dekker's (16) all-around tools made him a potential first-rounder before a disappointing spring and a $1 million asking price dropped him in the draft. He held firm to his price and returned to Florida. The Pirates made strong runs at Luquette (even after he had Tommy John surgery) and RHP Kyle Hooper (28), but Luquette attended Louisiana State and Hooper went to Santa Clara.

ASSESSMENT: Pittsburgh opted to heed MLB's guidelines with the No. 4 overall pick, choosing Sanchez over more expensive and more highly regarded players, and spend big money lower in the draft. It's hard to argue with Sanchez's performance, and the Pirates went well over the slot recommendations to land Dodson ($600,000), Von Rosenberg ($1.2 million) and Cain ($1,125,000).

2008   BONUSES: $9.8 MILLION

3B Pedro Alvarez (1) has been everything the Pirates hoped since they got him under contract. Chase d'Arnaud (4) could be their shortstop of the future. Signing RHP Tanner Scheppers (2) would have been a coup, but he wasn't healthy enough.

GRADE: A

2007   BONUSES: $4.5 MILLION

The decision to take LHP Daniel Moskos (1) over Matt Wieters with the No. 4 overall pick continues to look worse and worse. No other prospect has stepped up to lessen the sting, with SS Brian Friday (3) the best of the group.

GRADE: F

2006   BONUSES: $5.9 MILLION

RHP Brad Lincoln (1), who's making a strong comeback from Tommy John surgery, and draft-and-follow LHP Rudy Owens (28), are the only hope for this crop. 3B Lonnie Chisenall (11) may have been Pittsburgh's best pick, but he didn't sign until the Indians made him a first-round pick two years later.

GRADE: C

2005   BONUSES: $3.7 MILLION*

OF Andrew McCutchen (1) was BA's 2009 Rookie of the Year. Since-traded UT Brent Lillibridge (4) and 1B Steven Pearce (8) also have appeared in the majors.

GRADE: A

*Draft analysis by Jim Callis. Numbers in parentheses indicate draft rounds. *Bonuses for 2005 are first 10 rounds only.*

PROSPECT 1

PEDRO ALVAREZ, 3B

Born: Feb. 6, 1987.
Height: 6-3. **Weight:** 234.
Bats: L. **Throws:** R.
Drafted: Vanderbilt,
2008 (1st round).
Signed by: Trevor Haley.

Alvarez starred for three seasons at Vanderbilt, winning Baseball America's Freshman of the Year award in 2006 and tying a school record with 49 career homers. The consensus top bat available in a hitter-rich 2008 draft, he went second overall and became the first Pirates draftee ever signed to a major league contract. Following contentious negotiations between club president Frank Coonelly and agent Scott Boras, Alvarez agreed to a club-record $6 million bonus—two minutes after the Aug. 15 signing deadline expired. The MLB Players Association filed a grievance on Alvarez's behalf, and it was resolved about a month later, with Alvarez getting the same bonus as part of a $6.335 million deal. The best hitter drafted by the Pirates since they took Barry Bonds sixth overall in 1985, he didn't disappoint in his much-anticipated pro debut last season. Despite a slow start that saw him hitting just .200 five weeks into his career, Alvarez batted a combined .288/.378/.535 with a system-best 27 homers between high Class A Lynchburg and Double-A Altoona and was chosen as the Pirates' minor league player of the year. He finished the season by hitting five homers at the World Cup for the gold medal-winning United States team.

Alvarez has tremendous raw power to all fields. He opened eyes during the first days of spring training last year when he hit a batting-practice homer to dead center field that was estimated at 550 feet. He has good pitch-recognition skills and is usually willing to take a walk. He has a very strong arm and good hands at third base. The son of a livery cab driver in New York City, Alvarez has a blue-collar work ethic and is one of the first players at the ballpark and one of the last to leave. He is also an intelligent player, not surprising given his Vanderbilt pedigree.

Alvarez can be caught off balance by breaking balls from lefthanders, though he improved against them over the course of the season. He needs to get into better shape to stay at third base, as he has a thick body and was instructed by the Pirates to lose 10 pounds during the offseason. They hope the weight loss will improve his below-average quickness and range at third base. Many scouts don't think he'll be able to stay at the hot corner. He's a well-below-average runner, though smart enough not to take unnecessary risks.

Alvarez was playing so well by the end of the season that some scouts believe he's ready to step into Pittsburgh's Opening Day lineup for 2010. However, he'll begin the season at Triple-A Indianapolis and stay there until at least June to keep his arbitration and free agency clocks from starting. He should make an immediate impact and appears destined to become a big-time slugger for a franchise that hasn't had a 40-homer hitter since Willie Stargell in 1973. The only long-term question is what position Alvarez will play. If he keeps his weight in check, he'll be able to stay at third base. If not, he'll need to move across the diamond to first.

Year	Club (League)	Class	AVG	G	AB	R	H	2B	3B	HR	RBI	BB	SO	SB	OBP	SLG
2009	Lynchburg (CAR)	HiA	.247	66	243	38	60	14	1	14	55	37	70	1	.342	.486
	Altoona (EL)	AA	.333	60	222	42	74	18	0	13	40	34	59	1	.419	.590
MINOR LEAGUE TOTALS			.288	126	465	80	134	32	1	27	95	71	129	2	.378	.535

2 JOSE TABATA, OF Ch₁₁₁

BORN: Aug. 12, 1988. **B-T:** R-R. **HT.:** 5-11. **WT.:** 215. **SIGNED:** Venezuela, 2004. **SIGNED BY:** Ricardo Finol (Yankees).

The Pirates acquired Tabata (and Jeff Karstens, Daniel McCutchen and Ross Ohlendorf) in a July 2008 trade that sent Damaso Marte and Xavier Nady to the Yankees. After stalling in Double-A before the deal, Tabata regained his hitting form. His wife, 23 years his senior, was arrested in Florida last March on charges that she kidnapped a baby, but Tabata was not implicated. Tabata has a compact stroke and hits line drives to all fields. He has sound strike-zone judgment for a young hitter. He has enough range to play a passable center field but is better suited for right, where he can show off his above-average arm. He has slightly above-average speed. Tabata has yet to learn to put backspin on balls and hit them for power, though the Pirates are convinced he will. He has a thick lower half and will likely be a below-average runner once he's done filling out. The Yankees tired of his immature behavior, but he always has been one of the youngest players in his league and hasn't caused any problems for Pittsburgh. Tabata will begin 2010 back in Triple-A but figures to be in the majors at some point during the season. He has the potential to be an all-star right fielder if his power develops.

Year	Club (League)	Class	AVG	G	AB	R	H	2B	3B	HR	RBI	BB	SO	SB	OBP	SLG
2005	Yankees (GCL)	R	.314	44	156	30	49	5	1	3	25	15	14	22	.382	.417
2006	Charleston (SAL)	LoA	.298	86	319	50	95	22	1	5	51	30	66	15	.377	.420
2007	Tampa (FSL)	HiA	.307	103	411	56	126	16	2	5	54	33	70	15	.371	.392
2008	Trenton (EL)	AA	.248	79	294	40	73	9	0	3	36	26	49	10	.320	.310
	Pirates (GCL)	R	.455	4	11	4	5	1	0	2	7	2	0	0	.538	1.091
	Altoona (EL)	AA	.348	22	89	16	31	6	2	3	13	8	18	8	.402	.562
2009	Altoona (EL)	AA	.303	61	228	31	69	15	1	2	25	20	25	7	.370	.404
	Indianapolis (IL)	AAA	.276	32	134	21	37	7	1	3	10	10	18	4	.333	.410
MINOR LEAGUE TOTALS			.295	431	1642	248	485	81	8	26	221	144	260	81	.364	.402

3 TONY SANCHEZ, C ✝

BORN: May 20, 1988. **B-T:** R-R. **HT.:** 6-0. **WT.:** 220. **DRAFTED:** Boston College, 2009 (1st round). **SIGNED BY:** Chris Kline.

The Pirates took heat for overdrafting and overpaying Sanchez with the fourth overall pick in June, but he silenced critics who questioned his bat by hitting a combined .309/.439/.539 at three levels after signing for $2.5 million. He lost 30 pounds during his three seasons at Boston College and led the Eagles to their first NCAA tournament berth in 42 years last spring. Sanchez is an outstanding defensive catcher with soft hands, a strong arm and good ball-blocking skills. He threw out 33 percent of basestealers in his pro debut. Once he switched to wood bats in pro ball, he did a better job of keeping his swing under control and hitting the ball to the middle of the field. He should have solid-average power. He has good baseball instincts, a great deal of charisma and leadership skills. Sanchez can tighten up his footwork behind the plate and is still learning how to call games. He's a well-below-average runner, though that's typical for a catcher. Sanchez figures to reach Double-A at some point in 2010, though he may return to high Class A to start the season. A potential Gold Glover, he has a big league ETA of 2011.

Year	Club (League)	Class	AVG	G	AB	R	H	2B	3B	HR	RBI	BB	SO	SB	OBP	SLG
2009	State College (NYP)	SS	.308	4	13	2	4	1	0	0	1	1	2	0	.357	.385
	West Virginia (SAL)	LoA	.316	41	155	29	49	15	1	7	46	21	34	1	.415	.561
	Lynchburg (CAR)	HiA	.200	3	10	2	2	2	0	0	1	1	4	0	.385	.400
MINOR LEAGUE TOTALS			.309	48	178	33	55	18	1	7	48	23	40	1	.409	.539

4 BRAD LINCOLN, RHP ✝

BORN: May 25, 1985. **B-T:** L-R. **HT.:** 6-0. **WT.:** 215. **DRAFTED:** Houston, 2006 (1st round). **SIGNED BY:** Everett Russell.

After signing for $2.75 million as the fourth overall pick in 2006, Lincoln became yet another Pirates first-rounder who has been derailed by arm problems. But after losing 2007 to Tommy John surgery and using 2008 to rebuild his arm strength, he came back strong last season. Lincoln exceeded his previous career total by working 136 innings while reaching Triple-A, pitched in the Futures Game and won the gold-medal game for Team USA at September's World Cup. Lincoln has two plus pitches, a 90-93 mph fastball that reaches 95 with good late life and a curveball that breaks big and late. He's a fierce competitor who aggressively attacks both sides of the plate and wants the ball in big situations. A two-way star in college, he batted .308 last season. Lincoln's changeup is improving but still needs work. He challenges hitters too much at times, which made him prone to extra-base hits once he reached Triple-A, and he can be susceptible to home runs as well. Though he won six of his 12 starts at Indianapolis, Lincoln needs to return there to add some finishing touches to his game. He was added to the 40-man roster and should be in Pittsburgh by midseason. He will eventually settle in as a No. 3 starter, perhaps even a No. 2.

Year	Club (League)	Class	W	L	ERA	G	GS	CG	SV	IP	H	R	ER	HR	BB	SO	AVG
2006	Pirates (GCL)	R	0	0	0.00	2	2	0	0	8	6	1	0	0	1	9	.222
	Hickory (SAL)	LoA	1	2	6.75	4	4	0	0	16	25	15	12	2	6	10	.368
2007	Did not play—Injured																
2008	Hickory (SAL)	LoA	5	5	4.65	11	11	0	0	62	72	34	32	8	6	46	.288
	Lynchburg (CAR)	HiA	1	5	4.75	8	8	1	0	42	42	24	22	5	11	29	.259
2009	Altoona (EL)	AA	1	5	2.28	13	13	1	0	75	63	22	19	4	18	65	.228
	Indianapolis (IL)	AAA	6	2	4.70	12	12	0	0	61	72	37	32	7	10	42	.300
MINOR LEAGUE TOTALS			14	19	3.99	50	50	2	0	264	280	133	117	26	52	201	.274

5 CHASE D'ARNAUD, SS/2B ⤴

BORN: Jan. 21, 1987. **B-T:** R-R. **HT.:** 6-1. **WT.:** 175. **DRAFTED:** Pepperdine, 2008 (4th round). **SIGNED BY:** Rick Allen.

D'Arnaud played his first two seasons at Pepperdine as a third baseman, but he's on the fast track with the Pirates as a shortstop. He split his first full pro season between two Class A clubs and then played in the Arizona Fall League. He faced his younger brother Travis, a prime catching prospect in the Phillies system, in the South Atlantic League all-star game. With his good eye and slightly above-average speed, d'Arnaud fits well at the top of a batting order. Managers rated him the best defensive shortstop in the high Class A Carolina League after he displayed solid range and a strong arm. He possesses outstanding baseball savvy and a strong work ethic, which helps him perform above his tools. D'Arnaud doesn't have a standout tool to carry him. He has below-average power and strikes out a bit much for a hitter whose offensive strength is his on-base ability. Some scouts question whether d'Arnaud will have enough range to play shortstop in the major leagues. The Pirates will send d'Arnaud to Double-A to start 2010. He might not wow people with his physical gifts, but he has the look of a big league middle infielder who would be effective batting second in a lineup.

Year	Club (League)	Class	AVG	G	AB	R	H	2B	3B	HR	RBI	BB	SO	SB	OBP	SLG
2008	State College (NYP)	SS	.286	43	168	26	48	10	5	1	21	11	30	14	.333	.423
2009	West Virginia (SAL)	LoA	.291	62	213	32	62	14	3	3	31	30	31	17	.394	.427
	Lynchburg (CAR)	HiA	.295	54	210	45	62	19	4	4	26	30	41	14	.402	.481
MINOR LEAGUE TOTALS			.291	159	591	103	172	43	12	8	78	71	102	45	.381	.445

6 STARLING MARTE, OF ⤴

BORN: Oct. 9, 1988. **B-T:** R-R. **HT.:** 6-1. **WT.:** 170. **SIGNED:** Dominican Republic, 2007. **SIGNED BY:** Rene Gayo/Josue Herrera.

Marte is the first tangible result of the Pirates' renewed commitment to scouting Latin America. Signed for $85,000 in January 2007, he was the MVP of Pittsburgh's Rookie-level Dominican Summer League affiliate the following year. He made his U.S. debut in 2009, jumping from the Rookie-level Gulf Coast League to low Class A West Virginia after just two games. Marte is a potential five-tool talent. He stands out most with his plus-plus speed, which makes him a basestealing threat and a good defender in center and right field. He's a line-drive machine who should hit for power once he gets stronger. He also has an above-average arm. To be a threat at higher levels, Marte will need to get stronger and improve his pitch recognition and plate discipline. He seemed hesitant to turn on pitches in 2009, though that was partly a function of the Pirates asking him to concentrate on making contact. He makes tremendous plays in the outfield, but he also botches more than his share and made seven errors in 58 games last season. Marte has as much raw all-around ability as anybody in the system. He'll advance to high Class A Bradenton and work on refining his talent in 2010.

Year	Club (League)	Class	AVG	G	AB	R	H	2B	3B	HR	RBI	BB	SO	SB	OBP	SLG
2007	Pirates (DSL)	R	.220	45	132	27	29	4	1	1	11	10	29	16	.307	.288
2008	Pirates (DSL)	R	.296	65	257	53	76	10	2	9	44	16	53	20	.367	.455
2009	Pirates (GCL)	R	.000	2	7	1	0	0	0	0	0	0	1	0	.000	.000
	West Virginia (SAL)	LoA	.312	54	221	41	69	9	5	3	34	12	55	24	.377	.439
	Lynchburg (CAR)	HiA	1.000	1	2	0	2	0	0	0	1	0	0	0	1.000	1.000
MINOR LEAGUE TOTALS			.284	167	619	122	176	23	8	13	90	38	138	60	.355	.410

7 TIM ALDERSON, RHP

BORN: Nov. 3, 1988. **B-T:** R-R. **HT.:** 6-6. **WT.:** 217. **DRAFTED:** HS—Scottsdale, Ariz., 2007 (1st round). **SIGNED BY:** Lee Carballo (Giants).

The 22nd overall pick in the 2007 draft, Alderson signed with the Giants for $1.29 million. San Francisco included him in a trade for Freddie Sanchez last July. Some analysts wondered if Giants GM Brian Sabean overpaid because Alderson entered the season ranked at No. 45 on BA's Top 100 Prospects list, but his stuff and stock slipped during the year. Alderson is known for his control and command, though both deserted him at times after the trade. He throws two-seam and four-seam fastballs down in the strike zone. His curveball is an outstanding pitch at times, dropping off the table and tying up hitters. He didn't have any indications of arm trouble, but Alderson's fastball dipped from 88-92 mph to the high 80s last year, and his curveball wasn't as sharp. He still had success because he has a deceptive delivery, though the Pirates would like to smooth his mechanics out. He's reluctant to do so because he has had success throughout his career. At 21, Alderson will be one of the youngest pitchers in the Triple-A International League in 2010. The Pirates believe his post-trade struggles were a blip. If they're right, he should see Pittsburgh late in the season and eventually develop into a No. 3 starter.

Year	Club (League)	Class	W	L	ERA	G	GS	CG	SV	IP	H	R	ER	HR	BB	SO	AVG
2007	Giants (AZL)	R	0	0	0.00	3	2	0	0	5	4	0	0	0	0	12	.211
2008	San Jose (CAL)	HiA	13	4	2.79	26	26	0	0	145	125	48	45	4	34	124	.235
2009	San Jose (CAL)	HiA	1	1	4.15	5	5	0	0	26	31	12	12	4	3	20	.292
	Connecticut (EL)	AA	6	1	3.47	13	13	0	0	73	76	31	28	5	14	46	.265
	Altoona (EL)	AA	3	1	4.66	7	7	0	0	39	39	23	20	4	13	18	.257
MINOR LEAGUE TOTALS			23	7	3.29	54	53	0	0	288	275	114	105	17	64	220	.251

8 ZACK VON ROSENBERG, RHP

BORN: Sept. 24, 1990. **B-T:** R-R. **HT.:** 6-5. **WT.:** 205. **DRAFTED:** HS—Zachary, La., 2009 (6th round). **SIGNED BY:** Jerome Cochran.

Von Rosenberg became a high school hero in Louisiana after winning four state championship baseball games in four years as well as earning all-state honors as a punter. His talent dictated selection in the first two rounds of the 2009 draft, but teams shied away because of what was perceived as an airtight commitment to Louisiana State. However, the Pirates lured him into pro ball with a $1.2 million bonus. Von Rosenberg has good command of a three-pitch arsenal. His fastball sits at 88-91 mph and the velocity could increase as his body matures and he focuses on pitching after also playing shortstop in high school. He also has good depth on his curveball, a deceptive changeup and an uncanny feel for pitching for a teenager. Von Rosenberg has no glaring weak points, other than the fact he has pitched only one pro inning. He'll need to learn how to adjust to pitching every fifth day and to the grind of a full pro season. He has yet to physically mature. Von Rosenberg is so advanced that the Pirates will push him to low Class A if he performs well in spring training. Despite his youth, he could reach the major leagues quickly, and he projects as a solid No. 3 starter.

Year	Club (League)	Class	W	L	ERA	G	GS	CG	SV	IP	H	R	ER	HR	BB	SO	AVG
2009	Pirates (GCL)	R	0	0	0.00	1	1	0	0	1	0	0	0	0	0	1	.000
MINOR LEAGUE TOTALS			0	0	0.00	1	1	0	0	1	0	0	0	0	0	1	.000

9 RUDY OWENS, LHP

BORN: Dec. 18, 1987. **B-T:** L-L. **HT.:** 6-3. **WT.:** 215. **DRAFTED:** Chandler-Gilbert (Ariz.) CC, D/F 2006 (28th round). **SIGNED BY:** Ted Williams.

One of the last draft-and-follows left in the system, Owens was undoubtedly the Pirates' breakout player of 2009. After going 4-10, 5.06 in his first two pro seasons, he went 11-2, 2.10 with a 113-17 K-BB ratio in 124 innings. He was the organization's minor league pitcher of the year and most outstanding pitcher in the low Class A South Atlantic League, where he had a 32-inning scoreless streak. Thanks to a simple delivery that he repeats easily, Owens has pinpoint command. He can spot each of his pitches on both sides of the plate and in all four quadrants of the strike zone. He's aggressive with his four-seam fastball, which sits at 87-90 mph. His changeup grades out as his best pitch, and he has made improvements with his slurvy curveball. Owens' stuff is far from overpowering, and high Class A hitters batted .305 against him in his short stint there. He's a classic crafty lefthander, but he has much to prove against more advanced competition. Owens will likely begin 2010 back at high Class A Bradenton and finish the season in Double-A. How he performs there will provide a clearer picture of his future.

PITTSBURGH PIRATES

Year	Club (League)	Class	W	L	ERA	G	GS	CG	SV	IP	H	R	ER	HR	BB	SO	AVG
2007	Pirates (GCL)	R	1	4	5.32	6	4	0	0	22	20	13	13	1	8	17	.238
2008	State College (NYP)	SS	3	6	4.97	15	13	0	0	58	63	37	32	2	13	45	.269
2009	West Virginia (SAL)	LoA	10	1	1.70	19	19	0	0	101	71	22	19	8	15	91	.197
	Lynchburg (CAR)	HiA	1	1	3.86	6	6	0	0	23	29	10	10	3	2	22	.305
MINOR LEAGUE TOTALS			15	12	3.26	46	42	0	0	204	183	82	74	14	38	175	.236

10 GORKYS HERNANDEZ, OF

JASON SIPES

BORN: Sept. 7, 1987. **B-T:** R-R. **HT.:** 6-0. **WT.:** 175. **SIGNED:** Venezuela, 2005. **SIGNED BY:** Ramon Pena (Tigers).

After winning the Gulf Coast League batting title and the low Class A Midwest League MVP award in his first two seasons in the United States, Hernandez was traded twice in 20 months. The Tigers sent him to the Braves in a trade for Edgar Renteria in October 2007, and Atlanta shipped him to the Pirates in a deal for Nate McLouth last June. Hernandez is an outstanding defensive center fielder. He plays shallow and covers a lot of ground with his exceptional first-step quickness. His plus speed also makes him a threat on the bases. His line-drive swing has enabled him to hit .284 as pro. Primarily a slap hitter, Hernandez, who was added to the 40-man roster, needs to get stronger or risk having major league pitchers knock the bat out of his hands. His control of the strike zone has slipped, and he needs to do a better job of getting on base. He also needs to improve his jumps and reads after getting caught in 16 of his 35 steal attempts in 2009. Twice after the trade last summer, he was removed from games for disciplinary reasons. His defensive prowess and speed are enticing, but Hernandez needs to show more with the bat in Triple-A in 2010. Andrew McCutchen blocks his path to Pittsburgh's center-field job, so Hernandez could get traded again.

Year	Club (League)	Class	AVG	G	AB	R	H	2B	3B	HR	RBI	BB	SO	SB	OBP	SLG
2005	Tigers (DSL)	R	.265	63	211	44	56	10	0	4	19	30	38	10	.377	.370
2006	Tigers (GCL)	R	.327	50	205	41	67	9	2	5	23	10	27	20	.356	.463
2007	West Michigan (MWL)	LoA	.293	124	481	84	141	25	5	4	50	36	69	54	.344	.391
2008	Myrtle Beach (CAR)	HiA	.264	100	406	75	107	23	6	5	42	48	79	20	.348	.387
2009	Mississippi (SL)	AA	.316	52	212	33	67	11	2	0	19	15	54	10	.361	.387
	Altoona (EL)	AA	.262	86	344	45	90	14	2	3	31	24	76	9	.312	.340
MINOR LEAGUE TOTALS			.284	475	1859	322	528	92	17	21	184	163	343	123	.346	.386

11 COLTON CAIN, LHP

BORN: Feb. 5, 1991. **B-T:** L-L. **HT.:** 6-3. **WT.:** 225. **DRAFTED:** HS—Waxahachie, Texas, 2009 (8th round). **SIGNED BY:** Mike Leuzinger.

Cain would have been taken earlier than the eighth round in the 2009 draft based strictly on talent, but his signability was an issue with most clubs. Some saw him as a sandwich-round talent but few felt they could buy him out of his commitment to Texas. A year after luring Robbie Grossman away from the Longhorns, the Pirates did the same with Cain, giving him an eighth-round record $1.15 million bonus. Some teams liked Cain for his abilities as a power-hitting first baseman, but the Pirates are convinced he can become an above-average major-league starting pitcher. He throws his fastball in the low 90s and his curveball shows flashes of becoming a plus pitch. Like a lot of high school pitchers, he'll need to become more consistent, develop a changeup and smooth out his delivery now that he's in pro ball. He eats chicken for every pregame meal because he feels it gives him energy. Cain signed too late to make his pro debut last summer but attended instructional league. He'll probably open 2010 in extended spring training, then head to the Gulf Coast League.

Year	Club (League)	Class	W	L	ERA	G	GS	CG	SV	IP	H	R	ER	HR	BB	SO	AVG
2009	Did Not Play—Signed Late																

12 VICTOR BLACK, RHP

BORN: May 23, 1988. **B-T:** R-R. **HT.:** 6-3. **WT.:** 185. **DRAFTED:** Dallas Baptist, 2009 (1st round supplemental). **SIGNED BY:** Mike Leuzinger.

Black put himself into first-round contention when he outperformed two top Texas A&M pitching prospects, Brooks Raley and Alex Wilson, in front of several scouts in late April. Though some clubs cooled on Black after he lost his last three starts, the Pirates took him with the supplemental first-round pick they received for failing to sign Tanner Scheppers in 2008. They signed Black for $717,000 and limited his pitch counts at short-season State College. Black's fastball sits at 91-95 mph and registers a tick higher when he reaches back for more. He throws his slider at 84 mph and it completely locks up hitters when he has command of it. His changeup is lacking, which leads some scouts to wonder if his hard stuff would better serve him as a late-inning reliever. He had a poor sophomore season when he lost his delivery and control, and he still needs to throw strikes more consistently. He also could stand to add some upper-body strength to go with his solid lower half. The Pirates want to keep Black in the starting rotation for now, and he could begin his first full season in high Class A.

Year	Club (League)	Class	W	L	ERA	G	GS	CG	SV	IP	H	R	ER	HR	BB	SO	AVG
2009	State College (NYP)	SS	1	2	3.45	13	7	0	1	31	26	17	12	0	15	33	.213
MINOR LEAGUE TOTALS			1	2	3.45	13	7	0	1	31	26	17	12	0	15	33	.213

13 JEFF LOCKE, LHP

BORN: Nov. 20, 1987. **B-T:** L-L. **HT.:** 6-2. **WT.:** 180. **DRAFTED:** HS—Conway, N.H., 2006 (2nd round). **SIGNED BY:** Lonnie Goldberg (Braves).

Pirates fans were up in arms last June when the club traded Nate McLouth, who had played in the All-Star Game and won a Gold Glove the year before, then signed a $15.5 million contract in spring training. In return, the Braves sent Gorkys Hernandez, Locke and Charlie Morton to Pittsburgh. Locke got hit around early in high Class A after the trade, but settled in to go 3-0, 2.75 in his last nine starts and pitch 6⅔ scoreless innings in the finals as Lynchburg won the Carolina League title. Nicknamed the Redstone Rocket in high school because he lived he lived in the Redstone section of Conway, N.H., Locke is a hard-throwing lefthander. He pitches off a 91-94 mph fastball that has heavy sink and induces grounders. He also has a decent curveball and is making progress with his changeup. He has a herky-jerky delivery that adds deception. Like most high school pitchers from New England, Locke is relatively inexperienced, and he's trying to make up ground. Locke will begin 2010 in Double-A. Based on how he finished last season, he could be in the major leagues as soon as the second half of the season. He projects as a mid-rotation starter.

Year	Club (League)	Class	W	L	ERA	G	GS	CG	SV	IP	H	R	ER	HR	BB	SO	AVG
2006	Braves (GCL)	R	4	3	4.22	10	5	0	0	32	38	18	15	4	5	38	.299
2007	Danville (APP)	R	7	1	2.66	13	11	0	1	61	48	23	18	2	8	74	.213
2008	Rome (SAL)	LoA	5	12	4.06	25	24	1	0	140	150	75	63	6	38	113	.269
2009	Myrtle Beach (CAR)	HiA	1	4	5.52	10	10	0	0	46	47	31	28	1	26	43	.272
	Lynchburg (CAR)	HiA	4	4	4.08	17	17	0	0	82	98	44	37	4	18	56	.305
MINOR LEAGUE TOTALS			21	24	4.03	75	67	1	1	360	381	191	161	17	95	324	.271

14 QUINTON MILLER, RHP

BORN: Nov. 28, 1989. **B-T:** R-R. **HT.:** 6-1. **WT.:** 185. **DRAFTED:** HS—Medford, N.J., 2008 (20th round). **SIGNED BY:** Buddy Paine.

Another of the Pirates' several above-slot signings from the last two years, Miller slid to the 20th round of the 2008 draft because he was strongly committed to North Carolina. He signed for $900,000, a record for his round, and made his pro debut last season. He spent most of 2009 in low Class A, where he struggled early against older competition before going 1-0, 2.13 in his final six starts. Miller's fastball velocity is inconsistent, ranging from 86-94 mph, and he throws with a maximum-effort delivery. However, he made strides in refining his mechanics last year and continued to improve his quality slider. He's still trying to develop his changeup. Miller had shoulder problems in high school, which scared some teams away, but he showed no signs of arm problems in 2009. After his strong finish, he could push for a spot in high Class A with a good spring training. His raw ability makes him a potential No. 2 starter.

Year	Club (League)	Class	W	L	ERA	G	GS	CG	SV	IP	H	R	ER	HR	BB	SO	AVG
2009	State College (NYP)	SS	0	1	3.86	2	2	0	0	7	10	5	3	0	3	4	.345
	West Virginia (SAL)	LoA	2	3	4.47	12	12	0	0	56	50	35	28	5	25	40	.245
MINOR LEAGUE TOTALS			2	4	4.41	14	14	0	0	63	60	40	31	5	28	44	.258

15 BRYAN MORRIS, RHP

BORN: March 28, 1987. **B-T:** L-R. **HT.:** 6-3. **WT.:** 200. **DRAFTED:** Motlow State (Tenn.) CC, 2006 (1st round). **SIGNED BY:** Marty Lamb (Dodgers).

Morris was part of a huge three-way deal at the 2008 trading deadline. The Red Sox sent Manny Ramirez to the Dodgers while receiving Jason Bay from the Pirates, and Pittsburgh got four youngsters: Craig Hansen and Brandon Moss from Boston, and Andy LaRoche and Morris from Los Angeles. The only one of the four who has yet to appear in the majors, Morris could be the jewel of the package for the Pirates—if he can stay healthy. After signing for $1.325 million as the 26th overall pick in the 2006 draft, he missed all of 2007 while recovering from Tommy John surgery. He has pitched just 87 innings since joining Pittsburgh. Biceps tendinitis cut short his 2008 season, and he missed the first two months of 2009 following surgery to repair a torn ligament in his foot. On top of that, the Pirates suspended Morris for 10 days in early August when he berated an umpire after being removed from a game. Morris, who was added to the 40-man roster, has the ability to be a frontline starter. When he's physically sound and at his best, he has a 91-93 mph fastball that touches 95 and has good life. He also has a plus curveball with big break and a serviceable changeup. However, he has gone 4-11, 5.48 in 18 starts since the trade. His mechanics lack smoothness, which has contributed to his injuries and detracts from his control. Though he's only 22, Morris needs to start turning his potential into results.

Year	Club (League)	Class	W	L	ERA	G	GS	CG	SV	IP	H	R	ER	HR	BB	SO	AVG
2006	Ogden (PIO)	R	4	5	5.13	14	14	0	0	60	64	44	34	3	40	79	.267
2007	Did not play—Injured																
2008	Great Lakes (MWL)	LoA	2	4	3.20	17	17	1	0	82	74	34	29	5	31	72	.247
	Hickory (SAL)	LoA	0	2	5.02	3	3	0	0	14	17	9	8	2	12	11	.288
2009	Lynchburg (CAR)	HiA	4	9	5.57	15	15	0	0	73	87	58	45	2	34	32	.295
MINOR LEAGUE TOTALS			10	20	4.57	49	49	1	0	228	242	145	116	12	117	194	.271

16 JOHN RAYNOR, OF

BORN: Jan. 4, 1984. **B-T:** R-R. **HT.:** 6-2. **WT.:** 185. **DRAFTED:** UNC Wilmington, 2006 (9th round). **SIGNED BY:** Joel Matthews (Marlins).

The Pirates made Raynor the second overall pick in the major league Rule 5 draft in December. They'll have to keep him on their big league roster throughout 2010, or else place him on waivers and offer him back to the Marlins for half his $50,000 draft price. He'll compete for a reserve outfield job in spring training. Signed for $17,500 as a college senior in 2006, Raynor won the South Atlantic League MVP award in his first full season. He had no trouble skipping a level to Double-A in 2008, but more experienced pitchers got him out time after time with soft stuff away in Triple-A last year. He couldn't stop from pulling off pitches, and his plate discipline and production declined noticeably. It's possible he developed some bad habits after suffering a hairline fracture in his left hand while at the Arizona Fall League in 2008. Raynor's best tool is his speed, as he regularly runs to first base in 4.1 seconds from the right side of the plate, and he needs to get on base more often to take advantage of his basestealing prowess. He has succeeded in 83 percent of his steal attempts as a pro, though his 19 swipes last year were his lowest total in four seasons. Raynor even struggled somewhat defensively, though he improved as the year went on. His speed gives him the range to play center, but his below-average arm probably will keep him in left.

Year	Club (League)	Class	AVG	G	AB	R	H	2B	3B	HR	RBI	BB	SO	SB	OBP	SLG
2006	Jamestown (NYP)	SS	.286	54	199	36	57	8	4	4	21	17	51	21	.356	.427
2007	Greensboro (SAL)	LoA	.333	116	445	110	148	28	8	13	57	66	98	54	.429	.519
2008	Carolina (SL)	AA	.312	126	452	104	141	29	6	13	51	62	122	48	.402	.489
2009	New Orleans (PCL)	AAA	.257	123	447	63	115	24	2	6	36	42	121	19	.327	.360
MINOR LEAGUE TOTALS			.299	419	1543	313	461	89	20	36	165	187	392	142	.383	.452

17 RAMON AGUERO, RHP

BORN: Dec. 21, 1984. **B-T:** R-R. **HT.:** 6-4. **WT.:** 185. **SIGNED:** Dominican Republic, 2005. **SIGNED BY:** Rene Gayo/Jose Herrera.

Aguero was known as Samuel Vasquez during his first two pro seasons in the Dominican Summer League. However, when he tried to get a visa to come to the United States in 2008, it was found that he was using a false birth certificate and was actually 39 months older than the Pirates thought. He was allowed to enter the country, but his baseball future appeared in doubt when he got pounded as a 23-year-old starter at State College. However, Aguero was the most improved Pittsburgh farmhand last season, advancing from low Class A to Double-A after becoming a full-time reliever. The hardest thrower in the system, he routinely sits at 95-97 mph with his fastball. He complements his heater with a changeup that makes him tough on lefthanders. He also has a slider, but it's fringy. Aguero's lack of an effective third pitch and his tendency to lose steam on his fastball after a few innings make him strictly a short reliever. The Pirates placed him on the 40-man roster in November, quite an accomplishment for someone who went 1-10, 6.75 in short-season ball the previous year. Aguero likely will return to Altoona to start 2010 and could make a quick ascent to the big league bullpen because Pittsburgh craves hard-throwing relievers.

Year	Club (League)	Class	W	L	ERA	G	GS	CG	SV	IP	H	R	ER	HR	BB	SO	AVG
2006	Pirates (DSL)	R	1	1	3.41	8	4	0	0	29	28	15	11	1	9	19	.259
2007	Pirates (DSL)	R	5	2	2.26	16	13	1	0	76	64	31	19	5	22	81	.222
2008	State College (NYP)	SS	1	10	6.75	15	10	0	0	49	64	47	37	3	22	35	.308
2009	West Virginia (SAL)	LoA	1	2	4.71	20	3	0	0	50	58	31	26	5	16	40	.294
	Lynchburg (CAR)	HiA	1	0	2.49	11	0	0	0	22	20	10	6	1	9	22	.241
	Altoona (EL)	AA	0	2	2.84	8	0	0	4	13	8	4	4	0	6	13	.182
MINOR LEAGUE TOTALS			9	17	3.89	78	30	1	4	238	242	138	103	15	84	210	.261

18 ROBBIE GROSSMAN, OF

BORN: Sept. 16, 1989. **B-T:** B-L. **HT.:** 6-1. **WT.:** 190. **DRAFTED:** HS—Cypress, Texas, 2008 (6th round). **SIGNED BY:** Greg Hopkins.

After a disappointing senior season, Grossman dropped to the sixth round of the 2008 draft and appeared to be a lock to play college ball at Texas. But the Pirates won that recruiting war after inviting him to PNC Park for a private workout and offering him a $1 million bonus. Pittsburgh aggressively pushed Grossman to low Class A last season, though he had just 16 Rookie-ball at-bats in his pro debut. He did a decent job, with the exception of striking out 164 times. His good eye, patience and slightly above-average speed make him a potential top-of-the-order hitter if he can make more contact. He also shows flashes of power and could develop more pop as his body matures. Grossman gets into trouble by being too selective at times, especially in two-strike counts. He's an above-average outfielder with a playable arm. While he can play center field, he projects as more of a corner guy in the major leagues. Grossman wins high marks for his baseball IQ and is the type of player who figures to get the most of his ability. He'll move up to high Class A this season and is on track to reach the majors by the end of 2012.

Year	Club (League)	Class	AVG	G	AB	R	H	2B	3B	HR	RBI	BB	SO	SB	OBP	SLG
2008	Pirates (GCL)	R	.188	5	16	3	3	1	0	0	1	4	7	1	.381	.250
2009	West Virginia (SAL)	LoA	.266	116	451	83	120	21	2	5	42	75	164	35	.373	.355
MINOR LEAGUE TOTALS			.263	121	467	86	123	22	2	5	43	79	171	36	.373	.351

19 HUNTER STRICKLAND, RHP

BORN: Sept. 24, 1988. **B-T:** R-R. **HT.:** 6-5. **WT.:** 200. **DRAFTED:** HS—Zebulon, Ga., 2007 (18th round). **SIGNED BY:** Rob English (Red Sox).

It will be hard for Strickland to top his debut in the Pirates organization. Acquired from the Red Sox along with slick-fielding shortstop Argenis Diaz in a trade for Adam LaRoche last July, Strickland started for low Class A West Virginia five days later and pitched the first six innings of a combined no-hitter with Diego Moreno. Strickland was lifted because his pitch count reached 90. He added velocity to his fastball last season after adding weight to his lanky frame, touching 94 mph and usually sitting at 88-92. Besides his four-seam fastball, he also relies on a two-seamer and a curveball. His changeup is in the rudimentary stages, as he didn't begin throwing it until he began his pro career. Strickland has complex mechanics that include a high leg kick, but he's working on smoothing out his delivery. He does a fine job of throwing strikes but needs to improve his location because he's too hittable. He'll begin this season in high Class A, and if he can develop a swing-and-miss pitch, he'll jump on the fast track to Pittsburgh.

Year	Club (League)	Class	W	L	ERA	G	GS	CG	SV	IP	H	R	ER	HR	BB	SO	AVG
2007	Red Sox (GCL)	R	0	2	6.04	9	6	0	0	25	40	21	17	3	4	22	.357
2008	Lowell (NYP)	SS	5	3	3.18	15	10	0	0	71	67	32	25	5	17	59	.249
2009	Greenville (SAL)	LoA	5	4	3.35	18	12	0	1	83	85	39	31	11	13	51	.264
	West Virginia (SAL)	LoA	4	2	3.77	8	8	0	0	43	42	23	18	3	6	23	.250
MINOR LEAGUE TOTALS			14	11	3.68	50	36	0	1	222	234	115	91	22	40	155	.269

20 JAREK CUNNINGHAM, 3B/SS

BORN: Dec. 25, 1989. **B-T:** R-R. **HT.:** 6-1. **WT.:** 185. **DRAFTED:** HS—Mead, Wash., 2008 (18th round). **SIGNED BY:** Greg Hopkins.

After starring in his pro debut and looking like one of the steals of the 2008 draft, Cunningham missed all of last season when he tore the anterior cruciate ligament in his left knee during a conditioning drill. He also missed his high school senior year in 2008 with the same issue, but in a medical rarity, the ACL reattached itself without surgery. He couldn't avoid an operation the second time, however. Cunningham's draft stock plunged after the original injury, and the Pirates were able to take him in the 18th round and sign him away from an Arizona State commitment for $300,000. He has a short stroke, makes consistent hard contact and figures to develop at least slightly above-average power. He has a solid approach for a young player, so he should hit for average as well. Cunningham is a good athlete with above-average speed, range and arm strength. Pittsburgh played him mostly at third base in his pro debut to increase his versatility and take stress off his knee, but Cunningham was a shortstop in high school and has the tools to play there if the knee surgery doesn't cost him any quickness. The Pirates will see how he looks in spring training before determining where to send him for 2010.

Year	Club (League)	Class	AVG	G	AB	R	H	2B	3B	HR	RBI	BB	SO	SB	OBP	SLG
2008	Pirates (GCL)	R	.318	43	148	20	47	11	1	5	22	14	26	2	.385	.507
2009	Did Not Play—Injured															
MINOR LEAGUE TOTALS			.318	43	148	20	47	11	1	5	22	14	26	2	.385	.507

21 DANIEL McCUTCHEN, RHP

BORN: Sept. 26, 1982. **B-T:** R-R. **HT.:** 6-2. **WT.:** 215. **DRAFTED:** Oklahoma, 2006 (13th round). **SIGNED BY:** Mark Batchko (Yankees).

One of four players acquired from the Yankees in a July 2008 trade for Damaso Marte and Xavier Nady, McCutchen failed in his bid to win a big league rotation spot in spring training last year. He responded by leading the International League in wins and earning a September callup. Originally scheduled to pitch for the United States in the World Cup, he made six outings for the Pirates, turning in four quality starts and beating the Reds for his first big league win. McCutchen succeeds by throwing strikes with a three-pitch arsenal. He throws his four-seam fastball at 90-93 mph and also has a hard curveball and a much-improved changeup. An extreme flyball pitcher throughout his pro career, he allowed six homers in 36 major league innings. He's almost around the plate too much and doesn't have a true swing-and-miss pitch. McCutchen is what he is, a 27-year-old who projects as a No. 4 or 5 starter, but he should open 2010 in Pittsburgh's rotation.

Year	Club (League)	Class	W	L	ERA	G	GS	CG	SV	IP	H	R	ER	HR	BB	SO	AVG
2006	Staten Island (NYP)	SS	1	0	1.13	2	2	0	0	8	4	1	1	1	1	11	.148
	Charleston, SC (SAL)	LoA	1	0	2.14	7	0	0	1	21	13	5	5	2	5	18	.186
2007	Tampa (FSL)	HiA	11	2	2.50	17	16	0	0	101	86	29	28	7	21	67	.236
	Trenton (EL)	AA	3	2	2.41	7	7	0	0	41	30	11	11	2	12	36	.205
2008	Trenton (EL)	AA	4	3	2.55	9	9	0	0	53	43	16	15	4	18	52	.219
	Scranton/W-B (IL)	AAA	4	6	3.58	11	11	2	0	70	73	32	28	10	11	58	.265
	Indianapolis (IL)	AAA	3	3	4.69	8	8	0	0	48	49	25	25	12	7	41	.261
2009	Indianapolis (IL)	AAA	13	6	3.47	24	24	0	0	143	145	63	55	10	29	110	.264
	Pittsburgh (NL)	MAJ	1	2	4.21	6	6	0	0	36	38	17	17	6	11	19	.271
MAJOR LEAGUE TOTALS			1	2	4.21	6	6	0	0	36	38	17	17	6	11	19	.271
MINOR LEAGUE TOTALS			40	22	3.12	85	77	2	1	485	443	182	168	48	104	393	.244

22 JORDY MERCER, SS/3B

BORN: Aug. 27, 1986. **B-T:** R-R. **HT.:** 6-3. **WT.:** 191. **DRAFTED:** Oklahoma State, 2008 (3rd round) **SIGNED BY:** Matt Bimeal.

Mercer comes from Leedy, Okla., the same small town that produced Monty Fariss, the sixth overall pick in the 1988 draft. Like Fariss, Mercer is a tall shortstop who went on to stardom at Oklahoma State. He made the all-Big 12 Conference team at three different positions during his career: shortstop, utility player and pitcher. He topped the Carolina League with 36 doubles last season while helping Lynchburg win the league title. Mercer is an offense-first shortstop who has good gap power and the size and strength to eventually turn some of those doubles into homers. His biggest weakness as a hitter is his plate discipline, as he has particular trouble with off-speed pitches. Mercer's strong arm enabled him to hit 95 mph and close games in college, and also led the Pirates to experiment with him at third base late last season. His speed and range are average at shortstop, and he'll likely wind up at the hot corner in the long run. Headed to Double-A, he could begin making the full-time transition to third base because Pittsburgh's top shortstop prospect, Chase d'Arnaud, also figures to be with the Curve.

Year	Club (League)	Class	AVG	G	AB	R	H	2B	3B	HR	RBI	BB	SO	SB	OBP	SLG
2008	State College (NYP)	SS	.250	6	24	5	6	1	1	1	2	1	3	1	.280	.500
	Hickory (SAL)	LoA	.250	50	192	21	48	7	0	4	18	12	44	4	.300	.349
2009	Lynchburg (CAR)	HiA	.255	131	513	64	131	36	4	10	83	41	93	10	.314	.400
MINOR LEAGUE TOTALS			.254	187	729	90	185	44	5	15	103	54	140	15	.309	.390

23 EVAN CHAMBERS, OF

BORN: March 24, 1989. **B-T:** R-R. **HT.:** 5-9. **WT.:** 215. **DRAFTED:** Hillsborough (Fla.) CC, 2009 (3rd round). **SIGNED BY:** Matt Wondolowski.

Chambers began his collegiate career at Florida but got just eight at-bats as a freshman in 2008. After hitting seven homers in the summer New England Collegiate League, he transferred to Hillsborough (Fla.) CC, making him eligible for the 2009 draft. The Pirates saw enough in his all-around game to select him in the third round and sign him for $423,900. He's a short, stocky center fielder with good speed and home run potential, so he has drawn inevitable comparisons to Kirby Puckett. While it takes quite the optimist to project Chambers as a future star, he showed good offensive potential late in his first pro season. He has a quick bat, though his swing can get choppy and he struggles with pitch recognition. He works so hard to take pitches and show good discipline that he lets too many hittable offering go by. Chambers has the tools to become an above-average defender with good range and a playable arm. He'll begin his first full season in low Class A and try to push his way through an increasingly deep pool of center-field prospects in the system.

Year	Club (League)	Class	AVG	G	AB	R	H	2B	3B	HR	RBI	BB	SO	SB	OBP	SLG
2009	State College (NYP)	SS	.245	58	200	45	49	15	0	4	22	50	78	6	.393	.380
MINOR LEAGUE TOTALS			.245	58	200	45	49	15	0	4	22	50	78	6	.393	.380

24 DONNIE VEAL, LHP

BORN: Sept. 18, 1984. **B-T:** L-L. **HT.:** 6-4. **WT.:** 230. **DRAFTED:** Pima (Ariz.) CC, 2005 (2nd round). **SIGNED BY:** Steve McFarland (Cubs).

Veal went from being one of baseball's best lefty pitching prospects in 2006, when he led the minors with a .175 opponent average, to unprotected on the Cubs' 40-man roster after the 2008 season, allowing the Pirates to claim him in the major league Rule 5 draft. Pittsburgh held onto him by keeping him on its major league roster in 2009, finding him extra work by sending him to the minors on a couple of rehab assignments for a strained groin and a strained index finger. Veal's control fell apart in his last two years in the Chicago system, and was dreadful while he pitched sparingly last season. But he seemed to turn a corner in the Arizona Fall League, where he issued just seven walks in 21 innings. There's no doubting Veal's pure stuff, as he can carve hitters up with either a low-90s fastball that touches 95 or a hammer curveball. The problem comes when he can't maintain his funky delivery and loses the strike zone. He has yet to develop a feel for the changeup, and he might be best off focusing on two pitches and working in shorter stints out of the bullpen. Veal won points for his work ethic as he threw numerous side sessions in the bullpen under the watch of pitching coach Joe Kerrigan last season. The Pirates haven't given up on Veal as a starter and will use him in their Triple-A rotation this season.

Year	Club (League)	Class	W	L	ERA	G	GS	CG	SV	IP	H	R	ER	HR	BB	SO	AVG
2005	Cubs (AZL)	R	0	1	5.06	4	3	0	0	11	8	6	6	2	5	14	.205
	Boise (NWL)	SS	1	2	2.48	7	6	0	0	29	18	11	8	2	15	34	.180
2006	Peoria (MWL)	LoA	5	3	2.69	14	14	0	0	74	45	26	22	4	40	86	.179
	Daytona (FSL)	HiA	6	2	1.67	14	14	0	0	81	46	18	15	3	42	88	.170
2007	Tennessee (SL)	AA	8	10	4.97	28	27	0	0	130	126	80	72	11	73	131	.256
2008	Tennessee (SL)	AA	5	10	4.52	29	29	0	0	145	150	89	73	19	81	123	.276
2009	Indianapolis (IL)	AAA	0	1	6.43	9	1	0	0	14	6	10	10	0	16	13	.136
	Altoona (EL)	AA	0	0	1.35	7	5	0	0	13	5	2	2	0	10	18	.116
	Pittsburgh (NL)	MAJ	1	0	7.16	19	0	0	0	16	18	13	13	2	20	16	.281
MAJOR LEAGUE TOTALS			1	0	7.16	19	0	0	0	16	18	13	13	2	20	16	.281
MINOR LEAGUE TOTALS			25	29	3.77	112	99	0	0	497	404	242	208	41	282	507	.227

25 BRETT LORIN, RHP

BORN: March 31, 1987. **B-T:** L-R. **HT.:** 6-7. **WT.:** 245. **DRAFTED:** Long Beach State, 2008 (5th round). **SIGNED BY:** Tim Reynolds (Mariners).

One of the five players the Mariners sent to the Pirates for Jack Wilson and Ian Snell last July, Lorin pitched brilliantly for West Virginia following the trade, giving up six earned runs in seven starts. He's less experienced than most college pitchers because he worked just 58 innings in three seasons between Arizona and Long Beach State. He has made up for lost time by logging 175 innings in 1½ pro seasons, posting a 2.72 ERA and 177 strikeouts. A big-bodied righthander who has drawn comparisons to Carl Pavano, Lorin uses his frame to throw downhill with a lively 87-91 mph fastball. He has the potential for three average or better pitches, because both his hard slurve and his changeup have their moments. He improved his control last season, adding more fuel for the belief that he'll eventually pitch in the back of a big league rotation. After dominating the lower minors, Lorin will face tougher tests in 2010, when he'll start the year in high Class A with a chance to end it in Double-A.

Year	Club (League)	Class	W	L	ERA	G	GS	CG	SV	IP	H	R	ER	HR	BB	SO	AVG
2008	Everett (NWL)	SS	1	0	2.82	5	5	0	0	22	17	10	7	1	9	29	.207
	Wisconsin (MWL)	LoA	0	2	4.80	8	6	0	0	30	30	17	16	1	16	32	.275
2009	Clinton (MWL)	LoA	5	4	2.44	16	16	0	0	89	61	29	24	9	25	87	.192
	West Virginia (SAL)	LoA	3	1	1.57	7	7	0	0	34	33	10	6	2	10	29	.264
MINOR LEAGUE TOTALS			9	7	2.72	36	34	0	0	175	141	66	53	13	60	177	.222

26 NEIL WALKER, 3B

BORN: Sept. 10, 1985. **B-T:** B-R. **HT.:** 6-3. **WT.:** 215. **DRAFTED:** HS—Gibsonia, Pa., 2004 (1st round). **SIGNED BY:** Jon Mercurio.

Walker made his major league debut last September, five years after he was drafted with great fanfare from Pine-Richland High in Pittsburgh's northern suburbs. His father Tom and uncle Chip Lang also played in the big leagues. Picked 11th overall and signed for $1.95 million as a catcher, Walker moved to third base prior to the 2007 season. He seems to have a limited future with the Pirates at the hot corner, because they have Andy LaRoche starting there in the majors and top prospect Pedro Alvarez on the way. After going on the disabled list last June with a broken pinky and sprained knee, Walker hit .291/.319/.517 after returning to earn his callup. Pittsburgh was expecting that kind of power when it drafted him, but he hasn't shown it with any consistency. A switch-hitter, he undermines his offensive potential by lacking plate discipline. A good athlete who was recruited by college football programs as a wide receiver, Walker runs well for his size and has turned into an above-average defender at third base. He has quick reactions, solid range and a strong arm. Walker has expressed a willingness to become a super-utility player who could catch and play both infield and outfield corners. That may be his ticket to having a big league career of any length.

PITTSBURGH PIRATES

Year	Club (League)	Class	AVG	G	AB	R	H	2B	3B	HR	RBI	BB	SO	SB	OBP	SLG
2004	Pirates (GCL)	R	.271	52	192	28	52	12	3	4	20	10	33	3	.313	.427
	Williamsport (NYP)	SS	.313	8	32	2	10	3	0	0	7	2	1	1	.343	.406
2005	Hickory (SAL)	LoA	.301	120	485	78	146	33	2	12	68	20	71	7	.332	.452
	Lynchburg (CAR)	HiA	.262	9	42	4	11	2	1	0	12	0	12	0	.244	.357
2006	Lynchburg (CAR)	HiA	.284	72	264	32	75	22	1	3	35	19	41	3	.345	.409
	Altoona (EL)	AA	.161	10	31	5	5	0	0	2	3	1	4	0	.188	.355
2007	Altoona (EL)	AA	.288	117	431	77	124	30	3	13	66	53	73	9	.362	.462
	Indianapolis (IL)	AAA	.203	19	64	7	13	3	0	0	0	2	13	1	.261	.250
2008	Indianapolis (IL)	AAA	.242	133	505	69	122	25	7	16	80	29	102	10	.280	.414
2009	Pirates (GCL)	R	.167	8	30	2	5	2	0	1	1	1	5	0	.219	.333
	Indianapolis (IL)	AAA	.264	95	356	38	94	31	2	14	69	26	60	5	.311	.480
	Pittsburgh (NL)	MAJ	.194	17	36	5	7	1	0	0	0	4	11	1	.275	.222
MAJOR LEAGUE TOTALS			.194	17	36	5	7	1	0	0	0	4	11	1	.275	.222
MINOR LEAGUE TOTALS			.270	643	2432	342	657	163	19	65	361	163	415	39	.317	.433

27 BROCK HOLT, SS/2B

BORN: June 11, 1988. **B-T:** L-R. **HT.:** 5-11. **WT.:** 165. **DRAFTED:** Rice, 2009 (9th round). **SIGNED BY:** Trevor Haley.

Holt hit .348 with 12 home runs in 250 at-bats for Rice last spring after spending the first two years of his collegiate career at Navarro (Texas) JC, and the Pirates were pleasantly surprised to find him available in the ninth round. After signing quickly for $125,000, Holt had a fine pro debut, leading State College in hitting (.299), runs (45), homers (six) and steals (nine in as many tries). He has surprising pop for a smaller guy and can hit mistakes out of the park. However, his offensive strength is his ability to make consistent contact and get on base. His instincts allow him to turn his good speed into stolen bases. A shortstop at Navarro, Holt played second base at Rice in deference to potential 2010 first-round pick Rick Hague, then saw most of his time at short in pro ball. Holt is a steady defender with decent range and a solid arm. Pittsburgh could challenge him with an assignment to high Class A if he has a strong spring.

Year	Club (League)	Class	AVG	G	AB	R	H	2B	3B	HR	RBI	BB	SO	SB	OBP	SLG
2009	State College (NYP)	SS	.299	66	254	45	76	14	3	6	33	26	31	9	.361	.449
MINOR LEAGUE TOTALS			.299	66	254	45	76	14	3	6	33	26	31	9	.361	.449

28 BRIAN FRIDAY, SS

BORN: Dec. 16, 1985. **B-T:** R-R. **HT.:** 5-11. **WT.:** 180. **DRAFTED:** Rice, 2007 (3rd round). **SIGNED BY:** Everett Russell.

Since a strong 2007 pro debut, Friday has yet to show the same performance, in part because he has had a hard time staying on the field. He missed a significant portion of 2008 with a strained lower back, then sat out nearly a month early last season with an inner-ear infection. The Pirats worried that he might have vertigo, and the infection affected him past his disabled list stay, though he did rebound to earn a selection to the Double-A Eastern League all-star game. Friday profiles as a classic No. 2 hitter. He works counts and takes his walks, and he controls the bat well enough to be an asset in hit-and-run and sacrifice situations. He has modest power and slightly above-average speed. Normally a reliable fielder, he has struggled defensively when he has been less than 100 percent the last two years. He has average range and a strong arm at shortstop. Friday will move up to Triple-A this season, and if he can get back on track, he could get an opportunity to stabilize Pittsburgh's unsettled shortstop situation.

Year	Club (League)	Class	AVG	G	AB	R	H	2B	3B	HR	RBI	BB	SO	SB	OBP	SLG
2007	State College (NYP)	SS	.295	40	156	31	46	10	1	2	13	10	33	6	.371	.410
2008	Pirates (GCL)	R	.182	7	22	2	4	0	1	0	3	2	3	0	.280	.273
	Lynchburg (CAR)	HiA	.287	85	341	59	98	20	4	2	29	34	56	16	.365	.387
2009	Altoona (EL)	AA	.265	110	407	48	108	22	3	7	46	51	69	7	.361	.386
MINOR LEAGUE TOTALS			.276	242	926	140	256	52	9	11	91	97	161	29	.362	.388

29 JOSH HARRISON, OF/2B/3B

BORN: July 8, 1987. **B-T:** R-R. **HT.:** 5-8. **WT.:** 175. **DRAFTED:** Cincinnati, 2008 (6th round). **SIGNED BY:** Lukas McKnight (Cubs).

Harrison came to the Pirates along with Jose Ascanio and Kevin Hart last July in a trade that sent Tom Gorzelanny and John Grabow to the Cubs. Harrison has baseball in his blood, as he's the nephew of former big leaguer and current Orioles first-base coach John Shelby and the brother of former Rays farmhand Vince Harrison. Josh has a track record of performance, sharing Big East Conference player of the year honors in 2008 and batting .323 through low Class A, but scouts still aren't sure what to make of him. Using a simple, repeatable swing, he makes consistent line-drive contact and brings energy to the ballpark. The question is what else he brings to the table. He makes contact so easily that he doesn't draw many walks, and while he has more pop than expected from a little guy, that's not a major part of his game. He has fringy speed out of the box and is better under way, but he won't be a big basestealing threat at higher levels. His defensive position is also uncertain. His range and hands are fringy for second base, his main position in college, and his arm and power are substandard for third base. He saw most of his time last season in left field, but doesn't profile well there either. Harrison hit just .275/.310/.374 once he got to high Class A in 2009, and he needs to get his bat going again in Double-A this year.

Year	Club (League)	Class	AVG	G	AB	R	H	2B	3B	HR	RBI	BB	SO	SB	OBP	SLG
2008	Boise (NWL)	SS	.351	33	114	27	40	11	2	1	25	23	12	12	.462	.509
	Peoria (MWL)	LoA	.262	31	122	15	32	4	1	1	4	3	11	6	.286	.336
2009	Peoria (MWL)	LoA	.337	79	303	51	102	17	7	4	33	16	25	16	.377	.479
	Daytona (FSL)	HiA	.286	18	70	10	20	3	1	1	9	6	7	10	.351	.400
	Lynchburg (CAR)	HiA	.270	34	141	15	38	8	1	1	13	1	19	4	.289	.362
MINOR LEAGUE TOTALS			.309	195	750	118	232	43	12	8	84	49	74	48	.359	.431

30 DANIEL MOSKOS, LHP

BORN: April 28, 1986. **B-T:** R-L. **HT.:** 6-1. **WT.:** 210. **DRAFTED:** Clemson, 2007 (1st round). **SIGNED BY:** Greg Schilz.

The eminently likeable Moskos is the prospect frustrated Pirates fans love to hate, through no fault of his own. The fans haven't forgotten that former general manager Dave Littlefield chose Moskos with the fourth overall pick in the 2007 draft, when Matt Wieters was still on the board. Littlefield feared that Wieters wouldn't sign for less than $12 million (though he ultimately took $6 million), and Pittsburgh landed Moskos for $2.475 million. While Wieters was establishing himself in the major leagues last season, Moskos was in the rotation at Double-A Altoona. He had a solid season, but his strikeout rate (4.7 per nine innings) shows how much his stuff has diminished since his days at Clemson. His formerly 95 mph fastball is down to the high 80s, and the wipeout slider no longer has the same bite. Instead, he gets by on moving the ball around the strike zone and pitching to contact. He also throws a curveball and changeup, though neither is anything special. The Pirates were encouraged that Moskos showed up to spring training in top shape last season after struggling with his conditioning in 2008. He'll begin this season in the Indianapolis rotation, but his role in the majors more likely will be as a reliever.

Year	Club (League)	Class	W	L	ERA	G	GS	CG	SV	IP	H	R	ER	HR	BB	SO	AVG
2007	Pirates (GCL)	R	0	0	0.00	2	0	0	0	3	4	0	0	0	0	3	.333
	State College (NYP)	SS	0	0	4.26	11	0	0	1	13	19	8	6	1	6	13	.328
2008	Lynchburg (CAR)	HiA	7	7	5.95	29	20	0	0	110	124	83	73	8	43	78	.284
2009	Altoona (EL)	AA	11	10	3.74	27	25	1	0	149	159	75	62	11	58	77	.279
MINOR LEAGUE TOTALS			18	17	4.61	69	45	1	1	275	306	166	141	20	107	171	.285

St. Louis Cardinals

BY DERRICK GOOLD

St. Louis dealt a bevy of major league-ready prospects in 2009, including Brett Wallace

The Cardinals didn't view their series of win-now trades in 2009 as a jarring change of direction. Rather, they presented the spree-spending of prospects as an offshoot of a deeper design.

For nearly five seasons, starting with the drafting of Colby Rasmus 28th overall in 2005, the St. Louis front office followed an ownership mandate to restock a threadbare farm system and become more self-sufficient. The payback was supposed to be a flow of players like Rasmus, who debuted as a big league regular in 2009. But the Cardinals also eyed an alternative return on gathering minor league talent: the depth to  pull off bigger deals. That's the same formula that former general manager Walt Jocketty used to build seven playoff clubs and one World Series champion in 13 seasons in St. Louis. Now it's GM John Mozeliak pulling the trigger.

In moves for Mark DeRosa and Matt Holliday, the Cardinals traded five prospects, four of whom were expected to be major league contributors as early as 2010. To land Holliday from Oakland, they dealt third baseman Brett Wallace, as well as righthander Clayton Mortensen and outfielder Shane Peterson. It cost them future closer Chris Perez and righty Jess Todd to get DeRosa from Cleveland.

Rasmus' promotion and those two trades stripped this list of five of its top six prospects from a year ago. The sixth, catcher Bryan Anderson, missed most of the last two months of the season with shoulder problems. In other words, it's time to restock a radically altered and diluted farm system again.

The impact of St. Louis' moves was immediate, as Holliday gave the lineup a second legitimate threat after Albert Pujols and DeRosa solidified third base. After a two-year absence, the Cardinals returned to the playoffs with a 91-71 record.

Despite having its roster plundered, Triple-A Memphis won the Pacific Coast League championship. The return of lefty Jaime Garcia and third baseman David Freese from surgeries spurred the Redbirds' success, and both players will be counted on at the big league level in 2010, possibly as starters.

While the Cardinals remain confident they can lean on their system to produce in-house contributors such as Rasmus and Brendan Ryan, some fissures appeared during 2009. Pitching coach Dave Duncan acknowledged his frustrations with a disconnect between his major league staff and minor league development. Mozeliak insisted there would be changes to increase

Duncan's influence and strengthen the overall bond between the big league club and rising young players.

St. Louis hopes that international signings will become major sources of talent, though they had a major setback in that area. After giving Dominican outfielder Wagner Mateo a franchise-record $3.1 million bonus in July, they voided the contract two months later because of concerns about his vision. The Cardinals acknowledge they'll have to repair their image in Latin America, starting by showcasing the development of players already in the system, such as Venezuelan righthander Eduardo Sanchez.

TOP 30 PROSPECTS

1. Shelby Miller, rhp	**16.** Adam Reifer, rhp
2. Jaime Garcia, lhp	**17.** Richard Castillo, rhp
3. Lance Lynn, rhp	**18.** Tyler Henley, of
4. Daryl Jones, of	**19.** Bryan Anderson, c
5. David Freese, 3b/1b	**20.** Sam Freeman, lhp
6. Eduardo Sanchez, rhp	**21.** Joe Kelly, rhp
7. Allen Craig, of/1b/3b	**22.** Scott Bittle, rhp
8. Blake Hawksworth, rhp	**23.** P.J. Walters, rhp
9. Daniel Descalso, 2b	**24.** Steven Hill, c/of/1b
10. Robert Stock, c	**25.** Ryan Jackson, ss
11. Adam Ottavino, rhp	**26.** Mark Hamilton, 1b
12. Francisco Samuel, rhp	**27.** Yunier Castillo, ss
13. Jon Jay, of	**28.** Ben Jukich, lhp
14. Tyler Greene, ss/3b	**29.** Trey Hearne, rhp
15. Pete Kozma, ss	**30.** Cesar Valera, ss

General Manager: John Mozeliak. Farm/**Scouting Director:** Jeff Luhnow.

Class	Team	League	W	L	PCT	Finish*	Manager(s)
Majors	St. Louis Cardinals	National	91	71	.562	4th (16)	Tony LaRussa
Triple-A	Memphis Redbirds	Pacific Coast	77	67	.535	†4th (16)	Chris Maloney
Double-A	Springfield Cardinals	Texas	71	69	.507	5th (8)	Ron Warner
High A	Palm Beach Cardinals	Florida State	61	77	.442	10th (12)	Tom Spencer
Low A	Quad Cities River Bandits	Midwest	61	78	.439	9th (14)	Steve Dillard
Short-season	Batavia Muckdogs	New York-Penn	37	39	.487	8th (14)	Mark DeJohn
Rookie	Johnson City Cardinals	Appalachian	37	30	.552	3rd (10)	Mike Shildt
Rookie	GCL Cardinals	Gulf Coast	25	31	.446	12th (16)	Steve Turco

Overall 2009 Minor League Record — 369 391 .486 — 24th (30)

*Finish in overall standings (No. of teams in league). †League champion.

LAST YEAR'S TOP 30

Player, Pos.		Status
1.	Colby Rasmus, of	Majors
2.	Brett Wallace, 3b	(Athletics)
3.	Chris Perez, rhp	(Indians)
4.	Jess Todd, rhp	(Indians)
5.	Bryan Anderson, c	No. 19
6.	Clayton Mortensen, rhp	(Athletics)
7.	Daryl Jones, of	No. 4
8.	Jason Motte, rhp	Majors
9.	David Freese, 3b	No. 5
10.	Pete Kozma, ss	No. 15
11.	Adam Reifer, rhp	No. 16
12.	Jon Jay, of	No. 13
13.	Jaime Garcia, lhp	No. 2
14.	Mitchell Boggs, rhp	Majors
15.	Lance Lynn, rhp	No. 3
16.	Tyler Greene, ss	No. 14
17.	P.J. Walters, rhp	No. 23
18.	Niko Vasquez, ss	Dropped out
19.	Roberto de la Cruz, 3b	Dropped out
20.	Fernando Salas, rhp	Dropped out
21.	Francisco Samuel, rhp	No. 12
22.	Adam Ottavino, rhp	No. 11
23.	Tyler Herron, rhp	(Pirates)
24.	Richard Castillo, rhp	No. 17
25.	Steven Hill, 1b/of/c	No. 24
26.	Allen Craig, 3b	No. 7
27.	Tony Cruz, c/3b	Dropped out
28.	Shane Robinson, of	Dropped out
29.	Luke Gregerson, rhp	(Padres)
30.	Nick Additon, lhp	Dropped out

BEST TOOLS

Best Hitter for Average	Jon Jay
Best Power Hitter	Allen Craig
Best Strike-Zone Discipline	Charles Cutler
Fastest Baserunner	Adron Chambers
Best Athlete	Daryl Jones
Best Fastball	Shelby Miller
Best Curveball	Jaime Garcia
Best Slider	Blake King
Best Changeup	P.J. Walters
Best Control	P.J. Walters
Best Defensive Catcher	Matt Pagnozzi
Best Defensive Infielder	Ryan Jackson
Best Infield Arm	Tyler Greene
Best Defensive Outfielder	Shane Robinson
Best Outfield Arm	Jon Edwards

PROJECTED 2013 LINEUP

Catcher	Yadier Molina
First Base	Albert Pujols
Second Base	Skip Schumaker
Third Base	David Freese
Shortstop	Brendan Ryan
Left Field	Daryl Jones
Center Field	Colby Rasmus
Right Field	Ryan Ludwick
No. 1 Starter	Adam Wainwright
No. 2 Starter	Chris Carpenter
No. 3 Starter	Shelby Miller
No. 4 Starter	Jaime Garcia
No. 5 Starter	Lance Lynn
Closer	Jason Motte

TOP PROSPECTS OF THE DECADE

Year	Player, Pos.	2009 Org.
2000	Rick Ankiel, lhp	Cardinals
2001	Bud Smith, lhp	Out of baseball
2002	Jimmy Journell, rhp	Out of baseball
2003	Dan Haren, rhp	Diamondbacks
2004	Blake Hawksworth, rhp	Cardinals
2005	Anthony Reyes, rhp	Indians
2006	Anthony Reyes, rhp	Indians
2007	Colby Rasmus, of	Cardinals
2008	Colby Rasmus, of	Cardinals
2009	Colby Rasmus, of	Cardinals

TOP DRAFT PICKS OF THE DECADE

Year	Player, Pos.	2009 Org.
2000	Shaun Boyd, of	Out of baseball
2001	Justin Pope, rhp	Yankees
2002	Calvin Hayes, ss (3rd round)	Out of baseball
2003	Daric Barton, c	Athletics
2004	Chris Lambert, rhp	Orioles
2005	Colby Rasmus, of	Cardinals
2006	Adam Ottavino, rhp	Cardinals
2007	Pete Kozma, ss	Cardinals
2008	Brett Wallace, 3b	Athletics
2009	Shelby Miller, rhp	Cardinals

LARGEST BONUSES IN CLUB HISTORY

J.D. Drew, 1998	$3,000,000
Shelby Miller, 2009	$2,875,000
Rick Ankiel, 1997	$2,500,000
Chad Hutchinson, 1998	$2,300,000
Brett Wallace, 2008	$1,840,000

ST. LOUIS CARDINALS

TOP 2010 ROOKIE: David Freese, 3b. A Missouri native who had his shot at the majors detoured by a foot injury in 2009, he'll get an opportunity to claim a starting job.

BREAKOUT PROSPECT: Adam Ottavino, rhp. If he truly has ditched his penchant for experimenting with his mechanics, then the 2006 first-round pick can tap into his power-pitching potential.

SOURCE OF TOP 30 TALENT			
Homegrown	28	Acquired	2
College	17	Trades	1
Junior college	0	Rule 5 draft	1
High school	5	Independent leagues	0
Draft-and-follow	1	Free agents/waivers	0
Nondrafted free agents	0		
International	5		

SLEEPER: Michael Swinson, of. The raw talent hinted at what he's capable of by batting .338/.425/.541 at Rookie-level Johnson City, though he stumbled after a promotion.

Numbers in parentheses indicate prospect rankings

LF
Allen Craig (7)
Jon Jay (13)
Aaron Luna
Chris Swauger

CF
Daryl Jones (4)
Tyler Henley (18)
Adron Chambers
Shane Robinson
James Rapoport
D'Marcus Ingram
Frederick Parejo
Virgil Hill

RF
Michael Swinson
Kyle Conley
Ryde Rodriguez

3B
David Freese (5)
Roberto de la Cruz
Matt Carpenter
Rich Racobaldo
Jermaine Curtis

SS
Tyler Greene (14)
Pete Kozma (15)
Ryan Jackson (25)
Yunier Castillo (27)
Cesar Valera (30)
Donovan Solano

2B
Daniel Descalso (9)
Jose Martinez
Jason Stidham
Niko Vasquez

1B
Steven Hill (24)
Mark Hamilton (26)
Andrew Brown
Matt Adams
Curt Smith
Xavier Scruggs
Matt Arburr

C
Robert Stock (10)
Bryan Anderson (19)
Matt Pagnozzi
Charles Cutler
Tony Cruz
Luis de la Cruz

RHP

Starters	Relievers
Shelby Miller (1)	Eduardo Sanchez (6)
Lance Lynn (3)	Blake Hawksworth (8)
Adam Ottavino (11)	Francisco Samuel (12)
Richard Castillo (17)	Adam Reifer (16)
P.J. Walters (23)	Joe Kelly (21)
Trey Hearne (29)	Scott Bittle (22)
Arquimedes Nieto	Fernando Salas
Scott Gorgen	Blake King
Nick McCully	Casey Mulligan
Travis Lawler	Pete Parise
David Kopp	David Kington
Scott Schneider	
Andrew Moss	

LHP

Starters	Relievers
Jaime Garcia (2)	Sam Freeman (20)
Nick Additon	Ben Jukich (28)
Brad Furnish	Tyler Norrick
Hector Hernandez	Justin Fiske
Anthony Ferrara	

DRAFT ANALYSIS

2009 — BONUSES: $5.4 MILLION

BEST PURE HITTER: 1B Matt Adams (23) set single-season (an NCAA Division II-leading .495) and career (.454) records for batting average at Slippery Rock (Pa.), then hit .355/.400/.547 between two teams in his pro debut.

BEST POWER HITTER: OF Kyle Conley (7), who holds the Washington career record with 42 homers, or Adams. After scuffling in low Class A, Conley hit .385/.452/.752 at short-season Batavia.

FASTEST RUNNER: OF Virgil Hill (6) has plus-plus speed, not surprising considering that his mother, Denean Howard-Hill, won a silver medal in the 1988 Olympics in the 4x400-meter relay.

BEST DEFENSIVE PLAYER: SS Ryan Jackson (5) was the draft's top college defender at his position. Though he's a slightly below-average runner, he has plus range thanks to his instincts and quick first step. His arm is a cannon and he has reliable hands. C Robert Stock (2) also has plenty of arm strength.

BEST FASTBALL: No high schooler in the 2009 draft had a better fastball than RHP Shelby Miller (1). He works at 92-93 mph and touches 97, and his heater plays up further because of its life and deception. RHP Joe Kelly (3) pitches at 94-95 mph and hits 98, but Miller's fastball package is better.

BEST SECONDARY PITCH: RHP Scott Bittle (4) dominated the Southeastern Conference for three years, thanks to an 84-86 mph cutter that hitters knew was coming but still couldn't do anything with.

BEST PRO DEBUT: The Cardinals like to draft proven college performers, and a number of them excelled in their first taste of pro ball. Adams and Conley were mentioned above, while RHP Scott Schneider (20) went 3-3, 2.04 with 76 strikeouts in 71 innings while reaching low Class A. RHP David Kington (34) led the Rookie-level Appalachian League with eight saves, while RHP Andy Moss (35) won the ERA crown at 2.28.

BEST ATHLETE: Hill. OF David Washington (15) was an all-league basketball guard in San Diego who averaged 14.7 points per game and won the city slam-dunk competition as a senior. Miller made the all-Texas 3-A state football second team as both a tight end and a punter last fall.

MOST INTRIGUING BACKGROUND: Stock was Baseball America's 2005 Youth Player of the Year and skipped his senior year to enroll at Southern California at age 16 a year later. The Brewers drafted his brother Richard in the 45th round in June but didn't sign him. Hill's father Virgil Sr. also won Olympic silver, as a middleweight boxer in 1984, and later held world light-heavyweight and cruiserweight titles. Unsigned SS Taylor Terrasas' (39) father Rudy is the Mets' scouting director.

CLOSEST TO THE MAJORS: Bittle has had shoulder problems off and on since 2006 and hasn't pitched since April. But if he can stay healthy, he may not need more than a year in the minors.

BEST LATE-ROUND PICK: Adams or Schneider.

THE ONE WHO GOT AWAY: St. Louis signed an MLB-high 43 players, but couldn't lure finesse LHP Daniel Bibona (16) away from his senior season at UC Irvine.

ASSESSMENT: Miller dropped because of signability concerns, and the Cardinals stole him with the No. 19 overall pick for $2.875 million. After that, they returned to their usual college focus and were pleased with the initial performances of several players.

2008 — BONUSES: $5.5 MILLION

3B/1B Brett Wallace (1) would be the best prospect in the system if the Cardinals hadn't used him and OF Shane Peterson (2) in a trade for Matt Holliday. RHP Lance Lynn (1s) is about a year away from St. Louis.
GRADE: B

2007 — BONUSES: $4.6 MILLION

The Cardinals rushed RHPs Clayton Mortensen (1s) and Jess Todd (2), then used them in deals for Holliday and Mark DeRosa. SS Pete Kozma (1) is developing slowly, but 2B Daniel Descalso (3) had a breakthrough 2009 season.
GRADE: C

2006 — BONUSES: $5.3 MILLION

More trades for St. Louis, which dealt the two best players from this crop, RHP Chris Perez (1s) in the DeRosa deal and RHP Luke Gregerson (28) for Khalil Greene. OF Shane Robinson (5) and RHP P.J. Walters (11) have had big league cups of coffee, and OFs Jon Jay (2) and Allen Craig (8) should get theirs soon.
GRADE: C

2005 — BONUSES: $5.6 MILLION*

OF Colby Rasmus (1) looks like a star, and LHP Jaime Garcia (22) is the system's top pitching prospect. SS/3B Tyler Greene (1), RHP Mitchell Boggs (5) and OF Nick Stavinoha (7) have reached the majors, and St. Louis still has hopes for OF Daryl Jones (3).
GRADE: B+

*Draft analysis by Jim Callis. Numbers in parentheses indicate draft rounds. *Bonuses for 2005 are first 10 rounds only.*

SHELBY MILLER, RHP

Born: Oct. 10, 1990.
Height: 6-3. **Weight:** 205.
Bats: R. **Throws:** R.
Drafted: HS—Brownwood, Texas, 2009 (1st round).
Signed by: Ralph Garr Jr.

Bomb

The Cardinals hadn't taken a high school pitcher in the first five rounds of the draft since 2005, when they took righthander Tyler Herron 46th overall. The perception that they were unduly leery of high school pitchers stung them when they bypassed Rick Porcello in the 2007 draft, and they didn't let history repeat itself when another elite prep arm slipped in 2009. St. Louis took Miller with the 19th overall pick, making him the first high school pitcher taken by the franchise in the first round since Brian Barber in 1991. Cardinals officials knew it would take an above-slot bonus to land the Texas fireballer, and he signed at the Aug. 17 deadline for $2.875 million. Miller profiles as the possible No. 1 starter that had been obviously absent in the Cardinals farm system, making him worth the risk St. Louis cited for avoiding Porcello's price tag two years earlier. For his part, Miller doesn't shrink from the expectations. He moved to Houston, five hours from his home in Brownwood, Texas, so he could work out at a baseball-specific facility and improve his conditioning while waiting for a deal with the Cardinals. Miller, who had committed to Texas A&M, worked out for the major league staff at Busch Stadium and made two brief appearances at low Class A Quad Cities after signing.

True to his Lone Star State roots, Miller describes himself as gleefully chucking Texas heat in the tradition of his heroes Nolan Ryan and Josh Beckett. He embraces the comparisons. Miller has a fastball that sits easily at 92-93 mph and touches 97. He has a power attitude and a muscular delivery that hints he'll veer into the mid-90s as he matures. His height, reach and deception increase the perceived velocity of his fastball, and it has heavy life that keeps it low in the zone. Taking in all those factors, some scouts thought he had the best fastball of any high school pitcher in the 2009 draft. Miller also snaps off a 12-to-6 curveball that has the potential to be a plus pitch. He has made significant improvements with his changeup over the last year. He's a quality athlete who made the Texas 3-A all-state second team in football last fall as a tight end and punter. His mechanics and durability also bode well for his durability.

Harnessing his stuff is Miller's top priority. His command comes and goes, and the Cardinals believe he'll more easily repeat his delivery and be more consistent from pitch to pitch with some fine-tuning of his mechanics. His curveball and especially his changeup need more work to become reliable secondary pitches. Learning how to exploit and not just use his stuff will come with experience.

Because of his work in Houston, Miller was ready to dip his toe into pro ball with three innings at Quad Cities in August. The cameo was calculated, as St. Louis wants him to start 2010 in low Class A. Despite his age, he could speed through the lower levels of the minors. With his pyrotechnic stuff, frame and confidence, Miller cuts the image of a top-of-the-rotation starter. This system hasn't seen a young gun with this much potential since Rick Ankiel.

Year	Club (League)	Class	W	L	ERA	G	GS	CG	SV	IP	H	R	ER	HR	BB	SO	AVG
2009	Quad Cities (MWL)	LoA	0	0	6.00	2	2	0	0	3	5	3	2	0	2	2	.357
MINOR LEAGUE TOTALS			0	0	6.00	2	2	0	0	3	5	3	2	0	2	2	.357

2 JAIME GARCIA, LHP $Saul$

BORN: July 8, 1986. **B-T:** L-L. **HT.:** 6-2. **WT.:** 230. **DRAFTED:** Mission, Texas, 2005 (22nd round). **SIGNED BY:** Joe Almaraz.

Garcia missed most of 2009 recovering from Tommy John surgery, but returned to become the ace for Triple-A Memphis as the team won the Pacific Coast League championship. His postseason performance included a scoreless six-inning, six-strikeout start in the first round of the palyoffs, which manager Chris Maloney described as good enough "to pitch anywhere that night, at any level." Garcia commands a biting 12-to-6 curveball that's a genuine swing-and-miss pitch. He sets it up with an 88-92 mph fastball that has late, downward movement. He used his rehab to add a pitch that's a cross between a cutter and slider. His minor league playoff performance validated his reputation for being unflappable. After his 2007 and 2008 seasons ended early because of elbow soreness, and he pitched just 38 innings last season, Garcia still has to prove his durability. He has battled his command at times, and those problems may be related to endurance as well. The Cardinals want to fill a spot in their 2010 rotation from within, and Garcia is a leading candidate to do so. He left a favorable impression in a brief callup in 2008, and should make the club if he has a strong spring. He projects as a No. 3 starter.

Year	Club (League)	Class	W	L	ERA	G	GS	CG	SV	IP	H	R	ER	HR	BB	SO	AVG
2006	Quad Cities (MWL)	LoA	5	4	2.90	13	13	1	0	78	67	28	25	1	18	80	.229
	Palm Beach (FSL)	HiA	5	4	3.84	12	12	0	0	77	84	33	33	3	16	51	.282
2007	Springfield, MO (TL)	AA	5	9	3.75	18	18	0	0	103	93	47	43	14	45	97	.245
2008	Springfield, MO (TL)	AA	3	2	2.06	6	6	1	0	35	26	10	8	0	16	41	.206
	Memphis (PCL)	AAA	4	4	4.44	13	12	0	0	71	74	41	35	6	26	59	.270
	St. Louis (NL)	MAJ	1	1	5.63	10	1	0	0	16	14	10	10	4	8	8	.233
2009	Cardinals (GCL)	R	0	1	4.50	2	2	0	0	4	4	2	2	0	1	3	.250
	Palm Beach (FSL)	HiA	0	1	0.71	3	2	0	0	13	4	1	1	0	4	16	.105
	Memphis (PCL)	AAA	2	0	3.86	4	4	0	0	21	17	14	9	5	9	22	.230
MAJOR LEAGUE TOTALS			1	1	5.63	10	1	0	0	16	14	10	10	4	8	8	.233
MINOR LEAGUE TOTALS			24	25	3.49	71	69	2	0	402	369	176	156	29	135	369	.246

3 LANCE LYNN, RHP +

BORN: May 12, 1987. **B-T:** R-R. **HT.:** 6-5. **WT.:** 250. **DRAFTED:** Mississippi, 2008 (1st round supplemental). **SIGNED BY:** Jay Catalano.

The Cardinals favor college pitchers with a track record of production and durability. Lynn aced those traits, and his sinker clinched St. Louis' decision to draft him 39th overall and sign him for $938,000 in 2008. In his first full season of pro ball, he was a Double-A Texas League all-star and the Cardinals' minor league pitcher of the year. Lynn throws a 90-92 mph fastball with sink, and he complements it with control of three other pitches. The rest of his arsenal consists of a sharp slider, workable curveball and improved changeup. Consistency is the bedrock of his game, and he relies on his defense with about half of the balls put in play against him going on the ground. Being able to rely on his breaking pitches and developing a second pitch that will miss bats will be crucial as Lynn nears the majors. He can't overpower batters with velocity, which makes command all the more important and limits his ceiling. He's viewed less as a dominant starter than an innings-gobbler. Lynn will continue a steady climb with a move to Triple-A. He should slide into the back of St. Louis' rotation by mid-2011, if not sooner.

Year	Club (League)	Class	W	L	ERA	G	GS	CG	SV	IP	H	R	ER	HR	BB	SO	AVG
2008	Batavia (NYP)	SS	1	0	0.96	6	4	0	0	19	12	5	2	0	4	22	.179
	Quad Cities (MWL)	LoA	0	1	2.25	2	2	0	0	8	8	2	2	2	2	7	.258
2009	Palm Beach (FSL)	HiA	0	0	2.30	5	2	0	0	16	16	4	4	0	3	17	.276
	Springfield, MO (TL)	AA	11	4	2.92	22	22	0	0	126	117	51	41	5	51	98	.251
	Memphis (PCL)	AAA	0	0	2.70	1	1	0	0	7	5	2	2	0	3	9	.200
MINOR LEAGUE TOTALS			12	5	2.62	36	31	0	0	175	158	64	51	7	63	153	.244

4 DARYL JONES, OF $B√\iota$

BORN: June 25, 1987. **B-T:** L-L. **HT.:** 5-11. **WT.:** 180. **DRAFTED:** HS—Spring, Texas, 2005 (3rd round). **SIGNED BY:** Joe Almaraz.

A raw athlete with intriguing tools coming out of high school, Jones turned down a football scholarship to play wide receiver at Rice. He has become a more refined ballplayer with far more than just the speed and hope that fueled his first few seasons. After a breakout season in 2008, he played in the Futures Game in 2009 and was added to the 40-man roster after the season. Jones is the finest all-around athlete in the organization. His feel for the strike zone has matured, eliminating the anxiousness that sabotaged him early in his career and replacing it with a keen eye fit for a spot high in the order. His speed allows him to turn line-drive singles into doubles and gap doubles in triples, and it gives him the range to play center field. With his lack of arm strength, Jones may fit best defensively in left field. His lack of power (26 homers in 1,475 pro at-bats) doesn't profile for the position, however. He still has a lot to learn as a baserunner and basestealer. Tendinitis in both knees hampered him in 2009, as did a strain in his quadriceps, and reinforced how essential his legs are to his success. The logjam of outfielders in the system has relaxed enough that Jones is primed for Triple-A. He's on pace to make his big league debut in September, though how exactly he fits in St. Louis' future isn't clear.

Year	Club (League)	Class	AVG	G	AB	R	H	2B	3B	HR	RBI	BB	SO	SB	OBP	SLG
2005	Johnson City (APP)	R	.209	61	182	36	38	6	1	2	10	15	41	10	.311	.286
2006	Johnson City (APP)	R	.265	20	68	15	18	3	1	3	13	8	8	3	.367	.471
	Quad Cities (MWL)	LoA	.235	26	81	15	19	5	1	1	7	6	23	2	.308	.358
2007	Quad Cities (MWL)	LoA	.217	127	419	71	91	15	3	4	31	41	94	22	.304	.296
2008	Palm Beach (FSL)	HiA	.326	87	307	43	100	11	7	7	35	33	67	18	.406	.476
	Springfield (TL)	AA	.290	36	124	19	36	6	1	6	14	22	30	6	.409	.500
2009	Springfield (TL)	AA	.279	80	294	50	82	14	3	3	29	33	65	7	.360	.378
MINOR LEAGUE TOTALS			.260	437	1475	249	384	60	17	26	139	158	328	68	.349	.377

5 DAVID FREESE, 3B/1B

BORN: April 28, 1983. **B-T:** R-R. **HT.:** 6-2. **WT.:** 220. **DRAFTED:** South Alabama, 2006 (9th round). **SIGNED BY:** Bob Filotei (Padres).

Freese made the Cardinals' 2009 Opening Day roster, but his stay was fleeting. An ankle injury from a January car accident caught up with him in the spring, prevented him from seizing the wide-open third-base job and led to surgery in May. Freese was arrested in December on suspicion of driving while intoxicated, the fourth time in less than three years that a member of the team faced drunken-driving allegations. The Cards acquired the St. Louis native from the Padres in a December 2007 trade for Jim Edmonds, and the club picked up more of Edmonds' salary to pry Freese away. Freese has been a consistent .300 hitter, while also showing the ability to drive the ball to the opposite field. Memphis won two playoff games by 1-0 scores, both times on Freese homers. His short swing and good bat speed already have translated well in a few major league at-bats. When healthy, he has been more than serviceable at third base, where he shows solid arm strength. Freese can bury himself in whiffs at times, such as when he struck out 24 times in 85 at-bats last August. It's not clear his power will translate immediately in the majors, though he figures to keep his average up. He's a below-average athlete and runner. Encouraged by Freese's production after his foot surgery, St. Louis will give him every chance to start at third base. He'll be 27, so he needs to seize the opportunity.

Year	Club (League)	Class	AVG	G	AB	R	H	2B	3B	HR	RBI	BB	SO	SB	OBP	SLG
2006	Eugene (NWL)	SS	.379	18	58	19	22	8	0	5	26	7	12	0	.465	.776
	Fort Wayne (MWL)	LoA	.299	53	204	27	61	13	3	8	44	21	44	1	.374	.510
2007	Lake Elsinore (CAL)	HiA	.302	128	503	104	152	31	6	17	96	69	99	6	.400	.489
2008	Memphis (PCL)	AAA	.306	131	464	83	142	29	3	26	91	39	111	5	.361	.550
2009	Cardinals (GCL)	R	.455	4	11	2	5	2	0	1	6	1	3	0	.500	.909
	Springfield, MO (TL)	AA	.375	4	16	3	6	1	0	1	5	2	2	0	.444	.625
	Memphis (PCL)	AAA	.300	56	200	34	60	15	0	10	37	22	51	1	.369	.525
	St. Louis (NL)	MAJ	.323	17	31	3	10	2	0	1	7	2	7	0	.353	.484
MAJOR LEAGUE TOTALS			.323	17	31	3	10	2	0	1	7	2	7	0	.353	.484
MINOR LEAGUE TOTALS			.308	394	1456	272	448	99	12	68	305	161	322	13	.384	.532

6 EDUARDO SANCHEZ, RHP

BORN: Feb. 16, 1989. **B-T:** R-R. **HT.:** 5-11. **WT.:** 155. **SIGNED:** Venezuela, 2005. **SIGNED BY:** Enrique Brito.

An unheralded acquisition from the Cardinals' expanding presence in Latin America, Sanchez wasn't big and his mechanics were raw when the Cardinals signed him. He threw 92-93 mph when he joined their Rookie-level Venezuelan Summer League affiliate in 2006. Three years later, he was the system's breakout prospect of 2009. After Double-A Springfield made him a full-time closer at the end of July, he had a 2.25 ERA and converted eight of 11 save opportunities. Despite his size, Sanchez is a true fireballer. His fastball consistently works at 95 mph and reaches 97. Unlike several other Cardinals relief prospects, he has the makings of good command to go with his velocity. His sharp slider gives him a second strikeout pitch and is especially tough on righthanders. He has the poise to handle the closer's role. Sanchez's build is a concern for some scouts, who wonder if he can hold up over the long grind of a season. He was able to maintain his velocity through 60 appearances last season, however. His control was an issue at times in Double-A. Sanchez is a candidate for a nonroster invitation to big league camp. While he may open the 2010 season by returning to Double-A, he could make the leap to the big leagues during the summer.

Year	Club (League)	Class	W	L	ERA	G	GS	CG	SV	IP	H	R	ER	HR	BB	SO	AVG
2006	Cardinals (VSL)	R	1	2	8.71	19	2	0	0	31	47	33	30	3	24	38	.351
2007	Cardinals (GCL)	R	0	1	1.50	7	0	0	3	6	2	2	1	0	6	7	.100
	Johnson City (APP)	R	2	1	1.17	12	0	0	5	15	8	2	2	0	3	22	.154
2008	Quad Cities (MWL)	LoA	5	1	2.86	24	5	0	1	57	40	23	18	1	25	55	.209
2009	Palm Beach (FSL)	HiA	0	1	1.44	19	0	0	3	25	12	4	4	2	5	26	.146
	Springfield, MO (TL)	AA	2	0	2.70	41	0	0	10	50	32	16	15	4	20	56	.187
MINOR LEAGUE TOTALS			10	6	3.42	122	7	0	22	184	141	80	70	10	83	204	.217

7 ALLEN CRAIG, OF/1B/3B _T. †_

BORN: July 18, 1984. **B-T:** R-R. **HT.:** 6-2. **WT.:** 210. **DRAFTED:** California, 2006 (8th round). **SIGNED BY:** Dane Walker.

A defensive hot potato since his days in college, Craig played shortstop, left field and first base for California and has seen time at all four infield positions and both outfield corners as a pro. In big league camp last spring, he hit well in exhibition games but didn't get a single inning at third base despite the position being wide open. He ranked third in the Pacific Coast League in homers (26) and fourth in hitting (.322) last season and was added to the 40-man roster. Craig has a level swing with good torque and bat speed. He generates the best and most consistent power, and he has hit at least .304 with at least 22 homers in each of his three full seasons. Scouts say his bat is major league ready. The Cardinals aren't sure where to play Craig and don't consider him an option to fill their hole at third base. His lack of range and arm strength, plus a quirky throwing motion, work against him at the hot corner. First base isn't an option with Albert Pujols in St. Louis, so Craig played mostly left field in 2009. His below-average speed and arm make him an adequate defender at best, but he works hard and his bat does profile for the position. Craig's hitting has forced the Cardinals to consider him for at least a big league bench role, even if they haven't figured out his position. He's also an option in case they don't re-sign Matt Holliday and don't find a more established left fielder.

Year	Club (League)	Class	AVG	G	AB	R	H	2B	3B	HR	RBI	BB	SO	SB	OBP	SLG
2006	State College (NYP)	SS	.257	48	175	21	45	13	0	4	29	13	28	0	.325	.400
2007	Palm Beach (FSL)	HiA	.312	112	423	77	132	25	2	21	77	35	79	8	.370	.530
	Springfield, MO (TL)	AA	.292	7	24	5	7	2	0	3	3	1	6	0	.320	.750
2008	Springfield, MO (TL)	AA	.304	129	506	84	154	30	0	22	85	48	87	2	.373	.494
2009	Memphis (PCL)	AAA	.322	126	472	78	152	26	1	26	83	37	95	3	.374	.547
MINOR LEAGUE TOTALS			.306	422	1600	265	490	96	3	76	277	134	295	13	.366	.513

8 BLAKE HAWKSWORTH, RHP

BORN: March 1, 1983. **B-T:** R-R. **HT.:** 6-3. **WT.:** 195. **DRAFTED:** Bellevue (Wash.) CC, D/F 2001 (28th round). **SIGNED BY:** Dane Walker.

Hawksworth signed for $1.475 million in May 2002, the third-highest bonus ever as part of the now-extinct draft-and-follow process, and ranked No. 1 on this list two years later. Then ankle and shoulder problems ruined his 2004 and '05 seasons and required surgery, and he missed time in '07 (toe) and '08 (knee) with other ailments. He stayed healthy in 2009 and emerged as a surprise boost for the big league bullpen. Hawksworth's fastball can still cook in the low 90s with late movement. His changeup gives him a second plus pitch. He has a hard-won and battle-tested poise along with a quick, consistent delivery. Hawksworth is best when he's aggressive, though he has lapses of confidence as a starter that lead to command trouble. Because he doesn't have a reliable breaking ball, he becomes changeup-happy when he decides he can't trust his fastball. He'll need a third pitch if he's going to make it as a starter. Though the Cardinals need a starter and may give Hawksworth a look in that role in spring training, some club officials believe he should remain in the role in which he blossomed. As one coach said, "We never saw him this good as a starter."

Year	Club (League)	Class	W	L	ERA	G	GS	CG	SV	IP	H	R	ER	HR	BB	SO	AVG
2002	Johnson City (APP)	R	2	4	3.14	13	12	0	0	66	58	31	23	8	18	61	.232
	New Jersey (NYP)	SS	1	0	0.00	2	2	0	0	10	6	0	0	0	2	8	.171
2003	Peoria (MWL)	LoA	5	1	2.30	10	10	0	0	55	37	16	14	0	12	57	.187
	Palm Beach (FSL)	HiA	1	3	3.94	6	6	0	0	32	28	14	14	2	11	32	.235
2004	Palm Beach (FSL)	HiA	1	0	5.91	2	2	0	0	11	10	7	7	2	3	11	.250
2005	New Jersey (NYP)	SS	0	3	7.98	7	6	0	0	15	18	18	13	0	10	12	.321
2006	Palm Beach (FSL)	HiA	4	2	2.47	14	14	0	0	84	75	23	23	0	19	55	.247
	Springfield (TL)	AA	4	2	3.39	13	13	0	0	80	72	34	30	8	31	66	.248
2007	Memphis (PCL)	AAA	4	13	5.28	25	25	0	0	130	150	82	76	24	41	88	.295
2008	Cardinals (GCL)	R	0	0	0.00	2	2	0	0	7	2	0	0	0	2	6	.091
	Memphis (PCL)	AAA	5	7	6.09	18	16	0	0	89	111	71	60	12	38	83	.307
2009	Memphis (PCL)	AAA	5	4	3.58	12	12	1	0	73	61	31	29	3	20	57	.222
	St. Louis (NL)	MAJ	4	0	2.03	30	0	0	0	40	29	10	9	2	15	20	.209
MAJOR LEAGUE TOTALS			4	0	2.03	30	0	0	0	40	29	10	9	2	15	20	.209
MINOR LEAGUE TOTALS			35	39	4.01	124	120	1	0	649	628	327	289	59	207	536	.255

9 DANIEL DESCALSO, 2B

BORN: Oct. 19, 1986. **B-T:** L-R. **HT.:** 5-10. **WT.:** 190. **DRAFTED:** UC Davis, 2007 (3rd round). **SIGNED BY:** Jay North.

Descalso hit a soft .258 in his first two years of pro ball before breaking out when he reached Double-A in 2009. He hit .385 in April and was leading the Texas League in total bases (153) when he was promoted to Triple-A in early July. He won a gold medal with Team USA at the World Cup in September. Descalso's quick, level swing is built for gap power and the occasional home run. He has good feel for the strike zone, which heightens his ability to get on base when he's not hitting. His average speed plays up on the bases because he has good instincts. He has a very strong arm for a second baseman, enhancing his ability to turn the double play. He also has reliable range and soft hands. His pop wasn't as evident once Descalso reached Triple-A. If he can't produce a steady supply of doubles, he's unlikely to be a regular. He's limited in a utility role because he doesn't cover enough ground to play much at shortstop. The Cardinals lost Jarrett Hoffpauir on waivers, marking Descalso's arrival at the top of the system's depth chart at second base. After his first trip to big league camp, he'll return to Memphis and hope his bat gets going again.

Year	Club (League)	Class	AVG	G	AB	R	H	2B	3B	HR	RBI	BB	SO	SB	OBP	SLG
2007	Batavia (NYP)	SS	.268	66	250	29	67	7	5	0	31	26	37	12	.346	.336
2008	Palm Beach (FSL)	HiA	.243	115	403	57	98	24	2	8	50	33	53	7	.313	.372
	Springfield (TL)	AA	.351	9	37	6	13	1	1	0	4	3	2	1	.405	.432
2009	Springfield (TL)	AA	.323	73	288	46	93	26	5	8	51	31	41	0	.396	.531
	Memphis (PCL)	AAA	.253	46	150	23	38	4	0	2	17	16	21	3	.327	.320
MINOR LEAGUE TOTALS			.274	309	1128	161	309	62	13	18	153	109	154	23	.346	.400

10 ROBERT STOCK, C

BORN: Nov. 21, 1989. **B-T:** L-R. **HT.:** 6-0. **WT.:** 175. **DRAFTED:** Southern California, 2009 (2nd round). **SIGNED BY:** Jamal Strong.

Stock was Baseball America's Youth Player of the Year in 2005, and a year later he graduated high school early so he could enroll at Southern California. His bat and defense tailed off after his freshman year with the Trojans, and scouts got more interested in him as a pitcher last spring. But he prefers to catch, and the Cardinals are giving him a chance to do that after drafting him as a 19-year-old junior. He signed for $525,000. Stock has a cannon for a right arm, and his fastball hit 95 mph in college. He has a quick transfer and makes accurate throws, nailing 29 percent of basestealers in his pro debut. He has good lefthanded power, makes consistent contact and had no problems hitting with wood in his first pro summer. Stock batted just .263 in college and still has to prove he can hit enough to be an everyday player. His supporters think his age mitigated his college performance, while his detractors think he'll wind up as a pitcher. His biggest need defensively is to improve his receiving. He has below-average speed but isn't bad for a catcher. St. Louis hopes to advance Stock and 2009 first-rounder Shelby Miller together through the minors, and they'll begin their first full pro season in low Class A.

Year	Club (League)	Class	AVG	G	AB	R	H	2B	3B	HR	RBI	BB	SO	SB	OBP	SLG
2009	Johnson City (APP)	R	.322	41	149	25	48	9	2	7	24	11	28	0	.386	.550
	Quad Cities (MWL)	LoA	.095	5	21	1	2	0	0	0	0	2	5	0	.208	.095
MINOR LEAGUE TOTALS			.294	46	170	26	50	9	2	7	24	13	33	0	.363	.494

11 ADAM OTTAVINO, RHP

BORN: Nov. 22, 1985. **B-T:** R-R. **HT.:** 6-5. **WT.:** 230. **DRAFTED:** Northeastern, 2006 (1st round). **SIGNED BY:** Kobe Perez.

Ottavino progressed nicely in his first three seasons after signing for $950,000 as a 2006 first-round pick. But he has been hammered in the upper minors the last two years, and some Cardinals coaches wonder if he bought too much into the organization's emphasis on a natural, fluid delivery and became too undisciplined. His 2009 highlight came when he shut out a stacked Venezuela lineup for three innings while pitching for Italy in the World Baseball Classic. With a strong build and quick arm, Ottavino cuts the image of a power pitcher. His four-seam fastball climbs into the high 90s, and he can command it in the mid-90s. He also throws a two-seamer in the low 90s, and he has tightened his once-slurvy breaking ball. Ottavino is experimental to a fault. He has tinkered with his delivery each year, adding a high hand swing, then subtracting it, speeding his leg lift, then slowing it, and so on. All of that has contributed to erratic command and the stunted development of his other pitches, such as his changeup. He's running out of believers who think he can stick in a big league rotation. After the Cardinals staged a delivery intervention, Ottavino showed improvement down the stretch, and was added to the 40-man roster after the season. He'll return to Triple-A in 2010, which is probably his last chance to prove he can cut it as a starter.

Year	Club (League)	Class	W	L	ERA	G	GS	CG	SV	IP	H	R	ER	HR	BB	SO	AVG
2006	State College (NYP)	SS	2	2	3.14	6	6	0	0	29	23	12	10	1	13	26	.211
	Quad Cities (MWL)	LoA	2	3	3.44	8	8	0	0	37	28	21	14	3	19	38	.211
2007	Palm Beach (FSL)	HiA	12	8	3.08	27	27	1	0	143	130	63	49	10	63	128	.239
2008	Springfield, MO (TL)	AA	3	7	5.23	24	24	1	0	115	133	75	67	16	52	96	.291
2009	Memphis (PCL)	AAA	7	12	4.75	27	27	0	0	144	141	80	76	12	82	119	.261
MINOR LEAGUE TOTALS			26	32	4.15	92	92	2	0	468	455	251	216	42	229	407	.255

12 FRANCISCO SAMUEL, RHP

BORN: Dec. 20, 1986. **B-T:** R-R. **HT.:** 6-2. **WT.:** 185. **SIGNED:** Dominican Republic, 2006. **SIGNED BY:** Rene Rojas.

Slight of build but strong-armed, Samuel has some of the most electric stuff in the system. If he's ever able to harness it, he's capable of bolting to the big leagues and possibly becoming a closer. The reed-thin reliever has become the headliner from the Cardinals' campus in the Dominican Republic, which the team opened in November 2005, and was added to the 40-man roster last fall. His fastball touches 98 mph regularly, but that's when he's just letting it loose. He has better control of his heater at 94-95, and control is the key to his future. He has walked 153 batters in 162 pro innings, and his inability to throw consistent strikes cost him the closer's job to Eduardo Sanchez in Springfield last summer. The combination of Samuel's high-energy fastball and his 85-90 mph slider makes him virtually unhittable. He has an easy, explosive delivery with none of the high-exertion mechanics of other fireballers. Sometimes his delivery wavers, causing him to leave his pitches up in the zone. But most believe his command troubles are mental rather than mechanical. As one club official said, "Someday it's going to click." That's the day Samuel speeds to the majors.

Year	Club (League)	Class	W	L	ERA	G	GS	CG	SV	IP	H	R	ER	HR	BB	SO	AVG
2006	Cardinals (DSL)	R	1	3	7.56	11	4	0	0	17	24	19	14	0	19	17	.364
2007	Cardinals (GCL)	R	0	4	9.53	13	6	0	0	34	43	42	36	2	35	40	.309
2008	Quad Cities (MWL)	LoA	2	0	1.23	5	0	0	1	7	4	3	1	0	5	9	.154
	Palm Beach (FSL)	HiA	4	6	3.04	54	0	0	29	56	39	20	19	3	48	85	.196
2009	Springfield, MO (TL)	AA	3	4	5.66	52	0	0	22	48	36	33	30	2	46	59	.208
MINOR LEAGUE TOTALS			10	17	5.56	135	10	0	52	162	146	117	100	7	153	210	.242

13 JON JAY, OF

BORN: March 15, 1985. **B-T:** L-L. **HT.:** 5-11. **WT.:** 200. **DRAFTED:** Miami, 2006 (2nd round). **SIGNED BY:** Steve Turco.

Back when Jay was a high-average hitter for Miami, some scouts winced at the trigger he used to set up and then ignite his swing. Rather than apologize for the bobbing hands and quick loop that started his stroke, he gave it a nickname: "helicopter hands." Jay hit .308 in his first three seasons in pro ball, but when he started slowly in 2009, he tried to ground his bat waggle. He hit .324 over the final two months, joined the 40-man roster and then headed to the Venezuelan League to continue fine-tuning his swing. Jay is built to hit for average. He makes consistent contact with a level, slashing swing and shows the ability to guide line drives to the outfield. He doesn't provide much power, and while he has good speed he doesn't steal many bases. He puts the bat on the ball so easily that he doesn't get many walks, either. Jay profiles as an extra outfielder who's capable of playing left, center or right with good range and a fringy arm. Jay could break into the majors as a lefthanded-hitting fourth outfielder, just like Skip Schumaker did. Schumaker became a regular by playing multiple positions and hitting .300, and Jay has the same upside.

Year	Club (League)	Class	AVG	G	AB	R	H	2B	3B	HR	RBI	BB	SO	SB	OBP	SLG
2006	Quad Cities (MWL)	LoA	.342	60	234	42	80	13	3	3	45	28	27	9	.416	.462
2007	Springfield, MO (TL)	AA	.235	26	102	17	24	4	2	2	11	11	19	4	.333	.373
	Cardinals (GCL)	R	.500	1	2	0	1	0	0	0	0	0	1	0	.500	.500
	Palm Beach (FSL)	HiA	.286	32	126	19	36	8	0	2	10	5	25	5	.321	.397
2008	Springfield, MO (TL)	AA	.306	96	372	57	114	17	3	11	47	39	46	10	.379	.457
	Memphis (PCL)	AAA	.345	16	58	8	20	4	1	1	10	6	10	0	.406	.500
2009	Memphis (PCL)	AAA	.281	136	505	72	142	23	2	10	54	34	64	20	.338	.394
MINOR LEAGUE TOTALS			.298	367	1399	215	417	69	11	29	177	123	192	48	.363	.425

14 TYLER GREENE, SS/3B

BORN: Aug. 17, 1983. **B-T:** R-R. **HT.:** 6-2. **WT.:** 190. **DRAFTED:** Georgia Tech, 2005 (1st round). **SIGNED BY:** Roger Smith.

The career surge that started in the second half of 2008 continued through last season for Greene, who signed for $1.1 million as the 30th overall pick in the 2005 draft. He caught the eye of the major league coaching staff in spring training and turned that into a 48-game stint with the Cardinals. Greene's athleticism is his most marketable tool and was on full display in his first full pro season, when he hit 20 homers and stole 33 bases. But in June 2007, he dislodged his right kneecap on a swing. It took time for him to regain trust in his knee, and it took longer to regain traction with his career. Greene has plus speed and good pop for a middle infielder, but he continues to fight his freewheeling, all-or-nothing approach at the plate. He has more than enough arm strength to play shortstop, but he can get erratic at times and may not be able to play there on an everyday basis in the big leagues. Greene played all four infield positions as well as center field for St. Louis last season, and he'll try to win a utility role in spring training.

Year	Club (League)	Class	AVG	G	AB	R	H	2B	3B	HR	RBI	BB	SO	SB	OBP	SLG
2005	New Jersey (NYP)	SS	.261	35	138	28	36	12	0	1	18	15	37	13	.352	.370
	Palm Beach (FSL)	HiA	.271	20	85	17	23	4	0	2	5	5	28	6	.326	.388
2006	Palm Beach (FSL)	HiA	.224	71	268	38	60	10	1	5	19	29	90	22	.308	.325
	Quad Cities (MWL)	LoA	.287	59	223	42	64	8	3	15	47	20	65	11	.375	.552
2007	Springfield, MO (TL)	AA	.244	65	221	41	54	17	2	8	25	16	62	10	.309	.448
2008	Springfield, MO (TL)	AA	.259	97	374	62	97	15	4	16	41	22	99	14	.307	.449
	Memphis (PCL)	AAA	.234	30	111	17	26	7	0	0	7	11	35	6	.325	.297
2009	Memphis (PCL)	AAA	.291	89	340	70	99	10	5	15	42	38	86	31	.369	.482
	St. Louis (NL)	MAJ	.222	48	108	9	24	5	0	2	7	4	32	3	.270	.324
MAJOR LEAGUE TOTALS			.222	48	108	9	24	5	0	2	7	4	32	3	.270	.324
MINOR LEAGUE TOTALS			.261	466	1760	315	459	83	15	62	204	156	502	113	.334	.431

15 PETE KOZMA, SS

BORN: April 11, 1988. **B-T:** R-R. **HT.:** 6-0. **WT.:** 170. **DRAFTED:** HS—Owasso, Okla. 2007 (1st round). **SIGNED BY:** Steve Gossett.

Perhaps Kozma put it best when he was asked to describe himself and said there was nothing flashy about his abilities. Though he was the 18th overall pick in the 2007 draft and signed for $1.395 million, not one of his tools sparkles likely the prototypical first-round pick. Rather, it's Kozma's steady play that defines him as a prospect. He's a well-rounded player whom managers rated as the best defensive infielder in the Texas League last summer. He isn't the high-wire act that some more athletic infielders are, preferring instinctual jumps, quick exchanges and reliable range to dirt stains, wild throws and highlight dives. Kozma's defense is good enough for the big leagues, but his bat has been slower to develop. When they drafted him, the Cardinals acknowledged then that his feel for hitting and line-drive swing might take time to provide results. He rarely chases bad balls, and the Cardinals believe his ability to hit for average and gap power will improve when he makes better contact with pitches in the zone. Kozma will return to Double-A in 2010, with St. Louis hoping that he'll improve the second time around. That was the case for him at high Class A Palm Beach, where he hit .130 in 24 games in 2008 but jumped to .315 in 18 games last April, earning a swift promotion to Springfield. He grows on people the more they see him play, but many scouts still see him as more of a utilityman than an everyday player.

Year	Club (League)	Class	AVG	G	AB	R	H	2B	3B	HR	RBI	BB	SO	SB	OBP	SLG
2007	Cardinals (GCL)	R	.154	4	13	4	2	0	0	0	2	2	0	.267	.154
	Johnson City (APP)	R	.264	30	106	16	28	8	0	2	9	12	21	3	.350	.396
	Batavia (NYP)	SS	.148	8	27	1	4	0	1	0	2	1	7	1	.179	.222
2008	Quad Cities (MWL)	LoA	.284	99	377	58	107	20	4	5	40	45	69	12	.363	.398
	Palm Beach (FSL)	HiA	.130	24	77	4	10	4	0	0	10	10	27	0	.231	.182
2009	Palm Beach (FSL)	HiA	.315	18	73	8	23	5	0	0	8	8	16	1	.381	.384
	Springfield, MO (TL)	AA	.216	113	407	52	88	15	3	6	37	42	88	4	.288	.312
MINOR LEAGUE TOTALS			.243	296	1080	143	262	52	8	13	106	120	230	21	.320	.342

16 ADAM REIFER, RHP

BORN: June 3, 1986. **B-T:** R-R. **HT.:** 6-2. **WT.:** 195. **DRAFTED:** UC Riverside, 2007 (11th round). **SIGNED BY:** Jeff Ishii.

Though he pitched just seven innings while battling bone spurs and elbow tendinitis as a UC Riverside junior, the Cardinals invested an 11th-round pick in the 2007 draft and a $100,000 bonus in Reifer. He rated as the best pitching prospect in the short-season New York-Penn League in his 2008 pro debut, then skipped a level and closed games in high Class A last season. He features one of the best fastballs in the system, hitting 96-97 mph consistently and peaking at 99. He also has a slider that grades as a plus-plus pitch at times. His control and command don't score as high, however. Reifer lacks life on his four-seam fastball and often struggles to find the strike zone, getting into more jams than someone with his stuff should. St. Louis will keep him in the closer's role as he advances, though he'll need more command and more cool under duress to succeed at higher levels.

Year	Club (League)	Class	W	L	ERA	G	GS	CG	SV	IP	H	R	ER	HR	BB	SO	AVG
2008	Batavia (NYP)	SS	2	1	2.97	32	0	0	22	30	18	14	10	2	15	41	.162
2009	Palm Beach (FSL)	HiA	4	7	4.47	54	0	0	21	48	51	28	24	2	24	50	.270
MINOR LEAGUE TOTALS			6	8	3.89	86	0	0	43	79	69	42	34	4	39	91	.230

17 RICHARD CASTILLO, RHP

BORN: Oct. 11, 1989. **B-T:** R-R. **HT.:** 5-11. **WT.:** 165. **SIGNED:** Venezuela, 2007. **SIGNED BY:** Gregorio Gonzalez.

The Cardinals aren't afraid to aggressively promote prospects, and they've pushed Castillo as fast as any of their recent international signings. He made his U.S. debut in high Class A as an 18-year-old in May 2008, coming over from extended spring training when Palm Beach needed a spot starter. He acquitted himself well for three weeks and then pitched well when he was sent to low Class A to start on a regular basis. Castillo returned to Palm Beach in 2009 and spent the entire season there as the youngest starting pitcher in the Florida State League. Though he's undersized, Castillo has a loose delivery and St. Louis expects that he'll add hop to his 90-91 mph fastball as he fills out. His curveball has good snap and can be a true swing-and-miss pitch. He also has made progress with his changeup. Though he's advanced for his age, Castillo still has a lot to work on. He needs to throw strikes more consistently, and the Cardinals would like to see his conditioning and between-start work habits improve. That should come with maturity. So too will another promotion.

Year	Club (League)	Class	W	L	ERA	G	GS	CG	SV	IP	H	R	ER	HR	BB	SO	AVG
2007	Cardinals (VSL)	R	2	2	1.72	17	8	0	2	63	40	20	12	3	22	60	.183
2008	Palm Beach (FSL)	HiA	1	0	1.13	6	2	0	0	16	12	3	2	0	8	19	.222
	Quad Cities (MWL)	LoA	8	4	2.62	13	13	0	0	79	64	26	23	11	20	69	.227
2009	Palm Beach (FSL)	HiA	6	13	3.87	29	26	1	0	149	155	77	64	4	66	105	.270
MINOR LEAGUE TOTALS			17	19	2.97	65	49	1	2	306	271	126	101	18	116	253	.240

18 TYLER HENLEY, OF

BORN: June 10, 1985. **B-T:** L-L. **HT.:** 5-10. **WT.:** 200. **DRAFTED:** Rice, 2007 (8th round). **SIGNED BY:** Joe Almaraz.

Henley sprinted to a .313/.370/.531 start in high Class A in April 2008 before he took his reputation for gritty, gutty play to an unlucky extreme. A fastball cut in on his hands as he squared to bunt, and his finger got pinched between the ball and bat with such force that it severed the tip. He had the finger sewn back together and missed seven weeks, but added oomph to his nickname "Psycho T." Given a full, healthy season in 2009, Henley cracked the dense thicket of outfielders in the system and emerged as one of the best. He earned Texas League all-star honors, showing an ability to hit for average (.303) and gap power (31 doubles). He has worked to improve his weight transfer so that he can develop more power, most consistently. An aggressive hitter, he rarely takes a strike and often pounces on the first pitch, but he makes consistent contact. With solid speed and arm strength, he's capable of playing all three spots in the outfield and fits best in right field. An invitation to the Arizona Fall League boosted his chance to show there's more to his game than grass stains. He'll advance to Triple-A in 2010.

Year	Club (League)	Class	AVG	G	AB	R	H	2B	3B	HR	RBI	BB	SO	SB	OBP	SLG
2007	Batavia (NYP)	SS	.281	18	57	14	16	2	1	0	7	8	9	4	.403	.351
	Quad Cities (MWL)	LoA	.156	12	32	4	5	2	0	2	5	1	9	0	.200	.406
2008	Cardinals (GCL)	R	.368	5	19	6	7	3	1	1	2	1	2	0	.429	.789
	Palm Beach (FSL)	HiA	.280	84	329	47	92	26	4	6	40	27	51	7	.342	.438
2009	Springfield, MO (TL)	AA	.303	123	423	62	128	31	3	13	63	40	64	9	.367	.482
MINOR LEAGUE TOTALS			.288	242	860	133	248	64	9	22	117	77	135	20	.355	.460

19 BRYAN ANDERSON, C

BORN: Dec. 16, 1986. **B-T:** L-R. **HT.:** 6-1. **WT.:** 200. **DRAFTED:** HS—Simi Valley, Calif., 2005 (4th round). **SIGNED BY:** Jay North.

Anderson was in the midst of the worst season of his five-year pro career when a June 25 collision at home plate left him with a dislocated left shoulder and two torn ligaments in the joint. Anderson originally thought he'd need season-ending shoulder surgery, but on the day the operation was scheduled, the Cardinals' team doctor suggested he try rest and rehab. Anderson returned to get in a few games in the Rookie-level Gulf Coast League at the end of the season and was able play in the Arizona Fall League. The Cardinals also added him to the 40-man roster. He's still young and still has the fluid lefthanded swing that enabled him to hit .299 as a pro. However, his bat may be his lone solid-average tool. He has yet to develop the gap power that St. Louis projected for him, and he's still shaky behind the plate despite special instruction from former Gold Glove winner Mike Matheny. Anderson has fringy arm strength and unorthodox mechanics that cost him accuracy, and he threw out just 28 percent of basestealers in Triple-A last season. He also needs to improve his receiving and blocking skills. Like most catchers, he's a below-average runner. Anderson will return to Memphis, possibly in a time share with the defensive-minded Matt Pagnozzi, and try to re-establish his worth within the organization.

ST. LOUIS CARDINALS

Year	Club (League)	Class	AVG	G	AB	R	H	2B	3B	HR	RBI	BB	SO	SB	OBP	SLG
2005	Johnson City (APP)	R	.331	51	154	28	51	8	1	6	36	15	29	6	.383	.513
2006	Quad Cities (MWL)	LoA	.302	109	381	50	115	29	3	3	51	42	66	2	.377	.417
2007	Springfield, MO (TL)	AA	.298	103	389	51	116	15	1	6	53	32	77	0	.350	.388
2008	Springfield, MO (TL)	AA	.388	19	80	12	31	5	0	2	14	4	12	0	.412	.525
	Memphis (PCL)	AAA	.281	73	235	27	66	13	2	2	27	32	46	2	.367	.379
2009	Memphis (PCL)	AAA	.245	53	163	22	40	7	3	4	11	10	42	1	.293	.399
	Cardinals (GCL)	R	.313	5	16	3	5	0	0	1	2	4	4	1	.450	.500
MINOR LEAGUE TOTALS			.299	413	1418	193	424	77	10	24	194	139	276	12	.362	.418

20 SAM FREEMAN, LHP

BORN: June 24, 1987. **B-T:** R-L. **HT.:** 5-11. **WT.:** 170. **DRAFTED:** Kansas, 2008 (32nd round). **SIGNED BY:** Joe Almaraz.

As a freshman at North Central Texas CC, Freeman stood out more as a fleet-footed outfielder than as a pitcher. He started to realize his arm was his ticket when he was a full-fledged two-way player as a sophomore, and he became a full-time pitcher after transferring to Kansas in 2008. The Cardinals failed to sign him as a 24th-round pick in 2007 but landed him in the 32nd round a year later, after he had posted an 8.53 ERA as a swingman for the Jayhawks. They believe he could scoot swiftly through their system as a lefty specialist or even a set-up man. Despite his relative inexperience, he reached Double-A at the end of his first full pro season. Wiry and athletic, he has a quick arm that generates 92-95 mph fastballs. He also throws a cutter/slider and has toyed with a changeup. He came out of college with a herky-jerky delivery that he has smoothed out with more experience and instruction. Freeman likes to pitch inside, sometimes almost to a fault, leading to walks. In short-burst relief, he has done well against lefthanders, who batted 9-for-60 (.150) with no extra-base hits and 15 strikeouts against him in 2009. A sprained elbow ended his season in late July, but the Cardinals think he'll be healthy for 2010, when he'll return to Double-A.

Year	Club (League)	Class	W	L	ERA	G	GS	CG	SV	IP	H	R	ER	HR	BB	SO	AVG
2008	Johnson City (APP)	R	4	1	3.70	20	0	0	2	24	23	15	10	2	12	34	.250
	Palm Beach (FSL)	HiA	0	0	0.00	1	0	0	0	2	0	0	0	0	1	4	.000
2009	Palm Beach (FSL)	HiA	2	1	1.64	26	0	0	1	33	18	7	6	0	13	30	.157
	Springfield, MO (TL)	AA	0	1	3.52	15	0	0	1	23	19	9	9	6	14	17	.241
MINOR LEAGUE TOTALS			6	3	2.73	62	0	0	4	82	60	31	25	8	40	85	.205

21 JOE KELLY, RHP

BORN: June 9, 1988. **B-T:** R-R. **HT.:** 6-1. **WT.:** 165. **DRAFTED:** UC Riverside, 2009 (3rd round). **SIGNED BY:** Jeff Ishii.

Kelly set a UC Riverside record with 24 career saves, and the Cardinals signed him for $341,000 as a 2009 third-round pick to be a reliever. But it didn't take long for the organization to decide to try him as a starter. He'll begin 2010 in a rotation, probably in low Class A. He may not cut the image of a power pitcher with his skinny 6-foot-1 frame, but Kelly has a 94-95 mph fastball that has been known to hit 98. He has an aggressive flair for using his fastball, which has biting sink and generates a lot of swings and misses and weak grounders. His hard slider and changeup both have a chance to be at least average pitches, which is why the Cardinals think he can make it as a starter. The biggest questions for Kelly in that role will be whether he'll have enough command to keep his pitch counts down and enough durability to log the heavier workload. He had shoulder problems early in his college career and throws with a lot of effort in his delivery. Scouts aren't in love with his mechanics because he has a big arm sweep in the back of his delivery that makes it difficult for his arm to catch up with the rest of his body. At the least, working out of the rotation will give him the opportunity to work on his secondary pitches.

Year	Club (League)	Class	W	L	ERA	G	GS	CG	SV	IP	H	R	ER	HR	BB	SO	AVG
2009	Batavia (NYP)	SS	2	3	4.75	16	2	0	1	30	33	23	16	0	11	30	.273
MINOR LEAGUE TOTALS			2	3	4.75	16	2	0	1	30	33	23	16	0	11	30	.273

22 SCOTT BITTLE, RHP

BORN: Aug. 27, 1986. **B-T:** R-R. **HT.:** 6-2. **WT.:** 195. **DRAFTED:** Mississippi, 2009 (4th round). **SIGNED BY:** Jay Catalano.

Every bit of scouting the Cardinals did on Bittle screamed "quick-moving college reliever" with a true out pitch, and then they got his medical records. Intelligence gathered about his problematic shoulder before the draft was a red flag and a team physical reinforced those concerns. The Yankees drafted Bittle in the second round in 2008 but didn't sign him because of worries about the wear and tear on his shoulder, and he missed the last six weeks of his senior season with a strain in his shoulder capsule. He also sat out the 2006 season at Northeast Texas CC with rotator-cuff tendinitis. After signing for $75,000 as a fourth-round pick, Bittle reported for rehab at the Cardinals' facility in Jupiter, Fla. St. Louis believed he could have pitched but didn't activate him. When healthy, Bittle owned the Southeastern Conference for three years with an 84-86 mph cutter. He averaged 14.6

strikeouts per nine innings at Mississippi, even though hitters were looking for the cutter. Bittle also throws an upper-80s sinker that tops out at 92, and an average changeup. Besides his shoulder, the only real concern is that his cutter moves so much it's often a ball if hitters lay off it. Ticketed to make his pro debut in high Class A, he has a lot of bite in his game as long as his shoulder doesn't bark.

Year	Club (League)	Class	W	L	ERA	G	GS	CG	SV	IP	H	R	ER	HR	BB	SO	AVG
2009	Did Not Play—Injured																

23 P.J. WALTERS, RHP

BORN: March 3, 1985. **B-T:** R-R. **HT.:** 6-4. **WT.:** 200. **DRAFTED:** South Alabama, 2006 (11th round). **SIGNED BY:** Scott Nichols.

It took one start at Wrigley Field for Walters to show both what he's capable of and what he has to do to win at the major league level. The righthander with the devilish changeup struck out seven Cubs in four innings during a spot start on April 17, but many of the whiffs came on pitches out of the zone, something coaches have told him won't always work in the big leagues. In his next four outings, Walters fell behind in the count and gave up four walks and three homers over six innings, earning a return to Triple-A. Walters has a serviceable fastball that he can crank up to 89-91 mph consistently. He has improved his breaking ball to give him a third pitch, but it's his changeup that's the key to his success. It has screwball life and rides in on righthanders, and his easy delivery masks the true speed of the pitch. Walters slashed his home run numbers down from 22 in 2008 to just six in Triple-A last season, though he gave up six longballs in 16 major league innings. If he can find a way to live on the fringes of the strike zone, he'll find regular work in St. Louis, most likely as a middle reliever.

Year	Club (League)	Class	W	L	ERA	G	GS	CG	SV	IP	H	R	ER	HR	BB	SO	AVG
2006	State College (NYP)	SS	2	1	3.56	26	0	0	8	30	29	15	12	1	9	31	.242
2007	Quad Cities (MWL)	LoA	6	1	2.62	17	10	0	1	69	59	25	20	2	12	73	.229
	Palm Beach (FSL)	HiA	3	1	2.67	5	5	0	0	34	29	10	10	2	6	37	.225
	Springfield, MO (TL)	AA	3	4	2.37	8	8	1	0	49	42	13	13	4	15	37	.228
2008	Springfield, MO (TL)	AA	1	2	3.25	6	6	0	0	36	35	17	13	5	8	34	.252
	Memphis (PCL)	AAA	9	4	4.87	23	23	0	0	122	123	71	66	17	62	122	.266
2009	St. Louis (NL)	MAJ	0	0	9.56	8	1	0	0	16	21	19	17	6	9	14	.304
	Memphis (PCL)	AAA	8	10	4.54	21	20	2	0	121	128	73	61	6	44	113	.271
MAJOR LEAGUE TOTALS			0	0	9.56	8	1	0	0	16	21	19	17	6	9	14	.304
MINOR LEAGUE TOTALS			32	23	3.81	106	72	3	9	461	445	224	195	37	156	447	.252

24 STEVEN HILL, C/OF/1B

BORN: March 14, 1985. **B-T:** R-R. **HT.:** 5-11. **WT.:** 200. **DRAFTED:** Stephen F. Austin State, 2007 (13th round). **SIGNED BY:** Joe Almaraz.

After three pro seasons, Hill still finds himself without a definite position, bouncing from catcher to first base to the outfield corners. The constant remains his bat. He has cracked 48 homers in 268 pro games, after hitting 31 homers in his lone season at Eastfield (Texas) JC and a school-record 38 longballs in two years at Stephen F. Austin State. The Cardinals drafted him 412th overall in 2007, intrigued by his power and his ability to play multiple positions. His bat speed and strength allow him to drive the ball to all fields. His aggressive approach may catch up to him at higher levels, but he has hit .298 in pro ball while reaching Double-A. Short and stocky, Hill is a below-average athlete and runner who would enhance his chances of carving out a big league role if he could handle the defensive responsibilities of catching. He has enough arm strength, but his inconsistent release undermines his throwing and he nabbed just 21 percent of basestealers last season. He has improved his footwork and intuition with more experience behind the plate, but his receiving still needs polish. He lacks the desired height of a first baseman and has below-average range in the outfield, so his ultimate role could be as a righthanded power bat off the bench, capable of filling in at catcher. He'll move up to Triple-A in 2010.

Year	Club (League)	Class	AVG	G	AB	R	H	2B	3B	HR	RBI	BB	SO	SB	OBP	SLG
2007	Batavia (NYP)	SS	.436	10	39	4	17	5	1	1	11	5	5	0	.511	.692
	Quad Cities (MWL)	LoA	.303	62	261	38	79	15	0	11	44	9	58	1	.330	.487
2008	Springfield, MO (TL)	AA	.303	26	99	13	30	3	1	5	9	3	31	0	.330	.505
	Cardinals (GCL)	R	.313	4	16	4	5	1	0	3	5	0	7	0	.313	.938
	Palm Beach (FSL)	HiA	.285	46	172	28	49	11	2	9	34	15	42	0	.339	.529
2009	Springfield, MO (TL)	AA	.282	120	464	62	131	26	2	19	64	36	106	1	.333	.470
MINOR LEAGUE TOTALS			.296	268	1051	149	311	61	6	48	167	68	249	2	.340	.502

25 RYAN JACKSON, SS

BORN: May 10, 1988. **B-T:** R-R. **HT.:** 6-3. **WT.:** 180. **DRAFTED:** Miami, 2009 (5th round). **SIGNED BY:** Charlie Gonzalez.

The best defensive shortstop in college baseball in 2009, Jackson lasted until the fifth round of the draft because of questions about his bat. After hitting .360 and helping Miami reach the College World Series as a sophomore, he saw his average plummet to .263 last spring. Signed for $157,500, he batted just .216/.297/.241 in his pro debut at short-season Batavia. Jackson is thin and lacks strength, and he'll never hit for much power. He's also a below-average runner, so all of his offensive value is going to come from getting on base. He does have good discipline, though advanced pitchers aren't going to be afraid to challenge him. Jackson's defense is asset enough to buy him opportunity to work on his swing. He's nimble and slick at shortstop, and his instincts and innate footwork give him plenty of range. He has a strong arm and the confidence to improvise when needed. If Jackson can hit .250 with a respectable on-base percentage, he's a good enough defender to play regularly in the majors.

Year	Club (League)	Class	AVG	G	AB	R	H	2B	3B	HR	RBI	BB	SO	SB	OBP	SLG
2009	Batavia (NYP)	SS	.216	67	245	29	53	4	1	0	14	29	37	4	.297	.241
MINOR LEAGUE TOTALS			.216	67	245	29	53	4	1	0	14	29	37	4	.297	.241

26 MARK HAMILTON, 1B

BORN: July 29, 1984. **B-T:** L-L. **HT.:** 6-3. **WT.:** 220. **DRAFTED:** Tulane, 2006 (2nd round). **SIGNED BY:** Scott Nichols.

Hamilton slugged his way out of Tulane and into the second round of the 2006 draft with a trove of honors in his wake. He was an All-American and the Conference USA player of the year in 2006, as well as a two-time Cape Cod League all-star. After hitting 20 homers in his final season with the Green Wave, he didn't show that kind of power in pro ball until last season. He staked his place as one of the top sluggers in the system by helping revive a pedestrian Memphis lineup in time for the Redbirds to make a Pacific Coast League title run. Hamilton has a stout, muscular frame and bat speed to go with the strength that allows him to catapult balls. He's comfortable working deep counts and isn't easily fooled. All his value lies in his bat because he's a limited athlete and defender who profiles best as a DH. He has below-average athleticism, speed and arm strength. He's a substandard first baseman and he's not going to dislodge Albert Pujols anyway. Hamilton headed to the Dominican League to try to play left field, but his team released him after he batted .191 in 15 games. The Cardinals added him to the 40-man roster, and he'll return to Triple-A in 2010 and try to force them to find a place for his bat.

Year	Club (League)	Class	AVG	G	AB	R	H	2B	3B	HR	RBI	BB	SO	SB	OBP	SLG
2006	State College (NYP)	SS	.264	30	106	18	28	3	1	8	24	13	24	1	.347	.538
	Quad Cities (MWL)	LoA	.254	38	142	16	36	8	0	3	25	10	32	0	.307	.373
2007	Palm Beach (FSL)	HiA	.290	60	221	31	64	12	0	13	49	20	48	1	.348	.520
	Springfield, MO (TL)	AA	.250	68	248	32	62	15	0	6	41	24	54	1	.318	.383
2008	Springfield, MO (TL)	AA	.241	70	245	27	59	11	0	8	29	35	67	0	.338	.384
2009	Springfield, MO (TL)	AA	.307	48	163	26	50	11	0	8	28	28	46	0	.421	.521
	Memphis (PCL)	AAA	.308	46	130	22	40	11	0	6	19	13	34	0	.375	.531
MINOR LEAGUE TOTALS			.270	360	1255	172	339	71	1	52	215	143	305	3	.348	.453

27 YUNIER CASTILLO, SS

BORN: May 15, 1989. **B-T:** B-R. **HT.:** 6-0. **WT.:** 160. **SIGNED:** Dominican Republic, 2008. **SIGNED BY:** Charlie Gonzalez.

While the Cardinals have dedicated hundreds of thousands of dollars to establishing a better toehold in the Dominican Republic, one of the finest prospects they've pulled from the island was in their backyard. Scouts first saw the wiry Castillo as a teen infielder playing at a baseball academy in Miami, a reasonable drive away from the Cardinals' training complex in Jupiter, Fla. There are coaches within the organization who believe Castillo is the finest defensive shortstop in the system. He brings the aggressiveness, surehanded play and spring-loaded arm needed at the position. His instincts, quick first step and plus speed give him plenty of range. Much like Ryan Jackson, his offensive potential is sketchy. Castillo is so raw at the plate that he didn't draw a single walk in 50 games at Rookie-level Johnson City in 2009. Farm and scouting director Jeff Luhnow visited him during the season to stress the need to take pitches and work some counts, then watched Castillo take several strikes. He has modest power and is still learning how to turn his speed into steals. If he can find a happy medium between his itchy trigger and patience this spring, he'll advance to low Class A.

Year	Club (League)	Class	AVG	G	AB	R	H	2B	3B	HR	RBI	BB	SO	SB	OBP	SLG
2008	Cardinals (GCL)	R	.256	40	129	16	33	3	1	1	12	6	29	5	.285	.318
	Johnson City (APP)	R	.130	6	23	3	3	0	0	0	2	0	7	0	.125	.130
2009	Johnson City (APP)	R	.259	50	170	19	44	8	2	2	10	0	39	2	.263	.365
MINOR LEAGUE TOTALS			.248	96	322	38	80	11	3	3	24	6	75	7	.262	.329

28 BEN JUKICH, LHP

BORN: Oct. 17, 1982. **B-T:** L-L. **HT.:** 6-5. **WT.:** 205. **DRAFTED:** Dakota Wesleyan (S.D.), 2006 (13th round). **SIGNED BY:** Kevin Mello (Athletics).

When the Reds set their 40-man roster for the offseason, they knew there was a decent chance they could lose someone in the major league Rule 5 draft. Cincinnati added seven minor leaguers to its roster but couldn't find room for Jukich, a lefty with average stuff. The Reds weren't shocked to see him picked after he had shown a solid feel for pitching in Triple-A. The first player ever drafted out of Dakota Wesleyan (S.D.), he led the NAIA in strikeouts (144) and strikeouts per nine innings (13.7) before the Athletics selected him in the 13th round in 2006. A year later, Oakland traded him and Marcus McBeth to Cincinnati for Chris Denorfia. Though Jukich has pitched primarily as a starter in pro ball, the Cardinals will use him as a lefty reliever. He doesn't have a plus pitch, but he has very good command of an average three-quarters breaking ball, an 87-90 mph fastball and a fringy changeup. He hides the ball well in his delivery and gets good downward plane on his pitches. If the Cardinals are looking for a lefty specialist, Jukich may not be able to stick, but if they employ him as a long reliever, he might be useful. Rule 5 guidelines dictate that he stay on the big league roster for a year, or else he has to be placed on waivers and offered back to the Reds for half of the $50,000 draft price.

Year	Club (League)	Class	W	L	ERA	G	GS	CG	SV	IP	H	R	ER	HR	BB	SO	AVG
2006	Vancouver (NWL)	SS	0	0	3.24	3	1	0	2	8	9	3	3	0	5	10	.273
	Kane County (MWL)	LoA	3	2	2.38	13	4	0	0	42	41	15	11	1	25	40	.261
2007	Stockton (CAL)	HiA	3	4	5.40	12	12	0	0	58	61	42	35	8	15	46	.261
	Sarasota (FSL)	HiA	8	2	3.55	14	14	2	0	76	59	33	30	2	27	71	.215
2008	Chattanooga (SL)	AA	10	4	3.82	23	23	1	0	139	147	68	59	6	54	111	.281
	Louisville (IL)	AAA	1	1	4.37	4	3	0	0	23	30	14	11	2	4	15	.309
2009	Louisville (IL)	AAA	9	6	4.10	29	17	0	0	123	125	64	56	16	40	106	.264
MINOR LEAGUE TOTALS			34	19	3.93	98	74	3	2	469	472	239	205	35	170	399	.263

29 TREY HEARNE, RHP

BORN: Aug. 19, 1983. **B-T:** R-R. **HT.:** 6-1. **WT.:** 195. **DRAFTED:** Texas A&M-Corpus Christi, 2005 (28th round). **SIGNED BY:** Joe Almaraz.

Hearne ranked second in the low Class A Midwest League with a 2.25 ERA in 2006, but after he got torched for a 5.95 ERA the following season in high Class A, the Cardinals loaned him to Minatitlan in the Mexican League for the 2008 season. He pitched well and was selected to pitch in the all-star game there, but his season ended in May when he came down with elbow tendinitis. In his return to the United States, he led Cardinals farmhands with 14 wins and ranked second with a 2.92 ERA. He began the year in Springfield's bullpen, but in his second start he set a franchise record with 13 strikeouts in six innings. Hearne doesn't delight the radar gun with velocity or defy gravity with his breaking ball. What he does is throw with uncanny control and enough movement and deception to make his assortment of pitches hard to read and harder to hit squarely. At its best, his fastball zips at 88-89 mph, but his smooth delivery and quick release allow the ball to get on hitters quickly. He also throws a curveball and changeup, teasing the edges of the strike zone with all of his offerings. Hearne projects as a middle reliever and could get a big league look in 2010 after opening the season in Triple-A.

Year	Club (League)	Class	W	L	ERA	G	GS	CG	SV	IP	H	R	ER	HR	BB	SO	AVG
2005	New Jersey (NYP)	SS	4	2	2.56	24	1	0	0	39	25	15	11	2	12	42	.181
2006	Quad Cities (MWL)	LoA	12	3	2.25	31	17	0	0	128	102	42	32	10	34	106	.210
2007	Palm Beach (FSL)	HiA	5	11	5.95	31	21	0	0	138	181	103	91	10	42	90	.323
2008	Minatitlan (MEX)	AAA	5	1	2.94	9	9	0	0	52	33	22	17	0	31	51	.180
2009	Memphis (PCL)	AAA	2	1	3.38	4	4	0	0	27	23	12	10	4	6	16	.219
	Springfield, MO (TL)	AA	12	3	2.82	24	18	1	0	128	113	44	40	7	43	81	.240
MINOR LEAGUE TOTALS			40	21	3.54	123	70	1	0	511	477	238	201	33	168	386	.254

30 CESAR VALERA, SS

BORN: March 8, 1992. **B-T:** R-R. **HT.:** 6-1. **WT.:** 180. **SIGNED:** Venezuela, 2008. **SIGNED BY:** Enrique Brito.

The Cardinals sought to make a big international splash this past summer with a $3.1 million bonus for Wagner Mateo, a highly sought after center fielder from the Dominican Republic. The deal was celebrated as a statement move, but it crumbled a month later when a check of Mateo's vision led St. Louis to void the deal. The development of other players such as Valera could soften the hit. When the Cardinals went scouting Yorman Rodriguez, a Venezuelan outfielder who got $2.5 million from the Reds in 2008, the Cardinals became enamored with Valera. He showed the ability to lay off bad pitches and a line-drive swing that could generate damage as he matures. He doesn't have the raw power potential of Dominican third baseman Roberto de la Cruz, a $1.1 million bonus baby, but Valera outperformed him in the Gulf Coast League last summer. He has solid speed and defensive tools, though it's possible that he may have to move off shortstop once he matures physically. The Cardinals project him as an offensive middle infielder and likely will promote him to Johnson City in 2010.

Year	Club (League)	Class	AVG	G	AB	R	H	2B	3B	HR	RBI	BB	SO	SB	OBP	SLG
2009	Cardinals (GCL)	R	.242	54	186	32	45	10	2	1	21	10	55	8	.304	.333
MINOR LEAGUE TOTALS			.242	54	186	32	45	10	2	1	21	10	55	8	.304	.333

San Diego Padres

BY MATT EDDY

The Padres' firing of longtime general manager Kevin Towers, who had presided over an unprecedented run of franchise success in his 14 years, occurred against a backdrop of recent player-development success.

Older San Diego clubs that failed to make the playoffs in 2007 and 2008 gave way to a younger cast of players in the second half of 2009. They peaked in August and September, going 33-25 to avoid a second straight last-place finish in the National League West.

The top two players on the Padres' prospect list a year ago were at the heart of the transformation. Kyle Blanks joined the big league team in mid-June and belted 10 homers in 54 games before a foot injury ended his season in August. Mat Latos ranked as the No. 1 prospect in the Double-A Texas League before settling into San Diego's rotation in mid-July, going 4-5, 4.62. Rookies Everth Cabrera, Wade LeBlanc and Will Venable also exhausted their prospect eligibility while helping in the second-half surge.

The front-office upheaval didn't begin or stop with Towers. In March, a new ownership group fronted by former agent and Diamondbacks minority owner Jeff Moorad bought a 33 percent stake in the club from John Moores, who was ensnared in a divorce proceeding. CEO Sandy Alderson resigned after Moorad came aboard.

In late October, Moorad settled on Red Sox assistant GM Jed Hoyer to replace Towers. The Padres then fired vice president of scouting and player development Grady Fuson, who had a leading role in the club's 2005-09 drafts and also served as farm director, and reassigned scouting director Bill Gayton.

In early December, the Padres hired Red Sox scouting director Jason McLeod as assistant general manager. A San Diego native, McLeod spent a decade working for the Padres in a variety of roles before joining the Red Sox. In five drafts as scouting director, he made a succession of strong picks, including Daniel Bard, Clay Buchholz and Jacoby Ellsbury.

Moorad had expressed displeasure with San Diego's efforts in scouting and player development. Many of the Padres' recent first-round picks either haven't lived up to expectations (Matt Bush, Matt Antonelli) or were saddled by serious injuries (Tim Stauffer, Cesar Carrillo, Nick Schmidt, Allan Dykstra).

Fuson and Gayton performed an about-face with their drafting approach in 2009, selecting two premium high school athletes in outfielders Donavan Tate (No.

First baseman Kyle Blanks shifted to left field and hit for encouraging power in Petco Park

JOHN WILLIAMSON

TOP 30 PROSPECTS

1. Donavan Tate, of	16. Kellen Kulbacki, of
2. Simon Castro, rhp	17. Blake Tekotte, of
3. James Darnell, 3b	18. Jeremy Hefner, rhp
4. Jaff Decker, of	19. Jerry Sullivan, rhp
5. Logan Forsythe, 3b	20. Craig Italiano, rhp
6. Cory Luebke, lhp	21. Chad Huffman, of/1b
7. Wynn Pelzer, rhp	22. Jorge Reyes, rhp
8. Everett Williams, of	23. Cedric Hunter, of
9. Edinson Rincon, 3b	24. Ryan Webb, rhp
10. Aaron Poreda, lhp	25. Luis Durango, of
11. Drew Cumberland, ss	26. Cesar Ramos, lhp
12. Keyvius Sampson, rhp	27. Matt Antonelli, 2b
13. Adys Portillo, rhp	28. Dexter Carter, rhp
14. Rymer Liriano, of	29. Matt Clark, 1b
15. Lance Zawadzki, ss/3b	30. Cole Figueroa, ss/2b

3 overall) and Everett Williams (second round) on the first day. In the past, the organization showed a clear preference for polished college hitters and pitchers who stood out more for their feel than their pure stuff.

Along the same lines, San Diego made a point of stockpiling strong-armed pitchers in trades. Sending Scott Hairston to the Athletics in early July netted righthanders Sean Gallagher, Craig Italiano and Ryan Webb. Shipping ace Jake Peavy to the White Sox at the July 31 trade deadline brought in big leaguer Clayton Richard and three hard-throwing minor leaguers in Dexter Carter, Aaron Poreda and Adam Russell.

General Manager: Jed Hoyer. **Farm Director:** Vacant. **Scouting Director:** Jaron Madison.

Class	Team	League	W	L	PCT	Finish*	Manager(s)
Majors	San Diego Padres	National	75	87	.463	11th (16)	Bud Black
Triple-A	Portland Beavers	Pacific Coast	60	84	.417	16th (16)	R. Ready/G. Jones
Double-A	San Antonio Missions	Texas	70	70	.500	6th (8)	Terry Kennedy
High A	Lake Elsinore Storm	California	73	67	.521	5th (10)	Carlos Lezcano
Low A	Fort Wayne TinCaps	Midwest	94	46	.671	†1st (14)	Doug Dascenzo
Short-season	Eugene Emeralds	Northwest	34	42	.447	t-6th (8)	Greg Riddoch
Rookie	AZL Padres	Arizona	28	28	.500	5th (11)	Jose Flores
Overall 2009 Minor League Record			359	337	.516	8th (30)	

*Finish in overall standings (No. of teams in league). †League champion.

LAST YEAR'S TOP 30

Player, Pos.		Status
1.	Kyle Blanks, 1b	Majors
2.	Mat Latos, rhp	Majors
3.	Jaff Decker, of	No. 4
4.	Kellen Kulbacki, of	No. 16
5.	Adys Portillo, rhp	No. 13
6.	Cedric Hunter, of	No. 23
7.	Will Venable, of	Majors
8.	Allan Dykstra, 1b	Dropped out
9.	Matt Antonelli, 2b	No. 27
10.	James Darnell, 3b	No. 3
11.	Logan Forsythe, 3b	No. 5
12.	Wade LeBlanc, lhp	Majors
13.	Josh Geer, rhp	Majors
14.	Simon Castro, rhp	No. 2
15.	Drew Cumberland, ss	No. 11
16.	Wynn Pelzer, rhp	No. 7
17.	Eric Sogard, 2b	Dropped out
18.	Will Inman, rhp	Dropped out
19.	Blake Tekotte, of	No. 17
20.	Cesar Carrillo, rhp	Dropped out
21.	Nick Schmidt, lhp	Dropped out
22.	Steve Garrison, lhp	Dropped out
23.	Chad Huffman, of	No. 21
24.	Everth Cabrera, 2b/ss	Majors
25.	Mitch Canham, c	Dropped out
26.	Drew Miller, rhp	Dropped out
27.	Jeremy Hefner, rhp	No. 18
28.	Cole Figueroa, ss/2b	No. 30
29.	Ernesto Frieri, rhp	Dropped out
30.	Ivan Nova, rhp	(Yankees)

BEST TOOLS

Best Hitter for Average	Jaff Decker
Best Power Hitter	Matt Clark
Best Strike-Zone Discipline	Logan Forsythe
Fastest Baserunner	Luis Durango
Best Athlete	Donavan Tate
Best Fastball	Wynn Pelzer
Best Curveball	Keyvius Sampson
Best Slider	Wynn Pelzer
Best Changeup	Jeremy Hefner
Best Control	Chris Fetter
Best Defensive Catcher	Luis Martinez
Best Defensive Infielder	Beamer Weems
Best Infield Arm	Lance Zawadzki
Best Defensive Outfielder	Donavan Tate
Best Outfield Arm	Rymer Liriano

PROJECTED 2013 LINEUP

Catcher	Nick Hundley
First Base	Adrian Gonzalez
Second Base	James Darnell
Third Base	Chase Headley
Shortstop	Everth Cabrera
Left Field	Kyle Blanks
Center Field	Donavan Tate
Right Field	Jaff Decker
No. 1 Starter	Mat Latos
No. 2 Starter	Simon Castro
No. 3 Starter	Chris Young
No. 4 Starter	Kevin Correia
No. 5 Starter	Cory Luebke
Closer	Wynn Pelzer

TOP PROSPECTS OF THE DECADE

Year	Player, Pos.	2009 Org.
2000	Sean Burroughs, 3b	Out of baseball
2001	Sean Burroughs, 3b	Out of baseball
2002	Sean Burroughs, 3b	Out of baseball
2003	Xavier Nady, of	Yankees
2004	Josh Barfield, 2b	Indians
2005	Josh Barfield, 2b	Indians
2006	Cesar Carrillo, rhp	Padres
2007	Cedric Hunter, of	Padres
2008	Chase Headley, 3b	Padres
2009	Kyle Blanks, 1b	Padres

TOP DRAFT PICKS OF THE DECADE

Year	Player, Pos.	2009 Org.
2000	Mark Phillips, lhp	Out of baseball
2001	Jake Gautreau, 2b	Out of baseball
2002	Khalil Greene, ss	Cardinals
2003	Tim Stauffer, rhp	Padres
2004	Matt Bush, ss	Out of baseball
2005	Cesar Carrillo, rhp	Padres
2006	Matt Antonelli, 3b	Padres
2007	Nick Schmidt, lhp	Padres
2008	Allan Dykstra, 1b	Padres
2009	Donavan Tate, of	Padres

LARGEST BONUSES IN CLUB HISTORY

Donavan Tate, 2009	$6,250,000
Matt Bush, 2004	$3,150,000
Mark Phillips, 2000	$2,200,000
Sean Burroughs, 1998	$2,100,000
Adys Portillo, 2008	$2,000,000

SAN DIEGO PADRES

TOP 2010 ROOKIE: Aaron Poreda, lhp. Part of the Jake Peavy trade with the White Sox, he could help as a starter or reliever.

BREAKOUT PROSPECT: Jorge Reyes, rhp. His strong showings in the Cape Cod League and his brief pro debut may mean that the enigmatic Oregon State product has turned a corner.

SLEEPER: Jonathan Galvez, ss. He knows the strike zone and his wiry strength translates into present power, though he's still seeking consistency on defense.

SOURCE OF TOP 30 TALENT			
Homegrown	26	Acquired	4
College	15	Trades	4
Junior college	0	Rule 5 draft	0
High school	6	Independent leagues	0
Draft-and-follow	0	Free agents/waivers	0
Nondrafted free agents	0		
International	5		

Numbers in parentheses indicate prospect rankings

LF
Jaff Decker (4)
Edinson Rincon (9)
Kellen Kulbacki (16)
Chad Huffman (21)
Luis Domoromo

CF
Donavan Tate (1)
Everett Williams (8)
Blake Tekotte (17)
Cedric Hunter (23)
Luis Durango (25)
Brad Chalk
Dan Robertson
Danny Payne
Cameron Monger

RF
Rymer Liriano (14)
Sawyer Carroll
Mike Baxter
Yefri Carvajal
Wande Olabisi

3B
James Darnell (3)
Logan Forsythe (5)
Vince Belnome

SS
Drew Cumberland (11)
Lance Zawadzki (15)
Beamer Weems
Alvaro Aristy

2B
Matt Antonelli (27)
Cole Figueroa (30)
Eric Sogard
Jonathan Galvez

1B
Matt Clark (29)
Allan Dykstra
Nate Freiman
Craig Cooper
Cody Decker

C
Mitch Canham
Luis Martinez
Jason Hagerty
Adam Zornes
Emmanuel Quiles
Robert Lara

RHP

Starters	Relievers
Simon Castro (2)	Craig Italiano (20)
Wynn Pelzer (7)	Ryan Webb (24)
Keyvius Sampson (12)	Ernesto Frieri
Adys Portillo (13)	Mike Ekstrom
Jeremy Hefner (18)	Cesar Carrillo
Jerry Sullivan (19)	Brad Brach
Jorge Reyes (22)	Brandon Gomes
Dexter Carter (28)	Aaron Breit
Anthony Bass	Evan Scribner
Chris Fetter	Mike DeMark
Jeremy McBryde	Matt Buschmann
Corey Kluber	Alexis Lara
Erik Davis	Rafael Arias
James Needy	Robert Poutier
Will Inman	Miles Mikolas
Kendall Korbal	Matt Lollis

LHP

Starters	Relievers
Cory Luebke (6)	Aaron Poreda (10)
Cesar Ramos (26)	Rob Musgrave
Nick Schmidt	Colt Hynes
Steve Garrison	Ryan Hinson
Nate Culp	
Nick Greenwood	
Michael Watt	

2009

BONUSES: $9.1 MILLION

BEST PURE HITTER: OF Everett Williams (2) had the best bat among the elite athletes in the 2009 draft.

BEST POWER HITTER: 1B Nate Freiman (8), who holds the Duke career record with 43 homers, has the most present power. OF Donavan Tate (1) and Williams both are loaded with raw power and could pass him in time.

FASTEST RUNNER: Tate, Williams and OFs Cameron Monger (27) and Wande Olabisi (30) all have plus-plus speed. Monger stole 29 bases in 34 attempts in the Rookie-level Arizona League.

BEST DEFENSIVE PLAYER: Tate oozes Gold Glove potential in center field, complementing his vast range with a plus arm.

BEST FASTBALL: RHP Keyvious Sampson (4) can sit at 94 mph and top out at 96. RHP Matt Lollis (15) can reach 95, and RHP Kendall Korbal (21) showed similar velocity before needing Tommy John surgery.

BEST SECONDARY PITCH: Sampson's curveball or RHP Jorge Reyes' (17) slider.

BEST PRO DEBUT: 1B Cody Decker (22) was old for the Rookie-level Arizona League at 22, but he still won league MVP honors and led the circuit in doubles (21), homers (15), extra-base hits (39), RBIs (63) and slugging (.717). Freiman topped the short-season Northwest League with 33 extra-base hits and 68 RBIs. Finesse LHP Nick Greenwood (14) led the NWL with a 1.71 ERA and was joined on the league all-star team by 2B/3B Vince Belnome (28), who finished the summer by going 16-for-32 in low Class A. RHP Chris Fetter (9) also finished strong in low Class A and went 4-1, 1.66 with 75 strikeouts in 65 innings overall.

BEST ATHLETE: Tate, Williams and Olabisi had some of the best power-speed combinations in the entire draft. Olabisi is more raw than the two high schoolers, so much so that he barely played at Stanford. Tate could have played quarterback at North Carolina.

MOST INTRIGUING BACKGROUND: Olabisi was born to a royal family in Nigeria and later moved to Saudi Arabia, for which he played in the 2000 Little League World Series. He's also a biomechanical engineering major. Tate's father Lars was an NFL running back. 2B Ryan Skube's (44) dad Bob played in the majors and coached him in the AZL. C Griffin Benedict's (16) father Bruce was an all-star catcher for the Braves. 2B/SS Kevin Winn's (26) dad Earl scouts for the Twins.

CLOSEST TO THE MAJORS: After an inconsistent career at Oregon State, which included the 2007 College World Series MVP award, Reyes showed a 90-94 mph fastball and plus slider in the Cape Cod League

during the summer. If he maintains that stuff and his command, he'll beat Fetter to San Diego. Fetter is 6-foot-8 and throws a low-90s fastball on a steep plane.

BEST LATE-ROUND PICK: Reyes.

THE ONE WHO GOT AWAY: 3B John Wooten (20) turned down third-round money to go to East Carolina. He generates easy power and has a strong arm.

ASSESSMENT: After years of targeting proven college performers, the Padres did a 180 and went after sheer upside. Tate cost $6.25 million, the second-highest bonus in draft history, but San Diego got relative bargains with Williams ($775,000), Sampson ($600,000) and Reyes ($200,000).

2008

BONUSES: $5.4 MILLION

1B Allan Dykstra (1) can't even crack our Padres Top 30 list, but OF Jaff Decker (1s) and 3Bs Logan Forsythe (1s) and James Darnell (2) rank among the system's top position prospects. OF Blake Tekotte (3), SS/2B Cole Figueroa (6) and 1B Matt Clark (12) also show some promise.

GRADE: B

2007

BONUSES: $5.9 MILLION

The Padres had six picks before the second round, and not one of them looks like a star. The best of that group are SS Drew Cumberland (1s) and LHP Cory Luebke (1s), and RHP Wynn Pelzer (9) might be better than any of them.

GRADE: C

2006

BONUSES: $6.3 MILLION

San Diego hopes to build its rotation around RHP Mat Latos (11), one of the last high-priced draft-and-follows. 3B Matt Antonelli (1) and LHP Wade LeBlanc (2) have played in the majors. The Padres may rue trading OF Kyler Burke (1s) and 3B David Freese (9) for Michael Barrett and Jim Edmonds, and unsigned Grant Green (14) was the first shortstop selected in 2009.

GRADE: B

2005

BONUSES: $3.0 MILLION*

San Diego's first five picks—RHPs Cesar Carrillo (1) and Josh Geer (3), LHP Cesar Ramos (1s), OF/3B Chase Headley (2), C Nick Hundley (2)—have played in the majors, but only Headley looks like a significant part of the club's future. OF Will Venable (7) may outperform them all.

GRADE: C+

*Draft analysis by Jim Callis. Numbers in parentheses indicate draft rounds. *Bonuses for 2005 are first 10 rounds only.*

DONAVAN TATE, OF

Born: Sept. 27, 1990.
Height: 6-3. **Weight:** 200.
Bats: R. **Throws:** R.
Drafted: HS—Cartersville, Ga., 2009 (1st round).
Signed by: Ash Lawson.

BRIAN BISSELL

The No. 3 overall selection in June, Tate nearly doubled the franchise bonus record held by the ill-fated Matt Bush when he signed for $6.25 million at the Aug. 17 signing deadline. Tate also set a new mark for a high school pick, surpassing the $6.15 million the Rays gave Tim Beckham a year earlier. Widely regarded as the top prep position player available in 2009, Tate starred as a quarterback for Cartersville (Ga.) High and had committed to play football as well as baseball at North Carolina. His father Lars was a standout running back at Georgia and spent three seasons in the NFL. Tate followed in the footsteps of Allan Dykstra and Nick Schmidt, the Padres' previous two first-rounders, when the revelation of an injury sucked some of the excitement out of his signing. In just his second day working out with the Rookie-level Arizona League club, he was immobilized with a sports hernia and had surgery to reattach an abdominal muscle to his pubic bone. As a result, he missed the balance of the season and spent his instructional league time rehabbing. Tate compounded matters when he had surgery in late November to repair a broken jaw he sustained in an ATV accident near his Georgia home. The Padres expect him to be healthy in time for his first spring training.

Tate's premium athleticism stands out as the best in the system. Unlike many two-sport amateurs, he features graceful, fluid actions on the diamond, and he isn't stiff and mechanical like some ex-footballers. Best of all, he shows natural baseball instincts and he makes in-game adjustments against better pitching. Tate's potential to develop five plus tools, highlighted by huge raw power and plus-plus range in center field, has the Padres justifiably excited. He also has plus-plus speed and an above-average arm. His feel for hitting is less refined, but he reacts well to the ball and maintains good balance at the plate. Tate played with intensity all spring, even when he wasn't being scrutinized by a throng of scouts, and his mature and passionate demeanor translates into what one club official deems special makeup.

The biggest question facing Tate remains his feel for hitting. Some scouts said his swing was better when he was a sophomore in high school and regressed over the next two seasons. Like most young hitters with strength, he can get pull-happy. Now that he has committed to baseball full-time, he can polish his batting approach and learn through repetition what works for him. While hitting with metal bats, he could afford to simply trust his hands and his natural bat speed. San Diego intends to work with him on lengthening his stride and separating his hands when he loads his swing. Tate's abdominal injury cost him valuable development time. He first felt a twinge in his abdomen during the spring, but because he played only a handful of games each week, he didn't feel inhibited by the injury.

The Padres envision Tate developing into a power/speed center fielder who combines the best attributes of Mike Cameron and Andruw Jones. A solid showing in spring training should earn him an assignment to low Class A Fort Wayne, and from there the speed at which his bat develops will dictate his pace.

Year	Club (League)	Class	AVG	G	AB	R	H	2B	3B	HR	RBI	BB	SO	SB	OBP	SLG
2009	Did Not Play—Signed Late															

2 SIMON CASTRO, RHP ✝

BORN: April 9, 1988. **B-T:** R-R. **HT.:** 6-5. **WT.:** 211. **SIGNED:** Dominican Republic, 2006. **SIGNED BY:** Randy Smith/Felix Francisco.

Castro intrigued the Padres with his raw arm strength even while posting a 5.46 ERA in Rookie ball in his first two pro seasons. He started refining his command in 2008 and took a huge step forward last season, when he led the low Class A Midwest League in strikeouts (157 in 140 innings) and threw a seven-inning no-hitter in August. He helped Fort Wayne win the league title, allowing only one run in two playoff starts. Castro throws a 92-93 mph fastball with life down in the zone. He can dial up his riding, four-seam fastball to 95-96 and blow the ball past hitters upstairs. He throws a nasty low-80s slider that features hard, late break and is tough on righthanders. He has made steady improvements to his delivery, staying online to the plate and improving his extension. He earns high marks for his work ethic. Castro's slider can get big on him at times, and he's still refining what figures to be an average changeup. With a true swing-and-miss fastball, he needs to make a concerted effort to emphasize his secondary weapons in game situations. Castro slashed his walk rate last season and if that trend continues, he has the stuff and durability to profile as at least a No. 3 starter. He also could make a dynamic closer if needed. He should reach Double-A San Antonio at some point in 2010.

Year	Club (League)	Class	W	L	ERA	G	GS	CG	SV	IP	H	R	ER	HR	BB	SO	AVG
2006	Padres (DSL)	R	1	3	4.63	12	12	0	0	47	40	33	24	2	21	58	.219
2007	Padres (AZL)	R	2	6	6.22	14	12	0	0	51	61	48	35	4	30	55	.298
2008	Eugene (NWL)	SS	2	3	3.99	15	15	0	0	65	54	35	29	3	29	64	.223
2009	Fort Wayne (MWL)	LoA	10	6	3.33	28	27	1	0	140	118	61	52	9	37	157	.226
MINOR LEAGUE TOTALS			15	18	4.16	69	66	1	0	303	273	177	140	18	117	334	.237

3 JAMES DARNELL, 3B

BORN: Jan. 19, 1987. **B-T:** R-R. **HT.:** 6-2. **WT.:** 198. **DRAFTED:** South Carolina, 2008 (2nd round). **SIGNED BY:** Anthony Byrd.

He's more athletic than the typical Padres college draft pick, but that's not to say Darnell is all projection and no production. Through 142 pro games, he has batted .319/.428/.542 with nearly as many walks as strikeouts. He ranked ninth in the minors with a .424 on-base percentage last season. Darnell controls the strike zone and shows a natural feel for hitting. He generates plus power thanks to natural strength and bat speed. Working with roving hitting instructor Tony Muser, he has learned to put more backspin and loft on the ball by bracing his right hand under the bat head at the point of contact. He's an average runner but not a basestealing threat. His arm is strong enough for third base. Some observers think Darnell's hands and feet will play at third, but others aren't convinced. He made 30 errors in 117 games in 2009, with 17 miscues coming on throws. He struggles with accuracy when he doesn't get his feet set and throws on the run. He checked out of instructional league early with lingering back soreness. Darnell has enough bat to play anywhere on the diamond, and he may one day receive an audition at second base because of the Padres' crowded third-base and corner-outfield situations. He's ready to tackle Double-A in 2010.

Year	Club (League)	Class	AVG	G	AB	R	H	2B	3B	HR	RBI	BB	SO	SB	OBP	SLG
2008	Eugene (NWL)	SS	.373	16	67	9	25	6	1	2	15	11	12	1	.462	.582
2009	Fort Wayne (MWL)	LoA	.329	66	222	40	73	17	2	7	38	57	51	5	.468	.518
	Lake Elsinore (CAL)	HiA	.294	60	235	40	69	18	2	13	43	30	38	3	.377	.553
MINOR LEAGUE TOTALS			.319	142	524	89	167	41	5	22	96	98	101	9	.428	.542

4 JAFF DECKER, OF

BORN: Feb. 23, 1990. **B-T:** L-L. **HT.:** 5-10. **WT.:** 212. **DRAFTED:** HS—Peoria, Ariz., 2008 (1st round supplemental). **SIGNED BY:** Dave Lottsfeldt.

After signing for $892,000, Decker won the Rookie-level Arizona League MVP award in his pro debut. He was even more impressive in his encore, becoming the first teenager to lead the Midwest League in OPS (.956) since Prince Fielder in 2003 and ranking second in the minors in on-base percentage (.442). He homered twice in the playoffs as Fort Wayne cruised to the MWL title. Decker recognizes pitches and controls the strike zone like a much more experienced hitter. He has incredible power to his pull side and hits with authority to all fields. He employs a short swing and won't chase pitches out of the zone, rare attributes for a young power hitter. He has an average arm, having touched 90-92 mph from the mound in high school. For all his positives as a hitter, Decker draws negative reviews for his lack of athleticism. He's a well-below-average runner who figures to slow down further as he ages, which would make him a less-than-adequate defender in left field. He initially resisted the Padres' overtures to get in better shape, but he relented after missing a month in 2009, first with a concussion coming out of spring training and then with a tweaked back. Decker profiles as a Nick Swisher type whose game centers on walks and power—but with a better feel for hitting and less athleticism. He's ticketed for high Class A Lake Elsinore in 2010.

Year	Club (League)	Class	AVG	G	AB	R	H	2B	3B	HR	RBI	BB	SO	SB	OBP	SLG
2008	Padres (AZL)	R	.352	49	159	51	56	11	2	5	34	55	36	9	.523	.541
	Eugene (NWL)	SS	.200	3	10	2	2	0	0	0	0	2	5	0	.333	.200
2009	Fort Wayne (MWL)	LoA	.299	104	358	78	107	25	2	16	64	85	92	10	.442	.514
MINOR LEAGUE TOTALS			.313	156	527	131	165	36	4	21	98	142	133	19	.466	.516

5 LOGAN FORSYTHE, 3B †

BORN: Jan. 14, 1987. **B-T:** R-R. **HT.:** 6-1. **WT.:** 206. **DRAFTED:** Arkansas, 2008 (1st round supplemental). **SIGNED BY:** Lane Decker.

A torn thumb ligament knocked Forsythe out of action just three games after he signed for $835,000 in 2008. Healthy last season, he ranked second in the minors in walks (102) and sixth in on-base percentage (.429). Drafted 23 places ahead of fellow college third baseman James Darnell, he has stayed one step ahead of him in pro ball. He's not overwhelming in any area, but Forsythe has a solid base of tools. He features a short, balanced swing and isn't afraid to wait for his pitch, even if he falls behind in the count. He has the natural strength to hit for average power for a third baseman. His range, hands and arm are all plus tools at the hot corner. He's a solid-average runner and earns praise for his calm demeanor. Some observes think Forsythe's line-drive stroke will translate more into doubles than homers. His power declined noticeably in Double-A, though that's partially attributable to San Antonio's unforgiving ballpark. In 33 Texas League road games, he batted a steady .316/.444/.439, posting an OPS more than 230 points higher than his home mark (.647). The Padres' logjam at third base might push Forsythe to another position—second base, the outfield or even catcher—but no move is imminent. He figures to be a top-of-the-order hitter wherever he lands, and he'll likely reach Triple-A Portland in 2010.

Year	Club (League)	Class	AVG	G	AB	R	H	2B	3B	HR	RBI	BB	SO	SB	OBP	SLG
2008	Eugene (NWL)	SS	.333	3	9	2	3	1	0	0	0	1	3	0	.455	.444
	Padres (AZL)	R	.231	9	26	2	6	0	0	0	0	5	8	0	.429	.231
2009	Lake Elsinore (CAL)	HiA	.322	66	236	46	76	13	3	8	30	61	48	6	.472	.504
	San Antonio (TL)	AA	.279	66	244	37	68	9	3	3	31	41	63	5	.384	.377
MINOR LEAGUE TOTALS			.297	144	515	87	153	23	6	11	61	108	122	11	.430	.429

6 CORY LUEBKE, LHP ⏦

BORN: March 4, 1985. **B-T:** R-L. **HT.:** 6-4. **WT.:** 215. **DRAFTED:** Ohio State, 2007 (1st round supplemental). **SIGNED BY:** Jeff Stewart.

Three months after signing for $515,000 in 2007, Luebke was pitching in the high Class A California League playoffs. Back in Lake Elsinore to begin his first full season, he scuffled to a 6.84 ERA, but righted the ship after a demotion to low Class A. He bounced back with a strong 2009, reaching Double-A and starting Team USA's gold-medal game victory against Cuba at the World Cup. In 2008, Luebke seemed unwilling to work inside against righthanders, who learned to take his pitches to the opposite field. Last season, he pitched inside with a vengeance and broke bats with a 90-92 mph fastball. His new approach opened up the outer half of the plate for his secondary stuff, particularly his solid slider. He has streamlined his motion and got more downhill plane by softening the landing of his front foot, resulting in improved command and finish of his pitches. As an added bonus, he more consistently repeated his arm slot. Tall and a bit gangly, Luebke sometimes struggles to coordinate the long levers in his delivery. His changeup features good action, but he still throws it a bit too hard at 84-86 mph. He has experimented with various circle change grips. Luebke's stuff and size give him a ceiling as a No. 3 starter. He should get his first taste of Triple-A in 2010, with a big league callup possible in September.

Year	Club (League)	Class	W	L	ERA	G	GS	CG	SV	IP	H	R	ER	HR	BB	SO	AVG
2007	Eugene (NWL)	SS	3	0	1.46	8	3	0	0	25	18	6	4	2	2	26	.194
	Fort Wayne (MWL)	LoA	1	2	3.33	5	5	0	0	27	29	13	10	2	5	30	.269
	Lake Elsinore (CAL)	HiA	1	1	7.71	2	1	0	0	7	10	6	6	1	1	5	.357
2008	Lake Elsinore (CAL)	HiA	3	6	6.84	17	15	0	0	72	97	61	55	8	23	60	.323
	Fort Wayne (MWL)	LoA	3	3	2.89	10	10	0	0	56	52	19	18	6	9	40	.265
2009	Lake Elsinore (CAL)	HiA	8	2	2.34	14	14	1	0	88	73	24	23	3	17	80	.227
	San Antonio (TL)	AA	3	2	3.70	9	9	0	0	41	38	21	17	3	15	32	.241
MINOR LEAGUE TOTALS			22	16	3.78	65	57	1	0	317	317	150	133	25	72	273	.263

7 WYNN PELZER, RHP ✝

BORN: June 23, 1986. **B-T:** R-R. **HT.:** 6-1. **WT.:** 205. **DRAFTED:** South Carolina, 2007 (9th round). **SIGNED BY:** Pete DeYoung.

Pelzer earned a $190,000 bonus as a ninth-round pick in 2007 despite having a knee-cap broken by a line drive in the Cape Cod League after the draft. He has established his credentials as a power pitching prospect, ranking second in the California League in strikeouts (147 in 151 innings) and fourth in opponent average (.244) last season. A strong athlete with a quick arm, Pelzer pounds the zone with a heavy 93-95 mph fastball that touches 97 in short stints. He maintains his velocity deep into games, meaning that opposing batters geared to hit his fastball have insufficient time to react to his secondary stuff. They can look downright foolish waving at his hard slider. His tenacity serves him well on the mound. Pelzer's changeup lags behind his other offerings, in part because he eschewed the pitch in college in favor of a high-80s splitter. He'll dust off the splitter occasionally to give lefties a different look. He falls out of rhythm in his delivery at times, with the rest of his body struggling to catch up to his quick arm, affecting his command. Pelzer's stuff would play up in a relief role, and it's not hard to imagine him as a closer, challenging hitters with his fastball and slider. He has worked hard at being a starter after mostly relieving in college, and the Padres have no plans to change his role in Double-A in 2010.

Year	Club (League)	Class	W	L	ERA	G	GS	CG	SV	IP	H	R	ER	HR	BB	SO	AVG
2008	Fort Wayne (MWL)	LoA	9	6	3.19	29	23	0	0	118	114	64	42	9	32	100	.248
	Lake Elsinore (CAL)	HiA	0	0	27.00	1	0	0	0	1	3	4	3	0	1	0	.500
2009	Lake Elsinore (CAL)	HiA	11	8	3.94	27	27	0	0	151	134	76	66	6	59	147	.244
MINOR LEAGUE TOTALS			20	14	3.70	57	50	0	0	270	251	144	111	15	92	247	.247

8 EVERETT WILLIAMS, OF ✝

BORN: Oct. 1, 1990. **B-T:** L-R. **HT.:** 5-10. **WT.:** 205. **DRAFTED:** HS—Austin, 2009 (2nd round). **SIGNED BY:** Tim Holt.

The finest hitter among the elite prep athletes in the 2009 draft, Williams slipped to the second round and signed at the Aug. 17 deadline for $775,000. Like Donavan Tate, he comes from a family with athletic bloodlines. His cousin Cedric Allen pitched in the Reds system and two aunts are enshrined in the softball hall of fame. Williams' excellent bat speed is the product of strong, quick hands. He's physical and can crush the ball to all fields with his aggressive lefthanded stroke. One area scout saw Williams hit a 500-foot blast. He's a gifted center fielder who goes back on the ball well. He's an above average runner out of the box and even quicker under way. Inexperience is Williams' biggest hurdle. It shows most in his management of the strike zone, particularly with identifying and hitting breaking balls. While his innate hitting ability is undeniable, he'll work to add separation when he loads his hands, which will give him more leverage in his swing. His arm strength is fringy. While he profiles as a center fielder, Williams may move in deference to Tate. If his bat develops as expected, he'll have no problem providing enough offense for an outfield corner. He'll spend his first full pro season in low Class A.

Year	Club (League)	Class	AVG	G	AB	R	H	2B	3B	HR	RBI	BB	SO	SB	OBP	SLG
2009	Padres (AZL)	R	.389	4	18	1	7	2	1	0	6	1	7	2	.421	.611
	Eugene (NWL)	SS	.200	6	25	1	5	2	0	1	3	4	11	0	.310	.400
MINOR LEAGUE TOTALS			.279	10	43	2	12	4	1	1	9	5	18	2	.354	.488

9 EDINSON RINCON, 3B

BORN: Aug. 11, 1990. **B-T:** R-R. **HT.:** 6-1. **WT.:** 202. **SIGNED:** Dominican Republic, 2007. **SIGNED BY:** Randy Smith/Felix Francisco.

Rincon signed at age 16 with little fanfare, but he has separated himself from the Padres' other international players not only with his rapid development but also by quickly learning English. He recovered from knee surgery in April 2008 to make his U.S. debut that summer before ranking as the No. 2 prospect in the short-season Northwest League in 2009. The Padres hold Rincon up as a model for their other Latin prospects to follow. He controls the strike zone and works deep counts. He maintains balance at the plate and hits breaking balls. Scouts project him to hit for high averages as he moves up, and his raw strength should translate into average power. His arm strength is his best defensive asset. He draws raves for his aptitude and toughness. Rincon is anything but fluid at third base, with hard hands and feet that don't work well in terms of timing hops. He made 22 errors in 44 games and spent about a third of his time at DH. His slinging arm action results in too many throwing errors. He's a below-average runner and figures to slow down more as he matures. Though Rincon may not be long for the infield, his bat will keep him in San Diego's plans. He should make the jump to full-season ball in 2010.

Year	Club (League)	Class	AVG	G	AB	R	H	2B	3B	HR	RBI	BB	SO	SB	OBP	SLG
2007	Padres (DSL)	R	.295	33	122	14	36	7	0	2	15	17	26	2	.383	.402
	Padres (AZL)	R	.178	15	45	6	8	1	0	0	0	7	11	0	.302	.200
2008	Padres (AZL)	R	.308	23	65	8	20	1	1	0	19	14	18	0	.429	.354
2009	Eugene (NWL)	SS	.300	70	267	47	80	18	3	7	47	46	60	5	.415	.468
MINOR LEAGUE TOTALS			.289	141	499	75	144	27	4	9	81	84	115	7	.400	.413

10 AARON POREDA, LHP

BORN: Oct. 1, 1986. **B-T:** L-L. **HT.:** 6-6. **WT.:** 240. **DRAFTED:** San Francisco, 2007 (1st round). **SIGNED BY:** Joe Butler/Adam Virchis (White Sox).

The 25th overall pick in the 2007 draft, Poreda signed with the White Sox for $1.2 million. He made his major league debut last June, then went to the Padres six weeks later in the trade for Jake Peavy. He played for five teams at three levels last season, losing his feel for the strike zone along the way. Poreda fires plus four-seam fastballs ranging from 90-95 mph from a low three-quarters arm slot. The Padres see promise in his 88-91 two-seamer, which features better life in the zone. He has made strides in commanding his heater to both sides of the plate. He'll flash a plus slider in the high 80s. Big and strong, he's built for durability. After switching organizations, Poreda's delivery fell apart, as did his control. He gets around his slider too often, flattening it into a slurve. He lacks feel for his well-below-average changeup, and he needs to throw it more to try to develop it. Switching between starting in the minors and relieving in the majors has left Poreda with a feeling of lingering uncertainty about his role. Unless he makes huge strides with his command, he probably fits best at the back of a bullpen, where he could be San Diego's version of Matt Thornton.

Year	Club (League)	Class	W	L	ERA	G	GS	CG	SV	IP	H	R	ER	HR	BB	SO	AVG
2007	Great Falls (PIO)	R	4	0	1.17	12	8	0	0	46	29	7	6	1	10	48	.181
2008	Winston-Salem (CAR)	HiA	5	5	3.31	12	12	1	0	73	67	31	27	1	18	46	.238
	Birmingham (SL)	AA	3	4	2.98	15	15	1	0	88	81	34	29	5	22	72	.249
2009	Birmingham (SL)	AA	5	4	2.38	11	11	1	0	64	47	20	17	1	35	69	.206
	Chicago (AL)	MAJ	1	0	2.45	10	0	0	0	11	9	3	3	0	8	12	.231
	Charlotte (IL)	AAA	0	0	3.60	2	2	0	0	10	8	4	4	0	3	9	.216
	Portland (PCL)	AAA	0	3	7.16	7	6	0	0	33	28	27	26	3	37	30	.239
	San Diego (NL)	MAJ	0	0	3.86	4	0	0	0	2	1	1	1	0	5	0	.143
MAJOR LEAGUE TOTALS			1	0	2.70	14	0	0	0	13	10	4	4	0	13	12	.217
MINOR LEAGUE TOTALS			17	16	3.12	59	54	3	0	314	260	123	109	11	125	274	.226

11 DREW CUMBERLAND, SS

BORN: Jan. 13, 1989. **B-T:** L-R. **HT.:** 5-10. **WT.:** 170. **DRAFTED:** HS—Pace, Fla., 2007 (1st round supplemental). **SIGNED BY:** Bob Filotei.

On a traditional development path, Cumberland would be competing in Double-A this season. But because of several injuries, he's still trying to put the Midwest League in his rearview mirror. He has logged just 130 games in two years of full-season ball, all in low Class A. A strained oblique and jammed finger cut into his playing time in 2008. Last year, an errant pitch struck the back of his hand, bruising ligaments, tendons and bones and knocking him out of the playoffs. Cumberland tried to return for instructional league but pain and swelling put the kibosh on that. His brother Shaun is an outfield prospect in the Reds system. An electrifying talent, Cumberland has performed well for Fort Wayne when healthy, batting .290 with 35 steals and nearly as many walks (57) as strikeouts (60). He has good feel for the strike zone and for putting the barrel on the ball. With his plus-plus speed and below-average power, he fits at the top of the order. Cumberland has improved his efficiency at shortstop and strengthened his arm as he has physically matured and pursued an aggressive long-toss program. He still grades as merely adequate in those departments and may face a shift to second base, but that's no longer a foregone conclusion. A 2010 season free of serious injury could return Cumberland to his normal trajectory, including his first glimpse of Double-A.

Year	Club (League)	Class	AVG	G	AB	R	H	2B	3B	HR	RBI	BB	SO	SB	OBP	SLG
2007	Padres (AZL)	R	.318	21	85	16	27	2	1	0	7	7	9	6	.389	.365
	Eugene (NWL)	SS	.333	4	18	6	6	1	0	0	0	2	2	0	.429	.389
2008	Fort Wayne (MWL)	LoA	.286	53	206	29	59	8	1	1	17	17	24	16	.348	.350
	Padres (AZL)	R	.500	3	10	3	5	1	2	0	2	0	1	0	.500	1.000
2009	Fort Wayne (MWL)	LoA	.293	77	290	57	85	18	5	2	40	40	36	19	.386	.410
MINOR LEAGUE TOTALS			.299	158	609	111	182	30	9	3	66	66	72	41	.377	.392

12 KEYVIUS SAMPSON, RHP

BORN: Jan. 6, 1991. **B-T:** R-R. **HT.:** 6-0. **WT.:** 185. **DRAFTED:** HS—Ocala, Fla., 2009 (4th round). **SIGNED BY:** Rob Sidwell.

A top two-rounds talent on merit, Sampson slipped in 2009 because his bonus demands scared away teams.

The Padres pounced quickly on day two, selecting him with the third pick in the fourth round after Sampson and his guardian, acting as his agent, softened their bonus demands. The day before the Aug. 17 signing deadline, San Diego bought him out of a Florida State commitment for $600,000. As an amateur, Sampson dealt head-on with adversity, which included his mother's death and a criminal case back in 2006 that stemmed from a felony gun charge leveled at a passenger in a car he was driving. Between the lines, Sampson is a scout's dream, featuring an effortless, fluid arm action, plenty of poise and a feel for changing speeds. He ran his fastball up to 95-96 mph early in the spring before settling at 90-92 after signing. His power curveball already ranks as the best in the system, and his overall control is strong for a prep pitcher. He has shown a feel for a changeup. Sampson's lean, athletic frame offers all kinds of projection, but he closes off his delivery at times, which causes him to throw slightly across his body. The Padres have no recent experience developing prep righthanders as talented as Sampson, so they may opt to begin slowly with an assignment to short-season Eugene in 2010.

Year	Club (League)	Class	W	L	ERA	G	GS	CG	SV	IP	H	R	ER	HR	BB	SO	AVG
2009	Padres (AZL)	R	0	0	3.00	2	1	0	0	3	1	1	1	0	0	3	.111
	Eugene (NWL)	SS	0	0	3.60	2	1	0	0	5	3	2	2	0	3	5	.176
MINOR LEAGUE TOTALS			0	0	3.38	4	2	0	0	8	4	3	3	0	3	8	.154

13 ADYS PORTILLO, RHP

BORN: Dec. 21, 1991. **B-T:** R-R. **HT.:** 6-2. **WT.:** 218. **SIGNED:** Venezuela, 2008. **SIGNED BY:** Yfrain Linares/Felix Feliz/Randy Smith.

While Portillo received significantly more money to sign with the Padres, he's at a similar stage in his development as Simon Castro was back in 2006. Making his pro debut in 2009, San Diego's $2 million man led the Arizona League with nine losses in 10 decisions and finished with a 5.13 ERA. Portillo's overall stuff was fine, but his control wavered and he visibly tired down the stretch. There was nothing wrong with his fastball, as he touched 93 mph in each of his 12 starts and usually pitched at 90-92. Tall and projectable with strong body control, he figures to add velocity as he learns to repeat his delivery. Portillo lacks feel for his curveball, but he'll flash a plus downer from time to time. At this stage, he has more feel for his changeup than he does for his curve. The Padres rebuilt Portillo's mechanics during the season, eliminating a pause in his delivery and adding more separation after he leaves his balance point. A bright pupil who has taken quickly to learning English, Portillo could advance rapidly when things begin to click. He'll tackle the Northwest League in 2010.

Year	Club (League)	Class	W	L	ERA	G	GS	CG	SV	IP	H	R	ER	HR	BB	SO	AVG
2009	Padres (AZL)	R	1	9	5.13	13	12	0	0	53	67	41	30	2	28	44	.321
MINOR LEAGUE TOTALS			1	9	5.13	13	12	0	0	53	67	41	30	2	28	44	.321

14 RYMER LIRIANO, OF

BORN: June 20, 1991. **B-T:** R-R. **HT.:** 6-0. **WT.:** 217. **SIGNED:** Dominican Republic, 2007. **SIGNED BY:** Felix Francisco/Randy Smith.

San Diego signed shortstop Jonathan Galvez for $750,000 and Liriano for $300,000 during the 2007 international signing period, heralding the organization's new focus on Latin America. Both players made their pro debuts in the Rookie-level Dominican Summer League a year later, helping to christen the Padres' new academy in Najayo. Liriano scuffled to a .198 average with 106 strikeouts in just 67 DSL games, but he made significant improvements in his U.S. debut, ranking as one of the Arizona League's most dynamic talents in 2009. The 18-year-old ranked in the top five in batting (.350), hits (69), homers (eight), RBIs (44) and total bases (103), and he also stole 14 bases in 19 attempts. Liriano separates himself from the pack with plus-plus raw power, and in a July 26 game he hit three home runs, one to each field. He has true five-tool potential and a lithe, athletic body that reminds San Diego of a young Sammy Sosa. Like Sosa, Liriano is a passionate player who craves attention. His ceiling as a hitter is compromised by an undisciplined approach and present trouble with offspeed pitches. Added maturity and enhanced pitch recognition will help him clear this hurdle. Liriano boasts the best arm strength and accuracy among position players in the system, and he gets good jumps and angles on the ball in center field. He's just an average runner, though, and likely will settle in right field. Liriano loves to play, and given time he could develop in to an impact right fielder. It may take him four or more years to reach that apex, with his climb continuing in low Class A this season.

Year	Club (League)	Class	AVG	G	AB	R	H	2B	3B	HR	RBI	BB	SO	SB	OBP	SLG
2008	Padres (DSL)	R	.198	67	232	34	46	13	1	9	37	28	106	9	.296	.379
2009	Padres (AZL)	R	.350	50	197	44	69	8	1	8	44	15	52	14	.398	.523
MINOR LEAGUE TOTALS			.268	117	429	78	115	21	2	17	81	43	158	23	.342	.445

15 LANCE ZAWADZKI, SS/3B

BORN: May 26, 1985. **B-T:** B-R. **HT.:** 5-11. **WT.:** 194. **DRAFTED:** Lee (Tenn.), 2007 (4th round). **SIGNED BY:** Ash Lawson.

Zawadzki graduated from sleeper to prospect in 2009, smacking 15 homers, streamlining his game and spending the second half of the season in Double-A. The Padres' surfeit of compensation picks in 2007 meant that even though Zawadzki was a fourth-round selection, he was the 11th player they picked. Despite his small frame, he has good power from both sides of the plate, the result of quick hands and wrists. He revamped his swing last offseason, working to keep his hands in the hitting zone longer, which helped him to drive the ball the other way. He improved his selectivity last season as well. Zawadzki runs and throws well—his arm rates as a 70 on the 20-80 scouting scale by some accounts—and he has enough range to make all the routine plays at shortstop. A free-spirited player, his concentration lapses at times and he'll flub the routine play. At the plate, his swing can get too big and he falls into prolonged slumps when he'll strike out in bunches. Zawadzki stands as one of the Padres' more skilled prospects and someone who may be able to fill in at shortstop if Everth Cabrera falters or at second if Matt Antonelli doesn't rebound. Ultimately, he might have the most value in a super-utility role, providing offense all around the infield.

Year	Club (League)	Class	AVG	G	AB	R	H	2B	3B	HR	RBI	BB	SO	SB	OBP	SLG
2007	Padres (AZL)	R	.433	10	30	8	13	3	0	1	5	3	8	0	.485	.633
	Eugene (NWL)	SS	.267	25	101	13	27	4	1	2	14	10	24	1	.339	.386
2008	Fort Wayne (MWL)	LoA	.273	119	454	66	124	26	5	7	58	54	101	28	.352	.399
	San Antonio (TL)	AA	.333	2	3	1	1	0	0	0	0	0	2	0	.333	.333
2009	Lake Elsinore (CAL)	HiA	.276	36	145	19	40	6	2	10	34	18	29	3	.360	.552
	San Antonio (TL)	AA	.289	92	346	59	100	19	5	5	43	44	74	14	.372	.416
MINOR LEAGUE TOTALS			.283	284	1079	166	305	58	13	25	154	129	238	46	.362	.430

16 KELLEN KULBACKI, OF

BORN: Nov. 21, 1985. **B-T:** L-L. **HT.:** 5-11. **WT.:** 185. **DRAFTED:** James Madison, 2007 (1st round supplemental). **SIGNED BY:** Ash Lawson.

Taken 40th overall in the 2007 draft, Kulbacki delivered on his potential in 2008 with a monster season in the California League, hitting for average and power and showing a discerning batting eye. In the playoffs that September, he tore the labrum in his right shoulder while crashing into the outfield wall, necessitating surgery. Kulbacki worked hard to rehab the injury, but with his lead hitting shoulder affected he appeared tentative to cut loose with his swing during spring training. He stayed behind in extended spring until May, but when he returned he got off to a slow start. In his first taste of Double-A, Kulbacki hit .201 and went homerless in 36 games before succumbing to an injury even more grisly than his performance. His hamstring detached from the bone, shutting him down for the remaining two months of the season. The injury precluded him from getting at-bats during the fall as well. With a sound shoulder and hitting base, Kulbacki employs a short, compact, low-maintenance swing that produces a solid average and average power production. While his bat speed is just average, his short arms ensure that he doesn't get tied up inside. He knows the strike zone and has a knack for making solid contact. A below-average runner, Kulbacki is a left fielder because his range and arm are fringy. Kulbacki will have to hit to make it to the big leagues, and he'll have to prove in his second shot at Double-A that 2009 was merely a lost year.

Year	Club (League)	Class	AVG	G	AB	R	H	2B	3B	HR	RBI	BB	SO	SB	OBP	SLG
2007	Eugene (NWL)	SS	.301	61	226	33	68	13	3	8	39	27	56	1	.382	.491
2008	Fort Wayne (MWL)	LoA	.164	18	61	9	10	2	0	2	9	9	19	0	.260	.295
	Lake Elsinore (CAL)	HiA	.332	84	304	62	101	18	0	20	66	47	52	1	.428	.589
2009	San Antonio (TL)	AA	.201	36	134	11	27	5	1	0	11	9	23	2	.257	.254
MINOR LEAGUE TOTALS			.284	199	725	115	206	38	4	30	125	92	150	4	.370	.472

17 BLAKE TEKOTTE, OF

BORN: May 24, 1987. **B-T:** L-R. **HT.:** 5-11. **WT.:** 179. **DRAFTED:** Miami, 2008 (3rd round). **SIGNED BY:** Rob Sidwell.

Tekotte began the 2009 season in low Class A in part because of a center-field logjam at Lake Elsinore, where Brad Chalk and Danny Payne roamed. When Tekotte batted just .211/.281/.292 in 47 games during April and May, he didn't exactly argue for a promotion. He righted the ship, batting .328/.429/.529 in June and July, after he shortened his bat path and improved his pitch selection. Tekotte could grow into average power, but much of his value will be tied to his contributions as a tablesetter and as a defender. He put his plus speed to good use, showing a more aggressive baserunning style and stealing 30 bases in 42 attempts last year. He has just enough power to get himself in trouble, and while he excels at turning on inside fastballs, his swing often looks long against offspeed stuff. Plus range in center field stands as Tekotte's strongest tool. He throws well enough for a center fielder and improved his accuracy in 2009. Midwest League observers were quick to credit him for strong makeup. He's agile and athletic with room to fill out. Tekotte will get a crack at Lake Elsinore to begin 2010.

Year	Club (League)	Class	AVG	G	AB	R	H	2B	3B	HR	RBI	BB	SO	SB	OBP	SLG
2008	Eugene (NWL)	SS	.285	47	193	43	55	15	0	6	29	27	45	7	.379	.456
2009	Fort Wayne (MWL)	LoA	.258	134	530	83	137	24	5	13	56	68	97	30	.345	.396
MINOR LEAGUE TOTALS			.266	181	723	126	192	39	5	19	85	95	142	37	.354	.412

18 JEREMY HEFNER, RHP

BORN: March 11, 1986. **B-T:** R-R. **HT.:** 6-4. **WT.:** 215. **DRAFTED:** Oral Roberts, 2007 (5th round). **SIGNED BY:** Lane Decker.

Hefner placed third in the Midwest League in 2008 with 144 strikeouts, and the Padres were hopeful that he'd break out in the California League in 2009. Pitching in the same Lake Elsinore rotation as Cory Luebke and Wynn Pelzer, he finished third in the league with 14 wins, fourth with 142 whiffs and eighth with a 4.12 ERA. A smart pitcher, he limited damage from walks (2.3 per nine innings, the fifth-lowest rate in the Cal League) and stolen bases (just 21 attempts, of which a league-leading 62 percent were caught). Hefner doesn't overpower batters, relying instead on plus movement on his 89-92 mph sinker and an outstanding fading changeup. After losing the depth on his slider after turning pro, he resuscitated a curveball he hadn't thrown regularly since high school. It flashes plus potential, though it wasn't the strikeout pitch San Diego has hoped for. In 2010, Hefner will continue refining his feel for his curveball in Double-A. As a 24-year-old with a strong frame and fine control, he could be a big league rotation option in the second half. A future as a No. 4 or 5 starter or middle reliever awaits.

Year	Club (League)	Class	W	L	ERA	G	GS	CG	SV	IP	H	R	ER	HR	BB	SO	AVG
2007	Eugene (NWL)	SS	2	5	3.90	17	11	0	0	62	51	33	27	3	20	74	.221
2008	Fort Wayne (MWL)	LoA	10	5	3.33	29	24	0	0	140	117	53	52	12	41	144	.228
	Lake Elsinore (CAL)	HiA	0	0	3.60	1	1	0	0	5	3	2	2	0	2	6	.167
2009	Portland (PCL)	AAA	0	0	3.38	1	1	0	0	5	7	2	2	0	2	5	.318
	Lake Elsinore (CAL)	HiA	14	9	4.12	27	27	0	0	151	165	81	69	13	38	142	.284
MINOR LEAGUE TOTALS			26	19	3.76	75	64	0	0	364	343	171	152	28	103	371	.251

19 JERRY SULLIVAN, RHP

BORN: Jan. 18, 1988. **B-T:** R-R. **HT.:** 6-4. **WT.:** 218. **DRAFTED:** Oral Roberts, 2009 (3rd round). **SIGNED BY:** Lane Decker.

Hailing from the same Oral Roberts program as Jeremy Hefner, Sullivan might have turned pro as an early pick out of high school if he hadn't had Tommy John surgery prior to his senior year. In each of his three years of college, he led the Golden Eagles to a Summit League championship and earned all-conference honors. He signed quickly for $430,200 as the Padres' third-round pick in 2009. With an ideal pitcher's frame, Sullivan showed a quality fastball and the potential for two solid secondary pitches during his pro debut. He delivers 91-92 mph fastballs from a steep downhill plane and touches 94 on occasion. His ball runs naturally to his arm side. He has a power slider that's a plus pitch at times and loopy at others. He'll continue refining his strong changeup now that he'll need to use it more in pro ball. Sullivan's clean delivery is a product of his athleticism, though like most all young pitchers, he'll fly open at times, pulling his pitches to his arm side. The Padres want to get him on line to the plate more consistently. A smart pitcher, he varies his time to the plate and stymies the running game just six runners attempted to steal when he was on the mound. Sullivan offers enough present stuff and future projectability to make him an intriguing mid-rotation prospect. He'll probably open his first full pro season in low Class A, with the chance for a midseason promotion.

Year	Club (League)	Class	W	L	ERA	G	GS	CG	SV	IP	H	R	ER	HR	BB	SO	AVG
2009	Eugene (NWL)	SS	5	3	4.02	16	9	0	0	54	44	26	24	5	27	58	.219
MINOR LEAGUE TOTALS			5	3	4.02	16	9	0	0	54	44	26	24	5	27	58	.219

20 CRAIG ITALIANO, RHP

BORN: July 22, 1986. **B-T:** R-R. **HT.:** 6-4. **WT.:** 210. **DRAFTED:** HS—Flower Mound, Texas, 2005 (2nd round). **SIGNED BY:** Blake Davis (Athletics).

In the wake of "Moneyball," the Athletics surprised the industry by selecting high school arms in the second through fourth rounds of the 2005 draft, starting with Italiano. His arm strength has long been evident, but injuries limited him to 35 combined innings in 2006 (when he had labrum surgery) and 2007 (when a line drive hit him and caused a skull fracture). Healthy again in 2008, Italiano hit the wall once he got to high Class A and struggled there again as a starter last season. After the Padres acquired him along with Sean Gallagher and Ryan Webb in a midseason trade for Scott Hairston, they made Italiano a full-time reliever and lowered his arm angle from over the top to high three-quarters. His power fastball/slider combo and spotty control had long suggested a bullpen role. With his new slot, he touched 96 mph and sat at 92-94 more consistently, while showing outstanding boring action and improved control. His slider showed more depth, and Cal League batters struggled to lift either of Italiano's pitches. He didn't allow a home run in 31 innings while generating a 5.71 groundout/airout ratio with Lake Elsinore. A physical mound presence with strong makeup, Italiano could be ready to for the big league bullpen at some point in 2010, especially after being added to the 40-man roster in the offseason. He'll likely start the year in Double-A.

Year	Club (League)	Class	W	L	ERA	G	GS	CG	SV	IP	H	R	ER	HR	BB	SO	AVG
2005	Athletics (AZL)	R	1	2	6.75	8	3	0	0	19	20	17	14	0	8	27	.267
2006	Kane County (MWL)	LoA	0	1	3.50	4	4	0	0	18	18	12	7	1	9	23	.261
2007	Kane County (MWL)	LoA	0	3	12.71	6	6	0	0	17	32	25	24	3	16	24	.416
2008	Kane County (MWL)	LoA	7	0	1.16	14	14	0	0	70	43	16	9	2	35	79	.177
	Stockton (CAL)	HiA	1	4	9.90	14	5	0	0	30	44	37	33	7	26	33	.333
2009	Stockton (CAL)	HiA	5	6	5.63	16	16	0	0	77	83	55	48	6	40	75	.280
	Lake Elsinore (CAL)	HiA	0	1	1.44	19	0	0	0	31	24	10	5	0	10	44	.209
MINOR LEAGUE TOTALS			14	17	4.82	81	48	0	0	262	264	172	140	19	144	305	.262

21 CHAD HUFFMAN, OF/1B

BORN: April 29, 1985. **B-T:** R-R. **HT.:** 6-1. **WT.:** 215. **DRAFTED:** Texas Christian, 2006 (2nd round).
SIGNED BY: Tim Holt.

In two seasons in Double-A, Huffman belted just 16 home runs in 168 games—including a mere four at home in San Antonio. Freed from an extremely tough park for righthanded power hitters, he slugged 20 homers and 30 doubles in Triple-A last season. Unfortunately, he showed many other limitations, including contact issues, a pull-centric approach and a susceptibility to offspeed offerings. A top college performer who won a Northwest League on-base percentage title (.439) in his pro debut, Huffman has a strong batting eye to go with the power to profile at an outfield corner. He can smoke quality fastballs, but righthanders with good breaking balls and lefties who work him soft away give him fits. His pull approach leaves him vulnerable on the outer half, and he hit just .185/.307/.323 in 130 at-bats against southpaws in 2009. He could hit for higher average if he committed to using center and right field. Huffman is a fringe-average runner and a merely adequate defender in left field or at first base. His arm is below-average. A high-energy player who exudes confidence, he looks like a future regular on his best days and a part-timer on his worst. He's likely facing at least another half-season in Triple-A after being added to the 40-man roster for the first time. His brother Royce, who like Chad played baseball and football at Texas Christian, has spent the last seven years in Triple-A, most recently with the Rangers.

Year	Club (League)	Class	AVG	G	AB	R	H	2B	3B	HR	RBI	BB	SO	SB	OBP	SLG
2006	Eugene (NWL)	SS	.343	54	198	41	68	17	1	9	40	25	34	2	.439	.576
	Fort Wayne (MWL)	LoA	.214	5	14	2	3	0	1	0	0	2	2	0	.313	.357
2007	Lake Elsinore (CAL)	HiA	.307	84	316	63	97	19	2	15	76	42	56	0	.402	.522
	San Antonio (TL)	AA	.269	49	167	28	45	4	1	7	28	22	44	0	.362	.431
2008	San Antonio (TL)	AA	.284	119	437	68	124	30	1	9	58	67	83	1	.383	.419
2009	Portland (PCL)	AAA	.269	135	469	65	126	30	2	20	68	57	115	8	.361	.469
MINOR LEAGUE TOTALS			.289	446	1601	267	463	100	8	60	270	215	334	11	.385	.474

22 JORGE REYES, RHP

BORN: Dec. 7, 1987. **B-T:** B-R. **HT.:** 6-3. **WT.:** 195. **DRAFTED:** Oregon State, 2009 (17th round).
SIGNED BY: Andrew Salvo.

Reyes defined inconsistency during his three seasons at Oregon State. As a freshman in 2007, he was the Most Outstanding Player at the College World Series as the Beavers won their second straight national title. His sophomore year was a disaster, as he posted a 7.08 ERA and was arrested for reckless endangerment after he and two teammates unlawfully discharged a rifle during a target-shooting incident. Last spring, Reyes went 6-2, 4.20 and fell to the 17th round of the draft because of his track record and his choice of Scott Boras as an agent. In some ways, Reyes' situation mirrors that of Wynn Pelzer, a Boras client whom San Diego drafted in the ninth round in 2007. Both pitchers used a strong Cape Cod League showing to persuade the Padres to dole out an above-slot bonus. Reyes signed at the Aug. 17 deadline for $200,000. Reyes' stuff is firm, headlined by a 90-91 mph sinker that touches 94. He mixes in a plus slider but lacks a third pitch. His command looked better this summer than it had at any time since his freshman year. He turned in three strong starts at Eugene after signing, paving the way for the jump to low Class A next year. He'll be developed as a starter, but his repertoire may fit better in the bullpen.

Year	Club (League)	Class	W	L	ERA	G	GS	CG	SV	IP	H	R	ER	HR	BB	SO	AVG
2009	Eugene (NWL)	SS	1	1	1.38	3	3	0	0	13	9	3	2	1	2	12	.214
MINOR LEAGUE TOTALS			1	1	1.38	3	3	0	0	13	9	3	2	1	2	12	.214

23 CEDRIC HUNTER, OF

BORN: March 10, 1988. **B-T:** L-L. **HT.:** 6-0. **WT.:** 185. **DRAFTED:** HS—Lithonia, Ga., 2006 (3rd round).
SIGNED BY: Pete DeYoung.

Hunter seems to perform well every other year. The Arizona League MVP in 2006, he struggled in the pitcher-friendly Midwest League in his first full pro season. He rebounded with a strong 2008 performance in high Class A, then turned in by far his worst season in 2009 in Double-A. While he led the Texas League in plate appearances per strikeout (13.4), his incredible hand-eye coordination has meant that he has never had to define his strike zone. Too often he'll put in play the first pitch he can get his bat on—leading to lot of groundouts and shanked flyballs from well-located pitches. His unorthodox swing is geared toward hitting line drives all over the field and not for power. The Padres would like to see Hunter add strength and hit for a bit more authority. He improved his routes and reads in center field, but because he's an average runner he might not have the pure speed to stay there in the majors. His below-average arm would dictate a move to left field, where his bat would have to take a big step forward to prevent him sinking in the morass of tweeners in Triple-A. After a tough year in which little went right, Hunter's attempt at redemption will begin with a repeat of Double-A.

Year	Club (League)	Class	AVG	G	AB	R	H	2B	3B	HR	RBI	BB	SO	SB	OBP	SLG
2006	Padres (AZL)	R	.371	52	213	46	79	13	4	1	44	40	22	17	.467	.484
	Eugene (NWL)	SS	.267	5	15	0	4	0	0	0	0	1	3	0	.313	.267
2007	Fort Wayne (MWL)	LoA	.282	129	496	53	140	20	2	7	58	47	78	8	.344	.373
	Portland (PCL)	AAA	.500	3	4	1	2	0	0	1	3	1	1	0	.600	1.250
2008	Lake Elsinore (CAL)	HiA	.318	134	584	98	186	33	3	11	84	42	47	12	.362	.442
2009	San Antonio (TL)	AA	.261	131	541	71	141	20	6	2	54	25	43	13	.294	.331
MINOR LEAGUE TOTALS			.298	454	1853	269	552	86	15	22	243	156	194	50	.352	.396

24 RYAN WEBB, RHP

BORN: Feb. 5, 1986. **B-T:** R-R. **HT.:** 6-6. **WT.:** 215. **DRAFTED:** HS—Clearwater, Fla., 2004 (4th round). **SIGNED BY:** Steve Barningham (Athletics).

Joining the Padres in the Scott Hairston trade with the Athletics that also netted Craig Italiano and Sean Gallagher, Webb provided San Diego with instant value, showing two plus pitches while making 28 big league appearances. Former Padres GM Kevin Towers made an art form in putting together effective, low-cost bullpens, and the club's September crew featured a host of promising recent acquisitions: Gallagher and Webb, Aaron Poreda and Adam Russell (Jake Peavy trade with the White Sox), Luke Gregerson (Khalil Greene trade with the Cardinals), Luis Perdomo (waiver claim from the Giants) and Edward Mujica (purchased from the Indians). Even rookies Greg Burke (signed out of independent leagues) and Ernesto Frieri (signed out of Colombia) sprang from modest beginnings. Much like Italiano, Webb featured undeniable arm strength while in the Oakland system but didn't thrive until moving to the bullpen. His fastball sat at 94-96 mph in September, and he also showed off a nasty mid-80s curveball that he can locate for strikes. Webb is working to refine his high-80s cutter to bust in on the hands of lefthanders, who tagged him for an .889 OPS and all three of the homers he allowed in his big league debut. He's a strong candidate to open 2010 back in the Padres' bullpen.

Year	Club (League)	Class	W	L	ERA	G	GS	CG	SV	IP	H	R	ER	HR	BB	SO	AVG
2004	Athletics (AZL)	R	1	1	4.87	8	7	0	0	20	18	11	11	2	1	23	.228
2005	Kane County (MWL)	LoA	5	11	4.76	24	23	0	0	129	139	82	68	16	41	84	.280
2006	Stockton (CAL)	HiA	8	9	5.28	23	23	0	0	118	160	75	69	9	37	96	.332
2007	Midland (TL)	AA	0	4	9.12	5	5	0	0	26	34	27	26	10	10	16	.324
	Stockton (CAL)	HiA	4	7	5.75	15	15	0	0	83	83	59	53	13	22	71	.255
2008	Midland (TL)	AA	9	8	5.19	25	22	0	0	130	165	86	75	12	44	94	.310
2009	Sacramento (PCL)	AAA	7	1	4.34	31	2	0	2	46	57	22	22	3	15	39	.313
	Portland (PCL)	AAA	0	0	3.00	3	0	0	0	3	3	1	1	0	1	0	.300
	San Diego (NL)	MAJ	2	1	3.86	28	0	0	0	26	27	14	11	3	11	19	.265
MAJOR LEAGUE TOTALS			2	1	3.86	28	0	0	0	26	27	14	11	3	11	19	.265
MINOR LEAGUE TOTALS			34	41	5.28	134	97	0	2	554	659	363	325	65	171	423	.289

25 LUIS DURANGO, OF

BORN: April 23, 1986. **B-T:** B-R. **HT.:** 5-9. **WT.:** 158. **SIGNED:** Panama, 2003. **SIGNED BY:** Robert Rowley.

The diminutive Durango has come a long way since signing as a 17-year-old, steadily adding to his list of admirers with each minor league level he successfully completes. He won batting titles in his first two seasons in the United States, batting .378 in the Arizona League in 2006 and then .367 in the Northwest League as part of an MVP campaign in 2007. Durango started in left field for Panama in the World Baseball Classic last spring and then hit the ground running in Double-A, finishing the year ranked second in the Texas League with 44 stolen bases and 81 walks and third with his .390 on-base percentage. That snapshot provides a summary of Durango's offensive value. A switch-hitter, he can get his bat on most pitches, either slapping them for singles or fouling them off until the pitcher throws ball four. He's a plus-plus runner who has dramatically improved his instincts both on the bases and in center field. With a modest 70 percent success rate in full-season ball, he needs to be more efficient stealing bases. With San Antonio, Durango split time in center field with Cedric Hunter, limiting his repetitions at the position where he profiles as an average defender. He has improved his arm strength to average through dedication to his throwing program. With virtually no power—he has three career homers in four years in the U.S.—Durango will have to rely on his legs to carry him. Tighter team defenses and pitchers with more refined control figure to diminish his on-base ability in the big leagues. Added to the 40-man roster following the 2008 season, Durango received a September callup to San Diego last year. He has two options remaining, but he could make the Padres as a reserve as early as 2010.

SAN DIEGO PADRES

Year	Club (League)	Class	AVG	G	AB	R	H	2B	3B	HR	RBI	BB	SO	SB	OBP	SLG
2004	Universidad (VSL)	R	.227	50	132	28	30	1	0	0	8	16	16	10	.333	.235
2005	Red Sox/Padres (VSL)	R	.342	59	190	44	65	6	1	0	13	37	25	19	.473	.384
2006	Padres (AZL)	R	.378	39	143	35	54	2	4	0	14	23	16	17	.470	.448
2007	Eugene (NWL)	SS	.367	69	300	60	110	6	8	2	32	29	32	17	.422	.460
2008	Fort Wayne (MWL)	LoA	.305	93	334	56	102	11	3	1	25	49	43	14	.395	.365
	Lake Elsinore (CAL)	HiA	.431	17	72	20	31	4	1	0	10	13	7	1	.506	.514
2009	San Antonio (TL)	AA	.281	129	456	78	128	9	2	0	25	81	70	44	.390	.309
	San Diego (NL)	MAJ	.545	9	11	3	6	0	0	0	0	2	2	2	.615	.545
MAJOR LEAGUE TOTALS			.545	9	11	3	6	0	0	0	0	2	2	2	.615	.545
MINOR LEAGUE TOTALS			.320	456	1627	321	520	39	19	3	127	248	209	122	.415	.372

26 CESAR RAMOS, LHP

BORN: June 22, 1984. **B-T:** L-L. **HT.:** 6-2. **WT.:** 205. **DRAFTED:** Long Beach State, 2005 (1st round supplemental). **SIGNED BY:** Brendan Hause.

The Padres opted not to call up Ramos in September 2008, though he had been just as effective as Portland rotation-mates Josh Geer and Wade LeBlanc, both of whom received promotions. The oversight apparently provided ample motivation for Ramos. He rededicated himself in the winter prior to the 2009 season, getting in better shape, polishing his curveball and surviving in big league camp until the final cut. He would have been recalled in June if not for shoulder inflammation that knocked him out for two months, but he recovered to make his big league debut in September. Ramos has better raw stuff than either Geer or LeBlanc. The problem rests with the deployment of his fastball, changeup and cutter. He sits at 90-91 mph and touches 93 in every outing, but his heater lacks life and his fringy slider lacks finish. He compensates a bit with a plus changeup, and he works inside on righthanders with a high-80s cutter. The return of his curveball gave Ramos a surprise weapon last season, something he could throw for a called strike as a get-me-over offering early or as a back-door pitch later in the count. Ramos' ceiling is strictly that of fifth starter, but he's ready when the Padres need him.

Year	Club (League)	Class	W	L	ERA	G	GS	CG	SV	IP	H	R	ER	HR	BB	SO	AVG
2005	Eugene (NWL)	SS	0	1	6.53	6	4	0	0	21	27	21	15	3	7	13	.303
	Fort Wayne (MWL)	LoA	3	2	4.19	7	7	1	0	39	42	19	18	0	7	32	.282
2006	Lake Elsinore (CAL)	HiA	7	8	3.70	26	24	0	0	141	161	72	58	9	44	70	.292
2007	San Antonio (TL)	AA	13	9	3.41	27	27	2	0	164	153	69	62	15	43	90	.249
2008	Portland (PCL)	AAA	9	11	5.29	28	27	0	0	150	183	108	88	17	57	105	.306
2009	Padres (AZL)	R	0	1	2.25	4	2	0	0	8	8	3	2	0	0	8	.250
	Lake Elsinore (CAL)	HiA	1	0	1.00	2	1	0	0	9	9	1	1	0	5	6	.250
	Portland (PCL)	AAA	5	6	3.99	15	15	1	0	77	84	42	34	7	31	45	.274
	San Diego (NL)	MAJ	0	1	3.07	5	2	0	0	15	19	5	5	0	4	10	.328
MAJOR LEAGUE TOTALS			0	1	3.07	5	2	0	0	15	19	5	5	0	4	10	.328
MINOR LEAGUE TOTALS			38	38	4.12	115	107	4	0	607	667	335	278	51	194	369	..280

27 MATT ANTONELLI, 2B

BORN: April 8, 1985. **B-T:** R-R. **HT.:** 6-0. **WT.:** 205. **DRAFTED:** Wake Forest, 2006 (1st round). **SIGNED BY:** Ash Lawson.

Few prospects who have performed as well as Antonelli did in Double-A have played as poorly as he has in Triple-A. Signed for $1.575 million as the 17th overall pick in 2006, he has batted a miserable .209/.325/.327 with 11 home runs in 187 games with Portland over the past two seasons. The Padres yanked him from the Pacific Coast League in mid-August so he could rework his swing with hitting coordinator Tony Muser in Arizona. Antonelli put in three hours a day, examining old Wake Forest video and incorporating a stride and more load in his swing in an effort to keep his bat in the hitting zone longer. He took his rebuilt approach to the auxiliary fall league in Arizona and began hitting the ball where it was pitched, instead of hooking his swing in an effort to pull pitches and generate power. Antonelli shed some of the bulk he carried in 2008 and came to spring training lighter and leaner. But he banged up his right knee and didn't report to Portland until mid-May. Though his offense has gone backward, Antonelli has improved his defensive play so much that he's become a solid-average defender at second base. His first step was quicker and his double-play pivot was cleaner in 2009. He always has shown above-average arm strength. The Padres believe that he'll forge a big league role, either as starting second baseman or utilityman capable of also playing third base and center field.

Year	Club (League)	Class	AVG	G	AB	R	H	2B	3B	HR	RBI	BB	SO	SB	OBP	SLG
2006	Eugene (NWL)	SS	.286	55	189	38	54	12	1	0	22	46	31	9	.426	.360
	Fort Wayne (MWL)	LoA	.125	5	16	3	2	1	1	0	0	2	6	0	.222	.313
2007	Lake Elsinore (CAL)	HiA	.314	82	347	89	109	14	4	14	54	53	58	18	.409	.499
	San Antonio (TL)	AA	.294	49	187	34	55	11	1	7	24	30	36	10	.395	.476
2008	Portland (PCL)	AAA	.215	128	451	62	97	19	4	7	39	76	86	6	.335	.322
	San Diego (NL)	MAJ	.193	21	57	6	11	2	0	1	3	5	11	0	.292	.281
2009	Portland (PCL)	AAA	.196	59	189	25	37	11	2	4	22	26	30	1	.300	.339
MAJOR LEAGUE TOTALS			.193	21	57	6	11	2	0	1	3	5	11	0	.292	.281
MINOR LEAGUE TOTALS			.257	378	1379	251	354	68	13	32	161	233	247	44	.369	.394

28 DEXTER CARTER, RHP

BORN: Feb. 5, 1987. **B-T:** R-R. **HT.:** 6-6. **WT.:** 205. **DRAFTED:** Old Dominion, 2008 (13th round). **SIGNED BY:** Chuck Fox (White Sox).

After posting an 8.76 ERA as an Old Dominion junior, Carter lasted 13 rounds in the 2008 draft and signed with the White Sox for $32,500. He led the Rookie-level Pioneer League with a 2.23 ERA in his pro debut, helping Great Falls to the league title. He continued to dominate in low Class A last season, averaging 10.9 strikeouts per nine innings before the White Sox traded him, Aaron Poreda, Clayton Richard and Adam Russell to the Padres for Jake Peavy in July. Carter got roughed up after the deal, though he still managed to rank fifth in the minors with 166 strikeouts. The Padres attributed his poor performance after the trade to a tendency to work uphill, causing his stuff flatten out. Carter's frame, raw arm strength and lean, loose delivery remained intact, so San Diego used instructional league to get him throwing downhill. He sits at 90-92 mph and touches 93 with his fastball. He flashes a strong curveball, but too often he doesn't locate his breaker in the strike zone. He has the same problem with his changeup. Destined for high Class A in 2010, Carter projects as a possible No. 3 starter if he can make the necessary adjustments.

Year	Club (League)	Class	W	L	ERA	G	GS	CG	SV	IP	H	R	ER	HR	BB	SO	AVG
2008	Great Falls (PIO)	R	6	1	2.23	15	12	0	0	69	44	23	17	3	25	89	.179
2009	Kannapolis (SAL)	LoA	6	2	3.13	19	19	0	0	118	103	44	41	9	32	143	.236
	Fort Wayne (MWL)	LoA	1	4	12.86	6	6	0	0	21	34	30	30	3	15	23	.370
MINOR LEAGUE TOTALS			13	7	3.81	40	37	0	0	208	181	97	88	15	72	255	.234

29 MATT CLARK, 1B

BORN: Dec. 10, 1986. **B-T:** L-R. **HT.:** 6-5. **WT.:** 215. **DRAFTED:** Louisiana State, 2008 (12th round). **SIGNED BY:** David Francia.

Clark led NCAA Division I with 28 home runs at Louisiana State in 2008, one year after leading the California junior college ranks with 15 bombs while at Riverside CC. He's the son of Rangers Triple-A pitching coach and former big leaguer Terry Clark. The Padres committed a $150,000 bonus to Clark, a 12th-round pick, and he led the organization with 24 homers and 101 RBIs in his full-season debut in 2009. He hit so well with Fort Wayne that he advanced to high Class A, leapfrogging 2008 first-round pick Allan Dykstra on the organizational depth chart. A physical 6-foot-5, Clark generates natural loft and leverage with his lefthanded stroke, showing consistent plus-plus raw power to all fields. He has enough juice to hit the ball out of any park. He swings and misses too much to hit for anything but a modest average, but he hits the ball where it's pitched and excelled in RBI situations in 2009. He'll take his walks when pitchers work him carefully. Clark played third base as an amateur, but he's not mobile enough to play there in the pro ranks. He's a below-average runner and adequate first baseman. His bat will have to carry him. Clark's power production ought to get him to Triple-A at least, and he could get there at some point this season.

Year	Club (League)	Class	AVG	G	AB	R	H	2B	3B	HR	RBI	BB	SO	SB	OBP	SLG
2008	Eugene (NWL)	SS	.279	38	140	18	39	8	0	5	32	23	38	0	.384	.443
2009	Fort Wayne (MWL)	LoA	.266	64	252	41	67	22	0	11	55	33	72	0	.352	.484
	Lake Elsinore (CAL)	HiA	.292	67	250	44	73	13	3	13	46	28	62	2	.367	.524
MINOR LEAGUE TOTALS			.279	169	642	103	179	43	3	29	133	84	172	2	.365	.491

30 COLE FIGUEROA, SS/2B

BORN: June 30, 1987. **B-T:** L-R. **HT.:** 5-10. **WT.:** 180. **DRAFTED:** Florida, 2008 (6th round). **SIGNED BY:** Rob Sidwell.

The Padres followed Figueroa, their 2008 sixth-round pick, in the Cape Cod League before signing him in late July for $400,000. His father Bien played briefly for the Cardinals in 1992 and later served as a minor league manager. As such, Cole plays above his tools and has "instincts coming out of both pockets," in the words of one Padres official. Because of his natural feel for hitting, Figueroa began his first full pro season in high Class A, but he aggravated the surgically repaired meniscus in his right knee and missed all of May. He spent three months rehabbing the injury the previous offseason. After batting .187 with no power in high Class A, Figueroa was demoted and played well for Fort Wayne. He works the count, hits all types of pitching and uses the whole field, so he should hit for average. He struggles with pitches on the inner half, however, and has below-average power. Figueroa's thickening lower half translates into well-below-average speed, and he lacks the quickness to handle the demands of shortstop in the big leagues. He has great hands and an average arm, so he probably will wind up at second base, where he saw some action in 2009. Evaluators are mixed on his ultimate ceiling. Some see him as a potential regular, while others see an organizational player. He'll resume his career in high Class A in 2010.

Year	Club (League)	Class	AVG	G	AB	R	H	2B	3B	HR	RBI	BB	SO	SB	OBP	SLG
2008	Eugene (NWL)	SS	.289	32	114	23	33	6	0	5	16	24	16	7	.410	.474
2009	Lake Elsinore (CAL)	HiA	.187	21	75	5	14	3	0	0	9	6	14	5	.256	.227
	Fort Wayne (MWL)	LoA	.319	70	238	32	76	15	1	1	34	37	38	10	.408	.403
MINOR LEAGUE TOTALS			.288	123	427	60	123	24	1	6	59	67	68	22	.384	.391

San Francisco Giants

BY ANDY BAGGARLY

Following four consecutive losing seasons, the Giants witnessed a return to respectability in 2009 and surprised many by contending into September. Their 88-74 record was a 16-game improvement over the previous year and it came just in time for general manager Brian Sabean and manager Bruce Bochy, who got two-year contracts (plus a club option for 2012) one week after the season ended.

San Francisco did miss the playoffs for a sixth consecutive year. And there's no guarantee they'll continue their upward trajectory in 2010, especially if they're unable to fortify a lineup that ranked last in the National League in on-base percentage and 15th in slugging. Hitting coach Carney Lansford took the fall after the season.

Aside from Pablo Sandoval, the runner-up for the NL batting title, all of the Giants' highlights came on the mound. Randy Johnson won his 300th game, Jonathan Sanchez tossed the club's first no-hitter in 33 years and Tim Lincecum led the major leagues with 261 strikeouts en route to his second straight Cy Young Award. Matt Cain was a first-time all-star while nearly matching Lincecum start for start. And for the first time, Barry Zito performed like he wasn't fretting over being called a $126-million failure.

The Giants defied their own pronouncements when they called up lefthander Madison Bumgarner and catcher Buster Posey for the stretch run. Posey got only 17 at-bats in September as San Francisco faded, and perhaps the club's most important offseason decision will be if he's ready to start on Opening Day.

Bochy and Sabean have reputations for favoring veterans and giving short leashes to unestablished players, so their extensions were unpopular with some Giants fans. Their critics will monitor the Posey situation carefully.

Managing partner Bill Neukom lauded the farm system's 411-286 (.590) record, by far the best among major league organizations. Four of San Francisco's six U.S.-based affiliates reached the playoffs, with high Class A San Jose and short-season Salem-Keizer winning league titles.

Neukom said the Giants would continue to invest in player development and emphasize homegrown talent. They committed $3.3 million to high school righthander Zack Wheeler, whom they tabbed with the sixth overall pick in the draft. Scouting director John Barr also drafted a couple of power hitters in

Pablo Sandoval emerged as San Francisco's offensive leader, and fan favorite, in 2009

BILL NICHOLS

TOP 30 PROSPECTS

1. Buster Posey, c	**16.** Henry Sosa, rhp
2. Madison Bumgarner, lhp	**17.** Conor Gillaspie, 3b
3. Zack Wheeler, rhp	**18.** Chris Dominguez, 3b/1b
4. Thomas Neal, of	**19.** Eric Surkamp, lhp
5. Dan Runzler, lhp	**20.** Steve Johnson, rhp
6. Tommy Joseph, c	**21.** Brett Pill, 1b
7. Roger Kieschnick, of	**22.** Johnny Monell, c
8. Ehire Adrianza, ss	**23.** Clayton Tanner, lhp
9. Brandon Crawford, ss	**24.** Matt Graham, rhp
10. Francisco Peguero, of	**25.** Mike McBryde, of
11. Nick Noonan, 2b	**26.** Craig Clark, lhp
12. Rafael Rodriguez, of	**27.** Jose Casilla, rhp
13. Darren Ford, of	**28.** Aaron King, lhp
14. Waldis Joaquin, rhp	**29.** Brock Bond, 2b
15. Jason Stoffel, rhp	**30.** Angel Villalona, 1b

high school catcher Tommy Joseph and Louisville third baseman Chris Dominguez. Two prolific sluggers at San Jose, outfielders Thomas Neal and Roger Kieschnick, offered further hope at striking a balance in a traditionally pitching-heavy system.

For years, club officials felt pressure to take advantage of Barry Bonds' presence to take annual shots at the World Series. Now a different window is opening, which should bring its own sense of urgency in 2010. Lincecum will no longer work cheap after gaining arbitration status, and Cain is one year closer to free agency.

General Manager: Brian Sabean. **Farm Director:** Fred Stanley. **Scouting Director:** John Barr.

Class	Team	League	W	L	PCT	Finish*	Manager(s)
Majors	San Francisco Giants	National	88	74	.543	5th (16)	Bruce Bochy
Triple-A	Fresno Grizzlies	Pacific Coast	71	73	.493	t-10th (16)	Dan Rohn
Double-A	#Connecticut Defenders	Eastern	83	59	.585	2nd (12)	Steve Decker
High A	San Jose Giants	California	93	47	.664	†1st (10)	Andy Skeels
Low A	Augusta GreenJackets	South Atlantic	76	63	.547	3rd (16)	Dave Machemer
Short-season	Salem-Keizer Volcanoes	Northwest	49	27	.645	†1st (8)	Tom Trebelhorn
Rookie	AZL Giants	Arizona	39	17	.696	1st (11)	Mike Goff
Overall 2009 Minor League Record			411	286	.590	1st (30)	

#Double-A affiliate will move to Richmond (Eastern) in 2010.

LAST YEAR'S TOP 30

Player, Pos.		Status
1.	Madison Bumgarner, lhp	No. 2
2.	Buster Posey, c	No. 1
3.	Angel Villalona, 1b	No. 30
4.	Tim Alderson, rhp	(Pirates)
5.	Nick Noonan, 2b	No. 11
6.	Ehire Adrianza, ss	No. 8
7.	Conor Gillaspie, 3b	No. 17
8.	Rafael Rodriguez, of	No. 12
9.	Scott Barnes, lhp	(Indians)
10.	Sergio Romo, rhp	Majors
11.	Waldis Joaquin, rhp	No. 14
12.	Wendell Fairley, of	Dropped out
13.	Henry Sosa, rhp	No. 16
14.	Roger Kieschnick, of	No. 7
15.	Kevin Pucetas, rhp	Dropped out
16.	Jackson Williams, c	Dropped out
17.	Travis Ishikawa, 1b	Majors
18.	Alex Hinshaw, lhp	Majors
19.	Mike McBryde, of	No. 25
20.	Clayton Tanner, lhp	No. 23
21.	Aaron King, lhp	No. 28
22.	Francisco Peguero, of	No. 10
23.	Thomas Neal, 1b/of	No. 4
24.	Matt Downs, inf/of	Dropped out
25.	Edwin Quirarte, rhp	Dropped out
26.	Osiris Matos, rhp	Dropped out
27.	Charlie Culberson, ss	Dropped out
28.	Luis Perdomo, rhp	(Padres)
29.	Billy Sadler, rhp	(Astros)
30.	Joey Martinez, rhp	Dropped out

BEST TOOLS

Best Hitter for Average	Buster Posey
Best Power Hitter	Chris Dominguez
Best Strike-Zone Discipline	Buster Posey
Fastest Baserunner	Darren Ford
Best Athlete	Mike McBryde
Best Fastball	Dan Runzler
Best Curveball	Eric Surkamp
Best Slider	Dan Runzler
Best Changeup	Craig Clark
Best Control	Madison Bumgarner
Best Defensive Catcher	Buster Posey
Best Defensive Infielder	Brandon Crawford
Best Infield Arm	Brian Bocock
Best Defensive Outfielder	Mike McBryde
Best Outfield Arm	Mike McBryde

PROJECTED 2013 LINEUP

Catcher	Buster Posey
First Base	Tommy Joseph
Second Base	Nick Noonan
Third Base	Pablo Sandoval
Shortstop	Brandon Crawford
Left Field	Thomas Neal
Center Field	Francisco Peguero
Right Field	Roger Kieschnick
No. 1 Starter	Tim Lincecum
No. 2 Starter	Matt Cain
No. 3 Starter	Madison Bumgarner
No. 4 Starter	Zack Wheeler
No. 5 Starter	Jonathan Sanchez
Closer	Brian Wilson

TOP PROSPECTS OF THE DECADE

Year	Player, Pos.	2009 Org.
2000	Kurt Ainsworth, rhp	Out of baseball
2001	Jerome Williams, rhp	Athletics
2002	Jerome Williams, rhp	Athletics
2003	Jesse Foppert, rhp	Giants
2004	Merkin Valdez, rhp	Giants
2005	Matt Cain, rhp	Giants
2006	Matt Cain, rhp	Giants
2007	Tim Lincecum, rhp	Giants
2008	Angel Villalona, 3b/1b	Giants
2009	Madison Bumgarner, lhp	Giants

TOP DRAFT PICKS OF THE DECADE

Year	Player, Pos.	2009 Org.
2000	Boof Bonser, rhp	Twins
2001	Brad Hennessey, rhp	Orioles
2002	Matt Cain, rhp	Giants
2003	David Aardsma, rhp	Mariners
2004	Eddy Martinez-Esteve, of (2nd round)	Giants
2005	Ben Copeland, of (4th round)	Giants
2006	Tim Lincecum, rhp	Giants
2007	Madison Bumgarner, lhp	Giants
2008	Buster Posey, c	Giants
2009	Zack Wheeler, rhp	Giants

LARGEST BONUSES IN CLUB HISTORY

Buster Posey, 2008	$6,200,000
Zack Wheeler, 2009	$3,300,000
Rafael Rodriguez, 2008	$2,550,000
Angel Villalona, 2006	$2,100,000
Tim Lincecum, 2006	$2,025,000

SAN FRANCISCO GIANTS

TOP 2010 ROOKIE: Buster Posey, c. He eventually should become the Giants' first homegrown all-star position player since Matt Williams in 1996.

BREAKOUT PROSPECT: Johnny Monell, c. His lefthanded power and improving skills behind the plate could take him from the 30th round of the draft to San Francisco.

SLEEPER: Ydwin Villegas, ss. The Venezuelan teenager must gain strength and is just learning how to hit, but he's a defensive star in the making.

SOURCE OF TOP 30 TALENT			
Homegrown	29	Acquired	1
College	12	Trades	1
Junior college	2	Rule 5 draft	0
High school	7	Independent leagues	0
Draft-and-follow	1	Free agents/waivers	0
Nondrafted free agents	0		
International	7		

Numbers in parentheses indicate prospect rankings

LF
Thomas Neal (4)
Wendell Fairley
Eddy Martinez-Esteve
Gus Benusa

CF
Francisco Peguero (10)
Darren Ford (13)
Mike McBryde (25)
Ben Copeland
Evan Crawford

RF
Roger Kieschnick (7)
Rafael Rodriguez (12)

3B
Conor Gillaspie (17)
Chris Dominguez (18)
Ryan Rohlinger
Charlie Culberson
Drew Biery

SS
Ehire Adrianza (8)
Brandon Crawford (9)
Ydwin Villegas
Brian Bocock
Ryan Cavan

2B
Nick Noonan (11)
Brock Bond (29)
Matt Downs
Juan Carlos Perez
Nick Liles
Sharlon Schoop

1B
Brett Pill (21)
Angel Villalona (30)
Brandon Belt
Brian Horwitz
Jesus Guzman
Andy D'Alessio
Josh Mazzola
C.J. Ziegler

C
Buster Posey (1)
Tommy Joseph (6)
Johnny Monell (22)
Jackson Williams
Hector Sanchez

RHP

Starters	Relievers
Zack Wheeler (3)	Waldis Joaquin (14)
Henry Sosa (16)	Jason Stoffel (15)
Steve Johnson (20)	Jose Casilla (27)
Matt Graham (24)	Steve Edlefsen
Joe Martinez	Edwin Quirarte
Kevin Pucetas	Daniel Turpen
Jorge Bucardo	Andrew Reichard
Cameron Lamb	T.J. Brewer
Jeremy Toole	Kaohi Downing
Edward Concepcion	
Wilber Bucardo	
Garrett Broshuis	
Kyle Nicholson	

LHP

Starters	Relievers
Madison Bumgarner (2)	Dan Runzler (5)
Eric Surkamp (19)	Aaron King (28)
Clayton Tanner (23)	Joe Paterson
Craig Clark (26)	Ryan Verdugo
Paul Oseguera	Wilmin Rodriguez
Ari Ronick	

2009   BONUSES: $6.3 MILLION

BEST PURE HITTER: C Tommy Joseph (2) was one of the best high school hitters in the draft and plays a premium position, so the Giants were thrilled to get him with the 55th pick.

BEST POWER HITTER: 3B/1B Chris Dominguez (3) has 80 raw power on the 20-80 scouting scale, though making contact is an issue. He won four conference or summer league home run titles while at Louisville, and he set a school record with 25 homers as a junior before launching 11 more in his pro debut. Joseph hit a 465-foot blast at the 2009 International Power Showcase, a high school home run derby.

FASTEST RUNNER: OFs Evan Crawford (9) and Jonathan White (40) both have plus-plus speed.

BEST DEFENSIVE PLAYER: 1B Brandon Belt (5) is slick around the bag. Dominguez has jaw-dropping arm strength to match his power, but his range is fringy.

BEST FASTBALL: RHPs Zack Wheeler (1), Jason Stoffel (4) and Matt Graham (6) all touch 95. Stoffel is the lone reliever of the group and does it more consistently, while Wheeler has the most projection. Wheeler also spots his heater well down in the zone.

BEST SECONDARY PITCH: Stoffel's slider is unhittable at times.

BEST PRO DEBUT: 3B Drew Biery (22) won short-season Northwest League MVP honors after hitting .326/.406/.484. Stoffel posted a 0.90 ERA and 19-1 K-BB ratio in 20 innings between two clubs. RHP Craig Westcott's (30) deceptive delivery helped him go 7-0, 2.48 with 63 strikeouts in 43 innings.

BEST ATHLETE: Crawford.

MOST INTRIGUING BACKGROUND: RHP Shawn Sanford (13) has a second-degree black belt in taekwondo.

CLOSEST TO THE MAJORS: A candidate for the first round before an inconsistent junior season, Stoffel righted himself in pro ball and could join the Giants by mid-2011.

BEST LATE-ROUND PICK: RHP Jeremy Toole (10) needs to tone down his delivery and improve his command, but there's nothing wrong with his 88-94 mph fastball and 12-to-6 curveball. Biery and SS Ryan Cavan (16) impressed with their bats and gloves in the NWL. While watching his son Alex play at Point Loma Nazarene (Calif.), area scout Brad Cameron spotted RHP Kaohi Downing (50), who was primarily an outfielder for the Sea Lions. Now a full-time pitcher, Downing has run his fastball up to 94 mph.

THE ONE WHO GOT AWAY: C Jonathan Walsh (18), a switch-hitter with power, opted to attend Texas. RHP Mitch Mormann (20), who throws in the mid-90s but is raw, transferred from Des Moines Area CC to Louisiana State.

ASSESSMENT: The Giants were pleasantly surprised to find talents such as Wheeler, Joseph and Stoffel available where they drafted them. Joseph and Dominguez were welcome additions to a system lacking in power hitters.

2008   BONUSES: $9.1 MILLION

C Buster Posey (1) is ready to start in the major leagues, and he and 3B Conor Gillaspie (1s) both have received big league cups of coffee. OF Roger Kieschnick (3), SS Brandon Crawford (4) and LHP Eric Surkamp (7) had strong first full pro seasons. So did LHP Scott Barnes (8), who was traded for Ryan Garko.

GRADE: A

2007   BONUSES: $7.4 MILLION

LHP Madison Bumgarner (1) reached San Francisco shortly after turning 20 and looks like another Giants ace in the making. RHP Tim Alderson (1), since dealt for Freddie Sanchez, and 2B Nick Noonan (1s) regressed last year, but they're still on the prospect map—unlike OF Wendell Fairley (1), C Jackson Williams (1s) and 3B Charlie Culberson (1s). LHP Dan Runzler (5) shockingly rose from low Class A to the majors in 2009.

GRADE: A

2006   BONUSES: $4.4 MILLION

RHP Tim Lincecum's (1) size and delivery helped him fall to the Giants at No. 10, but they haven't been liabilities as he has won two Cy Young Awards. He's the only standout player in this crop, though 2B Emmanuel Burriss (1s), 3B Ryan Rohlinger (6), SS Brian Bocock (9) and 2B Matt Downs (36) have played in the big leagues.

GRADE: A

2005   BONUSES: $0.5 MILLION*

In a surreal draft effort, the Giants didn't have picks before the fourth round and spent only $500,000 on the first 10 rounds. Yet they still came up with a big league reliever in RHP Sergio Romo (28) and one of their best hitting prospects in draft-and-follow OF Thomas Neal (36). RHP Joe Martinez (12) and LHP Alex Hinshaw (15) also have pitched in the majors.

GRADE: C

*Draft analysis by Jim Callis. Numbers in parentheses indicate draft rounds. *Bonuses for 2005 are first 10 rounds only.*

BUSTER POSEY, C

Born: March 27, 1987.
Height: 6-1. **Weight:** 205.
Bats: R. **Throws:** R.
Drafted: Florida State, 2008 (1st round).
Signed by: Sean O'Connor.

LARRY GOREN

Posey won Baseball America's College Player of the Year and the Golden Spikes awards in his final season at Florida State in 2008, and he's certainly the golden boy in a system that hasn't developed an all-star position player in two decades. Not since Will Clark and Matt Williams has a hitting prospect been so eagerly anticipated in San Francisco. Since receiving the largest up-front bonus in major league history ($6.2 million, since surpassed by Stephen Strasburg) as the fifth overall pick in the 2008 draft, Posey has worn seven uniforms in parts of two pro seasons—including a major league jersey when the club promoted him Sept. 2. He watched more than he played, though, after Bengie Molina's strained quad healed. Fans voiced their disapproval as manager Bruce Bochy sat Posey down the stretch, and they figure to be even more upset if he isn't the Giants' catcher on Opening Day.

Posey draws legitimate comparisons to Joe Mauer. He's a pure hitter with terrific strike-zone awareness, and his clean, unfettered swing allows him to drive pitches from pole to pole. For a team full of impatient hitters, his sound, disciplined approach will be a most welcome tonic. No hyperbole: He's a better two-strike hitter than anyone on the major league roster. Power isn't his best tool, but he had 18 homers and 50 extra-base hits in the minors last season. His approach allows him to get into counts where he can get pitches to drive. Posey has tremendous baseball athleticism. He once played all nine positions in a game for the Seminoles, and flashed a 94 mph fastball as an occasional reliever. Not surprisingly, his arm strength and accuracy grade well-above-average. He threw out 46 percent of basestealers in the minors in 2009. He's an average runner—well-above-average for a catcher—who maximizes his opportunities on the bases. Posey's mental acuity is off the charts and he's a leader on the field. He carries himself like a veteran and seems immune to the immense expectations that follow him.

For all the strides Posey has made as a catcher, the mechanics of the position haven't become second nature yet. He's still working to improve his receiving and has problems handling quality fastballs with late life. Passed balls have been an issue, and he has committed 15 in 120 pro games. The Giants want him to get stronger in order to handle the grind of a full season.

Ideally, the Giants would like Posey to log another 150 games at Triple-A Fresno before handing him a pair of major league shinguards for keeps. But San Francisco has a need behind the plate, so Posey's spring training began in October. Though he was coming off a full season, he headed to the Arizona Fall League to get more game experience while also allowing the Giants to evaluate his readiness. Eventually, Posey should be a perennial all-star and another high-average hitter to pair with Pablo Sandoval in the middle of their lineup.

Year	Club (League)	Class	AVG	G	AB	R	H	2B	3B	HR	RBI	BB	SO	SB	OBP	SLG
2008	Giants (AZL)	R	.385	7	26	8	10	3	1	1	4	5	4	0	.484	.692
	Salem-Keizer (NWL)	SS	.273	3	11	2	3	2	0	0	2	3	0	0	.429	.455
2009	San Jose (CAL)	HiA	.326	80	291	63	95	23	0	13	58	45	45	6	.428	.540
	Fresno (PCL)	AAA	.321	35	131	21	42	8	1	5	22	17	23	0	.391	.511
	San Francisco (NL)	MAJ	.118	7	17	1	2	0	0	0	0	0	4	0	.118	.118
MAJOR LEAGUE TOTALS			.118	7	17	1	2	0	0	0	0	0	4	0	.118	.118
MINOR LEAGUE TOTALS			.327	125	459	94	150	36	2	19	86	70	72	6	.421	.538

2 MADISON BUMGARNER, LHP *Busch*

BORN: Aug, 1, 1989. **B-T:** R-L. **HT.:** 6-4. **WT.:** 215. **DRAFTED:** HS—Hudson, N.C., 2007 (1st round). **SIGNED BY:** Pat Portugal.

Bumgarner ranked third in the minors with a 1.85 ERA last season after leading the minors with a 1.46 mark in 2008. Nevertheless, his heady stock dipped slightly as his velocity waned. The 10th overall pick in 2007, he signed for $2 million. At his best, Bumgarner shows a mid-90s fastball, a slider with good tilt and an average changeup. His heater has late giddy-up and he has advanced command of it. His easy, three-quarters delivery adds deception. He works the ladder, loves to throw upstairs and gets the ball inside against lefties and righties alike. He's an ornery competitor in the mold of Kevin Brown, and when the Giants needed him to make his major league debut on an hour's notice, he showed zero fear. He's a good athlete who helps himself with the bat. Bumgarner pitched at 88-90 mph for most of the second half of last season. A perfectionist, he may have lost velocity because he threw too much on the side. His slider still isn't a finished product and his changeup isn't entirely trustworthy. He defaults to his fastball when he gets in jams. He must learn to control his emotions and trust his catcher. Bumgarner has No. 1 starter potential, and his stuff would play against big leaguers now. He's just 20, so they'd prefer to let him work in Triple-A to start 2010.

Year	Club (League)	Class	W	L	ERA	G	GS	CG	SV	IP	H	R	ER	HR	BB	SO	AVG
2008	Augusta (SAL)	LoA	15	3	1.46	24	24	1	0	142	111	28	23	3	21	164	.216
2009	San Jose (CAL)	HiA	3	1	1.48	5	5	0	0	24	20	10	4	0	4	23	.217
	Connecticut (EL)	AA	9	1	1.93	20	19	1	0	107	80	28	23	6	30	69	.209
	San Francisco (NL)	MAJ	0	0	1.80	4	1	0	0	10	8	2	2	2	3	10	.229
MAJOR LEAGUE TOTALS			0	0	1.80	4	1	0	0	10	8	2	2	2	3	10	.229
MINOR LEAGUE TOTALS			27	5	1.65	49	48	2	0	273	211	66	50	9	55	256	.213

3 ZACK WHEELER, RHP

BORN: May 30, 1990. **B-T:** R-R. **HT.:** 6-3. **WT.:** 180. **DRAFTED:** HS—Dallas, Ga., 2009 (1st round). **SIGNED BY:** Sean O'Connor.

Wheeler looked better every time the Giants scouted him, so they selected him with the sixth overall pick in June—the highest they've taken a pitcher since Jason Grilli at No. 4 in 1997—and signed him at the Aug. 17 deadline for $3.3 million, a franchise-record bonus for a pitcher. Wheeler's older brother Adam was a 13th-round pick in 2001 and pitched four seasons in the Yankees system. Wheeler is projectable with broad shoulders, long arms, huge hands and loose arm action. He throws an easy fastball with explosive late life, sitting in the low 90s and topping out at 95 mph. He'll show three plus pitches at times. His hard, three quarters breaking ball has sharp finish, and his changeup is advanced for his age. He sells it well and it has nice fade. Wheeler is still growing into his body and is getting stronger, but he'll need to work on his flexibility as well. Though he's usually around the plate with his fastball, his command isn't pinpoint. He still needs a more consistent feel for his changeup. Wheeler projects as a frontline starter in the big leagues. He's expected to begin his pro career close to home at low Class A Augusta. San Francisco doesn't need to rush him, but it's worth noting that Wheeler is more advanced than Madison Bumgarner was coming out of high school.

Year	Club (League)	Class	W	L	ERA	G	GS	CG	SV	IP	H	R	ER	HR	BB	SO	AVG
2009	Did Not Play—Signed Late																

4 THOMAS NEAL, OF *5/03*

BORN: Aug. 17, 1987. **B-T:** R-R. **HT.:** 6-1. **WT.:** 205. **DRAFTED:** Riverside (Calif.) CC, D/F 2005 (36th round). **SIGNED BY:** Lee Carballo.

Neal was a draft-and-follow who signed for $220,000 after a huge season at Riverside (Calif.) CC in 2006. His development stalled when he dislocated his throwing shoulder, and reconstructive surgery forced him to miss nearly all of 2007. He split time between DH and first base in 2008 and successfully returned to the outfield last season, when he led the high Class A California League with a .431 on-base percentage. Neal became a more complete hitter in 2009. He seldom strays from his plan at the plate and takes aggressive swings on mistakes. He has the bat speed to turn on quality fastballs and shows extra-base power from pole to pole. His arm strength has returned and he racked up 15 assists from left field last season. Neal is a below-average runner and his outfield range isn't the greatest. While he has good plate coverage, he's still learning to spoil two-strike pitches as opposed to putting them in play. As he moves up, more advanced pitchers will look to disrupt his timing with better breaking balls. A strong Arizona Fall League reinforced the notion that Neal could hit in the middle of the Giants' lineup. Time remains on his side even though he has missed a lot of baseball, as he's still just 22. Because his arm is playable in right field, he and Roger Kieschnick could switch corners at the Giants' new Double-A Richmond outpost in 2010.

Year	Club (League)	Class	AVG	G	AB	R	H	2B	3B	HR	RBI	BB	SO	SB	OBP	SLG
2006	Salem-Keizer (NWL)	SS	.250	50	176	26	44	6	2	4	20	7	44	1	.289	.375
2007	Giants (AZL)	R	.308	10	39	7	12	3	0	1	4	5	7	0	.413	.462
2008	Augusta (SAL)	LoA	.276	117	428	69	118	25	1	15	81	48	103	3	.359	.444
2009	San Jose (CAL)	HiA	.337	129	475	102	160	41	4	22	90	65	98	3	.431	.579
MINOR LEAGUE TOTALS			.299	306	1118	204	334	75	7	42	195	125	252	7	.382	.491

5 DAN RUNZLER, LHP _Leg_

BORN: March 30, 1985. **B-T:** L-L. **HT.:** 6-4. **WT.:** 230. **DRAFTED:** UC Riverside, 2007 (9th round). **SIGNED BY:** Ray Krawczyk.

Runzler is believed to be the first player ever to appear at each of the Giants' four full-season affiliates and graduate to the big league club in the same season. He clicked with his pitching coach at Augusta, former major leaguer Steve Kline, and took off from there. Between his five stops, he had a 0.80 ERA and struck out 83 in 59 innings. Runzler throws an explosive mid-90s fastball on a downhill plane and seldom misses up in the zone. He complements his heater with a late-breaking hammer curveball that he hadn't thrown consistently for strikes in the past. His stuff shuts down lefties and righties. He's aggressive and works quickly. Runzler isn't a tremendous athlete and doesn't field his position well. He must work at holding runners. He could be lethal with a changeup, but he seldom uses one. There's little doubt that Runzler would have been on San Francisco's playoff roster had the team advanced that far. He's a lock to make the team in 2010 and because he has closer stuff, the Giants might entertain offers for all-star Brian Wilson.

Year	Club (League)	Class	W	L	ERA	G	GS	CG	SV	IP	H	R	ER	HR	BB	SO	AVG
2007	Giants (AZL)	R	1	2	3.44	15	0	0	4	18	15	8	7	1	6	24	.242
	Salem-Keizer (NWL)	SS	0	0	9.00	1	0	0	0	1	2	1	1	0	2	1	.400
2008	Augusta (SAL)	LoA	0	1	5.47	20	0	0	0	25	25	18	15	2	19	26	.269
	Salem-Keizer (NWL)	SS	0	1	2.10	27	0	0	0	30	19	8	7	1	21	43	.184
2009	Augusta (SAL)	LoA	1	1	0.68	19	0	0	11	26	8	2	2	0	13	45	.093
	San Jose (CAL)	HiA	1	0	0.84	19	0	0	5	21	8	3	2	1	4	26	.104
	Connecticut (EL)	AA	3	0	0.96	7	0	0	1	9	5	1	1	1	7	11	.172
	Fresno (PCL)	AAA	0	0	0.00	2	0	0	0	2	2	0	0	0	0	1	.286
	San Francisco (NL)	MAJ	0	0	1.04	11	0	0	0	9	6	1	1	1	5	11	.188
MAJOR LEAGUE TOTALS			0	0	1.04	11	0	0	0	9	6	1	1	1	5	11	.188
MINOR LEAGUE TOTALS			6	5	2.37	110	0	0	21	133	84	41	35	6	72	177	.182

6 TOMMY JOSEPH, C †

BORN: July 16, 1991. **B-T:** R-R. **HT.:** 6-1. **WT.:** 210. **DRAFTED:** HS—Scottsdale, Ariz., 2009 (2nd round). **SIGNED BY:** Chuck Hensley.

Joseph came out of the same Horizon High (Scottsdale, Ariz.) program that produced Angels third baseman Brandon Wood and 2007 Giants first-round pick Tim Alderson, who was traded to the Pirates in the Freddy Sanchez deal last July. Originally a first base-man, Joseph moved behind the plate his senior year and was one of the best power-hitting prep prospects in the 2009 draft. Delighted to get him in the second round, San Francisco signed him for $712,500. Joseph matches muscle with a functional swing. He loads easily, his hands snap through the hitting zone, he's direct to the ball and he keeps his head down the barrel. It's no wonder he consistently generates backspin. He peppered the upper deck at Tropicana Field with 400-foot shots in a high school home run derby. He has above-average arm strength and accuracy. His defensive skills are raw, and Joseph needs to work on his feet and flexibility behind the plate. First base is always an option, especially with Buster Posey ahead of him. Joseph's bat would play there just fine. He's a well-below-average runner. Nobody inspired more buzz among Giants coaches in instructional league than Joseph, who put on a tape-measure show in Arizona. His adjustment to wood bats shouldn't be significant, and because he stays back so well, he should be able to handle breaking pitches. He's likely to see a full season in low Class A in 2010.

Year	Club (League)	Class	AVG	G	AB	R	H	2B	3B	HR	RBI	BB	SO	SB	OBP	SLG
2009	Did Not Play—Signed Late															

7 ROGER KIESCHNICK, OF ⊬

BORN: Jan. 21, 1987. **B-T:** L-R. **HT.:** 6-3. **WT.:** 215. **DRAFTED:** Texas Tech, 2008 (3rd round). **SIGNED BY:** Todd Thomas.

Kieschnick is a first cousin of former major leaguer Brooks Kieschnick, who became a rare two-way player to extend his big league career. Roger probably won't have to resort to such measures after ranking second in the California League in RBIs (110) and fifth in extra-base hits (68) in his pro debut at high Class A San Jose. A strapping power hitter, Kieschnick drives the ball to all fields. He employs a short stroke and actually hit better against lefthanders (.320 average/.943 OPS) than righties (.283/.842) last season. He has surprising speed and athleticism for a big man. He has plenty of arm to handle right field. He plays a throwback style, running out every ball and sliding hard into second base. The Giants knew Kieschnick would rack up his share of strikeouts, and he did. His aggressive approach, open stance and long swing make him susceptible to offspeed stuff on the outer half. Whiffs are an acceptable tradeoff for his power, but he has to be careful not to get himself out against more advanced pitching. AT&T Park isn't an inviting place for lefthanded power hitters, so Kieschnick must continue his overall development as a multidimensional threat. If all goes well at Double-A in 2010, he could push for a major league outfield job at some point the following season.

Year	Club (League)	Class	AVG	G	AB	R	H	2B	3B	HR	RBI	BB	SO	SB	OBP	SLG
2009	San Jose (CAL)	HiA	.296	131	517	86	153	37	8	23	110	36	130	9	.345	.532
MINOR LEAGUE TOTALS			.296	131	517	86	153	37	8	23	110	36	130	9	.345	.532

8 EHIRE ADRIANZA, SS ⊣

BORN: Aug. 21, 1989. **B-T:** B-R. **HT.:** 6-1. **WT.:** 155. **SIGNED:** Venezuela, 2007. **SIGNED BY:** Ciro Villalobos.

Adrianza quickly developed a following after signing as a 16-year-old. While on a rehab assignment in 2008, Omar Vizquel watched Adrianza field grounders and said his glove would get him to the big leagues. Though he was a career .224 hitter who missed most of 2008 with a broken foot, Adrianza jumped to low Class A last season and held his own as one of the youngest regulars in the South Atlantic League. Adrianza gobbles up slow rollers and makes accurate throws from every angle, and his premium range is especially impressive when he goes up the middle. His superb hands allow him to stay with bad hops even on baked surfaces. A natural righthanded hitter, he has developed a well-rounded approach from both sides and flashes gap power. An average runner, he has a quick first step and good instincts on the basepaths. Because Adrianza is so eager to please, he sometimes takes his fastballs at the plate into the field. He must get stronger so better pitchers won't just knock the bat out of his hands. He needs to tighten up his strike zone and avoid breaking balls off the plate. The Giants don't need to fast-track Adrianza, which is good because he'll need plenty of at-bats. He's expected to team with newly converted second baseman Charlie Culberson in the middle infield at high Class A San Jose in 2010.

Year	Club (League)	Class	AVG	G	AB	R	H	2B	3B	HR	RBI	BB	SO	SB	OBP	SLG
2006	Giants (DSL)	R	.156	44	122	17	19	2	1	0	7	24	31	3	.311	.189
2007	Giants (DSL)	R	.241	66	249	44	60	17	2	0	30	41	31	23	.351	.325
2008	Fresno (PCL)	AAA	.500	2	6	2	3	1	0	0	0	0	2	1	.625	.667
	Giants (AZL)	R	.255	15	55	13	14	4	0	1	6	7	4	0	.349	.382
	Salem-Keizer (NWL)	SS	.400	1	5	3	2	0	0	0	0	0	1	0	.400	.400
2009	Augusta (SAL)	LoA	.258	117	388	54	100	15	3	2	46	42	66	7	.333	.327
MINOR LEAGUE TOTALS			.240	245	825	133	198	39	6	3	89	116	134	33	.339	.313

9 BRANDON CRAWFORD, SS

BORN: Jan. 21, 1987. **B-T:** L-R. **HT.:** 6-2. **WT.:** 200. **DRAFTED:** UCLA, 2008 (4th round). **SIGNED BY:** Michael Kendall.

Considered a potential first-rounder for the 2008 draft, Crawford slid to the fourth round after a disappointing Cape Cod League and lukewarm junior season. He played just five games in his pro debut, then jumped to high Class A to begin 2009, destroying Cal League pitching and earning a promotion to Double-A after barely a month. An all-around talent, Crawford has a good blend of skills and field awareness. His positioning and first-step quickness allow him to make tough plays look easy. He's solid around the bag and has an accurate arm. Even when he struggled against Double-A pitching, it didn't affect his defense. He has the potential to hit 15-20 homers a year and shows power to the opposite field. His slightly above-average speed plays even better on the bases. Double-A pitchers fed Crawford a lot of breaking balls and he had trouble adjusting. Coaches didn't want to overwhelm him in his first full season, but he'll need to adjust the position of his feet and head to handle stuff on the inner half. Crawford might not have the bat control to be a No. 2 hitter in the big leagues, but he's gifted enough to make contributions in the lower third of the lineup. The Giants would be thrilled if he develops along the lines of J.J. Hardy.

Year	Club (League)	Class	AVG	G	AB	R	H	2B	3B	HR	RBI	BB	SO	SB	OBP	SLG
2008	Giants (AZL)	R	.429	4	14	3	6	1	1	0	3	0	3	0	.429	.643
	Salem-Keizer (NWL)	SS	.000	1	2	0	0	0	0	0	0	0	0	0	.000	.000
2009	San Jose (CAL)	HiA	.371	25	105	21	39	2	2	6	17	10	32	2	.445	.600
	Connecticut (EL)	AA	.258	108	392	38	101	26	2	4	31	20	100	11	.294	.365
MINOR LEAGUE TOTALS			.285	138	513	62	146	29	5	10	51	30	135	13	.329	.419

10 FRANCISCO PEGUERO, OF

BORN: June 1, 1988. **B-T:** R-R. **HT.:** 6-0. **WT.:** 175. **SIGNED:** Dominican Republic, 2006. **SIGNED BY:** Pablo Peguero.

Few players excite Giants minor league coaches more than Peguero, but a hernia forced him to spend most of the first two months of the 2009 season in extended spring training. When he finally got back on the field, he needed just a handful of games to show he didn't belong in short-season ball. After an impressive run in low Class A, he was called up to San Jose for the Cal League postseason and won playoff MVP honors. Peguero's high-energy play, enthusiasm, lightning-quick bat and ability to make contact remind San Francisco of Pablo Sandoval. Unlike the pudgy Kung Fu Panda, Peguero is a quality athlete who covers ground in center field and has a plus-plus arm. He's an above-average runner who will sprint to first on a checked-swing roller to the mound. Peguero likes to take an inside-out swing and won't hit for more power until he gets his hands inside the ball. Like Sandoval, he's hyperaggressive and sometimes does himself a disservice by failing to wait for a better pitch to hit. Peguero won an award as the most inspirational player in the Giants' instructional league camp and should become a fan favorite at San Jose. Peguero was added to the 40-man roster this winter and if he continues to develop at this pace, he could be ready for a big league opportunity by the end of 2011.

Year	Club (League)	Class	AVG	G	AB	R	H	2B	3B	HR	RBI	BB	SO	SB	OBP	SLG
2006	Giants (DSL)	R	.275	56	182	24	50	10	3	4	16	6	37	3	.307	.429
2007	Giants (DSL)	R	.294	69	235	51	69	12	2	1	17	15	39	25	.341	.374
2008	Augusta (SAL)	LoA	.261	50	180	23	47	2	4	2	15	12	43	15	.309	.350
	Salem-Keizer (NWL)	SS	.307	50	202	33	62	11	4	2	28	9	43	10	.349	.431
2009	Salem-Keizer (NWL)	SS	.394	17	71	14	28	3	1	0	12	3	9	7	.421	.465
	Augusta (SAL)	LoA	.340	58	238	28	81	12	4	1	34	5	39	15	.359	.437
MINOR LEAGUE TOTALS			.304	300	1108	173	337	50	18	10	122	50	210	75	.341	.409

11 NICK NOONAN, 2B

BORN: May 4, 1989. **B-T:** L-R. **HT.:** 6-0. **WT.:** 185. **DRAFTED:** HS—San Diego, 2007 (1st round supplemental). **SIGNED BY:** Ray Krawczyk.

Noonan is the only promising prospect out of the Giants' three sandwich picks in 2007, as the others (catcher Jackson Williams, infielder Charlie Culberson) didn't even make their top 30. Signed for $915,750, Noonan has gained a reputation as a clutch hitter after providing big hits for league championship teams the last two years in Augusta and San Jose. Though he hasn't put up big numbers, he has been young for his leagues, and his lefthanded swing and ability to make contact have earned him comparisons to Robin Ventura. Noonan has terrific plate coverage that gets him into trouble at times, because he'll put a borderline pitch into play more often than he'll work a count. He hit .198 against lefties in 2009, and tended to let his lower half collapse while flipping at pitches. Coaches had to remind him to keep a solid front side and stay back on breaking balls. If he makes the necessary adjustments, he could become an above-average hitter for a second baseman, producing for average with gap power. He provided a thrill in spring training last year, filling out a major league roster for a road game and delivering a ninth-inning grand slam against the Cubs. With solid-average speed, Noonan is an asset on the bases and can steal an occasional bag. Considered a below-average defender in the past, Noonan has improved his angles to grounders and has become much more dependable around the bag. Though he has a fringy arm, he's good at turning double plays. His field awareness, poise and work ethic are all points in his favor. San Francisco almost jumped Noonan past high Class A last year before deciding not to rush their second baseman of the future any further. He'll make the move to Double-A in 2010.

Year	Club (League)	Class	AVG	G	AB	R	H	2B	3B	HR	RBI	BB	SO	SB	OBP	SLG
2007	Giants (AZL)	R	.316	52	206	33	65	11	4	3	40	12	20	18	.357	.451
2008	Augusta (SAL)	LoA	.279	119	499	79	139	27	7	9	68	23	98	29	.315	.415
2009	San Jose (CAL)	HiA	.259	124	459	82	119	26	8	7	64	48	97	9	.330	.397
MINOR LEAGUE TOTALS			.277	295	1164	194	323	64	19	19	172	83	215	56	.329	.414

12 RAFAEL RODRIGUEZ, OF

BORN: July 13, 1992. **B-T:** R-R. **HT.:** 6-5. **WT.:** 198. **SIGNED:** Dominican Republic, 2008. **SIGNED BY:** Felix Peguero/Pablo Peguero.

Rodriguez's frame and athleticism draw comparisons to a young Vladimir Guerrero or Dave Winfield. Suitably impressed, the Giants spent $2.55 million—a franchise record for an international player—to sign him out of the Dominican Republic in 2008. Some evaluators weren't sure he'd be able to cover his huge strike zone against pro pitchers, but he had an encouraging pro debut, hitting .299 with a .392 on-base percentage in the Rookie-level Arizona League. San Francisco tried to reduce the pressure on Rodriguez by mostly batting him in the lower half. He maintained a controlled approach and made plenty of line-drive contact. Though he didn't homer in the AZL, he has considerable raw power that he'll begin to tap into as he gets stronger, develops better balances and chases fewer pitches out of the zone. Rodriguez runs a tick above-average, though he figures to slow down as he fills out and still has a lot of learning to do on the basepaths. He has plenty of arm to play right field, but mostly patrolled left in the Arizona heat. He'll deal with more sweltering conditions in 2010, this time in Augusta. He may be the youngest player in the South Atlantic League, opening the season at age 17.

Year	Club (League)	Class	AVG	G	AB	R	H	2B	3B	HR	RBI	BB	SO	SB	OBP	SLG
2009	Giants (AZL)	R	.299	35	127	25	38	8	0	0	19	16	23	5	.392	.362
MINOR LEAGUE TOTALS			.299	35	127	25	38	8	0	0	19	16	23	5	.392	.362

13 DARREN FORD, OF

BORN: Oct. 1, 1985. **B-T:** R-R. **HT.:** 5-11. **WT.:** 195. **DRAFTED:** Chipola (Fla.) JC, D/F 2004 (18th round). **SIGNED BY:** Tony Blengino (Brewers).

Ford had the ultimate tale of two halves in 2009. He batted .207/.341/.293 before the all-star break, then hit a scorching .354/.414/.563 afterward. What made the difference? He got healthy after spending time on the disabled list with biceps tendinitis, but more important, the Giants allowed him to drop a switch-hitting experiment that started in instructional league the previous fall. One of the fastest players in the minor leagues, Ford stopped trying to slap his way on base and began to believe in himself as a hitter. He didn't merely boost his average with infield singles. He drove the ball more consistently than he ever had in the past. Acquired from the Brewers along with lefthander Steve Hammond in a July 2008 trade for Ray Durham, Ford earned a place on San Francisco's 40-man roster in November. He was old for high Class A at age 23, but he could become a premium center fielder if he proves he can hit more advanced pitching. His speed changes games, allowing him to terrorize pitchers and catchers—and even score from first base on singles, which he has accomplished twice. He's a defensive standout, too. "There isn't a center fielder in the minor leagues who covers more ground north, south, east and west," San Jose manager Andy Skeels said. Ford's arm is below-average.

Year	Club (League)	Class	AVG	G	AB	R	H	2B	3B	HR	RBI	BB	SO	SB	OBP	SLG
2005	Helena (PIO)	R	.271	61	236	57	64	4	3	1	24	33	70	18	.365	.326
2006	West Virginia (SAL)	LoA	.283	125	491	93	139	24	3	7	54	56	133	69	.361	.387
2007	West Virginia (SAL)	LoA	.335	51	224	48	75	15	4	5	33	23	56	31	.398	.504
	Brevard County (FSL)	HiA	.231	72	273	46	63	7	1	4	27	35	67	36	.317	.308
2008	Brevard County (FSL)	HiA	.230	91	343	57	79	13	3	2	27	46	88	48	.322	.303
	San Jose (CAL)	HiA	.219	38	128	21	28	4	1	0	7	23	42	14	.346	.266
2009	San Jose (CAL)	HiA	.300	101	380	81	114	17	9	9	50	49	97	35	.386	.463
MINOR LEAGUE TOTALS			.271	539	2075	403	562	84	24	28	222	265	553	251	.357	.375

14 WALDIS JOAQUIN, RHP

BORN: Dec. 25. 1986. **B-T:** R-R. **HT.:** 6-2. **WT.:** 190. **SIGNED:** Dominican Republic, 2003. **SIGNED BY:** Rick Ragazzo/Pablo Peguero.

Scouts sat on the edge of their seats as Joaquin threw consistent 96-97 mph gas in Cactus League games last spring. His stuff was good enough to overcome command issues in Double-A and earn him big league callups in August and September. Three years earlier, he had missed the entire 2006 season while recovering from Tommy John surgery. Joaquin just rares back and throws the ball, usually sitting in the mid-90s with his fastball. He's wild in the strike zone and lacks the location to set up hitters inside and out, something he'll have to address to miss bats in the big leagues. His hard slider has plus action, and he's working to add a power two-seam fastball to his repertoire. Joaquin got so predictable in his patterns—first-pitch fastball, followed by a slider—that Connecticut manager Dave Machemer had him watch tape of closers such as Mariano Rivera and Jonathan Papelbon to see how they worked hitters. Joaquin's pure stuff could allow him to force his way into the San Francisco bullpen if he throws enough strikes in spring training. His inconsistency likely will make him more of a sixth- or seventh-inning option than a future set-up man or closer.

Year	Club (League)	Class	W	L	ERA	G	GS	CG	SV	IP	H	R	ER	HR	BB	SO	AVG
2004	Giants (DSL)	R	6	1	1.61	14	13	0	0	61	51	21	11	0	28	44	.229
2005	Giants (AZL)	R	1	1	3.64	10	5	0	1	30	28	17	12	1	10	37	.241
2006	Did Not Play—Injured																
2007	Salem-Keizer (NWL)	SS	3	0	2.84	15	5	0	0	38	24	13	12	2	16	30	.176
2008	Augusta (SAL)	LoA	1	2	4.33	27	3	0	2	52	49	32	25	1	20	49	.247
	San Jose (CAL)	HiA	0	1	4.66	9	4	0	0	19	20	13	10	2	11	23	.274
2009	Connecticut (EL)	AA	4	5	2.67	36	0	0	1	54	36	17	16	0	28	40	.190
	Fresno (PCL)	AAA	1	0	0.00	8	0	0	1	10	5	0	0	0	2	16	.143
	San Francisco (NL)	MAJ	0	0	4.22	10	0	0	0	11	10	5	5	1	7	12	.238
MAJOR LEAGUE TOTALS			0	0	4.22	10	0	0	0	11	10	5	5	1	7	12	.238
MINOR LEAGUE TOTALS			16	10	2.93	119	30	0	5	264	213	113	86	6	115	239	.220

15 JASON STOFFEL, RHP

BORN: Sept. 15 1988. **B-T:** R-R. **HT.:** 6-2. **WT.:** 215. **DRAFTED:** Arizona, 2009 (4th round). **SIGNED BY:** Chuck Hensley.

Though Arizona's 2008 bullpen included Ryan Perry and Daniel Schlereth, who would go in the first round of that draft and reached the majors less than a year later, it was Stoffel who served as the Wildcats' closer. Pegged to go in the first round as well in 2009, Stoffel saw his stock fall after an inconsistent junior season. The Giants believe they got a steal when they snagged him in the fourth round for $254,700. Stoffel overwhelmed hitters in his pro debut, going right after them with a 92-93 mph fastball that touches 95 and a plus slider with plenty of tilt. He also has a changeup but wasn't compelled to throw it much. Stoffel is a quick worker who doesn't like hitters to get comfortable in the box. He repeats his high three-quarters delivery well and issued just one walk in 19 pro innings. He maintains his stuff when asked to pitch on consecutive days. Stoffel is the best college closer to enter the system since former first-rounder David Aardsma, who was pushed through the minors but didn't learn to succeed until he'd passed through four organizations. Stoffel, who has better stuff, should move quickly as well. It would be no surprise if he ascends to Double-A by the end of 2010 and reaches San Francisco by the middle of the next season.

Year	Club (League)	Class	W	L	ERA	G	GS	CG	SV	IP	H	R	ER	HR	BB	SO	AVG
2009	Giants (AZL)	R	0	0	1.86	9	0	0	2	10	8	2	2	0	0	6	.211
	Salem-Keizer (NWL)	SS	1	0	0.00	8	0	0	2	10	6	1	0	0	1	13	.158
MINOR LEAGUE TOTALS			1	0	0.90	17	0	0	4	20	14	3	2	0	1	19	.184

16 HENRY SOSA, RHP

BORN: July 28, 1985. **B-T:** R-R. **HT.:** 6-2. **WT.:** 197. **SIGNED:** Dominican Republic, 2004. **SIGNED BY:** Rick Ragazzo/Pablo Peguero.

Sosa represented the Giants at the Futures Games in 2007, but he hasn't been as dominant or healthy since. He had arthroscopic knee surgery that October, which cost him most of the first two months in 2008. He also missed time with a pectoral strain in 2008, and a strained muscle in his upper back ended his 2009 season after 14 starts. After averaging a strikeout per inning before last year, he didn't miss as many bats in Double-A. He did compete well, going 6-0, 2.36. When Sosa is healthy, he has a mid-90s fastball that should play in the big leagues. He still needs something to complement his heat, as his curveball is just a get-me-over pitch and he tends to push his changeup. The only way to develop those pitches is to stay on the mound. Sosa has a high-energy personality and has been known to do a few hundred pushups after a start. He might not be durable enough to make 30 starts, but the Giants don't have much upper-level rotation depth, so they don't figure to try him as a reliever yet. He should advance to Triple-A in 2010.

Year	Club (League)	Class	W	L	ERA	G	GS	CG	SV	IP	H	R	ER	HR	BB	SO	AVG
2004	Giants (DSL)	R	0	5	5.30	13	7	0	0	36	40	28	21	2	19	25	.282
2005	Giants (DSL)	R	5	6	3.58	13	12	0	0	55	53	30	22	4	8	46	.250
2006	Giants (AZL)	R	2	1	3.90	9	6	0	0	32	20	15	14	3	12	41	.177
2007	Augusta (SAL)	LoA	6	0	0.73	13	10	0	1	62	30	8	5	2	25	61	.144
	San Jose (CAL)	HiA	5	5	4.38	14	14	0	0	64	66	36	31	8	36	78	.262
2008	San Jose (CAL)	HiA	3	4	4.31	12	12	0	0	56	62	28	27	6	18	58	.283
	Augusta (SAL)	LoA	0	0	0.00	2	0	0	0	1	1	1	0	0	2	0	.250
2009	Connecticut (EL)	AA	6	0	2.36	14	14	0	0	72	61	22	19	4	25	44	.231
MINOR LEAGUE TOTALS			27	21	3.30	90	75	0	1	379	333	168	139	29	145	353	.236

17 CONOR GILLASPIE, 3B

BORN: July 18, 1987. **B-T:** L-R. **HT.:** 6-1. **WT.:** 200. **DRAFTED:** Wichita State, 2008 (1st round supplemental). **SIGNED BY:** Hugh Walker.

Gillaspie was the first player from the 2008 draft to reach the majors, getting a September callup that year as a fringe benefit because he accepted a slot $970,000 bonus as the 37th overall pick. He spent all of last season quietly toiling in the hitter-friendly California League, where his .286/.364/.386 line was a disappointment. Gillaspie's advanced knowledge of the strike zone actually might have worked against him. "Unfortunately for him, it was a lot better than the umpires," San Jose manager Andy Skeels said. "The bat was literally taken out of his hands. He easily could've walked 30 more times." Gillaspie has good pitch recognition and plate coverage to go with quick hands, enabling him to make consistent line-drive contact. But some scouts question whether the former Cape Cod League MVP and batting champ ever will hit for the power desired from a third baseman. His biggest challenge is to stay at the position. He led Cal League third basemen with 27 errors, doesn't have good hands and struggles to get in a good throwing position. He has average arm strength and speed. Gillaspie volunteered to go to instructional league to overhaul his footwork, and coaches there praised his progress and attitude. He'll move up to Double-A this season.

Year	Club (League)	Class	AVG	G	AB	R	H	2B	3B	HR	RBI	BB	SO	SB	OBP	SLG
2008	Giants (AZL)	R	.273	6	22	2	6	3	0	0	7	3	1	0	.360	.409
	Salem-Keizer (NWL)	SS	.268	18	71	4	19	4	0	0	8	9	13	2	.350	.324
	San Francisco (NL)	MAJ	.200	8	5	1	1	0	0	0	0	2	0	0	.429	.200
2009	San Jose (CAL)	HiA	.286	126	469	62	134	31	2	4	67	55	68	2	.364	.386
MAJOR LEAGUE TOTALS			.200	8	5	1	1	0	0	0	0	2	0	0	.429	.200
MINOR LEAGUE TOTALS			.283	150	562	68	159	38	2	4	82	67	82	4	.362	.379

18 CHRIS DOMINGUEZ, 3B/1B

BORN: Nov. 22, 1986. **B-T:** R-R. **HT.:** 6-4. **WT.:** 240. **DRAFTED:** Louisville, 2009 (3rd round). **SIGNED BY:** Kevin Christman.

For years, the Giants drafted with a bias against big-bodied softball types. But things are changing under scouting director John Barr, and Dominguez is more than a one-dimensional slugger. A two-time Big East Conference player of the year, he turned down the Rockies as a sophomore-eligible fifth-round pick in 2008 before signing for $411,300 as a third-rounder last June. He has prodigious raw power that helped him win four conference or summer league home run titles while at Louisville, and he set a school record with 25 last spring. He's an all-or-nothing hitter with a big swing reminiscent of Troy Glaus', but Dominguez will need to make his swing more direct to the ball if he's going to make enough contact. He hit seven homers in his first month of pro ball before pitchers realized they could get him out with breaking balls. His arm strength is just as impressive as his power, and he threw in the mid-90s as a freshman reliever in college. San Francisco hopes he can stay at third base despite his lack of range and agility, but he made six errors in 31 pro games there. He also saw time at first base, which could be his future home. Dominguez likes to be the aggressor, even on the basepaths, where he showed enough quickness and instincts to steal 12 bases in 14 attempts. He's already 23, so he may spend his first full season in high Class A, where he could put up huge power numbers in the hitter's haven that is the California League.

Year	Club (League)	Class	AVG	G	AB	R	H	2B	3B	HR	RBI	BB	SO	SB	OBP	SLG
2009	Giants (AZL)	R	.306	9	36	8	11	2	0	2	8	3	9	1	.375	.528
	Salem-Keizer (NWL)	SS	.254	47	181	31	46	5	1	9	32	9	57	11	.298	.442
MINOR LEAGUE TOTALS			.263	56	217	39	57	7	1	11	40	12	66	12	.311	.456

19 ERIC SURKAMP, LHP

BORN: July 16, 1987. **B-T:** L-L. **HT.:** 6-5. **WT.:** 220. **DRAFTED:** North Carolina State, 2008 (6th round). **SIGNED BY:** Pat Portugal.

A product of Cincinnati's famed Moeller High—the alma mater of Buddy Bell, Ken Griffey Jr. and Barry Larkin—Surkamp impressed with Team USA and in the Cape Cod League before an up-and-down junior season at North Carolina State hurt his draft stock in 2008. Stolen as a sixth-round pick for $135,000, he ranked third in the minors and first in the system in strikeouts (169) and strikeouts per nine innings (11.6) in his first full pro season. He fanned 12 more in the Calfornia League championship clincher over High Desert after a promotion for the playoffs. Surkamp is a three-quarters slinger whose upper-80s fastball appears harder because he hides it well and it looks like it's coming out of his shirt. He's a good athlete whose best pitch is a curveball with plus depth and snap. He also commands an average changeup. He often struggles in the first two innings before settling down, which probably will dissuade club officials from trying him in relief. He has enough stuff and ability to remain a starter, and he could reach Double-A at some point this season.

SAN FRANCISCO GIANTS

Year	Club (League)	Class	W	L	ERA	G	GS	CG	SV	IP	H	R	ER	HR	BB	SO	AVG
2008	Giants (AZL)	R	0	0	2.70	2	0	0	0	3	3	1	1	0	0	7	.231
	Salem-Keizer (NWL)	SS	0	2	6.43	5	4	0	0	14	20	10	10	1	5	16	.351
2009	Augusta (SAL)	LoA	11	5	3.30	23	23	2	0	131	129	57	48	6	39	169	.257
MINOR LEAGUE TOTALS			11	7	3.58	30	27	2	0	148	152	68	59	7	44	192	.266

20 STEVE JOHNSON, RHP

BORN: Aug. 31, 1987. **B-T:** R-R. **HT.:** 6-1. **WT.:** 200. **DRAFTED:** HS—Brooklandville, Md., 2005 (13th round). **SIGNED BY:** Clair Rierson (Dodgers).

Johnson did a lot of traveling in 2009, and the end result is that he'll compete for a major league job in spring training. He opened the season with the Dodgers, earning a promotion from high Class A to Double-A at midyear, then was sent to the Orioles along with third baseman Josh Bell in a deadline deal for George Sherrill. Johnson is the son of Baltimore broadcaster and former big leaguer Dave Johnson, who reportedly teared up when announcing the trade on the air. But the reunion didn't last long, as the pitching-rich Orioles left Johnson off their 40-man roster and lost him to San Francisco in the major league Rule 5 draft. Johnson features a four-seam fastball that sits at 88-91 mph and has three other solid-average pitches in his slider, curveball and changeup. He isn't overpowering but he has a good feel for pitching and goes after hitters. His stuff profiles for the back of a rotation or middle relief, and San Francisco will try to use him in the latter role in 2010. If he doesn't stick on the Giants' big league roster all season, he'll have to pass through waivers and be offered back to the Orioles for half his $50,000 drafting price

Year	Club (League)	Class	W	L	ERA	G	GS	CG	SV	IP	H	R	ER	HR	BB	SO	AVG
2005	Dodgers (GCL)	R	0	2	9.53	6	3	0	0	11	18	12	12	1	4	14	.360
2006	Jacksonville (SL)	AA	0	0	0.00	2	0	0	0	5	2	0	0	0	2	3	.133
	Ogden (PIO)	R	5	5	3.89	14	14	0	0	79	79	37	34	4	25	86	.267
2007	Great Lakes (MWL)	LoA	3	6	4.85	18	16	0	0	82	90	57	44	2	40	65	.280
2008	Great Lakes (MWL)	LoA	9	2	2.34	13	13	0	0	73	59	21	19	4	25	57	.223
	Inland Empire (CAL)	HiA	3	6	7.10	11	11	0	0	52	68	47	41	9	21	55	.318
2009	Inland Empire (CAL)	HiA	8	4	3.82	18	16	0	1	97	94	50	41	14	42	102	.260
	Chattanooga (SL)	AA	1	1	1.69	2	2	0	0	11	8	5	2	1	3	15	.205
	Bowie (EL)	AA	3	2	2.84	7	7	0	0	38	24	13	12	3	17	37	.179
MINOR LEAGUE TOTALS			32	28	4.13	91	82	0	1	447	442	242	205	38	179	434	.261

21 BRETT PILL, 1B

BORN: Sept. 9, 1984. **B-T:** R-R. **HT.:** 6-4. **WT.:** 211. **DRAFTED:** Cal State Fullerton, 2006 (7th round). **SIGNED BY:** Ray Krawczyk.

Pill wasn't a front-burner prospect, but the Giants couldn't forget the 47 doubles he hit while playing in a pitcher's park at Augusta in 2007. He inspired more chin-rubbing last summer after a banner season in another hitter's graveyard. Despite driving in just five runs in April, Pill led the Eastern League with 109 RBIs. His 37 doubles weren't a surprise, but his 19 homers exceeded expectations. He showed more power after standing more upright, moving closer to the plate and opening his stance. As a result, he was able to "turn and burn" on offspeed mistakes. Pill will have to keep developing pull power if he hopes to be a run producer at AT&T Park. Some worry that his swing is too long for him to hit consistently enough to be a big league regular. He doesn't draw a lot of walks, in part because he makes contact easily. Tall and rangy, Pill has terrific hands and is the best defensive first baseman in the system. He doesn't look pretty when he throws, but his arm is accurate and he gets rid of the ball quickly. He's a below-average runner but isn't a liability on the bases. After adding him to its 40-man roster, San Francisco is eager to see what he'll do in the lively Triple-A Pacific Coast League in 2010.

Year	Club (League)	Class	AVG	G	AB	R	H	2B	3B	HR	RBI	BB	SO	SB	OBP	SLG
2006	Salem-Keizer (NWL)	SS	.220	60	223	37	49	16	0	5	35	22	39	3	.296	.359
2007	Augusta (SAL)	LoA	.269	137	536	72	144	47	1	10	91	38	81	4	.321	.416
2008	San Jose (CAL)	HiA	.266	131	458	73	122	32	0	9	65	33	85	5	.321	.395
2009	Connecticut (EL)	AA	.298	139	527	71	157	37	1	19	109	37	72	6	.348	.480
MINOR LEAGUE TOTALS			.271	467	1744	253	472	132	2	43	300	130	277	18	.326	.423

22 JOHNNY MONELL, C

BORN: March 27, 1986. **B-T:** L-R. **HT.:** 5-11. **WT.:** 205. **DRAFTED:** Seminole (Fla.) CC, 2007 (30th round). **SIGNED BY:** Glenn Tufts.

Monell's father Johnny Sr. was an outfielder who reached Triple-A in the Mets system before continuing his career in Taiwan and several independent leagues. Johnny Jr. followed his dad around and received plenty of exposure to the game as a result. The Giants were intrigued by his lefthanded power as early as 2005, when they drafted him in the 27th round out of a Bronx high school. He turned them down to attend Seminole (Fla.) CC, then spurned the Mets as a 49th-rounder in 2006 before signing with San Francisco as a 30th-rounder in 2007. Monell's power potential could allow him to reach the big leagues as a platoon player, and he may be more than that because he hasn't been overmatched by lefthanded pitching. He has a good grasp of the strike zone. Monell has an above-average arm as well, leading the South Atlantic League by erasing 42 percent of basestealers in 2009. Though he has improved, he still hasn't mastered the art or receiving and committed 18 passed balls in 84 games last season. Pitchers like throwing to him, and his game-calling skills draw praise. The Giants need to accelerate his development because he'll enter the 2010 season as a 24-year-old who hasn't played above low Class A.

Year	Club (League)	Class	AVG	G	AB	R	H	2B	3B	HR	RBI	BB	SO	SB	OBP	SLG
2007	Giants (AZL)	R	.240	28	75	11	18	3	1	3	19	15	16	3	.376	.427
2008	Giants (AZL)	R	.405	11	42	13	17	7	0	1	10	4	5	3	.479	.643
	Salem-Keizer (NWL)	SS	.267	43	161	21	43	17	0	5	25	11	36	1	.330	.466
2009	Augusta (SAL)	LoA	.273	91	293	46	80	21	0	8	44	33	45	4	.355	.427
MINOR LEAGUE TOTALS			.277	173	571	91	158	48	1	17	98	63	102	11	.361	.454

23 CLAYTON TANNER, LHP

BORN: Dec. 5, 1987. **B-T:** R-L. **HT.:** 6-1. **WT.:** 202. **DRAFTED:** HS—Concord, Calif., 2006 (3rd round). **SIGNED BY:** Keith Snider.

If Tanner was disillusioned to repeat the California League after ranking sixth in the circuit with a 3.69 ERA in 2008, he didn't show it. His fastball location improved, his slider got tighter and his changeup became a swing-and-miss pitch in the second half. This time he finished third in the league with a 3.17 ERA, and he was brilliant in two playoff starts as San Jose won the championship. Tanner's improved command came from a cleaner delivery that allowed him to stay back better and finish his pitches. His 88-90 mph fastball won't turn heads, but he pops 93 mph on occasion and gets grounders with his two-seamer. He did less nibbling than in the past, didn't get down on himself and showed the ability to avoid big innings. After surrendering just seven homers in 278 previous pro innings, Tanner gave up 18 last year. Seventeen were hit by righthanders, an indication that he needs more consistency with his changeup. A bright and chatty Bay Area native, Tanner loves doing his homework on hitters and fields his position well. Double-A will be a good test for him in 2010.

Year	Club (League)	Class	W	L	ERA	G	GS	CG	SV	IP	H	R	ER	HR	BB	SO	AVG
2006	Salem-Keizer (NWL)	SS	2	2	3.46	13	0	0	1	26	17	11	10	1	8	25	.183
2007	Augusta (SAL)	LoA	12	8	3.59	27	23	1	0	135	147	61	54	5	44	104	.282
2008	San Jose (CAL)	HiA	10	8	3.69	24	24	0	0	117	124	61	48	1	39	84	.274
2009	San Jose (CAL)	HiA	12	6	3.17	26	23	0	0	139	132	62	49	18	42	121	.254
MINOR LEAGUE TOTALS			36	24	3.47	90	70	1	1	418	420	195	161	25	133	334	.265

24 MATT GRAHAM, RHP

BORN: May 1, 1990. **B-T:** R-R. **HT.:** 6-4. **WT.:** 225. **DRAFTED:** HS—Spring, Texas, 2009 (6th round). **SIGNED BY:** Todd Thomas.

Graham had an up-and-down high school career in Texas, flashing first-round stuff but not with the consistency to go that high in the 2009 draft. The Giants considered him as early as the third round, and when he lasted until the sixth he clearly ranked as the top player on their board. They gave him $500,000 to turn down a scholarship to play at North Carolina. Graham has a strong, projectable frame and when he's at his best, his fastball sits in the low 90s with heavy sink. Because he doesn't repeat his delivery, his velocity tends to be all over the map. He has outstanding arm strength and was touching 95 mph in instructional league after missing time with a flu bug. Graham throws a hard curveball that has good action at times and flattens out at others. He has feel for a changeup and earns points for his competitive makeup. He's a perfect project for vice president of player personnel/pitching guru Dick Tidrow and pitching coordinator Bert Bradley. Graham's stuff and high-effort delivery scream short relief, but he'll get every chance to develop as a starter. Unless he bombs in spring training, he should make his pro debut in low Class A.

Year	Club (League)	Class	W	L	ERA	G	GS	CG	SV	IP	H	R	ER	HR	BB	SO	AVG
2009	Did Not Play—Signed Late																

25 MIKE McBRYDE, OF

BORN: March 22, 1985. **B-T:** R-R. **HT.:** 6-1. **WT.:** 215. **DRAFTED:** Florida Atlantic, 2006 (5th round). **SIGNED BY:** Steve Arnieri.

If McBryde puts everything together, he could have a career like Steve Finley's as an athletic, Gold Glove center fielder with the ability to beat opponents in several ways. McBryde remains an unfinished product at the plate, however, which is why the Giants chose not to protect him on their 40-man roster this offseason. He hit a career-high .308 in Double-A last year, but it was a mostly empty average and he tended to disappear for stretches. He also fared poorly when San Francisco sent him to Triple-A for the first month of the season. McBryde hits balls far in batting practice, but he often takes tentative swings in games. Coaches told McBryde that instead of trying to direct the ball and use his speed, he should turn it loose more often in hitter's counts. He still produced little power, and while he cut down his strikeouts in 2009, he didn't draw many walks. McBryde isn't an efficient basestealer despite his speed, which is breathtaking when he's running down balls in the gaps. A former two-way player at Florida Atlantic, he has the best outfield arm in the system. Ticketed for another shot at Triple-A this year, McBryde would be a perfect fit in the wide expanses of AT&T Park if his bat allows him to get there.

Year	Club (League)	Class	AVG	G	AB	R	H	2B	3B	HR	RBI	BB	SO	SB	OBP	SLG
2006	Salem-Keizer (NWL)	SS	.276	71	225	38	62	9	5	3	34	22	59	16	.344	.400
2007	Augusta (SAL)	LoA	.276	119	417	71	115	17	4	7	61	27	100	14	.328	.386
2008	San Jose (CAL)	HiA	.295	125	420	73	124	10	6	5	46	37	84	31	.368	.383
2009	Fresno (PCL)	AAA	.224	15	58	7	13	1	1	0	1	1	10	6	.250	.276
	Connecticut (EL)	AA	.308	90	318	62	98	21	2	5	41	17	53	16	.347	.434
MINOR LEAGUE TOTALS			.287	420	1438	251	412	58	18	20	183	104	306	83	.344	.394

26 CRAIG CLARK, LHP

BORN: July 9, 1984. **B-T:** L-L. **HT.:** 6-2. **WT.:** 200. **DRAFTED:** Penn State, 2007 (14th round). **SIGNED BY:** John DiCarlo Jr.

Clark's fastball doesn't touch 88 mph, but it's hard to argue with his results last season. San Jose went 22-3 in his starts and he didn't lose after May 7, setting a franchise mark with 15 consecutive winning decisions. The California League pitcher of the year, he ranked second in the minor leagues with 16 victories. "People say winning's not everything," San Jose manager Andy Skeels said. "Oh really? OK, who says, 'Give me the guy who knows how to lose.' The greatest skill any athlete can have is knowing how to win and Clarkie knows how to do that." Clark is the kind of pitcher who makes hitters mutter as they walk to the dugout, but he isn't your average finesse guy. He tied a Cal League record when he struck out 10 consecutive batters in a June 1 victory over Stockton. He's able to bust a mid-80s fastball in on a hitter's hands without any fear of missing over the plate. He also throws a high-70s slider, a low-70s curveball and a changeup. None of his offerings is an out pitch, but he mixes them well. His competitiveness is off the charts, he holds runners well and makes adjustments quickly. Clark finds creative ways to attack hitters, often following a slow breaking ball with a slower one. Promoted to Double-A for the Eastern League playoffs in September, he may be advanced enough to proceed to Triple-A to start 2010.

Year	Club (League)	Class	W	L	ERA	G	GS	CG	SV	IP	H	R	ER	HR	BB	SO	AVG
2007	Salem-Keizer (NWL)	SS	5	3	2.98	12	12	0	0	54	46	20	18	5	23	55	.232
2008	Augusta (SAL)	LoA	8	4	3.51	23	21	0	0	115	96	51	45	5	23	111	.224
2009	San Jose (CAL)	HiA	16	2	2.86	26	25	0	0	148	131	53	47	19	36	135	.237
MINOR LEAGUE TOTALS			29	9	3.12	61	58	0	0	317	273	124	110	29	82	301	.232

27 JOSE CASILLA, RHP

BORN: May 21, 1989. **B-T:** R-R. **HT.:** 6-1. **WT.:** 180. **SIGNED:** Dominican Republic, 2006. **SIGNED BY:** Pablo Peguero.

Casilla's brother Santiago has been a mainstay in the Athletics bullpen over the past three seasons. Jose bears similarities to his brother, who's nine years his elder, but the Giants aren't ruling out developing him as a starter. Casilla usually pitches at 92-94 mph coming out of the bullpen, but as with many young relievers, his velocity tends to vary from day to day. He dominated short-season Northwest League hitters last summer with his devastating slider, but he tends to fall in love with the pitch. Casilla gets distracted by runners and is less consistent from the stretch. He averaged 2.8 groundouts for every airout in 2009, which portends good things, and has given up just two homers in 131 pro innings. He has the most upside among an intriguing group of young Giants international pitchers that also includes the Bucardo brothers, Jorge and Wilber, and Edward Concepcion. San Francisco will test Casilla's durability and consistency in low Class A this year.

Year	Club (League)	Class	W	L	ERA	G	GS	CG	SV	IP	H	R	ER	HR	BB	SO	AVG
2006	Giants (DSL)	R	1	0	2.00	2	2	0	0	9	8	2	2	1	4	11	.235
2007	Giants (DSL)	R	6	3	3.76	16	14	0	0	69	58	32	29	0	22	58	.223
2008	Giants (AZL)	R	3	1	1.59	6	5	0	0	23	19	10	4	1	1	19	.216
	Salem-Keizer (NWL)	SS	0	0	2.70	2	0	0	0	3	4	1	1	0	1	4	.308
2009	Salem-Keizer (NWL)	SS	1	1	1.67	25	0	0	12	27	22	8	5	0	9	31	.210
MINOR LEAGUE TOTALS			11	5	2.81	51	21	0	12	131	111	53	41	2	37	123	.222

28 AARON KING, LHP

BORN: April 27, 1989. **B-T:** L-L. **HT.:** 6-4. **WT.:** 205. **DRAFTED:** Surry (N.C.) CC, 2008 (7th round). **SIGNED BY:** Pat Portugal.

After seeing King pitch on tape, Giants vice president of player personnel Dick Tidrow made King his "priority guy" in the 2008 draft. He has the size and arm action that the organization prizes, and he lasted seven rounds because he's something of a long-term project. King struggled in his first full pro season as San Francisco tried to hone his mechanics and give him a delivery he could repeat without difficulty. He's still figuring that out, as evidenced by his average of 4.5 walks per nine innings. There's nothing wrong with his pure stuff, however. His fastball sits in the low 90s and has been clocked as high as 97 mph. He managed to develop a nice changeup that he could throw for strikes. His breaking ball is less refined, a slurve that the Giants hope to turn into a true slider. The Giants will continue to develop him as a starter to get him innings, but King projects more as a reliever unless he makes drastic improvements to his command and breaking ball. He'll advance to high Class A this year.

Year	Club (League)	Class	W	L	ERA	G	GS	CG	SV	IP	H	R	ER	HR	BB	SO	AVG
2008	Giants (AZL)	R	4	1	2.84	11	6	0	0	32	24	10	10	1	15	41	.216
	Salem-Keizer (NWL)	SS	0	1	5.40	2	0	0	0	2	1	1	1	0	4	4	.200
2009	Augusta (SAL)	LoA	7	6	3.70	22	22	0	0	105	90	54	43	9	52	88	.234
MINOR LEAGUE TOTALS			11	8	3.52	35	28	0	0	138	115	65	54	10	71	133	.230

29 BROCK BOND, 2B

BORN: Sept. 11, 1985. **B-T:** B-R. **HT.:** 5-10. **WT.:** 195. **DRAFTED:** Missouri, 2007 (24th round). **SIGNED BY:** Todd Thomas.

Bond hit .333 to win the Eastern League batting title last year, and he led the prospect-rich league with a .429 on-base percentage. You could say the Giants found themselves a steal in the 24th round of the 2007 draft—except they actually meant to take Lipscomb outfielder Casey Bond (who's unrelated) and picked Brock by mistake. They did select Casey in the next round, and while he's now out of baseball Brock is working his way up the ladder. He plays hard every day, setting a great tone from the leadoff spot, and controls the strike zone. He doesn't have much power, but he has a career .324 batting average and .419 on-base percentage in three pro seasons. A fringe-average runner who got caught stealing (15) more than he succeeded (13) last season, he's aggressive running the bases and breaking up double plays. His so-so range and below-average arm limit him to second base. He has dabbled at third base and in left field in pro ball, and if he can show more versatility, he could make it as a big league utilityman. Bond already has exceeded expectations and will try to continue to do so in Triple-A this season.

Year	Club (League)	Class	AVG	G	AB	R	H	2B	3B	HR	RBI	BB	SO	SB	OBP	SLG
2007	Giants (AZL)	R	.227	18	44	4	10	0	2	0	6	6	3	2	.345	.318
	Salem-Keizer (NWL)	SS	.342	42	158	41	54	10	2	0	19	26	21	7	.453	.430
2008	Augusta (SAL)	LoA	.333	42	150	28	50	6	0	1	24	13	20	6	.401	.393
	San Jose (CAL)	HiA	.297	45	155	26	46	6	0	0	19	20	31	9	.394	.335
2009	Connecticut (EL)	AA	.333	122	450	93	150	21	5	1	33	67	69	13	.429	.409
MINOR LEAGUE TOTALS			.324	269	957	192	310	43	9	2	101	132	144	37	.419	.394

30 ANGEL VILLALONA, 1B

BORN: Aug. 13, 1990. **B-T:** R-R. **HT.:** 6-3. **WT.:** 230. **SIGNED:** Dominican Republic, 2006. **SIGNED BY:** Rick Ragazzo/Pablo Peguero.

The news couldn't have been more shocking. On the night San Jose clinched the Cal League title Sept. 19, their Opening Day first baseman was accused of fatally shooting a bar patron in the Dominican Republic. Villalona, a quiet but affable teenage power hitter, had taken leave from the team after straining his quadriceps in July. He was rehabbing the injury in Arizona when the Giants let him go home to visit his mother in the rough coastal town of La Romana. Instead of returning to the United States for instructional league, Villalona surrendered to authorities and was jailed awaiting trial on murder charges. If guilty, he could face a 20-year sentence. Details were sketchy and club officials weren't sure what to think, and during the offseason it appeared that Villalona might have the charges dismissed and make a restitution payment to the victim's family. If Villalona can resume his career, his elite power potential would make him one of the top five prospects in the system. But even if he's exonerated, the U.S. Embassy in the Dominican Republic has revoked his visa, so there's no guarantee he'll ever be able to get back into the country. Villalona's ability to crush balls earned him a $2.1 million bonus in 2006, a franchise record at the time. San Francisco has pushed him aggressively, as he was the youngest player in the South Atlantic League in 2008 and the youngest regular in the California League last season. Older pitchers have been able to exploit his lack of strike-zone awareness and patience. Villalona is a below-average athlete and a poor runner who hasn't exhibited the best conditioning habits. Though he has arm strength and surprising agility for a player with his build, he moved from third base after his first pro season and needs to work on his defense at first base.

Year	Club (League)	Class	AVG	G	AB	R	H	2B	3B	HR	RBI	BB	SO	SB	OBP	SLG
2007	Giants (AZL)	R	.285	52	200	40	57	12	3	5	37	15	42	1	.344	.450
	Salem-Keizer (NWL)	SS	.167	5	12	1	2	0	0	0	1	0	2	1	.231	.167
2008	Augusta (SAL)	LoA	.263	123	464	64	122	29	0	17	64	18	118	1	.312	.435
2009	San Jose (CAL)	HiA	.267	74	292	47	78	11	0	9	42	9	73	0	.306	.397
MINOR LEAGUE TOTALS			.268	254	968	152	259	52	3	31	144	42	235	3	.316	.424

Seattle Mariners

BY MATT EDDY

Year one of general manager Jack Zduriencik's tenure with the Mariners registered as a major success. The big league team won 85 times, improving its showing from 2008 by 24 games, while benefiting from a new focus on defense and starting pitching, particularly of the lefthanded variety.

Formerly scouting director for the Brewers, Zduriencik assumed control of the Mariners in October 2008 and made his first significant move two months later when he shipped former all-star J.J. Putz and two other players to the Mets in a three-team, 12-player deal. The transaction netted Franklin Gutierrez, who

had a career year both at the plate and in center field, three other big leaguers and three prospects—including first baseman Mike Carp, who made his big league debut during the 2009 season, and outfielder Ezequiel Carrera, who won the Double-A Southern League batting title.

Furthering their search for pitching and defense, the Mariners snagged Ian Snell and Jack Wilson during the Pirates' fire sale last July. The deal cost the organization several early-round draft picks made by former GM Bill Bavasi and scouting director Bob Fontaine, including Jeff Clement, the third overall choice in 2005.

Seattle buttressed its prospect depth with summer trades of Yuniesky Betancourt to the Royals and Jarrod Washburn to the Tigers. The swaps netted power righthander Danny Cortes and young lefties Luke French (who made seven uneven starts for the big league clubs and lost his prospect eligibility), Mauricio Robles and Derrick Saito.

As special assistant to the GM Tony Blengino helped identify acquisition targets through performance analysis, new scouting director Tom McNamara helped stock the system with talent through a productive draft. Both came to Seattle from Milwaukee with Zduriencik.

McNamara and his scouting department used the No. 2 overall pick in the draft on Dustin Ackley, the best pure hitter available. The sweet-swinging lefty signed late but played in the Arizona Fall League, where he batted .315/.412/.425, and Seattle will try to move him from first base to center field or second base. With two other picks among the top 33 (compensation for losing free agent Raul Ibanez to the Phillies), Seattle continued to stress defensive chops by taking shortstop Nick Franklin and catcher Steve Baron, two talented prep players from Florida.

Between the draft, the continued international effort—headlined in 2009 by the signing of slugging Dominican outfielder Guillermo Pimentel for $2 mil-

Astute trade acquisition Franklin Gutierrez shined as Seattle's everyday center fielder

BILL NICHOLS

TOP 30 PROSPECTS

1. Dustin Ackley, of/1b	16. Josh Fields, rhp
2. Michael Saunders, of	17. Steven Hensley, rhp
3. Adam Moore, c	18. J.C. Ramirez, rhp
4. Phillippe Aumont, rhp	19. Matt Tuiasosopo, 3b/2b
5. Alex Liddi, 3b	20. James Jones, of
6. Carlos Triunfel, ss/2b	21. Dennis Raben, 1b
7. Michael Pineda, rhp	22. Julio Morban, of
8. Tyson Gillies, of	23. Mike Carp, 1b
9. Nick Franklin, ss	24. Gabriel Noriega, ss
10. Greg Halman, of	25. Steve Baron, c
11. Danny Cortes, rhp	26. Kanekoa Texeira, rhp
12. Mario Martinez, 3b/1b	27. Ricky Orta, rhp
13. Mauricio Robles, lhp	28. Rich Poythress, 1b
14. Nick Hill, lhp	29. Guillermo Pimentel, of
15. Ezequiel Carrera, of	30. Kyle Seager, 2b/3b

lion—and trade acquisitions, the new regime breathed life into a farm system that Baseball America ranked 24th entering the season.

Down on the farm, high Class A High Desert went 83-57 and lost in the California League finals to San Jose. The Mavericks scored more runs than any minor league team and finished second in homers (to Seattle's Triple-A Tacoma affiliate). Third baseman Alex Liddi led the minors in hitting at .345, while outfielder Jamie McOwen hit safely in a league-record 45 straight games, a string no minor leaguer has surpassed in more than half a century.

General Manager: Jack Zduriencik. **Farm Director:** Pedro Grifol. **Scouting Director:** Tom McNamara.

Class	Team	League	W	L	PCT	Finish*	Manager(s)
Majors	Seattle Mariners	American	85	77	.525	7th (14)	Don Wakamatsu
Triple-A	Tacoma Rainiers	Pacific Coast	74	70	.514	7th (16)	Daren Brown
Double-A	West Tenn Diamond Jaxx	Southern	62	78	.443	10th (10)	Phil Plantier
High A	High Desert Mavericks	California	83	57	.593	2nd (10)	Jim Horner
Low A	Clinton LumberKings	Midwest	69	68	.504	7th (14)	Scott Steinmann
Short-season	Everett AquaSox	Northwest	39	37	.513	3rd (8)	John Tamargo
Rookie	Pulaski Mariners	Appalachian	28	36	.438	7th (10)	Jose Moreno
Rookie	AZL Mariners	Arizona	33	22	.600	†3rd (11)	Andy Bottin
Overall 2009 Minor League Record			388	368	.513	10th (30)	

*Finish in overall standings (No. of teams in league). †League champion.

LAST YEAR'S TOP 30

Player, Pos.		Status
1.	Greg Halman, of	No. 10
2.	Michael Saunders, of	No. 2
3.	Phillippe Aumont, rhp	No. 4
4.	Carlos Triunfel, ss/2b	No. 6
5.	J.C. Ramirez, rhp	No. 18
6.	Adam Moore, c	No. 3
7.	Mario Martinez, 3b	No. 12
8.	Jharmidy DeJesus, 3b	Dropped out
9.	Dennis Raben, of	No. 21
10.	Michael Pineda, rhp	No. 7
11.	Carlos Peguero, of	Dropped out
12.	Julio Morban, of	No. 22
13.	Rob Johnson, c/of	Majors
14.	Shawn Kelley, rhp	Majors
15.	Matt Tuiasosopo, 3b	No. 19
16.	Maikel Cleto, rhp	Dropped out
17.	Mike Carp, 1b	No. 23
18.	Cesar Jimenez, lhp	Majors
19.	Gabriel Noriega, ss	No. 24
20.	Tyson Gillies, of	No. 8
21.	Gaby Hernandez, rhp	Dropped out
22.	Denny Almonte, of	Dropped out
23.	Justin Thomas, lhp	(Pirates)
24.	Nathan Adcock, rhp	(Pirates)
25.	Edward Paredes, lhp	Dropped out
26.	Jose Lugo, lhp	(Twins)
27.	Aaron Pribanic, rhp	(Pirates)
28.	Brett Lorin, rhp	(Pirates)
29.	Danny Carroll, of	Dropped out
30.	Nolan Gallagher, rhp	Dropped out

BEST TOOLS

Best Hitter for Average	Dustin Ackley
Best Power Hitter	Greg Halman
Best Strike-Zone Discipline	Ezequiel Carrera
Fastest Baserunner	Tyson Gillies
Best Athlete	Tyson Gillies
Best Fastball	Phillippe Aumont
Best Curveball	Josh Fields
Best Slider	Steven Hensley
Best Changeup	Nick Hill
Best Control	Michael Pineda
Best Defensive Catcher	Steve Baron
Best Defensive Infielder	Gabriel Noriega
Best Infield Arm	Carlos Triunfel
Best Defensive Outfielder	Michael Saunders
Best Outfield Arm	Tyson Gillies

PROJECTED 2013 LINEUP

Catcher	Adam Moore
First Base	Dustin Ackley
Second Base	Jose Lopez
Third Base	Chone Figgins
Shortstop	Nick Franklin
Left Field	Michael Saunders
Center Field	Franklin Gutierrez
Right Field	Ichiro Suzuki
Designated Hitter	Alex Liddi
No. 1 Starter	Felix Hernandez
No. 2 Starter	Brandon Morrow
No. 3 Starter	Michael Pineda
No. 4 Starter	Ian Snell
No. 5 Starter	Ryan Rowland-Smith
Closer	Phillippe Aumont

TOP PROSPECTS OF THE DECADE

Year	Player, Pos.	2009 Org.
2000	Ryan Anderson, lhp	Out of baseball
2001	Ryan Anderson, lhp	Out of baseball
2002	Ryan Anderson, lhp	Out of baseball
2003	Rafael Soriano, rhp	Braves
2004	Felix Hernandez, rhp	Mariners
2005	Felix Hernandez, rhp	Mariners
2006	Jeff Clement, c	Pirates
2007	Adam Jones, of	Orioles
2008	Jeff Clement, c	Pirates
2009	Greg Halman, of	Mariners

TOP DRAFT PICKS OF THE DECADE

Year	Player, Pos.	2009 Org.
2000	Sam Hays, lhp (4th round)	Out of baseball
2001	Michael Garciaparra, ss (1st round supp.)	Brewers
2002	*John Mayberry Jr., of	Phillies
2003	Adam Jones, ss/rhp (1st round supp.)	Orioles
2004	Matt Tuiasosopo, ss (3rd round)	Mariners
2005	Jeff Clement, c	Pirates
2006	Brandon Morrow, rhp	Mariners
2007	Phillippe Aumont, rhp	Mariners
2008	Josh Fields, rhp	Mariners
2009	Dustin Ackley, of/1b	Mariners

*Did not sign.

LARGEST BONUSES IN CLUB HISTORY

Dustin Ackley, 2009	$6,000,000
Ichiro Suzuki, 2000	$5,000,000
Jeff Clement, 2005	$3,400,000
Brandon Morrow, 2006	$2,450,000
Matt Tuiasosopo, 2004	$2,290,000

SEATTLE MARINERS

TOP 2010 ROOKIE: Michael Saunders, of. The athletic outfielder's all-around skills should play well in his second exposure to big leagues.

BREAKOUT PROSPECT: Mario Martinez, 3b/1b. He has the tools to hit for average and power while providing quality defense at the hot corner.

SLEEPER: Juan Diaz, ss. A standout defender, he also added strength and drove the ball more consistently last season.

SOURCE OF TOP 30 TALENT

Homegrown	25	Acquired	5
College	10	Trades	4
Junior college	0	Rule 5 draft	1
High school	4	Independent leagues	0
Draft-and-follow	2	Free agents/waivers	0
Nondrafted free agents	0		
International	9		

Numbers in parentheses indicate prospect rankings

LF
Julio Morban (22)
Guillermo Pimentel (29)
Jamie McOwen
Kuo-Hui Lo

CF
Dustin Ackley (1)
Tyson Gillies (8)
Greg Halman (10)
Ezequiel Carrera (15)
Denny Almonte
Matt Cerione
Danny Carroll

RF
Michael Saunders (2)
James Jones (20)
Carlos Peguero
Jose Rivero

3B
Alex Liddi (5)
Carlos Triunfel (6)
Mario Martinez (12)
Matt Tuiasosopo (19)
Jharmidy DeJesus
Matt Mangini
Vinnie Catricala

SS
Nick Franklin (9)
Gabriel Noriega (24)
Juan Diaz
Anthony Phillips

2B
Kyle Seager (30)
Edilio Colina
Shaver Hansen

1B
Dennis Raben (21)
Mike Carp (23)
Rich Poythress (28)
Joe Dunigan

C
Adam Moore (3)
Steve Baron (25)
Travis Scott
Juan Fuentes
Trevor Coleman

RHP

Starters	Relievers
Michael Pineda (7)	Phillippe Aumont (4)
Danny Cortes (11)	Josh Fields (16)
Steven Hensley (17)	Kanekoa Texeira (26)
J.C. Ramirez (18)	Ricky Orta (27)
Maikel Cleto	Anthony Varvaro
Tyler Blandford	Jake Wild
Kenn Kasparek	John Housey
Brandon Maurer	
Gaby Hernandez	
Andrew Carraway	
Erasmo Ramirez	
Luke Burnett	
Nolan Gallagher	

LHP

Starters	Relievers
Mauricio Robles (13)	Nick Hill (14)
Donnie Hume	Edward Paredes
Jimmy Gillheeney	John Hesketh
Anthony Fernandez	Brian Moran
	Bobby LaFromboise
	Derrick Saito

2009 BONUSES: $10.9 MILLION

BEST PURE HITTER: OF/1B Dustin Ackley (1) was the best hitter in the draft and one of the best to come out of college in years. He's a line-drive machine who batted .412 over three seasons at North Carolina.

BEST POWER HITTER: Ackley, who hit 22 homers this spring, could develop plus power. OF Matt Cerione (13) has surprised Seattle with his plus raw power, but he'll have to be more selective to tap into it.

FASTEST RUNNER: Ackley, who flashes 70 speed and is a consistent 60 runner.

BEST DEFENSIVE PLAYER: C Steve Baron (1s) and SS Nick Franklin (1) went as high as they did because the Mariners see them as difference makers with their defense. Baron was rated the best defensive high school catcher in the draft by many clubs, thanks to his plus-plus arm and above-average receiving skills. Franklin should stay at short thanks to his athleticism and good actions.

BEST FASTBALL: The Mariners saw RHP Tyler Blandford (5) reach 98 mph this summer, and his fastball sits at 93-95 mph. It's notable more for its velocity than its life.

BEST SECONDARY PITCH: LHPs Jimmy Gillheeney (8) and John Hesketh (20) both have shown plus changeups. Hesketh dominated with his, striking out 64 in 43 pro innings.

BEST PRO DEBUT: RHP Andrew Carraway (12) went 8-0, 2.09 with a 70-9 K-BB ratio in 65 innings between short-season Everett and low Class A Clinton. 3B Vinnie Catricala (10) batted .301/.363/.493 and led Rookie-level Pulaski with eight homers.

BEST ATHLETE: Ackley and OF James Jones (4) stand out. Jones has the power and arm strength to play right field, and many teams thought he had a brighter future as a pitcher.

MOST INTRIGUING BACKGROUND: LHP Brian Moran (7), a teammate of Ackley and INF Kyle Seager (3) at North Carolina, is the nephew of Tar Heels great and 1985 No. 1 overall pick B.J. Surhoff. One of his high school coaches was the younger brother of Seattle scouting director Tom McNamara. 3B Evan Sharpley (50) was a backup quarterback at Notre Dame. Unsigned RHP David Holman's (47) father Brian and uncle Brad both pitched for the Mariners, with Brian getting one out away from a perfect game in 1990.

CLOSEST TO THE MAJORS: Ackley should rush to the big leagues, though he may be slowed down by learning a new position as the Mariners plan on trying him in center field and at second base.

BEST LATE-ROUND PICK: RHP John Housey (36), whose father Joe scouts for the Cubs, pitched just 76 innings in three seasons at Miami. He struck out 79 in 72 pro innings in his debut, throwing three pitches for strikes, led by a potential plus curveball.

THE ONE WHO GOT AWAY: The Mariners signed their first 15 picks and most of their targets. They hoped to have more of a shot at 1B Regan Flaherty (28), who has lefthanded power and comes from a baseball family in Maine. His father Ed coaches at Southern Maine, and his brother Ryan is a Cubs farmhand.

ASSESSMENT: Ackley could make scouting director Tom McNamara's first draft worthwhile all by himself. This crop could be remembered by how well Franklin and Baron—who were consensus prospects but not consensus top 33 picks—turn out.

2008 BONUSES: $4.3 MILLION

RHP Josh Fields (1) and 1B Dennis Raben (2) had physical woes in their first full pro seasons, with Raben missing all of 2009 after having knee surgery. RHPs Aaron Pribanic (3) and Brett Lorin (5) were part of the Ian Snell/Jack Wilson trade with the Pirates.
GRADE: D

2007 BONUSES: $4.5 MILLION

Seattle made RHP Phillippe Aumont (1) a reliever last year, which should keep him healthier but also reduces his value. RHP Shawn Kelley (13) exceeded expectations by contributing in the big league bullpen in just his third year as a pro.
GRADE: C

2006 BONUSES: $4.8 MILLION

This was the Mariners' best draft in years, but they undercut it by trading RHPs Chris Tillman (2) and Kam Mickolio (18) in the regrettable Erik Bedard deal. RHP Brandon Morrow (1) made the majors almost immediately, while C Adam Moore (6) should start for Seattle in 2010. RHP Doug Fister (7) was surprisingly effective in the rotation last year, and OF Tyson Gillies (25) had a breakout season in the minors.
GRADE: A

2005 BONUSES: $4.1 MILLION*

C/1B Jeff Clement (1) probably won't catch and may not hit, but Seattle got some use out of him in the Snell/Wilson deal. LHP Justin Thomas (4) got a cup of coffee with the Mariners in 2008.
GRADE: F

*Draft analysis by John Manuel (2009) and Jim Callis (2005-08). Numbers in parentheses indicate draft rounds. *Bonuses for 2005 are first 10 rounds only.*

PROSPECT 1

DUSTIN ACKLEY, OF/1B

Born: Feb. 26, 1988.
Height: 6-1. **Weight:** 185.
Bats: L. **Throws:** R.
Drafted: North Carolina,
2009 (1st round).
Signed by: Rob Mummau.

Undrafted out of a small high school in central North Carolina because he had a balky elbow and had faced low-level prep competition, Ackley starred for three seasons at North Carolina. Baseball America's 2007 Freshman of the Year, he led the Tar Heels to College World Series appearances in all three of his years, making the all-tournament team each time and setting the CWS record with 28 hits in 15 games. In NCAA postseason play, he batted 55-for-134 (.410) over 31 games, finishing with a 22-game hitting streak. Ackley finished as North Carolina's all-time leader in batting (.412), hits (346), runs (227) and total bases (544). He cracked 22 homers in 2009 after combining to hit 17 during his first two seasons, and earned first-team All-America honors as well as the nod as Atlantic Coast Conference player of the year. Selected second overall by Seattle, Ackley signed a five-year major league contract at the Aug. 17 deadline, a deal that included a $6 million bonus and a $7.5 million guarantee. Dustin's father John spent seven seasons as a catcher in the Red Sox system, topping out in Triple-A.

Ask any scout about Ackley and they'll focus immediately on his pure lefthanded stroke and his awe-inspiring feel for hitting. He combines all the necessary ingredients to win batting titles in the big leagues, including supreme hand-eye coordination, bat speed and a balanced, all-fields approach. He recognizes pitches and barrels up those in the strike zone. Most evaluators predict average power for Ackley, whose wiry strength is concentrated in his hands and forearms. Though he's not an overly physical player, he can turn on inside fastballs and pull them for home runs, and he can launch bombs to center field during batting practice. In games, however, he focuses on hitting the ball up the middle and to the opposite field, projecting as more of a gap-to-gap hitter. Ackley is a strong athlete who grades as an above-average runner and flashes 70 speed on the 20-80 scouting scale. He gets out of the box quickly and down the line in a shade under four seconds. Under way, he appears to glide despite his short running stride, and he aggressively seeks the extra base.

Ackley injured his throwing arm while pitching as a prep senior and had Tommy John surgery following his sophomore year at North Carolina, which precluded him from playing more than a handful of games in center field in 2009, as had been planned. He spent the majority of his time at first base, where he rated as a solid defender. His arm strength rates as below-average, and he has yet to prove he can handle any position but first base on a daily basis.

A unique talent, Ackley draws no natural comparisons. The Mariners haven't decided his future position. He played a bit of center field but mostly left in the Arizona Fall League, and Seattle planned to try him out at second base in January workouts. Wherever Ackley settles on the diamond, he should hit. He ought to reach Double-A West Tenn, at the very least, by the end of his first pro season.

Year	Club (League)	Class	AVG	AB	R	H	2B	3B	HR	RBI	BB	SO	SB	OBP	SLG
2009	Did Not Play—Signed Late														

2 MICHAEL SAUNDERS, OF

BORN: Nov. 19, 1986. **B-T:** L-R. **HT.:** 6-4. **WT.:** 210. **DRAFTED:** Tallahassee (Fla.) CC, D/F 2004 (11th round). **SIGNED BY:** Wayne Norton.

After recovering from arthroscopic shoulder surgery in the offseason, Saunders joined Triple-A Tacoma in late April and he turned in his finest pro season to date. Seattle rewarded him with a callup in late July, whereupon he faced lefties in five of his first six starts and Roy Halladay in the other. Not coincidentally, he got off to a 4-for-27 (.148) start. Saunders shows all five tools, scoring average marks across the board. He has quality bat speed and can pull the ball for power, though he didn't homer in 46 big league games. He can bunt for hits, controls the strike zone and hits offspeed pitches to left field, showing the ingredients necessary to hit for average. He runs well and has more than enough range and arm strength to handle a corner outfield post. Because he works deep counts, Saunders likely will continue to strike out at a healthy pace. The Mariners sat Saunders down for a stretch in September to address mechanical issues in his swing. Hitting coach Alan Cockrell helped him create more leverage and power in his stroke by incorporating his legs more efficiently. Gauging by how well Saunders hit in the Venezuelan League this winter, the lesson seemed to take. Saunders' steady development through the minors underscores his aptitude and dedication to his craft. He should be the Mariners' regular left fielder for 2010 and beyond.

Year	Club (League)	Class	AVG	G	AB	R	H	2B	3B	HR	RBI	BB	SO	SB	OBP	SLG
2005	Everett (NWL)	SS	.270	56	196	24	53	13	3	7	39	27	74	2	.361	.474
2006	Wisconsin (MWL)	LoA	.240	104	359	48	86	10	8	4	39	48	103	22	.329	.345
2007	High Desert (CAL)	HiA	.299	108	431	91	129	25	4	14	77	60	116	27	.392	.473
	West Tenn (SL)	AA	.288	15	52	8	15	1	2	1	7	7	20	2	.373	.442
2008	West Tenn (SL)	AA	.290	67	248	46	72	18	3	8	30	30	66	11	.375	.484
	Tacoma (PCL)	AAA	.242	24	95	12	23	4	1	3	16	9	30	1	.308	.400
2009	Tacoma (PCL)	AAA	.310	64	248	58	77	15	2	13	32	25	48	6	.378	.544
	Seattle (AL)	MAJ	.221	46	122	13	27	1	3	0	4	6	40	4	.258	.279
MAJOR LEAGUE TOTALS			.221	46	122	13	27	1	3	0	4	6	40	4	.258	.279
MINOR LEAGUE TOTALS			.279	438	1629	287	455	86	23	50	240	206	457	71	.364	.452

3 ADAM MOORE, C

BORN: May 8, 1984. **B-T:** R-R. **HT.:** 6-3. **WT.:** 220. **DRAFTED:** Texas-Arlington, 2006 (6th round). **SIGNED BY:** Mark Lummus.

Considered more of a slugger coming out of Texas-Arlington, Moore has significantly polished his defensive game, working relentlessly with catching instructor Roger Hansen on improving his footwork and technique. That effort paid off when the Mariners traded Jeff Clement to the Pirates in July, clearly making Moore their catcher of the future. He got his first big league exposure in September. Moore has a balanced approach and compact, line-drive stroke, allowing him to make consistent contact and wait on offspeed pitches. He's strong and generates plus power for the catching position. Agile for his size, he has cleaned up his blocking and receiving to the point where he can now count them as assets. He has a plus arm and ranked second in the Triple-A Pacific Coast League by throwing out 31 percent of basestealers last year. Moore has no notable shortcomings, though like most catchers, he's a well below-average runner. Despite his minor league performance, he doesn't have premium bat speed. With natural leadership skills, Moore possesses all the tools to catch regularly in the big leagues. He logged a career-high 113 games behind the plate last season and stands first in line on Seattle's big league depth chart for 2010.

Year	Club (League)	Class	AVG	G	AB	R	H	2B	3B	HR	RBI	BB	SO	SB	OBP	SLG
2006	Everett (NWL)	SS	.317	16	63	8	20	9	0	0	9	2	10	0	.348	.460
	Wisconsin (MWL)	LoA	.267	44	165	21	44	6	0	7	24	14	38	0	.342	.430
2007	High Desert (CAL)	HiA	.307	115	433	74	133	30	3	22	102	41	84	1	.371	.543
2008	West Tenn (SL)	AA	.319	119	429	60	137	34	2	14	71	40	77	0	.396	.506
2009	West Tenn (SL)	AA	.263	27	95	14	25	5	0	3	13	16	21	0	.371	.411
	Tacoma (PCL)	AAA	.294	91	340	41	100	19	0	9	43	26	51	1	.346	.429
	Seattle (AL)	MAJ	.217	6	23	4	5	1	0	1	2	0	7	1	.250	.391
MAJOR LEAGUE TOTALS			.217	6	23	4	5	1	0	1	2	0	7	1	.250	.391
MINOR LEAGUE TOTALS			.301	412	1525	218	459	103	5	55	262	139	281	2	.369	.483

4 PHILLIPPE AUMONT, RHP

BORN: Jan. 7, 1989. **B-T:** L-R. **HT.:** 6-7. **WT.:** 220. **DRAFTED:** HS—Gatineau, Quebec, 2007 (1st round). **SIGNED BY:** Wayne Norton.

The Mariners greeted Aumont with a surprise in spring training, telling the towering righthander that he'd continue his career in relief. They reasoned that the move not only would accelerate his timetable, but also would help him stay healthy after elbow soreness limited him to 56 innings in 2008. The recipient of a $1.9 million bonus as the 11th overall pick in 2007, he converted 12 of 14 save opportunities at high Class A High Desert before running into resistance in Double-A. Aumont wowed observers of the World Baseball Classic with his arm strength, imposing physique and tenacity as he guided Canada out of a none-out, bases-loaded jam against Team USA. His heavy sinker ranges from 92-95 mph with plus-plus life down in the zone. He dials his four-seamer up to 98 mph and savors challenging batters. His mid-70s curveball features occasional plus 12-to-6 break, especially when he repeats his high three-quarters arm slot and gets extension on the front side of his delivery. Aumont's high adrenaline levels can work against him at times. He missed the final three weeks of the season after breaking his non-pitching hand when he punched his locker. The biggest thing holding him back is an overall lack of command. His changeup is too firm, though it has some splitter action. If everything falls into place, Aumont has closer potential. He didn't exactly allay concerns by walking eight batters and allowing 18 runs in 12 Arizona Fall League innings. He'll get another crack at Double-A in 2010.

Year	Club (League)	Class	W	L	ERA	G	GS	CG	SV	IP	H	R	ER	HR	BB	SO	AVG
2008	Wisconsin (MWL)	LoA	4	4	2.75	15	8	0	2	56	46	22	17	4	19	50	.224
2009	High Desert (CAL)	HiA	1	2	3.24	29	0	0	12	33	24	14	12	3	12	35	.195
	West Tenn (SL)	AA	1	4	5.09	15	0	0	4	18	21	15	10	1	11	24	.292
MINOR LEAGUE TOTALS			6	10	3.29	59	8	0	18	107	91	51	39	8	42	109	.228

5 ALEX LIDDI, 3B

BORN: Aug. 14, 1988. **B-T:** R-R. **HT.:** 6-4. **WT.:** 176. **SIGNED:** Italy, 2005. **SIGNED BY:** Wayne Norton/Mario Mazzotti.

The first Italian position player to play pro ball in the United States, Liddi hit .313 in an encouraging 2006 pro debut but then limped through two years in the low Class A Midwest League as a teenager, batting .240/.306/.365 over 249 games. A promotion to a hitter's paradise in High Desert helped him unlock his significant offensive potential. Liddi hit .345 to lead all minor leaguers and also won California League MVP honors. He participated in the World Baseball Classic in March and the Futures Game in July. Most evaluators agree that Liddi's huge 2009 season was no mirage. With strong wrists, he generates natural power to center and right-center, and he did a better job of pulling the ball for power. Though he remains tall and lanky, he's beginning to add muscle to his frame. He has a feel for hitting, with his smooth stroke and solid plate coverage. His pitch selectivity improved in the second half, coinciding with a toe tap he added to his stance. He rates as a strong defender at third base, featuring soft hands and above-average arm strength. Liddi's athletic actions are not exactly graceful, and he already rates as a below-average runner. Some observers think his 2009 season was a product of his home ballpark, and he hit a more representative .308/.351/.498 with six homers on the road. With his breakout performance, Liddi cleared a giant hurdle in 2009. How well he makes the transition to a less favorable hitting environment in Double-A this year will reveal a lot about his future.

Year	Club (League)	Class	AVG	G	AB	R	H	2B	3B	HR	RBI	BB	SO	SB	OBP	SLG
2006	Mariners (AZL)	R	.313	47	182	31	57	13	6	3	25	12	48	9	.355	.500
	Wisconsin (MWL)	LoA	.184	38	4	7	1	0	0	2	1	8	0	.200	.211
2007	Wisconsin (MWL)	LoA	.240	113	400	41	96	28	3	8	52	36	123	5	.308	.385
2008	Wisconsin (MWL)	LoA	.244	125	447	65	109	26	4	6	53	42	115	17	.313	.360
2009	High Desert (CAL)	HiA	.345	129	493	97	170	44	5	23	104	53	122	10	.411	.594
MINOR LEAGUE TOTALS			.281	425	1560	238	439	112	18	40	236	144	416	41	.346	.453

6 CARLOS TRIUNFEL, SS/2B

BORN: Feb. 27, 1990. **B-T:** R-R. **HT.:** 5-11. **WT.:** 205. **SIGNED:** Dominican Republic, 2006. **SIGNED BY:** Patrick Guerrero/Bob Engle.

Triunfel signed for $1.3 million in 2006 and moved rapidly to high Class A in his pro debut a year later. After returning there in 2008, he missed most of last season when he fractured his fibula and tore ankle ligaments in his left leg during a grisly baserunning collision. Triunfel combines pure bat speed, coordination and barrel awareness to profile as a plus hitter. His impatient approach cuts into his production, but on the flip side he can hit all types of pitches to all fields. His strong, accurate arm rates at least a 70 on the 20-80 scouting scale and makes him a natural fit for the left side of the infield. His hands are soft enough to play shortstop. A bat wrap inhibits Triunfel's ability to turn on quality stuff on the inner half of the plate, which artificially caps his average power potential. He's a below-average runner who lacks the quickness and range to be an everyday shortstop, and his arm would be wasted at second base. His weight ballooned to near 220 pounds while he rehabbed his leg injuries. As a result, the Mariners hired a nutritionist to formulate a strict diet for him and he got his weight back down while playing in the Arizona Fall League. Triunfel still hasn't found a defensive home. He'll head back to Double-A, where he'll continue to play multiple positions while learning to trust his surgically repaired ankle.

Year	Club (League)	Class	AVG	G	AB	R	H	2B	3B	HR	RBI	BB	SO	SB	OBP	SLG
2007	Wisconsin (MWL)	LoA	.309	43	152	18	47	8	2	0	14	5	23	4	.342	.388
	Mariners (AZL)	R	.273	3	11	1	3	0	0	0	3	0	1	0	.231	.273
	High Desert (CAL)	HiA	.288	50	208	32	60	10	2	0	22	12	31	3	.333	.356
2008	High Desert (CAL)	HiA	.287	108	436	75	125	20	4	8	49	30	52	30	.336	.406
2009	Mariners (AZL)	R	.250	4	16	0	4	1	0	0	4	0	2	1	.250	.313
	West Tenn (SL)	AA	.231	7	26	2	6	1	0	0	4	1	2	0	.286	.269
MINOR LEAGUE TOTALS			.289	215	849	128	245	40	8	8	96	48	111	38	.332	.383

7 MICHAEL PINEDA, RHP

BORN: Jan. 18, 1989. **B-T:** R-R. **HT.:** 6-5. **WT.:** 250. **SIGNED:** Dominican Republic, 2005. **SIGNED BY:** Patrick Guerrero/Franklin Taveras.

Pineda toyed with Midwest League batters in 2008, ranking second in the circuit in ERA (1.95) and opponent average (.216). He picked up right where he left off last season, paying little heed to the tough pitching environments of High Desert and the California League as a whole. Mavericks Stadium didn't undermine him, but his elbow did, as lingering soreness sent him to the disabled list and limited him to 47 innings. Pineda's velocity returned when he pitched in the Cal League playoffs, with his fastball sitting at 91-92 mph and touching 94. It has good armside run, allowing him to tie up righthanders. He works the other side of the plate with an 86-91 mph cutter, and also shows advanced feel for a changeup. The natural movement he imparts on his pitches makes them difficult to square up. Pineda's elbow pain is cause for concern. He struggled to hold his velocity into the late innings last year. He'll snap off a true slider in the high 70s on occasion, but when he overthrows, the pitch is more of a cut fastball with short break. Having added 60-70 pounds to his frame since signing, Pineda has a strong build suited for the rotation—if his elbow holds up. Not many Mariners farmhands can match his upside, so the organization may opt to challenge Pineda with a ticket to Double-A in 2010.

Year	Club (League)	Class	W	L	ERA	G	GS	CG	SV	IP	H	R	ER	HR	BB	SO	AVG
2006	Mariners (DSL)	R	2	1	0.44	8	3	0	0	20	14	4	1	0	7	14	.189
2007	Mariners (DSL)	R	6	1	2.29	15	12	0	0	59	70	25	15	2	11	48	.286
2008	Wisconsin (MWL)	LoA	8	6	1.95	26	21	1	0	138	109	38	30	7	35	128	.216
2009	Mariners (AZL)	R	0	0	0.00	2	2	0	0	3	2	0	0	0	0	4	.200
	High Desert (CAL)	HiA	4	2	2.84	10	8	0	0	44	29	16	14	3	6	48	.190
MINOR LEAGUE TOTALS			20	10	2.04	61	46	1	0	265	224	83	60	12	59	242	.227

8 TYSON GILLIES, OF

BORN: Oct. 31, 1988. **B-T:** L-R. **HT.:** 6-2. **WT.:** 190. **DRAFTED:** Iowa Western CC, D/F 2006 (25th round). **SIGNED BY:** Wayne Norton.

A native of Vancouver, Gillies joins fellow Canadians Michael Saunders and Phillippe Aumont on this Top 10 list. Gillies skipped over low Class A on his way to High Desert last year, when he led the California League with 44 steals and ranked third in the minors in hitting (.341) and triples (14), fourth in runs (104) and fifth in on-base percentage (.430). Hearing deficiencies require him to wear hearing aids in both ears, and he has adapted by learning to read lips proficiently. A high-energy sparkplug, Gillies burst onto the national scene by stealing two bases at the Futures Game, where he also blazed a 3.4-second trail to first base on a bunt attempt. The top athlete in the system, his speed earns 80 grades on the 20-80 scouting scale from some evaluators. His quickness, hand-eye coordination and feel for the strike zone give him a chance to hit .280 or better. His speed translates into well above-average range in center field, where he boasts the system's top outfield arm. After Gillies was thrown out 19 times last season, the Mariners had him work on his basestealing technique during a two-week tutorial in Arizona. At the plate, he deploys a slap-and-run approach that rules out power almost completely. He homered only once away from High Desert. Hungry and talented, Gillies is eager to tackle the Double-A Southern League, where a combination of better defenses and more neutral ballpark conditions will put his tools to the test.

Year	Club (League)	Class	AVG	G	AB	R	H	2B	3B	HR	RBI	BB	SO	SB	OBP	SLG
2007	Mariners (AZL)	R	.221	35	86	20	19	3	2	0	6	6	23	9	.337	.302
	Everett (NWL)	SS	.625	4	8	3	5	0	0	0	2	0	1	2	.625	.625
2008	High Desert (CAL)	HiA	.233	11	30	4	7	0	1	0	1	1	6	1	.281	.300
	Everett (NWL)	SS	.313	61	192	36	60	6	5	2	22	35	46	24	.439	.427
2009	High Desert (CAL)	HiA	.341	124	498	104	170	17	14	9	42	60	81	44	.430	.486
MINOR LEAGUE TOTALS			.321	235	814	167	261	26	22	11	73	102	157	80	.419	.447

9 NICK FRANKLIN, SS

GAINES DUVALL

BORN: March 2, 1991. **B-T:** B-R. **HT.:** 6-1. **WT.:** 175. **DRAFTED:** HS—Altamonte Springs, Fla., 2009 (1st round). **SIGNED BY:** Chuck Carlson.

Franklin helped Lake Brantley High (Altamonte Springs, Fla.) win the Florida 6-A title in 2008, then bashed 10 homers to lead it back to the playoffs last spring. The 27th overall pick in the draft, he passed on an Auburn commitment to sign at the Aug. 17 deadline for $1.28 million. The Mariners received the choice from the Phillies as compensation for free agent Raul Ibanez, whose signing six years ago cost Seattle its top pick in the 2004 draft. The Mariners drafted Franklin as high as they did because of his strong defensive tools, which include plus range to both sides as well as good actions and hands. He has the instincts to stick in the middle infield. A switch-hitter, he possesses a short, compact stroke from both sides, projecting as more of a singles and doubles hitter than a true home run threat. His lefthanded swing is more refined than his righthanded stroke thanks to repetition. He's a tick above-average runner. A thin, wiry athlete, Franklin turned around good velocity while using metal bats, but he might top out near 10 homers annually with wood. Evaluations of his arm strength vary from below-average to a tick above, and his three-quarters arm slot costs him crispness and accuracy. He has less range going into the hole than to his glove side. The sum of Franklin's game is greater than the individual parts, and his gritty, enthusiastic style of play wins over most observers. Because his bat is more advanced, the Mariners may opt to send Franklin to low Class A Clinton in order to find playing time at shortstop for both him and Gabriel Noriega.

Year	Club (League)	Class	AVG	G	AB	R	H	2B	3B	HR	RBI	BB	SO	SB	OBP	SLG
2009	Mariners (AZL)	R	.302	10	43	6	13	2	0	1	4	1	6	0	.318	.419
	Everett (NWL)	SS	.400	6	20	4	8	2	1	0	2	1	2	1	.429	.600
MINOR LEAGUE TOTALS			.333	16	63	10	21	4	1	1	6	2	8	1	.354	.476

10 GREG HALMAN, OF

BORN: Aug. 26, 1987. **B-T:** R-R. **HT.:** 6-4. **WT.:** 190. **SIGNED:** Netherlands, 2004. **SIGNED BY:** Wayne Norton/Bob Engle/Peter Van Dalen.

Halman's showing in the World Baseball Classic—1-for-11 with nine strikeouts while playing for the Netherlands—was a harbinger of things to come. A year after finishing a homer shy of a 30-30 season and ranking No. 1 on this list, he endured long stretches void of productivity. He tied for the Southern League lead with 25 home runs, yet ranked last in average (.210), on-base percentage (.278), strikeouts (183) and K-BB ratio (6.3). Halman's game is centered on quick-twitch athleticism. It lends him explosive power at the plate and long, graceful strides in center field, where he's a solid defender with a strong arm. Plus-plus power is attainable with his whip-like bat speed and strong forearms. Lean and long-limbed, Halman draws physical comparisons to Andre Dawson and Alfonso Soriano. Though he's a tick above-average runner, he attempted just 16 steals in 2009 after swiping 31 in each of the previous two seasons. Eaten alive by a poor hitting approach, Halman was on target to set the SL's strikeout record before a bruised heel knocked him out for two weeks in June. He still wound up leading the minors with 191 over two stops. In contrast to years past, he struggled to put pitches in play early in counts, then seemed incapable of recognizing and maintaining enough balance to hit breaking balls. The Mariners have stressed to him the need for consistency and improved self-discipline. Halman stopped by instructional league to put in extra work. He remained upbeat after a tough year, perhaps because he's been there before. A year before his 2008 breakthrough, he bombed in the Midwest League. The ultimate boom or bust prospect, he'll return to Double-A to begin 2010.

Year	Club (League)	Class	AVG	G	AB	R	H	2B	3B	HR	RBI	BB	SO	SB	OBP	SLG
2005	Mariners (AZL)	R	.258	26	89	17	23	2	3	3	11	10	19	1	.350	.449
2006	Everett (NWL)	SS	.259	28	116	19	30	6	4	5	15	3	32	10	.295	.509
2007	Wisconsin (MWL)	LoA	.182	52	187	26	34	5	0	4	15	8	77	15	.234	.273
	Everett (NWL)	SS	.307	62	238	37	73	19	1	16	37	21	85	16	.371	.597
2008	High Desert (CAL)	HiA	.268	67	257	52	69	15	3	19	53	16	76	23	.320	.572
	West Tenn (SL)	AA	.277	61	235	43	65	14	2	10	30	16	66	8	.332	.481
2009	Mariners (AZL)	R	.182	3	11	1	2	0	1	0	2	2	8	0	.308	.364
	West Tenn (SL)	AA	.210	121	457	64	96	17	2	25	72	29	183	9	.278	.420
MINOR LEAGUE TOTALS			.247	420	1590	259	392	78	16	82	235	105	546	82	.307	.470

11 DANNY CORTES, RHP

BORN: March 4, 1987. **B-T:** R-R. **HT.:** 6-6. **WT.:** 215. **DRAFTED:** HS—Pomona, Calif., 2005 (7th round). **SIGNED BY:** Dan Ontiveros (White Sox).

Cortes was the Royals' top-ranked pitching prospect entering the 2009 season, but his stuff seemed flat by comparison when he repeated Double-A. An arrest for public urination in July was the final straw for Kansas City, which traded him for Yuniesky Betancourt, who had fallen out of favor in Seattle. Cortes pitched much better for West Tenn after the trade, striking out a batter per inning and going 1-2, 2.70 in his final six starts. In some ways, Cortes resembles Phillippe Aumont as a tall, physical righthander who boasts arm strength and intensity on the mound. At his best, he sits at 92-94 mph with late life down in the zone. He reels off a hard, sharp curveball for his finishing pitch, and also mixes in a loopy slider as a get-me-over offering. He has developed more feel for an average changeup. Cortes came to the Mariners with a max-effort delivery and didn't consistently throw strikes. He toned down his mechanics, and his composure and strikeout rate improved noticeably. He still walks too many batters, handing out 5.7 walks per nine innings last season. He already has been traded twice, a rare trick for a pitcher with such a good arm. Cortes' command has to take a major step forward for him to profile as a starter, but even with fringy command he has the weapons to work as a late-inning reliever. After two full seasons in Double-A, he's ready for Triple-A.

Year	Club (League)	Class	W	L	ERA	G	GS	CG	SV	IP	H	R	ER	HR	BB	SO	AVG
2005	Bristol (APP)	R	1	4	5.17	15	7	0	0	38	44	23	22	2	13	38	.289
2006	Kannapolis (SAL)	LoA	3	9	4.01	20	19	0	0	108	109	61	48	6	38	96	.260
	Burlington (MWL)	LoA	1	2	6.69	7	7	0	0	35	40	27	26	7	17	30	.284
2007	Wilmington (CAR)	HiA	8	8	3.07	24	24	0	0	123	102	50	42	7	45	120	.226
2008	NW Arkansas (TL)	AA	10	4	3.78	23	23	0	0	117	103	51	49	13	55	109	.241
2009	NW Arkansas (TL)	AA	6	6	3.92	16	15	0	0	80	77	43	35	3	50	57	.258
	West Tenn (SL)	AA	1	5	4.94	10	10	0	0	55	51	33	30	4	35	55	.248
MINOR LEAGUE TOTALS			30	38	4.08	115	105	0	0	556	526	288	252	42	253	505	.251

12 MARIO MARTINEZ, 3B/1B

BORN: Nov. 13, 1989. **B-T:** R-R. **HT.:** 6-3. **WT.:** 190. **SIGNED:** Venezuela, 2006. **SIGNED BY:** Bob Engle/Emilio Carrasquel

Signed as a shortstop for $600,000, Martinez outgrew his natural position after his first pro season in 2007. Since moving to third base, he has hit .313 over 553 at-bats in short-season ball the past two years. He paced the short-season Northwest League with 93 hits and ranked third with 20 doubles in 2009, though that came after he flunked the Midwest League during the first three months of the season. Martinez's level swing, all-fields approach and knack for contact should allow him to hit for average. He has cranked five home runs in each of the past two seasons, but his natural strength and the bat speed to turn around high velocity portend at least average power. He's an average runner who figures to slow down as he matures. Martinez already has a big league body, with surprising agility for his size. He ranges well to both sides, has soft hands and shows consistent above-average arm strength. Martinez speaks fluent English, having learned it during his first instructional league, and he mentors and translates for Spanish-speaking teammates. He'll tackle the MWL again in 2010.

Year	Club (League)	Class	AVG	G	AB	R	H	2B	3B	HR	RBI	BB	SO	SB	OBP	SLG
2007	Mariners (AZL)	R	.281	53	196	36	55	9	1	1	26	6	31	3	.311	.352
2008	Pulaski (APP)	R	.319	64	251	43	80	15	3	5	32	10	47	2	.344	.462
2009	Clinton (MWL)	LoA	.214	61	229	20	49	13	2	2	24	11	51	1	.264	.314
	Everett (NWL)	SS	.308	71	302	45	93	20	5	3	33	11	59	4	.340	.437
MINOR LEAGUE TOTALS			.283	249	978	144	277	57	11	11	115	38	188	10	.317	.398

13 MAURICIO ROBLES, LHP

BORN: March 5, 1989. **B-T:** L-L. **HT.:** 5-10. **WT.:** 160. **SIGNED:** Venezuela, 2006. **SIGNED BY:** German Robles (Tigers).

The Tigers surrendered Robles and Luke French to the Mariners in late July when they wanted Jarrod Washburn to slot behind Justin Verlander and Edwin Jackson in the rotation. An outfielder prior to signing, Robles jumped from the Rookie-level Venezuelan Summer League to full-season ball in 2008. He's short but strong, especially in the lower half, and he made strides in repeating his delivery in 2009. He sat at 90-91 mph and touched 95, and he also held his velocity deeper into games. Robles throws a power curveball in the low 80s, a pitch that rates as below-average now but flashes plus potential. He tends to slow his arm down to throw his breaking ball and changeup. If he develops a better feel for his changeup, he could mature into a No. 4 or 5 starter. He certainly has the bulldog demeanor required. Robles finished the year with six strong starts for High Desert and then blitzed through two California League playoff outings, whiffing 13 in 11 innings. He'll likely return to high Class A to start the year.

SEATTLE MARINERS

Year	Club (League)	Class	W	L	ERA	G	GS	CG	SV	IP	H	R	ER	HR	BB	SO	AVG
2006	Tigers/Marlins (VSL)	R	0	1	3.38	14	0	0	0	16	17	7	6	0	16	20	.279
2007	Tigers (VSL)	R	3	6	3.26	14	14	0	0	69	60	33	25	4	27	83	.237
2008	West Michigan (MWL)	LoA	5	3	2.66	23	16	0	0	91	54	27	27	2	54	79	.176
2009	West Michigan (MWL)	LoA	4	4	4.63	11	11	0	0	56	45	29	29	6	27	71	.221
	Lakeland (FSL)	HiA	4	2	3.60	7	7	0	0	35	34	16	14	3	14	40	.256
	High Desert (CAL)	HiA	3	2	2.78	7	6	0	0	32	23	14	10	1	19	34	.202
MINOR LEAGUE TOTALS			19	18	3.33	76	54	0	0	300	233	126	111	16	157	327	.218

14 NICK HILL, LHP

BORN: Jan. 30, 1985. **B-T:** L-L. **HT.:** 6-0. **WT.:** 190. **DRAFTED:** Army, 2007 (7th round). **SIGNED BY:** Rob Mummau.

The Red Sox first drafted Hill in 2006, but U.S. Military Academy rules at the time prohibited the 47th-round pick from signing. The Mariners made him the highest-drafted player ever from Army the following year, signing him for $70,000 as a seventh-round senior. He started his pro career that summer under the military's alternative-service option, which allowed him to forgo active duty. He has participated in recruiting efforts in the minor league cities where he was assigned, and he has spent his offseasons meeting with prospective student-athlete cadets. Hill completed his two-year service commitment last summer, taking leave from West Tenn for a month to do so. To make up for lost time, the Mariners sent him to the Arizona Fall League. Hill works effectively as both a reliever and starter, sitting at 87-89 mph with good sink and reaching as high as 91-92 with his four-seam fastball. He throws an 83-84 mph slider with solid depth and tilt. Add in his changeup, and he has the weaponry to attack lefthanders and righthanderrs. With his work ethic and competitiveness, Seattle envisions him making a big league impact at some point in 2010, most likely in the bullpen.

Year	Club (League)	Class	W	L	ERA	G	GS	CG	SV	IP	H	R	ER	HR	BB	SO	AVG
2007	Everett (NWL)	SS	1	3	0.51	18	0	0	2	35	24	6	2	0	9	45	.197
2008	West Tenn (SL)	AA	0	1	10.13	9	0	0	0	8	11	10	9	2	7	7	.306
	High Desert (CAL)	HiA	2	7	4.48	35	10	0	1	94	106	63	47	10	32	69	.278
2009	West Tenn (SL)	AA	5	6	3.10	36	9	3	2	96	84	44	33	5	24	100	.232
MINOR LEAGUE TOTALS			8	17	3.52	98	19	3	5	233	225	123	91	17	72	221	.250

15 EZEQUIEL CARRERA, OF

BORN: June 11, 1987. **B-T:** L-L. **HT.:** 5-10. **WT.:** 179. **SIGNED:** Venezuela, 2005. **SIGNED BY:** Gregorio Machado/Junior Alfonzo/Robert Alfonzo (Mets).

Carrera stood in the shadow of the other two minor leaguers acquired from the Mets in the December 2008 trade of J.J. Putz, but the slight center fielder passed Maikel Cleto and Mike Carp by winning the Southern League's batting (.337) and on-base percentage (.441) titles in 2009. In fact, his OBP ranked third in the minors. While in the Mets system, he revered fellow Venezuelan Endy Chavez, whose game Carrera emulates. He excels as a defensive outfielder because of his first-step quickness and proper angles to the ball. He doesn't throw well, but he improved his release time and accuracy in 2009. An above-average runner, Carrera is adept at bunting for hits, stretching singles into doubles and stealing bases late in games. The definition of a pesky hitter, he can outlast pitchers for walks by fouling off even quality offerings. He offers little power, and none against lefthand-ers, against whom he still looks uncomfortable. He also doesn't read lefties well on stolen-base attempts, and his success rate fell from 81 percent versus righthanders to 43 percent against southpaws. He spent time on the disabled list with a high ankle sprain and sprained thumb last year, both sustained while chasing down balls in the outfield. Farm director Pedro Grifol describes Carrera as having a compact game, excelling in all aspects of small ball. It's difficult to see him supplanting any of Seattle's starting outfielders, but Carrera profiles as a valuable reserve.

Year	Club (League)	Class	AVG	G	AB	R	H	2B	3B	HR	RBI	BB	SO	SB	OBP	SLG
2005	Mets (VSL)	R	.227	45	150	19	34	3	2	0	8	15	47	7	.308	.273
2006	Mets (VSL)	R	.301	57	216	41	65	4	5	1	19	16	28	22	.365	.380
2007	Mets (GCL)	R	.341	45	179	41	61	8	3	1	26	26	29	16	.430	.436
	Brooklyn (NYP)	SS	.300	20	70	11	21	2	0	0	6	4	13	6	.347	.329
2008	St. Lucie (FSL)	HiA	.263	114	430	61	113	11	12	7	29	46	86	28	.344	.393
2009	West Tenn (SL)	AA	.337	91	329	68	111	12	4	2	38	59	62	27	.441	.416
MINOR LEAGUE TOTALS			.295	372	1374	241	405	40	26	11	126	166	265	106	.379	.386

16 JOSH FIELDS, RHP

BORN: Aug. 19, 1985. **B-T:** R-R. **HT.:** 6-0. **WT.:** 185. **DRAFTED:** Georgia, 2008 (1st round). **SIGNED BY:** Chuck Carlson.

Former scouting director Bob Fontaine's final first-round pick for the Mariners, Fields finally signed on Feb. 16, 2009. He agreed to a bonus of $1.75 million—the midpoint between his $2 million asking price and the Mariners' longstanding $1.5 million offer. The Aug. 15 signing deadline didn't apply to Fields because he was a college senior with no eligibility remaining. In a four-year run as closer for Georgia, he set a Southeastern Conference record with 41 saves and helped pitch the Bulldogs to a runner-up finish in the 2008 College World Series. Though he's not physical, Fields has incredible arm speed, enabling him to fire fastballs at a consistent 93-96 mph. His low-80s power curveball features quality depth and rates as the best in the system. He really doesn't throw a changeup, having started only one game since high school. Fields' max-effort delivery is both deceptive and difficult to repeat, which makes throwing strikes a challenge. He wore down in 2009 after his long layoff and under the strain of a higher workload. He twice landed on the disabled list, first with a dead arm and then a strained oblique. A pair of plus-plus pitches gives him the upside as a late-inning reliever, possibly a closer, but first Fields must prove he can throw enough strikes. He'll get that chance with another run at Double-A.

Year	Club (League)	Class	W	L	ERA	G	GS	CG	SV	IP	H	R	ER	HR	BB	SO	AVG
2009	West Tenn (SL)	AA	2	2	6.48	31	0	0	1	33	33	33	24	2	22	36	.254
MINOR LEAGUE TOTALS			2	2	6.48	31	0	0	1	33	33	33	24	2	22	36	.254

17 STEVEN HENSLEY, RHP

BORN: Dec. 27, 1986. **B-T:** R-R. **HT.:** 6-3. **WT.:** 195. **DRAFTED:** Elon, 2008 (4th round). **SIGNED BY:** Rob Mummau.

Elon's career strikeout leader and the highest draft pick (fourth round) in school history, Hensley had his 2008 pro debut cut short by a partially torn elbow ligament. He opted for rest and rehab rather than surgery and made a full recovery in 2009, logging 148 innings—the majority of them in pitching-hostile High Desert—while pacing the organization with 135 strikeouts. Hensley aggressively throws strikes with his 88-92 mph fastball and plus hard slider. His fastball hit 94 during most starts, and more consistently in the second half of the season. His changeup, which he didn't use much in college, shows solid potential. He also throws a curveball, but it flattens out, as do his other pitches, when he drops from his usual high three-quarters arm slot. He's not overpowering, but he balances that by being a top competitor. Hensley could develop into a durable innings-eater or a setup reliever. The next step is conquering Double-A, where he got hit hard in three starts last year.

Year	Club (League)	Class	W	L	ERA	G	GS	CG	SV	IP	H	R	ER	HR	BB	SO	AVG
2008	Everett (NWL)	SS	2	1	5.22	8	6	0	0	29	28	20	17	3	9	32	.243
2009	Clinton (MWL)	LoA	4	0	0.00	4	3	0	0	20	18	4	0	0	0	16	.250
	West Tenn (SL)	AA	0	1	7.20	3	3	0	0	15	19	12	12	1	10	11	.322
	High Desert (CAL)	HiA	9	3	4.21	20	19	1	0	113	104	57	53	16	30	108	.246
MINOR LEAGUE TOTALS			15	5	4.16	35	31	1	0	177	169	93	82	20	49	167	.253

18 J.C. RAMIREZ, RHP

BORN: Aug. 16, 1988. **B-T:** R-R. **HT.:** 6-3. **WT.:** 175. **SIGNED:** Nicaragua, 2005. **SIGNED BY:** Luis Molina/Nemesio Porras.

Ramirez concluded his English training following the 2008 season and took a step toward making his name sound more Americanized by shortening it from Juan (or Juan Carlos) to J.C. One thing remained unchanged: He's a physical, durable pitcher who increased his workload again in 2009. The Mariners added him to the 40-man roster, though Ramirez remains raw and unrefined. His stuff is top-shelf, beginning with a lively 92-94 mph fastball that he can dial up to 96-97 when necessary. Even with present spotty command, his heater reminds Jaime Navarro, his pitching coach for two years running, of Kevin Brown's: "Just hard and down." Ramirez puts good spin on his high-70s slider, but the pitch lacks consistent tilt because he often drops his hands during delivery, which lowers his arm slot. He tends to slow his motion when not throwing a fastball, hindering his feel for his below-average changeup as well as his slider. He shows a tendency toward overthrowing, where he'll fly open and not incorporate his lower half. He also needs to do a better job of concentrating on the mound. Ramirez has mid-rotation potential and more than enough raw stuff to pitch in a big league bullpen if he can't remain a starter. His results away from High Desert were fine last year—3.09 ERA with two homers allowed in 11 starts—meaning he could graduate to Double-A in 2010.

Year	Club (League)	Class	W	L	ERA	G	GS	CG	SV	IP	H	R	ER	HR	BB	SO	AVG
2006	Mariners (VSL)	R	5	1	1.66	14	13	1	0	65	43	16	12	0	35	56	.191
2007	Everett (NWL)	SS	3	7	4.30	15	15	0	0	75	61	49	36	3	43	73	.211
2008	Wisconsin (MWL)	LoA	6	9	4.14	25	22	0	0	124	112	68	57	9	38	113	.239
2009	High Desert (CAL)	HiA	8	10	5.12	28	27	1	0	142	153	93	81	18	53	111	.276
MINOR LEAGUE TOTALS			22	27	4.12	82	77	2	0	407	369	226	186	30	169	353	.240

19 MATT TUIASOSOPO, 3B/2B

BORN: May 10, 1986. **B-T:** R-R. **HT.:** 6-2. **WT.:** 225. **DRAFTED:** HS—Woodinville, Wash., 2004 (3rd round). **SIGNED BY:** Phil Geisler.

When the Mariners signed free agents Eddie Guardado and Raul Ibanez five years ago, they forfeited their top two draft choices in 2004. They generously paid their top pick—Tuiasosopo at No. 93 overall—and his $2.29

million bonus still stands as the third-round record. An amateur quarterback whose father Manu and brother Marques both played in the NFL, Tuiasosopo turned down a football scholarship to Washington. He struggled mightily during his first three full seasons but has made steady improvements the last two years. His slugging percentage has climbed from .343 in Double-A to .460 in Triple-A as he has learned to identify and turn on his pitch. Raw strength never has been an issue. His strikeout rate soared in 2009 as he dealt with a sore right elbow that required surgery to remove a bone spur and knocked him out for two months. When healthy, he has solid plate coverage and above-average bat speed. Tuiasosopo hasn't played shortstop regularly since 2006, but he returned to his middle-infield roots last season, appearing in 27 games at second base between Tacoma and Seattle. A quality defender with a strong arm, he was adequate at second—though he doesn't look the part with his tall, muscled frame—after playing there during spring training over the years. He runs and moves well for his size. Tuiasosopo continues to succeed because of his top-notch competitive makeup. He has two minor league options remaining, so while he's in the mix for big league time at third base, he'll likely head to Triple-A to polish his second-base play and learn the corner outfield.

Year	Club (League)	Class	AVG	G	AB	R	H	2B	3B	HR	RBI	BB	SO	SB	OBP	SLG
2004	Mariners (AZL)	R	.412	20	68	18	28	5	2	4	12	13	14	1	.528	.721
	Everett (NWL)	SS	.248	29	101	18	25	6	1	2	14	10	36	4	.336	.386
2005	Wisconsin (MWL)	LoA	.276	107	409	72	113	21	3	6	45	44	96	8	.359	.386
2006	Inland Empire (CAL)	HiA	.306	59	232	31	71	14	0	1	34	14	58	5	.359	.379
	San Antonio (TL)	AA	.185	62	216	16	40	4	0	1	10	20	64	2	.259	.218
2007	West Tenn (SL)	AA	.260	129	446	74	116	27	5	9	57	76	113	4	.371	.404
2008	Tacoma (PCL)	AAA	.281	111	437	87	123	32	2	13	73	47	104	4	.364	.453
	Seattle (AL)	MAJ	.159	14	44	1	7	2	1	0	2	2	16	0	.213	.250
2009	Mariners (AZL)	R	.407	9	27	9	11	0	0	1	3	4	6	0	.500	.519
	Tacoma (PCL)	AAA	.261	59	226	43	59	15	0	11	35	36	83	3	.368	.473
	Seattle (AL)	MAJ	.227	7	22	2	5	1	0	1	2	2	5	0	.280	.409
MAJOR LEAGUE TOTALS			.182	21	66	3	12	3	1	1	4	4	21	0	.236	.303
MINOR LEAGUE TOTALS			.271	585	2162	368	586	124	13	48	283	264	574	31	.361	.407

20 JAMES JONES, OF

BORN: Sept. 24, 1988. **B-T:** L-L. **HT.:** 6-4. **WT.:** 195. **DRAFTED:** Long Island, 2009 (4th round). **SIGNED BY:** David May.

The Mariners defied scouting convention in preferring Jones as a position player. It's rare that a club walks away from low-90s velocity from the left side, but Jones went just 1-9, 7.40 in the second-tier Northeast Conference in 2009. Seattle signed him as a fourth-round pick for $267,300 and installed him as a right fielder at short-season Everett, where observers lauded the quality of his at-bats. Jones recognizes breaking balls, seldom chases pitches out of the zone and generates above-average bat speed with quick hands and wrists. He added more than 50 pounds to his lanky, long-limbed frame in three years at Long Island, and he still has projection remaining in his upper body. His high, tapered waist masks a strong lower half. Jones can drive the ball to all fields and is still growing into his power, which likely will grade as average when all's said and done. He's also a tick above-average runner who reads the ball well off the bat and covers more than enough ground in right. Jones touched 95 mph on the mound in college, and his quick, accurate arm rates as plus-plus in the outfield. He also has experience playing first base. Evaluators unanimously credit him with outstanding makeup. Given time to develop, Jones could develop into a solid regular in right field, though he'll always have pitching in his back pocket if needed.

Year	Club (League)	Class	AVG	G	AB	R	H	2B	3B	HR	RBI	BB	SO	SB	OBP	SLG
2009	Everett (NWL)	SS	.311	45	164	28	51	12	2	3	24	19	40	0	.392	.463
MINOR LEAGUE TOTALS			.311	45	164	28	51	12	2	3	24	19	40	0	.392	.463

21 DENNIS RABEN, 1B

BORN: July 31, 1987. **B-T:** L-L. **HT.:** 6-3. **WT.:** 220. **DRAFTED:** Miami, 2008 (2nd round). **SIGNED BY:** Mike Tosar.

Raben didn't have the chance to build on his promising 2008 pro debut, when he slugged .560 in the Northwest League despite a nagging finger injury. He missed all of last season after having microfracture surgery in April to help aid his body in replacing cartilage in his chronically sore right knee. Raben will return with the same offensive profile, though his decreased mobility will now limit him to first base. His range in left field was nothing special, though his arm is average. Raben stands out in the batter's box, where his résumé as a lefthanded power source is bolstered by his track record with wood. He shined in the Cape Cod League in 2007 and might have been a first-round pick in 2008 if not for a back injury during his junior year. Raben's plus power to all fields comes at a cost. He strikes out a lot and never hit higher than .292 in three college campaigns, so expecting him to hit for average in the major leagues is a stretch. He wasn't a factor on the bases even before his knee surgery. Raben turns 23 in July and has yet to play a game in a full-season league, so reaching high Class A in 2010 is imperative.

Year	Club (League)	Class	AVG	G	AB	R	H	2B	3B	HR	RBI	BB	SO	SB	OBP	SLG
2008	Everett (NWL)	SS	.275	27	91	24	25	11	0	5	14	19	24	1	.411	.560
2009	Did Not Play—Injured															
MINOR LEAGUE TOTALS			.275	27	91	24	25	11	0	5	14	19	24	1	.411	.560

22 JULIO MORBAN, OF

BORN: Feb. 13, 1992. **B-T:** L-L. **HT.:** 6-1. **WT.:** 190. **SIGNED:** Dominican Republic, 2008. **SIGNED BY:** Patrick Guerrero/Bob Engle.

Few if any clubs scout Latin America more efficiently than the Mariners, who snagged Morban for $1.1 million in July 2008. Though he doesn't have the explosive power of fellow Dominican outfielder Guillermo Pimentel, Morban has a better feel for hitting, more speed and a stronger defensive profile. Seattle intended to challenge him in the Rookie-level Appalachian League last season, but a left shoulder sprain grounded him in the Arizona League for all but four games. At 17, he still ranked as one of the AZL's youngest players, though the bum shoulder limited him to just six games in the field. A pure hitter with a compact stroke, Morban shows above-average bat speed and the willingness to hit to all fields. He ought to be an above-average hitter in time. Despite his youth, Morban's mature frame doesn't leave much room for projection, but he already has enough thunder in his bat to hit for average or better power. He runs and throws well, but perhaps not well enough to hold down center field on a daily basis. His instincts enhance his game on both sides of the ball. If Morban's bat develops, he profiles as a starting corner outfielder.

Year	Club (League)	Class	AVG	G	AB	R	H	2B	3B	HR	RBI	BB	SO	SB	OBP	SLG
2009	Pulaski (APP)	R	.333	4	9	3	3	1	0	0	0	0	3	0	.400	.444
	Mariners (AZL)	R	.266	42	154	28	41	9	7	5	23	7	49	8	.303	.513
MINOR LEAGUE TOTALS			.270	46	163	31	44	10	7	5	23	7	52	8	.309	.509

23 MIKE CARP, 1B

BORN: June 30, 1986. **B-T:** L-R. **HT.:** 6-2. **WT.:** 215. **DRAFTED:** HS—Lakewood, Calif., 2004 (9th round). **SIGNED BY:** Steve Leavitt (Mets).

Carp made his big league debut with the Mariners last June, after joining the organization the previous offseason in the three-team, 12-player blockbuster trade involving the Mets and Indians. Playing every other day for the Mariners in September, Carp batted .315 with moderate power and a good batting eye. The plate discipline is real, but his offensive ceiling more closely mirrors his performance in Triple-A, where he hit .271 with 15 home runs. That equates to fringe-average production for an everyday first baseman. Carp bats from an open stance and can really go down and get the ball. His swing plane is flat and his bat speed is no better than average, though, so he's most effective hitting the ball gap to gap. An adequate defender at first base, Carp hasn't shown much aptitude for left field because he's a below-average runner and athlete. He has big league potential as a hitter, but his overall offensive package may not be enough to secure his future as a regular. He has two minor league options remaining, giving the Mariners flexibility as they sift through their options for 2010.

Year	Club (League)	Class	AVG	G	AB	R	H	2B	3B	HR	RBI	BB	SO	SB	OBP	SLG
2004	Mets (GCL)	R	.267	57	191	30	51	12	0	4	26	22	51	2	.358	.393
2005	Hagerstown (SAL)	LoA	.249	89	313	49	78	12	1	19	63	35	96	2	.358	.476
2006	St. Lucie (FSL)	HiA	.287	137	491	69	141	27	1	17	88	51	107	2	.379	.450
2007	St. Lucie (FSL)	HiA	.250	1	4	0	1	0	0	0	0	0	0	0	.250	.250
	Binghamton (EL)	AA	.251	97	359	55	90	16	0	11	48	39	75	2	.337	.387
2008	Binghamton (EL)	AA	.299	134	478	67	143	29	1	17	72	79	88	1	.403	.471
2009	Tacoma (PCL)	AAA	.271	110	413	66	112	25	1	15	64	58	99	0	.372	.446
	Seattle (AL)	MAJ	.315	21	54	7	17	3	1	1	5	8	10	0	.415	.463
MAJOR LEAGUE TOTALS			.315	21	54	7	17	3	1	1	5	8	10	0	.415	.463
MINOR LEAGUE TOTALS			.274	625	2249	336	616	121	4	83	361	284	516	9	.371	.442

24 GABRIEL NORIEGA, SS

BORN: Sept. 13, 1990. **B-T:** R-R. **HT.:** 6-2. **WT.:** 170. **SIGNED:** Venezuela, 2007. **SIGNED BY:** Bob Engle/Pedro Avila/Emilio Carrasquel.

Noriega connected for his first four pro home runs in 2009, while improving his average by 73 points in a return to Rookie-level Pulaski. But his bat isn't what netted him an $800,000 bonus on the international market in 2007. An instinctual shortstop with the tools to play the position at the highest level, Noriega has an uncanny ability to slow the game down and make all the plays. He led all Appalachian League shortstops with a .960 fielding percentage last year. A smooth athlete but below-average runner, he features plus range and arm strength. Long-limbed and lanky, Noriega is a free swinger who sprays the ball to center and right field. A bat wrap limits the damage he inflicts to his pull side. Even the most optimistic power projection would peg him at well below-average, so he'll need to rein in the strikeouts and focus on situational hitting. Noriega will move up because of his fine defensive ability, but his low grades for power and speed limit his ceiling. He's ready for low Class A.

Year	Club (League)	Class	AVG	G	AB	R	H	2B	3B	HR	RBI	BB	SO	SB	OBP	SLG
2008	Mariners (AZL)	R	.421	9	38	7	16	0	0	0	2	1	6	3	.439	.421
	Pulaski (APP)	R	.238	41	151	11	36	4	2	0	18	6	43	6	.266	.291
2009	Pulaski (APP)	R	.311	61	206	27	64	14	2	4	26	16	6	8	.360	.456
MINOR LEAGUE TOTALS			.294	111	395	45	116	18	4	4	46	23	109	17	.333	.390

25 STEVE BARON, C

BORN: Dec. 7, 1990. **B-T:** R-R. **HT.:** 6-0. **WT.:** 195. **DRAFTED:** HS—Miami, 2009 (1st round supplemental). **SIGNED BY:** Mike Tosar.

The first pick of the sandwich round in 2009, Baron eschewed a Duke scholarship to sign for $980,000. The Mariners skipped him past the Arizona League, challenging him with an assignment in the Appalachian League. Baron's bat didn't respond, but his catching skills worked fine. He shut down running games, flashing a crisp, plus-plus arm and leading Appy League catchers by throwing out 54 percent of basestealers. Baron had no trouble running a pro pitching staff at age 18, having called his own games in high school. He has soft hands, and he blocks and receives the ball expertly. But like Pulaski teammate Gabriel Noriega, Baron projects as a strong defensive player with a below-average bat. He has the strength to hit for average or better power, but his rhythmic swing and contact issues—especially against breaking balls—likely will result in lengthy slumps and poor batting averages. Still, if he reaches his ceiling as a catcher who hits .250 with 12-15 homers per year while stifling the running game, he would have a spot on most every big league club. Baron may not be ready to hit low Class A pitching, so he could open 2010 in extended spring before joining Everett in June.

Year	Club (League)	Class	AVG	G	AB	R	H	2B	3B	HR	RBI	BB	SO	SB	OBP	SLG
2009	Pulaski (APP)	R	.179	30	106	12	19	6	0	2	13	7	38	0	.241	.292
MINOR LEAGUE TOTALS			.179	30	106	12	19	6	0	2	13	7	38	0	.241	.292

26 KANEKOA TEXEIRA, RHP

BORN: Feb. 6, 1986. **B-T:** R-R. **HT.:** 6-0. **WT.:** 210. **DRAFTED:** Saddleback (Calif.) CC, 2006 (22nd round). **SIGNED BY:** Danny Ontiveros (White Sox).

Mariners general manager Jack Zduriencik has drafted Texeira twice. As Brewers scouting director, he selected Texeira out of a Hawaii high school in the 31st round of the 2004 draft. Texeira declined to sign and turned pro with the White Sox after two years at Saddleback (Calif.) CC. Their paths intersected again in December, when the Mariners took Texeira from the Yankees in the major league Rule 5 draft. He'll have to stick on Seattle's roster all season, or else clear waivers and be offered back to the Yankees for $25,000. A strikeout pitcher who keeps the ball on the ground, Texeira could occupy a middle-relief role with the Mariners. Over the course of the past three seasons, he has fanned 8.6 batters per nine innings while generating 2.4 groundouts for every flyout—and he shows no platoon split. Texeira gets results with a deceptive short-arm delivery and a nifty 78-80 mph slider, which he fires repeatedly at the opposition. The pitch breaks sharply and dives toward the knees and ankles of lefthanders. His high-80s fastball features fair life and some sink from his high three-quarters slot. Like any sinker/slider reliever, Texeria gets hit when he leaves his pitches up and over the plate. He dusts off a low-80s changeup on occasion. While he's too homer-prone to work as closer or set-up man, he could have value in a lower-leverage role.

Year	Club (League)	Class	W	L	ERA	G	GS	CG	SV	IP	H	R	ER	HR	BB	SO	AVG
2006	Bristol (APP)	R	1	2	0.76	19	0	0	3	24	15	3	2	0	5	29	.179
	Kannapolis (SAL)	LoA	0	0	4.50	4	0	0	0	6	8	3	3	1	1	2	.333
2007	Kannapolis (SAL)	LoA	5	2	3.69	39	0	0	16	54	49	24	22	0	22	58	.239
2008	Winston-Salem (CAR)	HiA	3	1	0.93	36	0	0	20	39	28	10	4	0	14	36	.194
	Birmingham (SL)	AA	3	2	2.01	15	0	0	1	22	18	5	5	2	7	24	.225
2009	Trenton (EL)	AA	9	6	2.84	41	6	0	2	101	90	39	32	7	43	88	.236
MINOR LEAGUE TOTALS			21	13	2.49	154	6	0	42	246	208	84	68	10	92	237	.227

27 RICKY ORTA, RHP

BORN: Nov. 6, 1984. **B-T:** R-R. **HT.:** 6-2. **WT.:** 195. **DRAFTED:** Miami, 2006 (4th round). **SIGNED BY:** Mike Tosar.

Working as a starter in his first three pro seasons, Orta showed strikeout stuff but struggled to prevent runs or work deep into games. A reliever in college at Miami, he thrived when he returned to that role full-time in 2009. He was a key cog in West Tenn's high-octane bullpen, which also featured Phillippe Aumont, Nick Hill, Josh Fields and Anthony Varvaro. Orta has plenty of velocity—he sits at 92-94 mph—but his out pitch is his 83 mph slider. It features late break and tilt, neutralizing lefties and righties. He loves throwing the slider, both early in the count for called strikes and then later as a chase pitch. Orta's delivery features a pause as he separates his hands over the rubber, which adds deception but slows his times to the plate. His breakthrough was interrupted by blisters that necessitated three trips to the disabled list. To make up for lost time, Orta pitched in the Arizona Fall League, where he continued to dominate and secured his place on the 40-man roster. He's poised for a role in the big league bullpen in 2010, though he may put in some Triple-A time first.

Year	Club (League)	Class	W	L	ERA	G	GS	CG	SV	IP	H	R	ER	HR	BB	SO	AVG
2006	Everett (NWL)	SS	4	5	5.20	13	11	0	0	54	54	34	31	6	14	45	.265
2007	Wisconsin (MWL)	LoA	4	6	4.74	22	19	1	0	93	84	55	49	12	43	102	.242
2008	High Desert (CAL)	HiA	3	5	5.05	22	15	0	0	71	80	47	40	14	27	74	.279
2009	West Tenn (Sl)	AA	3	2	1.94	24	3	0	3	42	29	14	9	1	18	41	.196
MINOR LEAGUE TOTALS			14	18	4.47	81	48	1	3	260	247	150	129	33	102	262	.251

28 RICH POYTHRESS, 1B

BORN: Aug. 11, 1987. **B-T:** R-R. **HT.:** 6-4. **WT.:** 235. **DRAFTED:** Georgia, 2009 (2nd round). **SIGNED BY:** Garrett Ball.

Poythress slugged 25 home runs as a Georgia junior in 2009, ranking him fifth in NCAA Division I. He also drove in 86 runs, erasing Gordon Beckham's single-season school record. He signed for $694,800 as the 51st overall pick, then reported to Double-A, as negotiated in his contract, after a tune-up in the Arizona League. Though Poythress didn't set the Southern League on fire, he showed the same polished approach from his amateur days. Power is his standout tool, and he generates it not with pure bat speed but with strength and leverage in a handsy swing. Because he controls the strike zone and doesn't try to pull everything, he ought to hit for a decent average. Some scouts who saw him in college wonder if his power will play against better velocity. Poythress dallied at third base in college, but his below-average range and fringy arm make him better suited for first base. He doesn't have much speed. Poythress figures to head back to Double-A on merit in 2010. He has the potential to develop into a regular, but his bat will have to carry him.

Year	Club (League)	Class	AVG	G	AB	R	H	2B	3B	HR	RBI	BB	SO	SB	OBP	SLG
2009	Mariners (AZL)	R	.300	6	20	4	6	0	0	1	6	5	6	0	.462	.450
	West Tenn (SL)	AA	.230	26	87	11	20	2	0	1	9	15	24	1	.337	.287
MINOR LEAGUE TOTALS			.243	32	107	15	26	2	0	2	15	20	30	1	.362	.318

29 GUILLERMO PIMENTEL, OF

BORN: Oct. 5, 1992. **B-T:** L-L. **HT.:** 6-1. **WT.:** 180. **SIGNED:** Dominican Republic, 2009. **SIGNED BY:** Patrick Guerrero/Bob Engle/Luis Scheker.

The Mariners' prized international acquisition last summer, Pimentel turned down the Rangers to sign with Seattle for $2 million in July. International scouts raved about his power, grading it as a potential future 70 tool on the 20-80 scouting scale. While he has yet to play in a pro game, he hit balls out to all fields during instructional league. His present strength in his hands and wrists is impressive, and his lean frame hints at even more muscle down the road. That's a scary thought because Pimentel's whip-quick bat already produces plus-plus bat speed and excellent loft. That power may not play initially due to his aggressive, unrefined approach in which he looks to yank everything to right field. He hits the ball hard and shows rare glimpses of using the opposite field, so he could hit for average once he matures—even with low contact rates. His value rests entirely with his bat, and his indifferent approach to defense would limit him to left field, first base or even DH. A well below-average runner, Pimentel shows poor instincts in the outfield whether he's fielding or throwing the ball. His arm is below average. With a good spring, he could make his pro debut in the Appalachian League.

Year	Club (League)	Class	AVG	G	AB	R	H	2B	3B	HR	RBI	BB	SO	SB	OBP	SLG
2009	Did Not Play—Signed 2010 Contract															

30 KYLE SEAGER, 2B/3B

BORN: Nov. 3, 1987. **B-T:** L-R. **HT.:** 5-10. **WT.:** 175. **DRAFTED:** North Carolina, 2009 (3rd round). **SIGNED BY:** Rob Mummau.

Like No. 2 overall pick Dustin Ackley, Seager started for three years at North Carolina and was a major factor in the Tar Heels' three consecutive College World Series runs. Seager played second base as freshman and sophomore before shifting to third base in 2009. He signed for $436,500 as a third-round pick. He had open-heart surgery as a 2-year-old but has had no lingering health concerns. Seager's bat is his lone standout tool. He knows the strike zone and can hit all kinds of pitching. His smooth, balanced lefthanded swing produces line drives up the middle and to left field. With modest bat speed and a flat swing plane, he produces average power, specializing in doubles. A grinder with a thick lower half, he's a below-average runner whose future position likely will depend on the makeup of the club. Though his hands are fine, he doesn't have the thunder in his bat to profile as a true third baseman, and he lacks the athleticism to profile as an ideal second baseman. He also logged time at shortstop last summer, but he has no realistic future there. After holding his own in low Class A during his debut, Seager will begin 2010 at High Desert.

Year	Club (League)	Class	AVG	G	AB	R	H	2B	3B	HR	RBI	BB	SO	SB	OBP	SLG
2009	Mariners (AZL)	R	.000	1	3	0	0	0	0	0	0	0	1	0	.000	.000
	Clinton (MWL)	LoA	.275	41	153	17	42	8	0	1	22	22	20	4	.360	.346
	High Desert (CAL)	HiA	.000	2	5	1	0	0	0	0	0	0	0	0	.000	.000
MINOR LEAGUE TOTALS			.261	44	161	18	42	8	0	1	22	22	21	4	.344	.329

Tampa Bay Rays

BY BILL BALLEW

At first glance, 2009 looks like a disappointment for the defending American League champion Rays.

Not only did they fail to repeat, but they also finished a distant third in the AL East. A strict budget kept them from making a major move at the trading deadline. Two weeks later, their refusal to go much over MLB's bonus recommendations kept them from signing their top two draft picks, LeVon Washington and Kenny Diekroeger. At the end of August, they dealt Scott Kazmir, the best pitcher in franchise history, to the Angels in a money-saving move.

In the grand scheme of things, however, Tampa Bay believes it remains on course for long-term success. The Rays' 84 wins represented their second-highest total ever. While they lost out on Washington and Diekroeger, they paid over-slot bonuses to lock up four gifted high school draftees. Trading Kazmir—whose deteriorating command and inability to reach the 200-inning plateau convinced the front office that Wade Davis was a better fit for the rotation—yielded three promising youngsters, headlined by infielder Sean Rodriguez.

By exercising financial restraint last year, Tampa Bay should be able to keep its nucleus together in 2010. After Jason Bartlett, Matt Garza, B.J. Upton and others receive significant raises via arbitration, the major league payroll will rise to the low $60 million range, the highest in club history. Carl Crawford and Carlos Pena are on the verge of free agency, and general manager Andrew Friedman hopes to sign both to long-term deals.

Other than adding a couple of relievers, the Rays are mostly set for the upcoming season. Without making a major move, they should have a more potent offense and better pitching than they did a year ago. They have a young, talented rotation with James Shields, Garza, Jeff Niemann, David Price and Davis, with Jeremy Hellickson waiting in the wings.

While the system remains deep in pitching, Tampa Bay isn't as strong in position prospects, especially power hitters. Center fielder Desmond Jennings and shortstop Reid Brignac are on the verge of helping the Rays, but there's a steep dropping in big league-ready players behind them. Shortstop Tim Beckham, the No. 1 overall pick in the 2008 draft, isn't on the fast track after a mildly disappointing first full pro season.

With that need in mind, Tampa Bay took high

DAVID SCHOFIELD

Jeff Niemann spent two years in Triple-A before his breakout rookie season in 2009

TOP 30 PROSPECTS

1. Desmond Jennings, of	**16.** Todd Glaesmann, of
2. Jeremy Hellickson, rhp	**17.** Wilking Rodriguez, rhp
3. Wade Davis, rhp	**18.** Shawn O'Malley, ss
4. Matt Moore, lhp	**19.** Jeff Malm, 1b
5. Reid Brignac, ss	**20.** Albert Suarez, rhp
6. Tim Beckham, ss	**21.** Alex Cobb, rhp
7. Alex Colome, rhp	**22.** Cody Rogers, of
8. Jake McGee, lhp	**23.** David Newmann, lhp
9. Alex Torres, lhp	**24.** Matt Sweeney, 3b
10. Nick Barnese, rhp	**25.** Jason McEachern, rhp
11. Kyle Lobstein, lhp	**26.** Frank de los Santos, lhp
12. Luke Bailey, c	**27.** Aneury Rodriguez, rhp
13. Joe Cruz, rhp	**28.** Matt Gorgen, rhp
14. Ty Morrison, of	**29.** Jake Jefferies, c
15. Fernando Perez, of	**30.** Kevin James, lhp

school bats with its first five selections in the 2009 draft and signed outfielder Todd Glaesmann, catcher Luke Bailey and first baseman Jeff Malm. The Rays will have extra choices to work with in 2010, getting compensation picks for not signing Washington and Diekroeger and for losing Gregg Zaun as a free agent. They'll add another choice if Brian Shouse signs elsewhere.

To boost the quality of its development efforts, Tampa Bay brought back all of its minor league coaches from 2009 and added three more minor league coordinators for 2010.

General Manager: Andrew Friedman. **Farm Director:** Mitch Lukevics. **Scouting Director:** R.J. Harrison.

Class	Team	League	W	L	PCT	Finish*	Manager(s)
Majors	Tampa Bay Rays	American	84	78	.519	8th (14)	Joe Maddon
Triple-A	Durham Bulls	International	83	61	.576	†2nd (14)	Charlie Montoyo
Double-A	Montgomery Biscuits	Southern	65	74	.468	t-6th (10)	Billy Gardner
High A	Charlotte Stone Crabs	Florida State	71	66	.518	4th (12)	Jim Morrison
Low A	Bowling Green Hot Rods	South Atlantic	64	74	.464	14th (16)	Matt Quatraro
Short-season	Hudson Valley Renegades	New York-Penn	38	37	.507	6th (14)	Brady Williams
Rookie	Princeton Rays	Appalachian	36	31	.537	4th (10)	Jared Sandberg
Rookie	GCL Rays	Gulf Coast	19	36	.345	15th (16)	Joe Alvarez
Overall 2009 Minor League Record			376	379	.498	17th (30)	

*Finish in overall standings (No. of teams in league). †League champion.

LAST YEAR'S TOP 30

Rank	Player, Pos.	Status
1.	David Price, lhp	Majors
2.	Tim Beckham, ss	No. 6
3.	Wade Davis, rhp	No. 3
4.	Reid Brignac, ss	No. 5
5.	Desmond Jennings, of	No. 1
6.	Matt Moore, lhp	No. 4
7.	Nick Barnese, rhp	No. 10
8.	Jeremy Hellickson, rhp	No. 2
9.	Jake McGee, lhp	No. 8
10.	Jeff Niemann, rhp	Majors
11.	Kyle Lobstein, lhp	No. 11
12.	Albert Suarez, rhp	No. 20
13.	John Jaso, c	Dropped out
14.	Fernando Perez, of	No. 15
15.	Heath Rollins, rhp	Dropped out
16.	Mitch Talbot, rhp	Dropped out
17.	Alex Cobb, rhp	No. 21
18.	Jake Jefferies, c	No. 29
19.	Ryan Royster, of	Dropped out
20.	Reid Fronk, of	Dropped out
21.	Mike Sheridan, 1b	Dropped out
22.	Chris Luck, rhp	Dropped out
23.	Joe Cruz, rhp	No. 13
24.	Alex Colome, rhp	No. 7
25.	Mayo Acosta, c	Dropped out
26.	Mike McCormick, c	Dropped out
27.	K.D. Kang, of	Dropped out
28.	Ty Morrison, of	No. 14
29.	Jason McEachern, rhp	No. 25
30.	Shawn O'Malley, ss	No. 18

BEST TOOLS

Best Hitter for Average	Desmond Jennings
Best Power Hitter	Matt Sweeney
Best Strike-Zone Discipline	Desmond Jennings
Fastest Baserunner	Fernando Perez
Best Athlete	Desmond Jennings
Best Fastball	Jeremy Hellickson
Best Curveball	Matt Moore
Best Slider	Alex Torres
Best Changeup	Jeremy Hellickson
Best Control	Jeremy Hellickson
Best Defensive Catcher	Nevin Ashley
Best Defensive Infielder	Reid Brignac
Best Infield Arm	Tim Beckham
Best Defensive Outfielder	Desmond Jennings
Best Outfield Arm	Todd Glaesmann

PROJECTED 2013 LINEUP

Catcher	Kelly Shoppach
First Base	Carlos Pena
Second Base	Reid Brignac
Third Base	Evan Longoria
Shortstop	Jason Bartlett
Left Field	Carl Crawford
Center Field	Desmond Jennings
Right Field	B.J. Upton
Designated Hitter	Ben Zobrist
No. 1 Starter	David Price
No. 2 Starter	James Shields
No. 3 Starter	Matt Garza
No. 4 Starter	Jeremy Hellickson
No. 5 Starter	Jeff Niemann
Closer	Wade Davis

TOP PROSPECTS OF THE DECADE

Year	Player, Pos.	2009 Org.
2000	Josh Hamilton, of	Rangers
2001	Josh Hamilton, of	Rangers
2002	Josh Hamilton, of	Rangers
2003	Rocco Baldelli, of	Red Sox
2004	B.J. Upton, ss	Rays
2005	Delmon Young, of	Twins
2006	Delmon Young, of	Twins
2007	Delmon Young, of	Twins
2008	Evan Longoria, 3b	Rays
2009	David Price, lhp	Rays

TOP DRAFT PICKS OF THE DECADE

Year	Player, Pos.	2009 Org.
2000	Rocco Baldelli, of	Red Sox
2001	Dewon Brazelton, rhp	Camden (Atlantic)
2002	B.J. Upton, ss	Rays
2003	Delmon Young, of	Twins
2004	Jeff Niemann, rhp	Rays
2005	Wade Townsend, rhp	Rays
2006	Evan Longoria, 3b	Rays
2007	David Price, lhp	Rays
2008	Tim Beckham, ss	Rays
2009	*LeVon Washington, of	Chipola (Fla.) JC

*Did not sign.

LARGEST BONUSES IN CLUB HISTORY

Matt White, 1996	$10,200,000
Rolando Arrojo, 1997	$7,000,000
Tim Beckham, 2008	$6,150,000
David Price, 2007	$5,600,000
B.J. Upton, 2002	$4,600,000

TAMPA BAY RAYS

TOP 2010 ROOKIE: Wade Davis, rhp. His development paved the way for the Rays to trade Scott Kazmir.

BREAKOUT PROSPECT: Luke Bailey, c. With his power and arm strength, he might have been a first-round pick last June if he hadn't had Tommy John surgery.

SLEEPER: Zach Quate, rhp. The 14th-round pick from 2009 has reinvented himself and become an intriguing closer prospect.

SOURCE OF TOP 30 TALENT			
Homegrown	27	Acquired	3
College	4	Trades	3
Junior college	3	Rule 5 draft	0
High school	16	Independent leagues	0
Draft-and-follow	0	Free agents/waivers	0
Nondrafted free agents	0		
International	4		

Numbers in parentheses indicate prospect rankings

LF
K.D. Kang
Reid Fronk
D.J. Jones

CF
Desmond Jennings (1)
Ty Morrison (14)
Fernando Perez (15)
Cody Rogers (22)
Anthony Scelfo
Chris Murrill

RF
Todd Glaesmann (16)
Edward Dorville
Ryan Royster
Brett Nommensen

3B
Matt Sweeney (24)
Julio Cedeno

SS
Reid Brignac (5)
Tim Beckham (6)
Shawn O'Malley (18)
Hector Guevara

2B
Elliot Johnson
Cody Cipriano
Tyler Bortnick

1B
Jeff Malm (19)
Mike Sheridan
Matt Fields
Ryan Wiegand

C
Luke Bailey (12)
Jake Jefferies (29)
Nevin Ashley
Mike McCormick
Omar Narvaez
John Jaso
Mayo Acosta

RHP

Starters	Relievers
Jeremy Hellickson (2)	Matt Gorgen (28)
Wade Davis (3)	Zach Quate
Alex Colome (7)	Scott Shuman
Nick Barnese (10)	Heath Rollins
Joe Cruz (13)	Paul Phillips
Wilking Rodriguez (17)	Chris Luck
Albert Suarez (20)	Tyree Hayes
Alex Cobb (21)	
Jason McEachern (25)	
Aneury Rodriguez (27)	
Mitch Talbot	
Trevor Shull	
Wilmer Almonte	
Chris Andujar	
Brad Furdal	
Devin Fuller	
Marcus Proctor	
Matt Swilley	
Andrew Bellatti	

LHP

Starters	Relievers
Matt Moore (4)	Frank de los Santos (26)
Jake McGee (8)	Armando Zerpa
Alex Torres (9)	Darin Downs
Kyle Lobstein (11)	Josh Satow
David Newmann (23)	Neil Schenk
Kevin James (30)	

2009 — BONUSES: $4.0 MILLION

BEST PURE HITTER: 1B Jeff Malm (5) has done two things consistently in his baseball career—win and hit. He has a good swing and feel for the strike zone, and he should get better as he strengthens his body.

BEST POWER HITTER: C Luke Bailey (4) had a tough spring, including Tommy John surgery, but that shouldn't keep him from tapping into his plus raw power. He has a bit more pop than OF Todd Glaesmann (3).

FASTEST RUNNER: OF Chris Murrill (35) has built his game around his speed, which rates a 70 on the 20-80 scouting scale.

BEST DEFENSIVE PLAYER: Bailey will be an asset behind the plate if his arm bounces back from elbow surgery. Glaesmann may stick in center field and would be a premium defender in right. OF Cody Rogers (7) has athletic ability and plus speed that could make him a quality center fielder.

BEST FASTBALL: RHP Scott Shuman (19) walked 57 in 75 career innings at Auburn, but the Rays got him throwing more strikes while sitting at 93-95 mph. He struck out 29 and walked nine at Rookie-level Princeton. LHP Kevin James (9), who signed for $625,000, sits at 90-91 mph and has a projectable 6-foot-4, 190-pound frame. With its life, his fastball could surpass Shuman's.

BEST SECONDARY PITCH: RHP Zach Quate (14) developed a plus slider this year from a lower three-quarters slot. It helped him post a 1.09 ERA at Appalachian State this spring and a 0.35 ERA at short-season Hudson Valley as a pro.

BEST PRO DEBUT: Quate, who commands his average fastball with good life, had a 34-4 K-BB ratio in 26 innings while saving 13 games for the Renegades. Murrill hit .306/.360/.363 with 29 stolen bases at Hudson Valley, where SS/3B Tyler Bortnick (16) batted .300/.386/.470 with 24 steals.

BEST ATHLETE: Rogers, a plus runner with some explosiveness, gets the nod over Glaesman, a fellow Texas A&M recruit.

MOST INTRIGUING BACKGROUND: SS Dan Rhault (26) has overcome a childhood bout with leukemia, which has been in remission for 15 years. RHP Marcus Proctor (30) is the son of ex-big leaguer Marcus Jensen, who managed Oakland's Rookie-level Arizona League team in 2009. Unsigned SS Kalani Brackenridge's (44) brother Tyron plays cornerback for the NFL's Jacksonville Jaguars.

CLOSEST TO THE MAJORS: Quate, especially if he commands his stuff.

BEST LATE-ROUND PICK: Quate and Shuman.

THE ONE WHO GOT AWAY: The Rays were optimistic they'd get OF LeVon Washington (1) done and knew SS Kenny Diekroeger (2), a Stanford signee, would be a challenge. They considered both first-round talents and wound up losing both, with Washington choosing Chipola (Fla.) JC and a shot at the 2010 draft. SS Derek Dennis (10), another potential future first-rounder, is now at Michigan.

ASSESSMENT: It's hard to have a productive draft without signing your top two draft picks, but that's what the Rays pulled off this year. They still signed plenty of quality athletes and found some intriguing arms in the later rounds.

2008 — BONUSES: $9.9 MILLION

SS Tim Beckham (1), the first overall pick, didn't tear up pro ball in his first full season, but the Rays still hope for big things from him, as well as LHP Kyle Lobstein (2) and OF Ty Morrison (4).

GRADE: B

2007 — BONUSES: $8.0 MILLION

Even if LHP David Price (1) gets derailed on the road to stardom, his postseason heroics in 2008 more than justified his selection at No. 1 overall. LHP Matt Moore (8) and RHP Joe Cruz (30) were outright steals, and RHP Nick Barnese (3) and LHP David Newmann (4) could be as well.

GRADE: A

2006 — BONUSES: $5.6 MILLION

3B Evan Longoria (1) swiftly became a big league superstar, and OF Desmond Jennings (10) might attain the same status some day. RHP Josh Butler (2) reached the big leagues after a trade to the Brewers.

GRADE: A

2005 — BONUSES: $6.3 MILLION*

The Rays blew the No. 8 overall choice on RHP Wade Townsend (1) and failed to sign five future first-round or sandwich picks, including 1B Ike Davis (19). At least they landed RHP Jeremy Hellickson (4).

GRADE: C+

*Draft analysis by John Manuel (2009) and Jim Callis (2005-08). Numbers in parentheses indicate draft rounds. *Bonuses for 2005 are first 10 rounds only.*

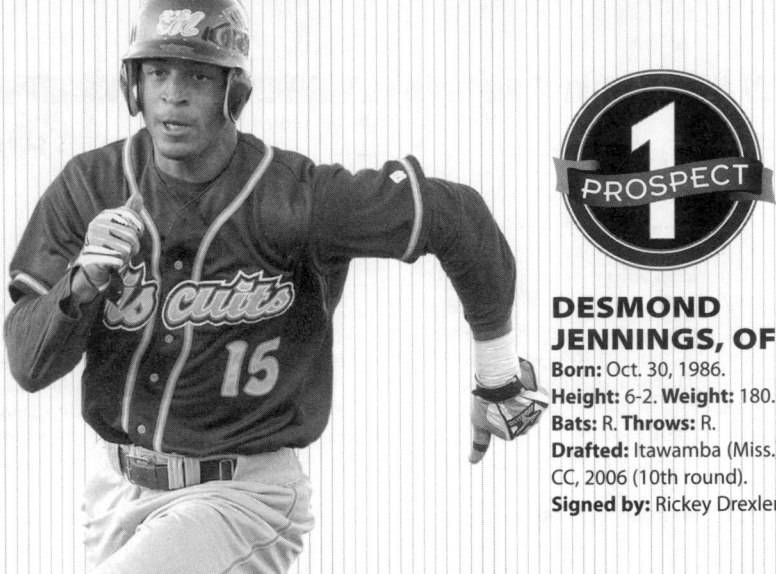

PROSPECT 1

DESMOND JENNINGS, OF

Born: Oct. 30, 1986.
Height: 6-2. **Weight:** 180.
Bats: R. **Throws:** R.
Drafted: Itawamba (Miss.)
CC, 2006 (10th round).
Signed by: Rickey Drexler.

A football and baseball standout in high school, Jennings turned down Alabama in order to attend Itawamba (Miss.) CC, where he earned juco all-America recognition as a wide receiver. Signed for $150,000 as a 10th-round pick in 2006, he rated as the No. 1 prospect in the low Class A South Atlantic League in 2007 but missed the final month after having arthroscopic knee surgery. He played in just 24 games in 2008, missing time with back and shoulder injuries, with the latter requiring surgery. Finally healthy last season, Jennings turned in one of the best campaigns in the minors. He earned Double-A Southern League MVP honors after ranking second in hitting (.316), third in steals (37), fourth in on-base percentage (.395) and fifth in slugging (.486). His numbers improved after a late-July promotion to Triple-A, where he tied an International League record with a 7-for-7 game. He helped Durham win the league title as well as the Triple-A national championship. Jennings was the only minor leaguer to post 50 extra-base hits and 50 steals in 2009.

Jennings has a lethal combination of speed and power that, combined with an aggressive approach and impressive overall knowledge, makes him a true game-changer. Managers rated Jennings as the best and fastest baserunner in the Southern League, as well as the best defensive outfielder and most exciting player. He has a live, athletic frame and five-tool talent that should continue to improve with experience. He has more power than most leadoff hitters, with at least 15-homer potential, and even better, he understands that his pop is secondary in importance to getting on base. He has exceptional strike-zone judgment and stays within himself by putting balls on the ground and using his speed to beat them out. With his outstanding speed and basestealing savvy, he swiped 52 bases in 59 attempts last year, including a steal of home, and took three bags in as many tries during the Futures Game. As a center fielder, he can run down balls from gap to gap. His arm is his lowest-rated tool, but it's average and he gets to balls quickly.

Despite his success at the highest levels of the minors, Jennings has relatively little game experience. He didn't dedicate himself to baseball until he signed in June 2006, and his injuries have limited him to 311 regular-season games since then. Additional reps will help him improve his ability to hit the ball to the opposite field as well as his reads in center field. He simply needs to continue to refine his skills against top-flight competition.

Given the Rays' conservative approach to development, Jennings could spend at least the first half of the 2010 season back in Triple-A. He looks ready to make the jump to Tampa Bay and could land there if he has a convincing showing in spring training. Regardless of his immediate future, Jennings is the club's long-term answer in center field, a potential all-star who will push B.J. Upton to right. When he arrives in the majors, Jennings will team with Carl Crawford and Upton to give Tampa Bay the most tooled-up set of outfielders in baseball.

Year	Club (League)	Class	AVG	G	AB	R	H	2B	3B	HR	RBI	BB	SO	SB	OBP	SLG
2006	Princeton (APP)	R	.277	56	213	48	59	10	1	4	20	22	39	32	.360	.390
2007	Columbus (SAL)	LoA	.315	99	387	75	122	21	5	9	37	45	53	45	.401	.465
2008	Vero Beach (FSL)	HiA	.259	24	85	17	22	5	1	2	6	14	16	5	.360	.412
2009	Montgomery (SL)	AA	.316	100	383	69	121	25	8	8	45	48	52	37	.395	.486
	Durham (IL)	AAA	.325	32	114	23	37	6	2	3	17	19	15	15	.419	.491
MINOR LEAGUE TOTALS			.305	311	1182	232	361	67	17	26	125	148	175	134	.391	.457

2 JEREMY HELLICKSON, RHP

BORN: April 8, 1987. **B-T:** R-R. **HT.:** 6-1. **WT.:** 185. **DRAFTED:** HS—Des Moines, Iowa, 2005 (4th round). **SIGNED BY:** Tom Couston.

After leading Rays farmhands with a 2.96 ERA and 162 strikeouts in 2008, "Hellboy" was even better last season. He was much better in his second stint at Double-A Montgomery, struck out 12 in six innings in the International League playoffs and was MVP of the Triple-A national championship after working five shutout innings. Hellickson rarely gives hitters a chance to gain the upper hand. He works ahead in the count with impeccable command of his low-90s fastball, which touches 94 mph and has nice sink. His changeup has become a plus pitch as he has added late fade over the past two years. He can throw his solid curveball for strikes or get hitters to chase it out of the zone. He throws strikes and creates deception by delivering all of his pitches from the same arm angle. Hellickson occasionally lacks movement on his fastball, which makes him more hittable. With further improvement to his curveball, he could have three above-average pitches. The biggest concerns with Hellickson entering 2009 was his command, but he improved it significantly. Hellickson has little to prove in the upper minors, but also no clear opportunity in Tampa Bay to open 2010. Added to the 40-man roster in November, he'll likely start the season in Triple-A and make his big league debut later in the year.

Year	Club (League)	Class	W	L	ERA	G	GS	CG	SV	IP	H	R	ER	HR	BB	SO	AVG
2005	Princeton (APP)	R	0	0	6.00	4	0	0	0	6	6	4	4	1	1	11	.240
2006	Hudson Valley (NYP)	SS	4	3	2.43	15	14	0	0	78	55	24	21	3	16	96	.193
2007	Columbus (SAL)	LoA	13	3	2.67	21	21	1	0	111	87	36	33	7	34	106	.214
2008	Vero Beach (FSL)	HiA	7	1	2.00	14	14	0	0	77	64	19	17	7	5	83	.224
	Montgomery (SL)	AA	4	4	3.94	13	13	0	0	75	84	36	33	15	15	79	.292
2009	Montgomery (SL)	AA	3	1	2.38	11	11	0	0	57	41	16	15	4	14	62	.198
	Durham (IL)	AAA	6	1	2.51	9	9	0	0	57	31	19	16	4	15	70	.157
MINOR LEAGUE TOTALS			37	13	2.71	87	82	1	0	461	368	154	139	41	100	507	.217

3 WADE DAVIS, RHP

BORN: Sept. 7, 1985. **B-T:** R-R. **HT.:** 6-5. **WT.:** 220. **DRAFTED:** HS—Lake Wales, Fla., 2004 (3rd round). **SIGNED BY:** Kevin Elfering.

With Scott Kazmir continually battling his command and injuries, the Rays dealt him to the Angels last August and inserted Davis into his rotation spot. He pitched a complete-game shutout with 10 strikeouts against the Orioles for his first big league win and looked very comfortable in the majors. Davis throws a heavy 93-94 mph fastball with above-average sink. His 11-to-5 curveball is also a plus pitch, arriving at 77-81 mph. He has a tall, strong frame that produces an easy delivery and an outstanding downhill plane on his pitches. The Rays also like his mental and physical toughness. Davis also throws a changeup and slider, neither of which is as consistent as his two plus offerings. If he can command one of those secondary pitches and throw a few more strikes, he could be dominant at the major league level. Barring something unexpected, Davis should be a fixture in the Tampa Bay rotation for the foreseeable future. He has the upside of a No. 2 starter, and the Rays also could be tempted to make him a closer down the road as they try to figure out how to get all of their talented young pitchers on the big league staff.

Year	Club (League)	Class	W	L	ERA	G	GS	CG	SV	IP	H	R	ER	HR	BB	SO	AVG
2004	Princeton (APP)	R	3	5	6.09	13	13	0	0	58	71	46	39	8	19	38	.301
2005	Hudson Valley (NYP)	SS	7	4	2.72	15	15	0	0	86	75	35	26	5	23	97	.234
2006	SW Michigan (MWL)	LoA	7	12	3.02	27	27	1	0	146	124	61	49	5	64	165	.234
2007	Vero Beach (FSL)	HiA	3	0	1.84	13	13	1	0	78	54	20	16	5	21	88	.196
	Montgomery (SL)	AA	7	3	3.15	14	14	0	0	80	74	37	28	3	30	81	.249
2008	Montgomery (SL)	AA	9	6	3.85	19	19	0	0	108	104	49	46	7	42	81	.261
	Durham (IL)	AAA	4	2	2.72	9	9	0	0	53	39	16	16	5	24	55	.205
2009	Durham (IL)	AAA	10	8	3.40	28	28	0	0	159	139	71	60	14	60	140	.231
	Tampa Bay (AL)	MAJ	2	2	3.72	6	6	1	0	36	33	19	15	2	13	36	.243
MAJOR LEAGUE TOTALS			2	2	3.72	6	6	1	0	36	33	19	15	2	13	36	.243
MINOR LEAGUE TOTALS			50	40	3.28	138	138	2	0	767	680	335	280	52	283	745	.239

4 MATT MOORE, LHP

BORN: June 18, 1989. **B-T:** L-L. **HT.:** 6-2. **WT.:** 200. **DRAFTED:** HS—Edgewood, N.M., 2007 (8th round). **SIGNED BY:** Jack Powell.

Stolen in the eighth round of the 2007 draft and signed for $115,000, Moore keeps getting better. After leading all pitchers in short-season leagues in strikeouts per innings (12.8) and opponent average (.154) in 2008, he topped the minors in the same categories (12.9 K/9, .195 average) as well as strikeouts (176) in his first taste of full-season ball last year. Moore's 90-92 mph fastball touches 94 and has impressive movement. His hard, late-breaking curveball generates awkward swings and misses. He does a great job of keeping his pitches, including a changeup with screwball-like action, down in the strike zone. He made impressive strides last year in his ability to reduce his pitch counts and work out of jams. Overall control and command of the strike zone is all Moore needs to become one of the premier prospects in the minors. He walked 33 batters in his first 35 innings last season before recovering. His changeup could use some more fade. He can work both sides of the plate with more consistency. If Moore can locate his pitches better, he can be a frontline starter. Only 19, he's headed to high Class A and the Rays may not be able to hold him back much longer.

Year	Club (League)	Class	W	L	ERA	G	GS	CG	SV	IP	H	R	ER	HR	BB	SO	AVG
2007	Princeton (APP)	R	0	0	2.66	8	3	0	0	20	12	6	6	1	16	29	.160
2008	Princeton (APP)	R	2	2	1.66	12	12	0	0	54	30	22	10	0	19	77	.154
2009	Bowling Green (SAL)	LoA	8	5	3.15	26	26	0	0	123	86	51	43	6	70	176	.195
MINOR LEAGUE TOTALS			10	7	2.69	46	41	0	0	198	128	79	59	7	105	282	.180

5 REID BRIGNAC, SS

BORN: Jan. 16, 1986. **B-T:** L-R. **HT.:** 6-3. **WT.:** 180. **DRAFTED:** HS—St. Amant, La., 2004 (2nd round). **SIGNED BY:** Benny Latino.

With the Rays drafting Tim Beckham No. 1 overall in 2008 and Jason Bartlett blossoming into an all-star in 2009, it might be easy to overlook other shortstops in the organization. But Brignac hasn't let that happen. He has been an International League all-star and received big league cups of coffee in each of the last two years, playing capably for the Rays when needed. Considered an offensive-minded player early in his career, Brignac has worked hard with the leather and become one of the top defensive shortstops in the minors. He has excellent quickness and above-average arm strength, and he does an excellent job of directing the defense. He has good pop for a middle infielder and uses the entire field. Brignac is an aggressive hitter who needs to show more plate discipline. He starts trying to pull the ball during slumps, which usually exacerbates the problem. More quick than fast, he's not an effective basestealer, getting caught in half of his 14 attempts in 2009. The lone complaint about his defense is that his range to the right is merely average. After two years of Triple-A seasoning, Brignac is ready to prove himself at the game's top level. Blocked by Bartlett, he'll probably have to settle for serving the Rays in a utility role this year.

Year	Club (League)	Class	AVG	G	AB	R	H	2B	3B	HR	RBI	BB	SO	SB	OBP	SLG
2004	Princeton (APP)	R	.361	25	97	16	35	4	2	1	25	9	10	2	.413	.474
	Charleston, SC (SAL)	LoA	.500	3	14	3	7	1	0	0	5	1	2	0	.533	.571
2005	SW Michigan (MWL)	LoA	.264	127	512	77	135	29	2	15	61	40	131	5	.319	.416
2006	Visalia (CAL)	HiA	.326	100	411	82	134	26	3	21	83	35	82	12	.382	.557
	Montgomery (SL)	AA	.300	28	110	18	33	6	2	3	16	7	31	3	.355	.473
2007	Montgomery (SL)	AA	.260	133	527	91	137	30	5	17	81	55	94	15	.328	.433
2008	Tampa Bay (AL)	MAJ	.000	4	10	1	0	0	0	0	0	1	5	0	.091	.000
	Durham (IL)	AAA	.250	97	352	43	88	26	2	9	43	25	93	5	.299	.412
2009	Durham (IL)	AAA	.282	96	415	51	117	28	2	8	44	27	69	5	.327	.417
	Tampa Bay (AL)	MAJ	.278	31	90	10	25	8	2	1	6	3	20	2	.301	.444
MAJOR LEAGUE TOTALS			.250	35	100	11	25	8	2	1	6	4	25	2	.279	.400
MINOR LEAGUE TOTALS			.281	609	2438	381	686	150	18	74	358	199	512	47	.337	.449

6 TIM BECKHAM, SS

BORN: Jan. 27, 1990. **B-T:** R-R. **HT.:** 6-0. **WT.:** 190. **DRAFTED:** HS—Griffin, Ga., 2008 (1st round). **SIGNED BY:** Milt Hill.

The first overall pick in the 2008 draft and the recipient of a then-record $6.15 million bonus, Beckham made steady improvements during a solid if unspectacular first full season in pro ball. After rating as the No. 1 prospect in Rookie-level Appalachian League in his pro debut, he ranked fifth in South Atlantic League last year. His older brother Jeremy played with him at low Class A Bowling Green. Despite hitting only five homers in 2009, Beckham has the raw strength and hitting ability to be one of the better power hitters in the system. He has plus bat speed with strong hands and wrists, and he uses his muscular legs to his advantage while staying back on the ball. Defensively, he has fluid actions, soft hands and a strong arm. He's a good baserunner with average speed but doesn't project as a basestealer. He has an outstanding work ethic. Several scouts believe Beckham's athleticism has started to decline because his lower half is getting bigger, which could necessitate a move to third base or an outfield corner. He made 43 errors last season, many because of inaccurate throws caused in part by lackadaisical footwork. His aggressive approach is a long way from being ready for the majors. The Rays' present plan is to keep Beckham at shortstop, and third base isn't much of an option with Evan Longoria already in Tampa Bay. Beckham will spend 2010 in high Class A at age 19.

Year	Club (League)	Class	AVG	G	AB	R	H	2B	3B	HR	RBI	BB	SO	SB	OBP	SLG
2008	Princeton (APP)	R	.243	46	177	30	43	12	0	2	14	13	43	5	.297	.345
	Hudson Valley (NYP)	SS	.333	2	6	5	2	1	0	0	0	2	1	1	.556	.500
2009	Bowling Green (SAL)	LoA	.275	125	491	58	135	33	4	5	63	34	116	13	.328	.389
MINOR LEAGUE TOTALS			.267	173	674	93	180	46	4	7	77	49	160	19	.323	.378

7 ALEX COLOME, RHP

BORN: Dec. 31, 1988. **B-T:** R-R. **HT.:** 6-2. **WT.:** 185. **SIGNED:** Dominican Republic, 2007. **SIGNED BY:** Eddy Toledo.

Deemed a raw prospect with considerable promise, Colome went 1-11, 5.04 in his first two pro seasons before blossoming as the Rays hoped last summer. He led the short-season New York-Penn League in strikeouts (94 in 76 innings) and ranked second in ERA (1.66). He's the nephew of former Tampa Bay reliever Jesus Colome. Colome has electric stuff and tremendous upside. He has a good frame and loose arm action, and the ball jumps out of his hand when he's relaxed. His fastball has been clocked as high as 97 mph and sits at 94-95. He also throws a hard curveball with 11-to-5 break and late bite. Though he has started to harness his stuff, Colome is still in the process of controlling his pitches and commanding them in the strike zone. He has displayed a decent feel for a lively changeup, but he often throws it too hard. He tends to overthrow when behind in the count, which hurts his ability to throw strikes. The sky is the limit for Colome once he realizes his strengths and uses them to his advantage. Even now, hitters rarely get good swings against him. Provided his changeup comes around, he has the ability to be a frontline starter. A move up to low Class A awaits.

Year	Club (League)	Class	W	L	ERA	G	GS	CG	SV	IP	H	R	ER	HR	BB	SO	AVG
2007	Devil Rays (DSL)	R	1	6	2.97	14	11	0	0	39	30	18	13	1	31	50	.208
2008	Princeton (APP)	R	0	5	6.80	12	11	0	0	46	50	45	35	5	26	52	.272
2009	Hudson Valley (NYP)	SS	7	4	1.66	15	15	2	0	76	46	22	14	0	32	94	.174
MINOR LEAGUE TOTALS			8	15	3.45	41	37	2	0	162	126	85	62	6	89	196	.212

8 JAKE McGEE, LHP

BORN: Aug. 6, 1986. **B-T:** L-L. **HT.:** 6-3. **WT.:** 230. **DRAFTED:** HS—Sparks, Nev., 2004 (5th round). **SIGNED BY:** Fred Repke.

McGee was one of the best lefthanded pitching prospects in the minors when he blew out his elbow in June 2008 and had Tommy John surgery. He returned to the mound a year later, showing flashes of his former stuff while working short stints. Prior to his injury, McGee had a mid-90s fastball that touched 98 mph and a hard three-quarters breaking ball with good tilt. If last summer is any indication, he should get those pitches back. He also has shown good feel for a changeup that has the makings of a plus pitch. McGee struggled with his control prior to the injury, and control is often the last thing to come back following Tommy John surgery. The consistency of his release point has fluctuated throughout his career. From a command standpoint, he needs to pound the bottom half of strike zone better. If he can't improve his ability to locate his pitches, his future may be as a reliever. The Rays were thrilled McGee got in some innings in 2009, which should allow this season to be devoted to development instead of rehabilitation. Ticketed for Double-A, he's still just 23 and has time to become a significant part of Tampa Bay's big league pitching staff.

Year	Club (League)	Class	W	L	ERA	G	GS	CG	SV	IP	H	R	ER	HR	BB	SO	AVG
2004	Princeton (APP)	R	4	1	3.97	12	12	0	0	57	49	30	25	5	25	53	.244
2005	Hudson Valley (NYP)	SS	5	4	3.64	15	14	0	0	77	64	32	31	4	23	89	.226
2006	SW Michigan (MWL)	LoA	7	9	2.96	26	26	0	0	134	103	54	44	7	65	171	.211
2007	Vero Beach (FSL)	HiA	5	4	2.93	21	21	0	0	117	86	45	38	8	39	145	.203
	Montgomery (SL)	AA	3	2	4.24	5	5	0	0	23	19	11	11	2	13	30	.224
2008	Montgomery (SL)	AA	6	4	3.94	15	15	0	0	78	65	38	34	6	37	65	.230
2009	Rays (GCL)	R	0	2	3.52	5	5	0	0	8	5	4	3	0	3	14	.172
	Charlotte (FSL)	HiA	0	2	6.45	11	11	0	0	22	26	16	16	2	9	26	.299
MINOR LEAGUE TOTALS			30	28	3.53	110	109	0	0	515	417	230	202	34	214	593	.222

9 ALEX TORRES, LHP

BORN: Dec. 8, 1987. **B-T:** L-L. **HT.:** 5-10. **WT.:** 160. **SIGNED:** Venezuela, 2005.
SIGNED BY: Carlos Porte (Angels).

The Rays acquired Torres, Sean Rodriguez and third-base prospect Matt Sweeney when
they traded Scott Kazmir to the Angels last August. After spending most of his first four
pro seasons in Rookie ball, Torres made a huge jump last year, winning the high Class A
Calfiornia League ERA (2.74) and performing well after a promotion to Double-A. Torres
rarely throws the ball straight or employs the same arm angle on consecutive pitches, keeping hitters on edge. His 89-91 mph fastball has plus movement and he does a good job
of using both sides of the plate. He also throws a curveball and slider, both of which are
tight, sharp breaking pitches. He's an aggressive pitcher with plenty of confidence. While most observers consider
Torres to be effectively wild, he needs to improve the command of all his pitches, particularly his offspeed stuff.
His changeup remains a work in progress, and refining it would give him four different offerings for hitters to
think about. He's undersized and runs up high pitch counts, so there are some concerns about his durability as
a starter. An offseason addition to the 40-man roster, Torres has the repertoire to be a quality big league starter.
He'll likely get some more Double-A seasoning at the start of 2010, with a second-half promotion to Triple-A
a possibility.

Year	Club (League)	Class	W	L	ERA	G	GS	CG	SV	IP	H	R	ER	HR	BB	SO	AVG
2005	Angels (DSL)	R	4	2	1.52	9	9	1	0	53	23	20	9	2	23	87	.122
2006	Angels (AZL)	R	2	5	4.29	14	9	0	1	50	42	28	24	1	36	47	.235
2007	Angels (AZL)	R	1	0	4.76	4	0	0	0	6	4	6	3	0	8	3	.190
2008	Angels (AZL)	R	4	0	1.54	4	4	0	0	23	11	4	4	1	10	24	.153
	R. Cucamonga (CAL)	HiA	3	2	3.91	10	10	0	0	53	52	26	23	1	29	62	.264
2009	R. Cucamonga (CAL)	HiA	10	3	2.74	21	19	0	0	121	93	43	37	4	63	124	.217
	Arkansas (TL)	AA	3	1	2.77	5	5	0	0	26	23	10	8	0	17	25	.245
	Montgomery (SL)	AA	0	2	3.12	2	2	0	0	9	7	6	3	1	5	7	.219
MINOR LEAGUE TOTALS			27	15	2.92	69	58	1	1	342	255	143	111	10	191	379	.210

10 NICK BARNESE, RHP

BORN: Jan. 11, 1989. **B-T:** R-R. **HT.:** 6-2. **WT.:** 170. **DRAFTED:** HS—Simi Valley,
Calif., 2007 (3rd round). **SIGNED BY:** Robbie Moen.

Shoulder tendinitis caused Barnese to miss the first two months of last season, but he
made up for lost time with a solid showing at Bowling Green. He has performed consistently while the Rays have moved him slowly, going 13-10, 2.64 with 183 strikeouts
in 177 pro innings. Barnese is a bulldog who will challenge any hitter at any time. He
uses whip-like arm action to deliver fastballs that sit at 91-92 mph and touch 94. When
he stays on top of his hard slurve, it's a two-plane pitch with a sharp break. The bottom
falls out of his changeup when it's at its best, and it could become a plus pitch with more
consistency. He creates good deception with his over-the-head windup, high leg kick and three-quarters arm
slot. He controls the running game with a quick pickoff move and good athleticism. Barnese needs to throw his
breaking ball down and in more often. When he learns to command all of his pitches on the inner half of the
plate, he'll be even more effective. He has strong makeup but can be his own worst enemy when he gets down
on himself. Some minor refinements and more consistency will enable Barnese to emerge as a No. 2 or 3 starter
in the big leagues. Tampa Bay can continue to be patient with his development, which will continue in high
Class A this year.

Year	Club (League)	Class	W	L	ERA	G	GS	CG	SV	IP	H	R	ER	HR	BB	SO	AVG
2007	Princeton (APP)	R	2	2	3.22	9	8	0	0	36	30	19	13	1	4	37	.216
2008	Hudson Valley (NYP)	SS	5	3	2.45	13	13	0	0	66	52	26	18	1	24	84	.212
2009	Bowling Green (SAL)	LoA	6	5	2.53	15	15	0	0	75	56	30	21	3	25	62	.202
MINOR LEAGUE TOTALS			13	10	2.64	37	36	0	0	177	138	75	52	5	53	183	.209

11 KYLE LOBSTEIN, LHP

BORN: Aug. 12, 1989. **B-T:** L-L. **HT.:** 6-3. **WT.:** 200. **DRAFTED:** HS—Flagstaff, Ariz., 2008 (2nd round).
SIGNED BY: Jason Durocher.

After bringing in Lobstein for a $1.5 million bonus at the signing deadline in 2008, the Rays received their
first significant look at the lefthander last summer. They were pleased with the early returns. Lobstein seemed to
get stronger as the season progressed, tossing a pair of seven-inning shutouts in August. A former two-way player
who had committed to Arizona before he signed with Tampa Bay, Lobstein has an ideal pitcher's frame with an
easy arm action and flawless mechanics. He has an advanced feel for pitching, good overall command and impressive mound presence, which reminds some scouts of a young Andy Pettitte. Lobstein's fastball is inconsistent,
fluctuating from 85-88 mph to 89-91, but either way it's effective because of its movement and deception. The

Rays believe his velocity will settle in the low 90s once his body matures. His curveball features a sharp downhill break in the upper 70s. He shows good feel for the changeup but is working to improve its depth and fade. If the complete package comes together, Lobstein will be a solid middle-of-the-rotation starter in the major leagues. He'll open 2010 in low Class A.

Year	Club (League)	Class	W	L	ERA	G	GS	CG	SV	IP	H	R	ER	HR	BB	SO	AVG
2009	Hudson Valley (NYP)	SS	3	5	2.58	14	14	0	0	73	55	23	21	4	23	74	.204
MINOR LEAGUE TOTALS			3	5	2.58	14	14	0	0	73	55	23	21	4	23	74	.204

12 LUKE BAILEY, C

BORN: March 11, 1991. **B-T:** R-R. **HT.:** 6-0. **WT.:** 198. **DRAFTED:** HS—LaGrange, Ga., 2009 (4th round). **SIGNED BY:** Milt Hill.

Regarded as one of the top high school catchers in the 2009 draft heading into the spring, Bailey strained an elbow ligament while pitching and had Tommy John surgery. Given the success rate of elbow reconstructions, the Rays saw little risk in using their fourth-round pick on Bailey, who passed up a scholarship to Auburn and signed for $750,000. He has above-average raw power and makes consistent contact. His power production dropped during his senior year, but scouts believe he was tinkering too much with his timing mechanisms while trying to make a good impression. Bailey has solid athleticism and surprising speed, and he also has played the infield corners in addition to catching. Before his injury, he had above-average arm strength with excellent carry and accuracy on his throws. He moves well behind the plate with steady footwork and soft hands. His makeup is considered a strength as well, and he showed his toughness by playing with a broken rib as a junior. Bailey's rehab has gone well and Tampa Bay expects him to make his pro debut during the summer. While the start of his pro career has been delayed, he has the raw tools to emerge as the top catcher in the organization.

Year	Club (League)	Class	AVG	G	AB	R	H	2B	3B	HR	RBI	BB	SO	SB	OBP	SLG
2009	Did Not Play—Signed Late															

13 JOE CRUZ, RHP

BORN: July 20, 1988. **B-T:** R-R. **HT.:** 6-4. **WT.:** 195. **DRAFTED:** East Los Angeles JC, 2007 (30th round). **SIGNED BY:** Robbie Moen.

Cruz is behind in his development compared to pitchers ranked ahead of him on this list, but his upside is impressive, particularly considering how far he has already come. The lanky hurler, whose 6-foot-4 frame still offers projectability, has a smooth delivery with a loose, fluid arm action. He gets good extension that makes his pitches look as if they're jumping out of his hand. Cruz throws his fastball at 92-94 mph and touches 96. He's still learning how to throw his offspeed pitches, a decent curveball with some bite and a fringy changeup. While his control is good, he needs to throw more quality strikes. He also must manage his emotions on the mound. When Cruz keeps his pitches down in the zone he can be close to unhittable, with several Rays officials comparing him to a young Matt Garza. That makes Cruz a steal as a former 30th-round pick who signed for $100,000. Ticketed for high Class A Charlotte in 2010, he can become a solid major league starter if his secondary pitches develop. If not, his live arm could work well out of the bullpen.

Year	Club (League)	Class	W	L	ERA	G	GS	CG	SV	IP	H	R	ER	HR	BB	SO	AVG
2007	Princeton (APP)	R	2	0	0.00	3	0	0	0	9	5	0	0	0	3	13	.161
2008	Princeton (APP)	R	1	3	3.17	13	13	0	0	54	61	29	19	5	14	62	.270
2009	Bowling Green (SAL)	LoA	5	8	4.04	21	21	0	0	98	110	54	44	5	26	99	.284
MINOR LEAGUE TOTALS			8	11	3.52	37	34	0	0	161	176	83	63	10	43	174	.273

14 TY MORRISON, OF

BORN: July 22, 1990. **B-T:** L-R. **HT.:** 6-2. **WT.:** 170. **DRAFTED:** HS—Tigard, Ore., 2008 (4th round). **SIGNED BY:** Paul Kirsch.

As an amateur, Morrison played in Virginia and Hawaii before finishing high school in Oregon. He signed with the Rays for $500,000 at the deadline in 2008 as a fourth-round pick, and has spent his first two pro seasons at Rookie-level Princeton. A fast-twitch athlete with broad shoulders and a frame that should allow him to get bigger and stronger as he matures, Morrison has excellent baseball instincts and aptitude. The Rays envision him developing into a top-of-the-order threat. He impressed with his keen batting eye during extended spring training, though he struck out too much during the season. He has excellent quickness and plus speed, and he is adept at stealing bases and beating out bunts. He also has decent pull power from the left side of the plate, and should have slightly above-average bat speed once he adds strength. Morrison covers a lot of ground in center field, though he still needs work on getting better jumps and taking more direct routes to balls. His arm is his worst tool, grading at slightly below average. Morrison made as much progress as any prospect in the organization last year, and Tampa Bay hopes for more of the same when he plays in low Class A in 2010.

Year	Club (League)	Class	AVG	G	AB	R	H	2B	3B	HR	RBI	BB	SO	SB	OBP	SLG
2008	Princeton (APP)	R	.265	10	34	2	9	0	0	0	1	2	12	3	.297	.265
2009	Princeton (APP)	R	.271	59	225	34	61	9	2	3	18	27	61	20	.365	.369
MINOR LEAGUE TOTALS			.270	69	259	36	70	9	2	3	19	29	73	23	.357	.355

15 FERNANDO PEREZ, OF

BORN: April 23, 1983. **B-T:** B-R. **HT.:** 6-1. **WT.:** 195. **DRAFTED:** Columbia, 2004 (7th round). **SIGNED BY:** Brad Matthews.

After playing with the Rays down the stretch in 2008 and earning a spot on their postseason roster, Perez entered last year as a strong candidate to be their fourth outfielder. That plan unraveled in late March when he dislocated his left wrist and had surgery. The highest player ever drafted out of Columbia (seventh round), he traveled with the big league club throughout the season in order to get better acclimated to the big leagues, and got into 18 games in September. Perez's game is centered on speed, with several scouts saying he's as close to an 80 runner on the 20-80 scouting scale as anyone in professional baseball. He has an incredible first step, which allows him to get great jumps in center field as well as on the basepaths. He has improved his technique by getting bigger leads on stolen-base attempts and taking better routes on balls in the gaps. His arm strength rates as average and he makes accurate throws. A switch-hitter since 2006, Perez must reduce his high strikeout totals and make more consistent contact, particularly from the left side. He also needs to continue honing a small-ball approach, with a focus on improving his bunting. He has a little pop and can hit an occasional home run. While Perez would be a big league starter for some teams, his future with Tampa Bay is unclear with the emergence of Desmond Jennings and presence of Carl Crawford and B.J. Upton. He should land a big league job this year as a backup outfielder and pinch-runner.

Year	Club (League)	Class	AVG	G	AB	R	H	2B	3B	HR	RBI	BB	SO	SB	OBP	SLG
2004	Hudson Valley (NYP)	SS	.232	69	267	46	62	8	5	2	20	30	70	24	.314	.322
2005	SW Michigan (MWL)	LoA	.289	134	522	93	151	17	13	6	48	58	80	57	.361	.406
2006	Visalia (CAL)	HiA	.307	133	547	123	168	19	9	4	56	78	134	33	.398	.397
2007	Montgomery (SL)	AA	.308	102	393	84	121	24	10	8	33	76	104	32	.423	.481
2008	Durham (IL)	AAA	.288	129	511	86	147	17	11	5	36	58	156	43	.361	.393
	Tampa Bay (AL)	MAJ	.250	23	60	18	15	2	0	3	8	8	16	5	.348	.433
2009	Rays (GCL)	R	.000	1	3	0	0	0	0	0	0	0	3	0	.000	.000
	Charlotte (FSL)	HiA	.200	3	10	1	2	0	0	0	0	1	1	2	.273	.200
	Durham (IL)	AAA	.278	13	36	10	10	3	0	0	2	7	17	8	.395	.361
	Tampa Bay (AL)	MAJ	.206	18	34	4	7	0	0	0	2	0	11	0	.206	.206
MAJOR LEAGUE TOTALS			.234	41	94	22	22	2	0	3	10	8	27	5	.301	.351
MINOR LEAGUE TOTALS			.289	584	2289	443	661	88	48	25	195	308	565	199	.375	.402

16 TODD GLAESMANN, OF

BORN: Oct. 24, 1990. **B-T:** R-R. **HT.:** 6-4. **WT.:** 205. **DRAFTED:** HS—Waco, Texas, 2009 (3rd round). **SIGNED BY:** Pat Murphy.

Because the Rays couldn't reach deals with their first- and second-round picks, Glaesmann emerged as their top signee from the 2009 draft. An athletic outfielder who had an impressive senior high school season, he signed for $930,000 while turning down an opportunity to play at Texas A&M. He didn't stand out during the showcase circuit in the summer of 2008, then tore a thumb ligament in the fall while playing football. The package came together, however, as the baseball season progressed, and Glaesmann now rates at least average with all five tools. At 6-foot-4 and 205 pounds, he has a frame that should produce power once he learns to add loft to his line-drive swing. His speed is also above average, both on the basepaths and in the field. So is his arm strength, which will allow him to make the move from center to right field if needed. Glaesmann will need to shorten his swing in order to make more consistent contact at higher levels, but otherwise he just needs to polish the tools he has. He'll play the entire 2010 season at 19, so he'll probably spend the summer at Princeton.

Year	Club (League)	Class	AVG	G	AB	R	H	2B	3B	HR	RBI	BB	SO	SB	OBP	SLG
2009	Rays (GCL)	R	.278	5	18	1	5	1	0	0	2	0	3	1	.278	.333
MINOR LEAGUE TOTALS			.278	5	18	1	5	1	0	0	2	0	3	1	.278	.333

17 WILKING RODRIGUEZ, RHP

BORN: March 2, 1990. **B-T:** R-R. **HT.:** 6-1. **WT.:** 160. **SIGNED:** Venezuela, 2007. **SIGNED BY:** Ronnie Blanco.

After two years of relieving in the Rookie-level Venezuelan Summer League, Rodriguez made an impressive step forward in 2009 as he made the transition to starting at Princeton. With some of the best all-around stuff in the Appalachian League, he rated as the circuit's No. 3 prospect despite winning only once in 13 starts. Rodriguez has a quick arm that produces a fastball that parks at 92-93 mph and touches 96. He also has a plus power curveball with tight spin and late bite. With a thick lower half and the ability to drive off his strong legs, Rodriguez could be an innings-eater at higher levels. He tends to overthrow on occasion, which hurts his control, and he has a habit of relying too much on his curve. He's working on his changeup, which shows promise despite a lack of fade and depth at this point. Rodriguez's mechanics are clean. He shows excellent poise and above-average command for his age. The Rays rarely push young players, particularly pitchers, but Rodriguez could jump to low Class A with a strong showing in spring training.

Year	Club (League)	Class	W	L	ERA	G	GS	CG	SV	IP	H	R	ER	HR	BB	SO	AVG
2007	Devil Rays/Reds (VSL)	R	3	2	1.95	17	0	0	2	32	23	7	7	1	14	28	.200
2008	Rays (VSL)	R	0	1	3.71	10	8	0	0	27	26	11	11	3	6	29	.260
2009	Princeton (APP)	R	1	6	3.21	13	13	0	0	56	44	24	20	5	12	52	.213
MINOR LEAGUE TOTALS			4	9	2.97	40	21	0	2	115	93	42	38	9	32	109	.220

18 SHAWN O'MALLEY, SS

BORN: Dec. 28, 1987. **B-T:** B-R. **HT.:** 5-11. **WT.:** 170. **DRAFTED:** HS—Kennewick, Wash., 2006 (5th round). **SIGNED BY:** Paul Kirsch.

O'Malley put together his best season as a pro last year, turning a corner in his development as a hitter. A career .237 hitter through his first three seasons, he batted .268 in high Class A and .313 in the Arizona Fall League. At the plate, the switch-hitting O'Malley focuses on making line-drive contact and using his speed. Despite having little power, he will turn on pitches, and he also hit to the opposite field with more consistency in 2009. His plate discipline improved dramatically, as he led the Florida State League with a .388 on-base percentage and ranked third in the AFL with a .470 OBP. He has become an excellent basestealer, succeeding on 40 of 52 attempts last year. A hustle player who comes to the ballpark ready to play every day, O'Malley has a strong arm at shortstop, along with above-average range and soft hands. With his athleticism and defensive savvy, he'll be able to play shortstop at higher levels and could be valuable as a utilityman. Jason Bartlett, Reid Brignac and Tim Beckham are ahead of him on Tampa Bay's depth chart, so O'Malley has his work cut out for him to become a starting shortstop for the Rays. He'll spend 2010 honing his skills in Double-A.

Year	Club (League)	Class	AVG	G	AB	R	H	2B	3B	HR	RBI	BB	SO	SB	OBP	SLG
2006	Princeton (APP)	R	.213	50	160	28	34	4	1	1	10	16	38	10	.310	.269
2007	Hudson Valley (NYP)	SS	.242	48	161	21	39	6	4	0	10	20	40	12	.344	.329
2008	Columbus (SAL)	LoA	.237	91	334	48	79	14	3	0	23	34	77	28	.325	.296
2009	Charlotte (FSL)	HiA	.268	103	366	73	98	9	2	1	27	58	80	40	.388	.311
MINOR LEAGUE TOTALS			.245	292	1021	170	250	33	10	2	70	128	235	90	.349	.303

19 JEFF MALM, 1B

BORN: Oct. 31, 1990. **B-T:** L-L. **HT.:** 6-3. **WT.:** 225. **DRAFTED:** HS—Las Vegas, 2009 (5th round). **SIGNED BY:** Jason Durocher.

While most teams thought Malm was headed to Southern California to play for head coach and family friend Chad Kreuter, Tampa Bay was able to sign him last August for $680,000 as a fifth-round pick, adding a much-needed big bat with power potential into the organization. Malm was a fixture on the national youth circuit for years. He was the youngest player on the U.S. junior national team in 2007 and the only underclassman to earn a spot in the Cape Cod High School Classic that summer. Playing for powerhouse Bishop Gorman High in Las Vegas, Malm helped the team to state championships in all four of his seasons and tied a national high school record with 277 career hits. He draws comparisons to Travis Hafner with his big build and ability to swing the bat. He has a sweet lefthanded stroke and manages the strike zone well. The only question some scouts have about his offensive potential is how much pop he'll have with wood bats, but he has the size and strength to develop at least average power. Malm has a strong arm and was clocked at 87-89 mph off the mound, but his lack of overall athleticism is expected to limit him to first base, where his defense is a tick above average. He's a below-average runner but could improve as he loses some of the baby fat on his 6-foot-3, 225-pound frame. After a seven-game debut last summer, Malm will get his first extended pro experience at either Princeton or Hudson Valley in 2010.

Year	Club (League)	Class	AVG	G	AB	R	H	2B	3B	HR	RBI	BB	SO	SB	OBP	SLG
2009	Rays (GCL)	R	.240	7	25	2	6	0	0	0	0	1	4	1	.296	.240
MINOR LEAGUE TOTALS			.240	7	25	2	6	0	0	0	0	1	4	1	.296	.240

20 ALBERT SUAREZ, RHP

BORN: Oct. 8, 1989. **B-T:** R-R. **HT.:** 6-2. **WT.:** 186. **SIGNED:** Venezuela, 2006. **SIGNED BY:** Ronnie Blanco.

Suarez was the winning pitcher on Opening Night for Hudson Valley last season, and he was pitching well in his second start against Staten Island before departing in the fifth inning. A week later he found out he needed Tommy John surgery. A product of the Rays' recent focus on Venezuela, he drew comparisons to Freddy Garcia during his 2008 pro debut. Prior to his injury, Suarez showed a fluid delivery and threw the ball on a sharp downhill plane, generating a 93-94 mph fastball and improving offspeed pitches. Though somewhat inconsistent, his curveball had good break, and he made strides with a promising changeup. Suarez has impressive control for a youngster, with just nine walks in 53 minor league innings. His makeup is considered a major asset as well. He has made a concerted effort to learn English in order to communicate better and hasten his development. Suarez has made steady progress in his rehabilitation, and Tampa Bay thinks his injury will be little more than a minor bump on his road to the majors. The Rays hope he'll be able to pitch in games late in the 2010 season.

Year	Club (League)	Class	W	L	ERA	G	GS	CG	SV	IP	H	R	ER	HR	BB	SO	AVG
2008	Princeton (APP)	R	0	2	3.92	11	9	0	0	44	41	28	19	3	7	37	.232
2009	Hudson Valley (NYP)	SS	1	0	2.79	2	2	0	0	10	8	3	3	1	2	4	.222
MINOR LEAGUE TOTALS			1	2	3.71	13	11	0	0	53	49	31	22	4	9	41	.230

21 ALEX COBB, RHP

BORN: Oct. 7, 1987. **B-T:** R-R. **HT.:** 6-1. **WT.:** 180. **DRAFTED:** HS—Vero Beach, Fla., 2006 (4th round). **SIGNED BY:** Kevin Elfering.

His stuff doesn't blow scouts away, but Cobb continues to make steady improvements in all phases of his game. A high school quarterback who had scholarship offers from several college programs, he has an advanced feel for pitching. His best pitch is an 11-to-5 curveball that he'll throw at any time in the count. In fact, there are occasions when Cobb uses his curve too much at the expense of his other pitches. His fastball sits in the low 90s and plays up because his breaking ball is so effective. His changeup has good sinking action and looks like a splitter at times. While he has very good control, Cobb needs to improve his fastball command and use his heater to get ahead of hitters. His climb through the system should continue in Double-A this year, and he has the ability to start in the middle of a major league rotation.

Year	Club (League)	Class	W	L	ERA	G	GS	CG	SV	IP	H	R	ER	HR	BB	SO	AVG
2006	Princeton (APP)	R	0	0	5.19	6	1	0	0	9	9	7	5	3	3	8	.265
2007	Hudson Valley (NYP)	SS	5	6	3.54	16	16	0	0	81	78	36	32	4	31	62	.259
2008	Columbus (SAL)	LoA	9	7	3.29	25	25	0	0	140	113	59	51	16	35	97	.224
2009	Charlotte (FSL)	HiA	8	5	3.03	24	23	0	0	125	116	49	42	6	31	107	.249
MINOR LEAGUE TOTALS			22	18	3.30	71	65	0	0	354	316	151	130	29	100	274	.242

22 CODY ROGERS, OF

BORN: Sept. 13, 1986. **B-T:** L-R. **HT.:** 6-2. **WT.:** 175. **DRAFTED:** Panola (Texas) JC, 2009 (7th round). **SIGNED BY:** Pat Murphy.

The Rays ruined Texas A&M's outfield plans by signing two of their recruits, third-round pick Todd Glaesmann and seventh-rounder Rogers, out of the 2009 draft. Rogers agreed to a $125,000 bonus, then earned Appalachian League all-star honors with a strong all-around effort. A lefthanded hitter, he has solid hitting ability with good bat speed, a natural feel for making contact and decent power. Tampa Bay is impressed with his strong wrists and solid approach at the plate, believing that he'll add extra-base pop as he matures and gets stronger. Employing an open stance, he gets in trouble when he becomes too pull-conscious, and he needs to use the opposite field when pitchers work him on the outer half. While he's a good athlete with the range to play center field, Rogers' lack of arm strength could make him a left fielder. His game is raw in many respects, but the Rays think he'll make steady progress as he continues to play every day. He's expected to play at short-season Hudson Valley in 2010, though a strong spring could land him in low Class A.

Year	Club (League)	Class	AVG	G	AB	R	H	2B	3B	HR	RBI	BB	SO	SB	OBP	SLG
2009	Princeton (APP)	R	.303	52	198	33	60	7	6	6	37	20	54	14	.364	.490
MINOR LEAGUE TOTALS			.303	52	198	33	60	7	6	6	37	20	54	14	.364	.490

23 DAVID NEWMANN, LHP

BORN: June 24, 1985. **B-T:** R-L. **HT.:** 6-2. **WT.:** 200. **DRAFTED:** Texas A&M, 2007 (4th round). **SIGNED BY:** Pat Murphy.

Newmann didn't make his pro debut until nearly five years after he was first drafted, but he looks like he might be worth the wait. The Indians took him in the 24th round in 2004, when he led San Jacinto (Texas) to the finals of the Junior College World Series by pitching a one-hitter in the opener and recording three subsequent saves. He missed the next two seasons after Tommy John surgery, but bounced back to go 11-1, 2.98 for Texas A&M in 2007. The Rays took him in the fourth round that year, but he signed too late to play that summer and then missed the 2008 season after tearing a knee ligament during spring training. He finally made his pro debut in 2009 in high Class A, turning in a solid regular-season showing before excelling in the Florida State League play-offs. Newmann gets heavy sink on his 89-92 mph fastball. His curveball can be an out pitch when it's on, though it still has room for improvement. He also throws a solid-average changeup. His command can be inconsistent, but he competes well and hitters rarely make hard contact against him. At this point, Newmann just needs to stay healthy and log innings in order to fulfill his potential. His next challenge will come in Double-A this year.

Year	Club (League)	Class	W	L	ERA	G	GS	CG	SV	IP	H	R	ER	HR	BB	SO	AVG
2009	Charlotte (FSL)	HiA	9	6	3.44	24	24	2	0	131	108	59	50	6	46	128	.223
MINOR LEAGUE TOTALS			9	6	3.44	24	24	2	0	131	108	59	50	6	46	128	.223

24 MATT SWEENEY, 3B

BORN: April 14, 1988. **B-T:** L-R. **HT.:** 6-3. **WT.:** 210. **DRAFTED:** HS—Rockville, Md., 2006 (8th round). **SIGNED BY:** Dan Radcliff (Angels).

Overlooked in the 2006 draft, Sweeney signed with the Angels for $75,000 as an eighth-rounder and quickly established himself as one of the top power hitters in their system. But he hurt his ankle when he was hit by a pitch at the end of the 2007 season, and subsequent surgery to remove bone chips and repair ligament damage cost him all of 2008. His bat was as potent as ever when he returned last season, though he missed two months with a chipped bone in his hip. His injury history didn't scare off the Rays, who acquired him as part of the Scott Kazmir trade in August. With his strength and balance and the loft in his swing, Sweeney is primed to do a lot of damage at the plate. He has good pitch-recognition skills, though he can get very aggressive at the plate. He had below-average speed, agility and defensive ability before he got hurt, and the injuries haven't helped. He has enough arm to play third base, but he has a career .860 fielding percentage at the hot corner and most scouts project him as a first baseman. Tampa Bay wants to see him play a full, healthy season in Double-A before determining his defensive home.

Year	Club (League)	Class	AVG	G	AB	R	H	2B	3B	HR	RBI	BB	SO	SB	OBP	SLG
2006	Angels (AZL)	R	.341	44	170	38	58	11	7	5	39	23	27	4	.431	.576
	Orem (PIO)	R	.167	2	6	0	1	0	0	0	0	0	2	0	.286	.167
2007	Cedar Rapids (MWL)	LoA	.260	119	439	64	114	29	2	18	72	38	88	7	.324	.458
2009	Angels (AZL)	R	.267	4	15	3	4	1	0	0	0	2	4	0	.389	.333
	R. Cucamonga (CAL)	HiA	.299	58	211	39	63	17	1	9	44	26	37	2	.379	.517
	Charlotte (FSL)	HiA	.158	6	19	1	3	1	0	0	3	3	8	0	.273	.211
MINOR LEAGUE TOTALS			.283	233	860	145	243	59	10	32	155	92	166	13	.359	.486

25 JASON McEACHERN, RHP

BORN: Oct. 12, 1990. **B-T:** R-R. **HT.:** 6-2. **WT.:** 185. **DRAFTED:** HS—Hickory, N.C., 2008 (13th round). **SIGNED BY:** Brad Matthews.

Some scouts in the organization see McEachern as a righthanded version of Kyle Lobstein. The lanky hurler has shown excellent overall control and the ability to control the tempo and get hitters out. He has a career 2.12 ERA in two pro seasons since signing for $90,000 as a 13th-round pick. He didn't attract much attention in the 2008 draft because he threw in the low 80s in the summer before his senior year and teams thought he'd be tough to sign away from Wingate (N.C.), an NCAA Division II school. McEachern arrived in spring training last year looking bigger, stronger and more mature, exactly what the Rays had hoped to see. He also has shown gradual improvement with all of his pitches. His fastball resides at 89-91 mph, and he backs it up with a solid curveball and changeup. He works both sides of the plate, keeps his offerings down in the strike zone and can get batters to chase pitches up. Expected to be part of the Bowling Green rotation at age 19 this season, he simply needs experience against better competition in order to maintain his progress.

Year	Club (League)	Class	W	L	ERA	G	GS	CG	SV	IP	H	R	ER	HR	BB	SO	AVG
2008	Princeton (APP)	R	3	0	1.44	9	2	0	0	25	17	5	4	2	8	16	.193
2009	Princeton (APP)	R	0	0	1.06	3	3	0	0	17	11	2	2	1	0	15	.190
	Hudson Valley (NYP)	SS	2	3	2.75	11	11	1	0	56	56	23	17	3	12	47	.260
MINOR LEAGUE TOTALS			5	3	2.12	23	16	1	0	98	84	30	23	6	20	78	.233

26 FRANK DE LOS SANTOS, LHP

BORN: Nov. 17, 1987. **B-T:** L-L. **HT.:** 6-0. **WT.:** 165. **SIGNED:** Dominican Republic, 2006. **SIGNED BY:** Junior Ramirez.

De los Santos may not have as high a ceiling as other pitchers in the system, but that doesn't detract from his solid 2009 season and overall steady progress. He has a live arm and works well off his 91-93 mph fastball. He labored diligently on his hard slider and changeup last year and threw strikes with both pitches, and his overall command improved considerably. His slider needs more consistency and sharper break, and he has flirted with switching to more of a cutter. Even without a quality breaking ball, lefthanders rarely take good cuts against him and posted a .485 OPS against him last season. The Rays like de los Santos' fearless, competitive approach and his outgoing personality. He has made a strong effort to become fluent in English and has shown the willingness to do whatever it takes to reach the big leagues. He's undersized but has good mound presence and challenges hitters. Most likely a situational reliever at the major league level, de los Santos must continue to refine his complementary pitches this year in high Class A.

Year	Club (League)	Class	W	L	ERA	G	GS	CG	SV	IP	H	R	ER	HR	BB	SO	AVG
2007	Princeton (APP)	R	4	5	3.64	13	13	0	0	64	64	30	26	5	16	43	.257
2008	Hudson Valley (NYP)	SS	4	5	5.40	11	11	0	0	57	73	40	34	2	16	44	.320
2009	Bowling Green (SAL)	LoA	4	10	3.65	27	27	1	0	136	136	69	55	7	45	81	.258
MINOR LEAGUE TOTALS			12	20	4.03	51	51	1	0	257	273	139	115	14	77	168	.272

27 ANEURY RODRIGUEZ, RHP

BORN: Dec. 13, 1987. **B-T:** R-R. **HT.:** 6-3. **WT.:** 180. **SIGNED:** Dominican Republic, 2005. **SIGNED BY:** Felix Feliz (Rockies).

Acquired from the Rockies for righthander Jason Hammel at the end of spring training last year, Rodriguez struggled with his mechanics shortly after joining the Rays but gradually made adjustments. In addition to cleaning up his delivery, he developed his changeup, dramatically improving the fade on the pitch. He also tightened the spin on his curveball, which allowed him to throw both of his offspeed offerings for strikes. Montgomery pitching coach Neil Allen worked with Rodriguez to create a hesitation in his delivery, allowing him to stay over the rubber better and generate more downhill plane with his pitches. The lingering concern with Rodriguez centers on the velocity of his fastball. Clocked at 92-94 mph with the Rockies, he sat at 89-91 mph with his fastball and didn't miss as many bats last year. He tends to overthrow when he gets in jams but has made progress in going from a thrower to a pitcher. Rodriguez should reach Triple-A at some point in 2010.

Year	Club (League)	Class	W	L	ERA	G	GS	CG	SV	IP	H	R	ER	HR	BB	SO	AVG
2005	Casper (PIO)	R	3	4	7.55	15	15	0	0	62	77	54	52	7	26	47	.309
2006	Tri-City (NWL)	SS	4	4	4.14	15	15	1	0	76	78	42	35	2	30	69	.261
2007	Asheville (SAL)	LoA	9	9	5.15	28	28	1	0	152	182	105	87	19	48	160	.298
2008	Modesto (CAL)	HiA	9	10	3.74	27	27	2	0	156	148	78	65	12	40	139	.251
2009	Montgomery (SL)	AA	9	11	4.50	27	27	1	0	142	122	78	71	17	59	111	.231
MINOR LEAGUE TOTALS			34	38	4.74	112	112	5	0	588	607	357	310	57	203	526	.267

28 MATT GORGEN, RHP

BORN: Jan. 27, 1987. **B-T:** R-R. **HT.:** 6-0. **WT.:** 210. **DRAFTED:** California, 2008 (16th round). **SIGNED BY:** Carlos Delgado.

Gorgen has made a seamless transition from college to the minors. He has 32 saves and a 1.35 ERA since signing for $125,000 as a 16th-round pick in 2008. He's the twin brother of Cardinals rigthhander Scott Gorgen, and while both are fearless on the mound, their styles are totally different. Scott relies heavily on his changeup, while Matt is a classic hard-charging reliever. His 91-92 mph fastball has been clocked as high as 95, and his 80-81 mph slider can be an out pitch. He has been working on a changeup, but it's still inconsistent and not nearly as good as his brother's. Gorgen needs to command his pitches better after posting a 10.38 ERA in the Arizona Fall League. He projects as a middle reliever or set-up man at the major league level. A return to Double-A, where he pitched well at the end of 2009, is next on his agenda.

Year	Club (League)	Class	W	L	ERA	G	GS	CG	SV	IP	H	R	ER	HR	BB	SO	AVG
2008	Hudson Valley (NYP)	SS	1	1	1.96	22	0	0	13	23	7	5	5	2	5	35	.093
2009	Charlotte (FSL)	HiA	4	0	0.57	28	0	0	15	48	24	4	3	1	16	59	.151
	Montgomery (SL)	AA	3	1	2.38	16	0	0	4	23	18	7	6	2	13	18	.214
MINOR LEAGUE TOTALS			8	2	1.35	66	0	0	32	93	49	16	14	5	34	112	.154

29 JAKE JEFFERIES, C

BORN: Oct. 30, 1987. **B-T:** L-R. **HT.:** 6-3. **WT.:** 200. **DRAFTED:** UC Davis, 2008 (3rd round). **SIGNED BY:** Carlos Delgado.

Jefferies shared Big West Conference player of the year honors in 2008, then had a solid pro debut after the Rays drafted him in the third round. An offensive-minded catcher, he's a contact-oriented hitter who should improve as he learns the nuances of how pitchers are trying to attack him. After being tough to strike out in college, he often went out of the strike zone early in the count last year, which took a toll on his batting average and overall production. He uses the entire field and could hit for more power as his approach improves. Jefferies arrived in spring training last year too bulky and tight after an offseason of weight training, which affected his throwing. Once he reduced his bulk and his entire body became looser, he made steady strides, dropping his pop times from a well below-average 2.3 seconds to a fringy 2.0. He threw out 26 percent of basestealers. Jefferies has focused on becoming more agile, and his footwork, blocking ability and overall quickness behind the plate improved. He works well with pitchers and calls a good game. Though he has below-average speed, he runs well for a catcher and has good instincts. Jefferies successfully made several adjustments last year, setting up for a solid season in high Class A in 2010.

Year	Club (League)	Class	AVG	G	AB	R	H	2B	3B	HR	RBI	BB	SO	SB	OBP	SLG
2008	Hudson Valley (NYP)	SS	.315	66	238	32	75	16	3	2	41	21	22	1	.379	.433
2009	Bowling Green (SAL)	LoA	.261	116	440	54	115	17	1	8	50	37	35	7	.326	.359
MINOR LEAGUE TOTALS			.280	182	678	86	190	33	4	10	91	58	57	8	.345	.385

30 KEVIN JAMES, LHP

BORN: Oct. 1, 1990. **B-T:** L-L. **HT.:** 6-4. **WT.:** 190. **DRAFTED:** HS—Milwaukee, 2009 (9th round). **SIGNED BY:** Tom Couston.

When Tampa Bay failed to sign its top two picks in the 2009 draft, James wound up as one of the beneficiaries. The Rays drafted James in the ninth round and became determined to sign him after scouting him over the summer. With unspent money in the draft budget, they found $625,000 to steer him away from attending Boston College. Easily the best draft prospect in Wisconsin last year, James showed flashes of ability but often struggled against weak competition. He has a lightning-quick arm that produces fastballs that sit at 90-91 mph and touch 93. His curveball is an above-average pitch when he stays on line to the plate, while his changeup shows enough promise that he could have three solid offerings. He has outstanding body control, particularly for such a tall pitcher, as well as above-average athleticism. He has wide shoulders with a frame reminiscent of a young Jake McGee, and the chance to fill out. In addition to honing his command and the quality of all his pitches, James needs to mature and control his emotions better on the mound. The Rays believe he has a high ceiling and will be patient with his development. After working just one inning in his pro debut, he'll pitch in Rookie ball in 2010.

Year	Club (League)	Class	W	L	ERA	G	GS	CG	SV	IP	H	R	ER	HR	BB	SO	AVG
2009	Rays (GCL)	R	0	0	0.00	1	0	0	0	1	1	0	0	0	0	1	.250
MINOR LEAGUE TOTALS			0	0	0.00	1	0	0	0	1	1	0	0	0	0	1	.250

Texas Rangers

BY AARON FITT

The Rangers farm system ranked as the best in game entering 2009, and it began bearing fruit immediately. The major league team's young core returned it to contention sooner than expected. Texas was just two games out of the wild card as late as Sept. 9 before fading down the stretch, but that slide couldn't obscure a season of positive stories on the major and minor league diamonds.

Elvis Andrus stepped into the everyday shortstop job as a 20-year-old, delivering often-spectacular defense and finishing second in American League rookie of the year voting. Julio Borbon added some  speed on the bases and in the outfield when he became a regular over the final seven weeks of the season, while Neftali Feliz, Derek Holland and Tommy Hunter provided sparks on the mound.

The Rangers also got breakout seasons from young veterans Scott Feldman, who won a franchise-record 12 games on the road and 17 overall, and Nelson Cruz, who bashed a team-high 33 homers.

The picture off the field wasn't as sunny, however, as owner Tom Hicks' financial problems essentially ceded fiscal control of the team to Major League Baseball. MLB extended a $15 million line of credit to the Rangers in the middle of the season, and the commissioner's office limited how high the club could go in its efforts to sign first-round pick Matt Purke. The team reportedly offered $4 million, which the righthander turned down to attend Texas Christian.

Three groups pursued efforts to buy the team in the offseason, and the Rangers selected a group led by Pennsylvania lawyer Chuck Greenberg to negotiate with exclusively. If that deal goes through, team president Nolan Ryan would remain in his role and would be a minority owner in the team, as would Hicks.

The new ownership group will take over an organization loaded with young talent. Even after graduating Andrus, Borbon, Holland, Hunter and Taylor Teagarden to the majors last season, Texas still has one of the deepest systems in baseball.

No team has a more talented trio of prospects than the Rangers have in Feliz, who hasn't exhausted his rookie/prospect eligibility; first baseman Justin Smoak, who tore up Double-A in his first full season; and 18-year-old lefthander Martin Perez, who established himself as one of the top pitching prospects in the minors. Texas is flush with power arms throughout the system, though it's thinner in position players.

Texas tried to make up for losing Purke by adding

Elvis Andrus played brilliant defense and held his own with the bat as a rookie

TOP 30 PROSPECTS

1. Neftali Feliz, rhp	**16.** Michael Kirkman, lhp
2. Justin Smoak, 1b	**17.** Blake Beavan, rhp
3. Martin Perez, lhp	**18.** Tommy Mendonca, 3b
4. Tanner Scheppers, rhp	**19.** Guillermo Moscoso, rhp
5. Jurickson Profar, ss	**20.** Omar Poveda, rhp
6. Kasey Kiker, lhp	**21.** Michael Main, rhp
7. Robbie Ross, lhp	**22.** Miguel Velazquez, of
8. Mitch Moreland, of/1b	**23.** Pedro Strop, rhp
9. Danny Gutierrez, rhp	**24.** Neil Ramirez, rhp
10. Wilmer Font, rhp	**25.** Jake Brigham, rhp
11. Max Ramirez, c	**26.** Tomas Telis, c
12. Joe Wieland, rhp	**27.** Wilfredo Boscan, rhp
13. Luis Sardinas, ss	**28.** Craig Gentry, of
14. Engel Beltre, of	**29.** Andrew Doyle, rhp
15. Leury Garcia, ss	**30.** Richard Alvarez, rhp

electric righthander Tanner Scheppers in the supplemental first round of the draft. The Rangers also continued to spend money in Latin America, doling out seven-figure bonuses to switch-hitting shortstops Jurickson Profar and Luis Sardinas.

A.J. Preller, formerly the head of the productive international scouting department, was promoted in the fall to lead all of the club's scouting efforts. Kip Fagg, Josh Boyd and Mike Daly were promoted to direct the organization's amateur, pro and international scouting departments. Former scouting director Ron Hopkins became a special assistant to the GM.

General Manager: Jon Daniels. **Farm Director:** Scott Servais. **Scouting Director:** Kip Fagg.

Class	Team	League	W	L	PCT	Finish*	Manager(s)
Majors	Texas Rangers	American	87	75	.537	4th (14)	Ron Washington
Triple-A	Oklahoma City RedHawks	Pacific Coast	69	75	.479	12th (16)	Bobby Jones
Double-A	Frisco RoughRiders	Texas	72	68	.514	4th (8)	Mike Micucci
High A	Bakersfield Blaze	California	75	65	.536	t-3rd (10)	Steve Buechele
Low A	Hickory Crawdads	South Atlantic	63	76	.453	15th (16)	Hector Ortiz
Short-season	Spokane Indians	Northwest	37	39	.487	4th (8)	Tim Hulett
Rookie	AZL Rangers	Arizona	25	31	.446	t-6th (11)	Bill Richardson
Overall 2009 Minor League Record			341	354	.491	20th (30)	

*Finish in overall standings (No. of teams in league). †League champion.

LAST YEAR'S TOP 30

Player, Pos.		Status
1.	Neftali Feliz, rhp	No. 1
2.	Derek Holland, lhp	Majors
3.	Justin Smoak, 1b	No. 2
4.	Elvis Andrus, ss	Majors
5.	Martin Perez, lhp	No. 3
6.	Taylor Teagarden, c	Majors
7.	Engel Beltre, of	No. 14
8.	Michael Main, rhp	No. 21
9.	Julio Borbon, of	Majors
10.	Max Ramirez, c	No. 11
11.	Wilfredo Boscan, rhp	No. 27
12.	Blake Beavan, rhp	No. 17
13.	Eric Hurley, rhp	Dropped out
14.	Warner Madrigal, rhp	Dropped out
15.	Neil Ramirez, rhp	No. 24
16.	Joe Wieland, rhp	No. 12
17.	Tommy Hunter, rhp	Majors
18.	Jose Vallejo, 2b	(Astros)
19.	Kasey Kiker, lhp	No. 6
20.	Wilmer Font, rhp	No. 10
21.	Kennil Gomez, rhp	Dropped out
22.	Tim Murphy, lhp	Dropped out
23.	Guillermo Moscoso, rhp	No. 19
24.	Omar Poveda, rhp	No. 20
25.	Robbie Ross, lhp	No. 7
26.	Greg Golson, of	Dropped out
27.	Joaquin Arias, ss	Dropped out
28.	Thomas Diamond, rhp	(Cubs)
29.	Clark Murphy, 1b	Dropped out
30.	John Bannister, rhp	(Royals)

BEST TOOLS

Best Hitter for Average	Justin Smoak
Best Power Hitter	Justin Smoak
Best Strike-Zone Discipline	Justin Smoak
Fastest Baserunner	Leury Garcia
Best Athlete	Greg Golson
Best Fastball	Neftali Feliz
Best Curveball	Tanner Scheppers
Best Slider	Robbie Ross
Best Changeup	Kasey Kiker
Best Control	Blake Beavan
Best Defensive Catcher	Leonel de los Santos
Best Defensive Infielder	Leury Garcia
Best Infield Arm	Leury Garcia
Best Defensive Outfielder	Craig Gentry
Best Outfield Arm	Greg Golson

PROJECTED 2013 LINEUP

Catcher	Taylor Teagarden
First Base	Justin Smoak
Second Base	Ian Kinsler
Third Base	Michael Young
Shortstop	Elvis Andrus
Left Field	Josh Hamilton
Center Field	Julio Borbon
Right Field	Nelson Cruz
Designated Hitter	Chris Davis
No. 1 Starter	Neftali Feliz
No. 2 Starter	Martin Perez
No. 3 Starter	Derek Holland
No. 4 Starter	Scott Feldman
No. 5 Starter	Tommy Hunter
Closer	Tanner Scheppers

TOP PROSPECTS OF THE DECADE

Year	Player, Pos.	2009 Org.
2000	Ruben Mateo, of	Reynosa (Mexican)
2001	Carlos Pena, 1b	Rays
2002	Hank Blalock, 3b	Rangers
2003	Mark Teixeira, 3b	Yankees
2004	Adrian Gonzalez, 1b	Padres
2005	Thomas Diamond, rhp	Cubs
2006	Edinson Volquez, rhp	Reds
2007	John Danks, lhp	White Sox
2008	Elvis Andrus, ss	Rangers
2009	Neftali Feliz, rhp	Rangers

TOP DRAFT PICKS OF THE DECADE

Year	Player, Pos.	2009 Org.
2000	Scott Heard, c	Out of baseball
2001	Mark Teixeira, 3b	Yankees
2002	Drew Meyer, ss	Astros
2003	John Danks, lhp	White Sox
2004	Thomas Diamond, rhp	Cubs
2005	John Mayberry Jr., of	Phillies
2006	Kasey Kiker, lhp	Rangers
2007	Blake Beavan, rhp	Rangers
2008	Justin Smoak, 1b	Rangers
2009	*Matt Purke, lhp	Texas Christian

*Did not sign.

LARGEST BONUSES IN CLUB HISTORY

Mark Teixeira, 2001	$4,500,000
Justin Smoak, 2008	$3,500,000
John Danks, 2003	$2,100,000
Vincent Sinisi, 2003	$2,070,000
Thomas Diamond, 2004	$2,025,000

TEXAS RANGERS

TOP 2010 ROOKIE: Neftali Feliz, rhp. A sensation for the Rangers as a reliever last summer, he has the stuff to be an elite starter and will get a chance to prove it this year.

BREAKOUT PROSPECT: Richard Alvarez, rhp. With an advanced feel for a three-pitch mix, he reminds Texas of a righthanded Martin Perez at the same age.

SLEEPER: Chad Bell, lhp. Signed for $450,000 as a 14th-round pick last year, he's reminiscent of Matt Harrison with his 89-92 mph fastball, good changeup and feel for pitching.

SOURCE OF TOP 30 TALENT			
Homegrown	24	Acquired	6
College	5	Trades	5
Junior college	0	Rule 5 draft	0
High school	9	Independent leagues	0
Draft-and-follow	0	Free agents/waivers	1
Independent/drafted	1		
International	9		

Numbers in parentheses indicate prospect rankings

LF
Mike Bianucci
Cristian Santana

CF
Engel Beltre (14)
Craig Gentry (28)
Greg Golson
David Paisano
Braxton Lane

RF
Miguel Velazquez (22)
Joey Butler
Ruben Sierra Jr.
Riley Cooper
Guillermo Pimentel

3B
Tommy Mendonca (18)
Erik Morrison
Johnny Whittleman
Matt West

SS
Jurickson Profar (5)
Luis Sardinas (13)
Leury Garcia (15)
Joaquin Arias
Edwin Garcia

2B
Marcus Lemon
Oduber Herrera
Edward Martinez

1B
Justin Smoak (2)
Mitch Moreland (8)
Chad Tracy
Clark Murphy
Jared Bolden
Michael Ortiz

C
Max Ramirez (11)
Tomas Telis (26)
Leonel de los Santos
Doug Hogan
Vin DiFazio
Jose Felix

RHP

Starters	Relievers
Neftali Feliz (1)	Pedro Strop (23)
Tanner Scheppers (4)	Evan Reed
Danny Gutierrez (9)	Warner Madrigal
Wilmer Font (10)	Tanner Roark
Joe Wieland (12)	Fabio Castillo
Blake Beavan (17)	Tyler Tufts
Guillermo Moscoso (19)	Justin King
Omar Poveda (20)	Justin Miller
Michael Main (21)	Reinier Bermudez
Neil Ramirez (24)	Andrew Laughter
Jacob Brigham (25)	Brennan Garr
Wilfredo Boscan (27)	Johnny Gunter
Andrew Doyle (29)	Kevin Castner
Richard Alvarez (30)	
Braden Tullis	
Kennil Gomez	
Eric Hurley	
Matt Thompson	
Carlos Pimentel	
Shawn Blackwell	
Nick McBride	
Carlos Melo	

LHP

Starters	Relievers
Martin Perez (3)	Ben Snyder
Kasey Kiker (6)	Zach Phillips
Robbie Ross (7)	Corey Young
Michael Kirkman (16)	Yoon-Hee Nam
Robbie Erlin	Beau Jones
Chad Bell	Geuris Grullon
Richard Bleier	Miguel de los Santos
Tim Murphy	
Paul Strong	
Edwin Escobar	

DRAFT ANALYSIS

2009

BEST PURE HITTER: The Rangers didn't draft a pure bat. They have faith that 3B Tommy Mendonca (3) will make the adjustments in his swing to be an average major league hitter.

BEST POWER HITTER: Mendonca ranked third in NCAA Division I with 27 homers last spring and has plus raw power. He has adjustments to make but his raw juice is undeniable.

FASTEST RUNNER: The Rangers signed a pair of plus-plus runners in OFs Ruben Sierra Jr. (6) and Braxton Lane (7).

BEST DEFENSIVE PLAYER: Mendonca has good range at third to go with soft hands and a plus arm.

BEST FASTBALL: RHP Tanner Scheppers' (1s) fastball has rated as the second-best in each of the last two drafts. Even this year, coming back from a shoulder injury, he sat at 93-96 mph and touched 99.

BEST SECONDARY PITCH: Scheppers has a plus hard curveball that gives him a swing-and-miss pitch, and LHP Robbie Erlin (3) has a hammer curve as well. LHP Paul Strong (17) got a $300,000 bonus thanks in part to his potential plus curve, and LHP Chad Bell (14), who signed for $450,000, features a promising changeup.

BEST PRO DEBUT: Mendonca reached high Class A after hitting .309/.361/.537 with nine home runs at shortseason Spokane. C Vin DiFazio (15), 23, hit .278/.417/.526 with 12 homers between Spokane and low Class A Hickory. RHP Braden Tullis (8) used a heavy 88-92 mph sinker to go 4-3, 3.04 at Spokane.

BEST ATHLETE: OF Riley Cooper (25) signed for $250,000 and an agreement that he'd be allowed to finish his football career at Florida. He led the Gators in receiving yards and touchdowns during the regular season. In baseball, he has above-average tools in his raw power, speed and arm.

MOST INTRIGUING BACKGROUND: Sierra's father was a four-time all-star (three times with the Rangers) and hit 306 big league homers. Lane's uncle MacArthur was an NFL running back for 11 seasons, leading the league in rushing touchdowns in 1970 and receptions in 1976. Unsigned OF Reggie Williams Jr.'s (32) father was a big league outfielder. Unsigned OF Anthony Hutting (38) is a cousin of Aaron Rowand and James Shields.

CLOSEST TO THE MAJORS: Scheppers.

BEST LATE-ROUND PICK: The Rangers were aggressive late, as Bell, Strong, RHP Shawn Blackwell (24; $300,000) and Cooper got above-slot bonuses. The best of the lot may be Bell, who has pitchability and three average to plus pitches.

THE ONE WHO GOT AWAY: Financial issues with ownership contributed to the Rangers' failure to sign LHP Matt Purke (1), who turned down a reported $4 million. He'll be draft-eligible again as a sophomore in 2011.

ASSESSMENT: Scheppers makes up a bit for the loss of Purke, and this draft crop has pitching depth. It may take a while for any position players other than Mendonca to make an impact.

2008

They weren't cheap at a combined cost of $5.075 million, but the Rangers may have gotten steals in 1B Justin Smoak (1) and LHP Robbie Ross (2). RHP Joe Wieland (4) has the makings of a workhorse starter.

GRADE: B+

2007

OF Julio Borbon (1s) and RHP Tommy Hunter (1s) already have found roles in Texas, while the club's early high school picks—RHPs Blake Beavan (1), Michael Main (1) and Neil Ramirez (1s)—have been slower to develop. OF/1B Mitch Moreland (17) ended thoughts of moving him to the mound by hitting .331 with 18 homers in 2009. The two best pitchers in this draft might turn out to be RHP Anthony Ranaudo (11) and LHP Drew Pomeranz (12), who didn't sign and project as early first-rounders in 2010.

GRADE: B+

2006

1B Chris Davis (5) and draft-and-follow LHP Derek Holland (25) took their lumps in the majors last year, but they're two players the Rangers are building around. So is the top pick from this draft, LHP Kasey Kiker (1). Part of the Josh Hamilton trade, LHP Danny Herrera (45) had a solid rookie season with the Reds. OF Craig Gentry (10) reached the majors last September.

GRADE: B+

2005

No player from this crop stands out as a slam-dunk big league regular, though OF John Mayberry Jr. (1; since traded to the Phillies), C Taylor Teagarden (3), 2B German Duran (6) and RHP Doug Mathis (13) all have reached the majors.

GRADE: C

*Draft analysis by John Manuel (2009) and Jim Callis (2005-08). Numbers in parentheses indicate draft rounds. *Bonuses for 2005 are first 10 rounds only.*

NEFTALI FELIZ, RHP

Born: May 2, 1988.
Height: 6-3. **Weight:** 180.
Bats: R. **Throws:** R.
Signed: Dominican
Republic, 2005.
Signed by: Julian Perez/
Roberto Aquino (Braves).

JOHN WILLIAMSON

Originally signed by the Braves for $100,000 out of the Dominican Republic, Feliz came to the Rangers in a five-prospect package for Mark Teixeira and Ron Mahay in July 2007. At the time, he hadn't pitched above Rookie ball, but Feliz since has made a name for himself as one of the most exciting young pitchers in baseball. Texas also received Elvis Andrus, Jarrod Saltalamacchia, Matt Harrison and Beau Jones in one of the best trades in franchise history. Feliz reached Double-A Frisco at age 20 and led the minors with 10.8 strikeouts per nine innings in his first full season in the Rangers system in 2008. He opened last season working as a starter at Triple-A Oklahoma, moving to the bullpen in late June to prepare him for a big league callup, which came in early August. Feliz electrified the home crowd in his major league debut, becoming the first Ranger ever to strike out four straight batters to start his career and touching 100 mph six times in 30 pitches over two perfect innings. He took the American League by storm over the next two months, dominating in 20 relief appearances.

An exceptional athlete with a fluid arm action, Feliz generates premium velocity with minimal effort, and scouts constantly comment that it looks like he's playing catch from the mound. His fastball explodes on hitters, sitting at 93-98 mph and touching triple digits. His fastball also has good late life and he commands it well, making it a true 80 pitch on the 20-80 scouting scale. Feliz made great strides with his changeup in 2009, and it now ranks as his No. 2 pitch. He maintains his arm speed on his changeup, and it can be a plus offering though it's as hard as some pitchers' fastballs at 89-90 mph. His athletic, physical frame should help him hold up under a starter's workload. He has a confident, aggressive mound presence and doesn't get rattled easily.

Feliz is still working on improving his feel for his breaking ball. In Triple-A, one of every three or four was a quality big league pitch, and he actually was more consistent and comfortable with it after his callup. At its best, the pitch is an 82-85 mph power curveball with 11-to-5 break, but it tends to flatten out at times and will probably turn into more of a slider. When he worked as a starter, Feliz had a tendency to work at 92-93 mph with his fastball in the early innings, then peak in the high 90s in the middle to late innings. In relief, he had to learn to dial up his stuff from the start of his outings. Feliz still is refining his command, particularly with his secondary stuff.

Because of his ability to hold his exceptional fastball velocity deep into games, Feliz profiles as a potential No. 1 starter if he can improve his breaking ball. The Rangers plan to break him in as a starter in 2010, but if he struggles they could move him back into the bullpen, where he could be a shutdown closer.

Year	Club (League)	Class	W	L	ERA	G	GS	CG	SV	IP	H	R	ER	HR	BB	SO	AVG
2005	Braves1 (DSL)	R	0	0	3.60	10	0	0	0	10	7	4	4	0	11	8	.184
2006	Braves (GCL)	R	0	2	4.03	11	5	0	2	29	20	13	13	0	14	42	.192
2007	Danville (APP)	R	2	0	1.98	8	7	0	0	27	18	8	6	0	12	28	.191
	Spokane (NWL)	SS	0	2	3.60	8	1	0	0	15	13	8	6	2	12	27	.228
2008	Clinton (MWL)	LoA	6	3	2.52	17	17	0	0	82	55	25	23	2	28	106	.193
	Frisco (TL)	AA	4	3	2.98	10	10	0	0	45	34	16	15	1	23	47	.217
2009	Oklahoma City (PCL)	AAA	4	6	3.49	25	13	0	0	77	69	36	30	2	30	75	.240
	Texas (AL)	MAJ	1	0	1.74	20	0	0	2	31	13	6	6	2	8	39	.124
MAJOR LEAGUE TOTALS			1	0	1.74	20	0	0	2	31	13	6	6	2	8	39	.124
MINOR LEAGUE TOTALS			16	16	3.05	89	53	0	2	286	216	110	97	7	130	333	.211

2 JUSTIN SMOAK, 1B

BORN: Dec. 5, 1986. **B-T:** B-L. **HT.:** 6-4. **WT.:** 220. **DRAFTED:** South Carolina, 2008 (1st round). **SIGNED BY:** Jim Cuthbert.

A high school teammate of Orioles catcher Matt Wieters in Goose Creek, S.C., Smoak mashed a school-record 62 career homers at South Carolina before signing for $3.5 million as the 11th overall pick. Smoak's first full pro season got off to a good start in Double-A before he missed a month at midseason with a ribcage injury. He struggled initially after a promotion to Triple-A, then made adjustments and finished on fire at IBAF World Cup, where he hit nine home runs in 14 games to capture MVP honors and help Team USA win the gold medal. The switch-hitting Smoak has plus-plus power potential from both sides of the plate. He has a mature, patient approach and the ability to use all fields. A potential plus defender at first base, he has good hands and digs balls out of the dirt well. Smoak isn't a finished product offensively yet, as he needs to stay back more consistently and get better extension out front. He also must improve his lateral range at first base, where his arm is merely adequate. Smoak figures to start 2010 back in Triple-A, but he could be ready for the big leagues sometime later in the year. He has a chance to be a switch-hitting slugger in the Mark Teixeira mold.

Year	Club (League)	Class	AVG	G	AB	R	H	2B	3B	HR	RBI	BB	SO	SB	OBP	SLG
2008	Clinton (MWL)	LoA	.304	14	56	9	17	3	0	3	6	5	10	0	.355	.518
2009	Rangers (AZL)	R	.667	2	6	3	4	0	1	2	5	1	1	0	.714	2.000
	Frisco (TL)	AA	.328	50	183	30	60	10	0	6	29	39	35	0	.449	.481
	Oklahoma City (PCL)	AAA	.244	54	197	25	48	11	0	4	23	35	45	0	.363	.360
MINOR LEAGUE TOTALS			.292	120	442	67	129	24	1	15	63	80	91	0	.403	.452

3 MARTIN PEREZ, LHP

BORN: April 4, 1991. **B-T:** L-L. **HT.:** 6-0. **WT.:** 178. **SIGNED:** Venezuela, 2007. **SIGNED BY:** Rafic Saab/Manny Batista/Don Welke.

The Rangers saw enough feel for pitching and competitiveness in a 16-year-old Perez to sign him for a $580,000 bonus in 2007, when his fastball sat in the mid-80s. Since then his velocity has jumped, and he ranked as the South Atlantic League's No. 1 prospect in 2009. His dominance earned him a mid-August promotion to Double-A, where he was pounded in his debut before settling down in his last four starts. Dubbed "The Venezuelan Gator" shortly after signing for his similarity to undersized former all-star Ron Guidry, Perez is more often compared to Johan Santana nowadays for his size, delivery, moxie and electric arm. He attacks hitters with a 91-95 mph fastball, and he's still maturing physically. He has exceptional feel for his sharp 1-to-7 curveball, which he can add and subtract from at will, throwing it anywhere from 68-81 mph. The Rangers directed Perez to throw a preponderance of changeups in the first half of the season to help him refine the pitch. He still doesn't turn the pitch over well and needs more consistency with it, but he'll flash a plus 78-82 mph changeup with good arm speed. When he got to Double-A, he got nervous, overthrew and didn't repeat his delivery as well. Perez has top-of-the-rotation upside, and he might not be far from the majors. He'll likely start 2010 in Double-A, where the Rangers plan to let him pitch deeper into games for the first time in his career.

Year	Club (League)	Class	W	L	ERA	G	GS	CG	SV	IP	H	R	ER	HR	BB	SO	AVG
2008	Spokane (NWL)	SS	1	2	3.65	15	15	0	0	62	66	32	25	3	28	53	.274
2009	Hickory (SAL)	LoA	5	5	2.31	22	14	0	1	94	82	35	24	3	33	105	.236
	Frisco (TL)	AA	1	3	5.57	5	5	0	0	21	29	16	13	2	5	14	.326
MINOR LEAGUE TOTALS			7	10	3.16	42	34	0	1	176	177	83	62	8	66	172	.261

4 TANNER SCHEPPERS, RHP

ST. PAUL SAINTS BASEBALL CLUB

BORN: Jan. 17, 1987. **B-T:** R-R. **HT.:** 6-4. **WT.:** 200. **DRAFTED:** St. Paul (American Association), 2009 (1st round supplemental). **SIGNED BY:** Derek Lee.

Scheppers projected as a top 10 pick in the 2008 draft before a shoulder injury caused him to miss Fresno State's improbable College World Series title run and dropped him to the Pirates at No. 48. Initially reported as a stress fracture, the injury was later described as significant wear and tear, so he opted for rehab over surgery. He turned down Pittsburgh and pitched for the independent St. Paul Saints in 2009, but he still lasted 44 picks because of concerns about his health. He signed for $1.25 million and posted a 5.73 ERA in the Arizona Fall League. Scheppers has an electric fastball that ranges from 93-99 mph and has excellent downhill angle. He complements it with a plus 82-84 mph curveball that could become plus-plus as he refines his command. He has an aggressive, competitive demeanor and a good work ethic. Scheppers can be wild with all his stuff and must do a better job getting ahead in counts. He has feel for a changeup but must develop the pitch to stick as a starter. He has a hitch in the back of his delivery, but his arm works well and the Rangers don't plan to mess much with his mechanics. They want him to add 10-15 pounds and continue strengthening his shoulder. Scheppers earns comparisons to Brandon Morrow, and as with Morrow, it could take some time to figure out if he fits best as a starter or closer. Scheppers is ticketed for a spot in the crowded Frisco rotation in 2010.

Year	Club (League)	Class	W	L	ERA	G	GS	CG	SV	IP	H	R	ER	HR	BB	SO	AVG
2009	Did Not Play—Signed Late																

5 JURICKSON PROFAR, SS

BILL MITCHELL

BORN: Feb. 20, 1993. **B-T:** B-R. **HT.:** 5-11. **WT.:** 165. **SIGNED:** Curacao, 2009. **SIGNED BY:** Mike Daly/Chu Halabi/Jose Felomina.

Profar made a name for himself in the Little League World Series, leading Curacao to the championship as an 11-year-old and back to the title game as a 12-year-old. With a fastball that touches 93 mph, he generated plenty of interest on the international market as a pitcher last summer, but Texas was the only organization that would accede to his wishes to be an everyday player. They signed him right after July 2 for $1.55 million, a franchise record for an international signee. Profar dazzled the Rangers with his savvy and presence during instructional league and at their Dominican academy later in the fall. His advanced instincts, keen field awareness, dogged work ethic and outgoing personality remind them of Elvis Andrus—whom Profar idolizes. He has a chance to be a plus defender at shortstop thanks to his sure hands, plus arm and average range. He also has a knack for putting the barrel on the ball from both sides of the plate, and his offensive approach is advanced for a 16-year-old. His average speed plays up on the basepaths because of his intelligence. More than anything, Profar just needs experience. As he fills out, he could develop fringe to solid-average power, but he needs to add strength to his thin, wiry frame. Many international scouts with other clubs aren't sold that he'll hit enough or stick at shortstop. The Rangers vehemently disagree. The precocious Profar could follow in Andrus' footsteps and start his first full pro season at low Class A Hickory as a 17-year-old.

Year	Club (League)	Class	AVG	G	AB	R	H	2B	3B	HR	RBI	BB	SO	SB	OBP	SLG
2009	Did Not Play—Signed 2010 Contract															

6 KASEY KIKER, LHP

BORN: Nov. 19, 1987. **B-T:** L-L. **HT.:** 5-10. **WT.:** 170. **DRAFTED:** HS—Seale, Ala., 2006 (1st round). **SIGNED BY:** Jeff Wood.

Shoulder soreness hampered Kiker in 2008, but he stayed healthy last year and led the Double-A Texas League in strikeouts per nine innings (8.6) while finishing second in opponent average (.231). His velocity and command faded late in the year, as he posted a 9.47 ERA in August, then issued 14 walks in 13 innings for Team USA in the World Cup. Kiker no longer flashes the 95-96 mph fastball that made him the 12th overall pick and earned him a $1.6 million bonus in 2006, but he attacks hitters with a 90-93 mph heater. The riding life on his fastball gets strikeouts up in the zone. His 79-80 mph changeup has blossomed into a plus pitch over the last two years. He's a fearless competitor who loves to work inside. Kiker's mid-70s curveball still has good shape and depth at times, but his command of the pitch has taken a step backward. He needs to throw it with tighter break more consistently. Durability will always be a question because of his size, and his fastball dropped to 85-89 mph late in the year. Some Rangers officials believe Kiker's stuff will play up in relief, and he could get some work in the bullpen in major league camp this spring. Ultimately, his future might be as a middle reliever or set-up man, but he'll open 2010 in the Oklahoma City rotation.

Year	Club (League)	Class	W	L	ERA	G	GS	CG	SV	IP	H	R	ER	HR	BB	SO	AVG
2006	Spokane (NWL)	SS	0	7	4.13	16	15	0	0	52	44	34	24	5	35	51	.232
2007	Clinton (MWL)	LoA	7	4	2.90	20	20	0	0	96	84	35	31	10	41	112	.237
2008	Bakersfield (CAL)	HiA	5	5	4.73	23	21	0	0	122	138	72	64	14	37	111	.292
2009	Frisco (TL)	AA	7	7	3.86	25	23	0	0	126	108	63	54	9	66	120	.231
MINOR LEAGUE TOTALS			19	23	3.93	84	79	0	0	396	374	204	173	38	179	394	.252

7 ROBBIE ROSS, LHP

BORN: June 24, 1989. **B-T:** L-L. **HT.:** 5-11. **WT.:** 185. **DRAFTED:** HS—Lexington, Ky., 2008 (2nd round). **SIGNED BY:** Jon Poloni.

The Rangers bought Ross out of a Kentucky commitment with a $1.575 million bonus just hours before the 2008 signing deadline. They were mildly disappointed by his lack of arm speed and fastball life in instructional league that fall, but he dominated in his pro debut last year. He ranked second in strikeouts per nine innings (9.2) and fourth in ERA (2.66) in the short-season Northwest League. Ross makes up for his lack of size with his tenacity and quick arm. He pitches down in the zone to both sides of the plate with a 90-93 mph fastball that bumps 94. The pitch plays up because of its late life—he can cut it and sink it, though he doesn't always know how he's doing it. He hides the ball well and eats up lefthanders, holding them to a .228 average in 2009. He also flashes an above-average, late-breaking slider at 82-83 mph. Ross' changeup is a work in progress, though he does have some feel for it. Because of his size, he sometimes gets underneath the ball, which cause his pitches to rise in the zone. He still must add strength to improve his stamina. Ross will move on to low Class A in 2010. Texas will develop him as a starter, and some club officials envision him as a mid-rotation starter in the mold of former all-star Danny Jackson.

Year	Club (League)	Class	W	L	ERA	G	GS	CG	SV	IP	H	R	ER	HR	BB	SO	AVG
2009	Spokane (NWL)	SS	4	4	2.66	15	15	0	0	74	68	28	22	5	17	76	.240
MINOR LEAGUE TOTALS			4	4	2.66	15	15	0	0	74	68	28	22	5	17	76	.240

8 MITCH MORELAND, OF/1B

BORN: Sept. 6, 1985. **B-T:** L-L. **HT.:** 6-2. **WT.:** 230. **DRAFTED:** Mississippi State, 2007 (17th round). **SIGNED BY:** Jeff Wood.

Moreland was a gritty two-way star for Mississippi State, hitting 10 homers and making 16 relief appearances for the Bulldogs' 2007 College World Series team. His plus lefthanded power helped him win the Cape Cod League home run derby in 2006 and finish as the runner-up in 2007, when the Rangers signed him late in the summer for $60,000. Thanks to his low-90s fastball and feel for a tight slider, they dabbled with the notion of using Moreland on the mound heading into 2009, but he mashed his way to Double-A and ended those plans. His .331/.391/.527 season was cut short in mid-August when he fouled a ball off his foot and broke a bone, but he recovered in time to post an .855 OPS in the Arizona Fall League. Moreland has above-average power, especially to left-center field. He's an intelligent hitter who makes adjustments from at-bat to at-bat, and he hangs in well against lefthanders. Club officials say he's the best natural leader in their system. Though he's better at first base, he showed solid instincts and a plus arm when he played right field in deference to Justin Smoak at Frisco last year. Moreland has a funky swing with some holes in it, but he has worked to shorten his stroke and pull the ball with more authority. He's a below-average runner whose range is lacking in the outfield. Given the organization's glut of first basemen, Moreland's best route to an everyday big league job is in right field. He figures there in Triple-A this year and could be a solid regular in the Brad Hawpe mold before too long.

Year	Club (League)	Class	AVG	G	AB	R	H	2B	3B	HR	RBI	BB	SO	SB	OBP	SLG
2007	Spokane (NWL)	SS	.259	27	108	10	28	7	1	2	15	8	25	1	.308	.398
2008	Clinton (MWI)	LoA	.324	123	466	64	151	37	4	18	99	60	67	2	.400	.536
2009	Bakersfield (CAL)	HiA	.341	43	170	34	58	19	0	8	26	21	26	1	.421	.594
	Frisco (TL)	AA	.326	73	301	51	98	19	3	8	59	23	42	1	.373	.488
MINOR LEAGUE TOTALS			.321	266	1045	159	335	82	8	36	199	112	160	5	.387	.518

9 DANNY GUTIERREZ, RHP

BORN: March 8, 1987. **B-T:** R-R. **HT.:** 6-1. **WT.:** 180. **DRAFTED:** Riverside (Calif.) CC, D/F 2005 (33rd round). **SIGNED BY:** John Ramey (Royals).

After blossoming into one of the Royals' top pitching prospects, Gutierrez was held back in extended spring training last April while recovering from a minor shoulder injury. The club wound up sending him home over a disagreement about his rehab. It wasn't the first off-field issue for Gutierrez, who has had three brushes with the law in the last two years, including an assault charge last June. Fed up, Kansas City dealt him to Texas in September for catcher Manny Pina and outfielder Tim Smith. Gutierrez has an athletic frame and a live arm. He has excellent command of a 91-95 mph fastball, and his 71-75 mph overhand curveball rates as a second plus offering. He changes speeds well and has a good feel for pitching. Gutierrez flashes a quality changeup at times, but it's inconsistent. His fastball is rather straight and could make him susceptible to homers against advanced hitters. His makeup is a major concern, but the Rangers believe he's maturing and that a fresh start will do him good. Gutierrez will open the season in Double-A and looks on track to compete for a big league job at some point in 2011. His electric repertoire gives him a chance to be a frontline starter—one evaluator compares him to Darryl Kile—if everything comes together.

Year	Club (League)	Class	W	L	ERA	G	GS	CG	SV	IP	H	R	ER	HR	BB	SO	AVG
2006	Idaho Falls (PIO)	R	0	4	6.57	14	9	0	0	49	74	42	36	6	21	36	.359
2007	Royals (AZL)	R	0	0	0.00	1	1	0	0	3	1	0	0	0	1	3	.100
	Burlington (MWL)	LoA	1	2	4.88	7	7	0	0	31	32	18	17	2	12	27	.264
2008	Burlington (MWL)	LoA	4	4	2.70	19	18	0	0	90	83	38	27	7	25	104	.246
2009	Wilmington (CAR)	HiA	1	0	1.65	8	4	0	0	27	17	5	5	0	7	25	.173
	Frisco (TL)	AA	0	0	3.60	1	1	0	0	5	3	2	2	1	0	3	.158
MINOR LEAGUE TOTALS			6	10	3.80	50	40	0	0	206	210	105	87	16	66	198	.265

10 WILMER FONT, RHP

BORN: May 24, 1990. **B-T:** R-R. **HT.:** 6-4. **WT.:** 240. **SIGNED:** Venezuela, 2006. **SIGNED BY:** Manny Batista/Andres Espinosa.

After his solid U.S. debut in 2007, Font was limited to four innings by shoulder soreness and knee tendinitis in 2008. The Rangers closely monitored his workload last year—he pitched more than five innings just once in 29 outings—and he stayed healthy all season, making one of the biggest jumps in the system. The hulking Font always has had an explosive fastball and has touched 100 mph in the past, but he focused on improving his command of the pitch last year and worked mostly at 93-98 mph. His fastball has heavy life to go with its velocity. His changeup made considerable strides in 2009 and rates as an average pitch at times, with a chance to be plus in the future. He also matured considerably last year, demonstrating a better understanding of the importance of between-starts routines and workouts. Font has long struggled to harness his mechanics, and though he's making progress, he still must do a better job repeating his delivery. The Rangers are trying to keep him online and going downhill instead of spinning off too quickly and leaving his arm dragging behind. They hope his secondary stuff will improve as his mechanics do. He's still trying to improve his feel for his breaking ball, which is currently a hard curve but could wind up as a slider. Font has a chance to start because he can maintain his plus-plus fastball velocity deep into games, but he could wind up in the bullpen because of his questionable command and secondary stuff. He'll continue working as a starter at high Class A Bakersfield for now, but he also has upside as a closer.

Year	Club (League)	Class	W	L	ERA	G	GS	CG	SV	IP	H	R	ER	HR	BB	SO	AVG
2007	Rangers (AZL)	R	2	3	4.53	14	10	0	0	46	41	33	23	2	24	61	.238
2008	Rangers (AZL)	R	1	0	10.38	3	0	0	0	4	1	5	5	1	1	6	.071
2009	Hickory (SAL)	LoA	8	3	3.49	29	24	0	0	108	93	51	42	4	59	105	.231
MINOR LEAGUE TOTALS			11	6	3.98	46	34	0	0	158	135	89	70	7	84	172	.229

11 MAX RAMIREZ, C

BORN: Oct. 11, 1984. **B-T:** R-R. **HT.:** 5-11. **WT.:** 175. **SIGNED:** Venezuela, 2002. **SIGNED BY:** Rolando Petit (Braves).

Ramirez, who was traded from Atlanta to Cleveland for Bob Wickman in 2006 and shipped to Texas for Kenny Lofton in 2007, almost got dealt for the third time in December. The Rangers and Red Sox reached an agreement to swap Ramirez for Mike Lowell, but Texas cancelled the deal after discovering Lowell needed surgery on his right thumb. Against the Rangers' wishes, Ramirez opened 2009 by playing for Venezuela in the World Baseball Classic, where he got little playing time. His season was hampered by tendinitis in his left wrist and soreness in his right wrist. When completely healthy, Ramirez is a plus hitter who works the count and drives the ball to all fields. He has shown some of his above-average power potential in the Venezuela League over the last two winters, but he's still working to unlock his power. He has a big leg kick and a lot of hand movement in his setup, which can hinder his timing. He tended to be late on fastballs and out in front of breaking balls in 2009. He's a below-average defensive catcher with below-average arm strength. Though he's a fairly accurate thrower, he erased just 23 percent of basestealers last season. He's a well below-average runner. Texas wants Ramirez to take his defense more seriously and work harder on staying in shape. He has a chance to be an offensive catcher/first baseman/DH and his bat is ready for a big league role in 2010, though he may not get that opportunity with the Rangers.

Year	Club (League)	Class	AVG	G	AB	R	H	2B	3B	HR	RBI	BB	SO	SB	OBP	SLG
2003	Braves2 (DSL)	R	.305	52	177	27	54	16	1	5	43	20	27	5	.386	.492
2004	Braves (GCL)	R	.275	57	204	20	56	16	1	8	35	19	50	1	.339	.480
2005	Danville (APP)	R	.347	63	239	45	83	19	0	8	47	31	41	1	.424	.527
2006	Rome (SAL)	LoA	.285	80	267	50	76	17	0	9	37	54	72	2	.408	.449
	Lake County (SAL)	LoA	.307	37	127	19	39	6	1	4	26	30	27	0	.435	.465
2007	Kinston (CAR)	HiA	.303	77	277	46	84	20	0	12	62	53	63	1	.418	.505
	Bakersfield (CAL)	HiA	.307	32	114	16	35	10	0	4	20	21	39	1	.420	.500
2008	Frisco (TL)	AA	.354	69	243	49	86	16	2	17	50	37	56	2	.450	.646
	Rangers (AZL)	R	.800	2	5	4	4	2	0	0	1	2	0	0	.857	1.200
	Oklahoma (PCL)	AAA	.243	10	37	5	9	1	0	2	6	3	13	0	.293	.432
	Texas (AL)	MAJ	.217	17	46	8	10	1	0	2	9	6	15	0	.345	.370
2009	Rangers (AZL)	R	.154	4	13	1	2	2	0	0	2	1	8	0	.214	.308
	Oklahoma City (PCL)	AAA	.234	76	274	29	64	13	0	5	43	35	85	1	.323	.336
MAJOR LEAGUE TOTALS			.217	17	46	8	10	1	0	2	9	6	15	0	.345	.370
MINOR LEAGUE TOTALS			.299	559	1977	311	592	138	5	74	372	306	481	14	.397	.487

12 JOE WIELAND, RHP

BORN: Jan. 21, 1990. **B-T:** R-R. **HT.:** 6-3. **WT.:** 175. **DRAFTED:** HS—Reno, Nev., 2008 (4th round). **SIGNED BY:** Butch Metzger.

The athletic Wieland committed to San Diego State as a two-way player but chose instead to sign with the

Rangers for $263,000 as a fourth-round pick in 2008. He opened his first full pro season throwing once a week in extended spring training so the Rangers could keep his innings down—an approach they also used with Kasey Kiker two years earlier. He reported to low Class A in late May, getting off to a strong start before tiring down the stretch. At his best, Wieland pitches with a 91-93 mph fastball with boring life, but his velocity dipped to 87-91 over the course of the season. He's projectable and should add velocity as he gets stronger. His sharp over-hand curveball is a power pitch at 82-83 mph, giving him two above-average offerings at times. Wieland worked hard in extended spring to develop his changeup, and the pitch has become much more consistent. He also is improving his fastball location against lefties, as he has a tendency to open up in his delivery, causing his heater to run over the middle of the plate. As Wieland matures physically, his stamina should improve and he could develop into a workhorse with three average or better pitches. He's likely to return to Hickory to start 2010, with a midseason promotion to high Class A likely.

Year	Club (League)	Class	W	L	ERA	G	GS	CG	SV	IP	H	R	ER	HR	BB	SO	AVG
2008	Rangers (AZL)	R	5	1	1.44	13	7	0	0	44	32	8	7	2	8	41	.200
2009	Hickory (SAL)	LoA	4	6	5.31	19	18	0	0	83	102	67	49	7	24	73	.299
MINOR LEAGUE TOTALS			9	7	3.98	32	25	0	0	127	134	75	56	9	32	114	.267

13 LUIS SARDINAS, SS

BORN: May 16, 1993. **B-T:** B-R. **HT.:** 6-0. **WT.:** 150. **SIGNED:** Venezuela, 2009. **SIGNED BY:** Mike Daly/Rafic Saab/Pedro Avila.

The Rangers believe Jurickson Profar and Sardinas are two of the best shortstop prospects that have appeared on the international market in the last five years, and they signed both for seven-figure bonuses in 2009. Sardinas showed a propensity for hitting better in games than in batting practice as an amateur, and he appeared in the Perfect Game National Showcase in Minneapolis in mid-June before signing with Texas for $1.2 million. Sardinas is a true shortstop with a wiry, athletic frame that evokes that of former all-star Tony Fernandez. He has smooth infield actions, sure hands, excellent range and above-average arm strength at shortstop. He projects as an above-average defender as he gains experience. Sardinas ran a 6.83-second 60-yard dash at the Perfect Game showcase and has been clocked as low as 6.6 seconds, making him an above-average runner. Offensively, he has a loose, wristy swing and a slap approach from both sides of the plate. He has decent plate discipline for his age and has shown an ability to work the count and take walks. He has started to gain weight and strength since signing, and the Rangers envision him as a solid line-drive hitter in time. He'll always have below-average power, however. Sardinas will start 2010 in extended spring training before making his pro debut in the Rookie-level Arizona League. He has a chance to be a slick-fielding everyday shortstop with speed and the ability to get on base.

Year	Club (League)	Class	AVG	G	AB	R	H	2B	3B	HR	RBI	BB	SO	SB	OBP	SLG
2009	Did Not Play—Signed 2010 Contract															

14 ENGEL BELTRE, OF

BORN: Nov. 1, 1989. **B-T:** L-L. **HT.:** 6-1. **WT.:** 169. **SIGNED:** Dominican Republic, 2006. **SIGNED BY:** Pablo Lantigua (Red Sox).

The Red Sox signed Beltre for $600,000 in 2006 and traded him to Texas along with Kason Gabbard and David Murphy for Eric Gagne at the 2007 trade deadline. Beltre led the Midwest League in runs (87) and hits (160) in 2008, but he hit .227/.281/.317 as a 19-year-old in high Class A last year. He's a premium athlete with the most exciting all-around tools package in the system, but his bat is a question mark. Beltre has yet to unlock the raw power potential in his wiry frame, partly because he's a free swinger who struggles to make consistent contact. The Rangers instructed him to focus on seeing more pitches in 2009, and the adjustment seemed to help, but every time he experienced success he would revert to hacking away early in counts. Beltre's above-average speed makes him a basestealing threat and translates into good range in center field, where he plays shallow and has the ability to track down balls over his head. He has a strong, accurate arm and good instincts, and he could be an elite defender as he matures. Beltre is a high-energy player who wants to be great, and he needs to do a better job slowing the game down. Still, he has progressed further than most players his age and has plenty of time to develop into the five-tool star he shows glimpses of now and then. Beltre will return to Bakersfield to start 2010.

Year	Club (League)	Class	AVG	G	AB	R	H	2B	3B	HR	RBI	BB	SO	SB	OBP	SLG
2007	Red Sox (GCL)	R	.208	34	125	20	26	3	3	5	13	12	44	6	.310	.400
	Rangers (AZL)	R	.310	22	84	19	26	3	4	4	15	8	21	3	.388	.583
	Spokane (NWL)	SS	.211	9	38	3	8	0	0	0	1	2	10	2	.250	.211
2008	Clinton (MWL)	LoA	.283	130	566	87	160	26	9	8	47	15	105	31	.308	.403
2009	Bakersfield (CAL)	HiA	.227	84	357	44	81	13	5	3	23	17	77	17	.281	.317
	Rangers (AZL)	R	.300	3	10	4	3	1	1	0	0	0	3	2	.364	.600
	Frisco (TL)	AA	.071	4	14	1	1	1	0	0	1	0	2	1	.133	.143
MINOR LEAGUE TOTALS			.255	286	1194	178	305	47	22	20	100	54	262	62	.303	.382

15 LEURY GARCIA, SS

BORN: March 18, 1991. **B-T:** B-R. **HT.:** 5-7. **WT.:** 153. **SIGNED:** Dominican Republic, 2007. **SIGNED BY:** Jesus Ovalle.

Garcia made his debut in 2008 as one of the youngest players in the Arizona League. The Rangers planned to start him at short-season Spokane last year but wound up jumping him to low Class A to fill a hole. As an 18-year-old facing much older competition, he held his own for a month and a half before batting .215 in the second half. Garcia is short but his raw tools are loud, earning him the nickname "Furcalito" (little Furcal) from teammates in 2008. He can be spectacular at shortstop, as his lightning-quick first step leads to exceptional range. His athleticism helps him make acrobatic plays from deep in the hole or up the middle. He has plus-plus arm strength, though he must be more consistent with his throws, especially on routine plays. He made 42 errors last year, and the Rangers estimate that about two-thirds were throwing miscues. Garcia has well above-average speed and good instincts on the basepaths. He's a switch-hitter who fares similarly against righties and lefties. Garcia is a spray hitter with well below-average power, though the Rangers say he will be strong enough as he matures to hit the ball into the gaps and keep defenses honest. He could become a serviceable bottom-of-the-order hitter if he can learn the strike zone better, and that would be enough to make him an everyday player thanks to his defensive wizardry and speed. Garcia is likely to repeat low Class A in 2010, though he could earn a promotion if he shows progress.

Year	Club (League)	Class	AVG	G	AB	R	H	2B	3B	HR	RBI	BB	SO	SB	OBP	SLG
2008	Rangers (AZL)	R	.209	41	129	17	27	3	3	0	14	8	40	12	.250	.279
2009	Hickory (SAL)	LoA	.232	83	276	28	64	6	3	1	18	18	64	19	.288	.286
MINOR LEAGUE TOTALS			.225	124	405	45	91	9	6	1	32	26	104	31	.276	.284

16 MICHAEL KIRKMAN, LHP

BORN: Sept. 18, 1986. **B-T:** L-L. **HT.:** 6-4. **WT.:** 195. **DRAFTED:** HS—Lake City, Fla., 2005 (5th round). **SIGNED BY:** Guy DeMutis.

Baseball America rated Kirkman as the No. 3 prep pitching prospect in Florida for the 2005 draft, behind Marlins first-rounder Chris Volstad and Cardinals sandwich-rounder Tyler Herron, but his career has taken twists and turns since then. After a strong pro debut, Kirkman pulled his hamstring early in 2006, and it took him two years to get his mechanics back together. He lost the ability to throw strikes and saw his velocity drop into the low 80s. He showed dramatically improved mechanics, command and stuff in 2008, then truly re-established himself as a prospect last season, dominating the hitter-friendly California League and holding his own after a promotion to Double-A. He posted a 2.51 ERA over his last seven starts at Frisco, capped by seven scoreless innings of two-hit ball in his last outing. Kirkman's quality four-pitch repertoire is highlighted by a 90-94 mph fastball. He has the ability to throw strikes with a solid-average slider, an average change and a promising overhand curveball that he rediscovered last season. Kirkman's big, durable frame, solid delivery and repertoire remind some Rangers officials of Jeremy Affeldt. He's still refining his feel for pitching and must prove that he's mentally tough enough to handle pressure situations, but he has all the ingredients to become a workhorse starter or a quality big league reliever, perhaps by 2011. Added to the 40-man roster in November, he's slated to start this season back in the Frisco rotation.

Year	Club (League)	Class	W	L	ERA	G	GS	CG	SV	IP	H	R	ER	HR	BB	SO	AVG
2005	Rangers (AZL)	R	3	1	3.44	14	9	0	0	52	51	28	20	0	19	58	.249
2006	Clinton (MWL)	LoA	0	3	6.98	6	6	0	0	19	23	17	15	0	24	22	.303
	Rangers (AZL)	R	1	2	13.20	8	4	0	0	15	21	27	22	0	27	8	.333
2007	Spokane (NWL)	SS	1	4	7.00	9	6	0	0	27	33	30	21	2	25	24	.306
	Clinton (MWL)	LoA	0	1	7.43	5	2	0	0	13	17	12	11	1	12	12	.304
2008	Spokane (NWL)	SS	1	1	0.00	2	2	0	0	10	7	4	0	0	2	9	.184
	Clinton (MWL)	LoA	4	3	4.36	15	14	0	0	74	78	43	36	8	23	58	.269
2009	Bakersfield (CAL)	HiA	4	1	2.06	8	7	0	0	48	43	16	11	1	18	54	.244
	Frisco (TL)	AA	5	7	4.19	18	18	0	0	97	93	54	45	9	43	64	.254
MINOR LEAGUE TOTALS			19	23	4.58	85	68	0	0	356	366	231	181	21	193	309	.266

17 BLAKE BEAVAN, RHP

BORN: Jan. 17, 1989. **B-T:** R-R. **HT.:** 6-7. **WT.:** 250. **DRAFTED:** HS—Irving, Texas, 2007 (1st round). **SIGNED BY:** Jay Eddings.

Pitching just once a week in high school, Beavan routinely ran his fastball up to 95-96 mph, helping him capture Baseball America's 2006 Youth Player of the Year award as he anchored the U.S. junior national team's pitching staff. But after signing for $1,497,500 as the 17th overall pick in the 2007 draft, his velocity was down to 89-91 for much of his pro debut in 2008. He learned how to succeed without his best stuff and ranked fourth in the Midwest League with a 2.37 ERA. He regained a bit of his velocity last year, touching 93 while pitching his way to Frisco, which is 30 miles from his hometown of Irving, Texas. Beavan has a mammoth, durable frame and a tenacious demeanor to match. He pounds the bottom of the strike zone without fear of contact. His four-seam fastball has good run, and he mixes in a two-seamer with decent sink. He has developed an average changeup, but his slider lacks depth and lateness, making it a fringy offering at best. The Rangers still hope Beavan will throw harder, and even if he doesn't he can be a strike-throwing innings-eater at the back of a big league rotation. He is scheduled to open 2010 in Double-A.

Year	Club (League)	Class	W	L	ERA	G	GS	CG	SV	IP	H	R	ER	HR	BB	SO	AVG
2008	Clinton (MWL)	LoA	10	6	2.37	23	23	0	0	122	105	42	32	12	20	73	.234
2009	Bakersfield (CAL)	HiA	5	4	4.30	12	12	1	0	73	75	44	35	6	16	51	.264
	Frisco (TL)	AA	4	4	4.01	15	15	0	0	90	113	47	40	4	13	34	.309
MINOR LEAGUE TOTALS			19	14	3.38	50	50	1	0	285	293	133	107	22	49	158	.267

18 TOMMY MENDONCA, 3B

BORN: April 12, 1988. **B-T:** L-R. **HT.:** 6-1. **WT.:** 200. **DRAFTED:** Fresno State, 2009 (2nd round). **SIGNED BY:** Butch Metzger.

Mendonca's dazzling glovework and record-tying four home runs earned him Most Outstanding Player honors at the 2008 College World Series as a sophomore, as he led longshot Fresno State to the national title. He finished that year with 19 home runs, though he also set a Division I record with 99 strikeouts, illustrating his feast-or-famine approach. Mendonca slugged 27 home runs as a junior in 2009 and cut his strikeouts to 64, albeit in 15 fewer games. He signed for a $587,700 bonus after Texas drafted him in the second round, giving him time to make adjustments in his pro debut at Spokane. Scouts questioned Mendonca's bat in college because he would over-rotate his upper half, bury his hands and bar his front arm, giving him a long path to the ball and making him vulnerable to pitches above the knees. He was hitting just .200 after 15 games at Spokane before he started working with Rangers coaches to revamp his hitting mechanics. He made progress with shortening his swing and improving his timing, and he finished with an .898 OPS at Spokane. Mendonca's power projects as above average, so he could be a solid offensive player even if he's a below-average hitter. He's an aggressive hitter who must become more patient. Defensively, he has excellent hands and instincts at third base, and he excels at coming in on slow rollers. He'll be a plus defender with a plus arm if he can improve his lateral range and agility by getting in better shape. He's a below-average runner. Mendonca is a down-and-dirty baseball rat who works hard at his craft. The Rangers envision him as a solid everyday third baseman in the Graig Nettles mold. He'll likely open 2010 in low Class A but figures to finish the season in Bakersfield, where he spent 11 games at the end of his pro debut.

Year	Club (League)	Class	AVG	G	AB	R	H	2B	3B	HR	RBI	BB	SO	SB	OBP	SLG
2009	Spokane (NWL)	SS	.309	49	188	33	58	12	2	9	26	9	66	0	.361	.537
	Bakersfield (CAL)	HiA	.209	11	43	5	9	3	0	0	2	1	12	1	.261	.279
MINOR LEAGUE TOTALS			.290	60	231	38	67	15	2	9	28	10	78	1	.343	.489

19 GUILLERMO MOSCOSO, RHP

BORN: Nov. 14, 1983. **B-T:** R-R. **HT.:** 6-1 **WT.:** 165. **SIGNED:** Venezuela, 2003. **SIGNED BY:** Ramon Peña (Tigers).

Moscoso's path through the minor leagues has been interrupted twice by shoulder issues. He had shoulder surgery in 2005 and missed the first six weeks in 2008 with soreness. He has shown flashes of brilliance when healthy, including a perfect game in 2007 at short-season Oneonta. The Rangers got him from the Tigers when they traded catcher Gerald Laird in December 2008, and Moscoso had a strong first season in his new organization, excelling in Triple-A as a starter and reaching the majors in a relief role. His best asset is his ability to pound the bottom of the strike zone with a low-90s fastball. He throws across his body a bit, giving him deception and adding to the excellent late life on his heater. His No. 2 pitch is an average changeup, but his slurvy breaking ball is fringe-average at best. He needs to tighten it and learn to throw it harder. At 26, Moscoso is ready for a big league role, either as a back-of-the-rotation starter, a long reliever or a swingman. His lively fastball and aggressive, confident mentality might be all he needs to carve out a living in a big league bullpen, but he must hone his secondary stuff if he wants to be a starter.

Year	Club (League)	Class	W	L	ERA	G	GS	CG	SV	IP	H	R	ER	HR	BB	SO	AVG
2003	Tigers (DSL)	R	2	0	1.85	12	2	0	1	39	29	9	8	2	7	44	.200
2004	Tigers (DSL)	R	6	3	1.90	15	11	3	2	90	58	23	19	2	16	102	.181
2005	Oneonta (NYP)	SS	2	2	4.37	11	10	0	0	47	49	27	23	4	11	44	.261
2006	Tigers (GCL)	R	3	2	2.50	13	3	0	0	36	37	14	10	3	8	33	.264
2007	Lakeland (FSL)	HiA	0	0	0.00	1	1	0	0	3	2	0	0	0	1	4	.182
	West Michigan (MWL)	LoA	0	0	1.13	1	1	0	0	8	5	1	1	1	0	7	.185
	Oneonta (NYP)	SS	8	2	2.37	14	14	2	0	80	75	25	21	3	15	68	.248
2008	Lakeland (FSL)	HiA	2	3	2.42	15	6	0	1	52	36	16	14	4	13	72	.196
	Erie (EL)	AA	3	1	3.12	6	6	0	0	35	24	17	12	4	8	50	.190
2009	Frisco (TL)	AA	3	1	4.46	9	7	0	0	42	41	23	21	1	14	36	.246
	Oklahoma City (PCL)	AAA	5	4	2.31	12	11	0	0	70	56	20	18	2	15	60	.218
	Texas (AL)	MAJ	0	0	3.21	10	0	0	0	14	15	7	5	1	6	12	.268
MAJOR LEAGUE TOTALS			0	0	3.21	10	0	0	0	14	15	7	5	1	6	12	.268
MINOR LEAGUE TOTALS			34	18	2.64	109	72	5	4	502	412	175	147	26	108	520	.221

TEXAS RANGERS

20 OMAR POVEDA, RHP

BORN: Sept. 28, 1987. **B-T:** R-R. **HT.:** 6-4. **WT.:** 215. **SIGNED:** Venezuela, 2004. **SIGNED BY:** Andres Espinosa/Manny Batista.

Poveda has climbed steadily through the system since signing in 2004. He missed time with a shoulder injury in 2008 and with a hand injury last year, but he held his own as a 21-year-old in Double-A. Poveda isn't a glamorous prospect, but he has a quality three-pitch repertoire, good command, a clean delivery and a strong, durable frame. His fastball sits at 88-92 mph and touches 93. He pitches with a good downward angle and has integrated a solid two-seamer with a bit more movement into his arsenal. His best pitch has long been his changeup, an above-average offering that he throws in any count against lefties or righties. He has also developed an average downer curveball. Poveda doesn't overpower hitters, but he throws strikes and gives his defense a chance. The Rangers would like to see him do a better job pitching out of trouble in the middle innings. He'll advance to Triple-A in 2010 and could earn some spot starts in the big leagues. He profiles as a back-of-the-rotation starter.

Year	Club (League)	Class	W	L	ERA	G	GS	CG	SV	IP	H	R	ER	HR	BB	SO	AVG
2005	Rangers (AZL)	R	2	6	5.71	14	9	0	0	52	64	38	33	1	12	56	.305
2006	Frisco (TL)	AA	0	1	1.80	1	1	0	0	5	4	2	1	0	5	1	.222
	Clinton (MWL)	LoA	4	13	4.88	26	26	0	0	149	167	92	81	12	37	133	.286
2007	Clinton (MWL)	LoA	11	4	2.79	21	21	0	0	126	94	44	39	10	32	120	.208
	Bakersfield (CAL)	HiA	1	2	5.14	5	5	0	0	28	27	18	16	4	13	33	.250
2008	Bakersfield (CAL)	HiA	4	4	4.47	17	17	0	0	91	82	56	45	10	40	97	.241
2009	Oklahoma City (PCL)	AAA	0	1	5.14	1	1	0	0	7	5	4	4	0	4	3	.208
	Rangers (AZL)	R	0	0	0.00	1	1	0	0	3	2	0	0	0	0	2	.182
	Frisco (TL)	AA	11	5	4.14	22	22	2	0	130	133	73	60	11	48	73	.263
MINOR LEAGUE TOTALS			33	36	4.25	108	103	2	0	591	578	327	279	48	191	518	.257

21 MICHAEL MAIN, RHP

BORN: Dec. 14, 1988. **B-T:** R-R. **HT.:** 6-2. **WT.:** 170. **DRAFTED:** HS—Deland, Fla., 2007 (1st round). **SIGNED BY:** Guy DeMutis.

Rated as the top 15-year-old player in the nation in 2004 by Baseball America, Main has established a reputation as an instructional league superstar who can't stay healthy during the season. Even before he was drafted, Main missed most of his junior year of high school with a rotator-cuff injury. He signed for $1,237,500 as the 24th overall pick in the 2007 draft, and a cracked rib derailed his first full pro season in 2008. He missed two months last year with mononucleosis that resulted in significant weight loss. He returned to Bakersfield in September and regained his weight by instructional league, when he showed a 92-94 mph fastball. In the past he has touched 96-97 mph and flashed a plus curveball and average changeup, but his breaking ball hasn't developed as hoped. It has morphed into more of a slider, and his command of it is inconsistent. Main has struggled to throw quality strikes with all his pitches, and he too frequently works from behind in the count. He's still a premium athlete with a quick arm and good makeup, but he needs to get stronger and stay healthy for a full season. He'll return to high Class A as a 21-year-old in 2010, and the Rangers hope he pitches his way to Frisco during the season.

Year	Club (League)	Class	W	L	ERA	G	GS	CG	SV	IP	H	R	ER	HR	BB	SO	AVG
2007	Rangers (AZL)	R	0	1	1.42	5	5	0	0	13	9	2	2	1	6	16	.196
	Spokane (NWL)	SS	2	0	4.70	5	5	0	0	15	14	11	8	1	7	18	.237
2008	Rangers (AZL)	R	1	1	3.38	3	3	0	0	13	9	8	5	1	5	15	.188
	Clinton (MWL)	LoA	2	2	2.58	10	10	0	0	45	38	16	13	4	13	50	.228
2009	Rangers (AZL)	R	0	0	0.00	2	2	0	0	3	3	0	0	0	0	5	.231
	Bakersfield (CAL)	HiA	4	6	6.83	14	12	0	0	58	72	48	44	9	37	49	.313
MINOR LEAGUE TOTALS			9	10	4.39	39	37	0	0	148	145	85	72	16	68	153	.258

22 MIGUEL VELAZQUEZ, OF

BORN: May 15, 1988. **B-T:** R-R. **HT.:** 6-2. **WT.:** 205. **DRAFTED:** HS—San Juan, P.R., 2006 (19th round). **SIGNED BY:** Frankie Thon.

Velazquez was projected as a top-three-rounds pick out of high school in Puerto Rico, but his stock plummeted when he was involved in a shooting with his brother in March 2006. Velazquez has told reporters that he was with his brother when his brother shot and seriously injured their neighbor, who they say was trying to kill their sister. The Rangers looked into the case and decided to take Velazquez in the 19th round that June, signing him for $72,000. He made a strong pro debut in 2007 but missed all of 2008 because of a parole violation that required him to spend time in a juvenile detention center. He returned to action last summer and picked up where he left off, showing true five-tool potential. Texas compares him to Nelson Cruz for his plus power potential, plus arm and average speed. Velazquez has a quick bat that produces hard line drives to all fields, and he could be an average or better hitter if he improves against breaking balls and refines his setup. The Rangers are working with Velazquez to lower his hands and quiet down his big leg kick. He also must improve his jumps on the bases and in right field. He has matured off the field, but he's still learning to be a good teammate. Velazquez will advance to low Class A in 2010.

Year	Club (League)	Class	AVG	G	AB	R	H	2B	3B	HR	RBI	BB	SO	SB	OBP	SLG
2007	Rangers (AZL)	R	.330	24	94	18	31	5	2	2	21	7	27	7	.381	.489
2008	Did Not Play—Suspended															
2009	Rangers (AZL)	R	.294	9	34	7	10	0	2	1	6	4	11	1	.385	.500
	Spokane (NWL)	SS	.297	54	209	33	62	12	2	10	40	19	43	9	.359	.517
MINOR LEAGUE TOTALS			.306	87	337	58	103	17	6	13	67	30	81	17	.368	.507

23 PEDRO STROP, RHP

BORN: June 13, 1985. **B-T:** R-R. **HT.:** 6-0. **WT.:** 160. **SIGNED:** Dominican Republic, 2002. **SIGNED BY:** Rolando Fernandez/Felix Feliz (Rockies).

Strop originally signed with the Rockies as a shortstop, but they moved him to the mound after he hit just .212 with 231 strikeouts in 221 games over four pro seasons. He averaged 12.3 strikeouts per nine innings in his first full year as a pitcher at high Class A Modesto in 2007, though his season was cut short by elbow tendinitis. His violent delivery puts stress on his arm, and he was limited to just seven innings in 2008 because of a stress fracture in his elbow. The Rockies designated him for assignment that fall, and the Rangers signed him to a minor league deal. He had a rough April in Triple-A last year, so Texas sent him down to Frisco to work on throwing more strikes. He improved each month and eventually earned a late-season cup of coffee in the majors, where four of his seven one-inning outings were perfect. Strop's three-pitch arsenal is explosive. His fastball sits at 94-96 mph and touches 98. He has developed an 87-mph splitter that can be unhittable when it's on, and he throws a power slider in the mid-80s. Strop is a gifted athlete who fields his position well. He still needs to fine-tune his command, and his mechanics make him an injury risk and make it more difficult for him to throw strikes, but his progress in 2009 was encouraging. He'll compete for a big league bullpen job this spring.

Year	Club (League)	Class	AVG	G	AB	R	H	2B	3B	HR	RBI	BB	SO	SB	OBP	SLG
2002	Rockies (DSL)	R	.227	60	194	28	44	9	3	0	20	12	32	6	.286	.304
2003	Casper (PIO)	R	.172	40	128	13	22	4	1	1	11	15	43	1	.284	.242
2004	Tri-City (NWL)	SS	.200	55	190	20	38	6	1	3	20	17	64	2	.286	.289
2005	Asheville (SAL)	LoA	.167	4	12	2	2	0	0	0	0	0	6	0	.167	.167
	Tri-City (NWL)	SS	.236	62	229	26	54	11	2	3	25	6	86	7	.261	.341
2007	Modesto (CAL)	HiA	.000	1	1	0	0	0	0	0	0	0	0	0	.000	.000
2008	Tulsa (TL)	AA	.000	8	1	1	0	0	0	0	0	0	1	0	.000	.000
MINOR LEAGUE TOTALS			.212	230	755	90	160	30	7	7	76	50	232	16	.276	.298

Year	Club (League)	Class	W	L	ERA	G	GS	CG	SV	IP	H	R	ER	HR	BB	SO	AVG
2006	Casper (PIO)	R	1	0	2.08	11	0	0	0	13	9	3	3	1	2	22	.188
	Asheville (SAL)	LoA	2	1	4.72	11	0	0	0	13	10	7	7	3	5	13	.213
2007	Modesto (CAL)	HiA	5	2	4.28	48	0	0	7	55	43	28	26	4	29	75	.215
2008	Tulsa (TL)	AA	0	0	2.57	7	0	0	3	7	6	2	2	0	4	7	.231
2009	Frisco (TL)	AA	5	5	4.38	36	0	0	4	51	48	28	25	1	29	48	.245
	Oklahoma City (PCL)	AAA	1	1	7.82	11	0	0	1	13	13	11	11	2	4	13	.271
	Texas (AL)	MAJ	0	0	7.71	7	0	0	0	7	6	6	6	0	4	9	.231
MAJOR LEAGUE TOTALS			0	0	7.71	7	0	0	0	7	6	6	6	0	4	9	.231
MINOR LEAGUE TOTALS			14	9	4.38	124	0	0	15	152	129	79	74	11	73	178	.228

24 NEIL RAMIREZ, RHP

BORN: May 25, 1989. **B-T:** R-R. **HT.:** 6-4. **WT.:** 190. **DRAFTED:** HS—Kempsville, Va., 2007 (1st round supplemental). **SIGNED BY:** Russ Ardolina.

The Rangers knew Ramirez would a long-term project when they signed him for $1 million as a sandwich pick in 2007, and they continue to stress patience as he slowly develops. He made his full-season debut at Hickory last June, getting his feet wet with four relief outings before sliding into a starting role. He settled in as the season progressed, peaking in August, when he posted a 2.86 ERA and a 28-13 K-BB ratio in 22 innings. Ramirez has a lightning-quick arm and the makings of an overpowering repertoire. He works at 92-96 mph with his fastball, and his overhand power curveball can be a swing-and-miss pitch at times. He's also making progress with his changeup, though it still has a long way to go. Ramirez did a much better job harnessing his emotions in 2009. But he still struggles from serious lapses in his command, often because he has trouble repeating his delivery and staying in rhythm. He tends to throw across his body and often fights to throw the ball to his glove side. Ramirez flashes frontline-starter stuff, but he's far from a safe bet to reach the majors. The Rangers might send him back to Hickory to work with pitching coach Brad Holman, who has earned praise for his patient approach with young pitchers like Martin Perez, Joe Wieland, Wilmer Font and Jake Brigham.

Year	Club (League)	Class	W	L	ERA	G	GS	CG	SV	IP	H	R	ER	HR	BB	SO	AVG
2008	Spokane (NWL)	SS	1	2	2.66	13	13	0	0	44	25	15	13	5	29	52	.166
2009	Hickory (SAL)	LoA	3	6	4.75	18	14	0	0	66	58	40	35	8	41	56	.235
MINOR LEAGUE TOTALS			4	8	3.92	31	27	0	0	110	83	55	48	13	70	108	.209

25 JAKE BRIGHAM, RHP

BORN: Feb. 10, 1988. **B-T:** R-R. **HT.:** 6-3. **WT.:** 210. **DRAFTED:** HS—Ococee, Fla., 2006 (6th round). **SIGNED BY:** Guy DeMutis.

Brigham looked like a potential top-two-rounds pick heading into his senior year of high school, but he took a big step backward in the spring, and the Rangers signed him for a $200,000 bonus as a sixth-round pick in 2006. His velocity jumped in instructional league in 2007, when he touched 97 mph in short stints, but he had Tommy John surgery that fall and missed all of 2008. He started throwing bullpen sessions again that August and spent the next four months working on calming down his delivery and using his lower half better. By the time he got to spring training last year, he was comfortable with his new delivery, and the Rangers used him in tandem starts with Martin Perez at Hickory. Brigham has serious arm strength, and he sat at 92-96 mph touched 97 in 2009. He also flashes a plus downer curveball, a power pitch in the low 80s. His command is inconsistent, and sometimes he takes his hand out of his glove too late, throwing off his timing. His nascent changeup has a long way to go, but he might not need it if he winds up in the bullpen, where some club officials believe his power two-pitch repertoire and attacking mentality would be a good fit. For now he'll continue to work as a starter, and Texas likely will send him back to low Class A to work on his control and learn how to win games.

Year	Club (League)	Class	W	L	ERA	G	GS	CG	SV	IP	H	R	ER	HR	BB	SO	AVG
2006	Rangers (AZL)	R	2	6	3.70	14	11	0	0	58	54	37	24	5	19	58	.236
2007	Spokane (NWL)	SS	5	4	3.16	15	15	0	0	77	69	43	27	9	34	65	.248
2009	Hickory (SAL)	LoA	2	11	5.52	25	17	0	1	90	104	70	55	10	38	81	.292
MINOR LEAGUE TOTALS			9	21	4.24	54	43	0	1	225	227	150	106	24	91	204	.263

26 TOMAS TELIS, C

BORN: June 18, 1991. **B-T:** B-R. **HT.:** 5-8. **WT.:** 175. **SIGNED:** Venezuela, 2007. **SIGNED BY:** Edgar Suarez.

Telis signed for $130,000 in July 2007, and the Rangers wasted no time converting him from shortstop to catcher because of his stocky build. He had a solid pro debut in the Rookie-level Dominican Summer League in 2008, winning the league's all-star game MVP award. He turned 18 just three days before making his U.S. debut in the Rookie-level Arizona League last June, and hit well enough against older competition to earn a late-season taste of Spokane. Telis is a pure line-drive hitter from both sides of the plate—he hit .313 against lefties and .325 against righties in the AZL. He makes consistent contact and has average raw power, though he has yet to tap into it in games. He has a chance to be an above-average hitter if he can learn to command the strike zone better. Telis is raw behind the plate, however. He has a fringe-average arm and a quick release, but he threw out just 19 percent of AZL basestealers last year. He must improve his footwork, receiving skills and transfer. He has below-average speed but isn't bad for a catcher. In time, Telis could be an offensive catcher with fringy defensive skills, which would make him a solid big league regular. He'll likely open 2010 at Spokane but could earn a promotion to low Class A at some point.

Year	Club (League)	Class	AVG	G	AB	R	H	2B	3B	HR	RBI	BB	SO	SB	OBP	SLG
2008	Rangers 1 (DSL)	R	.299	62	234	44	70	14	1	1	36	25	16	10	.374	.380
2009	Rangers (AZL)	R	.322	46	183	30	59	11	5	2	28	4	15	8	.333	.470
	Spokane (NWL)	SS	.400	7	20	4	8	1	0	2	2	0	4	0	.400	.750
MINOR LEAGUE TOTALS			.314	115	437	78	137	26	6	5	66	29	35	18	.358	.435

27 WILFREDO BOSCAN, RHP

BORN: Oct. 26, 1989. **B-T:** R-R. **HT.:** 6-2. **WT.:** 187. **SIGNED:** Venezuela, 2007. **SIGNED BY:** Manny Batista.

The Rangers signed Boscan for a bargain-basement $15,000 when he was a skinny 17-year-old with a low-80s fastball. His velocity jumped to 86-92 mph during his breakout 2008, and he followed up with a solid season as a 19-year-old in low Class A. Boscan pitched at 88-92 mph last year, and his loose, clean arm action suggests he could add another tick or two as he matures. He has started to fill out his wiry frame and improve his stamina. Boscan's best assets are his control and feel for pitching. He can attack hitters' weaknesses with two-seam and four-seam fastballs, an above-average changeup and a curveball that projects as an average pitch. He still struggles to throw his curve for strikes at times, but it did start to become more consistent at Hickory. Boscan is a younger, less physical version of Omar Poveda, and he projects similarly as a command-and-control starter at the back of a big league rotation. He's likely to start 2010 back in low Class A, with a promotion to Bakersfield likely by midseason.

Year	Club (League)	Class	W	L	ERA	G	GS	CG	SV	IP	H	R	ER	HR	BB	SO	AVG
2007	Rangers (DSL)	R	2	1	1.75	13	8	0	0	57	42	14	11	1	13	61	.210
2008	Spokane (NWL)	SS	9	1	3.12	15	12	0	0	69	66	30	24	4	11	70	.251
2009	Hickory (SAL)	LoA	6	8	3.59	23	21	0	0	105	105	57	42	7	19	59	.254
MINOR LEAGUE TOTALS			17	10	3.00	51	41	0	0	231	213	101	77	12	43	190	.243

28 CRAIG GENTRY, OF

BORN: Nov. 29, 1983. **B-T:** R-R. **HT.:** 6-2. **WT.:** 190. **DRAFTED:** Arkansas, 2006 (10th round). **SIGNED BY:** Jay Eddings.

After spending the first two years of his college career at Arkansas-Fort Smith JC, Gentry transferred to Arkansas. He wasn't drafted after his junior year, mostly because he had Tommy John surgery, but he worked his way back in time for his senior season and signed with the Rangers for $10,000 as a 10th-round pick in 2006. He put together a career season in Double-A last year to earn a September callup to Texas. Gentry's game is built around his speed, which rates as a 65 on the 20-80 scouting scale. He's an exceptional defensive center fielder thanks to his speed, jumps, routes and above-average arm. He also has good baserunning instincts, with 128 career stolen bases in 158 tries, and he was 49-for-55 in the minors last year. Offensively, Gentry does a good job working counts and making contact, and he's a good bunter. He has a bit of strength in his swing, too, but he has below-average power. Gentry's speed, defense and baserunning will make him a valuable extra outfielder in the big leagues, and he has an outside chance to be an everyday center fielder if his bat continues to improve. He figures to compete for a fourth outfielder job in spring training, but he'll likely start the season in Triple-A.

Year	Club (League)	Class	AVG	G	AB	R	H	2B	3B	HR	RBI	BB	SO	SB	OBP	SLG
2006	Spokane (NWL)	SS	.281	56	221	27	62	15	4	0	13	9	37	20	.350	.385
2007	Rangers (AZL)	R	.273	3	11	4	3	0	0	0	1	1	3	2	.385	.273
	Clinton (MWL)	LoA	.274	55	223	40	61	15	0	3	12	15	37	24	.335	.381
	Bakersfield (CAL)	HiA	.272	51	213	31	58	16	1	1	18	12	46	16	.325	.371
2008	Frisco (TL)	AA	.276	76	301	43	83	17	0	4	33	17	55	16	.333	.372
	Oklahoma (PCL)	AAA	.203	18	59	6	12	1	0	0	1	9	18	1	.309	.220
2009	Frisco (TL)	AA	.303	127	512	100	155	21	7	8	53	49	64	49	.378	.418
	Texas (AL)	MAJ	.118	11	17	4	2	1	0	0	1	2	5	0	.211	.176
MAJOR LEAGUE TOTALS			.118	11	17	4	2	1	0	0	1	2	5	0	.211	.176
MINOR LEAGUE TOTALS			.282	386	1540	251	434	85	12	16	131	112	260	128	.349	.384

29 ANDREW DOYLE, RHP

BORN: Nov. 12, 1987. **B-T:** R-R. **HT.:** 6-3. **WT.:** 200. **DRAFTED:** Oklahoma, 2009 (4th round). **SIGNED BY:** Jay Eddings.

After spending his freshman year at Oklahoma in the bullpen, Doyle spent the next two seasons in the weekend rotation, emerging as the staff ace by the end of his sophomore year. He went 17-8 in two seasons as a starter and climbed into the fourth round of the draft, signing for $234,000. He cruised through the Northwest League in a relief role in his pro debut, but fatigue took a toll on him after he was promoted to Hickory at the end of the season. A physical sinkerballer with an easy delivery, Doyle makes his living by pounding the bottom corners of the strike zone with an 89-91 mph two-seam fastball that features plus life. He can run his four-seamer up to 93-94 mph when he needs to, and he mixes in an average changeup with good sink. His slider was a below-average pitch that lacked depth in his pro debut, but he had some success using it to keep hitters off balance and induce groundouts in college. Though the Rangers used Doyle in relief during his debut like they did with Tommy Hunter in 2007, he profiles as an innings-eating starter like Hunter. He's likely to start 2010 in high Class A and could move quickly.

Year	Club (League)	Class	W	L	ERA	G	GS	CG	SV	IP	H	R	ER	HR	BB	SO	AVG
2009	Spokane (NWL)	SS	2	0	1.89	14	0	0	1	19	22	5	4	1	4	24	.282
	Hickory (SAL)	LoA	1	1	9.45	5	0	0	0	7	11	10	7	0	2	9	.367
MINOR LEAGUE TOTALS			3	1	3.86	19	0	0	1	26	33	15	11	1	6	33	.306

30 RICHARD ALVAREZ, RHP

BORN: Aug. 14, 1992. **B-T:** R-R. **HT.:** 6-2. **WT.:** 180. **SIGNED:** Venezuela, 2008. **SIGNED BY:** Rafic Saab/Manny Batista.

The Rangers say Alvarez's early development has followed the track of another precocious Venezuelan, Martin Perez. Like Perez, Alvarez showed below-average fastball velocity but a very advanced feel for pitching and a loose arm action when he signed with the Rangers in 2008. He spent most of his 2009 pro debut as a 16-year-old facing much older competition in the Arizona League, where he demonstrated impressive polish despite posting lackluster numbers. He pitched at 86-87 mph and topped out at 88, but Texas believes he'll add velocity as he matures, just as Perez did. Alvarez's three-pitch arsenal is highlighted by a plus changeup with good arm speed, deception and fade. He flashes an average curveball and does a good job mixing speeds and locations will all his stuff. For a young pitcher, he also does a good job fielding his position and controlling the running game. Alvarez has a clean arm action and a good delivery that he repeats well. He has already added 15-20 pounds since he first signed, and he could become an elite prospect if his stuff improves as he gets stronger. His command and feel for pitching could be enough to get him to the big leagues if he can develop just a fringe-average fastball.

Year	Club (League)	Class	W	L	ERA	G	GS	CG	SV	IP	H	R	ER	HR	BB	SO	AVG
2009	Rangers (AZL)	R	2	3	5.49	11	9	0	0	41	42	29	25	1	19	35	.268
MINOR LEAGUE TOTALS			2	3	5.49	11	9	0	0	41	42	29	25	1	19	35	.268

Toronto Blue Jays

BY NATHAN RODE

While Blue Jays fans spent much of the season wondering when or where Roy Halladay would get traded, 2009 actually marked the end of another long run in Toronto.

J.P. Ricciardi took over as general manager after the 2001 season and talked about taking down the Red Sox and Yankees. But the best he could muster was an 87-75 record and second-place finish in 2006—the only time the Blue Jays have finished better than third since winning the World Series in 1992-93. Toronto sank back below .500 in 2009, finishing 75-87 for the second-worst record of Ricciardi's tenure.

Toronto has been unable to build around one of baseball's best and most durable pitchers during his peak years. Ricciardi certainly tried, but his administration didn't develop enough premium talent. His drafts leaned heavily on low-ceiling college players, and his Jays didn't take a high school player in the first round until 2006 (outfielder Travis Snider). They returned to the college route in the first round the last two years, with their 2009 effort torpedoed by a failure to sign three of their first four picks.

Ricciardi's regime did provide building blocks such as Aaron Hill, Adam Lind and Ricky Romero, but it wasn't enough. He tried to fill holes with free agents, with some modest successes (A.J. Burnett, though he opted out of the last two seasons of his five-year, $55 million deal) and some expensive mistakes (B.J. Ryan, who was released last July with roughly $15 million remaining on a five-year, $47 million contract).

Ricciardi also overpaid to keep two of the organization's best development success stories in Toronto. He signed Vernon Wells to a seven-year, $126 million contract extension after the 2006 season, then locked up Alex Rios with a seven-year, $69.8 million deal in April 2008. Both players sank under the weight of those contracts, though the Jays were able to shed Rios' salary when the White Sox claimed him on waivers last summer.

Blue Jays interim president Paul Beeston fired Ricciardi on the last day of the season and tapped vice president of baseball operations Alex Anthopoulos to replace him. Beeston later decided to drop the "interim" from his title and assume control of the franchise again. Beeston was the Jays' first employee when the franchise was born in 1976.

In addition to replacing Ricciardi, the Jays also fired farm director Dick Scott and reassigned scouting director Jon Lalonde as a pro scout. Manager of minor

Roy Halladay's best wasn't good enough for the Blue Jays to win under J.P. Ricciardi

TOP 30 PROSPECTS

1. Zach Stewart, rhp	16. Ryan Schimpf, 2b
2. J.P. Arencibia, c	17. Tyler Pastornicky, ss
3. Chad Jenkins, rhp	18. Eric Thames, of
4. David Cooper, 1b	19. Tim Collins, lhp
5. Henderson Alvarez, rhp	20. Daniel Webb, rhp
6. Jake Marisnick, of	21. Johermyn Chavez, of
7. Josh Roenicke, rhp	22. Trystan Magnuson, rhp
8. Brad Mills, lhp	23. Brian Dopirak, 1b
9. Justin Jackson, ss	24. Ryan Goins, ss
10. Carlos Perez, c	25. Brad Emaus, 2b
11. Moises Sierra, of	26. Andrew Liebel, rhp
12. Kevin Ahrens, 3b	27. John Tolisano, 2b
13. K.C. Hobson, 1b	28. Kenny Wilson, of
14. Danny Farquhar, rhp	29. Gustavo Pierre, ss
15. Luis Perez, lhp	30. Rei Gonzalez, rhp

league operations Charlie Wilson was promoted to fill Scott's position, while assistant scouting director Andrew Tinnish moved up to take over for Lalonde.

Beeston and Anthopoulos seem intent on relying on player development to get the Jays out of mediocrity. In addition to a huge shuffle in the baseball department, Anthopoulos has nearly doubled the size of the team's scouting staff.

The Jays recognize that they need to sign and develop their own premium talent, particularly now that their corporate ownership has become more focused on the bottom line in recent years.

General Manager: Alex Anthopoulos. **Farm Director:** Charlie Wilson. **Scouting Director:** Andrew Tinnish.

Class	Team	League	W	L	PCT	Finish*	Manager(s)
Majors	Toronto Blue Jays	American	75	87	.463	t-10th (14)	Cito Gaston
Triple-A	Las Vegas 51s	Pacific Coast	71	73	.493	t-10th (16)	Mike Basso
Double-A	New Hampshire Fisher Cats	Eastern	64	78	.451	10th (12)	Gary Cathcart
High A	Dunedin Blue Jays	Florida State	67	67	.500	5th (12)	Omar Malave
Low A	Lansing Lugnuts	Midwest	54	84	.391	14th (14)	Clayton McCullough
Short-season	Auburn Doubledays	New York-Penn	26	49	.347	14th (14)	Dennis Holmberg
Rookie	GCL Blue Jays	Gulf Coast	30	28	.517	7th (16)	John Schneider
Overall 2009 Minor League Record			312	379	.452	28th (30)	

*Finish in overall standings (No. of teams in league). †League champion.

LAST YEAR'S TOP 30

Rank	Player, Pos.	Status
1.	Travis Snider, of	Majors
2.	J.P. Arencibia, c	No. 2
3.	Brett Cecil, lhp	Majors
4.	Justin Jackson, ss	No. 9
5.	David Cooper, 1b	No. 4
6.	Kevin Ahrens, 3b	No. 12
7.	Brad Mills, lhp	No. 8
8.	Ricky Romero, lhp	Majors
9.	Marc Rzepczynski, lhp	Majors
10.	Brad Emaus, 2b/3b	No. 25
11.	Scott Campbell, 2b	Dropped out
12.	Brian Jeroloman, c	Dropped out
13.	John Tolisano, 2b	No. 27
14.	Alan Farina, rhp	Dropped out
15.	Robert Ray, rhp	Dropped out
16.	Eric Eiland, of	Dropped out
17.	Luis Perez, lhp	No. 15
18.	Gustavo Pierre, ss	No. 29
19.	Mark Sobolewski, 3b	Dropped out
20.	Scott Richmond, rhp	Majors
21.	Kenny Wilson, of	No. 28
22.	Andrew Liebel, rhp	No. 20
23.	Tyler Pastornicky, ss	No. 17
24.	Danny Farquhar, rhp	No. 14
25.	Trystan Magnuson, rhp	No. 22
26.	Markus Brisker, of	Dropped out
27.	Curtis Thigpen, c/1b	(Athletics)
28.	Balbino Fuenmayor, 3b	Dropped out
29.	Henderson Alvarez, rhp	No. 5
30.	Tim Collins, lhp	No. 19

BEST TOOLS

Best Hitter for Average	David Cooper
Best Power Hitter	J.P. Arencibia
Best Strike-Zone Discipline	Brad Emaus
Fastest Baserunner	Kenny Wilson
Best Athlete	Jake Marisnick
Best Fastball	Zach Stewart
Best Curveball	Tim Collins
Best Slider	Chad Jenkins
Best Changeup	Henderson Alvarez
Best Control	Henderson Alvarez
Best Defensive Catcher	Brian Jeroloman
Best Defensive Infielder	Justin Jackson
Best Infield Arm	Kevin Ahrens
Best Defensive Outfielder	Kenny Wilson
Best Outfield Arm	Moises Sierra

PROJECTED 2013 LINEUP

Catcher	J.P. Arencibia
First Base	David Cooper
Second Base	Aaron Hill
Third Base	Kevin Ahrens
Shortstop	Justin Jackson
Left Field	Travis Snider
Center Field	Vernon Wells
Right Field	Jake Marisnick
Designated Hitter	Adam Lind
No. 1 Starter	Roy Halladay
No. 2 Starter	Chad Jenkins
No. 3 Starter	Ricky Romero
No. 4 Starter	Brett Cecil
No. 5 Starter	Marc Rzepczynski
Closer	Zach Stewart

TOP PROSPECTS OF THE DECADE

Year	Player, Pos.	2009 Org.
2000	Vernon Wells, of	Blue Jays
2001	Vernon Wells, of	Blue Jays
2002	Josh Phelps, c	Giants
2003	Dustin McGowan, rhp	Blue Jays
2004	Alex Rios, of	White Sox
2005	Brandon League, rhp	Blue Jays
2006	Dustin McGowan, rhp	Blue Jays
2007	Adam Lind, of	Blue Jays
2008	Travis Snider, of	Blue Jays
2009	Travis Snider, of	Blue Jays

TOP DRAFT PICKS OF THE DECADE

Year	Player, Pos.	2009 Org.
2000	Miguel Negron, of	White Sox
2001	Gabe Gross, of	Rays
2002	Russ Adams, ss	Padres
2003	Aaron Hill, ss	Blue Jays
2004	David Purcey, lhp	Blue Jays
2005	Ricky Romero, lhp	Blue Jays
2006	Travis Snider, of	Blue Jays
2007	Kevin Ahrens, 3b	Blue Jays
2008	David Cooper, 1b	Blue Jays
2009	Chad Jenkins, rhp	Blue Jays

LARGEST BONUSES IN CLUB HISTORY

Ricky Romero, 2005	$2,400,000
Felipe Lopez, 1998	$2,000,000
Gabe Gross, 2001	$1,865,000
Russ Adams, 2002	$1,785,000
Travis Snider, 2006	$1,700,000

TORONTO BLUE JAYS

TOP 2010 ROOKIE: Josh Roenicke, rhp. His power arm and competitive attitude could make him a closer one day.

BREAKOUT PROSPECT: Eric Thames, of. Injuries have marred his young career, but he was healthy enough in 2009 to give a glimpse of his hitting potential.

SLEEPER: Drew Hutchison, rhp. Signed for $400,000 as a 15th-rounder in August, he's a polished, athletic high school pitcher.

SOURCE OF TOP 30 TALENT			
Homegrown	27	Acquired	3
College	11	Trades	2
Junior college	2	Rule 5 draft	0
High school	7	Independent leagues	0
Draft-and-follow	0	Free agents/waivers	1
Nondrafted free agents	1		
International	6		

Numbers in parentheses indicate prospect rankings

LF
Eric Thames (18)
Johermyn Chavez (21)
Brian Van Kirk
Michael Crouse

CF
Jake Marisnick (6)
Kenny Wilson (28)
Darin Mastroianni
Markus Brisker
Eric Eiland

RF
Moises Sierra (11)

3B
Kevin Ahrens (12)
Mark Sobolewski
Balbino Fuenmayor

SS
Justin Jackson (9)
Tyler Pastornicky (17)
Gustavo Pierre (29)

2B
Ryan Schimpf (16)
Ryan Goins (24)
Brad Emaus (25)
John Tolisano (27)
Scott Campbell

1B
David Cooper (4)
K.C. Hobson (13)
Brian Dopirak (23)
Mike McDade

C
J.P. Arencibia (2)
Carlos Perez (10)
Brian Jeroloman
Sean Ochinko
A.J. Jimenez
Yan Gomes

RHP

Starters	Relievers
Zach Stewart (1)	Josh Roenicke (7)
Chad Jenkins (3)	Danny Farquhar (14)
Henderson Alvarez (5)	Trystan Magnuson (22)
Daniel Webb (20)	Dirk Hayhurst
Andrew Liebel (26)	Zeth Zinicola
Rei Gonzalez (30)	Bobby Bell
Drew Hutchison	Matt Daly
Robert Ray	Dustin Antolin
Chuck Huggins	Zach Dials
Ryan Tepera	Alan Farina
Joel Carreno	Brian Slover

LHP

Starters	Relievers
Brad Mills (8)	Tim Collins (19)
Luis Perez (15)	Frank Gailey
John Anderson	Aaron Loup
Carlos Pina	
Egan Smith	

DRAFT ANALYSIS

2009   BONUSES: $4.9 MILLION

BEST PURE HITTER: The Jays didn't draft a pure bat, but believe former Louisiana State teammates 2B Ryan Schimpf (5) and C/1B Sean Ochinko (11) have good swings and the strength to hit immediately. Both got off to good starts at short-season Auburn, with Ochinko batting .324 and Schimpf .287.

BEST POWER HITTER: 1B K.C. Hobson (6) signed for $500,000, and the Jays were paying for his plus raw power. He has an advanced idea at the plate and good hitting fundamentals.

FASTEST RUNNER: OF Jake Marisnick (3) has five-tool potential, though his bat is raw. He's a plus runner.

BEST DEFENSIVE PLAYER: SS Ryan Goins (4) lacks classic shortstop range, but his arm is plus and his instincts help him make plenty of plays. He has the hands and actions to stay at the position for now.

BEST FASTBALL: RHP Chad Jenkins (1) sits at 91-94 mph and can run his fastball up to 96, and he pounds the strike zone regularly. RHP Daniel Webb (18) has touched 96 since signing.

BEST SECONDARY PITCH: Jenkins' slider can be a plus power pitch when it's on, and Toronto has seen it scrape 87 mph. RHP Drew Hutchison (15) impressed the Jays with his changeup, which he throws with good arm speed and which features a little fade.

BEST PRO DEBUT: Ochinko ranked second in the New York-Penn League in batting. Fellow C Yan Gomes (10) led the NY-P with 44 RBIs and 23 doubles while batting .296/.363/.444. RHP Shawn Griffith (37) dominated as a college senior should in the Rookie-level Gulf Coast League, going 2-2, 0.66 with a 43-6 K-BB ratio in 27 innings.

BEST ATHLETE: Marisnick got a $1 million bonus, thanks to his power-speed combination and physicality that earns comparisons to Dale Murphy and Jeff Francoeur.

MOST INTRIGUING BACKGROUND: Hobson is the son of ex-Red Sox infielder and manager Butch. 1B Lance Durham's (14) father Leon and 2B Jonathan Fernandez's (34) dad Tony were big league all-stars, with the elder Fernandez one of the greatest players in franchise history. Unsigned RHP Brandon Kaye (45) is the half-brother of Jays starter Scott Richmond, while RHP Zach Outman's (29) brother Josh pitches for the Athletics.

CLOSEST TO THE MAJORS: Jenkins has the command and makeup to move very quickly.

BEST LATE-ROUND PICK: Recruited by Stetson as a two-way player, Hutchinson signed for $400,000 and reminds some Jays officials of Shawn Marcum,

who also was a shortstop/pitcher when Toronto drafted him. Webb had a poor year in junior college, but his raw ability made him one of the best high school righthanders available in the 2008 draft.

THE ONE WHO GOT AWAY: Toronto had an epic failure at the top of its draft, failing to sign its second, third and fourth picks in LHPs James Paxton (1s) and Jake Eliopoulos (2) and RHP Jake Barrett (3). Paxton returned to Kentucky, Eliopoulos went to Chipola (Fla.) JC and Barrett is attending Arizona State.

ASSESSMENT: There's a big hole at the top of this draft, a shame for an organization that has a strong track record for developing pitchers. The firing of GM J.P. Ricciardi pushed Jon Lalonde to a pro scouting position in October, making this his last Toronto draft.

2008   BONUSES: $4.4 MILLION

After a rousing pro debut, 1B David Cooper (1) came back to earth last season in Double-A. SS Tyler Pastornicky (5), OF Eric Thames (7) and RHP Danny Farquhar (10) are intriguing sleepers.

GRADE: C

2007   BONUSES: $6.6 MILLION

LHPs Brett Cecil (1s) and Mark Rzepcinski (5) already have staked out spots in Toronto's rotation, and LHP Brad Mills (4) has made two big league starts as well. All five of the hitters the Jays drafted in the first two rounds struggled in 2009, though C J.P. Arencibia (1) hit 21 homers and is the system's top position prospect.

GRADE: B

2006   BONUSES: $3.4 MILLION

OF Travis Snider (1) is the only pick with any promise from this draft, but at least it's considerable promise. Toronto gave up its second- and third-round choices as free-agent compensation.

GRADE: B

2005   BONUSES: $3.6 MILLION*

The Jays took LHP Ricky Romero (1) over Troy Tulowitzki, Andrew McCutchen and Jay Bruce with the No. 6 pick, but Romero redeemed himself last year after a slow start to his pro career. RHP Robert Ray (7) has pitched briefly in Toronto. The Jays failed to sign the best player they drafted, 1B Brett Wallace (42).

GRADE: C

*Draft analysis by John Manuel (2009) and Jim Callis (2005-08). Numbers in parentheses indicate draft rounds. *Bonuses for 2005 are first 10 rounds only.*

ZACH STEWART, RHP

Born: Sept. 28, 1986.
Height: 6-2. **Weight:** 205.
Bats: R. **Throws:** R.
Drafted: Texas Tech, 2008
(3rd round).
Signed by: Jerry Flowers
(Reds).

MIKE JANES

Zach Stewart's baseball career has taken several twists and turns. He made stops at Angelo State (Texas) and North Central Texas CC before transferring to Texas Tech for his junior season in 2008. The Red Raiders' pitching staff fell apart as the season wore on, and Stewart went from being their closer to their Friday-night starter. He generated some first-round buzz early in the spring, but his role changes caused his performance to suffer somewhat. The Reds drafted him in the third round, signed him for $450,000 and returned him to the bullpen for his pro debut. Though Stewart was electric as a reliever, Cincinnati moved him back to the rotation at the start of the 2009 season, in part to make him use his secondary pitches. He dominated hitters in high Class A and Double-A before the Reds shifted him to their Triple-A bullpen to keep his innings down. Soon thereafter, they traded him, Edwin Encarnacion and Josh Roenicke for Scott Rolen as the Blue Jays gladly shed some payroll. Toronto kept Stewart in relief in August, again in an attempt to manage his workload.

Stewart's bread and butter is his hard sinker, which sits at 92-94 mph and touches 95. He also offers a sharp 82-85 mph slider that generates more swings and misses than his fastball, which induces plenty of weak ground-outs. He has given up just three homers in 138 pro innings. After rarely using his changeup as a reliever, he developed more trust in the pitch last season. He also improved the life on his changeup, imparting more sink after it had cutting action in the past. A compact athlete with a strong build, Stewart has the durability to remain in the rotation if the Jays desire. He did a better job of maintaining the quality of his stuff as a starter last year than he had in college. He also has the makeup to handle the pressure of closing games. He throws strikes and stays on top of the ball well from a three-quarters arm slot.

Stewart must continue to refine his secondary pitches if he's going to be an effective big league starter. His slider can make hitters look silly but still needs more consistency, as does his changeup. His slider has the potential to go from average to plus, while his changeup has the makings of a solid-average pitch. He can get too competitive on the mound, resulting in him overthrowing and losing his ability to locate his pitches. His command isn't as advanced as his control.

In his first full pro season, Stewart wasn't fazed switching organizations and roles. Another change is in store for him in 2010, when he'll open the season in the Triple-A Las Vegas rotation. He should make his big league debut later in the year. The Blue Jays haven't determined their final plan for Stewart. If he gets the most out of his secondary pitches, he has the upside of a frontline starter. He also could be a force as a setup man or closer.

Year	Club (League)	Class	W	L	ERA	G	GS	CG	SV	IP	H	R	ER	HR	BB	SO	AVG
2008	Dayton (MWL)	LoA	1	2	0.55	11	0	0	3	16	10	2	1	0	3	13	.175
	Sarasota (FSL)	HiA	0	2	1.62	13	0	0	2	17	16	5	3	0	11	23	.262
2009	Sarasota (FSL)	HiA	1	1	2.13	7	7	1	0	42	47	17	10	1	8	32	.283
	Carolina (SL)	AA	3	0	1.46	7	7	0	0	37	29	7	6	1	10	31	.218
	Louisville (IL)	AAA	0	0	0.73	9	0	0	2	12	11	2	1	0	8	16	.234
	Las Vegas (PCL)	AAA	0	0	3.38	11	0	0	0	13	18	8	5	1	6	14	.327
MINOR LEAGUE TOTALS			5	5	1.70	58	14	1	7	138	131	41	26	3	46	129	.252

2 J.P. ARENCIBIA, C

BORN: Jan. 5, 1986. **B-T:** R-R. **HT.:** 6-0. **WT.:** 215. **DRAFTED:** Tennessee, 2007 (1st round). **SIGNED BY:** Matt Briggs.

The No. 2 college catching prospect behind Matt Wieters in 2007, Arencibia signed for $1,327,500 as the 21st overall pick. After struggling in his pro debut, in part because a pitch hit him on his left wrist, he has hit 27 and 21 homers in his two full seasons. Arencibia's ability to hit for power is his most attractive asset. He also has made strides behind the plate, boosting his overall value. He has a slightly above-average arm and has worked hard to shore up his once-shaky receiving skills. His game-calling has impoved as well. Scouts question how much Arencibia will hit in the major leagues because his swing is long and his bat speed is ordinary. His overly aggressive approach caught up to him in Triple-A. He still needs more polish defensively, as he threw out just 25 percent of basestealers and committed 14 passed balls in 2009. Like most catchers, he's a below-average runner. Even if he never hits for a high average, Areniciba could provide 20-25 homers on an annual basis and solid defense. With only John Buck, Raul Chavez and Ramon Castro standing in his way, he'll take over in Toronto as soon as he's ready. Arencibia will return to Las Vegas to begin 2010.

Year	Club (League)	Class	AVG	G	AB	R	H	2B	3B	HR	RBI	BB	SO	SB	OBP	SLG
2007	Auburn (NYP)	SS	.254	63	228	31	58	17	1	3	25	14	56	0	.309	.377
2008	Dunedin (FSL)	HiA	.315	59	248	38	78	22	0	13	62	11	46	0	.344	.560
	New Hampshire (EL)	AA	.282	67	262	32	74	14	0	14	43	7	55	0	.302	.496
2009	Las Vegas (PCL)	AAA	.236	116	466	67	110	32	1	21	75	26	114	0	.284	.444
MINOR LEAGUE TOTALS			.266	305	1204	168	320	85	2	51	205	58	271	0	.305	.467

3 CHAD JENKINS, RHP

BORN: Dec. 22, 1987. **B-T:** R-R. **HT.:** 6-4. **WT.:** 235. **DRAFTED:** Kennesaw State, 2009 (1st round). **SIGNED BY:** Matt Briggs.

As scouts flocked north of Atlanta to see Kennesaw State righthander Kyle Heckathorn last spring, they took notice of another weekend starter in Jenkins. He threw 41 consecutive scoreless innings and surpassed Heckathorn as a prospect, becoming the highest draft pick in school history when the Blue Jays selected him 20th overall. He signed late for $1.359 million and reported to instructional league. Jenkins draws comparisons to Joe Blanton because he's a physical workhorse, but he has better stuff. His fastball sits comfortably at 91-94 mph and touches 96, and its plus life allows him to pile up strikeouts and groundouts. With 83-84 mph velocity and late three-quarters tilt, his slider has the potential to be an above-average pitch. He maintains good arm speed on a changeup that has some fade. He commands all three of his pitches. Jenkins has toned up his body, but it's still soft and he'll have to maintain his conditioning. Both his slider and changeup need more work, but have the chance to improve by a full grade. He's still learning to incorporate his changeup more often after he didn't need it much in college. With his stuff, command and makeup, Jenkins should move quickly through the minors. His road to being a solid No. 3 starter should begin in high Class A Dunedin this season.

Year	Club (League)	Class	W	L	ERA	G	GS	CG	SV	IP	H	R	ER	HR	BB	SO	AVG
2009	Did Not Play—Signed Late																

4 DAVID COOPER, 1B

BORN: Feb. 12, 1987. **B-T:** L-L. **HT.:** 6-0. **WT.:** 200. **DRAFTED:** California, 2008 (1st round). **SIGNED BY:** Chris Becerra.

The first first-rounder from the 2008 draft to sign, Cooper agreed to a slightly below-slot $1.5 million bonus as the 17th overall pick. He hit .333/.399/.502 in his pro debut, but found the going much tougher at Double-A New Hampshire in his first full season. Cooper has the sweet swing and hand-eye coordination to hit for a high average. He made adjustments over the course of the 2009 season, shortening his swing and tinkering with some mechanics, allowing him to finish strong. He has solid gap power and is a doubles machine, with 61 in 197 pro games. It remains to be seen whether Cooper will develop the home run power teams traditionally want from their first basemen, He had trouble driving the ball against lefthanders last season, slugging just .326 against them. He's a bat-only player who has poor speed and subpar athleticism. He put more effort into improving his defense in 2009, but he's still a below-average first baseman. Despite his struggles, Cooper remains the best hitting prospect in the system. The Jays will slow him down by sending him back to Double-A at the start of the year and give him the chance to earn a midseason promotion to Triple-A. He could be ready to take over in Toronto when Lyle Overbay's contract expires after the 2010 season.

TORONTO BLUE JAYS

Year	Club (League)	Class	AVG	G	AB	R	H	2B	3B	HR	RBI	BB	SO	SB	OBP	SLG
2008	Auburn (NYP)	SS	.341	21	85	10	29	10	1	2	21	10	16	0	.411	.553
	Lansing (MWL)	LoA	.354	24	96	15	34	10	0	2	17	10	14	0	.415	.521
	Dunedin (FSL)	HiA	.304	24	92	10	28	9	0	1	13	10	16	0	.373	.435
2009	New Hampshire (EL)	AA	.258	128	473	62	122	32	0	10	66	59	92	0	.340	.389
MINOR LEAGUE TOTALS			.286	197	746	97	213	61	1	15	117	89	138	0	.361	.430

5 HENDERSON ALVAREZ, RHP

BORN: April 18, 1990. **B-T:** R-R. **HT.:** 6-0. **WT.:** 190. **SIGNED:** Venezuela, 2006.
SIGNED BY: Rafael Moncada.

Signed out of Venezuela as a 16-year-old, Alvarez posted a 5.63 ERA in two years in Rookie ball before breaking out at low Class A Lansing in 2009. He went 9-6, 3.47 for a last-place team, leading the Midwest League in fewest walks (1.4) and homers (0.1) allowed per nine innings. Managers rated his changeup as the MWL's best. All three of Alvarez's pitches have a chance to be average or better. His best offering is his changeup, which has splitter action. When he's at his best, his fastball sits at 89-92 mph and touches 94. He commands his fastball and changeup very well, and complements them with a three-quarters breaking ball. Alvarez needs to polish his breaking ball into a true slider or curveball. His velocity fluctuates, as there are games where he works at 86-89 mph, and adding more strength would help. He's not overpowering, so he'll have little margin for error against more advanced hitters. He has some recoil and falls off to first base in his delivery, and he tends to rush his mechanics with runners on base. The Blue Jays' want to be conservative with Alvarez because of his youth, and they shut him down last August because of his innings total. Projected as a No. 4 starter, he'll step up to high Class A in 2010.

Year	Club (League)	Class	W	L	ERA	G	GS	CG	SV	IP	H	R	ER	HR	BB	SO	AVG
2007	Blue Jays 1 (DSL)	R	1	2	5.61	8	7	0	0	26	36	18	16	0	8	20	.324
2008	Blue Jays (GCL)	R	1	4	5.63	12	11	0	0	46	63	41	29	3	6	34	.310
2009	Lansing (MWL)	LoA	9	6	3.47	23	23	1	0	124	121	54	48	1	19	92	.251
MINOR LEAGUE TOTALS			11	12	4.26	43	41	1	0	196	220	113	93	4	33	146	.276

6 JAKE MARISNICK, OF

BORN: March 30, 1991. **B-T:** R-R. **HT.:** 6-4. **WT.:** 200. **DRAFTED:** HS—Riverside, Calif., 2009 (3rd round). **SIGNED BY:** Rick Ingalls.

After turning in the highest score in the SPARQ physical testing at the 2008 Area Code Games, Marisnick established himself as one of the best pure athletes available in the 2009 draft. After a mediocre spring with the bat, he lasted until the third round. One of just two players to sign out of the Blue Jays' first five picks, he received a $1 million bonus at the Aug. 17 signing deadline. Marisnick's long frame is packed with raw strength and speed. He has the ingredients to develop above-average power. A plus runner, he can get down the line in 4.25 seconds from the right side of the plate. Currently a center fielder, he has a strong arm and makes accurate throws, so he'd be a good fit in right field if he has to move. If teams believed more in his bat, Marisnick could have been a first-round pick. A wrist cock in his load hinders timing and prevents him from driving the ball with authority. He needs to iron out that flaw to deliver on his five-tool potential. Marisnick gained strength between the draft and instructional league, so he could move to right field in the near future if he loses a step. For now, he'll stay in center and focus on improving at the plate. Rather than push him, Toronto will probably send him to extended spring training and have him make his pro debut at short-season Auburn in June.

Year	Club (League)	Class	AVG	G	AB	R	H	2B	3B	HR	RBI	BB	SO	SB	OBP	SLG
2009	Did Not Play—Signed Late															

7 JOSH ROENICKE, RHP

BORN: Aug. 4, 1982. **B-T:** R-R. **HT.:** 6-3. **WT.:** 195. **DRAFTED:** UCLA, 2006 (10th round). **SIGNED BY:** Rex de la Nuez (Reds).

Roenicke went to UCLA on a football scholarship as a quarterback/wide receiver before walking on to the baseball team and becoming the Bruins' closer. He also was a plus defender in center field, though his bat was short for pro ball. He signed with the Reds for $20,000 as a fifth-year senior drafted in the 10th round, and came to the Blue Jays in the Scott Rolen trade last summer. Roenicke made it to the big leagues quickly thanks to his power arm out of the bullpen. His fastball sits at 93-95 mph and peaks at 98 with some natural life. He also mixes in a high-80s cutter that runs and sinks. A tough competitor, he's not afraid to challenge hitters. Roenicke mostly works off his four-seam and cut fastballs. He also throws a hard slider that's inconsistent, and an adequate changeup that he rarely uses. He can fall in love with the radar gun and sometimes asks for his readings after coming off the mound. He may have tried too hard after the trade, overthrowing and battling his control. Though he scuffled with Toronto, Roenicke has nothing left to prove in Triple-A. A potential closer, the Blue Jays will give him the opportunity to make the big league bullpen in spring training.

Year	Club (League)	Class	W	L	ERA	G	GS	CG	SV	IP	H	R	ER	HR	BB	SO	AVG
2006	Reds (GCL)	R	1	0	1.17	7	0	0	0	8	8	2	1	0	3	9	.258
	Billings (PIO)	R	1	0	6.32	14	0	0	6	16	10	11	11	1	12	24	.179
2007	Sarasota (FSL)	HiA	2	1	3.25	27	0	0	16	28	23	10	10	1	15	41	.225
	Chattanooga (SL)	AA	1	1	0.95	19	0	0	8	19	12	3	2	0	6	15	.185
2008	Chattanooga (SL)	AA	4	2	3.27	22	0	0	10	22	21	10	8	2	12	28	.253
	Louisville (IL)	AAA	2	0	2.54	35	0	0	3	39	34	11	11	2	14	43	.234
	Cincinnati (NL)	MAJ	0	0	9.00	5	0	0	0	3	6	3	3	0	2	6	.400
2009	Louisville (IL)	AAA	1	0	2.57	27	0	0	12	28	30	9	8	0	6	32	.268
	Cincinnati (NL)	MAJ	0	0	2.70	11	0	0	0	13	13	4	4	0	4	14	.260
	Toronto (AL)	MAJ	0	0	7.13	13	0	0	0	18	19	15	14	2	12	19	.271
MAJOR LEAGUE TOTALS			0	0	5.56	29	0	0	0	34	38	22	21	2	18	39	.281
MINOR LEAGUE TOTALS			12	4	2.89	151	0	0	55	159	138	56	51	6	68	192	.232

8 BRAD MILLS, LHP

BORN: March 5, 1985. **B-T:** L-L. **HT.:** 5-11. **WT.:** 185. **DRAFTED:** Arizona, 2007 (4th round). **SIGNED BY:** Dan Cholowsky.

A 22nd-round pick by the Blue Jays in 2006, Mills returned to Arizona to complete his civil-engineering degree. He went 18 rounds higher in 2007, made it to Double-A in his first full season and reached the majors in his second. He got hammered in two big league starts, went down to Triple-A and threw eight shutout innings before spending the rest of the season on the disabled list with bruised ribs. Though he's far from overpowering, Mills has averaged more than a strikeout per inning as a pro via deception. His herky-jerky delivery throws hitters off, and his ability to mix his pitches keeps them off balance. He disguises his well above-average changeup with quality arm speed. He also gets outs with his solid 12-to-6 curveball. When he commands his 87-90 mph fastball, it's effective as well. Mills' below-average velocity and his tendency to pitch up in the strike zone with his high-three-quarters delivery created problems when he faced big league hitters. He's going to have to spot his fastball more precisely in the bottom of the zone to succeed in a major league rotation. Unless he overwhelms the Jays in spring training, Mills likely will open the season back in Las Vegas. Toronto has a number of young lefthanded starter candidates, so his future with the club may lie in long relief.

Year	Club (League)	Class	W	L	ERA	G	GS	CG	SV	IP	H	R	ER	HR	BB	SO	AVG
2007	Auburn (NYP)	SS	2	0	2.00	6	2	0	0	18	9	4	4	0	6	21	.143
2008	Lansing (MWL)	LoA	6	3	2.53	15	15	0	0	81	71	30	23	3	28	92	.233
	New Hampshire (EL)	AA	3	2	1.10	6	6	0	0	33	24	11	4	2	12	32	.205
	Dunedin (FSL)	HiA	4	0	1.35	6	6	0	0	33	25	9	5	2	12	35	.210
2009	Toronto (AL)	MAJ	0	1	14.09	2	2	0	0	8	14	12	12	4	6	9	.400
	Las Vegas (PCL)	AAA	2	8	4.06	14	14	1	0	84	83	43	38	6	35	72	.263
MAJOR LEAGUE TOTALS			0	1	14.09	2	2	0	0	8	14	12	12	4	6	9	.400
MINOR LEAGUE TOTALS			17	13	2.67	47	43	1	0	250	212	97	74	13	93	252	.230

9 JUSTIN JACKSON, SS

BORN: Dec. 11, 1988. **B-T:** R-R. **HT.:** 6-1. **WT.:** 186. **DRAFTED:** HS—Asheville, N.C., 2007 (1st round supplemental). **SIGNED BY:** Marc Tramuta.

Two seasons after the Tigers drafted Roberson High (Asheville, N.C.) teammate Cameron Maybin 10th overall, Jackson went 45th to the Blue Jays in the 2007 draft. Signed for $675,000, he has been slow to adjust to pro ball, hitting .221/.322/.315 in three seasons. Bothered by a torn labrum in his non-throwing shoulder in 2009, he was in an 0-for-27 slump when Toronto shut him down in late July to have surgery. Jackson is one of the best athletes in the system and profiles as a true shortstop. His range, hands and arm strength are better than those of most shortstops, and he's making nice progress with his reads and footwork. He draws walks and uses his solid speed to steal bases. He has some strength in his wiry frame and could fit as a No. 2 hitter if he gets going at the plate. The Jays blame his shoulder and youth for his struggles, but scouts with other organizations question Jackson's bat speed. While he's not afraid to take pitches, he often falls behind in the count and strikes out excessively. He won't ever hit for a lot of home run power, so he needs to focus on making much more contact. Tyler Pastornicky is starting to push Jackson for the title of top shortstop prospect in the system. Toronto will give Jackson a mulligan on 2009 and hope he starts to hit when he gets another crack at high Class A this season.

TORONTO BLUE JAYS

Year	Club (League)	Class	AVG	G	AB	R	H	2B	3B	HR	RBI	BB	SO	SB	OBP	SLG
2007	Blue Jays (GCL)	R	.187	42	166	20	31	1	1	2	13	20	44	7	.274	.241
2008	Lansing (MWL)	LoA	.238	121	454	74	108	26	6	7	47	62	154	17	.340	.368
2009	Dunedin (FSL)	HiA	.213	78	249	44	53	12	1	0	17	39	87	17	.321	.269
MINOR LEAGUE TOTALS			.221	241	869	138	192	39	8	9	77	121	285	41	.322	.315

10 CARLOS PEREZ, C

BORN: Oct. 27, 1990. **B-T:** R-R. **HT.:** 6-0. **WT.:** 193. **SIGNED:** Venezuela, 2008. **SIGNED BY:** Rafael Moncada.

The Jays signed Perez as a 17-year-old out of Venezuela in 2008 and were thrilled with his performance in his U.S. debut last season. He ranked as the No. 5 prospect in the Rookie-level Gulf Coast League and showed the potential to be a fine all-around catcher. Perez stands out most with his defensive skills. He has a plus arm, consistently records pop times around 1.9 seconds and led GCL catchers by throwing out 49 percent of basestealers. He shows a good feel for hitting, as his bat stays in the zone for a long time and he has better plate discipline than most teenagers. He's a good runner for a catcher and makes smart decisions on the basepaths. His receiving and blocking skills need more polish, but Perez is still young and has made notable improvements over the last year. He should develop gap power as he adjusts his contact-oriented approach and does a better job of incorporating his lower half in his swing. Because Perez is only 19 and hasn't played above Rookie ball, the Jays will take things slow with him. He probably will get some time in extended spring training and at Auburn this season before getting his first taste of full-season ball in 2011.

Year	Club (League)	Class	AVG	G	AB	R	H	2B	3B	HR	RBI	BB	SO	SB	OBP	SLG
2008	Blue Jays 1 (DSL)	R	.306	58	196	27	60	10	2	0	29	52	28	7	.459	.378
2009	Blue Jays (GCL)	R	.291	43	141	17	41	11	3	1	21	16	23	2	.364	.433
MINOR LEAGUE TOTALS			.300	101	337	44	101	21	5	1	50	68	51	9	.422	.401

11 MOISES SIERRA, OF

BORN: Sept. 24, 1988. **B-T:** R-R. **HT.:** 6-0. **WT.:** 225. **SIGNED:** Dominican Republic, 2005. **SIGNED BY:** Hilario Soriano.

Sierra's breakout 2009 season was a bright spot on a rather uninspiring Dunedin team. The Blue Jays threw him into the fire in high Class A at age 20, and he responded well after hitting .241/.304/.366 in his first three pro seasons. He has a strong, sturdy frame, prompting one Blue Jays official to note that he would have been a linebacker had he been born in the United States. Sierra's best asset is his arm, which rates as a 70 on the 20-80 scouting scale. He has solid-average power, which is still developing, and his swing stays on a good path through the ball. He doesn't show a lot of patience at the plate, but he doesn't strike out excessively either. Sierra is a solid-average runner and can take an extra base, though he figures to slow down a little as he fills out. His overall package fits the right-field profile, provided he realizes his power potential. He'll probably spend 2010 in Double-A, where he hit .353 in eight games at the end of last season.

Year	Club (League)	Class	AVG	G	AB	R	H	2B	3B	HR	RBI	BB	SO	SB	OBP	SLG
2006	Blue Jays (DSL)	R	.253	69	245	35	62	16	1	4	26	24	50	17	.345	.376
2007	Blue Jays (GCL)	R	.203	43	143	17	29	5	1	5	15	5	39	2	.248	.357
2008	Lansing (MWL)	LoA	.246	130	451	50	111	16	5	9	39	26	114	12	.297	.364
2009	Dunedin (FSL)	HiA	.286	110	405	56	116	24	2	5	56	34	66	10	.360	.393
	New Hampshire (EL)	AA	.353	8	34	1	12	1	0	1	6	1	8	0	.361	.471
MINOR LEAGUE TOTALS			.258	360	1278	159	330	62	9	24	142	90	277	41	.323	.377

12 KEVIN AHRENS, 3B

BORN: April 26, 1989. **B-T:** B-R. **HT.:** 6-1. **WT.:** 195. **DRAFTED:** HS—Houston, 2007 (1st round). **SIGNED BY:** Andy Beene.

The Blue Jays spent the 16th overall pick in the 2007 draft and a $1.44 million bonus on Ahrens, banking on his ability to hit for power from both sides of the plate. But like several other of Toronto's premium picks from that draft, he struggled in last season. His minor league career has been unimpressive as well, producing a .238/.313/.335 line in 275 games. Ahrens shows good swing mechanics in batting practice and has a mature, all-fields approach, and he has the raw strength to hit 15-20 homers annually in the big leagues. But his bat speed is just ordinary and while he did a better job of making contact in 2009, he didn't do much damage. A shortstop in high school, Ahrens has the athleticism, range and strong, accurate arm to play third base. He's still working on improving his reactions at the hot corner. He'll repeat high Class A in 2010 in an attempt to jump-start his bat. For all his struggles, he still has a lot of upside and is easily the best third-base prospect in the system.

Year	Club (League)	Class	AVG	G	AB	R	H	2B	3B	HR	RBI	BB	SO	SB	OBP	SLG
2007	Blue Jays (GCL)	R	.230	48	165	19	38	6	0	3	21	25	47	3	.339	.321
2008	Lansing (MWL)	LoA	.259	122	460	54	119	25	5	5	42	45	135	5	.329	.367
2009	Dunedin (FSL)	HiA	.215	105	377	35	81	17	2	4	36	37	76	1	.282	.302
MINOR LEAGUE TOTALS			.238	275	1002	108	238	48	7	12	99	107	258	9	.313	.335

13 K.C. HOBSON, 1B

BORN: Aug. 22, 1990. **B-T:** L-L. **HT.:** 6-2. **WT.:** 210. **DRAFTED:** HS—Bakersfield, Calif., 2009 (6th round). **SIGNED BY:** Tim Rooney.

The son of former big league player and manager Butch Hobson, K.C. has his father's physical strength, with big hands and forearms. He also takes after his dad with a bulldog, edgy kind of personality. The Blue Jays lured him from a commitment to Texas A&M with a $500,000 bonus after drafting him in the sixth round last June, but he signed too late to play in 2009. Hobson has a fundamentally sound and simple swing that produces big raw power. His mechanics are traditional, but he can get overaggressive at times, with his stroke getting long and his lower half opening up too soon. Hobson threw 90-91 mph off the mound and also saw action in left field as a high schooler, but he'll likely settle at first base as a pro because he has below-average speed. His feet work well around the bag and he has more arm than most first basemen. Toronto thinks he'll have the bat to profile at the position. He'll like begin 2010 in extended spring training before beginning his pro career at Auburn or in the Gulf Coast League.

Year	Club (League)	Class	AVG	G	AB	R	H	2B	3B	HR	RBI	BB	SO	SB	OBP	SLG
2009	Did Not Play—Signed Late															

14 DANNY FARQUHAR, RHP

BORN: Feb. 17, 1987. **B-T:** R-R. **HT.:** 5-10. **WT.:** 170. **DRAFTED:** Louisiana-Lafayette, 2008 (10th round). **SIGNED BY:** Rob St. Julien.

Toronto took a $112,500 gamble on Farquhar in 2008, drafting him in the 10th round after he struggled as Louisiana-Lafayette's ace that spring. Originally a swingman in college, Farquhar returned to the bullpen and had an outstanding pro debut, posting a 1.95 ERA while reaching low Class A. He was even better in his first full pro season, saving 22 games between two stops and having no trouble handling Double-A hitters. Farquhar has good stuff, but his delivery is what sets him apart. He uses a couple of different arm angles to keep hitters off balance. From his higher slot he sits at 93-94 mph and can bump 95-96 with his four-seam fastball. He also can drop down and offer an 88-91 mph two-seamer with sink. His secondary stuff consists of a curveball from the higher slot, as well as a slurvy breaker from down low. He has good life on his pitches thanks to his long arms and is incredibly tough on righthanders. The downside of the different arm slots is that Farquhar battles his command. Farquhar may never locate his pitches well enough to be a big league closer, but he's an asset out of the bullpen and could press for a job in Toronto this year.

Year	Club (League)	Class	W	L	ERA	G	GS	CG	SV	IP	H	R	ER	HR	BB	SO	AVG
2008	Auburn (NYP)	SS	2	2	2.39	12	0	0	0	26	20	10	7	1	6	27	.215
	Lansing (MWL)	LoA	0	0	0.00	3	0	0	0	6	0	1	0	0	2	4	.000
2009	Dunedin (FSL)	HiA	1	0	0.53	17	0	0	7	17	10	4	1	0	11	23	.164
	New Hampshire (EL)	AA	1	4	2.36	37	0	0	15	46	31	15	12	1	30	51	.193
MINOR LEAGUE TOTALS			4	6	1.89	69	0	0	22	95	61	30	20	2	49	105	.183

15 LUIS PEREZ, LHP

BORN: Jan. 20, 1985. **B-T:** L-L. **HT.:** 6-0. **WT.:** 205. **SIGNED:** Dominican Republic, 2003. **SIGNED BY:** Hilario Soriano.

Perez hasn't made the quickest climb through the system since signing in 2003, but he has come on strong in the last few years and claimed a spot on the 40-man roster after the 2008 season. It took him three years to get out of the Rookie-level Dominican Summer League before he finally made his U.S. debut in 2007. He made a successful jump to Double-A and made an appearance in the Futures Game last year. Perez's 89-91 mph fastball is his out pitch, a heavy sinker that touches 93. Hitters drive the pitch into the ground, as evidenced by his 2.15 groundout/airout ratio at New Hampshire. His secondary offerings are inconsistent but are quality pitches when they're on. His slider can be slurvy at times, and he's still learning to use his changeup more often. Perez could be a back-of-the-rotation starter, but it may be more realistic to project him as a reliever at this point. He'll add some final polish in Triple-A before pitching in Toronto at some point in 2010.

Year	Club (League)	Class	W	L	ERA	G	GS	CG	SV	IP	H	R	ER	HR	BB	SO	AVG
2004	Blue Jays (DSL)	R	0	0	1.69	6	1	0	0	5	3	3	1	0	7	7	.176
2005	Blue Jays (DSL)	R	2	3	4.96	12	11	0	0	53	42	37	29	3	28	68	.206
2006	Blue Jays (DSL)	R	4	0	1.38	14	14	0	0	85	47	19	13	0	23	107	.158
2007	Auburn (NYP)	SS	3	3	3.70	16	16	0	0	75	73	37	31	1	38	71	.252
2008	Lansing (MWL)	LoA	5	12	3.60	28	23	0	0	137	136	68	55	4	51	137	.264
2009	New Hampshire (EL)	AA	9	11	3.55	28	27	2	0	162	145	78	64	11	67	112	.239
MINOR LEAGUE TOTALS			23	29	3.35	104	92	2	0	518	446	242	193	19	214	502	.232

16 RYAN SCHIMPF, 2B

BORN: March 11, 1988. **B-T:** L-R. **HT.:** 5-9. **WT.:** 181. **DRAFTED:** Louisiana State, 2009 (5th round). **SIGNED BY:** Rob St. Julien.

Schimpf's size and style of play leads to obvious comparisons to Dustin Pedroia, another diminutive second baseman who wreaks havoc on offense. Schimpf signed for $155,700 as a fifth-round pick last summer after helping Louisiana State to a College World Series title. He spent most of the spring in left field for the Tigers, but he fits best at second base. After hitting .336/.449/.668 in 262 college at-bats, Schimpf continued to produce in his pro debut. He's a good athlete with a knack for hitting. He has a short stroke and surprising power for a guy his size. He projects to hit lots of doubles, and the Jays think he could produce 15 or more homers per season. He should also steal 15 or more bases annually with his tick above-average speed. Schimpf is reliable if not spectacular at second base. He has a fringy arm and needs to get a better feel for the position, starting with turning double plays. He could open his first full pro season in high Class A.

Year	Club (League)	Class	AVG	G	AB	R	H	2B	3B	HR	RBI	BB	SO	SB	OBP	SLG
2009	Blue Jays (GCL)	R	.500	2	4	1	2	0	1	0	0	2	0	1	.667	1.000
	Auburn (NYP)	SS	.287	34	129	25	37	7	1	3	14	15	24	4	.369	.426
MINOR LEAGUE TOTALS			.293	36	133	26	39	7	2	3	14	17	24	5	.381	.444

17 TYLER PASTORNICKY, SS

BORN: Dec. 13, 1989. **B-T:** R-R. **HT.:** 5-11. **WT.:** 170. **DRAFTED:** HS—Bradenton, Fla., 2008 (5th round). **SIGNED BY:** Joel Grampietro.

The Blue Jays went to the Florida high school ranks for two of their top five picks in the 2008 draft, and fifth-rounder Pastornicky has surpassed second-round outfielder Kenny Wilson in the early stages of their development. He's the son of Cliff Pastornicky, who played with the 1983 Royals and now scouts for Kansas City. An athletic infielder, Pastornicky doesn't have flashy tools but gets the most out of what he has. He has good instincts at shortstop, along with plus range and an average arm. He's an above-average runner and basestealer, which opposing catchers quickly figured out as he swiped 57 bases between two Class A stops in 2009. Pastornicky has a line-drive stroke and projects as a .275 hitter in the big leagues. The only thing he lacks is power, as he has hit just two homers in 636 pro at-bats. But as a potential top-of-the-order hitter who provides sound defense, he may not need it. Pastornicky got a taste of high Class A at the end of last season and likely will return there to begin 2010. If he doesn't end up as an everyday shortstop, he could be a very useful utilityman.

Year	Club (League)	Class	AVG	G	AB	R	H	2B	3B	HR	RBI	BB	SO	SB	OBP	SLG
2008	Blue Jays (GCL)	R	.263	50	160	32	42	6	3	1	17	21	21	27	.349	.356
2009	Lansing (MWL)	LoA	.269	109	413	63	111	11	9	1	31	39	50	51	.336	.346
	Dunedin (FSL)	HiA	.270	15	63	9	17	3	0	0	3	3	7	6	.303	.317
MINOR LEAGUE TOTALS			.267	174	636	104	170	20	12	2	51	63	78	84	.336	.346

18 ERIC THAMES, OF

BORN: Nov. 10, 1986. **B-T:** L-L. **HT.:** 6-0. **WT.:** 205. **DRAFTED:** Pepperdine, 2008 (7th round). **SIGNED BY:** Tim Rooney.

Thames' draft stock skyrocketed when he hit .407 with 13 homers during his redshirt junior season at Pepperdine in 2008. But he tore a quadriceps muscle in his right leg shortly before the draft, causing him to fall to the Blue Jays in the seventh round. After signing for $150,000, he had surgery to repair his quad and didn't make his pro debut in 2009. He pounded high Class A pitching, but missed all of July and a couple of weeks in August when his quad flared up on him again. Thames has a rock-solid build and is very strong. He has plus bat speed, a sound stroke and solid plate discipline. When he's healthy and not holding back, he shows average speed. His arm is average as well, and he fits best defensively in left field. Assuming Thames is healthy in spring training, he could get a crack at making the Double-A roster.

Year	Club (League)	Class	AVG	G	AB	R	H	2B	3B	HR	RBI	BB	SO	SB	OBP	SLG
2009	Blue Jays (GCL)	R	.286	7	21	4	6	3	0	0	1	3	5	0	.360	.429
	Dunedin (FSL)	HiA	.313	52	195	33	61	15	5	3	38	21	40	1	.386	.487
MINOR LEAGUE TOTALS			.310	59	216	37	67	18	5	3	39	24	45	1	.384	.481

19 TIM COLLINS, LHP

BORN: Aug. 29, 1989. **B-T:** L-L. **HT.:** 5-7. **WT.:** 155. **DRAFTED:** HS—Worcester, Mass., NDFA, 2007. **SIGNED BY:** J.P. Ricciardi.

Collins led his Worcester Technical High team to the Massachusetts Division 2 title in 2007, sporting a 7-0, 0.17 record on the mound and a league-leading .472 average at the plate. But because he stands just 5-foot-7, he went undrafted and was ready to attend CC of Rhode Island. Former Jays general manager J.P. Ricciardi, a native of Worcester, saw Collins pitch, however, and had him work out for the club. Toronto signed him as a free agent and has watched him scrap his way up the ladder to Double-A. He gets outs with a solid fastball that tops out at 93 mph and a true 12-to-6 curveball that he spins really well. His quirky delivery helps him as well. He has a high three-quarters arm slot and does an especially good job of staying on top of the ball and driving down despite his height. He has a high leg kick and stands as far to the third-base side of the rubber as possible. Working exclusively out of the bullpen, Collins hasn't used a changeup much. As he moves up he'll need to command his pitches better. Pro hitters didn't touch him until he got to New Hampshire at the end of 2009, and he'll return to Double-A to begin the 2010 season.

Year	Club (League)	Class	W	L	ERA	G	GS	CG	SV	IP	H	R	ER	HR	BB	SO	AVG
2007	Blue Jays (GCL)	R	0	0	4.50	7	0	0	0	6	6	3	3	0	2	7	.273
2008	Lansing (MWL)	LoA	4	2	1.58	39	0	0	14	68	36	13	12	3	32	98	.156
2009	Dunedin (FSL)	HiA	7	4	2.37	40	0	0	3	65	47	21	17	2	28	99	.199
	New Hampshire (EL)	AA	2	3	5.68	9	0	0	0	13	12	9	8	1	7	17	.255
MINOR LEAGUE TOTALS			13	9	2.37	95	0	0	17	152	101	46	40	6	69	221	.188

20 DANIEL WEBB, RHP

BORN: May 18, 1989. **B-T:** R-R. **HT.:** 6-3. **WT.:** 210. **DRAFTED:** Northwest Florida State JC, 2009 (18th round). **SIGNED BY:** Joel Grampietro.

Webb was one of the top high school righthanders available in the 2008 draft, but he scared teams off with his asking price and fell to the Diamondbacks in the 12th round. Arizona couldn't sign him and Webb's commitment to Kentucky fell through when he didn't qualify academically, so he ended up at Northwest Florida State JC. He didn't have much success there and went in the 18th round in 2009. When the Jays couldn't reach agreements with several of their top picks, they took some of that money and signed him for $450,000 at the Aug. 17 deadline. Webb has a good pitcher's frame and a live arm. His fastball sits in the low 90s, touched 94 last spring and peaked at 96 after he turned pro. He has a good feel for a changeup that could be an average to plus pitch once he polishes it. His curveball isn't what it was in high school and needs to be tightened up. He also can be erratic with a slinging arm action. Webb could be an effective starter with his fastball/changeup combination and his ability to hold his velocity deep into games. But he'll have to move into a relief role if he can't improve his command and curve. He signed too late to make his pro debut in 2009 but got some work in during instructional league. He could head to low Class A if he has a good spring.

Year	Club (League)	Class	W	L	ERA	G	GS	CG	SV	IP	H	R	ER	HR	BB	SO	AVG
2009	Did Not Play—Signed Late																

21 JOHERMYN CHAVEZ, OF

BORN: Jan. 26, 1989. **B-T:** R-R. **HT.:** 6-3. **WT.:** 220. **SIGNED:** Venezuela, 2005. **SIGNED BY:** Rafael Moncada.

Chavez hasn't progressed as quickly as the Blue Jays hoped he would after signing him as 16-year-old out of Venezuela in 2005, but he showed signs of tapping into his potential last year. Returning to Lansing after a dismal 2008 there, he had his best season as a pro, increasing his OPS by 225 points. He put in lots of work in the batting cage and finally seemed comfortable at the plate. Chavez already is maxed out physically, with a strong 6-foot-3, 220-pound frame. He tapped into his raw power last season, hitting 21 home runs in a pitcher-friendly league. He still needs to develop a more consistent approach and improve his plate discipline. Chavez has an above-average arm, but his fringy range and defensive instincts probably will relegate him to left field. He's an average runner. He'll head to high Class A in 2010.

TORONTO BLUE JAYS

Year	Club (League)	Class	AVG	G	AB	R	H	2B	3B	HR	RBI	BB	SO	SB	OBP	SLG
2006	Pulaski (APP)	R	.276	36	105	19	29	9	0	0	18	9	23	1	.371	.362
2007	Blue Jays (GCL)	R	.301	50	176	29	53	12	2	6	21	20	50	7	.389	.494
2008	Lansing (MWL)	LoA	.211	115	402	40	85	20	2	7	39	25	128	9	.272	.323
2009	Lansing (MWL)	LoA	.283	134	508	87	144	22	6	21	89	40	137	10	.346	.474
MINOR LEAGUE TOTALS			.261	335	1191	175	311	63	10	34	167	94	338	27	.331	.416

22 TRYSTAN MAGNUSON, RHP

BORN: June 6, 1985. **B-T:** L-R. **HT.:** 6-8. **WT.:** 210. **DRAFTED:** Louisville, 2007 (1st round supplemental). **SIGNED BY:** Steve Miller.

The nephew of former NHL defenseman Keith Magnuson, Trystan walked on the baseball team at Louisville and became the closer on the Cardinals' 2007 College World Series team as a fifth-year senior. The Blue Jays drafted him 56th overall that June and signed him for $462,500, though his pro debut was pushed back until 2008 because he had a sore elbow. Toronto toyed with the idea of making him a starter but kept him on tight pitch counts. He didn't have much success in the rotation, and he looked much more comfortable when he returned to the bullpen last year. With his tall, thin frame, Magnuson generates good velocity. His fastball sits at 90-92 mph and can get up to 94. He throws downhill and has confidence working in relief. Roving pitching instructor Dane Johnson helped him with a two-seam grip, improving the life on his fastball. Magnuson also throws a mid-80s slider that can be a plus pitch but sometimes lack depth. He's also working on a splitter. After reaching Double-A at the tail end of 2009, he'll return there this season and could push for a big league callup in September if all goes well.

Year	Club (League)	Class	W	L	ERA	G	GS	CG	SV	IP	H	R	ER	HR	BB	SO	AVG
2008	Lansing (MWL)	LoA	0	9	5.40	24	24	0	0	82	91	57	49	6	35	49	.282
2009	Dunedin (FSL)	HiA	4	1	2.77	38	0	0	1	62	56	23	19	2	27	45	.248
	New Hampshire (EL)	AA	1	0	0.00	5	0	0	0	10	4	0	0	0	1	7	.118
MINOR LEAGUE TOTALS			5	10	3.99	67	24	0	1	153	151	80	68	8	63	101	.259

23 BRIAN DOPIRAK, 1B

BORN: Jan. 20, 1983. **B-T:** R-R. **HT.:** 6-4. **WT.:** 230. **DRAFTED:** HS—Dunedin, Fla., 2002 (2nd round). **SIGNED BY:** Tom Shafer.

In the 2002 high school draft crop, Dopirak's raw power was considered comparable to Prince Fielder's. Eight years later, Fielder has 160 homers in the major leagues, while Dopirak has 145—all in the minors. He ranked as the Cubs' No. 1 prospect after a 2004 season in which he hit 39 homers and won Midwest League MVP honors, but he got off to a slow start the next year and messed up his swing and plate discipline trying desperately to hit for power. Released by the Cubs at the end of spring training in 2008, he signed with the Blue Jays, in part because they sent him to Dunedin, his hometown. In two seasons in the Toronto system, Dopirak has batted .313/.372/.554 and led the Eastern League with a .576 slugging percentage last year. His success has come with a change in approach. Previously a dead-pull, all-or-nothing hitter, he now uses the entire field without sacrificing any of his considerable power. In batting practice, he exclusively works up the middle and to right-center. He still takes a big hack and probably won't hit for a high average, but his strength is undeniable. He's a below-average runner and first baseman, so all of his value comes from his bat. Dopirak has shown enough to warrant a spot on the 40-man roster and could get his first big callup in 2010, though he'll see some more time in Triple-A first.

Year	Club (League)	Class	AVG	G	AB	R	H	2B	3B	HR	RBI	BB	SO	SB	OBP	SLG
2002	Cubs (AZL)	R	.253	21	79	10	20	4	0	0	6	6	23	0	.306	.304
2003	Boise (NWL)	SS	.240	52	192	25	46	4	0	13	37	24	58	0	.330	.464
	Lansing (MWL)	LoA	.269	19	78	8	21	3	0	2	10	2	22	0	.305	.385
2004	Lansing (MWL)	LoA	.307	137	541	94	166	38	0	39	120	48	123	4	.363	.593
2005	Daytona (FSL)	HiA	.235	132	507	53	119	26	0	16	76	37	107	1	.289	.381
2006	West Tenn (SL)	AA	.257	52	179	16	46	12	0	1	23	16	41	0	.322	.341
2007	Tennessee (SL)	AA	.218	21	78	2	17	1	0	1	4	3	19	0	.247	.269
	Daytona (FSL)	HiA	.277	94	347	49	96	23	0	17	64	23	91	1	.325	.490
2008	Dunedin (FSL)	HiA	.308	106	409	77	126	25	2	27	88	47	100	0	.382	.577
	New Hampshire (EL)	AA	.287	22	87	5	25	6	0	2	13	2	10	1	.297	.425
2009	New Hampshire (EL)	AA	.308	87	328	44	101	29	1	19	68	35	75	1	.374	.576
	Las Vegas (PCL)	AAA	.330	52	218	33	72	13	1	8	34	13	44	0	.366	.509
MINOR LEAGUE TOTALS			.281	795	3043	416	855	184	4	145	543	256	713	8	.339	.487

24 RYAN GOINS, SS

BORN: Feb. 13, 1988. **B-T:** L-R. **HT.:** 5-10. **WT.:** 170. **DRAFTED:** Dallas Baptist, 2009 (4th round). **SIGNED BY:** Aaron Jersild.

Goins hit 22 homers at Dallas Baptist last spring, propelling him into the fourth round of the draft and earning him a $216,000 bonus. Though he didn't go deep in his pro debut, he hit his way to low Class A. He's in the Brian Roberts mold and plays with a lot of energy, often getting dirty even in pregame drills. Despite showing power in college, Goins isn't expected to produce a lot of homers with wood bats. He'll be better off driving doubles to the gaps than trying to hit balls out of the park. He has a short, compact swing that stays in the zone a long time, and he has a knack for barreling balls. While he has a plus arm, Goins may not be an everyday shortstop because he has below-average speed and range. He projects better as an offensive second baseman. He should return to Lansing, at least for the start of the 2010 season.

Year	Club (League)	Class	AVG	G	AB	R	H	2B	3B	HR	RBI	BB	SO	SB	OBP	SLG
2009	Blue Jays (GCL)	R	.111	3	9	1	1	0	0	0	0	0	2	0	.111	.111
	Auburn (NYP)	SS	.297	24	101	15	30	5	1	0	8	8	23	2	.349	.366
	Lansing (MWL)	LoA	.198	19	81	6	16	4	0	0	9	7	23	1	.258	.247
MINOR LEAGUE TOTALS			.246	46	191	22	47	9	1	0	17	15	48	3	.300	.304

25 BRAD EMAUS, 2B

BORN: March 28, 1986. **B-T:** R-R. **HT.:** 5-11. **WT.:** 200. **DRAFTED:** Tulane, 2007 (11th round). **SIGNED BY:** Matt Briggs.

An ankle injury slowed Emaus during his junior year at Tulane, causing him to slide to the 11th round of the 2007 draft. He made his full-season debut in high Class A in 2008 and impressed the Blue Jays with his all-around skills, then carried that over to big league spring training last year, hitting .306/.370/.694 in 49 at-bats. He couldn't continue his momentum in Double-A, however. Emaus has solid tools across the board but gets higher marks for his moxie and approach to the game. He has a consistent swing and can pepper the gaps. He has good plate discipline and puts together quality at-bats. He got overanxious at the plate last season and got away from his usual stroke, which contributed to his struggles. Emaus projects to hit 10-15 homers annually in the big leagues and could use more strength down the road. Though he has slightly below-average speed, he has good baserunning instincts. Emaus' defense is improving at second base after he played third base in his first pro summer. He turns double plays well and has plenty of arm for second base. He'll return to Double-A and try to get back on track in 2010.

Year	Club (League)	Class	AVG	G	AB	R	H	2B	3B	HR	RBI	BB	SO	SB	OBP	SLG
2007	Auburn (NYP)	SS	.228	39	136	21	31	6	0	2	14	12	26	2	.298	.316
2008	Dunedin (FSL)	HiA	.302	124	473	87	143	34	3	12	71	60	56	12	.380	.463
2009	New Hampshire (EL)	AA	.253	137	505	67	128	28	2	10	67	59	69	10	.336	.376
MINOR LEAGUE TOTALS			.271	300	1114	175	302	68	5	24	152	131	151	24	.350	.406

26 ANDREW LIEBEL, RHP

BORN: March 22, 1986. **B-T:** R-R. **HT.:** 6-1. **WT.:** 180. **DRAFTED:** Long Beach State, 2008 (3rd round). **SIGNED BY:** Demerius Pittman.

Liebel spent most of his first three seasons at Long Beach State as a reliever before getting a chance to start. He went 8-4, 2.22 as a senior, pitching his way into the third round of the 2008 draft and signing for $340,000. He has more polish than stuff, with enough savvy that the Blue Jays sent him to high Class A for his first full pro season and promoted him to Double-A at the end of the year. Liebel's fastball sits at 88-89 mph and maxes out at 91, but he gets good movement and relies on his control. He sells his plus changeup well and does a nice job of mixing in an overhand curveball and a slider, though both breaking balls are fringy at this point. He can't overpower hitters but aggressively goes after them anyway. He doesn't have a huge ceiling, but he could be a back-of-the-rotation option after another year in the minors. He'll go back to New Hampshire to start 2010.

Year	Club (League)	Class	W	L	ERA	G	GS	CG	SV	IP	H	R	ER	HR	BB	SO	AVG
2008	Auburn (NYP)	SS	1	2	3.68	7	1	0	0	15	19	6	6	2	2	19	.311
2009	Dunedin (FSL)	HiA	5	13	3.63	27	27	2	0	156	155	74	63	13	42	118	.262
	New Hampshire (EL)	AA	1	0	2.08	2	2	0	0	13	10	3	3	2	2	12	.213
MINOR LEAGUE TOTALS			7	15	3.53	36	30	2	0	184	184	83	72	17	46	149	.263

27 JOHN TOLISANO, 2B

BORN: Oct. 7, 1988. **B-T:** B-R. **HT.:** 5-11. **WT.:** 190. **DRAFTED:** HS—Estero, Fla., 2007 (2nd round). **SIGNED BY:** Joel Grampietro.

One of the four high schoolers the Blue Jays drafted in the first two rounds in 2007, Tolisano led the Gulf Coast League with 10 homers in his pro debut. Like the rest of those premium picks, he has struggled to hit since. Tolisano's bat is supposed to be his strong suit. He has a compact body and swing, showing surprising power for his size. A switch-hitter, his swing is solid from both sides, albeit slightly better from the left. He made more contact in 2009, but he still needs further improvement on his plate discipline. Though Tolisano has slightly above-average speed, he's not a basestealing threat. He's an average defender at second with an average arm, and he has made improvements on the angles he takes to balls. He's a slightly above-average runner. He's a hard worker, but he needs to improve his conditioning after wilting in the heat of the Florida State League toward the end of last season. He'll return there to open 2010.

Year	Club (League)	Class	AVG	G	AB	R	H	2B	3B	HR	RBI	BB	SO	SB	OBP	SLG
2007	Blue Jays (GCL)	R	.246	49	183	35	45	5	0	10	33	26	40	7	.336	.437
2008	Lansing (MWL)	LoA	.229	120	432	64	99	20	8	6	47	56	110	5	.315	.354
2009	Dunedin (FSL)	HiA	.232	106	401	53	93	19	2	12	58	44	78	5	.305	.379
MINOR LEAGUE TOTALS			.233	275	1016	152	237	44	10	28	138	126	228	17	.315	.379

28 KENNY WILSON, OF

BORN: Jan. 30, 1990. **B-T:** B-R. **HT.:** 6-0. **WT.:** 165. **DRAFTED:** HS—Tampa, 2008 (2nd round). **SIGNED BY:** Joel Grampietro.

The Blue Jays signed Wilson away from a Florida commitment with a $644,000 bonus in 2008, and he immediately established himself as one of the best athletes and runners in the organization. If he doesn't do a better job of getting on base, though, he won't get the most out of his ability. Wilson began working on switch-hitting in instructional league after the 2008 season and gave it a try in games toward the end of 2009. He has a simple swing and can get down the line in less than 4.0 seconds on a swing from his natural right side, and Toronto wants to see what he may be capable of from the left side. He has good instincts on the bases and has stolen 65 bases in 146 pro games. Wilson never will hit for much power, but he can become a bigger threat at the plate if he improves his pitch recognition and plate discipline. He gets good jumps and has plus range in center field. His arm is average. Wilson missed six weeks with a hip injury last year, so he'll likely return to low Class A to get his feet under him at the start of 2010.

Year	Club (League)	Class	AVG	G	AB	R	H	2B	3B	HR	RBI	BB	SO	SB	OBP	SLG
2008	Blue Jays (GCL)	R	.210	51	162	25	34	6	2	0	12	20	60	25	.319	.272
2009	Blue Jays (GCL)	R	.200	8	25	6	5	2	1	0	0	3	8	3	.310	.360
	Lansing (MWL)	LoA	.212	87	321	51	68	12	3	4	27	35	99	37	.306	.305
MINOR LEAGUE TOTALS			.211	146	508	82	107	20	6	4	39	58	167	65	.311	.297

29 GUSTAVO PIERRE, SS

BORN: Dec. 28, 1991. **B-T:** R-R. **HT.:** 6-2. **WT.:** 183. **SIGNED:** Dominican Republic, 2008. **SIGNED BY:** Miguel Bernard/Hilario Soriano.

While the Blue Jays' recent history of signing expensive international free agents hasn't worked out well, they're optimistic about a pair of 2008 signees, catcher Carlos Perez and Pierre. Perez took a bigger step forward last season and ranks higher on this list, but Pierre may have a higher ceiling. Signed for $700,000 out of the Dominican Republic, he has a great body with plenty of physical projection remaining. He's long and lean with fast-twitch muscles. Pierre has above-average speed and has the frame to develop solid power. He's still raw at the plate and swings at everything, but he's also just 18 and has plenty of time to make adjustments. There was a lot of disagreement about his arm strength before he signed, but it turned out that Pierre had an injured elbow that required Tommy John surgery. He has an average arm and good actions at shortstop, but he may have to move off the position as he fills out. Pierre figures to spend time in extended spring training before shipping out to Auburn in June.

Year	Club (League)	Class	AVG	G	AB	R	H	2B	3B	HR	RBI	BB	SO	SB	OBP	SLG
2009	Blue Jays (GCL)	R	.259	48	174	22	45	10	4	4	22	3	45	8	.272	.431
MINOR LEAGUE TOTALS			.259	48	174	22	45	10	4	4	22	3	45	8	.272	.431

30 REI GONZALEZ, RHP

BORN: Nov. 1, 1985. **B-T:** R-R. **HT.:** 5-9. **WT.:** 215. **DRAFTED:** St. Petersburg (Fla.) JC, 2005 (19th round). **SIGNED BY:** Joel Grampietro.

Gonzalez doesn't exactly have the profile of a major league pitcher. He's a stocky 5-foot-9 and 215 pounds, and he's a righthanded finesse pitcher. Though a groin injury limited him to 17 starts in 2009, he posted a 2.90 ERA in Double-A, continuing his steady progression through the minors since signing as a 19th-round pick in 2005. Gonzalez succeeds via command of four pitches. He works both sides of the plate with his 89-92 mph four-seam fastball, and uses a two-seamer to get grounders. He also mixes in an average curveball and changeup. Gonzalez keeps the ball down in the zone and minimizes the walks and homers he allows, but he doesn't have a swing-and-miss pitch. He projects as more of a middle reliever than a starter in the big leagues, though the Blue Jays protected him on their 40-man roster this offseason rather than expose him to the Rule 5 draft. He'll get his first shot at Triple-A in 2010.

Year	Club (League)	Class	W	L	ERA	G	GS	CG	SV	IP	H	R	ER	HR	BB	SO	AVG
2005	Pulaski (APP)	R	2	0	1.63	7	6	0	0	28	26	9	5	0	6	24	.243
2006	Pulaski (APP)	R	3	5	4.26	13	13	0	0	61	75	41	29	2	16	50	.301
2007	Lansing (MWL)	LoA	9	7	3.53	20	20	1	0	115	121	55	45	4	30	71	.271
2008	Dunedin (FSL)	HiA	12	4	3.14	27	20	1	1	138	155	56	48	6	30	74	.287
2009	New Hampshire (EL)	AA	4	6	2.90	17	17	0	0	93	82	36	30	4	25	67	.236
MINOR LEAGUE TOTALS			30	22	3.25	84	76	2	1	434	459	197	157	16	107	286	.272

Washington Nationals

BY AARON FITT

The Nationals endured a whirlwind 2009. By the end of the summer, the signing of No. 1 overall pick Stephen Strasburg to a record contract and the installation of Mike Rizzo as general manager generated some actual excitement, even with the club headed toward its second straight 100-loss season. But the road to that optimism was bumpy.

Washington's year got off to an ugly start when it came out in February that shortstop Esmailyn Gonzalez, who signed for $1.4 million out of the Dominican Republic in 2006, actually was Carlos Alvarez. While his listed age was 19, he actually was 23 years old.

The next week, the Nationals fired special assistant Jose Rijo, who had signed Gonzalez, and moved out of their Dominican academy, which was owned by Rijo. On March 1, general manager Jim Bowden resigned amid a federal probe into Latin American bonus skimming. Rizzo was promoted from assistant GM to interim GM, and later to full-time GM.

With the major league season lost by the end of April, after Washington dropped 16 of its first 21 games, Rizzo's priority became the No. 1 pick in the draft. To no one's surprise, the Nationals selected Strasburg, the most hyped and perhaps the best prospect in the history of the draft. Agent Scott Boras made it clear Strasburg sought a precedent-setting contract, and the Nationals inked him to a record-shattering $15.1 million deal—including a $7.5 million bonus—scant minutes before the Aug. 17 deadline.

Washington also had the No. 10 choice as compensation for its failure to sign 2008 first-rounder Aaron Crow. The Nats used that pick on another college righty, Drew Storen, who signed for $1.6 million on draft day and quickly reached Double-A. Headlined by the Strasburg and Storen deals, Washington doled out a record $11,511,500 on draft bonuses in 2009.

The low point of the dismal big league season might have been when Jordan Zimmermann, who ranked No. 1 on this list a year ago, was lost to Tommy John surgery halfway through his rookie season as a member of Washington's rotation. The Nationals ended the year with the worst record in the majors (59-103) and will have the No. 1 draft pick for the second straight year, giving them another chance to infuse their mediocre farm system with impact talent.

Catcher Derek Norris and shortstops Ian Desmond and Danny Espinosa took major steps forward in 2009, but there were few other bright spots in the minor

RODGER WOOD

Drafted after Stephen Strasburg, Drew Storen should also help in Washington soon

TOP 30 PROSPECTS

1. Stephen Strasburg, rhp	16. Brad Peacock, rhp
2. Derek Norris, c	17. Juan Jaime, rhp
3. Drew Storen, rhp	18. Marco Estrada, rhp
4. Ian Desmond, ss	19. Graham Hicks, lhp
5. Danny Espinosa, ss	20. Luis Atilano, rhp
6. Chris Marrero, 1b	21. Jack McGeary, lhp
7. Jeff Kobernus, 2b	22. Roger Bernadina, of
8. Justin Maxwell, of	23. Will Atwood, lhp
9. Michael Burgess, of	24. Atahualpa Severino, lhp
10. Destin Hood, of	25. Adrian Nieto, c
11. Eury Perez, of	26. Hassan Pena, rhp
12. Aaron Thompson, lhp	27. Jeff Mandel, rhp
13. J.R. Higley, of	28. Steve Lombardozzi, 2b
14. Brad Meyers, rhp	29. J.P. Ramirez, of
15. A.J. Morris, rhp	30. Danny Rosenbaum, lhp

leagues, as many of Washington's top prospects turned in disappointing seasons. In the fall, Rizzo replaced farm director Bobby Williams with former Indians scout Doug Harris. Longtime scouting director Dana Brown left to take a job with the Blue Jays and was replaced by assistant scouting director Kris Kline.

Rizzo hired Braves scouting director Roy Clark, who consistently brought in quality talent in Atlanta, as vice president of player personnel. The Nats also brought in former Red Sox international scouting coordinator Johnny DiPuglia to revamp the organization's beleaguered international department.

General Manager: Mike Rizzo. **Farm Director:** Doug Harris. **Scouting Director:** Kris Kline.

Class	Team	League	W	L	PCT	Finish*	Manager(s)
Majors	Washington Nationals	National	59	103	.364	16th (16)	M. Acta/J. Riggleman
Triple-A	Syracuse Chiefs	International	76	68	.528	5th (14)	Tim Foli
Double-A	Harrisburg Senators	Eastern	70	72	.493	7th (12)	John Stearns
High A	Potomac Nationals	Carolina	79	58	.577	2nd (8)	Trent Jewett
Low A	Hagerstown Suns	South Atlantic	56	78	.418	16th (16)	Matthew LeCroy
Short-season	Vermont Lake Monsters	New York-Penn	34	41	.453	10th (14)	Jeff Garber
Rookie	GCL Nationals	Gulf Coast	36	19	.655	†2nd (16)	Bob Henley
Overall 2009 Minor League Record			351	336	.511	11th (30)	

*Finish in overall standings (No. of teams in league). †League champion.

LAST YEAR'S TOP 30

Rank	Player, Pos.	Status
1.	Jordan Zimmermann, rhp	Majors
2.	Ross Detwiler, lhp	Majors
3.	Chris Marrero, 1b	No. 6
4.	Michael Burgess, of	No. 9
5.	Jack McGeary, lhp	No. 21
6.	Derek Norris, c	No. 2
7.	Destin Hood, of	No. 10
8.	Adrian Nieto, c	No. 25
9.	J.P. Ramirez, of	No. 29
10.	Carlos Alvarez, ss	Dropped out
11.	Justin Maxwell, of	No. 8
12.	Garrett Mock, rhp	Majors
13.	Shairon Martis, rhp	Majors
14.	Danny Espinosa, ss	No. 5
15.	Graham Hicks, lhp	No. 19
16.	Leonard Davis, of/3b	Dropped out
17.	Bill Rhinehart, 1b	Dropped out
18.	Roger Bernadina, of	No. 22
19.	Ian Desmond, ss	No. 4
20.	Craig Stammen, rhp	Majors
21.	Marco Estrada, rhp	No. 18
22.	Mike Hinckley, lhp	(Orioles)
23.	Stephen King, 3b	Dropped out
24.	Will Atwood, lhp	No. 23
25.	Josh Smoker, lhp	Dropped out
26.	Colton Willems, rhp	Dropped out
27.	Luis Atilano, rhp	No. 20
28.	Cory Van Allen, lhp	Dropped out
29.	Luke Montz, c	Dropped out
30.	Terrell Young, rhp	(Reds)

BEST TOOLS

Best Hitter for Average	Derek Norris
Best Power Hitter	Derek Norris
Best Strike-Zone Discipline	Derek Norris
Fastest Baserunner	Roger Bernadina
Best Athlete	Justin Maxwell
Best Fastball	Stephen Strasburg
Best Curveball	Stephen Strasburg
Best Slider	Drew Storen
Best Changeup	Josh Wilkie
Best Control	Stephen Strasburg
Best Defensive Catcher	Sandy Leon
Best Defensive Infielder	Danny Espinosa
Best Infield Arm	Ian Desmond
Best Defensive Outfielder	Roger Bernadina
Best Outfield Arm	Michael Burgess

PROJECTED 2013 LINEUP

Catcher	Derek Norris
First Base	Chris Marrero
Second Base	Danny Espinosa
Third Base	Ryan Zimmerman
Shortstop	Ian Desmond
Left Field	Josh Willingham
Center Field	Nyjer Morgan
Right Field	Adam Dunn
No. 1 Starter	Stephen Strasburg
No. 2 Starter	Jordan Zimmermann
No. 3 Starter	Ross Detwiler
No. 4 Starter	John Lannan
No. 5 Starter	Collin Balester
Closer	Drew Storen

TOP PROSPECTS OF THE DECADE

Year	Player, Pos.	2009 Org.
2000	Tony Armas, rhp	Braves
2001	Donnie Bridges, rhp	Out of baseball
2002	Brandon Phillips, ss	Reds
2003	Clint Everts, rhp	Nationals
2004	Clint Everts, rhp	Nationals
2005	Mike Hinckley, lhp	Rangers
2006	Ryan Zimmerman, 3b	Nationals
2007	Collin Balester, rhp	Nationals
2008	Chris Marrero, 1b	Nationals
2009	Jordan Zimmermann, rhp	Nationals

TOP DRAFT PICKS OF THE DECADE

Year	Player, Pos.	2009 Org.
2000	Justin Wayne, rhp	Out of baseball
2001	Josh Karp, rhp	Out of baseball
2002	Clint Everts, rhp	Nationals
2003	Chad Cordero, rhp	Mariners
2004	Bill Bray, lhp	Reds
2005	Ryan Zimmerman, 3b	Nationals
2006	Chris Marrero, of	Nationals
2007	Ross Detwiler, lhp	Nationals
2008	*Aaron Crow, rhp	Royals
2009	Stephen Strasburg, rhp	Nationals

*Did not sign.

LARGEST BONUSES IN CLUB HISTORY

Stephen Strasburg, 2009	$7,500,000
Ryan Zimmerman, 2006	$2,975,000
Justin Wayne, 2000	$2,950,000
Josh Karp, 2001	$2,650,000
Clint Everts, 2002	$2,500,000

WASHINGTON NATIONALS

TOP 2010 ROOKIE: Stephen Strasburg, rhp. The most celebrated prospect in draft history might zoom to the majors without ever throwing a pitch in the minors.

BREAKOUT PROSPECT: Brad Peacock, rhp. With three slightly above-average pitches and plenty of athleticism, Peacock will take off if he can fine-tune his command.

SLEEPER: Brandon King, rhp. A 27th-round pick out of a West Virginia high school, he was former scouting director Dana Brown's favorite draft sleeper, a physical bulldog who garners comparisons to Joe Blanton.

SOURCE OF TOP 30 TALENT			
Homegrown	28	Acquired	2
College	11	Trades	2
Junior college	3	Rule 5 draft	0
High school	9	Independent leagues	0
Draft-and-follow	1	Free agents/waivers	0
Nondrafted free agents	0		
International	4		

Numbers in parentheses indicate prospect ranking.

LF
Destin Hood (10)
J.P. Ramirez (29)
Leonard Davis
Mike Daniel
Marvin Lowrance

CF
Justin Maxwell (8)
Eury Perez (11)
Roger Bernadina (22)
Boomer Whiting
Naoya Washiya
Chris Curran
Marcus Jones

RF
Michael Burgess (9)
J.R. Higley (13)
Edgardo Baez

3B
Michael Taylor
Stephen King
Steven Souza
Justin Bloxom
Ofilio Castro

SS
Ian Desmond (4)
Danny Espinosa (5)
Roberto Perez
Jesus Valdez

2B
Jeff Kobernus (7)
Steve Lombardozzi (28)
Seth Bynum
Michael Martinez

1B
Chris Marrero (6)
Bill Rhinehart
Tyler Moore

C
Derek Norris (2)
Adrian Nieto (25)
Sean Rooney
Sandy Leon
Brian Peacock

RHP

Starters	Relievers
Stephen Strasburg (1)	Drew Storen (3)
Brad Meyers (14)	Juan Jaime (17)
A.J. Morris (15)	Hassan Pena (26)
Brad Peacock (16)	Jeff Mandel (27)
Marco Estrada (18)	Dean Weaver
Luis Atilano (20)	Nathan Karns
Paul Demny	Luis Garcia
Marcos Frias	Dustin Crane
Brandon King	Josh Wilkie
Trevor Holder	Adrian Alaniz
Taylor Jordan	Adam Carr
Kyle Morrison	Cole Kimball
Pat Lehman	Johan Figuereo
Colton Willems	Carlos Peralta

LHP

Starters	Relievers
Aaron Thompson (12)	Atahualpa Severino (24)
Graham Hicks (19)	Chad Jenkins
Jack McGeary (21)	Patrick McCoy
Will Atwood (23)	Yunior Novoa
Danny Rosenbaum (30)	Ricardo Pecina
Josh Smoker	Jack Spradlin
Tommy Milone	
Mitchell Clegg	
Paul Applebee	
Cory Van Allen	
Bobby Hansen	

2009

BEST PURE HITTER: 2B Jeff Kobernus (2) makes consistent contact with a line-drive, all-fields approach. His pro debut was cut short after 10 games when an old knee injury required minor surgery.

BEST POWER HITTER: The Nationals didn't sign any sluggers. Kobernus has the most power among the signees, though he primarily drives balls into the gap and figures to top out at 15-20 homers per season.

FASTEST RUNNER: OF Naoya Washiya (14) has well above-average speed and went 12-for-12 stealing bases in the Rookie-level Gulf Coast League. Kobernus and OF J.J. Sferra (31) are plus runners.

BEST DEFENSIVE PLAYER: Kobernus has excellent hands, good athleticism and range, and solid arm strength. Washington thinks he can be an above-average defender at second or third base.

BEST FASTBALL: RHP Stephen Strasburg (1), the best pitching prospect since the draft began in 1965, maintains his mid- to upper-90s fastball late into games and has peaked at 102 mph. RHP Drew Storen (1) sits at 92-94 mph and tops out at 97, while RHPs Dean Weaver (7) and Nathan Karns (12) have reached 96 and RHP Dustin Crane (24) has hit 95.

BEST SECONDARY PITCH: Strasburg's power curveball is as unhittable as his fastball. When he doesn't stay on top of it, it morphs into a tough 83-85 mph slider. Storen's sharp slider has similar velocity.

BEST PRO DEBUT: Storen pitched for three full-season clubs, ending in Double-A with a 1.95 ERA, 11 saves and a 49-8 K-BB ratio in 37 innings.

BEST ATHLETE: Kobernus has average or better tools across the board, and the versatility to play second base, third base or center field.

MOST INTRIGUING BACKGROUND: Washiya is the second Japanese-born player ever drafted, following OF Mitsuru Sakamoto, a Rockies 24th-rounder in 2002. (The Padres made RHP Shuhei Fujiya the third, four rounds after Washiya.) RHP Shane McCatty's (34) father Steve led the American League in wins in 1981 and is Washington's big league pitching coach. Storen's dad Mark Patrick is a former baseball commentator with XM Radio.

CLOSEST TO THE MAJORS: Strasburg's first pro pitch could come in the big leagues, and Storen could join him on the Opening Day 2010 roster.

BEST LATE-ROUND PICK: Washington thinks LHP Danny Rosenbaum (22) could ride his feel for three pitches to their big league bullpen as soon as September. Also keep an eye on Karns, who had difficulty harnessing his power stuff at Texas Tech, and 6-foot-4, 235-pound RHP Brandon King (27).

King can dial his fastball up to 93 mph and flashes a promising breaking ball.

THE ONE WHO GOT AWAY: As a backup plan in case they couldn't sign Strasburg, the Nationals drafted several Texas high school players who could be early picks in 2012, including C Josh Elander (37, now at Texas Christian), RHP Cohl Walla (43, Texas), LHP Hoby Milner (44, Texas) and SS Michael Ratterree (45, Rice).

ASSESSMENT: Washington set a record by spending $11,511,500 on bonuses, including an unprecedented $7.5 million on Strasburg. He represents the future of the franchise, and the Nationals also have high hopes for Storen and Kobernus.

2008

Not signing RHP Aaron Crow (1) was a major blunder, though they did recoup a 2009 compensation pick that turned into Drew Storen. SS Danny Espinosa (3) is a good defender with a better bat than anticipated, while OF Destin Hood (2) offers upside.

GRADE: D

2007

LHP Ross Detwiler (1) and RHP Jordan Zimmermann (2) already have had some big league success, though Zimmermann now is recovering from Tommy John surgery. C Derek Norris (4) had a breakthrough 2009 season, and OF Michael Burgess (1s) has intriguing raw power. But the Nationals were hoping for more out of LHPs Josh Smoker (1s) and Jack McGeary (6).

GRADE: B+

2006

1B Chris Marrero (1) has hit when healthy, but he's all Washington will get out of this draft. RHP Colton Willems' (1) mechanics have fallen apart completely. RHP Sean Black (2) was the highest unsigned pick in the whole draft.

GRADE: D

2005

3B Ryan Zimmerman (1) is the franchise's biggest star, and LHP John Lannan (11) has been its most effective starting pitcher. OF Justin Maxwell (4) and RHPs Marco Estrada (6) and Craig Stammen (12) also have surfaced in Washington.

GRADE: A

*Draft analysis by Jim Callis. Numbers in parentheses indicate draft rounds. *Bonuses for 2005 are first 10 rounds only.*

1 PROSPECT

STEPHEN STRASBURG, RHP

Born: July 20, 1988.
Height: 6-4. **Weight:** 220.
Bats: Right. **Throws:** Right.
Drafted: San Diego State, 2009 (1st round).
Signed by: Mark Baca.

Strasburg went undrafted out of high school in 2006 because of questions about his conditioning, work ethic and maturity. Three years later, he was the No. 1 overall pick and regarded by many scouts as the best prospect in draft history. Strasburg's transformation began his freshman year, when he worked hard to get into better shape and posted a 2.43 ERA and seven saves out of San Diego State's bullpen. His coming-out party came in the summer of 2007, when he ranked as the No. 1 prospect in the New England Collegiate League and dominated in an exhibition against Team USA. As a sophomore, he struck out 23 batters in a game against Utah on his way to first-team All-America honors, then served as the ace for USA Baseball's collegiate national and Olympics teams that summer. While withstanding a relentless maelstrom of hype and national media attention, Strasburg posted one of the most dominant seasons in college baseball history in 2009, going 13-1, 1.32 with 195 strikeouts and 19 walks in 109 innings to lead the Aztecs to regionals for the first time since 1991 and capture Baseball America's College Player of the Year award. The Nationals drafted Strasburg in spite of agent Scott Boras' proclaimed desire to net Strasburg the largest contract in draft history, and he signed just minutes before the Aug. 17 deadline for a record $15.1 million major league deal, including an unprecedented $7.5 million bonus.

Strasburg is a once-in-a-generation talent. His plus-plus fastball sits in the mid- to upper 90s and the Nationals have seen him hit 102 mph. His breaking ball rates as a second plus-plus offering, a power 81-84 mph curveball that he can throw for strikes or use as a chase pitch. Even when he doesn't stay on top of it, it's a tough pitch, becoming more of a hard slider. He also flashes a plus changeup, though he seldom needed the pitch to dominate in college. Strasburg has excellent control with all of his pitches, and he also has very advanced command within the strike zone. He's athletic, physical and durable, and he earns raves for his makeup both on and off the field.

The only thing Strasburg doesn't have is pro experience. The general consensus is that there are no red flags in his delivery, as his arm action is fairly loose and he uses his legs well. But it should be noted that there are some within the organization who are concerned that he eventually could break down because he locks out his elbow on his follow through, putting torque on his shoulder. Still, even those with reservations say they wouldn't tinker with his mechanics.

Strasburg got his first taste of pro ball in the Arizona Fall League, where he topped out at 98 mph in his first outing and posted a 4.26 ERA with 23 strikeouts in 16 innings. He tweaked his left knee while shagging flies at the end of the AFL season, but the injury wasn't serious. Strasburg figures to compete for a job in the major league rotation in spring training, and he might never throw a pitch in the minors, though Washington might also choose to ease him into pro ball with an assignment to Double-A or Triple-A. He projects as a true No. 1 starter and a Cy Young Award winner, and anything less will be a disappointment.

Year	Club (League)	Class	W	L	ERA	G	GS	CG	SV	IP	H	R	ER	HR	BB	SO	AVG
2009	Did Not Play—Signed Late																

2 DEREK NORRIS, C *Leg*

BORN: Feb. 14, 1989. **B-T:** R-R. **HT.:** 6-0. **WT.:** 210. **DRAFTED:** HS—Goddard, Kan., 2007 (4th round). **SIGNED BY:** Ryan Fox.

Norris ranked as the No. 4 prospect in the short-season New York-Penn League in 2008 and the No. 4 prospect in the low Class A South Atlantic League in 2009, when he led the circuit in walks (90) and on-base percentage (.413). Two days before he was scheduled to leave instructional league for the Arizona Fall League, Norris broke the hamate bone in his hand while fouling a ball off, sidelining him for the rest of the winter. Norris has a strong, compact swing and the ability to make consistent, hard contact to all fields. He has a mature, patient offensive approach, excellent pitch recognition and advanced strike-zone awareness. He has above-average power to the pull side and also good power the other way. Behind the plate, he has good agility and blocking skills, solid-average arm strength and a quick release, helping him throw out 36 percent of basestealers last season. The Nationals kept him in the Sally League all year to improve his receiving skills, and he led SAL catchers with 18 errors and 28 passed balls. Converted from third base as high school senior, he's still working on his setup, specifically keeping his hands back and his knees out of the way. He sometimes loses focus on his defense. Norris projects as an above-average offensive player in the big leagues, and if he can become an average defender, he can be an all-star. He should be fully healthy for spring training and will start 2010 at high Class A Potomac.

Year	Club (League)	Class	AVG	G	AB	R	H	2B	3B	HR	RBI	BB	SO	SB	OBP	SLG
2007	Nationals (GCL)	R	.203	37	123	16	25	6	2	4	15	25	38	2	.344	.382
2008	Vermont (NYP)	SS	.278	70	227	42	63	12	0	10	38	63	56	11	.444	.463
2009	Hagerstown (SAL)	LoA	.286	126	437	78	125	30	0	23	84	90	116	6	.413	.513
MINOR LEAGUE TOTALS			.271	233	787	136	213	48	2	37	137	178	210	19	.412	.478

3 DREW STOREN, RHP *Tit*

BORN: Aug. 11, 1987. **B-T:** B-R. **HT.:** 6-2. **WT.:** 180. **DRAFTED:** Stanford, 2009 (1st round). **SIGNED BY:** Ryan Fox.

The son of former XM Radio host Mark Patrick, Storen racked up 15 saves in two seasons as Stanford's closer. The Nationals took him with the 10th overall pick in June, compensation for failing to sign 2008 first-rounder Aaron Crow, and signed him for a below-slot $1.6 million bonus as a draft eligible sophomore. He zoomed to Double-A in his pro debut, then led the Arizona Fall League with a 0.66 ERA. Storen's aggressive mentality and power repertoire are perfect for the late innings. He attacks hitters with a 92-94 mph fastball that touches 97, and he complements it with a pair of hard breaking balls. Some evaluators like his slider better, and others prefer his curve, but both have good depth. He also worked on a changeup in the AFL. He pounds the strike zone and doesn't get rattled easily. Storen's fastball is rather straight and he can be homer-prone when he leaves it up in the zone. Baserunners tended to get good jumps against him during his debut, so the Nationals worked with him on quickening his times to the plate. He already has cut his time from 1.4 seconds to about 1.25, showing good aptitude for adjustments. Storen is on the fast track and figures to reach the majors by 2010, perhaps as soon as Opening Day. He profiles as a closer or setup man and could be closing games in Washington by the end of the season.

Year	Club (League)	Class	W	L	ERA	G	GS	CG	SV	IP	H	R	ER	HR	BB	SO	AVG
2009	Hagerstown (SAL)	LoA	0	1	3.68	11	0	0	0	15	11	6	6	2	0	26	.193
	Potomac (CAR)	HiA	1	0	1.80	7	0	0	2	10	7	2	2	0	2	11	.206
	Harrisburg (EL)	AA	1	0	0.00	10	0	0	9	12	3	0	0	0	6	12	.077
MINOR LEAGUE TOTALS			2	1	1.95	28	0	0	11	37	21	8	8	2	8	49	.162

4 IAN DESMOND, SS *Leg*

BORN: Sept. 20, 1985. **B-T:** R-R. **HT.:** 6-2. **WT.:** 210. **DRAFTED:** HS—Sarasota, Fla., 2004 (3rd round). **SIGNED BY:** Russ Bove.

Though Desmond never had hit better than .264 at any minor league stop heading into 2009, Nats officials still believed he was close to taking off. After missing nearly two months early in the season following surgery to remove the hamate bone in his left hand, Desmond rewarded their faith by hitting .330 in the minors, then getting 10 hits in his first 17 at-bats following a September callup. If Desmond's bat continues to develop, he has a chance for average or better tools across the board. His quick hands and strong forearms generate plus bat speed and average power, and he has done a good job shortening his swing and becoming more patient at the plate. At shortstop, he has good range and a 65 arm on the 20-80 scouting scale. He is live-bodied and athletic, and he plays with plenty of energy. He has average speed and is a smart baserunner. Desmond is capable of making spectacular plays, but he must improve his concentration to cut down on errors on routine plays. He's not a finished product at the plate and still chases pitches out of the zone at times. Desmond will compete for a big league middle-infield job in spring training, but he figures to open the year back at Triple-A Syracuse.

Year	Club (League)	Class	AVG	G	AB	R	H	2B	3B	HR	RBI	BB	SO	SB	OBP	SLG
2004	Expos (GCL)	R	.227	55	216	28	49	11	0	1	27	10	40	13	.272	.292
	Vermont (NYP)	SS	.250	4	12	2	3	0	0	1	1	0	2	0	.308	.500
2005	Savannah (SAL)	LoA	.247	73	296	37	73	10	2	4	23	13	60	20	.291	.334
	Potomac (CAR)	HiA	.256	55	219	37	56	13	3	3	15	21	53	13	.325	.384
2006	Harrisburg (EL)	AA	.182	37	121	8	22	4	1	0	3	5	35	4	.214	.231
	Potomac (CAR)	HiA	.244	92	365	50	89	20	2	9	45	29	79	14	.313	.384
2007	Potomac (CAR)	HiA	.264	129	458	69	121	30	4	13	45	57	99	27	.357	.432
2008	Nationals (GCL)	R	.385	3	13	1	5	1	0	0	2	0	2	3	.385	.462
	Harrisburg (EL)	AA	.251	93	323	42	81	14	0	12	44	31	78	12	.318	.406
2009	Harrisburg (EL)	AA	.306	42	170	29	52	12	1	6	18	16	40	13	.372	.494
	Syracuse (IL)	AAA	.354	55	178	25	63	12	2	1	14	20	31	8	.428	.461
	Washington (NL)	MAJ	.280	21	82	9	23	7	2	4	12	5	14	1	.318	.561
MAJOR LEAGUE TOTALS			.280	21	82	9	23	7	2	4	12	5	14	1	.318	.561
MINOR LEAGUE TOTALS			.259	638	2371	328	614	127	15	50	237	202	519	127	.326	.388

5 DANNY ESPINOSA, SS ┼

RODGER WOOD

BORN: April 25, 1987. **B-T:** B-R. **HT.:** 6-0. **WT.:** 190. **DRAFTED:** Long Beach State, 2008 (3rd round). **SIGNED BY:** Mark Baca.

Espinosa is the latest shortstop prospect from Long Beach State, following Bobby Crosby, Troy Tulowitzki and Evan Longoria. After signing for an above-slot bonus of $525,000 as a third-round pick, he had a strong pro debut in 2008, then skipped a level last season and continued to produce in high Class A. Espinosa is a gamer with excellent instincts and solid tools across the board. He stands out most for his defense, with good range, sure hands and an above-average arm. He's a good athlete with excellent body control and agility and solid-average speed. Offensively, he's a switch-hitter who can drive the ball from both sides of the plate, though his OPS was .133 points higher while batting lefthanded in 2009. Espinosa has some length and leverage in his swing, which helps him hit for average power but also leads to strikeouts. He tends to get caught on his front foot and could drive the ball more consistently if he learned to stay back and use his legs more. Questions still linger about how Espinosa's bat will play at higher levels, and he will get a chance to address them at Double-A Harrisburg in 2010. Even if he doesn't hit for average, he should do enough things well to eventually earn a job as an everyday big leaguer. Espinosa and Ian Desmond look like Washington's double-play combination of the future.

Year	Club (League)	Class	AVG	G	AB	R	H	2B	3B	HR	RBI	BB	SO	SB	OBP	SLG
2008	Vermont (NYP)	SS	.328	19	64	8	21	2	0	0	4	17	17	2	.476	.359
2009	Potomac (CAR)	HiA	.264	133	474	90	125	31	4	18	72	74	129	29	.375	.460
MINOR LEAGUE TOTALS			.271	152	538	98	146	33	4	18	76	91	146	31	.388	.448

6 CHRIS MARRERO, 1B ✗ℯℓ

RODGER WOOD

BORN: July 2, 1988. **B-T:** R-R. **HT.:** 6-3. **WT.:** 210. **DRAFTED:** HS—Opa Locka, Fla., 2006 (1st round). **SIGNED BY:** Tony Arango.

No. 1 on this list two years ago, Marrero had his march through the system sidetracked when he broke his fibula and tore ligaments in his right ankle sliding into home plate in 2008. He returned to high Class A for a third straight season in 2009, and he made strides offensively and defensively to earn a mid-August promotion to Double-A. He batted .349/.402/.542 in the Arizona Fall League. Marrero's best tool is his plus-plus raw power to all fields, though he's still learning to tap into it. He arrived at spring training in the best shape of his life and worked hard to shorten his bat path and get himself into good hitting position. He did a good job using the middle of the field, and he could be an average or better hitter as he matures. Despite Washington's efforts to improve his stride at the plate, Marrero still has a tendency to step in the bucket, making him vulnerable to offspeed stuff away. He is big and long-levered, so his swing always will have some holes. Marrero lacks athleticism and speed and is a below-average defender at first base, though he's working at improving his agility, hands and ability to pick balls out of the dirt. Marrero will return to Double-A as a 21-year-old in 2010, and if all goes well he could break into the big leagues by 2012. His bat will have to carry him, but he has a chance to be a middle-of-the-order power hitter.

Year	Club (League)	Class	AVG	G	AB	R	H	2B	3B	HR	RBI	BB	SO	SB	OBP	SLG
2006	Nationals (GCL)	R	.309	22	81	10	25	9	0	0	16	8	19	0	.374	.420
2007	Hagerstown (SAL)	LoA	.293	57	222	31	65	14	0	14	53	14	39	0	.337	.545
	Potomac (CAR)	HiA	.259	68	255	40	66	11	3	9	35	32	63	0	.338	.431
2008	Potomac (CAR)	HiA	.250	70	256	40	64	15	2	11	38	25	55	0	.325	.453
2009	Potomac (CAR)	HiA	.287	112	414	58	119	21	2	16	65	42	97	2	.360	.464
	Harrisburg (EL)	AA	.267	23	75	9	20	6	0	1	11	8	18	0	.345	.387
MINOR LEAGUE TOTALS			.276	352	1303	188	359	76	7	51	218	129	291	2	.345	.462

7 JEFF KOBERNUS, 2B

RODGER WOOD

BORN: June 30, 1988. **B-T:** R-R. **HT.:** 6-2. **WT.:** 210. **DRAFTED:** California, 2009 (2nd round). **SIGNED BY:** Ryan Fox.

The son of a former Athletics minor leaguer of the same name, Kobernus was a three-year starter at California, playing mostly third base his first two seasons before moving to second as a junior. After signing for $705,500 as a second-round pick in June, he had his pro debut cut short after 10 games by an old knee injury that required minor surgery. The Nationals expected him to be fully healthy by the middle of the fall. Versatile and athletic, Kobernus has a well-rounded game. He makes consistent contact with a line-drive, gap-to-gap swing, and he has an advanced offensive approach. He has above-average speed and outstanding baserunning instincts, helping him rack up 44 steals in three years at Cal. His hands, feet and arm all work well at second base, and he has a chance to be a plus defender there, or at third base if Washington desired. He's a baseball rat with a good work ethic. Kobernus still is learning the subtleties of his relatively new position, refining his footwork, pivots and feeds. He has fringe-average power, though he can run into occasional homers and the Nationals believe he could hit as many as 15-20 per year. Kobernus could move quickly through the system, starting with a likely assignment to low Class A Hagerstown in 2010. He profiles as a solid big league regular, perhaps as soon as 2012.

Year	Club (League)	Class	AVG	G	AB	R	H	2B	3B	HR	RBI	BB	SO	SB	OBP	SLG
2009	Vermont (NYP)	SS	.220	10	41	8	9	1	0	0	2	2	5	4	.273	.244
MINOR LEAGUE TOTALS			.220	10	41	8	9	1	0	0	2	2	5	4	.273	.244

8 JUSTIN MAXWELL, OF

BORN: Nov. 5, 1983. **B-T:** R-R. **HT.:** 6-5. **WT.:** 235. **DRAFTED:** Maryland, 2005 (4th round). **SIGNED BY:** Alex Smith.

The injury-prone Maxwell stayed healthy in 2009, when he scuffled through his first season in Triple-A. He also had three stints in the big leagues, going 0-for-16 in seven games in May but rebounding with a .306/.370/.551 line in September. A physical specimen with plus athleticism, Maxwell has above-average power potential and a patient offensive approach. Nats hitting coach Rick Eckstein and first-base coach Marquis Grissom got the idea to lower his hands to chest level after watching video of other long-levered sluggers like Willie Stargell and Dave Winfield, and the adjustment fueled Maxwell's September surge by getting him in a stronger position to drive the ball more consistently. He's a plus runner who stole 41 bases in 50 tries last season. He's also an above-average defender in center field with excellent range and instincts. Maxwell still must prove he can make consistent contact and hit in the majors over a full season. He also must become more aggressive against pitches away. He has a below-average arm. Injuries have marred four of his last six seasons, and he'll be 26 in 2010. The Nationals will likely give Maxwell a chance to win a starting outfield job in spring training. If he hits, he can be a valuable four-tool player.

Year	Club (League)	Class	AVG	G	AB	R	H	2B	3B	HR	RBI	BB	SO	SB	OBP	SLG
2006	Savannah (SAL)	LoA	.172	17	58	8	10	2	2	1	7	8	23	1	.294	.328
	Vermont (NYP)	SS	.269	74	271	36	73	11	3	4	33	27	61	20	.346	.376
2007	Hagerstown (SAL)	LoA	.301	56	209	51	63	12	2	14	40	26	57	14	.389	.579
	Potomac (CAR)	HiA	.263	58	228	35	60	13	0	13	43	24	65	21	.338	.491
	Washington (NL)	MAJ	.269	15	26	5	7	0	0	2	5	1	8	0	.296	.500
2008	Harrisburg (EL)	AA	.233	43	146	35	34	6	3	7	28	31	28	13	.367	.459
2009	Syracuse (IL)	AAA	.242	111	384	68	93	10	5	13	42	54	136	35	.344	.396
	Washington (NL)	MAJ	.247	40	89	13	22	4	1	4	9	12	32	6	.343	.449
MAJOR LEAGUE TOTALS			.252	55	115	18	29	4	1	6	14	13	40	6	.333	.461
MINOR LEAGUE TOTALS			.257	359	1296	233	333	54	15	52	193	170	370	104	.351	.442

9 MICHAEL BURGESS, OF

RODGER WOOD

BORN: Oct. 20, 1988. **B-T:** L-L. **HT.:** 5-11. **WT.:** 195. **DRAFTED:** HS—Tampa, 2007 (1st round supplemental). **SIGNED BY:** Paul Tinnell.

Burgess comes from the same Hillsborough High (Tampa) program that spawned Dwight Gooden, Gary Sheffield and Elijah Dukes. He reached high Class A in his first full pro season in 2008 but struggled with the bat there last year. Burgess packs enormous strength into his thick, compact build, giving him plus-plus raw power. He has worked with a personal trainer to keep his weight in check, and he's very motivated to improve his game. His plus arm is very accurate, helping him lead the minors with 26 outfield assists in 2008. Fewer baserunners challenged him in 2009, but he still tied for fourth in the Carolina League with nine assists. He has become a solid overall defender in right field as well. Though the Nationals are encouraged that he's finally learning to shorten his swing and cut down his load, his progress hasn't been reflected in his numbers and he may never hit for average. He still chases a lot of breaking balls in the dirt, and his swing still has some length. He's a below-average runner. At the least, Burgess should have a chance to be a power bat off the bench. Whether he ever reaches his potential as a slugger depends upon the development of his bat, which is far from a sure thing. Still just 21, he'll get a crack at Double-A in 2010.

Year	Club (League)	Class	AVG	G	AB	R	H	2B	3B	HR	RBI	BB	SO	SB	OBP	SLG
2007	Nationals (GCL)	R	.336	36	128	22	43	6	3	8	32	25	37	1	.442	.617
	Vermont (NYP)	SS	.286	19	70	10	20	1	1	3	10	10	23	1	.383	.457
2008	Hagerstown (SAL)	LoA	.249	112	401	60	100	26	4	18	60	46	136	5	.335	.469
	Potomac (CAR)	HiA	.225	19	71	12	16	3	0	6	19	9	26	0	.325	.521
2009	Potomac (CAR)	HiA	.235	131	480	63	113	23	2	19	71	54	135	12	.325	.410
MINOR LEAGUE TOTALS			.254	317	1150	167	292	59	10	54	192	144	357	19	.345	.463

10 DESTIN HOOD, OF

BORN: April 30, 1990. **B-T:** R-R. **HT.:** 6-1. **WT.:** 225. **DRAFTED:** HS—Mobile, Ala., 2008 (2nd round). **SIGNED BY:** Eric Robinson.

The Nationals knew Hood was a long-term project when they signed him away from an Alabama football scholarship for a $1.1 million bonus, and they were pleased with his development in 2009. He added muscle in the offseason and quickly hit his way to short-season Vermont, where he held his own against older competition. Physical and athletic, Hood stands out most for his lightning-quick hands, which should lead to above-average power as he matures. He showed a more balanced offensive approach in his second pro season, doing a better job staying back and driving balls to all fields, though most of his power is still to the pull side. Hood's strike-zone awareness and pitch recognition are still developing. He has some arm strength, but he's still learning basic throwing mechanics and exchanges, so his arm plays below average. He's a fringe-average runner who will be limited to left field, where he's currently a below-average defender. The Nationals are betting on Hood's bat. If he develops as they hope, he could be an average or better hitter with plus power and serviceable defensive skills, though he's a long way off yet. He'll get his first taste of low Class A in 2010.

Year	Club (League)	Class	AVG	G	AB	R	H	2B	3B	HR	RBI	BB	SO	SB	OBP	SLG
2008	Nationals (GCL)	R	.256	25	86	18	22	6	1	0	14	8	19	5	.333	.349
2009	Nationals (GCL)	R	.330	25	88	18	29	10	3	3	24	8	19	3	.388	.614
	Vermont (NYP)	SS	.246	38	138	12	34	4	1	2	24	11	45	2	.302	.333
MINOR LEAGUE TOTALS			.272	88	312	48	85	20	5	5	62	27	83	10	.334	.417

11 EURY PEREZ, OF

BORN: May 30, 1990. **B-T:** R-R. **HT.:** 6-0. **WT.:** 180. **SIGNED:** Dominican Republic, 2007. **SIGNED BY:** Dana Brown/Moises de la Mota.

Perez showed a patient approach and the ability to make solid contact in two seasons in the Rookie-level Dominican Summer League. Near the end of spring training in 2009, the Nationals gave him a spot start in a Triple-A game against the Braves and Tommy Hanson, and Perez made a positive impression with a multihit performance. He kept on hitting in the Rookie-level Gulf Coast League, batting .381 to lead the league as well as all players in short-season circuits. Perez has a wiry, athletic frame and plus-plus speed. Though he's not overly physical, he does have quick hands and strong wrists, and he can drive the ball to the middle of the field. He doesn't project to have much power but profiles as a quality tablesetter, especially as he improves his basestealing skills. He was thrown out in a third of his 24 attempts in 2009. He's a good bunter who gets on base by working walks and beating out infield hits. Perez is a plus defender in center field with excellent range and an average-to-plus arm, helping him rank second in the GCL with seven outfield assists. He figures to start 2010 in extended spring training before moving up to Vermont. If Perez keeps hitting like he did in 2009, he could force his way up the organization ladder quickly.

Year	Club (League)	Class	AVG	G	AB	R	H	2B	3B	HR	RBI	BB	SO	SB	OBP	SLG
2007	Nationals 1 (DSL)	R	.253	51	158	41	40	5	1	0	14	32	39	15	.399	.297
2008	Nationals 1 (DSL)	R	.324	60	213	51	69	9	2	4	44	32	36	28	.428	.441
2009	Nationals (GCL)	R	.381	47	181	38	69	3	5	3	24	15	20	16	.443	.503
MINOR LEAGUE TOTALS			.322	158	552	130	178	17	8	7	82	79	95	59	.424	.420

12 AARON THOMPSON, LHP

BORN: Feb. 28, 1987. **B-T:** L-L. **HT.:** 6-3. **WT.:** 195. **DRAFTED:** HS—Houston, 2005 (1st round). **SIGNED BY:** Dennis Cardoza (Marlins).

After the Marlins signed him away from a commitment to Texas A&M with a $1.225 million bonus in 2005, Thompson progressed slowly but steadily through their system until 2008, when he missed two months with a minor shoulder injury. He returned to Double-A in 2009 and turned a corner after Jacksonville pitching coach Reid Cornelius taught him a cutter in mid-July. Four days after learning the pitch, he used it to rack up nine of his 10 strikeouts over six innings in his penultimate start as a member of the Florida organization. The Nationals acquired him at the July 31 trade deadline for first baseman Nick Johnson, and he posted a 3.31 ERA in six starts after the deal. At his best, Thompson shows a fastball that sits at 90-91 and touches 93 with good movement. He has good feel for a four-seamer, a two-seamer and a solid-average changeup in addition to his newfound cutter. His slurvy breaking ball is still a work in progress but shows sharp, hard break at times. At others, his breaking ball deserts him and his fastball velocity dips, so he must become more consistent. Thompson figures to start 2010 in Triple-A and could push for a job in Washington's rotation during the season. He projects as a No. 4 or 5 starter.

Year	Club (League)	Class	W	L	ERA	G	GS	CG	SV	IP	H	R	ER	HR	BB	SO	AVG
2005	Marlins (GCL)	R	2	4	4.50	8	8	0	0	32	42	20	16	1	10	41	.316
	Jamestown (NYP)	SS	1	2	3.10	5	5	0	0	20	25	13	7	1	10	17	.301
2006	Greensboro (SAL)	LoA	8	8	3.63	24	24	0	0	134	139	68	54	12	35	114	.270
2007	Jupiter (FSL)	HiA	4	6	3.37	20	19	0	0	115	121	64	43	2	35	84	.266
2008	Marlins (GCL)	R	0	0	2.00	2	2	0	0	9	8	2	2	0	1	9	.242
	Carolina (SL)	AA	2	5	5.62	16	16	0	0	82	111	61	51	9	40	53	.331
2009	Jacksonville (SL)	AA	5	9	4.11	20	20	0	0	114	121	63	52	7	43	75	.268
	Harrisburg (EL)	AA	0	3	3.31	6	6	0	0	33	32	18	12	3	11	27	.254
MINOR LEAGUE TOTALS			22	37	3.96	101	100	0	0	539	599	309	237	35	185	420	.281

13 J.R. HIGLEY, OF

BORN: June 21, 1988. **B-T:** R-R. **HT.:** 6-3. **WT.:** 210. **DRAFTED:** Sacramento CC, 2008 (9th round). **SIGNED BY:** Ryan Fox.

A teammate of Red Sox prospect Lars Anderson at Jesuit High in Carmichael, Calif., Higley redshirted at Loyola Marymount in 2007 and transferred to Sacramento CC in 2008. A shortstop in high school, he shifted to first base in junior college and then to the outfield in pro ball. The Nationals signed him for a $150,000 bonus. Higley was slated to start his first full pro season in low Class A before straining ligaments in his wrist late in the spring. He wound up spending most of 2009 at Vermont, but homered twice in his second game after a late-August promotion to Hagerstown. Higley has athletic bloodlines—his father was a wrestler at Iowa—and a frame to match. He's a line-drive, gap-to-gap hitter, but it's uncertain if he'll ever have enough pop to hold down an everyday job as a corner outfielder. Washington projects him to grow into average or better power down the road, but right now all his pop is to the pull side. He's an aggressive hitter who needs to improve his plate discipline and get better against offspeed stuff. His slightly above-average speed and arm strength are assets in the outfield, and he has excellent instincts in both right and center. He's a gamer with an aggressive mentality and a good work ethic. If his bat develops, Higley has a chance for average or better tools across the board. If it doesn't, he still could have value as an extra outfielder with premium defensive skills. He'll start 2010 back at Hagerstown.

Year	Club (League)	Class	AVG	G	AB	R	H	2B	3B	HR	RBI	BB	SO	SB	OBP	SLG
2008	Nationals (GCL)	R	.346	35	107	17	37	12	0	0	16	21	32	6	.486	.458
2009	Vermont (NYP)	SS	.271	53	192	22	52	6	3	3	20	12	52	6	.327	.380
	Hagerstown (SAL)	LoA	.300	11	40	7	12	3	1	2	6	4	12	0	.391	.575
MINOR LEAGUE TOTALS			.298	99	339	46	101	21	4	5	42	37	96	12	.391	.428

14 BRAD MEYERS, RHP

BORN: Sept. 13, 1985. **B-T:** R-R. **HT.:** 6-6. **WT.:** 195. **DRAFTED:** Loyola Marymount, 2007 (5th round). **SIGNED BY:** Craig Kornfeld.

Meyers opened his pro career by pitching 24 consecutive scoreless innings in 2007 and led the minor leagues with a 1.72 ERA last season, but the road in between was rocky. He came down with a dead arm in the second half of his pro debut and saw his fastball dip to 82-85 mph during a rough 2008 campaign. He improved his mechanics, velocity and fastball command to post a dominant 2009, reaching Double-A and capturing the organization's pitcher of the year award. Long and lanky with a high three-quarters arm slot, Meyers pitches downhill with an 88-90 mph fastball that tops out at 92. He locates the pitch very well to both sides of the plate, and he induces swings and misses thanks to its life and deception. Meyers' four-pitch mix also includes an average 82-84 mph slider, an average changeup with some fade and a short curveball that he uses as a show pitch. Meyers pounds the zone, but his stuff is not overpowering and his upside is limited to the back of a big league rotation. He also must overcome lingering questions about his durability. Even in his breakout 2009 season, he missed a few starts in July with a heel injury. Meyers should get a crack at Triple-A in 2010, though he could start the year back in Harrisburg.

Year	Club (League)	Class	W	L	ERA	G	GS	CG	SV	IP	H	R	ER	HR	BB	SO	AVG
2007	Nationals (GCL)	R	0	0	0.00	3	3	0	0	9	2	0	0	0	0	9	.067
	Hagerstown (SAL)	LoA	1	1	0.44	4	4	0	0	21	13	4	1	1	8	9	.178
	Potomac (CAR)	HiA	0	0	5.06	3	3	0	0	11	15	6	6	1	9	7	.357
2008	Hagerstown (SAL)	LoA	9	7	4.79	22	21	0	0	107	129	66	57	8	34	94	.299
2009	Potomac (CAR)	HiA	6	2	1.43	15	14	0	0	88	71	17	14	1	21	65	.222
	Harrisburg (EL)	AA	5	1	2.25	9	9	1	0	48	40	14	12	2	11	43	.225
MINOR LEAGUE TOTALS			21	11	2.86	56	54	1	0	284	270	107	90	13	83	227	.251

15 A.J. MORRIS, RHP

BORN: Dec. 1, 1986. **B-T:** R-R. **HT.:** 6-2. **WT.:** 200. **DRAFTED:** Kansas State, 2009 (4th round). **SIGNED BY:** Kerrick Jackson.

Morris arrived at Kansas State as a skinny, 164-pound Texas kid who wasn't ready for the Big 12 Conference, so he redshirted in 2006. After two up-and-down seasons, he had a breakout summer in the West Coast League in 2008, leading the circuit in strikeouts and drawing free-agent interest from scouts after having gone unpicked as a draft-eligible sophomore. He returned to Kansas State for his junior year and exploded onto the national scene, setting school records for wins (14) and strikeouts (100 in 116 innings) en route to first-team All-America honors. In the process, he led the Wildcats to their first NCAA tournament appearance ever. After signing him for $270,000 as a fourth-rounder, the Nationals sent Morris to the Gulf Coast League to focus on adding muscle, and he's now up to 200 pounds. In college, Morris dominated exclusively with a 90-91 mph fastball that touches 94 and an average slider. His fastball cuts, sinks and rides, and he commands it on the corners and at the knees. He worked on his changeup in his pro debut and instructional league, and it has the makings of giving him a third average pitch. He also repeated his low three-quarters arm slot more consistently in instructs and improved onto his ability to hold baserunners, reducing his times to the plate from 1.6 to 1.3 seconds. Morris still must add strength and refine his changeup if he is to stick as a starter, but his competitiveness and ability to pound the strike zone should make him a big leaguer even if he's relegated to a relief role. Morris could begin 2010 in high Class A and move quickly.

Year	Club (League)	Class	W	L	ERA	G	GS	CG	SV	IP	H	R	ER	HR	BB	SO	AVG
2009	Nationals (GCL)	R	0	0	0.00	2	2	0	0	5	0	0	0	0	0	4	.000
	Hagerstown (SAL)	LoA	0	4	3.82	8	8	0	0	38	44	23	16	2	8	36	.297
MINOR LEAGUE TOTALS			0	4	3.38	10	10	0	0	43	44	23	16	2	8	40	.270

16 BRAD PEACOCK, RHP

BORN: Feb. 2, 1988. **B-T:** R-R. **HT.:** 6-1. **WT.:** 175. **DRAFTED:** Palm Beach (Fla.) CC, D/F 2006 (41st round). **SIGNED BY:** Tony Arango.

An excellent athlete, Peacock played mostly shortstop in high school and the Nationals selected him in the 41st round of the 2006 draft as a catcher. He was impressive on the mound at Palm Beach (Fla.) CC in the spring of 2007, throwing two-seam fastballs that topped out at 94 mph and flashing an above-average knuckle-curve. After signing him for $110,000 as a draft-and-follow, the Nationals tweaked his arm slot and had him to throw a four-seamer and a conventional curve. He struggled with the adjustments and got bombed in low Class A in 2008, but once he was demoted to Vermont, he went back to his three-quarters arm-slot and college repertoire. Peacock has a quick arm and a smooth arm action, and he maintained a 90-94 mph fastball throughout last season. His knuckle-curve and changeup also rate as slightly above-average pitches when they're on. Peacock could take off once he learns to be a little more aggressive and do a better job attacking the bottom of the strike zone. He figures to return to high Class A to start 2010 but could reach Double-A by midseason.

Year	Club (League)	Class	W	L	ERA	G	GS	CG	SV	IP	H	R	ER	HR	BB	SO	AVG
2007	Nationals (GCL)	R	1	1	3.89	13	7	0	0	39	38	23	17	1	15	34	.242
2008	Hagerstown (SAL)	LoA	0	5	9.09	8	8	0	0	34	38	38	34	8	21	23	.284
	Vermont (NYP)	SS	4	7	3.12	14	14	2	0	75	67	38	26	3	27	54	.235
2009	Hagerstown (SAL)	LoA	5	8	4.05	19	17	0	0	100	104	49	45	10	32	77	.272
	Potomac (CAR)	HiA	3	3	4.34	8	7	0	0	48	46	26	23	4	10	27	.253
MINOR LEAGUE TOTALS			13	24	4.41	62	53	2	0	296	293	174	145	26	105	215	.257

17 JUAN JAIME, RHP

BORN: Aug. 2, 1987. **B-T:** R-R. **HT.:** 6-1. **WT.:** 180. **SIGNED:** Dominican Republic, 2004. **SIGNED BY:** Ismael Cruz/Sandi Rosario.

In his second season in the United States, Jaime had a breakout year at Vermont and Hagerstown. He always had explosive arm strength, but he was extremely raw when he arrived in the United States in 2008. He had too much baby fat, poor feel for his secondary stuff and a delivery that needed tightening. Now Jaime is stronger and more athletic. He's learning to throw strikes and repeat his delivery more consistently, though he still rushes it at times and it still has a bit of violence. Jaime's best pitch is a 92-96 mph fastball that routinely touches 98. He generally can throw it for strikes but still is working on commanding it within the strike zone. He flashes an above-average downer curveball, but most of the time it remains a below-average slurve. The Nationals used him as a starter in 2009 and forced him to throw his breaking ball and nascent changeup, but he still has very little feel for the change and his future is undoubtedly as a power arm in the bullpen. Jaime has the best pure arm in the system outside of Stephen Strasburg, and he eventually could become a major league closer if everything clicks. He remains quite a ways off from that ceiling, however, and could return to low Class A to start 2010.

Year	Club (League)	Class	W	L	ERA	G	GS	CG	SV	IP	H	R	ER	HR	BB	SO	AVG
2005	Nationals (DSL)	R	1	0	2.51	9	0	0	0	14	9	7	4	1	11	14	.176
2006	Nationals 2 (DSL)	R	0	0	2.61	6	0	0	1	10	5	7	3	0	8	13	.135
2007	Nationals 1 (DSL)	R	3	0	1.35	14	0	0	0	27	11	7	4	0	14	34	.121

Year	Club (League)	Class	W	L	ERA	G	GS	CG	SV	IP	H	R	ER	HR	BB	SO	AVG
2008	Nationals (GCL)	R	2	1	4.74	8	2	1	0	19	16	12	10	1	18	23	.232
2009	Vermont (NYP)	SS	2	1	1.88	6	5	0	0	24	15	6	5	0	15	36	.183
	Hagerstown (SAL)	LoA	3	1	2.27	8	7	0	0	32	22	15	8	2	16	40	.193
MINOR LEAGUE TOTALS			11	3	2.43	51	14	1	1	126	78	54	34	4	82	160	.176

18 MARCO ESTRADA, RHP

BORN: July 5, 1983. **B-T:** R-R. **HT.:** 6-0. **WT.:** 195. **DRAFTED:** Long Beach State, 2005 (6th round). **SIGNED BY:** Brian Hunter/Brian Parker.

Estrada's career has progressed in fits and starts since he transferred from Glendale (Calif.) CC to Long Beach State in 2005. His stock rose that spring when he went 8-3, 2.43 for the Dirtbags, sank when he broke his collarbone before the 2006 season, increased again in Hawaii Winter Baseball that fall, then fell again when he struggled through a rough 2007. He spent most of the last two years in Triple-A, where he held his own before tiring down the stretch both seasons, just in time for a pair of lackluster big league callups. Estrada is undersized but has a quick arm, capable of producing a low-90s fastball that tops out at 94. He has one of the best changeups in the system, an above-average pitch with good arm speed and tumbling action. He also throws a solid-average 78-81 mph curveball with some sharpness to it. The Nationals would like to see Estrada become more aggressive and attack hitters more, because he has a tendency to nibble. He also runs into trouble with his fastball because his size and low arm slot give the pitch a flat plane. Estrada's lack of physicality could make him a better fit in a big league bullpen, but his three-pitch mix does give him a chance to be a back-end starter. He'll compete for a big league job in spring training.

Year	Club (League)	Class	W	L	ERA	G	GS	CG	SV	IP	H	R	ER	HR	BB	SO	AVG
2005	Vermont (NYP)	SS	1	3	5.08	9	6	0	1	34	31	21	19	4	16	37	.231
2006	Nationals (GCL)	R	2	0	1.52	5	4	0	0	24	14	4	4	1	6	27	.165
	Savannah (SAL)	LoA	1	4	5.59	8	8	0	0	37	44	23	23	6	14	29	.301
2007	Hagerstown (SAL)	LoA	1	5	5.25	8	8	0	0	36	39	24	21	4	17	35	.279
	Nationals (GCL)	R	0	0	3.18	4	4	0	0	11	19	6	4	1	3	13	.365
	Potomac (CAR)	HiA	5	3	4.94	11	11	0	0	58	67	32	32	7	17	54	.291
2008	Harrisburg (EL)	AA	6	3	2.66	13	13	1	0	74	62	27	22	5	32	67	.223
	Columbus (IL)	AAA	3	3	3.58	12	12	0	0	65	73	28	26	3	21	52	.287
	Washington (NL)	MAJ	0	0	7.82	11	0	0	0	13	17	13	11	4	5	10	.304
2009	Syracuse (IL)	AAA	9	5	3.63	27	25	0	0	136	133	61	55	10	33	98	.256
	Washington (NL)	MAJ	0	1	6.14	4	1	0	0	7	6	6	5	1	4	9	.214
MAJOR LEAGUE TOTALS			0	1	7.20	15	1	0	0	20	23	19	16	5	9	19	.274
MINOR LEAGUE TOTALS			28	26	3.89	97	91	1	1	476	482	226	206	41	159	412	.262

19 GRAHAM HICKS, LHP

BORN: Feb. 19, 1990. **B-T:** L-L. **HT.:** 6-5. **WT.:** 170. **DRAFTED:** HS—Lakeland, Fla., 2008 (4th round). **SIGNED BY:** Paul Tinnell.

After his star turn at the 2008 Florida high school all-star game in Sebring, Fla., Hicks climbed into the fourth round of the draft. He turned down a scholarship offer from Central Florida to sign with Washington for an above-slot $475,000 bonus. After making two appearances in his pro debut, Hicks broke his left middle finger during a fielding drill at the end of his first day in instructional league but was completely healthy by spring training in 2009. He spent the offseason working on making his legs stronger and showed up in minor league camp more than a month early. But Hicks struggled with his consistency and command at Vermont, so he was sent back to the Gulf Coast League, where he finished strong. Hicks garners frequent comparisons to Nationals lefthander Ross Detwiler for his tall, skinny frame and electric arm, and like a young Detwiler he must continue to add strength. He currently sits at 88-90 mph and touches 91 with his fastball, but he projects to add velocity as he matures. He flashes an average-to-plus curveball and an average changeup, but he's still working on his feel for both pitches. Hicks is a tough competitor and a good athlete. He has a tendency to open up his front side too quickly, and his command should improve as he learns to make his delivery more efficient. Hicks has as much upside as any pitcher in the system outside of Stephen Strasburg, but he has a long way to go. He figures to start 2010 in low Class A.

Year	Club (League)	Class	W	L	ERA	G	GS	CG	SV	IP	H	R	ER	HR	BB	SO	AVG
2008	Nationals (GCL)	R	0	0	0.00	1	1	0	0	2	1	0	0	0	0	2	.143
	Vermont (NYP)	SS	0	1	3.00	1	1	0	0	3	3	3	1	0	2	1	.250
2009	Hagerstown (SAL)	LoA	0	0	5.40	1	1	0	0	5	6	3	3	2	3	6	.300
	Vermont (NYP)	SS	2	5	7.12	9	9	0	0	37	53	37	29	2	21	18	.338
	Nationals (GCL)	R	3	0	3.60	3	3	0	0	15	13	6	6	1	3	14	.245
MINOR LEAGUE TOTALS			5	6	5.69	15	15	0	0	62	76	49	39	5	29	41	.305

20 LUIS ATILANO, RHP

BORN: May 10, 1985. **B-T:** R-R. **HT.:** 6-2. **WT.:** 220. **DRAFTED:** HS—San Juan, P.R., 2003 (1st round supplemental). **SIGNED BY:** Julian Perez (Braves).

The 35th overall pick in the 2003 draft, Atilano never unlocked his potential with the Braves after signing for $950,000. Washington took a low-risk gamble in August 2006, trading Daryle Ward for him shortly after Atilano had Tommy John surgery. After missing nearly all of 2007, he has re-established himself as a prospect over the last two years. He got off to a rough start in 2009, posting an 0-3, 8.79 mark in April, and the Nationals noticed he was opening up too much in his delivery, decreasing his deception and sink. He took off after correcting the problem and finished the year with two strong starts in Triple-A and a 3-0, 2.21 showing in the World Cup, helping Puerto Rico finish in fourth place, equaling its best finish since 1976. Atilano attacks hitters with an 89-92 mph fastball with heavy sink and fools them with an above-average changeup. He has improved his conditioning over the last year and is a good athlete for his size. Washington believes Atilano is a breaking ball away from being a real good major league pitcher. He'll flash an average curveball at times, but at others the pitch is just a short spinner waiting to be crushed. The Nationals have a glut of back-of-the-rotation candidates, and he could force his way into that mix in spring training. He's more likely to start the year in Triple-A.

Year	Club (League)	Class	W	L	ERA	G	GS	CG	SV	IP	H	R	ER	HR	BB	SO	AVG
2003	Braves (GCL)	R	3	2	3.83	12	12	1	0	54	61	25	23	5	7	24	.288
2004	Danville (APP)	R	5	1	4.20	13	13	0	0	64	64	32	30	7	10	54	.260
2005	Rome (SAL)	LoA	8	9	4.17	24	24	1	0	136	138	77	63	17	32	66	.261
2006	Myrtle Beach (CAR)	HiA	6	7	4.50	19	18	2	0	116	134	63	58	16	27	45	.298
2007	Nationals (GCL)	R	0	0	6.75	1	0	0	0	1	1	1	1	0	1	2	.200
2008	Hagerstown (SAL)	LoA	0	0	3.16	7	3	0	1	26	29	14	9	1	7	13	.276
	Harrisburg (EL)	AA	0	1	1.50	2	1	0	0	6	6	3	1	0	2	3	.300
	Potomac (CAR)	HiA	5	2	2.32	15	11	0	0	62	50	21	16	5	14	39	.229
2009	Harrisburg (EL)	AA	7	8	4.16	21	20	0	0	115	143	58	53	12	27	61	.308
	Syracuse (IL)	AAA	2	0	2.45	2	2	0	0	11	11	3	3	2	1	5	.262
MINOR LEAGUE TOTALS			36	30	3.91	116	104	4	1	591	637	297	257	65	128	312	.278

21 JACK McGEARY, LHP

BORN: March 19,1989. **B-T:** L-L. **HT.:** 6-3. **WT.:** 195. **DRAFTED:** HS—West Roxbury, Mass., 2007 (6th round). **SIGNED BY:** Mike Alberts.

The Nationals signed McGeary for a sixth-round-record $1.8 million bonus and agreed to pay for him to attend classes at Stanford from September through early June for the first three years of his career. While living with three Cardinal pitchers (including Drew Storen), McGeary took 20 credit hours per week to get on track to graduate by June 2010. He decided to skip the spring quarter in 2009 to be with the Nationals from spring training through the end of the minor league season, before returning to Stanford for the fall and winter. But McGeary's first season as a full-time pro pitcher didn't go as planned. He struggled mightily with his control, even after a demotion to Vermont, and averaged a jarring 6.9 walks per nine innings. Mechanical problems largely accounted for McGeary's wildness. He has a tendency to get too deep on the back side of his delivery, causing him to get under the ball and throw uphill. He also struggles to repeat his release point and stay in sync. All of that took a toll on his fastball command, and his velocity wavered between 85-91 mph. He still shows good finish on his downer curveball at times, but his feel for the pitch comes and goes. He continues to develop his changeup, and at his best it gives him a third average or better pitch. McGeary is still young and has the potential to be a middle-of-the-rotation starter someday, but 2010 is a crucial year for him. The Nationals have seen other high-profile arms get derailed similarly in recent years (Colton Willems, Mike Hinckley, Clint Everts, Josh Smoker), and they need McGeary to get back on track to avoid that sort of wandering path through the minors.

Year	Club (League)	Class	W	L	ERA	G	GS	CG	SV	IP	H	R	ER	HR	BB	SO	AVG
2007	Vermont (NYP)	SS	0	1	13.50	2	1	0	0	3	3	5	4	0	5	4	.273
2008	Nationals (GCL)	R	2	2	4.07	12	12	0	0	60	61	34	27	2	13	64	.258
	Vermont (NYP)	SS	0	0	4.50	1	1	0	0	4	6	2	2	0	3	5	.375
2009	Hagerstown (SAL)	LoA	0	6	6.79	13	13	0	0	56	58	48	42	4	45	44	.280
	Vermont (NYP)	SS	2	6	4.31	13	13	0	0	56	61	43	27	5	41	45	.274
MINOR LEAGUE TOTALS			4	15	5.15	41	40	0	0	178	189	132	102	11	107	162	.273

22 ROGER BERNADINA, OF

BORN: June 12, 1984. **B-T:** L-L. **HT.:** 6-2. **WT.:** 200. **SIGNED:** Netherlands, 2001. **SIGNED BY:** Fred Ferreira.

It took Bernadina five full years just to reach Double-A, but his career finally picked up some momentum in 2007, when his strong play for the Netherlands in the European Olympic qualifier earned him a spot on the Nationals' 40-man roster. He carried that momentum into 2008, posting his best offensive season and earning major league callups in June and September. After starting last season in Triple-A, Bernadina returned to the majors in mid-April but broke his ankle in his third game when his foot got jammed at the bottom of the outfield wall as he was making a highlight-reel catch. He returned in time to play two rehab games in late August and was completely healthy in instructional league, where he made significant progress with his bunting. Bernadina's best tool is his plus-plus speed, which plays very well on the basepaths thanks to his solid instincts. He also has excellent range and a strong, accurate arm in center field, where he's an above-average defender. Bernadina has shortened his swing significantly over the last year, and he has average raw power, but he might never hit enough to hold down an everyday job in the majors. His speed and defense give him value as an extra outfielder, and if he continues to mature offensively he could become a Nyjer Morgan-type player. He should compete for a big league job in the spring.

Year	Club (League)	Class	AVG	G	AB	R	H	2B	3B	HR	RBI	BB	SO	SB	OBP	SLG
2002	Expos (GCL)	R	.276	57	196	22	54	7	0	3	18	19	25	1	.348	.357
2003	Savannah (SAL)	LoA	.237	77	278	36	66	12	3	4	39	19	53	11	.292	.345
2004	Savannah (SAL)	LoA	.238	129	450	67	107	24	7	7	66	60	113	24	.338	.369
2005	Savannah (SAL)	LoA	.233	122	417	64	97	15	3	12	54	75	92	35	.356	.369
2006	Potomac (CAR)	HiA	.270	123	434	60	117	19	3	6	42	56	98	28	.355	.369
2007	Columbus (IL)	AAA	.167	13	42	6	7	3	0	0	1	9	11	0	.327	.238
	Harrisburg (EL)	AA	.270	97	371	58	100	15	2	6	36	38	80	40	.340	.369
2008	Harrisburg (EL)	AA	.323	73	266	47	86	11	7	5	38	31	64	26	.398	.474
	Columbus (IL)	AAA	.351	47	191	33	67	13	3	4	16	16	37	15	.404	.513
	Washington (NL)	MAJ	.211	26	76	10	16	1	1	0	2	9	21	4	.294	.250
2009	Syracuse (IL)	AAA	.167	5	18	1	3	0	0	0	0	4	5	1	.318	.167
	Washington (NL)	MAJ	.250	3	4	1	1	1	0	0	0	1	1	1	.400	.500
	Nationals (GCL)	R	.250	2	4	0	1	0	0	0	0	0	1	0	.250	.250
MAJOR LEAGUE TOTALS			.213	29	80	11	17	2	1	0	2	10	22	5	.300	.263
MINOR LEAGUE TOTALS			.264	745	2667	394	705	119	28	47	310	327	579	181	.350	.383

23 WILL ATWOOD, LHP

BORN: Jan. 13, 1987. **B-T:** L-L. **HT.:** 6-2. **WT.:** 180. **DRAFTED:** South Carolina, 2008 (12th round). **SIGNED BY:** Bob Hamelin.

Atwood posted a 5.21 ERA in three years at South Carolina, but the Nationals believed they had found a sleeper in the 12th round of the 2008 draft after his strong pro debut. They skipped him a level to high Class A to start 2009, and he struggled mightily out of the gate, going 0-3, 11.65 in April, before settling down to go 6-3, 2.92 over the next three months. He tired down the stretch, however, and his velocity dropped. At his best, Atwood has good command of a solid three-pitch mix. His fastball sits at 88-90 and touches 92, and he spots it well to both sides of the plate. His best pitch is a solid-average changeup with fade, sink and good arm speed. His slow curveball has tight spin and a chance to give him a third average pitch. He has a lean frame and a clean, whippy arm action that reminds several Nats officials of John Lannan. Atwood's mechanics are sound, though he sometimes opens up too early in his delivery. He needs to improve his pickoff move and fine-tune his overall command, but he should be ready to take on Double-A in 2010. He profiles as a back-of-the-rotation starter.

Year	Club (League)	Class	W	L	ERA	G	GS	CG	SV	IP	H	R	ER	HR	BB	SO	AVG
2008	Vermont (NYP)	SS	2	1	2.41	12	12	0	0	52	40	17	14	2	9	60	.205
2009	Potomac (CAR)	HiA	8	8	4.61	26	26	0	0	137	142	76	70	10	40	118	.269
MINOR LEAGUE TOTALS			10	9	4.00	38	38	0	0	189	182	93	84	12	49	178	.252

24 ATAHUALPA SEVERINO, LHP

BORN: Nov. 6, 1984. **B-T:** L-L. **HT.:** 5-9. **WT.:** 170. **SIGNED:** Dominican Republic, 2004. **SIGNED BY:** Ismael Cruz/Sandi Rosario.

The Expos had a virtually nonexistent international budget when Major League Baseball owned the franchise prior to its move to Washington, and Severino—signed for $6,000 in February 2004—might go down as their most significant international acquisition during that period. After making his pro debut that summer, Severino had Tommy John surgery that sidelined him for all of 2005, and he spent the next two years dominating the Dominican Summer League. He has moved fairly quickly since arriving in the United States in 2007, climbing to Double-A in 2009, then following up with a strong winter with Licey in the Dominican League. Severino is undersized but makes up for it with his fearlessness and quick arm. He attacks the strike zone with an 89-93 mph fastball that touches 94, and he pitches inside very well with both his four-seamer and his two-seamer. His 76-82 mph breaking ball has 11-to-5 action and is still a work in progress. Sometimes it's an average pitch with sharp break, but at other times he gets around it and it's sweepy. He seldom throws his breaking ball to righthanders but does mix in a workable changeup. Severino is generally sound mechanically, though he flies open on occasion. He garners comparisons to J.C. Romero for his size, delivery and stuff, and his future is likely as a lefty specialist in the Romero mold. He could push his way to the majors at some point in 2010.

Year	Club (League)	Class	W	L	ERA	G	GS	CG	SV	IP	H	R	ER	HR	BB	SO	AVG
2004	Expos (DSL)	R	2	5	4.46	15	4	0	3	38	36	22	19	7	15	47	.248
2005	Did Not Play																
2006	Nationals 1 (DSL)	R	2	0	0.99	13	8	0	1	45	18	5	5	0	17	79	.121
2007	Nationals 1 (DSL)	R	3	0	0.48	3	3	0	0	19	14	2	1	0	2	31	.212
	Nationals (GCL)	R	1	0	2.94	13	5	0	0	34	25	12	11	3	10	28	.208
2008	Hagerstown (SAL)	LoA	4	2	4.05	15	0	0	1	33	28	17	15	2	17	34	.235
	Potomac (CAR)	HiA	0	4	3.96	26	0	0	0	39	31	18	17	2	20	31	.221
2009	Potomac (CAR)	HiA	4	0	2.54	29	0	0	13	46	35	14	13	4	14	39	.211
	Harrisburg (EL)	AA	6	0	2.78	15	0	0	2	23	19	8	7	1	14	27	.235
MINOR LEAGUE TOTALS			22	11	2.86	129	20	0	20	277	206	98	88	19	109	316	.209

25 ADRIAN NIETO, C

BORN: Nov. 12, 1989. **B-T:** B-R. **HT.:** 6-0. **WT.:** 200. **DRAFTED:** HS—Plantation, Fla., 2008 (5th round). **SIGNED BY:** Tony Arango.

Nieto and his parents came to the United States from Cuba on a makeshift raft when he was 8. He began catching shortly thereafter and joined a travel team with future No. 3 overall pick Eric Hosmer when he was 11, and the duo eventually led American Heritage High to BA's final No. 1 national ranking as seniors in 2008. A fifth-round pick that June, Nieto signed three days before the Aug. 15 deadline for a $376,000 bonus. He missed half of his first full pro season in 2009 after pulling a hamstring, and when he returned, he looked lost at the plate. Nieto's bat was his best tool in high school. The switch-hitter showed solid-average power to all fields from both sides of the plate and had a good feel for hitting. But he was a mess mechanically last summer, as his stroke was too long and his approach was inconsistent and passive. Nieto did make some strides defensively and threw out 44 percent of basestealers in 2009, but he still has a long way to go with his receiving, footwork and game-calling skills. He has a slightly above-average arm with good accuracy and a quick release. Nieto needs to get his body in better shape and add strength. He still has the ability to become an everyday big leaguer, but his regression in 2009 was discouraging. Nieto must reset and start fresh in 2010, likely at Vermont after beginning the season in extended spring training.

Year	Club (League)	Class	AVG	G	AB	R	H	2B	3B	HR	RBI	BB	SO	SB	OBP	SLG
2008	Nationals (GCL)	R	.217	8	23	1	5	3	0	0	3	2	7	0	.308	.348
2009	Nationals (GCL)	R	.228	42	136	22	31	6	1	0	17	20	30	1	.337	.287
MINOR LEAGUE TOTALS			.226	50	159	23	36	9	1	0	20	22	37	1	.333	.296

26 HASSAN PENA, RHP

BORN: March 25, 1985. **B-T:** R-R. **HT.:** 6-2. **WT.:** 210. **DRAFTED:** Palm Beach (Fla.) CC, 2006 (13th round). **SIGNED BY:** Tony Arango.

Pena defected from Cuba and spent a year at Palm Beach (Fla.) CC before the Nationals signed him as a 13th-rounder in 2006 for $149,500. His pro career has been marked by shoulder issues. Tendinitis delayed his pro debut in 2006, and he had minor offseason surgery to shave off a small spur near his rotator cuff before 2007. Shoulder soreness continued to hamper him in 2008, and he had another cleanup surgery before last season. When Pena has been healthy, he has shown electric stuff. He attacks hitters with a 90-94 mph fastball with good life, and his above-average power curveball is one of the best in the system. He also features an average changeup. Some of Pena's shoulder issues have been caused by his mechanics. In the past, his arm dragged behind in his delivery, putting stress on his shoulder. His arm action is still a little long in the back, but he has made progress cleaning it up. Pena worked as a closer in Cuba prior to defecting, and the Nationals tried to make him a starter for the first few years of his career before moving him to the bullpen last year. He thrived there, going 2-0, 0.49 in 10 appearances, and the Nationals will keep him in a relief role moving forward. Pena will advance to Double-A in 2010. If he can stay healthy, he could jump to the big leagues quickly as a reliever. He has the stuff to be a power setup man in the majors.

Year	Club (League)	Class	W	L	ERA	G	GS	CG	SV	IP	H	R	ER	HR	BB	SO	AVG
2007	Vermont (NYP)	SS	4	5	4.25	13	13	0	0	59	55	36	28	3	33	36	.256
2008	Hagerstown (SAL)	LoA	2	2	2.08	6	6	0	0	26	24	9	6	0	5	24	.245
	Potomac (CAR)	HiA	2	2	4.15	8	8	0	0	43	42	25	20	4	24	30	.266
2009	Nationals (GCL)	R	0	1	2.70	2	2	0	0	7	6	3	2	0	3	3	.261
	Hagerstown (SAL)	LoA	1	0	1.13	3	3	0	0	16	8	2	2	0	4	11	.151
	Potomac (CAR)	HiA	2	1	2.39	12	2	0	0	26	16	7	7	1	12	21	.174
MINOR LEAGUE TOTALS			11	11	3.29	44	34	0	0	178	151	82	65	8	81	125	.236

27 JEFF MANDEL, RHP

BORN: April 30, 1985. **B-T:** B-R. **HT.:** 6-3. **WT.:** 190. **DRAFTED:** Baylor, 2007 (19th round). **SIGNED BY:** Bob Laurie.

Mandel's stock soared after he posted a 1.91 ERA as a reliever during his sophomore year at Baylor, but he struggled to repeat that success as a junior and went undrafted in 2006. He moved into a starting role as a senior, going 7-8, 4.55, and the Nationals scooped him up and kept him in the rotation. Physical and athletic, Mandel filled in at first base and in the outfield while at Baylor. He has emerged as an innings-eating workhorse over the last two years. Mandel is a classic sinker/slider pitcher, and he also features an average changeup. He works at 86-91 mph with a late-sinking two-seamer, and he commands the pitch well. Mandel's slider is a slightly below-average pitch that can get loopy at times, but it's workable. Mandel never will be overpowering, but he has good feel for pitching and is a safe bet to induce plenty of groundballs in the majors, whether in a middle-relief role or as a starter. He should get a shot in Triple-A in 2010, with a big league callup possible by season's end.

Year	Club (League)	Class	W	L	ERA	G	GS	CG	SV	IP	H	R	ER	HR	BB	SO	AVG
2007	Vermont (NYP)	SS	0	0	4.50	1	0	0	0	2	2	1	1	0	1	1	.286
	Hagerstown (SAL)	LoA	4	7	6.71	14	13	0	0	62	87	49	46	6	17	49	.333
2008	Hagerstown (SAL)	LoA	4	3	5.21	11	11	0	0	57	73	35	33	5	16	45	.313
	Potomac (CAR)	HiA	6	6	3.68	17	17	1	0	95	103	47	39	7	26	58	.277

Year	Club (League)	Class	W	L	ERA	G	GS	CG	SV	IP	H	R	ER	HR	BB	SO	AVG
2009	Potomac (CAR)	HiA	8	4	3.61	17	17	1	0	100	94	52	40	7	31	54	.249
	Harrisburg (EL)	AA	4	2	2.94	8	8	0	0	52	47	18	17	5	12	35	.253
MINOR LEAGUE TOTALS			26	22	4.31	68	66	2	0	368	406	202	176	30	103	242	.283

28 STEVE LOMBARDOZZI, 2B

BORN: Sept. 20, 1988. **B-T:** B-R. **HT.:** 6-0. **WT.:** 170. **DRAFTED:** St. Petersburg (Fla.) JC, 2008 (19th round). **SIGNED BY:** Paul Tinnell.

Lombardozzi's father, also named Steve, hit .412 in the 1987 World Series to help the Twins topple the Cardinals. The younger Lombardozzi is built just like his dad and plays with the same hard-nosed style. A shortstop at St. Petersburg (Fla.) JC, he moved to second base after turning pro in 2008, and he posted a .987 fielding percentage at the new position last season. He has good infield actions, and his range and arm strength are fine for second base. Lombardozzi's excellent baseball instincts make all of his tools play up, including his solid-average speed. Offensively, he makes good contact from both sides of the plate, hitting .292 last season against lefthanders and .298 against righties. He also draws walks and is an adept bunter. Hagerstown hitting coach Tony Tarasco helped Lombardozzi increase his strength, and the addition of a leg kick helped him drive the ball into the gaps more often, though he'll always have below-average power. Lombardozzi lacks any standout tools, but he does all the little things to help teams win and could have a big league future as a sparkplug in the Nick Punto mold. He'll advance to high Class A in 2010.

Year	Club (League)	Class	AVG	G	AB	R	H	2B	3B	HR	RBI	BB	SO	SB	OBP	SLG
2008	Nationals (GCL)	R	.283	48	152	23	43	4	1	0	24	21	32	4	.371	.322
2009	Hagerstown (SAL)	LoA	.296	128	496	90	147	26	7	3	58	62	80	16	.375	.395
MINOR LEAGUE TOTALS			.293	176	648	113	190	30	8	3	82	83	112	20	.374	.378

29 J.P. RAMIREZ, OF

BORN: Sept. 29, 1989. **B-T:** L-L. **HT.:** 5-10. **WT.:** 185. **DRAFTED:** HS—New Braunfels, Texas, 2008 (15th round). **SIGNED BY:** Tyler Wilt.

Widely regarded as the best pure hitter in the Texas draft crop in 2008, Ramirez bypassed a Tulane scholarship to sign for $1 million right before the Aug. 15 deadline. The Nats had the money to meet his asking price after negotiations broke down with first-rounder Aaron Crow. Ramirez's first full season in pro ball was disappointing, as his bat revealed itself to be considerably less advanced than previously thought. He does have a smooth, compact lefthanded swing and textbook hitting mechanics, but hitting is his lone potential plus tool and his offensive approach needs plenty of work. He's a very aggressive hitter who chases high fastballs and breaking balls in the dirt. He struggled mightily against lefthanders in 2009, batting just .200/.264/.263. Ramirez has a flat, line-drive swing, and while some scouts believe his bat speed will eventually lead to average power potential, others doubt he'll hit enough homers to be an everyday left fielder. Though he played a few games in right field last season, his below-average speed, arm strength and defense will anchor him to left as he moves through the minors. Ramirez will have to hit his way to the majors, and his bat is years away from being big league-ready. He'll get a shot at low Class A in 2010.

Year	Club (League)	Class	AVG	G	AB	R	H	2B	3B	HR	RBI	BB	SO	SB	OBP	SLG
2008	Nationals (GCL)	R	.364	5	11	2	4	0	0	0	8	4	0	0	.533	.364
2009	Vermont (NYP)	SS	.264	72	295	35	78	18	6	4	39	14	45	6	.306	.407
MINOR LEAGUE TOTALS			.268	77	306	37	82	18	6	4	47	18	45	6	.316	.405

30 DANNY ROSENBAUM, LHP

BORN: Oct. 10, 1987. **B-T:** R-L. **HT.:** 6-1. **WT.:** 210. **DRAFTED:** Xavier, 2009 (22nd round). **SIGNED BY:** Alex Smith.

Rosenbaum began his college career at Indiana, where he threw just 20 innings as a freshman in 2007 before transferring to Xavier. He led the Musketeers in strikeouts in each of his two seasons with them, and in 2009 he helped Xavier reach its first NCAA regional playoff, where he struck out nine and allowed just two runs over 6 2/3 innings in a win against Sam Houston State. After signing for $20,000 as a 22nd-round pick, he dominated younger competition in his pro debut, then made a strong impression in instructional league. He pounds the strike zone with an 88-91 mph fastball that touches 92, and he can cut and sink the pitch effectively. His slurvy breaking ball has good depth, and the Nationals envision it as an average slider after he tightens it up a little. He also has good feel for a changeup, which he continued to develop in instructional league, but he needs to refine the pitch. The Nationals compare Rosenbaum to Will Atwood and John Lannan, and he could move just as quickly as they have. He might skip two levels and start 2010 in high Class A Potomac. Some club officials believe he could reach the big leagues by September if he shifts to a relief role. Washington will leave him in a starting role for now, but his future could be as a middle reliever.

Year	Club (League)	Class	W	L	ERA	G	GS	CG	SV	IP	H	R	ER	HR	BB	SO	AVG
2009	Nationals (GCL)	R	4	1	1.95	11	8	0	0	37	29	14	8	1	9	38	.215
MINOR LEAGUE TOTALS			4	1	1.95	11	8	0	0	37	29	14	8	1	9	38	.215

Two prominent Cuban defectors were on the market this offseason but hadn't completed deals before the Prospect Handbook went to press. Lefthander Aroldis Chapman, who showed a triple-digits fastball at the World Baseball Classic, could command a $20 million major league contract. Fellow lefty Noel Arguelles agreed to terms with the Royals on a five-year, $7 million big league contract in early December, but the paperwork was expected to take a few weeks to finalize.

Chapman would rank as the No. 1 prospect for roughly half of Major League Baseball's 30 organizations. Arguelles would have ranked No. 3 on our Royals list, between Aaron Crow and Wil Myers, had his contract been completed in time.

AROLDIS CHAPMAN, LHP

BORN: Sept. 11, 1987. **B-T:** L-L. **HT.:** 6-4. **WT.:** 190.

Chapman was expected to be the ace pitcher Cuba had been searching for to replace the aging Pedro Lazo and Norge Vera and the long-departed Jose Contreras on its national team. But Chapman's focus was elsewhere. He was thwarted in his first attempt to defect in 2008, which led Cuba to leave him off its team for the Beijing Olympics. He was reinstated to the national team for the World Baseball Classic, where he went 0-1, 5.68 in two starts. At the World Port Tournament in the Netherlands last July, Chapman fled the team, and Major League Baseball declared him a free agent in September when he established residency in the Pyranees principality of Andorra. In international play, he showed one of the world's more electric arms, though control troubles mean he's not yet a finished product. He struggled to establish his fastball as he lasted only two innings in a 6-0 loss to Japan at the World Baseball Classic. Chapman impressed scouts at the WBC by showing a fastball that touched 100 mph and sometimes sat in the mid-90s, prompting some to grade his heater as a top-of-the-scale 80 pitch. If Chapman can smooth out his still rough mechanics, he has potential that few pitchers can come close to matching. He sits at 94-95 mph from the left side and set a record in the Serie Nacional, Cuba's premier league, by hitting 102 mph. He also throws a changeup, slider and curveball, though none is nearly as good as his fastball. His long, lanky build and his long fingers are reminiscent of Brien Taylor, the No. 1 pick in the 1991 draft. Chapman's raw stuff is exceptional, but he's not likely to step right in and dominate big leaguers due to his wildness. He also will have to adjust to life in the United States, and he did raise some concerns when he switched agents within months of defecting. But Chapman's stuff is good enough that the worst-case scenario is that he ends up as a power lefty out of the bullpen. If he can improve his command, he has the potential to be a frontline starter.

NOEL ARGUELLES, LHP

BORN: Jan. 12, 1990. **B-T:** L-L. **HT.:** 6-3. **WT.:** 195.

Arguelles had an impressive international baseball pedigree before defecting at the World Junior Championships in Edmonton in July 2008. He had pitched the championship game at the Pan America 18-and-under tournament earlier in the year, striking out 11 in eight innings to beat Mexico. He defected along with shortstop Jose Iglesias, who signed an $8.25 million contract with the Red Sox last September. Though he's still only 20 years old, Arguelles does have some experience in the Serie Nacional. He went 0-5, 7.23 as a 16-year-old with Havana in 2006-2007 and 3-2, 5.82 in limited action in 2007-2008. While he's not nearly as polished as older Cuban defectors, Arguelles' stuff needs little projection. He has touched 93 mph with his fastball and sat around 90 mph in the Serie Nacional. His curveball and changeup both have chances to be average to a tick-above-average pitches. A scout who saw him in Canada compared Arguelles' body to Francisco Liriano's and said he would have been a first-round pick if he had been part of the draft. He avoided the draft and became a free agent by establishing residency in the Dominican Republic. As with any Cuban defector, Arguelles' biggest hurdle will be adjusting to life in the United States. A number of Cuban defectors have struggled to keep their weight in check. He has gained roughly 15 pounds of relatively solid weight since defecting, but he'll have to work hard to make sure he doesn't get too heavy. Arguelles sometimes struggled with his control in Cuba, but that wasn't a problem in his workouts for clubs. Arguelles is more polished than the average 20-year-old pitcher, but he's still at least a full year away from the big leagues.

2009 DRAFT

Bonuses and estimated slot recommendations by Major League Baseball for the first five rounds of the 2009 draft. MLB establishes guidelines for every pick through the first five rounds, and set a $150,000 ceiling (roughly equivalent to the final choice in the fifth round) for subsequent rounds. Asterisks indicate bonuses that were part of a major league contract, and crosses signify a two-sport contract, which allows the club to spread the bonus over as many as five years.

FIRST ROUND

Pick. Team: Player, Pos.	Bonus	Slot
1. Was: Stephen Strasburg, rhp	*$7,500,000	$4,000,000
2. Sea: Dustin Ackley, of	*$6,000,000	$3,250,000
3. SD: Donavan Tate, of	+$6,250,000	$2,925,000
4. Pit: Tony Sanchez, c	$2,500,000	$2,700,000
5. Bal: Matt Hobgood, rhp	$2,422,000	$2,520,000
6. SF: Zack Wheeler, rhp	$3,300,000	$2,340,000
7. Atl: Mike Minor, lhp	$2,420,000	$2,178,000
8. Cin: Mike Leake, rhp	$2,270,000	$2,043,000
9. Det: Jacob Turner, rhp	*$4,700,000	$1,962,000
10. Was: Drew Storen, rhp	$1,600,000	$1,863,000
11. Col: Tyler Matzek, lhp	$3,900,000	$1,791,000
12. KC: Aaron Crow, rhp	*$1,500,000	$1,719,000
13. Oak: Grant Green, ss	$2,750,000	$1,656,000
14. Tex: Matt Purke, lhp	Did Not Sign	$1,602,000
15. Cle: Alex White, rhp	$2,250,000	$1,557,000
16. Ari: Bobby Borchering, 3b	$1,800,000	$1,512,000
17. Ari: A.J. Pollock, of	$1,400,000	$1,467,000
18. Fla: Chad James, lhp	$1,700,000	$1,422,000
19. StL: Shelby Miller, rhp	+$2,875,000	$1,386,000
20. Tor: Chad Jenkins, rhp	$1,359,000	$1,359,000
21. Hou: Jiovanni Mier, ss	$1,358,000	$1,332,000
22. Min: Kyle Gibson, rhp	$1,850,000	$1,287,000
23. CWS: Jared Mitchell, of	$1,200,000	$1,260,000
24. LAA: Randal Grichuk, of	$1,242,000	$1,242,000
25. LAA: Mike Trout, of	$1,215,000	$1,215,000
26. Mil: Eric Arnett, rhp	$1,197,000	$1,197,000
27. Sea: Nick Franklin, ss	$1,280,000	$1,161,000
28. Bos: Reymond Fuentes, of	$1,134,000	$1,134,000
29. NYY: Slade Heathcott, of	$2,200,000	$1,107,000
30. TB: LeVon Washington, 2b	Did Not Sign	$1,080,000
31. ChC: Brett Jackson, of	$972,000	$972,000
32. Col: Tim Wheeler, of	$900,000	$954,000

SUPPLEMENTAL FIRST ROUND

Pick. Team: Player, Pos.	Bonus	Slot
33. Sea: Steven Baron, c	$980,000	$936,000
34. Col: Rex Brothers, lhp	$969,000	$918,000
35. Ari: Matt Davidson, 3b	$900,000	$900,000
36. LAD: Aaron Miller, lhp	$889,200	$889,200
37. Tor: James Paxton, lhp	Did Not Sign	$873,000
38. CWS: Josh Phegley, c	$858,600	$858,600
39. Mil: Kentrail Davis, of	$1,200,000	$844,200
40. LAA: Tyler Skaggs, lhp	$1,000,000	$829,800
41. Ari: Chris Owings, ss	$950,000	$815,400
42. LAA: Garrett Richards, rhp	$802,800	$802,800
43. Cin: Brad Boxberger, rhp	$857,000	$789,300
44. Tex: Tanner Scheppers, rhp	$1,250,000	$776,700
45. Ari: Mike Belfiore, lhp	$725,000	$764,100
46. Min: Matt Bashore, lhp	$751,500	$751,500
47. Mil: Kyle Heckathorn, rhp	$776,000	$739,800
48. LAA: Tyler Kehrer, lhp	$728,100	$728,100
49. Pit: Victor Black, rhp	$717,000	$717,000

SECOND ROUND

Pick. Team: Player, Pos.	Bonus	Slot
50. Was: Jeff Kobernus, 2b	$705,500	$705,600
51. Sea: Rich Poythress, 1b	$694,800	$694,800
52. SD: Everett Williams, of	$775,000	$684,000
53. Pit: Brooks Pounders, rhp	$670,000	$673,200
54. Bal: Mychal Givens, ss	$800,000	$663,300
55. SF: Tommy Joseph, c	$712,500	$653,400
56. LAD: Blake Smith, of	$643,500	$643,500
57. Cin: Billy Hamilton, ss	+$623,600	$634,500
58. Det: Andrew Oliver, lhp	$1,495,000	$624,600
59. Col: Nolan Arenado, 3b	$625,000	$614,700
60. Ari: Eric Smith, rhp	$605,700	$605,700
61. CWS: Trayce Thompson, of	$625,000	$596,700
62. Tex: Tommy Mendonca, 3b	$587,700	$587,700
63. Cle: Jason Kipnis, of	$575,000	$579,600
64. Ari: Marc Krauss, of	$550,000	$570,600
65. LAD: Garrett Gould, rhp	$900,000	$562,500
66. Fla: Bryan Berglund, rhp	$572,500	$554,400
67. StL: Robert Stock, c	$525,000	$545,400
68. Tor: Jake Eliopoulos, lhp	Did Not Sign	$537,300
69. Hou: Tanner Bushue, rhp	$530,000	$530,100
70. Min: Billy Bullock, rhp	$522,000	$522,000
71. CWS: David Holmberg, lhp	$514,000	$514,800
72. NYM: Steve Matz, lhp	$895,000	$506,700
73. Mil: Max Walla, of	$499,000	$499,500
74. Mil: Cameron Garfield, c	$492,200	$492,300
75. Phi: Kelly Dugan, of	$485,000	$485,100
76. NYY: J.R. Murphy, c	$1,250,000	$477,900
77. Bos: Alex Wilson, rhp	$470,700	$470,700
78. TB: Kenny Diekroeger, ss	Did Not Sign	$463,500
79. ChC: D.J. LeMahieu, 2b	$508,000	$457,200
80. LAA: Pat Corbin, lhp	$450,000	$450,000

THIRD ROUND

Pick. Team: Player, Pos.	Bonus	Slot
81. Was: Trevor Holder, rhp	$200,000	$442,800
82. Sea: Kyle Seager, 2b	$436,500	$436,500
83. SD: Jerry Sullivan, rhp	$430,200	$430,200
84. Pit: Evan Chambers, of	$423,900	$423,900
85. Bal: Tyler Townsend, 1b	$417,600	$417,600
86. SF: Chris Dominguez, 3b	$411,300	$411,300
87. Atl: David Hale, rhp	$405,000	$405,000
88. Cin: Donnie Joseph, lhp	$398,000	$398,700
89. Det: Wade Gaynor, 3b	$392,400	$392,400
90. Col: Ben Paulsen, 1b	$391,000	$387,000
91. KC: Wil Myers, c/3b	$2,000,000	$380,700
92. Oak: Justin Marks, lhp	$375,300	$375,300
93. Tex: Robbie Erlin, lhp	$425,000	$369,000
94. Cle: Joe Gardner, rhp	$363,000	$363,600
95. Ari: Keon Broxton, of	$358,000	$358,000
96. LAD: Brett Wallach, rhp	$351,900	$351,900
97. Fla: Marquise Cooper, of	$345,000	$346,500
98. StL: Joe Kelly, rhp	$341,000	$341,100
99. Tor: Jake Barrett, rhp	Did Not Sign	$335,700
100. Hou: Telvin Nash, of	$330,300	$330,300
101. Min: Ben Tootle, rhp	$324,900	$324,900
102. CWS: Bryan Morgado, lhp	Did Not Sign	$319,500
103. NYM: Robbie Shields, ss	$315,000	$315,000
104. Tor: Jake Marisnick, of	$1,000,000	$309,600
105. Mil: Josh Prince, ss	$304,200	$304,200

106. Phi: Kyrell Hudson, of	+$475,000	$299,700
107. Bos: David Renfroe, ss	+$1,400,000	$294,300
108. TB: Todd Glaesmann, of	+$930,000	$289,800
109. ChC: Austin Kirk, lhp	$320,000	$284,400
110. LAA: Josh Spence, lhp	Did Not Sign	$279,900

SUPPLEMENTAL THIRD ROUND

Pick. Team: Player, Pos.	Bonus	Slot
111. Hou: Jonathan Meyer, 3b	$274,500	$274,500

FOURTH ROUND

Pick. Team: Player, Pos.	Bonus	Slot
112. Was: A.J. Morris, rhp	$270,000	$270,000
113. Sea: James Jones, of	$267,300	$267,300
114. SD: Keyvius Sampson, rhp	$600,000	$263,700
115. Pit: Zack Dodson, lhp	$600,000	$261,000
116. Bal: Randy Henry, rhp	$365,000	$258,300
117. SF: Jason Stoffel, rhp	$254,700	$254,700
118. Atl: Mycal Jones, ss	$252,000	$252,000
119. Cin: Mark Fleury, c	$249,300	$249,300
120. Det: Edwin Gomez, ss	$245,700	$245,700
121. Col: Kent Matthes, of	$200,000	$243,000
122. KC: Chris Dwyer, lhp	$1,450,000	$240,300
123. Oak: Max Stassi, c	$1,500,000	$236,700
124. Tex: Andrew Doyle, rhp	$234,000	$234,000
125. Cle: Kyle Bellows, 3b	$230,000	$231,300
126. Ari: David Nick, ss	$225,000	$227,700
127. LAD: Angelo Songco, of	$225,000	$225,000
128. Fla: Dan Mahoney, rhp	$222,300	$222,300
129. StL: Scott Bittle, rhp	$75,000	$218,700
130. Tor: Ryan Goins, ss	$216,000	$216,000
131. Hou: B.J. Hyatt, rhp	$200,000	$213,300
132. Min: Derek McCallum, 2b	$209,700	$209,700
133. CWS: Matt Heidenreich, rhp	$200,000	$207,000
134. NYM: Darrell Ceciliani, of	$204,300	$204,300
135. NYY: Adam Warren, rhp	$195,000	$200,700
136. Mil: Brooks Hall, rhp	$700,000	$198,000
137. Phi: Adam Buschini, 2b	$195,000	$195,300

138. Bos: Jeremy Hazelbaker, of	$191,700	$191,700
139. TB: Luke Bailey, c	$750,000	$189,000
140. ChC: Chris Rusin, lhp	$140,000	$186,300
141. LAA: Wes Hatton, 2b	$182,700	$182,700

FIFTH ROUND

Pick. Team: Player, Pos.	Bonus	Slot
142. Was: Miguel Pena, lhp	Did Not Sign	$180,000
143. Sea: Tyler Blandford, rhp	$325,000	$179,100
144. SD: Jason Hagerty, c	$177,300	$177,300
145. Pit: Nate Baker, lhp	$176,000	$176,400
146. Bal: Ashur Tolliver, lhp	$200,000	$174,600
147. SF: Brandon Belt, 1b	$200,000	$173,700
148. Atl: Thomas Berryhill, rhp	$160,000	$171,900
149. Cin: Daniel Tuttle, rhp	$200,000	$171,000
150. Det: Austin Wood, lhp	$100,000	$169,200
151. Col: Joseph Sanders, 3b	$168,300	$168,300
152. KC: Louis Coleman, rhp	$100,000	$166,500
153. Oak: Steve Parker, 3b	$165,600	$165,600
154. Tex: Nick McBride, rhp	$325,000	$163,800
155. Cle: Austin Adams, rhp	$70,000	$162,900
156. Ari: Ryan Wheeler, 1b	$160,000	$161,100
157. LAD: J.T. Wise, c	$130,000	$160,200
158. Fla: Chase Austin, ss	$155,000	$158,400
159. StL: Ryan Jackson, ss	$157,500	$157,500
160. Tor: Ryan Schimpf, 2b	$155,700	$155,700
161. Hou: Brandon Wikoff, ss	$154,000	$154,800
162. Min: Tobias Streich, c	$150,000	$153,000
163. CWS: Kyle Bellamy, rhp	$147,500	$152,100
164. NYM: Damien Magnifico, rhp	Did Not Sign	$150,300
165. NYY: Caleb Cotham, rhp	$675,000	$149,400
166. Mil: D'Vontrey Richardson, of	+$400,000	$147,600
167. Phi: Matt Way, lhp	$40,000	$146,700
168. Bos: Seth Schwindenhammer, of	$140,000	$144,900
169. TB: Jeff Malm, 1b	$680,000	$144,000
170. ChC: Wes Darvill, ss	$142,200	$142,200
171. LAA: Casey Haerther, 1b	$141,300	$141,300

SIGNING BONUSES

2008 DRAFT

Bonuses and estimated slot recommendations by Major League Baseball for the top 100 picks of the 2008 draft. Asterisk indicates the bonus was part of a major league contract, and a cross signifies a two-sport contract, allowing the club to spread the bonus over as many as five years.

FIRST ROUND

Pick. Team: Player, Pos.	Bonus	Slot
1. TB: Tim Beckham, ss	+$6,150,000	$4,000,000
2. Pit: Pedro Alvarez, 3b	*$6,000,000	$3,500,000
3. KC: Eric Hosmer, 1b	$6,000,000	$3,250,000
4. Bal: Brian Matusz, lhp	*$3,200,000	$3,000,000
5. SF: Buster Posey, c	$6,200,000	$2,800,000
6. Fla: Kyle Skipworth, c	$2,300,000	$2,600,000
7. Cin: Yonder Alonso, 1b	*$2,000,000	$2,420,000
8. CWS: Gordon Beckham, ss	$2,600,000	$2,270,000
9. Was: Aaron Crow, rhp	Did Not Sign	$2,150,000
10. Hou: Jason Castro, c	$2,070,000	$2,070,000
11. Tex: Justin Smoak, 1b	$3,500,000	$1,990,000
12. Oak: Jemile Weeks, 2b	$1,910,000	$1,910,000
13. StL: Brett Wallace, 3b/1b	$1,840,000	$1,840,000
14. Min: Aaron Hicks, of	$1,780,000	$1,780,000
15. LAD: Ethan Martin, rhp	$1,730,000	$1,730,000
16. Mil: Brett Lawrie, c/3b	$1,700,000	$1,680,000
17. Tor: David Cooper, 1b	$1,500,000	$1,630,000
18. NYM: Ike Davis, 1b	$1,575,000	$1,580,000
19. ChC: Andrew Cashner, rhp	$1,540,000	$1,540,000
20. Sea: Joshua Fields, rhp	$1,750,000	$1,500,000
21. Det: Ryan Perry, rhp	$1,480,000	$1,480,000
22. NYM: Reese Havens, ss	$1,419,000	$1,430,000
23. SD: Allan Dykstra, 1b	$1,150,000	$1,400,000
24. Phi: Anthony Hewitt, 3b	$1,380,000	$1,380,000
25. Col: Christian Friedrich, lhp	$1,350,000	$1,350,000
26. Ari: Daniel Schlereth, lhp	$1,330,000	$1,330,000
27. Min: Carlos Gutierrez, rhp	$1,290,000	$1,290,000
28. NYY: Gerrit Cole, rhp	Did Not Sign	$1,260,000
29. Cle: Lonnie Chisenhall, ss	$1,100,000	$1,230,000
30. Bos: Casey Kelly, rhp/ss	+$3,000,000	$1,200,000

SUPPLEMENTAL FIRST ROUND

Pick. Team: Player, Pos.	Bonus	Slot
31. Min: Shooter Hunt, rhp	$1,080,000	$1,080,000
32. Mil: Jake Odorizzi, rhp	$1,060,000	$1,060,000
33. NYM: Brad Holt, rhp	$1,040,000	$1,040,000
34. Phi: Zach Collier, of	$1,020,000	$1,020,000
35. Mil: Evan Frederickson, lhp	$1,010,000	$1,010,000
36. KC: Mike Montgomery, lhp	$988,000	$988,000
37. SF: Conor Gillaspie, 3b	$970,000	$970,000
38. Hou: Jordan Lyles, rhp	$930,000	$954,000
39. StL: Lance Lynn, rhp	$938,000	$938,000
40. Atl: Brett DeVall, lhp	$1,000,000	$922,000
41. ChC: Ryan Flaherty, ss	$906,000	$906,000
42. SD: Jaff Decker, of	$892,000	$892,000
43. Ari: Wade Miley, lhp	$877,000	$877,000
44. NYY: Jeremy Bleich, lhp	$700,000	$863,000
45. Bos: Bryan Price, rhp	$849,000	$849,000
46. SD: Logan Forsythe, 3b	$835,000	$835,000

SECOND ROUND

Pick. Team: Player, Pos.	Bonus	Slot
47. TB: Kyle Lobstein, lhp	$1,500,000	$822,000
48. Pit: Tanner Scheppers, rhp	Did Not Sign	$809,000
49. KC: Johnny Giavotella, 2b	$787,000	$796,000
50. Bal: Xavier Avery, of	+$900,000	$784,000
51. Phi: Anthony Gose, of	$772,000	$772,000
52. Fla: Brad Hand, lhp	$760,000	$760,000
53. Mil: Seth Lintz, rhp	$900,000	$748,000
54. Mil: Cutter Dykstra, of	$737,000	$737,000
55. Was: Destin Hood, of	+$1,100,000	$726,000
56. Hou: Jay Austin, of	$715,000	$715,000
57. Tex: Robbie Ross, lhp	$1,575,000	$705,000
58. Oak: Tyson Ross, rhp	$694,000	$694,000
59. StL: Shane Peterson, of	$683,000	$683,000
60. Min: Tyler Ladendorf, ss	$673,000	$673,000
61. LAD: Josh Lindblom, rhp	$663,000	$663,000
62. Mil: Cody Adams, rhp	$653,000	$653,000
63. Tor: Kenny Wilson, of	$644,000	$644,000
64. Atl: Tyler Stovall, lhp	$750,000	$634,000
65. ChC: Aaron Shafer, rhp	$625,000	$625,000
66. Sea: Dennis Raben, of	$616,000	$616,000
67. Det: Cody Satterwhite, rhp	$606,000	$606,000
68. NYM: Javier Rodriguez, of	$585,000	$597,000
69. SD: James Darnell, 3b	$740,000	$589,000
70. Atl: Zeke Spruill, rhp	$600,000	$580,000
71. Phi: Jason Knapp, rhp	$590,000	$572,000
72. Col: Charlie Blackmon, of	$563,000	$563,000
73. Ari: Bryan Shaw, rhp	$553,000	$553,000
74. LAA: Tyler Chatwood, rhp	$547,000	$547,000
75. NYY: Scott Bittle, rhp	Did Not Sign	$539,000
76. Cle: Trey Haley, rhp	$1,250,000	$531,000
77. Bos: Derrik Gibson, ss	$600,000	$523,000

THIRD ROUND

Pick. Team: Player, Pos.	Bonus	Slot
78. TB: Jake Jefferies, c	$515,000	$515,000
79. Pit: Jordy Mercer, ss	$508,000	$508,000
80. KC: Tyler Sample, rhp	$500,000	$500,000
81. Bal: L.J. Hoes, 2b	$490,000	$492,000
82. SF: Roger Kieschnick, of	$525,000	$485,000
83. Fla: Edgar Olmos, lhp	$478,000	$478,000
84. Cin: Zach Stewart, rhp	$450,000	$471,000
85. Bos: Stephen Fife, rhp	$464,000	$464,000
86. CWS: Brent Morel, 3b	$440,000	$457,000
87. Was: Danny Espinosa, ss	$525,000	$450,000
88. Hou: Chase Davidson, 1b	Did Not Sign	$443,000
89. Tex: Tim Murphy, lhp	$436,000	$436,000
90. Oak: Petey Paramore, c	$430,000	$430,000
91. StL: Niko Vasquez, ss	$423,000	$423,000
92. Min: Bobby Lanigan, rhp	$417,000	$417,000
93. LAD: Kyle Russell, of	$410,000	$410,000
94. Mil: Logan Schafer, of	$404,000	$404,000
95. Tor: Andrew Liebel, rhp	$340,000	$397,000
96. Atl: Craig Kimbrel, rhp	$391,000	$391,000
97. ChC: Chris Carpenter, rhp	$385,000	$385,000
98. Sea: Aaron Pribanic, rhp	$390,000	$379,000
99. Det: Scott Green, rhp	$373,000	$373,000
100. NYM: Kirk Nieuwenhuis, of	$360,000	$367,000

SIGNING BONUSES

2007 DRAFT

Bonuses and estimated slot recommendations by Major League Baseball for the top 100 picks in the 2007 draft. Asterisks indicate bonuses that were part of a major league contract.

FIRST ROUND

Pick. Team: Player, Pos.	Bonus	Slot
1. TB: David Price, lhp	*$5,600,000	$3,600,000
2. KC: Mike Moustakas, ss/3b	$4,000,000	$3,150,000
3. ChC: Josh Vitters, 3b	$3,200,000	$2,700,000
4. Pit: Daniel Moskos, lhp	$2,475,000	$2,475,000
5. Bal: Matt Wieters, c	$6,000,000	$2,250,000
6. Was: Ross Detwiler, lhp	$2,150,000	$2,160,000
7. Mil: Matt LaPorta, of/1b	$2,000,000	$2,070,000
8. Col: Casey Weathers, rhp	$1,800,000	$1,980,000
9. Ari: Jarrod Parker, rhp	$2,100,000	$1,890,000
10. SF: Madison Bumgarner, lhp	$2,000,000	$1,800,000
11. Sea: Phillippe Aumont, rhp	$1,900,000	$1,710,000
12. Fla: Matt Dominguez, 3b	$1,800,000	$1,620,000
13. Cle: Beau Mills, 3b/1b	$1,575,000	$1,575,000
14. Atl: Jason Heyward, of	$1,700,000	$1,530,000
15. Cin: Devin Mesoraco, c	$1,400,000	$1,485,000
16. Tor: Kevin Ahrens, ss/3b	$1,440,000	$1,440,000
17. Tex: Blake Beavan, rhp	$1,497,500	$1,417,500
18. StL: Pete Kozma, ss	$1,395,000	$1,395,000
19. Phi: Joe Savery, lhp	$1,372,500	$1,372,500
20. LAD: Chris Withrow, rhp	$1,350,000	$1,350,000
21. Tor: J.P. Arencibia, c	$1,327,500	$1,327,500
22. SF: Tim Alderson, rhp	$1,290,000	$1,282,500
23. SD: Nick Schmidt, lhp	$1,260,000	$1,260,000
24. Tex: Michael Main, rhp	$1,237,500	$1,237,500
25. CWS: Aaron Poreda, lhp	$1,200,000	$1,215,000
26. Oak: James Simmons, rhp	$1,192,500	$1,192,500
27. Det: Rick Porcello, rhp	*$3,580,000	$1,170,000
28. Min: Ben Revere, of	$750,000	$1,080,000
29. SF: Wendell Fairley, of	$1,000,000	$990,000
30. NYY: Andrew Brackman, rhp	*$3,350,000	$945,000

SUPPLEMENTAL FIRST ROUND

Pick. Team: Player, Pos.	Bonus	Slot
31. Was: Josh Smoker, lhp	$1,000,000	$922,500
32. SF: Nick Noonan, ss/2b	$915,750	$915,750
33. Atl: Jon Gilmore, 3b	$900,000	$900,000
34. Cin: Todd Frazier, ss	$825,000	$877,500
35. Tex: Julio Borbon, of	*$800,000	$855,000
36. StL: Clayton Mortensen, rhp	$650,000	$855,000
37. Phi: Travis d'Arnaud, c	$832,500	$832,500
38. Tor: Brett Cecil, lhp	$810,000	$810,000
39. LAD: James Adkins, lhp	$787,500	$787,500
40. SD: Kellen Kulbacki, of	$765,000	$765,000
41. Oak: Sean Doolittle, 1b	$742,500	$742,500
42. NYM: Eddie Kunz, rhp	$720,000	$720,000
43. SF: Jackson Williams, c	$708,750	$708,750
44. Tex: Neil Ramirez, rhp	$1,000,000	$697,500
45. Tor: Justin Jackson, ss	$675,000	$675,000
46. SD: Drew Cumberland, ss	$661,500	$661,500
47. NYM: Nathan Vineyard, lhp	$657,000	$657,000
48. ChC: Josh Donaldson, c	$652,500	$652,500

Pick. Team: Player, Pos.	Bonus	Slot
49. Was: Michael Burgess, of	$630,000	$630,000
50. Ari: Wes Roemer, rhp	$620,000	$621,000
51. SF: Charlie Culberson, ss	$607,500	$607,500
52. Sea: Matt Mangini, 3b	$603,000	$603,000
53. Cin: Kyle Lotzkar, rhp	$594,000	$594,000
54. Tex: Tommy Hunter, rhp	$585,000	$585,000
55. Bos: Nick Hagadone, lhp	$571,500	$571,500
56. Tor: Trystan Magnuson, rhp	$462,500	$567,000
57. SD: Mitch Canham, c	$552,500	$562,500
58. LAA: Jon Bachanov, rhp	$553,300	$553,500
59. Oak: Corey Brown, of	$544,500	$544,500
60. Det: Brandon Hamilton, rhp	$540,000	$540,000
61. Ari: Ed Easley, c	$531,000	$531,000
62. Bos: Ryan Dent, ss	$571,000	$526,500
63. SD: Cory Luebke, lhp	$515,000	$522,000
64. SD: Danny Payne, of	$517,500	$517,500

SECOND ROUND

Pick. Team: Player, Pos.	Bonus	Slot
65. TB: Will Kline, rhp	$513,000	$513,000
66. KC: Sam Runion, rhp	$504,000	$504,000
67. Was: Jordan Zimmermann, rhp	$495,000	$495,000
68. Pit: Duke Welker, rhp	$477,000	$477,000
69. Atl: Joshua Fields, rhp	Did Not Sign	$472,500
70. Was: Jake Smolinski, 3b	$452,500	$463,500
71. StL: David Kopp, rhp	$459,000	$459,000
72. Col: Brian Rike, of	$450,000	$450,000
73. Ari: Barry Enright, rhp	$441,000	$441,000
74. Oak: Grant Desme, of	$432,000	$432,000
75. Sea: Denny Almonte, of	$427,500	$427,500
76. Fla: Mike Stanton, of	$475,000	$418,500
77. NYM: Scott Moviel, rhp	$414,000	$414,000
78. Atl: Freddie Freeman, 1b	$409,500	$409,500
79. Cin: Zack Cozart, ss	$407,250	$407,250
80. Tex: Matt West, inf	$405,000	$405,000
81. SD: Eric Sogard, 2b	$400,000	$400,500
82. StL: Jess Todd, rhp	$400,000	$400,500
83. Phi: Travis Mattair, 3b	$395,000	$396,000
84. Bos: Hunter Morris, 3b	Did Not Sign	$393,750
85. Tor: John Tolisano, 2b	$391,500	$391,500
86. LAD: Michael Watt, lhp	$389,000	$389,250
87. SD: Brad Chalk, of	$300,000	$387,000
88. Tor: Eric Eiland, of	$384,750	$384,750
89. CWS: Nevin Griffith, rhp	$382,500	$382,500
90. Oak: Josh Horton, ss	$380,250	$380,250
91. Det: Danny Worth, ss	$378,000	$378,000
92. Min: Danny Rams, c	$375,000	$375,750
93. NYM: Brant Rustich, rhp	$373,500	$373,500
94. NYY: Austin Romine, c	$500,000	$369,000

THIRD ROUND

Pick. Team: Player, Pos.	Bonus	Slot
95. TB: Nick Barnese, rhp	$366,000	$366,750
96. KC: Danny Duffy, lhp	$365,000	$364,500
97. ChC: Tony Thomas, 2b	$360,000	$360,000
98. Pit: Brian Friday, ss	$355,500	$355,500
99. NYM: Eric Niesen, lhp	$351,000	$351,000
100. Was: Steven Souza, 3b	$346,000	$346,500

COLLEGE TOP 100

Rank	Player	Pos.	Class	B-T	Ht.	Wt.	School
1.	Bryce Harper	c	Fr.	L-R	6-3	205	CC of Southern Nevada
2.	Anthony Ranaudo	rhp	Jr.	R-R	6-7	225	Louisiana State
3.	Deck McGuire	rhp	Jr.	R-R	6-6	228	Georgia Tech
4.	LeVon Washington	of/2b	Fr.	L-R	5-11	170	Chipola (Fla.) JC
5.	Chris Sale	lhp	Jr.	L-L	6-5	175	Florida Gulf Coast
6.	Christian Colon	ss	Jr.	R-R	6-1	190	Cal State Fullerton
7.	James Paxton	lhp	Sr.	L-L	6-4	215	Kentucky
8.	Zack Cox	3b	So.	L-R	6-1	215	Arkansas
9.	Alex Wimmers	rhp	Jr.	L-R	6-2	195	Ohio State
10.	Rick Hague	ss	Jr.	R-R	6-2	185	Rice
11.	Drew Pomeranz	lhp	Jr.	R-L	6-5	230	Mississippi
12.	Jedd Gyorko	2b/3b	Jr.	R-R	5-10	195	West Virginia
13.	Bryan Morgado	lhp	Jr.	L-L	6-3	205	Tennessee
14.	Chad Bettis	rhp	Jr.	R-R	6-1	185	Texas Tech
15.	Bryce Brentz	of/rhp	Jr.	R-R	6-1	185	Middle Tennessee State
16.	Brandon Workman	rhp	Jr.	R-R	6-5	220	Texas
17.	Sam Dyson	rhp	Jr.	R-R	6-2	195	South Carolina
18.	Jesse Hahn	rhp	Jr.	R-R	6-5	190	Virginia Tech
19.	Brett Eibner	rhp/of	Jr.	R-R	6-3	195	Arkansas
20.	Todd Cunningham	of	Jr.	B-R	6-1	200	Jacksonville State
21.	Kyle Blair	rhp	Jr.	R-R	6-4	200	San Diego
22.	Jarrett Parker	of	Jr.	L-L	6-4	210	Virginia
23.	Justin Grimm	rhp	Jr.	R-R	6-4	195	Georgia
24.	Gary Brown	of/3b	Jr.	R-R	6-1	180	Cal State Fullerton
25.	Rob Brantly	c	So.	L-R	6-2	200	UC Riverside
26.	Michael Choice	of	Jr.	R-R	6-1	190	Texas-Arlington
27.	Matt Harvey	rhp	Jr.	R-R	6-4	210	North Carolina
28.	Kevin Jacob	rhp	Jr.	R-R	6-6	235	Georgia Tech
29.	Leon Landry	of	Jr.	L-R	5-11	195	Louisiana State
30.	Austin Wates	of	Jr.	R-R	6-1	175	Virginia Tech
31.	Cameron Rupp	c	Jr.	R-R	6-2	235	Texas
32.	Micah Gibbs	c	Jr.	B-R	5-11	210	Louisiana State
33.	Rob Rasmussen	lhp	Jr.	L-L	5-11	170	UCLA
34.	Yasmani Grandal	c	Jr.	L-R	6-2	210	Miami
35.	Andrew Triggs	rhp	So.	R-R	6-3	210	Southern California
36.	Cole Cook	rhp	So.	R-R	6-6	210	Pepperdine
37.	Martin Viramontes	rhp	So.	R-R	6-5	225	Loyola Marymount
38.	Derek Dietrich	ss/3b	Jr.	L-R	6-1	195	Georgia Tech
39.	Chad Jones	lhp/of	Jr.	L-L	6-3	222	Louisiana State
40.	Nick Tepesch	rhp	Jr.	R-R	6-5	225	Missouri
41.	Tony Thompson	3b	Jr.	R-R	6-5	220	Kansas
42.	Sammy Solis	lhp	Jr.	R-L	6-5	210	San Diego
43.	Hunter Morris	1b/of	Jr.	L-R	6-2	220	Auburn
44.	Daniel Tillman	rhp	Jr.	R-R	6-1	195	Florida Southern
45.	Ross Wilson	2b/ss	Jr.	R-R	5-11	185	Alabama
46.	Dallas Gallant	rhp	Jr.	R-R	6-2	185	Sam Houston State
47.	Ryan LaMarre	of	Jr.	R-L	6-2	210	Michigan
48.	Kolbrin Vitek	3b/rhp	Jr.	R-R	6-3	195	Ball State
49.	Dixon Anderson	rhp	So.	R-R	6-5	225	California
50.	Brandon Cumpton	rhp	Jr.	R-R	6-2	196	Georgia Tech

51.	Kevin Munson	rhp	Jr.	R-R	6-2	200	James Madison
52.	Michael Kvasnicka	c/of	Jr.	B-R	6-2	210	Minnesota
53.	Patrick Cooper	rhp	Jr.	R-R	6-3	205	Bradley
54.	Mathew Price	rhp	So.	R-R	6-2	190	Virginia Tech
55.	Mickey Wiswall	3b/1b	Jr.	L-R	6-1	195	Boston College
56.	Barret Loux	rhp	Jr.	R-R	6-5	200	Texas A&M
57.	Tyler Holt	of	Jr.	R-R	6-1	175	Florida State
58.	Addison Reed	rhp	Jr.	L-R	6-3	215	San Diego State
59.	Josh Spence	lhp	Sr.	L-L	6-1	170	Arizona State
60.	Seth Rosin	rhp	Jr.	R-R	6-6	245	Minnesota
61.	Brian Dupra	rhp	Jr.	R-R	6-3	200	Notre Dame
62.	Jake Eliopoulos	lhp	Fr.	L-L	6-4	185	Chipola (Fla.) JC
63.	Alex McRee	lhp	Sr.	L-L	6-6	230	Georgia
64.	Andy Wilkins	1b/3b	Jr.	L-R	6-2	230	Arkansas
65.	Jake Thompson	rhp	Jr.	R-R	6-3	205	Long Beach State
66.	Victor Sanchez	3b	Jr.	R-R	6-1	175	San Diego
67.	Michael Olt	3b/ss	Jr.	R-R	6-2	190	Connecticut
68.	Cody Wheeler	lhp	Jr.	L-L	5-11	160	Coastal Carolina
69.	Asher Wojciechowski	rhp	Jr.	R-R	6-4	205	The Citadel
70.	Cory Vaughn	of	Jr.	R-R	6-3	225	San Diego State
71.	Kyle Parker	of	Jr.	R-R	6-1	200	Clemson
72.	Tyler Lyons	lhp	Sr.	B-L	6-2	205	Oklahoma State
73.	Daniel Renken	rhp	Jr.	R-R	6-4	195	Cal State Fullerton
74.	Joey Terdoslavich	1b	So.	B-R	6-2	200	Long Beach State
75.	Tyler Hanks	rhp	So.	R-R	6-2	195	CC of Southern Nevada
76.	Brooks Pinckard	rhp	So.	L-R	6-1	175	Baylor
77.	Logan Darnell	lhp	Jr.	L-L	6-2	200	Kentucky
78.	Cody Stanley	c	Jr.	L-R	5-10	190	UNC Wilmington
79.	Matt Miller	rhp	Jr.	R-R	6-6	217	Michigan
80.	Josh Mueller	rhp	Jr.	R-R	6-4	215	Eastern Illinois
81.	Blake Hassebrock	rhp	Jr.	R-R	6-5	205	UNC Greensboro
82.	Josh Rutledge	ss	Jr.	R-R	6-1	190	Alabama
83.	Chris Hernandez	lhp	Jr.	L-L	6-1	195	Miami
84.	Tyler Wilson	rhp	Jr.	R-R	6-2	185	Virginia
85.	Cole Green	rhp	Jr.	R-R	6-1	210	Texas
86.	Blake Forsythe	c	Jr.	R-R	6-2	220	Tennessee
87.	Tommy Kahnle	rhp	So.	R-R	6-2	220	Lynn (Fla.)
88.	Miles Hamblin	c	Jr.	L-R	6-0	190	Mississippi
89.	T.J. Walz	rhp	Jr.	R-R	6-1	175	Kansas
90.	Mike Nesseth	rhp	Jr.	R-R	6-5	215	Nebraska
91.	Devin Harris	of	Jr.	R-R	6-3	220	East Carolina
92.	Matt den Dekker	of	Sr.	L-L	6-1	205	Florida
93.	Kevin Keyes	of	Jr.	R-R	6-4	225	Texas
94.	Daniel Bibona	lhp	Sr.	L-L	6-0	170	UC Irvine
95.	Trent Mummey	of	Jr.	L-L	5-9	165	Auburn
96.	Taylor Ard	1b	So.	R-R	6-2	225	Mount Hood (Ore.) CC
97.	Rafael Neda	c	Jr.	R-R	6-1	215	New Mexico
98.	Mark Canha	of	So.	R-R	6-1	180	California
99.	Rob Segedin	3b/rhp	Jr.	R-R	6-3	220	Tulane
100.	Josh Osich	lhp	Jr.	L-L	6-3	195	Oregon State

HIGH SCHOOL TOP 100

Rk.	Player, Pos.	B-T	Ht.	Wt.	School	College Commitment
1.	Jameson Taillon, rhp	R-R	6-7	230	The Woodlands (Texas) HS	Rice
2.	Karsten Whitson, rhp	R-R	6-3	195	Chipley (Fla.) HS	Florida
3.	A.J. Cole, rhp	R-R	6-5	185	Oviedo (Fla.) HS	Miami
4.	Manny Machado, ss	R-R	6-2	180	Brito HS, Miami	Florida International
5.	Josh Sale, of	L-R	6-0	205	Bishop Blanchet HS, Seattle	Gonzaga
6.	Dylan Covey, rhp	R-R	6-2	200	Maranatha HS, Pasadena, Calif.	San Diego
7.	Kevin Gausman, rhp	L-R	6-4	180	Grandview HS, Aurora, Colo.	Louisiana State
8.	Stetson Allie, rhp/3b	R-R	6-2	215	St. Edward Prep, Cleveland	North Carolina
9.	Austin Wilson, of	R-R	6-4	200	Harvard-Westlake HS, Los Angeles	Stanford
10.	Nick Castellanos, 3b	R-R	6-3	190	Archbishop McCarthy HS, SW Ranches, Fla.	Miami
11.	Yordy Cabrera, ss	R-R	6-2	200	Lakeland (Fla.) HS	Miami
12.	Stefan Sabol, of/c	R-R	6-2	205	Aliso Niquel HS, Aliso Viejo, Calif.	Oregon
13.	Chevez Clarke, of	B-R	5-11	185	Marietta (Ga.) HS	Georgia Tech
14.	Kaleb Cowart, 3b/rhp	B-R	6-3	190	Cook HS, Adel, Ga.	Florida State
15.	Garin Cecchini, ss	L-R	6-2	200	Barbe HS, Lake Charles, La.	Louisiana State
16.	Michael Lorenzen, of/rhp	R-R	6-2	175	Union HS, Fullerton, Calif.	Cal State Fullerton
17.	Drew Cisco, rhp	L-R	6-1	190	Wando HS, Mount Pleasant, S.C.	Georgia
18.	DeAndre Smelter, rhp	R-R	6-2	220	Tattnall Square Academy, Macon, Ga.	Georgia Tech
19.	Jordan Shipers, lhp	R-L	5-11	170	South Harrison HS, Bethany, Mo.	Missouri State
20.	Kevin Ziomek, lhp	R-L	6-2	180	Amherst (Mass.) Regional HS	Vanderbilt
21.	Tony Wolters, ss	L-R	5-10	165	Rancho Buena Vista HS, Vista, Calif.	San Diego
22.	A.J. Vanegas, rhp	R-R	6-3	205	Redwood Christian HS, San Lorenzo, Calif.	Stanford
23.	Taijuan Walker, rhp	B-R	6-4	190	Yucaipa (Calif.) HS	Uncommitted
24.	Peter Tago, rhp	R-R	6-1	160	Dana Hills HS, Dana Point, Calif.	UCLA
25.	Aaron Sanchez, rhp	R-R	6-3	170	Barstow (Calif.) HS	Oregon
26.	Justin O'Conner, ss/c/rhp	R-R	6-0	180	Cowan HS, Muncie, Ind.	Arkansas
27.	Drew Vettleson, of/rhp/lhp	L-B	6-1	185	Central Kitsap HS, Silverdale, Wash.	Oregon State
28.	Cam Bedrosian, rhp	R-R	6-0	205	East Coweta HS, Sharpsburg, Ga.	Louisiana State
29.	Robbie Aviles, rhp	L-R	6-4	195	Suffern (N.Y.) HS	Florida
30.	Brian Ragira, of	R-R	6-2	175	Martin HS, Arlington, Texas	Stanford
31.	Chad Lewis, 3b	R-R	6-3	195	Marina HS, Huntington Beach, Calif.	San Diego State
32.	Marcus Littlewood, ss	B-R	6-3	190	Pineview HS, St. George, Utah	San Diego
33.	Jesse Biddle, lhp	L-L	6-4	225	Germantown Friends School, Philadelphia	Oregon
34.	Will Swanner, c	R-R	6-2	185	La Costa Canyon HS, Carlsbad, Calif.	Pepperdine
35.	Ty Linton, of	R-R	6-2	195	Charlotte Christian School	North Carolina
36.	Zach Alvord, ss	R-R	5-10	175	South Forsyth HS, Cumming, Ga.	Auburn
37.	Reggie Golden, of	R-R	5-10	200	Wetumpka (Ala.) HS	Alabama
38.	Jacoby Jones, ss	R-R	6-3	190	Richton (Miss.) HS	Louisiana State
39.	Kevin Jordan, of	L-R	6-0	190	Northside HS, Columbus, Ga.	Wake Forest
40.	John Simms, rhp	R-R	6-3	190	College Park HS, The Woodlands, Texas	Rice
41.	Kris Bryant, 3b	R-R	6-5	205	Bonanza HS, Las Vegas	San Diego
42.	Robby Rowland, rhp	R-R	6-6	205	Cloverdale (Calif.) HS	Oregon
43.	Ryan Bolden, of	R-L	6-2	195	Central HS, Madison, Miss.	Mississippi
44.	Sean Coyle, ss	R-R	5-9	175	Germantown Academy, Ft. Washington, Pa.	North Carolina
45.	Krey Bratsen, of	R-R	6-0	160	Bryan (Texas) HS	Texas A&M
46.	Dominic Ficociello, ss	B-R	6-3	155	Union HS, Fullerton, Calif.	Arkansas
47.	Joc Pederson, of	L-L	6-1	185	Palo Alto (Calif.) HS	Southern California
48.	Kendrick Perkins, of	L-L	6-3	225	LaPorte (Texas) HS	Texas A&M
49.	Christian Yelich, of/1b	L-R	6-4	190	Westlake HS, Thousand Oaks, Calif.	Miami
50.	Zach Lee, rhp	R-R	6-3	190	McKinney (Texas) HS	Louisiana State (FB)

#	Name	B-T	Ht	Wt	School	Commitment
51.	Robbie Ray, lhp	L-L	6-2	170	Brentwood (Tenn.) HS	Vanderbilt
52.	Delino DeShields Jr., 2b/of	R-R	5-9	180	Norcross (Ga.) HS	Uncommitted
53.	Gabriel Encinas, rhp	R-R	6-4	200	Saint Paul HS, Santa Fe Springs, Calif.	Loyola Marymount
54.	Michael Foltynewicz, rhp	R-R	6-4	190	Minooka (Ill.) HS	Texas
55.	Matt Lipka, ss	R-R	6-1	192	McKinney (Texas) HS	Alabama
56.	Mike Antonio, ss	R-R	6-1	170	Washington HS, New York	St. John's
57.	Angelo Gumbs, of	R-R	5-11	185	Torrance (Calif.) HS	Southern California
58.	Adam Plutko, rhp	R-R	6-3	180	Glendora (Calif.) HS	UCLA
59.	Jesus Valdez, rhp	R-R	6-3	185	Hueneme HS, Oxnard, Calif.	Arizona
60.	John Barbato, rhp	R-R	6-2	185	Varela HS, Miami	Florida
61.	Cody Buckel, rhp	R-R	6-2	180	Royal HS, Simi Valley, Calif.	Pepperdine
62.	Kellin Deglan, c	L-R	6-2	200	Langley (B.C.) HS	Florida International
63.	Bobby Wahl, rhp	R-R	6-2	185	West HS, Springfield, Va.	Mississippi
64.	Connor Mason, rhp	R-R	6-1	185	Suwanee, Ga. (home schooled)	Rice
65.	Justin Nicolino, lhp	L-L	6-3	160	University HS, Orlando	Virginia
66.	Tyler Austin, c	R-R	6-2	200	Heritage HS, Conyers, Ga.	Kennesaw State
67.	Jacob Felts, c	R-R	6-1	195	Orangefield HS, Orange, Texas	Texas
68.	Corey Hahn, of	L-L	5-10	160	Mater Dei HS, Santa Ana, Calif.	Arizona State
69.	Adam Duke, rhp	R-R	6-2	180	Spanish Fork (Utah) HS	Oregon State
70.	Alex Lavisky, c	R-R	6-0	195	St. Edward HS, Cleveland	Georgia Tech
71.	Luke Jackson, rhp	R-R	6-2	180	Calvary Christian HS, Clearwater, Fla.	Miami
72.	Eric Arce, c	L-R	5-9	205	North Oconee HS, Bogart, Ga.	Florida State
73.	Connor Narron, ss	B-R	6-3	190	Aycock HS, Pikeville, N.C.	North Carolina
74.	Kellen Sweeney, ss/of	L-R	6-0	180	Jefferson HS, Cedar Rapids, Iowa	San Diego
75.	Evan Grills, lhp	L-L	6-4	183	Sinclair SS, Whitby, Ont.	Uncommitted
76.	Deshun Dixon, lhp/of	R-L	5-10	175	Terry (Miss.) HS	Uncommitted
77.	Taylor Morton, rhp	R-R	6-2	195	Bartlett (Tenn.) HS	Tennessee
78.	Matt Roberts, c	R-R	6-1	195	Graham (N.C.) HS	North Carolina
79.	Andrew Smith, rhp	R-R	6-2	190	Roswell (Ga.) HS	North Carolina
80.	Daryl Norris, rhp	R-R	6-1	210	Fairhope (Ala.) HS	Mississippi State
81.	Austin Southall, 1b	L-R	6-1	215	University HS, Baton Rouge	Louisiana State
82.	Shane Rowland, c	L-R	5-9	170	Tampa Catholic HS	Miami
83.	Case Nixon, c/rhp	R-R	6-2	185	Hillcrest HS, Tuscaloosa, Ala.	Alabama
84.	Cito Culver, ss	B-R	6-1	175	Irondequoit HS, Rochester, N.Y.	Uncommitted
85.	Keenan Kish, rhp	L-R	6-2	170	Germantown Academy, Ft. Washington, Pa.	Florida
86.	Matthew Kirkland, 3b/c	R-R	6-2	210	South-Doyle HS, Knoxville	Tennessee
87.	Mason Williams, of	L-R	6-1	150	West Orange (Fla.) HS	South Carolina
88.	Lonnie Kaupilla, ss	R-R	6-1	170	Burbank (Calif.) HS	Stanford
89.	Tyler Shreve, rhp	R-R	6-4	215	East Valley HS, Redlands, Calif.	Colorado State (FB)
90.	Daniel Gibson, lhp	L-L	6-2	220	Tampa Jesuit HS	Florida
91.	Mark Podlas, of	L-L	6-2	190	Westhampton Beach (NY) HS	Virginia
92.	Austin Kubitza, rhp	L-R	6-5	185	Heritage HS, Colleyville, Texas	Rice
93.	Tyrell Jenkins, rhp	R-R	6-4	180	Henderson (Texas) HS	Uncommitted
94.	Scott Frazier, rhp	R-R	6-6	205	Upland (Calif.) HS	Pepperdine
95.	Evan Rutckyj, lhp	L-L	6-5	190	St. Josephs HS, St. Thomas, Ont.	Uncommitted
96.	Ryan Brett, ss	B-R	5-9	180	Highline HS, Seattle	Gonzaga
97.	Cameron Booser, lhp	L-L	6-4	215	Fife HS, Tacoma	Oregon State
98.	Jordan Haseltine, lhp	L-L	6-5	215	Wood HS, Vacaville, Calif.	San Francisco
99.	Tyler Skulina, rhp	R-R	6-5	250	Walsh Jesuit HS, Cuyahoga Falls, Ohio	Virginia
100.	Trey Griffin, of/1b	R-R	6-1	190	King HS, Lithonia, Ga.	Oklahoma State

FROM EVERY MINOR LEAGUE

As a complement to our organization prospect rankings, Baseball America also ranks prospects in each minor league at the end of their seasons. Like the organization lists, they place more weight on potential than performance and should not be regarded as all-star teams. Unlike the organization lists, which are from more of a scouting perspective, the minor league lists reflect the views of minor league managers, who give more weight to what a player does on the field now. We think both perspectives are useful, so we give you both, even though they don't always match up. For a player to qualify for a league prospect list, he must have spent at least one-third of the season in a league. Also unlike the organization lists, players can make the league lists even if they exhausted their rookie eligibility during the 2009 season.

TRIPLE-A

INTERNATIONAL LEAGUE
1. Matt Wieters, c, Norfolk (Orioles)
2. Tommy Hanson, rhp, Gwinnett (Braves)
3. Andrew McCutchen, of, Indianapolis (Pirates)
4. Chris Tillman, rhp, Norfolk (Orioles)
5. Wade Davis, rhp, Durham (Rays)
6. Jeremy Hellickson, rhp, Durham (Rays)
7. Austin Jackson, of, Scranton/Wilkes-Barre (Yankees)
8. Matt LaPorta, of/1b, Columbus (Indians)
9. Hector Rondon, rhp, Columbus (Indians)
10. Reid Brignac, ss, Durham (Rays)
11. Jake Arrieta, rhp, Norfolk (Orioles)
12. Fernando Martinez, of, Buffalo (Mets)
13. Jose Tabata, of, Indianapolis (Pirates)
14. Drew Stubbs, of, Louisville (Reds)
15. Michael Brantley, of, Columbus (Indians)
16. Jon Niese, lhp, Buffalo (Mets)
17. Carlos Carrasco, rhp, Lehigh Valley (Phillies)/Columbus (Indians)
18. Ross Detwiler, lhp, Syracuse (Nationals)
19. Ian Desmond, ss, Syracuse (Nationals)
20. Chris Heisey, of, Louisville (Reds)

PACIFIC COAST LEAGUE
1. Buster Posey, c, Fresno (Giants)
2. Neftali Feliz, rhp, Oklahoma City (Rangers)
3. Travis Snider, of, Las Vegas (Blue Jays)
4. Michael Saunders, of, Tacoma (Mariners)
5. Cameron Maybin, of, New Orleans (Marlins)
6. Alcides Escobar, ss, Nashville (Brewers)
7. Brett Wallace, 3b/1b, Memphis (Cardinals)/Sacramento (Athletics)
8. Kyle Blanks, 1b/of, Portland (Padres)
9. Justin Smoak, 1b, Oklahoma City (Rangers)
10. Vin Mazzaro, rhp, Sacramento (Athletics)
11. Bud Norris, rhp, Round Rock (Astros)
12. Esmil Rogers, rhp, Colorado Springs (Rockies)
13. Mat Gamel, 3b, Nashville (Brewers)
14. Brandon Allen, 1b, Reno (Diamondbacks)
15. Gio Gonzalez, lhp, Sacramento (Athletics)
16. Jeff Samardzija, rhp, Iowa (Cubs)

17. Adam Moore, c, Tacoma (Mariners)
18. Angel Salome, c, Nashville (Brewers)
19. Adrian Cardenas, 2b, Sacramento (Athletics)
20. Gaby Sanchez, 1b/3b, New Orleans (Marlins)

DOUBLE-A

EASTERN LEAGUE
1. Pedro Alvarez, 3b, Altoona (Pirates)
2. Madison Bumgarner, lhp, Connecticut (Giants)
3. Kyle Drabek, rhp, Reading (Phillies)
4. Carlos Santana, c, Akron (Indians)
5. Jesus Montero, c, Trenton (Yankees)
6. Domonic Brown, of, Reading (Phillies)
7. Junichi Tazawa, rhp, Portland (Red Sox)
8. Wilson Ramos, c, New Britain (Twins)
9. Michael Taylor, of, Reading (Phillies)
10. Brad Lincoln, rhp, Altoona (Pirates)
11. Hector Rondon, rhp, Akron (Indians)
12. Josh Reddick, of, Portland (Red Sox)
13. Ike Davis, 1b, Binghamton (Mets)
14. Marc Rzepczynski, lhp, New Hampshire (Blue Jays)
15. Jose Tabata, of, Altoona (Pirates)
16. Scott Sizemore, 2b, Erie (Tigers)
17. Jake Arrieta, rhp, Bowie (Orioles)
18. Nick Weglarz, of, Akron (Indians)
19. Zach McAllister, rhp, Trenton (Yankees)
20. Brandon Snyder, 1b, Bowie (Orioles)

SOUTHERN LEAGUE
1. Jason Heyward, of, Mississippi (Braves)
2. Gordon Beckham, ss, Birmingham (White Sox)
3. Desmond Jennings, of, Montgomery (Rays)
4. Mike Stanton, of, Jacksonville (Marlins)
5. Jarrod Parker, rhp, Mobile (Diamondbacks)
6. Tyler Flowers, c, Birmingham (White Sox)
7. Logan Morrison, 1b, Jacksonville (Marlins)
8. Freddie Freeman, 1b, Mississippi (Braves)
9. Jeremy Hellickson, rhp, Montgomery (Rays)
10. Josh Bell, 3b, Chattanooga (Dodgers)
11. Jay Jackson, rhp, Tennessee (Cubs)
12. Todd Frazier, of/2b/1b, Carolina (Reds)
13. Jonathan Lucroy, c, Huntsville (Brewers)
14. Chris Heisey, of, Carolina (Reds)
15. Dan Hudson, rhp, Birmingham (White Sox)
16. Jordan Danks, of, Birmingham (White Sox)
17. Sean West, lhp, Jacksonville (Marlins)
18. Andrew Lambo, of, Chattanooga (Dodgers)
19. Daniel Schlereth, lhp, Mobile (Diamondbacks)
20. Travis Wood, lhp, Carolina (Reds)

TEXAS LEAGUE
1. Mat Latos, rhp, San Antonio (Padres)
2. Justin Smoak, 1b, Frisco (Rangers)
3. Chris Carter, 1b, Midland (Athletics)
4. Jhoulys Chacin, rhp, Tulsa (Rockies)
5. Brett Wallace, 3b, Springfield (Cardinals)
6. Jason Castro, c, Corpus Christi (Astros)
7. Esmil Rogers, rhp, Tulsa (Rockies)
8. Trevor Reckling, lhp, Arkansas (Angels)
9. Peter Bourjos, of, Arkansas (Angels)
10. Hank Conger, c, Arkansas (Angels)
11. Kasey Kiker, lhp, Frisco (Rangers)
12. Lance Lynn, rhp, Springfield (Cardinals)

13. Daniel Descalso, 2b, Springfield (Cardinals)
14. Michael McKenry, c, Tulsa (Midland)
15. Adrian Cardenas, 2b/3b, Midland (Athletics)
16. Jeff Bianchi, ss, Northwest Arkansas (Royals)
17. Logan Forsythe, 3b, San Antonio (Padres)
18. Danny Cortes, rhp, Northwest Arkansas (Royals)
19. Corey Brown, of, Midland (Athletics)
20. Samuel Deduno, rhp, Tulsa (Rockies)

HIGH CLASS A

CALIFORNIA LEAGUE
1. Buster Posey, c, San Jose (Giants)
2. Christian Friedrich, lhp, Modesto (Rockies)
3. Jason Castro, c, Lancaster (Astros)
4. Chris Withrow, rhp, Inland Empire (Dodgers)
5. Phillipe Aumont, rhp, High Desert (Mariners)
6. Alex Liddi, 3b, High Desert (Mariners)
7. Pedro Figueroa, lhp, Stockton (Athletics)
8. Wynn Pelzer, rhp, Lake Elsinore (Padres)
9. Thomas Neal, of, San Jose (Giants)
10. James Darnell, 3b, Lake Elsinore (Padres)
11. Roger Kieschnick, of, San Jose (Giants)
12. Cory Luebke, lhp, Lake Elsinore (Padres)
13. Tyson Gillies, of, High Desert (Mariners)
14. Alex Torres, lhp, Rancho Cucamonga (Angels)
15. Trayvon Robinson, of, Inland Empire (Dodgers)
16. Grant Desme, of, Stockton (Athletics)
17. Logan Forysthe, 3b, Lake Elsinore (Padres)
18. Jemile Weeks, 2b, Stockton (Athletics)
19. Craig Italiano, rhp, Stockton (Athletics)/
Lake Elsinore (Padres)
20. Darren Ford, of, San Jose (Giants)

CAROLINA LEAGUE
1. Jason Heyward, of, Myrtle Beach (Braves)
2. Brian Matusz, lhp, Frederick (Orioles)
3. Pedro Alvarez, 3b, Lynchburg (Pirates)
4. Freddie Freeman, 1b, Myrtle Beach (Braves)
5. Lonnie Chisenhall, 3b, Kinston (Indians)
6. Casey Kelly, rhp, Salem (Red Sox)
7. Mike Montgomery, lhp, Wilmington (Royals)
8. Mike Moustakas, 3b, Wilmington (Royals)
9. Ryan Kalish, of, Salem (Red Sox)
10. Danny Espinosa, ss, Potomac (Nationals)
11. Danny Duffy, lhp, Wilmington (Royals)
12. Anthony Rizzo, 1b, Salem (Red Sox)
13. Chase d'Arnaud, ss/2b, Lynchburg (Pirates)
14. Jordan Danks, of, Winston-Salem (White Sox)
15. Zach Britton, lhp, Frederick (Orioles)
16. David Lough, of, Wilmington (Royals)
17. Luis Exposito, c, Salem (Red Sox)
18. Che-Hsuan Lin, of, Salem (Red Sox)
19. Jeff Bianchi, ss, Wilmington (Royals)
20. Brent Morel, 3b, Winston-Salem (White Sox)

FLORIDA STATE LEAGUE
1. Mike Stanton, of, Jupiter (Marlins)
2. Jesus Montero, c, Tampa (Yankees)
3. Domonic Brown, of, Clearwater (Phillies)
4. Yonder Alonso, 1b, Sarasota (Reds)
5. Kyle Drabek, rhp, Clearwater (Phillies)
6. Starlin Castro, ss, Daytona (Cubs)
7. Jenrry Mejia, rhp, St. Lucie (Mets)
8. Ben Revere, of, Fort Myers (Twins)
9. Ike Davis, 1b, St. Lucie (Mets)
10. Austin Romine, c, Tampa (Yankees)
11. Carlos Gutierrez, rhp, Fort Myers (Twins)
12. Matt Dominguez, 3b, Jupiter (Marlins)
13. Kirk Nieuwenhuis, of, St. Lucie (Mets)
14. Josh Vitters, 3b, Daytona (Cubs)

15. David Bromberg, rhp, Fort Myers (Twins)
16. Caleb Gindl, of, Brevard County (Brewers)
17. Chris Parmelee, 1b/of, Fort Myers (Twins)
18. Shane Peterson, of, Palm Beach (Cardinals)
19. Freddy Galvis, ss, Clearwater (Phillies)
20. Mark Rogers, rhp, Brevard County (Brewers)

LOW CLASS A

MIDWEST LEAGUE
1. Aaron Hicks, of, Beloit (Twins)
2. Dee Gordon, ss, Great Lakes (Dodgers)
3. Josh Vitters, 3b, Peoria (Cubs)
4. Brett Lawrie, 2b, Wisconsin (Brewers)
5. Mike Montgomery, lhp, Burlington (Royals)
6. Casey Crosby, lhp, West Michigan (Tigers)
7. Simon Castro, rhp, Fort Wayne (Padres)
8. Jaff Decker, of, Fort Wayne (Padres)
9. Cody Scarpetta, rhp, Wisconsin (Brewers)
10. Ethan Martin, rhp, Great Lakes (Dodgers)
11. Tim Melville, rhp, Burlington (Royals)
12. Eric Hosmer, 1b, Burlington (Royals)
13. A.J. Pollock, of, South Bend (Diamondbacks)
14. Wily Peralta, rhp, Wisconsin (Brewers)
15. James Darnell, 3b, Fort Wayne (Padres)
16. Chris Archer, rhp, Peoria (Cubs)
17. Kyle Russell, of, Great Lakes (Dodgers)
18. Grant Desme, of, Kane County (Athletics)
19. Pedro Figueroa, lhp, Kane County (Athletics)
20. Chris Carpenter, rhp, Peoria (Cubs)

SOUTH ATLANTIC LEAGUE
1. Martin Perez, lhp, Hickory (Rangers)
2. Casey Kelly, rhp/ss, Greenville (Red Sox)
3. Matt Moore, lhp, Bowling Green (Rays)
4. Derek Norris, c, Hagerstown (Nationals)
5. Tim Beckham, ss, Bowling Green (Rays)
6. Jordan Lyles, rhp, Lexington (Astros)
7. Jason Knapp, rhp, Lakewood (Phillies)/
Lake County (Indians)
8. Jared Mitchell, of, Kannapolis (White Sox)
9. Manny Banuelos, lhp, Charleston (Yankees)
10. Wilmer Flores, ss, Savannah (Mets)
11. Rudy Owens, lhp, West Virginia (Pirates)
12. Tony Sanchez, c, West Virginia (Pirates)
13. Anthony Gose, of, Lakewood (Phillies)
14. Tim Federowicz, c, Greenville (Red Sox)
15. Dexter Carter, rhp, Kannapolis (White Sox)
16. Nick Barnese, rhp, Bowling Green (Rays)
17. Travis d'Arnaud, c, Lakewood (Phillies)
18. Alex Perez, rhp, Lake County (Indians)
19. Trevor May, rhp, Lakewood (Phillies)
20. Melky Mesa, of, Charleston (Yankees)

SHORT-SEASON

NEW YORK-PENN LEAGUE
1. Ryan Westmoreland, of, Lowell (Red Sox)
2. Alex Colome, rhp, Hudson Valley (Rays)
3. Arodys Vizcaino, rhp, Staten Island (Yankees)
4. Sebastian Valle, c, Williamsport (Phillies)
5. Jason Kipnis, of, Mahoning Valley (Indians)
6. Victor Black, rhp, State College (Pirates)
7. Ramon Benjamin, lhp, Jamestown (Marlins)
8. Arquimedes Caminero, rhp, Jamestown (Marlins)
9. Alex Wilson, rhp, Lowell (Red Sox)
10. Kyle Lobstein, lhp, Hudson Valley (Rays)
11. Anthony Hewitt, 3b, Williamsport (Phillies)
12. Adam Warren, rhp, Staten Island (Yankees)
13. Destin Hood, of, Vermont (Nationals)
14. Jimmy Paredes, 2b, Staten Island (Yankees)
15. Derrik Gibson, ss/2b, Lowell (Red Sox)

16. Leandro Castro, of, Williamsport (Phillies)
17. Kyle Conley, of, Batavia (Cardinals)
18. Neil Medchill, of, Staten Island (Yankees)
19. Michael Almanzar, 3b, Lowell (Red Sox)
20. Jim Fuller, lhp, Brooklyn (Mets)

NORTHWEST LEAGUE
1. Hak-Ju Lee, ss, Boise (Cubs)
2. Edinson Rincon, 3b, Eugene (Padres)
3. Brett Jackson, of, Boise (Cubs)
4. Mario Martinez, 3b, Everett (Mariners)
5. Tim Wheeler, of, Tri-City (Rockies)
6. Ryan Wheeler, 3b, Yakima (Diamondbacks)
7. Robbie Ross, lhp, Spokane (Rangers)
8. Francisco Peguero, of, Salem-Keizer (Giants)
9. Matt Davidson, 3b, Yakima (Diamondbacks)
10. Miguel Velazquez, of, Spokane (Rangers)
11. Tommy Mendonca, 3b, Spokane (Rangers)
12. James Jones, of, Everett (Mariners)
13. Chris Dominguez, 3b, Salem-Keizer (Giants)
14. Julio Ramos, lhp, Vancouver (Athletics)
15. Rob Scahill, rhp, Tri-City (Rockies)
16. Ben Paulsen, 1b, Tri-City (Rockies)
17. Jerry Sullivan, rhp, Eugene (Padres)
18. Connor Hoehn, rhp, Vancouver (Athletics)
19. Logan Watkins, 2b, Boise (Cubs)
20. Braden Tullis, rhp, Spokane (Rangers)

ROOKIE

APPALACHIAN LEAGUE
1. Julio Teheran, rhp, Danville (Braves)
2. Jiovanni Mier, ss, Greeneville (Astros)
3. Wilking Rodriguez, rhp, Princeton (Rays)
4. Matt Hobgood, rhp, Bluefield (Orioles)
5. Gabriel Noriega, ss, Pulaski (Mariners)
6. David Holmberg, lhp, Bristol (White Sox)
7. John Lamb, lhp, Burlington (Royals)
8. Robert Stock, c, Johnson City (Cardinals)
9. Cesar Puello, of, Kingsport (Mets)
10. Juri Perez, rhp, Greeneville (Astros)
11. Trayce Thompson, of, Bristol (White Sox)
12. Tyler Ladendorf, ss, Elizabethton (Twins)
13. Steve Baron, c, Pulaski (Mariners)
14. Ty Morrison, of, Princeton (Rays)
15. Santos Rodriguez, lhp, Bristol (White Sox)
16. Tyler Stovall, lhp, Danville (Braves)
17. Mycal Jones, ss, Danville (Braves)
18. Jonathan Meyer, 3b, Greeneville (Astros)
19. Cody Rogers, of, Princeton (Rays)
20. Brett Oberholtzer, lhp, Danville (Braves)

PIONEER LEAGUE
1. Wil Myers, c, Idaho Falls (Royals)
2. Jake Odorizzi, rhp, Helena (Brewers)
3. Bobby Borchering, 3b, Missoula (Diamondbacks)
4. Garrett Richards, rhp, Orem (Angels)
5. Pat Corbin, lhp, Orem (Angels)
6. Jean Segura, 2b, Orem (Angels)

7. Chris Owings, ss, Missoula (Diamondbacks)
8. Nolan Arenado, 3b, Casper (Rockies)
9. Chris Balcom-Miller, rhp, Casper (Rockies)
10. Eric Arnett, rhp, Helena (Brewers)
11. Yorman Rodriguez, of, Billings (Reds)
12. Mike Belfiore, lhp, Missoula (Diamondbacks)
13. Tyler Kehrer, lhp, Orem (Angels)
14. Carlos Ramirez, c, Orem (Angels)
15. John Lamb, lhp, Idaho Falls (Royals)
16. Brett Wallach, rhp, Ogden (Dodgers)
17. Nick Bucci, rhp, Helena (Brewers)
18. Mariekson Gregorius, ss, Billings (Reds)
19. David Nick, 2b, Missoula (Diamondbacks)
20. Salvador Perez, c, Idaho Falls (Royals)

ARIZONA LEAGUE
1. Mike Trout, of, Angels
2. Fabio Martinez, rhp, Angels
3. Allen Webster, rhp, Dodgers
4. Rymer Liriano, of, Padres
5. Randal Grichuk, of, Angels
6. Julio Morban, of/dh, Mariners
7. Adys Portillo, rhp, Padres
8. Rafael Rodriguez, of, Giants
9. Jonathan Garcia, of, Dodgers
10. Jon Bachanov, rhp, Angels
11. Maverick Lasker, rhp, Brewers
12. Richard Alvarez, rhp, Rangers
13. Edward Concepcion, rhp, Giants
14. Jesus Brito, 3b, Indians
15. Hector Sanchez, c, Giants
16. Tomas Telis, c, Rangers
17. Rolando Gomez, ss, Angels
18. Jonathan Galvez, ss/2b, Padres
19. Danny Danielson, rhp, Dodgers
20. Max Walla, of, Brewers

GULF COAST LEAGUE
1. Christian Bethancourt, c, Braves
2. Kelvin DeLeon, of, Yankees
3. Reymond Fuentes, of, Red Sox
4. Jarred Cosart, rhp, Phillies
5. Carlos Perez, c, Blue Jays
6. Adrian Salcedo, rhp, Twins
7. Jonathan Singleton, 1b, Phillies
8. Destin Hood, of, Nationals
9. Tanner Bushue, rhp, Astros
10. Domingo Santana, of, Phillies
11. B.J. Hermsen, rhp, Twins
12. Roman Mendez, rhp, Red Sox
13. Billy Hamilton, ss, Reds
14. Eury Perez, of, Nationals
15. Brooks Pounders, rhp, Pirates
16. Yorman Rodriguez, of, Reds
17. Caleb Brewer, rhp, Braves
18. Jonathan Villan, ss, Phillies
19. Melvin Mercedes, rhp, Tigers
20. Daniel Tuttle, rhp, Reds

A

Abad, Fernando (Astros) 199
Abreu, Abner (Indians) 139
Abreu, Juan (Braves) 41
Ackley, Dustin (Mariners) 418
Adams, David (Yankees) 314
Adams, Ryan (Orioles) 60
Adduci, James (Cubs) 93
Adrianza, Ehire (Giants) 405
Aguero, Ramon (Pirates) 360
Ahrens, Kevin (Blue Jays) 470
Alburquerque, Al (Rockies) 154
Alderson, Tim (Pirates) 357
Allen, Brandon (Diamondbacks) 19
Allen, Kyle (Mets) 295
Alonso, Yonder (Reds) 115
Alvarez, Henderson (Blue Jays) 468
Alvarez, Pedro (Pirates) 354
Alvarez, Richard (Rangers) 461
Amarista, Alexi (Angels) 232
Anderson, Bryan (Cardinals) 377
Anderson, Lars (Red Sox) 67
Angle, Matt (Orioles) 59
Antigua, Jeffry (Cubs) 89
Antonelli, Matt (Padres) 396
Anundsen, Evan (Brewers) 267
Archer, Chris (Cubs) 87
Arcia, Oswaldo (Twins) 281
Arenado, Nolan (Rockies) 150
Arencibia, J.P. (Blue Jays) 467
Arnett, Eric (Brewers) 259
Arrieta, Jake (Orioles) 51
Atilano, Luis (Nationals) 489
Atwood, Will (Nationals) 491
Augenstein, Bryan (Diamondbacks) 22
Aumont, Phillippe (Mariners) 420
Austin, Jay (Astros) 197
Avery, Xavier (Orioles) 55
Avila, Alex (Tigers) 164
Axford, John (Brewers) 266

B

Bachanov, Jon (Angels) 233
Baez, Pedro (Dodgers) 247
Bailey, Luke (Rays) 439
Baker, Craig (Rockies) 154
Balcom-Miller, Chris (Rockies) 152
Banuelos, Manny (Yankees) 308
Barnes, Scott (Indians) 141
Barnese, Nick (Rays) 438
Barney, Darwin (Cubs) 88
Baron, Steve (Mariners) 428
Bashore, Matt (Twins) 284
Bastardo, Antonio (Phillies) 341
Beaulac, Eric (Mets) 299
Beavan, Blake (Rangers) 456
Beckham, Tim (Rays) 436
Belfiore, Mike (Diamondbacks) 20
Bell, Josh (Orioles) 51
Bell, Trevor (Angels) 230
Bellamy, Kyle (White Sox) 107
Beltre, Engel (Rangers) 455
Benson, Joe (Twins) 279
Beresford, James (Twins) 285
Berger, Eric (Indians) 141
Berglund, Bryan (Marlins) 185

Bernadina, Roger (Nationals) 490
Berry, Ryan (Orioles) 59
Betances, Dellin (Yankees) 316
Bethancourt, Christian (Braves) 36
Bianchi, Jeff (Royals) 214
Bittle, Scott (Cardinals) 378
Black, Victor (Pirates) 358
Blackmon, Charlie (Rockies) 151
Bleich, Jeremy (Yankees) 309
Boesch, Brennan (Tigers) 171
Bogusevic, Brian (Astros) 201
Bond, Brock (Giants) 413
Bonilla, Jose (Royals) 218
Borchering, Bobby (Diamondbacks) 19
Boscan, Wilfredo (Rangers) 460
Bourjos, Peter (Angels) 227
Bowden, Michael (Red Sox) 71
Boxberger, Brad (Reds) 118
Brackman, Andrew (Yankees) 310
Braddock, Zach (Brewers) 260
Brantley, Michael (Indians) 132
Brewer, Caleb (Braves) 42
Brigham, Jake (Rangers) 460
Brignac, Reid (Rays) 436
Brito, Jesus (Indians) 139
Britton, Drake (Red Sox) 72
Britton, Zach (Orioles) 51
Bromberg, David (Twins) 277
Brothers, Rex (Rockies) 149
Brown, Corey (Athletics) 326
Brown, Domonic (Phillies) 338
Brown, Jordan (Indians) 135
Broxton, Keon (Diamondbacks) 24
Bucci, Nick (Brewers) 268
Bullock, Billy (Twins) 279
Bumgarner, Madison (Giants) 403
Burgess, Michael (Nationals) 485
Burgos, Enrique (Diamondbacks) 27
Burke, Kyler (Cubs) 86
Burnett, Alex (Twins) 280
Burns, Greg (Marlins) 189
Bushue, Tanner (Astros) 197
Butler, Josh (Brewers) 267

C

Cain, Colton (Pirates) 358
Cain, Lorenzo (Brewers) 261
Cales, David (Cubs) 92
Cardenas, Adrian (Athletics) 325
Caridad, Esmailin (Cubs) 90
Carignan, Andrew (Athletics) 331
Carp, Mike (Mariners) 427
Carpenter, Chris (Cubs) 85
Carrasco, Carlos (Indians) 133
Carrera, Ezequiel (Mariners) 424
Carson, Robert (Mets) 296
Carter, Chris (Athletics) 322
Carter, Dexter (Padres) 397
Cashner, Andrew (Cubs) 83
Casilla, Jose (Giants) 412
Cassevah, Bobby (Athletics) 332
Castillo, Richard (Cardinals) 377
Castillo, Welington (Cubs) 92
Castillo, Yunier (Cardinals) 380
Castro, Jason (Astros) 194
Castro, Leandro (Phillies) 347
Castro, Simon (Padres) 387

Castro, Starlin (Cubs) 82
Cavazos-Galvez, Brian (Dodgers) 251
Ceda, Jose (Marlins) 183
Chacin, Jhoulys (Rockies) 147
Chaffee, Ryan (Angels) 234
Chambers, Evan (Pirates) 362
Chatwood, Tyler (Angels) 231
Chavez, Johermyn (Blue Jays) 473
Chirinos, Robinson (Cubs) 92
Chisenhall, Lonnie (Indians) 131
Ciriaco, Pedro (Diamondbacks) 28
Cisco, Mike (Phillies) 346
Clark, Craig (Giants) 412
Clark, Matt (Padres) 397
Cleary, Delta (Rockies) 153
Clemens, Koby (Astros) 201
Clemens, Paul (Braves) 44
Cobb, Alex (Rays) 442
Coffey, Cameron (Orioles) 57
Cofield, Kyle (Braves) 43
Coleman, Casey (Cubs) 91
Coleman, Louis (Royals) 214
Collier, Zach (Phillies) 349
Collins, Tim (Blue Jays) 473
Collmenter, Josh (Diamondbacks) 26
Collop, Justin (White Sox) 109
Colome, Alex (Rays) 437
Colvin, Brody (Phillies) 343
Colvin, Tyler (Cubs) 88
Conger, Hank (Angels) 226
Cooney, Brandon (Orioles) 57
Cooper, David (Blue Jays) 467
Corbin, Pat (Angels) 231
Correa, Heitor (Phillies) 345
Cortes, Danny (Mariners) 423
Cosart, Jarred (Phillies) 341
Cotham, Caleb (Yankees) 314
Cousins, Scott (Marlins) 181
Cowan, Jake (Orioles) 59
Cowgill, Collin (Diamondbacks) 21
Cozart, Zack (Reds) 118
Craig, Allen (Cardinals) 373
Crawford, Brandon (Giants) 405
Crosby, Casey (Tigers) 163
Crow, Aaron (Royals) 211
Cruz, Joe (Rays) 439
Cumberland, Drew (Padres) 390
Cunningham, Jarek (Pirates) 361
Cuthbert, Cheslor (Royals) 216

D

Danielson, Danny (Dodgers) 252
Danks, Jordan (White Sox) 100
d'Arnaud, Chase (Pirates) 356
d'Arnaud, Travis (Phillies) 339
Darnell, James (Padres) 387
Davidson, Matt (Diamondbacks) 22
Davis, Ike (Mets) 292
Davis, Kentrail (Brewers) 260
Davis, Wade (Rays) 435
de la Cruz, Kelvin (Indians) 135
de los Santos, Estarlin (Twins) 282
de los Santos, Fautino (Athletics) 328
de los Santos, Frank (Rays) 443
Decker, Jaff (Padres) 387
Deduno, Samuel (Rockies) 151
DeFratus, Justin (Phillies) 349

DeJesus Jr., Ivan (Dodgers)	245	Franklin, Nick (Mariners)	422	Hall, Brooks (Brewers)	268
del Rosario, Enerio (Reds)	121	Frazier, Parker (Rockies)	154	Halman, Greg (Mariners)	422
DeLeon, Kelvin (Yankees)	313	Frazier, Todd (Reds)	114	Hamilton, Billy (Reds)	118
Delgado, Dimasther (Braves)	39	Freeman, Freddie (Braves)	35	Hamilton, Mark (Cardinals)	380
Delgado, Randall (Braves)	37	Freeman, Sam (Cardinals)	378	Hand, Brad (Marlins)	184
DeLome, Collin (Astros)	203	Freese, David (Cardinals)	372	Harrell, Lucas (White Sox)	105
Dent, Ryan (Red Sox)	77	Friday, Brian (Pirates)	364	Harrison, Josh (Pirates)	365
Descalso, Daniel (Cardinals)	374	Friedrich, Christian (Rockies)	147	Harvey, Kris (Marlins)	187
Desme, Grant (Athletics)	325	Fuentes, Reymond (Red Sox)	69	Havens, Reese (Mets)	293
Desmond, Ian (Nationals)	483	Fuld, Sam (Cubs)	90	Hawksworth, Blake (Cardinals)	373
DeVall, Brett (Braves)	41	Fuller, Clay (Angels)	237	Hayenga, Keaton (Royals)	219
Diamond, Scott (Braves)	44			Hayes, Brett (Marlins)	187
Dolis, Rafael (Cubs)	87	**G**		Hearne, Trey (Cardinals)	381
Dominguez, Chris (Giants)	409			Heathcott, Slade (Yankees)	307
Dominguez, Matt (Marlins)	179	Gallagher, Austin (Dodgers)	250	Heckathorn, Kyle (Brewers)	262
Donald, Jason (Indians)	136	Galloway, Isaac (Marlins)	181	Hefner, Jeremy (Padres)	393
Donaldson, Josh (Athletics)	327	Galvis, Freddy (Phillies)	343	Heisey, Chris (Reds)	115
Doolittle, Sean (Athletics)	326	Gamboa, Eddie (Orioles)	61	Hellickson, Jeremy (Rays)	435
Dopirak, Brian (Blue Jays)	474	Gamel, Mat (Brewers)	259	Helm, Matt (Diamondbacks)	25
Dotson, Zach (Mets)	297	Garcia, Avisail (Tigers)	168	Henley, Tyler (Cardinals)	377
Doubront, Felix (Red Sox)	73	Garcia, Edgar (Phillies)	347	Hensley, Steven (Mariners)	425
Doyle, Andrew (Rangers)	461	Garcia, Jaime (Cardinals)	371	Heredia, Jairo (Yankees)	316
Drabek, Kyle (Phillies)	339	Garcia, Jonathan (Dodgers)	251	Hermsen, Brad (Twins)	282
Drake, Oliver (Orioles)	58	Garcia, Leury (Rangers)	456	Hernandez, Gorkys (Pirates)	358
Duffy, Danny (Royals)	213	Gartrell, Stefan (White Sox)	103	Herrera, Kelvin (Royals)	217
Dugan, Kelly (Phillies)	348	Gaston, Jon (Astros)	197	Hester, John (Diamondbacks)	27
Dunn, Mike (Yankees)	310	Gaub, John (Cubs)	87	Heyward, Jason (Braves)	34
Duran, Juan (Reds)	121	Gayhart, Jared (Tigers)	169	Hicks, Aaron (Twins)	274
Durango, Luis (Padres)	395	Gaynor, Wade (Tigers)	171	Hicks, Brandon (Braves)	41
Dwyer, Chris (Royals)	213	Gee, Dillon (Mets)	298	Hicks, Graham (Nationals)	489
Dydalewicz, Brad (Astros)	204	Gentry, Craig (Rangers)	461	Higley, J.R. (Nationals)	487
		Gervacio, Sammy (Astros)	195	Hill, Nick (Mariners)	424
E		Giavotella, Johnny (Royals)	216	Hill, Steven (Cardinals)	379
		Gibson, Derrik (Red Sox)	70	Hobgood, Matt (Orioles)	52
Eichhorn, Kevin (Diamondbacks)	25	Gibson, Kyle (Twins)	275	Hobson, K.C. (Blue Jays)	471
Elbert, Scott (Dodgers)	244	Giles, Tommy (Dodgers)	252	Hodges, Wes (Indians)	140
Ely, John (White Sox)	103	Gillaspie, Conor (Giants)	409	Hoehn, Connor (Athletics)	330
Emaus, Brad (Blue Jays)	475	Gillespie, Cole (Diamondbacks)	24	Hoes, L.J. (Orioles)	58
Englebrook, Evan (Astros)	202	Gillies, Tyson (Mariners)	421	Hoffman, Jamie (Yankees)	317
Eovaldi, Nathan (Dodgers)	247	Gindl, Caleb (Brewers)	264	Holmberg, David (White Sox)	101
Erbe, Brandon (Orioles)	53	Givens, Mychal (Orioles)	53	Holt, Brad (Mets)	292
Erickson, Gorman (Dodgers)	253	Glaesmann, Todd (Rays)	440	Holt, Brock (Pirates)	364
Escalona, Edgmer (Rockies)	156	Goins, Ryan (Blue Jays)	475	Hood, Destin (Nationals)	486
Escobar, Alcides (Brewers)	258	Goldschmidt, Paul (Diamondbacks)	23	Hoover, J.J. (Braves)	38
Escobar, Eduardo (White Sox)	105	Gomez, Edwin (Tigers)	173	Hosmer, Eric (Royals)	212
Espinosa, Danny (Nationals)	484	Gomez, Hector (Rockies)	148	House, T.J. (Indians)	135
Estrada, Marco (Nationals)	489	Gomez, Jeanmar (Indians)	130	House, Tyreace (Athletics)	332
Everidge, Tommy (Athletics)	329	Gomez, Rolando (Angels)	235	Howell, Del (Brewers)	266
Exposito, Luis (Red Sox)	75	Gonzalez, Miguel (White Sox)	102	Hudson, Dan (White Sox)	99
		Gonzalez, Rei (Blue Jays)	477	Hudson, Kyle (Orioles)	58
F		Gordon, Dee (Dodgers)	242	Hudson, Kyrell (Phillies)	343
		Gorgen, Matt (Rays)	444	Huffman, Chad (Padres)	394
Familia, Jeurys (Mets)	296	Gose, Anthony (Phillies)	340	Hunter, Brett (Athletics)	333
Farquhar, Danny (Blue Jays)	471	Gould, Garrett (Dodgers)	246	Hunter, Cedric (Padres)	394
Farris, Eric (Brewers)	265	Graham, Connor (Indians)	140		
Federowicz, Tim (Red Sox)	74	Graham, Matt (Giants)	411	**I**	
Feliz, Neftali (Rangers)	450	Green, Grant (Athletics)	323		
Fellhauer, Josh (Reds)	124	Green, Scott (Tigers)	172	Iglesias, Jose (Red Sox)	70
Fields, Daniel (Tigers)	165	Green, Taylor (Brewers)	265	Iorg, Cale (Tigers)	167
Fields, Josh (Mariners)	424	Greene, Tyler (Cardinals)	375	Italiano, Craig (Padres)	393
Fien, Casey (Tigers)	172	Greenwalt, Kyle (Astros)	205		
Fife, Stephen (Red Sox)	73	Gregorius, Mariekson (Reds)	120	**J**	
Figaro, Alfredo (Tigers)	168	Grichuk, Randal (Angels)	229		
Figueroa, Cole (Padres)	397	Griffith, Nevin (White Sox)	106	Jackson, Austin (Tigers)	163
Figueroa, Pedro (Athletics)	324	Grossman, Robbie (Pirates)	360	Jackson, Brett (Cubs)	83
Flaherty, Ryan (Cubs)	85	Guerra, Deolis (Twins)	282	Jackson, Jay (Cubs)	84
Flande, Yohan (Phillies)	344	Guerra, Javy (Dodgers)	248	Jackson, Justin (Blue Jays)	469
Flores, Wilmer (Mets)	291	Gutierrez, Carlos (Twins)	277	Jackson, Ryan (Cardinals)	379
Florimon, Pedro (Orioles)	55	Gutierrez, Danny (Rangers)	453	Jacobs, Brandon (Red Sox)	77
Flowers, Tyler (White Sox)	99			Jacobson, Brett (Orioles)	56
Font, Wilmer (Rangers)	454	**H**		Jaime, Juan (Nationals)	488
Ford, Darren (Giants)	407			James, Chad (Marlins)	179
Forsythe, Logan (Padres)	388	Hagadone, Nick (Indians)	131	James, Jiwan (Phillies)	342
Francisco, Juan (Reds)	116	Hale, David (Braves)	39	James, Kevin (Rays)	445

Jansen, Kenley (Dodgers)	247	Link, Jon (White Sox)	109	Miley, Wade (Diamondbacks)	24
Jay, Jon (Cardinals)	375	Liriano, Rymer (Padres)	391	Miller, Aaron (Dodgers)	243
Jefferies, Jake (Rays)	444	Lo, Chia-Jen (Astros)	196	Miller, Jai (Marlins)	188
Jeffress, Jeremy (Brewers)	266	Lobstein, Kyle (Rays)	438	Miller, Quinton (Pirates)	359
Jenkins, Chad (Blue Jays)	467	Locke, Jeff (Pirates)	359	Miller, Shelby (Cardinals)	370
Jennings, Dan (Marlins)	183	Lombardozzi, Steve (Nationals)	493	Milligan, Adam (Braves)	38
Jennings, Desmond (Rays)	434	Lopez, Robinson (Braves)	40	Mills, Beau (Indians)	139
Jimenez, Jorge (Marlins)	186	Lopez, Wilton (Astros)	202	Mills, Brad (Blue Jays)	469
Joaquin, Waldis (Giants)	407	Lorin, Brett (Pirates)	363	Minor, Mike (Braves)	35
Johnson, Chris (Astros)	200	Lotzkar, Kyle (Reds)	122	Mitchell, Bryan (Yankees)	310
Johnson, Cody (Braves)	37	Lough, David (Royals)	214	Mitchell, D.J. (Yankees)	312
Johnson, Graham (Marlins)	186	Lucroy, Jonathan (Brewers)	260	Mitchell, Jared (White Sox)	98
Johnson, Steve (Giants)	410	Luebke, Cory (Padres)	388	Mitchell, Matt (Royals)	220
Jones, Daryl (Cardinals)	371	Lutz, Zach (Mets)	297	Monell, Johnny (Giants)	410
Jones, James (Mariners)	426	Lyles, Jordan (Astros)	195	Montero, Jesus (Yankees)	306
Jones, Mycal (Braves)	40	Lynn, Lance (Cardinals)	371	Montgomery, Mike (Royals)	210
Jones, Nate (White Sox)	108			Moore, Adam (Mariners)	419
Joseph, Caleb (Orioles)	54	**M**		Moore, Matt (Rays)	436
Joseph, Corban (Yankees)	311			Morales, Angel (Twins)	277
Joseph, Donnie (Reds)	122	Magnuson, Trystan (Blue Jays)	474	Morales, Jose (Twins)	284
Joseph, Jonathan (Athletics)	331	Main, Michael (Rangers)	458	Morban, Julio (Mariners)	427
Joseph, Tommy (Giants)	404	Malm, Jeff (Rays)	441	Morel, Brent (White Sox)	100
Judy, Josh (Indians)	137	Maloney, Matt (Reds)	117	Moreland, Mitch (Rangers)	453
Jukich, Ben (Cardinals)	380	Mandel, Jeff (Nationals)	492	Morris, A.J. (Nationals)	488
		Manship, Jeff (Twins)	281	Morris, Bryan (Pirates)	359
K		Manzella, Tommy (Astros)	198	Morrison, Logan (Marlins)	179
		Marisnick, Jake (Blue Jays)	468	Morrison, Ty (Rays)	439
Ka'aihue, Kila (Royals)	216	Marks, Justin (Athletics)	332	Mortensen, Clayton (Athletics)	328
Kalish, Ryan (Red Sox)	68	Marrero, Chris (Nationals)	484	Moscoso, Guillermo (Rangers)	457
Keating, Patrick (Royals)	219	Marrero, Christian (White Sox)	106	Mosebach, Bobby (Angels)	235
Kehrer, Tyler (Angels)	233	Marson, Lou (Indians)	134	Moskos, Danny (Pirates)	365
Kelly, Casey (Red Sox)	67	Marte, Jefry (Mets)	295	Mount, Ryan (Angels)	236
Kelly, Joe (Cardinals)	378	Marte, Starling (Pirates)	356	Moustakas, Mike (Royals)	211
Kepler, Max (Twins)	278	Martin, Ethan (Dodgers)	243	Moviel, Scott (Mets)	296
Keuchel, Dallas (Astros)	203	Martinez, Fabio (Angels)	228	Mowdy, Ashton (Astros)	204
Kieschnick, Roger (Giants)	405	Martinez, Fernando (Mets)	291	Murphy, J.R. (Yankees)	309
Kiker, Kasey (Rangers)	452	Martinez, Jhan (Marlins)	182	Myers, Wil (Royals)	211
Kimbrel, Craig (Braves)	36	Martinez, Jose (White Sox)	109		
King, Aaron (Giants)	412	Martinez, Mario (Mariners)	423	**N**	
Kipnis, Jason (Indians)	134	Martinez, Osvaldo (Marlins)	189		
Kirkman, Michael (Rangers)	456	Massey, Tyler (Rockies)	157	Nash, Telvin (Astros)	200
Knapp, Jason (Indians)	131	Mateo, Marcos (Cubs)	91	Navarro, Reynaldo (Diamondbacks)	22
Kobernus, Jeff (Nationals)	485	Mathieson, Scott (Phillies)	344	Navarro, Yamaico (Red Sox)	71
Kohn, Michael (Angels)	237	Matthes, Kent (Rockies)	153	Neal, Thomas (Giants)	403
Kozma, Pete (Cardinals)	376	Matusz, Brian (Orioles)	50	Nelson, Chris (Rockies)	157
Krauss, Marc (Diamondbacks)	21	Matz, Steve (Mets)	294	Nevarez, Matt (Astros)	199
Kroenke, Zach (Diamondbacks)	29	Matzek, Tyler (Rockies)	146	Newmann, David (Rays)	442
Krol, Ian (Athletics)	328	Maxwell, Justin (Nationals)	485	Nicasio, Juan (Rockies)	152
Kulbacki, Kellen (Padres)	392	May, Lucas (Dodgers)	248	Nick, David (Diamondbacks)	25
Kunz, Eddie (Mets)	299	May, Trevor (Phillies)	340	Niese, Jon (Mets)	292
		McAllister, Zach (Yankees)	308	Niesen, Eric (Mets)	298
L		McBryde, Mike (Giants)	411	Nieto, Adrian (Nationals)	492
		McCutchen, Daniel (Pirates)	361	Nieuwenhuis, Kirk (Mets)	295
Lake, Junior (Cubs)	93	McEachern, Jason (Rays)	443	Noesi, Hector (Yankees)	315
Lamb, John (Royals)	212	McGeary, Jack (Nationals)	490	Noonan, Nick (Giants)	406
Lambo, Andrew (Dodgers)	244	McGee, Jake (Rays)	437	Norberto, Jordan (Diamondbacks)	28
Lasker, Maverick (Brewers)	269	McKenry, Michael (Rockies)	151	Noriega, Gabriel (Mariners)	427
Lawrie, Brett (Brewers)	259	McNutt, Trey (Cubs)	88	Norris, Derek (Nationals)	483
Leake, Mike (Reds)	115	Mejia, Jenrry (Mets)	290	Nova, Ivan (Yankees)	312
Lebron, Luis (Orioles)	54	Melancon, Mark (Yankees)	312	Nunez, Eduardo (Yankees)	311
Lee, Chen-Chang (Indians)	138	Melville, Tim (Royals)	212	Nunez, Gustavo (Tigers)	165
Lee, Hak-Ju (Cubs)	84	Mendez, Roman (Red Sox)	75	Nunez, Jhonny (White Sox)	106
Leesman, Charlie (White Sox)	108	Mendonca, Tommy (Rangers)	457		
LeMahieu, D.J. (Cubs)	86	Mercedes, Melvin (Tigers)	170	**O**	
Leon, Arcenio (Astros)	201	Mercedes, Roque (Diamondbacks)	28		
Leon, Arnold (Athletics)	329	Mercer, Jordy (Pirates)	362	Oberholtzer, Brett (Braves)	39
Leroux, Chris (Marlins)	185	Mesa, Melky (Yankees)	313	Odorizzi, Jake (Brewers)	261
Leyland, Josh (Athletics)	333	Mesoraco, Devin (Reds)	125	Ohlman, Michael (Orioles)	56
Liddi, Alex (Mariners)	420	Meszaros, Danny (Astros)	198	Oliver, Andy (Tigers)	163
Liebel, Andrew (Blue Jays)	475	Meyer, Jonathan (Astros)	200	Olmos, Edgar (Marlins)	184
Lin, Che-Hsuan (Red Sox)	74	Meyers, Brad (Nationals)	487	O'Malley, Shawn (Rays)	441
Lincoln, Brad (Pirates)	355	Mickolio, Kam (Orioles)	53	Ondrusek, Logan (Reds)	119
Lindblom, Josh (Dodgers)	244	Middlebrooks, Will (Red Sox)	73	Orta, Ricky (Mariners)	428
Lindsay, Shane (Rockies)	155	Mier, Jiovanni (Astros)	195	Ortegano, Jose (Braves)	43

Ortiz, Ryan (Athletics) 330
Osuna, Edgar (Royals) 220
Ottavino, Adam (Cardinals) 374
Owens, Rudy (Pirates) 357
Owings, Chris (Diamondbacks) 20
Ozuna, Marcell (Marlins) 183

P

Pacheco, Jordan (Rockies) 153
Parker, Blake (Cubs) 89
Parker, Jarrod (Diamondbacks) 18
Parmelee, Chris (Twins) 279
Parraz, Jordan (Royals) 217
Pastornicky, Tyler (Blue Jays) 472
Patton, Troy (Orioles) 55
Paul, Xavier (Dodgers) 250
Peacock, Brad (Nationals) 488
Peguero, Francisco (Giants) 406
Pelzer, Wynn (Padres) 389
Pena, Hassan (Nationals) 492
Peralta, Wily (Brewers) 263
Perez, Alexander (Indians) 138
Perez, Carlos (Blue Jays) 470
Perez, Eury (Nationals) 486
Perez, Fernando (Rays) 440
Perez, Luis (Blue Jays) 471
Perez, Martin (Rangers) 451
Perez, Rossmel (Diamondbacks) 26
Perez, Salvador (Royals) 217
Periard, Alex (Brewers) 267
Petersen, Bryan (Marlins) 182
Petersen, Curtis (Marlins) 188
Pettit, Chris (Angels) 232
Phegley, Josh (White Sox) 102
Phelps, David (Yankees) 315
Pierre, Gustavo (Blue Jays) 476
Pill, Brett (Giants) 410
Pimentel, Guillermo (Mariners) 429
Pimentel, Stolmy (Red Sox) 70
Pineda, Michael (Mariners) 421
Plouffe, Trevor (Twins) 283
Pollock, A.J. (Diamondbacks) 19
Poreda, Aaron (Padres) 390
Portillo, Adys (Padres) 391
Posey, Buster (Giants) 402
Poveda, Omar (Rangers) 458
Poythress, Rich (Mariners) 429
Price, Bryan (Indians) 140
Profar, Jurickson (Rangers) 452
Puckett, Cody (Reds) 125
Puello, Cesar (Mets) 296
Putkonen, Luke (Tigers) 169
Putnam, Zach (Indians) 136

R

Raben, Dennis (Mariners) 426
Raley, Brooks (Cubs) 90
Ramirez, Carlos (Angels) 233
Ramirez, J.C. (Mariners) 425
Ramirez, Jose (Yankees) 313
Ramirez, J.P. (Nationals) 493
Ramirez, Max (Rangers) 454
Ramirez, Neil (Rangers) 459
Ramirez, Wilkin (Tigers) 165
Ramos, Cesar (Padres) 396
Ramos, Julio (Athletics) 331
Ramos, Wilson (Twins) 275
Ratliff, Sean (Mets) 298
Raynor, John (Pirates) 360
Reckling, Trevor (Angels) 227
Reddick, Josh (Red Sox) 67
Reifer, Adam (Cardinals) 376

Remenowsky, Dan (White Sox) 107
Renfroe, David (Red Sox) 72
Retherford, C.J. (White Sox) 104
Revere, Ben (Twins) 276
Reyes, Jorge (Padres) 394
Reynolds, Matt (Rockies) 156
Rhee, Dae-Eun (Cubs) 86
Richards, Garrett (Angels) 228
Richardson, Dustin (Red Sox) 76
Richardson, D'Vontrey (Brewers) 265
Richardson, Hilton (Royals) 221
Rincon, Edinson (Padres) 389
Rivas, Amaury (Brewers) 264
Rivero, Carlos (Indians) 137
Rizzo, Anthony (Red Sox) 69
Robbins, James (Tigers) 173
Robertson, Tyler (Twins) 280
Robinson, Derrick (Royals) 218
Robinson, Trayvon (Dodgers) 245
Robles, Mauricio (Mariners) 423
Rodriguez, Aneury (Rays) 444
Rodriguez, Henry (Athletics) 327
Rodriguez, Rafael (Angels) 234
Rodriguez, Rafael (Giants) 407
Rodriguez, Santos (White Sox) 105
Rodriguez, Wilking (Rays) 440
Rodriguez, Yorman (Reds) 116
Roe, Chaz (Rockies) 155
Roenicke, Josh (Blue Jays) 468
Rogers, Cody (Rays) 442
Rogers, Esmil (Rockies) 150
Rogers, Mark (Brewers) 262
Rohrbough, Cole (Braves) 42
Rojas, Miguel (Reds) 121
Roling, Kiel (Rockies) 157
Romine, Andrew (Angels) 236
Romine, Austin (Yankees) 307
Rondon, Daiguro (Dodgers) 252
Rondon, Hector (Indians) 133
Rosa, Carlos (Royals) 215
Rosa, Garabez (Orioles) 60
Rosario, Wilin (Rockies) 147
Rosenbaum, Danny (Nationals) 493
Rosenberg, B.J. (Phillies) 347
Ross, Robbie (Rangers) 452
Ross, Tyson (Athletics) 324
Rowell, Billy (Orioles) 61
Runzler, Dan (Giants) 404
Russell, Kyle (Dodgers) 246
Russo, Kevin (Yankees) 316
Rustich, Brant (Mets) 300
Ryan, Dusty (Tigers) 171

S

Salcedo, Adrian (Twins) 278
Salome, Angel (Brewers) 263
Sample, Tyler (Royals) 215
Sampson, Keyvius (Padres) 390
Samuel, Francisco (Cardinals) 375
Sanchez, Eduardo (Cardinals) 372
Sanchez, Gaby (Marlins) 180
Sanchez, Gary (Yankees) 309
Sanchez, Tony (Pirates) 355
Sands, Jerry (Dodgers) 251
Sano, Miguel (Twins) 275
Santana, Carlos (Indians) 130
Santana, Daniel (Twins) 283
Santana, Domingo (Phillies) 342
Santeliz, Clevelan (White Sox) 101
Santos, Sergio (White Sox) 103
Sardinas, Luis (Rangers) 455
Satterwhite, Cody (Tigers) 167
Saunders, Michael (Mariners) 419

Savery, Joe (Phillies) 346
Sborz, Jay (Tigers) 170
Scarpetta, Cody (Brewers) 263
Schafer, Logan (Brewers) 262
Scheppers, Tanner (Rangers) 451
Schimpf, Ryan (Blue Jays) 472
Schlereth, Daniel (Tigers) 164
Schuster, Patrick (Diamondbacks) 26
Seager, Kyle (Mariners) 429
Seaton, Ross (Astros) 196
Segura, Jean (Angels) 231
Septimo, Leyson (Diamondbacks) 27
Serrano, Mark (Reds) 123
Severino, Atahualpa (Nationals) 491
Shelby, John (White Sox) 108
Shields, Robbie (Mets) 297
Shuck, J.B. (Astros) 199
Sierra, Moises (Blue Jays) 470
Silverio, Alfredo (Dodgers) 249
Simmons, Crawford (Royals) 220
Singleton, Jonathan (Phillies) 345
Sinkbeil, Brett (Marlins) 187
Sizemore, Scott (Tigers) 166
Skaggs, Tyler (Angels) 229
Skipworth, Kyle (Marlins) 181
Slama, Anthony (Twins) 281
Smith, Blake (Dodgers) 250
Smith, Eric (Diamondbacks) 23
Smith, Jordan (Reds) 120
Smith, Will (Angels) 232
Smoak, Justin (Rangers) 451
Smolinski, Jake (Marlins) 184
Snyder, Brandon (Orioles) 52
Sosa, Henry (Giants) 408
Soto, Neftali (Reds) 119
Souza, Justin (Athletics) 330
Spanjer-Furstenburg, Riaan (Braves) 45
Spoone, Chorye (Orioles) 60
Spruill, Zeke (Braves) 37
Stanton, Mike (Marlins) 178
Stassi, Max (Athletics) 373
Steele, T.J. (Astros) 198
Stewart, Zach (Blue Jays) 466
Stinson, Josh (Mets) 299
Stock, Robert (Cardinals) 374
Stoffel, Jason (Giants) 408
Stohr, Tyler (Tigers) 170
Stoneburner, Graham (Yankees) 314
Stoner, Tobi (Mets) 300
Storen, Drew (Nationals) 483
Stovall, Tyler (Braves) 40
Strasburg, Stephen (Nationals) 482
Strickland, Hunter (Pirates) 361
Strieby, Ryan (Tigers) 166
Strop, Pedro (Rangers) 459
Stutes, Mike (Phillies) 344
Suarez, Albert (Rays) 441
Sucre, Jesus (Braves) 44
Sulbaran, Juan Carlos (Reds) 124
Sullivan, Jerry (Padres) 393
Sullivan, Richard (Braves) 42
Surkamp, Eric (Giants) 409
Sweeney, Matt (Rays) 443

T

Tabata, Jose (Pirates) 355
Tanner, Clayton (Giants) 411
Tate, Donavan (Padres) 386
Taylor, Michael (Phillies) 339
Tazawa, Junichi (Red Sox) 68
Teheran, Julio (Braves) 35
Tejada, Ruben (Mets) 294
Tekotte, Blake (Padres) 392

Telis, Tomas (Rangers)	460	Van Mil, Loek (Twins)	285	Webster, Allen (Dodgers)	246
Texeira, Kanekoa (Mariners)	428	Van Slyke, Scott (Dodgers)	249	Weeks, Jemile (Athletics)	325
Thames, Eric (Blue Jays)	472	Vargas, Jonathan (Rockies)	156	Weglarz, Nick (Indians)	132
Thole, Josh (Mets)	293	Veal, Donnie (Pirates)	362	Weiland, Kyle (Red Sox)	76
Thompson, Aaron (Nationals)	486	Velazquez, Miguel (Rangers)	458	Weinhardt, Robbie (Tigers)	167
Thompson, Trayce (White Sox)	100	Venters, Jonny (Braves)	45	Wells, Casper (Tigers)	168
Tobin, Mason (Angels)	235	Viciedo, Dayan (White Sox)	101	Westmoreland, Ryan (Red Sox)	66
Todd, Jess (Indians)	137	Villalona, Angel (Giants)	413	Wheeler, Ryan (Diamondbacks)	21
Tolisano, John (Blue Jays)	476	Villan, Jonathan (Phillies)	346	Wheeler, Tim (Rockies)	149
Tootle, Ben (Twins)	284	Villar, Henry (Astros)	204	Wheeler, Zack (Giants)	403
Torres, Alex (Rays)	438	Villarreal, Brayan (Tigers)	169	White, Alex (Indians)	134
Torres, Carlos (White Sox)	104	Vinicio, Jose (Red Sox)	77	White, Cole (Royals)	221
Tosoni, Rene (Twins)	278	Viola, Pedro (Reds)	122	Wieland, Joe (Rangers)	454
Trinidad, Polin (Astros)	203	Vitters, Josh (Cubs)	83	Wiley, Byron (Reds)	125
Triunfel, Carlos (Mariners)	420	Vizcaino, Arodys (Yankees)	307	Williams, Everett (Padres)	389
Trout, Mike (Angels)	227	Von Rosenberg, Zack (Pirates)	357	Wilson, Alex (Red Sox)	74
Trumbo, Mark (Angels)	230	Voss, Jay (Marlins)	186	Wilson, Bobby (Angels)	236
Tucker, Ryan (Marlins)	180			Wilson, Kenny (Blue Jays)	476
Tuiasosopo, Matt (Mariners)	425			Withrow, Chris (Dodgers)	243
Turner, Jacob (Tigers)	162	**W**		Wood, Blake (Royals)	219
Tuttle, Daniel (Reds)	124	Wagner, Mark (Red Sox)	75	Wood, Tim (Marlins)	185
		Walden, Jordan (Angels)	229	Wood, Travis (Reds)	117
U		Walker, Neil (Pirates)	363	Worley, Vance (Phillies)	345
Urbina, Juan (Mets)	294	Walla, Max (Brewers)	268		
		Wallace, Brett (Athletics)	323	**Y**	
V		Wallach, Brett (Dodgers)	249		
		Walters, P.J. (Cardinals)	379	Ynoa, Michael (Athletics)	326
Valaika, Chris (Reds)	119	Waring, Brandon (Orioles)	57	Young Jr., Eric (Rockies)	148
Valdespin, Jordany (Mets)	301	Warren, Adam (Yankees)	315	Younginer, Madison (Red Sox)	72
Valencia, Danny (Twins)	276	Watkins, Logan (Cubs)	84		
Valera, Cesar (Cardinals)	381	Way, Matt (Phillies)	348	**Z**	
Valiquette, Phillippe (Reds)	123	Weathers, Casey (Rockies)	152		
Valle, Sebastian (Phillies)	341	Webb, Daniel (Blue Jays)	473	Zawadzki, Lance (Padres)	391
		Webb, Ryan (Padres)	395		